An Introduction To The Critical Studp And Knowledge Of The Holly Scriptures

FAC SIMILE of the BIBLIA PAUPERUM

Supposed to have been executed between A.D. 1420 and 1435

CONTENTS

OF

THE SECOND VOLUME.

PART I.

ON SCRIPTURE-CRITICISM

	Page
CHAPTER I. *On the Original Languages of Scripture.*	
SECTION I. *On the Hebrew Language.*	
Introductory Remarks on the Oriental or Shemitish Languages	2
I. Origin of the Hebrew Language	3
II. Historical Sketch of the Hebrew Language	5
III. Antiquity of the Hebrew Characters	6
IV. Antiquity of the Hebrew Vowel-Points	8—12
SECTION II. *On the Greek Language.*	
I. Similarity of the Greek Language of the New Testament with that of the Alexandrian or Septuagint Greek Version	13
II. The New Testament, why written in Greek	13—18
III. Examination of the Style of the New Testament	18—22
IV. Its Dialects	22
Hebraisms	23—27
Rabbinisms	27
Aramæisms, or Syriasms and Chaldaisms	27
Latinisms	28
Persisms and Cilicisms	29
SECTION III. *Of the Cognate or Kindred Languages*	
I. Aramæan with its two Dialects, 1. The Chaldee, 2. The Syriac	30
II. The Arabic, with its Derivative, the Ethiopic	31
III. Use and Importance of the Cognate Languages to Sacred Criticism	31
CHAPTER II. *On the Antient Versions of the Scriptures*	
SECTION I. *On the Targums or Chaldee Paraphrases of the Old Testament*	
I. Targum of Onkelos	34
II. Targum of the Pseudo-Jonathan	35
III. The Jerusalem Targum	ibid
IV. The Targum of Jonathan Ben Uzziel	36
V. The Targum on the Hagiographa	37
VI. The Targum on the Megilloth	ibid.
VII. VIII. IX. Three Targums on the Book of Esther	ibid.
X. A Targum on the Books of Chronicles	ibid.
XI. Real Value of the different Targums	ibid.

CONTENTS.

SECTION II. *On the Antient Greek Versions of the Old Testament.* Page

I. The Septuagint — 39
    1. History of it — 39—42
    2. A Critical Account of its Execution — 42—44
    3. What Manuscripts were used by its Authors — 44—46
    4. Account of the Biblical Labours of Origen — 47—50
    5. Notice of the Recensions or Editions of Eusebius and Pamphilus, of Lucian and Hesychius — 50, 51
    6. Importance of the Septuagint Version in the Criticism and Interpretation of the New Testament — 51
II. Account of other Greek Versions of the Old Testament — 52
    1. Version of Aquila — 52
    2. Version of Theodotion — 52
    3. Version of Symmachus — 53
    4, 5, 6. Anonymous Versions — 54
III. References in Antient Manuscripts to other Versions — 54, 55

SECTION III. *On the Antient Oriental Versions of the Old and New Testaments.*

I. Syriac Versions — 56
    1. Peschito, or Literal Version — 56—59
    2. Philoxenian Version — 59, 60
    3. Syro-Estrangelo and Palæstino-Syriac Version — 60, 61
II. Egyptian Versions — 61
    Coptic and Sahidic Versions — 62
    Ammonian and Basmuric Versions — 63
III. Ethiopic Version — 64—66
IV. Arabic Versions — 67, 68
V. Armenian Version — 68
VI. Persian Versions — 69

SECTION IV. *On the Antient Western Versions of the Scriptures*

I. Antient Latin Versions of the Scriptures — 69
    1. Old Italic or Ante-Hieronymian Version — 69
    2. Biblical Labours and Latin Version of Jerome — 70
    3. Vulgate Version and its Revisions — 71—74
    4. Critical Value of the Latin Vulgate Version — 74, 75
II. The Gothic Version — 75
III. The Sclavonic Version — 76
IV. Anglo-Saxon Version — 77, 78

CHAPTER III. *On the Manuscripts of the Bible.*

SECTION I. *On the Hebrew Manuscripts of the Old Testament.*

I. Different Classes of Hebrew Manuscripts — 80
II. The Rolled Manuscripts of the Synagogue — ibid
III. The Square Manuscripts used by the Jews in private Life — 81
IV. Antient Recensions or Editions of Hebrew Manuscripts — 82
V. Age of Hebrew Manuscripts — 83
VI. Of the Order in which the Sacred Books are arranged in Manuscripts — 84
VII. Modern Families or Recensions of Hebrew Manuscripts — 85, 86
VIII. Notice of the most Antient Manuscripts — 86—89
IX. Brief Notice of the Manuscripts of the Indian Jews — 89—91

SECTION II. *On the Manuscripts of the Samaritan Pentateuch.*

I. Origin of the Samaritans — 93
II. Account of the Samaritan Pentateuch. — Manuscripts of it — 94
III. Variations of the Samaritan Pentateuch from the Hebrew — 95
IV. Versions of the Samaritan Pentateuch — 96, 97

SECTION III. *On the Manuscripts of the Greek Scriptures*

§ 1. *General Observations on Greek Manuscripts.*

I. On what Materials written — 97
II. Form of Letters — 98

CONTENTS.

	Page
III. Abbreviations	98,
IV Codices Palimpsesti or Rescripti	1(
V. Account of the different Families, Recensions, or Editions of Manuscripts of the New Testament	100—1
1. The System of Dr Griesbach and Michaelis	101—1(
2. The System of M. Matthæi	1(
3. The System of Mr. Nolan	104—1
4. The System of Prof Hug	1
5. The System of Prof. Scholz	111—1
VI On the Fœdus cum Græcis, or Coincidence between many Greek Manuscripts and the Vulgate Latin Version	1

§ 2. Account of Greek Manuscripts containing the Old and New Testaments.

I The Alexandrian Manuscript	116—12
II The Vatican Manuscript	122—12

§ 3. Account of Manuscripts (entire or in part) containing the Septuagint or Greek Version of the Old Testament.

I. The Codex Cottonianus	125—12
II. III The Codices, Sarravianus and Colbertinus	12
IV The Codex Cæsareus	12
V The Codex Ambrosianus	12
VI. The Codex Coislinianus	1
VII The Codex Basilio-Vaticanus	13
VIII The Codex Turicensis	13

§ 4. Account of the principal Manuscripts containing the New Testament, entire or in part.

I The Codex Cottonianus (Titus C. XV.)	13
II. The Codex Bezæ or Cantabrigiensis	133—13
III The Codex Ephremi	13
IV The Codex Claromontanus	13
V The Codex Argenteus	138, 13
MSS of the Gothic Version, discovered by signor Mai	140, 14
VI. The Codex Rescriptus of St Matthew's Gospel in Trinity College, Dublin	14
VII The Codex Laudianus, 3.	142, 14
VIII The Codex Coislinianus	14
IX. The Codex Boernerianus	14
X The Codex Cyprius	14
XI The Codex Basiliensis E.	14
XII. The Codex San-Germanensis	14
XIII. The Codex Augiensis	14
XIV. The Codex Harleianus, 5598	14
XV. The Codex Regius, or Stephani η	14
XVI. The Codex Uffenbachianus	14
XVII The Codices Manners-Suttoniani	15(
XVIII. The Codices Mosquenses	151
XIX. The Codex Brixiensis	151
XX. Other MSS written in small characters, and deserving of especial notice; viz.	
1. The Codex Basileensis, 1.	152
2 The Codex Berolinensis	152
3. The Codex Corsendoncensis	152
4. The Codex Montfortianus	153
5. The Codex Meermannianus	154
6. The Codex Regius, 50	155
7 The Codex Leicestrensis	155
8 The Codex Vindobonensis	156
9. The Codex Ebnerianus	156
10. The Codex Ottobonianus	157
XXI. Notices of the Collations of the Barberini and Velesian Manuscripts	157, 158

CONTENTS.

CHAPTER IV. *On the Divisions and Marks of Distinction, occurring in Manuscripts and printed Editions of the Scriptures.*

SECTION I. *On the Divisions and Marks of Distinction, occurring in the Old Testament.*

	Page
I. Different Appellations given to the Scriptures	159
II. General Divisions of the Canonical Books	159
III. Particularly of the Old Testament	160
1. The Law	162
2. The Prophets	162
3. The Cetubim or Hagiographa	162
IV. Account of the Masora	163—167
V. Modern Divisions of the Books of the Old Testament. — Chapters and Verses	167, 168

SECTION II. *On the Divisions and Marks of Distinction, occurring in the New Testament.*

I. Antient Divisions of Τιτλοι and Κεφαλαια	169
Ammonian, Eusebian, and Euthalian Sections. — Modern Division of Chapters	170
II. Account of the Antient and Modern Punctuation of the New Testament	171
Antient Στιχοι and Modern Verses	172, 173
III. Of the Titles to each Book	173
IV. Subscriptions to the different Books	174

CHAPTER V. *Of the Various Readings occurring in the Old and New Testaments.*

I. The Christian Faith not affected by Various Readings	175
II. Nature of Various Readings. — Difference between them and mere Errata	177
III. Causes of Various Readings	177
1. The Negligence or Mistakes of Transcribers	177—180
2. Errors or Imperfections in the Manuscript copied	181
3. Critical Conjecture	181, 182
4. Wilful Corruptions of a Manuscript from Party Motives	183
IV. Sources, whence a true Reading is to be determined	183
1. Manuscripts	183—185
2. Antient Editions	185
3. Antient Versions	186—190
4. Parallel Passages	190—192
5. Quotations in the Writings of the Fathers	192—195
6. Critical Conjecture	195, 196
V. General Rules for judging of Various Readings	196—203

CHAPTER VI. *On the Quotations from the Old Testament in the New. — Quotations in the New Testament from the Apocryphal Writers, and from Profane Authors* — 204

SECTION I. *On the External Form of the Quotations from the Old Testament in the New.*

I. Tables of the Quotations from the Hebrew Scriptures and from the Septuagint Version, in the Order in which they occur in the New Testament	205—246
II. Classification of the Quotations from the Hebrew Scriptures in the New Testament	247—251
III. Classification of the Quotations from the Septuagint Version in the New Testament	251—256
IV. Considerations on the probable Causes of the seeming Discrepancies in the Quotations from the Old Testament in the New	256—259

CONTENTS.

Page

SECTION II. *On the Internal Form of Quotations, or the Mode in which Citations from the Old Testament are applied in the New.*

    General Observations on the Rabbinical and other Modes of quoting the Old Testament. — Classification of the Quotations in the New Testament - - - - - - 260—263
    I. Quotations from the Old Testament in the New, in which the Predictions are literally accomplished - - - 263
    II. Quotations, in which that is said to have been done, of which the Scriptures have not spoken in a literal, but in a spiritual, Sense - 264
    III. Quotations made by the Sacred Writers, in the Way of Illustration - 265—268
    IV. Quotations, and other Passages in the Old Testament, which are alluded to in the New - - - - - 269

SECTION III. *Of Apocryphal Passages, supposed to be quoted in the New Testament.* — *Quotations from Profane Authors* - 270—272

CHAPTER VII. *On Harmonies of Scripture.*

    I. Occasion and Design of Harmonies of Scripture - - 272
    II. Harmonies of the Four Gospels - - - 273
    III. Observations on the different Schemes of Harmonisers, and on the Duration of the Public Ministry of Jesus Christ - - 275—280

PART II.

ON THE INTERPRETATION OF SCRIPTURE.

BOOK I.

GENERAL PRINCIPLES OF INTERPRETATION.

CHAPTER I. *On the Sense of Scripture.*

SECTION I. *On the Meaning of Words.*
    I. Nature of Words - - - - 28
    II. Sense of Scripture defined - - - 28
        1. The Literal Sense - - - 282, 28
        2. The Allegorical, Typical, and Parabolic Sense - 28
        3. The Moral Sense of Professor Kant shown to be without Foundation - - - - 28

SECTION II. *General Rules for investigating the Meaning of Words* - - - - - 286—29

SECTION III. *Of Emphases.*
    I. Nature of Emphasis — its different kinds - - 2(
    II. Verbal Emphases - - - - 2(
        1. Emphases of the Greek Article - - 293—2(
        2. Emphases of other words - - - 2(
        3. Emphatic Adverbs - - - 2(
    III. Real Emphases - - - - 2(
    IV. General Rules for the Investigation of Emphases - 296—2(

CHAPTER II. *On the Subsidiary Means for ascertaining the Usus Loquendi.*

SECTION I. *Direct Testimonies for ascertaining the Usus Loquendi.*
    § 1. THE TESTIMONY OF CONTEMPORARY WRITERS. — SOURCES OF THIS TESTIMONY -
    I. Definition of Words - - - - 2
    II. Examples, and the Nature of the Subject - - 3
    III. Comparison of Similar or Parallel Passages - - 300—3

CONTENTS.

SECTION I. *Direct Testimonies for ascertaining the Usus Loquendi*, continued.

§ 2. ANTIENT VERSIONS —
    Importance of Antient Versions as an hermeneutical Aid — 310, 311
    Observations on the respective Merits of the several Antient Versions — 312
    Rules for consulting them to the best advantage — 313, 314

§ 3. SCHOLIASTS AND GLOSSOGRAPHERS —
    I. Nature of Scholia — 314
    II. And of Glossaries — 315
    III. Rules for consulting them to advantage in the Interpretation of the Scriptures — 315, 316

§ 4. ON THE TESTIMONY OF FOREIGNERS WHO HAVE ACQUIRED A LANGUAGE — 316—318

SECTION II. *Indirect Testimonies for ascertaining the Usus Loquendi.*

§ 1. OF THE CONTEXT — 318
    I. The Context defined and illustrated — 318—320
    II. Rules for ascertaining the Context — 320—324

§ 2. OF THE SUBJECT-MATTER — 325

§ 3. OF THE SCOPE — 326
    I. The Scope defined — Importance of investigating the Scope of a Book or Passage of Scripture — 326
    II. Rules for investigating it — 327—330

§ 4. ANALOGY OF LANGUAGES — 330
    I. Analogy of Languages defined. — Its different Kinds — ibid.
    II. Use of Grammatical Analogy — 331
    III. Analogy of Kindred Languages — ibid
    IV. Hints for consulting this Analogy in the Interpretation of Scripture — 332—334
    V. Foundation of Analogy in all Languages — 334

§ 5. OF THE ANALOGY OF FAITH — 335
    I. Analogy of Faith, defined and illustrated — 335
    II. Its Importance in studying the Sacred Writings — 336
    III. Rules for investigating the Analogy of Faith — 337—340

§ 6. ON THE ASSISTANCE TO BE DERIVED FROM JEWISH WRITINGS IN THE INTERPRETATION OF THE SCRIPTURES —
    I. The Apocryphal Books of the Old Testament — 341
    II. The Talmud — 341
        1. The Misna — ibid.
        2. The Gemara or Commentary — 342
        Jerusalem and Babylonish Talmuds — ibid.
    III. The Writings of Philo and Josephus — 344
        1. Account of Philo — ibid.
        2. Account of Josephus — 345, 346

§ 7. ON THE ASSISTANCE TO BE DERIVED FROM THE WRITINGS OF THE GREEK FATHERS IN THE INTERPRETATION OF THE SCRIPTURES — 347—350

§ 8. ON HISTORICAL CIRCUMSTANCES —
    I. Order of the Different Books of Scripture — 351
    II. Their Titles — ibid.
    III. Their Authors — 352
    IV. Their Dates — ibid.
    V. The Place where written — 353
    VI. Occasion on which they were written — 354
    VII. Antient Sacred and Profane History — ibid.
    VIII. Chronology — 356
    IX. Biblical Antiquities, including
        1. The Political and Ecclesiastical State of the Jews and other Nations mentioned in the Scriptures — ibid.
        2. Coins, Medals, and other antient Remains — 357
        Cautions in the Investigation of Biblical Antiquities — 358—360
        3. Geography — 361
        4. Genealogy — ibid.
        5. Natural History — 361, 362
        6. Philosophical Sects and Learning — 362

§ 9. ON COMMENTARIES —
    I. Different Classes of Commentators — 362

CONTENTS.

II. Nature of Scholia
III. Of Commentators, strictly so called
IV. Paraphrases
V. Collections of Observations on Holy Writ
VI. The Utility and Advantage of Commentaries
VII. Design to be kept in View when consulting them
VIII. Rules for consulting Commentators to the best Advantage — 366—3

BOOK II

ON THE SPECIAL INTERPRETATION OF SCRIPTURE.

CHAPTER I. *On the Interpretation of the Figurative Language of Scripture* — 36

SECTION I. *General Observations on the Interpretation of Tropes and Figures* — 371—37

SECTION II. *On the Interpretation of the Metonymies occurring in the Scriptures.*

Nature of a Metonymy
I. Metonymy of the Cause — 379—3
II. Metonymy of the Effect
III. Metonymy of the Subject — 382—3
IV. Metonymy of the Adjunct, in which the Adjunct is put for the Subject — 384—9

SECTION III. *On the Interpretation of Scripture Metaphors.*

Nature of a Metaphor — Sources of Scripture Metaphors — 886, 9
I. The Works of Nature
  1. Anthropopathy
  2. Prosopopœia
II. The Occupations, Customs, and Arts of Life
III. Sacred Topics, or Religion and Things connected with it
IV. Sacred History

SECTION IV. *On the Interpretation of Scripture Allegories.*

The Allegory defined. — Different Species of Allegory
Rules for the Interpretation of Scripture Allegories — 393—89

SECTION V. *On the Interpretation of Scripture Parables.*

I. Nature of a Parable
II. Antiquity of this Mode of Instruction
III. Rules for the Interpretation of Parables — 400—40
IV. Parables, why used by Jesus Christ — 406, 40
V. Remarks on the distinguishing Excellencies of Christ's Parables, compared with the most celebrated Fables of Antiquity — 407—41

SECTION VI. *On Scripture Proverbs.*

I. Nature of Proverbs. — Prevalence of this Mode of Instruction
II. Different Kinds of Proverbs
III. The Proverbs occurring in the New Testament, how to be interpreted — ibid

SECTION VII. *Concluding Observations on the Figurative Language of Scripture.*

I. Synechdoche
II. Irony
III. Hyperbole
IV. Paronomasia

CONTENTS.

Page

CHAPTER II. *On the Interpretation of the Poetical Parts of Scripture.*

 I. A large Portion of the Old Testament proved to be Poetical. — Cultivation of Poetry by the Hebrews - - - 419—421
 II. The Sententious Parallelism, the Grand Characteristic of Hebrew Poetry — Its Origin and Varieties - - 421—424
  1. Parallel Lines gradational - - - 424—426
  2. Parallel Lines antithetic - - - 426
  3. Parallel Lines constructive - - - 427—429
  4. Parallel Lines introverted - - - 429, 430
 III. The Poetical Dialect not confined to the Old Testament. — Reasons for expecting to find it in the New Testament - 430, 431
  Proofs of the Existence of the Poetical Dialect there —
  1. From simple and direct Quotations of single Passages from the Poetical Parts of the Old Testament - 432
  2. From Quotations of different Passages, combined into one connected whole - - - 432, 433
  3. From Quotations mingled with Original matter - 433, 434
 IV. Original Parallelisms occurring in the New Testament. —
  1. Parallel Couplets - - - 435
  2. Parallel Triplets - - - 435
  3. Quatrains - - - 436
  4, 5. Stanzas of Five and Six Lines - 436, 437
  6. Stanzas of more than Six Parallel Lines - 438
 V. Other Examples of the Poetical Parallelism in the New Testament —
  1. Parallel Lines gradational - - - 439
  2. The Epanodos - - - 440
 VI. Different kinds of Hebrew Poetry. —
  1. Prophetic Poetry - - - 441, 442
  2. Elegiac Poetry - - - 443
  3. Didactic Poetry - - - 443
  4. Lyric Poetry - - - 443
  5. The Idyl - - - 443
  6. Dramatic Poetry - - - 443
  7. Acrostic or Alphabetical Poetry - - - 444
 VII. General Observations for better understanding the Poetical Compositions of the Sacred Poets - - - 445, 446

CHAPTER III. *On the Spiritual Interpretation of the Scriptures.*

SECTION I. *General Observations on the Spiritual Interpretation of the Scriptures* - - - 446—449
SECTION II. *Canons for the Spiritual Interpretation of Scripture.*
SECTION III. *On the Interpretation of Types.* 449—454
 I. Nature of a Type - - - 455
 II. Different Species of Types —
  1. Legal Types - - - 456
  2. Prophetical Types - - - 457
  3. Historical Types - - - 457
 III. Rules for the Interpretation of Types - 458—460
 IV. Remarks on the Interpretation of Symbols - 460—462

CHAPTER IV. *On the Interpretation of the Scripture Prophecies.*

SECTION I. *General Rules for ascertaining the Sense of the Prophetic Writings* - - - 462—468
SECTION II. *Observations on the Accomplishment of Prophecy in general* - - - 468—472
SECTION III. *Observations on the Accomplishment of Prophecies concerning the Messiah in particular* - 473—475

CHAPTER V. *On the Doctrinal Interpretation of Scripture* 475—482

CONTENTS. xi
Page

CHAPTER VI. *Moral Interpretation of Scripture.*

SECTION I. *On the Interpretation of the Moral Parts of Scripture* - 482—488
SECTION II. *On the Interpretation of the Promises and Threatenings of Scripture* - 489—492

CHAPTER VII. *On the Interpretation, and Means of Harmonising Passages of Scripture, which are alleged to be contradictory.*

SECTION I. *Seeming Contradictions in Historical Passages.*
§ 1. Seeming Contradictions in the different Circumstances related - 495—502
§ 2. Apparent Contradictions from Things being related in a different Order by the Sacred Writers - 502—504
§ 3. Apparent Contradictions, arising from Differences in Numbers - 504—506
§ 4. Apparent Contradictions in the relation of Events in one Passage, and References to them in another - 507

SECTION II. *Apparent Contradictions in Chronology* - 507—511
SECTION III. *Apparent Contradictions between Prophecies and their Fulfilment* - 512—514
SECTION IV. *Apparent Contradictions in Doctrine.*
§ 1. Seeming Contradictions from a Mode of speaking, which, to our Apprehensions, is not sufficiently clear - 514—516
§ 2. Apparent Contradictions from the same Terms being used in different and even Contradictory Senses - 516, 517
§ 3. Apparent Contradictions, in Points of Doctrine, arising from the different Designs of the Sacred Writers - 517, 518
§ 4. Apparent Contradictions, arising from the different Ages in which the Sacred Writers lived, and the different Degrees of Knowledge which they possessed - 518, 519

SECTION V. *Seeming Contradictions to Morality* - 519—534
SECTION VI. *Apparent Contradictions between the Sacred Writers* 535—547
SECTION VII. *Seeming Inconsistencies between Sacred and Profane Writers* - 547—553
SECTION VIII. *Alleged Contradictions to Philosophy and the Nature of Things* - 553—560

CHAPTER VIII. *On the Inferential and Practical Reading of Scripture.*

SECTION I. *On the Inferential Reading of the Bible*
I. General Rules for the Deduction of Inferences - 561—564
II. Observations for ascertaining the Sources of Internal Inferences - 564, 565
III. Observations for ascertaining the Sources of External Inferences - 566—568

SECTION II. *On the Practical Reading of Scripture* - 568—574

BIBLIOGRAPHICAL APPENDIX, *containing a Concise Account of the Principal Editions of the Holy Scriptures, and of the Principal Philologers, Critics, and Commentators, who have elucidated the Text, History, and Antiquities of the Bible* 1—322
BIBLIOGRAPHICAL INDEX - 323—349

Lately published by the Author of this Work,

I. A COMPENDIOUS INTRODUCTION TO THE STUDY OF THE BIBLE, being an ANALYSIS OR Abridgement of the present Work. In one large volume 12mo, handsomely printed, and illustrated with Maps and other Engravings. Price 9s.

"We have no hesitation in affirming, that it is in reality — what its title imports — a Compendious Introduction to the Study of the Bible. It combines a multiplicity of subjects, yet methodically arranged; it is brief, yet comprehensive, touching upon most of the questions on which the less informed can desire instruction, and the whole is executed in a style simple, perspicuous, and unaffected. We therefore most earnestly recommend it to the youth of both sexes, also to those who have not the time nor means for consulting Mr Horne's larger Treatise, to those who are commencing their biblical studies, to all, in short, who wish to read the Bible with seriousness and attention, as at once the shortest and most complete Manual in the English Language."—CHRISTIAN REMEMBRANCER, *February,* 1827.

"Of the 'Compendious Introduction' before us, as might have been expected, it may be affirmed, with truth, that it preserves all that is most valuable in Mr Horne's more elaborate and voluminous Work, while at the same time it can never supplant its distinguished predecessor as a Book of Reference. The Compendious Introduction is the cheapest work in the language on the subject of Biblical Criticism."—EVANGELICAL MAGAZINE, *February,* 1827.

"It is quite an acquisition, as an analysis of his large Work, and as bringing many of its important points before us. It would form an admirable text-book to any theological professor, and the general scholar will find it to his advantage to consult it, if he has not time to go into the multifarious details of the Critical Introduction. It is beautifully printed, contains a large quantity of matter, and the maps and other illustrative engravings and vignettes are admirably executed."—CONGREGATIONAL MAGAZINE, *March,* 1827.

"To those who cannot afford to purchase Mr Horne's larger Work, and even to those who possess it, this volume will be found exceedingly valuable, as an epitome of information, selected with immense labour from a large number of resources."—HOME MISSIONARY MAGAZINE, *February,* 1827.

"We can cordially recommend it as a valuable compendium of information connected with the interpretation of Scripture."—WESLEYAN METHODIST MAGAZINE, *March,* 1827.

"The contents of a library, condensed into a single volume."—GENTLEMAN'S MAGAZINE, *April,* 1827.

"Ce livre est l'analyse d'un ouvrage en quatre volumes du même auteur, intitulé ' Introduction à l'Étude Critique et à la Science des Saintes Ecritures.' Il est écrit avec clarté et précision, et il peut éviter de longues et fastidieuses recherches. Ceux qui désirent connaître la vérité touchant la Religion Révélée pourront le consulter avec fruit, les preuves de la Religion Chrétienne s'y trouvent placées dans un meilleur ordre que dans beaucoup d'ouvrages du même genre, et sont accompagnées de documens et réflexions, que l'on ne trouve point ailleurs. Ce volume contient un Appendice et une Table des Matières qui en rendent la lecture plus facile."—REVUE ENCYCLOPÉDIQUE, *Juin,* 1827, p 670.

II. DEISM REFUTED, OR PLAIN REASONS FOR BEING A CHRISTIAN. Seventh Edition, corrected and enlarged; handsomely printed in 12mo. Price 5s.

"We recommend this Work, as an excellent manual for youth, and as a very suitable present to persons, who may, under any circumstances, be placed in contact with the opposers of revealed religion. It is especially deserving of notice, as refuting the very latest objections which have been devised."—CHRISTIAN GUARDIAN, *April,* 1826.

III. THE SCRIPTURE DOCTRINE OF THE TRINITY briefly stated and defended: and the Church of England vindicated from the Charge of Unchauntableness in retaining the Athanasian Creed. Second Edition, in one volume large 12mo. Price 5s.

"Mr Horne's treatise is excellently adapted for conveying information to the young, for establishing them in the first great principles of their Christian faith, and for satisfying the laudable curiosity of all who desire to know the scriptural grounds of their profession, and to give an answer and a defence to such as ask a reason of the hope that is in them."—CHRISTIAN REMEMBRANCER, or Churchman's Biblical, Ecclesiastical, and Literary Miscellany, *October,* 1820.

IV. ROMANISM CONTRADICTORY TO SCRIPTURE; or, the Peculiar Tenets of the Church of Rome as exhibited in her accredited Formularies, contrasted with the Holy Scriptures. A New Edition, 12mo. Price 1s.

"Mr Hartwell Horne has compressed a large portion of valuable information into a very narrow compass."—BRITISH CRITIC and Theol Rev *July,* 1827.

"Mr H might, in imitation of Leslie, have called this little publication 'A Short Method with the Catholics.' His method is, in each section, to show in Scripture language what are the tenets of Scripture, and then contrast them with the tenets of Popery — and a thorough contrast they are. His arguments are founded on facts against which there can be no appeal."—HOME MISSIONARY MAGAZINE, *March,* 1827.

*** TEN THOUSAND COPIES of this little Manual have been distributed in Ireland, at a very low price, at the expense of some gentlemen who take an interest in the moral and religious welfare of that country.

London Printed for T Cadell, Strand, W. Blackwood, Edinburgh, and R. Milliken, Dublin

INTRODUCTION

TO THE

CRITICAL STUDY AND KNOWLEDGE

OF

THE HOLY SCRIPTURES.

ON THE CRITICISM AND INTERPRETATION OF THE SCRIPTURES.

CRITICISM, in the more extensive sense of the term, is the art of forming a correct judgment concerning any object proposed to our consideration. In a more restricted sense, particularly with reference to the works of antient authors, it was fashionable, for a considerable time, among the literati on the continent of Europe, to employ this term as indicating merely that kind of labour and judgment, which was employed in settling the genuineness of the whole or part of the text of any author. But the term is now generally used in a much more enlarged sense, viz. to indicate any kind of labour or judgment, which is occupied either in the literary history of the text itself, or in settling or explaining it. To the former the German philosophers have given the appellation of *lower criticism;* while the latter has been termed *higher criticism*, because its objects and results are of a much more important nature.[1] In this latter sense, the term is taken in the present volume, which is devoted to the consideration of the Criticism and Interpretation of the Holy Scriptures.

The FIRST PART, which treats on Scripture Criticism, will be found to comprise a concise account of the languages in which the Sacred Volume is written; a sketch of its literary history, and of the several divisions and subdivisions of it, which have obtained at different times. The nature of various readings, and the means of determining genuine readings, will next be considered, together with the quotations from the Old Testament in the New, and the nature and different kinds of Harmonies of the Old and New Testament.

In the SECOND PART the principles and subsidiary means of Scripture Interpretation are discussed, together with the application of them to the exposition of the Sacred Volume, both exegetical and practical.

---

[1] Mantiughe, Brevis Expositio Critices Vet. Fœd. pp. 1, 2. Jahn's Dissertations, by Prof. Stuart, pp. 64, 65. Clarici Ars Critica, pp. 1, 2.

PART I.

ON SCRIPTURE CRITICISM.

CHAPTER I.

ON THE LANGUAGES IN WHICH THE OLD AND NEW TESTAMENTS ARE WRITTEN.

A KNOWLEDGE of the original languages of Scripture is of the utmost importance, and indeed absolutely necessary, to him who is desirous of ascertaining the genuine meaning of the Sacred Volume. Happily, the means of acquiring these languages are now so numerous and easy of access, that the student, who wishes to derive his knowledge of the Oracles of God from pure sources, can be at no loss for guides to direct him in this delightful pursuit.

SECTION I.

ON THE HEBREW LANGUAGE.

Introductory Remarks on the Oriental or Shemitish Languages. — I. *Origin of the Hebrew Language.* — II. *Historical Sketch of this Language.* — III. *And of its Characters.* — IV. *Of the Vowel Points.*

"THE languages of Western Asia, though differing in respect to dialect, are *radically* the same, and have been so, as far back as any historical records enable us to trace them. Palestine, Syria, Phœnicia, Mesopotamia, Babylonia, Arabia, and also Ethiopia are reckoned as the countries, where the languages commonly denominated *Oriental* have been spoken. Of late, many critics have rejected the appellation '*Oriental*,' as being too comprehensive, and substituted that of '*Shemitish*,' a denominative derived from *Shem*. To this, however, objections of a similar nature may be urged; for no inconsiderable portion of those, who spoke the languages in question, were not descendants of Shem. It is matter of indifference which appellation is used, if it be first defined.

The Oriental Languages may be divided into three principal dialects, viz. the Aramæan, the Hebrew, and the Arabic.

1. The Aramæan, spoken in Syria, Mesopotamia, and Babylonia or Chaldæa, is subdivided into the Syriac and Chaldee dialects; or, as they are sometimes called, the East and West Aramæan.

2. The Hebrew or Canaanitish (Isa. xix. 18.) was spoken in Palestine, and probably with little variation in Phœnicia, and the Phœnician colonies, as at Carthage and other places.

3 The Arabic, to which the Ethiopic bears a special resemblan has, in modern times, a great variety of dialects, as a spoken l guage, and is spread over a vast extent of country. But, so far we are acquainted with its former state, it appears more antiently have been principally limited to Arabia and Ethiopia.

The Arabic is very rich in forms and words; the Syriac, so as it is yet known, is comparatively limited in both; the Hebr holds a middle place between them, both as to copiousness of wor and variety of forms." [1]

Besides the preceding dialects, there are many slighter variatic of language, sometimes distinguished from the general names local appellations. Thus, the Ephraimites could not distingu between the letters ס (s) and שׁ (sh), as the Hebrews did, in spea ing: hence the Ephraimites pronounced S*ib*boleth instead of S*h*. boleth. (Judges xii. 6.) Nehemiah was indignant, that part his countrymen should speak the language of Ashdod. (Neh. x 23—25.)

The Samaritan dialect appears to be composed (as one mig expect, see 2 Kings xvii.) of Aramæan and Hebrew. and t slighter varieties of Arabic are as numerous as the provinces whe the language is spoken.

I. ORIGIN OF THE HEBREW LANGUAGE.

Of all the Oriental Languages, the HEBREW bears marks of bei the most antient: in this language the Old Testament is writte with the exception of a few words and passages that are in t Chaldæan dialect.[a] According to some critics, it derived its nar from Heber, one of the descendants of Shem (Gen. x. 21. 25. 14. 16, 17.): but other learned men are of opinion that it is d rived from the root עָבַר (ABER), *to pass over*, whence Abraham w denominated the *Hebrew* (Gen. xiv. 13.), having *passed over* t river Euphrates to come into the land of Canaan. This last o nion appears to be best founded, from the general fact that t most antient names of nations were appellative. "But, whatev extent of meaning was attached to the appellation *Hebrew*, befc the time of Jacob, it appears afterwards to have been limited or to his posterity, and to be synonymous with *Israelite*.

The origin of the Hebrew Language must be dated farther ba than the period, to which we can trace the appellation *Hebrew*. is plain, from the names of persons and places in Canaan, th wherever Abraham sojourned, he found a language in which could easily converse, viz. the Hebrew or Phœnician language That this was originally the language of Palestine, appears plain fro the names of nations being appellative, and from other facts in respe to the formation of this dialect. Thus, the *West* is, in Hebrew ב (YMM), which means the *sea*, that is, towards the Mediterranean S As the Hebrew has no other proper word for *west*, so it must

---

[1] Stuart's Hebrew Grammar, pp 1, 2.

[a] Besides some Chaldee words occasionally inserted in the historical and prophet books, after the Israelites became acquainted with the Babylonians, the following passa of the Old Testament are written in the Chaldee dialect, viz. Jer. x. 11. Dan. ii. 4 the end of chap vii. and Ezra iv. 8. to vi. 19. and vii. 12. to 17.

evident that the language, in its distinctive and peculiar forms, must have been formed in Palestine.[1]

The Jewish Rabbins, Jonathan the author of the Chaldee Paraphrase, Solomon Jarchi, and Aben-Ezra, have affirmed that Hebrew was the primitive language spoken in Paradise; and their opinion has been adopted by Origen, Jerome, Augustine, and some other fathers, as well as by some modern critics and philologers. Huet, however, and the majority of modern critics, are of opinion, that the language spoken by Adam perished in the confusion of tongues at Babel. But it seems highly probable, that if the original parents of mankind were placed in Western Asia, they spoke substantially the language which has for more than fifty centuries pervaded that country.[2] Without adopting, therefore, the hypothesis just stated, which rests only on bare probabilities, we may observe that the Hebrew is the most antient of all the languages in the world, at least we know of none that is older: that it is not improbable that it was the general language of men at the dispersion; and, however it might have subsequently been altered and improved, that it appears to be the original of all the languages, or rather dialects, which have since arisen in the world.[3]

Various circumstances, indeed, combine to prove that Hebrew is the original language, neither improved nor debased by foreign idioms. The words of which it is composed are very short, and admit of very little flexion, as may be seen on reference to any Hebrew grammar or lexicon. The names of persons and places are descriptive of their nature, situation, accidental circumstances, &c. The names of brutes express their nature and properties more significantly and more accurately than any other known language in the world. The names also of various antient nations are of Hebrew origin, being derived from the sons or grandsons of Shem, Ham, and Japhet; as the Assyrians from Ashur; the Elamites from Elam; the Aramæans from Aram; the Lydians from Lud; the Cimbrians or Cimmerians from Gomer; the Medians from Madai, the son of Japhet, the Ionians from Javan, &c.[4] Further, the names given to the heathen deities suggest an additional proof of the antiquity and originality of the Hebrew language; thus, Japetus is derived from Japhet; Jove, from JEHOVAH; Vulcan, from Tubal-Cain, who first discovered the use of iron and brass, &c. &c. Lastly, the traces of Hebrew which are to be found in very many other languages, and which have been noticed by several learned men, afford another argument in favour of its antiquity and priority. These vestiges are particularly conspicuous in the Chaldee, Syriac, Arabic, Persian, Phœnician, and other languages spoken by the people who dwelt nearest to Babylon, where the first division of languages took place.[5]

---

[1] Stuart's Heb. Gram. p. 5.
[2] Huet, Demonstr. Evang. Prop IV. c. 13. Alber, Hermeneut. Vet. Test. tom. i. p. 321. Stuart's Heb Gram, p 6
[3] Dr. Gr. Sharpe's Dissertations on the Origin of Languages, &c. pp. 22, et seq.
[4] Grotius de Veritate, lib. i. sect. 16. Walton's Prolegomena to the London Polyglott, prol. iii. § 6, (p. 76. ed. Dathii.) [5] Walton, Prol. iii. § 7, 8. (pp. 76, 77.)

On the Hebrew Language.

The knowledge of the Hebrew language was diffused very wi[de] by the Phœnician merchants, who had factories and colonie[s] almost every coast of Europe and Asia; that it was identically [the] same as was spoken in Canaan, or Phœnicia, is evident from being used by the inhabitants of that country from the tim[e of] Abraham to that of Joshua, who gave to places mentioned in the [Old] Testament, appellations which are pure Hebrew; such are, Kir[jath-]sepher, or the *city of books*, and Kiriath-sannah, or the *city of le[arn]ing*. (Josh. xv. 15. 49.) Another proof of the identity of the [two] languages arises from the circumstance of the Hebrews conver[sing] with the Canaanites without an interpreter; as the spies sent [by] Joshua with Rahab (Josh. ii.); the ambassadors sent by the Gibe[on]ites to Joshua (Josh. ix. 3—25.), &c. But a still stronger proo[f of] the identity of the two languages is to be found in the fragment[s of] the Punic tongue which occur in the writings of antient auth[ors.] That the Carthaginians (Pœni) derived their name, origin, [and] language from the Phœnicians, is a well-known and authentic [ated] fact; and that the latter sprang from the Canaanites might easil[y be] shown from the situation of their country, as well as from t[heir] manners, customs, and ordinances. Not to cite the testimonie[s of] profane authors on this point, which have been accumulated [by] Bishop Walton, we have sufficient evidence to prove that they [were] considered as the same people, in the fact of the Phœnicians [and] Canaanites being used promiscuously to denote the inhabitant[s of] the same country. Compare Exod. vi. 15. with Gen. xlvi. 10. [and] Exod. xvi. 33. with Josh. v. 12., in which passages, for the Heb[rew] words translated *Canaanitish* and *land of Canaan*, the Septua[gint] reads Phœnician and the country of Phœnicia.

II. HISTORICAL SKETCH OF THE HEBREW LANGUAGE.

The period from the age of Moses to that of David has [been] considered the *golden* age of the Hebrew language, which decl[ined] in purity from that time to the reign of Hezekiah or Manasseh, [hav]ing received several foreign words from the commercial and poli[tical] intercourse of the Jews and Israelites with the Assyrians and B[aby]lonians. This period has been termed the *silver* age of the Heb[rew] language. In the interval between the reign of Hezekiah and [the] Babylonish captivity, the purity of the language was neglected, [and] so many foreign words were introduced into it, that this period [has] not inaptly been designated its *iron* age. During the seventy y[ears'] captivity, though it does not appear that the Hebrews *entirely* [lost] their native tongue, yet it underwent so considerable a change [from] their adoption of the vernacular languages of the countries w[here] they had resided, that afterwards, on their return from exile, [they] spoke a dialect of Chaldee mixed with Hebrew words. On [this] account, it was, that, when the Hebrew Scriptures were read [it] was found necessary to interpret them to the people in the Chald[ee] language; as, when Ezra the scribe brought the book of the la[w of] Moses before the congregation, the Levites are said to have ca[used] the people to understand the law, because *they read in the book [of] the law of God, distinctly,* AND GAVE THE SENSE, AND CAUSED T[HEM]

TO UNDERSTAND THE READING (Neh. viii. 8.[1]). Some time after the return from the great captivity, Hebrew ceased to be spoken altogether: though it continued to be cultivated and studied, by the priests and Levites, as a learned language, that they might be enabled to expound the law and the prophets to the people, who, it appears from the New Testament, were well acquainted with their general contents and tenor; this last-mentioned period has been called the *leaden* age of the language.[2] "How long the Hebrew was retained, both in writing and conversation; or in writing, after it ceased to be the language of conversation, it is impossible to determine. The coins, stamped in the time of the Maccabees, are all the oriental monuments we have, of the period that elapsed between the latest canonical writers, and the advent of Christ; and the inscriptions on these are in Hebrew. At the time of the Maccabees, then, Hebrew was probably understood, at least, as the language of books; perhaps, in some measure, also, among the better informed, as the language of conversation. But soon after this, the dominion of the Seleucidæ, in Syria, over the Jewish nation, uniting with the former influence of the Babylonish captivity, in promoting the Aramaean dialect, appears to have destroyed the remains of proper Hebrew, as a living language, and to have universally substituted, in its stead, the Hebræo-Aramaean, as it was spoken, in the time of our Saviour. From the time when Hebrew ceased to be vernacular, down to the present day, a portion of this dialect has been preserved in the Old Testament. It has always been the subject of study among learned Jews. Before and at the time of Christ, there were flourishing Jewish academies at Jerusalem; especially under Hillel and Shammai. After Jerusalem was destroyed, schools were set up in various places, but particularly they flourished at Tiberias, until the death of R. Judah, surnamed *Hakkodesh* or *the Holy*, the author of the Mishna; about A. D. 230. Some of his pupils set up other schools in Babylonia, which became the rivals of these. The Babylonish academies flourished until near the tenth century."[3] From the academies at Tiberias and in Babylonia, we have received the Targums, the Talmud, the Masora (of all which an account will be found in the course of the present volume), and the written vowels and accents of the Hebrew language. The Hebrew of the Talmud and of the Rabbins has a close affinity with the later Hebrew.

III. ANTIQUITY OF THE HEBREW CHARACTERS.

The present Hebrew Characters, or Letters, are twenty-two in

---

[1] It is worthy of remark that the above practice exists at the present time, among the Karaite Jews, at Sympheropol, in Crim Tartary, where the Tartar translation is read together with the Hebrew Text (See Dr Pinkerton's Letter, in the Appendix to the Thirteenth Report of the British and Foreign Bible Society, p. 76.) A similar practice obtains among the Syrian Christians at Travancore, in the East Indies, where the Syriac is the learned language and the language of the church; while the *Malayalim* or Malabar is the vernacular language of the country. The Christian priests read the Scriptures from manuscript copies in the *former*, and expound them in the *latter* to the people. Owen's History of the British and Foreign Bible Society, vol. ii. p. 364.

[2] Walton, Prol. iii. § 15—24. (pp 84—97) Schleusner's Lexicon, voce, Ἑβραΐς. Jahn, Introd. ad Vet Fœdus, pp. 94—96. Parkhurst (Gr. Lex. voce, Ἑβραΐς) has endeavoured to show, but unsuccessfully, that no change from Hebrew to Chaldee ever took place.

[3] Stuart's Heb. Gram. p. 12.

number, and of a square form: but the antiquity of these letters is a point that has been most severely contested by many learned men. From a passage in Eusebius's Chronicle[1], and another in Jerome[2], it was inferred by Joseph Scaliger, that Ezra, when he reformed the Jewish church, transcribed the antient characters of the Hebrews into the square letters of the Chaldæans: and that this was done for the use of those Jews, who, being born during the captivity, knew no other alphabet than that of the people among whom they had been educated. Consequently, the old character, which we call the Samaritan, fell into total disuse. This opinion Scaliger supported by passages from both the Talmuds, as well as from rabbinical writers, in which it is expressly affirmed that such characters were adopted by Ezra. But the most decisive confirmation of this point is to be found in the antient Hebrew coins, which were struck before the captivity, and even previously to the revolt of the ten tribes. The characters engraven on all of them are manifestly the same with the modern Samaritan, though with some trifling variations in their forms, occasioned by the depredations of time. These coins, whether shekels or half shekels, have all of them, on one side, the golden manna-pot (mentioned in Exod. xvi. 32, 33.), and on its mouth, or over the top of it, most of them have a Samaritan Aleph, some an Aleph and Schin, or other letters, with this inscription, *The Shekel of Israel*, in Samaritan characters. On the opposite side is to be seen Aaron's rod with almonds, and in the same letters this inscription, *Jerusalem the holy*. Other coins are extant with somewhat different inscriptions, but the same characters are engraven on them all.[3]

The opinion originally produced by Scaliger, and thus decisively corroborated by coins, has been adopted by Casaubon, Vossius, Grotius, Bishop Walton, Louis Cappel, Dr. Prideaux, and other eminent biblical critics and philologers, and is now generally received: it was, however, very strenuously though unsuccessfully opposed by the younger Buxtorf, who endeavoured to prove, by a variety of passages from rabbinical writers, that *both* the square and the Samaritan characters were antiently used; the present square character being that in which the tables of the law, and the copy deposited in the ark, were written; and the other characters being employed in the copies of the law which were made for private and common use, and in civil affairs in general; and that, after the captivity, Ezra enjoined the former to be used by the Jews on all occasions, leaving the latter to the Samaritans and apostates. Independently, however, of the strong evidence against Buxtorf's hypothesis, which is afforded by the antient Hebrew coins, when we consider the implacable enmity that subsisted between the Jews and Samaritans, is it likely that the one copied from the other, or that the former preferred, to the beautiful letters used by their ancestors, the rude and inelegant characters of their most detested rivals? And when the vast difference between the Chaldee (or square) and the Samaritan letters,

---
[1] Sub anno 4740. [2] Præf. in 1 Reg.
[3] Walton, Prol. iii. §29—37. (pp. 103—125.) Carpzov, Critica Sacra, pp. 225—241. Bauer, Critica Sacra, pp. 111—127.

with respect to convenience and beauty, is calmly considered, it must be acknowledged that they never could have been used at the same time. After all, it is of no great moment which of these, or whether either of them, were the original characters, since it does not appear that any change of the words has arisen from the manner of writing them, because the Samaritan and Hebrew Pentateuchs almost always agree, notwithstanding the lapse of so many ages. It is most probable that the form of these characters has varied at different periods: this appears from the direct testimony of Montfaucon[1], and is implied in Dr. Kennicott's making the characters, in which manuscripts are written, one test of their age.[2] It is, however, certain that the Chaldee or square character was the common one: as in Matt. v 8. the yod is referred to as the smallest letter in the alphabet. It is highly probable that it was the common character, when the Septuagint version was made; because the departures in the Hebrew text from that version, so far as they have respect to the letters, can mostly be accounted for, on the ground, that the square characters were then used, and that the final letters which vary from the medial or initial form, were then wanting.[3]

IV. ANTIQUITY OF THE HEBREW VOWEL POINTS.

But however interesting these inquiries may be in a philological point of view, it is of far greater importance to be satisfied concerning the much litigated, and yet undecided, question respecting the antiquity of the Hebrew points, because, unless the student has determined for himself, after a mature investigation, he cannot with confidence apply to the study of this sacred language. Three opinions have been offered by learned men on this subject. By some, the origin of the Hebrew vowel points is maintained to be coeval with the Hebrew language itself: while others assert them to have been first introduced by Ezra after the Babylonish captivity, when he compiled the canon, transcribed the books into the present Chaldee characters, and restored the purity of the Hebrew text. A third hypothesis is, that they were invented, about five hundred years after Christ, by the doctors of the school of Tiberias, for the purpose of marking and establishing the genuine pronunciation, for the convenience of those who were learning the Hebrew tongue. This opinion, first announced by Rabbi Elias Levita in the beginning of the sixteenth century, has been adopted by Cappel, Calvin, Luther, Casaubon, Scaliger, Masclef, Erpenius, Houbigant, L'Advocat, Bishops Walton, Hare, and Lowth, Dr. Kennicott, Dr. Geddes, and other eminent critics, British and foreign, and is now generally received, although some few writers of respectability continue strenuously to advocate their antiquity. The *Arcanum Punctationis Revelatum* of Cappel was opposed by Buxtorf in a treatise *De Punctorum Vocalium Antiquitate*, by whom the controversy was almost exhausted. We shall briefly state the evidence on both sides.

---

[1] Hexapla Origenis, tom. 1 pp. 22. *et seq.*
[2] Dissertation on the Hebrew Text, vol. 1, pp. 310—314.
[3] Stuart's Hebrew Grammar, p. 16.

That the vowel points are of modern date, and of human invention, the anti-punctists argue from the following considerations:

1. "The kindred, Shemitish languages *anciently* had no written vowels. The most antient Estrangelo and Kufish characters, that is, the antient characters of the Syrians and Arabians, were destitute of vowels. The Palmyrene inscriptions, and nearly all the Phenician ones, are destitute of them. Some of the Maltese inscriptions, however, and a few of the Phenician have marks, which probably were intended as vowels. The Koran was confessedly destitute of them, at first. The punctuation of it occasioned great dispute among Mohammedans. In some of the older Syriac writings, is found a single point, which by being placed in different positions in regard to words, served as a diacritical sign. The present vowel system of the Syrians was introduced so late as the time of Theophilus and Jacob of Edessa (Cent. viii.) The Arabic vowels were adopted, soon after the Koran was written, but their other diacritical marks did not come into use, until they were introduced by Ibn Mokla, (about A.D. 900,) together with the Nishi character, now in common use."[1]

2. The Samaritan letters, which (we have already seen) were the same with the Hebrew characters before the captivity, have no points; nor are there any vestiges whatever of vowel points to be traced either in the shekels struck by the kings of Israel, or in the Samaritan Pentateuch. The words have always been read by the aid of the four letters Aleph, He, Vau, and Jod, which are called *matres lectionis*, or mothers of reading.

3. The copies of the Scriptures used in the Jewish synagogues to the present time, and which are accounted particularly sacred, are constantly written without points, or any distinctions of verses whatever: a practice that could never have been introduced, nor would it have been so religiously followed, if vowel points had been coeval with the language, or of divine authority. To this fact we may add, that in many of the oldest and best manuscripts, collated and examined by Dr. Kennicott, either there are no points at all, or they are evidently a *late* addition; and that all the antient various readings, marked by the Jews, regard only the letters, not one of them relates to the vowel points, which could not have happened if these had been in use.

4. Rabbi Elias Levita ascribes the invention of vowel points to the doctors of Tiberias, and has confirmed the fact by the authority of the most learned rabbins.

5. The antient Cabbalists[2] draw all their mysteries from the letters; but none from the vowel points, which they could not have neglected if they had been acquainted with them. And hence it is concluded, that the points were not in existence when the Cabbalistic interpretations were made.

6. Although the Talmud contains the determinations of the Jewish doctors concerning many passages of the law, it is evident that the points

---

[1] Stuart's Hebrew Grammar, p. 19.

[2] The Cabbalists were a set of rabbinical doctors among the Jews, who derived their name from their studying the *Cabbala*, a mysterious kind of science, comprising mystical interpretations of Scripture, and metaphysical speculations concerning the Deity and other beings, which are found in Jewish writings, and are said to have been handed down by a secret tradition from the earliest ages. By considering the numeral powers of the letters of the sacred text, and changing and transposing them in various ways, according to the rules of their art, the Cabbalists extracted senses from the sacred oracles, very different from those which the expressions seemed naturally to import, or which were even intended by their inspired authors. Some learned men have imagined, that the Cabbalists arose soon after the time of Ezra, but the truth is, that no Cabbalistic writings are extant but what are *posterior* to the destruction of the second temple. For an entertaining account of the Cabbala, and of the Cabbalistical philosophy, see Mr. Allen's Modern Judaism, pp. 65—94, or Dr. Enfield's History of Philosophy, vol. ii. pp. 199—221.

were not affixed to the text when the Talmud was composed; because there are several disputes concerning the sense of passages of the law, which could not have been controverted if the points had then been in existence. Besides, the vowel points are never mentioned, though the fairest opportunity for noticing them offered itself, if they had really then been in use. The compilation of the Talmud was not finished until the sixth century.[1]

7. The antient various readings, called Keri and Ketib, or Khetibh, (which were collected a short time before the completion of the Talmud,) relate entirely to consonants and not to vowel points; yet, if these had existed in manuscript at the time the Keri and Khetib were collected, it is obvious that some reference would directly or indirectly have been made to them. The silence, therefore, of the collectors of these various readings is a clear proof of the non-existence of vowel points in their time.

8. The antient versions, — for instance, the Chaldee paraphrases of Jonathan and Onkelos, and the Greek versions of Aquila, Symmachus, and Theodotion, but especially the Septuagint version,—*all* read the text, in many passages, in senses different from that which the points determine them to mean. Whence it is evident, that if the points had then been known, pointed manuscripts would have been followed as the most correct: but as the authors of those versions did not use them, it is a plain proof that the points were not then in being.

9. The antient Jewish writers themselves are totally silent concerning the vowel points, which surely would not have been the case if they had been acquainted with them. Much stress indeed has been laid upon the books of Zohar and Bahir, but these have been proved not to have been known for a thousand years after the birth of Christ. Even Buxtorf himself admits, that the book Zohar could not have been written till after the tenth century, and the rabbis Gedaliah and Zachet confess that it was not mentioned before the year 1290, and that it presents internal evidence that it is of a much later date than is pretended. It is no uncommon practice of the Jews to publish books of recent date under the names of old writers, in order to render their authority respectable, and even to alter and interpolate antient writers in order to subserve their own views.

10. Equally silent are the antient fathers of the Christian church, Origen and Jerome. In some fragments still extant, of Origen's vast biblical work, intitled the Hexapla (of which some account is given in a subsequent page), we have a specimen of the manner in which Hebrew was pronounced in the third century; and which, it appears, was widely different from that which results from adopting the Masoretic reading. Jerome also, in various parts of his works, where he notices the different pronunciations of Hebrew words, treats *only of the letters*, and nowhere mentions the points, which he surely would have done, had they been found in the copies consulted by him.

11. The letters א, ה, ו, י (Aleph, He, Vau, and Yod), upon the plan of the Masorites, are termed *quiescent*, because, according to them, they have no sound. At other times, these same letters indicate a variety of sounds, as the fancy of these critics has been pleased to distinguish them by points. This single circumstance exhibits the whole doctrine of points as the *baseless fabric of a vision*. To suppress altogether, or to render insignificant, a *radical* letter of any word, in order to supply its place by an *arbitrary dot or a fictitious mark*, is an invention fraught with the grossest absurdity.[2]

---

[1] For an account of the Talmud, see Part II Book I. Chap. II. Sect. I § 6, *infra*.
[2] Wilson's Elements of Hebrew Grammar, p. 49.

12 Lastly, as the *first* vestiges of the points that can be traced are to be found in the writings of Rabbi Ben Asher, president of the western school, and of Rabbi Ben Naphthali, chief of the eastern school, who flourished about the middle of the *tenth* century, we are justified in assigning that as the epoch when the system of vowel points was established.

Such are the evidences on which the majority of the learned rest their convictions of the modern date of the Hebrew points it now remains, that we concisely notice the arguments adduced by the Buxtorfs and their followers, for the antiquity of these points.

1. From the nature of all languages it is urged that they require vowels, which are in a manner the soul of words. This is readily conceded as an indisputable truth, but it is no proof of the antiquity of the vowel points: for the Hebrew language always had and still has vowels, independent of the points, without which it may be read. Origen, who transcribed the Hebrew Scriptures in Greek characters in his Hexapla, did not invent new vowels to express the vowels absent in Hebrew words, neither did Jerome, who also expressed many Hebrew words and passages in Latin characters. The Samaritans, who used the same alphabet as the Hebrews, read without the vowel points, employing the *matres lectionis*, Aleph, He or Hheth, Jod, Om, and Vau (a, e, i, o, u), for vowels; and the Hebrew may be read in the same manner, with the assistance of these letters, by supplying them where they are not expressed, agreeably to the modern practice of the Jews, whose Talmud and rabbinical commentators, as well as the copies of the law preserved in the synagogues, are to this day read without vowel points.

2. It is objected that the reading of Hebrew would be rendered very uncertain and difficult without the points, after the language ceased to be spoken. To this it is replied, that even after Hebrew ceased to be a vernacular language, its true reading might have been continued among learned men to whom it was familiar, and also in their schools, which flourished before the invention of the points. And thus daily practice in reading, as well as a consideration of the context, would enable them not only to fix the meaning of doubtful words, but also to supply the vowels which were deficient, and likewise to fix words to one determinate reading. Cappel[1], and after him Muscleff[2], have given some general rules for the application of the *matres lectionis*, to enable us to read Hebrew without points.

3. "Many Protestant writers have been led to support the authority of the points, by the supposed uncertainty of the unpointed text, which would oblige us to follow the direction of the church of Rome. This argument, however, makes against those who would suppose Ezra to have introduced the points: for in that case, from Moses to *his* day the text being unpointed must have been obscure and uncertain; and if this were not so, why should not the unpointed text have remained intelligible and unambiguous *after* his time, as it had done before it? This argument, moreover, grants what they who use it are not aware of: for if it be allowed that the unpointed text is ambiguous and uncertain, and would oblige us in consequence to recur to the church of Rome, the Roman Catholics may prove — at least with every appearance of truth — that it has always been unpointed, and that, therefore, we must have recourse to the church to explain it. Many writers of that communion have had the candour to acknowledge, that the unpointed Hebrew text can be read and understood like the Samaritan text; for although several words in Hebrew may, when

---

[1] Arcanum Punctationis revelatum, lib. 1. c. 18
[2] Grammatica Hebraica, vol. i. cap 1. § iv.

separate, admit of different interpretations, the context usually fixes their meaning with precision [1]; or, if it ever fail to do so, and leave their meaning still ambiguous, recourse may be had to the interpretations of antient translators or commentators. We must likewise remember, that the Masorites, in affixing points to the text, did not do so according to their own notions how it ought to be read; they followed the received reading of their day, and thus fixed unalterably that mode of reading which was authorised among them. and, therefore, though we reject these points as their invention, and consider that they never were used by any inspired writer, yet it by no means follows, that for the interpretation of Scripture we must go to a supposed infallible church; for we acknowledge the divine original of what the points express, namely, the sentiments conveyed by the letters and words of the sacred text." [2]

4. In further proof of the supposed antiquity of vowel points, some passages have been adduced from the Talmud, in which *accents* and *verses* are mentioned. The fact is admitted, but it is no proof of the existence of points; neither is mention of certain words in the Masoretic notes, as being irregularly punctuated, any evidence of their existence or antiquity: for the Masora was not finished by one author, nor in one century, but that system of annotation was commenced and prosecuted by various Hebrew critics through several ages. Hence it happened that the latter Masorites, having detected mistakes in their predecessors (who had adopted the mode of pronouncing and reading used in their day), were unwilling to alter such mistakes, but contented themselves with noting particular words as having been irregularly and improperly pointed. These notes, therefore, furnish no evidence of the existence of points before the time of the first compilers of the Masora [3]

The preceding are the chief arguments usually urged for and against the vowel points: and from an impartial consideration of them, the reader will be enabled to judge for himself. The weight of evidence, we apprehend, will be found to determine *against* them: nevertheless, " the points *seem* to have their uses, and these not inconsiderable; and to have this use among others — that, as many of the Hebrew letters have been corrupted since the invention of the points, and as the points subjoined originally to the true letters have been in many of these places regularly preserved, these points will frequently concur in proving the truth of such corruptions, and will point out the method of correcting them." [4]

A Bibliographical Account of the principal editions of the Hebrew Bible will be found in the Appendix to this volume, pp. 4 — 10., and of the principal Hebrew Grammars and Lexicons, both *with* and *without* points, in pp. 158—167.

---

[1] Thus the English verb *to skin* has two opposite meanings; but the context will always determine which it bears in any passage where it occurs.
[2] Hamilton's Introd. to the Study of the Hebrew Scriptures, pp 44, 45.
[3] Walton Prol. iii. §§ 38—56. (pp. 125—170.) Carpzov, Crit. Sacr. Vet. Test. part 1. c. v sect. vii pp. 242—274. Pfeiffer, Critica Sacra, cap iv. sect. ii. (Op. pp. 704—711.) Gerard's Institutes, pp 32—38. Jahn, Introd. ad Vet. Fœdus, pp. 129—131. Bauer, Critica Sacra, pp. 128—141. Prideaux's Connection, vol 1, part i. book 5. pp. 347— 361. 8th edition. Bishop Marsh (Lectures, part ii. pp. 136—140) has enumerated the principal treatises for and against the vowel points, some of which are also specified in pp. 157, 158. of the Appendix to this volume.
[4] Dr. Kennicott, Dissertation i. on Hebrew Text, p. 345.

SECTION II.

ON THE GREEK LANGUAGE.

I. *Similarity of the Greek Language of the New Testament with that of the Alexandrian or Septuagint Greek Version* — II. *The New Testament why written in Greek.* — III. *Examination of its Style.* — IV. *Its Dialects — Hebraisms — Rabbinisms — Aramæisms — Latinisms — Persisms and Cilicisms.*

I. SIMILARITY OF THE GREEK LANGUAGE OF THE NEW TESTAMENT WITH THAT OF THE ALEXANDRIAN OR SEPTUAGINT GREEK VERSION.

If a knowledge of Hebrew be necessary and desirable, in order to understand the Old Testament aright, an acquaintance with the Greek language is of equal importance for understanding the New Testament correctly. It is in this language that the Septuagint version of the Old Testament was executed: and as the inspired writers of the New Testament thought and spoke in the Chaldee or Syriac tongues, whose turns of expression closely corresponded with those of the antient Hebrew, the language of the apostles and evangelists, when they wrote in Greek, necessarily resembled that of the translators of the Septuagint. And as every Jew, who read Greek at all, would read the Greek Bible, the style of the Septuagint again operated in forming the style of the Greek Testament.[1] The Septuagint version, therefore, being a new source of interpretation equally important to the Old and New Testament, a knowledge of the Greek language becomes indispensably necessary to the biblical student.

II. A variety of solutions has been given to the question, WHY THE NEW TESTAMENT WAS WRITTEN IN GREEK.

The true reason is simply this, — that it was the language best understood both by writers and readers, being spoken and written, read and understood, throughout the Roman empire, and particularly in the eastern provinces. In fact, Greek was at that time as well known in the higher and middle circles as the French is in our day. To the universality of the Greek language, Cicero[2], Seneca[3], and Juvenal[4] bear ample testimony: and the circumstances of the Jews having had both political, civil, and commercial relations with the Greeks, and being dispersed through various parts of the Roman empire, as well as their having cultivated the philosophy of the

---

[1] Bishop Marsh's Lectures, part iii. pp. 30, 31. The question relative to the supposed Hebrew originals of Saint Matthew's Gospel, and of the Epistle to the Hebrews, is purposely omitted in this place, as it is considered in the subsequent part of this work.

[2] Orat. pro Archia Poeta, c. 10. *Græca leguntur in omnibus fere gentibus, Latina suis finibus, exiguis sane, continentur.* Julius Cæsar attests the prevalence of the Greek language in Gaul. De Bell Gall lib i. c. 29. lib vi. c. 14 (vol. i. pp. 23. 161 edit. Bipont.)

[3] In consolat. ad Helviam, c 6. *Quid sibi volunt in mediis barbarorum regionibus Græcæ urbes ? Quid inter Indos Persasque Macedonicus sermo ? Scythia et totus ille ferarum indomitarumque gentium tractus civitates Achaiæ, Ponticis impositas litoribus, ostentat*

[4] *Nunc totus Graias nostrasque habet orbis Athenas.* Sat xv. v 110 Even the female sex, it appears from the same satirist, made use of Greek as the language of familiarity and passion. See Sat. vi. v. 185—191.

Greeks, of which we have evidence in the New Testament, all sufficiently account for their being acquainted with the Greek language: to which we may add the fact, that the Septuagint Greek version of the Old Testament had been in use among the Jews upwards of two hundred and eighty years before the Christian æra: which most assuredly would not have been the case if the language had not been familiar to them. And if the eminent Jewish writers, Philo and Josephus, had motives for preferring to write in Greek (and the very fact of their writing in Greek proves that that language was vernacular to their countrymen), there is no reason — at least there is no general presumption — why the first publishers of the Gospel might not use the Greek language.[1] But we need not rest on probabilities. For,

1. It is manifest from various passages in the first book of Maccabees, that the Jews of all classes must at that time (B. C. 175—140) have understood the language of their conquerors and oppressors, the Macedonian Greeks under Antiochus, falsely named the Great, and his successors.

2. Further, when the Macedonians obtained the dominion of western Asia, they filled that country with Greek cities. The Greeks also possessed themselves of many cities in Palestine, to which the Herods added many others, which were also inhabited by Greeks. Herod the Great, in particular, made continual efforts to give a foreign physiognomy to Judæa; which country, during the personal ministry of Jesus Christ, was thus invaded on every side by a Greek population. The following particulars will confirm and illustrate this fact.

Aristobulus and Alexander built or restored many cities, which were almost entirely occupied by Greeks, or by Syrians who spoke their language. Some of the cities, indeed, which were rebuilt by the Asmonæan kings, or by the command of Pompey, were on the frontiers of Palestine, but a great number of them were in the interior of that country: and concerning these cities we have historical data which demonstrate that they were nearly, if not altogether, Greek. Thus, at Dora, a city of Galilee, the inhabitants refused to the Jews the right of citizenship which had been granted to them by Claudius.[2] Josephus expressly says that Gadara and Hippos *are Greek cities*, ἑλληνίδες εἰσι πολεις.[3] In the very centre of Palestine stood Bethshan, which place its Greek inhabitants called *Scythopolis*.[4] Josephus[5] testifies that Gaza, in the southern part of Judæa, was Greek: and Joppa, the importance of whose harbour induced the kings of Egypt and Syria successively to take it from the Jews[6],

---

[1] Josephus, de Bell. Jud. Proem § 2 says, that he composed his history of the Jewish war in the language of his country, and afterwards wrote it in Greek for the information of the Greeks and Romans The reader will find a great number of additional testimonies to the prevalence of the Greek language in the east, in Antonii Josephi Binterim Epistola Catholica Interlinealis de Lingua Originali Novi Testamenti non Latinâ, &c. pp 171—198. Dusseldorpii, 1820 It is necessary to apprise the reader, that the design of this volume is to support the absurd popish dogma, that the reading of the Holy Scriptures, in the vulgar tongue, ought not to be promiscuously allowed.
[2] Josephus, Ant. Jud. lib xix c. 6 § 5. [3] Ant. Jud. lib. xvi. c 11. § 4.
[4] Σκυθῶν Πολις, Judges i 27 (Septuagint Version.) Polybius, lib. v. c. 70. § 4.
[5] Josephus, Ant Jud. lib. xvii c 11 § 4.
[6] Diod. Sic. lib. xix. c 59. 93 1 Macc x. 75, xii. 33, 34. xiii. 11. xiv. 34. 2 Macc. xiii. 3. Josephus, Ant. Jud. lib. xiii. c. 9. § 2, and lib. xiv. c. 10. § 22.

most certainly could not remain a stranger to the same influence. Under the reign of Herod the Great, Palestine became still more decidedly Greek. That prince and his sons erected several cities in honour of the Cæsars. The most remarkable of all these, Cæsarea, (which was the second city in his kingdom,) was chiefly peopled by Greeks [1]; who after Herod's death, under the protection of Nero, expelled the Jews who dwelt there with them [2] The Jews revenged the affront, which they had received at Cæsarea, on Gadara, Hippos, Scythopolis, Askalon, and Gaza, — a further proof that the Greeks inhabited those cities jointly with the Jews.[3] After the death of Pompey, the Greeks being liberated from all the restraints which had been imposed on them, made great progress in Palestine under the protection of Herod; who by no means concealed his partiality for them [4], and lavished immense sums of money for the express purpose of naturalising their language and manners among the Jews. With this view he built a theatre and amphitheatre at Cæsarea [5]; at Jericho an amphitheatre, and a stadium [6]; he erected similar edifices at the very gates of the holy city, Jerusalem, and he even proceeded to build a theatre within its walls.[7]

3. The Roman government was rather favourable than adverse to the extension of the Greek language in Palestine, in consequence of Greek being the official language of the procurators of that country, when administering justice, and speaking to the people.

Under the earlier emperors, the Romans were accustomed frequently to make use of Greek, even at Rome, when the affairs of the provinces were under consideration.[8] If Greek were thus used at Rome, we may reasonably conclude that it would be still more frequently spoken in Greece and in Asia. In Palestine, in particular, we do not perceive any vestige of the official use of the Latin language by the procurators. We do not find a single instance, either in the books of the New Testament or in Josephus, in which the Roman governors made use of interpreters: and while use and the affairs of life accustomed the common people to that language, the higher classes of society would on many accounts be obliged to make use of it.

4. So far were the religious authorities of the Jews from opposing the introduction of Greek, that they appear rather to have *favoured* the use of that language.

They employed it, habitually, in profane works, and admitted it into official acts. An article of the Mischna prohibits the Jews from writing books in any other language, except the Greek.[9] Such a

---

[1] Josephus, de Bell Jud lib. iii. c. 9. compared with lib ii c 13. § 7.
[2] Bell. Jud lib. ii. c 14. § 4.   [3] Ibid. lib. ii. c. 18.
[4] Josephus, Ant. Jud lib xix c 7. § 5.
[5] Idem. lib xv. c 9. compared with lib xvi. c. 5
[6] Bell Jud lib. i. c. 33 § 6 8 Ant Jud. lib. xvii. c. 6
[7] Bell Jud. lib i. c 9. s 3 Ant. Jud. lib. xv. c. 8. Θεατρον εν 'Ιεροσολυμοις ωκοδομησεν Compare Eichhorn de Judæorum Re Scenica in Comment Soc. Reg. Scient Gotting Vol II. Class. Antiq pp. 10—13

[8] Thus will account for the Jewish king, Herod Agrippa, and his brother being permitted by the emperor Claudius to be present in the senate, and to address that assembly in Greek. Dion Hist. lib ix. c. 8.

[9] Mischna, Tract. Megill. c. 1. § 8.

prohibition would not have been given if they had not been accustomed to write in a foreign language. The act or instrument of divorce might, indifferently, be written and signed in Greek or Hebrew: in either language, and with either subscription, it was valid.[1] During the siege of Jerusalem, for the first time, some opposition was made to the use of the Greek language, when brides were forbidden to wear a nuptial crown, at the same time that fathers were commanded to prevent their children thenceforward from learning Greek.[2] This circumstance will enable us readily to understand why Josephus, when sent by Titus to address his besieged countrymen, spoke to them ἐβραιζων, that is, in the Hebrew dialect, and τη πατριω γλοσση, *in his native tongue*[3]: it was not that he might be better heard, but that he might make himself known to them as their fellow-countryman and brother.

5. The Greek language was spread through various classes of the Jewish nation by usage and the intercourse of life. The people, with but few exceptions, generally understood it, although they continued to be always more attached to their native tongue. There were at Jerusalem religious communities wholly composed of Jews who spoke Greek; and of these Jews, as well as of Greek proselytes, the Christian church at Jerusalem appears in the first instance to have been formed. An examination of the Acts of the Apostles will prove these assertions. Thus, in Acts xxi. 40. and xxii. 2. when Paul, after a tumult, addressed the populace in Hebrew, *they kept the more silence*. They, therefore, evidently expected that he would have spoken to them in another language, which they would have comprehended[4], though they heard him much better in Hebrew, which they preferred. In Acts vi. 9. and ix. 29. we read that there were at Jerusalem whole synagogues of Hellenist Jews, under the name of Cyrenians, Alexandrians, &c. And in Acts vi. 1. we find that these very Hellenists formed a considerable portion of the church in that city.[5] From the account given in John xii. 20. of certain Greeks, (whether they were Hellenistic Jews or Greek proselytes, it is not material to determine,) who through the apostle Philip requested an interview with Jesus, it may fairly be inferred that both Philip and Andrew understood Greek.[6]

6. Further, there are extant Greek monuments, containing epi-

---

[1] If the book of divorce be written in Hebrew, and the names of the witnesses in Greek, or *vice versa*, or the name of one witness be in Hebrew and the other in Greek; — if a scribe and witness wrote it, it is lawful. — Ibid. Tract. Gitin. c. 9. § 8.

[2] Ibid Tract Sotah. c 9. § 14.

[3] Bell Jud lib v c 9. § 2 lib. vi c. 2. § 1

[4] In like manner, it is well known, there are many hundred thousand natives of Ireland who *can* understand what is said to them in English, which language they will tolerate; but they LOVE their native Irish dialect, and will listen with profound attention to any one who kindly addresses them in it.

[5] Essai d'une Introduction Critique au Nouveau Testament, par J. E. Cellérier, fils, pp 242—248. Genève, 1823. 8vo. Dr. Wait's Translation of Hug's Introduction, vol. ii. pp. 32—53.

[6] A. Angler Hermeneutica Biblica, pp.74—79. Alber, Instit. Hermeneut. Nov. Test. tom. i. pp. 242, 243

taphs and inscriptions which were erected in Palestine and the neighbouring countries [1], as well as antient coins which were struck in the cities of Palestine, and also in the various cities of Asia Minor. [2] What purpose could it answer, to erect the one or to execute the other, in the Greek language, if that language had not been familiar — indeed vernacular to the inhabitants of Palestine and the neighbouring countries? There is, then, every reasonable evidence, amounting to demonstration, that Greek did prevail universally throughout the Roman empire, and that the common people of Judæa were acquainted with it, and understood it

Convincing as we apprehend the preceding facts and evidence will be found to the unprejudiced inquirer, two or three objections have been raised against them, which it may not be irrelevant here briefly to notice.

1. It is objected that, during the siege of Jerusalem, when Titus granted a truce to the factious Jews just before he commenced his last assault, he advanced towards them accompanied by an interpreter [3]: but the Jewish historian, Josephus, evidently means that the Roman general, confident of victory, from a sense of dignity, spoke first, and in his own maternal language, which we know was Latin. The interpreter, therefore, did not attend him in order to translate Greek words into Hebrew, but for the purpose of rendering into Hebrew or Greek the discourse which Titus pronounced in Latin.

2. It has also been urged as a strong objection to the Greek original of the gospels, that Jesus Christ spoke in Hebrew; because Hebrew words occur in Mark v. 41. (*Talitha cumi*); vii. 34. (*Ephphatha*); Matt. xxvii. 46. (*Eli, Eli ! Lama sabachthani*), and Mark xv. 34. But to this affirmation we may reply, that on this occasion the evangelists have noticed and transcribed these expressions in the original, because Jesus did not ordinarily and habitually speak Hebrew. But admitting it to be more probable, that the Redeemer did ordinarily speak Hebrew to the Jews, who were most partial to their native tongue, which they heard him speak with delight, we may ask — in what language but Greek did he address the multitudes, when they were composed of a mixture of persons of different countries and nations — proselytes to the Jewish religion, as well as heathen Gentiles? For instance, the Gadarenes (Matt. viii. 28—34. Mark v. 1. Luke viii. 26); the inhabitants of the borders of Tyre and Sidon (Mark vii. 24.); the inhabitants of the Decapolis; the Syrophœnician woman, who is expressly termed a *Greek*, ἡ γυνη Ἑλληνις, in Mark vii. 26.; and the *Greeks*, Ἑλληνες, who were desirous of seeing Jesus at the passover. (John xii. 20.) [4]

3. Lastly, it has been objected, that, as the Christian churches were in many countries composed chiefly of the common people, they did not and could not understand Greek. But not to insist on

---

[1] Antonii Jos. Binterim, Propempticum ad Molkenbuhru Problema Criticum, — Sacra Scriptura Novi Testamenti in quo idiomate originaliter ab apostolis edita fuit? pp 27—40. (Moguntiæ, 1822. 8vo)
[2] Ibid. pp. 40—44
[3] Josephus, de Bell. Jud. lib. vi c. 6.   [4] Cellérier Essai, p. 249 Hug, vol. ii. p 54.

the evidence already adduced for the universality of the Greek language, we may reply, that "in every church there were numbers of persons endowed with the gifts of tongues, and of the interpretation of tongues; who could readily turn the apostles' Greek epistles into the language of the church to which they were sent. In particular, the president, or the spiritual man, who read the apostle's Greek letter to the Hebrews in their public assemblies, could, without any hesitation, read it in the Hebrew language, for the edification of those who did not understand Greek. And with respect to the Jews in the provinces, Greek being the native language of most of them, this epistle was much better calculated for their use, written in the Greek language, than if it had been written in the Hebrew, which few of them understood." Further, "it was proper that all the apostolical epistles should be written in the Greek language; because the different doctrines of the Gospel being delivered and explained in them, the explanation of these doctrines could with more advantage, be compared so as to be better understood, being expressed in one language, than if, in the different epistles, they had been expressed in the language of the churches and persons to whom they were sent. Now, what should that one language be, in which it was proper to write the Christian Revelation, but the Greek, which was then generally understood, and in which there were many books extant, that treated of all kinds of literature, and on that account were likely to be preserved, and by the reading of which Christians, in after ages, would be enabled to understand the Greek of the New Testament? This advantage none of the provincial dialects used in the apostles' days could pretend to. Being limited to particular countries, they were soon to be disused: and few (if any) books being written in them which merited to be preserved, the meaning of such of the apostles' letters as were composed in the provincial languages could not easily have been ascertained."[1]

III. EXAMINATION OF THE STYLE OF THE NEW TESTAMENT.

The style of the New Testament has a considerable affinity with that of the Septuagint version, which was executed at Alexandria[2], although it approaches somewhat nearer to the idiom of the Greek language; but the peculiarities of the Hebrew phraseology are discernible throughout, the language of the New Testament being formed by a mixture of oriental idioms and expressions with those which are properly Greek. Hence it has by some philologers been termed *Hebraic-Greek*; and (from the Jews having acquired the Greek language, rather by practice than by grammar, among the Greeks, in whose countries they resided in large communities) *Hellenistic-Greek*. The propriety of this appellation was severely contested towards the close of the seventeenth and in the early part of the eighteenth cen-

---

[1] Dr. Macknight on the Epistles, Pref. to Hebrews, sect. 11. § 3 vol iv. p 336 4to. edit.
[2] Michaelis has devoted an entire section to show that the language of the New Testament has a tincture of the Alexandrian idiom Vol 1. pp. 143, *et seq.* Professor Winer has given an interesting historical sketch of the Greek Language of the New Testament, in his Greek Grammar of the New Testament, translated by Professor Stuart and Mr. Robinson, pp. 12—35. Andover [North America], 1825. 8vo.

I. Sect. II.]   *On the Greek Language.*   19

tury[1]· and numerous publications were written on both sides of the question, with considerable asperity, which, together with the con-

---

[1] The "controversy on this topic began, very soon after the revival of literature in Europe In the sixteenth century, Erasmus and Laurentius Valla ventured to assert publicly, that the Greek of the New Testament is Hellenistic Many learned men of that day were inclined to adopt this opinion. But Robert Stephens, in the preface to his celebrated edition of the New Testament (1576), took it into his head strenuously to contend for the Attic purity of its dialect. As his Testament was so widely circulated, the preface served to excite general attention to the subject in question, and to prepare the minds of critics for the mighty contest which followed. Sebastian Pforscher led the way, in his *Diatribe de Ling Græc. N Test. puritate*, published in 1629, at Amsterdam, in which he defends, with great warmth, the purity of the New Testament Greek His antagonist was J Jung, who published in 1640 his *Sententiæ doctissvirorum, de Hellenistis et Hellenistica Dialecto*. To this a reply was made, by J Grosse of Jena, styled *Trias propositionum theol stilum Nov Test. a barbaris criminationibus vindicantium*, in which the whole mass of Hellenists were consigned over to the most detestable heresy. In the same year, Wulfer wrote an answer to this in his *Innocentia Hellenistarum vindicata*, to which Grosse replied, in his *Observationes pro triade Observatt apologeticæ*. Musæus defended Wulfer (though not in all his positions) in his *Disquisitio de stilo Nov. Testamenti*, A. D. 1641, to which Grosse replied by a *Tertia defensio Triados*, 1641 In 1642, Musæus felt himself compelled to publish his *Vindiciæ Disquisitionis*, which however only excited Grosse to a *Quarta defensio Triados*

"About the same time, the controversy was briskly carried on in Holland. D Heinsius, in his *Aristarchus Sacer*, and his *Exercitt. sac in Nov. Testamentum*, had espoused the cause of Hellenism, and commented upon Pforscher's Diatribe In a plainer manner still did he do this, in his *Exercitatio de Lingua Hellenistica*, published in 1643. In the very same year, the celebrated Salmasius appeared as his antagonist, in three separate publications, the spirit and tone of which may be readily discerned from their titles. The first was inscribed *Commentarius controversiam de lingua Hellenistica decidens*, the second, *Funus linguæ Hellenisticæ;* the third, *Ossilegium linguæ Hellenisticæ*. In 1648, Gataker, in England, warmly espoused the cause of the Hellenists, in his *Dissert. de stilo Nov. Testamenti*. On the same side, about this time, appeared Werenfels, of Switzerland, in his essay *De stylo Script. Nov Testamenti;* and J Olearius, of Germany, in his book *De stilo Nov Testamenti*, also Böckler, in his Tract, *De ling. Nov. Test. originali*. In Holland, Vorstius published, in defence of the same side, his book *De Hebraismis Nov. Testamenti*, 1658; and in 1665, his *Comment. de Hebraismis, N. Test* The last was attacked by H. Vitringa, in his *Specimen annotatt. ad Philol Sac. Vorstii*. The best of these dissertations were collected and published by Rhenferd in his *Syntagma Diss. Philol. Theol. de Stilo Nov. Test* 1703, and also by Van Honert, about the same time, at Amsterdam.

"J H Michaelis, in his essay *De textu Nov. Test*. Halæ, 1707, and H. Blackwall in his *Sacred Classics illustrated and defended*, endeavoured to moderate the parties, and to show, that while it might safely be admitted that there are Hebraisms in the New Testament, it may at the same time be maintained, that the Greek of the sacred writers is entitled to the character of classic purity But all efforts at peace were defeated by Georgi of Wittemberg, who, in 1732, published his *Vindiciæ Nov Test* This was answered by Knapp and Dressing of Leipsic. In 1733, Georgi published his *Hierocriticus Sacer*, in three books; and at the end of the year, a second part, in as many more books, which were also answered by his Leipsic opponents. From this time, the cause of the Hellenists began to predominate throughout Europe And though many essays on this subject have since appeared, and it has been canvassed in a far more able manner than before, yet few of these essays have been controversial, almost all writers leaning to the side of Hellenism" Dissertations on the Importance and best Method of studying the Original Languages of the Bible, by Jahn and others, with Notes by Prof Stuart, (Andover, N America, 1821,) pp. 77, 78 The reader, who is desirous of investigating the controversy on the purity of the language of the New Testament, is referred to the Actiones Academicæ super Hermeneutica Novi Testamenti of Prof. Morus (vol i. pp. 202—233); in which he has enumerated the principal writers on each side of the question A similar list has been given by Beck (*Monogrammata Hermeneutices Novi Testamenti*, part I pp. 28—32.), by Rumpæus (Isagoge ad Lectionem N. T. pp 32. *et seq.*) and by Rambach. (Instit Herm Sacræ, pp 23, 399.) Dr Campbell has treated the subject very ably in the first of his Preliminary Dissertations, prefixed to his version of the four Gospels, and Wetstein (Libelli ad Crisin atque Interpretationem N T pp. 48—60.) has given some interesting extracts from Origen, Chrysostom, and other fathers, who were of opinion that the language of the New Testament was *not* pure Greek. Other writers might be mentioned, who have treated bibliographically on this

troversy, are now almost forgotten. The dispute, however interesting to the philological antiquarian, is, after all, a mere "strife of words[1]:" and as the appellation of Hellenistic or Hebraic Greek is sufficiently correct for the purpose of characterising the language of the New Testament, it is now generally adopted.

Of this Hebraic style, the Gospels of St. Matthew and St. Mark exhibit strong vestiges: the former presents harsher Hebraisms than the latter: and the Gospel of St. Mark abounds with still more striking Hebraisms. "The epistles of St. James and Jude are somewhat better, but even these are full of Hebraisms, and betray in other respects a certain Hebrew tone. St. Luke has, in several passages, written pure and classic Greek, of which the four first verses of his Gospel may be given as an instance. in the sequel, where he describes the actions of Christ, he has very harsh Hebraisms, yet the style is more agreeable than that of St. Matthew or St. Mark. In the Acts of the Apostles he is not free from Hebraisms, which he seems to have never studiously avoided; but his periods are more classically turned, and sometimes possess beauty devoid of art. St. John has numerous, though not uncouth, Hebraisms both in his Gospel and epistles: but he has written in a smooth and flowing language, and surpasses all the Jewish writers in the excellence of narrative. St. Paul again is entirely different from them all: his style is indeed neglected and full of Hebraisms, but he has avoided the concise and verse-like construction of the Hebrew language, and has, upon the whole, a considerable share of the roundness of Grecian composition. It is evident that he was as perfectly acquainted with the Greek manner of expression as with the Hebrew; and he has introduced them alternately, as either the one or the other suggested itself the first, or was the best approved."[2]

This diversity of style and idiom in the sacred writers of the New Testament affords an intrinsic and irresistible evidence for the authenticity of the books which pass under their names. If their style had been uniformly the same, there would be good reason for suspecting that they had all combined together when they wrote; or, else, that having previously concerted what they should teach, one of them had committed to writing their system of doctrine. In ordinary cases, when there is a difference of style in a work professing to be the production of *one* author, we have reason to believe that it was written by several persons. In like manner, and for the very same reason, when books, which pass under the names of *several* authors, are written in different styles, we are authorised to conclude that they were not composed by one person.

---

topic but the preceding foreign critics only are specified, as their works may be easily procured from the Continent.

[1]. Michaelis ascribes the disputes above noticed either to "a want of sufficient knowledge of the Greek, the prejudices of pedantry and school orthodoxy, or the injudicious custom of choosing the Greek Testament as the *first* book to be read by learners of that language; by which means they are so accustomed to its singular style, that in a more advanced age they are incapable of perceiving its deviation from the language of the classics." (Bp. Marsh's Michaelis, vol. i. p. 211.)

[2] Michaelis, vol. i. p. 112.

Further, If the New Testament had been written with classic purity; if it had presented to us the language of Isocrates, Demosthenes, Xenophon, or Plutarch, there would have been just grounds for suspicion of forgery; and it might with propriety have been objected, that it was impossible for Hebrews, who professed to be men of no learning, to have written in so pure and excellent a style, and, consequently, that the books which were ascribed to them must have been the invention of some impostor. The diversity of style, therefore, which is observable in them, so far from being any objection to the authenticity of the New Testament, is in reality a strong argument for the truth and sincerity of the sacred writers, and of the authenticity of their writings. "Very many of the Greek words, found in the New Testament, are not such as were adopted by men of education, and the higher and more polished ranks of life, but such as were in use with the common people. Now this shows that the writers became acquainted with the language, in consequence of an actual intercourse with those who spoke it, rather than from any study of books: and that intercourse must have been very much confined to the middling or even lower classes; since the words and phrases, most frequently used by them, passed current only among the vulgar. There are undoubtedly many plain intimations [1] given throughout these books, that their writers were of this lower class, and that their associates were frequently of the same description, but the character of the style is the strongest confirmation possible that their conditions were not higher than what they have ascribed to themselves." [2] In fact, the vulgarisms, foreign idioms, and other disadvantages and defects, which some critics imagine that they have discovered in the Hebraic Greek of the New Testament, " are assigned by the inspired writers as the reasons of God's preference of it, whose thoughts are not our thoughts, nor his ways our ways. Paul argues, that the success of the preachers of the Gospel, in spite of the absence of those accomplishments in language, then so highly valued, was an evidence of the divine power and energy with which their ministry was accompanied. He did not address them, he tells us (1 Cor. i. 17.) *with the wisdom of words*, — with artificial periods and a studied elocution, — *lest the cross of Christ should be made of none effect*, — lest to human eloquence that success should be ascribed, which ought to be attributed to the divinity of the doctrine and the agency of the Spirit, in the miracles wrought in support of it. There is hardly any sentiment which he is at greater pains to enforce. He *used none of the enticing or persuasive words of man's wisdom*. Wherefore? — ' That their faith

---

[1] It is obvious to cite such passages, as Mark i 16 ii. 14. John xxi 3. 7 where the occupations of the Apostles are plainly and professedly mentioned. It may be more satisfactory to refer to Acts iii 6 xviii. 3. xx 34. 2 Cor. viii. and ix. xi 6 8, 9. 27. xii. 14, &c. Phil. ii. 25. iv. 10, &c. 1 Thess. ii. 6 9 2 Thess iii 8. 10 Philem. 11. 18 In these, the attainments, occupations, and associates of the preachers of the Gospel are indirectly mentioned and alluded to; and afford a species of *undesigned* proof, which seems to repel the imputation of fraud, especially if the circumstance of style be taken into the account.

[2] Dr. Maltby's " Illustrations of the Truth of the Christian Religion," pp. 10—12

might not stand *in the wisdom of man, but in the power of God.*' (1 Cor. ii. 4, 5.) Should I ask what was the reason why our Lord Jesus Christ chose for the instruments of that most amazing revolution in the religious systems of mankind, men perfectly illiterate and taken out of the lowest class of the people? Your answer to this will serve equally for an answer to that other question, — Why did the Holy Spirit choose to deliver such important truths in the barbarous idiom of a few obscure Galilæans, and not in the politer and more harmonious strains of Grecian eloquence?—I repeat it, the answer to both questions is the same—That it might appear, beyond contradiction, that the excellency of the power was of God, and not of man."[1]

A large proportion, however, of the phrases and constructions of the New Testament is pure Greek; that is to say, of the same degree of purity as the Greek which was spoken in Macedonia, and that in which Polybius wrote his Roman History. Hence the language of the New Testament will derive considerable illustration from consulting the works of classic writers, and especially from diligently collating the Septuagint version of the Old Testament: the collections also of Raphelius, Palairet, Bos, Abresch, Ernesti, and other writers whose works are noticed in the Appendix to this volume, will afford the biblical student very essential assistance in explaining the pure Greek expressions of the New Testament according to the usage of classic authors. It should further be noticed, that there occur in the New Testament words that express both doctrines and practices which were utterly unknown to the Greeks; and also words bearing widely different interpretation from those which are ordinarily found in Greek writers.

IV. The New Testament contains examples of the various DIALECTS occurring in the Greek language, and especially of the Attic; which being most generally in use on account of its elegance, pervades every book of the New Testament. To these, some have added the poetic dialect, chiefly, it should seem, because there are a few passages cited by St. Paul from the antient Greek poets, in Acts xvii. 28. 1 Cor. xv. 33. and Tit. i. 12.[2] But the sacred writers of the New Testament being Jews, were consequently acquainted with the Hebrew idioms, and also with the common as well as with the *appropriated* or *acquired* senses of the words of that language. Hence, when they used a Greek word, as correspondent to a Hebrew one of like signification, they employed it as the Hebrew word was used, either in a common or appropriated sense, as occasion required. The whole arrangement of their periods " is regulated according to the Hebrew verses (not those in Hebrew poetry, but such as are found in the historical books); which are constructed in a manner directly opposite to the roundness of Grecian language, and for want

---

[1] Dr. Campbell's Preliminary Dissertations, Diss. i. (vol. i 3d edit.) p. 50. Bishop Warburton has treated this topic with his usual ability in his "Doctrine of Grace," book i chapters viii.—x. (Works, vol viii. pp. 279—302.) See also Michaelis's Introduction, vol. i. pp 116—123.

[2] J. B. Carpzov. Primæ Lineæ Hermeneuticæ, p. 16. Pfeiffer Herm. Sacra, c. vii. § 6. (Op. tom. ii p 652.)

of variety have an endless repetition of the same particles."[1] These peculiar idioms are termed *Hebraisms*, and their nature and classes have been treated at considerable length by various writers. Georgi, Pfochenius, Blackwall, and others, have altogether denied the existence of these Hebraisms; while their antagonists have, perhaps unnecessarily, multiplied them. Wyssius, in his Dialectologia Sacra, has divided the Hebraisms of the New Testament into thirteen classes; Vorstius[2] into thirty-one classes; and Viser into eight classes[3]; and Masclef has given an ample collection of the Hebraisms occurring in the sacred writings in the first volume of his excellent Hebrew Grammar.[4] The New Testament, however, contains fewer Hebrew grammatical constructions than the Septuagint, except in the book of Revelation; where we often find a nominative, when another case should have been substituted, in imitation of the Hebrew, which is without cases.[5] As the limits necessarily assigned to this section do not permit us to abridge the valuable treatises just noticed, we shall here adduce some instances of the Hebraisms found principally in the New Testament, and shall offer a few canons by which to determine them with precision.

1. Thus, *to be called, to arise,* and *to be found,* are the same as *to be*, with the Hebrews, and this latter is in the Old Testament frequently expressed by the former. Compare Isa. lx. 14. 18. lxi. 3 lxii. 12. Zech. viii. 8.

Accordingly, in the New Testament, these terms are often employed one for the other, as in Matt v. 9 *They shall be called the children of God* and ver. 19. *He shall be called the least in the kingdom of Heaven!*—1 John iii. 1 *That we should be called the sons of God.* *To be called* here and in other places is really *to be*, and it is so expressed according to the Hebrew way of speaking. There is the like signification of the word *arise*, as in 2 Sam xi 20 *if the king's wrath arise.* — Esth iv. 14 *Enlargement and deliverance shall arise to the Jews* Prov xxiv. 22 *their calamity shall arise suddenly.* — In all which places the word *arise* signifies no other than actual *being* or *existing*, according to the Hebrew idiom. And hence it is used in a similar manner in the New Testament, as in Luke xxiv. 38. *Why do thoughts arise in your hearts?* i e. Why are they there? — Matt. xxiv. 24. *There shall arise false Christs,* i e there shall actually be at that time such persons according to my prediction So, *to be found* is among the Hebrews of the same import with the above-mentioned expressions, and accordingly in the Old Testament one is put for the other, as in 1 Sam. xxv 28 *Evil hath not been found in thee* — 2 Chron. xix 3. *Good things are found in thee.* — Isa li 3 *Joy and gladness shall be found therein* — Dan. v. 12 *An excellent spirit was found* in Daniel. In these and other texts the Hebrew word rendered *found* is equivalent to *was* In imitation of this Hebraism, *to be found* is used for *sum* or *existo*, to be, in the New Testament, as in Luke xvii 18. *There are not found that returned to give glory to God, save this stranger.* — Acts v 39 *Lest haply ye be found to fight against God.* — 1 Cor. iv. 2 *That a man be found faithful.* — Phil. ii 8. *Being found in fashion as a man* — Heb. xi 5. *Enoch was not found* which is the same with Enoch was not, as is evident from comparing this place with Gen v, 24. to which it refers. The expression of St. Peter, 1 Ep ii. 22 *Neither was guile found in his mouth,* is taken from Isa. liii. 9. *Neither was there any deceit* (or guile) *in his mouth* Whence it appears, that in this, as well as the other texts above cited, *to be found* is equivalent to *was*

---

[1] Leusden de Dialectis, p. 20. Michaelis, vol i. p. 123.
[2] In his Philologia Sacra this work was originally published in 4to. but the best edition is that of M Fischer, in 8vo. Leipsic, 1778 Vorstius's treatise was abridged by Leusden in his Philologus Græcus, and Leusden's Abridgment was republished by Fischer, with valuable notes and other additions, in 8vo Leipsic, 1783.
[3] In his Hermeneutica Sacra Novi Testamenti, pars ii. vol. ii. pp. 1—62
[4] See particularly pp. 273—290. 301—307 and 338—352. See also Schaefer's Institutiones Scripturisticæ, pars ii. pp. 194—205.
[5] Michaelis, vol i. pp 125. Glassius has given several instances in his Philologia Sacra, canons xxviii. and xxix. vol. i. pp 67—79. edit. Dathe. Professor Winer divides the Hebraisms of the New Testament into two classes, *perfect* and *imperfect* Greek Grammar of the New Test. pp. 32—35 where he has given many important examples

2. Verbs expressive of a person's doing an action, are often used to signify his supposing the thing, or discovering and acknowledging the fact, or his declaring and foretelling the event, especially in the prophetic writings.

Thus, *He that findeth his life shall lose it* (Matt. x. 39.), means, *He that expects to save his life by apostacy, shall lose it* — So, *Let him become a fool* (1 Cor. iii 18.), is equivalent to, *Let him become sensible of his folly* — *Make the heart of this people fat* (Isa. vi. 9, 10.), i. e. *Prophesy that they shall be so.* — *What God hath cleansed* (Acts x. 15.), i. e. *What God hath declared clean.* — *But of that day and hour no man knoweth* (that is, maketh known), *not even the angels who are in heaven, neither the Son, but the Father* (Matt. xxiv 36.), that is, neither man, nor an angel, nor the Son, has permission to make known this secret.

3. Negative verbs are often put for a strong positive affirmation.

Thus, *No good thing will he withhold* (Psal. lxxxiv. 11.), means, *He will give them all good things.* — *Being not weak in the faith* (Rom. iv. 19.), i. e. *Being strong in the faith* — *I will not leave you comfortless* (John xiv. 18.), means, *I will both protect and give you the most solid comfort.*

4. The privileges of the first-born among the Jews being very great, that which is chief or most eminent in any kind, is called the first-born, Gen. xlix. 3.

So, in Job xviii. 13, the *first-born* of death is the most fatal and cruel death. — In Isa. xiv. 30. the *first-born* of the poor denotes those who are most poor and miserable (See also Psal. lxxxix. 27. Jer. xxxi. 9. Rom. viii. 29. Col. i. 15. 18. Heb. xii. 23.)

5. The word *son* has various peculiar significations. This word was a favourite one among the Hebrews, who employed it to designate a great variety of relations. The *son* of any thing, according to the oriental idiom, may be either what is closely connected with it, dependant on it, like it, the consequence of it, worthy of it, &c.

Thus, the *sons* or *children of Belial*, so often spoken of in the Old Testament, are wicked men, such as are good for nothing, or such as will not be governed. — *Children of light* are such as are divinely enlightened. (Luke xvi. 8. John xii. 36. Ephes. v. 8. 1 Thess. v. 5.) — *Children of disobedience* are disobedient persons. (Ephes. ii. 2.) Children of *Hell* (Matt. xxiii. 15.), — of *wrath* (Ephes. ii. 3.), and *Son of perdition* (John xvii. 12. 2 Thess. ii. 3.), are respectively such as are worthy thereof, or obnoxious thereto. — *A son of peace* (Luke x. 6.) is one that is worthy of it (See Matt. x. 13.) — The *children* of a place are the inhabitants of it (Ezra ii. 1. Psal. cxlix. 2. Jer. ii. 16. — So the word *daughter* is likewise used (2 Kings xix. 21. Psal. xlv. 12. cxxxvii. 8. Lam. ii. 13. Zech. ii. 10.), the *city* being as a *mother*, and the *inhabitants* of it taken collectively, as her *daughter*. The children of the *promise*, are such as embrace and believe the promise of the Gospel. (Gal. iv. 28.) — *Sons of men* (Psal. iv. 2.) are no more than men. And Christ is as often called the *son of man*, as he is man. The *sons of God* (Gen. vi. 2.) are those who professed to be pious, or the children of God.[1] (Matt. v. 45.) They are such as imitate him, or are governed by him. (1 John iii. 10.) On the same account are men called the *children of the devil*. So likewise (John viii. 44.) *father* is understood in a like sense; also those who are the *inventors* of any thing, or instruct others therein, are called their fathers. (Gen. iv. 20.)

6. *Name* is frequently used as synonymous with *persons*.

Thus, to believe on the *name* of Christ (John i. 12.) means to believe on him. See similar examples in John iii. 18. xx. 31. Rev. iii. 4. In like manner *soul* is put for person, in Matt. xii. 18. *In whom* my soul *is well pleased,* that is, in whom I am well pleased. See other examples in Gen. xii. 13. xix. 20. Psal. cvi. 15. Job xvi. 4. Prov. xxv. 25. Rom. xiii. 1. Heb. x. 38.

7. As the Jews had but few adjectives in their language, they had recourse to substantives, in order to supply their place.

Hence we find *kingdom* and *glory* used to denote a *glorious kingdom*. (1 Thess. ii. 12.) *Mouth* and *wisdom* for *wise discourse* (Luke xxi. 15.) the *patience of hope* for *patient expectation* (1 Thess. i. 3.) *glory of his power* for *glorious power*. (2 Thess. i. 9.) So cir-

---

[1] The various significations of the words "Son," and "Sons of God," according to the oriental idioms, are investigated and elucidated at considerable length by Professor Stuart, in his "Letters on the Eternal Generation of the Son of God," pp. 94—107. Andover (North America), 1822.

cumcision and uncircumcision mean circumcised and uncircumcised persons. Anathema (1 Cor. xvi. 22.) means, an excommunicated member. *The spirits of the prophets* (1 Cor. xiv. 32.), means, the *spiritual gifts of the prophets* When one substantive governs another, in the genitive, one of them is sometimes used as an adjective. *In the body of his flesh*, means, *in his fleshly body* (Col 1. 22.); *Bond of perfectness* (Col iii 14.), means, *a perfect bond.* In Eph vi 12. *spiritual wickedness*, means, *wicked spirits* *Newness of life* (Rom vii. 6.), is *a new life*. The *tree of the knowledge of good and evil* (Gen. ii. 9. compared with iii. 22.), means, *the tree of the knowledge of good*, or *of a pleasure which to taste is an evil*. When two substantives are joined together, by the copulative *and*, the one frequently governs the other, as in Dan. iii. 7 *All the people, the nations, and the languages*, mean, *people of all nations and languages* In Acts xxiii. 6. *the hope and resurrection of the dead*, means, *the hope of the resurrection of the dead*. In Col ii 8. *Philosophy and vain deceit*, denotes, *a false and deceitful philosophy* *Hath brought life and immortality to light* (2 Tim. i. 10.), means, to bring *immortal life to light*. But the expression, *I am the way, the truth, and the life*, (John xiv 6.) means, *I am the true and living way*. It is of importance to observe, that, in the original, nouns in the genitive case sometimes express the object, and sometimes the agent. In Matt ix 35. *the gospel of the kingdom*, means, *good news concerning the kingdom*. *Doctrines of devils*, (1 Tim. iv 1.) evidently mean, *doctrines concerning demons.* *The faith of Christ* often denotes the faith which the Lord Jesus Christ enjoins. The *righteousness of God* sometimes means, his personal perfection, and sometimes that righteousness which he requires of his people. In Col ii 11. *the circumcision of Christ*, means, *the circumcision enjoined by Christ* The Hebrews used the word *living*, to express the excellence of the thing to which it is applied. Thus *living water*, or *living fountain*, signifies, *running*, or *excellent water*. *Living stones, living way, living oracles*, mean, *excellent stones, an excellent way, and excellent oracles.*

8. The Jews, having no superlatives in their language, employed the words *of God* or *of the Lord*, in order to denote the greatness or excellency of a thing.

Thus, in Gen xiii 10, a beautiful garden is called the *garden of the Lord* In 1 Sam. xxvi 12 a *very deep sleep* is called *the sleep of the Lord* In 2 Chron xiv 14. and xvii. 10, the *fear of the Lord* denotes a very great fear. In Psal. xxxvi. 7. Heb (6. of English Bibles), the *mountains of God* are exceeding high mountains, and in Psal. lxxx. 10. (Heb.) the *tallest cedars* are termed *cedars of God*. The *voices of God* (Exod. ix. 28 Heb in our version properly rendered *mighty thunderings*) mean superlatively, loud thunder. Compare also the sublime description of the effects of thunder, or the voice of God, in Psal xxix. 3—8. The production of rain by the electric spark is alluded to, in a very beautiful manner, in Jer x. 13. *When he* (God) *uttereth his voice, there is a multitude of waters in the heavens* [1] In Jonah iii. 2. Nineveh is termed an *exceeding great city*, which in the original Hebrew is *a city great to God* The like mode of expression occurs in the New Testament Thus, in Acts vii 20. Moses is said to be ἀστειος τω Θεω, literally *fair to God*, or, as it is correctly rendered in our version, *exceeding fair*. And in 2 Cor x 4 the weapons of our warfare are termed δυνατα τω Θεω, literally, *mighty to God*, that is, *exceeding powerful*, — not mighty *through God*, as in our authorised translation.

9. According to the Hebrew idiom, a sword has a *mouth*, or the edge of the sword is called a *mouth*. (Luke xxi. 24.)

They shall fall by the mouth (or, as our translators have correctly rendered it, *the edge*) *of the sword* (Heb. xi. 34.) — *escaped the edge of the sword*, is in the Greek στομα, the *mouth* of the sword So, we read of a *two-mouthed sword* (Heb. iv. 12.), for it is διστομος in the Greek. That this is the Hebrew phraseology may be seen by comparing Judg iii. 16. Psal cxlix 6. Prov. v. 4.

10. The verb γινωσκω, *to know*, in the New Testament, frequently denotes *to approve*.

Thus, in Matt. vii. 23. *I never knew you*, means, I never approved you. A similar construction occurs in 1 Cor. viii 3. and in Rom. vii 15. (Gr.) which in our version is rendered *allow*. Compare also Psal. i. 6.

11. Lastly, to *hear* denotes to *understand*, to *attend to*, and to *regard what is said.*

In illustration of this remark, compare Deut. xviii. 15. with Acts iii. 23. and see also Matt. xvii. 5. and vi. 15 xiii. 9. and Luke viii. 8.

It were no difficult task to adduce numerous similar examples of

---

[1] Dr. A. Clarke on Exod. ix. 28.

the Hebraisms occurring in the Scriptures, and particularly in the New Testament; but the preceding may suffice to show the benefit that may be derived from duly considering the import of a word in the several passages of holy writ in which it occurs.

In order to understand the full force and meaning of the Hebraisms of the New Testament, the following canons have been laid down by the celebrated critic John Augustus Ernesti, and his annotator Professor Morus.

1. *Compare Hebrew words and forms of expressions with those which occur in good Greek formulæ, particularly in doctrinal passages.*

As all languages have some modes of speech which are common to each other, it sometimes happens that the same word or expression is both Hebrew, and good Greek, and affords a proper meaning, whether we take it in a Hebrew or a Greek sense. But, in such cases, it is preferable to adopt that meaning which a Jew would give, because it is most probable that the sacred writer had this in view rather than the Greek meaning, especially if the latter were not of very frequent occurrence. Thus, the expression, *ye shall die in your sins* (John viii. 24.), if explained according to the Greek idiom, is equivalent to *ye shall persevere in a course of sinful practice to the end of your lives* but, according to the Hebrew idiom, it not only denotes a physical or temporal death, but also eternal death, and is equivalent to *ye shall be damned on account of your sins,* in rejecting the Messiah. The latter interpretation, therefore, is preferably to be adopted, as agreeing best with the Hebrew mode of thinking, and also with the context.

This rule applies particularly to the doctrinal passages of the New Testament, which must in all cases be interpreted according to the genius of the Hebrew language. Thus, *to fear God,* in the language of a Jew, means to reverence or worship God generally *The knowledge of God,* which is so frequently mentioned in the New Testament, if taken according to the Hebrew idiom, implies not only the mental knowledge of God, but also the worship and reverence of Him which flows from it, and, consequently, it is both a *theoretical* and a *practical* knowledge of God. The reason of this rule is obvious. In the first place, our Saviour and his apostles, the first teachers of Christianity, were Jews, who had been educated in the Jewish religion and language, and who (with the exception of Paul) being unacquainted with the niceties of the Greek language at the time they were called to the apostolic office, could only express themselves in the style and manner peculiar to their country. Secondly, the religion taught in the New Testament agrees with that delivered in the Old Testament, of which it is a *continuation,* so that the ritual worship enjoined by the law of Moses is succeeded by a *spiritual* or *internal* worship, the legal dispensation is succeeded by the Gospel dispensation, in which what was imperfect and obscure is become perfect and clear. Now things that are continued are substantially the same, or of a similar nature. Thus the expression *to come unto God* occurs both in the Old and in the New Testament. In the former it simply means *to go up to the temple,* in the latter it is continued, so that what was imperfect becomes perfect, and it implies the *mental* or *spiritual approach unto the Most High,* i. e. the spiritual worshipping of God. In like manner, since the numerous particulars related in the Old Testament concerning the victims, priests, and temple of God are transferred, in the New Testament, to the atoning death of Christ, to his offering of himself to death, and to the Christian church, the veil of figure being withdrawn, the force and beauty of these expressions cannot be perceived, nor their meaning fully ascertained, unless we interpret the doctrinal parts of the New Testament, by the aid of the Old Testament.

2. *The Hebraisms of the New Testament are to be compared with the good Greek occurring in the Septuagint or Alexandrian version.*

As the Hebraisms occurring in the Old Testament are uniformly rendered, in the Septuagint version, in good Greek, this translation may be considered as a commentary and exposition of those passages, and as conveying the sense of the Hebrew nation concerning their meaning The Alexandrian translation, therefore, ought to be consulted in those passages of the New Testament in which the sacred writers have rendered the Hebraisms literally. Thus, in 1 Cor xv 54 death is said to be *swallowed up in victory,* which sentence is a quotation from Isaiah xxv 8 As the Hebrew word נֶצַח Netsach, with the ל prefixed, acquires the force of an adverb, and means *for ever, without end, or incessantly,* and as the Septuagint sometimes renders the word לנצח Lanetsach by εις νικος in victory, but most commonly by εις τελος, *for ever,* Michaelis is of opinion that this last meaning properly belongs to 1 Cor. xv. 54., which should therefore be rendered *death is swallowed up for ever.* And so it is translated by Bishop Pearce.

3. *In passages that are good Greek, which are common both to the Old and New Testament, the corresponding words in the Hebrew Old Testament are to be compared.*

Several passages occur in the New Testament, that are good Greek, and which are also to be found in the Alexandrian version. In these cases it is not sufficient to consult the Greek language only: recourse should also be had to the Hebrew, because such words of the Septuagint and New Testament have acquired a different meaning from what is given to them by Greek writers, and are sometimes to be taken in a more lax, sometimes in a more strict sense. Thus, in Gen v 24. and Heb xi 5. it is said that Enoch *pleased God* ευηρεστηκεναι τω Θεω, which expression in itself is sufficiently clear, and is also good Greek; but if we compare the corresponding expression in the Hebrew, its true meaning is, that *he walked with God* In rendering this clause by ευηρεστηκεναι τω Θεω, the Greek translator did not render the Hebrew *verbatim*, for in that case he would have said περιπατητε συν Θεω, but he translated t correctly as to the sense. Enoch *pleased God*, because he lived habitually as in the sight of God, setting him always before his eyes in every thing he said, thought, and did. In Psal ii 1. the Septuagint version runs thus, Ινατι εφρυαξαν εθνη, *why did the nations rage?* Now though this expression is good Greek, it does not fully render the original Hebrew, which means, *why do the nations furiously and tumultuously assemble together, or rebel?* The Septuagint therefore is not sufficiently close Once more, the expression ουκ οντες, *they are not*, is good Greek, but admits of various meanings, indicating those who are not yet in existence, those who are already deceased, or, figuratively, persons of no authority. This expression occurs both in the Septuagint version of Jer. xxxi 15. and also in Matt ii. 18 If we compare the original Hebrew, we shall find that it is to be limited to those who are dead. Hence it will be evident that the collation of the original Hebrew will not only prevent us from taking words either in too lax or too strict a sense, but will also guard us against uncertainty as to their meaning, and lead us to that very sense which the sacred writer intended

Besides the Hebraisms, which we have just considered, there are found in the New Testament various Rabbinical, Syriac, Persic, Latin, and other idioms and words, which are respectively denominated Rabbinisms, Syriasms, Persisms, Latinisms, &c. &c. on which it may not be improper to offer a few remarks.

1. *Rabbinisms.*—We have already seen that during, and subsequent to, the Babylonian captivity, the Jewish language sustained very considerable changes.[1] New words, new sentences, and new expressions were introduced, especially terms of science, which Moses or Isaiah would have as little understood, as Cicero or Cæsar would a system of philosophy or theology composed in the language of the schools. This New Hebrew language is called Talmudical, or Rabbinical, from the writings in which it is used; and, although these writings are of much later date than the New Testament, yet, from the coincidence of expressions, it is not improbable that, even in the time of Christ, this was the learned language of the Rabbins.[2] Lightfoot, Schoetgenius, Meuschen, and others, have excellently illustrated the Rabbinisms occurring in the New Testament.

2. *Aramæisms, or Syriasms and Chaldaisms.*—The vernacular language of the Jews, in the time of Jesus Christ, was the Aramæan; which branched into two dialects, differing in pronunciation rather than in words, and respectively denominated the *Chaldee* or East Aramæan, and the *Syriac*, or West Aramæan. The East Aramæan was spoken at Jerusalem and in Judæa; and was used by Christ

---

[1] See p. 5 *supra*.
[2] Michaelis, vol i. p 129., who has given some illustrative examples. Mori Acroases super Hermeneuticæ Novi Testamenti, vol i. p. 238. See also Olearius de Stylo Novi Testamenti, membr. iii. aphorism vii. (Thesaurus Theologicus Nov Test. tom. ii. pp. 23, 24.)

in his familiar discourses and conversations with the Jews; the West Aramæan was spoken in "Galilee of the Gentiles." It was therefore natural that numerous Chaldee and Syriac words, phrases, and terms of expression, should be intermixed with the Greek of the New Testament, and even such as are not to be found in the Septuagint: and the existence of these Chaldaisms and Syriasms, affords a strong intrinsic proof of the genuineness and authenticity of the New Testament. Were this, indeed, "free from these idioms, we might naturally conclude that it was not written either by men of Galilee or Judæa, and therefore was spurious; for, as certainly as the speech of Peter betrayed him to be a Galilæan, when Christ stood before the Jewish tribunal, so certainly must the written language of a man, born, educated, and grown old in Galilee, discover marks of his native idiom, unless we assume the absurd hypothesis, that God hath interposed a miracle, which would have deprived the New Testament of one of its strongest proofs of authenticity."[1]

The following are the principal Aramæan or Syriac and Chaldee words occurring in the New Testament: — Αββα (*Abba*), Father, (Rom. viii. 15.) — Ακελδαμα (*Aceldama*), the field of blood, (Acts i. 19.) — Αρμαγεδδων (*Armageddon*), the mountain of Megiddo, *or of the Gospel*, (Rev. xvi. 16.) — Βηθεσδα (*Bethesda*), the house of mercy, (John v. 2.) — Κηφας (*Cephas*), a rock or stone, (John i. 43) — Κορβαν (*Corban*), a gift or offering dedicated to God, (Mark vii. 11.) — Ελωι, Ελωι, λαμα σαβαχθανι (*Eloi, Eloi, lama sabachthani*), my God, my God! why hast thou forsaken me? (Matt xxvii. 46. Mark xv. 34.) — Εφφαθα (*Ephphatha*), be thou opened, (Mark vii. 34.) — Μαμμωνα (*Mammon*), riches, (Matt. vi. 24.) — Μαραν Αθα (*Maran Atha*), the Lord cometh, (1 Cor. xvi. 22.) — Ρακα (*Raca*), thou worthless fellow! (Matt. v. 22.) — Ταλιθα κουμι (*Talitha cumi*), maid arise! (Mark v. 41.)[2]

3. *Latinisms.* — "The sceptre having departed from Judah," (Gen. xlix. 10.) by the reduction of Judæa into a Roman province, the extension of the Roman laws and government would naturally follow the success of the Roman arms: and if to these we add the imposition of tribute by the conquerors, together with the commercial intercourse necessarily consequent on the political relations of the Jews with Rome, we shall be enabled readily to account for the Latinisms, or Latin words and phrases, that occur in the New Testament.

The following is a list of the principal Latinisms: — Ασσαριον (*assarion*, from the Latin word *assarius*), equivalent to about three quarters of a farthing of our money, (Matt. x. 29. Luke xii. 6.) — Κηνσος (*census*), as-

---

[1] Michaelis, vol. i. p. 135. Morus, vol. i p. 237. Angler, Hermeneuticæ Biblica, pp 83—88. Bishop Marsh, in his notes to Michaelis, states, that a new branch of the Aramæan language has been discovered by Professor Adler, which differs in some respects from the East and West Aramæan dialects. For an account of it, he refers to the third part of M. Adler's *Novi Testamenti Versiones Syriacæ, Simplex, Philoxeniana, et Hierosolymitana, denuo examinatæ*, &c. 4to Hafniæ, 1789, of which work we have not been able to obtain a sight. Pfeiffer has an amusing disquisition on the Galilæan dialect of Peter, which in substance corresponds with the above cited remark of Michaelis, though Pfeiffer does not seem to have known the exact names of the dialects then in use among the Jews. Op. tom i pp. 616—622.

[2] Additional examples of Chaldaisms and Syriasms may be seen in Olearius de Stylo Novi Testamenti, membr. iii aphorism vi. (Thesaurus Theologico-Philologicus, tom. ii. pp. 22, 23.)

sessment or rate, (Matt. xvii. 25.) — Κεντυριων (*centurio*), a centurion, (Mark xv. 39. 44, 45.) — Κολωνια (*colonia*), a colony, (Acts xvi 12) — Κουστωδια (*custodia*), a guard of soldiers, (Matt. xxvii. 65, 66. xxviii. 11.) — Δηναριος (*denarius*), a Roman penny, equivalent to about seven-pence halfpenny of our money, (Luke vii. 41.) — Φραγελλιον (*flagellum*), a scourge, (John ii. 15.); from this word is derived Φραγελλοω, to scourge with whips, (Matt. xxvii. 26. Mark xv. 15) As this was a Roman punishment, it is no wonder that we find it expressed by a term nearly Roman. — Ιουστος (*Justus*), (Acts i. 23.) — Λεγεων (*legio*), a legion, (Matt. xxvi. 53.) — Κοδραντης (*quadrans*) a Roman coin equivalent to about three fourths of an English halfpenny, (Matt. v. 26) — Λιβερτινος (*libertinus*), a freed man, (Acts vi. 9) — Λιτρα (*libra*), a pound, (John xii. 3.) — Λεντιον (*linteum*), a towel, (John xiii. 4) — Μακελλον (*macellum*), shambles, (1 Cor. x. 25.) — Μεμβρανα (*membrana*), parchment, (2 Tim. iv. 13.) — Μιλιον (*mille*), a mile; the Roman mile consisting of a thousand paces, (Matt. v. 41.) — Ξεστης (*sextarius*), a kind of pot, (Mark vii. 4. 8.) — Πραιτοριον (*prætorium*), a judgment hall, or place where the prætor or other chief magistrate heard and determined causes, (Matt. xxvii. 27.) — Σημικινθιον or Σιμικινθιον (*semicinctium*), an apron, (Acts xix. 12.) — Σικαριος (*sicarius*), an assassin, (Acts xxi. 38.) — Σουδαριον (*sudarium*), a napkin, or handkerchief, (Luke xix. 20) — Σπεκουλατωρ (*speculator*), a soldier employed as an *executioner*, (Mark vi. 27.) — Ταβερνα (*taberna*), a tavern, (Acts xxviii. 15.) — Τιτλος (*titulus*), a title, (John xix. 19, 20.)[1]

4. From the unavoidable intercourse of the Jews with the neighbouring nations, the Arabs, Persians (to whose sovereigns they were formerly subject), and the inhabitants of Asia Minor, numerous words, and occasional expressions may be traced in the New Testament, which have been thus necessarily introduced among the Jews. These words, however, are not sufficiently numerous to constitute so many entire dialects: for instance, there are not more than four or five Persian words in the whole of the New Testament. These cannot, therefore, be in strictness termed *Persisms;* and, though the profoundly learned Michaelis is of opinion that the Zend-avesta, or antient book of the Zoroastrian religion, translated by M. Anquetil du Perron, throws considerable light on the phraseology of Saint John's writings; yet, as the authenticity of that work has been disproved by eminent orientalists, it cannot (we apprehend) be with propriety applied to the elucidation of the New Testament. From the number of words used by Saint Paul in peculiar senses, as well as words not ordinarily occurring in Greek writers, Michaelis is of opinion (after Jerome) that they were provincial idioms used in Cilicia in the age in which he lived; and hence he denominates them *Cilicisms*.[2]

The preceding considerations and examples may suffice to convey

---

[1] Pritii Introductio ad Lectionem Novi Testamenti, pp. 320—322. Olearius, sect 2. memb. iii aph. ix. pp 24, 25. Aigler, Hermeneutica Biblica, p. 99. Michaelis, vol. i. pp 162—173. Morus, vol. i. pp. 235, 236. Olearius and Michaelis have collected numerous instances of Latinising phrases occurring in the New Testament, which want of room compels us to omit. Full elucidations of the various idioms above cited are given by Schleusner and Parkhurst in their Lexicons to the New Testament The Græco-Barbara Novi Testamenti (16mo. Amsterdam, 1649,) of Cheitomæus, may also be consulted when it can be met with.

[2] Michaelis, vol i. pp. 149—162.

some idea of the genius of the Greek language of the New Testament. For an account of the principal editions of the Greek Testament, see the Appendix to this Volume, pp. 10—27.; and for the most useful Lexicons that can be consulted, see pp. 168—172.

SECTION III.

ON THE COGNATE OR KINDRED LANGUAGES.

1. *The Aramæan, with its two dialects;* 1. *The Chaldee;* 2. *The Syriac.* — II. *The Arabic, with its derivative, the Ethiopic.* — III. *Use and importance of the Cognate Languages to Sacred Criticism.*

THE *Cognate* or *Kindred* Languages are those which are allied to the Hebrew, as being sister-dialects of the Shemitish languages, all of which preserve nearly the same structure and analogy. The principal cognate languages are the Aramæan, and the Arabic, with their respective dialects or derivatives.

I. The ARAMÆAN LANGUAGE (which in the authorised English version of 2 Kings xvii. 26., and Dan. ii. 4., is rendered the *Syrian* or *Syriack*) derives its name from the very extensive region of Aram, in which it was antiently vernacular. As that region extended from the Mediterranean sea through Syria and Mesopotamia, beyond the river Tigris, the language there spoken necessarily diverged into various dialects; the two principal of which are the Chaldee and the Syriac.

1. The *Chaldee,* but more correctly, the Babylonian, Assyrian, or *Eastern Aramæan* dialect was formerly spoken in Babylonia and Assyria, and was the vernacular dialect spoken in Judæa after the captivity of the Hebrews. Besides the portions of the Old Testament already stated in page 3, as being written in this tongue, numerous Chaldaic words occur in the book of Job, the Proverbs, and other parts of the sacred writings, for the correct understanding of which the knowledge of Chaldee is necessary. It is further of great use for enabling us to read the Chaldee paraphrases which show the sense put by the Jews themselves on the words of Scripture.[1]

2. The *Syriac* or *Western Aramæan* was spoken both in Syria and Mesopotamia; and, after the captivity, it became vernacular in Galilee. Hence, though several of the sacred writers of the New Testament expressed themselves in Greek, their ideas were Syriac; and they consequently used many Syriac idioms, and a few Syriac words.[2] The chief difference between the Syriac and Chaldee consists in the vowel-points or mode of pronunciation; and, notwithstanding the forms of their respective letters are very dissimilar, yet the correspondence between the two dialects is so close, that if the Chaldee be written in Syriac characters without points it becomes Syriac, with the exception of a single inflexion in the formation of

---

[1] Jahn, Elementa Aramaicæ Linguæ, p 2. Walton's Prolegomena, c. xii. § 2, 3. (pp 559—562. edit Dathii.)
[2] Masclef, Gramm. Hebr. vol. ii. p. 114. Wotton's Misna, vol. i. præf. p. xviii.

the verbs.[1] The great assistance, which a knowledge of this dialect affords to the critical understanding of the Hebrew Scriptures, is illustrated at considerable length by the elder Michaelis, in a philological dissertation, originally published in 1756, and reprinted in the first volume of MM. Pott's and Ruperti's "Sylloge Commentationum Theologicarum."[2]

II. Though more remotely allied to the Hebrew than either of the preceding dialects, the ARABIC LANGUAGE possesses sufficient analogy to explain and illustrate the former, and is not, perhaps, inferior in importance to the Chaldee or the Syriac; particularly as it is a living language, in which almost every subject has been discussed, and has received the minutest investigation from native writers and lexicographers. The Arabic language has many roots in common with the Hebrew tongue; and this again contains very many words which are no longer to be found in the Hebrew writings that are extant, but which exist in the Arabic language. The learned Jews who flourished in Spain from the tenth to the twelfth century under the dominion of the Moors, were the first who applied Arabic to the illustration of the Hebrew language: and subsequent Christian writers, as Bochart, the elder Schultens, Olaus Celsius, and others, have diligently and successfully applied the Arabian historians, geographers, and authors on natural history, to the explanation of the Bible.[3]

The *Ethiopic* language, which is immediately derived from the Arabic, has been applied with great advantage to the illustration of the Scriptures by Bochart, De Dieu, Hottinger, and Ludolph (to whom we are indebted for an Ethiopic Grammar and Lexicon)[4]: and Pfeiffer has explained a few passages in the books of Ezra and Daniel, by the aid of the *Persian* language.[5]

III. The *Cognate* or *Kindred Languages* are of considerable use in sacred criticism. They may lead us to discover the occasions of such false readings as transcribers unskilled in the Hebrew, but accustomed to some of the other dialects, have made by writing words in the form of that dialect instead of the Hebrew form. Further, the knowledge of these languages will frequently serve to prevent ill-grounded conjectures that a passage is corrupted, by showing that the common reading is susceptible of the very sense which such passage requires: and when different readings are found in copies of the Bible, these languages may sometimes assist us in determining which of them ought to be preferred.[6]

---

[1] Walton, Prol. c. xiii § 2, 3, 4, 5 (pp. 594—603.)

[2] D. Christiani Benedicti Michaelis Dissertatio Philologica, quâ Lumina Syriaca pro illustrando Ebraismo Sacro exibentur (Halæ, 1756), in Pott's and Ruperti's Sylloge, tom. i. pp. 170—241. The editors have inserted in the notes some additional observations from Michaelis's own copy

[3] Bauer, Herm. Sacr. pp. 82, 83. 106, 107. Walton, Prol. c. xiv. § 2—7 14. (pp. 635—641. 649.) Bishop Marsh's Divinity Lectures, part iii. p 28

[4] Bauer, Herm. Sacr p. 107 Walton, Prol c. xvi. § 6—8. (pp. 674—678.)

[5] Dubia Vexata, cent iv no. 66 (Op. tom i. pp. 420—422.) and Herm. Sacra, c. vi. § 9 (Ibid. tom. ii. p. 648.) Walton, Prol. c. xvi § 5 (pp. 691, 692.)

[6] Gerard's Institutes of Biblical Criticism, p. 63 — For Bibliographical Notices of the principal Grammars and Lexicons of the Cognate Languages, see the Appendix to this Volume, pp. 173—179.

CHAPTER II.

ON THE ANTIENT VERSIONS OF THE SCRIPTURES.

NEXT to the kindred languages, versions afford the greatest assistance to the criticism and interpretation of the Scriptures. "It is only by means of versions, that they, who are ignorant of the original languages, can at all learn what the Scripture contains: and every version, so far as it is just, conveys the sense of Scripture to those who understand the language in which it is written."

Versions may be divided into two classes, *antient* and *modern*. the former were made immediately from the original languages by persons to whom they were familiar; and who, it may be reasonably supposed, had better opportunities for ascertaining the force and meaning of words, than more recent translators can possibly have. Modern versions are those made in later times, and chiefly since the reformation: they are useful for explaining the sense of the inspired writers, while antient versions are of the utmost importance both for the criticism and interpretation of the Scriptures. The present chapter will, therefore, be appropriated to giving an account of those which are most esteemed for their antiquity and excellence.[1]

The principal antient versions, which illustrate the Scriptures, are the Chaldee Paraphrases, generally called Targums, the Septuagint, or Alexandrian Greek version, the translations of Aquila, Symmachus, and Theodotion, and what are called the fifth, sixth, and seventh versions, (of which latter translations fragments only are extant,) together with the Syriac, and Latin or Vulgate versions. Although the authors of these versions did not flourish at the time when the Hebrew language was spoken, yet they enjoyed many advantages for understanding the Bible, especially the Old Testament, which are not possessed by the moderns: for, living near the time when that language was vernacular, they could learn by tradition the true signification of some Hebrew words, which is now forgotten. Many of them also being Jews, and from their childhood accustomed to hear the rabbins explain the Scripture, the study of which they diligently cultivated, and likewise speaking a dialect allied to the Hebrew, — they could not but become well acquainted with the latter. Hence it may be safely inferred that the antient versions generally give the true sense of Scripture, and not unfrequently in passages where it could scarcely be discovered by any other means. All the antient versions, indeed, are of great importance both in the criticism, as well as in the interpretation, of the sacred writings, but they are not all witnesses of equal value; for the *authority* of the different versions depends partly on the age and country of their respective authors, partly on the text whence their translations were made, and partly on the ability and fidelity with which they were executed. It will therefore be not irrelevant to offer a short historical notice of

---

[1] For an account of the principal modern versions, the reader is referred to the Appendix, pp. 53—118.

the principal versions above mentioned, as well as of some other antient versions of less celebrity perhaps, but which have been beneficially consulted by biblical critics.

SECTION I.

ON THE TARGUMS, OR CHALDEE PARAPHRASES OF THE OLD TESTAMENT.

I. *Targum of Onkelos*; — II. *Of the Pseudo-Jonathan*, — III. *The Jerusalem Targum*, — IV. *The Targum of Jonathan Ben Uzziel*; — V. *The Targum on the Hagiographa*; — VI. *The Targum on the Megilloth*; — VII, VIII, IX. *Three Targums on the Book of Esther*, — X. *A Targum on the Books of Chronicles*; — XI. *Real value of the different Targums.*

THE Chaldee word תרגום Targum signifies, in general, any version or explanation; but this appellation is more particularly restricted to the versions or paraphrases of the Old Testament, executed in the East-Aramæan or Chaldee dialect, as it is usually called. These Targums are termed paraphrases or expositions, because they are rather comments and explications, than literal translations of the text: they are written in the Chaldee tongue, which became familiar to the Jews after the time of their captivity in Babylon, and was more known to them than the Hebrew itself: so that, when the law was "read in the synagogue every Sabbath day," in pure biblical Hebrew, an explanation was subjoined to it in Chaldee; in order to render it intelligible to the people, who had but an imperfect knowledge of the Hebrew language. This practice, as already observed, originated with Ezra [1]. as there are no traces of any written Targums prior to those of Onkelos and Jonathan, who are *supposed* to have lived about the time of our Saviour, it is highly probably that these paraphrases were at first merely oral; that, subsequently, the ordinary glosses on the more difficult passages were committed to writing; and that, as the Jews were bound by an ordinance of their elders to possess a copy of the law, these glosses were either afterwards collected together and deficiencies in them supplied, or new and connected paraphrases were formed.

There are at present extant ten paraphrases on different parts of the Old Testament, three of which comprise the Pentateuch, or five books of Moses: — 1. The Targum of Onkelos; 2. That falsely ascribed to Jonathan, and usually cited as the Targum of the Pseudo-

---

[1] See pp. 5, 6, *supra*. Our account of the Chaldee paraphrases is drawn up from a careful consideration of what has been written on them, by Carpzov, in his Critica Sacra, part ii c. 1. pp. 430—481, Bishop Walton, Prol. c 12 sect. ii. pp. 568—592.; Leusden, in Philolog. Hebræo-Mixt Diss v vi. and vii. pp 36—58. ; Dr. Prideaux, Connection, part ii. book viii. sub anno 97 b. c. vol iii pp. 531—555. (edit 1718.) Kortholt, De variis Scripturæ Editionibus, c. iii pp. 34—51. , Pfeiffer, Critica Sacra, cap. viii. sect. ii. (Op. tom, ii pp. 750—771.), and in his Treatise de Theologia Judaica, &c. Exercit ii (Ibid tom. ii pp. 862—889.) ; Bauer, Critica Sacra, tract iii pp 288 —308. ; Rambach. Inst. Herm Sacræ, pp 606—611. ; Pictet, Theologie Chretienne, tom. i. pp 145. *et seq*., Jahn, Introductio ad Libros Veteris Fœderis, pp. 69—75 , and Wæhner's Antiquitates Ebræorum, tom. i. pp 156—170.

Jonathan; and 3. The Jerusalem Targum; 4. The Targum of Jonathan Ben Uzziel, (i. e. the son of Uzziel) on the Prophets; 5. The Targum of Rabbi Joseph the blind, or one-eyed, on the Hagiographa; 6. An anonymous Targum on the five Megilloth, or books of Ruth, Esther, Ecclesiastes, Song of Solomon, and the Lamentations of Jeremiah; 7, 8, 9. Three Targums on the book of Esther; and, 10. A Targum or paraphrase on the two books of Chronicles. These Targums, taken together, form a continued paraphrase on the Old Testament, with the exception of the books of Daniel, Ezra, and Nehemiah (antiently reputed to be part of Ezra); which being for the most part written in Chaldee, it has been conjectured that no paraphrases were written on them, as being unnecessary; though Dr. Prideaux is of opinion that Targums were composed on these books also, which have perished in the lapse of ages.

The language, in which these paraphrases are composed, varies in purity according to the time when they were respectively written. Thus, the Targums of Onkelos and the Pseudo-Jonathan are much purer than the others, approximating very nearly to the Aramæan dialect in which some parts of Daniel and Ezra are written, except indeed that the orthography does not always correspond; while the language of the later Targums whence the rabbinical dialect derives its source, is far more impure, and is intermixed with barbarous and foreign words. Originally, all the Chaldee paraphrases were written without vowel-points, like all other oriental manuscripts: but at length some persons ventured to add points to them, though very erroneously, and this irregular punctuation was retained in the Venice and other early editions of the Hebrew Bible. Some further imperfect attempts towards regular pointing were made both in the Complutensian and in the Antwerp Polyglotts, until at length the elder Buxtorf, in his edition of the Hebrew Bible published at Basil, undertook the thankless task [1] of improving the punctuation of the Targums, according to such rules as he had formed from the pointing which he had found in the Chaldee parts of the books of Daniel and Ezra; and his method of punctuation is followed in Bishop Walton's Polyglott.

I. The *Targum of Onkelos.* — It is not known, with certainty, at what time Onkelos flourished, nor of what nation he was: Professor Eichhorn conjectures that he was a native of Babylon, first, because he is mentioned in the Babylonish Talmud; secondly, because his dialect is not the Chaldee spoken in Palestine, but much purer, and more closely resembling the style of Daniel and Ezra; and, lastly, because he has not interwoven any of those fabulous narratives to which the Jews of Palestine were so much attached, and from which they could with difficulty refrain. The generally received opinion is, that he was a proselyte to Judaism, and a disciple of the celebrated Rabbi Hillel, who flourished about fifty years before the Christian æra; and consequently that Onkelos was contemporary with our

---

[1] Père Simon, Hist. Crit du Vieux Test. liv. ii c. viii has censured Buxtorf's mode of pointing the Chaldee paraphrases with great severity; observing, that he would have done much better if he had more diligently examined manuscripts that were more correctly pointed.

Saviour: Bauer and Jahn, however, place him in the second century. The Targum of Onkelos comprises the Pentateuch or five books of Moses, and is justly preferred to all the others both by Jews and Christians, on account of the purity of its style, and its general freedom from idle legends. It is rather a version than a paraphrase, and renders the Hebrew text word for word, with so much accuracy and exactness, that being set to the same musical notes, with the original Hebrew, it could be read in the same tone as the latter in the public assemblies of the Jews. And this we find was the practice of the Jews up to the time of Rabbi Elias Levita; who flourished in the early part of the sixteenth century, and expressly states that the Jews read the law in their synagogues, first in Hebrew and then in the Targum of Onkelos. This Targum has been translated into Latin by Alfonso de Zamora, Paulus Fagius, Bernardinus Baldus, and Andrew de Leon of Zamora.[1]

II. The second Targum, which is a more liberal paraphrase of the Pentateuch than the preceding, is usually called the *Targum of the Pseudo-Jonathan*, being ascribed by many to Jonathan Ben Uzziel, who wrote the much-esteemed paraphrase on the Prophets. But the difference in the style and diction of this Targum, which is very impure, as well as in the method of paraphrasing adopted in it, clearly proves that it could not have been written by Jonathan Ben Uzziel, who indeed sometimes indulges in allegories, and has introduced a few barbarisms; but this Targum on the law abounds with the most idle Jewish legends that can well be conceived: which, together with the barbarous and foreign words it contains, render it of very little utility. From its mentioning the six parts of the *Talmud*, (on Exod. xxvi. 9.) which compilation was not written till two centuries after the birth of Christ;— *Constantinople*, (on Numb. xxiv. 19.) which city was always called Byzantium until it received its name from Constantine the Great, in the beginning of the fourth century; the *Lombards*, (on Numb. xxiv 24.) whose first irruption into Italy did not take place until the year 570; and the *Turks*, (on Gen. x. 2.) who did not become conspicuous till the middle of the sixth century,— learned men are unanimously of opinion that this Targum of the Pseudo-Jonathan could not have been written before the seventh, or even the eighth century. It has been translated into Latin by Anthony Ralph de Chevalier, an eminent French Protestant divine, in the sixteenth century.

III. The *Jerusalem Targum*, which also paraphrases the five books of Moses, derives its name from the dialect in which it is composed. It is by no means a connected paraphrase, sometimes omitting whole verses, or even chapters; at other times explaining only a single word of a verse, of which it sometimes gives a twofold interpretation; and at others, Hebrew words are inserted without any explanation whatever. In many respects it corresponds with the paraphrase of the Pseudo-Jonathan, whose legendary tales are here frequently repeated, abridged, or expanded. From the

---

[1] The fullest information, concerning the Targum of Onkelos, is to be found in the disquisition of G. B. Winer, entitled De Onkeloso ejusque Paraphrasi Chaldaica Dissertatio, 4to. Lipsiæ, 1820.

impurity of its style, and the number of Greek, Latin, and Persian words which it contains, Bishop Walton, Carpzov, Wolfius, and many other eminent philologers, are of opinion, that it is a compilation by several authors, and consists of extracts and collections. From these internal evidences, the commencement of the seventh century has been assigned as its probable date; but it is more likely not to have been written before the eighth or perhaps the ninth century. This Targum was also translated into Latin by Chevalier and by Francis Taylor.

IV. The *Targum of Jonathan Ben Uzziel.*— According to the talmudical traditions, the author of this paraphrase was chief of the eighty distinguished scholars of Rabbi Hillel the elder, and a fellow-disciple of Simeon the Just, who bore the infant Messiah in his arms: consequently he would be nearly contemporary with Onkelos. Wolfius[1], however, is of opinion that he flourished a short time before the birth of Christ, and compiled the work which bears his name, from more antient Targums, that had been preserved to his time by oral tradition. From the silence of Origen and Jerome concerning this Targum, of which they could not but have availed themselves if it had really existed in their time, and also from its being cited in the Talmud, both Bauer and Jahn date it much later than is generally admitted: the former, indeed, is of opinion, that its true date cannot be ascertained; and the latter, from the inequalities of style and method observable in it, considers it as a compilation from the interpretations of several learned men, made about the close of the third or fourth century. This paraphrase treats on the Prophets, that is (according to the Jewish classification of the sacred writings), on the books of Joshua, Judges, 1 & 2 Sam. 1 & 2 Kings, who are termed the *former* prophets; and on Isaiah, Jeremiah, Ezekiel, and the twelve minor prophets, who are designated as the *latter* prophets. Though the style of this Targum is not so pure and elegant as that of Onkelos, yet it is not disfigured by those legendary tales and numerous foreign and barbarous words which abound in the latter Targums. Both the language and method of interpretation, however, are irregular: in the exposition of the former prophets, the text is more closely rendered than in that on the latter, which is less accurate, as well as more paraphrastical, and interspersed with some traditions and fabulous legends. In order to attach the greater authority to the Targum of Jonathan Ben Uzziel, the Jews, not satisfied with making him contemporary with the prophets Malachi, Zachariah, and Haggai, and asserting that he received it from their lips, have related, that while Jonathan was composing his paraphrase, there was an earthquake for forty leagues around him; and that if any bird happened to pass over him, or a fly alighted on his paper while writing, they were immediately consumed by fire from heaven, without any injury being sustained either by his person or his paper. The whole of this Targum was translated into Latin by Alfonso de

---

[1] Bibliotheca Hebraicæ, tom. 1 p. 1160.

Zamora, Andrea de Leon, and Conrad Pellican; and the paraphrase on the twelve minor prophets, by Immanuel Tremellius.

V. The *Targum on the Cetubim, Hagiographa*, or Holy Writings, is ascribed by some Jewish writers to *Raf Jose*, or Rabbi Joseph, surnamed the one-eyed or blind, who is said to have been at the head of the academy at Sora, in the third century; though others affirm that its author is unknown. The style is barbarous, impure, and very unequal, interspersed with numerous digressions and legendary narratives on which account the younger Buxtorf, and after him Bauer and Jahn, are of opinion that the whole is a compilation of later times: and this sentiment appears to be the most correct. Dr. Prideaux characterises its language as the most corrupt Chaldee of the Jerusalem dialect. The translators of the preceding Targum, together with Arias Montanus, have given a Latin version of this Targum.

VI. The *Targum on the Megilloth*, or five books of Ecclesiastes, Song of Songs, Lamentations of Jeremiah, Ruth, and Esther, is evidently a compilation by several persons. the barbarism of its style, numerous digressions, and idle legends which are inserted, all concur to prove it to be of late date, and certainly not earlier than the sixth century. The paraphrase on the book of Ruth and the Lamentations of Jeremiah is the best executed portion: Ecclesiastes is more freely paraphrased; but the text of the Song of Solomon is absolutely lost amidst the diffuse *circumscription* of its author, and his dull glosses and fabulous additions.

VII, VIII, IX The *three Targums on the book of Esther*. —This book has always been held in the highest estimation by the Jews; which circumstance induced them to translate it repeatedly into the Chaldee dialect. Three paraphrases on it have been printed: one in the Antwerp Polyglott, which is much shorter and contains fewer digressions than the others; another in Bishop Walton's Polyglott, which is more diffuse, and comprises more numerous Jewish fables and traditions; and a third, of which a Latin Version was published by Francis Taylor; and which, according to Carpzov, is more stupid and diffuse than either of the preceding. They are all three of very late date.

X. A *Targum on the books of Chronicles*, which for a long time was unknown both to Jews and Christians, was discovered in the library at Erfurt, belonging to the ministers of the Augsburg confession, by Matthias Frederick Beck; who published it in 1680, 3, 4, in two quarto volumes. Another edition was published at Amsterdam by the learned David Wilkins (1715, 4to.), from a manuscript in the university library at Cambridge. It is more complete than Beck's edition, and supplies many of its deficiencies. This Targum, however, is of very little value; like all the other Chaldee paraphrases, it blends legendary tales with the narrative, and introduces numerous Greek words, such as οχλος, σοφισαι, αρχων, &c.

XI Of all the Chaldee paraphrases above noticed, the Targums of Onkelos and Jonathan Ben Uzziel are most highly valued by the Jews, who implicitly receive their expositions of doubtful passages. Shickhard, Mayer, Helvicus, Leusden, Hottinger, and Dr. Prideaux, have conjectured that some Chaldee Targum was in use in the synogogue where our Lord read Isa. lxi. 1, 2. (Luke iv. 17—19.); and that he quoted Psal. xxii. 1. when on the cross (Matt xxvii. 46.) not out of the Hebrew text, but out of a Chaldee paraphrase. But there does not appear to be sufficient ground for this hypothesis: for as the Chaldee or East Aramæan dialect was spoken at Jerusalem, it is at least as probable that Jesus Christ interpreted the Hebrew into the vernacular dialect in the first instance, as that he should have read from a Targum; and, when on the cross, it was perfectly natural that he should speak in the same language, rather than in the Biblical Hebrew; which, we have already seen, was cultivated and studied by the priests and Levites as a learned language. The Targum of Rabbi Joseph the Blind, in which the words cited by our Lord are to be found, is so long *posterior* to the time of his crucifixion, that it cannot be received as evidence. So numerous, indeed, are the variations, and so arbitrary are the alterations occurring in the manuscripts of the Chaldee paraphrases, that Dr. Kennicott has clearly proved them to have been designedly altered in compliment to the previously corrupted copies of the Hebrew text; or, in other words, that " alterations have been made wilfully in the Chaldee paraphrase to render that paraphrase, in some places, more conformable to the words of the Hebrew text, where those Hebrew words are supposed to be right, but had themselves been corrupted."[1] But notwithstanding all their deficiencies and interpolations, the Targums, especially those of Onkelos and Jonathan, are of considerable importance in the interpretation of the Scriptures, not only as they supply the meanings of words or phrases occurring but once in the Old Testament, but also because they reflect considerable light on the Jewish rites, ceremonies, laws, customs, usages, &c. mentioned or alluded to in both Testaments. But it is in establishing the genuine meaning of particular prophecies relative to the Messiah, in opposition to the false explications of the Jews and Antitrinitarians, that these Targums are pre-eminently useful. Bishop Walton, Dr. Prideaux, Pfeiffer, Carpzov, and Rambach, have illustrated this remark by numerous examples. Bishop Patrick, and Drs. Gill and Clarke, in their respective Commentaries on the Bible, have inserted many valuable elucidations from the Chaldee paraphrasts. Leusden recommends that no one should attempt to read their writings, nor indeed to learn the Chaldee dialect, who is not previously well-grounded in Hebrew: he advises the Chaldee text of Daniel and Ezra to be first read either with his own Chaldee Manual or with Buxtorf's Hebrew and Chaldee Lexicon; after which the Targums of Onkelos and Jonathan may be perused, with the help of Buxtorf's Chaldee and Syriac Lexicon, and of De Lara's work, *De Convenientia Vocabulorum Rabbinicorum cum Græcis et quibusdam aliis linguis Europæis*. Amstelodami, 1648, 4to.[2]

---

[1] Dr. Kennicott's Second Dissertation, pp 167—193.
[2] See a notice of the principal editions of the Chaldee Paraphrases in pp 32, 33. of the Appendix to this volume

SECTION II.

ON THE ANTIENT GREEK VERSIONS OF THE OLD TESTAMENT.

I. *The* SEPTUAGINT; — 1. *History of it;* — 2. *A Critical Account of its Execution;* — 3 *What Manuscripts were used by its Authors;* — 4. *Account of the Biblical Labours of Origen;* — 5. *Notice of the Recensions or Editions of Eusebius and Pamphilus, of Lucian, and of Hesychius;* — 6. *Peculiar Importance of the Septuagint Version in the Criticism and Interpretation of the New Testament;* — II. *Account of other Greek Versions of the Old Testament;* — 1 *Version of* AQUILA; — 2. *Of* THEODOTION; — 3. *Of* SYMMACHUS; — 4, 5, 6. *Anonymous Versions.* — III *References in Antient Manuscripts to other Versions.*

I. AMONG the Greek versions of the Old Testament, the ALEXANDRIAN or SEPTUAGINT, as it is generally termed, is the most antient and valuable; and was held in so much esteem both by the Jews and by the first Christians, as to be constantly read in the synagogues and churches. Hence it is uniformly cited by the early fathers, whether Greek or Latin, and from this version all the translations into other languages, which were antiently approved by the Christian Church, were executed (with the exception of the Syriac), as the Arabic, Armenian, Ethiopic, Gothic, and Old Italic or the Latin version in use before the time of Jerome: and to this day the Septuagint is exclusively read in the Greek and most other Oriental churches.[1] This version has derived its name either from the Jewish account of seventy-two persons having been employed to make it, or from its having received the approbation of the Sanhedrin, or great council of the Jews, which consisted of seventy, or, more correctly, of seventy-two persons. — Much uncertainty, however, has prevailed concerning the *real* history of this antient version: and while some have strenuously advocated its miraculous and divine origin, other eminent philologists have laboured to prove that it must have been executed by several persons and at different times.

1. According to one account, Ptolemy Philadelphus, king of Egypt, caused this translation to be made for the use of the library which he had founded at Alexandria, at the request and with the advice of the celebrated Demetrius Phalereus, his principal librarian. For this purpose, it is reported, that he sent Aristeas and Andreas, two distinguished officers of his court to Jerusalem, on an embassy to Eleazar,

---

[1] Walton, Prol c. ix (pp. 333—469), from which, and from the following authorities, our account of the Septuagint is derived, viz. Bauer, Critica Sacra, pp. 243—273. who has chiefly followed Hody's book, hereafter noticed, in the history of the Septuagint version Dr Prideaux, Connection, part ii. book i. sub anno 277. (vol. ii. pp. 27—49.); Masch's Preface to part ii. of his edition of Le Long's Bibliotheca Sacra, in which the history of the Septuagint version is minutely examined, Morus, in Ernesti, vol. ii. pp. 50 —81., 101—119., Carpzov, Critica Sacra, pp. 481—551., Masch and Boerner's edition of Le Long's Bibliotheca Sacra, part ii. vol. ii. pp. 216—220, 256—304., Thomas, Introductio in Hermeneuticam Sacrum utriusque Testamenti, pp 228—253. Harles, Brevior Notitia Litteraturæ Græcæ, pp 638—643., and Renouard, Annales de l'Imprimerie des Aldes, tom. i. p. 140 See also Origenis Hexapla, a Montfaucon, tom. i. Prœlim Diss. pp. 17—35 A *full* account of the manuscripts and editions of the Greek Scriptures is given in the preface to vol. i. of the edition of the Septuagint commenced by the late Rev. Dr. Holmes, of which an account is given in pp 37, 38, of the Appendix to this volume.

then high priest of the Jews, to request of the latter a copy of the Hebrew Scriptures, and that there might also be sent to him seventy-two persons (six chosen out of each of the twelve tribes), who were equally well skilled in the Hebrew and Greek languages. These learned men were accordingly shut up in the island of Pharos, where, having agreed in the translation of each period after a mutual conference, Demetrius wrote down their version as they dictated it to him: and thus, in the space of seventy-two days, the whole was accomplished. This relation is derived from a letter ascribed to Aristeas himself, the authenticity of which has been greatly disputed. If, as there is every reason to believe is the case, this piece is a forgery, it was made at a very early period: for it was in existence in the time of Josephus, who has made use of it in his Jewish Antiquities. The veracity of Aristeas's narrative was not questioned until the seventeenth or eighteenth century: at which time, indeed, biblical criticism was, comparatively, in its infancy. Vives [1], Scaliger [2], Van Dale [3], Dr. Prideaux, and, above all, Dr. Hody [4], were the principal writers in the seventeenth and eighteenth centuries who attacked the genuineness of the pretended narrative of Aristeas; and though it was ably vindicated by Bishop Walton [5], Isaac Vossius [6], Whiston [7], Brett [8], and other modern writers, the majority of the learned in our own time are fully agreed in considering it as fictitious.

Philo the Jew, who also notices the Septuagint version, was ignorant of most of the circumstances narrated by Aristeas, but he relates others which appear not less extraordinary. According to him, Ptolemy Philadelphus sent to Palestine for some learned Jews, whose number he does not specify: and these going over to the island of Pharos, there executed so many distinct versions, all of which so *exactly and uniformly* agreed in sense, phrases, and words, as proved them to have been not common interpreters; but men prophetically inspired and divinely directed, who had every word dictated to them by the Spirit of God throughout the entire translation. He adds that an annual festival was celebrated by the Alexandrian Jews in the isle of Pharos, where the version was made, until his time, to preserve the memory of it, and to thank God for so great a benefit. [9]

Justin Martyr, who flourished in the middle of the second century, about one hundred years after Philo, relates [10] a similar story, with the addition of the seventy interpreters being shut up each in his own separate cell (which had been erected for that purpose by order of Ptolemy Philadelphus); and that here they composed so many distinct versions, word for word, in the very same expressions, to the

---

[1] In a note on Augustine de Civitate Dei, lib. viii. c. 42.
[2] In a note on Eusebius's Chronicle, no. MDCCXXXIV.
[3] Dissertatio super Aristea, de LXX interpretibus, &c. Amst. 1705, 4to
[4] De Bibliorum Græcorum Textibus, Versionibus Græcis, et Latinâ Vulgatâ, libri iv. cui præmittitur Aristeæ Historia, folio, Oxon. 1705.
[5] Prol. c. ix. § 3—10. pp 338—359
[6] De LXX Interpretibus, Hag. Com. 1661, 4to.
[7] In the Appendix to his work on "The Literal Accomplishment of Scripture Prophecies," London, 1724, 8vo.
[8] Dissertation on the Septuagint, in Bishop Watson's Collection of Theological Tracts, vol. iii. p. 20. et seq.
[9] De Vita Mosis lib ii [10] Cohort ad Gentes

great admiration of the king; who, not doubting that this version was divinely inspired, loaded the interpreters with honours, and dismissed them to their own country, with magnificent presents. The good father adds, that the ruins of these cells were visible in his time. But this narrative of Justin's is directly at variance with several circumstances recorded by Aristeas; such, for instance, as the previous conference or deliberation of the translators; and, above all, the very important point of the version being dictated to Demetrius Phalereus. Epiphanius, a writer of the fourth century, attempts to harmonise all these accounts by shutting up the translators two and two, in thirty-six cells, where they might consider or deliberate, and by stationing a copyist in each cell, to whom the translators dictated their labours: the result of all which was the production of thirty-six inspired versions, agreeing most uniformly together.

It is not a little remarkable that the Samaritans have traditions in favour of their version of the Pentateuch, equally extravagant with those preserved by the Jews. In the Samaritan Chronicle of Abul Phatach, which was compiled in the fourteenth century from antient and modern authors both Hebrew and Arabic, there is a story to the following effect:—That Ptolemy Philadelphus, in the tenth year of his reign, directed his attention to the difference subsisting between the Samaritans and the Jews concerning the law; the former receiving only the Pentateuch, and rejecting every other work ascribed to the prophets by the Jews. In order to determine this difference, he commanded the two nations to send deputies to Alexandria. The Jews entrusted this mission to *Osar*, the Samaritans to *Aaron*, to whom several other associates were added. Separate apartments in a particular quarter of Alexandria, were assigned to each of these strangers; who were prohibited from having any personal intercourse, and each of them had a Greek scribe to write his version. Thus were the law and other Scriptures translated by the Samaritans; whose version being most carefully examined, the king was convinced that their text was more complete than that of the Jews. Such is the narrative of Abul Phatach, divested however of numerous marvellous circumstances, with which it has been decorated by the Samaritans; who are not surpassed even by the Jews in their partiality for idle legends.

A fact, buried under such a mass of fables as the translation of the Septuagint has been by the historians, who have pretended to record it, necessarily loses all its historical character, which indeed we are fully justified in disregarding altogether. Although there is no doubt but that some truth is concealed under this load of fables, yet it is by no means an easy task to discern the truth from what is false: the following, however, is the result of our researches concerning this celebrated version.

It is probable that the seventy interpreters, as they are called, executed their version of the Pentateuch during the joint reigns of Ptolemy Lagus, and his son Philadelphus. The Pseudo-Aristeas, Josephus, Philo, and many other writers, whom it were tedious to enumerate, relate that this version was made during the reign of Ptolemy II. or Philadelphus: Joseph Ben Gorion, however, among the Rabbins, Theodoret, and many other Christian writers, refer its date to the time of Ptolemy Lagus. Now these two traditions can be reconciled only by supposing the version to have been performed during the two years when Ptolemy Philadelphus shared the throne with his father; which date coincides with the third and fourth years of the hundred and twenty-third olympiad, that is, about the years 286 and 285, before the vulgar Christian æra. Further, this version was made neither by the command of Ptolemy, nor at the request nor under the superintendence of Demetrius Phalereus; but was voluntarily undertaken by the Jews for the use of their countrymen. It is well known, that, at the period above noticed, there was a great multitude of Jews settled in Egypt, particularly at Alexandria: these, being most strictly observant of the religious institutions and usages of their forefathers, had their Sanhedrin, or grand council composed of seventy or seventy-two members, and very numerous synagogues, in which the law was read to them on every sabbath; and as the bulk of the common people were no longer acquainted with biblical Hebrew (the Greek language alone being used in their ordinary intercourse), it became necessary to translate the Pentateuch into Greek for their use. This is a far more probable account of the origin of the Alexandrian version than the traditions above stated. If this translation had been made by public authority, it would unquestionably have been performed under the direction of the Sanhedrin, who would have examined, and perhaps corrected it, if it had been the work of a single individual, previously to giving it the stamp of their approbation, and introducing it into the synagogues. In either case the translation would, probably, be denominated the Septuagint, because the Sanhedrin was composed of seventy or seventy-two members. It is even possible that the Sanhedrin, in order to ascertain the fidelity of the work, might have sent to Palestine for some learned men, of whose assistance and advice they would have availed themselves in examining the version. This fact, if it could be proved (for it is offered as a mere conjecture), would account for the story of the king of Egypt's sending an embassy to Jerusalem. There is, however, one circumstance which proves that, in executing this translation, the synagogues were originally in contemplation, viz. that all the antient writers unanimously concur in saying that the Pentateuch was first translated. The five books of Moses, indeed, were the only books read in the synagogues until the time of Antiochus Epiphanes, king of Syria: who having forbidden that practice in Palestine, the Jews evaded his commands by substituting for the Pentateuch the reading of the prophetic books. When, afterwards, the Jews were delivered from the tyranny of the kings of Syria, they read the law and the prophets alternately in their synagogues: and the same custom was adopted by the Hellenistic or Græcising Jews.

2. But whatever was the real number of the authors of the version, their introduction of Coptic words, (such as οιφι, αχι, ρεμφαν, &c.) as well as their rendering of ideas purely Hebrew altogether in the Egyptian manner, clearly prove that they were natives of Egypt.

Thus they express the creation of the world, not by the proper Greek word ΚΤΙΣΙΣ, but by ΓΕΝΕΣΙΣ, a term employed by the philosophers of Alexandria to express the origin of the universe. The Hebrew word Thummim, (Exod. xxviii. 30.) which signifies perfections, they render ΑΛΗΘΕΙΑ, *truth* [1] The difference of style also indicates the version to have been the work not of one but of several translators, and to have been executed at different times. The best qualified and most able among them was the translator of the Pentateuch, who was evidently master of both Greek and Hebrew: he has religiously followed the Hebrew text, and has in various instances introduced the most suitable and best chosen expressions. From the very close resemblance subsisting between the text of the Greek version and the text of the Samaritan Pentateuch, Louis de Dieu, Selden, Whiston, Hassencamp, and Bauer, are of opinion that the author of the Alexandrian version made it from the Samaritan Pentateuch. And in proportion as these two correspond, the Greek differs from the Hebrew. This opinion is further supported by the declarations of Origen and Jerome, that the translator found the venerable name of Jehovah not in the letters in common use, but in very antient characters; and also by the fact that those consonants in the Septuagint are frequently confounded together, the shapes of which are similar in the Samaritan, but not in the Hebrew alphabet. This hypothesis, however ingenious and plausible, is by no means determinate: and what militates most against it is, the inveterate enmity subsisting between the Jews and Samaritans, added to the constant and unvarying testimony of antiquity that the Greek version of the Pentateuch was executed by Jews. There is no other way by which to reconcile these conflicting opinions, than by supposing either that the manuscripts used by the Egyptian Jews approximated towards the letters and text of the Samaritan Pentateuch, or that the translators of the Septuagint made use of manuscripts written in antient characters.

Next to the Pentateuch, for ability and fidelity of execution, ranks the translation of the book of Proverbs, the author of which was well skilled in the two languages. Michaelis is of opinion that, of all the books of the Septuagint, the style of the Proverbs is the best, the translators having clothed the most ingenious thoughts in as neat and elegant language as was ever used by a Pythagorean sage, to express his philosophic maxims. [2] The translator of the book of Job being acquainted with the Greek poets, his style is more elegant and studied: but he was not sufficiently master of the Hebrew language and literature, and consequently his version is very often erroneous. Many of the historical passages are interpolated: and in the poetical parts there are several passages wanting: Jerome, in

---

[1] The reason of this appears from Diodorus Siculus, who informs us that the president of the Egyptian courts of justice wore round his neck a golden chain, at which was suspended an image set round with precious stones, which was called TRUTH, ὃ προσηγορευον Αληθειαν, lib. i. c 75. tom. i. p 225. (edit. Bipont.) Bauer, (Crit. Sacr pp 244, 245) and Morus, (Acroases in Ernesti, tom. ii. pp. 67—81) have given several examples, proving from internal evidence that the authors of the Septuagint version were Egyptian.

[2] Michaelis, Introd. to New Test. vol. i. p. 113.

his preface to the book of Job, specifies as many as seventy or eighty verses. These omissions were supplied by Origen from Theodotion's translation. The book of Joshua could not have been translated till upwards of twenty years after the death of Ptolemy Lagus: for, in chapter viii. verse 18., the translator has introduced the word γαισος, a word of Gallic origin, denoting a short dart or javelin peculiar to the Gauls, who made an irruption into Greece in the third year of the 125th olympiad, or B.C. 278, and it was not till some time after that event that the Egyptian kings took Gallic mercenaries into their pay and service.

During the reign of Ptolemy Philometer, the book of Esther, together with the Psalms and Prophets, was translated. The subscription annexed to the version of Esther, expressly states it to have been finished on the fourth year of that sovereign's reign, or about the year 177 before the Christian æra: the Psalms and Prophets, in all probability, were translated still later, because the Jews did not begin to read them in their synagogues till about the year 170 before Christ. The Psalms and Prophets were translated by men every way unequal to the task. Jeremiah is the best executed among the Prophets; and next to this the books of Amos and Ezekiel are placed: the important prophecies of Isaiah were translated, according to Bishop Lowth, upwards of one hundred years after the Pentateuch, and by a person by no means adequate to the undertaking; there being hardly any book of the Old Testament so ill rendered in the Septuagint as this of Isaiah, (which together with other parts of the Greek version) has come down to us in a bad condition, incorrect, and with frequent omissions and interpolations: and so very erroneous was the version of Daniel, that it was totally rejected by the antient church, and Theodotion's translation was substituted for it. Some fragments of the Septuagint version of Daniel, which for a long time was supposed to have been lost, were discovered and published at Rome in 1772, from which it appears that its author had but an imperfect knowledge of the Hebrew language.

No date has been assigned for the translation of the books of Judges, Ruth, Samuel, and Kings, which appear to have been executed by one and the same author; who though he does not make use of so many Hebraisms as the translators of the other books, is yet not without his peculiarities.

3. Before we conclude the history of the Septuagint version, it may not be irrelevant briefly to notice a question which has greatly exercised the ingenuity of biblical philologers, viz. from what MANUSCRIPTS did the seventy interpreters execute their translation?. Professor Tyschen[1] has offered an hypothesis that they did not translate the Hebrew Old Testament into Greek, but that it has been transcribed in Hebræo-Greek characters, and that from this transcript their version was made this hypothesis has been examined by

---

[1] Tentamen de variis Codicum Hebraicorum Vet. Test MSS. Generibus, Rostock, 1772, 8vo. pp. 48—64. 81—124.

several German critics, and by none with more acumen than by Dathe, in the preface to his Latin version of the minor prophets¹: but as the arguments are not of a nature to admit of abridgment, this notice may perhaps suffice. The late eminently learned Bishop Horsley doubts whether the manuscripts from which the Septuagint version was made, would (if now extant) be entitled to the same degree of credit as our modern Hebrew text, notwithstanding their comparatively high antiquity. "There is," he observes, "certainly much reason to believe, that after the destruction of the temple by Nebuchadnezzar, perhaps from a somewhat earlier period, the Hebrew text was in a much worse state of corruption in the copies which were in private hands, than it has ever been since the revision of the sacred books by Ezra. These inaccurate copies would be multiplied during the whole period of the captivity, and widely scattered in Assyria, Persia, and Egypt; in short, through all the regions of the dispersion. The text, as revised by Ezra, was certainly of much higher credit than any of these copies, notwithstanding their greater antiquity. His edition succeeded, as it were, to the privileges of an autograph (the autographs of the inspired writers themselves being totally lost), and was henceforth to be considered as the only source of authentic text: insomuch that the comparative merit of any text now extant will depend upon the probable degree of its approximation to, or distance from, the Esdrine edition. Nay, if the translation of the LXX was made from some of those old manuscripts which the dispersed Jews had carried into Egypt, or from any other of those unauthenticated copies (which is the prevailing tradition among the Jews and is very probable, at least it cannot be confuted); it will be likely that the faultiest manuscript now extant differs less from the genuine Esdrine text, than those more antient, which the version of the LXX represents. But, much as this consideration lowers the credit of the LXX separately, for any various reading, it adds great weight to the consent of the LXX with later versions, and greater still to the consent of the old versions with manuscripts of the Hebrew, which still survive. And, as it is certainly possible that a true reading may be preserved in one solitary manuscript, it will follow, that a true reading may be preserved in one version: for the manuscript which contained the true reading at the time when the version was made, may have perished since; so that no evidence of the reading shall now remain, but the version."²

The Septuagint version, though originally made for the use of the Egyptian Jews, gradually acquired the highest authority among the Jews of Palestine, who were acquainted with the Greek language, and subsequently also among Christians. It appears, indeed, that the legend above confuted of the translators having been divinely inspired, was invented in order that the LXX might be held in the greater estimation. Philo the Jew, a native of Egypt, has evidently followed it in his allegorical expositions of the Mosaic law: and, though Dr. Hody

---
¹ Published at Halle, in 1790, in 8vo.
² Bishop Horsley's Translation of Hosea, Præf. pp. xxxvi. xxxvii. 2d edit

was of opinion that Josephus, who was a native of Palestine, corroborated his work on Jewish Antiquities from the Hebrew text, yet Salmasius, Bochart, Bauer, and others, have shown that he has adhered to the Septuagint throughout that work. How extensively this version was in use among the Jews, appears from the solemn sanction given to it by the inspired writers of the New Testament, who have in very many passages quoted the Greek version of the Old Testament.[1] Their example was followed by the earlier fathers and doctors of the church, who, with the exception of Origen and Jerome, were unacquainted with Hebrew: notwithstanding their zeal for the word of God, they did not exert themselves to learn the original language of the sacred writings, but acquiesced in the Greek representation of them; judging it, no doubt, to be fully sufficient for all the purposes of their pious labours. "The Greek Scriptures were the only Scriptures known to or valued by the Greeks. This was the text commented by Chrysostom and Theodoret, it was this which furnished topics to Athanasius, Nazianzen, and Basil. From this fountain the stream was derived to the Latin church, first, by the Italic or Vulgate translation of the Scriptures, which was made from the Septuagint, and not from the Hebrew; and, secondly, by the study of the Greek fathers. It was by this borrowed light, that the Latin fathers illuminated the western hemisphere: and, when the age of Cyprian, Ambrose, Augustine, and Gregory successively passed away, this was the light put into the hands of the next dynasty of theologists, the schoolmen, who carried on the work of theological disquisition by the aid of this luminary and none other. So that, either in Greek or in Latin, it was still the Septuagint Scriptures that were read, explained, and quoted as authority, for a period of fifteen hundred years."[2]

The Septuagint version retained its authority, even with the rulers of the Jewish synagogue, until the commencement of the first century after Christ: when the Jews, being unable to resist the arguments from prophecy which were urged against them by the Christians, in order to deprive them of the benefit of that authority, began to deny that it agreed with the Hebrew text. Further to discredit the character of the Septuagint, the Jews instituted a solemn fast, on the 8th day of the month Thebet (December), to execrate the memory of its having been made. Not satisfied with this measure, we are assured by Justin Martyr, who lived in the former part of the second century, that they proceeded to expunge several passages out of the Septuagint; and abandoning this, adopted the version of Aquila, a proselyte Jew of Sinope, a city of Pontus[3]: this is the translation mentioned in the Talmud and not the Septuagint, with which it has been confounded.[4]

4. The great use, however, which had been made by the Jews

---
[1] On the quotations from the Old Testament in the New, see Chapter VI. *infra*.
[2] Reeves's Collation of the Hebrew and Greek Texts of the Psalms, pp. 22, 23.
[3] On this subject the reader is referred to Dr. Owen's Inquiry into the present State of the Septuagint Version, pp. 29—87. (8vo London, 1769.) In pp. 126—138. he has proved the falsification of the Septuagint, from the versions of Aquila and Symmachus.
[4] Prideaux, Connection, vol. ii. p. 50. Lightfoot's Works, vol. ii. p. 806, 807.

previously to their rejection of the Septuagint, and the constant use of it by the Christians, would naturally cause a multiplication of copies; in which, besides the alterations designedly made by the Jews, numerous errors became introduced, in the course of time, from the negligence or inaccuracy of transcribers, and from glosses or marginal notes, which had been added for the explanation of difficult words, being suffered to creep into the text. In order to remedy this growing evil, ORIGEN, in the early part of the third century, undertook the laborious task of collating the Greek text then in use with the original Hebrew and with other Greek translations then extant, and from the whole to produce a new *recension* or revisal. Twenty-eight years were devoted to the preparation of this arduous work, in the course of which he collected manuscripts from every possible quarter, aided (it is said) by the pecuniary liberality of Ambrose, an opulent man, whom he had converted from the Valentinian heresy, and with the assistance of seven copyists and several persons skilled in caligraphy, or the art of beautiful writing. Origen commenced his labour at Cæsarea, A D. 231; and, it appears, finished his Polyglott at Tyre, but in what year is not precisely known.

This noble critical work is designated by various names among antient writers; as *Tetrapla, Hexapla, Octapla,* and *Enneapla.*

The *Tetrapla,* contained the four Greek versions of Aquila, Symmachus, the Septuagint, and Theodotion, disposed in four columns [1]: to these he added two columns more, containing the Hebrew text in its original characters, and also in Greek letters; these six columns, according to Epiphanius, formed the *Hexapla.* Having subsequently discovered two other Greek versions of *some parts* of the Scriptures, usually called the fifth and sixth, he added them to the preceding, inserting them in their respective places, and thus composed the *Octapla ,* and a separate translation of the Psalms, usually called the seventh version, being afterwards added, the entire work has by some been termed the *Enneapla.* This appellation, however, was never generally adopted. But, as the two editions made by Origen generally bore the name of the Tetrapla and Hexapla, Dr. Grabe thinks that they were thus called, not from the number of the columns, but of the versions, which were six, the seventh containing the Psalms only. [2] Bauer, after Montfaucon, is of opinion, that Origen edited only the Tetrapla and Hexapla; and this appears to be the real fact. The following specimens from Montfaucon will convey an idea of the construction of these two laborious works. [3]

---

[1] The late Rev Dr. Holmes, who commenced the splendid edition of the Septuagint noticed in pp. 37, 38 of the Appendix to this volume, was of opinion that the first column of the Tetrapla, contained the κοινη, or Septuagint text commonly in use, collated with Hebrew manuscripts by Origen, and that the other three columns were occupied by the versions of Aquila, Symmachus, and Theodotion.

[2] Dr. Holmes thinks that the text of the Septuagint in the Hexapla was not the Κοινη as then in use, but as corrected in the Tetrapla, and perhaps improved by further collations.

[3] Origenis Hexapla, Prœl, Diss. tom. 1. p. 16.

TETRAPLA.

Gen. i. 1.

ΑΚΥΛΑΣ.	ΣΥΜΜΑΧΟΣ.	Οἱ Ο	ΘΕΟΔΟΤΙΩΝ
Εν κεφαλαιω εκτισεν ὁ Θεος συν τον ουρανον και συν την γην.	Εν αρχη εκτισεν ὁ Θεος τον ουρανον και την γην	Εν αρχη εποιησεν ὁ Θεος τον ουρανον και την γην	Εν αρχη εκτισεν ὁ Θεος τον ουρανον και την γην.

In this specimen the version of Aquila holds the first place, as being most literal; the second is occupied by that of Symmachus, as rendering *ad sensum* rather than *ad literam*, the third by the Septuagint, and the fourth by Theodotion's translation

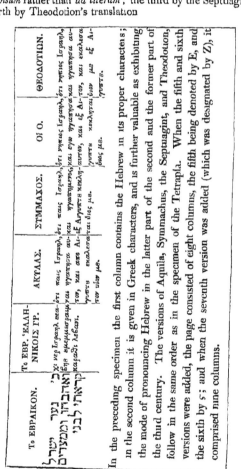

In the preceding specimen the first column contains the Hebrew in its proper characters; in the second column it is given in Greek characters, and is further valuable as exhibiting the mode of pronouncing Hebrew in the latter part of the second and the former part of the third century. The versions of Aquila, Symmachus, the Septuagint, and Theodotion, follow in the same order as in the specimen of the Tetrapla. When the fifth and sixth versions were added, the page consisted of eight columns, the fifth being denoted by E, and the sixth by ς; and when the seventh version was added (which was designated by Z), it comprised nine columns.

The original Hebrew being considered as the basis of the whole work, the proximity of each translation to the text, in point of closeness and fidelity, determined its rank in the order of the columns: thus Aquila's version, being the most faithful, is placed next to the sacred text; that of Symmachus occupies the fourth column; the Septuagint, the fifth; and Theodotion's, the sixth. The other three anonymous translations, not containing the entire books of the Old Testament, were placed, in the three last columns of the Enneapla, according to the order of time in which they were discovered by Origen. Where the same words occurred in all the other Greek versions, without being particularly specified, Origen designated them by Λ or ΛΟ, Λοιποι, the rest;—Οι Γ, or the three, denoted Aquila, Symmachus, and Theodotion;—Οι Δ, or the four, signified Aquila, Symmachus, the Septuagint, and Theodotion; and Π, Παντες, all the interpreters.

The object of Origen being to correct the differences found in the then existing copies of the Old Testament, he carefully noted the alterations made by him; and for the information of those who might consult his work, he made use of the following marks:—

1. Where any passages appeared in the Septuagint, that were not found in the Hebrew, he designed them by an *obelus* ÷ with two bold points : also annexed. This mark was also used to denote words not extant in the Hebrew, but added by the Septuagint translators, either for the sake of elegance, or for the purpose of illustrating the sense.

2. To passages wanting in the copies of the Septuagint, and supplied by himself from the other Greek versions, he prefixed an asterisk × with two bold points : also annexed, in order that his additions might be immediately perceived. These supplementary passages, we are informed by Jerome, were for the most part taken from Theodotion's translation; not unfrequently from that of Aquila; sometimes, though rarely, from the version of Symmachus; and sometimes from two or three together. But, in every case, the initial letter of each translator's name was placed immediately after the asterisk, to indicate the source whence such supplementary passage was taken. And in lieu of the very erroneous Septuagint version of Daniel, Theodotion's translation of that book was inserted entire.

3. Further, not only the passages wanting in the Septuagint were supplied by Origen with the asterisks, as above noticed; but also where that version does not appear accurately to express the Hebrew original, having noted the former reading with an obelus, ÷, he added the correct rendering from one of the other translators, with an asterisk subjoined. Concerning the shape and uses of the *lemniscus* and *hypolemniscus*, two other marks used by Origen, there is so great a difference of opinion among learned men, that it is difficult to determine what they were.[1] Dr. Owen, after Mont-

---

[1] Montfaucon, Prælim ad Hexapla, tom. i pp 36—42. Holmes, Vetus Testamentum Græcum, tom. i. Præfat cap i sect. i.—vii. The first book of Dr Holmes's erudite preface is translated into English in the Christian Observer for 1821, vol. xx. pp. 544—548 610—615. 676—683, 746—750

faucon, supposes them to have been marks of better and more accurate renderings.

In the Pentateuch, Origen compared the Samaritan text with the Hebrew as received by the Jews, and noted their differences. To each of the translations inserted in his Hexapla was prefixed an account of the author; each had its separate prolegomena; and the ample margins were filled with notes. A few fragments of these prolegomena and marginal annotations have been preserved; but nothing remains of his history of the Greek versions.[1]

Since Origen's time, biblical critics have distinguished two editions or exemplars of the Septuagint — the Κοινη or common text, with all its errors and imperfections, as it existed previously to his collation; and the Hexaplar text, or that corrected by Origen himself. For nearly fifty years was this great man's stupendous work buried in a corner of the city of Tyre, probably on account of the very great expense of transcribing forty or fifty volumes, which far exceeded the means of private individuals: and here, perhaps, it might have perished in oblivion, if Eusebius and Pamphilus had not discovered it, and deposited it in the library of Pamphilus the martyr at Cæsarea, where Jerome saw it about the middle of the fourth century. As we have no account whatever of Origen's autograph, after this time, it is most probable that it perished in the year 653, on the capture of that city by the Arabs; and a few imperfect fragments, collected from manuscripts of the Septuagint and the Catenæ of the Greek fathers, are all that now remain of a work, which in the present improved state of sacred literature would most eminently have assisted in the interpretation and criticism of the Old Testament.

5. As the Septuagint version had been read in the church from the commencement of Christianity, so it continued to be used in most of the *Greek* churches: and the text, as corrected by Origen, was transcribed for their use, together with his critical marks. Hence, in the progress of time, from the negligence or inaccuracy of copyists, numerous errors were introduced into this version, which rendered a new revisal necessary; and, as *all* the Greek churches did not receive Origen's biblical labours with equal deference, three principal recensions were undertaken nearly at the same time, of which we are now to offer a brief notice.

The first was the edition, undertaken by Eusebius and Pamphilus about the year 300, from the Hexaplar text, with the whole of Origen's critical marks: it was not only adopted by the churches of Palestine, but was also deposited in almost every library. By frequent

---

[1] The best edition, unhappily very rare, of the remains of Origen's Hexapla, is that of Montfaucon, in two volumes, folio, Paris, 1713. The first volume contains a very valuable preliminary disquisition on the Hebrew text and different antient Greek versions, of which we have liberally availed ourselves in the preceding and following pages, together with a minute account of Origen's biblical labours, and some inedited fragments of Origen, &c. To these succeed the remains of the Hexapla, from Genesis to the book of Psalms inclusive. The second volume comprises the rest of the Hexapla to the end of the twelve minor prophets, together with Greek and Hebrew Lexicons to the Hexapla. These fragments of Origen's great work were reprinted in two vols. 8vo. (Lipsiæ, 1769,) by C F. Bahrdt; whose edition has been most severely criticised by Fischer in his Prolusiones de Versionibus Græcis Librorum V T Litterarum Hebr. Magistris, p. 34. note (Lipsiæ, 1772, 8vo.) it is now but little valued.

transcriptions, however, Origen's marks or notes became, in the course of a few years, so much changed, as to be of little use, and were finally omitted: this omission only augmented the evil, since even in the time of Jerome it was no longer possible to know what belonged to the translators, or what were Origen's own corrections; and now it may almost be considered as a hopeless task to distinguish between them. Contemporary with the edition of Eusebius and Pamphilus was the recension of the Κοινη, or vulgate text of the Septuagint, conducted by Lucian, a presbyter of the church at Antioch, who suffered martyrdom A. D. 311. He took the Hebrew text for the basis of his edition, which was received in all the eastern churches from Constantinople to Antioch. While Lucian was prosecuting his biblical labours, Hesychius, an Egyptian bishop, undertook a similar work, which was generally received in the churches of Egypt. He is supposed to have introduced fewer alterations than Lucian; and his edition is cited by Jerome as the *Exemplar Alexandrinum.* Syncellus[1] mentions another revisal of the Septuagint text by Basil bishop of Cæsarea: but this, we have every reason to believe, has long since perished. All the manuscripts of the Septuagint now extant, as well as the printed editions, are derived from the three recensions above mentioned, although biblical critics are by no means agreed what particular recension each manuscript has followed.[2]

6. The importance of the Septuagint version for the right understanding of the sacred text, has been variously estimated by different learned men; while some have elevated it to an equality with the original Hebrew, others have rated it far below its real value. The great authority which it formerly enjoyed, certainly gives it a claim to a high degree of consideration. It was executed long before the Jews were prejudiced against Jesus Christ as the Messiah; and it was the means of preparing the world at large for his appearance, by making known the types and prophecies concerning him. With all its faults and imperfections, therefore, this version is of more use in correcting the Hebrew text than any other that is extant; because its authors had better opportunities of knowing the propriety and extent of the Hebrew language, than we can possibly have at this distance of time. The Septuagint, likewise, being written in the same dialect as the New Testament (the formation of whose style was influenced by it), it becomes a very important source of interpretation: for not only does it frequently serve to determine the genuine reading, but also to ascertain the meaning of particular idiomatic expressions and passages in the New Testament, the true import of which could not be known but from their use in the Septuagint.[3] Grotius, Keuchenius, Biel, and Schleusner, are the critics who have most successfully applied this version to the interpretation of the New Testament.

---

[1] Chronographia ab adamo usque ad Diocleswanum, p. 208.
[2] Dr. Holmes has given a copious and interesting account of the additions of Lucian and Hesychius, and of the sources of the Septuagint text in the manuscripts of the Pentateuch, which are now extant. Tom i. Præf. cap i sect. viii. *et seq.*
[3] In the Eclectic Review for 1806 (vol. ii part i. pp 337—347) the reader will find many examples adduced, confirming the remarks above offered, concerning the value and importance of the Septuagint version.

II. The importance of the Septuagint, in the criticism and interpretation of the Scriptures, especially of the New Testament[1], will justify the length of the preceding account of that celebrated version: it now remains that we briefly notice the other antient Greek translations, which have already been incidentally mentioned; viz. those of Aquila, Theodotion, Symmachus, and the three anonymous versions, usually cited as the fifth, sixth, and seventh versions, from which Origen compiled his Tetrapla and Hexapla.

1. *The Version of* AQUILA — The author of this translation was a native of Sinope in Pontus, who flourished in the second century of the Christian æra: he was of Jewish descent; and having renounced Christianity, he undertook his version to oblige the Jews, who then began to be disgusted with the Septuagint, as being too paraphrastic. It is certain that he lived during the reign of the emperor Adrian, and that his translation was executed before the year 160; as it is cited both by Justin Martyr, who wrote about that time, and by Irenæus between the years 170 and 176. The version of Aquila is extremely literal, and is made without any regard to the genius of the Greek language: it is, however, of considerable importance in the criticism of the Old Testament, as it serves to show the readings contained in the Hebrew MSS. of his time. Professor Dathe has collated several passages from this translation, and has applied them to the illustration of the prophet Hosea.[2] The fragments of Aquila and of the other Greek versions were collected and published, first by Flaminio Nobili, in his notes to the Roman edition of the Septuagint, and after him by Drusius, in his *Veterum Interpretum Græcorum Fragmenta* (Arnheim, 1622, 4to.)[3]; and also by Montfaucon in his edition of Origen's Hexapla above noticed. According to Jerome, Aquila published two editions of his version, the second of which was the most literal: it was allowed to be read publicly in the Jews' synagogues, by the hundred and twenty-fifth Novel of the emperor Justinian.

2. THEODOTION was a native of Ephesus, and is termed by Jerome and Eusebius an Ebionite or semi-Christian. He was nearly contemporary with Aquila, and his translation is cited by Justin Martyr, in his Dialogue with Tryphon the Jew, which was composed about the year 160. The version of Theodotion holds a middle rank be-

---

[1] "The Book," says the profound critic Michaelis, "most necessary to be read and understood by every man who studies the New Testament, is, without doubt, *the Septuagint*, which alone has been of more service than all the passages from the profane authors collected together It should be read in the public schools by those who are destined for the church, should form the subject of a course of lectures at the university, and be the constant companion of an expositor of the New Testament." Introduction to the New Test. vol. i p 177 —"About the year 1785," says Dr. A Clarke (speaking of his biblical labours), "I began to read the Septuagint regularly, in order to acquaint myself more fully with the phraseology of the New Testament. *The study of this version served more to expand and illuminate my mind than all the theological works I had ever consulted.* I had proceeded but a short way in it, before I was convinced that the prejudices against it were utterly unfounded, and that *it was of incalculable advantage towards a proper understanding of the literal sense of Scripture.*" Dr. Clarke's Commentary, vol. i General Preface, p. xv.

[2] Dissertatio Philologico-Critica in Aquilæ Reliquias Interpretationis Hoseæ, (Lipsiæ, 1757, 4to), which is reprinted in p. I. et seq. of Rosenmuller's Collection of his "Opuscula ad Crisin et Interpretationem Veteris Testamenti," Lipsiæ, 1796, 8vo.

[3] This work of Drusius's is also to be found in the sixth volume of Bishop Walton's Polyglott.

tween the servile closeness of Aquila and the freedom of Symmachus it is a kind of revision of the Septuagint made after the original Hebrew, and supplies some deficiencies in the Septuagint; but where he translates without help, he evidently shows himself to have been but indifferently skilled in Hebrew. Theodotion's translation of the book of Daniel was introduced into the Christian churches, as being deemed more accurate than that of the Septuagint.

3. SYMMACHUS, we are informed by Eusebius and Jerome, was a semi-Christian, or Ebionite: for the account given of him by Epiphanius, (that he was first a Samaritan, then a Jew, next a Christian, and last of all an Ebionite,) is generally disregarded as unworthy of credit. Concerning the precise time when he flourished, learned men are of different opinions. Epiphanius places him under the reign of Commodus II. an imaginary emperor: Jerome, however, expressly states, that his translation appeared after *that* of Theodotion: and as Symmachus was evidently unknown to Irenæus, who cites the versions of Aquila and Theodotion, it is probable that the date assigned by Jerome is the true one. Montfaucon accordingly places Symmachus a short time after Theodotion, that is, about the year 200. The version of Symmachus, who appears to have published a second edition of it revised, is by no means so literal as that of Aquila; he was certainly much better acquainted with the laws of interpretation than the latter, and has endeavoured, not unsuccessfully, to render the Hebrew idioms with Greek precision. Bauer [1] and Morus [2] have given specimens of the utility of this version for illustrating both the Old and New Testaments. Dr. Owen has printed the whole of the first chapter of the book of Genesis according to the Septuagint version, together with the Greek translations of Aquila, Theodotion, and Symmachus, in columns, in order to show their respective agreement or discrepancy. This we are obliged to omit, on account of its length; but the following observations of that eminent critic on their relative merits (founded on an accurate comparison of them with each other, and with the original Hebrew, whence they were made,) are too valuable to be disregarded. He remarks,

1. With respect to *Aquila*, (1) That his translation is close and servile — abounding in Hebraisms — and scrupulously conformable to the letter of the text. (2) That the author, notwithstanding he meant to disgrace and overturn the version of the Seventy, yet did not scruple to make use of it, and frequently to borrow his expressions from it.

2. With respect to *Theodotion*, (1) That he makes great use of the two former versions — following sometimes the diction of the one, and sometimes that of the other — nay, often commixing them both together in the compass of one and the same verse; and, (2) That he did not keep so strictly and closely to the version of the Seventy, as some have unwarily represented. [3] He borrowed largely from that of Aquila; but adapted it to his own style. And as his style was similar

---
[1] Critica Sacra, pp 277, 278. [2] Acroases Hermeneuticæ, tom. ii pp. 127, 128
[3] Theodotion, qui in cæteris cum lxx translatoribus facit. Hieron Ep ad Marcell. Licet autem Theodotio lxx Interpretum vestigio fere semper hæreat, &c. Montf Præl. in Hexapl. p. 57.

to that of the LXX, Origen, perhaps for the sake of uniformity, supplied the additions inserted in the Hexapla chiefly from this Version

3. With respect to *Symmachus*, (1) That his version, though concise, is free and paraphrastic — regarding the sense, rather than the words, of the original; (2) That he often borrowed from the three other versions — but much oftener from those of his immediate predecessors, than from the Septuagint; and, (3) It is observed by Montfaucon [1], that he kept close to the Hebrew original; and never introduced any thing from the Septuagint, that was not to be found in his Hebrew copy: but it evidently appears from verse 20. — where we read, και εγενετο ουτως — that either the observation is false, or that the copy he used was different from the present Hebrew copies. The 30th verse has also a reading — it may perhaps be an interpolation — to which there is nothing answerable in the Hebrew, or in any other of the Greek versions.[2]

4, 5, 6. — The three anonymous translations, usually called the *fifth*, *sixth*, and *seventh* versions, derive their names from the order in which Origen disposed them in his columns. The author of the *sixth* version was evidently a Christian: for he renders Habakkuk iii. 13. (*Thou wentest forth for the deliverance of thy people, even for the deliverance of thine anointed ones*[3],) in the following manner: Εξηλθες του σωσαι τον λαον σου δια Ιησου του Χριστου σου; i. e. *Thou wentest forth to save thy people through Jesus thy Christ*. The dates of these three versions are evidently subsequent to those of Aquila, Theodotion, and Symmachus: from the fragments collected by Montfaucon, it appears that they all contained the Psalms and minor prophets; the *fifth* and *sixth* further comprised the Pentateuch and Song of Solomon; and from some fragments of the *fifth* and *seventh* versions found by Bruns in a Syriac Hexaplar manuscript at Paris, it appears that they also contained the two books of Kings. Bauer is of opinion that the author of the seventh version was a Jew.

III. Besides the fragments of the preceding antient versions, taken from Origen's Hexapla, there are found in the margins of the manuscripts of the Septuagint some *additional* marks or notes, containing various renderings in Greek of some passages in the Old Testament: these are cited as the Hebrew, Syrian, Samaritan, and Hellenistic versions, and as the version of some anonymous author. The probable meaning of these references it may not be improper briefly to notice.

1. The *Hebrew* (ὁ Εβραιος) is supposed by some to denote the translation of Aquila, who closely and literally followed the Hebrew text. but this idea was refuted by Montfaucon and Bauer, who remark, that after the reference to the Hebrew, a reading follows, most widely differing from Aquila's rendering. Bauer more probably

---

[1] Ea tamen cautela ut Hebraicum exemplar unicum sequendum sibi proponeret, nec quidpiam ex editione τῶν Ο. ubi cum Hebraico non quadrabat, in interpretationem suam refunderet. Prælim. in Hexapl. p. 54
[2] Owen on the Septuagint, pp 124—126.
[3] Archbishop Newcome's version The authorised English translation runs thus — "Thou wentest forth for the salvation of thy people, even for the salvation of thine anointed."

conjectures, that the reference ὁ Εβραιος denotes the Hebrew text from which the Septuagint version differs.

2. Under the name of the *Syrian* (ὁ Συρος) are intended the fragments of the Greek version made by Sophronius, patriarch of Constantinople, from the very popular Latin translation of Jerome, who is supposed to have acquired the appellation of the Syrian, from his long residence on the confines of Syria. He is thus expressly styled by Theodore of Mopsuestia in a passage cited by Photius in his Bibliotheca.[1]

3. The *Samaritan* (το Σαμαρειτικον) is supposed to refer to the fragments of a Greek version of the Hebræo-Samaritan text, which is attributed to the ancient Greek scholiast so often cited by Flaminio Nobili, and in the Greek Scholia appended to the Roman edition of the Septuagint. Considerable doubts, however, exist concerning the identity of this supposed Greek version of the Samaritan text; which, if it ever existed, Bishop Walton thinks, must be long posterior in date to the Septuagint.[2]

4. It is not known to which version or author the citation ὁ Ελληνικος, or the Hellenic, refers:— the mark ὁ Αλλος, or ὁ Ανεπιγραφος, denotes some unknown author.

Before we conclude the present account of the antient Greek versions of the Old Testament, it remains that we briefly notice the translation preserved in St. Mark's Library at Venice, containing the Pentateuch, Proverbs, Ruth, Song of Solomon, Ecclesiastes, Lamentations of Jeremiah, and Prophecy of Daniel. The existence of this version, which was for a long time buried among other literary treasures deposited in the above-mentioned library, was first announced by Zanetti and Bongiovanni in their catalogue of its manuscripts. The Pentateuch was published in three parts, by M. Ammon, at Erlang, 1790, 1791, 8vo.: and the remaining books by M. Villoison at Strasburgh, 1784, 8vo. The original manuscript, Morelli is of opinion, was executed in the 14th century; and the numerous errors discoverable in it prove that it cannot be the autograph of the translator. By whom this version was made, is a question yet undetermined. Morelli thinks its author was a Jew; Ammon supposes him to have been a Christian monk, and perhaps a native of Syria of the eighth or ninth century; and Bauer, after Zeigler, conjectures him to have been a Christian grammarian of Constantinople, who had been taught Hebrew by a Western Jew. Whoever the translator was, his style evidently shows him to have been deeply skilled in the different dialects of the Greek language, and to have been conversant with the Greek poets. Equally uncertain is the date when this version was composed: Eichhorn, Bauer, and several other eminent biblical writers, place it between the sixth and tenth centuries: the late Dr. Holmes supposed the author of it to have been some Hellenistic Jew, between the ninth and twelfth centuries. "Nothing can be more completely happy, or more judicious, than the idea adopted by this author, of rendering the Hebrew

---

[1] Pape 205. edit. Hoeschelii. [2] Prol. c. xi § 22. pp. 552, 554.

text in the pure Attic dialect, and the Chaldee in its corresponding Doric."[1] Dr. Holmes has inserted extracts from this version in his edition of the Septuagint.[2]

SECTION III.

ON THE ANTIENT ORIENTAL VERSIONS OF THE OLD AND NEW TESTAMENTS.

I. SYRIAC VERSIONS. 1. *Peschito or Literal Version.* — 2. *Philoxenian Version.* — 3. *Syro-Estrangelo, and Palæstino-Syriac Version.* — II. EGYPTIAN VERSIONS. *Coptic, Sahidic, Ammonian, and Basmuric.* — III. ETHIOPIC VERSION. — IV. ARABIC VERSIONS. — V. ARMENIAN VERSION. — VI. PERSIC VERSIONS.

I. SYRIAC VERSIONS. — Syria being visited at a very early period by the preachers of the Christian faith, several translations of the sacred volume were made into the language of that country.

1. The most celebrated of these is the PESCHITO or *Literal* (VERSIO SIMPLEX), as it is usually called, on account of its very close adherence to the Hebrew and Greek texts, from which it was immediately made. The most extravagant assertions have been advanced concerning its antiquity; some referring the translation of the Old Testament to the time of Solomon and Hiram, while others ascribe it to Asa, priest of the Samaritans, and a third class to the apostle Thaddeus. This last tradition is received by the Syrian churches; but a more recent date is ascribed to it by modern biblical philologers. Bishop Walton, Carpzov, Leusden, Bishop Lowth, and Dr. Kennicott, fix its date to the first century; Bauer and some other German critics, to the second or third century; Jahn fixes it, at the latest, to the second century; De Rossi pronounces it to be very antient, but does not specify any precise date. The most pro-

---

[1] British Critic, O S. vol viii. p. 259.
[2] The preceding account of antient Greek versions is drawn from Carpzov, Critica Sacra, pp. 552—574., Bauer, Critica Sacra, pp. 273—288., Morus, Acroases Hermeneuticæ, tom. II. pp. 120—147.; Bishop Walton, Prolegom. c ix. § 19. pp. 385—387.; Jahn, Introductio in Libros Sacros Veteris Fœderis, pp. 66—70 ; and Masch's edition of Lelong's Bibliotheca Sacra, part II vol II. sect. i. pp. 220—229. Montfaucon, Præl. Diss ad Origenis Hexapla, tom. I pp. 46—73. In the fourth volume of the Commentationes Theologicæ, (pp. 195—263.) edited by MM. Velthusen, Kuinoel, and Ruperti, there is a specimen of a *Clavis Reliquiarum Versionum Græcarum, V T* by John Frederic Fischer it contains only the letter Α. A specimen of a new Lexicon to the antient Greek interpreters, and also to the apocryphal books of the Old Testament, so constructed as to serve as a Lexicon to the New Testament, was also lately published by M. E. G. A. Bockel, at Leipsic, intitled *Novæ Clavis in Græcos Interpretes Veteris Testamenti, Scriptoresque Apocryphos, ita adornatæ ut etiam Lexici in Novi Fœderis Libros usum præbere possit, atque editionis lax interpretum hexaplaris, specimina,* 4to. 1820. Cappel, in his Critica Sacra, has given a copious account, with very numerous examples, of the various lections that may be obtained by collating the Septuagint with the Hebrew (lib iv. pp. 491—766), and by collating the Hebrew text with the Chaldee paraphrases and the antient Greek versions (lib. v. cc. 1—6. pp. 767—844), tom. II. ed. Scharfenberg

bable opinion is that of Michaelis[1], who ascribes the Syriac version of *both* Testaments to the close of the first, or to the earlier part of the second century, at which time the Syrian churches flourished most, and the Christians at Edessa had a temple for divine worship erected after the model of that at Jerusalem. and it is not to be supposed that they would be without a version of the Old Testament, the reading of which had been introduced by the apostles. The Syriac version of the *New* Testament certainly must have been executed previously to the third century, because the text which it follows, according to Professor Hug, does not harmonise with the recension adopted by the churches of Palestine and Syria, subsequently to the third century.[2] It is independent, it belongs to no family, and sometimes presents the antient and peculiar readings of the *Vetus Itala*, or Old Italic version, or those occurring in the Codex Cantabrigiensis.

The *Old* Testament was evidently translated from the Original Hebrew, to which it most closely and literally adheres, with the exception of a few passages which appear to bear some affinity to the Septuagint: Jahn accounts for this by supposing, either that this version was consulted by the Syriac translator or translators, or that the Syrians *afterwards* corrected their translation by the Septuagint. Leusden conjectures, that the translator did not make use of the most correct Hebrew manuscripts, and has given some examples which appear to support his opinion. Dathe, however, speaks most positively in favour of its antiquity and fidelity, and refers to the Syriac version, as a certain standard by which we may judge of the state of the Hebrew text in the second century. and both Dr. Kennicott and Professor De Rossi have derived many valuable readings from this version. De Rossi, indeed, prefers it to all the other antient versions, and says, that it closely follows the order of the sacred text, rendering word for word, and is more pure than any other. As it is therefore probable that the Syriac version was made about the end of the first century, it might be made from Hebrew MSS. almost as old as those which were before transcribed into Greek, and from MSS. which might be in some places true where the others were corrupted. And it will be no wonder at all, if a version so very antient should have preserved a great variety of true readings, where the Hebrew manuscripts were corrupted afterwards. Dr. Boothroyd considers this version to be as antient, and in many respects as valuable, as the Chaldee Paraphrase[3]: and in the notes to his edition of the Hebrew Bible he was shown that this version has retained numerous and important various readings. To its general fidelity almost every critic of note bears unqualified approbation, although it

---

[1] Introd. to New Test. vol. ii part. i. pp. 29—38. Bishop Marsh, however, in his notes, has controverted the arguments of Michaelis, (ibid. part. ii. pp. 551—554) which have been rendered highly probable by the Rt. Rev Dr. Laurence, (Dissertation upon the Logos, pp. 67—75) who has examined and refuted the Bishop of Peterborough's objections.
[2] Hug's Introd. to the New Test. vol. i. pp. 357—360 Cellérier, Introd. au Nouv Test. p. 175.
[3] Biblia Hebraica, vol i. Pref. pp xv. xvi.

is not every where equal: and it is remarkably clear and strong in those passages which attribute characters of Deity to the Messiah. Jahn observes, that a different method of interpretation is adopted in the Pentateuch from that which is to be found in the Book of Chronicles; and that there are some Chaldee words in the first chapter of Genesis, and also in the Book of Ecclesiastes and the Song of Solomon: whence he infers that this version was the work not of one, but of several authors. The arguments prefixed to the Psalms were manifestly written by a Christian author.[1] The Syriac version of the New Testament comprises only the four Gospels, the Acts of the Apostles, the Epistles of Saint Paul (including the Epistle to the Hebrews), the first Epistle of Saint John, Saint Peter's first Epistle, and the Epistle of Saint James. The celebrated passage in 1 John v. 7., and the history of the woman taken in adultery (John viii. 2—11.), are both wanting. All the Christian sects in Syria and the East make use of this version exclusively, which they hold in the highest estimation. Michaelis pronounces it to be the very best translation of the Greek Testament which he ever read, for the general ease, elegance, and fidelity with which it has been executed. It retains, however, many Greek words, which might have been easily and correctly expressed in Syriac: in Matt. xxvii. alone there are not fewer than eleven words. In like manner some Latin words have been retained which the authors of the New Testament had borrowed from the Roman manners and customs. This version also presents some mistakes, which can only be explained by the words of the Greek text, from which it was immediately made. For instance, in rendering into Syriac these words of Acts xviii. 7., ONOMATI IOYΣTOY ΣEBOMENOY, the interpreter has translated *Titus* instead of *Justus*, because he had divided the Greek in the following manner — ONOMA TIIOYΣ TOY ΣEBOMENOY.[2]

An important accession to biblical literature was made, a few years since, by the late Rev. Dr. Buchanan, to whose assiduous labours the British church in India is most deeply indebted; and who, in his progress among the Syrian churches and Jews of India, discovered and obtained numerous antient manuscripts of the Scriptures, which are now deposited in the public library at Cambridge. One of these, which was discovered in a remote Syrian church near the mountains, is particularly valuable: it contains the Old and New Testaments, engrossed with beautiful accuracy in the *Estrangelo* (or old Syriac) character, on strong vellum, in large folio, and having three columns in a page. The words of every book are numbered: and the volume is illuminated, but not after the European manner, the initial letters having no ornament. Though somewhat injured by

---

[1] Carpzov, Critica Sacra, pp 623—626., Leusden, Philologus Hebræo-Mixtus, pp. 67.—71., Bishop Lowth's Isaiah, vol. i. p xci , Dr Kennicott, Diss ii p 355 ; Bauer, Critica Sacra, pp 308—320 , Jahn, Introd. ad Vet. Fœd pp. 75, 76., De Rossi, Variæ Lectiones ad Vet Test. tom. i. prol. p xxxii , Dathe, Opuscula ad Crisin et Interpretationem, Vet Test p. 171., Kortholt, de Versionibus Scripturæ, pp. 40—45 ; Walton, Proleg c 13 pp 593. et seq. Dr. Smith's Scripture Testimony of the Messiah, vol. i. pp. 396, 397.

[2] Hug's Introd. vol. i. pp. 342, 343.

time or neglect, the ink being in certain places obliterated, still the letters can in general be distinctly traced from the impress of the pen, or from the partial corrosion of the ink. The Syrian church assigns a high date to this manuscript, which, in the opinion of Mr. Yeates, who has published a collation of the Pentateuch [1], was written about the seventh century. In looking over this manuscript, Dr. Buchanan found the very first emendation of the Hebrew text proposed by Dr. Kennicott [2], which doubtless is the true reading.

The first edition of the Syriac version of the Old Testament appeared in the Paris Polyglott, but, being taken from an imperfect MS, its deficiencies were supplied by Gabriel Sionita, who translated the passages wanting from the Latin Vulgate, and has been unjustly charged with having translated the whole from the Vulgate. This text was reprinted in Bishop Walton's Polyglott, with the addition of some apocryphal books. There have been numerous editions of particular parts of the Syriac Old Testament, which are minutely described by Masch. [3] The principal editions of the Syriac Scriptures are noticed infra, in the Appendix, pp. 40, 41.

The Peschito Syriac version of the New Testament was first made known in Europe by Moses of Mardin, who had been sent by Ignatius, patriarch of the Maronite Christians, in 1552, to Pope Julius III., to acknowledge the papal supremacy in the name of the Syrian church, and was at the same time commissioned to procure the Syriac New Testament. This was accomplished at Vienna in 1555, under the editorial care of Moses and Albert Widmanstad, with the assistance of William Postell, and at the expense of the emperor Ferdinand I. This *Editio Princeps* is in quarto. The Syriac New Testament has since been printed several times.

There is also extant a Syriac version of the second Epistle of Saint Peter, the second and third Epistles of John, the Epistle of Jude, and the Apocalypse, which are wanting in the Peschito: these are by some writers ascribed to Mar Abba, primate of the East, between the years 535 and 552. The translation of these books is made from the original Greek; but the author, whoever he was, possessed but an indifferent knowledge of the two languages.

2. The PHILOXENIAN or SYRO-PHILOXENIAN Version derives its name from Philoxenus, or Xenayas, Bishop of Hierapolis or Mabug in Syria, A.D. 488—518, who employed his rural bishop (*Chorepiscopus*) Polycarp, to translate the Greek New Testament into Syriac. This version was finished in the year 508, and was afterwards revised by Thomas of Harkel or Heraclea, A.D. 616. Michaelis is of opinion, that there was a third edition; and a fourth is attributed

---

[1] In the Christian Observer, vol. xii pp 171—174 there is an account of Mr Yeates's Collation; and in vol ix of the same Journal, pp. 273—275. 348—350., there is given a very interesting description of the Syriac manuscript above noticed A short account of it also occurs in Dr. Buchanan's "Christian Researches," respecting the Syrians, pp 229—231 (edit. 1811.)

[2] Gen. iv. 8. *And Cain said unto Abel his brother, Let us go down into the plain.* It may be satisfactory to the reader to know, that this disputed addition is to be found in the Samaritan, Syriac, Septuagint, and Vulgate Versions, printed in Bishop Walton's Polyglott.

[3] Bibl Sacr. part ii. vol. i. sect. iv. pp. 64—71.

to Dionysius Barsalibæus, who was bishop of Amida from 1166 to 1177. It appears, however, that there were only two editions — the original one by Polycarp, and that revised by Thomas of Harkel; the single copy of the Four Gospels, with the alterations of Barsalibæus, in the twelfth century, being hardly intitled to the name of a new edition. This version was not known in Europe until the middle of the eighteenth century; when the Rev. Dr. Gloucester Ridley published a Dissertation on the Syriac Versions of the New Testament (in 1761), three manuscripts of which he had received thirty years before from Amida in Mesopotamia. Though age and growing infirmities, the great expense of printing, and the want of a patron, prevented Dr. Ridley from availing himself of these manuscripts; yet having, under circumstances of peculiar difficulty, succeeded in acquiring a knowledge of the Syriac language, he employed himself at intervals in making a transcript of the Four Gospels. These, being put into the hands of the late Professor White, were published by him with a literal Latin translation, in 1778, in two volumes 4to., at the expense of the delegates of the Clarendon press at Oxford. In 1779, Professor White published from the same press the Acts of the Apostles and the Catholic Epistles, and in 1804, the Epistles of Saint Paul, also in 4to. and accompanied with a Latin translation.

The Philoxenian version, though made immediately from the Greek, is greatly inferior to the Peschito, both in the accuracy with which it is executed, and also in its style. It is, however, not devoid of value, " and is of real importance to a critic, whose object is to select a variety of readings, with the view of restoring the genuine text of the Greek original; for he may be fully assured, that every phrase and expression is a precise copy of the Greek text as it stood in the manuscript from which the version was made. But, as it is not prior to the sixth century, and the Peschito was written either at the end of the first, or at the beginning of the second century, it is of less importance to know the readings of the Greek manuscript that was used in the former, than those of the original employed in the latter." [1]

3. Of the OTHER SYRIAC VERSIONS, the Syro-Estrangelo version of the Old Testament, and the Palæstino-Syriac version of part of the New Testament, are of sufficient importance to deserve a brief notice.

[i.] The SYRO-ESTRANGELO version is a translation of Origen's Hexaplar edition of the Greek Septuagint: it was executed in the former part of the seventh century, and its author is unknown. The late Professor De Rossi, who published the first specimen of it [2] does not decide whether it is to be attributed to Mar-Abba, James

---

[1] Michaelis's Introduction to the New Testament, vol. ii part i. p. 68. To Bishop Marsh's Notes, ibid. part ii. pp 533—585. we are chiefly indebted for the preceding account of the Syriac Versions of the New Testament. See also Hug's Introduction, vol. i. pp 372—386. Dr G. H Bernstein's Dissertation on Thomas of Harkel's revision of the Syro-Philoxenian Version, intitled De Versione Novi Testamenti Syriacâ Heracleensi Commentatio. Lipsiæ, 1822, 4to.

[2] M. De Rossi's publication is intitled Specimen ineditæ et Hexaplaris Bibliorum Versionis, Syro-Estranghelæ, cum simplici atque utriusque fontibus, Græco et Hebræo, collatæ cum duplici Latinâ versione et notis. Edidit, ac diatribam de rarissimo codice Ambrosiano, unde illud haustum est, præmisit Johannes Bern. Rossi 8vo Parmæ, 1778.

of Edessa, Paul Bishop of Tela, or to Thomas of Heraclea. Assemanni, ascribes it to Thomas, though other learned men affirm that he did no more than collate the Books of Scripture. This version, however, corresponds exactly with the text of the Septuagint, especially in those passages in which the latter differs from the Hebrew. A MS. of this version is in the Ambrosian Library at Milan, comprising the Books of Psalms, Job, Proverbs, Ecclesiastes, Song of Solomon, Wisdom, Ecclesiasticus, Hosea, Amos, Habakkuk, Zephaniah, Haggai, Zechariah, Malachi, Jeremiah, Daniel, and Isaiah: it also contains the obelus and other marks of Origen's Hexapla; and a subscription at the end states it to have been literally translated from the Greek copy, corrected by Eusebius himself, with the assistance of Pamphilus, from the books of Origen, which were deposited in the library at Cæsarea. The conformity of this MS. with the account given by Masius, in the preface to his learned Annotations on the Book of Joshua, affords strong grounds for believing that this is the second part of the MS. described by him as then being in his possession, and which, there is reason to fear, is irrecoverably lost. From this version M. Norberg edited the prophecies of Jeremiah and Ezekiel in 1787, 4to. Londini, Gothorum, and M. Bugati, the Book of Daniel, at Milan, 1788, 4to.[1]

[ii.] The PALÆSTINO-SYRIAC, or SYRIAC TRANSLATION OF JERUSALEM, was discovered in the Vatican Library at Rome by M. Adler, in a manuscript of the eleventh century. It is not an entire translation of the New Testament, but only a *Lectionarium*, or collection of detached portions, appointed to be read in the services of the church on Sundays and festival days. It is written in the Syriac or Chaldee dialect of Jerusalem, and was evidently made in a Roman province: for in Matt. xxvii. 27. the word στρατιωται, *soldiers*, is rendered by רומיא (ROMIA), as if the translator had never heard of any soldiers but Romans; and in the same verse σπειρα, *band* or *cohort*, is rendered by the Latin word *castra*, קסטרא. These and other indications afford reason to think, that the manuscript contains a translation made from the Greek, in Palestine; it was written at Antioch, and from all these circumstances, this version has been denominated the Jerusalem-Syriac Version. This manuscript has not yet been collated throughout, so that it is very uncertain to what recension it belongs. But, from what is known concerning it, there is reason to think that it combines the readings of different families.[2]

II. EGYPTIAN VERSIONS. — From the proximity of Egypt to Judæa, it appears that the knowledge of the Gospel was very early

---

The specimen consists of the first psalm printed in six columns. The first contains the Greek text of the Septuagint, the second, the Syro-Estrangelo text; the third, the Latin text translated from the Septuagint, the fourth, the Hebrew text; the fifth, the *Peschito* or old Syriac text above noticed, and the sixth, the Latin text translated from this latter version.

[1] Masch. part. ii vol. i pp 58—60. Jahn, Introd ad Vet. Fœd. pp 76—78. Monthly Review, O S vol lix pp 452—454 Some other Syriac versions of less note are described by Masch, ut supra, pp. 60—62

[2] Cellérier, Introd. au Nouv. Test. pp 180, 181. Hug's Introduction, vol 1. pp 386—389. A notice of the principal editions of the Syriac Version is given in the Appendix, pp 40, 41.

communicated to the inhabitants of that country, whose language was divided into three dialects — the *Coptic*, or dialect of Lower Egypt; the *Sahidic*, or dialect of Upper Egypt, and the *Basmuric*, or dialect of Middle Egypt.

The COPTIC language is a compound of the old Egyptian and Greek; into which the *Old Testament* was translated from the Septuagint, perhaps in the second or third century, and certainly before the seventh century. Of this version, the Pentateuch was published by Wilkins in 1731, and a Psalter, by the congregation *de Propagandâ Fide*, at Rome, in 1744 and 1749.[1]

In the SAHIDIC language the ninth chapter of Daniel was published by Münter at Rome in 1786; and Jeremiah, ch. ix. 17. to ch. xiii., by Mingarelli, in *Reliquiæ Egyptiorum Codicum in Bibliotheca Naniana asservatæ*, at Bologna, in 1785. The late Dr. Woide was of opinion that both the Coptic and Sahidic versions were made from the Greek. They express the phrases of the Septuagint version; and most of the additions, omissions, and transpositions, which distinguished the latter from the Hebrew, are discoverable in the Coptic and Sahidic versions.

The *Coptic* version of the *New Testament* was published at Oxford in 1716, in 4to., by Daniel Wilkins, a learned Prussian, who has endeavoured to prove that it must have been executed prior to the third century; but his opinion has been controverted by many learned men, and particularly by Louis Picques, who refers it to the fifth century. Professor Hug, however, has shown that it could not have been composed before the time of Hesychius, nor before the middle of the third century.[2] The celebrated passage (1 John v. 7.) is wanting in this version, as well as in the Syriac-Peschito, and Philoxenian translations. From the observations of Dr. Woide, it appears that the Coptic inclines more to the Alexandrian than the Sahidic — that no remarkable coincidence is to be found between the Coptic or Sahidic and the Vulgate, — and that we have no reason to suspect that the former has been altered or made to conform to the latter.

Concerning the age of the *Sahidic* version, critics are not yet agreed. Dr. Woide, however, has shown that it was most probably executed in the second century; and, consequently, it is of the utmost importance to the criticism of the Greek Testament. In a dissertation on this version, written in the German language, and abridged by Bishop Marsh[3], Dr. W. observes, that there are now in existence two Sahidic manuscripts, — one formerly in the possession of the late Dr. Askew, the other brought from Egypt by the celebrated traveller, Mr. Bruce. The former contains a work, intitled Sophia, and written by Valentinus, in the second century. This manuscript contains various passages both from the Old and New Testament, which coincide with the fragments of the Sahidic version now extant;

---

[1] Masch, part. ii. vol i pp 182—190. Jahn, p. 81. The *only* perfect copy of the Coptic Bible now in Europe is said to be in the possession of Monsieur Marcel. See M. Quatremère's Recherches sur la Langue et la Littérature d'Egypte, p. 118
[2] Hug's Introd vol 1 p 410.
[3] Marsh's Michaelis, vol. ii. part ii. pp. 595, 596

II. Sect. III.]   *The Ethiopic or Abyssinian Version.*   63

whence it is concluded that a Sahidic version of the whole Bible not only existed so early as the *beginning* of the second century, but that it was the same as that of which we have various fragments, and which, if put together, would form perhaps a complete Sahidic version of the Bible. The other manuscript to which Dr. Woide appeals, contains two books, the one intitled Βιβλος της γνωσεος, the other, Βιβλος λογου κατα μυστηριον. Now that this was written by a Gnostic, as well as the other manuscript, appears both from the title and the contents, and therefore it is concluded that the author lived in the second century. And as various passages are quoted in it both from the Old and New Testament, Dr. Woide deduces the same inference as from the foregoing. Of this version some fragments of the Gospels of Matthew and John have been published by Mingarelli, in a work intitled *Ægyptiorum Codicum Reliquiæ, Venetiis in Bibliothecâ Nianianâ asservatæ.* (Bononiæ, 1715, 4to.) But the completest collection of fragments of this version is that prepared for the press by the late Dr. Woide, who did not live to publish them. The work was completed and edited by the Rev. Dr. Ford, from the Clarendon press, at Oxford, in folio, 1799, as an appendix to Dr. W.'s fac-simile of the Codex Alexandrinus.

From the difference of their readings, and from the circumstance that additions in the one are omitted in the other, Bishop Marsh infers that the Coptic and Sahidic are independent versions, both made from the original Greek. Both, therefore, may be quoted as separate evidence for a reading in the Greek Testament.[1]

Besides the versions in the Coptic and Sahidic dialects, Father Georgi discovered, in a manuscript belonging to Cardinal Borgia, some fragments of a version written in a still different Egyptian dialect, which he calls the AMMONIAN DIALECT. It contains only 1 Cor. vii. 36.—ix. 16. and xiv. 33.—xv. 33. Some fragments of a BASMURICO-COPTIC Version of the Old and New Testament, discovered in the Borgian Museum at Velitri, were published by M. Engelbreth at Copenhagen, in 1816. Dr Frederick Munter has printed the Sahidic and Ammoniac texts of 1 Cor. ix. 10—16. in his *Commentatio de Indole Versionis Novi Testamenti Sahidicæ* (4to. Hafniæ, 1789), in parallel columns, in order to present the reader with a distinct view of the similarity or difference between the two versions. On account, however, of the chief difference consisting in the orthography of single words, he is not disposed to assign to the Ammoniac the name of a separate dialect. On considering the region where this dialect seemed to be vernacular, he was inclined for several reasons to fix upon the Oases, particularly the Ammonian Oasis, whence he called it the Ammonian Dialect: but Professor Hug, who has investigated the hypothesis of various learned men, is of opinion that the fragments in question may possibly exhibit the idiom of Middle Egypt. This version was probably executed in the latter part of the third century.[2]

III. The ETHIOPIC or ABYSSINIAN VERSION of the Old Testament was made from the Septuagint: although its author and date are

---

[1] Marsh's Michaelis, vol. ii part i. pp. 76—81 part ii. pp. 586—597

[2] Hug's Introduction, vol ii. pp. 417—425. For a notice of the editions or published fragments of the several Egyptian versions, see the Appendix to this volume, p 43.

unknown, yet, from the marks of unquestionable antiquity which it bears, there is every reason to believe that it was executed in the fourth century. Some peculiar readings occur in this translation: but, where it seems to be exact, it derives considerable authority from its antiquity. Only a few books and fragments of this version have been printed. The first portions of the Ethiopic Scriptures that appeared in print, were the Psalms, and the Song of Solomon; edited at Rome, by John Potken, A. D. 1513. The translation of the New Testament is supposed to have been made by Frumentius, who, about the year 330, first preached Christianity in Ethiopia. In 1548, the New Testament was printed at Rome by some Abyssinian priests, and was afterwards reprinted in the London Polyglott: but as the manuscripts used in the Roman edition were old and mutilated, the editors restored such chasms as appeared in the text, by translations from the Latin Vulgate. These editions, therefore, are not of much value, as they do not present faithful copies of the antient Ethiopic text; which, according to Professor Hug, exhibits the appearance either of several versions being united in one copy, or of several MSS. (belonging to different recensions) being quoted in the composition of this version.[1]

There is, however, reason to expect that, in no long time, the gift of the entire Ethiopic Scriptures will be imparted to Abyssinia. A manuscript copy of this version, in fine preservation, has been purchased by the committee of the Church Missionary Society. From a memoir on this manuscript by Professor Lee, we learn, that it contains the first eight books of the Old Testament, written on vellum, in a bold and masterly hand, in two columns on each page. The length of the page is that of a large quarto; the width is not quite so great. The volume contains 285 folios, of which the text covers 282, very accurately written, and in high preservation. On the first page is written, in Ethiopic, the invocation usually found in the books of the eastern Christians: "In the name of the Father, and of the Son, and of the Holy Ghost." Then follows an account of the contents of the book, written in Latin by some former possessor, and a date A. D. 1596, 20th September. On the reverse of the first folio is found a table, not unlike the tables of genealogy in some of our old English Bibles, which seems to be intended to show the hours appointed for certain prayers. Then follows the Book of Genesis, as translated from the Greek of the Septuagint. On the reverse of the third folio is the following inscription in Arabic: "The poor Ribea, the Son of Elias, wrote it: O wine! to which nothing can be assimilated, either in reality or appearance: O excellent drink! of which our Lord said, having the cup in his hand, and giving thanks, 'This is my blood for the salvation of men.'" Folios 7. & 8. have been supplied, in paper, by a more modern hand. On the reverse of folio 8. is a very humble attempt at drawing, in the

---

[1] Jahn, p 81. Masch, part II vol. I. pp 140—143. Michaelis, vol. II. pp. 95—98. 610—614. Hug, vol. I pp. 426—428. Walton, Prol. xv §§ 10—12. pp 679—685. Kortholt, pp. 298—301. In Mr Bruce's Travels, vol II. pp 416—420 (8vo. edit.) there is an interesting account of the Ethiopic biblical books. It is not known in whose possession the manuscript copy of the Ethiopic version now is, which was brought by Mr. B. from Abyssinia.

figure of a person apparently in prayer, accompanied by an inscription in Ethiopic, at the side of the figure: "In the prayers of Moses and Aaron, to [1] Abraham, Isaac, and Jacob, am I, thy servant, O Lord, presented in the power of the Trinity, a weak, infirm, and defiled sinner. Let them implore Christ." Under the drawing, in Ethiopic: "In the same manner, every slayer that slays Cain, will I repay in this; and, as he slew, so shall he be slain." On the reverse of folio 98., at the end of the Book of Exodus, are two figures, somewhat similar, but rather better drawn, and seemingly by the writer of the manuscript; and, in another place or two, there are marginal ornaments. At the end of Deuteronomy is this inscription, in Ethiopic: "The repetition of the law, which God spake to Moses. Numbered 5070 [2] (words). Intercede for your slave Isaac." — At the end of the volume: "Pray for those who laboured in this book; and for your slave Isaac, who gave this to Jerusalem, the Holy." Then follows an inscription, in Arabic: "In the name of the Father, and of the Son, and of the Holy Ghost, one God. O Lord, save thy people from every evil! O our God, Jesus Christ, the speaker to men! O holy people, remember your slave Isaac, the poor God shall remember you in the mercies of this book. Pray, if God be willing, that I may be permitted to see your face. And pray for me, the sinner. Pardon my sins, O Lord! and let my body be buried in Mount Sion." Then follows, in Ethiopic: "That our enemies may not say of us, 'We have conquered them:' be ye prudent. We have given you a lamp. Be ye the culture. — Sow ye the flock: reap and rejoice"..... A few lines have been erased. Then follows .... "me, Isaac, the poor, in your prayers. It was completed in Beth Gabbaza, of Axuma. In thy name, O Lord, have I planted, that thou place me not in any other place except Mount Sion; the mount of Christ; the house of Christians. Let them not be forgotten in your prayers, who have read and testified to you. Preserve, O Lord, this my offering for me thy servant, the poor; and preserve all these books which I offer, that the brethren, dwelling at Jerusalem, may be comforted. And pray for me [3], forget me not in the holy offices, and in prayer, that we may all stand before God in the terrible day and hours. That it might not be written that we were wanting, I have previously sent and given you this for the warfare of the testimony Intercede, and bless. And also for the refreshing of the record of the Fathers: and also for Cueskam [4], the

---

[1] As this inscription, which occurs on the supplied leaves, savours of the errors of the Romish Church, it was probably written by some Abyssinian Catholic. The inscriptions of Isaac, the writer of the MS., though mutilated, and sometimes obscure, seem free from these errors. The figure of St. Peter, mentioned below, was probably traced by the same hand

[2] It is customary among the Jews, Syrians, and Ethiopians, to number the words in the books of Scripture

[3] In most of the eastern churches, it is the practice to enumerate their Saints in a certain part of the Liturgy.

[4] The name of a region, a sea, and a mountain, in Ethiopia, so celebrated, as to be esteemed by the Ethiopians as preferable to even Sinai or Mount Olivet, and, as tradition

queen of the sons of Abyssinia; that they may be comforted, and thence convert our region — may, moreover, migrate into other regions, and restore Jerusalem: — and for the Calvary of Mary. Let them pray for me. Let it be preserved as the widow's mite, for ever and ever. Let them not sell or exchange; nor let them carry it away; nor let them cause it to be placed elsewhere. And....." the rest is wanting. Hence it appears, that the book was written at Axuma, the antient capital of Ethiopia; and that it was sent by Isaac to the Abyssinians residing in Jerusalem. No date appears in the manuscript itself. It is, probably, about 300 years old. On the reverse of fol. 285. is a drawing, intended to represent Andrew the Apostle, with the book of the Gospels in one hand, and the keys in the other. Some less ingenious draftsman, however, has, by means of the transparency of the vellum, traced out this figure on the first page of this folio, and given the name of Peter to his humble representation. He has thus succeeded in assigning to St. Peter the first place, and also in bestowing on him the keys. Against this picture of Peter is placed his age, 120 years.

The following fac-simile represents part of the remarkable prophecy of Balaam.[1]

Num. XXIV. 17.

[Ethiopic text]

---

says, whither Joseph and Mary, with the child Jesus, betook themselves, making it their residence for some time, after the flight into Egypt, *Castell*, sub voce. — *Ludolf*, sub voce, says it is the name of a monastery in Upper Egypt, which was always had in great veneration by the Copts and Ethiopians, and where Christ is said to have resided with his mother, when he fled from Herod.

[1] Eighteenth Report of the Church Missionary Society, pp. 188, 189. In p. 190, there

I shall see him, but not now: I shall call him blessed, but he is not near: there shall arise a star out of Jacob, and from Israel shall it arise: and he shall destroy the ambassadors of Moab, and shall take captive all the children of Seth.

This precious manuscript has been carefully transcribed, and is now printing with a fount of types, cast at the expense of the British and Foreign Bible Society, from the matrices (preserved at Frankfort) of the celebrated Ethiopic scholar John Ludolph; whose types, as used in his printed works, have been highly approved by the Abyssinians.[1]

IV. ARABIC VERSIONS. — Although the Christian religion was preached in Arabia, as well as in other countries of the East, at an early period, yet it never was the established religion of the country, as in Syria and Egypt; for even the temple at Mecca was a heathen temple till the time of Mohammed. Historical evidence, therefore, concerning the Arabic versions of the Old Testament, does not extend beyond the tenth century, when

1. Rabbi Saadias Gaon, a celebrated Jewish teacher at Babylon, translated, or rather paraphrased, the Old Testament into Arabic: of this version the Pentateuch was printed at Constantinople, in folio, in the year 1546, in Hebrew characters; and in the Paris and London Polyglotts, in Arabic letters. — The prophecy of Isaiah was published by Paulus in 8vo. at Jena, in 1790, 1791. The remaining books of this translation have not hitherto been discovered. Besides this, there are several other Arabic versions extant, made immediately from the Hebrew, either by Jews, Samaritans, or Christians, of which the following are the principal, viz.

2. The Arabic version of the Pentateuch, published by Erpenius at Leyden in 1622, 4to., appears to have been executed in the thirteenth century by some African Jew, who has very closely adhered to the Hebrew.

3. The Arabic version of the Book of Joshua, printed in the Paris and London Polyglotts, is, in the opinion of Bauer, made directly from the Hebrew. Its author and date are not known.

4. The Pentateuch, Psalms, and Prophecy of Daniel, were translated by Saadia Ben Levi Asnekot, who lived in the early part of the seventeenth century: they are extant only in MS. in the British Museum[2], and are of very little value.

Besides these versions, the Arab Christians have a translation of the Book of Job (printed in the Paris and London Polyglotts), and two versions of the Psalms, still in MS., which were respectively made from the Peschito or Old Syriac version. All the Arabic books of the Old Testament (with the exception of the Pentateuch and Job), which are printed in those Polyglotts, were executed from Hesy-

---

is an interesting notice of the Ethiopic MSS. of the Scriptures, in the Royal Library at Paris.

[1] For a notice of such parts of the Ethiopic Version of the Scriptures as have been printed, see the Appendix to this volume, p. 44.; and for other particulars relative to this Version, the reader is referred to Mr. Platt's "Catalogue of the Ethiopic Biblical Manuscripts in the Royal Library of Paris, and in the Library of the British and Foreign Bible Society," &c. London, 1823. 4to.

[2] Cat. Harl. MSS. vol. iii. num. 5505.

chius's recension of the Septuagint. The Psalms, inserted in Justinian's Polyglott Psalter, and Gabriel Sionita's Arabic Psalter, were made from Lucian's recension of that version: and the Arabic Psalter, printed at Aleppo in 1706, 4to., follows the Melchitic[1] recension of the LXX.[2]

There are many Arabic translations of the New Testament, besides those which have appeared in print: for since the Arabic language supplanted the Syriac and Egyptian, the inhabitants of the countries where these had been spoken, have been obliged to annex Arabic translations to the antient versions, which are no longer understood. These Arabic translations are supposed to have been made at different times between the seventh and the eleventh centuries: in general they were not all executed from the original text, but from the versions which they were intended to accompany. Thus some which are placed together with the Greek text, have been made from the Greek, while others have been made from the Syriac, the Coptic, and even from the Latin Vulgate.[3]

V. The ARMENIAN VERSION of the Old Testament was made from the Alexandrian Septuagint: its author was Miesrob, who invented letters fully expressive of the Armenian tongue, towards the close of the fourth or early in the fifth century. It is said to have been subsequently altered according to the Peschito or old Syriac version, and according to the Latin Vulgate, by Uscan, an Armenian bishop, who was specially sent to Amsterdam to superintend the edition there printed in 1666. The translation of the New Testament is ascribed jointly to Miesrob, and to the patriarch Isaac, at the end of the fourth or early in the fifth century. It was twice translated from the Syriac, and then from the Greek; and that the copies now extant were made from the latter language, is evident from their containing those books of the New Testament which were never admitted into the Peschito or antient literal Syriac version. This version, in the opinion of Semler, is of great importance, as faithfully representing the Greek MSS. whence it was made: but Michaelis observes, that it would be an inestimable treasure, had it descended to us unaltered by time and superstition. It has in several instances been made conformable to the Vulgate by Haitho or Hethom, sovereign of the Lesser Armenia from A. D. 1224 to 1270, who was attached to the Church of Rome, and skilled in the Latin language.[4]

---

[1] The *Melchites* were those Christians in Syria, Egypt, and the Levant, who, though not Greeks, followed the doctrines and ceremonies of the Greek Church. They were called Melchites, that is, Royalists, by their adversaries, by way of reproach, on account of their implicit submission to the edict of the emperor Marcian, in favour of the council of Chalcedon. Mosheim's Eccl. Hist vol ii p 188. note (*m*)

[2] Carpzov. Crit. Sacr pp 640—644 Bauer, Crit Sacr pp 321—324. Jahn, Introd. ad Vet. Fœd. pp 78—80. Masch, part ii. vol. i pp 103—110

[3] Michaelis (vol. ii part i. pp. 81—95) and Hug (vol i. pp. 430—454.) have gone fully into the history of the Arabic versions. For a notice of the principal editions of them, see the Appendix to this volume, pp. 41, 42

[4] Jahn, p. 82. Masch, pp 169—173 ; Kortholt, pp 304, 305. On the present state of the Armenian church in India, see Dr Buchanan's "Christian Researches," pp. 341—346. Semler, Apparatus ad Liberalem Novi Testamenti Interpretationem, p 69 Michaelis, vol. ii. pp 98—105. 614—617. Hug, vol. i. pp. 394—399.

VI PERSIC VERSIONS.—Although we have no authentic account of the conversion of the whole Persian nation to Christianity, yet we are informed by Chrysostom and Theodoret, that the Scriptures were very antiently translated into the Persian language. It does not appear, however, that any fragments of this antient version are extant. The translation of the Pentateuch, printed in the 4th volume of Bishop Walton's Polyglott, was executed by a Jew, for the benefit of the Jews, in the eleventh or twelfth century. The Hebrew text is, for the most part, faithfully rendered. Bishop Walton mentions two Persic versions of the Psalms—one by a Portuguese monk at Ispahan in the year 1618, and another by some Jesuits from the Vulgate Latin version.[1] These are yet in manuscript.

There are extant two *Persian Versions* of the four Gospels, the most antient and valuable of which was first printed in the London Polyglott, by Bishop Walton, from a manuscript in the possession of Dr. Pococke, dated A. D. 1314: it was made from the Syriac, having sometimes retained Syriac words, and subjoined a Persian translation. The other Persian translation was edited by Wheloc, and after his decease by Pierson, at London, in 1652–57, after a collation of three manuscripts. It is supposed to have been made from the Greek.[2]

SECTION IV.

ON THE ANTIENT WESTERN VERSIONS OF THE SCRIPTURES.

I. *Antient Latin Versions of the Scriptures.*—1. *Of the* OLD ITALIC *or* ANTE-HIERONYMIAN VERSION.—2. *Account of the Biblical Labours and Latin Version of* JEROME.—3. *Of the* VULGATE VERSION *and its Revisions.*—4. *Critical Value of the Latin Vulgate Version.*—II. GOTHIC VERSION. — III. SCLAVONIC VERSION.—IV. ANGLO-SAXON VERSION.

I ANTIENT LATIN VERSIONS OF THE SCRIPTURES — At the commencement of the Christian æra, the Latin was gradually supplanting the Greek as a *general* language, and it soon might be called the language of the western church. From the testimony of Augustine[a], it appears that the Latin church possessed a very great number of versions of the Scriptures, made at the first introduction of Christianity, and whose authors were unknown; and that, in the primitive times, as soon as any one found a Greek copy, and thought himself sufficiently versed in both languages, he attempted a translation of it.[4] In the course of time, this diversity of translation produced

---
[1] Walton, prol xvi §§ 6—8. pp. 692—695. Kortholt, c. xix. pp. 301—303. Jahn, p. 80. For an account of editions consult Masch, part ii. vol i. pp. 158—164.
[2] Michaelis, vol. ii. pp 105, 106. 617—619 Semler, p 69. Walton, Prol c. xvi. § 9. pp. 695, 696. Hug, vol i pp. 389—393
[3] Augustine, de Doctr Christ l. ii c 11.
[4] These various antient Latin versions, which are frequently termed *Ante-Hieronymian*, and of the manuscripts of which some valuable fragments have been preserved to us in the writings of the Fathers, were written in barbarous Latin, and frequently differed greatly. One single example, out of many that might be offered, will suffice Col ii, 15. as cited by Hilary (de Trin. lib i c 13), runs thus: "Exutus carnem ex potestates ostentui fecit, triumphatis iis cum fiducia in semet ipso." The same passage, as cited by Augustine,

much confusion, parts of separate versions being put together to form an entire composition, and marginal notes being inserted into the text: but one of these Latin translations appears to have acquired a more extensive circulation than the others, and for several ages was preferably used, under the name of the *Vetus Itala* or old Italic, on account of its clearness and fidelity.[1] This version, which in the time of Jerome was received as canonical, is by him termed sometimes the *Vulgate* and sometimes the *Old*, in opposition to the new translation undertaken by him. He mentions no other version. The Old Italic was translated from the Greek in the Old Testament as well as in the New, there being comparatively few members of the Western church, who were skilled in Hebrew. From the above cited expressions of Augustine, it has been inferred that the old Italic version was made in the *first* century of the Christian æra; but the New Testament could not have been translated into Latin before the canon had been formed, which was certainly not made in the first century: and the great number of Hebraisms and Syriasms observable in it, particularly in the Gospels of Matthew and Mark, have induced some eminent critics to conjecture that the authors of this translation were Jews converted to Christianity.[2] There is, however, every reason to believe, that it was executed in the early part of the second century: "at least it was quoted by Tertullian before the close of that century. But, before the end of the fourth century, the alterations, either designed or accidental, which were made by transcribers of the Latin Bible, were become as numerous as the alterations in the Greek Bible, before it was corrected by Origen."[3]

2. To remedy this growing evil, Jerome, at the request, and under the patronage of Pope Damasus, towards the close of the fourth century, undertook to revise this translation, and make it more conformable to the original Greek. He executed the revision of the Old Testament according to the Hexaplar text of Origen, which he went to Cæsarea to consult, and the New Testament after the original Greek; and completed his task A. D. 390 or 391. Of this revision, the Book of Job and the Psalms (which alone have been preserved to our times), together with the Chronicles, Proverbs, Ecclesiastes,

---

(contra Faustum, lib. xvi. c. 29.) stands thus: "Exutus se carnem principatus et potestates exemplavit, fiducialiter triumphatus eos in semet ipso." Other examples may be seen in Hug, vol. i. pp. 454—456.

[1] Augustine, de Doct. Christ. l. ii. c.15. This passage of Augustine is suspected to be incorrect, and Bishop Marsh, after Bentley, Ernesti, Lardner, and other critics, thinks that we ought to read *illa* for *Itala*. (Michaelis, vol ii. part ii. p. 623 See also Dr. Lardner's Works, vol. v. pp 115, 116.) But this conjecture is supported by no manuscript, and is also contradicted by the context of Augustine M. Breyther, who has examined the various conjectures and arguments, which have been alleged in support of the reading of *illa*, determines in favour of *Itala* as the genuine reading (Dissert. de vi quam antiquissimæ versiones, quæ extant, in crisin Evang. IV habeant, pp. 19—24.) Prof Hug also determines in favour of Itala. (Introd. to New Test. vol. i. pp 460, 461.)

[2] "The learned and ingenious Eichhorn, in his introduction to the Old Testament, supposes that the first Latin version of the Bible was made in Africa; where Latin alone being understood, a translation was more necessary; where the Latin version was held in the highest veneration; and where, the language being spoken with less purity, barbarisms might have been more easily introduced than in a provincial town in Italy." Bp. Marsh's Michaelis, vol. ii. part ii. p 628.

[3] Bishop Marsh's Divinity Lectures, part i. p. 66.

and Song of Solomon, are all that were ever published; Jerome's manuscripts, comprising the remaining books of Scripture, being lost or destroyed through the wilful negligence or fraud of some individual whom he has not named.[1] But before Jerome had finished his revisal, he had commenced a translation of the Old Testament from the Hebrew into Latin, in order that the Western Christians, who used this last language only, might know the real meaning of the Hebrew text, and thus be the better qualified to engage in controversial discussions with the Jews.

3. This version, which surpasses all former ones, was executed at different times, Jerome having translated particular books in the order requested by his friends. We learn from Augustine, that it was introduced into the churches by degrees, for fear of offending weak persons: at length it acquired so great an authority from the approbation it received from Pope Gregory I., that ever since the seventh century it has been exclusively adopted[2] by the Romish Church, under the name of the VULGATE version: and a decree of the Council of Trent, in the sixteenth century, commanded that the Vulgate alone should be used whenever the Bible is publicly read, and in all sermons, expositions, and disputations; and pronounced it to be *authentic*, — a very ambiguous term, which ought to have been more precisely defined, than the members of that Council chose to define it. " Upon this ground many contended, that the Vulgate version was dictated by the Holy Spirit, at least was providentially guarded against all error; was consequently of divine authority, and more to be regarded than even the original Hebrew and Greek texts. And, in effect, the decree of the Council, however limited and moderated by the explanation of some of their more judicious divines, has given to the Vulgate such a high degree of authority, that, in this instance at least, the translation has taken place of the original; for these translators, instead of the Hebrew and Greek texts, profess to translate the Vulgate. Indeed, when we find the Vulgate very notoriously deficient in expressing the sense, they do the original Scriptures the honour of consulting them, and take the liberty, by following them, of departing from their authentic guide; but, in general, the Vulgate is their original text; and they give us a translation of a translation; by which second transfusion of the Holy Scriptures into another tongue, still more of the original sense must be lost, and more of the genuine spirit must evaporate." [3]

The universal adoption of Jerome's new version throughout the Western church rendered a multiplication of copies necessary; and with them new errors were introduced in the course of time, by the intermixture of the two versions (the Old Italic, and Jerome's or the Vulgate) with each other. Of this confusion, Cassiodorus was the

---

[1] Jerome, Ep 64. ad Augustin.
[2] With the exception of the Psalms, which being daily chaunted to music in the church service, made it difficult to introduce alterations. The Old Italic Psalter, as corrected by Jerome, has therefore been used ever since the time of Gregory I. The apocryphal books of Baruch, Ecclesiasticus, Wisdom, and the two books of Maccabees, are also retained from the old Latin version.
[3] Bp Lowth's Translation of Isaiah, vol 1. Prel Diss. p lxxiu.

principal cause, who ordered them to be written in parallel columns, that the old version might be corrected by the Vulgate; and though Alcuin in the eighth century, by the command of Charlemagne, provided more accurate copies, the text again fell into such confusion, and was so disfigured by innumerable mistakes of copyists, — (notwithstanding the efforts made to correct it by Lanfranc archbishop of Canterbury in the eleventh century, and by Cardinal Nicholas, and some other divines, about the middle of the twelfth and in the thirteenth centuries)—that the manuscripts of the middle ages materially differ from the first printed editions.

Robert STEPHENS was the first who attempted to remedy this confusion, by publishing his critical editions of the Vulgate in 1528, 1532, 1534, 1540 [1], and particularly in 1545 and 1546. These, especially the last, having incurred the censures of the doctors of the Sorbonne, John Hentenius, a divine of Louvain, was employed to prepare a new edition of the Vulgate; this he accomplished in 1547 in folio, having availed himself of Stephens's previous labours with great advantage. A third corrected edition was published by Lucas Brugensis, with the assistance of several other divines of Louvain, in 1573, in three volumes, 8vo., which was also reprinted in 1586 in 4to. and 8vo, with the critical notes of Lucas Brugensis. The labours of the Louvain divines not being in every respect approved by Sixtus V., he commanded a new revision of the text to be made with the utmost care: to this work he devoted much time and attention, and corrected the proofs himself of the edition which was published at Rome in 1590, in folio. The text thus revised, Sixtus pronounced to be the authentic Vulgate, which had been the object of inquiry in the Council of Trent; and ordained that it should be adopted throughout the Romish Church. But, notwithstanding the labours of the Pope, this edition was discovered to be so exceedingly incorrect, that his successor Gregory XIV. caused it to be suppressed; and Clement VIII., the successor of Gregory in the pontificate, published another authentic Vulgate in 1592. This, however, differs more than any other edition, from that of Sixtus V., and mostly resembles that of Louvain. These fatal variances between editions, alike promulgated by pontiffs claiming infallibility, have not passed unnoticed by Protestant divines, who have taken advantage of them in a manner that sensibly affects the Church of Rome; especially Kortholt, who has at great length refuted the pretensions of Bellarmine in favour of the Vulgate in a mas-

---

[1] The edition of 1540 was Stephens's principal edition of the Latin Vulgate; as his edition of 1550 was his principal edition of the Greek. In *magnificence* it surpasses every edition of the Vulgate that ever was printed. and it is likewise of great value to a critic, as it contains a copious collection of readings from Latin manuscripts, and some of the early editions. Father Simon (Hist. Crit. des Versions du N. Test. ch. xi. p. 130.) calls it "*un chef-d'œuvre en fait de Bible;*" and (p. 131.) he terms this edition "*la meilleure des toutes*" Hentenius, in his preface to the Louvain edition, calls it "*accuratissima et castigatissima Biblia*" (See also the praises bestowed on it in Masch's edition of Le Long's Bibliotheca Sacra, part ii vol iii. p. 187) The title-page prefixed to the New Testament bears the date of 1539, though that which is prefixed to the Old Testament is dated 1540 (Marsh's Letters to Travis, p. 254 note) It is by this latter date, that Stephens's best edition of the Vulgate is usually known and cited.

terly manner¹, and our learned countryman Thomas James, in his *Bellum Papale, sive Concordia Discors Sixti V.* (London, 1600, 4to.) who has pointed out very numerous additions, omissions, contradictions, and other differences between the Sixtine and Clementine editions.² From this very curious and now rare volume, the following specimens of the differences between these two editions are selected, and arranged.

1. Clauses omitted in the Sixtine, but inserted in the Clementine Bible.

Num. xxx 11.	*Uxor in domo viri, &c.* to the end of the verse.
Prov. xxv 24	*Melius est sedere in angulo domatis, &c.*
Lev. xx. 9.	*Patri matrique maledixit.*
Jud. xvii 2, 3.	*Reddidit ergo eos matri suæ, &c*
1 Kings iv. 21.	*Quia capta est arca Dei.*
3 Kings (same as our first) xii 10	*Sic loqueris ad eos.*
2 Chron. ii 10	*Et vini vigenti millia metretas*
Matt. xxvii 35.	*Ut impleretur quod dictum est per prophetam dicentem, diviserunt sibi vestimenta mea, et super vestem meam miserunt sortem.*

2. Clauses or words introduced into the Sixtine, but omitted in the Clementine Bible.

1 Sam. xxiv. 8.	*Vivit dominus, quia nisi dominus percusserit eum, aut dies ejus venerit ut moriatur, aut descendens in prælium perirat; propitius mihi sit dominus ut non multam manum meam in Christum Domini.*
1 Sam. xxv 6	*Ex multis annis salvos faciens tuos et omnia tua*
2 Sam vi 12	*Dixitque David, ibo et reducam arcam.*
2 Sam viii 8	*De quo fecit Salomo omnia vasa ærea in templo et mare æneum et columnas et altare*
2 Sam xix 10	*Et concilium totius Israel venit ad regem.*
Prov. xxiv. ult.	*Usque quo piger dormis? usque quo de somno consurges.*
Hab 1. 3.	*Quare respicis contemptores et taces conculcante impio justiorem se? Et facies homines quasi pisces maris, et quasi reptilia non habentia ducem.*
Matt. xxiv. 41.	*Duo in lecto, unus assumetur, et unus relinquetur*
Acts xiv. 6.	*Et commota est omnis multitudo in doctrina eorum, Paulus autem, &c.*
xxiv. 18, 19.	*Et apprehenderunt me clamantes et dicentes, tolle inimicum nostrum.*

3 Manifest contradictions, or differences between the editions.

Ex xxiii. 18	Sixtine *Tuæ*, Clementine *meæ*.
Numb xxxiv 4	S *Ad meridiem*, C *A meridie*.
Deut xvii. 8.	S *Inter lepram et non lepram*, C *Inter lepram et lepram*.
Jos ii. 18.	S *Signum non fuerit*, C. *Signum fuerit*.
iv. 23.	S. *Deo nostro*, C *Vestro*
xi. 19.	S. *Quæ se non traderet*, C. *Quæ se traderet*.
xii 3.	S *Tuo*, C *Meo*.
1 Sam. iv 9.	S. *Nobis*, C. *Vobis*
xx. 9	S. *A me*, C. *A te*
1 Kings vii 9.	S. *Intrinsecus*, C. *Extrinsecus*
Hab. i 13.	S. *Quare non respicis*, C *Respicis*
Heb. v. 11.	S *Interpretabilis*, C. *Inuinterpretabilis*
2 Pet. i. 16.	S *Indoctas*, C *Doctas*.

4. Differences in numbers.

Ex xxiv. 5.	S *Vitulos duodecim*, C. *Vitulos*.
xxxii. 28.	S. *Trigenta tria millia*, C. *Vigenti millia*.
2 Sam xv. 7.	S. *Quatuor*, C. *Quadriginta*
1 Kings iv. 42	S *Quinque millia*, C. *Quinque et mille*.
2 Kings xiv 17	S. *Viginti Quinque*, C *Quindecim*
xxv. 19.	S. *Sex*, C *Sexaginta*.
2 Chron. xiii 17.	S. *Quinquaginta*, C. *Quingenta*.

---

¹ Korholt, de variis Scripturæ Editionibus, pp. 110—251.

² Additional instances of the contradictions between the above-mentioned papal editions, together with a defence of the *Bellum Papale*, may be seen in Mr. James's " Treatise of the Corruptions of Scripture, Councils, and Fathers, by the Prelates, Pastors, and Pillars of the Church of Rome, for the Maintenance of Popery," pp.272—358 London, 1688 8vo.

5. Other remarkable differences.

1 Sam. iii. 2, 3.	S *Nec poterat videre lucernam Dei antequam extingueretur.* C. *Nec poterat videre, lucerna Dei antequam extingueretur.*
1 Kings ii. 28.	S *Ad Salomonem,* C *Ad Joab.*
2 Kings xv. 19.	S. *In thersam,* C *In terram.*
Judith i. 2.	S. *Fecit, ejus muros in altitudinem* 70 *cubitus ·* this is one of those places where paper had been pasted on the text, the word first printed was *latitudinem,* and *altitudinem* was printed on a slip of paper, and put over it, C *Latitudinem*
Ibidem	S *Latitudinem,* 30 *cu.* C. *Altitudinem,* 30 *cubitus.*
Job xxxi. 7, 5.	S. *Si secutus est oculus meus cor meum,* C *Si secutum est oculos meus cor meum.*
Psa. xli. 3.	S. *Ad Deum fontem vivum,* C. *Ad Deum fortem, vivum.*
Prov xix. 26.	S *Qui affligit patrem et fugit matrem,* C. *Qui affigat, &c. et fugat, &c.*
xx. 25.	S *Devorare sanctos,* C *Devotare sanctos.*
Ezek xiv 22.	S. *Egredientur,* C *Ingredientur*
Sirach xxxviii 25.	S *Sapientiam scribæ,* C. *Sapientia scribæ.*
xlii. 9	S. *Adultera,* C *Adulta.*
Isaiah xlvi 12.	S. *Justum,* C. *Avem.*
Jer. xvii. 9.	S. *Cor hominis,* C. *Hominum.* [1]

Besides the preceding revisions by papal authority, there have been several others executed by private individuals; in which the Latin Vulgate has been so much corrected from the original Hebrew and Greek, that they have in some degree been considered (though erroneously) as new translations. Of this number are the Latin Bibles published by Clarius, Eber, and the Osianders.

[i.] Isidore CLARIUS's edition of the Vulgate first appeared at Venice in 1542, and is of extreme rarity: it was reprinted at the same place in 1557 and 1564. He has not only restored the antient Latin text, but has also corrected it in a great number of places which he conceived to be erroneously translated, so as to make them conformable to the Hebrew original. Although he corrected more than *eight thousand* places, as he states in his preface, yet he omitted some, lest he should offend the Roman Catholics by making too many alterations in the Vulgate version.

[ii.] The method of Clarius was followed by Paul EBER, who corrected the Vulgate from Luther's German version. His edition was published at Wittemberg, in 1565, with the addition of Luther's translation, under the authority of Augustus, Elector of Saxony; and was reprinted in 1574, in ten volumes, quarto.

[iii.] The edition of *Luke* OSIANDER appeared in 1578, and has since been very often reprinted; as also has a German translation of it, which was first published at Stutgard in 1600. *Andrew* Osiander's edition was also printed in 1600, and frequently since. They have both corrected the Vulgate, according to the Hebrew originals; and have occasioned some confusion to their readers, by inserting their emendations in a character different from that in which the Vulgate text is printed.

4. The Vulgate is regarded by Papists and Protestants in very different points of view: by the former it has been extolled beyond measure, while by most of the latter it has been depreciated as much below its intrinsic merit. Our learned countryman, John Bois (canon of Ely), was the first who pointed out the real value of this

---

[1] Hamilton's Introduction to the Hebrew Scriptures, pp. 163—166.

version, in his *Collatio Veteris Interpretis cum Bezâ aliisque recentionibus* (8vo. 1655). In this work, which is now of extreme rarity, the author has successfully shown that, in many places, the modern translators had unduly depreciated the Vulgate, and unnecessarily departed from it. Bois was followed by Father Simon, in his *Histoire Critique du Texte et des Versions du Nouveau Testament*, who has proved that the more antient the Greek manuscripts and other versions are, the more closely do they agree with the Vulgate: and in consequence of the arguments adduced by Simon, the Vulgate has been more justly appreciated by biblical critics of later times.

Although the Latin Vulgate is neither inspired nor infallible, as Morinus, Suarez, and other advocates of the Romish Church have attempted to maintain, yet it is allowed to be in general a faithful translation, and sometimes exhibits the sense of Scripture with greater accuracy than the more modern versions. for all those which have been made in modern times, by divines in communion with the Church of Rome, are derived from the Latin Vulgate, which, in consequence of the decree of the Council of Trent above noticed, has been substituted for the original Hebrew and Greek texts. The Latin Vulgate, therefore, is by no means to be neglected by the biblical critic: and since the Ante-Hieronymian Latin translations are unquestionably of great antiquity, both lead us to a discovery of the readings in very antient Greek manuscripts, which existed prior to the date of any now extant. Even in its present state, notwithstanding the variations between the Sixtine and Clementine editions, and that several passages are mistranslated, in order to support the peculiar dogmas of the Church of Rome, the Latin Vulgate preserves many true readings [1], where the modern Hebrew copies are corrupted. [2]

II. The GOTHIC VERSION of the Bible was made from the Greek, both in the Old and in the New Testament, by Ulphilas [3], a celebrated Bishop of the Mæso-Goths, who assisted at the council of Constantinople in 359, and was sent on an embassy to the emperor Valens about the year 378. He is said to have embraced Arianism, and to have propagated Arian tenets among his countrymen. Besides translating the *entire* Bible into the Gothic language, Ulphilas is said to have conferred on the Mæso-Goths the invention of the Gothic characters. The character, however, in which this version of the

---

[1] Cappell has given numerous examples in his Critica Sacra, lib. ii cc. vii.—ix. tom. ii. pp 858—898. (edit. Scharfenberg).

[2] The preceding account of the Latin versions has been compiled from Michaelis, vol. ii pp. 107—129. Semler, Apparatus ad Liberalem Vet Test. Interpretationem, pp. 308—314. Carpzov. Critica Sacra, pp. 671—706. Leusden, Philologus Hebræomixtus, pp 1—10 Bishop Walton, Prol c. xi. pp 470—507.; and Viser, Hermeneutica Sacra Novi Testamenti, vol ii. part iii. pp 73—96. See also Muntinghe's Expositio Critices Veteris Fœderis, pp. 149—156.; and Hug's Introduction, vol. i. pp. 464—483. For the principal editions of the Latin versions of the Scriptures, see the Appendix, pp. 44—46.

[3] " This," says Bishop Marsh, " is an original German name, and is a diminutive of the word Wolf · it is written in correct German, Wölfelein, but corruptly pronounced Wölfila or Wulfila, in the dialects of Switzerland, Bavaria, and Austria, to which that of the Mæso-Goths, who likewise inhabited the banks of the Danube, is nearly allied." Michaelis, vol ii part ii. p. 631.

New Testament is written, is, in fact, the Latin character of that age; and the degree of perfection, which the Gothic language had obtained during the time of Ulphilas, is a proof that it had then been written for some time.

The translation of Ulphilas (who had been educated among the Greeks) was executed from the Greek: but, from its coincidence in many instances with the Latin, there is reason to suspect that it has been interpolated, though at a remote period, from the Vulgate. Its unquestionable antiquity, however, and its general fidelity, have concurred to give this version a high place in the estimation of biblical critics: but, unfortunately, it has not come down to us entire. The only parts extant in print are, a fragment of the book of Nehemiah, a considerable portion of the four Gospels, and some portions of the apostolic epistles.[1]

III. The SCLAVONIC, or Old Russian Version, was also made from the Greek, both in the Old and New Testaments. It is ascribed to the two brothers, Cyril[2] (or Constantine, surnamed the Philosopher on account of his learning,) and Methodius, sons of Leo a Greek nobleman of Thessalonica, who, in the latter part of the ninth century, first preached the Gospel among the Moravo-Sclavonians: but it is questionable, whether these missionaries translated the whole of the sacred code, or whether their labours comprised only the books of the New Testament and the Psalms of David. M. Dobrowsky (who has bestowed more pains on the critical study of the Sclavonic Scriptures than any person now living) is of opinion " that, with the exception of the Psalms, no part of the Old Testament was translated at so early a period. So much, however, is certain, that the book of Proverbs must have been translated before, or in the twelfth century, as the frequent quotations made from it by Nestor (author of the Russian Chronicle, who died in 1156,) agree, on the whole, with the common text. The books of Job, on the other hand, the Prophets, and the apocryphal books of Wisdom and Ecclesiasticus, appear to have been done in Servia, in the thirteenth or fourteenth century; and the Pentateuch and remaining books in the fifteenth, either in Russia or Poland, at which time the whole were collected into one volume, and arranged according to the order of the books in the Bohemian Bible, printed in 1488 or 1489." The extreme rarity and recent date of MSS. of the entire Sclavonic Bible greatly corroborated this hypothesis of M. Dobrowsky, respecting the late execution of this version of the Old Testament.[3] Dr. Henderson has shown, by actual col-

---

[1] Michaelis, vol. ii part i pp. 130—153 149—152. Hug, vol. i. pp. 498—513.

[2] To this Cyril is ascribed the invention of the Sclavonic letters "But, it is manifest, this invention consisted in nothing more than the adaptation of the uncial characters of the Greek alphabet, so far as they went, to express the sounds of the new language, with the addition of certain other letters, borrowed or changed from other alphabets, to make up the deficiency. He also substituted Sclavonic for the Phenician names of the letters, on which account the alphabet has been called the Cyrillic, after his name." Dr. Henderson's Biblical Researches and Travels in Russia, p 67. (London, 1826.) In pp. 60—109. the learned traveller has given an extended and very interesting account of the Sclavonic language and sacred literature, from which the present notice of the Sclavonic version is abridged. [3] Ibid. pp. 73, 74.

lation, that the Sclavonic text of the Old Testament, in the editio princeps of the Bible printed at Ostrog in 1581, was made with the assistance of the Vulgate or some antient Latin MSS. found in the Bulgarian monasteries, or that it was at least revised and altered according to them; and he is of opinion that, if this edition were carefully collated, it would yield a rich harvest of various readings, some of which might prove of essential service to a future editor of the Septuagint.[1]

According to Professor Hug, the Sclavonic version exhibits the text of the Constantinopolitan recension. M. Dobrowsky pronounces it to be a very literal translation from the Greek, the Greek construction being very frequently retained, even where it is contrary to the genius of the Sclavonian language; and in general it resembles the most antient manuscripts, with which it agrees, even where their united evidence is against the common printed reading. "It contains at least *three fourths* of the readings which Griesbach has adopted into his text" [in his critical edition of the New Testament]. "Where he has few authorities, the Sclavonic mostly corroborates the authority of the textus receptus: and, where a great agreement obtains among the antient MSS. in favour of a reading, it joins them against the common editions. It varies from Theophylact as often as it agrees with him, and has neither been altered from him nor the Vulgate:"[2] and it possesses few or no *lectiones singulares*, or readings peculiar to itself.[3] From an edition of this version, printed at Moscow in 1614, M. Alter selected the readings of the Four Gospels, and from a manuscript in the imperial library, the readings of the Acts and Epistles, which are printed in his edition of the Greek New Testament. (Vienna, 1787, 2 vols. 8vo.) M. Dobrowsky states that these various lections are given with great accuracy, but that those which Matthai has selected from the Revelation are erroneous and useless. Griesbach has given a catalogue of the Sclavonic manuscripts collated for his edition of the New Testament, communicated to him by Dobrowsky.[4]

IV. ANGLO-SAXON VERSION.—Although Christianity was planted in Britain in the first century, it does not appear that the Britons had any translation of the Scriptures in their language earlier than the eighth century. About the year 706, Adhelm, the first bishop of Sherborn, translated the Psalter into Saxon: and at his earnest persuasion, Egbert or Eadfrid, bishop of Lindisfarne, or Holy Island, soon after executed a Saxon version of the Four Gospels.[5] Not

---

[1] Dr Henderson's Biblical Researches and Travels in Russia, p. 88.
[2] Ibid pp 89, 90.
[3] Dr Henderson corroborates this account of M Dobrowsky, and states that this version "may be considered as one of the most verbal ever executed Not only is every word and particle scrupulously expressed, and made, in general, to occupy the same place in the translation that it does in the original, but the derivation and compounds, as well as the grammatical forms, are all successfully imitated." (Ibid. pp 91, 92.)
[4] Michaelis, vol ii pp. 153—158 636, 637. Griesbach, Prolegomena, vol.1 pp cxxvii. —cxxxii Beck, Monogrammata Hermeneutices Novi Testamenti, pp. 108, 109 Hug, vol. i. pp 513—517.
[5] The manuscript of this translation is now deposited in the Cottonian Library in the British Museum (Nero, D. IV.). Mr. Astle has given a specimen of it in plate xiv. of his "Origin and Progress of Writing," and has described it in pp 100, 101.

many years after this, the learned and venerable Bede (who died A. D. 735) translated the entire Bible into that language. There were other Saxon versions, either of the whole or of detached portions of the Scriptures, of a later date. A translation of the book of Psalms was undertaken by the illustrious King Alfred, who died A. D 900, when it was about half finished: and Elfric, who was archbishop of Canterbury in 995, translated the Pentateuch, Joshua, Job, Judith, part of the book of Kings, Esther, and Maccabees. The *entire* Anglo-Saxon version of the Bible has never been printed: King Alfred's translation of the Psalms, with the interlineary Latin text, was edited by John Spelman, 4to. London, 1640; and there is another Saxon interlineary translation of the Psalter, deposited in the Archiepiscopal Library at Lambeth. Of the Four Gospels, there have been three editions printed: an account of which will be found in the Appendix, pp. 48, 49.

The Anglo-Saxon version being evidently translated from the Old Latin, Michaelis is of opinion that it may be of use in determining the readings of that version; and Semler has remarked, that it contains many readings which vary both from the Greek and Latin texts, of which he has given some examples. Dr. Mill selected various lections from this version; which, from the difference of style and inequalities observable in its execution, he ascribes to several authors: it is supposed to have been executed in the eighth century.[1] On the application of antient versions to the ascertaining of various readings, see Part I. Chap. V. of this volume; and on the benefit which may be derived from them in the interpretation of the Scriptures, see Part II. Book I. Chap. II. Sect. I. § 2.

---

[1] Johnson's Hist Account of English Translations of the Bible, in Bishop Watson's Collection of Theological Tracts, vol iii. pp. 61—63 Bp. Marsh's Michaelis, vol. ii. pp. 158. 637. Kortholt, pp 351—353. Semler, Apparatus ad Lib. Novi Test. Interp pp. 72, 73.

CHAPTER III.

ON THE MANUSCRIPTS OF THE BIBLE.

Form of a SYNAGOGUE ROLL of the Pentateuch.

SECTION I.

ON THE HEBREW MANUSCRIPTS OF THE OLD TESTAMENT.

I. *Different classes of Hebrew Manuscripts.* — II. *The Rolled Manuscripts of the Synagogues.* — III. *The Square Manuscripts used by the Jews in private life.* — IV. *Antient Recensions or Editions of Hebrew Manuscripts.* — V. *Age of Hebrew Manuscripts.* — VI. *Of the order in which the Sacred Books are arranged in Manuscripts. — Number of Books contained in different Manuscripts.* — VII. *Modern Families or Recensions of Hebrew Manuscripts.* — VIII. *Notice of the most antient Manuscripts.* — IX. *Brief notice of the Manuscripts of the Indian Jews.*

ALTHOUGH, as we have already seen, the Hebrew text of the Old Testament has descended to our times uncorrupted, yet, with all the care which the antient copyists could bestow, it was impossibe to preserve it free from mistakes, arising from the interchanging of the similar letters of the Hebrew alphabet, and other circumstances incident to the transcription of antient manuscripts. The Rabbins boldly asserted, and, through a credulity rarely to be paralleled, it was implicitly believed, that the Hebrew text was absolutely free from error, and that in all the manuscripts of the Old Testament not a single various reading of importance could be produced. Father Morin was the first person who ventured to impugn this notion in his *Exercitationes in utrumque Samaritanorum Pentateuchum*, published at Paris in 1631; and he grounded his opinion of the incorrectness of the Hebrew manuscripts on the differences between the Hebrew and the Samaritan texts in the Pentateuch, and on the differences between the Hebrew and the Septuagint in other parts of the Bible. Morinus was soon after followed by Louis Cappel, (whose *Critica Sacra* was published in 1650,) who pointed out a great number of errors in the printed Hebrew, and showed how they might be corrected by the antient versions and the common rules of criticism. He did not, however, advert to the most obvious and effectual means of emendation, namely, a collation of Hebrew manuscripts; and, valuable as his labours unquestionably are. it is certain that he neither used them himself, nor invited others to have recourse to them, in order to correct the sacred text. Cappel was assailed by various opponents, but chiefly by the younger Buxtorf in his *Anticritica*, published at Basil in 1653, who attempted, but in vain, to refute the principles he had established. In 1657 Bishop Walton, in his Prolegomena to the London Polyglott Bible, declared in favour of the principles asserted by Cappel, acknowledged the necessity of forming a critical apparatus for the purpose of obtaining a more correct text of the Hebrew Bible, and materially contributed to the formation of one by his own exertions. Subsequent biblical critics acceded to the propriety of their arguments, and since the middle of the seventeenth century, the importance and necessity of collating Hebrew manuscripts have been generally acknowledged.[1]

I. Hebrew manuscripts are divided into two CLASSES, viz. *autographs*, or those written by the inspired penmen themselves, which have long since perished; and *apographs*, or copies made from the originals, and multiplied by repeated transcription. These apographs are also divided into the *more antient*, which formerly enjoyed the highest authority among the Jews, but have in like manner perished long ago; and into the *more modern*, which are found dispersed in various public and private libraries. The manuscripts which are still extant, are subdivided into the *rolled* manuscripts used in the synagogues, and into the *square* manuscripts which are used by private individuals among the Jews.

II. The Pentateuch was read in the Jewish synagogues from the earliest times; and, though the public reading of it was intermitted during the Babylonish captivity, it was resumed shortly after the return of the Jews. Hence numerous copies were made from time to time; and as they held the books of Moses in the most superstitious veneration, various regulations were made for the guidance of the transcribers, who were obliged to conform to them in copying the ROLLS destined for the use of the synagogue. The date of these regulations is not known, but they are long posterior to the Talmud; and though many of them are the most ridiculous and useless that can be well conceived, yet the religious observance of them, which has continued for many centuries, has certainly contributed in a great degree to preserve the purity of the Pentateuch. The following are a few of the principal of these regulations.

The copies of the law must be transcribed from antient manuscripts of approved character only, with pure ink, on parchment prepared from the hide of a clean animal, for this express purpose, by a Jew, and fastened together by the strings of clean animals; every skin must contain a certain number of columns of prescribed length and breadth, each column comprising a given number of lines and words; no word must be written by heart or with points, or without

---

[1] Bishop Marsh's Lectures, part ii. p. 99

being first orally pronounced by the copyist; the name of God is not to be written but with the utmost devotion and attention, and previously to writing it, he must wash his pen. The want of a single letter, or the redundance of a single letter, the writing of prose as verse, or verse as prose, respectively vitiates a manuscript; and when a copy has been completed, it must be examined and corrected within thirty days after the writing has been finished, in order to determine whether it is to be approved or rejected. These rules, it is said, are observed to the present day by the persons who transcribe the sacred writings for the use of the synagogue.[1] The form of one of these rolled manuscripts (from the original among the Harleian MSS. in the British Museum, No. 7619.) is given in the vignette at the head of this section. It is a large double roll, containing the Hebrew Pentateuch; written with very great care on forty brown African skins. These skins are of different breadths, some containing more columns than others. The columns are one hundred and fifty-three in number, each of which contains about sixty-three lines, is about twenty-two inches deep, and generally more than five inches broad. The letters have no points, apices, or flourishes about them. The initial words are not larger than the rest; and a space, equal to about four lines, is left between every two books. Altogether, this is one of the finest specimens of the synagogue-rolls that has been preserved to the present time.

III. The SQUARE MANUSCRIPTS, which are in private use, are written with black ink, either on vellum or on parchment, or on paper, and of various sizes, folio, quarto, octavo, and duodecimo. Those which are copied on paper are considered as being the most modern; and they frequently have some one of the Targums or Chaldee Paraphrases, either subjoined to the text in alternate verses, or placed in parallel columns with the text, or written in the margin of the manuscript. The characters are, for the most part, those which are called the square Chaldee; though a few manuscripts are written with rabbinical characters, but these are invariably of recent date. Biblical critics, who are conversant with the Hebrew manuscripts, have distinguished three sorts of characters, each differing in the beauty of their form. The *Spanish* character is perfectly square, simple, and elegant: the types of the quarto Hebrew Bibles, printed by Robert Stephen and by Plantin, approach the nearest to this character. The *German*, on the contrary, is crooked, intricate, and inelegant, in every respect; and the *Italian* character holds a middle place between these two. The pages are usually divided into three columns of various lengths; and the initial letters of the manuscripts are frequently illuminated and ornamented with gold. In many manuscripts the Masora[2] is added; what is called the *larger Masora* being placed above and below the columns of the text, and the *smaller Masora* being inserted in the blank spaces between the columns.

IV. In the period between the sixth and the tenth centuries, the Jews had two celebrated academies, one at Babylon in the east, and

---

[1] Carpzov Critica Sacra Vet. Test. pp 371, 372.
[2] See an account of the Masora in Chap. IV. Sect. I. § IV. *infra*

another at Tiberias in the west; where their literature was cultivated, and the Scriptures were very frequently transcribed. Hence arose two RECENSIONS or editions of the Hebrew Scriptures, which were collated in the eighth or ninth century. The differences or various readings observed in them were noted, and have been transmitted to our time under the appellation of the oriental and occidental or eastern and western readings. They are variously computed at 210, 216, and 220, and are printed by Bishop Walton in the Appendix to his splendid edition of the Polyglott Bible. In the early part of the eleventh century, Aaron ben Asher, president of the academy at Tiberias, and Jacob ben Naphtali, president of the academy at Babylon, collated the manuscripts of the oriental and occidental Jews. The discrepancies observed by these eminent Jewish scholars amount to upwards of 864; with one single exception, they relate to the vowel points, and, consequently, are of little value; they are also printed by Bishop Walton. The western Jews, and our printed editions of the Hebrew Scriptures, almost wholly follow the recension of Aaron ben Asher.

Among the Jews five exemplars have been particularly celebrated for their singular correctness, and from them all their subsequent copies have been made. These standard copies bear the names of the Codex of Hillel, of Ben Asher, which is also called the Palestine or Jerusalem Codex, of Ben Naphtali, or the Babylonian Codex, the Pentateuch of Jericho, and the Codex Sinai.

1. The *Codex of Hillel* was a celebrated manuscript which Rabbi Kimchi (who lived in the twelfth century) says that he saw at Toledo, though Rabbi Zacuti, who flourished towards the close of the fifteenth century, states that part of it had been sold and sent into Africa. Who this Hillel was, the learned are by no means agreed; some have supposed that he was the very eminent Rabbi Hillel who lived about sixty years before the birth of Christ; others imagine that he was the grandson of the illustrious Rabbi Jehudah Hakkadosh, who wrote the Misna, and that he flourished about the middle of the fourth century. Others, again, suppose that he was a Spanish Jew, named Hillel; but Bauer, with greater probability, supposes the manuscript to have been of more recent date, and written in Spain, because it contains the vowel points, and all the other grammatical minutiæ; and that the feigned name of Hillel was inscribed on its title in order to enhance its value.

2, 3. The Codices of *Ben Asher* and *Ben Naphtali* have already been noticed. We may, however, state, on the authority of Maimonides, that the first of these was held in most repute in Egypt, as having been revised and corrected in very many places by Ben Asher himself, and that it was the exemplar which he (Maimonides) followed in copying the law, in conformity with the custom of the Jews.

4. The *Codex of Jericho* is highly commended by Rabbi Elias Levita, as being the most correct copy of the Law of Moses, and exhibiting the defective and full words.

5. The Codex *Sinai* was also a very correct manuscript of the Pentateuch, that presented some variation in the accents, in which respect it differed from the former. A sixth Codex, called *Sanbouki*,

is mentioned by Père Simon, as having been seen by him; but nothing certain is known respecting its date, or by whom it was written.

V. As the authority of manuscripts depends greatly on their antiquity, it becomes a point of considerable importance to ascertain their AGE as exactly as possible. Now this may be effected either by *external* testimony or by *internal* marks.

1. *External* testimony is sometimes afforded by the subscriptions annexed by the transcribers, specifying the time when they copied the manuscripts. But this criterion cannot always be depended upon for instances have occurred, in which *modern* copyists have added antient and false dates in order to enhance the value of their labours. As, however, by far the greater number of manuscripts have no subscriptions or other criteria by which to ascertain their date, it becomes necessary to resort to the evidence of

2. *Internal Marks*. Of these, the following are stated by Dr. Kennicott and M. De Rossi to be the principal · 1. The inelegance or rudeness of the character (Jablonski lays down the *simplicity* and *elegance* of the character as a criterion of antiquity); — 2. The yellow colour of the vellum; — 3. The total absence, or at least the very rare occurrence, of the Masora, and of the Keri and Ketib [1]; — 4. The writing of the Pentateuch throughout in one book, without any greater mark of distinction appearing at the beginning of books than at the beginning of sections; — 5. The absence of critical emendations and corrections; — 6. The absence of the vowel points; — 7. Obliterated letters, being written and re-written with ink; — 8. The frequent occurrence of the name Jehovah in lieu of Adonai; — 9. The infrequency of capital and little letters; — 10. The insertion of points to fill up blank spaces; — 11. The non-division of some books and psalms; — 12. The poetical books not being distinguished from those in prose by dividing them into hemistichs; — 13. Readings frequently differing from the Masoretic copies, but agreeing with the Samaritan text, with antient versions, and with the quotations of the fathers. The conjunction of all, or of several, of these internal marks, is said to afford certain criteria of the antiquity of Hebrew manuscripts. But the opinions of the eminent critics above named have been questioned by Professors Bauer and Tychsen, who have advanced strong reasons to prove that they are uncertain guides in determining the age of manuscripts. The most antient Hebrew manuscripts are *all* written without any divisions of words, as is evident not only from antient Hebrew coins and Palmyrene inscriptions, but also from various passages in the most antient translations, the authors of which frequently adopted a division of words, altogether different from that of the Masorites. This circumstance is also corroborated by the rabbinical tradition, that the law was formerly one verse and one word. It is impossible to determine the time, when the Hebrews began to divide words in manuscripts: we only know from the researches of Dr. Kennicott and other eminent Hebrew critics, that all the antient interpreters used manuscripts written in one continued series; that MSS. of more recent date (the

---

[1] For an account of these, see Chap. IV. Sect. I. § IV. *infra*.

thirteenth century) are still extant in which the same mode of writing appears, — for instance, the MSS. numbered 290. and 293. by Dr. Kennicott; and that some vestiges of the division of words are to be found in the Talmudical writings, and in Jerome.[1]

VI. A twofold ORDER of ARRANGEMENT of the sacred books is observable in Hebrew manuscripts, viz. the *Talmudical* and the *Masoretic*. Originally, the different books of the Old Testament were not joined together: according to Rabbi Elias Levita (the most learned Jewish writer on the subject), they were first joined together by the members of the great synagogue, who divided them into three parts, — the law, the prophets, and hagiographa, and who placed the prophets and hagiographa in a different order from that assigned by the Talmudists in the book intitled *Baba Bathra*.

The following is the Talmudical arrangement of the Old Testament: — Of the *Prophets*, Joshua, Judges, Samuel, Kings (1 and 2), Jeremiah, Isaiah, Ezekiel, and the Twelve Minor Prophets (in one book). Of the *Hagiographa*, Ruth, Psalms, Job, Ecclesiastes, Song of Solomon, Lamentations, Esther, Chronicles. By the Masorites, the Prophets are placed in the same order, with the exception of Isaiah, who precedes Jeremiah and Ezekiel, because he flourished before them. This arrangement is adopted in the manuscripts of the Spanish Jews, while the Talmudical order is preserved in those of the German and French Jews. In the Hagiographa the Masorites have departed from the arrangement of the Talmudists, and place the books comprised in that division thus: — Psalms, Job, Proverbs, Ruth, the Song of Solomon, Ecclesiastes, Lamentations of Jeremiah, Esther, Daniel, and Ezra. This mode of arrangement obtains in the Spanish manuscripts. But in the German MSS. they are thus disposed: Psalms, Proverbs, Job, the Five Megilloth (or books), Daniel, Ezra, and Chronicles; and the Five Megilloth (or books) are placed in the order in which they are usually read in their synagogues, viz. the Song of Solomon, Ruth, Lamentations of Jeremiah, Ecclesiastes, and Esther.

There are, however, several manuscripts extant, which depart both from the Talmudical and from the Masoretical order, and have an arrangement peculiar to themselves. Thus, in the Codex Norimbergensis 1. (No. 198. of Dr. Kennicott's catalogue), which was written A. D. 1291, the books are thus placed: the Pentateuch, Joshua, Judges, Samuel, Kings, Isaiah, Jeremiah, Ezekiel, the Twelve Minor Prophets, Ruth, Esther, Psalms, Job, Ecclesiastes, Song of Solomon, Lamentations, Proverbs, Daniel, Ezra, and Nehemiah (in one book), and Chronicles. In the Codex, No. 94., written A. D. 1285 (in the university library, at Cambridge), and also in No. 102., a manuscript in the British Museum, written early in the fourteenth century, the books of Chronicles precede the Psalms; Job is placed before the Proverbs; Ruth before the Song of Solomon; and Ecclesiastes before the Lamentations. In the Codex, No. 130., a manuscript of the same date (in the library of the Royal Society of London), Chronicles and Ruth precede the Psalms; and in the

---

[1] Muntinghoe, Expositio Crit. Vet. Fœd. pp. 40, 41.

Codex, No. 96., (in the library of St. John's College, Cambridge,) written towards the close of the fourteenth century, and also in many other MSS., Jeremiah takes precedence of Isaiah. In the Codex Regiomontanus 2. (No. 224.), written early in the twelfth century, Jeremiah is placed before Ezekiel, whose book is followed by that of Isaiah: then succeed the Twelve Minor Prophets. The Hagiographa are thus disposed: — Ruth, Psalms, Job, Proverbs, Ecclesiastes, Song of Solomon, Lamentations, Daniel, Esther, Ezra and Nehemiah (in one book), and the books of Chronicles (also in one book). The order pursued in the Codex Ebnerianus 2. is altogether different from the preceding. Samuel follows Jeremiah, who is succeeded by the two books of Kings, and by part of the prophecy of Ezekiel: then comes part of Isaiah. The Twelve Minor Prophets are written in one continued discourse; and are followed by Ruth, Psalms, Job, Proverbs with Ecclesiastes and the Song of Solomon, Lamentations, Daniel, Esther, Ezra, Nehemiah, and Chronicles.

Of the various Hebrew manuscripts which have been preserved, few contain the Old Testament entire: the greater part comprise only particular portions of it, as the Pentateuch, five Megilloth, and Haphtaroth, or sections of the prophets which are read on the sabbath-days; the Prophets or the Hagiographa. Some, indeed, are confined to single books, as the Psalms, the book of Esther, the Song of Solomon, and the Haphtaroth. This diversity in the contents of manuscripts is occasioned, partly by the design of the copyist, who transcribed the whole or part of the sacred writings for particular purposes; and partly by the mutilations caused by the consuming hand of time. Several instances of such mutilations are given in the account of the principal Hebrew MSS. now extant, in pp. 87—89. *infra*.

VII. As the Hebrew manuscripts which have been in use since the eleventh century have all been corrected according to some particular *recension* or edition, they have from this circumstance been classed into FAMILIES, according to the country where such recension has obtained. These *families* or recensions are three or four in number, viz.

1. The *Spanish Manuscripts*, which were corrected after the Codex of Hillel. They follow the Masoretic system with great accuracy, and are on this account highly valued by the Jews, though some Hebrew critics hold them in little estimation. The characters are written with great elegance, and are perfectly square: the ink is pale; the pages are seldom divided into three columns; the Psalms are divided into hemistichs; and the Chaldee paraphrases are not interlined, but written in separate columns, or are inserted in the margin in smaller letters. Professor Tychsen speaks in high terms of the caligraphy of the Spanish manuscripts. As the Spanish monks excelled in that art, he thinks the Jews, who abounded in Spain in the twelfth and thirteenth centuries, acquired it from them, and he appeals to manuscripts which he had seen, where the letters are throughout so equal, that the whole has the appearance of print.[1]

---

[1] Tychsen, Tentamen de variis Cod. Heb. MSS. pp. 302—308.

2. The *Oriental Manuscripts* are nearly the same as the Spanish manuscripts, and may be referred to the same class.

3. The *German Manuscripts* are written with less elegance than the Spanish codices: their characters are more rudely formed; the initial letters are generally larger than the rest, and ornamented; the ink is very black. They do not follow the Masoretic notation, and frequently vary from the Masoretic manuscripts, exhibiting important readings that are not to be found in the Spanish manuscripts, but which agree with the Samaritan text of the Pentateuch, and with the antient versions. The Chaldee paraphrases are inserted in alternate verses. This class of manuscripts is little esteemed by the Jews, but most highly valued by biblical critics.

4. The *Italian Manuscripts* hold a middle place between the Spanish and German codices, and sometimes have a nearer affinity to one class than to the other, both in the shape of the Hebrew characters, and also as it respects their adherence to or neglect of the Masoretic system. M. Bruns, the able assistant of Dr. Kennicott in collating Hebrew manuscripts, has given engraved specimens of the Spanish, German, and Italian manuscripts, in his edition of Dr. K.'s Dissertatio Generalis (8vo. Brunswick, 1783); and Professor Tychsen has given *fourteen* Hebrew alphabets, of various ages and countries, at the end of his Tentamen de variis Codicum Hebræorum Vet. Test. MSS. Generibus. Antient and unpointed Hebrew manuscripts, written for the use of the synagogues, and those Masoretic Spanish exemplars, which have been transcribed by a learned person, and for a learned person, from some famous and correct copy, are preferred by M. De Rossi to the copies written for private use, or even for the synagogue, from Masoretic exemplars, of which last the number is very great. But M. Bauer pronounces those manuscripts to be the best, whose various lections are most frequently confirmed by the antient versions, especially by the Alexandrian and Syriac, and also by the Samaritan Pentateuch and version.[1]

VIII. M. De Rossi has divided Hebrew manuscripts into three classes, viz. 1. *More antient*, or those written before the twelfth century; — 2. *Antient*, or those written in the thirteenth and fourteenth centuries; — 3. *More recent*, or those written at the end of the fourteenth, or at the beginning of the fifteenth century. The most recent, or those written since the fifteenth century, which are very numerous, and are those found in the synagogues, he pronounces to be of little or no use, unless it can be proved that they have been transcribed from antient apographs. The total number of Hebrew manuscripts collated by Dr. Kennicott for his critical edition of the Hebrew Bible is about six hundred and thirty. The total number collated by M. De Rossi for his Collection of Various Readings, is four hundred and seventy-nine manuscripts, besides two hundred

---

[1] Walton, Prolegom. c iv § 1—12 pp. 171—184 cc vii. viii. pp. 225—331. edit Dathii. Carpzov. Critica Sacra, pp 289—387. Dr. Kennicott, diss. i. pp. 315—317; also his Dissertatio Generalis, *passim* Jahn, Introd. ad Vet. Fœdus, pp. 153—170. Bauer, Critica Sacra, pp. 215—226. 343—407. De Rossi. Var Lect tom. 1 Prolegom. § xi.—xix pp xi.—xxii.

and eighty-eight printed editions. The following are the most antient manuscripts collated by Dr. Kennicott.

1. The CODEX LAUDIANUS, A. 172 and 162, and numbered 1. in Dr. Kennicott's list of Hebrew manuscripts. Though now in two folio parts, it is evident that they originally formed only one volume : each part consists of quinquernions, or gatherings of five sheets or ten leaves, and at the bottom of every tenth leaf is a catch-word beginning the next leaf, which is the first of the succeeding gathering of ten leaves. But at the end of the first part or volume, there is pasted on, one leaf of the next quinquernion, completing the book of Deuteronomy ; so that this volume concludes with five sheets and one leaf over. And the first gathering in the second volume consists of only four sheets and one leaf, which last is likewise pasted on, for want of its fellow-leaf. This manuscript is written on vellum, according to Dr. Kennicott, in the Spanish character, but in the opinion of Dr. Bruns it is in the Italic character, to which M. De Rossi assents. The letters, which are moderately large, are plain, simple, and elegant, but universally unadorned, and they were originally written without points, as is evident from the different colour of the ink in the letters and in the points. Some of the letters, having become obliterated by the lapse of ages, have been written over a second time ; and though such places were re-written in the same strong character, yet many of the words were becoming a second time invisible, when collated by Dr K. This eminent critic assigns it to the tenth century, but De Rossi refers it to the eleventh. The Laudian manuscript begins with Gen. xxvii. 31. It contains *fourteen thousand* variations from Vander Hooght's edition of the Hebrew Bible. More than two thousand are found in the Pentateuch, which confirm the Septuagint Greek version in one hundred and nine various readings; the Syriac, in ninety-eight ; the Arabic, in eighty-two ; the Vulgate or Latin Version, in eighty-eight , and the Chaldee Paraphrase, in forty-two : it also agrees with the Samaritan Pentateuch against the printed Hebrew, in seven hundred instances. What renders this manuscript the more valuable is, that it preserves a word of great importance for understanding 2 Sam. xxiii. 3—7., which word is confirmed by the Greek version, and thus recovers to us a prophecy of the Messiah.[1]

2. The CODEX CARLSRUHENSIS 1 (No. 154. of Dr. Kennicott's list of manuscripts,) formerly belonged to the celebrated and learned Reuchlin, whose efforts contributed so much towards the revival of literature in the fifteenth century. This manuscript is now preserved in the public library at Carlsruhe, and is the oldest that has a *certain* date. It is in square folio, and was written in the year of the world 4866, corresponding with 1106 of our æra. It contains the Prophets with the Targum.

3. The CODEX VIENNÆ (No. 590. of Kennicott) contains the Prophets and Hagiographa. It is written on vellum in folio, and if the date in its subscription be correct (A.D. 1018 or 1019), it is more antient than the preceding. Bruns collected two hundred important various readings from this manuscript. The points have been added by a later hand. According to Adler's enumeration, it consists of four hundred and seventy-one leaves, and two columns, each column containing twenty-one lines.

---

[1] Kennicott, Dissert. I pp. 315—319 Dissert. II. pp. 533, 534. Biblia Hebraica, tom. ii. Dissert Generalis, pp. 70, 71. De Rossi, Variæ Lectiones, tom. i. Proleg. p *LIX*.

4. The CODEX CÆSENÆ, in the Malatesta Library at Bologna (No. 536. of Kennicott), is a folio manuscript written on vellum, in the German character, towards the end of the eleventh century. It contains the Pentateuch, the Haphtaroth or sections of the Prophetical Books, and the Megilloth or five Books of Canticles, or the Song of Solomon, Ruth, the Lamentations of Jeremiah, Ecclesiastes, and Esther. De Rossi pronounces it to be a most antient and valuable manuscript, and states that in its margin are inserted some various readings of still more antient manuscripts.[1]

5. The CODEX FLORENTINUS 2. (No. 162. of Kennicott) is written on vellum, in quarto, in a square Spanish character, with points, towards the end of the eleventh, or at the latest, in the beginning of the twelfth century. It contains the books of Joshua, Judges, and Samuel. Very many of the letters, which were obliterated by time, have been renewed by a later hand.

6. The CODEX MEDIOLANENSIS, 9. (193. of Kennicott) is written on vellum, in octavo, in the German character, towards the close of the twelfth century. It has neither the points nor the Masora. This manuscript comprises the Pentateuch, the beginning of the book of Genesis, and the end of Leviticus and Deuteronomy, have been written by a later hand. Both erasures and alterations occur in this manuscript, and sometimes a worse reading is substituted in place of one that is preferable. Nevertheless it contains many good various readings

7. The CODEX NORIMBERGENSIS 4. (201 of Kennicott) is a folio manuscript, written on thin vellum, in the German character, and containing the Prophets and Hagiographa. It is mutilated in various parts. It is of great antiquity, and from the similarity of its character to that of the Codex Carlsruhensis, both Dr. Kennicott and M. De Rossi assign it to the beginning of the twelfth century.

8. The CODEX PARISIENSIS 27. (Regius 29. 210. of Kennicott) is a quarto manuscript of the entire Bible, written on vellum, in an elegant Italic character. The initial words are, with few exceptions, of the same size as the rest. The Masora and Keri are both wanting, and the Megilloth precede the books of Chronicles. It is highly valued by Kennicott and De Rossi, who refer it also to the beginning of the twelfth century.

9. Coeval with the preceding is the CODEX REGIOMONTANUS 2. (224. of Kennicott,) written in the Italic character, in small folio. This manuscript contains the Prophets and the Hagiographa, but it is mutilated in various places. The initial letters are larger than the others, and three of the poetical books are written in hemistichs.

10. To the beginning of the twelfth century likewise is to be referred the CODEX PARISIENSIS 24. (San-Germanensis 2. No. 366. of Kennicott): it is written on vellum, in large quarto. It is imperfect from Jer. xxix. 19. to xxxviii. 2., and from Hosea iv. 4. to Amos vi. 12. Isaiah follows Ezekiel according to the Talmudical Canon.[2]

The following are among the most antient of the manuscripts in the possession of the late M. De Rossi, and collated by him, viz.

1. The Codex, by him numbered 634., which is in quarto. It contains a fragment of the books of Leviticus and Numbers, — from Levit. xxi. 19. to Numb. i. 50., and exhibits every mark of the remotest antiquity. The vellum on which it is written is decayed by age; the character is intermediate, or Italic, — approaching to that of the German manuscripts. The letters are all of an uniform size; there is no trace of the Masora, or

---

[1] De Rossi, tom. i Proleg. p. LXXXVII
[2] Kennicott, Dissertatio Generalis, pp. 85. 87, 88, 89. 93 104.

of any Masoretic notes, nor is any space left before the larger sections; though sometimes, as in other very antient manuscripts, a few points are inserted between the words. M. De Rossi assigns this manuscript to the *eighth* century.

2. A manuscript of the Pentateuch (No. 503.), in quarto, and on vellum, containing from Gen. xii. 41. to Deut. xv. 12. It is composed of leaves of various ages, the most antient of which are of the *ninth* or tenth century. The character is semi-rabbinical, rude, and confessedly very antient. Points occur, in some of the more antient leaves, in the writing of the original copyist, but sometimes they are wanting. There are no traces of the Masora or of the Masoretic notes, and sometimes no space at all before the larger sections. It frequently agrees with the Samaritan text and antient versions.

3. A manuscript of the Pentateuch (No. 10.), with the Targum and Megilloth. It is written in the German character, on vellum, and in quarto, towards the end of the eleventh or in the beginning of the twelfth century. The Masora is absent. The character, which is defaced by time, is rudely formed, and the initial letters are larger than the rest. Coeval with this manuscript is,

4. A manuscript of the book of Job, in quarto, also on vellum, and in the German character. It is one of the most valuable manuscripts of that book. The pages are divided into two columns, the lines being of unequal length.

5. A manuscript of the Hagiographa (No. 379.), the size, character, and date of which correspond with the preceding. It begins with Psal. xlix.15. and ends with Neh. xl. 4. The Masora and Keri are absent; and the poetical books are divided into hemistichs.

6. A manuscript of the Pentateuch (No. 611.), on vellum, in octavo, and written in the German character, approaching somewhat to the Spanish, towards the close of the eleventh, or in the commencement of the twelfth century. The ink is frequently faded by age; there are no traces of the Masora; the Keri are very rarely to be seen, and the initial letters are larger than the others. There are frequent omissions in the text, which are supplied in the margin.[1]

Dr. Kennicott states that almost all the Hebrew manuscripts of the Old Testament, at present known to be extant, were written between the years 1000 and 1457, whence he infers that all the manuscripts written before the years 700 or 800 were destroyed by some decree of the Jewish senate, on account of their many differences from the copies then declared genuine. This circumstance is also alleged by Bishop Walton, as the reason why we have so few exemplars of the age of 600 years, and why even the copies of 700 or 800 years are very rare.

IX. It was long a desideratum with biblical scholars to obtain the Hebrew Scriptures from the Jews who are settled in India and other parts of the East. It was reasonably supposed, that, as these Jews had been for so many ages separated from their brethren in the west, their manuscripts might contain a text derived from the autographs of the sacred writers, by a channel independent of that through which the text of our printed Bibles has been transmitted to us. Dr. Kennicott was very anxious to obtain a copy, or at least a collation of a ma-

---

[1] De Rossi, Var. Lect. tom. i. Proleg. pp. cxvi. cvii. xcviii. cvii. cviii.

nuscript from India or China, for his edition of the Hebrew Bible, in the expectation that it would exhibit important variations from the Masoretic editions; but he was unsuccessful in his endeavours to procure it [1], and the honour of first bringing an Indian manuscript of the Hebrew Scriptures into Europe was reserved for the late Rev. Dr. Buchanan.

Among the biblical manuscripts brought from India by this learned and pious divine, and which are now deposited in the public library at Cambridge, there is a roll of the Pentateuch, which he procured from the black Jews in Malabar [2], who (there is strong reason to believe) are a part of the remains of the first dispersion of that nation by Nebuchadnezzar. The date of this manuscript cannot now be ascertained; but its text is supposed to be derived from those copies which their ancestors brought with them into India. Those Jews, on being interrogated, could give no precise account of it: some replied, that it came originally from Senna in Arabia; others of them said, it was brought from Cashmir. The Cabul Jews, who travel annually into the interior of China, remarked, that in some synagogues the Law is still found written on a roll of leather; not on vellum, but on a soft flexible leather, made of goat-skins, and dyed red. It is evident that the Jews, in the time of Moses, had the art of preparing and dyeing skins; for rams' skins dyed red, made a part of the covering for the tabernacle (Exod. xxvi. 14.); and it is not improbable, that the very autograph of the Law, written by the hand of Moses, was written on skins so prepared. The antient rules prescribed to the Jewish scribes direct, that the Law be so written, provided it be done on the skins of clean animals, such as sheep, goat, or calf-skins: therefore this MS., and many others in the hands of the Jews, agree in the same as an antient practice. The Cabul Jews, above noticed, show that copies of the Law, written on leather skins, are to be found among their people in India and China; and hence we have no doubt, that such are copies of very antient MSS. [3] The Cambridge Roll, or Indian

---

[1] According to the information collected from various sources, by Professor Bauer, it does not appear that the manuscripts of the Chinese Jews are of any remote antiquity, or are calculated to afford any assistance to biblical critics. Although Jews have resided in China for many centuries, yet they have no antient manuscripts, those now in use being subsequent to the fifteenth century. Critica Sacra, pp 405—407. See an account of the Hebræo-Chinese manuscripts in Koegler's Notitia S. S. Bibliorum Judæorum in Imperio Sinensi Edit. 2 8vo. Halæ ad Salam, 1805. Brotier, in his edition of Tacitus, (vol. iii. pp. 567. et seq) has given the best account that is extant of the Jews in China, a colony of whom settled in that country in the first century of the Christian æra. The reader will find an abridgment of it in Dr. Townley's Illustrations of Biblical Literature, vol. i. pp 83—89.

[2] See an account of these Jews in Dr Buchanan's "Christian Researches," pp. 224. et seq. 4th edit.

[3] Dr. Kennicott quotes from Wolfius, that a certain Jew, named Moses Pereyra, affirmed, he had found MS copies of the Hebrew text in Malabar; for that the Jews, having escaped from Titus, betook themselves through Persia to the Malabar coast, and arrived there safe in number about eighty persons Whence Wolfius concludes, that great fidelity is to be attached to the Malabar MSS The Buchanan MS. may fairly be denominated a Malabar copy, as having been brought from those parts. " Refert Moses Pereyra, se invenisse Manuscripta Exemplaria (Hebræi Textus) Malabarica. Tradit Judæos, a Tito fugientes, per Persiam se ad oras Malabaricas contulisse, ibique cum octoginta animis salvos advenisse. Unde constat, MStis Malabaricis multum fidei tribuendum esse " Wolf. 4. 97 See Dr. Kennicott's Dissertation the Second, p 532. Oxford, 1759.

copy of the Pentateuch, which may also be denominated *Malabaric*, is written on a roll of goat-skins dyed *red*, and was discovered by Dr. Buchanan in the record-chest of a synagogue of the black Jews, in the interior of Malayala, in the year 1806. It measures forty-eight feet in length, and in breadth about twenty-two inches, or a Jewish cubit. The book of Leviticus and the greater part of the book of Deuteronomy are wanting. It appears, from calculation, that the original length of the roll was not less than ninety English feet. In its present condition it consists of thirty-seven skins; contains one hundred and seventeen columns of writing perfectly clear and legible; and exhibits (as the subjoined fac-simile of Deut. iv. 1, 2. will show) a noble specimen of the manner and form of the most antient Hebrew manuscripts among the Jews.

ועתה ישראל שמע אל החקים ואל המשפטים
אשר אנכי מלמד אתכם לעשות למען תחיו
ובאתם וירשתם את הארץ אשר יהוה אלהי
אבתיכם נתן לכם לא תספו על הדבר אשר
אנכי מצוה אתכם ולא תגרעו ממנו לשמר

The columns are a palm of four inches in breadth, and contain from forty to fifty lines each, which are written without vowel points, and in all other respects according to the rules prescribed to the Jewish scribes or copyists. As some of the skins appear more decayed than others, and the text is evidently not all written by the same hand, Mr. Yeates (from whose Collation of this MS. the present account is abridged, and to whom the author is indebted for the preceding fac-simile,) is of opinion, that the roll itself comprises the fragments of at least *three* different rolls, of one common material, viz. dyed goat-skin, and exhibits three different specimens of writing. The old skins have been strengthened by patches of parchment on the back; and in one place four words have been renewed by the same supply. The text is written in the square character, and without the vowel points and accents; and the margin of the columns is every where plain, and free from writing of any sort. He has diligently examined and collated this manuscript with the printed text of Vander Hooght's edition of the Hebrew Bible; and the result of his investigation is, that the amount of variations in the whole does not exceed *forty*, and that none of them are found to differ from the common reading as to the sense and interpretation of the text, but are merely additions or omissions of a jod or vau letter, expressing such words to be *full* or deficient, according to the known usage of the Hebrew tongue. But even this small number of readings was considerably reduced, when compared with the text of Athias's edition, printed at Amsterdam in

1661; so that the integrity of the Hebrew text is confirmed by this valuable manuscript so far as it goes, and its testimony is unquestionably important. Four readings are peculiar to this copy, which are not to be found in Dr. Kennicott's edition of the Hebrew Bible; and many minute Masoretical distinctions, chiefly relative to the formation of the letters in certain words, show that the Masora of the Eastern Jews has its peculiarities not common with that of the Western Jews: whence it is certainly determined that the present roll is not a copy from any exemplar of the Jews in Europe; for no other synagogue rolls known in Europe are observed to have the same characteristics, at least as far as appears from any description of Hebrew manuscripts that is extant.[1]

"With respect to the several sorts of skins and hand-writing, the answer of some Indian Jews, when interrogated concerning this MS., is worthy of remark. By one account, it was brought from Senna in Arabia; and by another account, it came from Cashmir: which two accounts are cleared up on an examination of the MS., since, part of it being composed of brown skins, and the writing very similar to that seen in rolls of Arabian and African extraction, there is a possibility that such part is the fragment of an Arabian or African MS., as those Jews relate: and the other account, viz. that it was brought from Cashmir, may also be equally true; since that part consisting of red skins so well corresponds with their own description of copies found in the synagogues of the Eastern Jews. The consideration of this point attaches still greater consequences to the roll itself, which, as it is found to consist of fragments of copies purely Oriental, and seemingly unconnected with the Western Jewish copies, we may now conclude the same to be ample specimens of copies in those parts of the world. It is true, indeed, that a great part of the text is wanting, and the whole book of Leviticus; yet, notwithstanding the large deficencies of the MS., it ought to be a satisfaction to know, that herein are ample specimens of at least three antient copies of the Pentateuch, whose testimony is found to unite in the integrity and pure conservation of the Sacred Text, acknowledged by Christians and Jews in these parts of the world."[2]

The following testimony of Bishop Marsh to the value of the Codex Malabaricus is too valuable to be omitted: — "A manuscript Roll of the Hebrew Pentateuch, apparently of some antiquity, and found among the Black Jews in the interior of India, must be regarded at least as a literary curiosity, deserving the attention of the learned in general. And as this manuscript appears, on comparison, to have no important deviation from our common printed Hebrew text, it is of still greater value to a theologian, as it affords an additional argument for the integrity of the Pentateuch. The Hebrew manuscripts of the Pentateuch, preserved in the West of Europe, though equally derived, with the Hebrew manuscripts preserved in India, from the autograph of Moses, must have descended from it through very different channels; and therefore the close agreement of the former with the latter is a proof, that they have preserved the

---
[1] See Mr. Yeates's Collation of an Indian Copy of the Pentateuch, pp. 2, 3. 6, 7.
[2] Ibid. p. 8.

original text in great purity, since the circumstances, under which the MS. was found, forbid the explanation of that agreement on the principle of any immediate connexion. It is true that, as this manuscript (or rather the three fragments of which this manuscript is composed) was probably written much later than the time when the Masoretic text was established by the learned Jews of Tiberias, it may have been wholly derived from that Masoretic text: and in this case it would afford only an argument, that the Masoretic text had preserved its integrity, and would not affect the question, whether the Masoretic text itself were an accurate representative of the Mosaic autograph. But, on the other hand, as the very peculiar circumstances, under which the manuscript was found, render it at least possible, that the influence of the Masora, which was extended to the African and European Hebrew manuscripts by the settlement of the most distinguished Oriental Jews in Africa and Spain, never reached the mountainous district in the South of India; as it is possible, that the text of the manuscript in question was derived from manuscripts anterior to the establishment of the Masora, manuscripts even which might have regulated the learned Jews of Tiberias in the formation of their own text, the manuscript appears for these reasons to merit particular attention."[1] Such being the value of this precious manuscript, Mr. Yeates has conferred a great service on the biblical student by publishing his collation, of which future editors of the Hebrew Bible will doubtless avail themselves.

In the seventh and following volumes of the Classical Journal there is a catalogue of the biblical, biblico-oriental, and classical manuscripts at present existing in the various public libraries in Great Britain.

SECTION II.
ON THE MANUSCRIPTS OF THE SAMARITAN PENTATEUCH.

I. *Origin of the Samaritans* — II. *Account of the Samaritan Pentateuch.* — *Manuscripts of it* — III. *Variations of the Samaritan Pentateuch from the Hebrew.* — IV. *Versions of the Samaritan Pentateuch.*

I. ORIGIN OF THE SAMARITANS.

The Samaritans being generally considered as a Jewish sect, the specification of their tenets properly belongs to the third volume of this work. At present, it will be sufficient to remark that they were descended from an intermixture of the ten tribes with the Gentile nations. This origin rendered them odious to the Jews, who refused to acknowledge them as Jewish citizens, or to permit them to assist in rebuilding the Temple, after their return from the Babylonish captivity. In consequence of this rejection, as well as of other causes of dissension, the Samaritans erected a temple on Mount Gerizim, and instituted sacrifices according to the prescriptions of the Mosaic law. Hence arose that inveterate schism and enmity between the two nations, so frequently mentioned or alluded to in the New Testament. The Samaritans (who still exist but are greatly reduced in

[1] See Yeates's Collation of an Indian Copy of the Pentateuch, &c. pp. 40, 41.

numbers) reject all the sacred books of the Jews except the PENTA-TEUCH, or five books of Moses. Of this they preserve copies in the antient Hebrew characters, which as there has been no friendly intercourse between them and the Jews since the Babylonish captivity, there can be no doubt were the same that were in use before that event, though subject to such variations as will always be occasioned by frequent transcribing. And so inconsiderable are the variations from our present copies (which were those of the Jews), that by this means we have a proof that those important books have been preserved uncorrupted for the space of nearly three thousand years, so as to leave no room to doubt that they are the same which were actually written by Moses.

II. ACCOUNT of the Samaritan Pentateuch.

Although the Samaritan Pentateuch was known to and cited by Eusebius, Cyril of Alexandria, Procopius of Gaza, Diodorus of Tarsus, Jerome, Syncellus, and other antient fathers, yet it afterwards fell into oblivion for upwards of a thousand years, so that its very existence began to be questioned. Joseph Scaliger was the first who excited the attention of learned men to this valuable relic of antiquity; and M. Peiresc procured a copy from Egypt, which, together with the ship that brought it, was unfortunately captured by pirates. More successful was the venerable Archbishop Usher, who procured six copies from the East; and from another copy, purchased by Pietro della Valle for M. de Sancy, (then ambassador from France to Constantinople, and afterwards Archbishop of St. Maloes,) Father Morinus printed the Samaritan Pentateuch, for the first time, in the Paris Polyglott. This was afterwards reprinted in the London Polyglott by Bishop Walton, who corrected it from three manuscripts which had formerly belonged to Archbishop Usher. A neat edition of this Pentateuch, in Hebrew characters, was edited by Dr. Blayney, in octavo, Oxford, 1790.

Seventeen manuscripts of the Samaritan Pentateuch are known to be extant, of which Dr. Kennicott has given a minute description. Six of these manuscripts are in the Bodleian Library at Oxford, and one in the Cotton Library in the British Museum: concerning a few of the most valuable of these, the following particulars may not be unacceptable. They are numbered according to Dr. Kennicott's notation.

1. Cod. 127. is preserved in the British Museum. (Bibl. Cotton. Claudius, B. 8.) It is one of the six MSS. procured by Archbishop Usher, by whom it was presented to Sir Robert Cotton. This very valuable manuscript is complete, and was transcribed entirely by one hand, on two hundred and fifty-four pages of vellum. It is in an excellent state of preservation, a leaf of fine paper having been carefully placed between every two leaves of the vellum. This MS. was written. A. D. 1362.

2. Cod. 62. is preserved in the Bodleian Library at Oxford; and was also purchased by Archbishop Usher, from whose heirs the curators of that library bought it, with many other MSS. This manuscript is in large quarto, and contains an Arabic version in Samaritan letters, placed in a column parallel to the Samaritan text. Unhappily there are many chasms in it. Dr Kennicott attributes a

high value to this manuscript, which was written about the middle of the thirteenth century.

Cod. 197. is a most valuable manuscript in the Ambrosian Library at Milan, which was collated for Dr. Kennicott by Dr. Branca, who is of opinion that it is certainly not later than the tenth century. It is imperfect in many places; and is very beautifully written on extremely thin vellum, in red characters.

Cod. 363. (No. 1. of the MSS. in the Library of the Oratory at Paris,) is the celebrated manuscript bought by Pietro della Valle of the Samaritans, in 1616, and printed by Morinus in 1631–33. It is written throughout by one hand; and, though no date is assigned to it, Dr. Kennicott thinks it was written towards the close of the eleventh century. It was collated for Dr. Kennicott by Dr. Bruns, in some select passages. [1]

III. VARIATIONS of the Samaritan Pentateuch from the Hebrew.

The celebrated critic, Le Clerc [2], has instituted a minute comparison of the Samaritan Pentateuch with the Hebrew text; and has, with much accuracy and labour, collected those passages in which he is of opinion that the former is more or less correct than the latter. For instance —

1. *The Samaritan text appears to be more correct than the Hebrew*, in Gen. ii. 4. vii. 2. xix. 19. xx. 2. xxiii. 16. xxiv. 14. xlix. 10, 11. 1. 26. Exod. i. 2. iv. 2

2. *It is expressed more conformably to analogy*, in Gen. xxxi. 39. xxxv. 26. xxxvii. 17. xli. 34. 43. xlvii. 3. Deut. xxxii. 5.

3. *It has glosses and additions* in Gen. xxix. 15. xxx. 36. xli. 16. Exod. vii 18. viii. 23. ix. 5. xxi. 20. xxii. 5. xxiii 10. xxxii. 9. Lev. i. 10. xvii. 4. Deut. v. 21.

4. *It appears to have been altered by a critical hand*, in Gen. ii. 2. iv 10. ix. 5. x. 19. xi 21. xviii. 3. xix. 12. xx. 16. xxiv. 38. 55. xxxv. 7. xxxvi. 6. xli. 50. Exod. i. 5. xiii. 6. xv. 5. Num. xxii. 32.

5. *It is more full than the Hebrew text*, in Gen. v. 8. xi. 31. xix. 9. xxvii. 34. xxxix. 4. xliii. 25. Exod. xii. 40. xl. 17. Num. iv. 14. Deut. xx. 16.

6. *It is defective* in Gen. xx. 16. and xxv. 14.

It agrees with the Septuagint version in Gen. iv. 8. xix. 12. xx. 16. xxiii. 2. xxiv. 55. 62. xxvi. 18. xxix. 27. xxxv. 29 xxxix 8 xli. 16. 43. xliii. 26. xlix. 26. Exod. viii. 3. and in many other passages. Though,

7. *It sometimes varies from the Septuagint*, as in Gen i. 7. v. 29. viii. 3. 7. xlix. 22. Num. xxii. 4.

The differences between the Samaritan and Hebrew Pentateuchs may be accounted for, by the usual sources of various readings, viz. the negligence of copyists, introduction of glosses from the margin into the text, the confounding of similar letters, the transposition of letters, the addition of explanatory words, &c. The Samaritan Pentateuch, however, is of great use and authority in establishing correct readings: in many instances it agrees remarkably with the Greek Septuagint, and it contains numerous and excellent various lections, which are in every respect preferable to the received Ma-

---

[1] Kennicott, Diss. II. pp 538—540, and Diss. Gen. pp 81. 76 88 98.
[2] Comment. in Pentateuch, Index, ii. See also some additional observations on the differences between the Samaritan and Hebrew Pentateuchs, in Dr. Kennicott's Remarks on Select Passages in the Old Testament, pp. 43—47.

soretic readings, and are further confirmed by the agreement of other antient versions.

The most material variations between the Samaritan Pentateuch and the Hebrew, which affect the authority of the former, occur, first, in the prolongation of the patriarchal generations; and, secondly, in the alteration of Ebal into Gerizim (Deut. xxvii.), in order to support their separation from the Jews. The chronology of the Samaritan Pentateuch has been satisfactorily vindicated by the Rev. Dr. Hales, whose arguments, however, will not admit of abridgment[1]; and with regard to the charge of altering the Pentateuch, it has been shown by Dr. Kennicott, from a consideration of the character of the Samaritans, their known reverence for the law, our Lord's silence on the subject in his memorable conversation with the woman of Samaria, and from various other topics; that what almost all biblical critics have hitherto considered as a wilful corruption by the Samaritans, is in all probability the *true* reading, and that the corruption is to be charged on the Jews themselves. In judging therefore of the genuineness of a reading, we are not to declare absolutely for one of these Pentateuchs against the other, but to prefer the true readings in both. "One antient copy," Dr. Kennicott remarks, with equal truth and justice, "has been received from the Jews, and we are truly thankful for it: another antient copy is offered by the Samaritans; let us thankfully accept that likewise. Both have been often transcribed; both therefore may contain errors. They differ in many instances, therefore the errors must be many. Let the two parties be heard without prejudice; let their evidences be weighed with impartiality; and let the genuine words of Moses be ascertained by their joint assistance. Let the variations of all the manuscripts on each side be carefully collected; and then critically examined by the context and the antient versions. If the Samaritan copy should be found in some places to correct the Hebrew, yet will the Hebrew copy in other places correct the Samaritan. *Each* copy therefore is invaluable; each copy therefore demands our pious veneration, and attentive study. The Pentateuch will never be understood perfectly, till we admit the authority of BOTH.[2]

IV. VERSIONS of the Samaritan Pentateuch.

Of the Samaritan Pentateuch two versions are extant; one in the proper Samaritan dialect, which is usually termed the Samaritan version, and another in Arabic.

1. The Samaritan version was made in Samaritan characters, from the Hebræo-Samaritan text into the Samaritan dialect, which is intermediate between the Hebrew and the Aramæan languages. This version is of great antiquity, having been made at least before the time of Origen, and not improbably before the commencement of the Christian æra. The author of the Samaritan version is unknown, but he has in general adhered very closely and faithfully to the original text; so that this version is almost exactly the counterpart of the original Hebrew-Samaritan codex with all its various

---

[1] Analysis of Chronology, vol. 1 pp. 80. *et seq.*
[2] Kennicott, Diss. II pp. 20—165.

readings. This shows, in a degree, really surprising, how very carefully and accurately the Hebrew Pentateuch has been copied and preserved by the Samaritans, from the antient times in which their version was made.[1]

2. The Arabic version of the Samaritan Pentateuch is also extant in Samaritan characters, and was executed by Abu Said, A.D. 1070, in order to supplant the Arabic translation of the Jewish Rabbi, Saadia Gaon, which had till that time been in use among the Samaritans. Abu Said has very closely followed the Samaritan Pentateuch, whose readings he expresses, even where the latter differs from the Hebrew text: in some instances, however, both Bishop Walton and Bauer have remarked, that he has borrowed from the Arabic version of Saadia. On account of the paucity of manuscripts of the original Samaritan Pentateuch, Bauer thinks this version will be found of great use in correcting its text. Some specimens of it have been published by Dr. Durell in the " Hebrew Text of the Parallel Prophecies of Jacob relating to the Twelve Tribes," &c. (Oxford, 1763, 4to.) and before him by Castell in the fourth volume of the London Polyglott; also by Hwiid, at Rome, in 1780, in 8vo., and by Paulus, at Jena, in 1789, in 8vo.[2]

SECTION III.

ON THE MANUSCRIPTS OF THE GREEK SCRIPTURES.

§ 1. GENERAL OBSERVATIONS ON GREEK MANUSCRIPTS.

I. *On what Materials written.* — II. *Form of Letters.* — III. *Abbreviations.* — IV. *Codices Palimpsesti or Rescripti.* — V. *Account of the different Families, Recensions, or Editions of Manuscripts of the New Testament* — 1. *The System of Dr. Griesbach and Michaelis.* — 2. *Of M. Matthæi* — 3. *Of Mr. Nolan.* — 4. *Of Prof. Hug* — 5. *Of Prof. Scholz.* — VI. *On the Fœdus cum Græcis, or Coincidence between many Greek Manuscripts and the Vulgate Latin Version.*

I. THE Greek manuscripts, which have descended to our time, are written either on vellum or on paper; and their external form and condition vary, like the manuscripts of other antient authors. The vellum is either purple-coloured or of its natural hue, and is either thick or thin. Manuscripts on very thin vellum were always held in the highest esteem. The paper also is either made of cotton, or the common sort manufactured from linen, and is either glazed, or *laid* (as it is technically termed), that is, of the ordinary roughness. Not more than six manuscript fragments on purple vellum are known to be extant; they are described in the following sections of this chapter. The Codex Claromontanus, of which a brief notice is also given in a subsequent page, is written on very thin vellum. All

---

[1] North American Review, New Series, vol xxii. p 313
[2] Bp Walton, Proleg c xi §§ 10—21. pp 527—553 Carpzov Critica Sacra, pp. 585—620. Leusden, Philologus Hebræus, pp 59—67 Bauer, Critica Sacra, pp. 325—335. Muntinghe, Expositio Critices Veteris Fœderis, pp. 148, 149.

manuscripts on paper are of a much later date; those on cotton paper being posterior to the ninth century, and those on linen subsequent to the twelfth century; and if the paper be of a very ordinary quality, Wetstein pronounces them to have been written in Italy, in the fifteenth and sixteenth centuries.

II. The letters are either capital (which in the time of Jerome were called *uncial*, i. e. initial) or *cursive*, i. e. small; the capital letters, again, are of two kinds, either unadorned and simple, and made with straight thin strokes, or thicker, uneven, and angular. Some of them are supported on a sort of base, while others are decorated, or rather burthened with various tops. As letters of the first kind are generally seen on antient Greek monuments, while those of the last resemble the paintings of semi-barbarous times, manuscripts written with the former are generally supposed to be as old as the fifth century, and those written with the latter are supposed to be posterior to the ninth century. Greek manuscripts were usually written in capital letters till the seventh century, and mostly without any divisions of words; and capitals were in general use until the eighth century, and some even so late as the ninth; but there is a striking difference in the forms of the letters after the seventh century. Great alterations took place in the eighth, ninth, and tenth centuries: the Greek letters in the manuscripts copied by the Latins in the ninth century, are by no means regular; the α, ε, and γ, being inflected like the *a*, *e*, and *y*, of the Latin alphabet. Towards the close of the tenth century, small or cursive letters were generally adopted; and Greek manuscripts written in and since the eleventh century are in small letters, and greatly resemble each other, though some few exceptions occur to the contrary. Flourished letters rarely occur in Greek manuscripts of the thirteenth, fourteenth, and fifteenth centuries.[1] The fac-similes of the Alexandrian and other manuscripts, given in the subsequent pages of this work, will furnish the reader with a tolerably correct idea of the various styles of Greek writing which obtained at different periods between the sixth and the fourteenth centuries.

The most antient manuscripts are written without accents, spirits, or any separation of the words; nor was it until after the ninth century that the copyists began to leave spaces between the words. Michaelis, after Wetstein, ascribes the insertion of accents to Euthalius, bishop of Sulca in Egypt, A. D. 458.[2]

III. Nearly the same mode of spelling obtains in antient manuscripts which prevails in Greek printed books; but, even in the earliest manuscripts, we meet with some words that are abbreviated by putting the first and last letters, and sometimes also the middle letter, for an entire word, and drawing a line over the top: thus ΘC, KC, IC, XC, ΥΣ, ΣHP, IHΛ, or ΙΣΗΛ, ΠΝΛ, ΠΗΡ, ΜΗΡ, ΟΥΝΟΣ,

---

[1] Wetstein's Prolegomena to his edition of the Greek Testament, vol i pp. 1—3. Astle on the Origin of Writing, pp 60—76. 2d edit. Wetstein has given an alphabet from various Greek manuscripts, and Astle has illustrated his observations with several very fine engravings.

[2] Wetstein, Proleg. p. 73. Michaelis, vol. ii pp. 519—524.

ΑΝΟΣ, ΙΛΗΜ, ΔΑΔ, respectively denote Θεος *God*, Κυριος *Lord*, Ιησους *Jesus*, Χριςος *Christ*, Υιος *a son*, Σωτηρ *Saviour*, Ισραηλ *Israel*, Πνευμα *spirit*, Πατηρ *father*, Μητηρ *mother*, Ουρανος *heaven*, Ανθρωπος *man*, Ιερουσαλημ *Jerusalem*, Δαυιδ *David*.[1] At the beginning of a new book, which always commences at the top of a page, the first three, four, or five lines are frequently written in vermilion; and, with the exception of the Alexandrian and Vatican manuscripts, all the most antient codices now extant have the Eusebian κεφαλαια and τιτλοι, of which we have given an account in a subsequent chapter.[2]

Very few manuscripts contain the whole either of the Old or of the New Testament. By far the greater part have only the four Gospels, because they were most frequently read in the churches; others comprise only the Acts of the Apostles and the Catholic Epistles; others, again, have the Acts, and St. Paul's Epistles; and a very few contain the Apocalypse. Almost all of them, especially the more antient manuscripts, are imperfect, either from the injuries of time, or from neglect.[3]

All manuscripts, the most antient not excepted, have erasures and corrections; which, however, were not always effected so dexterously, but that the original writing may sometimes be seen. Where these alterations have been made by the copyist of the manuscript, (*à primâ manu*, as it is termed,) they are preferable to those made by later hands, or *à secundâ manu*. These erasures were sometimes made by drawing a line through the word, or, what is tenfold worse, by the penknife. But, besides these modes of obliteration, the copyist frequently blotted out the old writing with a *sponge*, and wrote other words in lieu of it. nor was this practice confined to a single letter or word, as may be seen in the Codex Bezæ.[4] Authentic instances are on record, in which whole books have been thus obliterated, and other writing has been substituted in the place of the manuscript so blotted out: but where the writing has already faded through age, they preserved their transcriptions without further erasure.

IV. These manuscripts are termed *Codices Palimpsesti* or *Rescripti*. Before the invention of paper, the great scarcity of parchment in different places induced many persons to obliterate the works of antient writers, in order to transcribe their own, or those of some other favourite author in their place: hence, doubtless, the works of many eminent writers have perished, and particularly those of the greatest antiquity, for such, as were comparatively recent, were transcribed, to satisfy the immediate demand; while those, which

---

[1] Concerning Greek Abbreviations, see Montfaucon's Palæographia Græca, pp. 345. —370. Mr. Astle has also given a specimen of Greek abbreviations from two Psalters. — On Writing, p 76. plate vi

[2] See Chap IV Sect. II pp 169, 170 *infra*.

[3] The Codex Cottonianus, for instance, when perfect, contained only the Book of Genesis, the Codex Cæsareus contains only part of the same book, together with a fragment of the Gospel of St. Luke, the Alexandrian manuscript wants the first twenty-four chapters of St. Matthew's Gospel; and the Codex Bezæ contains only the four Gospels and the Acts of the Apostles.

[4] Wetstein's Prolegomena, pp 3—8. Griesbach has discovered the hands of FIVE *different correctors* in the Codex Claromontanus. See his Symbolæ Criticæ, tom. ii. pp. 32—52.

were already dim with age, were erased.¹ It was for a long time thought, that this destructive practice was confined to the eleventh, twelfth, thirteenth, and fourteenth centuries, and that it chiefly prevailed among the Greeks: it must, in fact, be considered as the consequence of the barbarism which overspread those dark ages of ignorance; but this destructive operation was likewise practised by the Latins, and is also of a more remote date than has usually been supposed.

In general, a Codex Rescriptus is easily known, as it rarely happens that the former writing is so completely erased, as not to exhibit some traces: in a few instances, *both* writings are legible. Many such manuscripts are preserved in the library of the British Museum. Montfaucon found a manuscript in the Colbert library, which had been written about the eighth century, and originally contained the works of St. Dionysius: new matter had been written over it, three or four centuries afterwards, and both continued legible.² Muratori saw in the Ambrosian library a manuscript comprising the works of the venerable Bede, the writing of which was from eight to nine hundred years old, and which had been substituted for another upwards of a thousand years old. Notwithstanding the efforts which had been made to erase the latter, some phrases could be deciphered, which indicated it to be an antient pontifical.³ The indefatigable researches of signor Angelo Mai (principal keeper of the Vatican Library at Rome) have discovered several valuable remains of biblical and classical literature in the Ambrosian Library at Milan⁴; and a short account of some of the principal Codices Rescripti of the New Testament, or of parts thereof, will be found in the sequel of this section.

V. The *total* number of manuscripts of the New Testament (whether they have been transmitted to us entire or in fragments), which are known to have been wholly or partially collated, amounts nearly to five hundred; but this number forms only a small part of the manuscripts found in public and private libraries. The result of these collations has shown that certain manuscripts have an affinity to each other, and that their text is distinguished from that of others by characteristic marks; and eminent critics, (particularly Griesbach, who devoted the whole of his life to sacred criticism,) after diligently comparing the quotations from the New Testament in the writings of Clement of Alexandria and of Origen with those made by Tertullian and Cyprian, have ascertained that, so early as the third century, there were in existence two *families*, *recensions*, or *editions*⁵ of ma-

---
¹ Peignot, Essai sur l'Histoire de Parchemin, pp 83 *et seq*.
² Palæogr. Græc pp 261. 236 The greater part of the manuscripts on parchment which Montfaucon had seen, he affirms, were written on parchment, from which some former treatise had been erased, except in those of a very antient date. Mem de l'Acad. de Inscript. tom ix p. 325.
³ Muratori. Antiq. Ital. tom. iii diss 43. col. 833, 834.
⁴ See a brief notice of Signor Mai's discovery of a Codex Rescriptus of Saint Paul's Epistles, in pp 140, 141. *infra*, of the present volume
⁵ Bengel expressed this relationship or affinity between manuscripts by the term *family* (Introd. ad Crisin N. T §§ 27–30.) Semler (Apparatus ad Liberalem Novi Testamenti Interpretationem, p 45) and Griesbach (Symbolæ Criticæ, tom i. p cxvii.) use the term *recensio, recension*, that is *edition*, which last term is adopted by Michaelis, vol. iL p. 173.

nuscripts, or, in other words, two entirely different texts of the New Testament.[1] Michaelis has observed that, as different countries had different versions according to their respective languages, their manuscripts naturally resembled their respective versions, as these versions, generally speaking, were made from such manuscripts as were in common use. *Five* different systems of recensions or editions have been proposed, viz. by Griesbach and Michaelis, by Matthæi, by Mr. Nolan, by Professor Hug, and by Professor Scholz.

1. The basis of Dr. GRIESBACH'S system is, the division of the Greek manuscripts of the New Testament into three classes, each of which is considered as an independent witness for the various readings which it contains. The value of a reading, so far as manuscript authority is regarded, is decided by Griesbach, not according to the individual manuscript in which it is found, but according to the number of classes by which it is supported. The classes, under which he arranges all the Greek manuscripts are the following; viz. 1. The Alexandrine; 2. The Occidental or Western; and 3. The Byzantine or Oriental, to which Michaelis has added, 4. The Edessene. To each of these are given the appellation of *recension* or *edition*, as we commonly say of printed books.

(1.) The first class, or ALEXANDRINE RECENSION, which is also called the EGYPTIAN Recension, comprises those manuscripts, which, in remarkable and characteristic readings, agree with the quotations of the early Alexandrine writers, particularly Origen and Clement of Alexandria. After them, this recension was adopted by the Egyptian Greeks.

To this class Griesbach refers the Codex Alexandrinus[2], noted by the letter A., but in the epistles of Saint Paul only; and also B. the Vatican manuscript. To this class also Dr. Scholz refers C., the Codex Ephremi; L. the Codex Regius 62., an imperfect manuscript of the four Gospels of the eighth century, collated by Wetstein and Griesbach, P. the Guelpherbytanus A., a Codex Rescriptus of the sixth century, comprising fragments of the four Gospels, Q the Guelpherbytanus B, also a Codex Rescriptus of the same date, and containing some fragments of Luke and John, T. the Codex Borgiæ I, containing a Greek Sahidic version of John vi. 28—67. vii. 6. viii. 31, executed in the fourth century; Griesb. 22., the Codex Regius 72., a fragment of Matt. i. 1. ii. 2., written in the eleventh century, Griesb. 33., the Codex Regius 14., a mutilated MS. of the Old and New Testament, of the eleventh century; Griesb. 102., the Codex Medicæus, which comprises from Matt. xxiv. to Mark viii. 1., and the Codex Regius 305, a MS. of the thirteenth century.[3] The Alexandrine Recension is followed by the Coptico-Memphitic, Coptico-Basmuric, Coptico-Sahidic, Ethiopic, Armenian, and the Syro-Philoxenian versions; and it is the text cited by the fathers, Eusebius,

---

[1] In the second volume of Griesbach's Symbolæ Criticæ (pp. 229—620) there is a laborious collation of the quotations from the New Testament, made by Origen and Clement of Alexandria, with the Vulgate or common Greek text.

[2] See an account of these and of the other MSS. mentioned in this Section in pp. 115—157 *infra*. The letters and figures, above used, are those employed by Griesbach, to denote the several manuscripts collated or consulted by him for his edition of the New Testament. They are explained in the Prolegomena to his first volume.

[3] The manuscripts in the Royal Library at Paris are generally known by the appellation of Codices Regii.

Anastasius, Ammonius, Didymus, Cyril of Alexandria, Marcus, Macarius, Cosmas Indicopleustes, Nonnus, Isidore of Pelusium, Theodore of Pelusium, and frequently also by Chrysostom.

(2.) The OCCIDENTAL or WESTERN RECENSION is that which was adopted by the Christians of Africa (especially by Tertullian and Cyprian), Italy, Gaul, and the west of Europe generally.

According to Griesbach, it is followed in A. the Codex Alexandrinus, in the Acts of the Apostles, and the Catholic Epistles; and according to Dr. Scholz, in D the Codex Bezæ or Cantabrigiensis; in the Codex Regius 314., a MS. of the eighth century, containing Luke ix. 36—47. and x. 12—22., Griesb. 1 (Basileensis); Griesb. 13. the Codex Regius 50., a mutilated MS. of the twelfth century, collated for Birch's edition of the four Gospels, Griesb. 28. the Codex Regius 379, a MS. of the eleventh century; Griesb. 69. the Codex Leicestrensis, and 124., the Codex Vindobonensis (Lambecii 31), Griesb. 131 the Codex Vaticanus 360, a MS. of the eleventh century, collated by Birch; Griesb. 157 the Codex Vaticanus 2, a MS. of the twelfth century, also collated by Birch; the Codex Regius 177. containing the four Gospels, with very copious scholia, written (Dr. Scholz thinks) in the eleventh century, and in the Codex Regius, 375, containing lessons from the New Testament, excepting the Revelation, and written early in the eleventh century: in the Gospels, it very seldom differs from the Codex Bezæ, but in the Acts of the Apostles and in the Epistles, it chiefly agrees with the Alexandrine recension. With these manuscripts sometimes harmonise the Sahidic Version, made in the fourth century, the Syriac Version of Jerusalem, and the readings in the margin of the Syro-Philoxenian Version; as also the Ante-Hieronymian or Old Latin Versions, which were in use before the Vulgate Version.

The Western Edition was cited by the African fathers, Tertullian, Cyprian, Lactantius, Victorinus, Augustine, and by the unknown author of the book against Fulgentius the Donatist, by the Italic fathers, Zeno of Verona, Gaudentius of Brescia, Chromatius of Aquileia, Ambrose, the author of certain pieces which are attributed to that writer, Rufinus, the author of the Opus Imperfectum on St Matthew, Gregory surnamed the Great, and Lucifer Bishop of Cagliari; and by the Gallic fathers, Irenæus, Hilary, Julius Firmicus Maternus, Phœbadius (a Spaniard) bishop of Agen, Juvencus, and by the Mozarabic Ritual. With this edition also coincides the Vulgate Latin version, which is followed by Isidore bishop of Seville, Remigius, Bede, Rabanus Maurus, Haymo, Anselm, Pietro Damiani, Bernard, and all subsequent writers in communion with the Latin church for the last thousand years, as well as by the Lectionaries, Breviaries, Antient Missals, Acts of the Martyrs, and other ecclesiastical books of that church.[1]

(3.) Towards the end of the fourth century, and during the fifth and sixth centuries, critics have observed a text differing from the two first, and which they call the BYZANTINE or ORIENTAL RECENSION or Edition, because it was in general use at Constantinople, after that city became the capital and metropolitan see of the eastern empire.

With this edition are closely allied those of the neighbouring provinces, whose inhabitants were subject to the spiritual jurisdiction of the patriarch of Constantinople.[2] The readings of the Byzantine Recension are those

---

[1] Scholz, Curæ Criticæ in Historiam Textûs Evangeliorum, pp 27—30.

[2] Michaelis remarks, that the greatest number of manuscripts written on Mount Athos are evidently of the Byzantine edition, and he thinks it probable that almost all the Moscow manuscripts, of which M. Matthæi has given extracts, belong to this edition. As

which are most commonly found in the Κοινη Εκδοσις, or printed Vulgate Greek Text, and are also most numerous in the existing manuscripts which correspond to it. Griesbach reckons upwards of one hundred manuscripts of this class, which minutely harmonise with each other. On account of the many alterations, that were unavoidably made in the long interval between the fourth and fifteenth centuries, Michaelis proposes to divide the Byzantine edition into antient and modern; but he does not specify any criteria by which we can determine the boundaries between these two classes. The Byzantine text is found in the four Gospels of the Alexandrian manuscript; it was the original of the Sclavonic or old Russian version, and was cited by Chrysostom and Theophylact bishop of Bulgaria.

As the Peschito, or Old Syriac Version of the New Testament differs from the three preceding recensions, Michaelis after Griesbach has instituted another, which he designates,

(4.) The EDESSENE EDITION, comprehending the special Asiatic instruments, as they were termed by Griesbach, or those Manuscripts from which that Version was made.

Of this edition no manuscripts are extant; which circumstance Michaelis accounts for, by the early prejudice of the Syrian literati in favour of whatever was Grecian, and also by the wars that devastated the East for many ages subsequent to the fifth century. But by some accident which is difficult to be explained, manuscripts are found in the west of Europe, accompanied even with a Latin translation, such as the Codex Bezæ, which so eminently coincide with the Old Syriac Version, that their affinity is indisputable.

Although the readings of the Western, Alexandrine, and Edessene editions sometimes differ, yet they very frequently harmonise with each other. This coincidence Michaelis ascribes to their high antiquity, as the oldest manuscripts extant belong to one of these editions, and the translations themselves are antient. A reading confirmed by three of them is supposed to be of the very highest authority; yet the true reading may sometimes be found only in the fourth.

Most of the Manuscripts now extant exhibit one of the texts above described; some are composed of two or three recensions. No individual manuscript preserves any recension in a pure state; but manuscripts are said to be of the Alexandrian or Western Recension, as the appropriate readings of each preponderate. The margins of these manuscripts, as well as those of the Ethiopic, Armenian, Sahidic, and Syro-Philoxenian versions, and the Syriac version of Jerusalem, contain the Alexandrian variations for the Western readings, or vice versâ; and some Byzantine manuscripts have the Alexandrian or Western various lections in their margins.[1]

Each of these recensions has characteristics peculiar to itself. The Occidental or Western preserves harsh readings, Hebraisms, and solecisms, which the Alexandrine has exchanged for readings more

---

the valuable manuscripts collected by the late learned Professor Carlyle were obtained in Syria, Constantinople, and the islands of the Levant, it is probable, whenever they shall be collated, that they will be found to coincide with the Byzantine Recension. These manuscripts are preserved in the Archiepiscopal Library at Lambeth, and are described *infra*, pp 150, 151.

[1] Michaelis, vol ii pp 163—177. Griesbach's Symbolæ Criticæ, tom i. pp cxvii.— cxxii. cxxxvii. clvii —clxiv tom ii. pp. 132—148. Griesbach's edit. of the New Test. vol. i. Proleg. pp. lxxiii.—lxxxi, edit. Halæ, 1796.

conformable to classic usage. The Western is characterised by readings calculated to relieve the text from difficulties, and to clear the sense: it frequently adds supplements to the passages adduced from the Old Testament; and omits words that appear to be either repugnant to the context or to other passages, or to render the meaning obscure. The Alexandrine is free from the interpretations and transpositions of the western recensions. An explanatory reading is therefore suspicious in the western recension, and a classical one in the Alexandrine. The Byzantine or Constantinopolitan recension (according to Griesbach's system) preserves the Greek idiom still purer than the Alexandrine, and resembles the Western in its use of copious and explanatory readings. It is likewise mixed, throughout, with the readings of the other recensions.

The system of recensions, above proposed by Bengel and Semler, and completed by the late celebrated critic Dr. Griesbach, has been subjected to a very severe critical ordeal; and has been formidably attacked, on the Continent by the late M. Matthæi, and in this country by the Rev. Dr. Laurence (now archbishop of Cashel)[1], and the Rev Frederic Nolan.

2. Totally disregarding Griesbach's system of recensions, Professor MATTHÆI recognises only one class or family of manuscripts, which he terms *Codices Textûs Perpetui*, and pronounces every thing that is derived from commentaries and scholia to be corrupt. As the manuscripts of the New Testament, which he found in the library of the Synod, came originally from Mount Athos, and other parts of the Greek empire, and as the Russian church is a daughter of the Greek church, those manuscripts consequently contain what Griesbach has called the *Byzantine Text*, which Matthæi admits to be the only authentic text, excluding the Alexandrine and Western recensions, and also rejecting all quotations from the fathers of the Greek church. To the class of manuscripts to which the Codex Bezæ, the Codex Claromontanus, and others of high antiquity belong, he gave, in the preface to his edition of Saint John's Gospel, the appellation of *Editio Scurrilis*, nor did he apply softer epithets to those critics who ventured to defend such manuscripts.[2]

3. The Rev. F. NOLAN's system of recensions is developed in his "*Inquiry into the Integrity of the Greek Vulgate or received Text of the New Testament.*" (London, 1815, 8vo.)[3] That integrity he has confessedly established by a series of proofs and connected arguments, the most decisive that can be reasonably desired or expected; but as these occupy nearly six hundred closely printed pages, the limits of this section necessarily restrict us to the following concise notice of his elaborate system.

---

[1] In his "Remarks on the Classification of Manuscripts adopted by Griesbach in his edition of the New Testament," Oxford, 1814. 8vo.

[2] Schoell, Hist. de la Littérature Grècque, tom. ii. p. 136. Bishop Marsh's Lectures, part ii p. 30.

[3] There is a copious analysis of this work in the British Critic, (N. S) vol v. pp. 1—24., from which, and from the work itself, the present notice of Mr. Nolan's system of recensions is derived.

It has been an opinion as early as the times of Bishop Walton, that the purest text of the Scripture canon had been preserved at Alexandria; the libraries of that city having been celebrated from an early period for their correct and splendid copies. From the identity of any MS. in its peculiar readings, with the Scripture quotations of Origen, who presided in the catechetical school of Alexandria, a strong presumption arises that it contains the Alexandrine recension: the supposition being natural, that Origen drew his quotations from the copies generally prevalent in his native country. This, as we have seen, was the basis of Dr. Griesbach's system of recensions. accordingly he ascribes the highest rank to the manuscripts of the Alexandrine class, the authority of a *few* of which in his estimation outweighs that of a multitude of the Byzantine. The peculiar readings, which he selects from the manuscripts of this class, he confirms by a variety of collateral testimony, principally drawn from the quotations of the antient fathers and the versions made in the primitive ages. To the authority of Origen, however, he ascribes a paramount weight, taking it as the standard by which his collateral testimony is to be estimated; and using their evidence merely to support his testimony, or to supply it when it is deficient. The readings which he supports by this weight of testimony, he considers genuine; and, introducing a number of them into the sacred page, he has thus formed his corrected text of the New Testament. The necessary result of this process, as obviously proving the existence of a great number of spurious readings, has been that of shaking the authority of the authorised English version, together with the foundation on which it rests.

In combating the conclusions of Griesbach, Mr. Nolan argues, from the inconstancy of Origen's quotations, that no certain conclusion can be deduced from his testimony; he infers from the history of Origen, who principally wrote and published in Palestine, that the text, quoted by that antient father, was rather the Palestine than the Alexandrine; and he proves, from the express testimony of Saint Jerome, that the text of Origen was really adopted in Palestine, while that of Hesychius was adopted at Alexandria.

Having thus opened the question, and set it upon the broader ground assumed by those critics, who confirm the readings of the Alexandrine text, by the coincidence of the antient versions of the Oriental and Western churches; Mr. N. combats this method, proposed for investigating the genuine texts, in two modes. He first shows that a coincidence between the Western and Oriental churches does not necessarily prove the antiquity of the text which they mutually support; as the versions of the former church were corrected, after the texts of the latter, by Jerome and Cassiodorus, who may have thus created the coincidence, which is taken as a proof of the genuine reading. In the next place, he infers, from the prevalence of a text published by Eusebius of Cæsarea, and from the comparatively late period at which the Oriental Versions were formed, that their general coincidence may be traced to the influence of Eusebius's edition. This position he establishes, by a proof deduced from the general prevalence of Eusebius's sections and canons in the Greek MSS. and antient versions, and by a presumption derived from the agreements of those texts and versions with each other, in omitting several passages contained in the Vulgate Greek, which were at variance with Eusebius's peculiar opinions.[1] And having thus established the general influence of Eusebius's text, he generally concludes against the stability of the critical principles on which the German critics have undertaken the correction of the Greek Vulgate.

The material obstacles being thus removed to the establishment of his plan, Mr. Nolan next proceeds to investigate the different classes of text which exist in the Greek manuscripts. Having briefly considered the Scripture quotations of the fathers, and shown that they afford no adequate criterion for reducing the text into classes, he proceeds to the consideration of the antient translations, and after an examination of the Oriental versions, more particularly of the Sahidic, he comes to the conclusion, that no version but the Latin can be taken as a safe guide in ascertaining the genuine text of Scripture. This point being premised, the author lays the foundation of his scheme of classification, in the following observations.

" In proceeding to estimate the testimony which the Latin translation bears to the state of the Greek text, it is necessary to premise, that this translation exhibits three varieties: — as corrected by Saint Jerome, at the desire of Pope Damasus, and preserved in the Vulgate; as corrected by Eusebius of Verceli, at the desire of Pope Julius, and preserved in the Codex Vercellensis; and as existing previously to the corrections of both, and preserved, as I conceive, in the Codex Brixianus. The first of these three editions of the Italic translation is too well known to need any description; both the last are contained in beautiful manuscripts, preserved at Verceli, and at Brescia, in Italy. The curious and expensive manner in which at least the latter of these manuscripts is executed, as written on purple vellum in silver characters, would of itself contain no inconclusive proof of its great antiquity; such having been the form in which the most esteemed works were executed in the times of Eusebius, Chrysostom, and Jerome. The former is ascribed, by immemorial tradition, to Eusebius Vercellensis, the friend of Pope Julius and Saint Athanasius, and, as supposed to have been written with his own hand, is deposited among the relics, which are preserved, with a degree of superstitious reverence, in the author's church at Verceli in Piedmont. By these three editions of the translation, we might naturally expect to acquire some insight into the varieties of the original; and this expectation is fully justified on experiment. The latter, not less than the former, is capable of being distributed into three kinds; each of which possesses an extraordinary coincidence with one of a correspondent kind, in the translation. In a word, the Greek manuscripts are capable of being divided into three principal classes, one

---

[1] In the course of this discussion, Mr Nolan assigns adequate reasons for the omission of the following remarkable passages Mark xvi. 9—20., John viii 1—11., and for the peculiar readings of the following celebrated texts, Acts xx. 28. 1 Tim. iii 16. 1 John v. 7. See his Inquiry, pp. 35—41.

of which agrees with the Italic translation contained in the Brescia manuscript; another with that contained in the Verceli manuscript; and a third with that contained in the Vulgate." [1]

Specimens of the nature and closeness of the coincidence of these three classes are annexed by Mr. Nolan, in separate columns, from which the four following examples are selected. He has prefixed the readings of the received text and authorised English version (from Matt. v. 38. 41. and 44.), in order to evince their coincidence with that text, to which the preference appears to be due, on account of its conformity to the Italic translation contained in the Codex Brixianus.

38. και οδοντα αντι οδοντος. *Rec.*
— and a tooth for a tooth. *Auth.*

οδοντα αντι οδοντος. *Cant.*	dentem pro dentem. *Verc.*
και οδοντα αντι οδοντος. *Vat.*	et dentem pro dente. *Vulg.*
και οδοντα αντι οδοντος *Mosc.*	et dentem pro dente. *Brix.*

41. ὑπαγε μετ' αυτου δυο. *Rec.*
— go with him twain. *Auth.*

ὑπαγε μετ' αυτου ετι αλλα δυο. *Cant.*	vade cum illo *adhuc alia* duo. *Verc.*
ὑπαγε μετ' αυτου δυο. *Vat.*	vade cum illo *et alia* duo. *Vulg.*
ὑπαγε μετ' αυτου δυο. *Mosc.*	vade cum illo duo. *Brix*

44. ευλογειτε τους καταρωμενους ὑμας. *Rec.*
— bless them that curse you. *Auth.*

ευλογειτε τους καταρωμενους ὑμας. *Cant.*	desunt. *Verc.*
	desunt. *Vulg.*
ευλογειτε τους καταρωμενους ὑμας. *Mosc.*	benedicite maledicentibus vos. *Brix.*

44. προσευχεσθε ὑπερ των επηρεαζοντων ὑμας, και διωκοντων ὑμας. *Rec.*
— pray for them who despitefully use you and persecute you. *Auth.*

προσευχεσθε ὑπερ των επηρεαζοντων και διωκοντων ὑμας. *Cant.*	orate pro calumniantibus et persequentibus vos. *Verc.*
προσευχεσθε ὑπερ των διωκοντων ὑμας, *Vat.*	orate pro persequentibus et calumniantibus vos. *Vulg.*
προσευχεσθε ὑπερ των επηρεαζοντων ὑμας, και διωκοντων ὑμας. *Mosc.*	orate pro calumniantibus *vobis* et persequentibus vos. *Brix.*

The preceding short specimen will sufficiently evince the affinity subsisting between the Latin and Greek manuscripts, throughout the different classes into which they may be divided. at the same time it will illustrate the dissimilarity which those classes exhibit among themselves, in either language, regarded separately. Still further to evince the affinity which in other respects they possess among themselves, Mr. Nolan exhibits a connected portion, comprising the first twelve verses of the fifth chapter of St. Matthew's Gospel, in the original and the translation: from which we select the six following examples:

CLASS I.

| *Codex Cantabrigiensis.* | *Codex Vercellensis.* |
| 1. Ιδων δε τους οχλους, ανεβη εις το ορος· και καθισαντος αυτου, προσηλθον αυτω οι μαθηται αυτου· | 1. Videns autem Jesus turbam, ascendit in montem, et cum sedisset, accesserunt ad eum discipuli ejus, |

---

[1] Nolan's Inquiry, pp. 58—61.

2. Καὶ ἀνοίξας τὸ στόμα αὐτοῦ, ἐδίδαξεν αὐτοὺς λέγων·
3. Μακάριοι οἱ πτωχοὶ τῷ πνεύματι· ὅτι αὐτῶν ἐστιν ἡ βασιλεία τῶν οὐρανῶν.
5. Μακάριοι οἱ πραεῖς· ὅτι αὐτοὶ κληρονομήσουσι τὴν γῆν.
4. Μακάριοι οἱ πενθοῦντες· ὅτι αὐτοὶ παρακληθήσονται.
6 Μακάριοι οἱ πεινῶντες καὶ διψῶντες τὴν δικαιοσύνην· ὅτι αὐτοὶ χορτασθήσονται.

2. Et aperuit os suum, et docebat eos dicens:
3. Beati pauperes spiritu: quoniam ipsorum est regnum cœlorum.
5. Beati mites: quoniam ipsi hereditate possidebunt terram.
4 Beati qui lugent. quoniam ipsi consolabuntur.
6 Beati qui esuriunt et sitiunt justitiam. quoniam ipsi saturabuntur.

CLASS II.

Codex Vaticanus.

1. Ἰδὼν δὲ τοὺς ὄχλους, ἀνέβη εἰς τὸ ὄρος· καὶ καθίσαντος αὐτοῦ, προσῆλθον [αὐτῷ] οἱ μαθηταὶ αὐτοῦ·
2. Καὶ ἀνοίξας τὸ στόμα αὐτοῦ, ἐδίδασκεν αὐτοὺς λέγων.
3. Μακάριοι οἱ πτωχοὶ τῷ πνεύματι· ὅτι αὐτῶν ἐστιν ἡ βασιλεία τῶν οὐρανῶν.
4. Μακάριοι οἱ πενθοῦντες· ὅτι αὐτοὶ παρακληθήσονται.
5 Μακάριοι οἱ πραεῖς· ὅτι αὐτοὶ κληρονομήσουσι τὴν γῆν
6. Μακάριοι οἱ πεινῶντες καὶ διψῶντες τὴν δικαιοσύνην· ὅτι αὐτοὶ χορτασθήσονται.

Versio Vulgata.

1. Videns autem turbas ascendit in montem, et cum sedisset accesserunt ad eum discipuli ejus:
2. Et aperiens os suum, docebat eos dicens:
3. Beati pauperes spiritu. quoniam ipsorum est regnum cœlorum.
4. Beati mites: quoniam ipsi possidebunt terram.
5. Beati qui lugent: quoniam ipsi consolabuntur.
6 Beati qui esuriunt et sitiunt justitiam: quoniam ipsi saturabuntur.

CLASS III.

Codex Moscuensis.

1. Ἰδὼν δὲ τοὺς ὄχλους, ἀνέβη εἰς τὸ ὄρος· καὶ καθίσαντος αὐτοῦ, προσῆλθεν αὐτῷ οἱ μαθηταὶ αὐτοῦ.
2. Καὶ ἀνοίξας τὸ στόμα αὐτοῦ, ἐδίδασκεν αὐτοὺς λέγων.
3. Μακάριοι οἱ πτωχοὶ τῷ πνεύματι· ὅτι αὐτῶν ἐστιν ἡ βασιλεία τῶν οὐρανῶν.
4. Μακάριοι οἱ πενθοῦντες· ὅτι αὐτοὶ παρακληθήσονται.
5. Μακάριοι οἱ πραεῖς· ὅτι αὐτοὶ κληρονομήσουσι τὴν γῆν
6. Μακάριοι οἱ πεινῶντες καὶ διψῶντες τὴν δικαιοσύνην· ὅτι αὐτοὶ χορτασθήσονται.

Codex Brixiensis.

1. Videns autem turbas ascendit in montem, et cum sedisset accesserunt ad eum discipuli ejus;
2. Et aperiens os suum, docebat eos dicens:
3. Beati pauperes spiritu: quoniam ipsorum est regnum cœlorum.
4 Beati qui lugent: quoniam ipsi consolabuntur.
5. Beati mansueti: quoniam ipsi hereditabunt terram.
6. Beati qui esuriunt et sitiunt justitiam: quoniam ipsi saturabuntur.

On these different classes of manuscripts in the Greek and Latin, Mr. Nolan remarks, that it must be evident, on the most casual inspection, that the manuscripts in both languages possess the same text, though manifestly of different classes. "They respectively possess that identity in the choice of terms and arrangement of the language, which is irreconcileable with the notion of their having descended from different archetypes. And though these classes, in either language, vary among themselves, yet, as the translation follows the varieties of the original, the Greek and Latin consequently afford each other mutual confirmation. The different classes of text in the Greek and Latin translation, as thus coinciding, may be regarded as the conspiring testimony of those churches, which were appointed the witnesses and keepers of Holy Writ, to the existence of three species of text in the original and in the translation."[1]

Having thus produced the testimony of the eastern and western churches to the existence of these classes, the learned inquirer proceeds to ascertain the *antiquity* of the classes: which he effects by the Latin translation.

"As the existence of a translation necessarily implies the priority of the original from which it was formed; this testimony may be directly referred to the close of the fourth century. The Vulgate must be clearly referred to that period, as it was then formed by St. Jerome; in its bare existence, of course, the correspondent antiquity of the Greek text, with which it agrees, is directly established. This version is, however, obviously less antient than that of the Verceli or Brescia manuscript; as they are of the old Italic translation, while it properly constitutes the new. In the existence of the antient version, the antiquity of the original text with that which it corresponds is consequently established. The three classes of text, which correspond with the Vulgate and Old Italic Version, must be consequently referred to a period not less remote than the close of the fourth century."[2]

The system of classification being thus carried up as high as the fourth century, Mr. Nolan justifies it by the testimony of Jerome; for this learned father, who lived at that period, asserts the existence of three classes of text in the same age, which respectively prevailed in Egypt, Palestine, and Constantinople. The identity of these classes with the different classes of text which still exist in the Greek original and Latin translation[3], our author then proceeds to establish. And this he effects by means of the manuscripts which have been written, the versions which have been published, and the collations which have been made, in the different countries to which St. Jerome refers his classes; founding every part of his proofs on the testimony of Adler, Birch, Woide, Munter, and other critics who have analysed the text and versions of the New Testament.

The result of this investigation is, that the three classes of text, which are discoverable in the Greek manuscripts, are nearly identical with the three editions, which existed in the age of Jerome; with which they are identified by their coincidence with the Latin translation which existed in the age of that Christian father. Of the *first class*, the *Codex Bezæ* or Cambridge manuscript, is an exemplar: it contains the text which Jerome refers to Egypt, and ascribes to Hesychius. Of the *second class*, the *Codex Vaticanus*, or Vatican manuscript, forms the exemplar, and contains the text which Jerome refers to Palestine, and ascribes to Eusebius; and of the *third class*,

---

[1] Nolan's Inquiry, p. 70. [2] Ibid. pp. 70, 71.
[3] To which is now to be added the Peschito or Old Syriac version. The identity above noticed Mr. Nolan purposes fully to illustrate, in a future edition of his "Inquiry."

the Moscow manuscript, collated by Matthæi, and by him noted with the letter V. and the Harleian manuscript in the British Museum, No 5684., noted G. by Griesbach, are the exemplars, and contain the text which Jerome attributes to Lucian, and refers to Constantinople. The result of Mr. Nolan's long and elaborate discussion is, that, as the Occidental or Western, Alexandrine, and Byzantine texts (according to Griesbach's system of recensions), respectively coincide with the Egyptian, Palestine, and Byzantine texts of Mr. N., we have only to substitute the term Egyptian for Western, and Palestine for Alexandrine, in order to ascertain the particular text of any manuscript which is to be referred to a peculiar class or edition. " The artifice of this substitution admits of this simple solution: the Egyptian text was imported by Eusebius of Verceli into the West, and the Palestine text republished by Euthalius at Alexandria, the Byzantine text having retained the place in which it was originally published by Lucianus In a word, a manuscript which harmonises with the Codex Cantabrigiensis, must be referred to the first class, and will contain the text of Egypt. One which harmonises with the Vatican manuscript, must be referred to the second class, and will contain the text of Palestine. And one which harmonises with the Moscow manuscript, must be referred to the third class, and will contain the text of Constantinople.[1]

The advantages resulting from the system of recensions just developed are twofold — In the first place, it leads not only to a more adequate method of classification, but also to the discovery of a more antient text, by means of the priority of the old Italic Version to the New or Vulgate Latin of Jerome. And, secondly, it coincides with the respective schemes of Dr. Griesbach and of M. Matthæi, and derives support from their different systems. It adopts the three classes of the former, with a slight variation merely in the name of the classes; and, in ascertaining the genuine text, it attaches the same authority to the old Italic translation, which the same distinguished critic has ascribed to that version. It likewise agrees with the scheme of Matthæi, in giving the preference to the Κοινη Εκδοσις, the Greek Vulgate or Byzantine text, over the Palestine and Egyptian; but it supports the authority of this text on firmer grounds than the concurrence of the Greek manuscripts. " Hence," it is observed, that " while it differs from the scheme of M. Matthæi, in building on the Old Italic Version, it differs from that of Dr. Griesbach, in distinguishing the copies of this translation, which are free from the influence of the Vulgate, from those which have been corrected since the times of Eusebius of Verceli, of Jerome, and Cassiodorus. And it affords a more satisfactory mode of disposing of the multitude of various readings, than that suggested by the latter, who refers them to the intentional or accidental corruptions of transcribers; or by that of the former, who ascribes them to the correction of the original Greek by the Latin translation : as it traces them to the influence of the text which was published by Eusebius, at the command of Constantine."

---

[1] Nolan's Inquiry, pp. 105, 106.

4. Widely different from all the preceding theories is the system of recensions proposed by the learned (Roman Catholic) Professor Hug, of Fribourg, who affirms the existence of three recensions or editions, and divides the history of the sacred text of the New Testament into three periods, viz.

(1.) The *First Period* comprises the text of the New Testament, from the time when its several books were written to the third century. That text, according to the testimony of Clement of Alexandria, Origen, Irenæus, and other Fathers, was early the object of imprudent or rash alterations; although their statements were greatly exaggerated, yet the fact is certain, that such alterations were actually made; and the text, thus altered, was, according to Hug, what is commonly termed ΚΟΙΝΗ ΕΚΔΟΣΙΣ, or the *common edition*. Though almost every where the same, this edition had two forms, a little different, one of which corresponds with Griesbach's Western Recension, and the other with his special Asiatic Instruments, and particularly with the Peschito or Old Syriac version.

(2.) *Second Period.*— The defects of the *common edition* having been perceived about the middle of the third century, three learned men, severally and independently, though nearly simultaneously, undertook the arduous task of purifying the text, and of restoring it to its first form, by the aid of manuscripts, viz. Origen in Palestine, Hesychius in Egypt, where he was a bishop, and Lucian, a priest at Antioch, in Syria. The work of *Hesychius* was generally received in Egypt, and became the source of the Alexandrine family: that of *Lucian*, which was better known, and has sometimes been termed the *Editio Vulgata*, or *Lucianus*, was introduced into divine worship in Syria, in Asia Minor, in Thrace, and at Constantinople; and that of Origen, having been made in his old age, and left for publication by his pupils, was confined within Palestine, where it was soon superseded by the edition of Lucian, and in no long time was entirely lost.

(3.) The *Third Period* of the history of the text of the New Testament embraces the variations made therein, from the threefold recension in the third century, to our own time.[1]

5. The system proposed by Professor Hug has been much and deservedly admired for its ingenuity, and for the solution which it affords to a great number of difficulties. It has, however, been materially modified by Dr. (now Professor) Scholz, a pupil of Hug's, of whose views he is by no means a servile follower.

Scholz has, in fact, proposed two systems of recensions.

(1.) The *first* of these systems was communicated to the public in 1820[2], and was the result of his examination of forty-eight manuscripts in the Royal Library at Paris; seventeen of which he collated entirely and with the utmost care, and nine of them had never before been examined by any person. In the opinion of Scholz, there

---

[1] Cellerier, Introduction au Nouv. Test. pp. 84—103. Hug's Introd. to the New Testament, vol i pp. 134—231.
[2] Curæ Criticæ in Historiam Textus Evangeliorum, Commentationibus Duis exhibitæ a Joh. M. Augustino Scholz. Heidelbergæ, 1820. 4to.

is nothing which indicates the existence of the Origenian Recension; and the labours of Hesychius and of Lucian had no more influence on the history of the text than those of their predecessors. He professes carefully to have examined every thing concerning them in the antient writers of the church; and he states that he has found nothing that could lead him to form a different idea. But, among the various instruments or manuscripts which he has compared, he thinks he has discovered vestiges of four distinct families; viz. two *African* or rather *Egyptian*, one of which corresponds with the Alexandrine Recension of Griesbach, and the other, with his Occidental Recension; and two *Asiatic*, one of which is particularly deserving of that name, and corresponds with the special Asiatic instruments of Griesbach, and the other under the appellation of *Byzantine*, is the *Constantinopolitan* Recension. To these he added a fifth recension, which he denominated the *Cyprian*, because it contains that text which is exhibited in the *Codex Cyprius*, a manuscript of the eighth century brought from the isle of Cyprus (whence it derives its name), which is described in a subsequent page. By a comparison of the readings of the Codex Cyprius with the received text, and with the Alexandrine and Constantinopolitan Recensions in nearly one hundred instances, Professor Scholz has shown, that it very frequently coincides with the two last, sometimes agreeing with both, sometimes following the one or the other of them, and sometimes holding a mean between them. In many instances it harmonises with but few manuscripts; and in some cases its readings are peculiar to itself. On these accounts, he is of opinion that the Codex Cyprius exhibits a family which has sprung from a collation of various manuscripts, some of which owe their origin to Egypt, others to Asia, and others to Cyprus.

The origin and history of the four African and Asiatic families above mentioned, are investigated at considerable length by Professor Scholz, who proceeds to form an estimate of their respective critical merits. In the two African families he finds an extremely corrupted text; but the two Asiatic families are very superior to them, approaching much nearer to the original purity of the antient text: and (which is a necessary consequence) they differ very little from each other, they present a text much more fixed, more uniform, and more generally approved.

It is proper to add that, subsequently to Scholz's publication of the preceding theory of recensions, Professor Hug, with a candour and modesty which reflect the highest honour upon him, announced that his pupil's labours had led him to entertain some doubts concerning his own system; and that he shall wait for the appearance of the critical edition of the New Testament which Scholz is preparing, before he offers any reply to his theory.

(2.) The theory of Prof. Scholz has been materially modified in consequence of the results obtained by him in his Biblical Researches in various parts of Europe and in Palestine; and in which he goes far towards overturning the bases of the systems of recensions generally adopted in Germany. Of these details he has published an interesting account (in German[1]), which does not admit of abridgment. It may, however, suffice here to state that from the differences which are sufficiently perceptible in the manuscripts and editions of the Greek Text of the New Testament, he concludes that these instruments naturally divide themselves into TWO great classes, which are constantly the same throughout the books of the New Testament. To the first of these classes belong all the editions and those numerous manuscripts, which were written within the limits of the patriarchate of Constantinople, or which were destined for liturgical use: the second class comprises certain manuscripts written in the south of France, in Sicily, Egypt, and elsewhere. Transcribed, unquestionably, from copies which were valuable on account of their age and beauty, they were intended only to preserve the contents of those copies. but, as they presented a different text from that which was generally received, they could not be employed in divine service: hence they were for the most part negligently written, with an incorrect orthography, and on leaves of vellum of different sizes and qualities. To this class, Prof. Scholz gives the appellation of *Alexandrine*, because its text originated in Alexandria. The other class he terms the *Constantinopolitan*, because its text was written within the precincts of the patriarchate of Constantinople: and he has endeavoured to show, by the actual collation of several hundred manuscripts (which is further confirmed by an induction of historical particulars), that the Constantinopolitan text is almost always faithful to the text now actually received, while the Alexandrine text varies from it in almost every verse. There are extant other manuscripts, which belong sometimes to one class, and sometimes to the other, and which also have some peculiar varieties: but repeated examinations of them enable him to state that they do not possess sufficient characters to constitute them distinct classes.'

In the subsequent part of his Biblico-Critical Travels, Professor Scholz proceeds to discuss the use of the terms, *recensio* and *textus recensus*, introduced by Griesbach, and formerly adopted by himself; which terms he is of opinion are now no longer applicable. According to Scholz, the Constantinopolitan text *never* underwent any general revision; and the Alexandrine text, which was corrupted in the three first centuries, has since that time remained without any further alteration.

Although Prof. Scholz's system of classing manuscripts seems, at first view, to contradict those of his predecessors in this department of sacred criticism, yet this contradiction is only apparent — not real: for he actually recognises the same facts as other critics, he only denies the importance of some, and explains others in a different way. With respect to the results, however, there is no difference. The grand, the final result of the principle of families, viz. the possibility

---

[1] Biblische Critische Reise, &c. i. e. Biblico-Critical Travels in France, Switzerland, Italy, Palestine, and the Archipelago, in 1818-1821 pp. 163—182 Leipzig, 1823 8vo There is an interesting account of these Travels in the Bibliothèque Universelle (Littérature) for 1823, tom. xxiv. pp. 335—355.

and certainty of the integrity of the sacred text is expressed more distinctly by Scholz than by any of his predecessors. Further, though not free from objections, this system appears generally to offer more than any other, a remarkable character of simplicity and universality: it is less complicated, and also possesses a greater degree of probability, than those of Griesbach and Hug, and it is supported by researches which are truly learned and laborious. Although the absolute certainty of Scholz's system can only be determined by the appearance of the critical edition of the Greek New Testament, which he is preparing for publication; yet he is allowed to have done much towards demonstrating the great pre-eminence of the Asiatic or Constantinopolitan text over the African or Alexandrine text, and consequently the real merit of the present received text of the New Testament. But, whatever may be the result of Scholz's projected edition, (and towards which *six hundred manuscripts*, unknown to Griesbach, have lent their aid,) the critical labours of Dr. Griesbach will not cease to possess high claims to the grateful attention of every student of sacred literature.

As a general and correct index to the great body of Greek manuscripts, they are an invaluable treasure to the scholar, and a necessary acquisition to the divine: at the same time, his collection of various readings is admirably calculated to satisfy our minds on a point of the highest moment, — the integrity of the Christian Records. Through the long interval of seventeen hundred years, — amidst the collision of parties, — the opposition of enemies, — and the desolations of time, — they remain the same as holy men read them in the primitive ages of Christianity. A very minute examination of manuscripts, versions, and fathers, proves the *inviolability* of the Christian Scriptures. "They all coincide in exhibiting the same Gospels, Acts, and Epistles, and among all the copies of them which have been preserved, there is not one which dissents from the rest either in the doctrines or precepts, which constitute Christianity. They ALL contain the same doctrines and precepts. For the knowledge of this fact, we are indebted to such men as Griesbach, whose zealous and persevering labours to put us in possession of it intitle them to our grateful remembrance. To the superficial, and to the novice, in theology, the long periods of life, and the patient investigation, which have been applied to critical investigation, may appear as mere waste, or, at the best, as only amusing employment: but to the serious inquirer, who, from his own conviction, can declare that he is not following cunningly devised fables, the time, the talents, and the learning, which have been devoted to critical collation, will be accounted as well expended, for the result which they have accomplished. The *real* theologian is satisfied from his own examination, that the accumulation of many thousands of various readings, obtained at the expense of immense critical labour, does not affect a single sentiment in the whole New Testament. And thus is criticism, — which some despise, and others neglect, — found to be one of those undecaying columns, by which the imperishable structure of Christian Truth is supported."[1]

---

[1] Eclectic Review, vol. v. part i. p. 189.

VI. From the coincidence observed between many Greek manuscripts and the Vulgate, or some other Latin version, a suspicion arose in the minds of several eminent critics, that the Greek text had been altered throughout to the Latin; and it has been asserted that at the council of Florence, (held in 1439 with the view of establishing an union between the Greek and Latin churches,) a resolution was formed, that the Greeks should alter their manuscripts from the Latin. This has been termed by the learned, *Fœdus cum Græcis*. The suspicion, concerning the altering of the Greek text, seems to have been first suggested by Erasmus, but it does not appear that he supposed the alterations were made before the fifteenth century: so that the charge of *Latinising* the manuscripts did not (at least in his notion of it) extend to the original writers of the manuscript, or as they are called, the writers *a prima manu;* since it affected only the writers *a secunda manu,* or subsequent interpolators. The accusation was adopted and extended by Father Simon and Dr. Mill, and especially by Wetstein. Bengel expressed some doubts concerning it; and it was formally questioned by Semler, Griesbach, and Woide. The reasonings of the two last-mentioned critics convinced Michaelis (who had formerly agreed with Erasmus) that the charge of Latinising was unfounded; and in the fourth edition of his Introduction to the New Testament (the edition translated by Bishop Marsh), with a candour of which there are too few examples, Michaelis totally abandoned his first opinion, and expressed his opinion that the pretended agreement in the *Fœdus cum Græcis* is a mere conjecture of Erasmus, to which he had recourse as a refuge in a matter of controversy. Carrying the proof to its utmost length, it only shows that the Latin translations and the Greek copies were made from the same exemplars; which rather proves the antiquity of the Latin translations, than the corruption of the Greek copies. It is further worthy of remark, that Jerome corrected the Latin from the Greek; a circumstance which is known in every part of the Western Church. Now, as Michaelis justly observes, when it was known that the learned father had made the Greek text the basis of his alterations in the Latin translation, it is scarcely to be imagined that the transcribers of the Western Church would alter the Greek by the Latin, and it is still less probable, that those of the Eastern Church would act in this manner.[1]

§ 2. ACCOUNT OF GREEK MANUSCRIPTS, CONTAINING THE OLD AND NEW TESTAMENTS.

I. *The Alexandrian Manuscript.* — II. *The Vatican Manuscript.*

OF the few manuscripts known to be extant, which contain the Greek Scriptures, (that is, the Old Testament, according to the Septuagint Version, and the New Testament,) there are two which pre-eminently demand the attention of the biblical student for their

[1] Michaelis's Introduction, vol. ii. part i pp. 163—179. Butler's Horæ Biblicæ, vol i. p. 1 &.

antiquity and intrinsic value, viz. The Alexandrian manuscript, which is preserved in the British Museum, and the Vatican manuscript, deposited in the library of the Vatican Palace at Rome.

I. The CODEX ALEXANDRINUS, or Alexandrian Manuscript, which is noted by the letter A. in Wetstein's and Griesbach's critical editions of the New Testament, consists of four folio volumes; the three first contain the whole of the Old Testament, together with the apocryphal books, and the fourth comprises the New Testament, the first epistle of Clement to the Corinthians, and the apocryphal Psalms ascribed to Solomon. In the New Testament there is wanting the beginning as far as Matt. xxv. 6. ο νυμφιος ερχεται; likewise from John vi. 50. to viii. 52. and from 2 Cor. iv. 13. to xii. 7. The Psalms are preceded by the epistle of Athanasius to Marcellinus, and followed by a catalogue, containing those which are to be used in prayer for each hour, both of the day and of the night; also by fourteen hymns, partly apocryphal, partly biblical, the eleventh of which is the hymn of the Virgin Mary, usually termed the Magnificat, (Luke i. 46—55.) and here intitled προσευχη Μαριας της Θεοτοκου, or, *the prayer of Mary the mother of God* · the arguments of Eusebius are annexed to the Psalms, and his canons to the Gospels. This manuscript is now preserved in the British Museum, where it was deposited in 1753. It was sent as a present to King Charles I. from Cyrillus Lucaris, a native of Crete, and patriarch of Constantinople, by Sir Thomas Rowe, ambassador from England to the Grand Seignior, in the year 1628. Cyrillus brought it with him from Alexandria, where, probably, it was written. In a schedule annexed to it, he gives this account; that it was written, according to tradition, by Thecla, a noble Egyptian lady, about thirteen hundred years ago, a little after the council of Nice. He adds, that the name of Thecla, at the end of the book, was erased; but that this was the case with other books of the Christians, after Christianity was extinguished in Egypt by the Mohammedans: and that recent tradition records the fact of the laceration and erasure of Thecla's name. The proprietor of this manuscript, before it came into the hands of Cyrillus Lucaris, had written an Arabic subscription, expressing that this book was said to have been written with the pen of Thecla the Martyr.

Various disputes have arisen with regard to the place whence it was brought, and where it was written, to its antiquity, and of course to its real value. Some critics have bestowed upon it the highest commendation, whilst it has been equally depreciated by others. Of its most strenuous adversaries, Wetstein seems to have been the principal. The place from which it was sent to England was, without doubt, Alexandria, and hence it has been called *Codex Alexandrinus*. As to the place where it was written, there is a considerable difference of opinion. Matthæus Muttis, who was a contemporary, friend, and deacon of Cyrillus, and who afterwards instructed in the Greek language John Rudolph Wetstein, uncle of the celebrated editor of the Greek Testament, bears testimony, in a letter written to Martin Bogdan, a physician in Berne, dated January 14. 1664, that it had been brought from one of the twenty-two monasteries in Mount Athos, which the Turks never destroyed, but allowed to continue upon the payment of tribute. Dr. Woide endeavours to weaken the evidence of Muttis, and to render the testimony of the elder Wetstein suspicious: but Spohn[1] shows that the objections of Woide are ungrounded. Allowing their reality, we cannot infer that Cyrillus found this manuscript in Alexandria. Before he went to Alexandria he spent some time on Mount Athos, the repository and manufactory of manuscripts of the New Testament, whence a great number have been brought into the West of Europe, and a still greater number has been sent to Moscow. It is therefore probable, independently of the evidence of Muttis, that Cyrillus procured it there either by purchase or by present, took it with him to Alexandria, and brought it thence on his return to Constantinople. But the question recurs, where was this copy written? The Arabic subscription above cited, clearly proves, that it had been in Egypt at some period or other, before it fell into the hands of Cyrillus. This subscription shows that it once belonged to an Egyptian, or that during some time it was preserved in Egypt, where Arabic has been spoken since the seventh century. Besides, it is well known that a great number of manuscripts of the Greek Bible have been written in Egypt. Woide has also pointed out a remarkable coincidence between the Codex Alexandrinus and the writings of the Copts. Michaelis alleges another circumstance as a probable argument of its having been written in Egypt. In Ezekiel xxvii. 18. both in the Hebrew and Greek text, the Tyrians are said to have fetched their wine from Chelbon, or, according to Bochart, Chalybon. But as Chalybon, though celebrated for its wine, was unknown to the writer of this manuscript, he has altered it by a fanciful conjecture to οινον εκ χεβρων, wine from Hebron. This alteration was probably made by an Egyptian copyist, because Egypt was formerly supplied with wine from Hebron. The subscription before mentioned ascribes the writing of it to Thecla, an Egyptian lady of high rank, who could not have been, as Michaelis supposes, the martyress Thecla, placed in the time of St. Paul: but Woide replies, that a distinction must be made between Thecla martyr, and Thecla proto-martyr. With regard to these subscriptions we may observe, with Bishop Marsh, that the true state of the case appears to be as follows "Some centuries after the Codex Alexandrinus had been written, and the Greek subscriptions, and perhaps those other parts where it is more defective, already lost, it fell into the hands of a Christian inhabitant of Egypt, who, not finding the usual Greek subscription of the copyist, added in Arabic, his native language, the tradition, either true or false, which had been preserved in the family or families to which the manuscript had belonged, 'Memorant hunc codicem scriptum esse calamo Theclæ martyris.' In the 17th century, when oral tradition respecting this manuscript had probably ceased, it became the property of Cyrillus Lucaris: but whether in Alexandria, or Mount Athos, is of no importance to the present inquiry. On examining the manuscript, he finds that the Greek subscription

---

[1] Caroli Godofredi Woidii Notitia Codicis Alexandrini, cum variis ejus lectionibus omnibus. Recudendum curavit, notasque adjecit Gottlieb Leberecht Spohn, pp. 10—13. (8vo. Lipsiæ, 1790.)

is lost, but that there is a tradition recorded in Arabic by a former proprietor, which simply related that it was written by one Thecla a martyress, which is what he means by 'memoria et traditio recens.' Taking therefore upon trust, that one Thecla a martyress was really the copyist, he consults the annals of the church to discover in what age and country a person of this name and character existed; finds that an Egyptian lady of rank, called Thecla, suffered martyrdom between the time of holding the council of Nicæa and the close of the fourth century; and concludes, without further ceremony, that she was the very identical copyist. Not satisfied with this discovery, he attempts to account for the loss of the Greek subscription, and ascribes it to the malice of the Saracens, being weak enough to believe that the enemies of Christianity would exert their vengeance on the name of a poor transcriber, and leave the four folio volumes themselves unhurt." Dr. Woide, who transcribed and published this manuscript, and must be better acquainted with it than any other person, asserts, that it was written by two different copyists; for he observed a difference in the ink, and, which is of greater moment, even in the strokes of the letters. The conjecture of Oudin, adopted by Wetstein, that the manuscript was written by an Accemet is, in the judgment of Michaelis, worthy of attention [1]; and he adds, that this conjecture does not contradict the account that Thecla was the copyist, since there were not only monks but nuns of this order.

The antiquity of this manuscript has also been the subject of controversy. Grabe and Schulze think that it might have been written before the end of the fourth century, which, says Michaelis, is the very utmost period that can be allowed, because it contains the epistles of Athanasius. Oudin places it in the tenth century. Wetstein refers it to the fifth, and supposes that it was one of the manuscripts collected at Alexandria in 615, for the Syriac version. Dr. Semler refers it to the seventh century. Montfaucon [2] is of opinion, that neither the Codex Alexandrinus, nor any Greek manuscript, can be said with great probability to be much prior to the sixth century. Michaelis apprehends, that this manuscript was written after Arabic was become the native language of the Egyptians, that is, one, or rather two centuries after Alexandria was taken by the Saracens, which happened in the year 640, because the transcriber frequently confounds M and B, which is often done in the Arabic: and he concludes, that it is not more antient than the eighth century. Woide, after a great display of learning, with which he examines the evidence for the antiquity of the Codex Alexandrinus, concludes, that it was written between the middle and the end of the fourth

---

[1] The Accemets were a class of monks in the antient church, who flourished, particularly in the East, during the fifth century. They were so called, because they had divine service performed, without interruption, in their churches. They divided themselves into three bodies, each of which officiated in turn, and relieved the others, so that their churches were never silent, either night or day. Wetstein adopts the opinion of Casimir Oudin, that the Codex Alexandrinus was written by an Accemet, because it contains a catalogue of the psalms that were to be sung at every hour both of the day and night. Proleg in Nov. Test. vol. 1 p 10.

[2] Palæog Græc p. 185.

century. It cannot be allowed a greater antiquity, because it has not only the τιτλοι or κεφαλαια majora, but the κεφαλαια minora, or Ammonian sections, accompanied with the references to the canons of Eusebius. Woide's arguments have been objected to by Spohn.[1] Some of the principal arguments advanced by those who refer this manuscript to the fourth or fifth centuries are the following: the epistles of Saint Paul are not divided into chapters like the gospels, though this division took place so early as 396, when to each chapter was prefixed a superscription. The Codex Alexandrinus has the epistles of Clement of Rome; but these were forbidden to be read in the churches, by the council of Laodicea, in 364, and that of Carthage, in 419. Hence Schulze has inferred, that it was written before the year 364; and he produces a new argument for its antiquity, deduced from the last of the fourteen hymns found in it after the psalms, which is superscribed υμνος εθινος, and is called the grand doxology; for this hymn has not the clause αγιος ο θεος, αγιος ισχυρος, αγιος αθανατος, ελεησον ημας, which was used between the years 434 and 446: and therefore the manuscript must have been written before this time. Wetstein thinks that it must have been written before the time of Jerome, because the Greek text of this manuscript was altered from the old Italic. He adds, that the transcriber was ignorant that the Arabs were called Hagarenes, because he has written (1 Chron. v. 20.) αγοραιοι for Αγαραιοι. Others allege that αγοραιοι is a mere erratum: because Αγαραιων occurs in the preceding verse, Αγαριτης in 1 Chron. xxvii. 31. and Αγαρηνοι in Psal. lxxxii. 7. These arguments, says Michaelis, afford no certainty, because the Codex Alexandrinus must have been copied from a still more antient manuscript; and if this were faithfully copied, the arguments apply rather to this than to the Alexandrian manuscript itself. It is the hand-writing alone, or the formation of the letters, with the want of accents, which can lead to any probable decision. The arguments alleged to prove that it is not so antient as the fourth century, are the following. Dr. Semler thinks, that the epistle of Athanasius, on the value and excellency of the Psalms, would hardly have been prefixed to them during his life. But it ought to be recollected, that Athanasius had many warm and strenuous advocates. From this epistle Oudin has attempted to deduce an argument, that the manuscript was written in the tenth century. This epistle, he says, is spurious, and could not have been forged during the life of Athanasius, and the tenth century was fertile in spurious productions. Again, the Virgin Mary, in the superscription of the Song of the Blessed Virgin, is styled θεοτοκος, a name which Wetstein says betrays the fifth century. Further, from the probable conjecture, that this manuscript was written by one of the order of the Acœmetæ, Oudin concludes against its antiquity; but Wetstein contents himself with asserting, that it could not have been written before the fifth century, because Alexander, who founded this order, lived about the year 420. From this statement, pursued more at large,

---

[1] Pp 42—109 of his edition of Woide's Notitia Codicis Alexandrini.

Michaelis deduces a reason for paying less regard to the Codex Alexandrinus than many eminent critics have done, and for the preference that is due, in many respects, to antient versions, before any single manuscript, because the antiquity of the former, which is in general greater than that of the latter, can be determined with more precision.

The value of this manuscript has been differently appreciated by different writers. Wetstein, though he denotes it by A, the first letter of the alphabet, is no great admirer of it, nor does Michaelis estimate it highly, either on account of its internal excellence or the value of its readings. The principal charge which has been produced against the Alexandrian manuscript, and which has been strongly urged by Wetstein, is its having been altered from the Latin version. It is incredible, says Michaelis, who once agreed in opinion with Wetstein, but found occasion to alter his sentiments, that a transcriber who lived in Egypt, should have altered the Greek text from a Latin version, because Egypt belonged to the Greek diocese, and Latin was not understood there. On this subject Woide has eminently displayed his critical abilities, and ably defended the Greek manuscripts in general, and the Codex Alexandrinus in particular, from the charge of having been corrupted from the Latin. Griesbach concurs with Woide [1], and both have contributed to confirm Michaelis in his new opinion. If this manuscript has been corrupted from a version, it is more reasonable to suspect the Coptic, the version of the country in which it was written. Between this manuscript and both the Coptic and Syriac versions, there is a remarkable coincidence. Griesbach has observed, that this manuscript follows three different editions: the Byzantine in the Gospels, the Western edition in the Acts of the Apostles, and the Catholic epistles, which form the middle division of this manuscript, and the Alexandrine in the epistles of Saint Paul. The transcriber, if this assertion be true, must have copied the three parts of the Greek Testament from three different manuscripts of three different editions. It is observable, that the readings of the Codex Alexandrinus coincide very frequently not only with the Coptic and the old Syriac, but with the new Syriac and the Ethiopic; and this circumstance favours the hypothesis, that this manuscript was written in Egypt, because the new Syriac version having been collated with Egyptian manuscripts of the Greek Testament, and the Ethiopic version being taken immediately from them, have necessarily the readings of the Alexandrine edition.

The Alexandrian manuscript is written in uncial or capital letters, without any accents or marks of aspiration, but with a few abbreviations nearly similar to those already noticed [2], and also with some others which are described by Dr. Woide [3], who has likewise explained the various points and spaces occurring in this manuscript.

---

[1] In his "Symbolæ Criticæ," vol. i. pp. 110—117. [2] See pp. 98, 99. *supra*.
[3] In the Preface to his fac-simile of the Alexandrian manuscript of the New Testament, §§ 27—34.

Sect. III. § 2.] *Containing the Old and New Testaments.* 121

A fac-simile of the Codex Alexandrinus, containing the New Testament, was published in folio by the late Dr. Woide, assistant librarian of the British Museum, with types cast for the purpose, line for line, without intervals between the words, precisely as in the original.[1] The following specimen will convey to the reader an idea of this most precious manuscript.

John i. 1—7.

ϹΝΑΡΧΗΗΝΟΛΟΓΟϹΚΑΙΟΛΟΓΟϹΗ
ΠΡΟϹΤΟΝΘΝ·ΚΑΙΘϹΗΝΟΛΟΓΟϹ·
ΟΥΤΟϹΗΝΕΝΑΡΧΗΠΡΟϹΤΟΝΘΝ
ΠΑΝΤΑΔΙΑΥΤΟΥΕΓΕΝΕΤΟ·ΚΑΙΧΩ
ΡΕΙϹΑΥΤΟΥΕΓΕΝΕΤΟΟΥΔΕΕΝ·
ΟΓΕΓΟΝΕΝΕΝΑΥΤΩΖΩΗΗΝ·
ΚΑΙΗΖΩΗΗΝΤΟΦΩϹΤΩΝΑΝΩΝ
ΚΑΙΤΟΦΩϹΕΝΤΗϹΚΟΤΙΑΦΑΙ
ΝΕΙ·ΚΑΙΗϹΚΟΤΙΑΑΥΤΟΟΥΚΑΤΕ
ΛΑΒΕΝ·   ΕΓΕΝΕΤΟΑΝΟϹΑΠΕ
ϹΤΑΛΜΕΝΟϹΠΑΡΑΘΥΟΝΟΜΑΑΥ
ΤΩΙΩΑΝΝΗϹ ΟΥΤΟϹΗΛΘΕΝ
ΕΙϹΜΑΡΤΥΡΙΑΝΙΝΑΜΑΡΤΥΡΗ
ϹΗΠΕΡΙΤΟΥΦΩΤΟϹ ΙΝΑΠΑΝ
ΤΕϹΠΙϹΤΕΥϹΩϹΙΝΔΙΑΥΤΟΥ

For this stereotype specimen we are indebted to the Rev. H. Baber, one of the librarians of the British Museum, who kindly favoured us with the use of the Alexandrian types, with which he printed the Codex Alexandrinus.[2] For the gratification of the English reader, the following extract is subjoined, comprising the first seven verses of Saint John's Gospel, rendered rather more literally than the idiom of our language will admit, in order to convey an exact idea of the original Greek (above given) of the Alexandrian manuscript.

---

[1] See a notice of Dr Woide's publication, in the Appendix to this volume, p. 19.

[2] See an account of this magnificent publication in the Appendix to this volume, pp. 38, 39. — The reader, who may be desirous of further information concerning the Alexandrian manuscript, is referred to Dr Grabe's prolegomena to his edition of the Greek Septuagint, and also to the prolegomena of Dr. Woide already cited, and to those of Dr Mill and Wetstein, prefixed to their editions of the New Testament. See also Michaelis's Introduction to the New Testament, vol ii, part i. pp. 186—209., and Bishop Marsh's notes in part ii pp. 648—660, and Hug's Introduction to the New Test. vol i pp 268—273. Dr. Lardner has given the table of contents of this manuscript in his Credibility of the Gospel History, part ii. chap. 147. (Works, 8vo. vol. v. pp. 253—256.; 4to. vol. iv. pp. 44—46.)

John i. 1—7.

INTHEBEGINNINGWASTHEWORDANDTHEWORDWAS
WITHG̅D̅·ANDG̅D̅WASTHEWORD·
HEWASINTHEBEGINNINGWITHG̅D̅
ALLWEREMADEBYHIMANDWITH
OUTHIMWASMADENOTONE*THING*·
THATWASMADEINHIMLIFEWAS·
ANDTHELIFEWASTHELIGHTOFM̅N̅
ANDTHELIGHTINDARKNESSSHIN
ETHANDTHEDARKNESSDIDNOTITCOMPRE
HEND·   THEREWASAM̅N̅SE

NTFROMGODWHOSENAME*WAS*
IOHN·THIS*PERSON*CAME
ASAWITNESSTHATHEMIGHTTESTI
FYCONCERNINGTHELIGHTTHATA
LLMIGHTBELIEVETHROUGHHIM·

II. The CODEX VATICANUS, No. 1209., which Wetstein and Griesbach have both noted with the letter B, contests the palm of antiquity with the Alexandrian manuscript. No fac-simile of it has ever been published. The Roman edition of the Septuagint, printed in 1590, professes to exhibit the text of this manuscript; and in the preface to that edition it is stated to have been written before the year 387, *i. e.* towards the close of the fourth century: Montfaucon and Blanchini refer it to the fifth or sixth century, and Dupin to the seventh century. Professor Hug has endeavoured to show that it was written in the early part of the fourth century; but, from the omission of the Eusebian κεφαλαια and τιτλοι, Bishop Marsh concludes with great probability that it was written before the close of the fifth century. The Vatican manuscript is written on parchment or vellum, in uncial or capital letters, in three columns on each page, all of which are of the same size, except at the beginning of a book, and without any divisions of chapters, verses, or words, but with accents and spirits. The shape of the letters, and colour of the ink, prove that it was written throughout by one and the same careful copyist. The abbreviations are few, being confined chiefly to those words which are in general abbreviated, such as Θ̅C̅, K̅C̅, I̅C̅, X̅C̅, for Θεος, Κυριος, Ιησους, Χριςος, *God, Lord, Jesus, Christ.* Originally this manuscript contained the entire Greek Bible, including both the Old and New Testaments; in which respect it resembles none so much as the Codex Alexandrinus, though no two manuscripts vary more in their readings. The Old Testament wants the first forty-six chapters of Genesis, and thirty-two psalms, viz. from Psal. cv. to cxxxvii. inclusive; and the New Testament wants the latter part of the epistle to the Hebrews, viz. all after chapter ix. verse 14. and also Saint Paul's other epistles to Timothy, Titus, and Philemon, and the whole Book of Revelation. It appears, however, that this last book, as well as the latter part of the epistle to the Hebrews, has been supplied by a modern hand in the fifteenth century, and, it is said, from some manuscript that had formerly belonged to Cardinal Bessarion. In many places the faded letters have also been retouched by a modern but careful hand: and when the person who made these amendments (whom Michaelis pronounces to have been a man of learning) found various readings in other manuscripts he has introduced them into the Codex Vaticanus, but has still preserved the original text, and in some few instances he has ventured to erase with a penknife. Various defects, both in orthography and language, indicate that this manuscript was executed by an Egyptian copyist. Instead of συλληψη, &c. he has written συλλημψη, λημψεσθε, λημφθησεται, which occurs only in Coptic or Græco-coptic MSS. He has also written εἶπαν for εἶπον, as may be seen in the celebrated Rosetta inscription; εἶδαν, ἔπεσαν, εισηλθαν, ἀνειλατο, and διεμαρτυρατο, as in the inscription of the Theban Memnon; and ἑωρακαν and γεγοναν, as the Alexandrians wrote according to the testimony of Sextus Empiricus. These peculiarities show that the Codex Vaticanus exhibits the Egyptian text, subsequent to the third century, according to the Alexandrine Recension of Griesbach, and the Hesychian Recension of Hug.

It has been supposed that this manuscript was collated by the editors of the Complutensian Polyglott, and even that this edition was almost entirely taken from it: but Bishop Marsh has shown by actual comparison that this was not the case.

The Vatican manuscript has been repeatedly collated by various eminent critics, from whose extracts Wetstein collected numerous various readings: but the latest and best collation is that by Professor Birch, of Copenhagen, in 1781. Although the antiquity of the Vatican manuscript is indisputable, it is by no means easy to determine between its comparative value and that of the Alexandrian manuscript; nor is there any absolute and universal standard by which their several excellencies may be estimated. With regard to the Old Testament, if any Greek manuscript were now extant, containing an *exact* copy of the several books as they were originally translated, such manuscript would be perfect, and, consequently, the most valuable. The nearer any copy comes to this perfection, the more valuable it must be, and *vice versâ*. In its present state the Hebrew Text cannot determine fully the value of these MSS. in their relation to one another; and yet as that text receives great assistance from both, it proves that both deserve our highest regard. It is worthy of remark, that neither of them has the asterisks of Origen, though both of them were transcribed in the fifth century; which, Dr. Kennicott observes [1], is one proof that they were not taken either mediately or immediately from the Hexapla. The Vatican and Alexandrian manuscripts differ from each other in the Old Testament chiefly in this;—that, as they contain books, which have been corrected by different persons, upon different principles; and as they differ greatly in some places in their interpolations,—so they contain many words which were either derived from different Greek versions, or else were translated by one or both of the transcribers themselves from the Hebrew text, which was consulted by them at the time of transcribing.

On the ground of its internal excellence, Michaelis preferred the Vatican manuscript (for the New Testament) to the Codex Alexandrinus. If, however, that manuscript be most respectable which comes the nearest to Origen's Hexaplar copy of the Septuagint, the Alexandrian manuscript seems to claim that merit in preference to its rival: but if it be thought a matter of superior honour to approach nearer the old Greek version, uncorrected by Origen, that merit seems to be due to the Vatican.[1]

The accompanying plate exhibits a specimen of the Vatican manuscript from a fac-simile traced in the year 1704 for Dr. Grabe, editor of the celebrated edition of the Septuagint, which is noticed in a subsequent part of this work. The author has reason to believe that it is *the most faithful* fac-simile ever executed of this MS. It was made by signor Zacagni, at that time principal keeper of the Vatican library, and is now preserved among Dr. Grabe's manuscripts in the Bodleian library at Oxford. This fac-simile has been most carefully and accurately copied, under the direction of the Rev. Dr. Bandinel, the keeper of that noble repository of literature, to whom the author now offers his acknowledgments for his kind assistance on this occasion. The passage represented in our engraving contains the first three verses of the first chapter of the prophet Ezekiel, of which the following is a literal English version:

IEZEKIEL.

+   +   +

NOWITCAMETOPASSINTHETHIR
INTHE
TIETHYEARFOURTH
MONTHONTHEFIFTHOFTHEMONTH
WHENIWASINTHEMIDST
OFTHECAPTIVESBYTHE
RIVERCHOBARAND
THEHEAVENSWEREOPENED
ANDISAWTHEVISIONSOFGDONTHEFI
FTHOFTHEMONTHTHIS
WASTHEFIFTHYEAROFTHE
CAPTIVITYOFTHEKI
NGJOACHIM ANDCA
METHEWORDOFTHELDTOE
ZEKIELTHESONOFBUZITHE
PRIESTINTHELANDOFTHECHALDEESB
YTHERIVERCHO
BARANDUPONMEWAS
THEHANDOFTHELDANDILOOKEDANDLO
AWHIRLWNDCAMEOUTOF
THENORTHANDAGREATCLOUD
WITHIT

---

[1] Signor Zacagni's Letter to Dr. Grabe, dated Rome, Nov. 29. 1704, in Dr. Kennicott's Diss. ii. pp. 408—411. Michaelis, vol. ii. part i. pp. 341—350. Part ii. pp. 810—820. Hug's Introd. to the New Test. vol. i. pp. 262—272.

+ Ἰεζεκιηλ̄

+   +   +

Κ ΚΑΙΕΓΕΝΕΤΟΕΝΤΩΤΡΙΑ
ΚΟΣΤΩΕΤΕΙ ΤΕ ΤΑΡΤΩ
ΜΗΝΙΠΕΜΠΤΗΤΟΥΜΗΝΟΣ
ΚΑΙ ΕΓΩΗΜΗΝ ΕΝ ΜΕΣΩ
ΤΗΣ ΑΙΧΜΑΛΩΣΙΑΣ ΕΠΙΤΟΥ
ΠΟΤΑΜΟΥ ΤΟΥ ΧΟΒΑΡ ΚΑΙ
ΗΝΟΙΧΘΗΣΑΝ ΟΙ ΟΥΡΑΝΟΙ
ΚΑΙ ΕΙΔΟΝ ΟΡΑΣΕΙΣ ΘΥ ΠΕΜ
ΠΤΗ ΤΟΥ ΜΗΝΟΣ ΤΟΥΤΟ
ΤΟ ΕΤΟΣ ΤΟ ΠΕΜΠΤΟΝ ΤΗΣ
ΑΙΧΜΑΛΩΣΙΑΣ ΤΟΥ ΒΑΣΙ
ΛΕΩΣ ΙΩΑΚΕΙΜ ΚΑΙ ΕΓΕ
ΝΕΤΟ ΛΟΓΟΣ ΚΥ ΠΡΟΣ ΙΕ
ΖΕΚΙΗΛ ΥΙΟΝ ΒΟΥΖΕΙ ΤΟΝ
ΙΕΡΕΑ ΕΝ ΓΗ ΧΑΛΔΑΙΩΝ ΕΠΙΤΟΥ ΠΟΤΑΜΟΥ ΤΟΥ ΧΟ
ΒΑΡ ΚΑΙ ΕΓΕΝΕΤΟ ΕΠΕΜΕ
ΧΕΙΡ ΚΥ ΚΑΙ ΙΔΟΝ ΚΑΙ ΙΔΟΥ
ΠΝΑ ΕΞΑΙΡΟΝ ΗΡΧΕΤΟ ΑΠΟ
ΒΟΡΡΑ ΚΑΙ ΝΕΦΕΛΗ ΜΕΓΑ
ΛΗ ΕΝ ΑΥΤΩ

FAC-SIMILE of Ezekiel, I v 1. 4. 5. of the CODEX
VATICANUS *made in the year 1704 by Sig.*
Zacagni for D. Grabe, and preserved among
his Manuscripts in the BODLEIAN LIBRARY

No fac-simile edition (like that of the Alexandrian New Testament edited by Dr. Woide, and of the Old Testament by the Rev. H. H. Baber) has ever been executed of the precious Vatican manuscript. During the pontificate of Pius VI. the Abate Spoletti contemplated the publication of it, for which purpose he delivered a memorial to the Pope. No *public* permission was ever given: and though the Pontiff's private judgment was not unfavourable to the undertaking, yet, as his indulgence would have been no security against the vengeance of the inquisition, Spoletti was obliged to abandon his design.[1] It is, however, but just to add, that no obstacles were thrown in the way of the collation of manuscripts in the Vatican, for Dr. Holmes's critical edition of the Septuagint version, of which some account will be found in pp. 37, 38. of the Appendix to this volume.

§ 3. ACCOUNT OF MANUSCRIPTS (ENTIRE OR IN PART) CONTAINING THE SEPTUAGINT OR GREEK VERSION OF THE OLD TESTAMENT.

I. *The Codex Cottonianus.* — II. *The Codex Sarravianus.* — III. *The Codex Colbertinus* — IV. *The Codex Cæsareus, Argenteus, or Argenteo-Purpureus.* — V *The Codex Ambrosianus.* — VI. *The Codex Coislinianus.* — VII. *The Codex Basiliano-Vaticanus.* — VIII. *The Codex Turicensis.*

IT is not precisely known what number of manuscripts of the Greek version of the Old Testament are extant. The highest number of those collated by the late Rev. Dr. Holmes, for his splendid edition of this version, is one hundred and thirty-five. *Nine* of them are described, as being written in uncial characters, and as having furnished him with the most important of the various readings, with which his first volume is enriched: besides these he has noticed *sixty-three* others, written in cursive or small characters, and which have likewise furnished him with various lections. Of these manuscripts the following are more particularly worthy of notice, on account of their rarity and value.[2]

I. The CODEX COTTONIANUS is not only the most antient but the most correct manuscript that is extant. It was originally brought from Philippi by two Greek bishops, who presented it to King Henry VIII. whom they informed that tradition reported it to have been the identical copy, which had belonged to the celebrated Origen, who lived in the former half of the third century. Queen Elizabeth gave it to Sir John Fortescue, her preceptor in Greek, who, desirous of preserving it for posterity, placed it in the Cottonian library. This precious manuscript was almost destroyed by the calamitous fire which consumed Cotton House at Westminster, in the year 1731. Eighteen fragments are all that now remain, and of these, both the leaves, and consequently the writing in a just proportion, are con-

---

[1] Michaelis, vol ii. part i p 181, part ii. pp. 644, 645.
[2] Our descriptions are chiefly abridged from Dr Holmes's Præfatio ad Pentateuchum, cap. ii prefixed to the first volume of his critical edition of the Septuagint version published at Oxford, in 1798, folio.

tracted into a less compass; so that what were large are now small capitals. These fragments are at present deposited in the British Museum.[1]

In its original state, the Codex Cottonianus contained one hundred and sixty-five leaves, in the quarto size; it is written on vellum, in uncial characters, the line running along the whole width of the page, and each line consisting, in general, of twenty-seven, rarely of thirty letters. These letters are almost every where of the same length, excepting that at the end of a line they are occasionally somewhat less, and in some instances are interlined or written over the line. Like all other very antient manuscripts, it has no accents or spirits, nor any distinction of words, verses, or chapters. The words are, for the most part, written at full length, with the exception of the well known and frequent abbreviations of $\overline{KC}$, $\overline{KN}$, $\overline{\Theta C}$, $\overline{\Theta N}$, for Κυριος and Κυριον, *Lord*, and Θεος, Θεον, *God*. Certain consonants, vowels, and diphthongs are also interchanged.[2] The coherence of the Greek Text is very close, except where it is divided by the interposition of the very curious paintings or illuminations with which this manuscript is decorated. These pictures were two hundred and fifty in number, and consist of compositions within square frames, of one or of several figures, in general not exceeding two inches in height; and these frames, which are four inches square, are occasionally divided into two compartments. The heads are perhaps too large, but the attitudes and draperies have considerable merit: and they are by competent judges preferred to the miniatures that adorn the Vienna manuscript, which is noticed in pp. 128, 129. *infra*. Twenty-one fragments of these illuminations were engraved, in 1744, on two large folio plates, at the expense of the Society of Antiquaries of London. It is observed by Mr. Planta, the present principal librarian of the British Museum, that more fragments must have been preserved than the eighteen which now remain, because none of those engraved are now to be met with.[3] On an examination of the Codex Cottonianus, with a view to take a fac-simile of some one of its fragments for this work, they were found in a nearly pulverised and carbonised state, so that no accurate copy could be made. The annexed engraving therefore is copied from that of the Antiquarian Society.[4] The subject on the right-hand of Plate II. is Jacob delivering his son Benjamin to his brethren, that they may go a second time into Egypt, and buy corn for himself and his family. The passage of Genesis, which it is intended to illustrate, is ch. xliii. 13, 14., of which the following is a representation in ordinary Greek characters; the words preserved being in capital letters.

---

[1] Catalogus Bibliothecæ Cottonianæ, p. 365. (folio, 1802.) Casley's Catalogue of MSS. in the King's library, pp. viii. ix.
[2] These permutations were a fruitful source of errors in manuscripts. Some instances of them are given *infra*, Chap V. § III.
[3] Catalogus Bibliothecæ Cottonianæ, p. 365.
[4] Vetusta Monumenta, quæ ad Rerum Britannicarum Memoriam Conservandam Societas Antiquariorum sumptu suo edenda curavit. Londini, 1747, folio, tom. i. Pl. LXVII. No VI et VII.

ἘΞΗΛΘΕΝ ΔΕ ΒΑϹΙΛΕΥϹ ϹΟΔΟΜΩΝ

FAC SIMILE

Sect. III. § 3.] *Containing the Septuagint Version.* 127

ΚΑΙΤΟΝΑΔΕΛΦΟΝΫ́ΜΩν λαβετε και ανα
ΣΤΑΝΤΕΣΚΑΤΑΒΗΤΕΠΡΟΣ τον ανϑρω
ΠΟΝ ΟΔΕ̄ΘΣΜΟΥΔΩΗ υμιν χαριν εναν
ΤΙΟΝΤΟΤΑΝΘΡΩΠΟΤ·ΚΑΙ αποστειλαι τον
ΑΔΕΛΦΟΝΫ́ΜΩΝΤΟΝ ενα και τον Βενι
ΑΜΕΙΝ ΕΓΩΜΕΝΓΑΡΚΑΘαπερ ἡ τεκνω
ΜΑΙΗΤΕΚΝΩΜΑΙ.

In English, thus:
ALSOYOURBROTHER take, and a
RISEGOAGAINUNTOthe ma
N·ANDMAYG͞DGIVE you favour be
FORETHEMANTHAT he may send back
YOURBROTHER and Benj
AMIN ASFORMEAS I have been be
REAVEDOFCHILDRENIAM bereaved.

The subject on the left-hand of the same plate is Joseph's interview with his brethren in his own house, on their return into Egypt. It illustrates Genesis xliii. 30, 31, and is as follows:

' ταραχϑη δε Ιωσηφ· συνεσ
ΤΡΕΦΕΤΟΓΑΡΤΑΕΝΤΕΡΑ αυτου
ΤΩΑΔΕΛΦΩΑΥΤΟΥ·ΚΑΙΕΖΗτει κλαυσχι·
ΕΙΣΕΛΘΩΝΔΕΕΙΣΤΟΤΑΜΕΙον εκλαυσ
ΕΝΕΚΕΙ·ΚΑΙΝΙΨΑΜΕΝΟΣΤΟ προσωπον
εΞΕΛΘΩΝΕΝΕΚΡΑΤΕΥΣΑΤΟ·και ιπε
Παραϑετε αρτους.

In English, thus:
And Joseph was discomposed·
FORhisBOWELSYEARNED
TOWARDSHISBROTHER·ANDheSOUGht *where* to weep·
ANDENTERINGINTOHISCHAMBeι, he we
PTTHERE·ANDWHENHEHADWASHED his face, *and*
cOMEFORTHHERESTRAINED himself· and said
set on bread.

The larger Greek characters at the foot of Plate I. are copied from the third plate of Mr. Astle's work on the Origin of Writing; they exhibit the four first words of Gen. xiv. 17. of the same size as in the Codex Cottonianus Geneseos, before the calamitous fire above noticed. The loss of the consumed parts of this precious manuscript would have been irreparable, had not extracts of its various readings been made by different learned men, which have been preserved to the present time. Thus the collations of it by Archbishop Usher and Patrick Young, in the middle of the seventeenth century, are printed in the sixth volume of Bishop Walton's Polyglott Edition of the Bible. Archbishop Usher's autograph collation is deposited in the Bodleian Library, among the other MSS. of that distinguished prelate. The principal various readings, noted by Dr. Gale, towards the close of the same century, are entered in the margin of an Aldine edition of the Greek Version, which subsequently belonged to the late Dr. Kennicott. But the most valuable collation is that made in the year 1703, by Dr. Grabe, who was deeply skilled in palæography, and bequeathed by him to the Bodleian Library, whence the late Rev. Dr. Owen published it at London, in 1778, in an octavo volume. Dr. Holmes has chiefly followed Grabe's extract of various readings, in his critical edition of the Septuagint, but he has occasionally availed himself of Archbishop Usher's collation.[1]

The Codex Cottonianus is the most antient manuscript of any part of the Old Testament that is extant. It is acknowledged to have been written towards the end of the *fourth*, or in the *beginning of the fifth* century; and it seldom agrees with any manuscript or printed edition, except the Codex Alexandrinus, which has been described in pp. 116—122. of the present volume. There are, according to Dr. Holmes, at least twenty instances in which this manuscript expresses the meaning of the *original* Hebrew more accurately than any other exemplars.

II. III. The Codices SARRAVIANUS (now in the Public Library of the Academy at Leyden), and COLBERTINUS, (formerly numbered 3084 among the Colbert MSS., but at present deposited in the Royal Library at Paris,) are distinct parts of the same manuscript, and contain the Pentateuch, and the books of Joshua and Judges. The Codex Sarravianus is defective in those very leaves, viz. seven in Exodus, thirteen in Leviticus, and two in Numbers, which are found in the Colbertine manuscript; the writing of which, as well as the texture of the vellum, and other peculiarities, agree so closely with those of the Codex Sarravianus, as to demonstrate their perfect identity. These manuscripts are neatly written on thin vellum, in uncial letters, with which some round characters are intermixed, the ink of which is beginning to turn yellow. The contractions or abbreviations, permutations of letters, &c. are the same which are found in the Codex Cottonianus. These two Codices, as they are termed, may be referred to the fifth or sixth century. To some paragraphs of the book of Leviticus, titles or heads have been prefixed, evidently by a later hand.

IV. The CODEX CÆSAREUS (which is also frequently called the CODEX ARGENTEUS, and CODEX ARGENTEO-PURPUREUS, because it is written in *silver letters* on *purple vellum*,) is preserved in the Imperial Library at Vienna. The letters are beautiful but thick, partly round and partly square. In size, it approximates to the quarto form: it consists of twenty-six leaves only, the first twenty-four of which contain a fragment of the book of Genesis, viz. from chapter iii 4. to chap. viii. 24.: the two last contain a fragment of St. Luke's Gospel, viz. chapter xxiv. verses 21—49. In Wetstein's critical edition of the Greek New Testament, these two leaves are denoted by the letter N. The first twenty-four leaves are ornamented with

---

[1] Another collation was made by the eminent critic, Crusius, who highly commended the Codex Cottonianus in two dissertations published by him at Gottingen in 1744 and 1745. Crusius's collation subsequently fell into the hands of Breitinger, the editor of the beautiful edition of the Septuagint published at Zurich in 1730—1733. It is not at present known what has become of this collation.

forty-eight curious miniature paintings, which Lambecius refers to the age of Constantine; but, from the shape of the letters, this manuscript is rather to be assigned to the end of the fifth or the beginning of the sixth century. In these pictures, the divine prescience and providence are represented by a hand proceeding out of a cloud: and they exhibit interesting specimens of the habits, customs, and amusements of those early times.[1] From the occurrence of the words κιτωνας (*Kitōnas*) instead of χιτωνας (*cHitōnas*), and Αβιμελεκ (*Abimeleκ*) instead of Αβιμελεχ (*AbimelecH*), Dr. Holmes is of opinion that this manuscript was written by dictation. Vowels, consonants, &c. are interchanged in the same manner as in the Codex Cottonianus, and similar abbreviations are likewise found in it. In some of its readings the Codex Cæsareus resembles the Alexandrian manuscript. In his letter to the Bishop of Durham, published in 1795, and containing a specimen of his proposed new edition of the Septuagint version with various lections[2], Dr. Holmes printed the *entire text* of this MS which had been collated and revised for him by Professor Alter, of Vienna ; and he also gave an engraved fac-simile of the whole of its seventh page. From this fac-simile our specimen is copied in Plate 5. No. 2. It is the seventeenth verse of the fourteenth chapter of the book of Genesis, and runs thus in ordinary Greek characters.

ΕΞΗΛΘΕΝΔΕΒΑΣΙΛΕΤΣΣΟΔΟΜΩΝΕΙΣΣΤΝ
ΑΝΤΗΣΙΝΑΥΤΩΜΕΤΑΤΟΑΝΑΣΤΡΕΨΑΙΑΥΤΟ
ΑΠΟΤΗΣΚΟΠΗΣΤΩΝΒΑΣΙΛΕΩΝ·ΕΙΣΤΗΝ
ΚΟΙΛΑΔΑΤΗΝΣΑΤΗ :

In English, thus, as nearly as the idiom of our language will allow :

ANDTHEKINGOFSODOMWENTOUT·TOME
ETHIMAFTERHISRETURN
FROMTHESLAUGHTEROFTHEKINGS·TOTHE
VALLEYOFSAVE :

V. The CODEX AMBROSIANUS derives its name from the Ambrosian Library at Milan, where it is preserved: it is probably as old as the seventh century. This manuscript is a large square quarto (by Montfaucon erroneously termed a folio), written in three columns in a

---

[1] The whole forty-eight embellishments are engraven in the third volume of Lambecius's Commentariorum de augustissima bibliotheca Cæsarea-Vindobonensi, libri viii. (Vindobonæ, 1665—1679, folio, 8 vols.) They are also republished in Nesselius's Breviarum et Supplementum Commentariorum Bibliothecæ Cæsareæ-Vindobonensis (Vindobonæ, 6 parts, in 2 vols folio), vol. i pp. 55—102. . and again in the third book or volume of Kollarius's second edition of Lambecius's Commentarii (Vindobonæ, 1766—1782, 8 vols. folio.) Montfaucon's fac-simile of the characters (Palæographia Græca, p. 194) has been made familiar to English readers by a portion of it, which has been copied by Mr. Astle (on the Origin of Writing, plate iii. p 70) but his engraver is said by Dr Dibdin (Bibliographical Decameron, vol i. p xliv) to have deviated from the original, and to have executed the fac-simile in too heavy a manner. Dr D has himself given a most beautiful fac simile of one of the pictures of this MS in the third volume of his Bibliographical and Antiquarian Tour in France and Germany

[2] Honorabili et admodum Reverendo, Shute Barrington, LL. D. Episcopo Dunelmensi, Epistola, complexa Genesin ex Codice Purpureo-Argenteo Cæsareo-Vindobonensi expressam, et Testamenti Veteris Græci, Versionis Septuaginta-viralis cum Variis Lectionibus denuo edendi, Specimen. Dedit Robertus Holmes, S. T. P e Collegio Novo, et nuperrime Publicus in Academia Oxoniensi Poetices Prælector. Oxonii, MDCCXCV folio.

round uncial character. The accents and spirits however have evidently been added by a later hand.

VI. The CODEX COISLINIANUS originally belonged to M. Seguier, Chancellor of France in the middle of the seventeenth century, a munificent collector of biblical manuscripts, from whom it passed, by hereditary succession, to the Duc de Coislin. From his library it was transferred into that of the monastery of Saint Germain-Des-Prez, and thence into the Royal Library at Paris, where it now is. According to Montfaucon, by whom it is particularly described [1], it is in quarto, and was written in a beautiful round uncial character, in the *sixth*, or at the latest in the *seventh* century. But the accents and spirits have been added by a comparatively recent hand. It consists of two hundred and twenty-six leaves of vellum, and formerly contained the *octateuch*, (that is the five books of Moses, and those of Joshua, Judges, and Ruth,) the two books of Samuel and the two books of Kings, but it is now considerably mutilated by the injuries of time. The copyist was totally ignorant of Hebrew, as is evident from the following inscription, which he has placed at the beginning of the book of Genesis:— Βαρησεθ παρα Εβραιοις, οπερ εστιν ερμενευομενον, λογοι ημερων,— that is, Βαρησεθ *in Hebrew, which being interpreted is* (or means) *the Words of Days*, or the *history of the days*, i. e the history of the six days' work of creation. This word Βαρησεθ (*Bareseth*) is no other than the Hebrew word בראשית (BERESHITH) *in the beginning*, which is the first word in the book of Genesis. Montfaucon further observed that this manuscript contained readings very similar to those of the Codex Alexandrinus; and his remark is confirmed by Dr. Holmes, so far as respects the Pentateuch.

VII. The CODEX BASILIANO-VATICANUS is the last of the MSS. in uncial characters collated by Dr. H. It formerly belonged to a monastery in Calabria, whence it was transferred by Pietro Memniti, superior of the monks of the order of Saint Basil at Rome into the library of his monastery; and thence it passed into the papal library of the Vatican, where it is now numbered 2,106. It is written on vellum, in oblong leaning uncial characters; and according to Montfaucon was executed in the ninth century. Dr. Holmes considers it to be a manuscript of considerable value and importance, which, though in many respects it corresponds with the other MSS. collated by him, yet contains some valuable lections which are no where else to be found. On this account it is to be regretted that the Codex Basiliano-Vaticanus is imperfect both at the beginning and end.

VIII. The CODEX TURICENSIS is numbered 262 in Mr. Parson's catalogue of MSS. collated for the book of Psalms, in his continuation of the magnificent edition of the Septuagint commenced by the late Rev. Dr. Holmes. It is a quarto manuscript of the book of Psalms, the writing of which proves it to have been executed at least in the eleventh century, if not much earlier; and consists of two hundred and twenty-two leaves of extremely thin purple vellum; and the silver characters and golden initial letters are in many parts so de-

---

[1] Bibliotheca Coisliniana, olim Seguieriana, folio, Paris, 1732.

cayed by the consuming hand of time, as to be with difficulty legible. The portions of the psalms wanting in this MS. are Psal. i.—xxv.; xxx. 1.—xxxvi. 20.; xli. 5.—xliii. 2.; lviii. 13.—lix. 4.; lxiv. 11. lxxi. 4.; xcii. 3.—xciii. 7.; and xcvi. 12.—xcvii. 8. Several of the antient ecclesiastical hymns, which form part of this MS., are also mutilated. It is, however, consolatory to know that those portions of the psalms which are deficient in the Codices Alexandrinus and Vaticanus, may be supplied from the Codex Turicensis [1]: and this circumstance, it should seem, occasioned the generally accurate traveller, Mr. Coxe (whose error has been implicitly copied by succeeding writers) to state that the MS. here described once formed part of the Codex Vaticanus.[2]

§ 4. ACCOUNT OF THE PRINCIPAL MANUSCRIPTS CONTAINING THE NEW TESTAMENT ENTIRE OR IN PART.

I. *The Codex Cottonianus.* (*Titus C. XV.*) — II. *The Codex Bezæ, or Cantabrigiensis.* — III. *The Codex Ephremi.* — IV. *The Codex Claromontanus.* — V. *The Codex Argenteus.* — *MSS. of the Gothic Version discovered by signor Mai.* — VI. *The Codex Rescriptus of St. Matthew's Gospel in Trinity College, Dublin.* — VII. *The Codex Laudianus, 3.* — VIII. *The Codex Coislinianus.* — IX. *The Codex Boernerianus* — X *The Codex Cyprius.* — XI *The Codex Basileensis E.* — XII. *The Codex San-Germanensis.* — XIII. *The Codex Augiensis.* — XIV. *The Codex Harleianus, 5598.* — XV. *The Codex Regius or Stephani η.* — XVI. *The Codex Uffenbachianus.* — XVII. *The Codices Manners-Suttoniani.* — XVIII. *The Codices Mosquenses.* — XIX. *The Codex Brixiensis.* — XX. *Other MSS. written in small characters and deserving of especial notice, viz.* 1. *The Codex Basileensis,* 1. — 2. *The Codex Berolinensis.* — 3. *The Codex Corsendoncensis.* — 4. *The Codex Montfortianus* — 5. *The Codex Meermannianus.* — 6. *The Codex Regius,* 50.—7. *The Codex Leicestrensis.*—8. *The Codex Vindobonensis.*— 9. *The Codex Ebnerianus.* — 10. *The Codex Ottobonianus.* — XXI. *Notice of the Collations of the Barberini and Velesian Manuscripts.*

THE autographs, or manuscripts of the New Testament, which were written either by the apostles themselves, or by amanuenses under their immediate inspection [3], have long since perished; and we have no information whatever concerning their history. The pretended autograph of St. Mark's Gospel at Venice is now known to be nothing more than a copy of the Latin version [4], and no existing manuscripts of the New Testament can be traced higher than the fourth century; and most of them are of still later date. Some contain the whole of the New Testament; others comprise particular

---

[1] The preceding description of the Codex Turicensis is abridged from Professor Breitinger's scarce tract, addressed to Cardinal Quirini, and intitled "De antiquissimo Turicensis Bibliothecæ Græco Psalmorum Libro, Epistola Turici. 1748." 4to.

[2] See Coxe's Travels in Switzerland, in Pinkerton's Collection of Voyages and Travels, vol vi p 672, 4to

[3] Saint Paul dictated most of his epistles to amanuenses; but, to prevent the circulation of spurious letters, he wrote the concluding benediction with his own hand. Compare Rom xvi. 22 Gal. vi. 11 and 2 Thess. iii. 17, 18. with 1 Cor. xvi. 21.

[4] See Vol. IV. Part II. Ch. II. Sect. III. § V. *infra*

books or fragments of books; and there are several which contain, not whole books arranged according to their usual order, but detached portions or lessons (αναγνωσεις), appointed to be read on certain days in the public service of the Christian church; from which again whole books have been put together. These are called *Lectionaria*, and are of two sorts: 1. *Evangelisteria*, containing lessons from the four Gospels; and, 2. *Apostolos*, comprising lessons from the Acts and Epistles, and sometimes only the Epistles themselves. When a manuscript contains both parts, Michaelis says that it is called *Apostolo-Evangelion*. Forty-six Evangelisteria were collated by Griesbach for the four Gospels of his edition of the New Testament, and seven Lectionaria or Apostoli, for the Acts and Epistles.[1] Some manuscripts, again, have not only the Greek text, but are accompanied with a version, which is either interlined, or in a parallel column; these are called *Codices Bilingues*. The greatest number is in Greek and Latin; and the Latin version is, in general, one of those which existed before the time of Jerome. As there are extant Syriac-Arabic and Gothic-Latin manuscripts, Michaelis thinks it probable that there formerly existed Greek-Syriac, Greek-Gothic, and other manuscripts of that kind, in which the original and some version were written together.[2] Where a transcriber, instead of copying from one and the same antient manuscript, selects from several those readings, which appear to him to be the best, the manuscript so transcribed is termed a *Codex Criticus*.

Besides the Alexandrian and Vatican manuscripts which have been already described, the following are the principal manuscripts of the New Testament, of every description, which are more peculiarly worthy of notice.

I. The Codex Cottonianus (Titus C. XV.), preserved in the Cottonian Library in the British Museum, is a most precious fragment of the four Gospels, written in silver letters on a faded purple ground. It is one of the oldest (if not the most antient) manuscript of any part of the New Testament that is extant;' and contains,

(1.) Part of Saint Matthew's Gospel, beginning at Chapter XXVI. v 57. and ending with v. 65. of the same Chapter.

(2.) Part of the same Gospel, beginning at Chapter XXVII. v. 26. and ending with v. 34 of the same Chapter.

(3.) Part of Saint John's Gospel, beginning at Chapter XIV v. 2. and ending with v. 10. of the same Gospel.

(4.) Part of the same Gospel, beginning at Chapter XV. v. 15. and ending with v. 22. of the same Chapter.

In the accompanying Plate 3. No. 1. we have given a fac-simile of John xiv. 6. from this manuscript, of which the following is a

---

[1] Griesbach, Proleg ad Nov Test tom. i. pp. cxix —cxxii. In the second volume of his Symbolæ Criticæ, (pp 3—30, Dr G. has described eleven important Evangelisteria, which had either been not collated before, or were newly examined and collated by himself Michaelis, vol ii. part i pp 161—163 part ii. 639, 640. The Rev. Dr. Dibdin has described a superb Evangelisterium, and has given fac-similes of its ornaments, in the first volume of his Bibliographical Decameron, pp xcii —xciv. This precious manuscript is supposed to have been written at the close of the eleventh, or early in the thirteenth century. The illuminations are executed with singular beauty and delicacy.

[2] Introduction to the New Test. vol. ii. part 1 p. 164.

FAC SIMILES.

1 Of the Codex Cottonianus (Titus CXV)
John XIV 6

ΛΕΓΕΙΑΥΤωΟΪ
ΕΓωΕΙΜΕΙΗΟ
ΔΟΣΚΑΙΗΑΛΗ
ΘΙΑΚΑΙΗΖωΗ
ΟΥΔΙΣΕΡΧΕΤα
ΠΡΟΣΤΟΝΠΡα
ΕΙΜΗΔΙΕΜΟΥ

2 Of the Codex N° 5

ΝΟ
ΡΑΚ
ΟΜΟΝ
ΟωΝΙ
ΠΟΝΤ
ΝΟΣΕΖ

3 Of the Codex Cyprius

ΟΨὲΔὲϹΑΒΒΑΤωΝ·ΤΗ ΙΙΦωϹΚΟΥϹΗΕ
ϹΑΒΒΑΤωΝ·ΗΛΦΕΝΜ ΡΙΑΗΜΑΓΔΑΛΗ

Fac-simile of the Codex Bezae a MS of the Four Gospels and Acts of the Apostles preserved in the University Library at Cambridge)   Matt chap V v 1,2,3

ΚΔ ΙΔωΝΔΕΤΟΥϹΟΧΛΟΥϹ·ΑΝΕΒΗΕΙϹΤΟΟΡΟϹ
ΚΑΙΚΑΘΙϹΑΝΤΟϹΑΥΤΟΥ·ΠΡΟϹΗΛΘΟΝΑΥΤω

ΚΕ ΟΙΜΑΘΗΤΑΙΑΥΤΟΥ·ΚΑΙΔΙΑΝΟΙΞΑϹΤΟϹΤΟΜΑΑΥΤΟΥ
ΕΔΙΔΑΞΕΝΑΥΤΟΥϹΛΕΓωΝ

Κϛ ΜΑΚΑΡΙΟΙΟΙΠΤωΧΟΙΠΝΙ·ΟΤΙΑΥΤωΝΕϹΤΙΝ
ΗΒΑϹΙΛΕΙΑΤωΝΟΥΡΑΝωΝ

---

uidensauteonturbasascenditinmonteon
etsedenteeo·accesseruntadeum
discipulieius·eraperiensossuum
docuiteosdicens

beatipauperesspu·quoniamipsorumest
regnumcaelorum

representation in ordinary Greek characters, with the corresponding literal English version.

ΛΕΓΕΙΑΥΤΩΟΙΣ	SAITHUNTOHIMJs
ΕΓΩΕΙΜΕΙΗΟ	IAMTHEW
ΔΟΣΚΑΙΗΑΛΗ	AYANDTHETRU
ΘΙΑΚΑΙΗΖΩΗ	THANDTHELIFE
ΟΥΔΙΣΕΡΧΕΤΑΙ	NOMANCOMETH
ΠΡΟΣΤΟΝΠΤΡΑ	UNTOTHEFTHR
ΕΙΜΗΔΙΕΜΟΥ	BUTBYME

The words ΙΗΣΟΥΣ (*Jesus*), ΘΕΟΣ (*God*), ΚΥΡΙΟΣ (*Lord*), ΥΙΟΣ (*Son*), and ΣΩΤΗΡ (*Saviour*), are written in letters of gold; the three first with contractions similar to those in the Codex Alexandrinus, and Codex Bezæ. This precious fragment is acknowledged to have been executed at the end of the fourth, or at the latest in the beginning of the fifth century.

II. The CODEX BEZÆ, also called the CODEX CANTABRIGIENSIS, is a Greek and Latin manuscript, containing the four Gospels and the Acts of the Apostles. It is deposited in the public library of the university of Cambridge, to which it was presented by the celebrated Theodore Beza, in the year 1581. Of this manuscript, which is written on vellum, in quarto, without accents or marks of aspiration, or spaces between the words, the accompanying fac-simile will convey an idea. It represents the first three verses of the fifth chapter of Saint Matthew's Gospel, which are copied from Dr. Kipling's facsimile edition of the Codex Bezæ, published at Cambridge in 1793, of which an account is given in pp. 20, 21. of the Appendix to this volume. We have placed the Latin *under* the Greek, in order to bring the whole within the compass of an octavo page. The following is a literal English version of this fac-simile.

Matt. V. 1—3.
ANDSEEINGTHEMULTITUDESHEWENTUPINTOAMOUNTAIN
ANDWHENHEWASSETDOWN·CAMETOHIM
HISDISCIPLES·ANDOPENINGHISMOUTH
HETAUGHTTHEMSAYING

BLESSED*ARE*THEPOORINSPT.†FORTHEIRSIS
THEKINGDOMOFHEAVEN.

Sixty-six leaves of this manuscript are much torn and mutilated, and ten of them have been supplied by a later transcriber.

The Codex Bezæ is noted with the letter D. by Wetstein and Griesbach. In the Greek it is defective, from the beginning to Matt. i. 20., and in the Latin to Matt. i. 12. In the Latin it has likewise the following chasms, viz. Matt. vi. 20.—ix. 2.; Matt. xxvii. 1—12.; John i. 16.—ii. 26.; Acts viii. 29.—x. 14.; xxii. 10—20.;

---

† Contracted for SPIRIT The Greek is ΠΝΙ, ΠΝΕΥΜΑΤΙ, and the Latin SPU, for SPIRITU.

and from xxii. 29. to the end. The Gospels are arranged in the usual order of the Latin manuscripts, Matthew, John, Luke, Mark. It has a considerable number of corrections, some of which have been noticed by Dr. Griesbach; and some of the pages, containing Matt. iii 8—16. John xviii. 13.—xx. 13. and Mark xv. to the end, are written by a later hand, which Wetstein refers to the tenth century, but Griesbach to the twelfth. The Latin version is that which was in use before the time of Jerome, and is usually called the Old Italic or Ante-Hieronymian version. In the margin of the Greek part of the manuscript there are inserted the Ammonian sections, evidently by a later hand; and the words αρχη, τελος, και λεγε, ωδε σηκε, are occasionally interspersed, indicating the beginning and end of the Αναγνωσματα, or lessons read in the church. The subjects discussed in the Gospels are sometimes written in the margin, sometimes at the top of the page. But all these notations are manifestly the work of several persons and of different ages. The date of this manuscript has been much contested. Those critics who give it the least antiquity, assign it to the sixth or seventh century. Wetstein supposed it to be of the fifth century. Michaelis was of opinion, that of all the manuscripts now extant, this is the most antient. Dr. Kipling, the editor of the Cambridge fac-simile, thought it much older than the Alexandrian manuscript, and that it must have been written in the second century. On comparing it with Greek inscriptions of different ages, Bishop Marsh is of opinion that it cannot have been written later than the sixth century, and that it may have been written even two or three centuries earlier: and he finally considers it prior to all the manuscripts extant, except the Codex Vaticanus, and refers it to the fifth century, which, perhaps, is the true date, if an opinion may be hazarded where so much uncertainty prevails.

Wetstein was of opinion, from *eleven* coincidences which he thought he had discovered, that this was the identical manuscript collated at Alexandria in 616, for the Philoxenian or later Syriac version of the New Testament; but this is a groundless supposition. It is, however, worthy of remark, that many of the readings by which the Codex Bezæ is distinguished are found in the Syriac, Coptic, Sahidic, and in the margin of the Philoxenian-Syriac version. As the readings of this manuscript frequently agree with the Latin versions before the time of St. Jerome, and with the Vulgate or present Latin translation, Wetstein was of opinion that the Greek text was altered from the Latin version, or, in other words, that the writer of the Codex Bezæ departed from the lections of the Greek manuscript or manuscripts whence he copied, and introduced in their stead, from some Latin version, readings which were warranted by no Greek manuscript. This charge Semler, Michaelis, Griesbach, and Bishop Marsh have endeavoured to refute; and their verdict has been generally received. Matthæi, however, revived the charge of Wetstein, and considered the text as extremely corrupt, and suspected that some Latin monk, who was but indifferently skilled in Greek, wrote in the margin of his New Testament various passages from the Greek and Latin fathers, which seemed to refer to particular passages. He further thought that this monk had noted the differences occurring in some Greek and Latin manuscripts of the New Testament, and added parallel passages of Scripture: and that from this *farrago* either the monk himself, or some other person, manufactured his text (whether foolishly or fraudulently is uncertain), of which the Codex Bezæ is a copy. But this *suspicion* of Matthæi has been little regarded in Germany, where he incurred the antipathy of the most eminent biblical critics, by vilifying the sources of various readings from which he had it not in his power to draw, when he began to publish his edition of the New Testament; giving to the Codex Bezæ, the Codex Claromontanus (noticed in pp. 137, 138. *infra*), and other manuscripts of unquestionable antiquity, the appellation of *Editio Scurrilis*.[1] Bishop Middleton considers the judgment of Michaelis as approximating very near to the truth, and has given a collation of numerous passages of the received text with the Codex Bezæ; and the result of his examination, which does not admit of abridgment, is, that the Codex Bezæ, though a most venerable remain of antiquity, is not to be considered, in a critical view, as of much authority. He accounts for the goodness of its readings, considered with regard to the *sense*, by the natural supposition of the great antiquity of the manuscript, which was the basis of the Codex Bezæ; but while its latinising is admitted, he contends that we have no reason to infer that its readings, considered in the same light, are therefore faulty. The learned prelate concludes with subscribing to the opinion of Matthæi somewhat modified. He believes that no fraud was intended; but only that the critical possessor of the basis filled its margin with glosses and readings chiefly from the Latin, being a Christian of the Western Church; and that the whole collection of Latin passages was translated into Greek, and substituted in the text by some one who had a high opinion of their value, and who was better skilled in caligraphy than in the Greek and Latin languages.[2] The arguments and evidences adduced by Bishop Middleton, we believe, are by many, at least in England, considered so conclusive, that, though the antiquity of the manuscript is fully admitted, yet it must be deemed a latinising manuscript, and, consequently, is of comparatively little *critical* value.

At the time Beza presented this manuscript to the university of Cambridge, it had been in his possession about nineteen years; and in his letter to that learned body he says, that it was found in the monastery of Saint Irenæus at Lyons, where it had lain concealed for a long time. But how it came there, and in what place it was written, are questions concerning which nothing certain is known. The most generally received opinion is, that it was written in the west of Europe.

The Cambridge manuscript has been repeatedly collated by critical editors of the New Testament. Robert Stephens made extracts from it, though with no great accuracy, under the title of Codex β, for his edition of the Greek Testament, of 1550; as Beza also did

---

[1] Bp Marsh's Lectures, part ii. pp 30, 31.
[2] Bishop Middleton on the Greek Article, pp 677—598., first edition.

for his own edition published in 1582. Since it was sent to the university of Cambridge, it has been more accurately collated by Junius, whose extracts were used by Curcellæus and Father Morin. A fourth and more accurate collation of it was made, at the instigation of Archbishop Usher, and the extracts were inserted in the sixth volume of the London Polyglott, edited by Bishop Walton. Dr. Mill collated it a fifth and sixth time; but that his extracts are frequently defective, and sometimes erroneous, appears from comparing them with Wetstein's New Testament, and from a new collation which was made, about the year 1733, by Mr. Dickenson of Saint John's College; which is now preserved in the library of Jesus' College, where it is marked O, Θ, 2. Wetstein's extracts are also very incorrect, as appears from comparing them with the manuscript itself.[1]

A splendid fac-simile of the Codex Bezæ was published by the Rev. Dr. Kipling at Cambridge, under the patronage and at the expense of the university, in 1793, in 2 vols. atlas folio. Dr. Harwood regulated the text of the Gospels and Acts, in his edition of the Greek Testament, chiefly according to the readings of the Codex Bezæ; which was so highly valued by the learned but eccentric divine, Whiston, that in his "Primitive New Testament in English," (8vo. Stamford and London, 1745,) he has translated the four Gospels and Acts literally from this manuscript. Dr. A. Clarke, in his Commentary on the New Testament, has paid very particular attention to the readings of the Codex Bezæ.

III. The CODEX EPHREMI, or CODEX REGIUS, 1905., (at present 9.) by Wetstein and Griesbach noted with the letter C., is an invaluable Codex Rescriptus, written on vellum, and is of very high antiquity. The first part of this manuscript contains several Greek works of Ephrem the Syrian, written over some more antient writings which had been erased, though the traces are still visible, and in most places legible. These more antient writings were the entire Greek Bible. In the New Testament, there are very numerous chasms, which are specified by Wetstein, from whom they have been copied by Michaelis and Griesbach. The text is not divided into columns; the uncial characters are larger than those of the Codex Alexandrinus, without accents, and the words are not divided. There are large initial letters at the beginning of each section; and the text is sometimes divided into articles, not much larger than our verses. A small cross indicates the end of a division; a full point below a letter is equivalent to a comma, and in the middle to a semi-colon. The Gospels follow the divisons of Ammonius, and also have the τιτλοι, *à prima manu*; the sections of the epistles sometimes agree with the αναγνωσις or lessons occurring in the MSS. which are known to have been written in Egypt. The titles and subscriptions to the several books are very brief, without any of the additions which are sometimes found in the Codex Alexandrinus. The Codex Ephremi exhibits the text of the Alexan-

---

[1] Milli Prolegomena, §§ 1268—1273. Griesbach, Symbolæ Criticæ, tom. i. pp lv.—lxiv. Michaelis, vol. ii. part i. pp 228—242 and part ii. pp. 679—721. Hug's Introd vol. i. pp. 275—278.

drine Recension in its greatest purity, and numerous other indications of its Egyptian origin. In this manuscript the disputed verse, John v. 4., is written, not in the text, but as a marginal scholion. Wetstein conjectured, that this was one of the manuscripts that were collated at Alexandria in 616 with the new Syriac version; but of this there is no evidence. From a marginal note to Heb. viii. 7. the same critic also argued, that it was written before the institution of the feast of the Virgin Mary: that is, before the year 542. But his arguments are not considered as wholly decisive by Michaelis, who only asserts its great antiquity in general terms. Bishop Marsh pronounces it to be at least as antient as the seventh century; and Professor Hug considers it to be even older than the Codex Alexandrinus. The readings of the Codex Ephremi, like those of all other very antient manuscripts, are in favour of the Latin; but there is no satisfactory evidence that it has been corrupted from the Latin version. It has been altered by a critical collator, who, according to Griesbach, must have lived many years after the time when the manuscript was written, and who probably erased many of the antient readings. Kuster was the first who procured extracts from this manuscript for his edition of Dr. Mill's Greek Testament. Wetstein has collated it with very great accuracy, and the numerous readings he has quoted from it greatly enhance the value of his edition.[1]

IV. The CODEX CLAROMONTANUS, or REGIUS 2245., is a Greek-Latin manuscript of St. Paul's Epistles, found in the monastery of Clermont, in the diocese of Beauvais, and used by Beza, together with the Codex Cantabrigiensis, in preparing his edition of the New Testament. It follows the Western Recension, and is noted D. by Wetstein and Griesbach in the second volumes of their respective editions of the Greek Testament. Sabatier supposes it to have been written in the sixth century; Montfaucon places it in the seventh century; Griesbach thinks it was written in the sixth or seventh century, and Hug, in the eighth century. This manuscript is written on vellum in uncial characters, and with accents and marks of aspiration added by another hand, but of great antiquity. As it contains the Epistle to the Hebrews, which has been added by a later hand, it is supposed to have been written in the west of Europe. Dr. Mill contended that the Codex Claromontanus was the second part of the Codex Bezæ; but this opinion has been confuted by Wetstein, who has shown that the former is by no means connected with the latter, as appears from the difference of their form, their orthography, and the nature of the vellum on which they are written. Bishop Marsh adds, on the authority of a gentleman who had examined both manuscripts, that the Codex Claromontanus contains only *twenty-one* lines in each page, while the Cambridge manuscript contains *thirty-three* lines in a page; the abbreviations in the two manu-

---

[1] Wetstenh Nov. Test. tom. i. Proleg. pp. 27, 28. Griesbach's Symb. Crit tom. i. pp. i.—liv. and Nov Test. tom. i. pp. ci. cii Michaelis, vol. ii. part i. pp 258—260. part ii pp. 737, 738. Hug's Introduction, vol. i. pp 271—273 See also the Palæographia Græca of Montfaucon (pp. 213, 214.) who has given a fac-simile of this manuscript, which Professor Hug says is not equal to the elegance of this codex.

scripts are also different. The Codex Claromontanus, like other Greek-Latin manuscripts, has been accused of having a Greek Text, that has been altered from the Latin; but this charge has been satisfactorily refuted by Dr. Semler. The *migrations* of this manuscript are somewhat remarkable. From the hands of Beza it went into the Putean library, which derived its name from the family of De Puy. Jacques De Puy, who was librarian to the king of France, and died in 1656, bequeathed it, together with his other manuscripts, to the Royal Library at Paris, where it is now preserved, and at present is marked 107. According to the accounts of Wetstein and Sabatier, thirty-six leaves were cut out of it at the beginning of the last century, (it is supposed by John Aymon, a notorious literary thief of that time,) and were sold in England, but they were sent back by the Earl of Oxford in 1729. The manuscript, therefore, is once more complete, as the covering only is wanting in which the stolen sheets had been enclosed, which is kept in the British Museum, and filled with the letters that passed on the occasion, as a monument of this infamous theft.[1]

V. The CODEX ARGENTEUS is a manuscript containing the four Gospels, in the Gothic version of Ulphilas[2], which is preserved in the university of Upsal. It is written on vellum, and has received the name of *Argenteus* from its silver letters; it is of a quarto size, and the vellum leaves are stained with a violet colour; and on this ground the letters, which are all *uncial* or capitals, were afterwards painted in silver, except the initial characters and a few other passages, which are in gold. The cover and back of the volume are of silver embossed. From the deep impression of the strokes, Ihre, Michaelis, and Hug are of opinion, that the letters were either imprinted with a warm iron, cut with a graver, or cast for the purpose, and afterwards coloured; but Mr. Coxe, (with whom the late eminent traveller Dr. E. D. Clarke seems to coincide,) after a very minute examination, was convinced that each letter was painted, and not formed in the manner supposed by those critics. Most of the silver letters have become green by time, but the golden letters are still in good preservation. We have no knowledge of this important manuscript prior to the discovery of it in the abbey of Werden in Westphalia, whence it was taken to Prague. In the year 1648, when that city was stormed by the Swedes, it fell into the hands of a Swedish count, who presented it to his sovereign, queen Christina. After remaining some time in her library, during the confusion which preceded her abdication of the throne of Sweden, it suddenly and unaccountably disappeared, and was again brought to light in the Netherlands. Some have supposed that the celebrated Isaac Vossius received it as a present from the Queen; others, that he brought it away by stealth. After his death, however, it was purchased for six hundred dollars by count Magnus Gabriel de la Gardie, who presented it to the university of Upsal, where it

---

[1] Michaelis, vol. ii. part i. pp 244—248. part ii. pp 724—728. Griesbach, Symbolæ Criticæ, tom. i. pp lv.—lxiv. Hug, vol. i pp 280—282.

[2] See an account of this version, *supra*, pp 75, 76.

at present remains. The following cut is a faithful fac-simile of the characters of the Codex Argenteus: it was traced from the manuscript itself for the late Dr. E. D Clarke, and is the most correct fac-simile known to be extant. It corresponds with our version of Luke xviii. 17. *Verily, I say unto you, Whosoever shall not receive the kingdom of God as a little child, shall in no wise enter therein.* It is worthy of remark, that, in the Codex Argenetus, the well known old Saxon or Gothic word *Barn*, is used to signify the original word Παιδίον, *a little child.*

𐌰𐌼𐌴𐌽 ⲟ𐌹𐍈𐌰 𐌹𐌶𐍅𐌹𐍃. 𐍃𐌰𐌴𐌹 𐌽𐌹
𐌰𐌽𐌳𐌰𐌽𐌹𐌼𐌹𐍈 𐍈𐌹𐌽𐌳𐌰𐌽𐍂𐌰𐌺𐌰𐌲𐌰
𐌲𐌿𐌸𐍃 𐍃𐍅𐌴 𐌱𐌰𐍂𐌽. 𐌽𐌹 𐌵𐌹𐌼𐌹𐍈
𐌹𐌽 𐌹𐌶𐌰𐌹:

Concerning the age of this venerable manuscript, critics are by no means agreed. Some of the zealous advocates for its antiquity have maintained that it is the very copy which Ulphilas wrote with his own hand. The librarian by whom it was exhibited to Dr. Clarke stated it to have been completed about the end of the fourth century, by a bishop of Thrace, in the Gothic language used at that time in Mœsia. This brings its age very nearly, if not quite, to the time when Ulphilas lived: but it is not likely—indeed it is utterly improbable—that the only copy of the Gothic translation of the Gospels, which is now extant, should be precisely the original. What proves that this cannot be the identical MS. of Ulphilas, is the fact, that several various readings have been discovered in the margin, a circumstance which clearly shows that it must have been written at a time when several transcripts had been already made.

Some fragments of the Gothic version of St. Paul's Epistle to the Romans were discovered by M. Knittel, in the year 1756, in a Codex Rescriptus belonging to the library of the Duke of Brunswick at Wolfenbüttel: they were published by him in 1762, and reprinted in 1763, in 4to., at Upsal, with notes by Ihre. The Brunswick manuscript contains the version of Ulphilas in one column, and a Latin translation in the other: it is on vellum, and is supposed to be of the sixth century. In the eighth or ninth century, the *Origines Isidori Hispalensis* were written over the translation of Ulphilas; but the ink had become so exceedingly pale as not to admit of deciphering the original manuscript without great difficulty.[1]

In the year 1817, a most important discovery was made among the Codices Rescripti, in the Ambrosian library at Milan, by signor

---

[1] Michaelis, vol ii. pp 140—153. 631—635. Semler, pp. 70—72. Viser, Hermeneut. Nov Test vol ii. part iii. pp. 56—58. Schoell, Histoire Abrégé de la Littérature Grecque, tom ii p 131. Hug, vol. i. pp. 488—498. Coxe's Travels in Russia, &c. vol iv. pp. 173—180. edit. 1802. Dr. E. D. Clarke's Travels, vol. vi. pp. 183, 184 4to.

Angelo Maï, who is at present keeper of the manuscript-department of the Vatican library. While this indefatigable explorer of antient literature was examining two Codices Rescripti in the Ambrosian library, he was surprised with the discovery of some Gothic writing in one of them; which on further investigation proved to be fragments of the books of Kings, Ezra, and Nehemiah. The discovery thus auspiciously made, stimulated him to further inquiries, which were rewarded with the discovery of *four* other Codices Rescripti containing portions of the Gothic version. He now associated in his researches, signor Carolo Ottavio Castillionei; and to their joint labours we are indebted for a specimen and account[1] of these manuscripts, from which the following particulars are abridged.

The *first* of these five Gothic MSS (which is noted S. 36) consists of 204 quarto pages on vellum, the later writing contains the homilies of Gregory the Great on the Prophecies of Ezekiel, which from their characters must have been executed before the eighth century. Beneath this, in a more antient Gothic hand, are contained the Epistles of St. Paul to the Romans, 1st and 2d Corinthians, Ephesians, Philippians, Colossians, 1st and 2d of Timothy, Titus, and Philemon, together with a fragment of the Gothic Calendar. The Epistles to the Romans, Corinthians, Ephesians, and to Timothy, are very nearly entire, and form the chief part of this MS.: of the other Epistles, considerable fragments only remain. The titles of the Epistles may be traced at the heads of the pages where they commence. This MS. appears to have been written by two different copyists, one of whom wrote more beautifully and correctly than the other: and various readings may be traced in some of the margins written in a smaller hand. Entire leaves have been turned upside down by the *rescribes* of this MS. A fac-simile specimen of this manuscript is given in the accompanying Plate 5. No. 1 It represents the commencement of Paul's Epistles to the Ephesians, and may be thus rendered: *The Epistle of Paul to the Ephesians beginneth. Paul, an apostle of Jesus Christ according to the will of God, to the saints who are at Ephesus*

. The *second* MS. also, in quarto, and noted S. 45., contains 156 pages of thinner vellum, the Latin writing on which is of the eighth or ninth century, and comprises Jerome's exposition of Isaiah. Under this has been discovered, (though with some difficulty, on account of the thickness of the Latin characters and the blackness of the ink,) the Gothic version of Saint Paul's two Epistles to the Corinthians, the Galatians, Ephesians, Philippians, Colossians, the two Epistles to the Thessalonians and to Titus What is deficient in the preceding MS. is found in this, which has some various readings peculiar to itself, and therefore is an independent codex.

In the *third* manuscript, noted G. 82., a quarto Latin volume, containing the plays of Plautus, and part of Seneca's Tragedies of Medea and Œdipus, signor Maï discovered fragments of the Books of Kings, Ezra, and Nehemiah. This discovery is peculiarly valuable, as not the smallest portion of the Gothic version of the Old Testament was known to be in existence, and, further, as it furnishes a complete refutation of the idle tale repeated by Gibbon after preceding writers, viz. that Ulphilas prudently suppressed the four Books of Kings, as they might tend to irritate the fierce and sanguinary spirit of his countrymen.[2] The date of the

---

[1] Ulphilæ Partium Ineditarum, in Ambrosianis Palimpsestis ab Angelo Maio repertarum, Specimen, conjunctis curis ejusdem Maii et Caroli Octavii Castillionæi editum, Mediolani, Regiis Typis, M. DCCC. XIX. 4to [2] Decline and Fall, vol. vi. p. 269.

LES.

vision of Saint Paul's Epistles —
Library at Milan

Tem plum
uang elio

Book of Genesis at Vienna

ϹΩΟΔΟΜΩΝ ΕΙϹϹΥΝ
ΑΤΟΑΝΑϹΤΡΕΨΑΙΑΥΤΟ
Ι ΒΑϹΙΛΕΩΝ ΕΙϹΤΗΝ

FAC[SIMILES.]

1. Of a Codex Rescriptus of the G[reek version of Saint] Dionised in the Am[brosian Library at Milan.]

quEas cendEras in-tem pLuo
orare Testan e euan̄ç elio

2. Of the Codex Cannon[ici ?] to Book of Genesis at

ΕΖΗΛΘΕΝΔΕ ΒΑϹΙΛ[ΕΥϹ] ΥϹϹΟΔΟΜΟ[Υ]
ΑΝΤΗϹΙΝΑΥ ΤΩΝ ΕΤΑΤΟΑΝΑϹ
ΑΠΟ ΤΗϹΚΟΙΙΗϹ Τ[Ο]ΥΝΒΑϹΙΛΕ
ΚΟΙΛΑΔΑ ΤΗΝϹΑΥΗ

Latin writing of this MS. which Mai deciphered with great difficulty, is not specified, but, on comparing his specimen of it with other engraved specimens, we are inclined to refer it to the eighth or ninth century.

The *fourth* specimen (noted I 61.) consists of a single sheet in small quarto, containing four pages of part of Saint John's Gospel in Latin, under which are found the very fragments of the twenty fifth, twenty-sixth, and twenty-seventh chapters of Matthew's Gospel, which are wanting in the celebrated manuscript of the Gothic Gospels preserved at Upsal, and usually known by the appellation of the *Codex Argenteus*.

The *fifth* and last manuscript, (noted G. 147.) which has preserved some remains of Gothic literature, is a volume of the proceedings of the Council of Chalcedon, under the later writing have been discovered some fragments of antient authors whose names Signor Mai has not specified, and also a fragment of a Gothic Homily, rich in biblical quotations, and the style of which he thinks shows that it was translated from some one of the fathers of the Greek church. The characters of this MS. bear a close resemblance to those of the Codex Argenteus, at Upsal, which was executed in the sixth century.

The manuscripts above described are written in broad and thick characters, without any division of words or of chapters, but with contractions of proper names, similar to those found in antient Greek MSS. Some sections, however, have been discovered, which are indicated by numeral marks or larger spaces, and sometimes by large letters. The Gothic writing is referred to the sixth century.

The portions of the Gothic version of the Old and New Testament, printed by signors Mai and Castillionei, are, I. Nehemiah, chap. v. verses 13—18. chap. vi. 14—19. and vii. 1—3. II. A Fragment of Saint Matthew's Gospel, containing chap. xxv. 38—46. xxvi. 1—3., 65—75. and xxvii. 1.: this fragment contains the *whole of the passages* which are wanting in the Upsal MS. of the four Gospels. III. Part of St. Paul's Epistle to the Philippians, chap. ii. 22—30. and iii. 1—16. IV. Saint Paul's Epistle to Titus, chap i. 1—16. ii. 1.; and V. verses 11—23. of his Epistle to Philemon. The Gothic text is exhibited on the left-hand page, and on the right-hand page the editors have given a literal Latin translation of it, together with the Greek original. These are succeeded by fragments of a Gothic Homily, and Calendar, with Latin translations, Gothic alphabet, and a glossary of new Gothic words which they have discovered in the passages which they have printed.

VI. A very valuable Codex Rescriptus was discovered nearly thirty years since by the (late) Rev. Dr. Barrett, senior fellow of Trinity College, Dublin. While he was examining different books in the library of that college, he accidentally met with a very antient Greek manuscript, on certain leaves of which he observed a twofold writing, one antient and the other comparatively recent, transcribed over the former. The original writing on these leaves had been greatly defaced, either by the injuries of time, or by art; on close examination he found, that this antient writing consisted of the three following fragments:—the Prophet Isaiah, the Evangelist Saint Matthew, and certain orations of Gregory Nazianzen. The fragment, containing Saint Matthew's Gospel, Dr. Barrett carefully transcribed; and the whole has been accurately engraved in fac-simile by the order and at the expense of the University, thus presenting to the reader a perfect resemblance of the original.[1] The accompanying engraving is copied from Dr. B.'s first plate. It represents the 18th and 19th verses of the first chapter of Saint Matthew's Gospel. We have subjoined the same verses in ordinary Greek types, with a literal version in parallel columns.

V 18. ΤΟΤΔΕΙΓΧΤΗΓΕΝΕΣΙΧΟΥ	V. 18. NOWTHEBIRTHOFJSCHITTII
ΤΩΣΗΝ ΜΝΗΣΤΕΥΘΕΙ	USWAS·BEINGESPOU
ΣΗΣΤΗΣΜΗΤΡΟΣΑΥΤΟ,	SEDHIISMOTHER
ΜΑΡΙΑΣΤΩΙΩΣΗΦΠΡΙΝ	MARYTOJOSEPHBEFORE
ΣΥΝΕΛΘΕΙΝΑΥΤΟΥΣΕΥ	THEYCAMETOGETHERSHEWAS
ΡΗΘΗΕΝΓΑΣΤΡΙΕΧΟΥΣΑ·	FOUNDWITHCHILD
ΕΚΠΝΣΑΓΙΟΥ	BYTHEHOLYSPT·
V. 19. ΙΩΣΗΦΔΕΟΑΝΗΡΑΥΤΗΣ	V. 19. JOSEPHrHENIIERHUSBAND
ΔΙΚΑΙΟΣΩΝΚΑΙΜΗΘΕΛ...	BEINGAJUSTMANANDNOTWILL...
ΑΥΤΗΝΔΕΙΓΜΑΤΕΙΣΑΙ	TOMAKEHERAPUBLICEXAMPLE
ΕΒΟΥΛΗΘΗΛΑΘΡΑΑΠΟΛΥ	WASMINDEDPRIVILYTOPUT
ΣΑΙΑΥΤΗΝ	HERAWAY.

Of the original writing of this manuscript, which Dr. Barrett calls the *Codex Vetus*, only sixty-four leaves remain, in a very mutilated state: each page contains one column; and the columns in general consist of twenty-one lines, and sometimes (though rarely) of twenty-two or twenty-three; the lines are nearly of equal lengths, and consist, ordinarily, of eighteen or twenty square letters, written on vellum originally of a *purple* colour, but without any points. From these two circumstances, as well as from the division of the text, the orthography, mode of pointing, abbreviations, and from some other considerations, Dr Barrett, with great probability, fixes its age to the sixth century. This manuscript follows the Alexandrian Recension. The *Codex Recens*, or later writing (which contains several tracts of some Greek fathers), he attributes to a scribe of the thirteenth century: about which time it became a general practice to erase antient writings, and insert others in their place.[2]

VII. The *Codex*[3] *Laudianus* 3., as it is noted by Dr. Mill, but noted by the letter E by Wetstein, and *E by Griesbach, is a Greek-Latin manuscript of the Acts of the Apostles, in which the Latin text is one of those versions which differ from Jerome's edition, having been altered from the particular Greek text of this manuscript. It is defective from chap. xxvi. 29. to xxviii. 26.

This manuscript is erroneously supposed to have been the identical book used by the venerable Bede in the seventh century, because it

---

[1] The title of this interesting (and comparatively little known) publication is as follows: "Evangelium Secundum Matthæum ex Codice Rescripto in Bibliotheca Collegii SSæ Trinitatis juxta Dublin Descriptum Opera et Studio Johannis Barrett, S. T. P. MDCCCI." 4to

[2] Dr. Barrett's Prolegomena, pp. 2—9.

[3] So called from Archbishop Laud, who gave this, among many other precious manuscripts, to the University of Oxford It is now preserved in the Bodleian Library, F. 82. No. 1119.

Fac Simile of a Codex Rescriptus of Saint Matthews Gospel in the Library of Trinity College Dublin

Matt Chap. 1 v. 18. 19.

ΤΟΥΔΕΙΥΧΥΗΓΕΝΕϹΙϹΟΥ
ΤΩϹΗΝ·ΜΝΗϹΤΕΥΘΕΙ
ϹΗϹΤΗϹΜΗΤΡΟϹΑΥΤΟ
ΜΑΡΙΑϹΤΩΙΩϹΗΦΠΡΙΝ
ϹΥΝΕΛΘΕΙΝΑΥΤΟΥϹΕΥ
ΡΕΘΗΕΝΓΑϹΤΡΙΕΧΟΥϹΑ
··ΕΚΠΝϹΑΓΙΟΥ·
ΙΩϹΗΦΔΕΟΑΝΗΡΑΥΤΗϹ
ΔΙΚΑΙΟϹΩΝΚΑΙΜΗΘΕΛ
ΑΥΤΗΝΔΕΙΓΜΑΤΕΙϹΑΙ
ΕΒΟΥΛΗΘΗΛΑΘΡΑΑΠΟΛΥ
ϹΑΙΑΥΤΗΝ·

Ο ΔΕΕΦΗ
ΑΝΔΡΕΣ
ΑΔΕΛΦΟΙ
ΚΑΙΠΑΤΕΡΕΣ
ΑΚΟΥΣΑΤΕ
ΟΘΣ
ΤΗΣΔΟΞΗΣ
ΩΦΘΗ
ΤΩΠΡΙ
ΗΜΩΝ
ΑΒΡΑΑΜ

ΑΔ ILLE AIT
UIRI
FRATRES
ETPATRES
AUDITE
DEUS
GLORIAE
UISUS EST
PATRI
NOSTRO
ABRAHAE

has all those irregular readings which, in his Commentaries on the Acts, he says were in *his* book; and no other manuscript is now found to have them. There is an extraordinary coincidence between it and the old Syriac version of the Acts of the Apostles. Wetstein conjectures, from an edict of a Sardinian prince, Flavius Pancratius, written at the end of this manuscript, and from several other circumstances, that it was written in Sardinia in the seventh century. To this conjecture Michaelis is disposed to accede, though Dr. Woide supposed it to have been written in the East, because its orthography has several properties observable in the Codex Alexandrinus. But as these peculiarities are also found in other very antient manuscripts, Bishop Marsh considers them as insufficient to warrant the inference, especially when we reflect on the great improbability that a *Greek* manuscript written in the *East* should be accompanied with a Latin translation. It will be seen from the annexed fac-simile [1], which represents the chief part of Acts vii. 2., that this Latin translation, contrary to the usual arrangement of the Greek-Latin manuscripts, occupies the first column of the page. Only one word (or at the utmost, two or three words, and that but seldom,) is written in a line, and in uncial or capital letters; and they are so written that each Latin word is always opposite to the correspondent Greek word. Hence it is evident, that the manuscript was written for the use of a person who was not well skilled in both languages; and as the Latin occupies the first column, this circumstance is an additional evidence that it was written in the West of Europe, where Latin only was spoken. For the satisfaction of the English reader, the verse in question is subjoined in common Roman and Greek capitals, with the corresponding literal English in a third column.

AD ILLE AIT	ΟΔΕ ΕΦΗ	AND HE SAID
UIRI	ΑΝΔΡΕΣ	MEN
FRATRES	ΑΔΕΛΦΟΙ	BRETHREN
ET PATRES	ΚΑΙ ΠΑΤΕΡΕΣ	AND FATHERS
AUDITE	ΑΚΟΥΣΑΤΕ	HEARKEN
DEUS	Ο ΘΣ	THE GD
GLORIÆ	ΤΗΣ ΔΟΞΗΣ	OF GLORY
UISUS EST	ΩΦΘΗ	APPEARED
PATRI	ΤΩΠΡΙ	UNTO THE FTHER
NOSTRO	ΗΜΩΝ	OF US
ABRAHAE.	ΑΒΡΑΑΜ.	ABRAHAM.

With regard to the date of this manuscript;— Mr. Astle refers it to the beginning of the fifth century; Griesbach to the seventh, or eighth; and Mr. Hearne to the eighth century. But from the shape of the letters and other circumstances, Bishop Marsh pronounces it to be less antient than the Codex Bezæ, which was written in the fifth century. Probably the end of the sixth or the former part of the seventh century may be assigned as the date of the Codex Laudi-

---

[1] It is copied from Mr. Astle's work on the Origin of Writing, Plate iv.

anus 3. This manuscript is of great value: Michaelis pronounces it to be indispensable to every man who would examine the important question, whether the Codices Græco-Latini have been corrupted from the Latin, and adds, that it was this manuscript which convinced him that this charge is without foundation.[1]

VIII. The CODEX COISLINIANUS, H. of Griesbach's notation is a very beautiful MS. of the sixth century, containing fragments of St. Paul's Epistles. It is written in uncial characters, with accents; and was formerly kept at mount Athos, where it was applied, as old parchment, to the binding of other books, in the year 1218; as appears in a note of the book to the binding of which it was applied.[2]

IX. The CODEX BOERNERIANUS derives its name from Dr. C. F. Boerner, to whom it formerly belonged, and is now deposited in the royal library at Dresden. It is noted by the letter G. 2 by Wetstein and Griesbach. It contains St. Paul's Epistles, with the exception of that to the Hebrews, which was formerly rejected by the church of Rome; and is written in Greek and Latin, the Latin or old Ante-Hieronymian version being interlined between the Greek, and written over the text, of which it is a translation. Semler supposed that the Latin was written since the Greek; but Professor Matthæi, who published a copy of this manuscript, suggests that the uniformity of the hand-writing, and similarity in the colour of the ink, evince that both the Greek and Latin texts proceeded from the same transcriber. It frequently agrees with the Codex Claromontanus (described in pp. 137, 138 *supra*), and with the Codex Augiensis, of which a notice is given in p. 147. *infra* The time when this manuscript was written has not been determined with precision. That it is antient, appears (says Michaelis) from the form of the characters, and the absence of accents and marks of aspiration. It seems to have been written in an age when the transition was making from uncial to small characters; and from the correspondence of the letters *r*, *s*, and *t*, in the Latin version to that form which is found in the Anglo-Saxon alphabet, Bishop Marsh infers, that this manuscript was written in the west of Europe, and probably between the eighth and tenth centuries. Kuster, who first collated this manuscript, supposed it to be *British*; Doederlein, Irish. The learned reviewer of Matthæi's edition of this manuscript, in the Jena Literary Gazette, decides that it could only be written in Germany or France; because in the margin many passages are noted *contra* γοδδισχαλκον, apparently because they are contradictory to the opinion of Gottschalk, a celebrated monk, who disputed concerning predestination in the ninth century, but whose tenets excited little attention except in those two countries. The writer in question thinks it probable that this manuscript was written by Johannes Scotus, who lived at the court of Charles the Bald, king of France, and was the most celebrated opponent of

---

[1] Griesbach, Symb Crit tom ii pp 181—183 Michaelis, vol ii part i pp. 269—274 part ii. pp. 747, 748. Di Wette Præfat ad Cod Alexandr pp xxvi —xxviii. §§ 76—81 Astle on the Origin of Writing, p 76. 2d edit. The Greek and Latin text of the Codex Laudianus was printed at Oxford in 8vo in 1715, by the celebrated antiquary, Thomas Hearne, with a specimen of the original characters

[2] Hug's Introduction, vol. i. p 288.

Gottschalk. The manuscript, however, could not have been written later than the ninth century, for in the beginning of the tenth, Gottschalk's dispute had lost all its importance. Griesbach and Hug accordingly refer the Codex Boernerianus to the ninth or tenth century. There is a transcript of this MS. in the library of Trinity College, Cambridge, among the books and manuscripts that were left by Dr. Bentley, who probably procured it for his intended edition of the Greek Testament. Professor Matthæi published a copy of this manuscript at Meissen in Saxony, in 1791, in quarto, which was reprinted at the same place in 1818, also in quarto.[1]

X. The CODEX CYPRIUS, or Colbertinus, 5149., noted K. in the first volume of Wetstein's and Griesbach's editions of the Greek Testament, is a copy of the four Gospels, brought from the island of Cyprus in the year 1637; and now deposited in the Royal Library at Paris, where it is at present numbered 83. This manuscript was first collated by Father Simon[2], whose extracts of various readings were inserted by Dr. Mill in his critical edition of the New Testament.[3] Wetstein charged this manuscript with latinising, but without sufficient evidence. Michaelis deemed it to be of great value, and expressed a wish for a more accurate collation of it. That wish was not realised until the year 1819, when Dr. J. M. A. Scholz, of Heidelberg, being at Paris, subjected this manuscript to a very rigorous critical examination, the results of which he communicated to the public in his *Curæ Criticæ in Historiam Textus Evangeliorum* (4to. Heidelbergæ, 1820): from this work the following particulars are abridged.

This manuscript is written on vellum, in an oblong quarto size, and in excellent preservation. The uncial characters are not round, as in most antient manuscripts, but leaning; they exhibit evident marks of haste and sometimes of carelessness in the transcriber, and they present the same abbreviations as occur in the Alexandrian, Vatican, and other manuscripts. In a few instances, accents are absent, but frequently they are incorrectly placed, the spirits (asper and lenis) are often interchanged; and the permutations of vowels and consonants are very numerous. Thus we meet with καικρυμμενω for κεκρυμμενω (Matt. xiii. 44.), ελθει for ελθη (Mark iv. 22.); ραββει for ραββι (Matt. xxiii. 7. xxvi. 25. 49, &c.); οκοδομητο for ωκοδομητο (Luke iv. 29.); τουτω for τουτο (Luke viii. 9.); Δαδδαιον for Θαδδαιον; εκαθευδον for εκαθευδον (Matt. xxv. 5.); Ναζαρεθ for Ναζαρετ (Mark i. 9.) &c. From the confused and irregular manner in which the accents and spirits are placed, Dr. Scholz conjectures that the Codex Cyprius was transcribed from a more antient copy that was nearly destitute of those distinctions. Some of the permutations are unquestionably errors of the transcriber, but the greater part of them, he is of opinion, must be referred to the orthography and pronun-

---

[1] Kuster's preface to his edition of Mill's Greek Testament, *sub finem*. Michaelis, vol ii part i. pp 225—227 part ii pp 672—677. Jena Algemeine Litteratur Zeitung, as abridged in the Analytical Review for 1793, vol. xvii. p. 231. Hug's Introduction, vol i pp. 283—286
[2] Histoire Critique du Texte du Nouveau Testament, ch. x. p 104.
[3] Nov Test Millii et Kusteri Prolegom. p. 162.

ciation which (it is well known) were peculiar to the Alexandrians. To this manuscript are prefixed a *synaxarium* or epitome of the lives of the Saints, who are venerated by the Greek church, and a *menologium* or martyrology, together with the canons of Eusebius: to each of the three last Gospels is also prefixed an index of the κεφαλαια or larger chapters. The numbers of the Ammonian sections and larger chapters [1], are marked in the inner margin; and the numbers of the other chapters, together with the titles, are placed either at the top or at the bottom of the page. The Gospel of St. Matthew comprises 359 Ammonian sections, and 68 chapters; that of St. Mark, 241 sections, and 48 chapters; that of St. Luke, 342 sections and 83 chapters; and the Gospel of St. John, 232 sections, and 19 chapters. The celebrated passage in John viii. 1—11., concerning the woman who had been taken in adultery, constitutes a distinct chapter. From the occasional notation of certain days, on which particular portions were to be read, as well as from the prefixing of the synaxarium and menologium, Dr. Scholz considers this manuscript as having originally been written, and constantly used, for ecclesiastical purposes.

A considerable difference of opinion prevails, respecting the age of the Codex Cyprius. Simon referred it to the tenth century: Hug, to the ninth century; Dr. Mill thought it still later, Montfaucon assigned it to the eighth century, and with his opinion Dr. Scholz coincides, from the general resemblance of the writing to that of other manuscripts of the same date. Specimens of its characters have been given by Montfaucon [2], Blanchini [3], and Dr. Scholz.[4] Our fac-simile in Plate 3. No. 3.[5] is copied from the last-mentioned writer: it contains part of the first verse of the twenty-eighth chapter of St. Matthew's Gospel, in English thus:

INTHEENDOFTHESABBATH ASITBEGANTODAWNTOWARDSTHEFIRST*DAY* OFTHEWEEK'CAMEMARYMAGDALENE.

This manuscript is of considerable importance in a critical point of view, particularly as it affords great weight to the readings of the best and most antient MSS., antient versions, and the fathers.[6]

XI. The CODEX BASILEENSIS, B. VI. 21., noted by Dr. Mill, B. 1., by Bengel, Bas. *a*, and by Wetstein and Griesbach, E., is a manu-

---

[1] See an account of these divisions in pp. 169, 170. *infra*.
[2] Palæographia Græca, p. 232.
[3] Evangeliarium Quadruplex, Part I p 492. plate 3 from that page.
[4] At the end of his Curæ Criticæ in Historiam Textus Evangeliorum In pp 80—90. Dr Scholz has given the *first entire* collation ever published, of the Various Readings contained in the Codex Cyprius
[5] This plate faces page 132 *supra*.
[6] Dr. Scholz (Cur Crit. pp. 63—65) has given several instances of such readings, one only of which we have room to notice In John vii 8 the Codex Cyprius reads ουκ αναβαινω, which in later manuscripts is altered to ουπω αναβαινω, because the celebrated antagonist of Christianity, Porphyry, had used it as a ground of objection. With the Codex Cyprius agree the Cambridge Manuscript, the Codices Regii, 14 (33 of Griesbach's notation,) and 55 (17 of Griesbach), several of the Moscow manuscripts cited by Matthæi, the Memphitic and Ethiopic versions, together with several of the Ante-Hieronymian versions, and, among the fathers, Jerome, Augustine, Cyril, Chrysostom, and Epiphanius. This reading alone proves that the Codex Cyprius has *not* been altered from the Latin, as Wetstein asserted without any authority.

script of the four Gospels, written in uncial letters, in the eighth or (more probably) ninth century. It is mutilated in Luke i. 69. — ii. 4., iii. 4—15., xii. 58.—xiii. 12, xv. 8—20.; and xxiv. 47. to the end of the Gospels: but the chasms in Luke i 69. — ii. 4., xii. 58. — xiii. 12., and xv. 8—20. have been filled up by a later hand. This manuscript was not used by Erasmus; but it was collated by Samuel Battier for Dr. Mill, who highly valued it; by Iselin, for Bengel's edition of the New Testament; and by Wetstein, who has given its readings in his edition.[1]

XII. The CODEX SAN-GERMANENSIS (noted E. 2. in the second volume of Wetstein's edition of the New Testament) is a Greek-Latin manuscript of St. Paul's Epistles, written in the seventh century, in uncial letters, and with accents and marks of aspiration, *à primâ manu*. It has been generally supposed to be a mere copy of the Codex Claromontanus (described in pp. 137. *supra*), but this opinion is questioned by Dr. Semler, in his critical examination of this manuscript, who has produced many examples, from which it appears that if the transcriber of it actually had the Clermont MS. before him, he must at least have selected various readings from other manuscripts. Bishop Marsh, therefore, considers the San-Germanensis as a kind of *Codex Eclecticus*, in writing which the Clermont MS. was principally but not at all times consulted. The manuscript now under consideration takes its name from the monastery of St. Germain-des-Prez, in Paris, in whose library it was formerly preserved. Dr. Mill first procured extracts from it, for his edition of the New Testament, where it is noted by the abbreviation Ger. for Germanensis. By Wetstein, it is noted E 2., and by Griesbach E.

According to Montfaucon, there is also extant another more antient Codex San-Germanensis of St. Paul's Epistles, which has never been collated. It is a fragment, containing only thirteen leaves; and is supposed to be as antient as the fifth century.[2]

XIII. The CODEX AUGIENSIS is a Greek-Latin manuscript of St. Paul's Epistles; it derives its name from the monastery of Augia major, at Rheinau, to which it belonged in the fifteenth century. After passing through various hands, it was purchased by the celebrated critic, Dr Richard Bentley, in 1718; and in 1787, on the death of the younger Bentley, it was deposited in the library of Trinity College, Cambridge. This manuscript is defective from the beginning to Rom. iii. 8., and the epistle to the Hebrews is found only in the Latin version. Hug assigns it to the latter half of the ninth, or to the tenth century, and Michaelis to the ninth century, which (Bishop Marsh remarks) is the utmost that can be allowed to its antiquity. The Greek text is written in uncial letters without accents, and the Latin in Anglo-Saxon characters: it has been col-

---

[1] Marsh's Michaelis, vol. ii. part i. pp. 217, 218. Hug's Introd. vol. i. pp. 289 —294.

[2] Michaelis, vol. ii. part i. p. 314. part ii. pp. 784, 785., Hug, vol i p 282. Montfaucon's Bibliotheca Bibliothecarum, tom. ii p. 1041. In his Palæographia Græca, he has given a fac-simile of the Greek and Latin characters of the Codex San-Germanensis. Another fac-simile of them is given by Blanchini, in his Evangeliarium Quadruplex, vol. i in the last of the Plates annexed to p 533.

lated by Wetstein, who has noted the Codex Augiensis with the letter F. in the second part of his edition of the New Testament. In many respects it coincides with the Codex Boernerianus, and belongs to the Western Recension. The words Χριϛος (*Christ*), and Ιησους (*Jesus*) are not abbreviated by $\overline{XC}$ and $\overline{IC}$, as in the common manuscripts, but by $\overline{XPC}$ and $\overline{IHC}$, as in the Codex Bezæ [1]

XIV. The CODEX HARLEIANUS, No. 5598, is a most splendid Evangeliarium, or collection of lessons from the four Gospels, unknown to Dr. Griesbach; it is written on vellum, in uncial Greek letters, which are gilt on the first leaf, and coloured and ornamented throughout the rest of the book. It consists of seven hundred and forty-eight pages; and according to an inscription on the last page, was written by one Constantine, a presbyter, A. D. 995. To several of the longer sections, titles are prefixed in larger characters. The passages of the Gospels are noted in the margin, as they occur, by a later hand, and between pages 726. and 729., there are inserted ten leaves of paper, containing the series of Lessons or Extracts from the Gospels, which are supposed to have been written by Dr. Covell, who was chaplain to the British Embassy at Constantinople A. D. 1670 —1677, and was a diligent collector of MSS. In Plate 3. No. 2. is given a fac-simile [2] of the third page of this precious manuscript. It represents the eighteenth verse of the first chapter of Saint John's Gospel. We have annexed the same passage in ordinary Greek types, together with a literal English Version, in parallel columns.

ΘΝΟΥΔΕΙΣΕΩ	G̅D̅NOMANHATHSE
ΡΑΚΕΠΩΠΟΤΕ·	ENATANYTIME
‘ΟΜΟΝΟΓΕΝΗΣΥ̅Σ̅	THEONLYBEGOTTENS̅N̅
‘ΟΩΝΕΙΣΤΟΝΚΟΛ	WHOISINTHEBO
ΠΟΝΤΟΥΠ̅ΡΣΕΚΕΙ	SOMOFTHEFH̅R̅H
ΝΟΣΕΞΗΓΗΣΑΤΟ·	EHATHMADEHIMKNOWN

The lines of this venerable MS. are not all of equal length, some containing ten, others ten or more letters in each line. The same contractions of $\overline{\Theta\Sigma}$ for Θεος (*God*), $\overline{\Pi P}$ for Πατηρ (*Father*), $\overline{Y\Sigma}$ for Υιος (*a son*), &c. which occur in all the most antient Greek manuscripts, are also to be seen in this evangeliarium. As it has *never* yet been collated, it is highly worthy of the attention of future editors of the New Testament.

XV. The CODEX REGIUS, 2861., at present 62 η, (or the eighth of the manuscripts collated by Robert Stephens,) is a quarto manuscript, on vellum, of the ninth century, and written in uncial letters of an oblong form. The accents are frequently wanting, and are often wrongly placed, even when they are inserted, from which circumstance Griesbach thinks that this manuscript was transcribed from another very antient one, which had no accents. Each page

---

[1] Michaelis, vol II part I. pp. 210, 211. part II pp 664, 665. Hug, vol I. pp. 286—288.
[2] This plate faces page 132. *supra*.

is divided into two columns, and the words follow, for the most part, without any intervals between them. The iota subscriptum, and postscriptum, are uniformly wanting: the usual abbreviations occur, and the letters ΑΥ and ΟΥ are sometimes written with contractions, as in the Codex Coislinianus 1. (a manuscript of the eighth century); and not seldom a letter is dropped in the middle of a word:— Thus, we read in it παραβλη for παραβολη, κλησεται for κληϑησεται, κατρωμενος for καταρωμενος, &c. &c. Errors in orthography appear in every page, and also permutations of vowels and consonants. This manuscript contains the four Gospels, with the following chasms, viz. Matt. iv. 21.—v. 14. and xxviii. 17. to the end of the Gospel; Mark x. 17—30. and xv. 10—20.; and John xxi. 15. to the end. The τιτλοι and the Ammonian sections with reference to the canons of Eusebius are written in the Codex Regius *à primâ manu*. It is noted L. by Wetstein, and also by Griesbach[1], who has given a very complete and accurate collation of its various readings in his Symbolæ Criticæ. This manuscript harmonises with the Alexandrine or Western Recension.

XVI. The CODEX UFFENBACHIANUS 2, (1. of Bengel's notation, and No. 53. of Wetstein's and Griesbach's catalogues of manuscripts,) is a fragment of the Epistle to the Hebrews, consisting of two leaves: it is at present preserved in the public library at Hamburgh. Having been very imperfectly described by Maius, Wetstein, and Bengel, Dr. H. P. C. Henke rendered an important service to biblical literature by subjecting it to a minute critical examination, the result of which he published at Helmstadt, in 1800, in a quarto tract, with a fac-simile of the writing.[2] According to this writer, the Codex Uffenbachianus originally consisted of one ternion, or six leaves, of which the four middle ones are lost. It is wholly written in *red* uncial characters, slightly differing from the square form observable in the most antient manuscripts. The accents and notes of aspiration are carefully marked, but the iota subscriptum nowhere occurs: nor are any stops or minor marks of distinction to be seen, except the full stop, which is promiscuously placed at the bottom, in the middle, or at the top of a page, to serve as a comma, a colon, or a full point. The note of interrogation occurs only once, viz. in Heb. iii. 17. after the word ρημω; but there are scarcely any abbreviations beside those which we have already noticed as existing in the Alexandrian and other antient manuscripts. It is remarkable, that the first verse of the second chapter is wanting in this manuscript, which is characterised by some peculiar readings. M. von Uffenbach, who was its first *known* possessor, referred it to the seventh or eight century. Wetstein asserted it to have been written in the eleventh century; but, on comparing it with the specimens of manuscripts engraved by Montfaucon and Blanchini, we are of opinion with Dr. Henke, that

---

[1] Griesbach's Symbolæ Criticæ, tom. i. pp. lxvi.—cxli. Michaelis, vol. ii. part i. pp 304—306. part ii. pp. 778, 779. Hug, vol. i. p 294.

[2] Dr. Henke's publication and fac-simile are reprinted by Pott and Ruperti, in their Sylloge Commentationum Theologicarum, vol. ii. pp. 1—82. Helmstadt, 1801, from which our account of the Codex Uffenbachianus is abridged.

it was executed in the ninth century. In its readings, the Codex Uffenbachianus sometimes approximates to the Alexandrine, and sometimes to the Western Recension.

XVII. The CODICES MANNERS-SUTTONIANI are a choice collection of manuscripts, in the archiepiscopal library at Lambeth, which have been purchased, and presented to that library by his Grace the present Archbishop. They are principally the collection made by the Rev. J. D. Carlyle, Professor of Arabic in the university of Cambridge, during his travels in the East, with a view to a critical edition of the New Testament, with various readings; which however was never undertaken, in consequence of his lamented decease.[1] Of these manuscripts (which are chiefly of the New Testament) the following are particularly worthy of notice, on account of the harvest of various lections which they may be expected to afford.

1. No. 1175 is a manuscript of the four Gospels, written on vellum, in quarto, towards the end of the eleventh or at the beginning of the twelfth century. The two first verses of the first chapter of Saint Matthew's Gospel are wanting. At the end of this manuscript, on a single leaf, there are part of the last verse of the seventh chapter of Saint John's Gospel and the first eleven verses of the eighth chapter.

2. No. 1176 is another manuscript of the four Gospels, on vellum, in quarto, written in the twelfth century. On the first leaf there are some figures painted and gilt, which have nearly disappeared from age. This is followed by the chapters of the four Gospels.

3. No. 1177 is a manuscript of the four Gospels, on vellum, of the twelfth century, which is very much mutilated in the beginning.

4. No. 1178 contains the four Gospels, most beautifully written on vellum, in quarto, in the tenth century. The first seven verses and part of the eighth verse of the first chapter of Saint Matthew's Gospel are wanting.

5. No. 1179 contains the four Gospels, mutilated at the beginning and end. It is on vellum, in quarto, of the twelfth century.

6—8. Nos. 1182, 1183, and 1185, are manuscripts, containing the Acts of the Apostles, the Catholic Epistles, and the whole of Saint Paul's Epistles. They are all written in quarto and on paper. No. 1182 is of the twelfth century: the conclusion of St. John's First Epistle, and the subsequent part of this manuscript to the end, have been added by a later hand. No. 1183 is of the fourteenth century. No. 1185 is of the fifteenth century, and is mutilated at the end.

9. No. 1186 is a quarto manuscript on vellum, written in the eleventh century, and contains the Epistles of Saint Paul and the Apocalypse. It is unfortunately mutilated at the beginning and end. It commences with Rom. xvi. 15. .... παν (that is, Ολυμπαν) και τους συν αυτοις παντας αγιους,— .... pas (that is, *Olympas*) *and all the saints which are with them* · and it ends with the words, επι τω θρονω λεγοντες Αμην, — *on the throne, saying, Amen.* Rev. xix. 4. The Rev. H. J. Todd has given a fac-simile of this precious manuscript in his catalogue of the manuscripts in the archiepiscopal library at Lambeth.

---

[1] Six of these precious MSS having been reclaimed by the Patriarch of Jerusalem, as having been lent only to Professor Carlyle, they were returned to him in 1817, by his Grace the ARCHBISHOP OF CANTERBURY. Full particulars relative to this transaction, so honourable to the noble and munificent character of the Primate of all England, may be seen in the Rev. H. J. Todd's "Account of Greek Manuscripts, chiefly Biblical, which had been in the possession of the late Professor Carlyle, the greater part of which are now deposited in the Archiepiscopal Library at Lambeth Palace." London [1818.] 8vo.

10—12. Nos. 1187—1189 are lectionaries from the four Gospels, written on vellum in the thirteenth century.

13. No. 1190 is a manuscript on vellum written with singular neatness, in the thirteenth century. Formerly it contained the Acts of the Apostles, and the Catholic Epistles, together with the whole of Saint Paul's Epistles. It is sadly mutilated and torn, both in the middle and at the end.

14. No. 1191 is a lectionary, from the Acts of the Apostles and the Epistles. It is on vellum, in quarto, of the thirteenth century. It is mutilated both at the beginning and end. All the preceding manuscripts were brought by Professor Carlyle from the Greek islands.

15—17. Nos 1194, 1195, and 1196 are lectionaries from the Acts of the Apostles and Epistles. They are on vellum, in quarto, and were written in the thirteenth century. No. 1194 is mutilated at the end: the writing of this manuscript is singularly neat, and many of the letters are gilt. No. 1195 is also mutilated at the beginning, and No. 1196 at the end.

18. No. 1192 is a very beautiful manuscript of the four Gospels, in quarto, written on vellum in the thirteenth century.

19. No. 1193 is a lectionary from the four Gospels, also written on vellum, in the thirteenth century. It is mutilated at the end. The six last manuscripts, Nos. 1191—1196 were brought from Syria.[1]

XVIII. The CODICES MOSQUENSES, or Moscow manuscripts, are fifty-five in number. They were discovered by M. Matthæi, while he was a professor in that city, principally in the library belonging to the Holy Synod, and were collated by him with great accuracy. The principal various readings, derived from them, are printed in his edition of the Greek Testament, of which a notice is given in p.18. of the Appendix to this volume. Though these MSS. are not of the highest antiquity, yet they are far from being modern, since some of them were written in the eighth, several in the tenth or eleventh, and many in the twelfth century. As the Russian is a daughter of the Greek church, Michaelis remarks that the Moscow manuscripts very frequently contain the readings of the Byzantine recension, though he has observed many readings that were usual not only in the west of Europe, but also in Egypt. Of the Codices Mosquenses, there are three, which Matthæi designates by the letters V. H. and B., and to which he gives a high character for antiquity, correctness, and agreement: they are all written in uncial characters. The manuscript V. contains the four Gospels; from John vii. 39. to the end is the writing of the twelve or thirteenth century the preceding part is of the eighth century. It is written with accents, and is regularly pointed throughout. B. is an Evangeliarium or collection of the four Gospels, of the same date: H. is also an Evangeliarium, and, in the judgment of Matthæi, the most antient manuscript known to be extant in Europe. V. and H. were principally followed by him in forming the text of his edition of the New Testament.[2]

XIX. The CODEX BRIXIENSIS or BRIXIANUS is a precious manu-

---

[1] Catalogue of the MSS. in the Archiepiscopal Library, at Lambeth, by the Rev H. J Todd, pp 261, 262. folio, London, 1812.

[2] Michaelis, vol. ii. part i. pp. 288, 289. part ii. pp. 763—767. In Beck's Monogrammata Hermeneutices Librorum Novi Testamenti (pp 67—71. 98) and Griesbach's second edition of the Greek Testament (pp cxxiii—cxxvi.), there are lists of the Moscow manuscripts. Prof. Matthæi has also given notices of them with occasional fac-similes, in the different volumes of his edition of the Greek Testament.

script of the Old Italic (Latin) Version executed in the eighth century, preserved at Brescia, in Lombardy. It is an oblong quarto, written in uncial characters, on purple vellum, which in the lapse of time has faded to a bluish tinge. The letters were written with ink, and subsequently silvered over. The initial words of each Gospel have been traced with gold, vestiges of which are still visible. The letters O. and V., T. and D., are frequently interchanged, and especially the letters B. and V. To the Gospels are prefixed the Eusebian Canons.[1] The Codex Brixiensis is very frequently referred to by Mr. Nolan in his " Inquiry into the Integrity of the Greek Vulgate or received Text of the New Testament," on account of its antiquity and importance, in vindicating the integrity of that text. It is printed by Blanchini in his Evangeliarum Quadruplex.

XX. Besides the preceding manuscripts, which (with few exceptions) are written in square or uncial characters, there are many others written in *small letters*, which are quoted by Griesbach and other critics, by Arabic numerals, 1, 2, 3, &c.; and which, though not equal in point of antiquity with several of those in uncial letters, are nevertheless of great value and importance, and frequently exhibit readings not inferior to those contained in the foregoing manuscripts. Of this description are the following; viz.

1. The CODEX BASILEENSIS, (noted by Bengel Bas. γ, and by Wetstein and Griesbach 1, throughout their editions,) contains the whole of the New Testament, except the Revelation, and is written on vellum with accents. On account of the subscriptions and pictures which are found in it, (one of which appears to be a portrait of the emperor Leo, surnamed the Wise, and his son Constantine Porphyrogennetus,) Wetstein conjectures that it was written in their time, that is, in the tenth century. Michaelis and Griesbach have acceded to this opinion. Erasmus, who made use of it for his edition of the Greek Testament, supposed it to be a latinising manuscript, and his supposition was subsequently adopted by Wetstein; but Michaelis has vindicated it from this charge, and asserts that it is intitled to very great esteem. According to Hug, the text of the Gospels is very different from the text of the other parts of the book.[2]

2. The CODEX BEROLINENSIS is a quarto manuscript, on vellum, of the tenth century, preserved in the Royal Library at Berlin. It contains the following fragments; viz. Matt. i. 1—21.; vi. 12—32.; and xxii. 6. to the end of that Gospel; Mark i. 1—5. 29.; ix. 21.— xiii. 12.; Luke viii. 27. to the end of the Gospel; John i. 1.—ix. 21. and xx. 15. to the end of the Gospel. The various readings comprised in this manuscript were published by M. Pappelbaum, archdeacon of Berlin, in his description of it; whence they have been inserted by M Dermout in his Collectanea Critica in Novum Testamentum[3], and by Dr. Schulz (who numbers it 239) in his third edition of Griesbach's Greek Testament.

3. The CODEX CORSENDONCENSIS, which is in the Imperial Li-

---

[1] Blanchini Evangeliarum Quadruplex, tom. i. Prolegomena, pp. 1—40.
[2] Hug, vol. i. pp. 297, 298.
[3] Dermout, Collectanea Critica, p. 22.

brary at Vienna, is noted 3 by Wetstein and Griesbach. It was used by Erasmus for his second edition, and contains the whole of the New Testament, except the book of Revelation. It appears to have been written in the twelfth century, and by an ignorant transcriber, who has inserted marginal notes into the text. Wetstein charges it with being altered from the Latin.

4. The CODEX MONTFORTIANUS or MONTFORTII, also called DUBLINENSIS (61 of Griesbach), is a manuscript containing the whole of the New Testament, preserved in the library of Trinity College, Dublin, to which it was presented by Archbishop Usher. It derives its name of Montfortianus from having belonged to Dr. Montfort, previously to coming into Usher's possession. It has acquired much celebrity as being supposed to be the only manuscript which has the much-contested clause in 1 John v. 7, 8, and is the same which was cited by Erasmus under the title of *Codex Britannicus*, who inserted the disputed passage in the third edition of his Greek Testament on its authority. It is written in small Greek characters on thick glazed paper, in duodecimo, and without folios. Dr. A. Clarke (to whom we are indebted for the fac-simile which is given in a subsequent part of this work [1]) is of opinion that it was most probably written in the *thirteenth* century, from the similarity of its writing to that of other manuscripts of the same time. He has no doubt but it existed before the invention of printing, and is inclined to think it the work of an unknown bold critic, who formed a text from one or more manuscripts in conjunction with the Latin Vulgate, and who was by no means sparing of his own conjectural emendations, as it possesses various readings which exist in no manuscript yet discovered. But how far the writer has in any place faithfully copied the text of any particular antient manuscript, is more than can be determined. In the early part of the last century Mr. Martin claimed for this manuscript so early a date as the eleventh century. But Bishop Marsh, after Griesbach, contends that it is at least as modern as the fifteenth or sixteenth century. The Codex Montfortianus, he observes, "made its appearance about the year 1520 and that the manuscript had just been written, when it first appeared, is highly probable, because it appeared at a critical juncture, and its appearance answered a particular purpose.[2] But, whether written for the occasion or not, it could not have been written *very long* before the sixteenth century;

---

[1] See Vol IV Part II. Chap. IV Sect. V. § VI. *infra*

[2] "Erasmus had published two editions of the Greek Testament, one in 1516, the other in 1519, both of which were without the words, that begin with εν τω ουρανω and end with εν τη γη, in the disputed clause in 1 John v. 7, 8 This *omission*, as it was called by those who paid more deference to the Latin translation than to the Greek original, exposed Erasmus to much censure, though, in fact, the complaint was for *non-addition*. Erasmus, therefore, very properly answered; 'Addendi de meo, quod Græcis deest, provinciam non susceperam' He promised, however, that though he could not insert in a Greek edition what he had never found in a Greek manuscript, he would insert the passage in his next edition, if in the mean time a Greek MS. could be discovered which had the passage In less than a year after that declaration, Erasmus was informed, that there was a Greek MS. in England which contained the passage. At the same time a copy of the passage, as contained in that MS., was communicated to Erasmus and Erasmus, as he had promised, inserted that copy in his next edition, which was published in 1522."

for this manuscript has the Latin chapters, though the κεφαλαια of Eusebius are likewise noted. Now the *Latin* chapters were foreign to the usage of the *Greek* Church, before the introduction of printed editions, in which the Latin chapters were adopted, as well for the Greek as for the Latin Testament. Whatever Greek manuscripts therefore were written with Latin Chapters, were written in the *West* of Europe, where the Latin Chapters were in use. They were written by the Greeks, or by the descendants of those Greeks, who fled into the West of Europe, after the taking of Constantinople, and who then began to divide their manuscripts according to the usage of the country, in which they fixed their abode.[1] The Dublin manuscript, therefore, if not written for the purpose to which it was applied in the third edition of Erasmus[2], could hardly have been written more than fifty years before. And how widely those critics have erred in their conjectures, who have supposed that it was written so early as the twelfth century, appears from the fact that the Latin Chapters were not *invented* till the 13th century.[3] But the influence of the Church of Rome in the composition of the Dublin manuscript, is most conspicuous in the *text* of that manuscript, which is a servile imitation of the Latin Vulgate. It will be sufficient to mention how it follows the Vulgate at the place in question. It not only agrees with the Vulgate, in the insertion of the seventh verse; it follows the Vulgate also at the end of the sixth verse, having χριστος, where all other Greek manuscripts have πνευμα: and in the eighth verse it omits the final clause which had *never* been omitted in the Greek manuscripts, and was not omitted even in the *Latin* manuscripts before the thirteenth century.[4] Such is the character of that solitary manuscript, which is opposed to the united evidence of all former manuscripts, including the Codex Vaticanus, and the Codex Alexandrinus."[5] Upon the whole, it does not appear that the date of the Codex Montfortianus *can* be earlier than the close of the fifteenth century. The uncollated parts of this manuscript were collated by the late Rev. Dr. Barrett, of Trinity College, Dublin, with Wetstein's edition of the Greek Testament; beginning with Rom. ii. and ending with the Apocalypse, including also a collation of the Acts of the Apostles, from chap. xxii. 27. to chap. xxviii. 2. This collation, comprising thirty-five pages, forms the third part of his fac-simile edition of the Codex Rescriptus of St. Matthew's Gospel.

5. The CODEX MEERMANNIANUS derives its name from its former

---

[1] "There are three Greek manuscripts with the Latin Chapters in the University Library at Cambridge, marked Hh 6. 12 Kk 5 35 and Ll. 2. 13. That which is marked Ll 2 13., and is evidently the oldest of the three, was written at Paris by Jerom of Sparta, for the use and at the expence of a person called Bodet, as appears from the subscription to it. Now Jerom of Sparta died at the beginning of the sixteenth century."
[2] "The third edition of Erasmus has 1 John v 7 *precisely* in the words of the Dublin MS."
[3] See p. 168 *infra*.
[4] "Here there is an additional proof, respecting the age of the Dublin MS."
[5] Bishop Marsh's Lectures, Part VI pp 25—26. See also his letters to Mr. Archdeacon Travis, (Leipzig, 1795, 8vo.) Pref pp xvii xviii. xxiii in the notes. Michaelis vol. ii. part i. pp 284—287 part ii. pp 755—759. Dr A. Clarke's Succession of Sacred Literature, pp 86—92

possessor M. Meerman, at the sale of whose library it was purchased by a private individual, but has since been deposited in the Library of the University of Leyden. It was written towards the close of the twelfth century, and contains the four Gospels, Acts, and all the Epistles; but it is defective in Acts i. 1—14. xxi. 14.—xxii. 28. Rom. i. — vii. 13. 1 John iv. 20. to the end, the second and third Epistles of John, and the Epistle of Jude. This manuscript was first collated by M. Dermout, in his Collectanea Critica in Novum Testamentum; and the various readings discovered by him are incorporated by Dr Schulz in his edition of Griesbach's Greek Testament, where it is numbered 246.[1]

6. The CODEX REGIUS, formerly 2244.[2] at present 50., (noted Paris. 6. by Kuster, 13. by Wetstein, and *13. by Griesbach,) is a manuscript of the four Gospels in the Royal Library at Paris. Though not more antient, probably, than the thirteenth century, it is pronounced by Michaelis to be of very great importance: it has the following chasms, which were first discovered by Griesbach, viz. Matt. i. 1.—ii. 21.; xxvi. 33—53.; xxvii. 26.—xxviii. 10.; Mark i. 2. to the end of the chapter; and John xxi. 2. to the end of the Gospel. The various readings from this manuscript given by Kuster and Wetstein are very inaccurate. Matt. xiii. xiv. and xv. were the only three chapters actually collated by Griesbach, who expresses a wish that the whole manuscript might be completely and exactly collated, especially the latter chapters of the Gospels of Luke and John. In consequence of this manuscript harmonising in a very eminent manner with the quotations of Origen, he refers it to the Alexandrine edition, though he says it has a certain mixture of the Western.[2]

7. The CODEX LEICESTRENSIS derives its name from being the property of the Corporation of Leicester [3]: it is a manuscript of the whole New Testament, written by a modern hand, partly on paper, and partly on vellum, chiefly the former, and is referred by Wetstein and Griesbach to the fourteenth century. It is noted by Dr. Mill by the letter L., in the first part of Wetstein's New Testament Codex, 69.; in the second, 37. in the third, 31.; and in the fourth, 14.; and by Griesbach, 69. The book of Acts is inserted between the epistle to the Hebrews and that of Saint James. This manuscript is defective from the beginning as far as Matt. xviii. 15., and has also the following chasms, viz. Acts x. 45.—xiv 7. Jude 7 to the end of that Epistle, and it concludes with part of Rev. xix. It has many peculiar

---

[1] Dermout, Collectanea Critica in N. T Pars I p 14
[2] Michaelis, vol i part i pp 502, 303 — Griesbach's Symbolæ Criticæ, vol. i. pp. cliv. —clxiv. Nov. Test vol. i p cv
[3] In a critique on the second edition of this work, in the Eclectic Review for January, 1822, (vol. xvii N S. p. 83.) it is stated, that when the writer of that article made enquiry respecting the Codex Leicestrensis, it was no longer to be found in the Library of the Town Hall at Leicester Anxious, for the interest of sacred literature, to ascertain the *real fact*, the author of the present work requested Mr Combe (an eminent bookseller at that place, to whom he thus gladly makes his acknowledgments,) to make the requisite investigation. The result of Mr. Combe's critical researches is, that *the Codex Leicestrensis is still carefully preserved*. Mr. C further collated the author's account of it (which had been drawn up from the notices of Wetstein and Michaelis,) with the manuscript itself, and this collation has enabled him to make the description above given *more complete* as well as *more correct*.

readings; and in those which are not confined to it, this manuscript chiefly agrees with D. or the Codex Cantabrigiensis: it also harmonises in a very eminent manner with the old Syriac version; and, what further proves its value, several readings, which Dr. Mill found in it alone, have been confirmed by other manuscripts that belong to totally different countries. The Codex Leicestrensis was first collated by him, and afterwards more accurately by Mr. Jackson, the learned editor of Novatian's works, whose extracts were used by Wetstein. There is another and still more accurate transcript of Mr. J.'s collation in his copy of Mill's edition of the Greek Testament, which is now preserved in the library of Jesus College, Cambridge, where it is marked O, Θ, 1.[1]

8. The CODEX VINDOBONENSIS, Lambecii 31. (124. of Griesbach,) is a manuscript of the four Gospels, written in the eleventh or twelfth century: it has been collated by Treschow, Birch, and Alter. It is of very great importance, and agrees with the Codex Cantabrigiensis in not less than eighty unusual readings; with the Codex Ephremi in upwards of thirty-five; with the Codex Regius 2861., or Stephani η, in fifty; with the Codex Basileensis in more than fifty, and has several which are found in that manuscript alone; with the Codex Regius 2244², in sixty unusual readings; and with the Codex Colbertinus 2844., in twenty-two.[2]

9. The CODEX EBNERIANUS is a very neat manuscript of the New Testament in quarto, formerly in the possession of Hieronymus Ebner Von Eschenbach of that city, from whom its appellation is derived: it is now the property of the University of Oxford, and is deposited among the other precious manuscripts preserved in the Bodleian Library. The Codex Ebnerianus contains 425 leaves of vellum, and was written in the year 1391. The whole of the New Testament is comprised in this volume, excepting the Book of Revelation: each page contains 27 lines, at equal distances, excepting those in which the different books commence, or which are decorated with illuminations. Besides the New Testament, the Eusebian Canons are introduced, together with the lessons for particular festivals, and a menologium used in the Greek church, &c. The book is bound in massy silver covers, in the centre of which the Redeemer of the World is represented sitting on a throne, and in the act of pronouncing a blessing. Above his head is the following inscription, in square letters, exhibiting the style in which the capitals are written:
—Δεσποτα ευλογησον τον δουλον σου ελαχιστον Ιερονυμον Ιουλιελμον και την οικιαν αυτου. "Lord, bless the least of thy servants, Hieronymus Gulielmus, and his family." Of the style of writing adopted in the body of the manuscript, the annexed engraving will afford a correct

---

[1] Michaelis, vol. ii. part i pp. 355—357. part ii pp. 749, 750. Bp Marsh adds, "This copy of Mill's Greek Testament, with Jackson's marginal readings, is a treasure of sacred criticism, which deserves to be communicated to the public It contains the result of all his labours in that branch of literature, it supplies many of the defects of Mill, and corrects many of his errors and, besides quotations from manuscripts and antient versions, it contains a copious collection of readings from many of the fathers, which have hitherto been very imperfectly collated, or wholly neglected " Ibid. p. 750

[2] Michaelis, vol ii part ii p. 870.

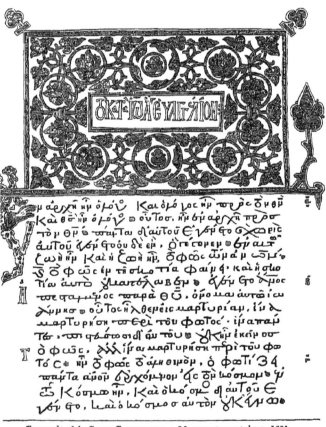

Fac-simile of the Codex Ebnerianus, a Manuscript executed A.D. 1391.

idea, and at the same time exemplify the abbreviations frequent in Greek manuscripts of the 12th and 13th centuries. Our specimen comprises the ten first verses of the first chapter of Saint John's Gospel; the abbreviations, though very numerous, being uniformly the same, do not interpose any material difficulty to the easy perusal of the manuscript. Wetstein, though he has admitted it into his catalogue, has made use of it only in the eighteenth chapter of Saint John's Gospel; Michaelis has classed it among the uncollated manuscripts of the New Testament.[1] It is to be hoped that some learned member of the University of Oxford will publish a collation of *all* the various readings which may be found in this manuscript.

10. The CODEX OTTOBONIANUS 298. is one of the manuscripts preserved in the Vatican Library, and was written in the fifteenth century. It contains the Acts and Apostolic Epistles, and was collated by Dr. Scholz for his intended critical edition of the New Testament. It is here noticed on account of its containing the disputed clause in 1 John v. 7, 8., in the following manner: οἱ μαρτυρουντες απο του ούρανο πατηρ λογος και πνευμα αγιον και οἱ τρεις εις το ἐν εισι και τρεις εισιν οἱ μαρτυρουντες απο της γης, το πνευμα, &c. &c. This manuscript has been altered in many places, in order to make it harmonise with the Latin Vulgate[2]; on this account, as well as its late date, it can be of little value in sacred criticism, except where it corroborates the readings of MSS. of better authority and of earlier date. Its principal readings are given by M. Dermout in his Collectanea Critica in Novum Testamentum.

XXI. The limits assigned to this work forbid any further detail respecting the other manuscripts of the New Testament. Referring the reader, therefore, to the elaborate volumes of Michaelis, who has given a catalogue raisonné of two hundred and ninety-two manuscripts, to which his annotator Bishop Marsh has added one *hundred and seventy-seven*[3], we proceed briefly to notice two collations of manuscripts, which in the seventeenth century produced a warm contest between biblical critics of different denominations.

1. In 1673, Pierre POUSSINES (Petrus Possinus), a learned Jesuit,

---

[1] See Wetstein's N T. Proleg. p. 58 Bp Marsh's Michaelis, vol ii. part i. p 258. De Murr's Memorabilia Bibliothecæ Norimb part ii pp 100—131. where the Codex Ebnerianus is minutely described and illustrated with thirteen plates of illuminations, &c. which are very curious in an antiquarian point of view. Our engraving is copied from one of De Murr's fac-similes.

[2] Scholz, Biblische Critische Reise, p 105

[3] Michaelis, vol ii part i. pp. 185—361 part ii. pp. 649—835. Professor Beck, in his Monogrammata Hermeneutices Librorum Novi Fœderis, (part i. pp 42—100.) has given a catalogue of all the manuscripts (394 in number) which are *certainly* known to have been collated, exclusive of Lectionaria, Euchologia, or prayer books of the Greek church, and Menologia or Martyrologies In pp. 91—93. he has specified, by numbers referring to his own catalogue, what manuscripts are written in uncial letters; what contain the entire New Testament, and how many contain the greater part, or particular books of the New Testament. It seems to be precisely that sort of catalogue which Michaelis recommends biblical students to make, in order that they may be enabled (when consulting Mill or Wetstein) to judge of the proportion of manuscripts which are in favour of a reading to those which decide against it. The total number of manuscripts collated by Griesbach for his edition of the New Testament, was *three hundred and fifty-five*. He has given a list of them in his Prolegomena, tom. i. pp ci —cxxvi and also critical accounts of the most important manuscripts in the two volumes of his Symbolæ Criticæ.

published[1] extracts from twenty-two manuscripts, which, he said, were in the library of Cardinal Barberini at Rome, and had been collated by order of Pope Urban VIII., by John Matthæus Caryophilus. Dr. Mill inserted these extracts among his various readings; but as it was not known for a long time what had become of the Barberini manuscripts, and as the readings of the Barberini collation are for the most part in favour of the Latin Vulgate version, Wetstein, Semler, and other Protestant divines, accused Poussines of a literary fraud. Of this, however, he was acquitted by Isaac Vossius, who found the manuscript of Caryophilus in the Barberini Library; and the imputation against the veracity of that eminent Greek scholar has been completely destroyed by M. Birch, a learned Danish divine, who recognised in the Vatican Library six of the manuscripts from which Caryophilus had made extracts.[2]

2. Another Jesuit, John Louis DE LA CERDA, inserted in his *Adversaria Sacra*, which appeared at Lyons in 1696, a collation of sixteen manuscripts (eight of which were borrowed from the library of the king of Spain) which had been made by Pedro Faxardo, Marquis of Velez. From these manuscripts, the marquis inserted various readings in his copy of the Greek Testament, but without specifying what manuscripts in particular, or even how many in general, were in favour of each quoted reading. The remarkable agreement between the Velesian readings and those of the Vulgate excited the suspicions of Mariana (who communicated them to De la Cerda) that Velez had made use only of interpolated manuscripts, that had been corrected agreeably to the Latin Vulgate, subsequently to the council of Florence. However this may be, the collation of Velez will never be of any utility in the criticism of the New Testament, unless the identical manuscripts, which he made use of, should hereafter be discovered in any Spanish library. But such a discovery must be considered as hopeless after the laborious and careful researches made by Bishop Marsh, relative to this collation of Velez, who (he has proved to demonstration) did NOT collate one single Greek or Latin manuscript, but took his various lections from Robert Stephens's edition of the *Latin* Vulgate, published at Paris in 1540; that the object which the marquis had in view, in framing this collection of readings, was to support, not the Vulgate in general, but the text of this edition in particular, wherever it varied from the text of Stephens's *Greek* Testament printed in 1550; and that with this view he translated into Greek the readings of the former, which varied from the latter, except where Stephens's Greek margin supplied him with the readings which he wanted, where he had only to transcribe, and not to translate.[3]

---

[1] At the end of his Catena Patrum Græcorum in Marcum Poussines prefixed to these extracts the title of *Collationes Græci Contextus omnium Librorum Novi Testamenti juxta editionem Antverpensem regiam, cum xxii Antiquis Codicibus Manuscriptis Ex Bibliotheca Barberina.*

[2] Michaelis, vol. ii. part i. pp. 212—216 part ii pp. 666, 667 Birch, Quatuor Evangelia, Prolegom. p 36. Ejusdem, Variæ Lectiones ad Text. N Evangel. Proleg. p xlii. Hafniæ, 1801, 8vo

[3] Michaelis, vol. ii. part i pp. 351—354, part ii. pp. 824, 825. Mr (now Bishop)

CHAPTER IV.

ON THE DIVISIONS AND MARKS OF DISTINCTION OCCURRING IN MANUSCRIPTS AND PRINTED EDITIONS OF THE SCRIPTURES.

SECTION I.

ON THE DIVISIONS AND MARKS OF DISTINCTION OCCURRING IN THE OLD TESTAMENT.

I. *Different Appellations given to the Scriptures* — II. *General Divisions of the Canonical Books* — III *Particularly of the Old Testament* — 1. *The Law.* — 2. *The Prophets.* — 3. *The Cetubim or Hagiographa.* — IV *Account of the Masora.* — V. *Modern Divisions of the Books of the Old Testament.* — *Chapters and Verses.*

I. THE collection of writings, which is regarded by Christians as the sole standard of their faith and practice, has been distinguished, at various periods, by different appellations. Thus, it is frequently termed the Scriptures, the Sacred or Holy Scriptures, and sometimes the Canonical Scriptures. This collection is called *The Scriptures*, as being the most important of all *Writings*, — the *Holy* or *Sacred Scriptures*, because they were composed by persons divinely inspired; and the *Canonical Scriptures*, either because they are a rule of faith and practice to those who receive them; or because, when the number and authenticity of these books were ascertained, lists of them were inserted in the ecclesiastical *canons* or catalogues, in order to distinguish them from such books as were *apocryphal* or of uncertain authority, and unquestionably not of divine origin. But the most usual appellation is that of the BIBLE — a word which in its primary import simply denotes a book, but which is given to the writings of the prophets and apostles, by way of eminence, as being the Book of Books, infinitely superior in excellence to every unassisted production of the human mind.[1]

II. The most common and general division of the canonical books is that of the Old and New Testament; the former containing those revelations of the divine will which were communicated to the Hebrews, Israelites, or Jews, before the birth of Christ, and the latter comprising the inspired writings of the evangelists and apostles. The appellation of Testament is derived from 2 Cor. iii. 6 14.; in which place the words η παλαια διαθηκη and η καινη διαθηκη are by the old Latin translators rendered *antiquum testamentum* and *novum testamentum*, old and new testament, instead of *antiquum fœdus* and *novum fœdus*, the *old and new covenant*, for although the Greek word διαθηκη signifies both testament and covenant, yet it uniformly corresponds with the Hebrew word *Berith*, which constantly signifies a covenant.[2] The term "old covenant," used by Saint Paul in

---

Marsh's Letters to Archdeacon Travis, p 67., and the Appendix to that work, (pp 253—344) in which a minute detail of the Velesian readings is given, as also in Christian Benedict Michaelis's Tractatio Critica de Variis Lectionibus Novi Testamenti, §§ 57—89 (pp 96—101.) 4to. Halæ Magdeburgicæ, 1749

[1] Lardner's Works, 8vo vol. vi pp 1—8 4to vol iii pp 137—140 Jahn, Introd. ad Vet Fœd. p. 7.

[2] Jerome, Comment. in Malachi, cap. ii. op. tom iii. p. 1816.

2 Cor. iii. 14., does not denote the entire collection of writings which we term the Bible, but those antient institutions, promises, threatenings, and, in short, the whole of the Mosaic dispensation, related in the Pentateuch, and in the writings of the prophets; and which in process of time were, by a metonymy, transferred to the books themselves. Thus we find mention made of the *book of the covenant* in Exodus (xxiv. 7.), and in the apocryphal book of Maccabees (Macc. i. 57.): and after the example of the apostle, the same mode of designating the sacred writings obtained among the first Christians, from whom it has been transmitted to modern times.[1]

III. The arrangement of the books comprising the Old Testament, which is adopted in our Bibles, is not always regulated by the exact time when the books were respectively written; although the book of Genesis is universally allowed to be the first, and the prophecy of Malachi to be the latest of the inspired writings. Previously to the building of Solomon's temple, the Pentateuch was deposited *in the side of the ark of the covenant* (Deut. xxxi. 24—26), to be consulted by the Israelites; and after the erection of that sacred edifice, it was deposited in the treasury, together with all the succeeding productions of the inspired writers. On the subsequent destruction of the temple by Nebuchadnezzar, the autographs of the sacred books are supposed to have perished: although some learned men have conjectured that they were preserved, because it does not appear that Nebuchadnezzar evinced any particular enmity against the Jewish religion; and in the account of the sacred things carried to Babylon (2 Kings xxv. 2 Chron. xxxvi. Jer. lii.), no mention is made of the sacred books. However this may be, it is a fact, that copies of these autographs were carried to Babylon: for we find the prophet Daniel quoting the law (Dan. ix. 11. 13.), and also expressly mentioning the prophecies of Jeremiah (ix 2), which he could not have done, if he had never seen them. We are further informed that on the rebuilding, or rather on the finishing, of the temple in the sixth year of Darius, the Jewish worship was fully re-established according *as it is written in the book of Moses* (Ezra vi. 18.): which would have been impracticable, if the Jews had not had copies of the law then among them. But what still more clearly proves that they must have had transcripts of their sacred writings during, as well as subsequent to, the Babylonish captivity, is the fact, that when the people requested Ezra to produce the law of Moses (Nehem. viii. 1.), they did not entreat him to get it dictated *anew* to them; but that he would bring forth *the book of the law of Moses, which the Lord had commanded to Israel.*

About fifty years after the rebuilding of the temple, and the consequent re-establishment of the Jewish religion, it is generally admitted that the canon of the Old Testament was settled; but by whom this great work was accomplished, is a question on which there is considerable difference of opinion. On the one hand it is contended, that it could not have been done by Ezra himself; because, though he has

---

[1] Dr. Lardner has collected several passages from early Christians writers, who thus metonymically use the word Testament Works, 8vo. vol. vi. p. 9. 4to. vol iii. p. 140.

related his zealous efforts in restoring the law and worship of Jehovah, yet concerning the settlement of the canon he is totally silent; and the silence of Nehemiah, who has recorded the pious labours of Ezra, as well as the silence of Josephus, who is diffuse in his encomiums on him, has further been urged as a presumptive argument why he could not have collected the Jewish writings. But to these hypothetical reasonings we may oppose the constant tradition of the Jewish church, uncontradicted both by their enemies and by Christians, that Ezra, with the assistance of the members of the great synagogue (among whom were the prophets Haggai, Zechariah, and Malachi), did collect as many copies of the sacred writings as he could, and from them set forth a correct edition of the canon of the Old Testament, with the exception of his own writings, the book of Nehemiah, and the prophecy of Malachi; which were subsequently annexed to the canon by Simon the Just, who is said to have been the last of the great synagogue. In this Esdrine text, the errors of the former copyists were corrected. and Ezra (being himself an inspired writer) added in several places, throughout the books of this edition, what appeared necessary to illustrate, connect, or complete them.[1] Whether Ezra's own copy of the Jewish Scriptures perished in the pillage of the temple by Antiochus Epiphanes, is a question that cannot now by ascertained: nor is it material, since we know that Judas Maccabæus repaired the temple, and replaced every thing requisite for the performance of divine worship (1 Macc. iv. 36—59.), which included a correct, if not Ezra's own, copy of the Scriptures.[2] It is not improbable, that in this latter temple an ark was constructed, in which the sacred books of the Jews were preserved until the destruction of Jerusalem and the subversion of the Jewish polity by the Romans under Titus, before whom the volume of the law was carried in triumph, among the other spoils which had been taken at Jerusalem.[3] Since that time, although there has been no certain standard edition of the Old Testament, yet, since both Jews and Christians have constantly had the *same* Hebrew Scriptures to which they have always appealed, we have every possible evidence to prove that the Old Testament has been transmitted to us entire, and free from any material or designed corruption.

The various books contained in the Old Testament, were divided by the Jews into three parts or classes — the *Law* — the *Prophets* — and the *Cetubim*, or *Hagiographa*, that is, the Holy Writings: which division obtained in the time of our Saviour[4],

---

[1] Prideaux's Connection, part i book v. sub anno 446. vol i. pp. 329—344 and the authorities there cited. Carpzov. Introd ad Libros Biblicos Vet. Test. pp. 24. 308, 309.
[2] Bishop Tomline's Elements of Christian Theology, vol i. p 11.
[3] Josephus de Bell. Jud. lib vii c 5. § 5
[4] *These are the words which I spake unto you, while I was yet with you, that all things might be fulfilled which are written in the* LAW, *and in the* PROPHETS, *and in the* PSALMS, *concerning me* (Luke xxiv 44) In which passage by the *Psalms* is intended the Hagiographa, which division beginning with the Psalms, the whole of it (agreeably to the Jewish manner of quoting) is there called by the name of the book with which it commences. Saint Peter also, when appealing to prophecies in proof of the Gospel, says — " All the prophets from Samuel, and those that follow after, as many as have spoken, have likewise foretold of these days." (Acts iii. 24) In which passaget he apostle plainly includes the books of Samuel in the class of prophets.

and is noticed by Josephus[1], though he does not enumerate the several books.

1. The LAW (so called, because it contains precepts for the regulation of life and manners) comprised the Pentateuch, or five books of Moses, which were originally written in one volume, as all the manuscripts are to this day, which are read in the synagogues. It is not known when the writings of the Jewish legislator were divided into *five* books: but, as the titles of Genesis, Exodus, Leviticus, Numbers, and Deuteronomy, are evidently of Greek origin, (for the tradition related by Philo, and adopted by some writers of the Romish church, that they were given by Moses himself, is too idle to deserve refutation,) it is not improbable that these titles were prefixed to the several books by the authors of the Alexandrian or Septuagint Greek version.

2. The PROPHETS, which were thus designated, because these books were written by inspired prophetical men, were divided into the *former* and *latter*[2], with regard to the time when they respectively flourished: the former prophets contained the books of Joshua, Judges, 1 and 2 Samuel, and 1 and 2 Kings, the two last being each considered as one book, the latter prophets comprised the writings of Isaiah, Jeremiah, Ezekiel, and of the twelve minor prophets, whose books were reckoned as one The reason why Moses is not included among the prophets, is, because he so far surpassed all those who came after him, in eminence and dignity, that they were not accounted worthy to be placed on a level with him: and the books of Joshua and Judges are reckoned among the prophetical books, because they are generally supposed to have been written by the prophet Samuel.

3. The CETUBIM or HAGIOGRAPHA, that is, the Holy Writings, comprehended the Psalms, Proverbs, Job, Song of Solomon, Ruth, Lamentations of Jeremiah, Ecclesiastes, Esther, Daniel, Ezra and Nehemiah (reckoned as one), and the two books of Chronicles, also reckoned as one book.[3] This third class or division of the Sacred Books has received its appellation of *Cetubim* or *Holy Writings*, because they were not orally delivered, as the law of Moses was; but the Jews affirm that they were composed by men divinely inspired, who, however, had no public mission as prophets: and the Jews conceive that they were dictated not by dreams, visions, or voice, or in other ways, as the oracles of the prophets were, but that they were more immediately revealed to the minds of their authors. It is remarkable that Daniel is excluded from the number of prophets, and that his writings, with the rest of the Hagiographa, were not publicly read in the synagogues as the Law and the Prophets were: this is ascribed to the singular minuteness with which he foretold the coming of the Messiah before the destruction of the city and sanctuary (Dan. ix.) and the apprehension of the Jews, lest the public reading of his predictions should lead any to embrace the doctrines of Jesus Christ[4]

The Pentateuch is divided into fifty or fifty-four *Paraschioth*, or

---

[1] Contr. Apion lib. i. § 8.

[2] This distinction, Carpzov thinks, was borrowed from Zech. i. 4.—" Be ye not as your fathers, unto whom the *former* prophets have cried."—Introd. ad Lib Bibl. Vet. Test p. 146.

[3] The Song of Solomon, Ruth, Lamentations, Ecclesiastes, and Esther, are, in the modern copies of the Jewish Scriptures, placed immediately after the Pentateuch; under the name of the five *Megilloth* or volumes. The Book of Ruth holds sometimes the first or second, and sometimes the fifth place.

[4] Hottinger's Thesaurus, p. 510. Leusden's Philologus Hebræus, Diss. ii. pp 13—22. Bishop's Cosin's Scholastical Hist of the Canon, c. ii pp. 10. et seq

larger sections, according as the Jewish lunar year is simple or intercalary; one of which sections was read in the synagogue every Sabbath-day: this division many of the Jews suppose to have been appointed by Moses, but it is by others attributed, and with greater probability, to Ezra. These paraschioth were further subdivided into smaller sections termed *Siderim*, or orders. Until the persecution of Antiochus Epiphanes, the Jews read only the law; but the reading of it being then prohibited, they substituted for it fifty-four *Haphtoroth*, or sections from the prophets. Subsequently, however, when the reading of the law was restored by the Maccabees, the section which had been read from the Law was used for the first, and that from the Prophets, for the second lesson.[1] These sections were also divided into *Pesukim*, or verses, which have likewise been ascribed to Ezra; but if not contrived by him, it appears that this subdivision was introduced shortly after his death: it was probably intended for the use of the Targumists or Chaldee interpreters. After the return of the Jews from the Babylonish captivity, when the Hebrew language had ceased to be spoken, and the Chaldee became the vernacular tongue, it was (as we have already remarked[2]) usual to read the law, first in the original Hebrew, and afterwards to interpret it to the people in the Chaldee dialect. For the purpose of exposition, therefore, these shorter periods were very convenient.[3]

IV. Originally, the text of the Sacred Books was written without any breaks or divisions into chapters or verses, or even into words; so that a whole book, as written in the antient manner, was, in fact, but one continued word. Many antient Greek and Latin manuscripts thus written are still extant. The sacred writings having undergone an infinite number of alterations by successive transcriptions, during the lapse of ages, whence various readings had arisen, the Jews had recourse to a canon, which they judged to be infallible, in order to fix and ascertain the reading of the Hebrew text, and this rule they called *Masora* or tradition, as if this critique were nothing but a tradition which they had received from their ancestors. Accordingly, they pretend, that, when God gave the law to Moses on Mount Sinai, he taught him, first, its *true reading*, and, secondly, its *true* interpretation; and that both these were handed down by oral tradition, from generation to generation, until at length they were committed to writing. The former of these, viz. the true reading, is the subject of the Masora; the latter or true interpretation

---

[1] Of these divisions we have evident traces in the New Testament; thus, the section (περιοχη) of the prophet Isaiah, which the Ethiopian eunuch was reading, was, in all probability, that which related to the sufferings of the Messiah (Acts viii 32.) When Saint Paul entered into the synagogue at Antioch in Pisidia, he stood up to preach *after the reading of the Law and the Prophets* (Acts xiii 15), that is, after reading the first lesson out of the Law, and the second lesson out of the Prophets. And in the very discourse which he then delivered, he tells the Jews that *the Prophets were read at Jerusalem on every Sabbath-day*, that is, in those lessons which were taken out of the Prophets. (Acts xiii. 27.)

[2] See pp. 5, 6. *supra*, of this volume.

[3] In Vol. III Part. Chap. III. Sect. IV. we have given a table of the *Paraschioth* or Sections of the Law, together with the *Haphtoroth* or Sections of the Prophets as they are read in the different Jewish synagogues for every sabbath of the year, and also showing the portions corresponding with our modern divisions of chapters and verses.

is that of the *Mishna* and *Gemara*, of which an account is given in a subsequent chapter of the present volume.

The Masoretic notes and criticisms relate to the books, verses, words, letters, vowel points, and accents. The *Masorites* or Massorets, as the inventors of this system were called, were the first who distinguished the books and sections of books into verses. They marked the number of all the verses of each book and section, and placed the amount at the end of each in numeral letters, or in some symbolical word formed out of them; and they also marked the middle verse of each book. Further, they noted the verses where something was supposed to be forgetten; the words which they believed to be changed; the letters which they deemed to be superfluous; the repetitions of the same verses; the different reading of the words which are redundant or defective; the number of times that the same word is found at the beginning, middle, or end of a verse; the different significations of the same word; the agreement or conjunction of one word with another; what letters are pronounced, and what are inverted, together with such as hang perpendicularly, and they took the number of each, for the Jews cherish the sacred books with such reverence, that they make a scruple of changing the situation of a letter which is evidently misplaced; supposing that some mystery has occasioned the alteration. They have likewise reckoned which is the middle letter of the Pentateuch, which is the middle clause of each book, and how many times each letter of the alphabet occurs in all the Hebrew Scriptures. The following table from Bishop Walton will give an idea of their laborious minuteness in these researches.

			Times				Times.
א	Aleph	occurs in the Hebrew Bible	42377	ל	Lamed	occurs in the Hebrew Bible	41517
ב	Beth		38218	מ	Mem		77778
ג	Gimel	-	29537	נ	Nun	-	41696
ד	Daleth	-	32530	ס	Samech	-	13580
ה	He	-	47554	ע	Ain	-	20175
ו	Vau	-	76922	פ	Pe	-	22725
ז	Zain	-	22867	צ	Tsaddi	-	21882
ח	Cheth	-	23447	ק	Koph	-	22972
ט	Teth	-	11052	ר	Resh	-	22147
י	Yod	-	66420	ש	Shin	-	32148
כ	Caph	-	48253	ת	Tau	-	59343*

* Bishop Walton's Prolegom. c. viii. § 8. p. 275. edit. Dathii. In the last century, an anonymous writer published the following calculation (copied from the Encyclopædia Perthensis) similar to that of the Masorites, for the ENGLISH VERSION of the Bible, under the title of the *Old and New Testament Dissected*. It is said to have occupied three years of the compiler's life, and is a singular instance of the trifling employments to which superstition has led mankind.

THE OLD AND NEW TESTAMENT DISSECTED.

Books in the Old	-	39	In the New	-	27	Total	-	66
Chapters	-	929	-	260	-	-	1,189
Verses	-	23,214	-	7,959	-	-	31,173
Words	-	592,439	-	181,253	-	-	773,692
Letters	-	2,728,800	-	838,380	-	-	3,567,180

Such is the celebrated Masora of the Jews. At first, it did not accompany the text; afterwards the greatest part of it was written in the margin. In order to bring it within the margin, it became necessary to abridge the work itself This abridgment was called the *little* Masora, *Masora parva*, but, being found too short, a more copious abridgment was inserted, which was distinguished by the appellation of the *great* Masora, *Masora magna*. The omitted parts were added at the end of the text, and called the *final* Masora, *Masora finalis*.[1]

Lastly, in Jewish manuscripts and printed editions of the Old Testament, a word is often found with a small circle annexed to it, or with an asterisk over it, and a word written in the margin of the same line. The former is called the *Ketib*, that is, *written*, and the latter, *Keri*, that is, *read* or reading, as if to intimate, write in this manner, but read in that manner. For instance, when they meet with certain words, they substitute others: thus, instead of the sacred name Jehovah, they substitute Adonai or Elohim, and in lieu of terms not strictly consistent with decency, they pronounce others less indelicate or more agreeable to our ideas of propriety.[2] The invention of these marginal corrections has been ascribed to the Masorites.

The age when the Masorites lived has been much controverted. Some ascribe the Masoretic notes to Moses; others attribute them to Ezra and the members of the great synagogue, and their successors after the restoration of the temple-worship, on the death of Antiochus Epiphanes. Archbishop Usher places the Masorites before the time of Jerome; Cappel, at the end of the fifth century;

Apocrypha.

Chapters	- -	183
Verses	- -	6,081
Words	- -	252,185

The middle chapter, and the least in the Bible, is Psalm 117.
The middle verse is the eighth of the 118th Psalm
The middle line 2d of Chronicles, 4th chapter, 16th verse.
The word *and* occurs in the Old Testament, 35,543 times.
The same word occurs in the New Testament, 10,684 times.
The word Jehovah occurs 6855 time.

Old Testament.

The middle book is Proverbs.
The middle chapter is Job 29th.
The middle verse is 2d Chronicles, 20th chapter, between the 17th and 18th verses.
The least verse is 1st Chronicles, 1st chapter and 25th verse.

New Testament.

The middle book is Thessalonians 2d.
The middle chapter is between the 13th and 14th Romans.
The middle verse is chapter 17th of Acts, 17th verse.
The least verse is 11th Chapter of John, verse 35.
The 21st verse of the 7th chapter of Ezra has all the Letters in the Alphabet except j.
The 19th chapter of the 2d of Kings and the 37th of Isaiah are alike.

[1] Butler's Horæ Biblicæ, vol. i. p. 61.
[2] The reader will find a learned and elaborate elucidation of the Keri in the Rev John Whittaker's Historical and Critical Inquiry into the Interpretation of the Hebrew Scriptures, pp. 114—178.

Bishop Marsh is of opinion, that they cannot be dated higher than the fourth or fifth century; Bishop Walton, Basnage, Jahn, and others, refer them to the rabbins of Tiberias in the sixth century, and suppose that they commenced the Masora, which was augmented and continued at different times by various authors; so that it was not the work of one man, or of one age. In proof of this opinion, which we think the most probable, we may remark, that the notes which relate to the variations in the pointing of particular words, must have been made *after* the introduction of the points, and consequently after the Talmud; other notes must have been made before the Talmud was finished, because it is from these notes that it speaks of the points *over* the letters, and of the variations in their size and position. Hence it is evident, that the *whole* was not the work of the Masorites of Tiberias; further, no good reason can be assigned to prove the Masora the work of Ezra, or his contemporaries; much appears to show it was not: for, in the *first* place, most of the notes relate to the vowel points, which, we have seen[1], were not introduced until upwards of fifteen hundred years after his time, and the remarks made about the shape and position of the letters are unworthy of an inspired writer, being more adapted to the superstition of the rabbins, than to the gravity of a divine teacher. *Secondly,* No one can suppose that the prophets collected various readings of their own prophecies, though we find this has been done, and makes part of what is called the Masora. *Thirdly,* The rabbins have never scrupled to abridge, alter, or reject any part of these notes, and to intermix their own observations, or those of others, which is a proof that they did not believe them to be the work of the prophets; for in that case they would possess equal authority with the text, and should be treated with the same regard. *Lastly,* Since all that is useful in the Masora appears to have been written since Ezra's time, it is impossible to ascribe to him what is useless and trifling; and from these different reasons it may be concluded that no part of the Masora was written by Ezra. And even though we were to admit that he began it, that would not lead us to receive the present system in the manner the Jews do, because, since we cannot now distinguish what he wrote, and since we find many things in it plainly unworthy of an inspired writer, we may justly refuse it the credit due to inspiration, unless his part were actually separated from what is the work of others. On the whole, then, it appears, that what is called the Masora is intitled to no greater reverence or attention than may be claimed by any other human compilation.[2]

Concerning the *value* of the Masoretic system of notation, the learned are greatly divided in opinion. Some have highly commended the undertaking, and have considered the work of the Masorites as a monument of stupendous labour and unwearied assiduity, and as an admirable invention for delivering the sacred text from a multitude of equivocations and perplexities to which it was liable, and for putting a stop to the unbounded licentiousness and

---

[1] See pp 8—12. of the present volume.
[2] Waehner's Antiquitates Hebræorum, vol i. pp. 93—137.

rashness of transcribers and critics, who often made alterations in the text on their own private authority. Others, however, have altogether censured the design, suspecting that the Masorites corrupted the purity of the text by substituting, for the antient and true reading of their forefathers, another reading more favourable to their prejudices, and more opposite to Christianity, whose testimonies and proofs they were desirous of weakening as much as possible.

Without adopting either of these extremes, Bishop Marsh observes, that "the text itself, as regulated by the learned Jews of Tiberias, was probably the result of a collation of manuscripts. But as those Hebrew critics were cautious of introducing *too many* corrections into the text, they noted in the margins of their manuscripts, or in their critical collections, such various readings derived from other manuscripts, either by themselves or by their predecessors, as appeared to be worthy of attention. This is the *real* origin of those marginal or Masoretic readings which we find in many editions of the Hebrew Bible. But the propensity of the later Jews to seek mystical meanings in the plainest facts gradually induced the belief that both textual and marginal readings proceeded from the sacred writers themselves; and that the latter were transmitted to posterity by *oral* tradition, as conveying some mysterious application of the *written* words. They were regarded, therefore, as materials, not of *criticism*, but of *interpretation*."[1] The same eminent critic elsewhere remarks, that notwithstanding all the care of the Masorites to preserve the sacred text without variations, "if their success has not been complete, either in *establishing* or *preserving* the Hebrew text, they have been guilty of the only fault which is common to every human effort."[2]

V. The divisions of the Old Testament, which now generally obtain, are four in number: namely, 1. The *Pentateuch*, or five books of Moses;— 2. The *Historical Books*, comprising Joshua to Esther inclusive;— 3. The *Doctrinal* or *Poetical Books* of Job, Psalms, the Proverbs, Ecclesiastes, and the Song of Solomon;— and, 4. The *Prophetical Books* of Isaiah, Jeremiah with his Lamentations, Ezekiel, Daniel, and the Twelve Minor Prophets. These are severally divided into chapters and verses, to facilitate reference, and not primarily with a view to any natural division of the multifarious subjects which they embrace: but by whom these divisions were originally made is a question, concerning which there exists a considerable difference of opinion.

That it is comparatively a modern invention is evident from its being utterly unknown to the antient Christians, whose Greek Bibles, indeed, had then Τιτλοι and Κεφαλαια (*Titles* and *Heads*); but the intent of these was, rather to point out the *sum* or contents of the text, than to divide the various books. They also differed greatly from the present chapters, many of them containing only a few verses, and some of them not more than one. The invention of chapters has by some been ascribed to Lanfranc, who was archbishop of

---

[1] Lectures on Divinity, part ii. p. 84. [2] Ibid. p 98.

Canterbury in the reigns of William the Conqueror and William II.; while others attribute it to Stephen Langton, who was archbishop of the same see in the reigns of John and Henry III. But the real author of this very useful division was cardinal Hugo de Sancto Caro, who flourished about the middle of the 13th century, and wrote a celebrated commentary on the Scriptures. Having projected a concordance to the Latin Vulgate version, by which any passage might be found, he divided both the Old and New Testaments into chapters, which are the same we now have: these chapters he subdivided into smaller portions, which he distinguished by the letters A, B, C, D, E, F, and G, which are placed in the margin at equal distances from each other, according to the length of the chapters.[1] The facility of reference thus afforded by Hugo's divisions, having become known to Rabbi Mordecai Nathan, (or Isaac Nathan, as he is sometimes called,) a celebrated Jewish teacher in the fifteenth century, he undertook a similar concordance for the Hebrew Scriptures; but instead of adopting the marginal letters of Hugo, he marked every fifth verse with a Hebrew numeral, thus, א 1. ה 5, &c., retaining, however, the cardinal's divisions into chapters. This concordance of Rabbi Nathan was commenced A. D. 1438, and finished in 1445. The introduction of verses into the Hebrew Bible was made by Athias, a Jew of Amsterdam, in his celebrated edition of the Hebrew Bible, printed in 1661, and reprinted in 1667. He marked every verse with the figures in common use, except those which had been previously marked by Nathan with Hebrew letters, in the manner in which they at present appear in Hebrew Bibles. By rejecting these Hebrew numerals, and substituting for them the corresponding figures, all the copies of the Bible in other languages have since been marked.[2] As, however, the modern divisions and sub-divisions are not always made with the strictest regard to the connexion of parts, it is greatly to be wished that all future editions of the Scriptures might be printed after the judicious manner adopted by Mr. Reeves in his equally beautiful and correct editions of the entire Bible; in which the numbers of the verses and chapters are thrown into the margin, and the metrical parts of Scripture are distinguished from the rest by being printed in verses in the usual manner.

---

[1] These divisions of cardinal Hugo may be seen in any of the older editions of the Vulgate, and in the earlier English translations of the Bible, which were made from that version, particularly in that usually called *Taverner's Bible*, folio, London, 1539. The *precise year*, in which Hugo divided the text of the Latin Vulgate into its present chapters, is not known. But as it appears from the preface to the Cologne edition of his works, that he composed his Concordance about the year 1248, and as his division of the Vulgate into its present chapters was connected with that Concordance, it could not have been done many years before the *middle* of the thirteenth century. Bp. Marsh's Lectures, part v. p. 25 note 15

[2] Buxtorf. Præf. ad Concordant. Bibliorum Hebræorum. Prideaux's Connexion, vol. i. pp. 332—342. Carpzov. Introd. ad Libros Biblicos Vet. Test. pp. 27, 28. Leusden, Philol. Hebr Diss. iii. pp. 23—31. Ackermann, Introd. in Libros Sacros Vet. Fœd pp. 100—104.

SECTION II.

ON THE DIVISIONS AND MARKS OF DISTINCTION OCCURRING IN THE NEW TESTAMENT.

I. *Antient Divisions of* Τιτλοι *and* Κεφαλαια. — *Ammonian, Eusebian, and Euthalian Sections.* — *Modern Division of Chapters.* — II. *Account of the Antient and Modern Punctuation of the New Testament.* — *Antient* Στιχοι *and Modern Verses.* — III *Of the Titles to each Book.* — IV. *Subscriptions to the different Books.*

IT is evident on inspecting the most antient manuscripts of the New Testament, that the several books were originally written in one continued series without any blank spaces between the words[1]; but in progress of time, when Christianity was established, and frequent appeals were made to the sacred writers, in consequence of the heresies that disturbed the peace of the church, it became necessary to contrive some mode by which to facilitate references to their productions.

I. The Jews, we have already seen[2], divided their law into paraschioth and siderim, or larger and smaller sections, and the prophets into haphtoroth or sections; and this division most probably suggested to the early Christians the idea of dividing the Books of the New Testament into similar sections. The early Christian teachers gave the name of Pericopæ to the sections read as lessons by the Jews[3]: and Clement of Alexandria applies the same appellation to larger sections of the Gospels and St. Paul's Epistles. These pericopæ then were Αναγνωσματα, church lessons or sections of the New Testament, which were read in the assemblies for divine worship after Moses and the Prophets.

Subsequently the antients divided the New Testament into two kinds of chapters, some longer and others shorter; the former were called in Greek τιτλοι, and in Latin *breves;* and the table of contents of each brevis, which was prefixed to the copies of the New Testament, was called *breviarium.* The shorter chapters were called κεφαλαια, *capitula,* and the list of them, *capitulatio.*

This method of dividing is of very great antiquity, certainly prior to the fourth century: for Jerome, who flourished towards the close of that century, expunged a passage from Saint Matthew's Gospel

---

[1] This is manifest from the strange manner in which the early fathers of the Christian church have sometimes separated and united words in the passages which they have quoted. Thus instead of δοξασατε δη ἄρα τε τον Θεον, *therefore glorify God* (1 Cor. vi 20), Chrysostom read δοξασατε δη ἄρατε τον Θεον, *glorify and carry God;* and in this erroneous reading he has been followed by the Latin translator, who has *glorificate et portate Deum.* In like manner, in Phil. ii. 4., instead of ἕκαστοι σκοπουντες, *looking every man,* the Codex Boernerianus reads ἑκαστοις κοπουντες, *toiling for every one.* Cellérier, Essai d'une Introduction Critique au Nouveau Testament, p. 112. Genève, 1823. 8vo. Hug's Introduction, vol. i. p. 235.

[2] See p. 163. *supra.*

[3] Justin. Dialog. cum Tryphone, cc. 65, 6. 72. cited in Hug's Introd vol i p. 253. Some vestiges of the same mode of division occur in Tertullian, ad ux. lib. ii. c. 2. p. 187 D. De Pudicitiâ, c. 16 *sub finem.* De Monogam c 11. p 683. The passages are given at length by Dr. Lardner, Works, 8vo. vol. ii. p. 283., 4to. vol. i. p. 433.

which forms an entire chapter, as being an interpolation.[1] These divisions were formerly very numerous; but, not being established by any ecclesiastical authority, none of them were ever received by the whole church. Saint Matthew's Gospel, for instance, according to the old breviaria, contained twenty-eight breves; but, according to Jerome, sixty-eight. The same author divides his Gospel into 355 capitula; others, into 74; others, into 88; others, into 117: the Syriac version, into 76; and Erpenius's edition of the Arabic, into 101. The most antient, and it appears the most approved of these divisions, was that of Tatian (A.D. 172), in his Harmony of the four Gospels, for the τιτλοι or breves: and that of Ammonius, a learned Christian of Alexandria in the third century, in his Harmony of the Gospels, for the κεφαλαια or capitula. From him they were termed the *Ammonian Sections*. As these divisions were subsequently adopted, and the use of them was recommended, by Eusebius the celebrated ecclesiastical historian, they are frequently called by his name. According to this division, Saint Matthew contains 68 breves, and 355 capitula; Saint Mark, 48 breves, and 234 capitula; Saint Luke, 83 breves, and 342 capitula; and St. John, 18 breves, and 231 capitula. All the evangelists together form 216 breves and 1126 capitula. In antient Greek manuscripts the τιτλοι or larger portions are written on the upper or lower margin, and the κεφαλαια or smaller portions are numbered on the side of the margin. They are clearly represented in Erasmus's editions of the Greek Testament, and in Robert Stephens's edition of 1550.

The division of the Acts of the Apostles, and of the Catholic Epistles, into chapters, was made by Euthalius bishop of Sulca in Egypt, in the fifth century; who published an edition of St. Paul's Epistles, that had been divided into chapters, in one continued series, by some unknown person in the fourth century, who had considered them as *one* book. This arrangement of the Pauline Epistles is to be found in the Vatican manuscript, and in some others; but it by no means prevails uniformly, for there are many manuscripts extant, in which a fresh enumeration commences with each epistle.[2]

Besides the divisions into chapters and sections above mentioned, the Codex Bezæ and other manuscripts were further divided into lessons, called Αναγνωσματα or Αναγνωσεις. Euthalius is said to have divided Saint Paul's Epistles in this manner, as Andrew Bishop of Cæsarea in Cappadocia divided the Apocalypse, at the beginning of the sixth century, into twenty-four lessons, which he termed λογοι (according to the number of elders before the throne of God, Rev. iv. 4.), and seventy-two titles, according to the number of parts, viz. body, soul, and spirit, of which the elders were composed!

The division of τιτλοι and κεφαλαια continued to be general both in the eastern and western churches, until cardinal Hugo de Sancto Caro in the thirteenth century introduced the chapters now in use,

---

[1] The paragraph in question is to be found in the Codex Bezæ, immediately after the twenty-eighth verse of the twenty-eighth chapter of St. Matthew's Gospel. Michaelis has printed it, together with two Latin translations of it, in his Introduction to the New Test. vol. i. pp. 293—295.

[2] Milln Prolegomena, §§ 354—360, 662—664. 739. *et seq.*

throughout the western church, for the New Testament as well as the Old: of which an account has already been given.[1] The Greek or eastern church, however, continued to follow the antient divisions; nor are any Greek manuscripts known to be extant, in which chapters are found, prior to the fifteenth century, when the Greek fugitives, after the taking of Constantinople, fled into the West of Europe, became transcribers for members of the Latin church, and of course adopted the Latin divisions.

II. Whether any points for marking the sense were used by the apostles, is a question that has been greatly agitated; Pritius, Pfaff, Leusden, and many other eminent critics, maintaining that they were in use *before* the time of the apostles, while Dr. Grabe, Fabricius, Montfaucon, Hoffman, John Henry Michaelis, Rogall, John David Michaelis, Moldenhawer, Ernesti, and a host of other critics, maintain that the use of points is *posterior* to the time of apostles.[2] The numerous mistakes of the fathers[3], or their uncertainty how particular passages were to be read and understood, clearly prove that there was no regular or accustomed system of punctuation in use, in the fourth century. The *majority* of the points or stops now in use are unquestionably of modern date. for although some full points are to be found in the Codex Alexandrinus, the Codex Vaticanus, and the Codex Bezæ (as they also are in inscriptions four hundred years before the Christian æra), yet it cannot be shown that our present system of punctuation was *generally* adopted earlier than the ninth century. In fact, it seems to have been a gradual improvement, commenced by Jerome, and continued by succeeding biblical critics. The punctuation of the manuscripts of the Septuagint, Ernesti observes from Cyril of Jerusalem[4], was unknown in the early part of the fourth century, and consequently (he infers) the punctuation of the New Testament was also unknown. About fifty years afterwards, Jerome began to add the comma and colon; and they were then inserted in many more antient manuscripts. About the middle of the fifth century, Euthalius (then a deacon of the church at Alexandria) published an edition of the four Gospels, and afterwards (when he was bishop of Sulca in Egypt) an edition of the Acts of the Apostles and of all the Apostolical Epistles, in which he divided the New Testament into στιχοι (*stichoi*), or lines regulated

---

[1] See p 168 *supra*, of this volume

[2] Rumpæus has given twelve closely printed quarto pages to the enumeration of these opinions. Com Crit. in Nov. Test pp. 165—176.

[3] Some of these mistakes and uncertainties of interpretation are sufficiently curious. Thus Jerome on Eph. i. 5 says · " Dupliciter legendum, ut caritas vel cum superioribus vel inferioribus copuletur." And on Philemon 4, 5. he says. Ambiguâ verò *dictum*, utrùm grates agat Deo suo *semper*, an memoriam ejus faciat in orationibus suis *semper*. Et utrumque intelligi potest." (Jerome, Homil IV, in Joh. pp 42, 43. edit Francofurti.) Epiphanius mentions a mark of punctuation used in the Old Testament, which he calls υποδιαστολη; but he takes notice of nothing of the kind in the New Testament, though he was warmly discussing the manner in which the sense ought to be divided in John i 3. The disputes which arose concerning this passage, prove to demonstration that there was no fixed punctuation at the period referred to. Chrysostom, for instance, branded as heretics those who placed a pause after the words ουδε ἐν and before γεγονεν, yet this mode of pointing was adopted by Irenæus, Clement of Alexandria, Origen, and even by Athanasius. Colléner, Introduction, p. 114. where other additional examples are given.

[4] Cyrilli Catechesis xiii, p 301. Ernesti, Inst Interp. Nov. Test. p. 159

by the sense, so that each terminated where some pause was to be made in reading. Of this method of division (which Euthalius devised in order to assist the clergy when reading the Word in public worship, and obviate the inconveniences and mistakes just noticed) the following extract from Tit. ii. 2, 3, according to the Codex H. Coislinianus 202., will give an idea to the reader:—

ΠΡΕΣΒΥΤΑΣ ΝΗΦΑΛΙΟΥΣ ΕΙΝΑΙ
ΣΕΜΝΟΥΣ
ΣΩΦΡΟΝΑΣ
ΥΓΙΑΙΝΟΝΤΑΣ ΤΗ ΠΙΣΤΕΙ
ΤΗι ΑΓΑΠΗι
ΠΡΕΣΒΥΤΙΔΑΣ ΩΣΑΥΤΩΣ
ΕΝ ΚΑΤΑΣΤΗΜΑΤΙ ΙΕΡΟΠΡΕΠΕΙΣ
ΜΗ ΔΙΑΒΟΛΟΥΣ
ΜΗ ΟΙΝΩι ΠΟΛΛΩι ΔΕΔΟΥΛΩΜΕΝΑΣ
ΚΑΛΟΔΙΔΑΣΚΑΛΟΥΣ.

In English, thus:
THAT THE AGED MEN BE SOBER
GRAVE
TEMPERATE
SOUND IN FAITH
IN LOVE
THE AGED WOMEN LIKEWISE
IN BEHAVIOUR AS BECOMETH HOLINESS
NOT FALSE ACCUSERS
NOT GIVEN TO MUCH WINE
TEACHERS OF GOOD THINGS.[1]

This mode of dividing the sacred text was called Στιχομετρια; and this method of writing στιχηδον γραψαι. At the end of each manuscript it was usual to specify the number of stichoi which it contained. When a copyist was disposed to contract his space, and therefore crowded the lines into each other, he placed a point where Euthalius had terminated the line. In the eighth century the stroke which we call a comma was invented. In the Latin manuscripts, Jerome's points were introduced by Paul Warnefrid, and Alcuin, at the command of the emperor Charlemagne; and in the ninth century the Greek note of interrogation (;) was first used. At the invention of printing, the editors placed the points arbitrarily, probably (Michaelis thinks) without bestowing the necessary attention; and Stephens in particular, it is well known, varied his points in every edition. The fac-similes given in the third chapter of this volume will give the reader an idea of the marks of distinction found in the more antient manuscripts.

The stichoi, however, not only assisted the public reader of the New Testament to determine its sense; they also served to measure

---

[1] Hug's Introduction, vol. i. p 241

the size of books; thus, Josephus's twenty books of Jewish Antiquities contained 60,000 stichoi, though in Ittigius's edition there are only 40,000 broken lines. And, according to an antient written list preserved by Simon, and transcribed by Michaelis, the New Testament contained 18,612 stichoi.[1]

The verses into which the New Testament is now divided, are much more modern, and are an imitation of those invented for the Old Testament by Rabbi Nathan in the fifteenth century.[2] Robert Stephens was their first inventor[3], and introduced them in his edition of the New Testament, published in the year 1551. This invention of the learned printer was soon introduced into all the editions of the New Testament; and the very great advantage it affords, for facilitating references to particular passages, has caused it to be retained in the majority of editions and versions of the New Testament, though much to the injury of its interpretation, as many passages are now severed that ought to be united, and *vice versâ*.[4] From this arrangement, however, Wetstein, Bengel, Bowyer, Griesbach, and other editors of the Greek Testament, have wisely departed, and have printed the text in continued paragraphs, throwing the numbers of Stephen's verses into the margin. Mr. Reeves also has pursued the same method in his beautiful and correct editions of the authorised English version, and of the Greek Testament in 12mo., 1803.

Besides the text in the different books of the New Testament, we meet with titles or inscriptions to each of them, and also with subscriptions at the end, specifying the writer of each *book*, the time and place, when and where it was written, and the person to whom it was written.

III. It is not known by whom the *Inscriptions* or TITLES of the various books of the New Testament were prefixed. In consequence of the very great diversity of titles occurring in manuscripts it is generally admitted that they were not originally written by the Apostles, but were subsequently added, in order to distinguish one book from another, when the canon of the New Testament was formed. It is however certain, that these titles are of very great antiquity; for we find them mentioned by Tertullian in the latter part of the second century[5], and Justin Martyr, in the early part of the same century, expressly states, that the writings of the four evangelists were in his day termed *Gospels*.[6]

---

[1] Introd. to the New Test. vol. II. pp. 526, 527. Michaelis, after Simon, uses the word *remata*, but this is evidently a mistake. On the subjects discussed in this section Pritius's Introductio in Nov. Test. pp. 338—346. 362—375. may be consulted.

[2] See p 168. *supra*, of this volume.

[3] He made this division when on a journey from Lyons to Paris, and, as his son Henry tells us, (in his preface to the Concordance of the New Testament) he made it *inter equitandum*, literally, while riding on horseback; but Michaelis rather thinks that the phrase means only, that when he was weary of riding, he amused himself with this work at his inn. Michaelis, vol. II. p. 527.

[4] Thus Col iv. 1 ought to have been united to the third chapter.

[5] Adversus Marcionem, lib. iv. c 2

[6] Apol. I. p. 98. Lardner's Works, 8vo. vol. II. p. 121.; 4to. vol. i. p. 344. Pritii Introd. in Nov. Test. pp. 331—333

IV. But the *Subscriptions* annexed to the Epistles are manifestly spurious: for, in the *first* place, some of them are, beyond all doubt, false, as those of the two Epistles to the Thessalonians, which purport to be written at Athens, whereas they were written from Corinth. In like manner, the subscription to the first epistle to the Corinthians states, that it was written from Philippi, notwithstanding St. Paul informs them (xvi. 8.) that he will *tarry at Ephesus until Pentecost;* and notwithstanding he begins his salutations in that Epistle, by telling the Corinthian Christians (xvi. 19.) *the Churches of Asia salute you,* a pretty evident indication that he himself was in Asia at that very time. Again, according to the subscription, the Epistle to the Galatians was written from Rome; yet, in the Epistle itself, the Apostle expresses his surprise (i. 6.) that they were so SOON *removed from him that called them;* whereas his journey to Rome was *ten years* posterior to the conversion of the Galatians. And what still more conclusively proves the falsehood of this subscription is, the total absence in this epistle of all allusions to his bonds or to his being a prisoner; which Saint Paul has not failed to notice in every one of the four epistles, written from that city and during his imprisonment.[1] *Secondly,* The subscriptions are altogether wanting in some antient manuscripts of the best note, while in others they are greatly varied. And, *thirdly,* The subscription annexed to the first Epistle to Timothy is evidently the production of a writer of the age of Constantine the Great, and could not have been written by the Apostle Paul: for it states that epistle to have been written to Timothy from Laodicea, the chief city of Phrygia Pacatiana; whereas the country of Phrygia was not divided into the two provinces of *Phrygia Prima,* or *Pacatiana,* and *Phrygia Secunda,* until the fourth century. According to Dr. Mill, the subscriptions were added by Euthalius bishop of Sulca in Egypt, about the middle of the fifth century. But, whoever was the author of the subscriptions, it is evident that he was either grossly ignorant, or grossly inattentive.

The various subscriptions and titles to the different books are exhibited in Griesbach's Critical Edition of the New Testament.

CHAPTER V.

OF THE VARIOUS READINGS OCCURRING IN THE OLD AND NEW TESTAMENTS.

I. *The Christian Faith not affected by Various Readings.* — II. *Nature of Various Readings.* — *Difference between them and mere errata.* — III. *Causes of various Readings;* — 1. *The negligence or mistakes of transcribers;* — 2. *Errors or imperfections in the manuscript copied;* —

---

[1] Paley's Horæ Paulinæ, pp. 378, 379.

3. *Critical Conjecture;* — 4. *Wilful Corruptions of a manuscript from party motives.* — IV. *Sources whence a true reading is to be determined;* — 1. *Manuscripts;* — 2. *Antient Editions;* — 3. *Antient Versions;* — 4. *Parallel Passages;* — 5. *Quotations in the Writings of the Fathers;* — 6. *Critical Conjecture;* — V. *General Rules for judging of Various Readings.*

I. THE Old and New Testaments, in common with all other antient writings, being preserved and diffused by transcription, the admission of mistakes was unavoidable: which increasing with the multitude of copies, necessarily produced a great variety of different readings. Hence the labours of learned men have been directed to the collation of manuscripts, with a view to ascertain the genuine reading; and the result of their researches has shown, that these variations are not such as to affect our faith or practice in any thing material: they are mostly of a minute, and sometimes of a trifling nature. "The real text of the sacred writers does not now (since the originals have been so long lost) lie in any single manuscript or edition, but is dispersed in them all. It is competently exact indeed, even in the worst manuscript now extant; nor is one article of faith or moral precept either perverted or lost in them."[1] It is therefore a very ungrounded fear that the number of various readings, particularly in the New Testament, may diminish the certainty of the Christian religion. The probability, Michaelis remarks, of restoring the genuine text of *any* author, increases with the increase of the copies; and the most inaccurate and mutilated editions of antient writers are precisely those of whose works the fewest manuscripts remain.[2] Above all, in the New Testament, the various readings show that there could have been no collusion; but that the manuscripts were written independently of each other, by persons separated by distance of time, remoteness of place, and diversity of opinions. This extensive independency of manuscripts on each other, is the effectual check of wilful alteration, which must have ever been immediately corrected by the agreement of copies from various and distant regions out of the reach of the interpolator. By far the greatest number of various readings relate to trifles, and make *no alteration whatever in the sense,* such as Δαβιδ for Δαυιδ; Σολομωντα for Σολομωνα; και for δε; καγω for και εγω (&ᶜ for *and I*); ελαττων for

---

[1] Dr. Bentley's remarks on Free-thinking, rem. xxxii. (Bp Randolph's Enchiridion Theologicum, vol. v. p 163.) The various readings that affect doctrines, and require caution, are extremely few, and easily distinguished by critical rules, and where they do affect a doctrine, other passages confirm and establish it. See examples of this observation in Michaelis, vol. i p. 266, and Dr. Nares's Strictures on the Unitarian Version of the New Testament, pp. 219—221.

[2] Michaelis's Introduction to the New Testament, vol. i pp. 263—268. "In profane authors," says Dr. Bentley, "(as they are called) whereof one manuscript only had the luck to be preserved, — as Velleius Paterculus among the Latins, and Hesychius among the Greeks — the faults of the scribes are found so numerous, and the defects so beyond all redress, that notwithstanding the pains of the learnedest and acutest critics for two whole centuries, those books still are, and are likely to continue, a mere heap of errors. On the contrary, where the copies of any author are numerous, though the various readings always increase in proportion, there the text, by an accurate collation of them made by skilful and judicious hands, is ever the more correct, and comes nearer to the true words of the author." Remarks on Free-thinking, in Enchirid. Theol. vol. v. p. 158.

ελασσων; Κυριος for Θεος; λαλωσιν for λαλησωσιν; Μωσης for Μωυσης; and γινεσθω for γενεσθω; all which in most cases may be used indifferently.

In order to illustrate the preceding remarks, and to convey an idea of their full force to the reader, the various readings of the first *ten* verses of Saint John's Gospel are annexed in Greek and English;— and they are particularly chosen because they contain one of the most decisive proofs of the divinity of our Lord and Saviour Jesus Christ.

Common Reading.	Various Reading.	Authorities.
Ver 1. 'O λογος ην ΠΡΟΣ τον Θεον. The Word was WITH God.	EN τω Θεω — IN God.	Clemens Alexandrinus.
2. Ουτος ην εν αρχη προς τον Θεον. The same was in the beginning with God	*omitted.*	The MSS. 47 and 64 of Griesbach's notation, Matthæi's 19.
4. Εν αυτω ζωη HN. In him wAs life.	ΕΣΤΙΝ — IS life.	The Codex Bezæ, Origen, Augustine, Hilary, and other Fathers.
4. Και η ζωη ην το φως των ανθρωπων. And the life was the light of men.	*omitted.*	The fragment of St. John's Gospel, edited by Aldus, Clemens Alexandrinus, and Origen.
— the light OF MEN.	The light was the life	B The Codex Vaticanus.
5. 'Η σκοτια ΑΥΤΟ ου κατελαβεν. The darkness comprehended IT not.	ΑυτοΝ — HIM not	B The Codex Vaticanus, the MSS. 13 and 114* of Griesbach, three other MSS. of less note, and Theodotus.
7 Ινα παντες πιςευσωσι δι' αυτου That all men might believe through him.	*omitted.*	The MS. 235 of Griesbach, the Aldine Fragment of St John's Gospel, Irenæus, and Hilary.
9. Ερχομενον εις ΤΟΝ κοσμον. That cometh into THE world.	*In* HUNC *mundum —* into THIS world.	The Vulgate and Italic (or old Ante-Hieronymian) Versions, Tertullian, Cyprian, Hilary, Ambrose, Augustine, and other fathers.
10. Εν ΤΩ κοσμω ην He was in THE world	HOC *mundo —* in THIS world.	The MSS of the old Latin Versions, denominated the Codices Veronensis, Vercellensis, Brixiensis, and Corbeiensis, edited by Blanchini and Sabatier; Irenæus, Cyprian, Ambrose, *once,* Augustine *repeatedly.*

On the whole, these various readings — though not selected from any single manuscript, but from all that have been collated, together with the antient versions and the quotations from the fathers, — no where contradict the sense of the evangelist; nor do they produce any material alteration in the text.[1]

---

[1] Christian Observer for 1807, vol. vi. p. 221.

The principal collators and collectors of various readings for the Old Testament, are Dr. Kennicott and M De Rossi, of whose labours an account is given in the Appendix, pp. 7, 8. 150. As the price of their publications necessarily places them out of the reach of very many biblical students, the reader, who is desirous of availing himself of the results of their laborious and learned researches, will find a compendious abstract of them in Mr. Hamilton's *Codex Criticus* (London, 1821, 8vo.). For the New Testament, the principal collations are those of Erasmus, the editors of the Complutensian and London Polyglotts, Bishop Fell, Dr. Mill, Kuster, Bengel, Wetstein, Dr. Griesbach, and Matthæi, whose editions are also described in the Appendix to this volume [1]; and for the Septuagint, the collations of the late Rev. Dr. Holmes, and his continuator, the Rev. J. Parsons.[2]

II. However plain the meaning of the term "*Various Reading*" may be, considerable difference has existed among learned men concerning its nature. Some have allowed the name only to such readings as may *possibly* have proceeded from the author; but this restriction is improper. Michaelis's distinction between mere errata and various readings appears to be the true one. "Among two or more different readings, one only can be the true reading: and the rest must be either wilful corruptions or mistakes of the copyist." It is often difficult to distinguish the genuine from the spurious; and whenever the smallest doubt can be entertained, they all receive the name of VARIOUS READINGS; but in cases where the transcriber has evidently written falsely, they receive the name of *errata*.

III. As all manuscripts were either dictated to copyists or transcribed by them, and as these persons were not supernaturally guarded against the possibility of error, different readings would naturally be produced. — 1. By the negligence or mistakes of the transcribers; to which we may add, 2. The existence of errors or imperfections in the manuscripts copied; 3. Critical emendations of the text; and 4. Wilful corruptions made to serve the purposes of a party. Mistakes thus produced in one copy would of course be propagated through all succeeding copies made from it, each of which might likkewise have peculiar faults of its own; so that various readings would thus be increased, in proportion to the number of transcripts that were made.

1. *Various readings have been occasioned by the* NEGLIGENCE or MISTAKES OF THE TRANSCRIBERS.

(1.) *When a manuscript is dictated, whether to one or to several copyists, the party dictating might not speak with sufficient clearness, he might read carelessly, and even utter words that were not in his manuscript; he might pronounce different words in the same manner. The copyist, therefore, who should follow such dictation, would necessarily produce different readings.* One or two examples will illustrate this remark.

In Eph iv. 19., Saint Paul, speaking of the Gentiles, while without the Gospel, says, that *being past feeling, they gave themselves over to lasciviousness*. For απηλγηκοτες past

---

[1] Michaelis has given a list of authors who have collected various readings, with the remarks on their labours Introd vol. ii. part i. pp 419—429. See also Pfaff's Dissertatio de Genuinis Novi Testamenti Lectionibus, pp 101—122.

[2] See an account of their edition of the Septuagint, in the Appendix, pp. 37, 38.

feeling (which the context shows to be the genuine reading), several manuscripts, versions, and fathers read απηλπικοτες, *being without hope*. Dr. Mill is of opinion, that this lection proceeded from some ignorant copyist who had in his mind Saint Paul's account of the Gentiles in Eph. ii. 12. where he said that they had no hope, ελπιδα μη εχοντες. But for this opinion there is no foundation whatever. The antient copyists were not in general men of such subtile genius. It is therefore most probable that the word απηλπικοτες crept in, from a mis-pronunciation on the part of the persons dictating. The same remark will account for the reading of νηπιοι, *young children*, instead of ηπιοι, *gentle*, in 1 Thess. ii. 7, which occurs in many manuscripts, and also in several versions and fathers. But the scope and context of this passage prove that νηπιοι cannot be the original reading. It is the Thessalonians, whom the apostle considers as *young children*, and himself and fellow-labourers as the *nurse*. He could not therefore with any propriety say that he was among them as a *little child*, while he himself professed to be *their nurse*.

(2.) *Further, as many Hebrew and Greek letters are similar both in sound and in form, a negligent or illiterate copyist might, and the collation of manuscripts has shewn that such transcribers did, occasion various readings by substituting one word or letter for another.*

The permutation, or interchanging, of vowel points, letters, and even entire words, which are to be found in Hebrew manuscripts are copiously treated by Muntinghe.[1] Of the permutations in Greek MSS., the Codex Cottonianus of the book of Genesis presents many very striking examples.

Thus, B and M are interchanged in Gen. xlii. 11. τερεμινθον is written for τερεβινθον, — Γ and K, as γυνηγος for κυνηγος, x 9.; and è contra φαλεκ for φαλεγ, xi. 16. — Γ and N, as συγκοψουσιν for συνκοψουσιν, xxxiv. 30. — Γ and X, as δραχματα for δραγματα, xxxvii. 6. — Δ and Λ as Κελμοναιους for Κεδμοναιους, xv. 19., and è contra Αιδαμ for Αιλωμ, xxxvi. 2. — Δ and N, as Νεβρων for Νεβρωδ, x. 9 — Δ and T, as Ατατ for Αταδ, x. 10, &c. — Z and Σ, as Χασαδ for Χαζαδ, xxii. 22.; and μακαριζουσιν for μακαρισουσιν, xxx. 13. — Θ and X, Οχοζαχ for Οχοζαδ, xxvi. 26. — Θ and T, αποστραφητι for αποστραφηδι, xvi 9. — K and X, as Καλακ for Χαλαχ, x 11.; and ουχ for ουκ, xlii. 9. — Π and Φ, as υφεξηρηται for υπεξηρηται, xxxix. 9. Sometimes *consonants* are added to the end of the words apparently for the sake of euphony, as Χωθαλ for Χωθα, xiv. 15.—γυναικαν for γυναικα, xi. 13 — Ευϊλατ for Ευϊλα, x. 7.—M is generally retained in the different flexions of the verb λαμβανω, in the future λημψολαι, λημψονται, xiv. 23, 24, &c. and in the aorist, λημφθητο, xviii. 4. And also in the word συμπαραλημφθης, xix 17. This also is common in the *Codex Vaticanus*. Sometimes a *double consonant* is expressed by a *single* one, and *vice versa*. for instance, ενενηκοντα for εννενηκοντα, v 9, and Σεννααρ for Σεναας, x. 10.; ψελια for ψελλια, xxiv. 47, &c.

The Vowels are often interchanged; for instance, A and E, as τεσσερακοντα for τεσσαρακοντα, vii. 4.; αναση for ανεση, xxi. 14. — A and H, as ανεωξεν for ηνεωξεν, viii. 6, μαχαιρη for μαχαιρα, xxvii 40. — E and H, as ευφεμα for ευημα, xxv. 29., ηνυπνιασθη for ενυπνιασθη, xxviii. 12. — H and I, as Κιτιοι for Κητιοι, x. 4., ελικη for ελικι, xlix. 11. H and T, as πηχυν for πηχυν, vi. 17. — Ρευμα for Ρευμα, xxii. 24. — O and T, as διωρυθα for διορφα, vi. 17. — O and Ω, as Ρωσοδ for Ρωσωδ, x. 11 — The *Vowels* are often interchanged with the *Diphthongs*; for instance, AI and E, as απελευσεθαι for απελευσεσθε, xix. 2., ανενεγκαι for ανενεγκε, xxii 2, παιδιον for πεδιον, xxxv. 27., καταξεται for καταξετε, xlii. 38. — EI and A, as γηρα for γηρα, xv. 15. — EI and E as εινεκεν for ενεκεν, xviii 5.,— EI and H, as ειδειν and ηδειν, xvii 19 — EI and I, as παρεισηκει for παρεισηκει, xviii. 8., γυναικαι for γυναικεια, xviii. 11., ουδις for ουδεις, xli. 41, κρειον for κριον, xv. 9, &c — OI and H, as λαθοις for λαθης, xxxi. 50 — OT and H, as πληρης for πληρους, xxvii. 27.; and lastly, OT and Ω, as καταρουμενους for καταρωμενους, xii. 13.[2]

The manuscripts of the New Testament abound with similar instances of permutations.

Thus we meet with Αμιναδαμ for Αμιναδαβ, in Matt i 4.; Ακειμ for Αχειμ, in Matt. i. 14; δια των μαθητων for δυο των μαθητων, in Matt. xi. 2.; Ματθαν for Ματθατ, in Luke iii. 24.; μαρανθη for μαρανθη, in Luke xiv 34; τοπον for τυπον, in John xx. 25., καιρος for κυριος, in Rom. xii. 11.; Δαυιδ for Δαβιδ, in Matt. i. 1., and in many other passages. The reader will find numerous other examples in the elder Michaelis's Dissertation on various readings.[3] Permutations of this kind are very frequent in antient manuscripts, and also in inscriptions on coins, medals, stones, pillars, and other monuments of antiquity.

---

[1] Brevis Expositio Critices Veteris Fœderis, pp. 87—108.
[2] Dr. Holmes's Edition of the Septuagint, vol. i. Præf. cap. ii. § I.
[3] D. Christiani Benedicti Michaelis Tractatio Critica de Variis Lectionibus Novi Testamenti, pp. 8—10. Halæ Magdeburgicæ, 1749, 4to.

(3.) *In like manner the transcribers might have mistaken the line on which the copy before them was written, for part of a letter; or they might have mistaken the lower stroke of a letter for the line; or they might have mistaken the true sense of the original, and thus have altered the reading; at the same time they were unwilling to correct such mistakes as they detected, lest their pages should appear blotted or defaced, and thus they sacrificed the correctness of their copy to the beauty of its appearance. This is particularly observable in Hebrew manuscripts.*

(4.) *A person having written one or more words from a wrong place, and not observing it; or not choosing to erase it, might return to the right line, and thus produce an improper insertion of a word or a clause.*

Of this we have a striking instance in John vii 26 — *Do the rulers know* INDEED (αληθως), *that this is the* VERY *Christ* (αληθως ὁ Χριστος, TRULY *the Christ*)? The second αληθως is wanting in the Codices Vaticanus, Cantabrigiensis (or Codex Bezæ), Cyprius, Stephani η, or Regius 62, Nanianus, and Ingolstadiensis, in numbers 1, 13, 28, 40, 69, 69, 116, 118, and 124, of Griesbach's notation, and nine other manuscripts of less note, which are not specified by him, it is also wanting in the manuscripts noted by Matthæi with the letters a, l, s, and 10, in all the editions of the Arabic version, in Wheeloc's edition of the Persian version, in the Coptic, Armenian, Sclavonic, and Vulgate versions; and in all the copies of the Old Italic version, except that of Brescia. Origen, Epiphanius, Cyril, Isidore of Pelusium, Chrysostom, and Nonnus, among the antient fathers; and Grotius, Mill, Bengel, Bishop Pearce, and Griesbach, among the modern writers, are all unanimous in rejecting the word αληθως. The sentence in 1 Cor. x. 28. Του γαρ Κυριου η γη και το πληρωμα αυτης, *The earth is the Lord's and the fulness thereof*, is wanting in the Codices Alexandrinus, Vaticanus, Cantabrigiensis, Basileensis, Boreeli, Harleianus No. 5864, and Seidelii, and in Nos 10, 17, 28, 46, 71*, 78, and 80, of Griesbach's notation it is also wanting in the Syriac version, in Erpenius's edition of the Arabic version, in the Coptic, Sahidic, Ethiopic, Armenian, Vulgate, and Old Italic versions, and in the quotations of the fathers Johannes Damascenus, Ambrosiaster, Augustine, Isidore of Pelusium, and Bede Griesbach has left it out of the text, as a clause that ought most undoubtedly to be erased There is, in fact, scarcely any authority to support it; and the clause is superfluous, in all probability it was inserted from the twenty-sixth verse, which is word for word the same.

(5.) *When a transcriber had made an omission, and afterwards observed it, he then subjoined what he had omitted, and thus produced a transposition.*[1]

Thus, Matt. v. 4. is *subjoined* to 5. in the Codex Bezæ, in the Vulgate version, and in the quotation of Jerome. Luke xxiii. 17. is omitted in the Codices Alexandrinus, Vaticanus, Cyprius, and Stephani η, in the Coptic and Sahidic versions, and in the Codex Vercellensis of the Old Italic version · and it is subjoined to the ninteenth verse in the Codex Bezæ.

In like manner, Rom i. 29. is very different in different copies.

In the Textus Receptus or common editions, we read, αδικια, πορνεια, πονηρια, πλεονεξια, κακια, — *unrighteousness, fornication, wickedness, covetousness, maliciousness*.

In the Codex Alexandrinus and Ethiopic version, we read, αδικια, πονηρια, κακια, πλεονεξια, — *unrighteousness, wickedness, maliciousness, covetousness*.

In the Codex Claromontanus, we read, αδικια, κακια, πορνεια, πλεονεξια, — *unrighteousness, maliciousness, covetousness*

In the Vulgate version, we read, *iniquitate, malitiâ, fornicatione, avaritiâ, nequitiâ*, whence it is evident that the authors of that translation read, αδικια, πονηρια, πορνεια, πλεονεξια, κακια And

The order of the words in the Syriac version shows that its authors read, αδικια, πορνεια, πονηρια, κακια, πλεονεξια, — *unrighteousness, fornication, wickedness, maliciousness, covetousness*.

(6.) *Another cause of various lections in Hebrew manuscripts, referable to this head, is the addition of letters to the last word in the lines in order to preserve their symmetry; and in Greek manuscripts omissions are frequently occasioned by what is called* ὁμοιοτελευτον (homoeoteleuton), *or when a word after a short interval occurs a second time in a passage. Here, the transcriber having written the word at the beginning of the passage, on*

---
[1] Dr. Gerard's Institutes of Biblical Criticism, p. 238.

looking at the book again from which he copies, his eye catches the same word at the end of the passage, and continuing to write what immediately follows, he of course omits intermediate words.

This fact will account for the *omission* of the concluding sentence of Matt. v 19, and the whole of verse 80, in the Codex Bezæ. Again, in Matt. xxviii. 9 the words απαγγειλαι τοις μαθηταις αυτου (*to tell his disciples*), are omitted from the same cause, in the Codices Vaticanus and Bezæ, in the MSS by Griesbach numbered 10, 33, 49, 59, 60, 69, 119, 142*, 225, 227, the Evangelisteria numbered 1, 13, 15, 17, 32, in the second of the Barberini MSS, and in those noted d and q by Matthæi, as well as in the Syriac, Arabic (as printed in the London Polyglott), Persic, Coptic, Armenian, Vulgate Latin, Saxon, and Old Italic Versions (except the manuscript of Brescia), and by the fathers Origen, Chrysostom, Jerome, and Augustine. And Mark ix. 26. is *omitted* in the Codices Vaticanus 1209, Stephani η, Vaticanus 854, and the MSS. by Griesbach numbered 2, 27, 63, 64, 121, 157, in Matthæi's 17, in the Coptic Version, the Codex San-germanensis 2 of the Italic Version, in the printed editions of Aldus and Frobenius, and by Theophylact.

(7.) *As all the most antient manuscripts were written in capital letters, and without any spaces between words, or even sentences, syllables are frequently omitted or repeated. So, careless or ignorant transcribers have very often mistaken the notes of abbreviation, which are of frequent occurrence in antient manuscripts. A few specimens of such abbreviations are given in the preceding part of this Volume.*

From this source probably originated the reading, in 1 Pet ii 3 of Χριϛοϛ (*Christ*) instead of Χρηϛοϛ (*gracious*), which occurs in the MSS. by Griesbach numbered 40, 68, and others of less note, in Matthæi's g, in some printed editions, and also in the verse as cited by Clemens Alexandrinus, Gregory Nazianzen, and Procopius, and by Theophylact in his commentary on this text. The reading in the manuscript whence the transcriber made his copy, must have been $\overline{Xs}$, which, not being understood by him, he altered into Χριϛοϛ.

(8.) *Lastly, the ignorance or negligence of transcribers has been a most fruitful source of various readings, by their having mistaken marginal notes or scholia for a part of the text. It was not unusual in antient manuscripts to write in the margin an explanation of difficult passages, or a word synonymous to that in the text, but more usual and more easily understood, or with the intent of supplying a seeming deficiency; any or all of which might, in the copies taken from the manuscript in which these notes were written, be easily obtruded on the text itself.*

Thus, to Matt. vi 33, some copies, as well as the fathers Clemens Alexandrinus, Origen, and Eusebius, add the following clause, as having been uttered by Jesus Christ Αιτειτε τα μεγαλα, και τα μικρα υμιν προστεθησεται και αιτειτε τα επουρανια και τα επιγεια προστεθησεται υμιν — *Seek ye great things, and little things shall be added unto you; and seek ye heavenly things, and earthly things shall be added unto you.* But this addition is manifestly a gloss.

So, in Mark vii. 35., after *he spake plain*, the following sentence is added in MS 90 of Griesbach's notation — και ελαλει ευλογων τον Θεον, — *and he spake, praising God* That the man did this, we may readily conclude, but this sentence was not added by the evangelist It was evidently a gloss

Again, in Luke vii. 16, after the sentence *God hath visited his people*, the words εις αγαθον, *for good*, are added in the manuscripts by Griesbach noted M. 13, 50, 69, 71, 106, 114, and eight others, in Matthæi's x, in the Syriac (as printed in the London Polyglott), in the Armenian, and in all the Arabic versions, and in the Codices Veronensis, Vercellensis, Corbeiensis, Colbertinus 4051, San-germanensis 1, and Forojuliensis, of the Old Italic Version. But it is manifestly a gloss, and is rejected as such by Dr Mill, and Griesbach

It is worthy of remark, that the differences caused by these or similar additions do in no respect whatever affect any point of faith or morality. Several eminent critics, for instance, are of opinion that the controverted clause in 1 John v. 7, 8 crept into the text in this manner, because it is not found in any antient manuscripts, nor in the writings of the fathers who disputed against the Arians The evidence for the passage in question is fully considered in Vol. IV Part II Chap IV Sect. V. § VI. But, for the sake of argument, let us suppose it to be an omission in the manuscripts where it is wanting or an addition to those where it occurs; it cannot in any way be prejudicial to the Christian faith; because, whatever sense we may put upon that passage, the same truth being most clearly and indisputably taught in other places of the New Testament, there is no more occasion for adding it, than there is inconvenience in omitting it.

2. ERRORS *or* IMPERFECTIONS *in the manuscript, from which a transcriber copied, are a further source of various readings.*

Besides the mistakes arising from the strokes of certain letters being faded or erased, others of a contrary nature may arise from the transparency of the paper or vellum, whence the stroke of a letter on one side of the leaf may seem to be a part of the letter on the other side of the leaf, and in this manner O may be taken for Θ.

According to Wetstein, this very accident happened to Mill, in examining the celebrated passage (1 Tim iii 16) in the Codex Alexandrinus. Mill had asserted in regard to the OC in this manuscript, that some remains of a stroke were still visible in the middle of the omicron, and concluded therefore that the word was properly ΘC. But Wetstein, who examined this manuscript more accurately, could discover no trace of any stroke in the omicron, but took notice of a circumstance which he supposes led Mill into error. On the other side of the leaf, directly opposite to O, is the letter Є, in the word ЄΤCЄBЄΙΑ, the middle stroke of which is visible on the former side, and occupies the hollow of O. Wetstein having made the discovery, called several persons to witness, who confirmed the truth of it. But this hypothesis of Wetstein's has been questioned by Dr Woide[1], and has been most clearly *disproved* by Dr. Berriman[2]. In order to discover the genuine reading of a manuscript where the letters are faded, Michaelis recommends the critic to have recourse to such as are related to it, either in time, place, or character, and if possible to those which were immediately copied from it while the letters were still legible. Velthusen and Griesbach are unanimous in regard to the propriety of this rule, but in their application of it to 1 Tim iii 16 they have drawn directly opposite conclusions. Those who endeavour to supply what time has destroyed, and venture to write anew the remnant, or seeming remnant, of a faded stroke, are guilty of an act that deserves the highest censure: the Codex Alexandrinus, Codex Ephrem, and Codex Claromontanus, have all suffered in this manner, but the authors of these amendments have deprived their successors of the means of judging for themselves, and have defeated the end which they intended to answer.

Again, the omission of a passage in an antient manuscript, which the writer added afterwards in the margin, might lead a copyist into error, unless it was particularly marked in what part of the text the passage ought to be inserted. Many manuscripts are still extant, in which omissions are in this manner supplied, especially in those preserved at Moscow, which Matthæi has extracted and accurately described in his critical edition of the New Testament.

3. *A third source of various readings is* CRITICAL CONJECTURE, *or an intended improvement of the original text.*

"In reading the works of an author of known literary reputation we ascribe grammatical or orthographical errors, if any are to be found, rather to a mistake of the printer than to a want of knowledge in the writer. In the same manner the transcriber of a manuscript attributes the faults of his original to the error of a former copyist, and alters them, as he supposes they were written by the author. But if he carries his critical conjectures too far, he falls himself into the error which he intended to avoid." This may be done in various ways.

(1) *Thus the transcriber may take an expression to be faulty which in reality is not so; or he may mistake the sense of the author, and suppose that he has discovered a grammatical error, when, in fact, he himself construes falsely:* — *or the grammatical error intended to be corrected actually proceeded from the author himself.*[3]

---

[1] Novum Testamentum Græcum, e Codice MS. Alexandrino, Præfat. § 87. p. xxxi.
[2] Critical Dissertation upon 1 Tim. iii. 16. pp 153—160
[3] With regard to those corrections of grammatical errors, Michaelis has laid down the four following rules, viz

"1. In those passages where we find only an apparent grammatical error, the seemingly erroneous reading may be generally considered as the genuine, and the other readings as corrections, and therefore spurious.

(2.) *Further, some critical copyists have not only corrected ungrammatical or inaccurate expressions, but have even converted inelegant into elegant phrases: and they have likewise omitted words that appeared to them superfluous, or the difference of which they did not understand.*

Thus, in Mark vii. 37 τους αλαλους, *the dumb*, is omitted as superfluous in Griesbach's MS. 28 (Colbertinus 4705, or Colbertinus 2. of Dr Mill's notation.) So, in Mark x. 19. Μη αποστηρησης, *defraud not*, is omitted in the Codices Vaticanus and Cyprius, and in eighteen other manuscripts, as well as in the Armenian version, and also in Theophylact. It seems included in μη κλεψης, *do not steal*, and does not occur in the other Gospels Once more, λεγοντος, *saying*, (Matt. i. 22.) is omitted, because the transcriber deemed it an unnecessary addition after the words, *that which was spoken of the Lord by the prophet.*

(3.) *But of all the sources of various lections which are referable to this head, the most ample, according to Michaelis, and the most productive of spurious passages in the New Testament, is the practice of altering parallel passages so as to render more perfect their conformity to each other. The Gospels in particular have suffered in this way, and Saint Paul's Epistles have very frequently been interpolated, in order to make his quotations from the Old Testament harmonise with the Septuagint version, where they differed from the exact words of the latter.*

Two or three instances of alterations from parallel passages will confirm this remark.

Thus, in Matt. xii 8 *For the son of man is lord even of the sabbath-day,* και, *even*, is omitted in eighty-seven manuscripts, and in several printed editions, as well as in the Syriac, Arabic, the Persic in Bp Walton's Polyglott, the Coptic, Armenian, Sclavonic, and Italic versions, and also in the passage as quoted by Tertullian, Cyprian, Origen, Chrysostom, Euthymius, and Theophylact. It has been added from the parallel passage in Mark ii. 28. or in Luke vi. 5.; and is justly rejected by Griesbach as an interpolation. In Matt. xii. 35 της καρδιας, *of the heart*, is wanting in one hundred and seven manuscripts as well as in several printed editions, and in the Arabic, Persic, Sclavonic, Anglo-Saxon, Old Italic, and Vulgate versions, it is also wanting in the passage as cited by Origen, the author of the Dialogue against the Marcionites, Gregory Nazianzen, Gregory of Nyssa, Chrysostom, Theophylact, Cyprian, Lucifer, Hilary, and Ambrosiaster. It has been inserted from the parallel place in Luke vi. 45.

The clause in Matt. xxvii. 35 Ινα πληρωθη το ρηθεν (*that it might be fulfilled which was spoken*), &c. to the end of that verse, is omitted in one hundred and sixty-one manuscripts in the Syriac MSS and also in some Syriac editions, in the Arabic version both MSS and also as printed in Bp. Walton's Polyglott, in the Persic version of the Polyglott, in all the manuscripts, and in most printed editions of the Coptic, Sahidic, Ethiopic, and Sclavonic versions, in most MSS. and editions of the Vulgate Latin version, in several MSS. of the old Italic version; and likewise in the verse as cited by Chrysostom, Titus of Bostra, Euthymius, Theophylact, Origen, the old Latin translator of Irenæus, Augustine, and Juvencus. This clause has been interpolated from John xix. 24. Griesbach justly omits it as decidedly spurious.

Numerous similar interpolations have been made in the Acts of the Apostles, by these supposed amendments, and where the same story is related more than once, transcribers, and more frequently translators, have supplied from the one what seemed to be deficient in the other. Not to multiply examples unnecessarily in illustration of this last remark, it will be sufficient to compare the narrative of Saint Paul's conversion, as related by Saint Luke (Acts ix.), with the apostle's own account of it in Acts xxii. and xxvi ; and also the two narratives of the conversion of Cornelius, described in Acts x. and xi.

(4.) *Lastly, some critics have altered the text of the New Testament in*

" 2. Real grammatical errors, in the works of a correct and classical writer, are justly ascribed to a mistake of the copyist, and the same sentiments may be entertained of an author of less eminence, when among several copies one or two only have the false-reading.

" 3. But when expressions that deviate from the strictness of grammar are found in the writings of an author who had not the advantage of a learned education, and was totally regardless of the accuracy of his style, not in single but repeated instances, and retained in a very great number of manuscripts, they must be attributed, not to the transcriber, but the author.

" 4. When one grammatical error in particular is frequently found in one and the same writing, as the improper use of the nominative in the book of Revelation, no doubt can be made that it proceeded from the author himself." — Michaelis, vol. i. p. 306.

conformity to the Vulgate version; but various readings, which are evidently derived from this source, are utterly undeserving of attention.

4. WILFUL CORRUPTIONS, *in order to serve the purposes of a party, whether orthodox or heterodox, are another source of various readings.*

Among the antient heretics no one has been more severely charged with falsifying the sacred text, in order to support his tenets, nor has any one more justly deserved the censure, which has been bestowed upon such unwarrantable conduct, than Marcion. Yet Michaelis has shown that all his deviations from the text in common use are not wilful corruptions, but that many of them are really various readings; and he has exculpated the Arians from the same charge. It is, however, well known that Marcion caused the two first chapters of Saint Luke's Gospel to disappear from his copy, as also Luke iv. 37, 38, 39. In Luke viii. 19 he also expunged the words η μητηρ και οι αδελφοι αυτου, *his mother and brethren* In Mark xv. 28. instead of μετα ανομων ελογισθη, *he was numbered with the transgressors,* the Eutychians read νεκρων, *dead,* in order to support their hypothesis, that Christs's body was an aerial form and not human.

On the other hand, it is a fact that some corruptions have been designedly made by those who are termed orthodox, and have subsequently been preferred when so made, in order to favour some received opinion, or to preclude an objection against it. As this is a source of various readings (we believe) but little known, and less considered, we shall adduce two or three examples from Pfaff's dissertation on various readings, who has considered the subject at length.

(1.) Mark xiii. 32 Ουδε ο υιος These words are omitted in some manuscripts, and rejected by some of the fathers, because they thought it favoured the Arians. Ambrose, who flourished in the fourth century, states that many manuscripts in his time omitted them

(2.) Luke i. 35 After γεννωμενον, the words εκ σου have been added in several manuscripts in the Syriac, Persic, Arabic, Ethiopic, and other translations, as well as in numerous quotations of the fathers, in opposition to the Eutychians, who denied the two natures of Jesus Christ.

(3.) Luke xxii. 43. The whole verse is omitted in the Alexandrian and some other manuscripts, because some orthodox Christians imagined that the mention of an angel's strengthening our Saviour during his agony in the garden detracted from his Deity.

(4.) 1 Cor. xv 5. Saint Paul asserts that Christ appeared after his resurrection *to the twelve,* τοις δωδεκα, though at that time two of the number were wanting, Thomas being absent, and Judas Iscariot being dead. Some manuscripts therefore read ενδεκα, *eleven,* lest the sacred historian should be charged with falsehood, though every attentive reader of the New Testament knows that the Apostle, in writing this, used the figure called *synecdoche,* in which a part is put for the whole

(5.) Matt. i 18. Πριν η συνελθειν αυτους (*before they came together*), and 25. αυτης τον πρωτοτοκον (*her first born*), are in some copies designedly omitted, lest any should doubt the perpetual virginity of Mary the mother of Christ.

IV. The causes of various readings being thus ascertained, the next step is to consider the sources whence the true reading is to be determined. The legitimate sources of emendation, are 1. Manuscripts; 2. The most antient and best Editions; 3. Antient Versions, (and, for the Old Testament in particular, the Samaritan text of the Pentateuch, together with the Masora, and the Talmud); 4. Parallel Passages; 5. Quotations from the Old and New Testament in the works of the Fathers; and 6. Critical Conjecture. But these various sources are all to be used with great judgment and caution, as being fallible criteria; nor is the common reading ever to be rejected but upon the most rational grounds.

1. MANUSCRIPTS. — Having already given some observations on the age of the manuscripts, together with an account of some of the most antient[1], it will only be necessary that we should in this place

---

[1] See an account of the principal Hebrew and Greek MSS. in pp. 87—93, 94, 95. 115—157. of the present volume.

offer a few hints concerning their relative value, and the application of them to the determination of various readings.

(1.) *In general, then, we may affirm that the present copies of the Scriptures of the Old and New Testament, under the guardianship of the Jewish, Samaritan, and Christian churches, agreeing in every thing essential, are of the same authenticity and authority with the original autographs; notwithstanding the errors that have crept into them, from whatever cause*

(2.) *The number of manuscripts however is not so much to be considered, as their quality, antiquity and agreement with the most antient interpreters; for the true reading may be preserved in a single manuscript.*

(3.) *Those manuscripts are to be accounted the best, which are most consonant with those used by the antient interpreters; and, with regard to the Old Testament, in particular, M de Rossi states, that those manuscripts are in every case preferable which have not been tampered with by the Masoretes, and which have the Chaldee paraphrase interjected, in alternate verses.*

(4.) *Although, other things being equal the more antiently and accurately written manuscripts are to be preferred, yet a recent and incorrect copy may often have the better reading, because it may have been transcribed from an excellent and antient copy.*

(5.) *An accurate manuscript is preferable to one that is negligently written.*

Various readings therefore, particularly in the Hebrew Scriptures, which are found in manuscripts transcribed by a learned person, or for a learned person, from some celebrated or corrected copy, are to be preferred to those written for private use, and the readings found in antient and unpointed manuscripts, written for the use of the synagogue, are better than those found in Masoretic exemplars.

(6.) *The first erased reading of a manuscript is not always an error of the copyist, nor is the second substituted one always the better reading. Both are to be tried by the touchstone of the antient versions, and in the Pentateuch by the Samaritan text also.*

(7.) *Other things being equal, Michaelis states, that a Lectionarium is not of equal value with a manuscript of the same antiquity that contains the books of the New Testament complete, because in the former the text was frequently altered, according to the readings which were most approved at the time when it was written; though Lectionaria sometimes have readings of great importance.*[1]

(8.) In reckoning up the number of manuscripts for or against any particular reading, it will be necessary,

FIRST, *To distinguish properly between one manuscript and another, that the same MS. be not counted twice over, and consequently* ONE *pass for* TWO.

This (it is now ascertained) was the case with the Codex Bezæ, which has been proved to be the same which was the second of Stephens's MSS. marked β, and not two distinct manuscripts. Wherever, therefore, a number of manuscripts bears evident marks of having been transcribed in succession, that is, each of them being first a copy taken from another, and then an original having a copy taken from it, or where all are taken from one common original, they are not to be considered as furnishing so many different instances of various reading, but should be estimated only as one, whose authority resolves itself into that of the first manuscript. Inattention to this circumstance has contributed to increase the number of various readings beyond what they really are. But though two manuscripts, one of which is copied from the other, can be admitted only as a single evidence, yet, if a word is faded in the more antient one, it may be supplied from that which is more modern. Manuscripts which, though not immediately copied from each other, exhibit a great uniformity in their readings, seem to be the produce of the same country, and to have, as it were, the usual readings of that country. A set of manuscripts of this kind is to be considered as the same edition, in which it is of no importance to the authenticity of a reading whether five hundred or five thousand copies be taken. Numbers alone, therefore, decide nothing in the present instance

---

[1] Introduction, Vol. II p 161.

SECONDLY, *We must carefully observe what part of the Scriptures the several manuscripts actually contain, and in what respects they are defective.*

There are few MSS. extant, which contain either the Old or the New Testament entire, and have been transmitted to us without loss and damage Of the MSS. of the Old Testament, which have been described in pp 87—89 *supra*, not one is complete, and with regard to the New Testament, we have already seen that the Codices Alexandrinus, Vaticanus, and Leicestrensis, are mutilated. Other MSS contain the Gospels, or the Gospels and Acts of the Apostles, others the Acts and Pauline Epistles, or the Catholic Epistles, or both, others have the Epistles by themselves, and there are several manuscripts which contain the whole of the New Testament except the Apocalypse; to which are to be added the Lectionaries, or select portions of the New Testament, which were read as lessons, or Epistles and Gospels in the service of the church. Now it is absolutely necessary that we observe the state and condition of MSS, in order that we may avoid false conclusions and inferences from the non production of a manuscript for a various reading by any editor of the New Testament, who professedly gives an account of the various readings of MSS., as if it therefore did not vary, when in reality the text itself was wanting therein, and also in order that we may not cite a MS. in favour of any reading, where in truth such MS has no reading at all. From inattention to this obvious rule, Amelotte [1] cited the first codex of Stephens, the Complutensian, Cardinal Ximenes's, Cisneros's, and that of Alcala, as so many different manuscripts, when, in fact, there was but one and the same printed edition.

THIRDLY, *we must also observe whether the MSS. have been entirely and exactly collated.*

Sometimes, perhaps, only the more noted and important texts have been consulted This was the case with the Codex Claromontanus, as collated by Beza, and also with the MSS. of the Apostolic Epistles in the Archiepiscopal Library at Lambeth, which have only been collated for the controverted clause in 1 John v 7 Sometimes also it happens that MSS. have come late into the hands of editors of the New Testament, after the printing was begun, and consequently only part of the various lections have been exhibited This was the case both with Dr Mill and with Griesbach in their critical editions. Again, it sometimes happens that a manuscript has been collated in the beginning, but, from some accident or other, the collation of it has not been completed. This was the case with the Codex Cyprius, of which we had no entire collation until Dr Scholz printed one at the end of his Dissertation on that manuscript [2], and also with the Codex Montfortianus, which was collated in the Gospels and most parts of the Acts of the Apostles, and in part of the Epistle to the Romans. Nor had we any complete collation of it, until the Rev. Dr. Barrett printed one at the end of his fac-simile of the Codex Rescriptus of Matthew's Gospels, now preserved in the library of Trinity College, Dublin. [3] It is therefore absolutely necessary that we should inquire into these particulars, that we may not be deceived ourselves, or deceive others, by alleging an authority that has never been examined.

2. *The best and most antient* PRINTED EDITIONS, an account of which is given in the Appendix to this volume, are so far only to be admitted in evidence, as they are *immediately* taken from manuscripts. The various readings, however, which they contain, are not to be neglected, particularly those of the Hebrew Bibles printed in Rabbi Ben Chaim's or Hajim's Masoretical edition. In the New Testament, as the readings found in all the printed editions rest on the authority of a few manuscripts which are not always the most antient, the concurrence of all these editions cannot confer great authority on the readings adopted by them, in opposition to others which appear to be well supported.

---

[1] Amelotte, the bitter enemy of the learned and pious Port-Royalists, published a French translation of the New Testament in four volumes, 8vo., in the years 1666—1668. In his notes he boasted of having consulted all the manuscripts in Europe, *which he afterwards confessed he had not seen !* Chalmers's Biographical Dictionary, vol. ii. pp. 95—97.
[2] Scholz, Curæ Criticæ in Historiam Textus Evangeliorum, pp 80—90.
[3] Barrett, Evangelium secundum Matthæum ex Codice Rescripto in Bibliotheca Collegii SS. Trinitatis juxta Dublin. Appendix, pp. 5—35.

3. The ANTIENT VERSIONS (of which an account has already been given), though not free from error, nevertheless afford important assistance towards determining the true readings of passages, as they show what readings their authors considered to be genuine: but it is necessary that we consult only correct texts of such versions.

(1.) *Antient Versions are a legitimate source of emendation, unless upon collation we have reason to conclude that the translators of them were clearly mistaken.*

One or two examples will illustrate this remark. In James v. 12 many MSS., the Arabic of the London Polyglott, the Armenian and the Sclavonic versions, as also the Monk Antiochus, Oecumenius, and Theophylact, read ἱνα μη εις ὑποκρισιν πεσητε, *lest ye fall into hypocrisy*. But the Codices Alexandrinus and Vaticanus, and several other manuscripts, besides the printed editions, and the Syriac, Arabic (as edited by Erpenius), Coptic, Ethiopic, Vulgate, and other versions, all read the clause as it appears in our authorised English version, which is unquestionably the true reading, viz ἱνα μη ὑπο κρισιν πεσητε, *lest ye fall into condemnation*. Again, in 1 Pet. v. 13 we read, ασπαζεται ὑμας ἡ εν Βαβυλωνι συνεκλεκτη. Here some word is evidently to be supplied, in order to complete the sense. Dr. Mill conjectures that Peter's wife was intended. But the word εκκλησια, *church*, is found in the margin of two manuscripts (4 and 33 of Griesbach's notation), and in the Syriac, Arabic, Armenian, and Vulgate versions. It ought therefore to be received into the text. It is very properly supplied in *Italic characters* by the learned and venerable translators of our authorised English version, who render the verse thus:— *The church that is at Babylon, elected together with you, saluteth you.* Once more, in 2 Pet. ii. 2. the apostle, predicting the false teachers who would corrupt the church by their destructive doctrines, says, that *many shall follow*, αυτων ταις απωλειαις, *their destructions*, that is, *their pernicious ways* (as our translators have rendered it), their *heresies of destruction* or *destructive opinions*, mentioned in the preceding verse. This reading, however, is only found in the MSS. 43 and 65 of Griesbach's notation (both of the twelfth century), and in a few others of no note. But instead of it, we read, ασελγειαις, that is, *lasciviousnesses* or *uncleannesses*, in the Codices A. B C (Alexandrinus, Vaticanus, and Ephremi) and in more than fifty other manuscripts, most of which are among the most antient, correct, and authentic. This is also the reading of both the Syriac, all the Arabic, the Coptic, Ethiopic, Armenian, Sclavonic, and Vulgate versions, and of the fathers Chrysostom, Theophilus, Oecumenius, and Jerome. The word ασελγειαις, *lasciviousnesses*, is, therefore, beyond all doubt, the true reading, and is very properly printed as such by Griesbach: and it points out the nature of the heresy intended by the apostle. It was a sort of antinomianism. The heretics alluded to, pampered and indulged the lusts of the flesh; and if the Nicolaitans are meant, it is very applicable to them, for they taught the community of wives, &c.

(2.) *Antient manuscripts, supported by some of the antient versions and by the sense, render a reading certainly right, though it be not found in the more modern.*

In Isa. lviii. 10. we read, *If thou draw out thy soul to the hungry.* This, Bishop Lowth remarks, is a correct rendering of the present Hebrew text, but it is an obscure phrase, and without example in any other place. Instead, however, of נפשך (naphshek) *thy soul*, eight manuscripts (three of which are antient) read לחמך (lahmek) *thy bread*, and so it is rendered in the Syriac version. The proper reading thereof is, *draw out* (or *bring forth*) *thy bread*. The Septuagint version expresses both words, τον αρτον εκ της ψυχης σου, *thy bread from thy soul*.[1]

(3.) *The concurrence of the antient versions is sufficient to establish a reading as certainly right, when the sense or parallel place shows both the propriety of that reading, and the corruption of what is found in the copies of the original.*

---

[1] Gerard's Institutes, p 271. Lowth's Isaiah, vol. ii. p. 348. Another eminent commentator, however, defends the common reading and rendering. He is of opinion, that the emendation above proposed is a gloss, and should not be adopted. "*To draw out the soul in relieving the poor*, is to do it not of constraint or necessity,— but cheerfully, and is both nervous and elegant. His *soul pities*, and his *hand gives*."— (Dr. A. Clarke on Isa. lviii. 10.)

Thus, in Prov xviii. 21. (22 of English version) we read, Whoso findeth *a wife, findeth a good* thing. This is not true in *every* instance; it contradicts other maxims of the inspired writer, as Dr. Kennicott has shown, who is sufficiently eloquent on this occasion. He therefore conjectured that Solomon originally expressed himself thus, *he that findeth a* GOOD *wife, findeth a good thing, and obtaineth favour from the* LORD. This reading derives a strong confirmation from the fact, that the epithet *for good* is uniformly found in the Septuagint Greek, the Syriac, Arabic, and Vulgate versions. It is likewise found in two antient manuscript Chaldee paraphrases of the Book of Proverbs (one of which is at Cambridge, and the other in the King of Prussia's library at Berlin). All these concurring testimonies, together with the necessary sense of the text itself, prove that the Hebrew originally read, and ought to be so restored, *He that findeth a good wife, findeth a good thing.*[1]

(4.) *The Samaritan Pentateuch, which is only a different copy of the same original text, being more antient than the Babylonish captivity, and religiously preserved in the antient Hebrew characters, is a legitimate source of emendation. Although it differs in many places from the present Hebrew text, and these differences have been made objections against its authority, because it has been taken for granted that it must be wrong wherever it is not conformable to the Hebrew; yet as this assumption proceeds on the erroneous supposition of the absolute integrity of the Masoretic copies, it ought not to be regarded.*

Bauer has given a considerable number of rules for the application of the Samaritan Pentateuch to the determination of various readings, which he has illustrated by examples, for the whole of which we have not room. The following are such of his remarks as are of most general application.

(1.) Where the Samaritan text has the larger sections repeated from the other chapters of the Pentateuch, it is interpolated, and the Hebrew text is on no account to be corrected from it.

(2.) Where the Samaritan text contains readings in support of the peculiar dogmas entertained by the Samaritans, there it is to be considered as altered by the fraud of that sect.

(3.) Where the Samaritan text more strictly follows the rules of grammar, avoiding enallages of number and gender, and on the other hand, where the Hebrew text departs from those rules, not frequently expressing the enallage both of number and gender;—in such cases the reading of the Hebrew text is preferable to that of the Samaritan.

(4.) Where the Samaritan text contains a clearer reading, which removes any difficulty or obscurity, by the addition of a single word or phrase, there it has evidently been corrected by the Samaritan doctors, and the reading of the Hebrew copies is to be preferred. The application of this and the preceding canon to most of the corrections which Houbigant conceived might be drawn from the Samaritan Pentateuch, will show that those corrections are of no value whatever.

(5.) Where a reading in the Samaritan text departs from that of the Hebrew text, in the guttural letters, the true reading is to be found in the latter.

(6.) A various reading in the Samaritan text, which appears to be derived from the resemblance of the shape of the letters, is to be rejected.

(7.) A reading in the Samaritan text which is entirely unsupported by the authority of the Masoretic copies, and of the antient versions, is not to be regarded as the true one, and is not preferable to the Masoretic reading.

(8.) If the Samaritan text agrees with the Septuagint version (as frequently is the case), their testimony is to be considered but as one, from the very close affinity subsisting between them.

(9.) A various reading of the Samaritan Pentateuch is of the greatest value when it is confirmed by the antient versions of Aquila, and Symmachus, by the Syriac version, the Chaldee paraphrase, and the best and most antient Hebrew MSS. Thus, in Gen. xxii. 13. instead of, *behold* BEHIND him אחר (ACHER), the Samaritan reads אחד (ACHAD) *one,* and with this reading agree the Septuagint and Syriac versions, the Targum or Chaldee paraphrase of Onkelos, and *twenty-nine* of the manuscripts collated by Dr. Kennicott, together with *thirteen* of those collated by De Rossi. The proper rendering therefore of this verse is, *And Abraham lifted up his eyes and looked, and behold a ram caught in a thicket by his horns.*

---

[1] Kennicott's Second Dissertation on the Hebrew Text, pp. 189—192 Dr. Gerard has given four additional instances of the above rule. Institutes, pp. 272, 273.

The two following canons are selected from Dr. Gerard's Institutes of Biblical Criticism, (pp. 270, 271) with a few corrections

(10.) Readings in the Pentateuch supported by the Samaritan copy, a few Hebrew MSS., the antient versions, parallel places, and the sense, are certainly right, though they are not found in the generality of Hebrew manuscripts nor in editions.

Thus in Gen 1 25. after *ye shall carry up my bones from hence*, the parallel text in Exod. xiii. 19. twelve manuscripts, the Samaritan Text, the Septuagint, Syriac, Arabic, and Vulgate versions, all add *with you*. These words, therefore, are part of the text, and are very properly incorporated in it by Dr. Boothroyd, in his new translation of the Scriptures.

In Lev. ix. 21. the common reading is, *as Moses commanded* but in thirty manuscripts the Samaritan text, the Septuagint and Arabic versions, and the Targum of Onkelos, we read, *As Jehovah commanded Moses* which unquestionably is the true reading, and is supported not only by these authorities, but also by the whole chapter itself

(11.) Readings in the Pentateuch, supported by the Samaritan text, antient versions, parallel places, and the sense, are certainly right, though they are not found in any (or in only one) Hebrew manuscript now extant.

Thus in Gen ii 24. we read, *And they shall be one flesh* , but it is *they* two in the Samaritan text, and in the Septuagint, Syriac, Old Italic, Vulgate, and Arabic versions compared with Matt. xix 5. Mark x 8. 1 Cor vi 16. Eph. v. 31 , Philo Judæus, Tertullian, Epiphanius, Jerome, and Augustine In Exod vi 20. after *she bare him Aaron and Moses*, "and Miriam their sister," is added in the Samaritan text, the Septuagint and Syriac versions, and in one manuscript. There is no doubt but that it forms part of the sacred text. Again, in Exod. xii. 40 we read, *The sojourning of the children of Israel, who dwelt in Egypt, was four hundred and thirty years*. But this is not true, for it was only *two hundred and fifteen years ;* and it contradicts Gal. iii 17. which says, that it was only four hundred and thirty years from the calling of Abraham. two hundred and fifteen of which elapsed before the going into Egypt. (Compare Gen xii 4. xvii 1, 21 xxv. 26. and xlvii. 9.) The following is the verse as it appears in all the MSS. and editions of the Samaritan Pentateuch, confirmed by the Alexandrian Manuscript of the Septuagint. *Now the sojourning of the children of Israel*, and of their fathers, *which they sojourned* in the land of Canaan and *in the land of Egypt, was four hundred and thirty years*. This is the true reading, and removes all doubt and obscurity. It is proper to remark, that the last three examples of additional passages from the Samaritan text are introduced by Dr. Boothroyd into the text of his translation of the Bible

(5.) *Such antient versions as were immediately made from the original are proper sources of emendation, when our present Hebrew and Greek manuscripts disagree ; and their respective value is in proportion to their priority of date, their being made from accurate exemplars, their being literal translations, and their being confirmed by one another, and, as far as respects the Pentateuch, by the Samaritan text ; for the sole dissent of versions, unsupported by other authorities, constitutes only a dubious lection.*

Before, however, we admit any various reading into the text on the authority of an antient version, we must be certain that the text of such version has not been corrupted. And no various reading can be derived from the modern *Latin Versions* of the Greek or Oriental versions, which are given in the Polyglotts, because the Latin translators have in some instances mistaken the sense of such Oriental versions.

(6.) *The Greek version of the Old Testament, called the Septuagint, being the most antient and illustrious, is preferable to the Old Syriac version of the same portion of Scripture ; but the Old Syriac version of the New Testament, being executed at the close of the apostolic age, and consequently the most antient of all the translations of the New Testament, is preferable to every other version of it.*

The readings pointed out by the Greek version are sometimes the genuine lections, even when they are not found in any Hebrew manuscripts now extant. For instance, in Gen. iv. 8 we read, *And Cain said to Abel his brother : And it came to pass, when they were in the field, &c.* Here there is a manifest deficiency in all the Hebrew MSS and printed editions. The translators of the authorised English version, not being able to find that any thing was said on this occasion, ventured to intimate that there was a conversation, indefinitely, and therefore rendered the first clause of the verse, *and Cain talked with Abel his brother*. The deficiency, which exists in all the MSS. and editions, is supplied in the Septuagint version, which is supported by the Samaritan text, the Syriac and Vulgate Latin versions, the two Chaldee Targums, the Greek translation of Aquila, and by the passage as

Ch. V.] In the Old and New Testaments. 189

cited by Philo all of which supply the deficient words, *Let us go out into the field.* There is no doubt, therefore, that they form part of the original text, and that the verse ought to be translated thus. *And Cain said unto Abel his brother,* Let us go out into the field. *And it came to pass, when they were in the field, that Cain rose up against Abel his brother, and slew him.*

Again, in Acts xiii 18. we read *about the time of forty years suffered he* (ἐτροποφορησεν) *their manners in the wilderness,* that is, he dealt indulgently with them. However the Israelites provoked Jehovah, he mercifully bore with and endured them. On which clause we find in the margin of our authorised version the following conjecture Gr. ἐτροποφορησεν, perhaps for ἐτροφοφορησεν, *bore* or *fed them as a nurse beareth* or *feedeth her child* This conjecture is confirmed by the Codices Alexandrinus, Ephremi, and Basileensis, and four others of less note, as well as by the Syriac, Arabic, Coptic, and Ethiopic versions, and the quotations in some of the fathers; all of which read ἐτροφοφορησεν, *he nourished and fed them,* or *bore them about in his arms as a tender nurse does her child.* This reading agrees excellently with the scope of the place, and is at least of equal value with that in the commonly received text Griesbach has therefore admitted it, and excluded the other. Both readings, indeed, when rightly understood, speak nearly the same sense, but the latter is the most expressive, and agrees best with St Paul's discourse, and with the history to which he alludes The same form of expression occurs in Exod. xix 4. Numb. xi. 12. Isa. xlvi 3, 4. and lxiii. 9.

(7) *The Oldest Latin Versions of the New Testament, being of very high antiquity, notwithstanding they contain some false readings, are nevertheless of great value, because they lead to a discovery of the readings in very antient Greek manuscripts, that existed prior to the date of any that are now extant.* The vulgate, for instance, in its present state, being (as we have already seen) a mixture of the Old Italic version, and that of Jerome, points out the state *of the original text partly in the first and partly in the fourth century, and it gives great authority to those readings which it clearly indicates it also contains several which are preferable to the present readings, and are supported by some of the best and oldest manuscripts.*

Thus the literal rendering of Jer. li 19. is — *He is the former of all things, and the rod of his inheritance,* which is unintelligible The venerable translators of our authorised version have supplied *Israel* is the rod, &c most probably from the parallel sentence in Jer x. 16 ; and that this is the true reading is evident from the Vulgate version, which reads *et Israel sceptrum hereditatis ejus,* and also from the Chaldee paraphrase, which is further supported by twenty-three manuscripts collated by Dr Kennicott.[1]

(8) *The Syriac version being very literal, ascertains clearly the readings which it followed, to which, on account of its antiquity, it gives great authority; and it has preserved some, that appear to be genuine.*

Thus in 2 Sam xv 7 we read, *It came to pass after forty years,* which is manifestly erroneous, though supported by the commonly printed Vulgate, the Septuagint, and the Chaldee David reigned only forty years, and if we follow the text, the rebellion of Absalom would follow long *after* the death of David. In order to obviate this difficulty, some commentators have proposed to date from the time when David was first anointed by the prophet Samuel But the Syriac version, (which is confirmed by the Arabic version, by Josephus, by the Sixtine edition of the Vulgate, by several manuscripts of the same version, and by Theodoret,) reads FOUR Most learned men are of opinion that ארבעים (ARBAYIM) *forty,* is an error for ארבע (ARBA) *four* Accordingly, Dr Boothroyd has adopted the reading of the Syriac version, and translates *at the end of* FOUR *years,* in his new version of the Old Testament.

(9.) *Every deviation in the antient versions, both of the Old and New Testaments, is not to be considered as a proof of a various reading in the original manuscript whence it was taken; for the translator may have mistaken the original word, or he may have given it a signification different from what it bears at present, and this is the case particularly with the Septuagint.*

(10.) *One or a few antient versions may render a reading probable, when it is strongly supported by the sense, connection, or parallel places, in oppo-*

---

[1] Gerard's Institutes, p. 87. Kennicott's Second Dissertation. pp. 439, 440. and his Dissertatio Generalis, § 41. at the end of the second volume of his Critical Edition of the Hebrew Bible.

sition to one that does not agree with these, though found in other versions and in manuscripts.

Thus, in Gen. xiv. 20. we read, *And he gave tithes of all* This leaves it uncertain whether Melchizedek or Abram gave tithes. It rather seems to be the former, but it was the latter. In Heb vii 4. as well as the Samaritan text, and the Septuagint version, we have *Abram gave to him a tithe of all*, ἔδωκεν αὐτῷ Ἄβραμ δεκάτην ἀπὸ πάντων; which is probably the genuine reading.

Again, in Isa. xl 5. we read, *All flesh shall see together*, which is an imperfect sentence. The translators of our authorised version have supplied *it*, referring to the glory of God mentioned in the preceding part of the verse. This omission is antient, being prior to the Chaldee, Syriac, and Vulgate versions but all the copies of the Septuagint version and the parallel passage in Isa. lu. 10. read, *shall see the salvation of our God*, which lection is acknowledged by Luke (iii. 6.). Bishop Lowth therefore considers it as genuine, and has admitted it into the text of his translation of Isaiah

(11.) *The concurrence of all or most of the antient versions, in a reading not found in manuscripts now extant, renders such reading probable, if it be agreeable to the sense. though not absolutely contrary to it.*[1]

Thus, in 1 Sam. ix. 7 we read, *What shall we bring the man* לאיש (LA-ISH)? In *one* of the manuscripts collated by Dr. Kennicott (No 182. a manuscript of the fourteenth century) we read לאיש האלהים (LA-ISH H-ELOHIM), *to the man of God?* which is confirmed by the Chaldee paraphrase, and by the Septuagint, Syriac, Vulgate, and Arabic versions, and is probably the genuine reading.

(12.) *Of the Chaldee paraphrases*[2], *when manuscripts vary, those are to be preferred which are the more antient, and which have not been corrected, according to the present Masoretic text.*

(13.) *The Masora*[3], *Talmud, and Talmudical writers are also sources of emendation, but of no great authority in readings of any moment.*

With regard to the Masora, that reading only is to be admitted from it which is supported by antient versions, and is in perfect harmony with the context, the analogy of language, and parallel passages.

In Isa. ix. 2. (Heb., 8 of English version) we read, *Thou hast multiplied the nation, and not the joy*. The Ketib has לא (LA) *not*, with which the Vulgate version, and that of Symmachus agree; but the Keri reads לו (LI) *to him, or it*, that is, *the nation*, and with this agree the Chaldee paraphrase, the Septuagint, the Vulgate version, the readings in the text of fifteen manuscripts collated by Dr Kennicott, and six of those collated by M De Rossi. The latter reading is not only best supported, but it is also excellently in unison with the preceding verse. Bishop Lowth has therefore adopted it, and translates thus. *Thou hast multiplied the nation, thou hast increased their joy.*

Readings derived from the Talmud and Talmudical writers are only to be admitted, when they expressly cite the Hebrew text, and when their readings are confirmed by manuscripts. In judging of the various lections obtained from the Jewish writers, those which are collated from the Talmud, (though few in number,) are of great value, and equal to those furnished by Aquila, Symmachus, the Syriac version, and the Chaldee paraphrase. But such as are derived from the commentaries and lexicons of the Rabbins, who lived between the tenth and thirteenth centuries, are (according to Prof. Bauer) to be accounted equal with the readings of manuscripts.[4]

4. PARALLEL PASSAGES afford a very material help in determining various readings, where all other assistance fails. Cappel[5] and

---

[1] Gerard's Institutes, pp 280, 281. where several additional examples are given, for which we have not room.
[2] See an account of the Chaldee paraphrases, pp. 33—38. of this volume.
[3] See an account of the Masora in pp. 163—166. *supra*, and of the Talmud in Part II. Book I. Chap. II. Sect. II. § 6 *infra*, of this volume.
[4] Bauer, Critica Sacra, pp. 444, 445.
[5] See his Critica Sacra, (lib. i. cc. iii.—xiv.) vol. i. pp. 14—135. 8vo. edition, with Professor Vogel's notes.

Dr. Kennicott [1] have shown at great length what use may be made of parallel passages, in order to ascertain the genuine reading where it may be dubious, or to restore it where it may be lost. Professor Bauer has given an abstract of Cappel's collection of parallel passages in pp. 235—238. of his *Critica Sacra:* and two or three instances will show the importance of them in ascertaining a true reading in the New Testament.

In Matt. i. 4. not fewer than fourteen manuscripts and two of the fathers read Αμιναδαμ, *Aminada*M, but the parallel passage in 1 Chron. ii. 10. has *Aminada*B, which therefore is the genuine reading of the Evangelist. Again, in Matt. xxvii. 46. instead of λαμα (*lama*), many MSS. read λειμα (*leima*), λιμα (*lima*), or λεμα (*lema*) ; but a reference to Psal. xxii. 2. (Heb., or 1. of English version), shows that λαμα is the proper reading. Once more, in Matt. ii. 23 the common reading is Ναζαρετ (*Nazare*T); but in the Codices C. E. K. (Ephremi, Basileensis B. VI. 21. and Cyprius,) and many other MSS. of less note, besides several printed editions, and the Coptic, Armenian, Italic, Vulgate, and Anglo-Saxon versions, and also in the quotations of Eusebius and Cyril, we read Ναζαρεθ (*Nazare*TH). And that this is the true reading is evident from comparing the numerous other passages of the four Gospels in which this place is called *Nazareth* and not *Nazaret*.

(1.) *Where Parallel Passages, together with the sense, support the reading of antient manuscripts, they show that such reading is perfectly right.*

Thus in Isa lxi 4. we read, *they shall build the old wastes* but the sentence is incomplete, as we know not who are the builders. After *they shall build,* four MSS. (two of which are antient) add ממך (MaMaCH) *they that spring from thee.* and this reading is confirmed by lviii. 12 where the sentence is the very same, this word being added. Bishop Lowth therefore receives it into the text, and translates the sentence thus

And they that spring from thee shall build up the ruins of old times.

(2.) *In a text evidently corrupted, a parallel place may suggest a reading perfectly genuine.* [2]

Thus, in the common printed editions of Judg. vii. 18 we read, *Say, of the Lord and of Gideon* This is defective. The venerable English translators have, with great propriety, supplied *the sword,* חרב (HEREB) from the successful exploit of Gideon, related in v. 20. The word which those learned but much traduced men thus supplied from a parallel place, proves to be right for it is found in ten manuscripts, besides the Chaldee Paraphrase, and the Syriac and Arabic Versions. In like manner they have supplied the word *fourth* in 2 Kings xxv. 3 from Jer. lii. 6. to complete the sense ; and this supply is also confirmed by the different versions

(3) *To determine with accuracy the authority of parallel passages in the Old Testament, they should be divided into four classes, viz.*

1. Passages containing the historical narration of an event which occurred *but once,* or the record of a prayer or speech *but once* uttered. Ex gr. Jos. xix. 50. xxiv. 30. comp. with Jud. ii. 9   2 Sam. xxii. with Ps. xviii.   The Book of Kings, with that of Chronicles. 2 Kings xxv. with Jer. lii. 2 Kings xviii. to xx. with Isa. xxxvi. to xxxix. Isa. ii 2. 4. with Micah iv. 1—3

2. Passages containing a command, and either a repetition of it, or a record of its being obeyed Ex xx. 2—17. with Deut v. 6—22. Ex. xxv. to xxix. with xxxvi. to xxxix. Levit. xi. 13—19 with Deut xiv. 12—18.   Ezekiel xli. 6. with 7.

3. Proverbial sayings, or expressions frequently repeated. Num. xxi. 28, 29. and xxiv. 17. with Jer. xlviii. 45, 46. Ezek. v. 7. with xi. 12. Jer. v. 9 and 29 with ix. 9. Psalm xlii. 5. 11 with xliii 5.   Jer. x. 25. with Psalm lxxix. 6, 7.   Jer. x. 16 with li 19. Isa. xxiv. 17, 18. with Jer. xlviii. 43, 44.

---

[1] In his first Dissertation on the Hebrew Text, pp. 13. 79. 198. 444. 457. 461. 481. 484. 502. 510.

[2] Gerard's Institutes, p. 273. Where the reader will find several additional illustrations of this canon.

4. Records of the same genealogies, 1 Chron with several chapters of Genesis, and Ezra, with Nehemiah.

In any such passages as these, where there is a difference in numbers or names — where there is more than a verbal difference in records of the same transaction — or where there is even a verbal difference in copies of the same prayer or speech, in the printed text, but not in manuscripts and versions, there it is erroneous, and ought to be corrected.[1]

5. QUOTATIONS *from the Old and New Testaments in the Writings of the Fathers* are an emendatory source which is by no means to be neglected: but only *correct* editions of their works should be consulted. Among the antient fathers of the church, those are particularly worthy of attention and collation who wrote in the Greek language; because they spoke, and read, and wrote that very language in which the sacred writings of the New Testament were originally composed. The phrase and diction of those writings was, therefore, familiar to them; they naturally expressed themselves in the Scripture style and language. When they referred to any texts of Scripture, or discoursed more at large upon them, they would of course be guided by the original *Greek* of the New Testament [2], and not by any version that had been made, and might possibly vary from it; whereas the Latin fathers being only accustomed to the *Latin version*, it is as much to be expected that they should conform their language, quotations, and comments to it; though, perhaps, upon some occasions, and according to their ability, taking notice also of the Greek original. A Latin father will be an evidence for the Latin version, where he takes no express notice of the Greek: and according to the clearness and fulness of that evidence, we may argue, that the Latin version, or some copy or copies of it, had that reading in his time, which is cited by him. And this may deserve to be attended to with regard to any omissions in the Greek MSS. which the Latin may be thought to have supplied: but still the testimony of the Latin father in this case will prove nothing more than the reading of a Latin version: by what authority that version is supported, is a matter of further enquiry. Indeed where it can be shown that a Latin father followed no particular version, but translated directly for himself (as Tertullian and Cyprian have frequently done); this brings us somewhat nearer to some manuscript in the original language, and may be considered, according as it shall happen to be circumstantiated, as a distinct testimony for the reading of some Greek MS. in particular.[3]

In order to judge of the true reading of any text of Scripture, from any quotation of it, with which we meet in the writings of the fathers, the following criteria have been laid down, principally by J. D. Michaelis.

(1.) *In considering the testimony of a single father, we are in the first place to enquire in what age he lived, and what were his abilities? Whether he was a person of learning and judgment, of accuracy and exactness, or*

---

[1] Hamilton's Codex Criticus of the Hebrew Bible, p. 18.
[2] It is to be observed that the Greek Fathers generally quote the Old Testament from the Septuagint version.
[3] Dr. Berriman's Dissertation on 1 Tim. iii. 16. pp. 28, 29.

otherwise? And also whether the treatise or work, in which the Scriptures are so quoted, be the genuine production of the writer whose name it bears?

(2.) *Wherever it is certain that the quotations were actually taken from manuscripts, they are of very great importance in deciding on the authenticity of a true reading, and are in general to be preferred to any manuscripts of the Greek Testament now extant, the oldest of which cannot be placed earlier than the end of the fourth or the commencement of the fifth century.*

If therefore a father, who flourished in the fifth and subsequent ages, has a particular reading, it is the same as if we found it in a manuscript of that time.

(3.) *As the fathers have frequently, though not always, quoted from memory, it is necessary to make a distinction between those passages which they expressly declare that they have taken literally from manuscripts, and those which they quote without any such assurance.*

(4.) *We are not therefore to reject the quotation of a father, because it differs from the common text, but must first examine whether it cannot be discovered in manuscripts of the New Testament; and to enable those who have access to manuscripts to make this comparison with as much ease as possible, we should endeavour to procure the most accurate and copious extracts from the writings of the fathers.*

If a reading, then, which had the appearance of being an error of memory, is actually discovered in manuscripts, we may without hesitation put it down in the list of various readings its antiquity will be determined by the age in which the father who quoted it lived and the manuscripts which contain it will afford a secondary evidence of its age and authenticity. But we must not judge of the writings of all the fathers, nor of all the writings of the same father, in the same manner. They may be divided into three different classes. 1 Commentaries, to which may be referred also those discourses which were written as expositions of parts of the Bible. 2. Works of Education. 3 Polemical writings. In the first it is evident that the book which is expounded is not quoted from memory, but the author, in writing his commentary, had lying before him a manuscript of the Greek Testament But with respect to the polemical writings of the fathers, those who are acquainted with their mode of disputation, and know that their principal object is sometimes to confound their adversaries rather than to support the truth, will refer the quotations which appear in these productions to the lowest class If a father was acquainted with more than one reading to a passage, he would certainly quote that which best suited his purpose, and with which he could most easily confute his opponents. It is therefore not sufficient to know what reading he quotes, but we must likewise consider where he quotes it and those therefore who collect various readings from the writings of the antient fathers, would do well to point out the book, chapter, edition, and page, in order to enable the reader to form a proper judgment.

(5.) *It is necessary to make an accurate distinction between a quotation properly so called, and a passage of Scripture introduced and applied as part of a discourse.*

For if a writer, in treating any known doctrine of the Bible, uses the words of Scripture, he is at liberty to add or subtract, to contract or dilate them in a manner that is best adapted to the tenor of his discourse But even such passages are not unworthy of notice, for if they are different in different manuscripts, and any one of these latter coincides with the former, the coincidence is not to be considered as a matter of chance. But when no manuscript corroborates the reading in such a passage, it is intitled to no voice in deciding on the text of the Greek Testament.

(6.) *In collecting readings from the works of the fathers, an accurate distinction must be made between those who wrote in Greek, and those who wrote in another language.*

Properly speaking, the former only are to be considered when we select readings for the Greek Testament, and the latter immediately relate to the text of the version from which they are quoted, unless particular mention be made of the Greek, or the writer, like Jerome, made a practice of correcting the translation of his country from the original.

(7.) *It must also be observed whether a father takes notice of a text only once, or but seldom, or very often.*

For a *frequent* repetition will make the slighter kinds of difference deserving of more attention; whereas a single instance or two of that sort will be the more easily imputed to a slip of the memory, or a casual mistake.

(8.) *It is necessary to observe whether an author be uniform and consistent with himself, or different and various.*

If a text be found differently expressed by the same author, we shall often be at a loss to know which he esteemed the right and sometimes, perhaps, he may be wrong in each; and yet sometimes, too, it may be easily discovered, that one passage was designed to express the text more exactly, and another was only a reference by memory, and from thence proceeded the variation. An example of this we have in Chrysostom. In his comment upon Acts xx. 28 he reads it εκκλησιαν του Θεου, *Church of God, three times* (though Dr. Mill cites him there for the reading of Κυριου (*Lord*) but in his comment on Eph. iv. 12 he casually refers to this text, and quotes it probably by memory, and there he puts it down εκκλησιαν του Κυριου, that is, *Church of the Lord*.

(9.) *The writings of the fathers are to be compared, one with another; and an inquiry must be instituted, what testimony arises from them upon the whole.*

If it be a point, of which they generally take notice, or in which they are agreed, if we meet with no contrary voice, or none worthy of being regarded, or with some who argue for it, while others criticise or comment upon it, this will afford the clearest and strongest testimony that can be either desired or obtained.

(10.) *We must compare the evidence arising from an examination of the writings of the fathers, with that which appears to be the reading of the Greek manuscripts in general, and see how well they agree together. Where the MSS in general and the fathers do agree, it must be something very extraordinary that will make it reasonable to believe that they are altogether in a mistake. Nay, that evidence from the fathers must be very strong, which will make it reasonable to think the Greek MSS. agreeing in general among themselves, are mistaken.*

A casual citation of a text will not be sufficient to prove them so mistaken, nor a bare comment upon a version, where it varies from the original much less will this do, where opposite testimonies can be produced from Greek writers, and especially where those opposite testimonies are so full upon the point, as supposes and implies that they found the reading which they mention in the Greek copies which were in use in their days. If any instance can be found in which it can be clearly proved from the writings of the fathers, that the general and allowed reading of the Greek copies, in the early ages of the church was different from the general reading of the Greek MSS in our days, we should without hesitation give up such general reading of our present MSS. But it is very questionable whether one single instance of this sort can any where be found and those persons who raise general clamours about the corruption of the manuscripts of the sacred writings, *unsupported by any solid proofs*, are no more to be heard, but still more to be condemned, than those who speak in this manner of the writings of the fathers. But in a matter of doubt and uncertainty, where the MSS. of the sacred writings in the original language are divided, the united testimony of the fathers will turn the scale in favour of the side for which they appear, and will more powerfully establish and confirm the general reading of the Scripture MSS. where they are agreed.[1]

(11.) *The Fathers having in general quoted the Scriptures very exactly, as they had it in their copies, whenever a reading followed by them agrees with any antient manuscript, it is in all probability the genuine reading.*

Thus, in most copies of Matt. vi. 1. we read, Take heed that you do not your ALMS (ελεημοσυνην) but in the Codices Vaticanus and Cantabrigiensis, and three or four other MSS of less antiquity, as also in the old Italic and Vulgate versions and most of the Fathers, we read δικαιοσυνην, *righteousness*, that is, acts of righteousness. This reading is most agreeable to the mode of speech which obtained among the Jews [2] and consequently is the genuine one. Griesbach has therefore inserted it in the text.

---

[1] Berriman's Dissertation, p. 38.

[2] That the Jews in the time of Christ understood the word צדקה, δικαιοσυνη, *righteousness*, in the sense of alms, is abundantly proved by Mr John Gregory, Works, pp. 59, 60. (London, 1684, 4to.) and especially by Dr Lightfoot, Works, vol. ii. pp. 153, 154. folio.

Again, in Luke x 1 we read that the *Lord appointed other seventy disciples* The Codices Vaticanus, Cantabrigiensis, and Medicæus (No. 42, of Griesbach's notation), together with the Persian, Armenian, Vulgate, and four copies of the Old Italic versions, read εβδομηκοντα δυο, seventy two; and in this reading they are supported by eleven Fathers principally of the Latin or Western Church On the contrary, all the other MSS. have simply εβδομηκοντα, *seventy*, in which reading they are supported by the learned Greek Fathers, Eusebius, Gregory Bishop of Nyssa, Cyril, Euthymius, Theophylact, and Theophanes, and by Irenæus, Tertullian, Ambrose, Jerome Damasus, and others among the Latin writers The common reading, therefore, is established as the genuine one by the concurrence of the Fathers with MSS

Once more, in John i 28. we read that *These things were done in Bethabara*. This lection is found in thirty-one manuscripts, in the printed editions, in the Armenian version, and a late exemplar of the Sclavonic version, and is preferred by Origen, and after him by Eusebius, Suidas, Jerome, and others But it is *certain* that, instead of Βηθαβαρα, we ought to read Βηθανια *Bethany*, which word is found in the Codices Alexandrinus, Vaticanus, Ephremi, Basileensis, Harleianus No 5684, Seidelii, Stephani η, Stephani π, Regius No 2243², (now 48) and Vaticanus 354, in B. and V. of Matthæi's notation, in upwards of one hundred other MSS. of less antiquity, and in the Syriac, Armenian, Persic, Coptic, and Vulgate versions, and in three MSS. of the Sclavonic version (one of the twelfth, the other two of the fourteenth century) The reading of Βηθανια, *Bethany*, is also confirmed by the most eminent of the primitive Fathers *prior to* the time of Origen (who is supposed to have first changed the reading); and is unquestionably the genuine one Griesbach has therefore inserted it in the text.

(12.) *The total silence of the Fathers concerning a reading, which would have confirmed their opinion in a controverted point, justly renders that reading suspicious, unless such total silence can be satisfactorily accounted for*

This negative argument against a reading will be of little weight where it respects the writings of one single author only and where it is founded only upon some particular part of his works, and such author has himself taken notice of the text in other places, it will be of no weight at all Nay, if but one or two only have made mention of a text, this will be a better proof that it was read in their days, than any omission of their contemporaries, or of those that lived after them, will be a proof that it was not. But let us take this argument in the strongest light, and let the utmost possible be made of it; it can only furnish matter of doubt and enquiry , it can at most amount to no more than probable and presumptive evidence, and nothing can be positively and certainly concluded from it One plain positive proof from the original MSS. or the antient versions, will be able to weigh it down, unless it can be shown that they have been altered and corrupted.

6. The fragments of HERETICAL WRITINGS are not to be overlooked in the search for various readings: for the supposition is rash, that they generally corrupted the text of *all* parts of the sacred Writings.[1]

7. CRITICAL CONJECTURE is not *alone* a legitimate source of emendation, nor is it at all to be applied, unless the text is manifestly corrupted, and in the most urgent necessity: for the conjectural criticism of an interested party, in his own cause, and in defiance of positive evidence, is little better than subornation of testimony in a court of law.

(1.) *Conjectural Readings, strongly supported by the sense, connection, the nature of the language, or similar texts, may sometimes be* probable, *especially when it can be shown that they would easily have given occasion to the present reading . and readings first suggested by conjecture have sometimes been afterwards found to be actually in manuscripts, or in some version.*

Thus, in Gen i 8. the clause, *And God saw that it was good*, is wanting to complete the account of the second day's work of creation, but it is found in the tenth verse in the middle of the narrative of the third day's work. Hence, many learned men have conjectured, either, 1 That the sentence, *And the evening and the morning were the second day*, has been transposed from verse 10. to verse 8 ; or 2 That the clause, *And God saw that it*

---

[1] Stuart's Elements of Interpretation, p. 119. (Andover, 1822)

was good, has been transposed from verse 8. to verse 10. The latter conjecture affords the most *probable* reading, and is to be preferred, being confirmed by the Septuagint version; the translators of which most evidently found this clause in the copies which they used.

(2.) *A Conjectural Reading, unsupported by any manuscripts, and unauthorised by similarity of letters, by the connection and context of the passage itself, and by the analogy of faith, is manifestly to be rejected.*

In the address of James to the apostles convened at Jerusalem, he gives it as his opinion that they should write to the believing Gentiles *that they abstain from pollutions of idols, and fornication, and things strangled, and blood.* (Acts xv. 20.) As the question related to the *ceremonial* and not to the *moral* law, the celebrated critic Dr. Bentley conjectured that for πορνειας, *fornication,* we should read χοιρειας, *swine's flesh;* and in this conjecture he has been followed by Mr. Reeves in the Scholia to his beautiful and useful editions of the Bible. But this reading is supported by *no* manuscript whatever, nor by any similarity of the letters, nor by the context of the passage; for in the encyclical letter of the Apostles (ver 25.) we read *fornication.* If χοιρειας had been the correct lection in the first instance, it would have been unquestionably retained in the second. And when it is recollected that the word πορνεια, which in our version is rendered *fornication,* means not only the crime against chastity usually so called, but also adultery and prostitution of *every* kind (for which very many of the feasts of the idolatrous Gentiles were notorious), the force of the apostolic prohibition will be evident, and the genuineness of the commonly received reading will be established in opposition to Bentley's arbitrary conjecture.[1]

No one should attempt this kind of emendation who is not most deeply skilled in the sacred languages; nor should critical conjectures ever be admitted into the text, for we never can be certain of the truth of merely conjectural readings. Were these indeed to be admitted into the text, the utmost confusion and uncertainty would necessarily be created. The diligence and modesty of the Masorites are in this respect worthy of our imitation: they invariably inserted their conjectures in the margin of their manuscripts, but most religiously abstained from altering the text according to their hypotheses: and it is to be regretted that their example has not been followed by some modern translators of the Old and New Testament (and especially of the latter); who, in order to support doctrines which have no foundation whatever in the sacred writings, have not hesitated to obtrude their conjectures into the text This is particularly the case with the Greek and English New Testament edited by Dr. Mace in 1729, whose bold and unhallowed emendations were exposed by Dr. Twells, and also with the editors of the (Unitarian) improved version of the New Testament, whose conjectures and erroneous criticisms and interpretations have been most ably exposed by the Rev. Drs. Nares and Laurence, the Quarterly and Eclectic Reviewers, and other eminent critics.

V. Having thus stated the causes of various readings, and offered a few cautions with regard to the sources whence the true lection is to be determined, it only remains that we submit to the reader's attention a few general rules, by which an accurate judgment may be formed concerning various readings.

1. *We must take care, that we do not attempt to correct that which does not require emendation.* The earlier *manuscript,* cæteris paribus, *is more likely to be right than the later, because every subsequent copy is liable to new errors.*

---

[1] Other examples of unsupported conjectural emendations may be seen in Pritii Introd. ad Lectionem Novi Testamenti, p. 393.; Clerici Ars Critica, tom. ii. part iii. sect. 1. c. 16. § 11.; and in Wetstein's Prolegom. ad Nov. Test. pp. 170. et seq.

This rule will prevent us from being misled by an immoderate desire of correcting what we may not understand, or what may at a first glance *appear* to be unsuitable to the genius of the Hebrew or Greek language, or to the design of an author. Wherever, therefore, any difficulty presents itself, it will be necessary previously to consider whether it may not be obviated in some other manner, before we have recourse to emendation; and even ingenuously to acknowledge our ignorance, rather than indulge a petulant licentiousness of making corrections. Examples are not wanting of critics on the sacred writings, who have violated this obvious rule, particularly Houbigant, in the notes to his edition of the Hebrew Bible.

2. *That reading in which all the recensions of the best copies agree, and which is supported by all the antient versions, is to be accounted genuine.*

3. *Readings are certainly right, and that in the very highest sense, at all consistent with the existence of any various reading, which are supported by several of the most antient manuscripts, or by the majority of them, — by all or most of the antient versions, — by quotations, — by parallel places (if there be any), — and by the sense; even though such readings should not be found in the common printed editions, nor perhaps in any printed edition.*[1]

Thus, in the common printed editions of 1 Kings i. 20. we read, *And thou, my Lord, O King, the eyes of all Israel are upon thee*, which is not sense. Instead of ואתה, *And* THOU, we have עתה, *And* NOW, in ninety-one of the manuscripts collated by Dr. Kennicott, in the Chaldee paraphrase, and in the Arabic and Vulgate versions. This is the genuine reading, and is required by the sense.

Again, in Matt. xxv. 29, we read, *From him that hath not shall be taken away even that which he* HATH, και Ὁ ΕΧΕΙ αρθησεται. This is found in all the antient copies, and in the majority of manuscripts, and in the Vulgate, as well as in some copies of the Syriac, Sclavonic, and Old Italic versions, and six Fathers, we read Ὁ ΔΟΚΕΙ ΕΧΕΙΝ, *that which he* SEEMETH TO HAVE. But it is wrong, and has been corrected from Luke viii. 18.

4. *Greater is the authority of a reading, found in only a few manuscripts of different characters, dates, and countries, than in many manuscripts of a similar complexion. But, of manuscripts of the same family or recension, the reading of the greater number is of most weight. The evidence of manuscripts is to be weighed, not enumerated: for the agreement of several manuscripts is of no authority, unless their genealogy (if we may be allowed the term) is known; because it is possible that a hundred manuscripts that now agree together may have descended from one and the same source.*

5. *Readings are certainly right, which are supported by a few antient manuscripts, in conjunction with the antient versions, quotations, parallel places (if any), and the sense; though they should not be found in most manuscript or printed editions, especially when the rejection of them in the latter can be easily accounted for.*

The common reading of Psalm xxviii. 8. is, *The* LORD *is their strength* למו (LAMO); but there is no antecedent. In six manuscripts and all the versions, however, we read, לעמו (LEAMMO) *of his people*, which completes the sense. This emendation is pronounced by Bp. Horsley, to be "unquestionable" he has therefore incorporated it in the text of his New Version of the Psalms, and has translated the sentence thus ·

Jehovah is the strength of his people.

In most manuscripts and printed editions of Eph v. 9. we read, *The fruit of the* SPIRIT (του πνευματος), *is in all goodness, and righteousness, and truth.* But it is *the fruit of the* LIGHT (του φωτος) in the Codices Alexandrinus, Vaticanus, and Claromontanus, Augiensis, San-germanensis, and Boernerianus, and six others of less note, as well as in the Syriac version, the Arabic version edited by Erpenius, the Coptic, Sahidic, Ethiopic, Armenian, Old Italic, and Vulgate versions; and it is so quoted by seven of the fathers. Φωτος, *light*, is therefore considered by most critics as the true reading, because the Spirit is not mentioned in any part of the context; and this reading is inserted in the text as genuine by Griesbach. The connection, indeed, shows that this last is the true reading, which was altered by some unknown copyist or critic, because it was uncommon, from Gal. v 22. As light (Eph. v. 8.) not only means the divine influence upon the soul, but

---

[1] Gerard's Institutes, pp. 266—268.

also the Gospel, the apostle Paul might with admirable propriety say, that *the fruit of the light* (that is, of the *Gospel*) *is in all goodness, and righteousness, and truth* — goodness, αγαθωσυνη, in the principle and disposition, — righteousness, δικαιοσυνη, the exercise of that goodness in the whole conduct of life, — and truth, αληθεια, the director of that principle and of its exercise to the glory of God and the good of mankind

6. *Of two readings, both of which are supported by manuscripts, the best is to be preferred; but if both of them exhibit good senses, then that reading which gives the best sense is to be adopted. But, in order to determine the nature of the whole passage, the genius of the writer, and not the mere opinions and sentiments of particular interpreters, are to be consulted.*

In Psalm ii. 6. there are two readings, one of which is found in the Masoretic copies, and the other in the Septuagint version. The former may be literally translated thus *Yet will I anoint my King upon my holy hill of Sion.* This reading is supported by weighty evidence, viz the Masora, the quotation of it in Acts iv 27, the Greek versions of Aquila and Symmachus, the Chaldee paraphrase, and Jerome. The other reading which is found in the Septuagint, may be thus rendered *But as for me, by him I am appointed king on Sion, his holy mountain.* Now here the authority for the two readings is nearly equal but if we examine their goodness, we shall see that the Masoretic lection is to be preferred, as being more grammatically correct, and more suited to the context

7. *A good various reading. though supported only by one or two witnesses of approved character, is to be preferred.*

8. *In the prophetical and poetical books of the Old Testament, as well as in the New Testament, that reading is best which accords with the poetical parallelism.*

The subject of poetical parallelism is fully considered in Part II. Book II Chap. II. *infra.* The application of this canon to the various readings of the Old Testament has long been recognised, but as its applicability to the New Testament is not so obvious, we shall illustrate it by an example drawn from the latter.

Thus in Matt. vii 2. we read,

Εν ω γαρ κρινετε, κριθησεσθε
Και εν ω μετρειτε, αντιμετρηθησεται ὑμιν.

For, with what judgment ye judge, ye shall be judged,
And with what measure ye mete, it shall be measured to you again

For αντιμετρηθησεται, *shall be measured again,* (which is the reading of the common printed editions, of the manuscript by Matthæi noted with the letter H, of the manuscript 13 of Griesbach's notation, of the Vulgate version, of some manuscripts of the Old Italic version, of Polycarp, of Clement of Alexandria, of Origen sometimes, and of the Latin Fathers), we read μετρηθησεται, *shall be measured,* in the Codices Vaticanus, Harleianus No 5684, Cyprius, Stephani η, Regius 2243[2] (now 48), and Vaticanus 354, all of which are manuscripts in uncial characters of great antiquity, in twelve manuscripts in smaller characters, by Griesbach, numbered 1, 17, 33, 77, 108, 114, 117, 131, 218, 236 of Professor Birch's Collation, the Evangelisteria, numbered 32 and 36, and seventy other manuscripts of inferior note, and by the manuscripts distinguished by Matthæi with the Letters B and V (both of the eighth century), a. c. and d. (all of the tenth or eleventh century), and by eight others of Matthæi's manuscripts of less note, by the Armenian and Ethiopic versions, by the copies of the Old Italic version preserved at Verona, Vercelli, Forli, and Toledo, by Clement of Rome, by Origen once, by the author of the dialogue against Marcion, by Theodoret, Theophylact, Euthymius, Chrysocephalus, and other Greek writers. The reading of μετρηθησεται, therefore, being supported by such an overwhelming body of evidence, is very properly introduced into the text by Griesbach as preferable to the common reading of αντιμετρηθησεται, and it is further demanded by the parallelism. For κριματι (judgment), κρινετε (ye judge), and κριθησεσθε (ye shall be judged), in the first line, require, in order to preserve the balance of the period, μετρω (measure), μετρειτε (ye measure), and μετρηθησεται (it shall be measured), in the second line [1]

9. *Of two readings of equal or nearly equal authority, that is to be preferred, which is most agreeable to the style of the sacred writer.*

If, therefore, one of two readings in the New Testament exhibits the Hebrew idiom, it is preferable to one that is good Greek, because the latter has the appearance of being a gloss of some Greek writer, which the former does not present. Thus in Jude 1,

---

[1] Bp Jebb's Sacred Literature, p 144 In pp 206 329—331, of the same work the reader will find other instructive examples of the canon above given

ηγιασμενοις, *sanctified*, is a better lection than ηγαπημενοις, *beloved*, because the former is more in unison with the usage of the apostles in their salutations, and in the commencement of their Epistles. In Acts xvii. 26. the reading, εξ ενος αίματος, *of one blood*, is preferable to εξ ενος, *of one* (which occurs in Rom. iv. 10.), because it is in unison with the Hebrew style of writing. In John vi. 69, the common reading, *Thou art the Christ, the Son of the living God*, Χριστος ὁ υἱος του Θεου του ζωντος, is preferable to that of *the holy one of God*, ὁ ἁγιος του Θεου, which Griesbach has admitted into the text, omitting του ζωντος, on the authority of the Codices Vaticanus, Ephremi, Cantabrigiensis, Stephani η, the Coptic version, and some other authorities of less note. That eminent critic, indeed, allows that the received lection is not to be despised, but we may observe that its genuineness is not only confirmed by the consentient testimonies of many MSS., versions, and fathers, but also from the fact and from the style of writing adopted by the Evangelists. For the appellation of *holy one of God* is no where applied to our Saviour, except in the confession of the demoniac. (Mark i. 24. Luke iv. 54.) In Acts iv. 27, 30, Jesus is termed ἁγιος παις, *holy child*, but not *holy one of God*. On the contrary, the appellation of Christ, *the Son of God*, occurs repeatedly in the New Testament, and especially in this Gospel of John (i. 50., 49. of English version, and xi. 27.), and is elsewhere expressly applied to him by Peter. See Matt. xvi. 16. The common reading, therefore, of John vi. 69. is to be preferred, in opposition to that adopted by Griesbach, as being most agreeable to the style of the sacred writer.

10. *That reading is to be preferred which is most agreeable to the context, and to the author's design in writing.*

Every writer, and much more a divinely inspired writer, is presumed to write in such a manner, as not to contradict himself either knowingly or willingly, and to write throughout with a due regard to the order and connection of things. Now in Mark i. 2, for εν τοις προφηταις, *in the prophets*, several manuscripts read εν Ησαια τω προφητη, *in the prophet Isaiah*. Both Mill and Griesbach reject the common reading. But as the context shows that the Evangelist cited not one but *two* prophets, viz. Mal iii. 1, and Isa. xl. 3, the common reading ought to be retained, especially as it is supported by the Codex Alexandrinus, the Ethiopic and Coptic versions, and the quotations of many fathers.

11. *A reading, whose source is clearly proved to be erroneous, must be rejected.*

12. *Of two readings, neither of which is unsuitable to the sense, either of which may have naturally arisen from the other, and both of which are supported by manuscripts, versions, and quotations in the writings of the fathers; the one will be more probable than the other, in proportion to the preponderance of the evidence that supports it: and that preponderance admits a great variety of degrees.*[1]

In Acts xx. 28. we read, *Feed the church of God, which he hath purchased with his own blood.* Of this sentence there are not fewer than six various readings, viz. 1. Την εκκλησιαν του Χριστου, *the church of Christ*; 2. Του Θεου, *of God*, which lection is expunged by Griesbach, who prefers, 3. Του Κυριου, *of the Lord*. This reading is also preferred by Wetstein; 4. Του Κυριου και Θεου, *of the Lord and God*, which Griesbach has inserted in his inner margin, 5. Του Θεου και Κυριου, *of the God and Lord*, and 6. Του Κυριου Θεου, *of the Lord God*. In order to determine which of these readings is to be adopted, it is necessary briefly to review the various authorities which have been adduced for each.

1. Του Χριστου — *Of Christ*. This reading is supported by no Greek MSS.; but it is found in the *printed* editions of the Peschito or old Syriac version, even in the Vatican copies of the Nestorians. This reading is also found in the Arabic version edited by Erpenius (which was made from the Syriac), and it seems to be supported by Origen (probably, for the passage is ambiguous), by Athanasius, the anonymous author of the first dialogue against the Macedonians, Theodoret, the interpolated Epistle of Ignatius, Basil, and Fulgentius. The popish synod of the Malabar Christians, held in 1599, under the direction of Mendoza, the Portuguese archbishop of Goa, states that the Nestorians inserted this reading at the instigation of the devil, *instigante diabolo!*

2. Του Θεου — *Of God*. This is the common reading. It is supported by that most antient and venerable MS., B, or the Codex Vaticanus[2], and by seventeen others, none

---

[1] Gerard's Institutes, p. 275.
[2] From Professor Birch (of Copenhagen) finding nothing noted in his collation of the Vatican MS. respecting the reading of Θεου, (though he expressly says, that if any variety of reading had taken place in that MS. it could not have escaped him, as he intended to examine this remarkable place above all others in all the MSS that came in his way,

of which indeed are older than the eleventh century, and many of them are more modern. It is also supported by two MSS of the Peschito or Old Syriac version, collated by Professor Lee for his edition of the Syriac New Testament, and which, he states, are much more antient than those upon which the printed text was formed. This reading is also found in a very antient Syriac MS. in the Vatican Library, in the Latin Vulgate, the Ethiopic, according to Dr. Mill, through Griesbach thinks it doubtful, and it is quoted or referred to by Ignatius, Tertullian, Athanasius, Basil, Epiphanius, Ambrose, Chrysostom, Celestine bishop of Rome, Oecumenius, Theophylact, and eleven other fathers of the Greek and Latin Church, besides the sixth Synod in Trullo (held A. D. 680), and the second Nicene Synod (held A. D. 787).

3. Του Κυριου — *Of the Lord.* This reading is supported by thirteen manuscripts, viz. the Codices Alexandrinus, Cantabrigiensis, Ephremi, and Laudianus, (all of which are written in uncial letters, of great and indisputed antiquity, and derived from different and independent sources), the Moscow MS. which formerly belonged to Chrysostom, according to Matthæi (on Eph. iv 9.), who has noted it with the letter B, and eight others of less note. This reading is also found in the Coptic, Sahidic, in the margin of the Philoxenian or later Syriac, in the Old Italic as contained in the Codex Cantabrigiensis, and as edited by Sabatier, and in the Armenian versions. The Ethiopic version has likewise been cited, as exhibiting the reading of Κυριου, *Lord*, but its evidence is indecisive, the *same* word being used therein for both *Lord* and *God.* Griesbach thinks it probable that this version reads Κυριου, from the consentient testimony of the Coptic and Armenian versions. Among the fathers, this reading is supported by Eusebius, Athanasius, Chrysostom, Ammonius, Maximus, Antonius, Ibas, Lucifer, Jerome, Augustine, Sedulius, Alcimus, the author of the pretended Apostolical Constitutions, and the second Council of Carthage (which, however, in the Greek, reads Θεου, *of God*).[1]

4. Του Κυριου και Θεου — *Of the Lord and God.* This reading is supported only by the Codex G. (Passionei, assigned by Blanchini to the eighth, but by Montfaucon to the ninth century,) and *sixty-three* other MSS.; none of which, though they form the majority in point of number, are among the most correct and authoritative. It is also found in the Sclavonic version, but it is not cited by one of the fathers; and is printed in the Complutensian and Plantin editions.

5. Του Θεου και Κυριου — *Of the God and Lord.* This reading occurs only in the MS. by Griesbach numbered 47. it is an apograph transcribed in the sixteenth century by John Faber of Deventer from one written in 1293.

6. Του Κυριου Θεου — *Of the Lord God.* This reading is found only in one MS. (95 of Griesbach's notation) of the fifteenth century, and the incorrect Arabic version printed in the Paris and London Polyglotts, and it is cited by Theophylact alone, among the fathers.

Of these six readings, No 2 Του Θεου, *Of God*, No 3. Του Κυριου, *Of the Lord*, and No. 4 Του Κυριου και Θεου, *Of the Lord and God*, are best supported by external testimony, and it is the preponderance of the evidence adduced for each, that must determine which of them is the genuine reading.

1. The testimony of manuscripts is pretty equally divided between these three readings. Though Κυριου is supported by the greater number of uncial MSS. (viz. the Codices Alexandrinus, Cantabrigiensis, Ephremi, and Laudianus,) yet Θεου is supported by the Codex Vaticanus, which is of the highest authority; and Κυριου και Θεου, though deficient in this respect (for G or the Codex Passionei, as we have noticed, is not earlier than the eighth or ninth century), yet it is most numerously supported by manuscripts of different families, and especially by the Moscow manuscripts, and by the Complutensian edition.

2. The antient versions, supporting Θεου and Κυριου, are equal to each other in number indeed, but those which support the former are superior in weight. For the Latin Vulgate, the Peschito or old Syriac, and the Ethiopic, in favour of Θεου, are of higher authority than their competitors, the Coptic, Sahidic, and Armenian. The compound reading Κυριου και Θεου is unsupported by any but the Sclavonic, which is closely connected with the Moscow manuscripts.

Griesbach endeavours to set aside the testimony furnished by the Vatican MS. But it is a FACT that Θεου is the reading of that manuscript for (1.) it WAS there in 1738, when it was collated by the very learned Thomas Wagstaffe, then at Rome, for Dr. Berriman, who was at that time engaged in preparing for publication his work on the genuineness of 1 Tim iii. 16., and (2.) Θεου IS the reading of the Vatican MS., for a *transcript of it was* obtained by Mr. R. Taylor from the keeper of the Vatican library for the second London edition of Griesbach's Greek Testament, printed by him in 1818, with equal beauty and accuracy.

[1] Irenæus is commonly cited as an authority for the reading του Κυριου. but Mr. Burton has shown that much use *cannot* be made of his authority in deciding this reading. (Testimonies of Ante-Nicene Fathers, p. 17.)

3. The testimony of the fathers is greatly in favour of Θεου. For though a considerable number of counter-testimonies in favour of Κυριου is named by Wetstein, and copied by Griesbach; yet no citations from thence are adduced by either, which leads us to suspect, that their testimony is either spurious, slight, or else refuted by the express citations on the other side. Thus, the objection of Athanasius to the phrase, "the blood of God," as "being no where used in Scripture, and to be reckoned among the daring fabrications of the Arians," recorded by Wetstein[1], is abundantly refuted by his own counter-testimony, citing the received reading of Acts xx. 28 and by the frequent use of the phrase by the orthodox fathers, Ignatius, Tertullian, Leontius, Fulgentius, Bede, Theophylact, and others above enumerated. The objection, therefore, was urged inconsiderately, and probably in the warmth of controversy; in which Athanasius was perpetually engaged with the Arians, his incessant persecutors.

Κυριου και Θεου, is unsupported by the fathers before Theophylact; and is contradicted by his testimony in favour of Θεου.

From this abstract, it appears to the writer of these pages, that the *external* evidence preponderates, upon the whole, in favour of Θεου, and this is further confirmed by the *internal* evidence. For, in the first place, the expression εκκλησια του Θεου, *church of God*, is in unison with the *style* of St. Paul[2]; and it occurs in not fewer than *eleven* passages of his epistles[3], while the phrase εκκλησια του Κυριου, *church of the Lord*, occurs *no where* in the New Testament. And, secondly, Θεου might easily give occasion to the other readings, though none of these could so easily give occasion to Θεου. If (as Michaelis remarks) the Evangelist Luke wrote Θεου, the origin of Κυριου and Χριτου may be explained either as corrections of the text or as marginal notes; because "the blood of God" is a very extraordinary expression; but if he had written Κυριου, it is inconceivable how any one should alter it into Θεου. And on this latter supposition, the great number of various readings is inexplicable. It seems as if different transcribers had found a difficulty in the passage, and that each corrected according to his own judgment.

Upon the whole, then, the received reading, εκκλησια του Θεου, *church of God*, is BETTER supported than any of the other readings, and, consequently, we may conclude that it was the *identical expression* uttered by Paul, and recorded by Luke.[4]

13. *Whenever two different readings occur, one of which seems difficult, and obscure, but which may be explained by the help of antiquity, and a more accurate knowledge of the language, whereas the other is so easy as to be obvious to the meanest capacity, the latter reading is to be suspected; because the former is more in unison with the style of the sacred writers, which, abounding with Hebraisms, is repugnant to the genius of the pure or strictly classical Greek language.*

No transcriber would designedly change a clear into an obscure reading, nor is it possible that an inadvertency should make so happy a mistake as to produce a reading that perplexes indeed the ignorant, but is understood and approved by the learned. This canon is the touchstone which distinguishes the true critics from the false. Bengel, Wetstein, and Griesbach, critics of the first rank, have admitted its authority; but those

---

[1] Nov Test. vol i p. 597. [2] See canon 9. pp 198,199. *supra*.
[3] Compare 1 Cor i 2. x 32. xi. 16. 22 xv. 9. 2 Cor i. 1. Gal i. 13 1 Thess ii. 14 2 Thess i 4. and 1 Tim iii. 5. 15   The phrase εκκλησια του Κυριου, *congregation of the Lord*, is of frequent occurrence in the Septuagint version, whence it might have crept into the text of the MSS. that support it, particularly of the Codex Alexandrinus, which was written in Egypt, where the Septuagint version was made.
[4] Nov. Test a Griesbach, tom ii. pp. 112—117. and Appendix, p. (34) 2d edit. (Halæ Saxonum, 1806.) Dr Hales, on Faith in the Trinity, vol. ii. pp. 105—131. Michaelis's Introduction to the New Testament, vol. i. p 335. Nolan's Inquiry into the Integrity of the Greek Vulgate, pp 286—289. 516—518. Mr. N. has given *at length* the quotations from the writings of the fathers in which Θεου is found. It is worthy of remark, that Mr. Wakefield, who was a professed and conscientious Unitarian, decides in favour of του Θεου, *of God*, as the *genuine* reading but instead of rendering the words του ιδιου αιματος, in the following sentence, "*with his own blood,*" he translates them by "*his own Son,*" and he adduces some passages from Greek and Roman writers, to show that *aima* and *sanguis* (blood) are used to signify a son or near relative. If, indeed, Acts xx. 27. were the only passage, where the phrase "purchasing with *his own blood*" occurred, we might receive this saying but as the redemption of man is, throughout the New Testament, ascribed exclusively to the vicarious and sacrificial death of Christ, it is not likely that this very *unusual* meaning should apply here. — (Dr. A. Clarke, in loc.)

of inferior order generally prefer the easy reading, for no other reason than because its meaning is most obvious.

14. *If for a passage, that is not absolutely necessary to the construction, various readings are found, that differ materially from each other, we have reason to suspect its authenticity; and likewise that all the readings are interpolations of transcribers who have attempted by different methods to supply the seeming deficiency of the original.*

This rule, however, must not be carried to the extreme, nor is a *single* variation sufficient to justify our suspicion of a word or phrase, though its omission affects not the sense, or even though the construction would be improved by its absence: for, in a book that has been so frequently transcribed as the New Testament, mistakes were unavoidable, and therefore a *single* deviation alone can lead us to no immediate conclusion.

15. *A reading is to be rejected, in respect to which plain evidence is found that it has undergone a* DESIGNED *alteration.*

Such alteration may have taken place (1.) From doctrinal reasons; — (2.) From moral and practical reasons, — (3.) From historical and geographical doubts, (Matt. viii. 28 compared with Mark v 1), — (4.) From the desire of reconciling passages contradictory with each other, — (5.) From the desire of making the discourse more intensive, hence many emphatic readings have originated, — (6.) From the comparison of many manuscripts, the readings of which have been amalgamated, — (7.) From a comparison of parallel passages. [1]

16. *Readings, which are evidently* glosses, *or* interpolations, *are invariably to be rejected.*

(1) *Glosses* are betrayed, 1. When the words do not agree with the scope and context of the passage; 2. When they are evidently foreign to the style of the sacred writer, 3. When there is evident tautology; 4 When words, which are best absent, are most unaccountably introduced; 5 When certain words are more correctly disposed in a different place; and, lastly, when phrases are joined together, the latter of which is much clearer than the former

(2. " An *interpolation* is sometimes betrayed by the circumstance of its being delivered in the language of a later church. In the time of the Apostles the word Christ was never used as the proper name of a person, but as an epithet expressive of the ministry of Jesus, and was frequently applied as synonymous to 'Son of God.' The expression, therefore, 'Christ is the Son of God,' Acts viii 37 is a kind of tautology, and is almost as absurd as to say Christ is the Messiah, that is, the anointed is the anointed. But the word being used in later ages as a proper name, this impropriety was not perceived by the person who obtruded the passage on the text."

(3.) " If one or more words that may be considered as an addition to a passage, are found only in manuscripts, but in none of the *most antient versions*, nor in the quotations of the early fathers, we have reason to suspect an interpolation." In Acts viii. 39. the Alexandrian manuscript reads thus: ΠΝΑ [ΑΓΙΟΝΕΠΕΣΕΝΕΠΙΤΟΝΕΥΝΟΥΧΟΝΑΝΓΕΛΟΣΔΕ] ΚΤΗΡΠΑΣΕΝΤΟΝΦΙΛΙΠΠΟΝ—*The Spi* [*holy fell upon the eunuch, but the Angel*] *of the Lord caught away Philip*. The words between brackets, Michaelis thinks, are spurious, and Griesbach decidedly pronounces them to be an emendation of the copyist. They are found in six manuscripts cited by him, but these are *not antient*, and they are also in the Armenian version executed in the end of the fourth, or early in the fifth century, and in the Sclavonic version executed in the ninth century. We are justified, therefore, in stating that they are not to be received into the sacred text.

17. *Expressions that are less emphatic, unless the scope and context of the sacred writer require emphasis, are more likely to be the genuine reading, than readings different from them, but which have, or seem to have, greater force or emphasis.* For copyists, like commentators, who have but a smattering of learning, are mightily pleased with emphases.

18. *That reading is to be preferred, which gives a sense apparently false, but which, on thorough investigation, proves to be the true one.*

19. *Various readings, which have most clearly been occasioned by the* **errors** *or negligence of transcribers, are to be rejected.* How such readings **may** *be caused, has already been shown in* pp. 177—180. *supra*.

---

[1] Stuart's Elements of Interpr p 113.

20. *Lectionaries, or Lesson Books, used in the early Christian church, are not admissible as evidence for various readings.*

Whenever, therefore, Ιησους, Jesus, αδελφοι, brethren, or similar words, (which were antiently prefixed to the lessons accordingly as the latter were taken from the Gospels or Epistles, and which are found only in lectionaries,) are found at the beginning of a lesson, they are to be considered as suspicious, and fifty manuscripts that contain them have no weight against the same number which omit them.

21. *Readings introduced into the Greek text from Latin versions are to be rejected.*

22. *A reading that is contradictory to history and geography is to be rejected, especially when it is not confirmed by manuscripts.*

In Acts xii. 25 we read that *Barnabas and Saul returned* FROM (εξ) *Jerusalem*, where seven manuscripts, two manuscripts (5 and 7) of the Sclavonic version, and the Arabic version in Bishop Walton's Polyglott, have εις, το *Jerusalem* This last reading has been added by some ignorant copyist, for Barnabas and Saul were returning from Jerusalem to Antioch with the money which they had collected for the poor brethren.

23. *That reading which makes a passage more connected is preferable,* all due allowance being made for abruptness in the particular case. Saint Paul is remarkable for the abruptness of many of his digressions.

24. *Readings, certainly genuine, ought to be restored to the text of the printed editions*, though hitherto admitted into none of them, that they may henceforth be rendered as correct as possible they ought likewise to be adopted in all versions of Scripture: and till this be done, they ought to be followed in explaining it.

25. *Probable readings may have so high a degree of evidence, as justly entitles them to be inserted into the text, in place of the received readings which are much less probable.* Such as have not considerably higher probability than the common readings, should only be put into the margin: but they, and all others, ought to be weighed with impartiality.

26. *Readings certainly, or very probably false, ought to be expunged from the editions of the Scriptures, and ought not to be followed in versions of them,* however long and generally they have usurped a place there, as being manifest corruptions, which impair the purity of the sacred books.

The preceding are the *most material* canons for determining various readings, which are recommended by the united wisdom of the most eminent biblical critics. They have been drawn up chiefly from Dr. Kennicott's Dissertations on the Hebrew text, De Rossi's Compendio di Critica Sacra, and the canons of the same learned author, in his Prolegomena so often cited in the preceding pages, and from the canons of Bauer in his Critica Sacra, of Ernesti, of Pfaff, Pritius, Wetstein, Griesbach, Beck, Muntinghe, and, above all, of Michaelis, with Bishop Marsh's annotations, often more valuable than the elaborate work of his author.

CHAPTER VI.

ON THE QUOTATIONS FROM THE OLD TESTAMENT IN THE NEW — QUOTATIONS IN THE NEW TESTAMENT FROM THE APOCRYPHAL WRITERS, AND FROM PROFANE AUTHORS.

IT is obvious, even on the most cursory perusal of the Holy Scriptures, that some passages are cited in other subsequent passages; and, in particular, that numerous quotations from the Old Testament are made in the New. In these references, there is frequently an apparent contradiction or difference between the original and the quotation; of which, as in the contradictions alleged to exist in the Scriptures, (which are considered and solved in the second part of this volume,) infidelity and scepticism have sedulously availed themselves. These seeming discrepancies, however, when brought to the touchstone of criticism, instantly disappear: and thus the entire harmony of the Bible becomes fully evident. The appearance of contradiction, in the quotations from the Old Testament that are found in the New, is to be considered in two points of view, namely, 1. As to the *external form*, or the words in which the quotation is made; and, 2. As to the *internal form*, or the manner or purpose to which it is applied by the sacred writers.

A considerable difference of opinion exists among some learned men, whether the Evangelists and other writers of the New Testament quoted the Old Testament from the Hebrew, or from the venerable Greek version, usually called the Septuagint. Others, however, are of opinion, that they did not confine themselves exclusively to either; and this appears most probable. The only way by which to determine this important question, is to compare and arrange the texts actually quoted. Drusius, Junius, Glassius, Cappel, Hoffman, Eichhorn, Michaelis, and many other eminent biblical critics on the Continent, have ably illustrated this topic; in our own country, indeed, it has been but little discussed. The only writers on this subject, known to the author, are the Rev. Dr. Randolph, formerly Regius Professor of Divinity in the University of Oxford, the Rev. Dr. Henry Owen, and the Rev. Thomas Scott (the titles of whose publications will be found in pp. 145, 146. of the Appendix to this volume); but they have treated it with so much ability and accuracy, that he has to acknowledge himself indebted to their labours for great part of his materials for the present chapter.[1]

---

[1] Besides the publications of the writers above mentioned, the author has constantly availed himself of the researches of Drusius (Parallela Sacra), in the 8th volume of the Critici Sacri, — of Cappel's Critica Sacra, lib. ii (in vol. i. pp 156—172. of Prof Vogel's edition), — of Glassius's Philologia Sacra, part ii. pp. 1387. et seq. (ed Dathii); and of Michaelis's Introduction to the New Testament, translated by Bishop Marsh (vol. i. pp. 200—246. 470—493). Dr. Gerard's Institutes of Biblical Criticism have also been occasionally referred to, as well as Schlegelius's Dissertatio De Agro sanguinis et Prophetâ circa eum allegatâ, in the Thesaurus Dissertationum Exegeticarum ad Nov. Test. tom. ii. pp. 309—340.

SECTION I.

ON THE EXTERNAL FORM OF THE QUOTATIONS FROM THE OLD TESTAMENT IN THE NEW.

§ 1. TABLES OF THE QUOTATIONS FROM THE HEBREW SCRIPTURES AND FROM THE SEPTUAGINT GREEK VERSION, IN THE ORDER IN WHICH THEY OCCUR IN THE NEW TESTAMENT.[1]

1.   Isa vii 14

הנה העלמה הרה וילדת בן וקראה שמו עמנואל:

Behold, a virgin shall conceive, and bear a son and shall call his name Immanuel.

Isa vii. 14.

Ιδου η παρθενος εν γαστρι ληψεται, και τεξεται υιον, και καλεσεις το ονομα αυτου Εμμανουηλ

Behold the virgin shall conceive and bear a son, and thou shalt call his name Emmanuel.

Matt. i. 23.

Ιδου η παρθενος εν γαστρι εξει, και τεξεται υιον, και καλεσουσι το ονομα αυτου Εμμανουηλ.

Behold, a virgin shall be with child, and shall bring forth a son, and they shall call his name Emmanuel.

2.   Micah v 2

ואתה בית־לחם אפרתה צעיר להיות באלפי יהודה ממך לי יצא להיות מושל בישראל

But thou, Bethlehem Ephratah, *though* thou be little among the thousands of Judah, *yet* out of thee shall he come forth unto me, *that is* to be ruler of Israel.

Micah v. 2.

Και συ Βηθλεεμ οικος Εφραθα, ολιγοστος ει του ειναι εν χιλιασιν Ιουδα; εκ σου μοι εξελευσεται, του ειναι εις αρχοντα του Ισραηλ.

But, as for thee, Bethlehem, thou house of Ephratha, art thou the least [or, too little], to become one of the thousands of Judah? Out of thee shall one come forth to me, to be the ruler of Israel

Matt. ii. 6.

Και συ Βηθλεεμ, γη Ιουδα, ουδαμως ελαχιστη ει εν τοις ηγεμοσιν Ιουδα· εκ σου γαρ εξελευσεται ηγουμενος, οστις ποιμανει τον λαον μου τον Ισραηλ.[2]

And thou, Bethlehem in the land of Judah, art not the least among the princes of Judah for out of thee shall come a governor that shall rule my people Israel.

3.   Hos. xi. 1

וממצרים קראתי לבי׃

I ...... called my son out of Egypt.

Hos xi 1.

Εξ Αιγυπτου μετεκαλεσα τα τεκνα αυτου

I called his children out of Egypt.

Matt ii. 15.

Εξ Αιγυπτου εκαλεσα τον υιον μου.

Out of Egypt have I called my son.

---

[1] In the first edition of this work, the author had simply given the references to these quotations They are now inserted at length, in order to save the student's *time*, and also to enable him more readily to compare the Hebrew and Greek together, and the English version of the passages is annexed for the convenience of the mere English reader. The text of the Septuagint is that termed the *Vatican*, and where there are any material variations in the *Alexandrine* text, they are briefly noticed. The English version of the Septuagint is given from Mr Thomson's Anglo-American translation (with the exception of two or three passages that have been altered to make them more literal), entitled " The Holy Bible, containing the Old and New Covenant, commonly called the Old and New Testament, translated from the Greek. Philadelphia, 1808." In four volumes, 8vo.

[2] This quotation agrees exactly neither with the Hebrew nor with the Septuagint. The only material difference is that the evangelist adds the negative ουδαμως, which is in neither of them. But the Syriac translation reads it with an interrogation, *Num parva es?* Art thou little? And so Archbishop Newcome has rendered it.

    And thou, Bethlehem Ephrata,
       Art thou too little to be among the leaders of Judah?
       Out of thee shall come forth unto me
       One *who is* to be a ruler in Israel

The question, he observes, implies the negative, which is inserted in Matt ii. 6. and also in the Arabic version. Both the Hebrew and the Greek, as they now stand, are capable of being pointed interrogatively. And it is worthy of remark, that the Codex Cantabrigiensis reads μη, *not*, interrogatively, instead of ουδαμως, in which it is followed by the Old Italic version, and by Tertullian, Cyprian, and other Latin fathers.

206 　　　　　　　　*Tables of Quotations from* 　　　　　　[Part I. Ch.

4.	Jer. xxxi. 15.	Jer xxxi 15.	Matt. ii 18
	קול ברמה נשמע נהי בכי תמרורים רחל מבכה על־בניה מאנה להנחם על־בניה כי איננו	Φωνη εν ‛Ραμα ηκουσθη θρηνου, και κλαυθμου, και οδυρμου ‛Ραχηλ αποκλαιομενη ουκ ηθελε παυσασθαι επι τοις υιοις αυτης, ὁτι ουκ εισιν	Φωνη εν ‛Ραμα ηκουσθη, θρηνος και κλαυθμος, και οδυρμος πολυς, ‛Ραχηλ κλαιουσα τα τεκνα αὑτης, και ουκ ηθελε παρακληθηναι, ὁτι ουκ εισι [1]
	A voice was heard in Ramah, lamentation, *and* bitter weeping, Rachel weeping for her children, refused to be comforted for her children, because they *were* not.	There was heard at Rama, a sound of lamentation, and weeping and wailing Rachel weeping for her children, refused to be comforted, because they are not.	In Rama was there a voice heard, lamentation, and weeping, and great mourning, Rachel weeping *for* her children, and would not be comforted, because they are not

5.	Psal xxii 6	lxix 9, 10.	
	Isa. liii. liii	Zech. xi. 12, 13.	

			Matt. ii. 23
			‛Οπως πληρωθῃ το ῥηθεν δια των προφητων, ὁτι Ναζωραιος κληθησεται. [2]
			That it might be fulfilled which was spoken by the prophets, He shall be called a Nazarene.

6	Isa. xl. 3–5.	Isa. xl 3–5	Matt iii 3 Mark i. 3 Luke iii 4–6
	קול קורא במדבר פנו דרך יהוה ישרו בערבה מסלה לאלהינו ׃ כל־גיא ינשא וכל־הר וגבעה ישפלו והיה העקב למישור והרכסים לבקעה ׃ ונגלה כבוד יהוה וראו כל־בשר יחדו כי פי יהוה דבר ׃	Φωνη βοωντος εν τῃ ερημῳ· ‛Ετοιμασατε την ὁδον Κυριου, ευθειας ποιειτε τας τριβους του Θεου ἡμων. Πασα φαραγξ πληρωθησεται, και παν ορος και βουνος ταπεινωθησεται και εσται παντα τα σκολια εις ευθειαν, και ἡ τραχεια εις πεδια. [3] Και οφθησεται ἡ δοξα Κυριου, και οψεται πασα σαρξ το σωτηριον του Θεου.	Φωνη βοωντος εν τῃ ερημῳ ‛Ετοιμασατε την ὁδον Κυριου, ευθειας ποιειτε τας τριβους αυτου Πασα φαραγξ πληρωθησεται, και παν ορος και βουνος ταπεινωθησεται και εσται τα σκολια εις ευθειαν, και αἱ τραχειαι εις ὁδους λειας Και οψεται πασα σαρξ το σωτηριον του Θεου. [4]
	The voice of him that crieth in the wilderness, Prepare ye	A voice of one crying in the wilderness, Prepare the way	The voice of one crying in the wilderness, Prepare ye the

---

[1] The quotation in Matthew agrees very nearly with the Hebrew, but not with the Septuagint. Dr. Randolph thinks it might possibly be taken from some other translation. (On the Quotations, p. 27.)

[2] As the evangelist cites *the Prophets* in the plural number, it is highly probable that this passage is not a quotation from any particular prophet, but a citation denoting the humble and despised condition of the Messiah, as described by the prophets in general, and especially by the prophet Isaiah. (See Dr Hunt's sermon on Matt. ii. 23, at the end of his "Observations on several Passages in the Book of Proverbs," pp. 170—193.) Though the words, *he shall be called a Nazarene*, are not to be found in the writings of the prophets, yet as the *thing* intended by them is of frequent occurrence, the application is made with sufficient propriety. The Israelites despised the Galileans in general, but especially the Nazarenes, who were so contemptible as to be subjects of ridicule even to the Galileans themselves. Hence, *Nazarene* was a term of reproach proverbially given to any despicable worthless person whatever Wherefore since the prophets (particularly those above referred to) have, in many parts of their writings, foretold that the Messiah should be rejected, despised, and traduced, they have in reality predicted that he should be called a *Nazarene*. And the Evangelist justly reckons Christ's dwelling in Nazareth, among other things, a completion of these predictions, because in the course of his public life, the circumstance of his having been educated in that town was frequently objected to him as a matter of scorn, and was one principal reason why his countrymen would not receive him (John i. 46 and vii. 41. 52.) Dr. Macknight's Harmony, vol. i. p. 53 8vo edit. See also Rosenmuller, Kuinoel, and other commentators on this text.

[3] Ὁδους λειας. (Alex.)

[4] This quotation agrees in sense, though not exactly, with the Hebrew, and also with the Septuagint. The whole of it occurs in Luke iii 4–6, and the first part in Matt. iii 3 and Mark i. 3.

the way of the Lord, make straight in the desert a highway for our God. Every valley shall be exalted, and every mountain and hill shall be made low and the crooked shall be made straight; and the rough places plain. And the glory of the Lord shall be revealed; and all flesh shall see *it* together	of the Lord, make straight the roads for our God. Every valley shall be filled up, and every mountain and hill be levelled And all the crooked *places* shall be made a straight *road*, and the rough *way* smooth plains. And the glory of the Lord will appear; and all flesh shall see the salvation of God.	way of the Lord, make his paths straight Every valley shall be filled, and every mountain and hill shall be brought low, and the crooked shall be made straight, and the rough ways shall be made smooth, and all flesh shall see the salvation of God.
7. Deut. viii. 3. לא על הלחם לבדו יחיה האדם כי על־כל־מוצא פי־יהוה	Deut. viii 3 Ουκ επ' αρτω μονω ζησεται ὁ ανθρωπος, αλλ' επι παντι ῥηματι τω εκπορευομενω δια στοματος Θεου	Matt. iv 4. Luke iv. 4. Ουκ επ' αρτω μονω ζησεται ανθρωπος, αλλ' επι παντι ῥηματι εκπορευομενω δια στοματος Θεου.
Man doth not live by bread only, but by every *word* that proceedeth out of the mouth of the Lord doth man live	Man shall not live by bread only, but by every word that proceedeth out of the mouth of God.	Man shall not live by bread alone, but by every word that proceedeth out of the mouth of God.
8. Psal. xci. 11, 12 כי מלאכיו יצוה־לך לשמרך בכל־דרכיך : על כפים ישאונך פן־תגוף באבן רגלך :	Psal. xci. 11, 12 Ὅτι τοις αγγελοις αυτου εντελειται περι σου, του διαφυλαξαι σε εν πασαις ταις ὁδοις σου Επι χειρων αρουσι σε, μη ποτε προσκοψης προς λιθον τον ποδα σου	Matt. iv. 6 Ὅτι .. τοις αγγελοις αυτου εντελειται περι σου, και επι χειρων αρουσι σε, μηποτε προσκοψης προς λιθον τον ποδα σου.
For he shall give his angels charge over thee, to keep thee in all thy ways They shall bear thee up in *their* hands, lest thou dash thy foot against a stone	For he will give his angels a charge concerning thee, to keep thee in all thy ways. With their hands they shall bear thee up, lest thou shouldest at any time strike thy foot against a stone	For .... he shall give his angels charge concerning thee, and in *their* hands they shall bear thee up, least at any time thou dash thy foot against a stone.
9. Deut vi 16 לא תנסו את־יהוה אלהיכם	Deut. vi. 16 Ουκ εκπειρασεις Κυριον τον Θεον σου.	Matt. iv. 7. Ουκ εκπειρασεις Κυριον τον Θεον σου.
Thou shalt not tempt the Lord thy God	Thou shalt not tempt the Lord thy God.	Thou shalt not tempt the Lord thy God.
10. Deut vi 13 את־יהוה אלהיך תירא ואתו תעבד	Deut. vi. 13. Κυριον τον Θεον σου φοβηθηση, και αυτω μονω λατρευσεις	Matt. iv. 10 Κυριον τον Θεον σου προσκυνησεις, και αυτω μονω λατρευσεις
Thou shalt fear the Lord thy God, and serve him.	Thou shalt fear the Lord thy God, and serve him alone.	Thou shalt worship the Lord thy God, and him only shalt thou serve.
11. Isa. ix. 1, 2. כעת הראשון הקל ארצה זבלון וארצה נפתלי והאחרון הכביד דרך הים עבר הירדן גליל הגוים : העם ההלכים בחשך ראו אור גדול ישבי בארץ צלמות אור נגה עליהם .	Isa ix 1, 2. Χωρα Ζαβουλων ἡ γη Νεφθαλειμ, και οἱ λοιποι οἱ την παραλιαν και περαν του Ιορδανου Γαλιλαια των εθνων Ὁ λαος ὁ πορευομενος εν σκοτει, ιδετε φως μεγα οἱ κατοικουντες εν χωρα σκια θανατου, φως λαμψει εφ' ὑμας.	Matt iv. 15, 16. Γη Ζαβουλων, και γη Νεφθαλειμ, ὁδον θαλασσης, περαν του Ιορδανου, Γαλιλαια των εθνων. Ὁ λαος ὁ καθημενος εν σκοτει ειδε φως μεγα, και τοις καθημενοις εν χωρα και σκια θανατου φως ανετειλεν αυτοις. [1]

---

[1] These words are not an exact translation of the Hebrew, and Dr. Randolph observes that it is difficult to make sense of the Hebrew or of the English in the order in which the words at present stand. But the difficulty, he thinks, may easily be obviated, by removing

		[Part I. Ch.
At the first he lightly afflicted the land of Zebulun, and the land of Naphtali, and afterwards did more grievously afflict her by the way of the sea, beyond Jordan, in Galilee of the nations. The people that walked in darkness have seen a great light, they that dwell in the land of the shadow of death, upon them hath the light shined.	With regard to the region of Zabulon, the land of Nephthalim, and the rest who inhabit the sea shore, and beyond Jordan, Galilee of the nations, ye people who walk in darkness, behold a great light¹ and ye who dwell in a region, the shade of death, on you a light shall shine.	The land of Zabulon, and the land of Nephthalim, by the way of the sea, beyond Jordan, Galilee of the Gentiles, the people which sat in darkness saw great light and to them which sat in the region and shadow of death, light is sprung up.
12. Isa. liii. 4. אכן חלינו הוא נשא ומכאבינו סבלם	Isa. liii. 4. Οὗτος τας ἁμαρτίας ἡμῶν φέρει, και περι ἡμῶν οδυνάται	Matt. viii. 17. Αυτος τας ασθενείας ἡμῶν ελαβε, και τας νοσους εβαστασεν
Our infirmities he hath borne. And our sorrows he hath carried them. (Bp Lowth.)	This man beareth away our sins, and for us he is in sorrow.	Himself took our infirmities, and bare our sicknesses.
13. Hos. vi. 6. כי חסד חפצתי ולא־זבח	Hos. vi. 6. Ελεος θελω η θυσιαν.	Matt. ix. 13. xii. 7. Ελεον θελω, και ου θυσιαν.
I desired mercy and not sacrifice.	I desire mercy rather than sacrifice.	I will have mercy, and not sacrifice
14. Mal. iii. 1. הנני שלח מלאכי ופנה־דרך לפני	Mal. iii. 1. Ιδου εξαποστελλω τον αγγελον μου, και επιβλεψεται ὁδον προ προσώπου μου.	Matt. xi 10 Mark i. 2. Luke vii 27 Ιδου, εγω αποστελλω τον αγγελον μου προ προσώπου σου ὁς κατασκευασει την ὁδον σου εμπροσθεν σου.¹
Behold I will send my messenger and he shall prepare the way before me.	Behold I send forth my messenger, and he will examine the way before me.	Behold I send my messenger before thy face, which shall prepare thy way before thee.
15. Isa xlii. 1–4. הן עבדי אתמך־בו בחירי רצתה נפשי נתתי רוחי עליו משפט לגוים יוציא : לא יצעק ולא ישא ולא ישמיע בחוץ קולו : קנה רצוץ לא ישבור ופשתה כהה לא יכבנה לאמת יוציא משפט : ולתורתו איים ייחלו :	Isa. xlii 1—4. Ιακωβ ὁ παις μου, αντιληψομαι αυτου Ισραηλ ὁ εκλεκτος μου· προσεδεξατο αυτον ἡ ψυχη μου· εδωκα το πνευμα μου επ' αυτον, κρισιν τοις εθνεσιν εξοισει. Ου κεκραξεται, ουδε ανησει, ουδε ακουσθησεται εξω ἡ φωνη αυτου. Καλαμον τεθλασμενον ου συντριψει, και λινον καπνιζομενον ου σβεσει, αλλα εις αληθειαν εξοισει κρισιν — Και επι τω ονοματι αυτου εθνη ελπιουσιν.	Matt. xii 18—21. Ιδου, ὁ παις μου, ὁν ἡρετισα· ὁ αγαπητος μου, εις ὁν ευδοκησεν ἡ ψυχη μου θησω το πνευμα μου επ' αυτον, και κρισιν τοις εθνεσιν απαγγελει. Ουκ ερισει, ουδε κραυγασει, ουδε ακουσει τις εν ταις πλατειαις την φωνην αυτου Καλαμον συντετριμμενον ου κατεαξει, και λινον τυφομενον ου σβεσει· έως αν εκβαλη εις νικος την κρισιν· Και εν τω ονοματι αυτου εθνη ελπιουσι.²

the first six words of Isa ix. and joining them to the former chapter, as they are in all the old versions And then the words may be thus rendered *As the former time made vile, or debased, the land of Zabulon, and the land of Nephtali, so the latter time shall make it glorious The way of the sea, &c.* A prophecy most signally fulfilled by our Saviour's appearance and residence in these parts. The evangelist, from the first part of the sentence, takes only *the land of Zabulon, and the land of Nephthalim* What follows is an exact, and almost literal translation of the Hebrew only for הלכים, *walked*, is put καθημενος, *sat*. How properly this prophecy is cited, and applied to our Saviour, see Mr Mede's Disc on Mark i. 14, 15. Mr Lowth's Comment on Isa. 9. and Bishop Lowth's translation. (Randolph on the Quotations, p. 28)

¹ This quotation differs from the Hebrew and all the old versions in these two particulars the words προ προσωπου σου are added, and what is in Hebrew לפני, *before* me, is rendered εμπροσθεν σου, *before* thee. For the reason of this difference it is not easy to account, but by supposing some corruptions crept into the antient copies, the sense is much the same (Dr Randolph on the Quotations, p. 28)

² This quotation by no means agrees with the Septuagint version, whose authors have ob-

VI. Sect. I. § 1.] *The Old Testament in the New.*

Behold my servant whom I uphold, mine elect in whom my soul delighteth I have put my spirit upon him, he shall bring forth judgment to the Gentiles. He shall not cry, nor lift up, nor cause his voice to be heard in the street A bruised reed shall he not break, and the smoking flax shall he not quench he shall bring forth judgment unto truth. He shall not fail nor be discouraged, till he have set judgment in the earth and the isles shall wait for his law	Jacob is my servant, I will uphold him, Israel is my chosen one, my soul hath embraced him I have put my spirit upon him, he will publish judgment to the nations· he will not cry aloud, nor urge with vehemence, nor will his voice be heard abroad. A bruised reed he will not break, nor will he quench smoking flax, but will bring forth judgment unto truth,—and in his name shall the nations trust (or hope).	Behold my servant whom I have chosen, my beloved in whom my soul is well pleased. I will put my spirit upon him, and he shall show judgment to the Gentiles. He shall not strive nor cry; neither shall any man hear his voice in the streets A bruised reed shall he not break, and smoking flax shall he not quench, till he send forth judgment unto victory. And in his name shall the Gentiles trust.

16. Isa. vi. 9, 10   Isa. vi. 9–11.   Matt. xiii. 14, 15. Acts xxviii. 26, 27 Mark iv 12. Luke viii. 10.

שמעו שמוע ואל־תבינו וראו ראו ואל־תדעו׃ השמן לב־העם הזה ואזניו הכבד ועיניו השע פן־ יראה בעיניו ובאזניו ישמע ולבבו יבין ושב ורפא לו	Ακοη ακουσετε, και ου μη συνητε, και βλεποντες βλεψετε, και ου μη ιδητε Επαχυνθη γαρ ἡ καρδια του λαου τουτου, και τοις ωσιν αυτων βαρεως ηκουσαν, και τους οφθαλμους εκαμμυσαν, μηποτε ιδωσι τοις οφθαλμοις, και τοις ωσιν ακουσωσι, και τη καρδια συνωσι, και επιστρεψωσι, και ιασομαι αυτους.	Ακοη ακουσετε, και ου μη συνητε και βλεποντες βλεψετε, γαρ ἡ καρδια του λαου τουτου, και τοις ωσι βαρεως ηκουσαν, και τους οφθαλμους αυτων εκαμμυσαν, μηποτε ιδωσι τοις οφθαλμοις, και τοις ωσιν ακουσωσι, και τη καρδια συνωσι, και επιστρεψωσι, και ιασωμαι αυτους. [1]
Hear ye indeed, but understand not And see ye indeed, but perceive not. Make the heart of this people fat, and make their eyes heavy, and shut their eyes, lest they see with their eyes, and hear with their ears, and understand with their heart, and convert, and be healed	By hearing, ye shall hear, though ye may not understand, and seeing, ye shall see, though ye may not perceive For the heart of this people is stupefied, and their ears are dull of hearing, and they have shut their eyes, that for a while they may not see with their eyes, and hear with their ears, and understand with their hearts, and return that I may heal them.	By hearing ye shall hear, and shall not understand · and seeing ye shall see, and shall not perceive · for this people's heart is waxed gross, and their ears are dull of hearing, and their eyes they have closed; lest at any time they should see with their eyes, and hear with their ears, and should understand with their heart, and should be converted, and I should heal them.

17   Psal. lxxviii. 2.   Psal. lxxviii. 2.   Matt xiii. 35.

אפתחה במשל פי אביעה חידות מני־קדם׃	Ανοιξω εν παραβολαις το στομα μου, φθεγξομαι προβληματα απ' αρχης	Ανοιξω εν παραβολαις το στομα μου, ερευξομαι κεκρυμμενα απο καταβολης κοσμου.

---

scured this prophecy by adding the words *Jacob and Israel*, which are not in the original Hebrew. It is probably taken from some old translation agreeing very nearly with the Hebrew. The only difficulty is in the words ἑως αν εκβαλη εις νικος την κρισιν. But if by לנצח משפט we understand *the cause under trial*, then *to send forth his cause unto truth*, will be to carry the cause, and vindicate its truth; which agrees in sense with εκβαλη εις νικος την κρισιν. (Dr. Randolph on the Quotations, p 28.)

[1] This quotation is taken almost verbatim from the Septuagint. In the Hebrew the sense is obscured by false pointing It, instead of reading it in the imperative mood, we read it in the indicative mood, the sense will be . *ye shall hear but not understand · and ye shall see but not perceive. This people hath made their heart fat, and hath made their ears heavy and shut their eyes*, &c. which agrees in sense with the Evangelist and with the Septuagint, as well as with the Syriac and Arabic Versions, but not with the Latin Vulgate. We have the same quotation, word for word, in Acts xxviii 26. Mark and Luke refer to the same prophecy, but quote it only in part. (Dr. Randolph, p. 29.)

I will open my mouth in a parable; I will utter dark sayings of old.	I will open my mouth in parables; I will utter dark sayings of old	I will open my mouth in parables, I will utter things which have been kept secret from the foundation of the world.
18. Isa xxix. 13. בי נגש העם הזה בפיו ובשפתיו כבדוני ולבו רחק ממני ותהי יראתם אתי מצות אנשים מלמדה	Isa xxix. 13. Εγγιζει μοι ὁ λαος οὑτος εν τω στοματι αυτου, και εν τοις χειλεσιν αυτων τιμωσι με, ἡ δε καρδια αυτων πορρω απεχει απ᾽ εμου ματην δε σεβονται με, διδασκοντες ενταλματα ανθρωπων και διδασκαλιας.	Matt xv 8, 9. Εγγιζει μοι ὁ λαος οὑτος τω στοματι αυτων, και τοις χειλεσι με τιμα ἡ δε καρδια αυτων πορρω απεχει απ᾽ εμου ματην δε σεβονται με, διδασκοντες διδασκαλιας, ενταλματα ανθρωπων. [1]
This people draw near me with their mouth, and with their lips do honour me, but have removed their heart far from me, and their fear towards me is taught by the precept of men.	This people draw near to me with their mouth, and with their lips they honour me, but their heart is far from me. And in vain do they worship me, teaching the commands and doctrines of men.	This people draweth nigh unto me with their mouth and honoureth me with *their* lips but their heart is far from me. But in vain do they worship me, teaching *for* doctrines the commandments of men.
19. Gen. ii. 24. על־כן יעזב־איש את־אביו ואת־אמו ודבק באשתו והיו לבשר אחד׃	Gen ii 24. Ἑνεκεν τουτου καταλειψει ανθρωπος τον πατερα αυτου και την μητερα, και προσκολληθησεται προς την γυναικα αυτου· και εσονται οἱ δυο εις σαρκα μιαν.	Matt xix 5. Ἑνεκεν τουτου καταλειψει ανθρωπος τον πατερα και την μητερα, και προσκολληθησεται τη γυναικι αυτου και εσονται οἱ δυο εις σαρκα μιαν [2]
Therefore shall a man leave his father and his mother, and shall cleave unto his wife, and they shall be one flesh.	Therefore a man shall leave *his* father and mother, and shall cleave to his wife; and they two shall be one flesh.	For this cause shall a man leave father and mother, and shall cleave to his wife, and they twain shall be one flesh.
20. Exod xx. 12-16. כבד את־אביך ואת־אמך לא תרצח לא תנאף לא תגנב לא תענה ברעך עד שקר׃	Exod xx 12-16 Τιμα τον πατερα σου, και την μητερα σου — Ου μοιχευσεις Ου κλεψεις· Ου φονευσεις Ου ψευδομαρτυρησεις	Matt. xix 18, 19 Ου φονευσεις. Ου μοιχευσεις· Ου κλεψεις Ου ψευδομαρτυρησεις· Τιμα τον πατερα σου και την μητερα
Honour thy father and thy mother. Thou shalt not kill. Thou shalt not commit adultery. Thou shalt not steal Thou shalt not bear false witness against thy neighbour.	Honour thy father and thy mother — Thou shalt not commit adultery — Thou shalt not steal. — Thou shalt not commit murder. — Thou shalt not bear false witness	Thou shalt do no murder: thou shalt not commit adultery thou shalt not steal. thou shalt not bear false witness honour thy father and thy mother.
21. Lev. xix. 18. ואהבת לרעך כמוך	Lev. xix 18. Και αγαπησεις τον πλησιον σου ὡς σεαυτον	Matt. xix 19 xxii. 39. Αγαπησεις τον πλησιον σου ὡς σεαυτον.
Thou shalt love thy neighbour as thyself.	And thou shalt love thy neighbour, as thyself.	Thou shalt love thy neighbour, as thyself.
22. Zech. ix. 9, (and see Isa. lxii 11) גילי מאד בת־ציון הריעי בת־ירושלם הנה מלכך יבוא לך צדיק	Zech ix. 9 Χαιρε σφοδρα, θυγατερ Σιων; κηρυσσε, θυγατερ Ἱερουσαλημ	Matt. xxi. 5. Ειπατε τη θυγατρι Σιων· Ιδου, ὁ Βασιλευς σου ερχεται

---

[1] The quotation in this passage of St Matthew's Gospel approaches nearer to the Septuagint than to the Hebrew text, especially in the clause ματην δε σεβονται με—in vain do they *worship me*, which is found in the Septuagint, but not in the Hebrew, and is retained by the Evangelist. The verbal differences, however, show that an *exact* quotation was not intended. (Scott.)

[2] This quotation agrees with the Hebrew, excepting that the word for *two* is there omitted. But it ought to be inserted in the Hebrew text, as we have already seen in p. 188. *supra*.

VI. Sect. I. § 1.] *The Old Testament in the New.*

ונושע הוא עני ורכב על־חמור
ועל־עיר בן־אתנות׃

Rejoice greatly, O daughter of Zion, shout, O daughter of Jerusalem, behold, thy king cometh unto thee. He is just and having salvation, lowly, and riding upon an ass even upon a colt the foal of an ass.

ιδου, ὁ Βασιλευς σου ερχεται σοι δικαιος και σωζων αυτος πραυς, και επιβεβηκως επι ὑποζυγιον και πωλον νεον.

Rejoice exceedingly, O daughter of Sion, make proclamation, O daughter of Jerusalem Behold, thy king is coming to thee, he is righteous, and having salvation He is meek, and mounted on an ass, even a young colt.

σοι πραυς, και επιβεβηκως επι ονον, και πωλον υἱον ὑποζυγιον. [1]

Tell ye the daughter of Sion, Behold thy king cometh unto thee, meek and sitting upon an ass, and (*more correctly*, even) a colt the foal of an ass.

23. Psal. viii. 3. (2 of English version.)

מפי עוללים ויונקים יסדת עז

Out of the mouths of babes and sucklings thou hast ordained strength.

Psal. viii 2.

Εκ στοματος νηπιων και θηλαζοντων κατηρτισω αινον.

Out of the mouth of babes and sucklings thou hast perfected praise

Matt. xxi. 16.

Εκ στοματος νηπιων και θηλαζοντων κατηρτισω αινον.

Out of the mouth of babes and sucklings thou hast perfected praise.

24. Psal. cxviii 22, 23.

אבן מאסו הבונים היתה לראש
פנה ׃ מאת יהוה היתה זאת היא
נפלאת בעינינו ׃

The stone *which* the builders refused, is become the head *stone* of the corner. This is the LORD's doing, and it is marvellous in our eyes.

Psal. cxviii 22, 23.

Λιθον ὁν απεδοκιμασαν οἱ οικοδομουντες, οὑτος εγεννηθη εις κεφαλην γωνιας παρα Κυριου εγενετο αὑτη, και εστι θαυμαστη εν οφθαλμοις ἡμων.

The stone, which the builders rejected, the same is become the head of the corner. This was from the Lord (or, the Lord's doing), and it is wonderful in our eyes

Matt. xxi 42. Mark xii 10. Luke xx 17 Acts iv. 11.

Λιθον ὁν απεδοκιμασαν οἱ οικοδομουντες, οὑτος εγεννηθη εις κεφαλην γωνιας παρα κυριου εγενετο αὑτη, και εστι θαυμαστη εν οφθαλμοις ἡμων.

The stone which the builders rejected, the same is become the head of the corner, this is the Lord's doing, and it is marvellous in our eyes.

25.   Exod iii. 6

אנכי אלהי אביך אלהי אברהם
אלהי יצחק ואלהי יעקב

I am the God of thy father, the God of Abraham, the God of Isaac, and the God of Jacob

Exod. iii. 6.

Εγω ειμι ὁ Θεος του πατρος σου, Θεος Αβρααμ, και Θεος Ισαακ, και Θεος Ιακωβ

I am the God of thy father, the God of Abraham, and the God of Isaac, and the God of Jacob.

Matt xxii 32. Mark xii. 26. Luke xx 37.

Εγω ειμι ὁ Θεος Αβρααμ, και ὁ Θεος Ισαακ, και ὁ Θεος Ιακωβ.

I am the God of Abraham, and the God of Isaac, and the God of Jacob.

26.   Deut. vi. 5

ואהבת את יהוה אלהיך בכל־
לבבך ובכל־נפשך ובכל־מאדך ׃

I am the God of thy father, the God of Abraham, the God of Isaac, and the God of Jacob

Deut. vi 5

Αγαπησεις Κυριον τον Θεον σου εξ ὁλης της διανοιας σου, και εξ ὁλης της ψυχης σου, και εξ ὁλης της δυναμεως σου.

Matt xxii. 37. Mark xii. 30. Luke x 27.

Αγαπησεις Κυριον τον Θεον σου ὁλη τη καρδια σου, και εν ὁλη τη ψυχη σου, και εν ὁλη τη διανοια σου [2]

---

[1] This quotation seems to be taken from two prophecies, viz Isa. lxii. 11 where we read *Say ye to the daughter of Zion, behold thy salvation cometh* — and from Zech ix. 9.   The latter part agrees more exactly with the Hebrew than with the Septuagint, only both Saint Matthew and the Septuagint seem to have read עני, *meek*, instead of עני, *afflicted*   (Dr Randolph on the Quotations, p. 29)

[2] The Vatican edition of the Septuagint here translates לבבך, by της διανοιας σου (*thy understanding*).   But the Alexandrian edition renders it της καρδιας σου (*thy heart*)   St Matthew takes in both, but puts ψυχη (*soul*) between, he also puts εν ὁλη for εξ ὁλης agreeably to the Hebrew ; and he leaves out the latter clause, *with all thy strength*. St. Mark and St Luke agree entirely with St. Matthew, only they add the latter clause   (Dr. Randolph)   The variation from the Septuagint and Hebrew does not in the least affect the meaning   Mr Scott thinks, with great probability, that the Evangelists, under the teaching of the Holy Spirit, gave the meaning of this first and great commandment in the most emphatical language, without intending either implicitly to quote the Septuagint, or literally to translate the Hebrew.

212 *Tables of Quotations from* [Part I. Ch.

Thou shalt love the Lord thy God with all thine heart, and with all thy soul, and with all thy might.	Thou shalt love the Lord thy God with thy whole understanding, and with thy whole soul, and with thy whole might.	Thou shalt love the Lord thy God with all thy heart, and with all thy soul, and with all thy mind.

27. Psal. cx. 1.

נאם יהוה לאדני שב לימיני עד־אשית איביך הדם רגליך׃

The LORD said unto my Lord, Sit thou at my right hand, until I make thine enemies thy footstool.

Psal. cx. 1

Ειπεν ὁ Κυριος τω Κυριω μου, Καθου εκ δεξιων μου, ἑως αν θω τους εχθρους σου ὑποποδιον των ποδων σου.

The Lord said unto my Lord, Sit at my right hand, until I make thine enemies thy footstool.

Matt. xxii. 44. Mark xii. 36. Luke xx. 42.

Ειπεν ὁ Κυριος τω Κυριω μου, Καθου εκ δεξιων μου, ἑως αν θω τους εχθρους σου ὑποποδιον των ποδων σου.

The Lord said unto my Lord, Sit thou on my right hand, until I make thine enemies thy footstool.

28. Zech. xiii. 7.

הך את־הרעה ותפוצין הצאן

Smite the shepherd, and the sheep shall be scattered.

Zech. xiii 7.

Παταξον τον ποιμενα, και διασκορπισθησονται τα προβατα της ποιμνης.¹

Smite the shepherd, and the sheep of the flock shall be scattered abroad.

Matt. xxvi. 31.

Παταξω τον ποιμενα, και διασκορπισθησεται τα προβατα της ποιμνης

I will smite the shepherd, and the sheep of the flock shall be scattered abroad.

29. Zech. xi. 13.

השליכהו אל־היוצר אדר היקר אשר יקרתי מעליהם ואקחה שלשים הכסף ואשליך אתו בית יהוה אל־היוצר׃

Zech. xi 13.

Καθες αυτους εις το χωνευτηριον, και σκεψομαι ει δοκιμον εστιν, ὁν τροπον εδοκιμασθην ὑπερ αυτων· και ελαβον τους τριακοντα αργυρους και ενεβαλον αυτους εις τον οικον Κυριου, εις το χωνευτηριον.

Matt. xxvii 9, 10.

Και ελαβον τα τριακοντα αργυρια, την τιμην του τετιμημενου, ὁν ετιμησαντο απο υἱων Ισραηλ. Και εδωκαν αυτα εις τον αγρον του κεραμεως, καθα συνεταξε μοι Κυριος.²

¹ This is the reading of the Alexandrine MS. of the Septuagint, excepting that the evangelist reads παταξω, *I will smite*, instead of παταξον The Arabic version agrees with Saint Matthew ; and Drs. Randolph and Owen both think it probable that the Hebrew ought to be read אך instead of הך, for it follows in the first person, *I will turn mine hand*, &c   See Houbigant in loc   Kennicott's Dissertatio Generalis, § 44. Randolph on the Quotations, p 80. Owen on the Modes of Quotation, p. 54

² This citation is attended with no small difficulty. The prophecy is cited from Jeremiah · but in that prophet no such prophecy is to be found. In Zech. xi. 13. such a prophecy *is* found, but neither do the words there perfectly agree with Saint Matthew's citation. Some critics are of opinion that an error has crept into Saint Matthew's copy , and that Ιερ has been written by the transcribers instead of Ζεχ. or that the word has been interpolated. And it is to be observed, that the word is omitted in the MSS. by Griesbach numbered 33 (of the eleventh or twelfth century), and 157 (of the twelfth century), in the later Syriac and in the modern Greek versions, one or two MSS. of the old Italic version, some manuscripts cited by Augustine, and one Latin MS. cited by Lucas Brugensis. Griesbach's MS 22. (of the eleventh century) reads Ζαχαριου, which word is also found in the margin of the later Syriac version, and in an Arabic exemplar cited by Bengel in his Critical Edition of the New Testament. Origen, and after him Eusebius, conjectured that this was the true reading. Other eminent critics have thought that the ninth, tenth, and eleventh chapters of what is called Zechariah's Prophecy were really written by Jeremiah, and they have certainly assigned very probable reasons for such opinion both from the matter and style (See Dr. Hammond on Heb. viii. 9 Mede's Works, pp. 786-838. Bp. Kidder's Demonst. of Messiah, part ii. p. 196 &c Lowth, Prælect. Poet. Lect xxi. See also Vol. IV. Part. I. Chap. VII. Sect II. § III , where reasons are assigned to show that these chapters were actually written by Zechariah.) It is, however, *most likely*, that the original reading of Matthew xxvii. 9. was simply, *that which was spoken* BY THE PROPHET, δια του προφητου, without naming any prophet : And this conjecture is confirmed by the fact that Saint Matthew often omits the name of the prophet in his quotations. (See Matt. i. 22, ii. 5. xiii. 35 and xxi. 4) Bengel approves of the omission. It was, as we have already shown (see pp. 161, 162. of this volume), the custom of the Jews, to divide the OLD Testament into three parts: the *first*, beginning with the Law, was called THE LAW, the second, commencing with the Psalms, was called THE PSALMS, and the third, beginning with the prophet in question, was called JEREMIAH. consequently, the

VI. Sect. I. § 1.] *The Old Testament in the New.*

Cast it unto the potter, a goodly price that I was prized at of them And I took the thirty *pieces* of silver, and cast them to the potter in the house of the LORD	Put them into the smelting furnace, and I will see whether it is proof, in like manner as I have been proved by them. So I took the thirty pieces of silver, and threw them down in the house of the Lord, for the smelting furnace.	And they took the thirty pieces of silver, the price of him that was valued, whom they of the children of Israel did value and gave them for the potter's field, as the Lord appointed me.
30. Psal. xxii. 19 (18. of English version.) יחלקו בגדי להם ועל לבושי יפילו גורל They part my garments among them, and cast lots upon my vesture.	Psal. xxi. 18 (xxii 18. of English Bible.) Διεμερισαντο τα ιματια μου έαυτοις, και επι τον ματισμον μου εβαλον κληρον. They have parted my garments among them, and for my vesture have cast lots.	Matt. xxvii. 35. John xix. 24. Διεμερισαντο τα ιματια μου έαυτοις, και επι τον ιματισμον μου εβαλον κληρον. They parted my garments among them, and upon my vesture did they cast lots.
31. Psal. xxii. 2. (1. of English version.) אלי אלי לכה עזבתני My God, my God, why hast thou forsaken me ?	Psal xxii. 1. Ὁ Θεος, ὁ Θεος μου, προσχες μοι, ἱνατι εγκατελιπες με; O God, my God, attend to me! Why hast thou forsaken me ?	Matt. xxvii. 46. Ηλι, Ηλι, λαμα σαβαχθανι; τουτ' εστι, Θεε μου, Θεε μου, ἱνατι με εγκατελιπες , [1] Eli, Eli lama sabachthani? That is to say, My God, my God, why hast thou forsaken me ?
32. Isa. liii 12 ואת־פשעים נמנה And he was numbered with the transgressors.	Isa. liii. 12 Και εν τοις ανομοις ελογισθη. And he was numbered among the transgressors.	Mark xv. 28. Luke xxii. 37. Και μετα ανομων ελογισθη And he was numbered with the transgressors.
33. Exod xiii. 2 קדש לי בל־בכור פטר כל־רחם Whatsoever openeth the womb — both of man and of beast, it is mine.	Exod xiii. 2. Ἁγιασον μοι παν πρωτοτοκον πρωτογενες, διανοιγον πασαν μητραν. Consecrate to me every first born, that openeth every womb.	Luke ii. 23. Παν αρσεν διανοιγον μητραν άγιον τω Κυριω κληθησεται. Every male that openeth the womb shall be called holy to the Lord.

---

writings of Zechariah, and of the other prophets, being included in that division which began with *Jeremiah*, all quotations from it would go under this prophet's name. This solution completely removes the difficulty. Dr. Lightfoot (who cites the Baba Bathra and Rabbi David Kimchi's Preface to the prophet Jeremiah as his authorities) insists that the word Jeremiah is perfectly correct, as standing at the head of that division from which the evangelist quoted, and which gave its denomination to all the rest. — With regard to the prophecy itself, if in Saint Matthew's Gospel, for εδωκαν, THEY gave, we read εδωκα, *I gave*, which is the reading of the Evangelisteria, 24 and 81, of Griesbach's notation (both of the eleventh century) and of both the Syriac versions, the evangelist's quotation will very nearly agree with the original. That we should read εδωκα, *I gave*, appears further to be probable from what follows,— καθα συνεταξε μοι Κυριος, as the Lord commanded me,— Και ελαβον τα τριακοντα αργυρια, και εδωκα αυτα εις τον αγρον του κεραμεως· *and I took the thirty pieces of silver, and I gave them for the potter's field.* The translation is literal, excepting only that היוצר is rendered αγρον του κεραμεως and בית יהוה is omitted , and the same is also omitted in some antient MSS. (See Kennicott's Dissertatio Generalis, § 49 p 21.) The words την τιμην του τετιμημενου ὁν ετιμησαντο απο υίων Ισραηλ and καθα συνεταξε μοι Κυριος are added to supply the sense, being taken in sense, and very nearly in words, from the former part of the verse ; this latter clause is in the Arabic version. Dr. Randolph on the Quotations, p 30. Novum Testamentum, à Griesbach, tom. i. p. 184. Dr. Lightfoot's Horæ Hebraicæ on Matt. xxvii. 9 (Works, vol. ii. p. 265.)

[1] This is taken from the Hebrew, but the words are Syriac or Chaldee. Sabachthani is the word now in the Chaldee Paraphrase. (Dr. Randolph, p. 30.)

34. Lev. xii. 8. שתי־תרים או שני בני יונה Two turtles or two young pigeons	Lev. xii 8. Δυο τρυγονας η δυο νεοσσους περιστερων Two turtle-doves or two young pigeons	Luke ii. 24. Ζευγος τρυγονων η δυο νεοσσους περιστερων A pair of turtle doves, or two young pigeons.
35. Isa. lxi. 1, 2. רוח אדני יהוה עלי יען משח יהוה אתי לבשר ענוים שלחני לחבש לנשברי־לב קרא לשבוים דרור ולאסורים פקח קוח. לקרא שנת־רצון ליהוה The Spirit of the LORD GOD is upon me, because the Lord hath anointed me to preach good tidings unto the meek, he hath sent me to bind up the broken-hearted, to proclaim liberty to the captives, and the opening of the prison to *them that are* bound. to proclaim the acceptable year of the LORD	Isa lxi. 1, 2. Πνευμα Κυριου επ' εμε, ου εἵνεκεν εχρισε με Ευαγγελιζεσθαι πτωχοις απεσταλκε με, ιασασθαι τους συντετριμμενους την καρδιαν, κηρυξαι αιχμαλωτοις αφεσιν, και τυφλοις αναβλεψιν Καλεσαι ενιαυτον Κυριου δεκτον. The Spirit of the Lord *is* upon me, for the business for which he hath anointed me He hath sent me to preach the Gospel to the poor, to heal the broken-hearted, to preach deliverance to the captives, and recovering *of sight* to the blind, to proclaim the acceptable year of the Lord.	Luke iv 18, 19. Πνευμα Κυριου επ' εμε, ου ἑνεκεν εχρισε με ευαγγελιζεσθαι πτωχοις· απεσταλκε με ιασασθαι τους συντετριμμενους την καρδιαν, κηρυξαι αιχμαλωτοις αφεσιν, και τυφλοις αναβλεψιν, αποστειλαι τεθραυσμενους εν αφεσει· Κηρυξαι ενιαυτον Κυριου δεκτον.[1] The Spirit of the Lord *is* upon me, because he hath anointed me to preach the Gospel to the poor, he hath sent me to heal the broken-hearted, to preach deliverance to the captives, and recovering of sight to the blind, to set at liberty them that are bruised, to preach the acceptable year of the Lord.
36. Psal. lxix. 10. (9. of English version.) כי־קנאת ביתך אכלתני The zeal of thine house hath eaten me up.	Psal. lxviii 9 (lxix. 9. of English Bible.) Ο ζηλος του οικου σου κατεφαγε με Zeal for thine house hath consumed me.	John ii. 17. Ὁ ζηλος του οικου σου κατεφαγε με The zeal of thine house hath eaten me up.
37 Psal. lxxviii. 24. ודגן־שמים נתן למו׃ And had given them of the corn of heaven.	Psal lxxviii. 24. Και αρτον ουρανου εδωκεν αυτοις And he gave them the bread of heaven.	John vi. 31 Αρτον εκ του ουρανου εδωκεν αυτοις φαγειν. He gave them bread from heaven to eat
38. Isa. liv. 13. וכל־בניך למודי יהוה And all thy children *shall be* taught of the LORD.	Isa. liv. 13. Και παντας τους υιους σου διδακτους Θεου Even thy sons, all instructed of God.	John vi. 45 Και εσονται παντες διδακτοι του Θεου. And they shall be all taught of God.

---

[1] This quotation is made exactly from the Septuagint, as far as the words αιχμαλωτοις αφεσιν, *deliverance to the captives* and it accords with the Hebrew, except that the word Jehovah twice occurs there, which is omitted in the Septuagint and by the Evangelist But, instead of the Hebrew clause, translated *the opening of the prison to them that are bound*, we read τυφλοις αναβλεψιν *recovering* of sight *to the blind*, which words are adopted by St. Luke, who adds, αποστειλαι τεθραυσμενους εν αφεσι, *setting at liberty them that are bruised*, which words do not appear in the Septuagint. The difference between this quotation as it appears in Luke iv. 18 and the original Hebrew is thus accounted for—Jesus Christ doubtless read the prophet Isaiah in Hebrew, which was the language constantly used in the Synagogue, but the Evangelist, writing for the use of the Hellenists (or Greek Jews) who understood and used only the Septuagint version, quotes that version, which on the whole gives the same sense as the Hebrew. Le Clerc, Dr Owen, and Michaelis, are of opinion that they are either a different version of the Hebrew, and inserted from the margin of the evangelical text, or else that they are a gloss upon it, taken from Isa lviii 6. where the very words occur in the Greek, though the Hebrew text is very different The Arabic version agrees nearly with the Evangelist. The Hebrew appears formerly to have contained more than we now find in the manuscripts and printed editions. (Scott, Randolph.)

39.	Isa. xii. 3.		John vii. 38
			Ὁ πιστευων εις εμε, καθως ειπεν ἡ γραφη, ποταμοι εκ της κοιλιας αυτου ρευσουσιν ὑδατος ζωντος.[1]
			He that believeth on me, as the Scripture hath said, out of his belly shall flow rivers of living water.
40	Psal. lxxxii. 6	Psal lxxxii 6	John x 34.
	אֲנִי־אָמַרְתִּי אֱלֹהִים אַתֶּם	Εγω ειπα, θεοι εστε.	Εγω ειπα, θεοι εστε
	I have said, Ye are gods	I said, Ye are gods	I said, Ye are gods.
41	Zech ix. 9	Zech ix. 9	John xii 15. (See Matt. xxi. 5. pp. 210, 211. supra.)
	See the passage, in No. 22 pp. 210, 211. supra	See the passage in No 22 pp 210, 211. supra	Μη φοβου, θυγατερ Σιων· ιδου ὁ Βασιλευς σου ερχεται, καθημενος επι πωλον ονου.[2]
			Fear not, daughter of Sion; behold thy king cometh, sitting on an ass's colt.
42.	Isa. liii. 1.	Isa liii 1	John xii 38 (and see Rom. x 16.)
	מִי הֶאֱמִין לִשְׁמֻעָתֵנוּ וּזְרוֹעַ יְהוָה עַל־מִי נִגְלָתָה	Κυριε, τις επιστευσε τη ακοη ἡμων, Και ὁ βραχων Κυριου τινι απεκαλυφθη,	Κυριε τις επιστευσε τη ακοη ἡμων; Και ὁ βραχιων Κυριου τινι απεκαλυφθη,
	Who hath believed our report? And to whom hath the arm of the Lord been revealed?	Lord. who hath believed our report? And to whom hath the arm of the Lord been revealed (or, made manifest)?	Lord, who hath believed our report? And to whom hath the arm of the Lord been revealed?
43	Isa. vi 9, 10.	Isa. vi. 9, 10	John xii 40. (See Matt. xiii. 14, 15 p. 209. supra.)
	See the passage, No 16. p. 209 supra.	See the passage in No 16. p 209 supra	Τετυφλωκεν αυτων τους οφθαλμους, και πεπωρωκεν αυτων την καρδιαν ινα μη ιδωσι τοις

---

[1] There are no words answering to these either in the Septuagint, or in the Hebrew. It is indeed no citation, but only a reference or allusion. The Jewish writers inform us that on the last day of the Feast of Tabernacles, it was usual to pour water on the altar, to denote their praying then for the blessing of rain, the latter rain, which was then wanted against their approaching seed time. This water they drew out of Siloah, and brought it with great pomp and ceremony to the temple, playing with their instruments, and singing, and repeating the words of the prophet *With joy shall ye draw water out of the wells of salvation* (Isa. xii. 3.) Our Lord, according to his usual custom, takes occasion from hence to instruct the people; and applies this ceremony and this scripture to himself. He signifies to them that the water here spoken of was to be had from him alone — *If any man thirst, let him come unto me, and drink. He that believeth in me, as the Scripture hath said, out of his belly shall flow rivers of living water.* — The word κοιλια, here translated belly, signifies a hollow receptacle, and may properly be used for such cisterns or reservoirs, as were usually built to receive the waters issuing from their fountains. The meaning then is, that every true believer shall, according to this scripture, repeated by the people on this occasion, abound with living water, have within him such a cistern, as will supply living water, both for his own and other's use: What is signified by water we are informed in the next verse, viz the gifts of the Spirit. The like metaphor our Lord makes use of, John iv 10. And in the prophetic writings (see Isa. xliv 3. lv 1 Ezek. xxxvi. 25–27. Zech xiv. 8) it is often peculiarly used to signify the gifts and graces of the Spirit to be conferred under the gospel dispensation. (Dr. Randolph, p 31.)

[2] This differs both from the Septuagint and the Hebrew, and also from the citation in Matt xxi 5. The evangelist either followed some other translation, or chose to express briefly the sense, but not the words of the prophet. (Ibid.)

216   *Tables of Quotations from*   [Part I. Ch.

οφθαλμοις, και νοησωσι τη καρδια, και επιστραφωσι, και ιασω-
μαι αυτους [1]

He hath blinded their eyes
and hardened their heart; that
they should not see with *their*
eyes, nor understand with *their*
heart, and be converted, and
I should heal them.

		John xii. 18
44. Psal. xli 9.	Psal. xli 9.	
איבל להמי הגדיל עלי עקב:	Ὁ εσθιων αρτους μου εμεγα-λυνεν επ' εμε πτερνισμον	Ὁ τρωγων μετ' εμου τον αρτον, επηρεν επ' εμε την πτερναν αυτου
Mine own familiar friend, ... which did eat of my bread, hath lift up *his* heel against me.	He, who ate of my bread, hath lifted up his heel against me.	He that eateth bread with me, hath lifted up his heel against me.
45. Psal. cix 3. (See Psal. xxxv. 19, and lxix 4.)	Psal cix 3	John xv. 25.
וילהמוני הנם:	Επολεμησαν με δωρεαν.	Εμισησαν με δωρεαν. [2]
They ... fought against me without a cause.	They fought against me without cause	They hated me without a cause
46. Psal. xxii. 19 (18. of English version)	Psal xxii. 18.	John xix 24.
יהלקו בגדי להם ועל־לבושי יפילו גורל	Διεμερισαντο τα ιματια μου έαυτοις, και επι τον ιματισμον μου εβαλον κληρον.	Διεμερισαντο τα ιματια μου έαυτοις, και επι τον ιματισμον μου εβαλον κληρον.
They part my garments among them, and cast lots upon my vesture.	They parted my raiment among them, and for my vesture they did cast lots.	They parted my raiment among them, and for my vesture they did cast lots
47. Exod xii. 46. (See Psal. xxxiv 20.)	Exod xii. 46.	John xix 36.
ועצם לא־תשברו־בו:	και οστουν ου συντριψετε απ' αυτου.	Οστουν ου συντριβησεται αυτου. [3]
Neither shall ye break a bone thereof.	And ye shall not break a bone thereof.	A bone of him shall not be broken
48. Zech xii. 10.	Zech xii. 10.	John xix. 37.
והביטו אלי את אשר־דקרו	Επιβλεψονται προς με, ανθ' ών κατωρχησαντο.	Ὀψονται εις ὁν εξεκεντησαν [4]

---

[1] The Evangelist has here given us the sense of the Prophet in short: If we suppose that λαος αυτος (as it is in the Hebrew העם הזה) is to be understood as the nominative case before τετυφλωκεν, (it being not unusual for words that signify a multitude to be joined with plural pronouns or adjectives) and read αὐτων with an aspirate, the citation will be a good translation of the original, only somewhat abridged   (Dr Randolph on Quotations, p. 31.)

[2] This quotation agrees both with the Septuagint and with the Hebrew, except that what the former renders επολεμησαν (*fought against*), is by the evangelist rendered εμισησαν (they hated) Or possibly the passage intended to be cited may be Psal. xxxiv. (xxxv. of English Bible) 19 where the Psalmist speaks of those who were his enemies wrongfully — μισουντες με δωρεαν *who hate me without cause*   (Randolph, Scott.)

[3] This gives the sense both of the Septuagint and the Hebrew, except that it expresses in the passive voice what is there spoken in the active. Or it may be taken from Psal xxxiv. 20. where it expressed passively, thus . Τα οστα αυτων ἑν εξ αυτων ου συντριβησεται. He keepeth *all their bones, not one of them shall be broken* — (Randolph, p. 32)

[4] It is evident that the Evangelist here plainly read אליו (*him*) instead of אלי (*me*) in the **Hebrew**: But so also read thirty-six Hebrew MSS. and two antient editions. And that this is the true reading appears by what follows— *and they shall mourn for him* On the authority of these manuscripts, Archbishop Newcome reads and translates אליו *him*. (Minor Prophets, p. 390, 8vo edit)

VI. Sect. I. § 1.]   *The Old Testament in the New.*   217

They shall look on him whom they pierced. (*Archbp. Newcome's version.*)	They will look to me instead of the things, concerning which (or against which) they have contemptuously danced.	They shall look on him whom they pierced.

49. Psal. lxix 26 (25. of English version.)
(And see Psal. cxix. 8.)

תהי־טירתם נשמה באהליהם אל־יהי ישב׃	Psal. lxix 25. Γενηθήτω ἡ ἐπαυλις αυτων ηρημωμενη, και εν τοις σκηνωμασιν αυτων μη εστω ὁ κατοικων	Acts i. 20. Γενηθήτω ἡ ἐπαυλις αυτου ερημος, και μη εστω ὁ κατοικων εν αυτη.[1]
Let their habitation be desolate, *and* let none dwell in their tents	Let their tent (or habitation) be desolate, and in their dwellings no inhabitant	Let his habitation be desolate, and let no man dwell therein.

50.

Psal cix 8. פקדתו יקח אחר׃	Psal cix. 8. Και την επισκοπην αυτου λαβοι ἑτερος.	Acts i 20. Την επισκοπην αυτου λαβοι ἑτερος.
Let another take his office.	And let another take his office, [or bishoprick]	His bishoprick let another take.

51. Joel iii. 1–5. (ii 28–32. of English version)

והיה אחרי־כן אשפוך את־רוחי על כל־בשר ונבאו בניכם ובנתיכם זקניכם חלמות יחלמון בחוריכם חזינות יראו׃ וגם על־העבדים ועל־השפחות בימים ההמה אשפוך את־רוחי׃ ונתתי מופתים בשמים ובארץ דם ואש ותמרות עשן׃ השמש יחפך לחשך והירח לדם לפני בוא יום יהוה הגדול והנורא׃ והיה כל אשר־יקרא בשם יהוה ימלט	Joel ii 28—32. Και εσται μετα ταυτα, και εκχεω απο του πνευματος μου επι πασαν σαρκα, και προφητευσωσιν οἱ υἱοι ὑμων, και αἱ θυγατερες ὑμων, και οἱ πρεσβυτεροι ὑμων ενυπνια ενυπνιασθησονται, και οἱ νεανισκοι ὑμων δρασεις οψονται. και επι τους δουλους μου και επι τας δουλας μου εν ταις ἡμεραις εκειναις εκχεω απο του πνευματος μου Και δωσω τερατα εν ουρανω, και επι της γης αἱμα και πυρ και ατμιδα καπνου ὁ ἡλιος μεταστραφησεται εις σκοτος, και ἡ σεληνη εις αἱμα, πριν ελθειν την ἡμεραν Κυριου την μεγαλην, και επιφανη Και εσται, πας ὁς αν επικαλεσηται το ονομα Κυριου σωθησεται	Acts ii. 17—21 (See Rom. x. 13) Και εσται εν ταις εσχαταις ἡμεραις (λεγει ὁ Θεος), εκχεω απο του πνευματος μου επι πασαν σαρκα και προφητευσουσιν οἱ υἱοι ὑμων και αἱ θυγατερες ὑμων, και οἱ νεανισκοι ὑμων δρασεις οψονται, και οἱ πρεσβυτεροι ὑμων ενυπνια ενυπνιασθησονται. Και γε επι τους δουλους μου και επι τας δουλας μου, εν ταις ἡμεραις εκειναις εκχεω απο του πνευματος μου, και προφητευσουσι. Και δωσω τερατα εν τω ουρανω ανω, και σημεια επι της γης κατω, αἱμα και πυρ και ατμιδα καπνου ὁ ἡλιος μεταστραφησεται εις σκοτος, και ἡ σεληνη εις αἱμα, πριν η ελθειν την ἡμεραν Κυριου την μεγαλην και επιφανη. Και εσται, πας ὁς αν επικαλεσηται το ονομα Κυριου, σωθησεται.
And it shall come to pass afterward, *that* I will pour out my spirit upon all flesh, and your sons and your daughters shall prophesy, your old men shall dream dreams, and your young men shall see visions And also upon the servants and the handmaids in those days will I pour out my spirit And I will show wonders in the heavens and in the earth,	And it shall come to pass after those things, that I will pour out *a portion* of my spirit upon all flesh, and your sons and your daughters shall prophesy, and your old men shall dream dreams, and your young men shall see visions. And on my servants and on my handmaids in those days I will pour out *a portion* of my spirit. And I will exhibit	And it shall come to pass in the last days (saith God), I will pour out of my spirit upon all flesh. and your sons and your daughters shall prophesy, and your young men shall see visions, and your old men shall dream dreams. And on my servants and on my handmaidens, I will pour out in those days of my spirit and they shall prophesy. And

---

[1] This agrees in sense, though not in words with the Septuagint, which is a literal translation of the Hebrew. The only difference is, that the apostle applies to a particular person, what was spoken by David of his enemies in the plural. (Dr. Randolph, p. 32)

218 Tables of Quotations from [Part I. Ch.

blood and fire, and pillars of smoke. The sun shall be turned into darkness and the moon into blood, before the great and the terrible day of the LORD come And it shall come to pass *that* whosoever shall call on the name of the LORD shall be delivered.	wonders in the heavens and on the earth, blood and fire, and smoky vapour. The sun shall be turned into darkness, and the moon into blood, before the coming of the great and illustrious day of the Lord. And it shall come to pass, *that* whosoever shall call on the name of the Lord shall be saved.	I will show wonders in heaven above, and signs in the earth beneath, blood and fire, and vapour of smoke. The sun shall be turned into darkness, and the moon into blood, before that great and notable day of the Lord come. And it shall come to pass *that* whosoever shall call on the name of the Lord shall be saved

52. Psal xvi 8—11	Psal. xvi. 8—11.	Acts ii. 25—28.
שויתי יהוה לנגדי תמיד כי מימיני בל־אמוט׃ לכן שמח לבי ויגל כבודי אף־בשרי ישכן לבטח׃ כי לא־תעזב נפשי לשאול לא־תתן חסידך לראות שחת׃ תודיעני ארח חיים שבע שמחות את־פניך	Προωρωμην τον Κυριον ενωπιον μου δια παντος, ότι εκ δεξιων μου εστιν, ίνα μη σαλευθω Δια τουτο ηυφρανθη ή καρδια μου, και ηγαλλιασατο ή γλωσσα μου ετι δε και ή σαρξ μου κατασκηνωσει επ' ελπιδι 'Οτι ουκ εγκαταλειψεις την ψυχην μου εις άδην, ουδε δωσεις τον όσιον σου ιδειν διαφθοραν Εγνωρισας μοι όδους ζωης πληρωσεις με ευφροσυνης μετα του προσωπου σου	Προωρωμην τον Κυριον ενωπιον μου δια παντος, ότι εκ δεξιων μου εστιν, ίνα μη σαλευθω Δια τουτο ευφρανθη ή καρδια μου, και ηγαλλιασατο ή γλωσσα μου· ετι δε και ή σαρξ μου κατασκηνωσει επ' ελπιδι· 'Οτι ουκ εγκαταλειψεις την ψυχην μου εις άδου, ουδε δωσεις τον όσιον σου ιδειν διαφθοραν Εγνωρισας μοι όδους ζωης· πληρωσεις με ευφροσυνης μετα του προσωπου σου. [1]
I have set the LORD always before me, because *he* is at my right hand I shall not be moved. Therefore my heart is glad, and my glory rejoiceth; my flesh also shall rest in hope For thou wilt not leave my soul in hell, nor suffer thy Holy One to see corruption. Thou wilt show me the path of life, in thy presence is fulness of joy	I foresaw the Lord continually before me, because he is at my right hand that I may not be moved Therefore my heart was gladdened, and my tongue exulted with joy, moreover my flesh also will dwell in hope. For thou wilt not leave my soul in Hades, (or, the mansion of dead,) nor suffer thine Holy One to see corruption Thou hast made known to me the ways of life Thou with thy presence wilt fill me with joy	I foresaw the Lord always before me face, for he is on my right hand, that I should not be moved. therefore did my heart rejoice, and my tongue was glad, moreover also my flesh shall rest in hope because thou wilt not leave my soul in hell, neither wilt thou suffer thine Holy One to see corruption. Thou hast made known to me the ways of life, thou shalt make me full of joy with thy countenance.

53. Deut. xviii. 15. 19.	Deut. xviii 15 19.	Acts iii. 22, 23
נביא מקרבך מאחיך כמני יקים לך יהוה אלהיך אליו תשמעון׃ והיה האיש אשר לא־ישמע אל־דברי אשר ידבר בשמי אנכי אדרש מעמו׃	Προφητην εκ των αδελφων σου, ως εμε, αναστησει σοι Κυριος ό Θεος σου· αυτου ακουσεσθε ——— Και ό ανθρωπος ός εαν μη ακουση όσα αν λα-	Προφητην ύμιν αναστησει Κυριος ό Θεος ύμων εκ των αδελφων ύμων, ως εμε· αυτου ακουσεσθε κατα παντα όσα αν λαληση προς ύμας Εσται δε,

[1] This quotation is taken from the Septuagint, but differs in several respects from the Hebrew. For שויתי is put προωρωμην The Vulgate here agrees with the Septuagint, the Syriac and Chaldee versions with the Hebrew. The Arabic differs from them all; for this difference it is not easy to account. Again, for כבודי, *my glory*, is put ἡ γλωσσα μου, *my tongue*. The Vulgate and Arabic, as well as the Septuagint, agree with the apostle, the Chaldee and Syriac with the Hebrew. For שבע is put πληρωσεις με. Here again the Vulgate, Arabic, and Septuagint agree The Syriac reads *satiabor:* the true reading, Dr. Randolph conjectures, might perhaps be אשבע, which the Septuagint might translate according to the sense πληρωσεις με These are but trifling differences; but what most important is that חסידיך *Holy Ones*, in the plural number, is translated by the Septuagint and cited by the apostle, and applied to our Saviour in the singular, τον όσιον σου, *Thine Holy One*. This reading is confirmed by the Keri, or marginal reading, by all the antient versions, and by one hundred and eighty of the best Hebrew MSS., and it is required by the sense. The Masorites have marked their own reading as doubtful. See Kennicott's Dissert. I. p. 496., and also his Dissertatio Generalis, § 17. Randolph, p. 32. Owen, p. 71.

VI. Sect. I. § 1.] *The Old Testament in the New.* 219

The LORD thy God will raise up unto thee a prophet from the midst of thee, of thy brethren, like unto me . unto him shall ye hearken ——— And it shall come to pass, that whosoever will not hearken unto my words, which he shall speak in my name, I will require it of him

λησῃ ὁ προφητης εκεινος επι τω ονοματι μου, εγω εκδικησω εξ αυτου.

The Lord thy God will raise up for thee, from among thy brethren, a prophet like unto me ; to him shall ye hearken. — And whosoever will not hearken to what that prophet shall speak in my name, I will execute vengeance on him

πασα ψυχη, ητις αν μη ακουσῃ του προφητου εκεινου, εξολοθρευθησεται εκ του λαου [1]

A prophet shall the Lord your God raise up unto you, of your brethren, like unto me · him shall ye hear in all things whatsoever he shall say unto you And it shall come to pass, that every soul which will not hear that prophet, shall be destroyed from among the people.

54. Gen xxii 18

והתברכו בזרעך כל גויי הארץ

And in thy seed shall all the nations of the earth be blessed.

Gen. xxii. 18

και ενευλογηθησονται εν τω σπερματι σου παντα τα εθνη της γης

And in thy seed shall all the nations of the earth be blessed

Acts iii 25

Και τω σπερματι σου ενευλογηθησονται πασαι αἱ πατριαι της γης

And in thy seed shall all the kindreds (i e *nations, as being derived from one common ancestor*) of the earth be blessed.

55. Psal. ii. 1, 2.

למה רגשו גוים ולאמים יהגו
ריק | יתיצבו מלכי־ארץ ורוזנים
נוסדו־יחד על־יהוה ועל־משיחו ׃

Why do the nations rage, and the people imagine a vain thing? The kings of the earth set themselves, and the rulers take counsel together, against the LORD, and against his Anointed.

Psal ii. 1, 2

'Ινατι εφρυαξαν εθνη, και λαοι εμελετησαν κενα, Παρεστησαν οἱ βασιλεις της γης, και οἱ αρχοντες συνηχθησαν επι το αυτο κατα του Κυριου, και κατα του Χριστου αυτου

Why did the nations rage, and the people imagine (or meditate) vain things? The kings of the earth stood up (or combined), and the rulers assembled together against the Lord and his Anointed.

Acts iv. 25, 26.

'Ινατι εφρυαξαν εθνη, και λαοι εμελετησαν κενα, Παρεστησαν οἱ βασιλεις της γης, και οἱ αρχοντες συνηχθησαν επι το αυτο κατα του Κυριου, και κατα του Χριστου αυτου.

Why did the heathen rage, and the people imagine vain things The kings of the earth stood up, and the rulers were gathered together, against the Lord and against his Christ (i. e. MESSIAH, or ANOINTED one)

56. Gen xii. 1.

לך־לך מארצך וממולדתך
ומבית אביך אל־הארץ אשר אראך ׃

Get thee out from thy country, and from thy kindred, and from thy father's house, unto a land that I will show thee.

Gen. xii. 1.

Εξελθε εκ της γης σου και εκ της συγγενειας σου, και εκ του οικου του πατρος σου· και δευρο εις την γην, ἡν αν σοι δειξω

Depart from thy land, and from thy kindred, and from the house of thy father, and come to the land which I will show thee.

Acts vii 3.

Εξελθε εκ της γης σου, και εκ της συγγενειας σου, και δευρο εις γην, ἡν αν σοι δειξω.

Get thee out of thy country, and from thy kindred, and come into the land which I shall show thee.

57. Gen xv 13, 14.

כי־גר יהיה זרעך בארץ לא להם
ועבדום וענו אחם ארבע מאות
שנה | וגם את־הגוי אשר יעברו
דן אנכי ואחרי־כן יצאו ברכש
גדול ׃

Gen xv. 13, 14.

Παροικον εσται το σπερμα σου εν γη ουκ ιδια, και δουλωσουσιν αυτους, και κακωσουσιν αυτους, και ταπεινωσουσιν αυτους, τετρακοσια ετη   To δε εθνος, ὡ εαν δουλευσωσι, κρινω

Acts vii. 6, 7.

'Οτι εσται το σπερμα αυτου παροικον εν γη αλλοτρια, και δουλωσουσιν αυτο, και κακωσουσιν ετη τετρακοσια. Και το εθνος, ὡ εαν δουλευσωσι, κρινω εγω, ειπεν ὁ Θεος· και

---

[1] This expresses the sense both of the Hebrew and Septuagint, but not the words; it may possibly be taken from some other translation or paraphrase. (Dr. Randolph. 33.)

220 *Tables of Quotations from* [Part I. Ch.

		εγω μετα δε ταυτα, εξελευσον- ται ώδε μετα αποσκευης πολλης.	μετα ταυτα εξελευσονται, και λατρευσουσι μοι εν τω τοπω τουτω.¹
	That thy seed shall be a stranger in a land *that is* not theirs, and shall serve them, and they shall afflict them four hundred years And also that nation whom they shall serve will I judge · and afterwards shall they come out with great substance.	Thy seed shall sojourn in a land not their own And they shall be enslaved and afflicted, and humbled, four hundred years. But the nation which they shall serve I will judge; and after that they shall come out hither with much wealth.	That his seed should sojourn in a strange land, and that they should bring them into bondage, and entreat *them* evil four hundred years And the nation, to whom they shall be in bondage, will I judge, said God . and after that shall they come forth, and serve me in this place
58.	Gen xlvi. 27. כל־הנפש לבית־יעקב הבאה מצרימה שבעים:	Gen. xlvi 27. Πασαι ψυχαι οικου Ιακωβ αἱ εισελθουσαι μετα Ιακωβ εις Αι- λυπτον, ψυχαι ἑβδομηκοντα- πεντε.	Acts vii. 14. Αποστειλας δε Ιωσηφ μετε- καλεσατο τον πατερα αυτου Ιακωβ και πασαν την συγγε- νειαν αυτου εν ψυχαις ἑβδομη- κονταπεντε
	All the souls of the house of Jacob, which came into Egypt, *were* threescore and ten souls.	All the souls of Jacob's house, that went with him into Egypt, *were* seventy-five souls	Then sent Joseph, and called his father Jacob to him, and all his kindred, threescore and fifteen souls.
59.	(See Josh. xxiv. 32.)		Acts vii 16 Ὁ ωνησατο Αβρααμ τιμης αργυριου παρα των υἱων Εμ- μορ του Συχεμ.² That Abraham bought for a sum of money, of the sons of Emmor, *the* father of Sychem.
60	Amos v. 25–27 הובאתים ומנחה הגשתם־לי במדבר ארבעים שנה בית ישראל ׃ ונשאתם את סכות מלככם ואת כיון צלמיכם כוכב אלהיכם אשר עשיתם לכם . והגליתי אתכם מהלאה לדמשק	Amos v. 25, 26. Μη σφαγια και θυσιας προσ- ηνεγκατε μοι, οικος Ισραηλ, τεσσαρακοντα ετη εν τη ερημω; Και ανελαβετε την σκηνην του Μολοχ, και το αστρον του θεου ὑμων Ῥαιφαν, τους τυπους αυ- των οὑς εποιησατε ἑαυτοις και μετοικιω ὑμας επεκεινα Δαμα- σκου.	Acts vii 42, 43. Μη σφαγια και θυσιας προσ- ηνεγκατε μοι ετη τεσσαρα- κοντα εν τη ερημω, οικος Ισραηλ, Και ανελαβετε την σκηνην του Μολοχ, και το ασ- τρον του θεου ὑμων Ῥεμφαν, τους τυπους οὑς εποιησατε προσκυνειν αυτοις· και μετοι- κιω ὑμας επεκεινα Βαβυλωνος.³

---

¹ It seems to have been Stephen's design to give a short account of the conduct of God towards the children of Israel. In this he does not confine himself to the words of Moses, but abridges his history, and sometimes adds a clause by way of explication. The present citation agrees very nearly with the Hebrew. It only adds, ειπεν ὁ Θεος, and again, και λατρευσουσι μοι εν τω τοπω τουτω, which seems to refer to v. 16. where it is said, *they shall come hither again*. (Dr Randolph on the Quotations, p. 33.)

² In this quotation there is a very considerable error in the copies of the New Testament; and some commentators have supposed that Abraham's purchase of a piece of land of the children of Heth, for a sepulchre, was alluded to But this is clearly a mistake. It is most probably as Bishop Pearce (in loc.) and Dr. Randolph (p. 33.) have conjectured, that Αβρααμ is an interpolation, which has crept into the text from the margin If therefore we omit this name, the sense will run very clearly thus. *So Jacob went down into Egypt and died, he and our fathers And they* (our fathers) *were carried over into Sychem, and laid in the sepulchre, which he* (Jacob) *bought for a sum of money of the sons of Emmor the father of Sychem*. See Josh. xxiv. 32 and Dr. Whitby, on Acts vii. 16.

³ This seems to be taken from the Septuagint, though with some variation. The only considerable difference is that we here read Βαβυλωνος, Babylon, instead of Δαμασκου, Damascus, in the Septuagint. The Hebrew and all the antient versions read Damascus, as also do one or two manuscripts; and this seems to be the true reading. The Septuagint agrees in sense, though not literally, with the Hebrew. Ῥαιφαν, or Ῥεμφαν, was the name of the same idol in Egypt, which was called כיון (CHIUN) in Syria, and represented the planet Saturn.

Have ye offered unto me sacrifices and offerings, in the wilderness, forty years, O house of Israel? But ye have borne the tabernacle of your Moloch and Chiun, your images, the star of your god which ye made to yourselves. Therefore I will cause you to go into captivity beyond Damascus.	Did you, O house of Israel, offer to me burnt offerings and sacrifices forty years in the wilderness? You have, indeed, taken up the tent of Moloch, and the star of your god Raiphan — those types of them which you have made for yourselves. Therefore I will remove you beyond Damascus.	O ye house of Israel, have ye offered to me slain beasts and sacrifices, forty years in the wilderness? Yea, ye took up the tabernacle of Moloch, and the star of your god Remphan, figures which ye made to worship them, and I will carry you away beyond Babylon.

61. Isa. lxvi 1, 2.

כה אמר יהוה השמים כסאי והארץ הדם רגלי אי־זה בית אשר תבנו־לי ואי־זה מקום מנוחתי ואת־כל־אלה ידי עשתה	Isa. lxvi 1, 2. Οὕτως λεγει Κυριος, Ὁ ουρανος μου ϑρονος, και ἡ γη ὑποποδιον των ποδων μου ποιον οικον οικοδομησετε μοι, και ποιος τοπος της καταπαυσεως μου, Παντα γαρ ταυτα εποιησεν ἡ χειρ μου.	Acts vii. 49, 50. Ὁ ουρανος μοι ϑρονος, ἡ δε γη ὑποποδιον των ποδων μου ποιον οικον οικοδομησετε μοι; λεγει Κυριος ἡ τις τοπος της καταπαυσεως μου. Ουχι ἡ χειρ μου εποιησε ταυτα παντα,
Thus saith the LORD, the heaven is my throne, and the earth is my footstool where is the house that ye build unto me? And where is the place of my rest? For all those things hath mine hand made.	Thus saith the Lord, The heaven is my throne, and the earth my footstool What sort of an house will ye build me? And of what sort shall be the place of my rest? For all these things my hand hath made	Heaven is my throne, and earth is my footstool what house will ye build me? saith the Lord or what is the place of my rest? Hath not my hand made all these things?

62. Isa. liii. 7, 8.

כשה לטבח יובל וכרחל לפני גוזזיה נאלמה ויא יפתח פיו מעצר וממשפט לקח ואת־דורו מי ישוחח כי נגזר מארץ חיים	Isa. liii 7. Ὡς προβατον επι σφαγην ηχϑη, και ὡς αμνος εναντιον του κειροντος αφωνος, οὑτως ουκ ανοιγει το στομα. Εν τῃ ταπεινωσει ἡ κρισις αυτου ηρϑη· την γενεαν αυτου τις διηγησεται, ὁτι αιρεται απο της γης ἡ ζωη αυτου.	Ὡς προβατον επι σφαγην ηχϑη, και ὡς αμνος εναντιον του κειροντος αυτου αφωνος, οὑτως ουκ ανοιγει το στομα αυτου. Εν τῃ ταπεινωσει αυτου ἡ κρισις αυτου ηρϑη την δε γενεαν αυτου τις διηγησεται; ὁτι αιρεται απο της γης ἡ ζωη αυτου.[1]
He is brought as a lamb to the slaughter; and as a sheep before her shearers is dumb, so he openeth not his mouth. He was taken from prison and from judgment; and who shall declare his generation, for he was cut off out of the land of the living	He was led as a sheep to the slaughter, and as a lamb before its shearer is dumb, so he openeth not his mouth. In his humiliation his legal trial was taken away. Who will declare his manner of life? Because his life was taken from the earth.	He was led as a sheep to the slaughter, and like a lamb dumb before his shearer, so opened he not his mouth. In his humiliation his judgment was taken away, and who shall declare his generation? for his life is taken from the earth.

63. (See Psal. lxxxix 20, and 1 Sam. xiii. 14.)

Acts. xiii. 22.

Εὑρον Δαβιδ τον του Ιεσσαι, ανδρα κατα την καρδιαν μου, ὁς ποιησει παντα τα ϑεληματα μου.

I have found David the son of Jesse, a man after my own heart, which shall fulfil all my will.

See Hammond, Lud. de Dieu, Annot. Lowth on Amos, v 25 Spencer de Leg Heb l. iii. c. 3 Michaelis, Supplem. ad Lex. Heb p 1225. (Randolph, p. 84.) The apparent variance between the prophet and Stephen is of no moment, as the prophecy was fulfilled by Salmaneser, king of Assyria, carrying the people of Israel both beyond Damascus and Babylon, into the cities of the Medes. See 2 Kings xvii 6. (Dr Randolph.)

[1] The quotation is here made from the Septuagint with no material variation, the pronouns αυτου and αυτου (him and his) are added by the sacred historian, the latter twice. The variation from the present Hebrew text is greater, but not so great as to affect the general import of the passage. (Scott, Randolph.)

64. Psal. ii. 7.	Psal. ii. 7.	Acts xiii. 33.
בני אתה אני היום ילדתיך׃	Υἱός μου ει συ, εγω σημερον γεγεννηκα σε.	Υἱός μου ει συ, εγω σημερον γεγεννηκα σε.
Thou art my Son, this day have I begotten thee.	Thou art my Son, this day have I begotten thee.	Thou art my Son, this day have I begotten thee.
65. Isa. lv. 3.	Isa. lv. 3.	Acts xiii. 34.
ואכרתה לכם ברית עולם חסדי דוד הנאמנים	Και διαθησομαι ὑμιν διαθηκην αιωνιον,—τα ὁσια Δαυιδ τα πιστα	Δωσω ὑμιν τα ὁσια Δαβιδ τα πιστα
I will make an everlasting covenant with you, even the sure mercies of David.	And I will make with you an everlasting covenant,—the gracious promises to David, which are faithful.	I will give you the sure mercies of David.
66. Hab. i. 5.	Hab. i. 5.	Acts xiii. 41.
ראו בגוים והביטו והתמהו תמהו כי־פעל פעל בימיכם לא תאמינו כי־יספר׃	Ιδετε οἱ καταφρονηται, και επιβλεψατε, και θαυμασατε θαυμασια, και αφανισθητε διοτι εργον εγω εργαζομαι εν ταις ἡμεραις ὑμων, ὁ ου μη πιστευσητε, εαν τις εκδιηγηται.	Ιδετε οἱ καταφρονηται, και θαυμασατε, και αφανισθητε· ὁτι εργον εγω εργαζομαι εν ταις ἡμεραις ὑμων, εργον ᾡ ου μη πιστευσητε, εαν τις εκδιηγηται ὑμιν
Behold ye, among the heathen, and regard, and wonder marvellously, for I will work a work in your days, which ye will not believe, though it be told you.	Behold, ye despisers, and view intently, and be amazed at wonderful things, and vanish (or perish) For in your days I am doing a work, which ye will not believe, though one tell you	Behold, ye despisers, and wonder and perish, for I work a work in your days, a work which you shall in no wise believe, though a man declare it unto you.
67. Isa. xlix. 6.	Isa. xlix. 6.	Acts xiii. 47.
ונתתיך לאור גוים להיות ישועתי עד־קצה הארץ׃	Τεθεικα σε εις φως εθνων, του ειναι σε εις σωτηριαν ἑως εσχατου της γης	Τεθεικα σε εις φως εθνων, του ειναι σε εις σωτηριαν ἑως εσχατου της γης [1]
I will also give thee for a light to the Gentiles, that thou mayest be my salvation unto the ends of the earth.	I have appointed thee for the light of the nations, that thou mayest be for salvation to the furthest parts of the earth.	I have set thee to be a light of the Gentiles, that thou shouldest be for salvation unto the ends of the earth.
68. Amos ix. 11, 12.	Amos ix. 11, 12.	Acts xv. 16, 17.
ביום ההוא אקים את־סכת דויד הנפלת וגדרתי את־פרציהן והרסתיו אקים ובניתיה כימי עולם׃ למען יירשו את־שארית אדום וכל־הגוים אשר־נקרא שמי עליהם נאם־יהוה עשה זאת׃	Εν τη ἡμερα εκεινη αναστησω την σκηνην Δαυιδ την πεπτωκυιαν, και ανοικοδομησω τα πεπτωκοτα αυτης, και τα κατεσκαμμενα αυτης αναστησω, και ανοικοδομησω αυτην, καθως αἱ ἡμεραι του αιωνος· Ὁπως εκζητησωσιν οἱ καταλοιποι των ανθρωπων, και παντα τα εθνη, εφ' οὑς επικεκληται το ονομα μου επ' αυτους, λεγει Κυριος ὁ ποιων παντα ταυτα	Μετα ταυτα αναστρεψω, και ανοικοδομησω την σκηνην Δαβιδ την πεπτωκυιαν, και τα κατεσκαμμενα αυτης ανοικοδομησω, και ανορθωσω αυτην· Ὁπως αν εκζητησωσιν οἱ καταλοιποι των ανθρωπων τον Κυριον, και παντα τα εθνη εφ' οὑς επικεκληται το ονομα μου επ' αυτης, λεγει Κυριος ὁ ποιων ταυτα παντα [2]

---

[1] This quotation is the reading of the Alexandrine copy of the Septuagint, and is a literal rendering of the Hebrew, merely omitting the pronoun *my*; *salvation*, instead of *my salvation*. The Vatican MS differs very much.

[2] This quotation, in general, seems to be taken from the Septuagint, but with several verbal variations The passage, however, varies more materially from the Hebrew, especially in the clause, *That the residue of men may seek after the Lord*, which, in the authorised English version from the Hebrew, is rendered, *That they may possess the remnant of Edom*. The Septuagint translators evidently read ידרשו (yidroshu), not יירשו (yiroshu) and אדם (adam), not אדום (edom); and the quotation of it by the apostle or the evangelical historian, according to that reading, gives great sanction to it. (Scott.)

VI. Sect. I. § 1.] *The Old Testament in the New.*

In that day will I raise up the tabernacle of David, that is fallen; and I will close up the breaches thereof, and I will raise up his ruins, and I will build it as in the days of old That they may possess the remnant of Edom, and of all the heathen, which are called by my name, saith the LORD, that doeth this.	In that day I will raise up the tabernacle of David, which hath fallen; I will rebuild those parts of it which have fallen to decay, and repair what have been demolished. I will indeed rebuild it as in the days of old, that the rest of mankind may seek [*the Lord*], even all the nations who are called by my name, saith the Lord, who doth all these things.	After this I will return and build again the tabernacle of David, which is fallen down, and I will build up again the ruins thereof, and I will set it up · that the residue of men might seek after the Lord, and all the Gentiles upon whom my name is called, saith the Lord, who doeth all these things.

69. Exod. xxii. 27 (28. of English version.)

ונשיא בעמך לא תאר.

Thou shalt not curse the ruler of thy people

Exod. xxii 28

Αρχοντα του λαου σου ου κακως ερεις.

Thou shalt not speak evil of the ruler of thy people.

Acts xxiii. 5.

Αρχοντα του λαου σου ουκ ερεις κακως

Thou shalt not speak evil of the ruler of thy people.

70. Hab. ii 4

וצדיק באמונתו יחיה:

The just shall live by his faith.

Hab. ii 4

Ὁ δε δικαιος εκ πιστεως μου ζησεται.

But the just shall live by faith in me

Rom i 17.

Ὁ δε δικαιος εκ πιστεως ζησεται.

The just shall live by faith.

71. Isa. lii 5.

ותמיד כל היום שמי מנאץ:

My name continually every day is blasphemed.

Isa. lii. 5.

Δι' ὑμας δια παντος το ονομα μου βλασφημειται εν τοις εθνεσι

On your account my name is continually reviled among the nations.

Rom ii. 24

Το γαρ ονομα του Θεου δι' ὑμας βλασφημειται εν τοις εθνεσι [1]

For the name of God is blasphemed among the Gentiles through you.

72. Psal. li 6. (4. of English version)

למען תצדק בדברך תזכה בשפטך:

That thou mightest be justified when thou speakest, *and* be clear when thou judgest.

Psal. li. 4.

Ὁπως αν δικαιωθης εν τοις λογοις σου, και νικησης εν τω κρινεσθαι σε.

So that thou mayest be justified in thy sayings, and overcome when thou art judged.

Rom. iii. 4.

Ὁπως αν δικαιωθης εν τοις λογοις σου, και νικησης εν τω κρινεσθαι σε. [2]

That thou mightest be justified in thy sayings, and mightest overcome when thou art judged.

73. Gen xv. 6.

והאמן ביהוה ויחשבה לו צדקה:

And he believed in the LORD, and he counted it to him for righteousness

Gen. xv. 6.

Και επιστευσεν Αβραμ τω Θεω, και ελογισθη αυτω εις δικαιοσυνην.

And Abram believed God, and it was counted to him for righteousness.

Rom iv. 3.

Επιστευσε δε Αβρααμ τω Θεω, και ελογισθη αυτω εις δικαιοσυνην

And Abraham believed God, and it was counted to him for righteousness.

74. Psal. xiv. 1—3.

אין עשה־טוב: יהוה משמים השקיף על־בני־אדם לראות היש משכיל דרש את־אלהים: הכל סר

Psal. xiv 1—3

Ουκ εστι ποιων χρηστοτητα, ουκ εστιν ἑως ἑνος Κυριος εκ του ουρανου διεκυψεν επι τους

Rom iii. 10—12.

Ουκ εστι δικαιος, ουδε εἱς Ουκ εστιν ὁ συνιων· ουκ εστιν ὁ εκζητων τον Θεον Παντες

---

[1] In this quotation from the Septuagint, του Θεου (*of God*), is substituted for μου (*my*), and the words εν τοις εθνεσι (*among the nations*), are added to the Hebrew in the Septuagint. (Scott, Randolph.)

[2] This is taken from the Septuagint, which agrees with the Hebrew. The Greek translators render תזכה (*tizkeh*) *thou mayest be clear* or *pure*, by νικησης, *thou mayest overcome*, for, "to be clear in judgment," or to be acquitted, is "to overcome." (Randolph, Scott.)

224 Tables of Quotations from [Part I. Ch.

Hebrew	Septuagint	New Testament
יחדו נאלחו אין עשה־טוב אין גם אחד ׃	υιους των ανθρωπων, του ιδειν ει εστι συνιων, η εκζητων τον Θεον. Παντες εξεκλιναν, ἅμα ηχρειωθησαν ουκ εστι ποιων χρηστοτητα, ουκ εστιν ἑως ἑνος	εξεκλιναν, ἁμα ηχρειωθησαν ουκ εστι ποιων χρηστοτητα, ουκ εστιν ἑως ἑνος.¹
There is none that doeth good. The LORD looked down from heaven upon the children of men; to see if there were any that did understand *and* seek God They are all gone aside, they are *all* together become filthy *there is* none that doeth good, no not one.	There is none who doeth good, no, not one. The Lord looked down from heaven on the children of men, to see if any had understanding, or were seeking God. They had all gone aside, they were altogether become vile. There is none who doth good, no, not one.	There is not one righteous; no, not one, there is none that understandeth, there is none that seeketh after God. They are all gone out of the way, they are altogether become unprofitable, there is none that doeth good; no, not one.
75. Psal. v 10. (9. of English version.)	Psal v 9.	Rom. iii. 13.
קבר־פתוח גרנם לשונם יחליקון	Ταφος ανεωγμενος ὁ λαρυγξ αυτων· ταις γλωσσαις αυτων εδολιουσαν.	Ταφος ανεωγμενος ὁ λαρυγξ αυτων ταις γλωσσαις αυτων εδολιουσαν
Their throat is an open sepulchre, they flatter with their tongue.	Their throat *is* an open sepulchre, with their tongue they have practised deceit.	Their throat is an open sepulchre, with their tongues they have used deceit.
76. Psal. cxl. 4. (3. of English version.)	Psal cxxxix. 3. (cxl. 8 of English Bible.)	Rom. iii 13.
חמת עכשוב תחת שפתימו	Ιος ασπιδων ὑπο τα χειλη αυτων	Ιος ασπιδων ὑπο τα χειλη αυτων
Adders' poison *is* under their lips.	The poison of asps *is* under their lips.	The poison of asps (*a venomous species of serpent*) *is* under their lips
77. Psal x. 7.	Psal. x 7.	Rom iii. 14.
אלה פיהו מלא ומרמות	Οὗ ἁρας το στομα αυτου γεμει και πικριας	Ὧν το στομα αρας και πικριας γεμει ²
His mouth is full of cursing and deceit	His mouth is full of cursing and bitterness.	Whose mouth is full of cursing and bitterness.
78. Isa lix, 7, 8.	Isa lix, 7, 8.	Rom. iii. 15-17.
רגליהם לרע ירצו וימהרו לשפך דם נקי ———— שד ושבר במסלותם ׃ דרך ש׳ ום לא ידעו	Οἱ δε ποδες αυτων επι πονηριαν τρεχουσι, ταχινοι εκχεαι αἱμα — Συντριμμα και ταλαιπωρια εν ταις ὁδοις αυτων Και ὁδον ειρηνης ουκ οιδασι.	Οξεις οἱ ποδες αυτων εκχεαι αἱμα Συντριμμα και ταλαιπωρια εν ταις ὁδοις αυτων· Και ὁδον ειρηνης ουκ εγνωσαν.
Their feet run to evil, and they make haste to shed innocent blood ———— Wasting and destruction *are* in their paths. The way of peace they know not.	Their feet run to evil, they are swift to shed blood. — Destruction and misery are in their ways, and the way of peace they do not know.	Their feet *are* swift to shed blood. Destruction and misery *are* in their ways, and the way of peace they have not known

---

¹ The former part of this quotation is an abridgment of the Septuagint, but agreeing in meaning with the Hebrew It is rather an abridgment. The latter part is exactly from the Septuagint. The Hebrew word rendered in our version *they are become filthy*, and which signifies *to be loathsome or putrid*, is in the Septuagint rendered ηχρειωθησαν, *they are become unprofitable*. This the apostle retains. It is not so forcible as the Hebrew, but is sufficient for his argument; and it cannot be supposed that many of the Christians at Rome had any other Scriptures except the Septuagint. (Scott.)

² This quotation agrees with the Septuagint, which also agrees with the Hebrew, excepting that the Greek translators have rendered מרמות (MIRMUTH,, deceit, by πικριας, bitterness. Dr. Randolph and Mr. Scott conjecture that they read מרורות (MERAROTH).

The Old Testament in the New.

79.

Psal. xxxvi 2. (1. of English version)	Psal. xxxv 1 (xxxvi. 1. of English Bible.)	Rom. iii. 18.
אין־פחד אלהים לנגד עיניו ׃	Ουκ εστι φοβος Θεου απεναντι των οφθαλμων αυτου	Ουκ εστι φοβος Θεου απεναντι των οφθαλμων αυτων.
There is no fear of God before his eyes.	There is no fear of God before his eyes.	There is no fear of God before their eyes.

80.

Psal. xxxii 1, 2	Psal. xxxi. 1, 2.	Rom iv 7, 8
אשרי נשוי־פשע כסוי חטאה ׃ אשרי־אדם לא יחשב יהוה לו עון	Μακαριοι ὡν αφεθησαν αἱ ανομιαι, και ὡν επεκαλυφθησαν αἱ ἁμαρτιαι· Μακαριος ανηρ ᾡ ου μη λογισηται Κυριος ἁμαρτιαν	Μακαριοι ὡν αφεθησαν αἱ ανομιαι, και ὡν επεκαλυφθησαν αἱ ἁμαρτιαι· Μακαριος ανηρ ᾡ ου μη λογισηται Κυριος ἁμαρτιαν
Blessed is he whose transgression is forgiven, whose sin is covered. Blessed is the man unto whom the Lord imputeth not iniquity	Happy are they whose iniquities are forgiven, and whose sins are covered. Happy is the man, to whom (to whose account) the Lord will not impute (or charge) sin	Blessed are they, whose sins are forgiven, and whose iniquities are covered. Blessed is the man to whom the Lord will not impute sin.

81.

Gen xvii. 5	Gen. xvii 5	Rom iv 17
אב־המון גוים נתתיך ׃	Πατερα πολλων εθνων τεθεικα σε	Πατερα πολλων εθνων τεθεικα σε
A father of many nations have I made thee	I have made thee the father of many nations	A father of many nations have I made thee.

82.

Gen. xv 5	Gen. xv 5.	Rom. iv. 18.
כה יהיה זרעך ׃	Οὑτως εσται το σπερμα σου.	Οὑτως εσται το σπερμα σου.
So shall thy seed be.	So shall thy seed be	So shall thy seed be.

83.

Psal. xliv. 22.	Psal. xliv 22	Rom. viii 36
כי־עליך הורגנו כל־היום נחשבנו כצאן טבחה ׃	Ὁτι ἑνεκα σου θανατουμεθα ὁλην την ἡμεραν· ελογισθημεν ὡς προβατα σφαγης	Ὁτι ἑνεκα σου θανατουμεθα ὁλην την ἡμεραν ελογισθημεν ὡς προβατα σφαγης
For thy sake we are killed all the day long, we are counted as sheep for the slaughter.	For, for thy sake we are killed all the day long, and accounted as sheep for the slaughter.	For thy sake we are killed all the day long, We are accounted as sheep for the slaughter.

84.

Gen xxi 12	Gen xxi. 12	Rom. ix 7.
כי ביצחק יקרא לך זרע.	Ὁτι εν Ισαακ κληθησεται σοι σπερμα.	Αλλ' εν Ισαακ κληθησεται σοι σπερμα
For, in Isaac, shall thy seed be called.	For in Isaac shall thy seed be called.	But, in Isaac shall thy seed be called

85.

Gen xviii 10	Gen. xviii 10	Rom ix 9.
שוב אשוב אליך כעת חיה והנה־בן לשרה אשתך	Επαναστρεφων ἡξω προς σε κατα τον καιρον τουτον εις ὡρας, και ἑξει υἱον Σαρῥα ἡ γυνη σου	Κατα τον καιρον τουτον ελευσομαι, και εσται τη Σαρῥα υἱος [1]
I will certainly return to thee according to the time of life, and lo, Sarah thy wife shall have a son.	I will return to thee about this time twelvemonth, and Sarah, thy wife, shall have a son	At this time will I come, and Sara shall have a son.

---

[1] St. Paul here seems to have made use of some other translation, different from any we now have; it agrees in sense both with the Septuagint and the Hebrew. The most remarkable difference from the Hebrew is, that כעת חיה is rendered κατα τον καιρον τουτον. They seem to have read it חזה, as the same thing is expressed Gen. xvii. 21. The Samaritan agrees with the Hebrew. The Vulgate, Syriac, and Arabic versions agree with the Septuagint. However, the sense of the prophecy, both ways, is much the same, that Sarah should have a son at the time of life, or at the return of time next year. (Dr. Randolph on the Quotations, p 86.)

226   *Tables of Quotations from*   [Part I. Ch.

86. Gen. xxv. 23. רב יעבד צעיר The elder shall serve the younger	Gen. xxv 23 Και ὁ μειζων δουλευσει τω ελασσονι And the elder shall serve the younger	Rom. ix. 12. Ὁ μειζων δουλευσει τω ελασσονι The elder shall serve the younger
87. Mal. i. 2, 3. ואהב את־יעקב ואת־עשו שנאתי׃ I loved Jacob, and I hated Esau.	Mal. i 2, 3 Και ηγαπησα τον Ιακωβ, τον δε Ησαυ εμισησα Yet I loved Jacob, and hated Esau.	Rom. ix 13. Τον Ιακωβ ηγαπησα τον δε Ησαυ εμισησα Jacob have I loved, but Esau have I hated
88. Exod xxxiii. 19 וחנתי את־אשר אחן ורחמתי את־אשר ארחם׃ I will be gracious to whom I will be gracious, and I will show mercy on whom I will show mercy.	Exod. xxxiii. 19 Και ελεησω ὁν αν ελεω, και οικτειρησω ὁν αν οικτειρω I will have mercy on whom I please to have mercy, and I will have compassion on whomsoever I compassionate.	Rom. ix 15. Ελεησω ὁν αν ελεω, και οικτειρησω ὁν αν οικτειρω I will have mercy on whom I will have mercy, and I will have compassion on whom I will have compassion.
89. Exod. ix. 16 ואולם בעבור זאת העמדתיך בעבור הראתך את־כחי ולמען ספר שמי בכל־הארץ׃ For this cause have I raised thee up, for to show in thee my power and that my name may be declared throughout all the earth.	Exod. ix. 16. Και ἑνεκεν τουτου διετηρηθης, ἱνα ενδειξωμαι εν σοι την ισχυν μου, και ὁπως διαγγελη το ονομα μου εν παση τη γη But thou hast been preserved for this purpose, that by thee I might display my power, and that my name may be celebrated throughout all the earth.	Rom. ix 17. Εις αυτο τουτο εξηγειρα σε, ὁπως ενδειξωμαι εν σοι την δυναμιν μου, και ὁπως διαγγελη το ονομα μου εν παση τη γη For this same purpose have I raised thee up, that I might show my power in thee, and that my name might be declared throughout all the earth
90. Hos. ii. 25. ורחמתי את־לא רחמה ואמרתי ללא־עמי עמי־אתה I will have mercy upon her that had not obtained mercy and I will say to them which were not my people, Thou art my people	Hos. ii. 23. Και αγαπησω την ουκ ηγαπημενην, και ερω τω ου λαω μου, λαος μου ει συ And I will love her who was not beloved, and to them who were not my people, I will say Thou art my people.	Rom. ix. 25. Καλεσω τον ου λαον μου, λαον μου και την ουκ ηγαπημενην, ηγαπημενην I will call them my people, which were not my people; and her beloved which was not beloved.
91. Hos. ii. 1. (i. 10. of English version.) והיה במקום אשר־יאמר להם לא־עמי אתם יאמר להם בני אל־חי׃ And it shall come to pass, that in the place where it was said unto them, ye are not my people, there it shall be said unto them, ye are the sons of the living God.	Hos. i. 10 Και εσται, εν τω τοπω, οὑ ερρηθη αυτοις, Ου λαος μου ὑμεις, κληθησονται και αυτοι υἱοι Θεου ζωντος But it shall come to pass that, in the place where it was said, "Ye are not my people," they shall be called children of the living God	Rom. ix 26 Και εσται, εν τω τοπω οὑ ερρηθη αυτοις, Ου λαος μου ὑμεις, εκει κληθησονται υἱοι Θεου ζωντος And it shall come to pass, that in the place where it was said unto them, Ye are not my people there shall they be called the children of the living God
92. Isa x 22, 23. כי אם־יהיה עמך ישראל כחול הים שאר ישוב בו כליון חרוץ שוטף צדקה׃ כי כלה ונחרצה אדני יהוה צבאות עשה בקרב כל־הארץ׃	Isa x. 22, 23 Και εαν γενηται ὁ λαος Ισραηλ ὡς ἡ αμμος της θαλασσης, το καταλειμμα αυτων σωθησεται Λογον συντελων και συντεμνων εν δικαιοσυνη ὁτι λογον συντετμημενον Κυριος ποιησει εν τη οικουμενη ὁλη	Rom. ix. 27, 28. Εαν η ὁ αριθμος των υἱων, Ισραηλ ὡς ἡ αμμος της θαλασσης, το καταλειμμα σωθησεται Λογον γαρ συντελων και συντεμνων εν δικαιοσυνη, ὁτι λογον συντετμημενον ποιησει Κυριος επι της γης [1]

---

[1] This quotation agrees nearly with the Septuagint, and still more nearly with the Arabic. They differ in several particulars from the Hebrew, but the general sense is the same. The

VI. Sect. I. § 1.] *The Old Testament in the New.* 227

For though thy people Israel be as the sand of the sea, *yet* a remnant of them shall return the consumption decreed shall overflow with righteousness For the Lord God of Hosts shall make a consumption, even determined in the midst of all the land.	Though the people of Israel be as the sand of the sea, a remnant of them shall be saved He is closing an account, and making a deduction with saving goodness Because with the whole land the Lord will make a reckoning from which a deduction hath been made.	Though the number of the children of Israel be as the sand of the sea, a remnant shall be saved for he will finish the work, and cut it short in righteousness because a short work will the Lord make upon the earth.

93   Isa. i. 9   Isa. i 9   Rom ix. 29.

לולי יהוה צבאות הותיר לנו
שריד כמעט כסדם היינו לעמרה
דמינו :

Και ει μη Κυριος Σαβαωθ εγκατελιπεν ἡμιν σπερμα, ὡς Σοδομα αν εγενηθημεν, και ὡς Γομορρα αν ὡμοιωθημεν

Ει μη Κυριος Σαβαωθ εγκατελιπεν ἡμιν σπερμα, ὡς Σοδομα αν εγενηθημεν, και ὡς Γομορρα αν ὡμοιωθημεν.

Except the Lord of Hosts had left us a very small remnant, we should have been as Sodom, and we should have been like unto Gomorrah.	Had not the Lord of Hosts left us a seed, we should have been as Sodom, and made like Gomorrah.	Except the Lord of Sabaoth had left us a seed, we had been as Sodoma, and been made like unto Gomorrha.

94   Isa viii. 14   Isa viii 14   Rom ix. 33.

ולאבן נגף ולצור מכשול לשני
בתי ישראל

Και ουχ ὡς λιθου προσκομματι συναντησεσθε, ουδε ὡς πετρας πτωματι.

Ιδου τιθημι εν Σιων λιθον προσκομματος, και πετραν σκανδαλου και πας ὁ πιστευων επ' αυτω ου καταισχυνθησεται.¹

He shall be... for a stone of stumbling, and a rock of offence to both the houses of Israel.	And ye shall not run against a stumbling stone, nor as under a falling rock.	Behold I lay in Sion a stumbling stone, and rock of offence, and whosoever believeh on him shall not be ashamed. See also Rom x. 11, and 1 Pet. ii 6, 7.

95   Isa xxviii 16   Isa xxviii 16.

הנני יסד בציון אבן אבן בחן
פנת יקרת מוסד מוסד המאמין
לא יחיש

Ιδου, εγω εμβαλλω εις τα θεμελια Σιων λιθον πολυτελη, εκλεκτον, ακρογωνιαιον, εντιμον, εις τα θεμελια αυτης, και ὁ πιστευων ου μη καταισχυνθη

Behold I lay in Zion for a foundation a stone, a tried stone, a precious corner stone, a sure foundation he that believeth shall not make haste (Be confounded, *Bp Lowth*)	Behold, I lay for the foundation of Sion a stone of inestimable worth—a chosen precious corner-stone for the foundations of it and he who believeth shall not be ashamed.

---

prophet foretells a great destruction of the children of Israel, but not a total one; a *remnant should return and be saved* the apostle very aptly applies this to the times of the Gospel, when some few of the Jews believed, and were saved, and a signal destruction came upon the rest It is worthy of observation, that the expressions here in Isaiah are the same as we find in Dan. ix where the destruction of Jerusalem is foretold See this prophecy and the application of it well explained by Bishop Newton, Dissertations on the Prophecies, vol. ii. p. 56. (Dr Randolph on the Quotations, p. 86.)

¹ The quotation in Rom ix. 33 is taken from two places in the prophecy of Isaiah. St. Paul, in order to prove that the Jews in general should be cast off, and only those among them who believed should be saved, refers to two passages in the prophet Isaiah, of which he quotes such parts as were sufficient to prove his point. The first citation agrees with the Hebrew. The Septuagint (as will be seen in a subsequent page) differs widely The other citation agrees nearly with the Septuagint: it differs from the Hebrew only in reading with the Septuagint καταισχυνθησεται, *shall be ashamed*, which is also the reading of the Arabic version. They seem to have read in the original (יבוש YABISH) instead of (יחיש YECHISH). (Dr Randolph on Quotations, p. 86.) The Quotation in Rom. x 13 agrees with the latter clause of Isa. xxviii. 16. with the whole of which also agrees the quotation in 1 Pet. ii. 6.

228　　　　　　　　　*Tables of Quotations from*　　　　　[Part I. Ch.

96. Lev. xviii. 5	Lev. xviii. 5	Rom. x. 5.
אשר יעשה אתם האדם וחי בהם	Ἁ ποιησας αυτα ανθρωπος, ζησεται εν αυτοις	Ὁ ποιησας αυτα ανθρωπος ζησεται εν αυτοις.
Judgments .. which if a man do, he shall live in them.	Which, if a man do, he shall live thereby	The man which doeth those things shall live by them.

97. Deut. xxx. 12—14	Deut. xxx. 12—14	Rom. x. 6—8.
לא בשמים הוא לאמר מי יעלה־לנו השמימה ויקחה לנו וישמענו אתה ונעשנה׃ ולא־מעבר לים הוא לאמר מי יעבר־לנו אל־עבר הים ויקחה לנו וישמענו אתה ונעשנה׃ כי־קרוב אליך הדבר מאד בפיך ובלבבך לעשתו׃	Ουκ εν τω ουρανω ανω εστι, λεγων, Τις αναβησεται ἡμιν εις τον ουρανον, και ληψεται ἡμιν αυτην, και ακουσαντες αυτην ποιησομεν; Ουδε περαν της θαλασσης εστι, λεγων, Τις διαπερασει ἡμιν εις το περαν της θαλασσης, και λαβῃ ἡμιν αυτην, και ακουστην ἡμ ν ποιηση αυτην και ποιησομεν, Ἐγγυς σου εστι το ῥημα σφοδρα εν τω στοματι σου, και εν τη καρδια σου, και εν ταις χερσι σου ποιειν αυτο	Μη ειπῃς εν τη καρδια σου Τις αναβησεται εις τον ουρανον, (τουτ' εστι, Χριστον καταγαγειν) Η, τις καταβησεται εις την αβυσσον, (τουτ' εστι Χριστον εκ νεκρων αναγαγειν)—— Ἐγγυς σου το ῥημα εστιν, εν τω στοματι σου, και εν τη καρδια σου ¹
It is not in heaven, that thou shouldest say, Who shall go up for us to heaven, and bring it unto us, that we may hear it and do it? Neither is it beyond the sea, that thou shouldest say, Who shall go over the sea for us, that we may hear it and do it? But the word *is* very nigh unto thee in thy mouth and in thy heart.	It is not in heaven above, that thou shouldest say, Who will ascend for us into heaven, and bring it to us, that we may hear and do it? Nor is it beyond the sea, that thou shouldest say, Who will cross the sea for us, and bring it to us, and let us hear it, and we will do it? The word is very near thee, in thy mouth and in thy heart, and in thy hand.	Say not in thine heart, Who shall ascend into heaven? (that is, to bring down Christ *from above*.) Or, who shall descend into the deep? (that is, to bring up Christ again from the dead.)...The word is nigh thee, *even* in thy mouth and in thy heart

98. Isa. lii. 7.	Isa. lii. 7.	Rom. x. 15
מה־נאוו אל־ההרים רגלי מבשר משמיע שלום מבשר טוב׃	Ὡς ὡρα επι των ὀρεων, ὡς ποδες ευαγγελιζομενου ακοην ειρηνης, ὡς ευαγγελιζομενος αγαθα	Ὡς ὡραιοι οἱ ποδες των ευαγγελιζομενων ειρηνην, των ευαγγελιζομενων τα αγαθα
How beautiful upon the mountains are the feet of him that bringeth good tidings, that publisheth peace; that bringeth good tidings of good!	Like beauty on the mountains, — like the feet of one proclaiming peace, like one proclaiming glad tidings.	How beautiful are the feet of them that preach the Gospel of Peace, *and* bring glad tidings of good things!

99. Psal. xix. 5. (4. of English version.)	Psal. xix. 4	Rom. x. 18.
בכל־הארץ יצא קום ובקצה תבל מליהם	Εις πασαν την γην εξηλθεν ὁ φθογγος αυτων, και εις τα περατα της οικουμενης τα ῥηματα αυτων	Εις πασαν την γην εξηλθεν ὁ φθογγος αυτων, και εις τα περατα της οικουμενης τα ῥηματα αυτων ²

---

¹ The apostle here, with some little alteration, accommodates what Moses says in the book of Deuteronomy to his present purpose. Moses there, speaking of the covenant made with the children of Israel, expresses the easiness of that covenant by proverbial phrases taken from the transactions of God with the children of Israel. *Who* (says he) *shall go up for us into Heaven, &c.* alluding to the delivery of the law from Heaven — *Who shall go over the sea for us, &c.* alluding to the passage of the Israelites over the Red Sea. St. Paul makes use of the like phrases, only altering the latter so as to allude to the descent of Christ into the grave. This is a most beautiful allusion; and the latter part, in which the main stress of the argument lies, agrees both with the Septuagint and with the Hebrew, omitting only a word or two. (Dr. Randolph on the Quotations, p. 37.)

² This quotation agrees verbatim with the Septuagint, and it agrees with the Hebrew, excepting that instead of קום (QUM), *a line or direction*, both the apostle and the Septuagint

[VI. Sect. I. § 1]   *The Old Testament in the New.*   229

Their line (more correctly, sound) is gone out through all the earth, and their words to the end of the world.	To every land their sound is gone forth, and their doctrines to the limits of the world.	Their sound went into all the earth, and their words unto the ends of the world.

100. Deut. xxxii 21	Deut. xxxii 21.	Rom. x. 19.
ואני אקניאם בלא־עם בגוי נבל אכעיסם	Κἀγω παραζηλωσω αυτοις επ' ουκ εθνει, επι εθνει ασυνετω παροργιω αυτους	Εγω παραζηλωσω ὑμας επ' ουκ εθνει, επι εθνει ασυνετω παροργιω ὑμας
I will move them to jealousy with *those which are* not a people, I will provoke them to anger by a foolish nation	I will provoke them by what is not a nation. By a foolish nation will I vex them.	I will provoke you to jealousy by *them that are* no people, and by a foolish nation will I anger you.

101 Isa lxv 1, 2	Isa lxv 1, 2	Rom. x. 20, 21.
נדרשתי ללוא שאלו נמצאתי ללא בקשני — פרשתי ידי כל היום אל־עם סורר	Εμφανης εγενηθην τοις εμε μη επερωτωσιν, εὑρεθην τοις εμε μη ζητουσιν — Εξεπετασα τας χειρας μου ὁλην την ἡμεραν προς λαον απειθουντα και αντιλεγοντα	Εὑρεθην τοις εμε μη ζητουσιν, εμφανης εγενομην τοις εμε μη επερωτωσι · Ὁλην την ἡμεραν εξεπετασα τας χειρας μου προς λαον απειθουντα και αντιλεγοντα
I am sought of *them that* asked not *for me*, I am found of *them that* sought me not —— I have spread out my hands all the day long unto a rebellious people.	I became manifest to them who inquired not for me, I was found by them who sought me not —— I stretched out my hands all the day long to a disobedient and gainsaying people	I was found of them that sought me not, I was made manifest unto them that asked not after me. —— All day long I have stretched forth my hands unto a disobedient and gainsaying people

102. 1 Kings xix. 14	1 Kings xix. 14	Rom. xi. 3
את־מזבחתיך הרסו ואת־נביאיך הרגו בחרב ואותר אני לבדי ויבקשו את־נפשי לקחתה׃	Τα θυσιαστηρια σου καθειλαν και τους προφητας σου απεκτειναν εν ῥομφαια και ὑπολελειμμαι εγω μονωτατος, και ζητουσι την ψυχην μου λαβειν αυτην	Κυριε, τους προφητας σου απεκτειναν, και τα θυσιαστηρια σου κατεσκαψαν· κἀγω ὑπελειφθην μονος, και ζητουσι την ψυχην μου.[1]
The children of Israel have thrown down thine altars, and slain thy prophets with the sword and I *even* I only am left and they seek my life to take it away	They have demolished thy altars, and slain thy prophets with the sword, and I only am left, and they seek my life to take it.	Lord, they have killed thy prophets, and digged down thine altars, and I am left alone, and they seek my life.

103. 1 Kings xix 18	1 Kings xix 18	Rom. xi 4
והשארתי בישראל שבעת אלפים כל־הברכים אשר לא־כרעו לבעל	Και καταλειψεις εν Ισραηλ ἑπτα χιλιαδας ανδρων, παντα γονατα ἁ ουκ ωκλασαν γονυ τω Βααλ	κατελιπον εμαυτω ἑπτακισχιλιους ανδρας, οἱτινες ουκ εκαμψαν γονυ τη Βααλ.
I have left *me* seven thousand in Israel, all the knees which have not bowed unto Baal, and every mouth which hath not kissed him	And thou shalt leave in Israel seven thousand men, even all the knees which have not bowed to Baal.	I have reserved to myself seven thousand men who have not bowed the knee to *the image of* Baal.

---

translators seem to have read קוֹלָם (qolam), φθογγος, *a sound:* Which last is doubtless the true reading, as it agrees best with the context, and is supported by the Chaldee Paraphrase, the Syriac, Arabic, and Vulgate Latin Versions, and by Jerome. Symmachus, in his Greek translation, renders the Hebrew by ηχος, *sound.* (Dr Randolph on the Quotations, p 37) Prof N. M. Berlin, Psalmi, ex Recensione Textus Hebræi et Versionum Antiquarum, Latine Versi, p. 31. (Upsaliæ, 1805)

[1] This quotation agrees in sense both with the Septuagint and the Hebrew, but seems to be taken from a different translation The words of the original are transposed, and somewhat abridged. (Dr. Randolph)

230 Tables of Quotations from [Part I. Ch.

104. Isa. xxix 10. (and see Isa. vi 9 Ezek xii 2) כי־נסך עליכם יהוה רוח תרדמה ויעצם את־עיניכם The Lord hath poured out upon you the spirit of deep sleep, and hath closed your eyes.	Isa. xxix. 10. (and see Isa vi 9. Ezek xii 2.) Ὅτι πεποτικεν ὑμας Κυριος πνευματι κατανυξεως, και καμμυσει τους οφθαλμους αυτων For the Lord hath drenched you with the spirit of stupefaction, and will close up the eyes of them.	Rom. xi. 8. Εδωκεν αυτοις ὁ Θεος πνευμα κατανυξεως, οφθαλμους του μη βλεπειν, και ωτα του μη ακουειν ¹ God hath given them the spirit of slumber, eyes that they should not see, and ears that they should not hear
105. Psal. lxix. 23, 24. (22, 23. of English version) יהי־שלחנם לפניהם לפח ולשלומים למוקש. תחשכנה עיניהם מראות ומתניהם תמיד המעד Let their table become a snare before them and that which should have been for their welfare, let it become a trap Let their eyes be darkened that they see not, and make their loins continually to shake.	Psal. lxix. 22, 23. Γενηθητω ἡ τραπεζα αυτων ενωπιον αυτων εις παγιδα, και εις ανταποδοσιν, και εις σκανδαλον Σκοτισθητωσαν οἱ οφθαλμοι αυτων του μη βλεπειν, και τον νωτον αυτων δια παντος συγκαμψον. Let their table before them become a snare, and a recompence, and a stumbling block. Let their eyes be darkened, that they may not see, and bow down their neck continually.	Rom. xi 9, 10. Γενηθητω ἡ τραπεζα αυτων εις παγιδα, και εις θηραν, και εις σκανδαλον, και εις ανταποδομα αυτοις Σκοτισθητωσαν οἱ οφθαλμοι αυτων του μη βλεπειν, και τον νωτον αυτων δια παντος συγκαμψον Let their table be made a snare and a trap, and a stumbling block, and a recompence unto them Let their eyes Le darkened that they may not see, and bow down their back alway.
106. Isa lix. 20, 21 (and see Isa. xxvii. 9.) ובא לציון גואל ולשבי פשע ביעקב נאם יהוה: ואני זאת בריתי אותם And the Redeemer shall come to Sion, and unto them that turn from transgression, saith the LORD. As for me, this is my covenant with them, saith the LORD.	Isa lix. 20, 21 (and see Isa. xxvii 9.) Ἡξει ἑνεκεν Σιων ὁ ῥυομενος, και αποστρεψει ασεβειας απο Ιακωβ Και αὑτη αυτοις ἡ παρ' εμου διαθηκη. For the sake of Sion, the Deliverer will come, and turn away ungodliness from Jacob. And this shall be my covenant with them.	Rom xi. 26, 27. Ἡξει εκ Σιων ὁ ῥυομενος, και αποστρεψει ασεβειας απο Ιακωβ Και αὑτη αυτοις ἡ παρ' εμου διαθηκη, ὁταν αφελωμαι τας ἁμαρτιας αυτων ² And the Redeemer shall come to Sion, and unto them that turn from transgression, saith the LORD As for me, this is my covenant with them saith the LORD.
107. Deut. xxxii 35. לי נקם ושלם To me *belongeth* vengeance and recompence.	Deut xxxii. 35 Εν ἡμερα εκδικησεως ανταποδωσω In the day of vengeance I will requite.	Rom xii. 19 (and see Heb. x. 30.) Εμοι εκδικησις εγω ανταποδωσω, λεγει Κυριος Vengeance is mine (literally *to me* belongeth *vengeance*); I will repay, saith the Lord.

---

¹ The first part of this quotation agrees with the Hebrew, only altering the person, *them* for *you*. The latter part seems to refer to some other Scripture, either Isa. vi 9 or Ezek xii 2, where the same thing is said (Dr. Randolph on the Quotations, p. 37)

² This quotation is taken from the Septuagint, except only that the apostle reads εκ instead of ἑνεκεν. Perhaps the copy of the Septuagint which he used had it so, or possibly the text of the apostle may have been altered by transcribers: the word ἑνεκεν (*for the sake of*), comes nearer to the Hebrew, and answers better the apostle's purpose. And again, at the end the apostle adds ὁταν αφελωμαι τας ἁμαρτιας αυτων — *when I shall take away their sins* This may possibly be taken from Isa xxvii 9. where we read in the Septuagint και τουτο εστιν ἡ ευλογια αυτου ὁταν αφελωμαι την ἁμαρτιαν αυτου — *and this is to him a subject of thanksgiving, when I take away his sin*. It is not easy to discover how the Septuagint translators read the Hebrew,

VI. Sect. I. § 1.]   *The Old Testament in the New.*   231

108 Prov xxv 21, 22	Prov. xxv 21, 22.	Rom. xii 20.
אם־רעב ש׳ אך האכילהו לחם ואם־צמא השקהו מים : כי גחלים אתה חתה על־ראשו	Εαν πεινα ὁ εχθρος σου, ψωμιζε αυτον εαν διψα, ποτιζε αυτον Τουτο γαρ ποιων ανθρακας πυρος σωρευσεις επι την κεφαλην αυτου	Εαν ουν πεινα ὁ εχθρος σου, ψωμιζε αυτον εαν διψα, ποτιζε αυτον τουτο γαρ ποιων ανθρακας πυρος σωρευσεις επι την κεφαλην αυτου
If thine enemy be hungry, give him bread to eat, and if he be thirsty, give him water to drink For thou shalt heap coals of fire upon his head	If thine enemy hunger, feed him, if he be thirsty, give him drink; for by doing thus, thou wilt heap coals of fire upon his head.	Therefore, if thine enemy hunger, feed him, if he thirst, give him drink, for in so doing, thou shalt heap coals of fire on his head
109 Isa xlv 23.	Isa xlv 23	Rom xiv 11.
בי נשבעתי יצא מפי צדקה דבר ולא ישוב כי־לי תכרע כל־ברך תשבע כל־לשון	Κατ' εμαυτου ομνυω, ει μη εξελευσεται εκ του στοματος μου δικαιοσυνη, οἱ λογοι μου ουκ αποστραφησονται ὁτι εμοι καμψει παν γονυ, και ομειται πασα γλωσσα τον Θεον	Ζω εγω, λεγει Κυριος, ὁτι εμοι καμψει παν γονυ, και πασα γλωσσα εξομολογησεται τω Θεω.¹
I have sworn by myself; the word is gone out of my mouth in righteousness and shall not return, that unto me every knee shall bow, every tongue shall swear.	By myself I swear righteousness shall proceed from my mouth, my words shall not be reversed), that to me every knee shall bow, and every tongue shall swear with respect to God	As I live, saith the Lord, every knee shall bow to me, and every tongue shall confess to God.
110 Psal lxix 10. (9. of English version)	Psal lxix 9	Rom xv 8.
וחרפות חורפיך נפלו עלי	Οἱ ονειδισμοι των ονειδιζοντων σε επεπεσον επ' εμε	Οἱ ονειδισμοι των ονειδιζοντων σε επεπεσον επ' εμε.
The reproaches of them that reproached thee, are fallen on me.	On me have fallen the reproaches of them that reproached thee.	The reproaches of them that reproached thee, fell on me.
111. Psal xviii. 50. (49 of English version)	Psal, xviii 49	Rom xv 9.
על־כן אודך בגוים יהוה ולשמך אזמרה :	Δια τουτο εξομολογησομαι σοι εν εθνεσι, Κυριε, και τω ονοματι σου ψαλω	Δια τουτο εξομολογησομαι σοι εν εθνεσι, και τω ονοματι σου ψαλω.
Therefore will I give thanks unto thee, O Lord, among the heathen, and sing praises unto thy name	For this cause I will praise thee, O Lord, among the nations, and sing melodiously unto thy name.	For this cause will I confess to thee among the Gentiles, and sing unto thy name.
112. Deut. xxxii. 42 (43. of English version.)	Deut xxxii. 43	Rom xv 10.
הרנינו גוים עמו	Ευφρανθητε εθνη μετα του λαου αυτου	Ευφρανθητε εθ.η μετα του λαου αυτου ²

¹ This does not exactly agree either with the Septuagint or with the Hebrew. Instead of Κατ' εμαυτου ομνυω, *By myself I swear*, the apostle gives us an equivalent expression often used in Scripture, Ζω εγω, *As I live* The rest of the citation agrees exactly with the Alexandrine copy of the Septuagint, which translates רבב הכל by εξομολογειται, *shall confess*. The Vatican translates it more literally,—ομειται, *shall swear*, but both of them agree in joining ביחוח, in the following verse, with ישבע, in this, leaving out אך and כי,—and to this the Arabic version agrees   (Dr Randolph on the Quotations, p 38)

² This is an exact quotation from the Septuagint The clause which we have given occurs in the *middle* of the verse, which some writers not having observed, they have supposed that the Septuagint is not quoted. The preceding words of this verse in the Septuagint,

Ευφρανθητε ουρανοι ἀμα αυτω,
Και προσκυνησατωσαν αυτω παντες αγγελοι Θεου.

Rejoice, O heavens, with him,
And let all the angels of God worship him—

are not in the Hebrew; and the clause, quoted from the Septuagint, evidently gives the

232 Tables of Quotations from [Part I. Ch.

Rejoice, O ye nations, *with* his people.	Rejoice, O nations, with his people.	Rejoice, ye Gentiles, with his people.
113. Psal. cxvii. 1. הללו את־יהוה כל־גוים שבחוהו כל־האמים׃	Psal. cxvii. 1 Αινειτε τον κυριον παντα τα εθνη, επαινεσατε αυτον παντες οἱ λαοι.	Rom. xv. 11. Αινειτε τον Κυριον παντα τα εθνη, και επαινεσατε αυτον παντες οἱ λαοι.
Praise the Lord all ye nations praise him all ye people	Praise the Lord, all ye nations Praise him, all ye peoples	Praise the Lord, all ye Gentiles, and laud him, all ye people
114 Isa. xi. 10. והיה ביום ההוא שרש ישי אשר עמד לנס עמים אליו גוים ידרשו	Isa. xi. 10 Εσται εν τη ημερα εκεινη ἡ ῥιζα του Ιεσσαι, και ὁ ανισταμενος αρχειν εθνων, επ' αυτω εθνη ελπιουσι	Rom. xv. 12 Εσται ἡ ῥιζα του Ιεσσαι, και ὁ ανισταμενος αρχειν εθνων, επ' αυτω εθνη ελπιουσιν
And in that day there shall be a root of Jesse, which shall be for an ensign of the people, to it shall the Gentiles seek	There shall be in that day the root of Jesse, even he who riseth up to rule nations, in him nations will put their trust	There shall be a root of Jesse, and he that shall rise to reign over the Gentiles, in him shall the Gentiles trust.
115 Isa. lii. 15 כי אשר לא־ספר להם ראו ואשר לא־שמעו התבוננו׃	Isa. lii. 15 Ὁτι οἱς ουκ ανηγγελη περι αυτου, οψονται, και οἱ ουκ ακηκοασι, συνησουσι.	Rom. xv. 21 Οἱς ουκ ανηγγελη περι αυτου, οψονται, και οἱ ουκ ακηκοασι, συνησουσι
That, which had not been told them, shall they see, and that which they had not heard, shall they consider	Because they, to whom no publication was made concerning him, shall see; and they, who had not heard, will understand	To whom he was not spoken of, they shall see, and they that have not heard shall understand
116 Isa. xxix. 14. ואבדה חכמת חכמיו ובינת נבניו תסתתר׃	Isa. xxix. 14 Και απολω την σοφιαν των σοφων, και την συνεσιν των συνετων κρυψω	1 Cor. i. 19 Απολω την σοφιαν των σοφων, και την συνεσιν των συνετων αθετησω
The wisdom of their wise men shall perish, and the understanding of their prudent men shall be hid.	And I will destroy the wisdom of the wise, and will hide the understanding of the prudent.	I will destroy the wisdom of the wise, and will bring to nothing the understanding of the prudent.
117. Isa. lxiv. 3. (4. of English version.) ומעולם לא־שמעו לא האזינו עין לא־ראתה אלהים זולתך יעשה למחכה־לו׃	Isa. lxiv. 4 Απο του αιωνος ουκ ηκουσαμεν, ουδε οἱ οφθαλμοι ἡμων ειδον Θεον, πλην σου, και τα εργα σου, ἁ ποιησεις τοις ὑπομενουσιν ελεον.	1 Cor. ii. 9 Ἁ οφθαλμος ουκ ειδε, και ους ουκ ηκουσε, και επι καρδιαν ανθρωπου ουκ ανεβη, ἁ ἡτοιμασεν ὁ Θεος τοις αγαπωσιν αυτον. 1
For since the beginning of the world, men have not heard nor perceived by the ear, neither hath the eye seen, O God, besides thee, *what* he hath prepared for him that waiteth for him	Never have we heard, nor have our eyes seen a God, besides thee, nor works such as thine, which thou wilt do for them who wait for mercy.	Eye hath not seen, nor ear heard, nor have entered into the heart of man, the things which God hath prepared for them that love him.

genuine meaning of the Hebrew, though, in the abrupt language of poetry, the preposition signifying *with* is omitted. (Scott.)

[1] This is a most difficult passage. It does not agree either with the Hebrew, or the Septuagint, nor any other translation now extant: nor is it possible either to make sense of the Hebrew, or to reconcile the old versions, either with the Hebrew or with one another. In the apostle's citation the sense is easy and consistent, and agreeable to the context in the prophet. No sense can be made of the Hebrew, but by a very forced construction. Some critics have imagined that the quotation was taken from some apocryphal book: but it is so near to the Hebrew here, both in sense and words, that we cannot suppose it to be taken from any other passage. Nor in this case would the apostle (it is presumed) have introduced it with—*as it*

#	Hebrew	Septuagint	New Testament
118	Isa xl. 13. מי־תכן את־רוח יהוה ואיש עצתו יודיענו׃ Who hath directed the spirit of the Lord, or *being* his counsellor, hath taught him?	Isa. xl. 13. Τις εγνω νουν Κυριου; και τις αυτου συμβουλος εγενετο, ὁς συμβιβα αυτον, Who hath known the mind of the Lord? and who hath been of his counsel to teach him?	1 Cor. ii. 16 (See also Rom. xi. 34) Τις γαρ εγνω νουν Κυριου, ὁς συμβιβασει αυτον, For who hath known the mind of the Lord, that he may instruct him?
119	Job v. 13. לכד חכמים בערמם He taketh the wise in their own craftiness.	Job v. 13 Ὁ καταλαμβανων σοφους εν τῃ φρονησει. Who entangleth the wise in their wisdom.	1 Cor. iii. 19. Ὁ δρασσομενος τους σοφους εν τῃ πανουργιᾳ αυτων He taketh the wise in their own craftiness.
120	Psal xciv 11. יהוה ידע מחשבות אדם כי־ המה הבל׃ The Lord knoweth the thoughts of men, that they are vanity	Psal xciii. 11. Κυριος γινωσκει τους διαλογισμους των ανθρωπων, ὁτι εισι ματαιοι The Lord knoweth the thoughts of men, that they are vain	1 Cor. iii 20. Κυριος γινωσκει τους διαλογισμους των σοφων, ὁτι εισι ματαιοι.[1] The Lord knoweth the thoughts of the wise, that they are vain
121	Deut xxv 4. לא־תחסם שור בדישו׃ Thou shalt not muzzle the ox when he treadeth out *the corn*	Deut xxv 4 Ου φιμωσεις βουν αλοωντα Thou shalt not muzzle an ox treading out corn	1 Cor ix. 9 Ου φιμωσεις βουν αλοωντα Thou shalt not muzzle the *mouth of the* ox that treadeth out the corn.
122	Exod xxxii. 6 וישב העם לאכל ושתו ויקמו לצחק׃ The people sat down to eat and to drink, and rose up to play.	Exod xxxii 6 Και εκαθισεν ὁ λαος φαγειν και πιειν, και ανεστησαν παιζειν. And the people sat down to eat and drink, and rose up to play.	1 Cor. x. 7 Εκαθισεν ὁ λαος φαγειν και πιειν, και ανεστησαν παιζειν. The people sat down to eat and drink, and rose up to play
123	Deut xxxii. 17. יזבחו לשדים לא אלה They sacrificed to devils, not to God.	Deut. xxxii. 17. Εθυσαν δαιμονιοις, και ου Θεῳ. They sacrificed to demons, and not to God	1 Cor x 20[2] Αλλ' ὁτι ἁ θυει τα εθνη, δαιμονιοις θυει, και ου Θεῳ. But the things which the Gentiles sacrifice, they sacrifice to devils and not to God.
124	Psal. xxiv 1. ליהוה הארץ ומלואה The earth is the Lord's, and the fulness thereof.	Psal xxiv. 1. Του Κυριου ἡ γη, και το πληρωμα αυτης The earth is the Lord's, and the fulness thereof	1 Cor. x 26. Του γαρ Κυριου ἡ γη, και το πληρωμα αυτης. For the earth is the Lord's, and the fulness thereof

is written. It is more reasonable to suppose that the Hebrew text has been here greatly corrupted, and that the apostle took his citation from some more correct copy. See Bishop Lowth's Note on Isa lxiv 4., and Dr Kennicott's Dissertatio Generalis, § 84 87. (Dr. Randolph on the Quotations, p. 39)

[1] This quotation agrees both with the Septuagint and with the Hebrew, except that it substitutes σοφων, *of the wise,* for ανθρωπων, *of men,* which however does not alter the sense. (Dr. Randolph)

[2] This does not appear to be any citation at all, though it agrees nearly both with the Septuagint and Hebrew of Deut. xxxii. 17. (Ibid)

125.	Isa. xxviii. 11, 12. כי בלעגי שפה ובלשון אחרת ידבר אל־העם הזה ---- ולא אבוא שמוע For with stammering lips and another tongue will he speak to his people ---- Yet they would not hear	Isa. xxviii. 11, 12. Διὰ φαυλισμὸν χειλέων, διὰ γλώσσης ἑτέρας ὅτι λαλήσουσι τῷ λαῷ τούτῳ — καὶ οὐκ ἠθέλησαν ἀκούειν On account of the mockery of their lips, because they will speak to this people with a strange tongue — yet they would not hear	1 Cor. xiv. 21 Ὅτι ἐν ἑτερογλώσσοις, καὶ ἐν χείλεσιν ἑτέροις, λαλήσω τῷ λαῷ τούτῳ, καὶ οὐδ᾽ οὕτως εἰσακούσονταί μου, λέγει Κύριος [1] With men of other tongues and other lips will I speak unto this people, and yet for all that will they not hear me, saith the Lord
126.	Psal. viii. 6 כל שתה תחת־רגליו: Thou hast put all things under his feet.	Psal. viii. 6 Πάντα ὑπέταξας ὑποκάτω τῶν ποδῶν αὐτοῦ. Thou hast put all things under his feet	1 Cor. xv. 27 Πάντα γὰρ ὑπέταξεν ὑπὸ τοὺς πόδας αὐτοῦ. For he hath put all things under his feet
127.	Isa. xxii. 13. אכול ושתו כי מחר נמות: Let us eat and drink, for to-morrow we die.	Isa. xxii. 13 Φάγωμεν καὶ πίωμεν· αὔριον γὰρ ἀποθνήσκομεν Let us eat and drink, for to-morrow we die.	1 Cor. xv. 32 Φάγωμεν καὶ πίωμεν· αὔριον γὰρ ἀποθνήσκομεν Let us eat and drink, for to-morrow we die
128.	Gen. ii. 7. ויהי האדם לנפש חיה: Man became a living soul.	Gen. ii. 7. Καὶ ἐγένετο ὁ ἄνθρωπος εἰς ψυχὴν ζῶσαν. And man became a living soul	1 Cor. xv. 45 Ἐγένετο ὁ πρῶτος ἄνθρωπος Ἀδὰμ εἰς ψυχὴν ζῶσαν [2] The first man, Adam, was made a living soul.
129.	Isa. xxv. 8. בלע המות לנצח He will swallow up death in victory	Isa. xxv. 8 Κατέπιεν ὁ θάνατος ἰσχύσας Mighty death had swallowed up	1 Cor. xv. 54. Κατεπόθη ὁ θάνατος εἰς νῖκος. Death is swallowed up in victory.
130.	Hos. xiii. 14. אהי דבריך מות אהי קטבך שאול O death, I will be thy plagues; O grave, I will be thy destruction.	Hos. xiii 14 Ποῦ ἡ δίκη σου, θάνατε; ποῦ τὸ κέντρον σου, ᾅδη, O death, where is thy punishment? Where thy sting, O grave?	1 Cor. xv. 55. Ποῦ σου, θάνατε, τὸ κέντρον, Ποῦ σου, ᾅδη, τὸ νῖκος, [3] O death, where is thy sting? O grave, where is thy victory?
131.	Psal. cxvi. 10. האמנתי כי אדבר I believed, therefore have I spoken.	Psal. cxvi. 10 Ἐπίστευσα, διὸ ἐλάλησα I believed; therefore I spake.	2 Cor. iv. 13 Ἐπίστευσα, διὸ ἐλάλησα I have believed, therefore have I spoken.
132.	Isa. xlix. 8. בעת רצון עניתיך וביום ישועה עזרתיך In an acceptable time I heard thee, and in a day of salvation have I helped thee.	Isa. xlix. 8. Καιρῷ δεκτῷ ἐπήκουσά σου, καὶ ἐν ἡμέρᾳ σωτηρίας ἐβοήθησά σοι In an acceptable time I have hearkened to thee, and in a day of salvation helped thee	2 Cor. vi. 2 Καιρῷ δεκτῷ ἐπήκουσά σου, καὶ ἐν ἡμέρᾳ σωτηρίας ἐβοήθησά σοι. I have heard thee in a time accepted, and in the day of salvation have I succoured thee.

---

[1] This is not quoted from the Septuagint, but agrees in *substance* with the Hebrew, excepting that it substitutes the *first* person for the *third*, and adds λέγει Κύριος — *saith the Lord*.

[2] This is taken from the Septuagint, which translates the Hebrew literally, but the apostle, by way of explanation, adds πρῶτος — *first*, and Ἀδὰμ — *Adam* (Scott.)

[3] Dr. Randolph is of opinion that the apostle either had a different reading of this passage of Hosea, or that he understood the words in a different sense from that expressed in the Hebrew Lexicons. But Bishop Horsley has shown that St. Paul only cited the prophet indirectly. (Translation of Hosea, Notes, pp. 163—167.)

VI. Sect. I. § 1.]   *The Old Testament in the New.*   235

133. Lev. xxvi 11, 12.	Lev xxvi 11, 12.	2 Cor. vi 16
ונתתי משכני בתוככם ── והתהלכתי בתוככם והייתי לכם לאלהים ואתם תהיו לי לעם׃	Και θησω την σκηνην μου εν ὑμιν ── Και εμπεριπατησω εν ὑμιν και εσομαι ὑμων Θεος, και ὑμεις εσεσθε μοι λαος	Ὅτι ενοικησω εν αυτοις, και εμπεριπατησω και εσομαι αυτων Θεος, και αυτοι εσονται μοι λαος [1]
I will set my tabernacle among you ── And I will walk among you, and will be you God, and ye shall be my people.	And I will fix my tabernacle among you ── And I will walk about among you, and be your God, and ye shall be my people	I will dwell in them, and walk in *them*, and I will be their God, and they shall be my people
134. Isa lii 11, 12	Isa lii 11, 12.	2 Cor vi 17
סורו סורו צאו משם טמא אל תגעו צאו מתוכה הברו נשאי כלי יהוה ׃	Αποστητε, αποστητε, εξελθατε εκειθεν, και ακαθαρτου μη ἁψησθε, εξελθετε εκ μεσου αυτης, αφορισθητε ── και ὁ επισυναγων ὑμας Θεος Ισραηλ	Διο εξελθετε εκ μεσου αυτων, και αφορισθητε, λεγει Κυριος και ακαθαρτου μη ἁπτεσθε κἀγω εισδεξομαι ὑμας [2]
Depart ye, depart ye, go ye out from thence, touch no unclean *things*, go ye out of the midst of her ── And the God of Israel will gather you up. (See the marginal rendering.)	Depart, depart, come out thence, and touch no polluted thing Come out of the midst of her, be clean. And the God of Israel will bring up your rear	Wherefore, come out from among them, and be ye separate, saith the Lord and touch not the unclean thing, and I will receive you.
135 (See 2 Sam vii. 14 in No 146 p. 237 *infra*.)		2 Cor vi. 18
		Και εσομαι ὑμιν εις πατερα, και ὑμεις εσεσθε μοι ε·ς υἱους και θυγατερας, λεγει Κυριος παντοκρατωρ [3]
		And I will be a father unto you, and ye shall be my sons and daughters, saith the Lord Almighty.
136. Exod xvi. 18	Exod xvi 18.	2 Cor viii. 15
ולא העדיף המרבה והממעיט לא החסיר	Ουκ επλεονασεν, ὁ το πολυ· και ὁ το ελαττον, ουκ ηλαττονησεν	Ὁ το πολυ, ουκ επλεονασε· και ὁ το ολιγον, ουκ ηλαττονησε
He that gathered much had nothing over, and he that gathered little had no lack.	He who gathered much had nothing over, and he who gathered little did not fall short	He *that had gathered* much, had nothing over, and he *that had gathered* little, had no lack.
137 Psal cxii. 9	Psal cxii 9	2 Cor. ix 9
פזר נתן לאביונים צדקתו עמדת לעד	Εσκορπισεν, εδωκε τοις πενησιν ἡ δικαιοσυνη αυτου μενει εις τον αιωνα του αιωνος	Εσκορπισεν, εδωκε τοις πενησιν ἡ δικαιοσυνη αυτου μενει εις τον αιωνα

---

[1] In this and the following verses, the apostle applies to the Christian church what was spoken of the Israelites, in different places, but with some little variation. This citation is taken from Lev xxvi. 11, 12., only altering the persons · נתתי משכני בתוככם *I will set my tabernacle among you*, is very properly translated ενοικησω εν αυτοις, *I will dwell in them* ── The clause following is left out, and the rest is translated according to the Septuagint, only with change of the person, and the Septuagint is an exact translation of the Hebrew. (Dr. Randolph on the Quotations.)

[2] The general sense of the prophet cited is given in this passage, but it is neither made from the Septuagint, nor is it a translation of the Hebrew. The Septuagint is, *verbally*, much more according to the Hebrew

[3] We cannot say, certainly, whence this quotation is taken; we have the substance of it in several parts of Scripture, where God promises to be a father to Israel, and calls Israel his son. Dr. Randolph thinks that it is most probably a reference to 2 Sam vii 14 where the very words are spoken of Solomon ── *I will be his father, and he shall be my son*, and this promise to David is introduced v 8. *Thus saith the Lord of Hosts* (in the Septuagint, Κυριος παντοκρατωρ, *the Lord Almighty*). The apostle applies this to Christians in general (Dr Randolph on the Quotations, p. 41.) But Mr Scott is of opinion, that the apostle seems rather to apply to Christians the general declarations made by Jehovah concerning Israel (Exod. iv. 22, 23. Jer. xxxi 1 9. and Hosea i. 9, 10.) See Christ. Observer, vol 2. p. 235

236   *Tables of Quotations from*   [Part I. Ch.

He hath dispersed, he hath given to the poor, his righteousness endureth for ever.	He hath dispersed, he hath given to the needy, his righteousness shall endure for ever	He hath dispersed abroad, he hath given to the poor, his righteousness endureth for ever
138. Deut. xix 15 על פי שני עדים או שלשה עדים יקום דבר. At the mouth of two witnesses, or at the mouth of three witnesses, shall the matter be established	Deut. xix. 15 Επι στοματος δυο μαρτυρων, και επι στοματος τριων μαρτυρων, στησεται παν ρημα By the mouth of two witnesses, or by the mouth of three witnesses, every thing shall be established	2 Cor xiii. 1. Επι στοματος δυο μαρτυρων και τριων σταθησεται παν ρημα[1] In the mouth of two or three witnesses shall every word be established
139. Gen. xii 3 (and see xviii. 18.) ונברכו בך כל משפחת האדמה: In thee shall all families of the earth be blessed	Gen. xii 3 (and see Gen xviii 18) Και ενευλογηθησονται εν σοι πασαι αι φυλαι της γης And in thee shall all the tribes of the earth be blessed	Gal iii. 8 Οτι ενευλογηθησονται εν σοι παντα τα εθνη In thee shall all nations be blessed.
140 Deut. xxvii 26 ארור אשר לא־יקים את־דברי התורה־הזאת לעשות אותם Cursed be he that confirmeth not *all* the words of this law to do them.	Deut. xxvii. 27 (26 of English version) Επικαταρατος πας ανθρωπος, ὁς ουκ εμμενει εν πασι τοις λογοις του νομου τουτου, ποιησαι αυτους Cursed be every man who will not persevere in all the words of this law to do them	Gal iii 10. Επικαταρατος πας ὁς ουκ εμμενει εν πασι τοις γεγραμμενοις εν τω βιβλιω του νομου, του ποιησαι αυτα.[2] Cursed is every one, that continueth not in all things, which are written in the book of the law, to do them
141. Deut. xxi 23 קללת אלהים תלוי He that is hanged is accursed of God	Deut xxi 23 Κεκατηραμενος ὑπο Θεου πας κρεμαμενος επι ξυλου Every one that is hanged on a tree [gibbet], is accursed of God	Gal iii 13. Επικαταρατος πας ὁ κρεμαμενος επι ξυλου[3] Cursed is every one that hangeth on a tree.
142. Isa. liv. 1 רני עקרה לא ילדה פצחי רנה וצהלי לא־חלה כי־רבים בני־שוממה מבני בעולה Sing, O barren, thou *that* didst not bear, break forth into singing and cry aloud, thou *that* didst not travail with child, for more are the children of the desolate, than of the married wife	Isa. liv 1. Ευφρανθητι στειρα ἡ ου τικτουσα ρηξον και βοησον ἡ ουκ ωδινουσα ὁτι πολλα τα τεκνα της ερημου μαλλον η της εχουσης τον ανδρα. Rejoice thou barren, who bearest not break forth with shouts of joy, thou who sufferest not the pangs of childbirth for many more are the children of the desolate than of her who hath an husband.	Gal. iv. 27. Ευφρανθητι στειρα ἡ ου τικτουσα ρηξον και βοησον, ἡ ουκ ωδινουσα ὁτι πολλα τα τεκνα της ερημου μαλλον η της εχουσης τον ανδρα. Rejoice, thou barren that bearest not break forth and cry, thou that travailest not, for the desolate hath many more children than she which hath an husband

---

[1] This is only an allusion it is taken, with a trifling abridgment, from the Alexandrine copy of the Septuagint, which is an exact translation of the Hebrew

[2] Both the apostle's quotation and the Septuagint version give the grand meaning of the Hebrew, but neither of them is a literal translation, and it is evident that the apostle did not studiously quote the Septuagint. (Scott)

[3] Neither the apostle nor the Septuagint gives a literal translation of the Hebrew. The word *was, every one*, is inserted, which has no corresponding word in the Hebrew; and the words ὑπο Θεου, *of God*, of the Septuagint, are omitted (Scott) Dr Randolph thinks that they are probably a corruption of the text

VI. Sect. I. § 1.] *The Old Testament in the New.* 237

143. Gen xxi 10

גרש האמה הזאת ואת־בנה כי
לא יירש בן־האמה הזאת עם־בני
עם־יצחק ׃

Cast out this bondwoman and her son, for the son of this bondwoman shall not be heir with my son, *even with* Isaac.

Gen xxi 10

Εκβαλε την παιδισκην ταυτην, και τον υιον αυτης· ου γαρ μη κληρονομησει ὁ υιος της παιδισκης ταυτης μετα του υιου μου Ισαακ.

Send away this girl and her son, for the son of the girl shall not inherit (or, be the heir) with my son Isaac.

Gal. iv 30.

Εκβαλε την παιδισκην, και τον υιον αυτης· ου γαρ μη κληρονομηση ὁ υιος της παιδισκης μετα του υιου της ελευθερας.[1]

Cast out the bondwoman and her son for the son of the bondwoman shall not be heir with the son of the free woman.

144 Psal lxviii 19 (18. of English version.)

עלית למרום שבית שבי לקחת
מתנות באדם

Thou hast ascended up on high, thou hast led captivity captive thou hast received gifts for men.

Psal lxviii. 8

Αναβας εις ὑψος, ηχμαλωτευσας αιχμαλωσιαν ελαβες δοματα εν ανθρωπω.

Having ascended on high, thou hast led captivity captive, and received gifts in the manner of men

Eph iv 8

Αναβας εις ὑψος, ηχμαλωτευσεν αιχμαλωσιαν, και εδωκε δοματα τοις ανθρωποις

When he ascended up on high, he led captivity captive, and gave gifts unto men.

145 Exod xx 12 (and see Deut v 16.)

כבד את־אביך ואת־אמך למען
יאריכן ימיך על האדמה

Honour thy father and thy mother, that thy days may be long upon the land

Exod xx 12 (and see Deut v 16.)

Τιμα τον πατερα σου, και την μητερα σου, ἱνα ευ σοι γενηται, και ἱνα μακροχρονιος γενῃ επι της γης

Honour thy father and thy mother, that it may be well with thee, and that thou mayest live long in the land.

Eph vi 2, 3

Τιμα τον πατερα σου και την μητερα — Ἱνα ευ σοι γενηται, και εσῃ μακροχρονιος επι της γης[2]

Honour thy father and thy mother — that it may be well with thee, and that thou mayest live long upon the earth.

146. 2 Sam vii. 14.

אני אהיה־לו לאב והוא יהיה־לי
לבן

I will be his father, and he shall be my son

2 Sam vii. 14.

Εγω εσομαι αυτω εις πατερα, και αυτος εσται μοι εις υιον.

I will be to him a father, and he shall be to me a son

Heb i 5.

Εγω εσομαι αυτω εις πατερα, και αυτος εσται μοι εις υιον.

I will be to him a father, and he shall be to me a son

147. Psal xcvii. 7.

השתחוו־לו כל־אלהים ׃

Worship him, all ye gods

Deut xxxii 43

Και προσκυνησατωσαν αυτω παντες αγγελοι Θεου.

And let all the angels of God worship him.

Heb. i 6.

Και προσκυνησατωσαν αυτω παντες αγγελοι Θεου[3]

And let all the angels of God worship him

148 Psal civ 4

עשה מלאכיו רוחות משרתיו
אש להט ׃

Ὁ ποιων τους αγγελους αυτου πνευματα, και τους λειτουργους αυτου πυρ φλεγον

Psal civ 4

Heb i 7.

Ὁ ποιων τους αγγελους αυτου πνευματα, και τους λειτουργους αυτου πυρος φλογα.

---

[1] This agrees with the Septuagint, except that the pronouns ταυτην and ταυτης (*this*) are omitted in the quotation, and that της ελευθερας (*of the free woman*) is substituted for μου Ισαακ (*my son Isaac.*) In both these respects the quotation varies from the Hebrew, though the sense is in no respect affected or altered by it. These alterations or accommodations were necessary to the apostle's argument (Randolph, Scott.)

[2] This quotation may be taken either from Exod xx 12. above given, or from Deut v. 16. which runs thus — *Honour thy father and thy mother, that thy days may be prolonged, and that it may go well with thee in the land which the LORD thy God giveth thee*

[3] It will be seen that these words are quoted exactly from the Septuagint of Deut xxxii 43. But there is something answering to them in the Hebrew Some other additions are made to the same verse which are not in the Hebrew. (Scott.)

Who maketh his angels spirits, his ministers a flaming fire

Who maketh winds his messengers, and flaming fire his ministers

Who maketh his angels spirits, and his ministers a flame of fire

149. Psal. xlv. 7, 8 (6, 7 of English version.)

כסאך אלהים עולם ועד שבט מישׁר שבט מלכותך: אהבת צדק ותשׂנא רשׁע על כן משׁחך אלהים אלהיך שׁמן שׂשׂון מחבריך:

Psal. xlv. 6, 7.

Ὁ θρονος σου, ὁ Θεος, εις αιωνα αιωνος ῥαβδος ευθυτητος ἡ ῥαβδος της βασιλειας σου· Ηγαπησας δικαιοσυνην, και εμισησας ανομιαν· δια τουτο εχρισε σε ὁ Θεος, ὁ Θεος σου, ελαιον αγαλλιασεως παρα τους μετοχους σου.

Heb. i. 8, 9

Ὁ θρονος σου, ὁ Θεος, εις τον αιωνα του αιωνος ῥαβδος ευθυτητος ἡ ῥαβδος της βασιλειας σου· Ηγαπησας δικαιοσυνην, και εμισησας ανομιαν· δια τουτο εχρισε σε ὁ Θεος, ὁ Θεος σου, ελαιον αγαλλιασεως παρα τους μετοχους σου.

Thy throne, O God, is for ever and ever the sceptre of thy kingdom is a right sceptre Thou lovest righteousness and hatest wickedness, therefore God, thy God, hath anointed thee with the oil of gladness above thy fellows

Thy throne, O God, is for ever and ever, the sceptre of thy kingdom is a sceptre of rectitude Thou didst love righteousness and hate iniquity, therefore God, thy God, hath anointed thee with the oil of joy above thy associates

Thy throne, O God, is for ever and ever; a sceptre of righteousness is the sceptre of thy kingdom Thou hast loved righteousness and hated iniquity, therefore God, thy God, hath anointed thee with the oil of gladness above thy fellows.

150. Psal. cii. 25—27.

לפנים הארץ יסדת ומעשׂה ידיך שׁמים. המה יאבדו ואתה תעמד וכלם כבגד יבלו כלבושׁ תחליפם ויחלפו: ואתה הוא ושׁנותיך לא יתמו:

Psal. cii. 25—27.

Κατ' αρχας την γην συ, Κυριε, εθεμελιωσας, και εργα των χειρων σου εισιν οἱ ουρανοι· Αυτοι απολουνται, συ δε διαμενεις και παντες ὡς ἱματιον παλαιωθησονται, και ὡσει περιβολαιον ἑλιξεις αυτους, και αλλαγησονται· Συ δε ὁ αυτος ει, και τα ετη σου ουκ εκλειψουσιν

Heb. i 10—12.

Συ κατ' αρχας, Κυριε, την γην εθεμελιωσας, και εργα των χειρων σου εισιν οἱ ουρανοι. Αυτοι απολουνται, συ δε διαμενεις και παντες ὡς ἱματιον παλαιωθησονται, και ὡσει περιβολαιον ἑλιξεις αυτους, και αλλαγησονται Συ δε ὁ αυτος ει, και τα ετη σου ουκ εκλειψουσι [1]

Of old hast thou laid the foundation of the earth, and the heavens are the work of thy hands. They shall perish, but thou shalt endure, yea, all of them shall wax old like a garment. As a vesture shalt thou change them, and they shall be changed but thou art the same and thy years shall not fail.

Thou, Lord, in the beginning, didst lay the foundations of the earth, and the heavens are the work of thy hands. They shall perish, but thou wilt endure they shall all wax old like a garment, and like a mantle thou wilt fold them up, and they shall be changed But thou art the same, and thy years shall have no end.

Thou, Lord, in the beginning hast laid the foundation of the earth, and the heavens are the works of thine hands. They shall perish, but thou remainest, and they shall all wax old as doth a garment; and as a vesture shalt thou fold them up, and they shall be changed but thou art the same, and thy years shall not fail.

151. Psal viii 4—6

מה־אנושׁ כי־תזכרנו ובן־אדם כי תפקדנו: ותחסרהו מעט מאלהים וכבוד והדר תעטרהו: תמשׁילהו במעשׂי ידיך כל שׁתה תחת רגליו:

Psal. viii. 4—6.

Τι εστιν ανθρωπος, ὁτι μιμνησκη αυτου, ἡ υἱος ανθρωπου, ὁτι επισκεπτη αυτον; Ηλαττωσας αυτον βραχυ τι παρ' αγγελους, δοξη και τιμη εστεφανωσας αυτον, και κατεστησας αυτον επι τα εργα των χειρων σου παντα ὑπεταξας ὑποκατω των ποδων αυτου

Heb. ii. 6—8.

Τι εστιν ανθρωπος, ὁτι μιμνησκη αυτου; ἡ υἱος ανθρωπου, ὁτι επισκεπτη αυτον; Ηλαττωσας αυτον βραχυ τι παρ' αγγελους δοξη και τιμη εστεφανωσας αυτον, και κατεστησας αυτον επι τα εργα των χειρων σου· παντα ὑπεταξας ὑποκατω των ποδων αυτου

---

[1] This quotation is taken from the Septuagint, which agrees exactly with the Hebrew; only for תחליפם (thou shalt change), is put ἑλιξεις (thou shalt fold up) Some manuscripts of this epistle have αλλαξεις, (thou shalt change), which is also the reading of the Vulgate version. Dr. Randolph, therefore, thinks it probable, that the original reading, both in the psalm and this epistle was αλλαξεις. It is so in the Alexandrine edition of the Septuagint, and in the clause immediately following, all copies read αλλαγησονται. On the Quotations, p 42.

VI. Sect. I. § 1.] *The Old Testament in the New.* 239

What is man that thou art mindful of him? And the son of man that thou visitest him? For thou hast made him a little lower than the angels, and hast crowned him with glory and honour. Thou madest him to have dominion over the works of thy hands thou hast put all *things* under his feet.

What is man that thou shouldest be mindful of him? or the son of man that thou shouldest visit him? Thou madest him a little lower than angels, with glory and honour hast thou crowned him, and set him over the works of thy hands. Thou hast put all things under his feet.

What is man, that thou art mindful of him? or the son of man, that thou visitest him? Thou madest him a little lower than the angels, thou crownedst him with glory and honour, and didst set him over the works of thy hands. thou hast put all things in subjection under his feet.

152. Psal xxii 23. (22 of English version.)

אספרה שמך לאחי בתוך קהל
אהלליך׃

I will declare thy name unto my brethren in the midst of the congregation will I praise thee

Psal. xxii. 22.

Διηγησομαι το ονομα σου τοις αδελφοις μου· εν μεσω εκκλησιας ὑμνησω σε

I will declare thy name to my brethren in the midst of the congregation I will sing praise to thee

Heb ii. 12.

Απαγγελω το ονομα σου τοις αδελφοις μου· εν μεσω εκκλησιας ὑμνησω σε

I will declare thy name unto my brethren in the midst of the church will I sing praise unto thee.

153. Isa. viii 17, 18

וקויתי לו׃ הנה אנכי והילדים אשר נתן־לי יהוה

I will look for him. — Behold, I and the children which the LORD hath given me.

Isa viii 17, 18

Και πεποιθως εσομαι επ' αυτω Ιδου εγω και τα παιδια ἁ μοι εδωκεν ὁ Θεος.

And I will trust in him Here am I, and the children whom God hath given me

Heb ii 13

Εγω εσομαι πεποιθως επ' αυτω — Ιδου εγω και τα παιδια ἁ μοι εδωκεν ὁ Θεος

I will put my trust in him. Behold I and the children which God hath given me.

154. Psal. xcv. 7—11.

היום אם־בקלו תשמעו׃ אל־תקשו לבבכם כמריבה כיום מסה במדבר׃ אשר נסוני אבותיכם בחנוני גם־ראו פעלי׃ ארבעים שנה אקוט בדור ואמר עם תעי לבב הם והם לא־ידעו דרכי׃ אשר־נשבעתי באפי אם־יבאון אל־מנוחתי׃

Psal. xcv. 7—11.

Σημερον, εαν της φωνης αυτου ακουσητε, μη σκληρυνητε τας καρδιας ὑμων, ὡς εν τω παραπικρασμω, κατα την ἡμεραν του πειρασμου εν τη ερημω· Οὑ επειρασαν με οἱ πατερες ὑμων, εδοκιμασαν, και ειδον τα εργα μου Τεσσαρακοντα ετη προσωχθισα τη γενεα εκεινη, και ειπα Αει πλανωνται τη καρδια, και αυτοι ουκ εγνωσαν τας ὁδους μου 'Ὡς ωμοσα εν τη οργη μου, ει εισελευσονται εις την καταπαυσιν μου

To-day, since ye have heard his voice, harden not your hearts as at the great provocation, — as in the day of the temptation in the desert, where your fathers tried me, they proved me, though they had seen my works. Forty years I was incensed with that generation, and said, They do always err in their heart, and have not known my ways. So I sware in my wrath, They shall not enter into my rest.

Heb. iii. 7—10.

Σημερον, εαν της φωνης αυτου ακουσητε, μη σκληρυνητε τας καρδιας ὑμων, ὡς εν τω παραπικρασμω, κατα την ἡμεραν του πειρασμου εν τη ερημω· Οὑ επειρασαν με οἱ πατερες ὑμων, εδοκιμασαν με, και ειδον τα εργα μου τεσσαρακοντα ετη· Διο προσωχθισα τη γενεα εκεινη, και ειπον Αει πλανωνται τη καρδια· αυτοι δε ουκ εγνωσαν τας ὁδους μου 'Ὡς ωμοσα εν τη οργη μου, ει εισελευσονται εις την καταπαυσιν μου·

To-day, if ye will hear his voice, harden not your hearts, as in the provocation, in the day of temptation in the wilderness; when your fathers tempted me, proved me, and saw my works forty years. Wherefore I was grieved with that generation, and said, They do always err in *their* hearts; and they have not known my ways. So I sware in my wrath, They shall not enter into my rest.

To-day, if ye will hear his voice, harden not your heart, as in the provocation, *and* as in the day of temptation in the wilderness When your fathers tempted me, proved me, and saw my work. Forty years long was I grieved with *this* generation, and said, It *is* a people that do err in their heart, and they have not known my ways unto whom I sware in my wrath, that they should not enter into my rest.

155. Gen. ii. 3.

ויברך אלהים את־יום השביעי

Gen. ii 3

Και ευλογησεν ὁ Θεος την

Heb. iv. 4.

Και κατεπαυσεν ὁ Θεος εν

240 Tables of Quotations from [Part I. Ch.

ויקדש אתו כי בו שבת מכל־
מלאכתו אשר־ברא אלהים לעשות ׃

ἡμεραν την ἑβδομην, και ἡγιασεν αυτην ὁτι εν αυτη κατεπαυσεν απο παντων των εργων αυτου, ὡν ηρξατο ὁ Θεος ποιησαι.

τη ἡμερα τη ἑβδομη απο παντων των εργων αυτου [1]

And God blessed the seventh day, and sanctified it, because that in it he had rested from all his work which God had created and made

And God blessed the seventh day, and hallowed it, because on it he rested from all these works of his, which God had taken occasion to make

And God did rest the seventh day from all his works

156. Psal. cx. 4

אתה־כהן לעולם על־דברתי
מלכי־צדק ׃

Psal. cx. 4.

Συ ἱερευς εις τον αιωνα κατα την ταξιν Μελχισεδεκ

Heb v 6

Συ ἱερευς εις τον αιωνα κατα την ταξιν Μελχισεδεκ

Thou art a priest for ever, after the order of Melchisedec.

Thou art a priest for ever, after the order of Melchisedek.

Thou art a priest for ever after the order of Melchisedec

157. Gen. xxii 16, 17

ויאמר בי נשבעתי נאם־יהוה
כי־ברך אברכך והרבה ארבה
את־זרעך

Gen xxii 16, 17

Λεγων, Κατ' εμαυτου ωμοσα, λεγει Κυριος — Ἡ μην ευλογων ευλογησω σε, και πληθυνων πληθυνω το σπερμα σου

Heb vi 13, 14.

Θεος .. ωμοσε καθ' ἑαυτου, λεγων· Η μην ευλογων ευλογησω σε, και πληθυνων πληθυνω σε

By myself have I sworn, saith the Lord, ... that in blessing I will bless thee, and in multiplying I will multiply thy seed

Saying, By myself have I sworn, saith the Lord, — with blessings, I will indeed bless thee, and I will multiply thy seed abundantly

God .. sware by himself, saying, Surely, blessing, I will bless thee, and multiplying, I will multiply thee

158 Exod xxv. 40.

וראה ועשה בתבניתם אשר־
אתה מראה בהר ׃

Exod. xxv 40.

Ὁρα, ποιησεις κατα τον τυπον τον δεδειγμενον σοι εν τω ορει

Heb viii 5.

Ὁρα γαρ, φησι, ποιησης παντα κατα τον τυπον τον δειχθεντα σοι εν τω ορει

And look, that thou make them after their pattern, which was showed thee in the mount

See that thou make them according to the pattern shown thee on this mount.

For, See, saith he, *that* thou make all things according to the pattern showed to thee in the mount.

159. Jer xxxi 31—34.

הנה ימים באים נאם־יהוה
וכרתי את־בית ישראל ואת־בית
יהודה ברית חדשה ׃ לא כברית
אשר כרתי את־אבותם ביום
החזיקי בידם להוציאם מארץ
מצרים אשר־המה הפרו את־
בריתי ואנכי בעלתי בם נאם־
יהוה ׃ כי זאת הברית אשר אכרת
את־בית ישראל אחרי הימים ההם
נאם־יהוה נתתי את־תורתי בקרבם
ועל־לבם אכתבנה והייתי להם
לאלהים והמה יהיו־לי לעם ׃ ולא
ילמדו עוד איש את־רעהו ואיש
את־אחיו לאמר דעו את־יהוה כי
כולם ידעו אותי למקטנם ועד־
גדולם נאם־יהוה כי אסלח לעונם
ולחטאתם לא אזכר־עוד ׃

Jer. xxxi. 31—34.

Ιδου, ἡμεραι ερχονται, φησι Κυριος, και διαθησομαι τω οικω Ισραηλ και τω οικω Ιουδα διαθηκην καινην ου κατα την διαθηκην ἡν διεθεμην τοις πατρασιν αυτων, εν ἡμερα επιλαβομενου μου της χειρος αυτων, εξαγαγειν αυτους εκ γης Αιγυπτου· ὁτι αυτοι ουκ ενεμειναν εν τη διαθηκη μου, και εγω ημελησα αυτων, φησι Κυριος· Ὁτι αὑτη ἡ διαθηκη μου, ἡν διαθησομαι τω οικω Ισραηλ, μετα τας ἡμερας εκεινας, φησι Κυριος· διδους δωσω νομους μου εις την διανοιαν αυτων, και επι καρδιας αυτων γραψω αυτους· και εσομαι αυτοις εις Θεον, και αυτοι εσονται μοι εις λαον. Και ου μη διδαξωσιν ἑκαστος τον πολιτην αυτου και ἑκαστος τον αδελφον αυτου, λεγων, Γνωθι τον Κυριον· ὁτι παντες ειδη-

Heb viii 8—12.

Ιδου, ἡμεραι ερχονται, λεγει Κυριος, και συντελεσω επι τον οικον Ισραηλ και επι τον οικον Ιουδα διαθηκην καινην ου κατα την διαθηκην ἡν εποιησα τοις πατρασιν αυτων, εν ἡμερα επιλαβομενου μου της χειρος αυτων, εξαγαγειν αυτους εκ γης Αιγυπτου· ὁτι αυτοι ουκ ενεμειναν εν τη διαθηκη μου, καγω ημελησα αυτων, λεγει Κυριος· Ὁτι αὑτη ἡ διαθηκη, ἡν διαθησομαι τω οικω Ισραηλ μετα τας ἡμερας εκεινας, λεγει Κυριος διδους νομους μου εις την διανοιαν αυτων, και επι καρδιας αυτων επιγραψω αυτους και εσομαι αυτοις εις Θεον, και αυτοι εσονται μοι εις λαον Και ου μη διδαξωσιν ἑκαστος τον πλησιον αυτου, και ἑκαστος τον αδελφον αυτου, λεγων, Γνωθι τον Κυριον· ὁτι παντες ειδη-

---

[1] This is an abridgment both of the Septuagint and the Hebrew.

	σουσι με, απο μικρου αυτων έως μεγαλου αυτων· ότι ίλεως εσομαι ταις αδικιαις αυτων, και των άμαρτιων αυτων ου μη μνησθω ετι	σουσι με, απο μικρου αυτων έως μεγαλου αυτων ότι ίλεως εσομαι ταις αδικιαις αυτων, και των άμαρτιων αυτων, και των ανομιων αυτων ου μη μνησθω ετι [1]
Behold, the days come, saith the Lord, that I will make a new covenant with the house of Israel and with the house of Judah, not according to the covenant that I made with their fathers, in the day that I took them by the hand to bring them out of the land of Egypt, (which my covenant they brake although I was an husband to them, saith the Lord) But this shall be the covenant that I will make with the house of Israel; after those days, saith the Lord, I will put my law in their inward parts, and will write it in their hearts; and will be their God, and they shall be my people And they shall teach no more every man his neighbour, and every man his brother, saying, know the Lord for they shall all know me from the least unto the greatest, saith the Lord for I will forgive their iniquity, and I will remember their sin no more.	Behold, the days are coming, saith the Lord, when I will make a new covenant with the house of Judah, not according to the covenant which I made with their fathers, in the day when I took them by the hand to bring them out of Egypt. Because they did not abide by this covenant of mine, therefore I took no care of them, saith the Lord For, this is my covenant which I will make with the house of Israel after those days, saith the Lord, I will adapt my laws to their understandings, and write them on their hearts, and I will be their God, and they shall be my people, and they shall no more teach every man his neighbour, and every man his brother, saying, Know the Lord, for all will know me from the greatest to the least of them, for I will be merciful to their iniquities, and no more remember their sins.	Behold, the days come, saith the Lord, when I will make a new covenant with the house of Israel and the house of Judah not according to the covenant that I made with their fathers, in the day when I took them by the hand to lead them out of the land of Egypt, because they continued not in my covenant, and I regarded them not, saith the Lord For this is the covenant that I will make with the house of Israel after those days, saith the Lord I will put my laws in their mind, and write them in their hearts, and I will be to them a God, and they shall be to me a people And they shall not teach every man his neighbour, and every man his brother, saying, Know the Lord for all shall know me from the least to the greatest For I will be merciful to their unrighteousness, and their sins and their iniquities will I remember no more

160. Exod. xxiv 8

הנה דם־הברית אשר יהוה
עמכם

Behold the blood of the covenant, which the Lord hath made with you

Exod xxiv. 8

Ιδου το αίμα της διαθηκης, ής διεθετο Κύριος προς ὑμας

Behold the blood of the covenant, which the Lord hath made with you.

Heb. ix 20

Τουτο το αίμα της διαθηκης, ής ενετειλατο προς ὑμας ὁ Θεος

This is the blood of the testament, which God hath enjoined unto you

161. Psal xl 7—9 (6–8 of English version)

זבח ומנחה לא חפצת אזנים
כרית לי עולה וחטאה לא שאלת׃

Θυσιαν και προσφοραν ουκ ηθελησας, σωμα δε κατηρτισω

Heb. x 5—7

Θυσιαν και προσφοραν ουκ ηθελησας, σωμα δε κατηρτισω

---

[1] This long quotation is in general made from the Septuagint, though with several verbal differences, which will be easily observed on collation, but which do not affect the meaning, though they seem to imply, that the apostle did not confine himself to the Septuagint. It is, however, manifest that he had that translation in his thoughts, because he exactly quotes it, where it differs most materially from the Hebrew The Septuagint is, almost throughout this passage, a close version of the Hebrew, but, instead of the clause, which in our authorised English translation is rendered — *although I was a husband to them*, the Septuagint reads, και εγω ημελησα αυτων, *therefore I took no care of them*, which lection is followed by the apostle. Whether the Hebrew was thus read differently, as Dr Randolph and other learned men suppose, or whether the apostle did not think the difference so material as to interrupt his argument on account of it, others must determine. Another variation is, that the Hebrew has the preterite in no place, where the Septuagint has the future, διδους δωσω, *I will put*, &c. But the Hebrew should doubtless be read with what the grammarians term the *convussive vau*, and be understood in a future sense, as the context requires (which both before and after speaks of a new and future covenant); as it is also rendered in all the antient versions, and in the Chaldee paraphrase; and as twenty of the Hebrew manuscripts collated by Dr. Kennicott read See his *Dissertatio Generalis*, § 66. (Dr. Randolph, Scott.)

242   Tables of Quotations from   [Part I. Ch.

או אמרתי הנה־באתי במגלת־ספר
כתוב עלי׃ לעשות־רצונך
אלהי חפצתי ותורתך בתוך מעי

μοι· Ὁλοκαυτωμα και περι ἁμαρτιας ουκ ᾐτησας Τοτε ειπον Ιδου, ἡκω (εν κεφαλιδι βιβλιου γεγραπται περι εμου) του ποιησαι το θελημα σου, ὁ Θεος μου, ηβουληθην, και τον νομον σου εν μεσω της καρδιας μου

μοι· Ὁλοκαυτωματα και περι ἁμαρτιας ουκ ευδοκησας Τοτε ειπον Ιδου, ἡκω (εν κεφαλιδι βιβλιου γεγραπται περι εμου) του ποιησαι, ὁ Θεος, το θελημα σου¹

Burnt offering and sin offering hast thou not required. Then said I, Lo, I come in the volume of the book it is written of me I delight to do thy will, O my God, yea thy law is within my heart.

Sacrifice and offerings thou didst not desire, but thou preparedst a body for me. Whole burnt offerings, and offerings for sin thou didst not require Then I said, Behold I come (in the volume of a book it is written respecting me) to perform, O my God, thy will, I was determined, even that law of thine, within my heart.

Sacrifice and offering thou wouldest not, but a body hast thou prepared me In burnt offerings and sacrifices for sin thou hast had no pleasure. Then said I, Lo, I come (in the volume of the book it is written of me) to do thy will, O God.

162. Deut xxxii 35 (36 of English version.)

כי־ידין יהוה עמו

The LORD shall judge his people

Deut. xxxii 36

Ὅτι κρινει Κυριος τον λαον αυτου.

Because the Lord will judge his people.

Heb x. 30

Κυριος κρινει τον λαον αυτου

The Lord shall judge his people

163.   Hab ii 3, 4.

כי־בא יבא לא יאחר׃ הנה
עפלה לא־ישרה נפשו בו וצדיק
באמונתו יחיה

Hab. ii. 3, 4.

Ὅτι ερχομενος ἡξει, και ου μη χρονιση Γαρ ὑποστειληται, ουκ ευδοκει ἡ ψυχη μου εν

Heb x 37, 38 (and see Rom. i. 17. Gal iii. 11.)

Ὁ ερχομενος ἡξει, και ου χρονιει Ὁ δε δικαιος εκ πιστεως ζησεται και εαν ὑπο-

---

¹ This quotation is taken from the Septuagint with a little variation, but although the general meaning is the same, they are widely different in verbal expression in the Hebrew. David's words are, "אזנים כרית לי *aznayim carita li*, which we translate, *my ears hast thou opened*, but they might be more properly rendered, *my ears hast thou bored, that is*, Thou hast made Me *thy servant for ever*, to dwell in thine own house for the allusion is evidently to the custom mentioned Exod xxi. 2, &c. " If thou buy a Hebrew servant, six years he shall serve, and in the seventh he shall go out free but if the servant shall positively say, I love my master, &c I will not go out free, then his master shall bring him to the door-post, and shall bore his ear through with an awl, and he shall serve him for ever." But how is it possible that the Septuagint and the apostle should take a meaning so totally different from the sense of the Hebrew? Dr Kennicott has a very ingenious conjecture here he supposes that the Septuagint and apostle express the meaning of the words as they stood in the copy from which the Greek translation was made, and that the present Hebrew text is corrupted in the word אזנים *aznayim* ears, which has been written through carelessness for נוה אז *az gevah*, THEN, a BODY. The first syllable אז, THEN, is the same in both, and the latter נים *nim*, which, joined to אז *az*, makes אזנים *aznayim*, might have been easily mistaken for גוה *gevah*, BODY ב *nun*, being very like ג *gimel*, ׳ *yod* like ו *vau*, and ח *he* like final ם *mem*, especially if the line on which the letters were written in the MS happened to be blacker than ordinary (which has often been a cause of mistake) it might have been easily taken for the under stroke of the *mem*, and thus give rise to a corrupt reading and to this the root כרה *carah* signifies as well to *prepare*, as to *open, bore, &c.* On this supposition the antient copy translated by the Septuagint, and followed by the apostle, must have read the text thus, לי כרית גוה אז *az geva carita li*, σωμα δε κατηρτισω μοι. then *a body thou hast prepared me* thus the Hebrew text, the Version of the Septuagint, and the apostle, will agree in what is known to be an indisputable fact in Christianity; namely, that Christ was incarnated for the sin of the world. The Æthiopic has nearly the same reading the Arabic has both, *A body hast thou prepared for me, and mine ears thou hast opened*. But the *Syriac*, the *Chaldee*, and the *Vulgate*, agree with the present Hebrew text, and none of the MSS collated by *Kennicott* and *De Rossi* have any various reading on the disputed words. (Dr. A Clarke's Commentary on the New Testament, note on Heb x. 5.)

For the vision is yet for an appointed time, but at the end, it shall speak and not lie though it tarry, wait for it, because it will surely come, it will not tarry Behold, his soul, which is lifted up, is not upright in him but the just shall live by his faith	αυτω ὁ δε δικαιος εκ πιστεως μου ζησεται For he will assuredly come, and will not fail If any one draw back, my soul hath no pleasure in him. But the just shall live by faith in me	στειληται, ουκ ευδοκει ἡ ψυχη μου εν αυτω [1] For yet a little while, and he that shall come, will come, and will not tarry Now the just shall live by faith but if any man draw back, my soul shall have no pleasure in him.

164 Gen. xlvii 31

וישתחו ישראל על־ראש המטה ׃

And Israel bowed himself upon the bed's head

Gen xlvii 31

Και προσεκυνησεν Ισραηλ επι το ακρον του ῥαβδου αυτου.

And Israel bowed down on the head of his staff.

Heb xi 21.

Και προσεκυνησεν επι το ακρον της ῥαβδου αυτου.

And worshipped, leaning upon the top of his staff

165. Prov iii. 11.

מוסר יהוה בני אל־תמאס ואל־תקץ בתוכחתו ׃

My son, despise not the chastening of the LORD, neither be weary of his correction.

Prov iii, 11.

Τἱε, μη ολιγωρει παιδειας Κυριου, μηδε εκλυου ὑπ' αυτου ελεγχομενος

My son, slight not the correction of the Lord, nor faint when reproved by him

Heb. xii. 5.

Υἱε μου, μη ολιγωρει παιδειας Κυριου, μηδε εκλυου ὑπ' αυτου ελεγχομενος.

My son, despise not thou the chastening of the Lord, nor faint when thou art rebuked of him.

166 Josh i 5 (and see Deut xxxi. 8)

לא ארפך ולא־אעזבך ׃

I will not fail thee, nor forsake thee.

Deut xxxi 8

Ουκ ανησει σε, ουδε μη σε εγκαταλιπη

(The Lord) .. . will not leave thee, nor forsake thee.

Heb. xiii. 5.

Ου μη σε ανω, ουδ' ου' μη σε εγκαταλιπω

I will never leave thee, nor forsake thee.

167 Psal. cxviii 6

יהוה לי לא אירא מה־יעשה לי אדם ׃

The LORD is on my side, I will not fear ; what can man do unto me ?

Psal cxviii. 6.

Κυριος εμοι βοηθος, και ου φοβηθησομαι τι ποιησει μοι ανθρωπος

The Lord is my helper, and I will not fear what man can do unto me.

Heb xiii. 6

Κυριος εμοι βοηθος, και ου φοβηθησομαι τι ποιησει μοι ανθρωπος.

The Lord is my helper, and I will not fear what man can do unto me.

168. Hag ii 6

עוד אחת מעט היא ואני מרעיש את־השמים ואת־הארץ

Yet once, it is a little while, and I will shake the heavens and the earth.

Hag ii 6

Ετι ἁπαξ εγω σεισω τον ουρανον, και την γην

Yet once more, I will shake the heaven and the earth.

Heb. xii. 26.

Ετι ἁπαξ εγω σειω ου μονον την γην, αλλα και τον ουρανον. [3]

Yet once more I shake, not the earth only, but also heaven.

---

[1] This quotation is nearly from the Septuagint both the apostle's citation and that version differ considerably from the Hebrew text , yet the general meaning is the same   (Scott.)

[2] This quotation is taken from the Septuagint version of Gen. xlvii 31 , omitting only the word Israel The variation from the Hebrew is merely in the vowel points הַמִּטָּה *a bed*, the Septuagint read הַמַּטֶּה *a staff*. And that this is the true reading seems probable, because it does not appear that Jacob was then confined to his bed, and because it is not easy to understand what can be meant by *worshipping* or bowing himself *on the head of his bed* In the other reading the sense is plain Jacob *worshipped God*, and, being old and feeble, supported himself by *leaning on the top of his staff*. (Dr. Randolph on the Quotations p 45)

[3] The apostle seems purposely to have varied from the Septuagint, in order to render the quotation more emphatical and suited to his purpose. The Septuagint well translates the Hebrew, omitting the words rendered in our version, *It is a little while*   (Scott)

169	Hos xiv. 3 (2. of English version) ושלמה פרים שפתינו׃	Hos xiv. 2. Και ανταποδωσομεν καρπον χειλεων ἡμων	Heb. xiii. 15 Δι' αυτου ουν αναφερωμεν θυσιαν αινεσεως δια παντος τω Θεω, τουτεστι, καρπον χειλεων ὁμολογουντων τω ονοματι αυτου.[1]
	So will we render the calves of our lips.	And we will render to thee the fruit of our lips	By him, therefore, let us offer the sacrifice of praise to God continually, that is, the fruit of our lips, confessing (*marginal rendering*) to his name.
170	(Gen. vi. 3. 5 ?)	(Gen. vi 3—5 ?)	James iv 5. Προς φθονον επιποθει το πνευμα ὁ κατωκησεν εν ἡμιν.[2]
			The spirit, that dwelleth in us, lusteth to envy
171	Prov. iii 34. אם־ללצים הוא יליץ ולענוים יתן־חן׃	Prov iii 34 Κυριος ὑπερηφανοις αντιτασσεται, ταπεινοις δε διδωσι χαριν.	James iv. 6. Ὁ Θεος ὑπερηφανοις αντιτασσεται, ταπεινοις δε διδωσι χαριν [3]
	Surely he scorneth the scorners, but giveth grace unto the lowly.	The Lord resisteth the proud, but he giveth grace unto the humble.	God resisteth the proud, but giveth grace unto the humble
172.	Lev xi 44 והייתם קדשים כי קדוש אני	Lev. xi. 44. Και ἁγιοι εσεσθε, ὁτι ἁγιος ειμι εγω Κυριος ὁ Θεος ὑμων.	1 Pet i 16 Ἁγιοι γενεσθε, ὁτι εγω ἁγιος ειμι
	Ye shall be holy, for I am holy.	And be ye holy, because I the Lord your God am holy.	Be ye holy, for I am holy

---

[1] This is not properly a citation, but only an allusion to an expression in Hos. xiv 3. The phrase καρπον χειλεων, *fruit of the lips*, is taken from the Septuagint. In the Hebrew, it is פרים שפתינו, which our English translation and the Vulgate version render *the calves of our lips*. This expression may refer primarily to the sacrifices, heifers, calves, &c which the Israelites had vowed to Jehovah, so that the *calves of their lips* were the sacrifices which they had promised. From the apostle and Septuagint rendering this word *fruit* (in which they are followed by the Syriac and Arabic versions) it is evident that their copies read פרי (FRUIT) the ם being omitted, and thus the word would be literally *fruit*, and not *calves*. This reading however is not found in any of the MSS hitherto collated.

[2] This, Dr. Randolph has observed, is a difficult passage. The apostle is generally thought to refer to Gen vi 3 5, where we have the like in sense, but, in expression, the apostle differs widely both from the Hebrew and the Septuagint. Dr Randolph and Mr. Scott, after some expositors, think it a general reference to the doctrine of Scripture, and not a direct quotation, as much as to say, it is the constant doctrine of Scripture, that *the spirit which dwelleth in us lusteth to envy, and is prone to all evil*. It ought however to be observed, that many eminent critics, as Whitby, Griesbach, Macknight, &c, divide this verse into two members, which they read and point, *interrogatively*, thus, Do ye think that the Scripture speaketh in vain? Doth the Spirit, which dwelleth in us, lust unto envy? Which mode of pointing removes the difficulty at once.

[3] This is taken from the Septuagint, only putting Ὁ Θεος instead of Κυριος. They differ from the Hebrew, with which the Vulgate agrees,—*illudet illusores*, he will scorn the scorners. The Arabic version agrees with the Septuagint — *resistet superbis*, he will resist the proud. The Syriac version renders it *destruet irrisores*, he will destroy the scorners, and the Chaldee paraphrase — *illusores propellet*, he will drive away the scorners. It is not easy to account for this difference, nor is it worth while to attempt it. the sense is much the same, as the *proud* and the *scorners* are equivalent expressions in Scripture language. (Dr. Randolph, p. 46.)

173 Isa xl. 6—8.	Isa xl 6—8	1 Pet. i. 24, 25.
כל־הבשר חציר וכל־חסדו כציץ השדה . יבש חציר נבל ציץ ... ודבר אלהינו יקום לעולם .	Πασα σαρξ χορτος, και πασα δοξα ανθρωπου ὡς ανθος χορτου Εξηρανθη ὁ χορτος, και το ανθος εξεπεσε. Το δε ῥημα του Θεου ἡμων μενει εις τον αιωνα.	Διοτι πασα σαρξ ὡς χορτος, και πασα δοξα ανθρωπου ὡς ανθος χορτου Εξηρανθη ὁ χορτος, και το ανθος αυτου εξεπεσε· Το δε ῥημα Κυριου μενει εις τον αιωνα
All flesh is grass, and all the goodliness thereof is as the flower of the field The grass withereth, the flower fadeth ... But the word of our God shall stand fast for ever.	All flesh is grass, and all the glory of man as a flower of grass The grass is withered, and the flower fallen, but the word of our God endureth for ever	For all flesh is as grass, and all the glory of man, as the flower of grass. The grass withereth, and the flower thereof falleth away. but the word of the Lord endureth for ever.
174 Isa xxviii. 16.	Isa xxviii. 16	1 Pet ii 6 (and see Rom. ix 33)
הנני יסד בציון אבן בחן פנת יקרת מוסד מוסד המאמין לא יחיש :	Ιδου, εγω εμβαλλω εις τα θεμελια Σιων λιθον πολυτελη, εκλεκτον, ακρογωνιαιον, εντιμον, εις τα θεμελια αυτης και ὁ πιστευων ου με καταισχυνθη	Ιδου, τιθημι εν Σιων λιθον ακρογωνιαιον, εκλεκτον, εντιμον· και ὁ πιστευων επ' αυτω ου μη καταισχυνθη
Behold I lay in Zion for a foundation, a stone, a tried stone, a precious corner stone, a sure foundation, he that believeth shall not make haste	Behold I lay for the foundation of Sion, a stone of inestimable worth, a chosen precious corner-stone for the foundations of it and he who believeth shall not be ashamed	Behold I lay in Sion a chief corner-stone, elect, precious, and he that believeth on him shall not be confounded
175. Exod xix. 6	Exod xix 6	1 Pet ii. 9.
ואתם תהיו־לי ממלכת כהנים וגוי קדוש	Ὑμεις δε εσεσθε μοι βασιλειον ἱερατευμα, και εθνος ἁγιον.	Ὑμεις δε... βασιλειον ἱερατευμα, εθνος ἁγιον
Ye shall be unto me a kingdom of priests, and an holy nation	And ye shall be to me a royal priesthood, and an holy nation.	But ye are ... a royal priesthood, a holy nation.
176 Isa liii. 9	Isa liii 9.	1 Pet ii 22.
לא־חמס עשה ולא מרמה בפיו :	Ανομιαν ουκ εποιησεν, ουδε δολον εν τω στοματι αυτου	Ὁς ἁμαρτιαν ουκ εποιησεν, ουδε ευρεθη δολος εν τω στοματι αυτου.
Because he had done no violence, neither was any deceit in his mouth	He committed no iniquity, nor practised guile with his mouth.	Who did no sin, neither was guile found in his mouth
177. Isa liii 5	Isa liii 5	1 Pet ii 24
ובחברתו נרפא־לנו :	Τω μωλωπι αυτου ἡμεις ιαθημεν	Ου τω μωλωπι αυτου ιαθητε.
With his stripes we are healed.	By his bruises we are healed.	By whose stripes ye were healed.
178. Psal xxxiv 13—17 (12—16. of English version.)	Psal. xxxiii 13—16.	1 Pet iii. 10—12.
מי־האיש החפץ חיים אהב ימים לראות טוב . נצר לשונך מרע ושפתיך מדבר מרמה : סור מרע ועשה־טוב בקש שלום ורדפהו : עיני יהוה אל־צדיקים ואזניו אל־שועתם : פני יהוה בעשי רע	Τις εστιν ανθρωπος ὁ θελων ζωην, αγαπων ἡμερας ιδειν αγαθας, Παυσον την γλωσσαν σου απο κακου, και χειλη σου του μη λαλησαι δολον· εκκλινον απο κακου, και ποιησον αγαθον ζητησον ειρηνην, και διωξον αυτην Οφθαλμοι Κυριου επι δικαιους, και ωτα αυτου εις δεησιν αυτων· προσωπον δε Κυριου επι ποιουντας κακα.	Ὁ γαρ θελων ζωην αγαπαν, και ιδειν ἡμερας αγαθας, παυσατω την γλωσσαν αυτου απο κακου, και χειλη αυτου του μη λαλησαι δολον εκκλινατω απο κακου, και ποιησατω αγαθον· ζητησατω ειρηνην, και διωξατω αυτην Ὁτι οἱ οφθαλμοι Κυριου επι δικαιους, και ωτα αυτου εις δεησιν αυτων· προσωπον δε Κυριου επι ποιουντας κακα.

246   *Quotations from the Old Testament in the New.*   [Part I. Ch.

What man desireth life, *and* loveth *many* days, that he may see good? Keep thy tongue from evil, and thy lips from speaking guile. Depart from evil and do good, seek peace and pursue it The eyes of the LORD *are* upon the righteous, and his ears *are* open unto their cry. The face of the LORD *is* against them that do evil.

What man soever desireth life, and loveth to see good days? Keep thy tongue from evil, and thy lips from speaking guile Depart from evil and do good, seek peace and pursue it The eyes of the Lord are upon the righteous, and his ears are open to their prayer. But the face of the Lord *is* against them that do evil

For he that will love life and see good days, let him refrain his tongue from evil, and his lips that they speak no guile. Let him eschew evil and do good, let him seek peace and pursue it For the eyes of the Lord *are* over the righteous, and his ears *are* open unto then prayers but the face of the Lord *is* against them that do evil

179   Isa. viii 12, 13.

ואת־מוראו לא־תיראו ולא תעריצו : את־יהוה צבאות אתו תקדישו :

Neither fear ye their fear nor be afraid
Sanctify the LORD of Hosts himself.

Isa. viii 12, 13.

Τον δε φοβον αυτου ου μη φοβηθητε, ουδε μη ταραχθητε κυριον αυτον άγιασατε.

Be not ye terrified with the fear of him, nor dismayed. Hallow the Lord himself.

1 Pet iii 14, 15

Τον δε φοβον αυτων μη φοβηθητε, μηδε ταραχθητε Κυριον δε τον Θεον άγιασατε.[1]

And be not afraid of their terror, neither be troubled, but sanctify the Lord God in your hearts.

180.   Prov x. 12

ועל כל־פשעים תכסה אהבה :

Love covereth all sins.

Prov. x. 12.

Παντας δε τους μη φιλονεικουντας καλυπτει φιλια

But friendship covereth all them who are not contentious

1 Pet iv. 8.

Ότι ή αγαπη καλυψει πληθος άμαρτιων [2]

For charity shall cover the multitude of sins.

181.   Psal ii 9

תרעם בשבט ברזל ככלי יוצר תנפצם :

Thou shalt break them with a rod of iron, thou shalt dash them in pieces like a potter's vessel

Psal. ii. 9.

Ποιμανεις αυτους εν ράβδω σιδηρᾳ· ώς σκευος κεραμεως συντριψεις αυτους.

Thou shalt rule them with a rod of iron. thou shalt break them to pieces like a potter's vessel

Rev ii. 27.

Και ποιμανει αυτους εν ράβδω σιδηρα ώς τα σκευη τα κεραμικα συντριβεται [3]

And he shall rule with a rod of iron as a potter's vessel, shall they be broken to shivers

---

[1] Both this quotation and the Septuagint give the meaning of the Hebrew; but the word αυτων (*their*), which is used by St. Peter, seems to give the sense better than the singular αυτου (*his*) of the Septuagint. The original Hebrew (which is JEHOVAH *Sabaoth*, Lord of Hosts) will admit of either. (Scott)

[2] This is a translation from the Hebrew, and widely different from the Septuagint; only for *all sins*, the apostle has *the multitude of sins* The Septuagint, Syriac, and Arabic versions differ strangely from each other (Dr Randolph, Scott)

[3] This is nearly a quotation of the Septuagint (which exactly translates the Hebrew), the person only being altered from the second to the third. (Dr. Randolph, Scott.)

SECTION II.

ON THE EXTERNAL FORM OF THE QUOTATIONS FROM THE OLD TESTAMENT IN THE NEW.

§ 1. CLASSIFICATION OF THE QUOTATIONS FROM THE HEBREW SCRIPTURES IN THE NEW TESTAMENT.

THE Quotations from the Hebrew Scriptures in the New Testament may be arranged under the nine following classes, viz. I. Quotations exactly agreeing with the Hebrew; — II. Those which agree *nearly* with the Hebrew; — III. Quotations, agreeing with the Hebrew in *sense* but not in words; — IV. Such as give the *general* sense; — V. Quotations, which are taken from *several* passages of Scripture; — VI. Quotations differing from the Hebrew, but agreeing with the Septuagint; — VII. Quotations in which there is reason to suspect a different reading in the Hebrew, or that the Apostles understood the words in a sense different from that expressed in our Lexicons; — VIII. Passages, in which the Hebrew seems to be corrupted; — and IX. Passages which are not properly citations, but mere references or allusions.

I. Quotations exactly agreeing with the Hebrew.

No.	Chap and Verse of O. T.		Chap and Verse of N. T.
3	Hos xi 1.	agrees with	Matt. ii 15.
7	Deut viii 3.	-	Matt. iv. 4 Luke iv. 4.
9	Deut vi. 16.	-	Matt. iv. 7.
12.	Isa. liii. 4.	-	Matt. viii. 17.
19.	Hos vi. 6.	-	Matt. ix 13 xii. 7.
21.	Lev. xix 18	-	Matt. xix. 19 xxii 39.
24	Psal. cxviii. 22, 23.	-	Matt. xxi. 42 Mark xii 10. Luke xx. 17. Acts iv. 11.
27.	Psal cx 1.	-	Matt. xxii. 44 Mark xii. 36. Luke xx. 42.
30.	Psal xxii. 19	-	Matt xxvii. 35.
31	Psal xxii 2.	-	Matt xxvii. 46
32.	Isa liii 12	-	Mark xv. 28 Luke xxii. 37.
34.	Lev. xii 8	-	Luke ii. 24.
36	Psal. lxix 10.	-	John ii. 17.
40.	Psal. lxxii. 6.	-	John x 34
42	Psal. liii 1	-	John xii. 38. See Rom x. 16
46.	Psal. xxii 19.	-	John xix 24.
50	Psal. cix 8.	-	Acts i. 20
54.	Gen xxii 18	-	Acts iii. 25
55.	Psal ii. 1, 2.	-	Acts iv 25, 26
64.	Psal ii. 7	-	Acts xiii 33.
69.	Exod. xxii 27.	-	Acts xxiii. 5
75	Psal v. 10.	-	Rom iii. 13.
76.	Psal cxl 4.	-	Rom. iii. 13.
79	Psal xxxvi. 2.	-	Rom iii. 18.
80	Psal. xxxii. 1, 2.	-	Rom. iv. 7, 8.
81	Gen. xvii. 5	-	Rom. iv. 17.
82.	Gen xv 5.	-	Rom. iv. 18
83.	Psal. xliv 22.	-	Rom. viii. 36.
84.	Gen. xxi. 7.	-	Rom ix. 7.
86.	Gen xxv 23.	-	Rom ix. 12
87.	Mal. i. 2, 3.	-	Rom. ix. 13.
88.	Exod xxxiii. 19.	-	Rom. ix. 15.
89.	Exod. ix. 16.	-	Rom. ix. 17.

No.	Chap. and Verse of O. T.		Chap. and Verse of N. T.
95.	Lev. xviii. 5.	agrees with	Rom. x. 5.
109.	Psal. lxix. 10.	- - -	Rom. xv. 3.
110.	Psal. xviii. 50.	- - -	Rom. xv. 9.
112.	Psal. cxvii. 1.	- - -	Rom. xv. 11.
114.	Isa. liii. 15.	- - -	Rom. xv. 21.
118.	Job v. 13.	- - -	1 Cor. iii. 19.
120.	Deut. xxv. 4.	- - -	1 Cor. ix. 9.
121.	Exod. xxxii. 6.	- - -	1 Cor. x. 7.
123.	Psal. xxiv. 1.	- - -	1 Cor. x. 26.
125.	Psal. viii. 6.	- - -	1 Cor. xv. 27.
126.	Isa. xxii. 13.	- - -	1 Cor. xv. 32.
128.	Isa. xxv. 8.	- - -	1 Cor. xv. 54.
130.	Psal. cxvi. 10.	- - -	2 Cor. iv. 13.
131.	Isa. xlix. 8.	- - -	2 Cor. vi. 2.
135.	Exod. xvi. 18.	- - -	2 Cor. viii. 15.
136.	Psal. cxii. 9.	- - -	2 Cor. ix. 9.
141.	Isa. liv. 1.	- - -	Gal. iv. 27.
145.	2 Sam. vii. 14.	- - -	Heb. i. 5.
146.	Psal. civ. 4.	- - -	Heb. i. 7.
147.	Psal. xlv. 7, 8.	- - -	Heb. i. 8, 9.
149.	Psal. viii. 4—6.	- - -	Heb. ii. 6—8.
150.	Psal. xxii. 23.	- - -	Heb. ii. 12.
151.	Isa. viii. 17, 18.	- - -	Heb. ii. 13.
152.	Gen. ii. 3.	- - -	Heb. iv. 4.
153.	Gen. xxii. 16, 17.	- - -	Heb. vi. 13, 14.
160.	Deut. xxxii. 35.	- - -	Heb. x. 30.
162.	Gen. xlvii. 31.	- - -	Heb. xi. 21.
163.	Prov. iii. 11.	- - -	Heb. xii. 5.
164.	Josh. i. 5.	- - -	Heb. xiii. 5.
170.	Lev. xi. 44.	- - -	1 Pet. i. 16.

II. *Quotations nearly agreeing with the Hebrew.*

These correspond nearly with the Hebrew, though not so literally as those in the preceding class, to which they are nearly equal in number. Thus,

1	Isa. vii. 14.	nearly agrees with	Matt. i. 23.
4.	Jer. xxxi. 15.	- - -	Matt. ii. 18.
8.	Psal. xci. 11, 12.	- - -	Matt. iv. 6.
10.	Deut. vi. 13.	- - -	Matt. iv. 10.
11.	Isa. ix. 1, 2.	- - -	Matt. iv. 15, 16.
16.	Isa. vi. 9, 10.	- - -	{ Matt. xiii. 14, 15. Acts xxviii. 26. Mark iv. 12. Luke viii. 10.
19.	Gen. ii. 24.	- - -	Matt. xix. 5.
20.	Exod. xx. 12—16.	- - -	Matt. xix. 18, 19.
23.	Exod. iii. 6.	- - -	Matt. xxii. 32. Mark xii. 26. Luke xx. 37.
26.	Deut. vi. 5.	- - -	Matt. xxii. 37. Mark xii. 30. Luke x. 27.
28.	Zech. viii. 7.	- - -	Matt. xxvi. 31.
37.	Psal. lxxviii. 24.	- - -	John vi. 31.
38.	Isa. liv. 13.	- - -	John vi. 45.
44.	Psal. xli. 9.	- - -	John xiii. 18.
45.	Psal. cix. 3.	- - -	John xv. 25.
47.	Exod. xii. 46.	- - -	John xix. 36.
48.	Zech. xii. 10.	- - -	John xix. 37.
51.	Joel ii 1—5.	- - -	Acts ii. 17. (See Rom. x. 11.)
56.	Gen. xii. 1.	- - -	Acts vii. 3.
61.	Isa. lxvi. 1, 2.	- - -	Acts vii. 49, 50.
67.	Isa. xlix. 6.	- - -	Acts xiii. 47.
70.	Hab. ii. 4.	- - -	Rom. i. 17.
71.	Isa. lii. 5.	- - -	Rom. ii. 24.

VI. Sect. II. § 1.] *Hebrew Scriptures in the New Testament.* 249

No.	Chap and Verse of O. T.	Chap and Verse of N. T.
72.	Psal. li 6. nearly agrees with	Rom. iii 4.
73.	Gen. xv. 6.	Rom. iv 3.
91.	Hos. ii. 1. (i. 10. of English Version)	Rom. ix. 26.
93.	Isa. i. 9.	Rom. ix. 29.
94.	Isa. viii. 14. Isa. xxviii. 16.	Rom. ix 33.
97.	Isa. lii 7.	Rom. x. 15
98.	Psal xix. 5. (4. of English Version)	Rom. x. 18
99.	Deut xxxii 21.	Rom. x. 19.
100	Isa. lxv. 1, 2	Rom. x 20, 21.
101	1 Kings xix. 14.	Rom. xi 3
102	1 Kings xix 18.	Rom xi 4.
106.	Deut xxxii. 25	Rom xii 19 Heb x. 30.
107.	Prov xxv. 21, 22.	Rom. xii. 20.
111	Deut. xxxii 42 (43. of English Version)	Rom xv. 10.
115.	Isa xxix. 14.	1 Cor i. 19
117	Isa xl 13	1 Cor. ii. 16.
119.	Psal. xciv. 11.	1 Cor iii 20.
124.	Isa. xxviii. 11, 12.	1 Cor. xiv. 21.
127.	Gen. ii 7	1 Cor. xv 45.
132.	Lev xxvi 11, 12.	2 Cor. vi 16.
142	Gen xxi 10.	Gal. iv 30
143.	Psal lxviii. 19.	Eph iv 8.
144.	Exod. xx 12.	Eph. vi. 2, 3.
145.*	Psal xcvii 7.	Heb i 6.
148.	Psal cii 25—27.	Heb. i 10—12
152.	Psal xcv 7—11.	Heb iii. 7—10.
156	Exod xxv 40.	Heb viii 5
157	Jer. xxxi 31 34.	Heb. viii 8—12.
158	Exod. xxiv. 8.	Heb ix 20
166	Psal. cxviii. 6	Heb xiii 6.
171.	Isa. xl. 6—8.	1 Pet. i 24, 25.
173	Exod. xix 6.	1 Pet ii. 9
174.	Isa liii. 9.	1 Pet. ii. 22.
175.	Isa. liii 5	1 Pet. ii 24.
176	Psal xxxiv. 13—17.	1 Pet. iii. 10—12.
177	Isa viii 12, 13.	1 Pet. iii. 14, 15.
178.	Prov. x. 12.	1 Pet. iv. 8.
179.	Psal. ii 9.	Rev. ii. 27.

III. *Quotations agreeing with the Hebrew in* SENSE *but* NOT *in words.*

6.	Isa. xl. 3—5. { agrees in sense, but not in words, with }	Matt iii. 3. Mark i. 3. and Luke iii. 46
15	Isa. xlii 1—4.	Matt xii 18—21.
17.	Psal. lxxviii. 2.	Matt xiii 35.
22.	Zech ix. 9.	Matt. xxi. 5.
23.	Psal. viii. 3.	Matt xxi. 16.
29.	Zech. xi 13.	Matt. xxvii. 9, 10.
33.	Exod xiii 2	Luke ii 23.
41.	Zech ix. 9	John xii. 15.
43.	Isa vi 9, 10	John xii. 40.
49.	Psal. lxix. 26.	Acts i 20.
53.	Deut. xviii. 15. 19.	Acts iii. 22, 23.
59.	(see Josh. xxiv. 32)	Acts vii 16
74.	Psal xiv. 1—3.	Rom. iii. 10—12.
78.	Isa. lix. 7, 8	Rom iii. 15—17.
85.	Gen. xviii 10.	Rom. ix. 9.
90.	Hos. ii. 23.	Rom. ix. 25.
92.	Isa. x. 22, 23.	Rom. ix. 27, 28.
104.	Psal. lxix. 23, 24.	Rom. xi. 9, 10.

250 Classification of Quotations from the [Part I. Ch.

No.	Chap. and Verse of O. T.		Chap. and Verse of N. T.
108.	Isa. xlv. 23.	{ agrees in sense, but not in words, with }	Rom. xiv. 11.
113.	Isa. xi 10.		Rom xv. 12.
133	Isa. liii. 11, 12		2 Cor. vi. 17.
138.	Gen xii. 3.		Gal. iii 8.
139.	Deut. xxvii 26.		Gal. iii 10.
165.	Hag ii. 6		Heb xii 26.

IV. *Quotations that give the general Sense, but which abridge or add to it.*

5.	(Psal. xxii. 6. lxix. 9, 10. Isa. lii. liii. Zech. xi 12, 13.)	compared with	Matt. ii. 23.
41.	Zech. ix. 9.		John xii. 15.
43.	Isa. vi. 9, 10.		{ John xii. 40. (and see Matt xiii. 14, 15 Mark iv 12. Luke viii. 10. Acts xxviii. 26.) }
57.	Gen. xv. 13, 14.		Acts vii. 6, 7
58.	Gen. xlvi. 27		Acts vii. 14.
68	Amos ix 11, 12.		Acts xv. 16, 17.
103.	Isa xxix 10.		Rom xi 8.
168.	(Gen. vi. 35. ?)		James iv 5.

V. *Quotations that are taken from several passages of Scripture.*

Sometimes there is such a change made in the quotation, that it is not easy to ascertain from what particular passage of the Old Testament it is taken. The instances of this description, however, in which the citation is made from *several* passages of Scripture, are very few. Dr. Randolph has mentioned only three, to which we have added two others.

63.	(See Psal lxxxix 20. and 1 Sam. xiii. 14)	compared with	Acts xiii 22.
94.	Isa. xxviii. 16. and viii. 14.		Rom. ix. 33
103.	Isa xxix 10. (and see Isa. vi 9. and Ezek. xii. 2.)		Rom xi 8
82.	Zech ix. 9. (and see Isa. lxii. 11.)		Matt. xxi. 5.
50.	Psal lxxi 26. and cix. 8.		Acts i. 20.

To this head also we may perhaps refer the quotation, No. 5. p. 206. relative to the Messiah being called a Nazarene

VI. *Quotations differing from the Hebrew, but agreeing with the Septuagint.*

18	Isa xxix 13.	compared with	Matt. xv 8, 9.
52	Psal. xvi. 8—11.		Acts ii 25—28.
60.	Amos v. 25—27.		Acts vii. 42, 43.
65.	Isa. lv. 3.		Acts xiii 34.
98.	Psal. xix. 5. (4. of English Version)		Rom x. 18.
169.	Prov. iii. 34.		James iv. 6.

VI. Sect. II. § 2.] *Septuagint Version in the New Testament.* 251

VII. *Quotations in which there is reason to suspect a different reading in the Hebrew, or that the Apostles understood the words in a sense different from that expressed in our Lexicons.*

No.	Chap. and Verse of O. T.		Chap. and Verse of N. T.
2.	Micah v. 2.	compared with	Matt. ii. 6.
14.	Mal. iii. 1.	-	Matt. xi. 10. Mark i. 2. Luke vii. 27.
35.	Isa. lxi. 1, 2.	-	Luke iv. 18, 19
62.	Isa. liii. 7, 8.	-	Acts viii. 32, 33.
66	Hab. i. 5.	-	Acts xiii. 41
68.	Amos ix. 11, 12.	-	Acts xv. 16, 17.
77	Psal. x. 7	-	Rom. iii. 14.
98.	Psal. xix. 5	-	Rom. x, 18
105	Isa. lix. 20, 21	-	Rom. xi. 26, 27
106.	Deut. xxxii. 35.	-	Rom. xii. 19
112.	Deut. xxxii. 16.	-	Rom. xv. 10.
116.	Isa. lxiv. 3.	-	1 Cor. ii. 9
161.	Hab. ii. 3, 4	-	Heb. x. 37, 38.
172.	Isa. xxviii. 16	-	1 Pet. ii. 6.

VIII. *Passages in which the Hebrew seems to be corrupted.*

2.	Micah v. 2.	compared with	Matt. ii. 6.
14.	Mal. iii. 1.	-	Matt. xi. 10 Mark i. 2. Luke vii. 27.
52.	Psal. xvi. 8—11	-	Acts ii. 25—28.
68.	Amos ix. 11, 12.	-	Acts xv. 16, 17
159.	Psal. xl. 7—9.	-	Heb. x. 5—7

IX. *Passages which are not properly Citations, but mere References or Allusions.*

39.	Isa. xii. 3	alluded to in	John vii. 38
96	Deut. xxx. 12—14.	-	Rom. v. 6—8.
122.	Deut. xxxii 17	-	1 Cor. x. 20
129.	Hos. xiii. 14	-	1 Cor. xv. 55.
137.	Deut. xix. 15.	-	2 Cor. xiii. 1.
167	Hos. xiv. 3.	-	Heb. xiii. 15.

To this class also we may most probably refer the allusions in 2 Cor. vi. 18. See p. 235. and note.

§ 2. CLASSIFICATION OF THE QUOTATIONS FROM THE SEPTUAGINT VERSION IN THE NEW TESTAMENT.

ALTHOUGH the sacred authors of the New Testament have in many instances quoted from the Hebrew Scriptures, as the preceding tables have shown; yet it is equally certain that they have very frequently made their citations from the Greek version usually denominated the Septuagint, even where this translation from the Hebrew is inaccurate, but where the errors are of such a nature as *not* to weaken the proofs for which they were alleged. In fact, as the apostles

wrote for the use of communities who were ignorant of Hebrew, it was necessary that they should refer to the Greek version, which was generally known and read. Had they given a new and more accurate translation according to the Hebrew, citing as they often did from memory, the reader would not have known what passage they intended to quote: and if, on the other hand, while they retained the words of the Septuagint, they had taken notice of each inaccuracy, they would have diverted the reader's attention from the main object to the consideration of trifles. It must, however, be remarked, that the writers of the New Testament appear to have been so careful to give the true sense of the Old Testament, that they forsook the Septuagint version, whenever it did not give that sense, so far as they had occasion to cite it, and these citations often correspond with the present Hebrew text. The quotations from the Septuagint in the New Testament may be classed under the five following heads: —
I. Such as agree verbatim with the Septuagint, or only change the person, number, &c.; — II. Quotations taken from the Septuagint, but with some variation, — III Quotations agreeing with the Septuagint in sense, but not in words; — IV. Quotations differing from the Septuagint, but agreeing exactly, or nearly, with the Hebrew; — and, V. Quotations which differ both from the Septuagint and from the Hebrew, and are probably taken from some other translation or paraphrase.

I. *Quotations agreeing verbatim with the Septuagint, or only changing the person, number, &c.*

No.	Chap. and Verse of O T.				Chap. and Verse of N. T.
7	Deut. viii. 3.		agrees with		Matt. iv 4. Luke iv 4.
9.	Deut. vi. 16.	-	-	-	Matt. iv 7
13.	Hos vi. 6	-	-	.	Matt ix. 13 xii 17.
20.	Exod. xx. 12—16.		-	-	Matt. xix 18, 19
21.	Lev xix. 18	-	-	-	Matt. xix. 19, xxii. 39
23.	Psal viii 2		-	-	Matt. xxi. 16.
24.	Psal. cxviii. 22, 23.		-	-	{ Matt xxi 42. Mark xii 10. Luke xx. 17. Acts iv. 11.
25.	Exod. iii 6.	-	-	-	Matt. xxii. 32. Mark xii. 26. Luke xx.37
27.	Psal. cx 1.	-	-	-	Matt. xxii. 44. Mark xii 36. Luke xx. 42.
28.	Zech xiii 7	-	-	-	Matt. xxvi. 31.
30.	Psal. xxi 18.		-	-	Matt. xxvii. 35. John xix. 24.
36.	Psal. lxviii 9.		-	-	John ii. 17.
40.	Psal. lxxxii. 6.		-	-	John x. 34.
42.	Isa. liii. 1.	-	-	-	John xii. 38.
49	Psal. cix. 8.		-	-	Acts i 20.
52.	Psal xvi 8—11.		-	-	Acts ii. 25—28.
55.	Psal. ii 1, 2.	-	-	-	Acts iv. 25, 26.
58	Gen. xlvi. 27.		-	-	Acts vii. 14
64.	Psal ii. 7.	-	-	-	Acts xiii. 33.
67.	Isa xlix. 6.	-	-	-	Acts xiii 47.
69.	Exod xxii. 28		-	-	Acts xxiii. 5.
72.	Psal li. 4.		-	-	Rom. iii 4
75.	Psal. v. 9	-	-	-	Rom. iii 13
76.	Psal cxxxix. 3. (cxl. 3. of English Bible)				Rom. iii 13
77.	Psal. x. 7.	-	-	-	Rom. iii 14.
79.	Psal. xxxv. 1. (xxxvi. 1. of English Bible)				Rom. iii. 18.
78.	Gen. xv. 6.		-	.	Rom. iv 3.
80.	Psal. xxxii. 1, 2.		-	-	Rom. iv. 7, 8

No	Chap and Verse of O. T.				Chap and Verse of N. T.
81.	Gen xvii 5.	-	agrees with		Rom. iv 17.
82.	Gen. xv. 5.	-	-	-	Rom. iv 18.
83	Psal xliv 22		-	-	Rom. viii 36.
84.	Gen xxi 12.	-	-	-	Rom ix 7.
86	Gen. xxv 3	-	-	-	Rom ix 12.
87	Mal i. 2, 3		-	-	Rom. ix 13.
88	Exod. xxxiii 19			-	Rom. ix 15
91	Hos i. 10.	-	-	-	Rom ix. 26.
93.	Isa i. 9.	-		-	Rom ix 29
95	Lev xviii 5.	-	-	-	Rom x 5
98.	Psal xix 4	-	-	-	Rom x 18
99.	Deut xxxii. 21.		-	-	Rom x 19
100	Isa lxv 1, 2	-	-	-	Rom x 20, 21.
107	Prov. xxv 21, 22		-	-	Rom xii 20.
109	Psal lxix 9.	-	-	-	Rom. xv. 3.
110	Psal xviii 49.		-	-	Rom xv. 9
111	Deut xxxii 43.	-	-	-	Rom. xv. 10.
112	Psal cxvii 1		-	-	Rom. xv 11.
114.	Isa lii 15	-	-	-	Rom xv 21.
120	Deut. xxxv. 4.	-	-	-	1 Cor. ix. 9
121	Exod. xxxii 6		-	-	1 Cor x 7
123.	Psal xxiv 1	-	-	-	1 Cor x 26
125.	Psal viii. 6.		-	-	1 Cor xv 27.
126	Isa. xxii. 13.	-	-	-	1 Cor xv 32
130.	Psal. cxvi 10	-	-	-	2 Cor iv 13.
131	Isa. xlix 8	-	-	-	2 Cor vi 2
136.	Psal cxii 9.	-	-	-	2 Cor ix 9
141	Isa liv 1	-	-	-	Gal iv 27.
145	2 Sam. vii 14	-	-	-	Heb i 5.
145*	Deut xxxii 43.		-	-	Heb. i 6
146.	Psal civ 4		-	-	Heb. i. 7.
147.	Psal. xlv. 6, 7.	-	-	-	Heb i. 8, 9
148.	Psal. cii 25—27.		-	-	Heb i 10—12
149.	Psal viii. 4—6	-	-	-	Heb ii 6—8.
153.	Gen ii 3	-	-	-	Heb iv 4
154	Psal cx 4	-	-	-	Heb v. 6.
155	Gen xxii. 16, 17.		-	-	Heb vi. 13, 14.
160.	Deut. xxxii 36	-	-	-	Heb x 30.
161.	Hab ii. 3, 4.	-	-	-	Heb. x 37, 38.
162	Gen. xlvii 31		-	-	Heb xi 21
163	Prov iii 11.	-	-	-	Heb xii. 5.
164	Deut xxxi 8		-	-	Heb xiii 5
166	Psal cxviii 6	-	-	-	Heb. xiii 6.
167	Hos xiv 2.	-	-	-	Heb xiii 15.
173	Exod xix 6	-	-	-	1 Pet ii 9.
175.	Isa liii 5	-	-	-	1 Pet. ii 24
176	Psal xxxiv 12—16.		-	-	1 Pet. iii. 10—12.

II. *Quotations taken from the Septuagint, but with some Variation.*

These variations, however, are immaterial, consisting occasionally, — 1. Of additions of words, to render the sense more explicit to the Gentiles, — 2. Of omissions of words, where the insertion of them was not necessary to prove the point for which they were adduced; — 3. Of synonymous changes, substituting other words of the same import for the exact words of the Septuagint, — which might easily be done, citing, as the Apostles sometimes did, from memory; — 4. Of transpositions of words; — 5. Of changes of proper names into appellatives; — and, 6. Of occasional alterations in the

254 *Classification of Quotations from the* [Part I. Ch.

divisions of sentences. But in all these sentences the sense is invariably given.

No.	Chap. and Verse of O. T.		Chap and Verse of N. T
1.	Isa. vii 14.	compared with	Matt. i 23
8	Psal. xci. 11, 12.	-	Matt iv 6.
10.	Deut. vi. 13.	-	Matt iv 10.
16.	Isa vi. 9—11.	-	Matt xiii 14, 15 Acts xxviii 26, 27. Mark iv. 12. Luke viii. 10.
18	Isa xxix. 13.	-	Matt xv. 8, 9.
19.	Gen. ii 24	-	Matt. xix 5.
29.	Zech xi 13	-	Matt xxvii 9, 10.
35	Isa lxi 1, 2.	-	Luke iv 18, 19.
37	Psal. lxxviii. 24.	-	John vi. 31.
47.	Exod. xii 46.	-	John xix 36.
51.	Joel ii 28—32.	-	Acts ii. 17—21.
54.	Gen. xxii 18	-	Acts iii 25.
56.	Gen 12. 1	-	Acts vii. 3.
60.	Amos v 25, 26.	-	Acts vii. 42, 43.
62	Isa. liii. 7.	-	Acts viii. 32, 33.
65.	Isa lv 3.	-	Acts xiii 34.
70.	Hab. ii. 4.	-	Rom. i 17
71.	Isa lii. 5.	-	Rom. ii. 24
74	Psal xiv 1—3.	-	Rom. iii 10—12.
84.	Exod. ix. 16.	-	Rom. ix. 17
94.	Isa. viii 44. xxviii. 16	-	Rom. ix 33.
104.	Psal lxix 22, 23.	-	Rom xi. 9, 10.
105.	Isa lix 20, 21.	-	Rom xi. 26, 27.
113.	Isa. xi. 10	-	Rom xv. 12
115.	Isa. xxix. 14	-	1 Cor i 19.
117.	Isa xl 13	-	1 Cor ii. 16
119.	Psal. xciv. 11.	-	1 Cor iii 20.
122.	Deut. xxxii 17.	-	1 Cor. x 20
127.	Gen ii. 7.	-	1 Cor. xv. 45
129.	Hos xiii 14.	-	1 Cor xv. 55
132.	Lev xxvi. 11, 12	-	2 Cor. vi 16
135.	Exod. xvi. 18	-	2 Cor. viii 15.
137.	Deut. xix. 15.	-	2 Cor. xiii 1
138.	Gen xii 3 xviii. 18.	-	Gal iii 8
142.	Gen. xxi 10.	-	Gal iv 30.
144	Exod xx. 12.	-	Eph vi 2, 3.
150	Psal xxii 22	-	Heb ii 12.
151.	Isa. viii. 17, 18.	-	Heb. ii. 13
152.	Psal xcv. 7—11	-	Heb iii 7—10.
156.	Exod xxv 40.	-	Heb viii. 5
159.	Psal. xl. 6—9.	-	Heb x 5—7.
169.	Prov. iii 34.	-	James iv. 6.
171.	Isa. xl. 6—8	-	1 Pet i. 24, 25
172.	Isa xxviii 16.	-	1 Pet. ii 6.
174.	Isa liii 9	-	1 Pet. ii. 22
177.	Isa. viii 12, 13.	-	1 Pet. iii. 14, 15.

III. *Quotations agreeing with the Septuagint in* SENSE *but* NOT *in Words.*

4.	Jer xxxi 15	agrees in sense, but not in words, with	Matt ii 18.
6	Isa xl 3—5.	-	Matt. iii. 3 Mark i. 3. Luke iii. 4—6.
17.	Psal lxxviii. 2	-	Matt xiii 35.
26.	Deut. vi 5.	-	Matt xxii. 37. Mark xii 30 Luke x. 27.
32.	Isa. liii. 12.	-	Mark xv 28. Luke xxii. 37.
33.	Exod. xiii. 2.	-	Luke ii 23.
34.	Lev. xii. 8.	-	Luke ii. 24.

No.	Chap. and Verse of O. T.				Chap. and Verse of N. T.
38	Isa. liv 13	{agrees in sense, but not in words, with}			John vi. 45.
41	Zech. ix 9	-	-	-	John xii. 15.
44	Psal. xli 9	-	-	-	John xiii. 18.
45	Psal. cix. 8.	-	-	-	John xv. 25.
48	Zech. xii 10.	-	-	-	John xix 37.
50	Psal. lxix 25.		-	-	Acts i 20
53	Deut. xviii 15, 19.		-	-	Acts iii 22, 23.
57	Gen xv. 13, 14.		-	-	Acts vii. 6, 7.
61	Isa lxii. 1, 2.	-	-	-	Acts vii 49, 50.
68	Amos ix. 11, 12.		-	-	Acts xv. 16, 17.
78	Isa lix 7, 8		-		Rom iii. 15—17.
85	Gen xviii 10.		-		Rom ix 9.
90	Hos. ii 23.			-	Rom. ix. 25.
92	Isa x 22, 23		-	-	Rom. ix 27, 28.
101	1 Kings xix 14.		-		Rom. xi. 3
103	Isa xxix 10.		-	-	Rom xi 8.
108	Isa xlv 23.		-	-	Rom. xiv 11
118	Job v 13.	-	-	-	1 Cor iii 19.
133	Isa. liii 11, 12.		-	-	2 Cor. vi, 17.
139	Deut. xxvii.27. (26 of English Version)				Gal. iii. 10
140	Deut. xxi. 23		-	-	Gal. iii 13.
157	Jer. xxxi 31—34.		-	-	Heb. viii. 8—12.
158	Exod xxiv 8.		-	-	Heb. ix 20.
165	Hag ii 6.	-	-	-	Heb xii. 26.
179	Psal. ii. 9.	-	-	-	Rev. ii 27.

IV. *Quotations differing from the Septuagint, but agreeing exactly, or nearly, with the Hebrew.*

There are several instances of an evidently *intentional* renunciation of the Septuagint version, in order to adhere to the Hebrew original: these instances occur when the Septuagint so materially differs from the Hebrew, as to render the passage unsuitable to the purpose for which the sacred writer produced the quotation, or where it is palpably erroneous. The number of these departures from the Septuagint is *eleven*, viz.

3.	Hos. xi 1.	-	cited in	Matt. ii. 15
4	Jer xxxi 15.	-	-	Matt. ii 18
12	Isa liii 4	-	-	Matt. viii. 17.
22.	Zech. ix. 9.	-	-	Matt. xxi. 5.
31.	Psal xxii 1.	-	-	Matt. xxvii. 46.
95.	Isa lii 7.	-	-	Rom. x. 15
102.	1 Kings xix 18.	-	-	Rom. xi 4
118.	Job v. 13	-	-	1 Cor iii. 19
128	Isa xxv. 8.	-	-	1 Cor xv. 54.
170.	Lev xi. 44.	-	-	1 Pet. i. 16.
178.	Prov. x. 12.	-	-	1 Pet. iv. 8.

V. *Quotations which differ both from the Septuagint and from the Hebrew, and are probably taken from some other translation, or paraphrase, or were so rendered by the sacred writers themselves.*

2.	Micah v 2.	-	cited in	Matt. ii 6.
6.	Isa xl. 3—5.	-	-	Matt. iii 3. Mark i 3. Luke iii. 4—6.
11.	Isa. ix. 1, 2.	-	-	Matt. iv. 15, 16

No.	Chap. and Verse of O. T.				Chap and Verse of N. T.
14.	Mal. in. 1.	-	cited in		Matt. xi 10 Mark i 2. Luke vii. 27.
15.	Isa. xlii. 1—4.	-	-	-	Matt xii. 18—21.
41.	Zech. ix. 9.				John xii. 15.
53.	Deut xviii. 15. 19.		-	-	Acts iii. 22, 23
66	Hab. i 5.	-	-	-	Acts xiii 41.
85	Gen. xviii. 10		-	-	Rom. ix 9.
90.	Hos li. 23.		-	-	Rom ix 25.
92	Isa x. 22, 23.		-	-	Rom ix, 27, 28
96	Deut. xxx. 12—14.		-	-	Rom. x. 6—8
101	1 Kings xix. 14.		-	-	Rom. xi. 3.
106	Deut. xxxii. 35.				Rom. xii. 19. (and see Heb. x 30.)
116.	Isa lxiv 4	-	-	-	1 Cor ii 9.
124.	Isa. xxviii. 11, 12.		-	-	1 Cor xiv. 21.
139	Deut xxvii. 27			-	Gal iii 10
143	Psal. lxviii 18.		-	-	Eph. iv, 8.
158.	Exod. xxiv 8.	-	-	-	Heb ix. 20.

§ 3. CONSIDERATIONS ON THE PROBABLE CAUSES OF THE SEEMING DISCREPANCIES IN THE QUOTATIONS FROM THE OLD TESTAMENT IN THE NEW.

ON a comparison of the quotations from the Old Testament in the New, it is obvious that in the *Epistles*, which were addressed generally to churches consisting of converted Hellenists (that is Greek Jews), or Gentiles, or of both, the quotations are uniformly made from the Septuagint version, or with express reference to it, except where some important reason induced the sacred writer to deviate from it: for the Septuagint was the only version generally known in those churches, whose members were mostly strangers to the Hebrew. There are, however, some apparent contradictions in the quotations from the Old Testament in the New, the reconciliation of which has much engaged the attention of learned men, who have assigned various causes to account for, or explain such discrepancies. These it may be useful briefly to consider, before we discuss the mode in which the sacred writers of the New Testament apply their quotations from the Old Testament. The causes of the differences in these quotations may be reduced to three, viz. 1. Sophistications or corruptions of the Hebrew text;— 2. Various Readings, or differences in copies;—and, 3. Our ignorance of the correct meaning of particular texts.

1. The instances of *Sophistication*, or corruption of the Hebrew text, are comparatively few, and are only nine in number, as we have already seen[1]; the comparison of manuscripts and versions alone can enable the critic to determine the true reading.

2. *Various Readings* in the manuscript copies of the Greek Bible, used by the sacred writers of the New Testament, are another cause of the apparent contradictions in the quotations made in it from the Old Testament; and these manuscripts might differ from those which we have at present. Professor Michaelis likewise thinks

---

[1] See § VIII. p 251. *supra*

it possible that, in those cases where the quotations are materially different, another translation might have been added in the Septuagint as a marginal note, in the same manner as we find in the Hexapla of Origen, under the name of αλλος. The Proverbs of Solomon, he observes, present instances where the same Hebrew words are twice translated; which can be explained on no other supposition, than that one of them was originally a marginal note, which has insensibly crept into the text itself.[1]

3. Another cause of the apparent discrepancy occurring in the quotations from the Old Testament in the New, may arise from our not understanding particular Hebrew texts or words: a few such instances have already been noticed.[2] But this is only a temporary cause — the researches of commentators and critics (which the preceding tables have tended to confirm) have shown that the writers of the New Testament express the true sense, though not the sense generally attributed to the Hebrew: and in proportion as such researches are more diligently prosecuted, and our knowledge of the original languages of the Scriptures is increased, these difficulties will gradually and certainly diminish.

4. It is further to be observed that the very same quotations are often *contracted* by some of the evangelists and as often enlarged by others. This difference in quoting may be accounted for by the different occasions on which they are introduced, and the different ends which they were intended to serve. Thus Luke, who wrote his Gospel for the instruction of *Gentile* converts, quotes (iii. 4—6.) not less than *three* verses from the prophet Isaiah[3]; while Matthew (iii. 3.) and Mark (i. 3.) quote only the *first* of them. But it was necessary to Luke's purpose that he should proceed so far, in order to assure the Gentiles, that they were destined to be partakers of the privileges of the Gospel, and to *see the salvation of God*. On the other hand, Matthew (xiii. 14, 15.) and Paul (Acts xxviii. 26, 27.) when reproving the Jews for their incredulity, which Isaiah had long before predicted, introduced the prophecy at full length, whereas Mark (iv. 11, 12.) and Luke (viii. 10.) only refer to it briefly. Mark, whose Gospel was written for a mixed society of Jewish and Gentile converts, has many peculiarities belonging to him, which are not specified by the other evangelists. Of these peculiarities, we have an instance in his manner of citing the passage of Isaiah just noticed. The verse in his Gospel runs thus:

Τοις εξω εν παραβολαις τα παντα γινεται· Ἱνα βλεποντες βλεπωσι, και μη ιδωσι, και ακουοντες ακουωσι, και μη συνιωσι, μηποτε επιστρεψωσι, και αφεθη αυτοις τα ἁμαρτηματα. *Unto them that are without all these things are done in parables: That seeing, they may see and not perceive; and hearing, they may hear and not understand; lest at any time they should be converted, and their sins should be forgiven them.*

In order to engage the Jews the more effectually to adopt and obey his Gospel, Mark has not only inserted in it more Hebrew or rather

---

[1] Marsh's Michaelis, vol. 1. p. 235.
[2] See § 2. VII. p. 251. *supra.*
[3] See the passages of Isaiah and Luke at length, in p 206. No. 6.

Syro-Chaldaic phrases than all the other evangelists together, but in the verse here given, he has forsaken both the Hebrew and Greek of Isa. vi. 11. (in our translation truly rendered *and I will heal them*[1]), and has quoted the Chaldee Paraphrase, which he translated for himself, και αφεθη αυτοις τα αμαρτηματα, *and their sins should be forgiven them;* and which thus probably became more intelligible to the Gentiles also. Now these particular variations are so far from being disparagements to the Gospels, that they are in reality the excellencies and ornaments of them. They are such variations only, as these different converts, of different conceptions, required to have made, for their obtaining a true and right knowledge of the Old Testament prophecies.[2] A similar mode of citation is pursued by the illustrious apostle, Paul, who does not mention or allege the law and the Prophets in one and the same manner to Jews and Gentiles. Thus, to Felix the Roman governor, he says of himself (Acts xxiv. 14.) *Believing all things which are written in the law and the prophets.* But to king Agrippa (xxvi. 22.) *Saying none other things than those which the prophets and Moses did say should come.* And thus he distinguishes in his Epistles. In that to the Hebrews are many passages from the Old Testament, but not a single instance in which it is quoted as *written.* But in his other Epistles he rarely uses any other form than, *It is written,* or *The Scripture saith.* Thus he cites it to the Romans; the chief variations from which mode to that of *He saith*, are in the three chapters, ix. x. xi. which principally relate to the Jews; and even there he seldom fails to name the prophet whose words are adduced. To the Galatians, and in both Epistles to the Corinthians, with one or two exceptions, he urges the words of the Old Testament as *written.* To the Philippians, Colossians, and Thessalonians, if we mistake not, he makes no direct quotation from it. In the Epistle to the Ephesians he refers to it twice, and there indeed in both places under the form of *He saith.* But he himself had spent above two years in teaching them with the utmost diligence and attention (Acts xix. 8. 10.), and wrote his Epistle to them some years after; when he might have full assurance that he spoke to those *who knew the law.* A passage in this epistle, compared with a similar one in that to the Colossians, seems to prove that he made a difference between them, and judged the Ephesians to be better versed in the sacred books. To these he proposes the precept of obedience to parents with a view to the Mosaic promise: (Eph. vi. 1—3.) *Children, obey your parents in the Lord; for this is right.* HONOUR THY FATHER AND MOTHER; WHICH IS THE FIRST COMMANDMENT WITH PROMISE. But he omits this reference to the words of the Decalogue, in giving the same precept to the Colossians; with whose proficiency in the Scriptures he was less acquainted, as having never been among them. He says only (Col. iii. 20.) *Children obey your parents in all things, for this is well pleasing unto the Lord.*

Thus we see that St. Paul has one mode of citing the Old Testament to the Hebrews, and another to the churches of which the

---

[1] See the passages of Isaiah and of the Evangelists cited, in p. 209 No 16
[2] Dr Owen, on the Modes of Quotation used by the Evangelical Writers, pp. 85—8 7

Gentiles were members; that in the former case he agrees with Matthew, in the latter with Mark and Luke. And in this respect there is so much uniformity in the Apostle and two Evangelists, that we may justly conclude, it was not accidental, but designed by him and them, for the same purpose of suiting their style to the small measure of scriptural knowledge which they might well suppose many of their readers to possess. By which means the unlearned or newly converted Gentiles were instructed, that what was offered to them as the word of God *which came in old time*, was to be found in the books of Scripture; and, if Judaisers crept in and perplexed them with doctrines of an oral or traditionary law, they were furnished with this reply to such teachers: "When the Apostles and Evangelists, who have been our more immediate guides, propose to us any part of the Mosaic economy, they allege only what is *written*, and what they carefully inform us to be so."[1]

We have dwelt the longer on this subject, not only on account of its importance in illustrating the external form of the quotations of the Old Testament by the Evangelists and Apostles, but also because it furnishes us with an additional instance of those simple notes of authenticity, with which the New Testament abounds, and which the genius of forgery could *never* have devised.

Upon the whole, then, as it respects the external form of quotations from the Old Testament, it may be observed that the writers of the New Testament did not make it a *constant* rule to cite from the Greek version, because there are many places in which their quotations differ from that version, and agree with the Hebrew.[2] And as their quotations now correspond with the Hebrew, very frequently in express words[3], and generally in the sense[4]; so it is highly probable that they uniformly agreed at first, and that, where the Hebrew was properly expressed in the Greek version, they used the words of that version. But where it materially varied from the meaning of the Hebrew Scriptures, they either gave the sense of the passage cited in their own words; or took as much of the Septuagint as suited their purpose, introducing the requisite alterations. Hence several passages are neither direct quotations from the Hebrew text, nor quotations from the Septuagint[5]; and some, as we have already seen, agree with the latter even where it varies from the former, but only where the deviation does not so affect the meaning of the passage as to interfere with the pertinency of the quotation for the purpose intended. "All this accords to what ordinary writers, in similar circumstances, would have done, and, in fact, have been authorised to do: but the sacred penmen, being themselves divinely inspired, might take liberties which we must not; because their comments were equally the *Word of God* with the texts commented on."[6]

---

[1] Dr. Townson's Discourses on the Four Gospels, disc. 4. sect. ii. (Works, vol. i. pp. 101, 102.)
[2] See § 3. IV. p. 255. *supra*.   [3] See § 2. I. and II. pp. 247—249 *supra*.
[4] See § 3 III, IV. pp. 249, 250. *supra*.   [5] See § 3 V. p. 255, 256 *supra*.
[6] The Rev. T. Scott, on the Authority of the Septuagint, in the Christian Observer for 1810, vol. ix. p. 102.

SECTION II.

ON THE INTERNAL FORM OF QUOTATIONS, OR THE MODE IN WHICH CITATIONS FROM THE OLD TESTAMENT ARE APPLIED IN THE NEW.

General Observations on the Rabbinical and other modes of quoting the Old Testament — Classification of the Quotations in the New Testament · — I. Quotations from the Old Testament in the New, in which the predictions are literally accomplished ; — II. Quotations in which that is said to have been done, of which the Scriptures have not spoken in a literal but in a spiritual sense ; — III. Quotations made by the Sacred Writers in the way of Illustration ; — IV. Quotations and other passages from the Old Testament which are alluded to in the New.

IN considering the passages of the Old Testament, which have been introduced by the apostles and evangelists into the writings of the New, "there is often a difficulty with respect to the *application* of such quotations; when they are applied to a purpose to which they seem to have no relation, according to their original design. This difficulty arises from the writers of the New Testament making quotations from the Old with very different views: and it can be removed only by attending to their real view in a particular quotation." An accurate distinction, therefore, must be made between such quotations as, being merely borrowed, are used as the words of the writer himself, and such as are quoted in proof of a doctrine, or the completion of a prophecy.

Michaelis[1] has remarked, that whenever a book is the subject of our daily reading, it is natural that its phrases should occur to us in writing — sometimes with a perfect recollection of the places whence they are taken, and at other times when the places themselves have totally escaped our memory. Thus, the lawyer quotes the maxims of the law · the scholar, his favorite classics; and the divine, the precepts of the Gospel. It is no wonder, therefore, if the same has happened to the writers of the New Testament; who being daily occupied in the study of the Old Testament, unavoidably adopted its modes of expression, and especially of the Greek Septuagint, which they have borrowed, and applied to their own use in various ways and for various purposes.

The quotations from the Old Testament in the New are generally introduced by certain formulæ, such as, *That it might be fulfilled — As it is written — Isaiah prophesied*, &c.; and various rules have been framed in order to account for their application. It has been observed by the same great philologist, that the writers of the New Testament quote in general like the Rabbins, without mentioning the place whence the quotation is taken; as they pre-suppose the reader to be so well acquainted with the Old Testament, as to be able to find it without particular direction. The Rabbins select some principal word out of each section, and apply that name to the

---

[1] Introduction to the New Testament, vol. i. pp. 200—203.

section itself, in the same manner as the Mohammedans distinguish the *suras* or chapters of their Koran, saying, in Eli, in Solomon, when they intend to signify the sections where those names are mentioned. For instance, Rashi, in his remarks on Hosea ix. 9. (*They have deeply corrupted* themselves, *as in the days of Gibeah*), says — "Some are of opinion that this is Gibeah of Benjamin *in the concubine*," that is, is mentioned in the chapter of the concubine, or Judges xix. And in this manner quotations are sometimes made in the New Testament. Thus, in Mark xii. 26. and Luke xx. 37. επι της βατου (*in* or *at* the bush), signifies, "in the section relating to the burning bush," which, according to the modern division, is the third chapter of Exodus. Again, in Rom. xi. 2. εν Ηλια (in Elias) signifies "in the section in which the actions of Elias are recorded;" which at present forms the seventeenth, eighteenth, and nineteenth chapters of the first book of Kings.[1]

Another very frequent practice of the Rabbins was, to produce only the initial words of a quoted passage, while those are omitted in which the force of the argument consists, or the absence of which destroys the connection. Of this description are the quotations in Rom. vii. 7. and xiii. 9. (Thou shalt not covet), in which the Apostle leaves us to supply the following words contained in Exod. xx. 17. *Thou shalt not covet thy neighbour's wife*, &c. Similar instances are to be found in Rom. xi. 27. and Heb. ii. 13.[2]

The formulæ (*as it is written, that it might be fulfilled, it hath been said*, &c. &c.) with which the quotations in the New Testament are generally introduced, have been supposed by Surenhusius[3], (to whose learned researches biblical students are most deeply indebted) to be the indications of the modes in which they are expressed; so that by attending to these formulæ, we may easily know why the evangelists allege the subsequent words in one certain manner rather than in another; and why they depart more or less from the Hebrew text. Agreeably to this hypothesis Surenhusius has, with infinite labour and industry, collected a great variety of rules[4] out of the Talmud

---

[1] Michaelis, vol. i pp. 243, 244. 133, 134. 492. Upon the same rule, Michaelis thinks the supposed contradiction between Mark ii 26 and 1 Sam. xxi 1 may be explained "in the chapter of Abiathar," or, in that part of the books of Samuel in which the history of Abiathar is related This explanation, Rosenmuller very justly remarks, would be preferable to any other, if Mark had added the expression *it is written*, or *the Scripture saith*. Scholia in N T tom 1. p 579. edit 1801. See also Kuinoel on Mark ii. 26. Comm. in Libros N. T. Historicos, tom. ii. p 32.

[2] Michaelis, vol. I pp. 244—246

[3] In the preface to his "Βιβλος Καταλλαγης in quo, secundum veterum Theologorum Hebræorum Formulas allegandi et modos interpretandi, conciliantur loca ex Veteri in Novo Testamento allegata." 4to. Amst. 1713 The words of Professor Surenhusius are as follow "*Etenim omni in loco ex V T in N. allegato recte conciliando, videndum est prius, quâ allegandi formulâ utantur Apostoli; ex qua statim dignoscere licet, quare sequentia verba hoc, et non alio modo, allegaverit, atque ad veterem Scripturam Hebræam plusve minusve attenderint. Sic alium sensum involvit illa allegandi formula* Ερρηθη; *alium* Γεγραπται; *alium, ινα πληρωθη το ρηθεν, alium* Επληρωθη η γραφη, &c.

[4] The following are the principal *theses* or rules laid down by Surenhusius, whose work, it may be proper to remark, deserves a place in the library of every biblical student, on account of its learned illustration of many passages of Scripture not immediately connected with the quotations from the Old Testament.

1. Sometimes the words are read, not according to the regular vowel-points, but agree-

and the Rabbinical writings, and has illustrated them with numerous extracts, in order to explain and justify all the quotations made from the Old Testament in the New. But what militates against this hypothesis is, that we find, that the very *same quotations*, expressed in the same words, and brought to prove the very same points, are introduced by *different* formulæ in different gospels. A further objection to the rules adduced by Surenhusius, is their number and their complexity, which render it difficult to refer all the quotations accurately to them. It is therefore not only more convenient, but more intrinsically useful, to refer the citations from the Old Testament in the New to the four following classes, which have been adopted, with some alteration, from Rosenmuller [1], after Gusset and Wolfius. According to these critics, the phrases, *that it might be fulfilled, as it is written*, &c. &c. may be properly applied in the New Testament, —

I. When the thing predicted is literally *accomplished*.

II. When that is done, of which the Scripture has spoken, not in a literal, but in a spiritual sense.

III. When a thing is done, neither in a literal nor in a spiritual sense, according to the fact referred to in the Scriptures; but is similar to that fact. The passages thus cited may, briefly, be termed quotations in the way of illustration.

---

ably to others substituted for them Instances of this sort, Surenhusius is of opinion, are to be found in Acts iii. 22, 23. and vii. 42, &c. 1 Cor xv. 54 and 2 Cor. viii. 15.

2. Sometimes letters are changed, as in Rom. ix. 33. 1 Cor ix 9, &c. Heb. viii. 9. and x 5.

3. Sometimes both letters and vowel-points are changed, as in Acts xiii 40, 41. and 2 Cor. viii. 15

4 Sometimes words are added from a parallel passage, or are changed in the quotation, which words appear as if the whole occurred in the cited text, as in Rom. xi. 3. xv. 10. 1 Cor. xv. 45. 2 Cor. vi. 16 Eph v. 14. and Heb xii. 12, 13.

5. Sometimes additional words are inserted to complete the sense, as in Matt. iv. 10. xxi. 5. John vi. 49. xii. 38. and Rom. x. 6

6. Sometimes several passages are abridged together, in order to make the subject more clear as in Matt. xxi 5. Luke iv 18, 19 John viii. 5, &c.

7. Sometimes the beginnings of verses are only added, for the sake of brevity, although the sacred writer refers to the whole passage, which he paraphrases. Instances of this sort occur in Acts i. 20. Rom xi. 27. Heb iii. and iv and x.

8. Some passages are cited, either allegorically, or by way of simple proof, in which case the subject cannot be proved, unless the passage cited be compared with others, and illustrated, as in Rom. ix. 12, 13. x 8. and Heb. iv. 5, 6.

9. Sometimes one and the same passage is cited to prove many things, and is applied to many persons, as in Matt. xiii 14. compared with John xii. 40. Rom. ix. 33. and x. 11. compared with 1 Pet. ii. 6.

10 Sometimes a subject is intended to be proved by several passages, though one only is adduced, the reader being left to find them out, as in Acts xv. 15, 16

11. The first and last clauses of a verse only are sometimes cited, the intermediate clauses being omitted. See Eph. v. 14., and 1 Pet. 1. 24, 25.

12. Sometimes a passage is simply adduced without any formula of quotation, and then another intervenes parenthetically, which being cited, the sacred writer returns to the first quoted passage, which is illustrated in a variety of particulars. Thus St. Paul, in Heb. iii. 7. first cites Psal xcv. 7., then he interposes references to Exod xvii. 2. Numb. ix. 13. xiv. 23. and Deut. i. 34 , and at length, in the 15th verse, he returns to Psal. xcv. 7.; which he explains, as if all the intermediately quoted passages were contained in one and the same text. Similar instances occur in Heb. iv. 15. and 1 Cor. iii. 7. Surenhusii Βιβλος Καταλλαγης, pp. 1—56.

[1] Scholia in Nov. Test. tom. i. p. 25.

IV. *When the sacred writers have made simple* allusions *to passages in the Old Testament.*[1]

In the following tables, the quotations are arranged under each class, to which they appear respectively to belong. Some of the references, perhaps, may be disputable; and in some, it is possible that the author may be mistaken: but as they are the result of a laborious and patient comparison of every prophecy or citation, in classifying which he could have but little assistance, he trusts he may be allowed to say, that he has exerted the best of his judgment, and to indulge the hope that he has not misapplied the quotations in any essential point.

I. *Of Quotations from the Old Testament in the New, in which the things predicted are* literally *accomplished.*

Direct prophecies are those which relate to Christ and the Gospel, and to them alone, and which cannot be taken in any other sense: and the Scripture is said to be *fulfilled* in the *literal sense*, when that event which it foretells is accomplished. The quotations from the Old Testament in the New, which belong to this class, are both numerous and highly important. Such are those which mention the calling of the Gentiles and the everlasting kingdom of Messiah: such also is the 110th Psalm, which, it has been well remarked, is as plain as a prophetic description ought to be. It is applicable to Christ alone, and it sets forth his exaltation, his royal dignity, his priestly office, the propagation of his Gospel, the obedience of his subjects, the destruction of his enemies, and of the Roman emperors who persecuted his church.[2]

Other examples of this description will be found in the following quotations, the references in which are made to the authorised English version of the Bible.[3]

Gen. xii 3 xviii. 18. xxii. 18. quoted in	Acts iii. 25. Gal. iii. 8.
Gen. xvii. 7. 19 xxii. 16, 17 — —	Luke i. 55. 72, 73, 74.
Deut. xviii 15 19. — — —	Acts iii 22, 23.
Psal. ii 1, 2. — — —	Acts iv 25, 26.
Psal. ii 7. — — —	Acts xiii 33 Heb i. 5. v. 5
Psal. viii 2 — — —	Matt xxi 16
Psal viii. 4—6 — —	Heb ii 6—8.
Psal xvi 8—11 — —	Acts ii 25—28 31.
Psal xvi 10 — —	Acts xiii 35.
Psal. xxii. 1 — —	Matt. xxvii 46. Mark xv 34.
Psal xxii. 18. — — —	{ Matt xxvii 35. Mark xv 24 Luke xxiii. 34 John xix. 24
Psal xxii 22. — — —	Heb ii 12
Psal. xxxi. 5 — — —	Luke xxiii 46.
Psal xli. 9 — — —	John xiii 18. Acts i. 16.
Psal. xlv 6, 7 — — —	Heb i 8, 9.
Psal lxviii. 18 — — —	Eph iv. 7, 8.
Psal. lxix. 21. — — —	{ John xix 28, 29. Matt. 27. 48. Mark xv. 36 and Luke xxiii. 36.

---

[1] The fourth class mentioned by Rosenmuller, Gusset, and Woltius, is as follows:— When that which has, in the Old Testament, been mentioned as formerly done, is accomplished, in a larger and more extensive sense, in the New Testament. But as the citations which appear to belong to this class may be referred to the first and third, we have substituted the preceding in lieu of it.

[2] Jortin's Remarks on Eccles. Hist. vol. i. p. 121, 2d edit. The best critical illustration of the prophetical sense of Psalm cx. is, perhaps, that given by Dr Gregory Sharpe, in his "Second Argument in Defence of Christianity, taken from the antient Prophecies," pp 275—311.

[3] As the passages from the prophetic writings have already been given at full length, they are here designedly omitted.

Psal. lxix 25. cix 8	quoted in	Acts i 20.
Psal. xcv. 7—11.		Heb iii. 7—11., iv 3. 5—7.
Psal. cii. 25—27		Heb. i. 10—12.
Psal. cx. 1.		{ Matt xxii. 44 Mark xii. 36 Luke xx 42. { Acts ii. 34, 35. Heb. i 13.
Psal. cx 4.		Heb v 6
Psal. cxviii. 22, 23.		{ Matt. xxi. 42. Mark xii. 10, 11 Luke xx. 17. { Acts iv 11
Psal. cxviii 25, 26.		Matt xxi 9 Mark xi. 9. John xii. 13.
Psal. cxxxii. 11. 17.		Luke i. 69. Acts ii. 30.
Isa. vii. 14.		Matt i 23.
Isa ix 1, 2.		Matt. iv. 15, 16.
Isa ix. 7. (with Dan. vii. 14. 27)		Luke i. 32, 33.
Isa. xi. 10.		Rom. xv. 12.
Isa. xxv 8.		1 Cor. xv. 54
Isa. xxvii. 9, and lix. 20, 21.		Rom xi. 26, 27.
Isa xxviii. 16. (with Joel ii. 32.)		Rom ix. 33. and 1 Pet ii. 5.
Isa. xl 3—5.		Matt. iii 3 Mark i 3 Luke iii. 4—6.
Isa xlii 1—4		Matt xii. 17—21.
Isa. xlix. 6.		Acts xiii 47, 48 and xxvi. 23 Luke ii. 32.
Isa liii. 1.		John xii. 38 Rom. x. 16
Isa. liii. 3—6.		Acts xxvi. 22, 23.
Isa liii 4—6 11.		1 Pet. ii 24, 25.
Isa. liii. 4		Matt viii 17.
Isa. liii 9		1 Pet ii 22.
Isa. liii. 12		Mark xv. 28. Luke xxii 37
Isa liv 13		John vi. 45.
Isa. lv. 3.		Acts xiii. 34.
Jer xxxi 31—34.		Heb. viii. 8—12 x. 16, 17.
Hosea i 10		Rom ix 26
Hosea ii. 23		Rom ix. 25. 1 Pet ii. 10.
Joel ii. 28—32.		Acts ii 16—21
Amos ix. 11, 12.		Acts xv 16, 17
Micah v. 2.		Matt. ii 5, 6. John vii. 42.
Habak i 5.		Acts xiii 40.
Haggai ii. 6.		Heb. xii 26
Zech ix 9		Matt. xxi. 4, 5 John xii 14 16.
Zech. xi. 13.		Matt. xxvii. 9, 10
Zech. xii 10.		John xix. 37.
Zech. xiii 7.		Matt xxvi 31. 56 Mark xiv. 27. 50.
Mal. iii. 1		Matt xi. 10. Mark i 2. Luke vii 27.
Mal. iv. 5, 6.		{ Matt. xi 13, 14. xvii 10—13. Mark ix. { 11—13. Luke i. 16, 17

II. *Of Quotations from the Old Testament in the New, in which that is said to have been done, of which the Scriptures have not spoken in a literal, but in a* spiritual *sense.*

There are citations out of the Old Testament in the New in a mediate and typical or spiritual sense, respecting Christ and his mystical body the church. The Scripture is therefore said to be fulfilled, when that is accomplished in the antitype which is written concerning the type. Thus, in John xix. 36. we read, these things were done that the *Scriptures should be fulfilled* — " a bone of him shall not be broken." These words, which were originally written of the paschal lamb (Exod. xii. 46. Numb. ix. 12), are said to be fulfilled in Christ, who is the antitype of that lamb. Additional examples of the same kind will be found in the annexed passages

Gen xiv 18. 20.	cited and applied in	Heb. vii. 1—10.
Gen. xv. 5.		Rom iv. 18.
Gen xvi 15.		Gal iv 22.
Gen. xvii. 4.		Rom iv. 17
Gen. xvii. 10.		Rom. ix. 9.
Gen. xxi 1—3.		Gal iv 22, &c.

cited and applied in	
Gen. xxi. 12.	Rom. ix. 7.
Gen. xxv. 23.	Rom. ix. 10.
Exod. xvi. 13—15.	John vi. 31. 49. 1 Cor. x. 3.
Exod. xvii. 6. Numb. xx. 11.	1 Cor. x. 4.
Exod. xix 6.	1 Pet. ii. 9
Exod. xxiv. 8.	Heb. ix. 20.
Levit xxvi 11, 12.	2 Cor. vi. 16
Numb xxi. 8, 9.	John iii. 14.
Deut xxi 23.	Gal iii 13.
Deut xxxii 21.	Rom. x. 19
2 Sam vii. 14.	Heb. i. 5.
Psal. ii 9	Rev ii. 27.
Psal viii 4—6	Heb ii 6—8.
Psal viii 6	1 Cor xv. 27
Psal xviii 49	Rom xv 9
Psal xxxv 19 lxix. 4 and cix 3	John xv. 25
Psal xl. 6—8.	Heb. x 5—7.
Psal. lxix. 9	John ii 17
Psal. civ 4.	Heb i. 7
Isa xl. 6, 7	1 Pet 1. 24, 25.
Isa. lii. 7 and Nahum i 15.	Rom. x. 15.
Isa liv, 1.	Gal iv. 27
Isa lxiv. 4	1 Cor. ii. 9.
Jonah i 17 ii. 1. and iii. 5	Matt xii. 40, 41 Luke xi. 30. 32.
Habak ii. 3.	Heb. x. 37
Habak ii 4	Rom. i 17 Gal iii. 11 Heb. x. 38

III. *Of Quotations from the Old Testament in the New, in which a thing is done neither in a literal nor in a spiritual sense, according to the fact referred to in the Scriptures, but is similar to that fact, — in other words, where the passages referred to are cited* in the way of illustration.

The attentive reader of the New Testament cannot fail to observe, that many passages of the Old Testament are cited and adapted by the writers of the New Testament to an occurrence which happened in their time, on account of their correspondence and similitude. These citations are not prophecies, though they are said sometimes to be fulfilled; for any thing may be said to be fulfilled when it can be pertinently applied. This method of explaining Scripture by the way of illustration will enable us to solve some of the greatest difficulties relating to the prophecies.

For the better understanding of this important subject, it should be recollected, that the writings of the Jewish Prophets, which abound in fine descriptions, poetical images, and sublime diction, were the classics of the later Jews, and, in subsequent ages, all their writers affected allusions to them, borrowed their images and descriptions, and very often cited their identical words when recording any event or circumstance that happened in the history of the persons whose lives they were relating; provided it was *similar* and parallel to one that occurred in the times, and was described in the books of the antient prophets. It was a familiar idiom of the Jews[1], when quoting the writings of the Old Testament, to say, — *that it might be fulfilled, which was spoken by such and such a prophet;* not intending to be understood that such a particular passage in one of the sacred books was ever designed to be a *real prediction* of what they were then relating, but signifying only, that the words of the Old Testament might be properly adapted to express their meaning and illustrate their ideas. And thus the Apostles, who were Jews by birth, and wrote and spoke in the Jewish idiom, have very frequently alluded to the sacred books, after the customary style of their nation, intending no more by this mode of speaking, than that the words of such an antient writer are happily descriptive of what was transacted in their time, and might, with equal propriety, be adapted to characterise such a particular circumstance as happened in their days: that there was a con-*similarity* of case and incidents, and that the expressive style and diction of the old inspired prophets were as justly applicable to the occurrences recorded by the apostles, as they were suitable to denote those events and facts in their times which they had commemorated

---

[1] The Talmud and Rabbinical writers abound with instances, great numbers of which are quoted by Surenhusius, in the work already cited, in p 261. note 3.

'Thus, our Lord, speaking of the insurmountable prepossessions and perverseness of the Jews to whom he preached, says — *Seeing they see not, and hearing they hear not, neither do they understand,* — that is, their stupidity is so gross, and their prejudices are so numerous, that though they have capacities proper for understanding and receiving my doctrine, they will neither understand nor receive it; so that in them is fulfilled the prophecy of Isaiah, — his words are perfectly applicable to the present age, and descriptive of their moral character and condition — *Hearing ye will hear, and will not understand; and seeing ye will see, and will not perceive. For this people's heart is waxed gross, and their ears are dull of hearing, and their eyes they have closed, lest at any time they should see with their eyes, and hear with their ears, and should understand with their heart, and should be converted, and I should heal them.* (Isa vi. 9, 10. cited in Matt. xiii. 14, 15.) The same passage of the evangelical prophet is cited by St. Paul (Rom. xi. 8), and applied to the invincible obstinacy of his countrymen, — not, indeed, as though they had then, and then only, received their precise accomplishment, but as beautifully expressive of the obduracy, determined infidelity, and impenitence of the Jews.

Again, the prophet Jeremiah, describing the miseries of captivity by a beautiful figure, represents Rachel as deploring the loss of her children, bathed in tears, piercing the air with loud lamentations, and indulging in inconsolable grief. When Herod imbrued his hands in the blood of the innocents in Bethlehem and its vicinity, how applicable were the prophet's words to such a cruel scene, and how happily are they cited by the evangelist, to exhibit to his reader the mourning and lamentation caused by that sanguinary tyrant! They are a beautiful quotation, and not a prediction of what then happened and yet, upon the murder of these babes, the sacred historian says, according to the Jewish phraseology, when they cited Scripture — *Then was fulfilled that which was spoken by the prophet Jeremiah; In Ramah there was a voice heard, lamentation and weeping, and great mourning, Rachel weeping for her children, and would not be comforted because they are not.* (Jer xxxi. 15. cited in Matt. ii 17, 18.)

Once more, — our Lord having delivered several parables, the sacred historian, after remarking that Jesus Christ chose to convey his religious and moral instruction to the Jews by means of parables, with which all his public discourses abounded, says: — *That it might be fulfilled which was spoken by the prophet,* " *I will open my mouth in parables, I will utter things which have been kept secret from the foundation of the world.*" (Psal. lxxviii 2. quoted in Matt. xiii. 35.)[1]

A similar instance occurs in St Paul's second Epistle to the Corinthians (vi. 2), where he cites the saying of the Prophet (Isa. xlix 8) — *I have heard thee in a time accepted, and in the day of salvation I have succoured thee.* In this passage the Apostle does not mean to declare that the prophet had the Corinthians in view, but he cites it as a parallel case intimating that they might collect from that saying that there was a certain *accepted time,* in which God would hear them, and which, therefore, it concerned them not to let pass without carefully improving it.

The following table presents a list of the passages thus quoted from the Old Testament by the writers of the New, in the way of illustration:—

Gen. xv. 5.	cited in	Rom iv. 18.
Gen. xv. 6.	-	Rom. iv. 3. Gal. iii. 6. and James ii. 23.
Gen. xviii. 10.	-	Rom ix. 9.
Gen. xix. 15 26.	-	Luke xvii. 28, 29. 32.
Gen xxi. 12.	-	Rom ix. 7.
Gen xxv 33.	-	Heb xii 16.
Gen xxvii. 28, &c.	-	Heb. xi. 20. xii. 17.
Exod. ix. 16	-	Rom ix. 17.
Exod. xxxii. 6.	-	1 Cor. x. 7.

---

[1] This mode of quoting passages by way of illustration was not confined to the inspired penmen. Pagan writers often cite passages from their old poets, to describe things of which these poets never thought; and this, Dr. Jortin remarks, is no fault, but rather a beauty in writing. and a passage, applied justly in a new sense, is ever pleasing to an ingenious reader, who loves to see a likeness and pertinency where he expected none. (Rem. on Eccl. Hist. vol. 1 p. 120.) In Ælian, Diogenes the Cynic philosopher is reported to have said, that "*he fulfilled* in himself all the curses of tragedy" and Olympiodorus, in his life of Plato, has this expression, "*that it might be true concerning him,*" and then cites the following verse from Homer·

Του και απο γλωσσης μελιτος γλυκιων ρεεν αυδη.
Words sweet as honey from his lips distill'd. POPE.

Which verse, however applicable to that great philosopher, is not to be considered as an oracle delivered by the poet, with a view to the particular use or accommodation of it by this biographer. (Sharpe's Second Argument in Defence of Christianity, p. 349.)

Exod. xxxiii. 19.	cited in	Rom. ix. 15.
Lev. xi. 45.	-	1 Pet. i. 16.
Lev xviii. 5.	-	Rom. x 5. Gal. iii. 12.
Deut. vii. 13	-	Matt. iv. 10. Luke iv. 8.
Deut. vi. 16.	-	Matt. iv. 7. Luke iv 12.
Deut. viii. 3.	-	Matt. iv. 4. Luke iv. 4.
Deut xxv 4.	-	1 Cor. ix. 9. 1 Tim. v. 18.
Deut. xxvii. 26.	-	Gal. iii. 10
Deut. xxxii 35.	-	Rom. xii. 19. Heb. x 30.
Deut xxxii 36	-	Heb x 30.
Deut. xxxii. 43.	-	Rom xv. 10.
Josh i 5	-	Heb. xiii. 5.
2 Sam. xxi. 6.	-	Matt. xii. 3, 4. Mark ii 25, 26. Luke vi. 3, 4.
1 Kings xix. 14. 18	-	Rom. xi. 3, 4.
Psal v 9. and cxl 3.	-	Rom iii. 13.
Psal. x 7.	-	Rom iii. 14
Psal. xiv 1—3. and liii. 1—3.	-	Rom. iii. 10—12.
Psal. xix 4.	-	Rom x 18.
Psal. xxiv. 1.	-	1 Cor. x. 26.
Psal. xxxii. 1, 2.	-	Rom. iv. 7, 8.
Psal. xxxiv. 12—16.	-	1 Pet. iii. 10—12.
Psal xxxvi. 1	-	Rom iii 18.
Psal. xliv. 22.	-	Rom viii. 36.
Psal. li. 4.	-	Rom iii. 4
Psal lxix. 9.	-	Rom. xv 3.
Psal. lxix. 22, 23.	-	Rom. xi 9, 10.
Psal. lxxviii 2	-	Matt. xiii 35.
Psal lxxxii. 6	-	John x. 34.
Psal cxii 9	-	2 Cor ix 9.
Psal cxvi. 10.	-	2 Cor. iv. 13
Psal cxvii. 1	-	Rom. xv. 11.
Psal cxviii 6	-	Heb. xiii. 6.
Prov. i. 16. Isa lix 7, 8	-	Rom. iii. 15—17.
Prov iii 11, 12.	-	Heb xii 5, 6
Prov. iii. 34.	-	James iv. 6.
Prov. x. 12.	-	1 Pet. iv 8.
Prov. xxv. 21, 22.	-	Rom. xii. 20.
Prov. xxvi. 11.	-	2 Pet. ii. 22.
Isa. i. 9.	-	Rom. ix. 29.
Isa. vi 9, 10.	-	{ John xii. 40. Matt. xiii. 14, 15. Luke viii. 10. Rom. xi. 8.
Isa. viii. 12, 13.	-	1 Pet. iii. 14, 15.
Isa. viii 17, 18.	-	Heb. ii 13.
Isa. x. 22, 23.	-	Rom. ix. 27, 28.
Isa. xxviii. 16	-	Rom. x. 11
Isa. xxix. 10.	-	Rom xi. 8.
Isa. xxix 13	-	Matt. xv. 8, 9. Mark vii 6.
Isa. xxiv 14.	-	1 Cor. i 19.
Isa. xxix. 16 and xlv. 9.	-	Rom. ix. 20, 21
Isa. xlv. 23.	-	Rom. xiv. 11. Phil. ii. 10.
Isa. xlix. 8.	-	2 Cor. vi. 2.
Isa. liii. 5. with Ezek xxxvi 20.	-	Rom. ii. 24.
Isa. lii. 7. and Nahum i. 15.	-	Rom. x. 15
Isa. liii. 11, 12.	-	2 Cor vi 17.
Isa. liii. 15.	-	Rom. xv. 21.
Isa. lvi. 7 (and Jer. vii. 11.)	-	Matt. xxi. 13. Mark xi. 17. Luke xix. 46.
Isa. lxi. 1, 2.	-	Luke iv. 18, 19.
Isa. lxv. 1, 2.	-	Rom x. 20, 21.
Isa. lxvi. 1, 2.	-	Acts vii. 49, 50.
Jer. xxxi. 15.	-	Matt. ii. 17, 18.
Jer. xxxi 33. and xxxii. 38. (with 2 Sam vii. 14.)	-	{ 2 Cor. vi 18.
Hosea xi. 1.	-	Matt. ii. 15.
Hab. ii. 4.	-	Rom. i. 17.
Joel ii. 32.	-	Rom. x. 13.
Mal. i. 2, 3	-	Rom. ix. 13

It cannot escape observation, that by far the larger portion of the preceding passages is cited and adapted to the purpose of illustration by the Apostle Paul. Dr. John Taylor[1] has some useful remarks (of which the following are an abstract), on the various designs with which St. Paul cited them : —

1. Sometimes his intention goes no further than using the *same strong expressions*, as being equally applicable to the point in hand. Thus, in Rom. x. 6—8 he uses the words of Moses (Deut. xxx. 12—14.), not to prove any thing, nor as if he thought Moses spoke of the same subject; but merely as intimating that the strong and lively expressions, used by Moses concerning the doctrine he taught, were equally applicable to the faith of the Gospel. So, in Rom. x. 18. he quotes Psal. xix. 4. though it is not unlikely that those expressions were used by the antient Jews in application to the Messiah, as the Apostle applies them.

2. Sometimes the design of the quotation is only to show that the *cases are parallel*. or that what happened in his times corresponded with what happened in former days. See Rom. ii. 24. viii. 36. ix. 27—29. xi. 2—5. 8—10. and xv. 21.

3. Sometimes the quotation is only intended to *explain a doctrinal point*. See Rom. i. 17. iv. 7, 8. 18—21. ix. 20, 21. x. 15. and xv. 3.

4. Sometimes the quotation is designed to *prove a doctrinal point*. See Rom. iii. 4. 10—18. iv. 3—17. v. 12—14. ix. 7. 9. 12, 13. 15. 17. x. 5. 11. 13. xii. 20. xiv. 11.

Lastly, when a passage of the Old Testament is quoted in the New, in order to prove a point of doctrine, the person or writer applies it, though not always in the precise words of the original, yet constantly according to its genuine sense as it stands there. Examples of such application will be found in Deut. viii. 3. compared with Matt. iv. 4. , Deut. vi. 16. compared with Matt. iv. 7., Deut. xxxiii. 35. and Prov. xxv. 21, 22. compared with Rom. xii. 19, 20. — The expression in Hos. vi. 6., *mercy and not sacrifice*, is applied to different purposes in Matt. ix. 13., but to both properly.

In applying passages cited from the Old Testament by way of illustration, Turretin has suggested the three following rules, which claim the attention of the biblical student.

1. In applications of this kind, we must not neglect the literal sense, which is the first and only genuine sense of Scripture.

2. Such applications ought not to be forced, or far-fetched; for those which were made by the Apostles were simple, and easy to be apprehended.

3. Too much stress ought not to be laid on these applications; which, it should be considered, are merely illustrations adduced by the sacred writers further to explain the subjects under their discussion.

Such being the nature of these illustrative quotations, it follows that no doctrines — at least such as are necessary to salvation — either can or ought to be deduced from them.[2]

---

[1] In his Paraphrase and Notes on Saint Paul's Epistle to the Romans, p. 339. 4th edit. 1769.

[2] Turretin, De Sacr. Script. Interpretatione, pp 118, 119. see also pp 107—117. The subject of Scripture quotations, which are made by way of illustration, is more fully discussed by Dr. Sharpe (Second Argument from Prophecy, pp 347—365), Dr. Hey (Norrisian Lectures, vol i pp. 260. 262.); Dr. Harwood (Introduction to the New Test. vol. i. pp 279—290.), Rumpæus (Comment Crit. ad Libros Nov. Test pp. 443. 449, 450.); Bishop Kidder (in his Demonstration of the Messias, chap iii. Boyle's Lectures, vol. i. pp. 150—152.), Dr. Nicholls (Conference with a Theist, part iii. vol. ii. pp. 10—13 ed. 1698); and especially by Dr. Sykes (On the Truth of the

IV. Of Quotations, and other Passages from the Old Testament, which are alluded to in the New.

Besides the passages mentioned in the preceding class, as citations by the writers of the New Testament in the way of illustration, there is a fourth class, nearly allied to them, and comprising a few quotations, together with a larger number of other passages not distinctly cited from the Old Testament; but which, on comparing them with the New Testament, appear most evidently to have been present to the minds of the sacred writers, who have *alluded* to them without expressly quoting them. A careful inspection of such passages, with reference to their scope and context, together with an application of the rules above suggested by Turretin, will readily enable the student to judge of the allusions which he may meet with in the New Testament: and in addition to those rules, Dr. Gerard has remarked, that when the inspired writers quote a passage from the Old Testament, *merely in the way of allusion*, it is enough that the words which they borrow emphatically express their own meaning. It is not necessary that they be precisely the same with those of the passage alluded to, nor that they be there used, either of the same subject or of a similar subject.[1] The following table presents a list of the *principal* passages thus alluded to in the New Testament.

Gen i 6 9. alluded to in	2 Pet. iii. 5
Gen i. 27.	Matt xix 4 Mark x. 6. 1 Cor. xi 7
	James iii. 9
Gen ii. 2, 3.	Heb. iv. 4
Gen. ii. 7.	1 Cor. xv. 45
Gen ii. 21, 22.	1 Cor xi 8. 1 Tim ii. 13.
Gen. ii. 24.	Matt xix 5 Mark x. 7. 1 Cor. vi. 16.
	Eph. v, 31.
Gen. iii. 6.	1 Tim. ii. 14.
Gen. iii. 4. 13.	2 Cor xi. 3.
Gen iii. 16	1 Cor. xiv. 34.
Gen. iv 4.	Heb xi 4
Gen. iv. 8	Matt xxiii. 35. Luke xi. 51. 1 John iii. 12.
	Jude, verse 11.
Gen. v. 24.	Heb xi 5.
Gen. vi vii.	Matt xxiv. 37, 38. Luke xvii 26, 27 Heb.
	xi 7 1 Pet iii. 19, 20. 2 Pet. ii. 5. iii. 6.
Gen. xii. 1—4.	Acts vii 3. Heb. xi. 8.
Gen. xiii. 15	Rom. iv 13.
Gen. xv. 13, 14	Acts vii 6, 7.
Gen xvii 10.	Acts vii 8
Gen xviii 3 xix 2	Heb. xiii. 2.
Gen. xviii 10	Heb. xi. 11.
Gen xviii 12.	1 Pet. iii 6.
Gen. xix 24.	2 Pet. ii, 6 Jude, verse 7.
Gen xxi. 12.	Heb. xi. 18.
Gen xlvi. 27.	Acts vii. 14.
Gen xlvii. 31	Heb. xi. 21.
Gen l 24	Heb. xi 22.
Exod ii 2 11.	Heb. xi. 23—27. Acts vii. 20—29.
Exod. iii. 6.	Mark xii 26. Acts vii. 31, 32.
Exod xii. 12. 18	Heb. xi 28.
Exod. xiv. 22.	1 Cor. x, 2. Heb. xi. 29.

Christian Religion, chapters xiii. xiv xv. pp. 206—296. edit. 1725.). The reader will also find some excellent remarks on the different modes of quotation, in Dr. Cook's Inquiry into the Books of the New Testament, pp 284—304.

[1] Institutes of Biblical Criticism, p. 422. § 195.

Exod. xix. 12. 16. 18, 19. alluded to in	Heb xii. 18—20.
Exod. xx. 12—16. Deut. v. 16—20. -	{ Matt xix 18, 19 Mark x. 19. Luke xviii. 20. Rom xiii. 9. James ii. 11.
Exod. xiii. 2. Numb. viii. 16, 17. xviii. 15. 17 - - - }	Luke ii. 23.
Lev. xiv 3, 4 10 - - -	Matt. viii 4. Mark i. 44. Luke v 14.
Lev. xix 12. - - -	Matt. v. 33.
Lev. xix. 18 - - -	Matt. v. 43. Gal. v 14.
Numb. xi 4. - - -	1 Cor x. 6.
Numb. xiv. 23. 29. 37. and xxvi 64, 65. -	Heb. iii. 16, 17. Jude, verse 5.
Numb. xxi 4—6. - - -	1 Cor. x. 9.
Numb. xxii. 23. 39. - -	2 Pet. ii 15, 16. Jude 5. 11
Deut xviii. 1. - - -	1 Cor ix. 13.
Deut. xxiv. 1. - - -	Matt v. 31. Mark x. 4 Luke xvi. 18.
Josh. ii. 1. vi. 22, 23. - -	Heb. xi 31. James ii. 25.
Josh vi. 20. - - -	Heb. xi. 30.
Judges, the whole book, generally -	Acts xiii. 20 Heb. xi. 32.
1 Sam. viii. 5. and x. 1. - -	Acts xiii. 21.
1 Sam. xiii 14. xv. 23. xvi. 12, 13. -	Acts xiii. 22.
1 Kings xvii 1. and xviii. 42—45. -	James v. 17, 18.
1 Chron. xxiii 13 - - -	Heb v. 4.
Psal. xc. 4. - - -	2 Pet. iii. 8
Prov. xxvii. 1. - - -	James iv. 13, 14.
Isa xii. 3. - - -	John vii. 38.
Isa. lxvi. 24. - - -	Mark ix 44.
Jer vi 16. - - -	Matt. xi. 29
Lam. iii. 45. - - -	1 Cor. iv 13.
Dan. iii. 23—25. - - -	Heb. xi. 34
Dan. ix 27. xii. 11. - - -	Matt. xxiv. 15 Mark xiii. 14.
Hos xiii. 14. - - -	1 Cor. xv 55.
Hos xiv. 2. - - -	Heb xiii. 15
Amos, v. 25, 26, 27. - - -	Acts vii. 42, 43.

SECTION III.

OF APOCRYPHAL PASSAGES, SUPPOSED TO BE QUOTED IN THE NEW TESTAMENT—QUOTATIONS FROM PROFANE AUTHORS.

IT was a practice of the antient Hebrew divines to cite, not only the Scriptures, as we have seen in the preceding sections, but also to quote histories, facts, and apophthegms or sayings of their early sages, which they had received by *oral tradition* from the time of Moses, in order to supply those passages which are wanting in the Pentateuch. Of this method of quotation we have three instances in the New Testament. The first is 2 Tim. iii. 8. where we meet with the name of Jannes and Jambres as the two Egyptian magicians who opposed Moses. Schickard and some other learned men are of opinion that Saint Paul, being deeply conversant in Jewish literature, derived his knowledge of these names from the Targum or Chaldee Paraphrase of Jonathan Ben Uzziel, on Exod. vii 11. But as there is reason to believe that this Targum is of too late a date to have been consulted by the Apostle, it is most probable that he alluded to an antient and generally received tradition relative to those men. What corroborates the latter conjecture is, that their names are mentioned by some antient profane writers, as Numenius the

Pythagorean[1], by Artapanus[2], and by Pliny.[3] The Jews affirm that they were princes of Pharaoh's magicians, and that they greatly resisted Moses.[4] Origen, who flourished in the second century, informs us, that there was extant, in his time, an apocryphal book concerning these magicians, inscribed *Jannes et Mambres Liber*.[5] The other two instances alluded to are the 9th verse of the Epistle of Jude, which cites the story of Michael the archangel, contending with Satan about the body of Moses, and the 14th verse of the same epistle, in which he quotes an apocryphal prophecy of Enoch. The first of these is borrowed from traditional accounts then received by the Jews, with whom the Apostle argues from their own authors and concessions.[6] The prophecy of Enoch is now known to have been cited from an apocryphal book, bearing that patriarch's name, which was extant at the time when Jude wrote, and of which we have given a short notice in p. 124. of the Appendix to this volume. The following is the passage, as translated by Archbishop Laurence from an Ethiopic version of this book:—

" Behold, he comes with ten thousand of his saints, to execute judgment upon them, and to reprove all the carnal for every thing which the sinful and ungodly have done and committed against him."[7]

Thus this much litigated point is now finally determined: but Jude's quotation of a single passage from the apocryphal book in question, will no more prove *his* approbation of the whole book, than Paul's quotations from certain heathen poets prove that apostle's approbation of every part of the compositions to which he referred.

On a reference to the passages of the Old Testament, which are cited in the way of illustration by the evangelical writers[8], it will be observed that by far the greater number of such quotations has been made by Saint Paul. But the same great apostle of the Gentiles, becoming all things to all men, and being deeply versed in the works of heathen authors, as well as in the sacred writings, did not confine himself *exclusively* to the inspired books: and, accordingly, we have three instances in the New Testament of the fine taste and ability with which he cited and applied passages from Pagan authors, when contending with the Gentiles, or writing to Gentile converts. The first is in Acts xvii. 28., where he cites part of a verse from the *Phænomena* of Aratus.

...... του γαρ και γενος εσμεν
..... for we his offspring are

The passage was originally spoken of the heathen deity Jupiter, and

---

[1] Apud Origen. contra Celsum, pp. 198, 199. edit. Spencer, and in Eusebius de Præp. Evang. l 8 c. 8.
[2] In Eusebius, l. 9. c. 27.   [3] Pliny, Hist Nat. l. 30 c. 1.
[4] Surenhusius, Βιβλος Καταλλαγης, pp 589, 590.
[5] Tract 35. in Matt. cited by Dr. Whitby on 2 Tim. iii. 8.
[6] Surenhusius (pp 699—703.) has given a long extract from the Jalkut Rubeni, fol. 76 col. 2. which details the history of Michael's conflict with the devil The same author (pp. 709—712) has also referred to many Rabbinical writers who take notice of Enoch's prophecy.
[7] The Apocryphal Book of Enoch the Prophet, (London, 1821, 8vo) ch 11 p 2. On the subject of the apocryphal quotations by Jude, see further, Vol. IV. Part II. Chap. IV. Sect. VII. § II.
[8] See pp. 265—267. supra.

is dexterously applied to the true God by Paul, who draws a very strong and conclusive inference from it.

The second instance alluded to is in 1 Cor. xv. 33., in which passage the Apostle quotes a senary iambic, which is supposed to have been taken from Menander's *lost* comedy of Thais,

Φθειρουσιν ηθη χρησθ' ὁμιλιαι κακαι.

rendered, in our translation, *Evil communications corrupt good manners.*

The last instance to be noticed under this head is Titus i. 12., where St. Paul quotes from Epimenides, a Cretan poet, the verse which has already been cited and illustrated in Vol. I. p. 185.; to which the reader is referred.

CHAPTER VII.

ON HARMONIES OF SCRIPTURE.

I. *Occasion and Design of Harmonies of the Scriptures.* — II. *Harmonies of the Four Gospels.* — III. *Observations on the different Schemes of Harmonisers, and on the Duration of the Public Ministry of Jesus Christ.*

I. THE several books of the Holy Scriptures, having been written at different times and on different occasions, necessarily treat on a great variety of subjects, historical, doctrinal, moral, and prophetic. The sacred authors also, writing with different designs, have not always related the same events in the same order: some are introduced by anticipation; and others again are related first which should have been placed last. Hence seeming contradictions have arisen, which have been eagerly seized by the adversaries of Christianity, in order to perplex the minds and shake the faith of those who are not able to cope with their sophistries. These contradictions, however, are not real, for they disappear as soon as they are brought to the test of candid examination.

The manifest importance and advantage of comparing the sacred writers with each other, and of reconciling apparent contradictions, have induced many learned men to undertake the compilation of works, which, being designed to show the perfect agreement of all parts of the sacred writings, are commonly termed HARMONIES. A multitude of works of this description has, at different times, been issued from the press; the execution of which has varied according to the different designs of their respective authors. They may, however, be referred to three classes; viz.—

1. Works which have for their object the RECONCILING OF APPARENT CONTRADICTIONS in the sacred writings. — These, in fact, are a sort of Commentaries; and a notice of the principal publications of this kind will be found in the Appendix to this volume among the commentators and expositors of Holy Writ.

2. HARMONIES OF THE OLD TESTAMENT. — The design of these

is, to dispose the historical, poetical, and prophetical Books in Chronological Order, so that they may mutually explain and authenticate one another Our learned countryman, Dr. Lightfoot, in the year 1647, published a " Chronicle" or Harmony of the Old Testament; on the basis of which the Rev. George Townsend constructed "The Old Testament arranged in Historical and Chronological Order;" but he has deviated from, and improved upon the plan of Lightfoot very materially. His work is noticed in the Appendix to this volume.[1]

3. HARMONIES OF THE NEW TESTAMENT are of two sorts; viz.

(1.) Harmonies of the ENTIRE New Testament, in which not only are the four Gospels chronologically disposed, but the Epistles are also placed in order of time, and interspersed in the Acts of the Apostles. Mr. Townsend's " New Testament arranged in Chronological and Historical Order," is the most complete work of this kind in the English language.[2]

(2.) Harmonies of the four GOSPELS, in which the narratives or memoirs of the four evangelists are digested in their proper chronological order.

II. The Memoirs or Narratives of the life of Jesus Christ, having been written with different designs, and for the use of particular classes of Christians; the importance and advantage of collating these relations with each other, and obtaining the clear amount of their various narratives, at a very early period suggested the plan of forming the Gospels into Harmonies, exhibiting completely their parallelisms and differences, or into a connected history, termed respectively *Monotessaron* and *Diatessaron*, in which the *four* accounts are blended into one, containing the substance of them all. Works of this description are extremely numerous. Mr. Pilkington has enumerated one hundred and four, which had come to his knowledge in 1747[3]; and Walchius has given a *select* list of one hundred and thirty, which had been published prior to the year 1765.[4] The indefatigable bibliographer Fabricius, and his editor, Professor Harles, have given a a list of those which were known to be extant, to the year 1795, which amounts to one hundred and seventy-two, but it is by no means complete.[5] Our notice must necessarily be confined to a few of the principal composers of harmonies.[6]

1. TATIAN, who wrote about the middle of the second century, composed a digest of the evangelical history, which was called το δια τεσσαρων, that is, *the Gospel of the four*, or Μονοτεσσαρον, *Monotessaron*, that is, *one narrative composed out of the four*. Tatian is the most antient harmonist on record: for, if Theophilus bishop of Antioch had before written on that subject (as Jerome insinuates), his work is long since lost. In the beginning of the third century, Ammonius, an Alexandrian, composed a harmony which was also

---
[1] See Appendix, p. 114 [2] Ibid. p 115.
[3] Pilkington's Evangelical History and Harmony, Preface, pp. xviii.—xx.
[4] Walchii Bibliotheca Selecta, vol iv. pp 863—900
[5] Bibliotheca Græca, vol. iv pp 882—889
[6] Our notices of Harmonies are chiefly derived from the three works just cited, and from Michaelis's Introduction to the New Testament, vol. iii. part 1, pp. 31—96 and part ii. pp 29—49.

called το δια τεσσαρων, or the Gospel of the four, of the execution of which Eusebius speaks with approbation. The works of Tatian and Ammonius have long ago perished; but attempts have been made to obtrude spurious compilations upon the world for them in both instances. Victor, who was bishop of Capua, in the sixth century, gave a Latin version of a harmony, which was published by Michael Memler at Mayence, in 1524, as a translation of *Ammonius's Harmony*, in consequence of Victor being undetermined to which of those writers it was to be ascribed, though he was disposed to refer it to Tatian. And Ottomar Luscinius published one at Augsburg in 1524, which he called that of Ammonius, though others have ascribed it to Tatian. It is not a harmony in the strict sense of the term, but a mere summary of the life of Christ delivered in the author's own words.

2. The diligent ecclesiastical historian EUSEBIUS, who wrote in the former part of the fourth century, composed a very celebrated harmony of the Gospels, in which he divided the evangelical history into *ten* canons or tables, which are prefixed to many editions and versions of the New Testament, particularly to Dr. Mill's critical edition of it. In the *first* canon he has arranged, according to the antient chapters, (which are commonly called the Ammonian Sections, from Ammonius, who made these divisions,) those parts of the history of Christ, which are related by all four evangelists. In the rest he has disposed the portions of history related by,

2. Matthew, Mark, and Luke.
3. Matthew, Luke, and John.
4. Matthew, Mark, and John.
5. Matthew and Luke.
6. Matthew and Mark.
7. Matthew and John.
8. Luke and Mark.
9. Luke and John.
10. Only one of the four evangelists.

Though these Eusebian canons are usually considered as a harmony, yet it is evident, from a bare inspection of them, that they are simply indexes to the four Gospels, and by no means form a harmony of the same nature as those, which have been written in modern times, and which are designed to bring the several facts recorded by the evangelists into chronological order, and to reconcile contradictions. On this account Walchius does not allow them a place in his bibliographical catalogue of harmonies.

3. About the year 330, JUVENCUS, a Spaniard, wrote the evangelical history in heroic verse. His method is said to be confused, and his verse is not of a description to ensure him that immortality which he promised himself. His work has fallen into oblivion.

5. The four books of AUGUSTINE, bishop of Hippo, in Africa, *De Consensu Quatuor Evangeliorum*, are too valuable to be omitted. They were written about the year 400, and are honourable to his industry and learning. Augustine wrote this work, with the express design of vindicating the truth and authority of the Gospels from the cavils of objectors.

From the middle ages until the close of the fifteenth century, various harmonies were compiled by Peter Comestor, Guido de Perpiniano, Simon de Cassia, Ludolphus the Saxon, (a German Carthusian monk, whose work was held in such high estimation that it passed through not fewer than thirty editions, besides being translated into French and Italian,) Jean Charlier de Gerson, chancellor of the university of Paris, Peter Lombard, Thomas Aquinas, and many others, which are now of little value, and which have long since fallen into disuse. Of the various harmonies published since the Reformation, by foreign authors, the Latin Harmony of Chemnitz (or Chemnitius) is the most esteemed: and among our British divines those of Drs. Doddridge and Macknight are most generally read on account of their valuable expositions and commentaries. But, for exhibiting the parallel passages of each evangelist, perhaps the columnar form of Archbishop Newcome is preferable; while he, who is desirous of perusing one connected and continuous narrative, in which all the shades of circumstances are judiciously interwoven, will find Mr. Townsend's "New Testament arranged in Historical and Chronological Order," &c. the most useful.[1]

III. In the construction of an Evangelical Harmony, two questions have presented themselves to the consideration of harmonisers; viz. first, what evangelist has preserved the true order of circumstances, to which all the others are to be reduced? And, secondly, what was the duration of the public ministry of Jesus Christ?

1. On the first of these topics, we may remark that all the modern harmonies of the Gospels may be divided into two classes; viz. 1. Harmonies, of which the authors have taken for granted, that all the facts recorded in all the four Gospels are arranged in chronological order; and, 2. Harmonies, of which the authors have admitted, that in one or more of the four Gospels the chronological order has been more or less neglected. At the head of the first class is Andrew Osiander, one of Luther's fellow-labourers, in promoting the reformation in Germany: his method is followed by Calovius, Sandhagen, and others, on the Continent, and in this country by Dr. Macknight. Chemnitz stands at the head of the other class, and also has many followers of his method of arrangement. " The harmonies of the former kind are very similar to each other, because, though the authors of them had to interweave the facts recorded in one Gospel with the facts recorded in another, yet, as they invariably retained the order which was observed in each Gospel, and consequently repeated whatever facts occurred in different places in different Gospels, as often as those facts presented themselves to the harmonists in their progress through the Gospels, there was less room for material deviations in their plan and method. But in the harmonies of the latter kind we meet with considerable variations, because, though the authors of them are unanimous in their principle, they are at variance in the applica-

---

[1] See the Appendix, pp. 116—122 for an account of these and of the Harmonies of the Gospel, or of particular Books of the New Testament.

tion of it: and, though they agree in making transpositions, by which they distinguish themselves from the harmonists of the first class, yet they do not always make the same transpositions. Some, for instance, have supposed, as Chemnitz, Archbishop Newcome, and other harmonists of this class have done, that St. Matthew has mostly neglected chronological order, while others, as Bengel and Bertling, have supposed, that he has in general retained it. Hence, though they have all the same object in view, namely, to make a chronological harmony, or to arrange the events, which are recorded in the Gospels, as nearly as possible according to the order of the time in which the events happened, they have adopted different modes of producing this effect. For in some harmonies the order of St. Matthew is inverted, and made subservient to that of St. Mark, while in other harmonies St. Mark's order is inverted, and made subservient to that of St. Matthew. Some harmonists again suppose, that all the evangelists have neglected chronological order, while others make an exception in favour of one or more of them, though the question, which of the evangelists should be excepted, likewise affords matter of debate. And even those harmonists, who agree as to the Gospel or Gospels, in which transpositions should be made, differ in respect to the particular parts where these transpositions ought to take place."[1]

A late excellent writer on the evidences and criticisms of the New Testament[2], however, is of opinion that the evangelists did not design to adhere to the order of time in writing their respective memoirs of the life of Jesus Christ. The purpose with which the four Gospels were written, he remarks, appears to have been, not a regular chronologically disposed history of the life, ministry, and sufferings of Jesus Christ, but the collection of such a body of well-authenticated facts, as might disclose the nature, and form sufficient proof of the truth of Christianity. This, he thinks, is obvious from the manner in which the evangelists generally place together the facts narrated. "That manner is such as completely to effect the latter, but not the former purpose. There are no marks of an intention, on the part of any of the evangelists, to give to their narratives a regular chronological order. While, in general, there are no indications of the succession, and proximity of the events narrated, but from their being prior, or posterior, and contiguous in the narrative, or from such indefinite expressions as τότε, πάλιν, εν ταῖς ἡμέραις ἐκείναις, ἐν ἐκείνῳ τῷ καιρῷ, ἐν τῷ καθεξῆς, μετὰ ταῦτα; on the other hand, it sometimes occurs, that the events which one evangelist relates as in immediate succession, are noticed by himself to be not contiguous in time, and are put down by another, with some of the intervening transactions interposed. Than evidence of this kind, as to the purpose of a history, no declaration by the writer can be more satisfactory. Such declaration, unless perfectly explicit, may require to be modified by what his work bears within itself of its purpose. But

---

[1] Michaelis's Introduction, vol. iii. part ii. p. 45.
[2] The Rev. Dr. Cook, in his Inquiry into the Books of the New Testament.

there can be no ambiguity in the evidence, deduced from such facts as we have noticed, in the Gospel narratives.

Against this evidence, too, there is no contrary declaration to be weighed. The Evangelist, John, (xx. 30, 31.) expressly asserts that the purpose of his writing was to make such a selection of facts as might be good ground of faith in the divine mission of Jesus Christ; but he no where affirms the chronological order of the selection. Luke, also, thus declares the purpose of his writing to Theophilus, 'Ινα επιγνως περι ών κατηχηθης λογων την ασφαλειαν, (Luke i. 4.) and the expression in the preceding verse, Εδοξε κᾀμοι, παρηκολουθηκοτι ανωθεν πασιν ακριβως, καθεξης σοι γραψαι, is to be interpreted according to that purpose. For this purpose, thus distinctly expressed by two of the evangelists, and evident from the manner of writing common to them all, it was assuredly necessary that, either directly or indirectly, they should furnish us with such information, as might enable us to refer the facts in the Gospel history to a certain country, and a certain period in the history of the world. Without this, the Gospels would not have afforded the proper means for distinguishing them from fictitious histories; and hence, could not have answered the purpose of furnishing evidence to the truth of Christianity. This it was possible to do, either formally by dates, such as are found in the beginning of the 2d and 3d chapters of Luke's Gospel; or by allusions to known places, persons, and circumstances, to be learnt from other histories. Of these two modes, the evangelists, with a few exceptions, follow the latter; natural to men writing immediately for contemporaries, upon or near the scene of the events; and conformable to the usual simplicity by which their whole style is pervaded. But for this purpose, it was not in the least necessary to frame regular chronological narratives; and accordingly what was not necessary, has not been effected; the connections carrying forward the arrangement of events in the Gospels, being not merely those of time, but of the various associations, such as similarity in the facts themselves, vicinity of place, &c. by which it is possible that the human mind may be guided, in recollecting and classifying things that are past. And such, perhaps, upon the whole, is the impression made on most readers by the narratives of the evangelists. As we read them, we have a general feeling that they are carrying us ultimately forward, from preceding to subsequent events, yet, occasionally, over intervals of time concerning which nothing has been recorded, or with deviations from the chronological order; thus rendering it difficult, or impossible, to make one harmonious arrangement of the whole Gospel history, in which each event shall obtain, in perfect consistency with the account of each Evangelist, its proper chronological place." [1]

Amid this diversity of opinions, supported as each is by the most ingenious arguments which its author could produce, it is extremely difficult to decide. By the adoption of the very probable hypothesis last stated, concerning the purpose for which the evangelists wrote,

---

[1] Dr. Cook's Inquiry, pp 211—214.

we certainly get rid, and in the fairest way, of all the difficulties with which the two classes of authors of Harmonies of the Gospels above noticed have to combat. As the evidence laid before the reader will enable him to determine for himself, which of these hypotheses to adopt, we shall only remark, that Bishop Marsh recommends Griesbach's Synopsis of the three first Gospels as preferable to every other harmony extant.[1]

2. Very different opinions have been entertained by the compilers of Harmonies, with regard to the duration of Christ's public ministry; whence a corresponding diversity has necessarily arisen in the disposition of their respective harmonies. During the three first centuries, the common opinion was, that Christ's ministry lasted only one year, or at furthest one year and four months. Early in the fourth century, Eusebius the ecclesiastical historian, maintained that it continued between three and four years: this opinion was generally received, though the antient opinion was retained by Augustine. During the middle ages, no further inquiries appear to have been made on this subject: and, after the Reformation, all the harmonisers of the sixteenth and seventeenth centuries assumed it for certain that Christ's ministry lasted between three and four years. Bengel, however, in his German Harmony of the Gospels, published at Tubingen in 1736, reduced it to two years; and, three years before, Mr. Mann in his essay "Of the true Years of the Birth and Death of Christ," (London, 1733, 8vo.) revived the antient opinion that it lasted only one year. This was also followed by Dr. Priestley in his Greek and English Harmonies. The hypothesis of Eusebius was adopted by Archbishop Newcome, who maintained that one year was by far too short a period for the several progresses of Jesus Christ in Galilee, and the transactions connected with them: and Bishop Marsh observes, that the Gospel of John presents almost insuperable obstacles to the opinion of those who confine Christ's ministry to one year. For, in order to effect this purpose, it is necessary to make omissions and transpositions in St. John's Gospel, which are not warranted by the laws of criticism, but are attempted merely to support a previously assumed hypothesis. On the other hand, he thinks that the opinion, which makes Christ's ministry to have continued three years (and which receives no support whatever from the three first Gospels) cannot be satisfactorily proved even

---

[1] Michaelis's Introduction, vol. iii. part ii. p. 47. Michaelis has given a harmonised table of the four Gospels (Introd vol. iii part i pp. 37—83), which Bishop Marsh (part ii p. 67.) pronounces to be a very useful one, considered as a general index to the four Gospels. Dr A. Clarke has reprinted Michaelis's harmonised table at the end of his Commentary on the Gospels; observing that it is useful to the reader of them, in pointing out *where* the same transaction is mentioned by the evangelists, what they have in *common*, and what is *peculiar to each*. Michaelis has generally followed Matthew's account, with which the narratives of the other evangelists are collated. In 1821, an English Harmony was compiled by, and printed at the expence of, Thomas Bowles, Esq (for private distribution only), intitled "Diatessaron, or the History of our Lord Jesus Christ, compiled from the four Gospels, according to the Translation of Dr Campbell, and in the order adopted by John David Michaelis, London,' 8vo. In this beautifully executed volume, the compiler has made some slight variations from the order of time followed by Michaelis in the harmonised table just mentioned.

from the Gospel of Saint John, who at the utmost has noticed, or at least named, only three distinct passovers.[1]

Another opinion has lately been announced, with equal modesty and learning, in a dissertation on " The Chronology of our Saviour's Life," by the Rev. C. BENSON, M. A. (Cambridge, 1819, 8vo.) The results of his investigation (which depends on minute chronological and critical discussions that do not admit of abridgment) are, that Herod died in the year of the Julian period 4711; and, consequently, that the birth of Christ took place A.J.P. 4709, in the spring (probably in the month of April or May); that his baptism was performed in or about the month of November, A. J. P. 4739, during the procuratorship of Pontius Pilate, that, agreeably to the indications of time contained in Saint John's Gospel, the ministry of Jesus Christ lasted through three passovers, or *two years and a half*, and that he was crucified on the fifteenth day of the month Nisan (April 15th), A. J. P. 4742.

From the difficulty of producing a harmony, complete in all its parts, some eminent critics (and among them the elegant and accomplished expositor, Gilpin) have maintained that we ought to peruse the four several memoirs of Jesus Christ written by the evangelists, separately and distinctly; and that, by explaining them separately, the *whole* becomes more uniform. Archbishop Newcome, however, has ably vindicated, and proved, the utility and advantage of harmonies; and with his observations, the present chapter shall conclude. A harmony, he remarks, has the following uses: —

By the juxta-position of parallel passages, it is often the best comment; and it cannot but greatly alleviate the reader's trouble, in his attempts to illustrate the phraseology and manner of the evangelists. It also shows that Mark, who inserts much new matter, did not epitomise the Gospel of Matthew: and it affords plain indications, from the additions and omissions in John's Gospel, that his was designed to be a supplemental history Further, a harmony in many instances illustrates the propriety of our Lord's conduct and works. Thus, previously to the call of the four Apostles (Mark i. 16—20.) Andrew had been the Baptist's disciple, and had received his testimony to Jesus (John i. 35 40.): Peter had been brought to Jesus by Andrew his brother (John i. 42.), and Jesus had shown more than human knowledge and more than human power (John i. 48. ii. 11. 23. iii. 2. iv. 29. 49, 50.) than what had probably fallen within the experience of these disciples, or at least must have gained their belief on the firmest grounds. So, the words of Christ (John v. 21. 25.) are prophetically spoken *before* he had raised any from the dead; and his reproofs (Matt. xii. 34. Mark vii. 6.) are uttered *after* he had wrought miracles, during two feasts at Jerusalem. Nor was the jealousy of the Jewish rulers early awakened by the call of the twelve apostles to a stated attendance. This event took place after our Lord had celebrated his second passover at Jerusalem, and when he was about to absent himself from that city for so long a

---

[1] Michaelis's Introduction, vol. iii. part ii p 66.

period as eighteen months. In like manner,
sent forth to show, throughout a wide tract
wisdom and power their Master endued then
months of our Lord's crucifixion: and the sce
a kind of miracle which would have exasperat
portion as it tended to exalt his prophetic char
Jerusalem, till the last passover approached.
sumptions of the inspiration of the evangelists
comparison of the Gospels, from their being :
mental to each other, in passages reconcilabl
tion of a seemingly indifferent circumstance
agreement in the midst of a *seeming disagre*
honesty, often neglects appearances: hypocri
always guarded." [1]

---

[1] West on the Resurrection, p. 278. (London

PART II.

ON THE INTERPRETATION OF SCRIPTURE.

BOOK I.

GENERAL PRINCIPLES OF INTERPRETATION.

CHAPTER I.

ON THE SENSE OF SCRIPTURE.

SECTION I.

ON THE MEANING OF WORDS.

I. *Nature of Words.* — II. *The Sense of Scripture defined:* 1. *The Literal Sense;* — 2. *The Allegorical, Typical, and Parabolical Sense;* — 3. *The Moral Sense of Professor Kant, shown to be destitute of Foundation.*

MAN, being formed for society, has received from his Creator the faculty of communicating to his fellow-men, by means of certain signs, the ideas conceived in his mind. Hence, his organs of speech are so constructed, that he is capable of forming certain articulate sounds, expressive of his conceptions; and these, being fitly disposed together, constitute discourse which, whether it be pronounced or written, must necessarily possess the power of declaring to others what he wishes they should understand.

I. The vehicles, or signs, by which men communicate their thoughts to each other, are termed WORDS; whether these are orally uttered, or described by written characters; the idea, or notion, attached to any word, is its SIGNIFICATION; and the ideas which are expressed by several words connected together, — that is, in entire sentences and propositions, and which ideas are produced in the minds of others, — are called the SENSE or proper meaning of words. Thus, if a person utter certain words, to which another individual attaches the same idea as the speaker, he is said to *understand* the latter, or to comprehend the *sense* of his words. If we transfer this to sacred subjects, we may define the *sense of Scripture* to be that conception of its meaning, which the Holy Spirit presents to the understanding of man, by means of the words of Scripture, and by means of the ideas comprised in those words.[1]

---

[1] Stuart's Elements of Interpretation, p. 7. (Andover. 1822.)

EVERY WORD MUST HAVE SOME MEANING.

Although in every language there are very many words which admit of several meanings, yet in common parlance there is only *one true sense* attached to any word; which sense is indicated by the connection and series of the discourse, by its subject-matter, by the design of the speaker or writer, or by some other adjuncts, unless any ambiguity be purposely intended. That the same usage obtains in the Sacred Writings there is no doubt whatever. In fact, the perspicuity of the Scriptures requires this unity and simplicity of sense, in order to render intelligible to man the design of their Great Author, which could never be comprehended if a multiplicity of senses were admitted. In all other writings, indeed, besides the Scriptures, before we sit down to study them, we expect to find one single determinate sense and meaning attached to the words; from which we may be satisfied that we have attained their true meaning, and understand what the authors intended to say. Further, in common life, no prudent and *conscientious* person, who either commits his sentiments to writing or utters any thing, intends that a diversity of meanings should be attached to what he writes or says: and, consequently, neither his readers, nor those who hear him, affix to it any other than the true and obvious sense. Now, if such be the practice in all fair and upright intercourse between man and man, is it for a moment to be supposed that God who has graciously vouchsafed to employ the ministry of men in order to make known his will to mankind, should have departed from this way of simplicity and truth? Few persons, we apprehend, will be found, in this enlightened age, sufficiently hardy to maintain the affirmative.[1]

II. The SENSE OF SCRIPTURE DEFINED.

1. The LITERAL SENSE of any place of Scripture is that which the words signify, or require, in their natural and proper acceptation, without any trope, metaphor, or figure, and abstracted from any mystic meaning: Thus, in

Gen. i. 1 We read that *God created the heaven and the earth.* These words mean what they literally import, and are to be interpreted according to the letter. So, in John x. 30. we read, *I and the Father are one;* in which passage the deity of Christ, and his equality with God the Father, are so distinctly and unequivocally asserted, that it is difficult to conceive how any other than its proper and literal meaning could ever be given to it.

The literal sense has also been termed the *grammatical* sense; the term *grammatical* having the same reference to the Greek language as the term *literal* to the Latin, both referring to the elements of a word. Words may also be taken properly and physically, as in John i. 6. *There was a man whose name was John* · this is called the proper literal sense. When, however, words are taken metaphorically and figuratively, that is, are diverted to a meaning which they

---

[1] Keilii Elementa Hermeneut Nov Test p. 12. On this subject the reader may consult M Winterberg's " Prolusio de interpretatione unica, unica, et certæ persuasionis de doctrinæ religionis veritate et amicæ consensionis causâ," in Velthusen's and Kuinoel's *Commentationes Theologicæ*, vol. iv. pp. 420—438.

do not *naturally* denote, but which they nevertheless intend under some figure or form of speech,—as when the properties of one person or thing are attributed to another,—this is termed the *tropical* or *figurative* sense.[1]

"Thus, when hardness is applied to *stone*, the expression is used literally, in its proper and natural signification:—when it is applied to the *heart*, it is used *figuratively*, or in an improper acceptation. Yet the sense, allowing for the change of subject, is virtually the same, its application being only transferred from a physical to a moral quality."[2] An example of this kind occurs in Ezek. xxxvi. 26. and xi. 19., where the *heart of stone* denotes a hard obdurate heart, regardless of divine admonitions, and the *heart of flesh* signifies a tender heart, susceptible of the best and holiest impressions. In like manner, in Zech. vii. 12, the obdurate Jews are said to have made their hearts as *an adamant stone*. Numerous similar expressions occur in the New as well as in the Old Testament, as in Luke xiii. 32. John i. 29. and xv 5., where Herod, for his craftiness and cruelty, is termed a *fox;* the Saviour of the world is called the *Lamb of God*, because to his great atoning sacrifice for the sins of the whole world, the lamb, which was offered every morning and evening, had a typical reference, he is also called a *vine*, as all true Christians are designated the *branches*, to intimate that Christ is the support of the whole church, and of every particular believer,—that, in the language of the New Testament, they are all implanted and grafted into him, that is, united to him by true faith and sincere love, and that they all derive spiritual life and vigour from him. It were unnecessary to multiply examples of this kind, as every diligent reader of the Word of God will doubtless be able to recollect them.

Further, the literal sense has been called the HISTORICAL SENSE, as conveying the meaning of the words and phrases used by a writer at a certain time.

Thus, in the more antient books of the Old Testament, the word *isles* or *islands* signifies every inhabited region, particularly all the western coasts of the Mediterranean Sea, and the seats of Japhet's posterity, viz. the northern part of Asia, Asia Minor, and Europe, together with some other regions. Of this sense of the word we have examples in Gen. x. 5. Isa. xi 11. xx. 6. xxiii. 6. xxiv. 15. xlii. 15. lxvi. 19. Ezekiel xxvi. 15. 18. xxvii. 3—7. 15. 35. But, in a later age, it denotes islands properly so called, as in Esther x. 1, and, perhaps, Jer. xlvii. 4. (marginal rendering)[3] Again, the phrase, to *possess* or *inherit the land*, which is of very frequent occurrence in the Old Testament, if we consider it *historically*, that is, with reference to the history of the Jewish nation, means simply, to hold the secure and undisturbed possession of the promised land; and in the New Testament, the phrase to "*follow Christ*" must in like manner be understood *historically* in some passages of the

---

[1] "The *tropical* sense is no other than the *figurative* sense As we say, in language derived from the Greek, that a trope is used when a word is turned from its literal or grammatical sense so we say, in language derived from the Latin, that a *figure* is there used, because in such cases the meaning of the word assumes a new *form*. The same opposition, therefore, which is expressed by the terms *literal* sense and *figurative* sense, is expressed also by the terms *grammatical* sense and *tropical* sense." Bishop Marsh's Lect part iii. p 67
[2] Bishop Vanmildert's Bamp Lect p 222
[3] Jahn, Enchiridion Hermeneuticæ Generalis, p 24, who cites Michaelis's Spicilegium Geographiæ Hebrææ Exteræ, part i pp. 131—143., and also his Supplementum ad Lexica Hebraica, pp 68, 69.

Gospels, implying no more than that the persons there mentioned followed the Lord Jesus Christ in his progresses, and were auditors of his public instructions, precisely as the apostles followed him from place to place, and heard his doctrine.[1]

Interpreters now speak of the true sense of a passage, by calling it the GRAMMATICO-HISTORICAL SENSE: and exegesis, founded on the nature of language, is called grammatico-historical. The object in using this compound name is, to show that both grammatical and historical considerations are employed in making out the sense of a word or passage.

2. Where, besides the direct or immediate signification of a passage, whether literally or figuratively expressed, there is attached to it a more remote or recondite meaning, this is termed the MEDIATE, SPIRITUAL, or MYSTICAL SENSE[2]: and this sense is founded, not on a transfer of words from one signification to another, but on the entire application of the matter itself to a different subject.

Thus, what is said *literally* in Exod xxx. 10. and Levit. xvi. concerning the High Priest's entrance into the most holy place on the day of expiation, with the blood of the victim, we are taught by St. Paul to understand *spiritually* of the entrance of Jesus Christ into the presence of God with his own blood. (Heb. ix. 7—20.)

The spiritual sense of Scripture has frequently been divided into *allegorical*, *typical*, and *parabolical*. The reason of this mode of classifications, as well as of some other minor distinctions, does not sufficiently appear. Since, however, it has obtained a place in almost every treatise on the interpretation of the Scriptures, it may not be irrelevant to define and illustrate these senses by a few examples.

(1.) The ALLEGORICAL SENSE is, when the Holy Scriptures, besides the literal sense, signify any thing belonging to faith or *spiritual doctrine*.

Such is the sense which is required rightly to understand Gal. iv. 24. ἅ τινα ἐστιν ἀλληγορούμενα, *which things are allegorically spoken*, or, *which things are thus allegorised by me;* that is, under the veil of the literal sense they further contain a spiritual or mystical sense.

(2.) The TYPICAL SENSE is, when, under external objects or prophetic visions, secret things, whether present or future, are represented; especially when certain transactions recorded in the Old Testament presignify or adumbrate those related in the New Testament.

Thus, in Psal. xcv. 11, the words "*they should not enter into my rest,*" literally understood, signify the entrance of the Israelites into the promised land; but, spiritually and typically, the entering into the rest and

---

[1] Many additional instances might be offered, if the limits of this work would permit The reader, who is desirous of fully investigating the *historic sense* of Scripture, will derive much solid benefit from Dr. Storr's Disquisition de Sensu Historico, in vol. i. (pp. 1—88) of his "Opuscula Academica ad Interpretationem Librorum Sacrorum pertinentia," 8vo Tubingen, 1796

[2] "Dicitur mysticus," says a learned and sensible Roman Catholic writer, "a μύω, *claudo;* quia licet non semper fidei mysteria comprehendat, magis tamen occultus, et clausus est, quam literalis, qui *per verba rite intellecta* facilius innotescit." Adami Viser, Hermeneutica Sacra Novi Testamenti, pars ii. pp. 51, 52. See also Jahn's Enchiridion Hermeneuticæ Generalis, pp 41, 42 ; and Bishop Vanmildert's Bampton Lectures, p 222.

enjoyment of heaven, through the merits and mediation of Christ, as is largely shown in the epistle to the Hebrews, chapters iii. and iv.

(3.) The PARABOLICAL SENSE is, when, besides the plain and obvious meaning of the thing related, an occult or spiritual sense is intended. As this chiefly occurs in passages of a moral tendency, the parabolic has by some writers been termed the *moral* or *tropological* sense.

Of this description is the parable of the talents: the design of which is to show that the duties which men are called to perform are suited to their situations and the talents which they severally receive; that whatever a good man possesses he has received from God, as well as the ability to improve that good; and that the grace and temporal mercies of God are suited to the power which a man has of improving them. Thus, also, the injunction in Deut. xxv. 4., relative to muzzling the ox while treading out the corn, is explained by St. Paul with reference to the right of maintenance of ministers of the Gospel. (1 Cor. ix. 9—11.)

It were easy to multiply examples of each of the different senses here mentioned; but as they have all one common foundation, and as we shall have occasion to adduce others in the course of the following pages, when stating the rules for interpreting the sense of Scripture after it has been ascertained, the instances above quoted may suffice to illustrate the distinctions subsisting between them.[1]

3. The MORAL SENSE or interpretation, advocated by the late Professor Kant, of Berlin, (whose philosophical system has obtained many followers on the Continent) consists in setting aside the laws of grammatical and historical interpretation, and attributing a moral meaning to those passages of Scripture; which, agreeably to grammatical interpretation, contain nothing coincident with the moral dictates of unassisted reason. According to this hypothesis, nothing more is necessary, than that it be *possible* to attach a moral meaning to the passage; — it is of little moment, how forced or unnatural it may be. Against this mode of interpretation (which is here noticed in order to put the student on his guard) the following weighty objections have been urged: —

(1.) Such a mode of explaining Scripture, does not deserve the name of an interpretation: for this moral interpreter does not inquire, what the Scriptures actually *do* teach by their own declarations, but what they *ought* to teach, agreeably to his opinions.

(2.) The principle is incorrect, which is assumed as the basis of this mode of interpretation: viz. that the grammatical sense of a passage of Scripture cannot be admitted, or at least is of no use in

---

[1] Bauer, Herm Sacr pp. 13—44. Viser, Hermeneutica Sacra, Nov. Test. pars ii. pp. 1—150. J E. Pfeiffer, Institutiones Hermeneuticæ Sacræ, pp 122—132 Aug. Pfeiffer, Herm Sacr cap III. (Op. tom. ii pp. 633—638.) Ernesti Institutio Interpretis Novi Test pp 14—30. (4th edit.) Mori Acroases Academicæ super Hermeneutica Nov Test tom. i. pp. 27—78. J B. Carpzovii, Primæ Lineæ Herm. Sac p. 24. Alber, Institutiones Hermeneuticæ Nov Test tom. 1. pp. 44—46. Bishop Middleton on the Greek Article, pp 580—590. Bishop Marsh's Lect. part III. lect xv. and xvi pp 42 —78; and Bishop Vanmildert's Bampton Lectures, Serm vii. pp 217—232. and notes, pp 385—396. The two writers, last cited, have illustrated the sense of Scripture, by applying it to the discussion of some important controversial points between Protestants and Romanists, which the limits of a practical work will not admit of being noticed.

ethics, whenever it contains a sentiment, which reason alone could not discover and substantiate.

(3.) Such a mode of interpretation is altogether unnecessary: for the Bible is abundantly sufficient for our instruction in religion and morality, if its precepts are construed as applying directly or by consequence to the moral necessities of every man. And, although there are passages of difficult explanation in the Bible, as might naturally be expected from the antiquity and peculiar languages of the Scriptures; yet, in most instances these passages do not relate to doctrines; and, when they do, the doctrines in question are generally taught in other and plainer passages.

(4.) As, on this plan, the mere possibility of attaching a moral import to a text is regarded as sufficient for considering it as a true signification; almost every passage must be susceptible of a multitude of interpretations, as was the case during the reign of the mystical and allegorical mode of interpretation, which has long since been exploded. This must produce confusion in religious instruction, want of confidence in the Bible, and, indeed, a suspicion as to its divine authority: for this must be the natural effect of the moral of interpretation on the majority of minds.

(5.) Lastly, if such a mode of interpreting the doctrines of Christianity should prevail, it is not seen how insincerity and deceit, on the part of interpreters, are to be detected and exposed.[1]

SECTION II

GENERAL RULES FOR INVESTIGATING THE MEANING OF WORDS.

SINCE words compose sentences, and from these, rightly understood, the meaning of an author is to be collected, it is necessary that we ascertain the individual meaning of words before we proceed further to investigate the sense of Scripture. In the prosecution of this important work, we may observe, generally, that as the same method and the same principles of interpretation are common both to the sacred volume and to the productions of uninspired man, consequently the signification of words in the Holy Scriptures must be sought precisely in the same way in which the meaning of words in other works usually is or ought to be sought. Hence also it follows, that the method of investigating the signification of words in the Bible is no more arbitrary than it is in other books, but is in like manner regulated by certain laws, drawn from the nature of languages. And since no text of Scripture has more than one meaning, we must endeavour to find out that *one true sense* precisely in the same manner as we would investigate the sense of Homer or any other antient writer; and in that sense, when so ascertained, we

---

[1] Schmucker's Elementary Course of Biblical Theology, vol. i. pp 272, 273. (Andover, North America, 1827.) Alber, Institutiones Hermeneut. Nov. Test. vol. i. pp. 90—98.

ought to acquiesce, unless, by applying the just rules of interpretation, it can be shown that the meaning of the passage had been mistaken, and that another is the only just, true, and critical sense of the place. This principle, duly considered, would alone be sufficient for investigating the sense of Scripture; but as there are not wanting persons who reject it altogether, and as it may, perhaps, appear too generally expressed, we shall proceed to consider it more minutely in the following observations.[1]

1. *Ascertain the* usus loquendi, *or notion affixed to a word by the persons in general by whom the language either is now or formerly was spoken, and especially in the particular connection in which such notion is affixed.*

The meaning of a word used by any writer, is the meaning affixed to it by those for whom he *immediately* wrote. For there is a kind of natural compact between those who write and those who speak a language, by which they are mutually bound to use words in a certain sense he, therefore, who uses such words in a different signification, in a manner violates that compact, and is in danger of leading men into error, contrary to the design of God, "who will have all men to be saved, and to come unto the knowledge of the truth." (1 Tim. ii. 4.) The aids for investigating the usus loquendi being considered in the ensuing chapter, it will be sufficient to observe in illustration of the present canon, that

(1.) The books of the Old and New Testament, are, each, to be frequently and carefully read, and the subjects therein treated are to be compared together, in order that we may ascertain the meaning of what the authors thought and wrote

They, who wish to attain an accurate knowledge of the philosophical notions of Plato, Aristotle, or any other of the antient Grecian sages, will not consult the later Platonic writers, or the scholastic authors who depended wholly on the *authority* of Aristotle, and whose knowledge of his works was frequently very imperfect, but will rather peruse the writings of the philosophers themselves — in like manner, the books of the Old and New Testament are to be constantly and carefully perused and weighed by him, who is sincerely desirous to obtain a correct knowledge of their important contents For, while we collate the expressions of each writer, we shall be enabled to harmonise those passages which treat on the same topics; and may reasonably hope to discover their true sense Some foreign biblical critics, however, (who, in their zeal to accommodate the immutable truths of Scripture to the standard of the present age, would divest the Christian dispensation of its most important doctrines,) have asserted that, in the interpretation of the Old Testament, all reference to the New Testament is to be excluded But, unless we consult the latter, there are passages in the Old Testament, whose meaning *cannot* be fully apprehended. To mention only one instance, out of many that might be adduced — in Gen i 26, 27. God is said to have created man after his own image · this passage (which, it should be recollected, describes man in his primeval state of spotless innocence, before he became corrupted by the fall,) the divines in question affirm, must be interpreted according to the crude and imperfect notions entertained by the antient heathen nations concerning the Deity![2] But, if we avail ourselves of the information communicated in the New Testament (as we are fully warranted to do by the example of Christ and his inspired apostles), we shall be enabled to form a correct notion of the divine image intended by the sacred historian viz that it consisted in righteousness, true holiness, and knowledge. See Eph iv 24 and Col iii 10

(2.) It is also indispensable that we lay aside, in many instances, that more accurate knowledge which we possess of natural things, in order that we may fully enter into the meaning of different parts of the sacred writings.

---

[1] The following rules are chiefly drawn from Chladenius's Institutiones Exegeticæ, pp. 238—242., Jahn's Enchiridion Hermeneuticæ Sacræ, pp 34—38. Langit Hermeneutica Sacra, pp 16 et seq Rambachii Institutiones Hermeneuticæ Sacræ, p. 53. et seq., and Semler's Apparatus ad Liberalem Novi Testamenti Interpretationem, p.179. et seq See also J E Pfeiffer's Inst. Herm Sacr. p 349 et seq

[2] How crude, imperfect, and erroneous these views of the Heathens were respecting the Almighty, has been shown at great length by various eminent advocates for the truth of the divine origin of Revelation; but no one has discussed it more elaborately than Dr. Leland, in his "Advantage and Necessity of the Christian Revelation, as shown from the state of Religion in the Heathen World." 1768. 8vo. Reprinted at Glasgow in 1819, in 2 vols. A compendious notice of the heathen notions respecting the Deity is given in Vol. I. pp. 1—8.

The antient Hebrews being altogether ignorant of, or imperfectly acquainted with many things, the nature of which is now fully explored and well known, it were absurd to apply our more perfect knowledge to the explanation of things which are related according to the limited degrees of knowledge they possessed. Hence it is not necessary that we should attempt to illustrate the Mosaic account of the creation according to the Copernican system of the universe, which the experiments of philosophers have shown to be the true one. As the Scriptures were composed with the express design of making the divine will known to man, the sacred authors might, and did, make use of popular expressions and forms of speech, then in use among the persons or people whom they addressed, the philosophical truth of which they neither affirmed nor denied.

2. *The received signification of a word is to be retained, unless weighty and necessary reasons require that it should be abandoned or neglected.*

We shall be justified in rejecting the received meaning of a word in the following cases, viz

(1.) If such meaning clash with any doctrine revealed in the Scriptures

Thus, according to our authorised English version, Eli's feeble reproaches of his profligate sons served only to lull them into security, *because the Lord would slay them* (1 Sam. ii. 25), the meaning of which rendering is, to make their continuance in sin the *effect of* Jehovah's determination to destroy them, and thus apparently support the horrid tenet, that God wills his creatures to commit crimes, because he is determined to display his justice in their destruction. It is true that the ordinarily received meaning of the Hebrew particle כי (ki) is, *because*, but in this instance it ought to be rendered *therefore*, or *though*[1], which makes their wilful and impenitent disobedience the cause of their destruction, and is in unison with the whole tenor of the Sacred Writings. The proper rendering, therefore, of this passage is, *Notwithstanding, they hearkened not unto the voice of their father.* THEREFORE *the Lord would slay them*

(2) If a certain passage *require* a different explanation from that which it appears to present as Mal iv. 5, 6 compared with Luke i 17. and Matt xi. 14.

(3.) If the thing itself will not admit of a tropical or figurative meaning being affixed to the word.

3. *Where a word has several significations in common use, that must be selected which best suits the passage in question, and which is consistent with an author's known character, sentiments, and situation, and the known circumstances under which he wrote.*

For instance, the word BLOOD, which in various accounts is very significant in the Sacred Writings, denotes—our *natural descent* from one common family, in Acts xvii. 26.; —*death* in Heb. xii. 4., the *Sufferings and Death of Christ*, considered as an atonement for the souls of sinners, in Rom v 9 and Eph i 7, and also as the procuring cause of our justification in Rom. v. 9, and of our sanctification in Heb ix. 14 [2]

4 *Although the force of particular words can only be derived from etymology, yet too much confidence must not be placed in that frequently uncertain science*

5 *The distinctions between words, which are apparently synonymous, should be carefully examined and considered*

In the Latin language many words are accounted perfectly synonymous, which, however, only partially accord together Thus, a person whose discourse is cut short, is said to be *silent* (silere), and one, who has not begun to speak, is said to *hold his tongue* (tacere). Cicero, speaking of beauty, observes, that there are two kinds of it, the one *dignified and majestic* (dignitas), the other *soft and graceful* (venustas), the *latter* to be considered proper to *women*, the *former* to men [3] The same remark will apply to the language of Scripture. For instance, in the 119th Psalm there are not fewer than ten different words, pointing out the word of God, viz Law, Way, Word, Statutes, Judgments, Commandments, Precepts, Testimonies, Righteousness, and Truth or Faithfulness. Now all these words, though usually considered as synonymous, are not *literally* synonymous, but refer to some latent and distinguishing properties of the Divine Word, whose manifold excel-

---

[1] Noldius, in his work on Hebrew particles, has shown that כי (ki) has the meaning of *therefore*, in a great number of instances, among which he quotes this very passage He has also adduced others, where it evidently means *though* Purver adopts the latter, and thus translates the clause in question — *Notwithstanding they would not hearken to the voice of their father,* THOUGH *the Lord should slay* them.

[2] For the various meanings of the word *blood*, see the Index of the Symbolical Language of Scripture, voce BLOOD, in the fourth volume of this work.

[3] Cum autem pulchritudinis duo genera sint, quorum in altero *venustas* sit, in altero *dignitas*, venustatem muliebrem ducere debemus, dignitatem virilem. Cicero de Officiis, lib. i. c. xxxvi. (op. tom xii. p. 57. ed Bipont)

lencies and perfections are thus illustrated with much elegant variety of diction. In the New Testament we meet with similar instances, as in Col. ii. 22. ενταλματα και διδασκαλιας ανθρωπων, *the commandments and doctrines of men*. *Doctrines* in this passage include truths propounded to be believed or known; *Commands* imply *laws*, which direct what is to be done or avoided: the latter depend upon and are derived from the former. The apostle is speaking of the *traditions taught* by the elders, and the *load of cumbrous ceremonies commanded* by them, in addition to the significant rites prescribed in the law of Moses. In Rom. xiv. 13. προσκομμα, a *stumbling block*, means a slighter cause of offence, viz. that which wounds and disturbs the conscience of another; σκανδαλον, an *occasion to fall*, means a more weighty cause of offence, that is, such as may cause any one to apostatise from the Christian faith. Similar examples occur in 1 Tim. iii. 1. and 1 Pet. iv. 3.[1]

6. *The epithets introduced by the sacred writers, are also to be carefully weighed and considered, as all of them have either a declarative or explanatory force, or serve to distinguish one thing from another, or unite these two characters together.*

The epithets of Scripture then are:

(1.) *Exegetical* or *Explanatory*, that is, such as declare the nature and properties of a thing.

Thus, in Tit. ii. 11. the *grace of God* is termed *saving*, not indeed as if there were any other divine grace bestowed on man, that was not saving; but because the grace of God revealed in the Gospel is the primary and true source of eternal life. Similar epithets occur in 2 Tim. i. 9. in which our *calling* is styled *holy*; in 1 Pet. iv. 3. where *idolatry* is termed abominable, and in 1 Pet. ii. 9. where the Gospel is called the mavellous light of God, because it displays so many amazing scenes of divine wonders.

(2.) *Diacritical* or *Distinctive*, that is, such as distinguish one thing from another.

For instance, in 1 Pet. v. 4. the *crown* of future glory is termed a *never-fading crown*, αμαραντινος, to distinguish it from that *corruptible* crown which, in the Grecian games, was awarded to the successful candidate. In like manner, genuine faith, in 1 Tim. i. 5. is called *undissembled*, ανυποκριτος; God, in the same chapter, (v. 17.) is designated the *King incorruptible*, Βασιλευς αφθαρτος, and in Rom. xii. 1. Christians dedicating themselves to God, is termed a *reasonable service*, λατρεια λογικη, in contradistinction to the Jewish worship, which chiefly consisted in the sacrifice of *irrational creatures*.

(3.) *Both Explanatory and Distinctive*, as in Rom. ix. 5.

Where Christ is called *God blessed for ever*. By which epithet both his divine nature is *declared*, and he is eminently *distinguished* from the Gentile deities. Similar examples occur in John xvii. 11. (compared with Luke xi 11—13.) where God is termed *Holy Father*, in 1 John v 20. where Christ is styled the *true God*, as also the *Great God* in Tit. ii 13. and Heb ix. 14. where the Holy Spirit is denominated the *Eternal Spirit*.

7. *General terms are used sometimes in their whole extent, and sometimes in a restricted sense, and whether they are to be understood in the one way or in the other, must depend upon the scope, subject-matter, context, and parallel passages.*

Thus, in 1 Thess iii 8. St. Paul, speaking to the Thessalonians, says, *Now we live, if* (more correctly, when) *ye stand fast in the Lord*. The word *live*, in this passage, is not to be understood in its whole extent, as implying that the apostle's physical life or existence depended on their standing fast in the Lord, but must be understood in a limited sense. It is as if he had said, "Your steadfastness in the faith gives me new life and comfort. I now feel that I live to some purpose — I relish and enjoy life — since my labour in the Gospel is not in vain." That this is the true meaning of the apostle, is evident both from the subject-matter and from the context: for Saint Paul, filled with deep anxiety lest the Thessalonians should have been induced to depart from the faith by the afflictions which they had to endure, had sent Timothy to raise and comfort them. Having heard of their constancy in the faith, he exclaims, Now *we live, if ye stand fast in the Lord*.

8. *The most simple sense is always that which is the genuine meaning.*

This remark is so obvious as to require no illustrative example. Where indeed two meanings or senses present themselves, without doing any violence to the words or to their

---

[1] On the subject of words commonly thought synonymous, see Dr Campbell's Dissertation prefixed to his translation of the Gospels, vol. i. pp. 164—240. edit. 1807.

scope and connection, and to the subject-matter, &c in such case the different arguments for and against each meaning must be carefully discussed, and that meaning which is supported by the most numerous and weighty arguments, and is found to be the most probable, must be preferred, as being the genuine sense. Yet, simple and obvious as this canon confessedly is, it is perpetually violated by the modern school of interpreters in Germany, at the head of which stand the names of Professors Semler, Bauer, Paulus, Wegscheider, Eichhorn, and others, against whose tenets the unwary student cannot be sufficiently put upon his guard, on account of the great celebrity which some of these writers have justly acquired for their profound philological attainments. The teachers of this school assert that there is no such thing as a divine revelation in the sense attached to this word by Christians; and that the miracles recorded in the Scriptures are merely natural occurrences, exaggerated and embellished by those who have related them. According to these anti-supernaturalists, the whole of the doctrines of Scripture consist either of the precepts of nature clothed in obscure expressions, or of absolutely false doctrines invented by the sacred writers, who were men subject to error like ourselves, and (what they say is still worse) who were deprived of that mass of knowledge which constitutes the glory of our age. To confirm the preceding observations by a few examples.

(1.) According to Eichhorn, the account of the creation and fall of man is merely a poetical, philosophical speculation of some ingenious person, on the origin of the world and of evil.[1] So, in regard to the offering up of Isaac by Abraham, he says, "The Godhead could not have required of Abraham so horrible a crime, and there can be no justification, palliation, or excuse for this pretended command of the Divinity." He then explains it. "Abraham *dreamed* that he must offer up Isaac, and according to the superstition of the times, regarded it as a divine admonition. He prepared to execute the mandate, which his dream had conveyed to him. A lucky accident (probably the rustling of a ram who was entangled in the bushes) hindered it; and this, according to antient idiom, was also the voice of the divinity."[2]

(2.) The same writer represents the history of the Mosaic legislation, at mount Sinai, in a curious manner. Moses ascended to the top of Sinai, and kindled a fire there, (how he found wood on this barren rock, or raised it to the top, Eichhorn does not tell us,) a fire consecrated to the worship of God, before which he prayed. Here an unexpected and tremendous thunder-storm occurred. He seized the occasion, to proclaim the laws which he had composed in his retirement, as the statutes of Jehovah, leading the people to believe that Jehovah had conversed with him. Not that he was a deceiver, but he really believed, that the occurrence of such a thunder-storm was a sufficient proof of the fact, that Jehovah had spoken to him, or sanctioned the work in which he had been engaged..[3] The prophecies of the Old Testament are, according to him, patriotic wishes, expressed with all the fire and elegance of poetry, for the future prosperity, and a future deliverer of the Jewish nation.[4]

(3.) In like manner, C. F. Ammon, who was formerly professor of theology at Erlangen, tells us, in respect to the miracle of Christ's walking on the water, that "to walk on the sea, is not to stand on the waves, as on the solid ground, as Jerom *dreams*, but to walk through the waves so far as the shoals reached, and then to swim."[5] So, in regard to the miracle of the loaves and fishes[6], he says, that Jesus probably distributed some loaves and fishes which he had, to those who were around him; and thus excited, by his example, others among the multitude, who had provisions, to distribute them in like manner.[7]

(4.) Thiess, in his commentary on the Acts, explains the miraculous effusion of the Spirit on the day of Pentecost[8], in the following manner. — "It is not uncommon," says he, "in those countries, for a violent gust of wind to strike on a particular spot or house. Such a gust is commonly accompanied by the electric fluid, and the sparks of this are scattered all around. These float about the chamber, become apparent, and light upon the disciples. They kindle into enthusiasm at this, and believe the promise of their Master is now to be performed. This enthusiasm spectators assemble to witness; and instead of preaching as before in Hebrew, each one uses his own native tongue to proclaim his feelings."

(5.) The same Thiess[9], represents the miraculous cure by Peter, of the man who was lame from his birth, in a very singular way. "This man," says he, "was lame only according to report. He never walked at all; so, the people believed that he could not walk ...Peter and John, being more sagacious, however, *threatened* him. ' In the name of the Messiah,' said they, ' Stand up.' The word *Messiah* had a magical power. He stood up. Now they saw that he could walk. To prevent the compassion of men from being turned

---

[1] Urgeschichte passim.   [2] Bibliothek Band. i. s. 45, &c.
[3] Bibliothek. Band. 1. Theil 1. s 76, &c.
[4] Prophetem, Bibliothek. Einleit passim.
[5] Pref. to edit. of Ernesti Inst. Interpret p. 12.
[7] P. 16.   [8] Acts ii.   [6] Matt. xiv. 15.
[9] Comm. on chap. iii.

into rage (at his deceit), he chose the most sagacious party, and connected himself with the apostles."

(6.) The case of Ananias falling down dead, is thus represented by the same writer: "Ananias fell down terrified, but probably he was carried out and buried while still alive." Heinrichs, however, who produces this Comment of Thiess, relates another mode of explaining the occurrence in question, viz. that *Peter stabbed Ananias;* "which does not at all disagree with the vehement and easily-exasperated temper of Peter." It is, however, but just to Heinrichs to state that he has expressed his decided disapprobation of this pretended interpretation.[1]

(7.) Professor De Wette, in his treatise *De Morte Christi Expiatoria*, (on the atonement of Christ,) represents Christ as disappointed, that the Jews would not hearken to him as a moral teacher simply, which was the first character he assumed. Christ then assumed the character of a prophet, and asserted his divine mission, in order that the Jews might be induced to listen to him. Finding that they would not do this, and that they were determined to destroy him, in order not to lose the whole object of his mission, and to convert necessity into an occasion of giving himself credit, he gave out, that his death itself would be *expiatory!*[2]

9. *Since it is the design of interpretation to render in our own language the same discourse which the sacred authors originally wrote in Hebrew or Greek, it is evident that our interpretation or version, to be correct, ought not to affirm or deny more than the inspired penmen affirmed or denied at the time they wrote; consequently we should be more willing to take a sense from Scripture than to bring one to it.*

This is one of the most antient laws of interpretation extant, and cannot be sufficiently kept in mind, lest we should *teach for doctrines the commandments of men*, and impose our *narrow* and *limited* conceptions instead of the *broad* and *general* declarations of Scripture. For want of attending to this simple rule, how many forced and unnatural interpretations have been put upon the Sacred Writings! — interpretations alike contradictory to the *express* meaning of other passages of Scripture, as well as derogatory from every idea we are taught to conceive of the justice and mercy of the Most High. It will suffice to illustrate this remark by one single instance. In John iii. 16, 17. we read that "*God so loved the* WORLD, *that he gave his only begotten Son, that whosoever believeth in him shall not perish but have everlasting life: for God sent not his Son to condemn the world, but that the world through him might be saved.*" The plain, obvious, and literal sense of this passage, as well as of its whole context, is, that the whole of mankind, including both Jews and Gentiles, without any exception in favour of individuals, were in a ruined state, about to perish everlastingly and utterly without the power of rescuing themselves from destruction; that God provided for their rescue and salvation by giving his Son to die for them, and that all who *believe* in him, that is, who believe what God has spoken concerning Christ, his sacrifice, the end for which it was offered, and the way in which it is to be applied in order to become effectual, that *all who thus believe* shall not only be exempted from eternal perdition, but shall also ultimately *have everlasting life*, in other words, be brought to eternal glory. Yet how are these "good tidings of great joy to all people," narrowed and restricted by certain expositors, who adopt the hypothesis that Jesus Christ was given for the *elect alone!* How, indeed, could God be said to love those, to whom he denies the means of salvation, and whom he destines by an irrevocable decree to eternal misery? And what violence are such expositors compelled to do to the passage in question in order to reconcile it to their preconceived notions! They are obliged to interpret that comprehensive word, the *world*, by a synecdoche of a part for the whole, and thus say, that it means the nobler portion of the world, namely the *elect*, without calling to their aid those other pa-

---

[1] Nov. Test. Koppianum, vol. iii. Partic. ii. pp. 355—357, &c.

[2] For the preceding examples, the absurdity and extravagance of which are too obvious to require any comment, the author is indebted to the researches of Professor Stuart in his letters to the Rev. W. E. Channing (pp. 144, 145. 147.) Andover (North America), 1819. 12mo. On the topic above discussed, the reader will find some painfully-interesting details in Mr Jacob's Agricultural and Political Tour in Germany (London, 1820, 4to.), pp. 208—212, in the Magasin Evangélique, (Génève, 1820, 8vo.) tome ii. pp. 26—32, in Dr. J. P. Smith's Scripture Testimony to the Messiah, vol. ii. part ii. pp. 634, 635, and Mr Rose's Discourses on the State of the Protestant Religion in Germany. It is proper to add, that the system of obscurity and impiety above noticed has met with able refutations; and Kuinoël, whose commentary on the historical books of the New Testament (noticed in another part of this work) was composed principally for Germans, has given abstracts of these refutations. — On the subject of the *Mythical Interpretation of Scripture*, as it is termed, see the NOTE at the end of this volume.

rallel passages of Scripture, in which the above consolatory truth is explicitly affirmed in other words. A similar instance occurs in Matt xviii. 11, where Jesus Christ is said to have " come to save that which was lost," το απολωλος; which word, as its meaning is not restricted by the Holy Spirit, is not to be interpreted in a restricted sense, and consequently must be taken in its most obvious and universal sense. In this way we are to understand Deut xxvii 26 and Isa. lxiv. 6.

10. *Before we conclude upon the sense of a text, so as to prove any thing by it, we must be sure that such sense is not repugnant to natural reason.*

If such sense be repugnant to natural reason, it cannot be the true meaning of the Scripture, for God is the original of natural truth, as well as of that which comes by particular revelation No proposition, therefore, which is repugnant to the fundamental principles of reason, can be the sense of any part of the word of God, and that which is false and contrary to reason, can no more be true and agreeable to the revelations contained in the Sacred Writings, than God (who is the author of one as well as the other) can contradict himself. Whence it is evident that the words of Jesus Christ, — *This is my body,* and *This is my blood*, — (Matt xxvi 26 28) are not to be understood in that sense, which makes for the doctrine of transubstantiation because it is impossible that contradictions should be true, and we cannot be more certain that any thing is true, than we are that *that* doctrine is false

---

SECTION III.

OF EMPHASES.

I. *Nature of Emphasis. — Its different Kinds.* — II. VERBAL EMPHASES. 1. *Emphases of the Greek Article.* — 2. *Emphases of other Words.* — 3. *Emphatic Adverbs.* — III. REAL EMPHASES. — IV. *General Rules for the Investigation of Emphases.*

I. NATURE OF EMPHASIS:—its different kinds.

In the use of language, cases arise where the ordinary signification of a word receives a certain accession (*auctarium*) or idea, which such word has not of itself. This accession may be effected in two ways; the first consists in an honorary or in a degrading sense, according to the usage and opinion of men; of this kind of accession it would be irrelevant to treat in this place. The second class of words comprises those which receive an accession or augmentation in the *extent* or *force of meaning*. These constitute what may with propriety be called EMPHATIC WORDS. Emphasis, therefore, may be thus defined: —*An accession to the ordinary signification of a word, either as to the extent or force of its meaning.*

Thus, when the Jews speak of Moses, they simply term him *the Prophet*. In like manner, the antient Greeks call Demosthenes, *the Orator;* Plato, *the Philosopher;* Homer, *the Poet*, by way of eminence. These respective appellations are emphatic. The title of — *the Prophet* — given by the Jews to Moses, signifies that he was the first of the Jewish prophets, and of such distinguished dignity, that there *arose* no subsequent *prophet in Israel like unto Moses, whom the Lord knew face to face,* and conversed *mouth to mouth.* (Deut. xxxiv. 10. Numb. xii. 8.)[1]

Emphases are either *verbal*, that is, such as occur in *words* both separately and together, or *real*, that is, such as appear in the magnitude and sublimity of the *thing* described by words. The

---

[1] Ernesti, Inst. Interp. Nov Test pp 40, 41. Mori Hermeneut Nov. Test. Acroases, tom. i. pp. 323, 324. Stuart's Elements of Interpretation, p. 27.

propriety of this division has been contested by Huet, Ernesti[1], and some others, who affirm that emphases subsist in words only, and not in things, and that in things grandeur and sublimity alone are to be found. On this clasification, however, there is a difference of opinion: and Longinus himself, who has placed emphases among the sources of the sublime, seems to have admitted that they exist also in things. In the first instance, unquestionably, they are to be sought in words, sometimes in particles, and also in the Greek article; and when their force is fully apprehended, they enable us to enter into the peculiar elegances and beauties of the sacred style. A few examples illustrative of this remark must suffice.

II. VERBAL EMPHASES.

1. *Emphases of the Greek Article.*

In Matt. xxvi. 28 our Saviour having instituted the sacrament of the Lord's supper, after giving the cup to his disciples, adds "For this is my blood of the New Testament which is shed for many for the remission of sins." Almost every syllable of the original Greek, especially the articles, is singularly emphatic. It runs thus — Τουτο γαρ εςι ΤΟ αιμα μου, ΤΟ της καινης διαθηκης, ΤΟ περι πολλων εκχυνομενον εις αφεσιν αμαρτιων. The following literal translation and paraphrase do not exceed its meaning —"*For this is* THAT *blood of mine*, which was pointed out by all the sacrifices under the Jewish law, and particularly by the shedding and sprinkling of the blood of the paschal lamb, THAT BLOOD of the sacrifice slain for the ratification *of the new covenant*, THE *blood* ready to be *poured out for the multitudes*, the whole Gentile world as well as the Jews, *for the taking away of sins*; sin, whether original or actual, in all its power and guilt, in all its energy and pollution?" In Matt. xvi. 16 the following sentence occurs —Συ εις 'Ο Χριςος 'Ο υιος ΤΟΥ Θεου ΤΟΥ ζωντος, "*Thou art* THE *Christ*, THE SON OF THE *living God*." In this passage, also, every word is highly emphatic, agreeably to a rule of the Greek language, which is observed both by the sacred writers, as well as by the most elegant profane authors, viz. that when the article is placed before a noun, it denotes a certain and definite object; but when it is omitted, it in general indicates any person or thing indefinitely. The apostle did not say, "Thou art Christ, Son of God," without the article: but, "*Thou art* THE *Christ*, the Messiah, THE SON," that very son, thus positively asserting his belief of that fundamental article of the Christian religion, the divinity and office of the Redeemer of the world — "*Of the living God*, or *of God* THE *living one*." Similar instances occur in John i. 21. 'Ο προφητης ει συ, "*art thou* THAT *Prophet*" whom the Jewish nation have so long and so anxiously expected, and who had been promised by Moses (Deut xviii 15 18)? and also in John x. 11 Εγω ειμι 'Ο ποιμην 'Ο καλος, *I am* THAT *good Shepherd*, or *the shepherd*, THAT *good one*, of whom Isaiah (xl 11) and Ezekiel (xxxiv 23) respectively prophesied

Another very important rule in the construction of the Greek article is the following, which was first completely illustrated by the late eminently learned Granville Sharp; though it appears not to have been unknown to former critics and commentators.[3]

"*When two or more personal nouns of the same gender, number, and case, are connected by the copulative και* (and), *if the first has the definitive article, and the second, third, &c. have not, they both relate to the same person.*"

---

[1] Ernesti (Inst Interp Nov Test p 41) and after him Bauer (Herm. Sacra, p 282.) and Morus (Hermeneut. Nov. Test. Acroases, tom i pp. 323—326) have distinguished emphases into *temporary* and *permanent*. The *former* are found in words at a certain time and place, and arise from the feelings of the party speaking, or from the importance of the thing. The *latter* or permanent emphases are those, in which a word receives from custom a greater signification than it has of itself, and which it retains under certain forms of speech. The knowledge of both these is to be derived from a consideration of the context and subject-matter. But the examples adduced in defence of this definition concur to make it a distinction without a difference, when compared with the ordinary classification of emphases into verbal and real, which we have accordingly retained

[2] Dr. A Clarke's Discourse on the Eucharist, pp. 61, 62.

[3] Venema, in an admirable dissertation on the true reading of Acts xx 28. has adverted to it. (See the passage in the British Critic (N S.), vol. xi. p 612), and also Mr De Gols, in his valuable, though now neglected, Vindication of the Worship of Jesus Christ. (London, 1726. 8vo.) p 37.

This rule Mr. S. has illustrated by the eight following examples:—

1. Ὁ Θεος και πατηρ Κυριου ἡμων. 2 Cor. i. 8.
2. Τῳ Θεῳ και πατρι. 1 Cor. xv. 24.

These examples are properly rendered, in the authorised translation, and according to the preceding rule,

1. The God and Father of our Lord.
2. To God *even* the Father.
3. Εν τη βασιλεια του Χριστου και Θεου. Eph v 5.

Common Version.	Corrected Version.
In the Kingdom of Christ and of God.	In the Kingdom of Christ, *even* of God.

4. Καἰα χαριν του Θεου ἡμων και Κυριου Ιησου Χριστου   2 Thess. i. 12.

Common Version.	Corrected Version.
According to the grace of our God and the Lord Jesus Christ.	According to the grace of Jesus Christ, *our God and Lord*.

5. Ενωπιον του Θεου και Κυριου Ιησου Χριστου   1 Tim. v. 21.

Common Version	Corrected Version.
Before God and the Lord Jesus Christ	Before Jesus Christ, *the God and Lord*, or, *our God and Lord*. (*For the definitive Article has sometimes the power of a possessive Pronoun.*)

6. Επιφανειαν της δοξης του μεγαλου Θεου και σωτηρος ἡμων Ιησου Χριστου,   Titus ii. 13.

Common Version.	Corrected Version
The glorious appearing of the great God and our Saviour Jesus Christ.	The glorious appearing *of our great God and Saviour Jesus Christ*.

7. Εν δικαιοσυνη του Θεου ἡμων και σωτηρος Ιησου Χριστου   2 Pet. i. 1.

Common Version.	Corrected Version
Through the righteousness of God, and of our Saviour Jesus Christ.	Through the righteousness of Jesus Christ, *our God and Saviour*.

8. Και τον μονον δεσποτην Θεον και Κυριον ἡμων Ιησουν Χριστον αρνουμενοι. Jude 4.

Common Version	Corrected Version.
And denying the only Lord God, and our Lord Jesus Christ.	And denying our only *Master*, *God*, *and Lord Jesus Christ*.[1]

The above rule and examples are further confirmed by the researches of Bishop Middleton; and altogether furnish a most striking body of evidence in behalf of the divinity of our Saviour. That fundamental and most important doctrine of the Christian faith does not indeed depend upon the niceties of grammatical construction: but when these are eagerly seized by those who deny the divinity of the Son of God, in order to support their interpretation, we are amply justified in combating them with the same weapons. On this account the reader will be gratified by the addition of a few examples, both from classic authors, as well as from two or three of the fathers of the Christian church, in which Mr. Sharp's rule is completely exemplified. They are selected from Mr. Boyd's supplementary researches on the Greek article, annexed to Dr. A. Clarke's Commentary on Eph vi. and on the Epistle to Titus.

Ὁπα τας Τηρειας
Μητιδος οικτρας αλοχου
Κιρκηλατου τ' αηδονος.   Æschyli Supplices, v. 62—64.

The voice of the wretched wife of Tereus, the nightingale, pursued by the falcon.

Ὁ δυστυχης δαιμον, ὁ σος καμος.   Sophoclis Electra.
Mine and thine evil genius.

Ὁ εμος γενετας και σος.
My son and thine.

Οἱα τε πασχομεν εκ της μυσαρας,
Και παιδοφονου της δε λεαινης   Euripidis Ion, v. 1389. 1403.

What things we suffer from this execrable lioness, and slayer of children!

---

[1] Sharp on the Greek article, pp. xxxix. xl 1—56

Του μακαριου και ενδοξου Παυλου. — Of the blessed and illustrious Paul. (Polycarp, Epist ad Philipp)

Αγαπην του Χριϛου, του Θεου ἡμων. — The love of Christ our God (Ignatius, Epist. ad Romanos.)

Τον Κτιϛην, και Δημιουργον — The Creator and Maker. (Irenæus adv Hæres. lib iv. p. 48. edit. Oxon 1702.)

Του κουφαιοτατου παρ' ὑμων και πρωτου των ποιητων, Ὁμηρου — Homer the most distinguished among you, and first of the poets (Justin Martyr, Cohortatio ad Græcos)

Ὁ Αρχιϛρατηγος και Ποιμην των κατ' ουρανον, ᾡ παντα πειθονται. — The great Ruler and Shepherd of them in heaven, whom all things obey (Methodius)

Αμφι τον αναρχον και ανωλεθρον Βασιλεα. — Around the King, without beginning and immortal. (Ibid)

Ἱνα τον Βασιλεα γεραιρη παντων και Ποιητην. — That he may venerate the King and Maker of all. (Ibid)

Ὁ ϛρατηγος ἡμων και ποιμην Ιησους, και αρχων, και νυμφιος — Jesus, our leader, and shepherd, and governor, and bridegroom. (Ibid)

Τον Θεον μονον αρνεισθε, τον δεσποτην και δημιουργον του παντος. — Ye deny the only God, the Lord and Creator of all. (Chrysostom. Orat. de non anathem vivis aut defunctis.)

Εν ἡμερα επιφανειας και αποκαλυψεως του μεγαλου Θεου και Αρχιποιμενος ἡμων, Ιησου Χριϛου. — In the day of the appearing and revelation of Jesus Christ, the Great God and Chief Shepherd of us (Gregor. Nazianzen. Orat. 4. adv. Julian in fine)

2. *Emphases of other Words.*

John 1 14. *The word was made flesh and dwelt among us,* εσκηνωσεν εν ἡμιν, literally *tabernacled among us.* The verb σκηνοω (from σκηνη) signifies to erect a booth, tabernacle, or temporary residence, and not a permanent habitation or dwelling-place. It was therefore fitly applied to the human nature of Christ; which, like the antient Jewish tabernacle, was to be only for a temporary residence of the Eternal Divinity.

Matt. ix. 36 *When Jesus saw the multitudes, he had compassion on them,* — Εσπλαγχνισθη (from Σπλαγχνον, a bowel), the antients generally, and the Jews in particular, accounting the bowels to be the seat of sympathy and the tender passions, applied the organ to the sense[1]. The proper meaning, therefore, of this phrase is, that our Lord was moved with the deepest sympathy and commiseration for the neglected Jews.

Heb iv. 13 *All things are naked and opened,* τετραχηλισμενα, *to the eyes of him with whom we have to account.* The emphasis is here derived from the manner in which sacrifices were antiently performed

3. *Emphatic Adverbs.*

[i.] *Sometimes* ADVERBS OF TIME *are emphatic; and a careful notation of the time indicated by them will materially illustrate the force and meaning of the Sacred Writings.*

Thus, in Mal. iii 16. we read, THEN *they that feared the Lord, spake often one to another, &c* The word THEN is here peculiarly emphatic, and refers to the time when the last of the prophets wrote, and when many bold infidels and impious persons were found among the Jews, who spake "stout words" against God, and vindicated them. They considered all the time spent by them in his service as lost; they attended his "ordinances" with many expressions of self-denial and humiliation, but they derived no benefit from them, and they concluded that those haughty rebels who cast off all religion, and tempted God by their presumptuous wickedness, were the most prosperous and happy persons (v. 13—15.) THEN, viz *at this season of open wickedness,* there was a remnant of pious Jews, who "spake often one to another," met together from time to time that they might confer on religious subjects, animate each other to their duty, and consult how to check the progress of impiety Of these persons, and their pious designs and discourses, we are told that Jehovah took especial notice, and that "a book of remembrance was written before him for them that feared the Lord, and that thought upon his name"

[ii.] *A knowledge of historical circumstances, however, is requisite, lest we ascribe the emphasis to a wrong source; as in Acts ix. 31.*

THEN *had the churches rest* (ειρηνην, literally, peace or prosperity). The cause of this peace has by some commentators been ascribed to the conversion of Saul, who had previously "made havoc of the church" but this is not likely, as *he* could not be a cause of *universal* persecution and distress, whatever activity and virulence he might have shown during the time of his enmity to the Christian church. Besides, his own persecution (as

---

[1] Kuinoel in loc. who has given illustrations from classical writers, and also from the Apocrypha.

the context shows) proves that the opposition to the Gospel continued with considerable virulence three years after *his* conversion. If we advert to the political circumstances of the Jewish nation at that time, we shall find the true cause of this rest. The emperor Caligula had ordered his statue to be erected in the temple at Jerusalem, and, in pursuance of his mandate, Petronius, the president of Syria, was on his march with an army for that purpose. Filled with consternation, the Jews met him in vast multitudes in the vicinity of Ptolemais or Acre, and ultimately prevailed on him to abandon his design. It was this persecution of the Jews by the Romans, that the sacred writer had in view, which diverted the Jews from persecuting the Christians and "THEN *had the churches rest throughout all Judea and Galilee and Samaria*," the terror occasioned by the imperial decree having spread itself throughout those regions.¹

III. REAL EMPHASES.

The knowledge of these can only be derived from an acquaintance with the manners, customs, &c. of antient nations, which are noticed by writers on biblical antiquities and by commentators, so far as they are necessary to illustrate the sacred writings. Two or three instances of these also will suffice to explain their nature.

1. Rom. xi 17. In this verse we have a very beautiful illustration taken from the ingrafting of trees; an art with which we find St Paul was well acquainted. The point to be explained was, the union of the Gentiles with the Jews under the Gospel dispensation. The Jews were the olive tree, the grafts were both Gentiles and Jews, and the act of ingrafting was, the initiation of both into the Christian religion. The Jews are informed that olive branches may with greater ease be ingrafted into their own original stock, which is more natural and congenial to them. The Gentiles are again reminded, that, if the natural branches were not spared because of their unfruitfulness, much less would they be spared who were aliens to the Jewish stock, if they should prove unfruitful.

2. The *prize*, βραβειον, mentioned in 1 Cor ix 24, is the crown awarded to the victor in the olympic games; whence καταβραβευειν, rendered *beguile you of your reward* (Col ii. 18.), means to deprive any one of a reward or prize, either by partial judgment or in any way impeding him in his Christian course. In 1 Cor. ix 24 the apostle illustrates the necessity of being in earnest in the Christian race, by a beautiful allusion to the games of the heathen. As the racers and wrestlers in those games fitted themselves for their different exercises, and each strove zealously for the victory, so should the Christian prepare himself for his religious course, and strive for the victory in his great contest with the world.

3 1 Cor iv 13. *We are made the filth of the earth,* περικαθαρματα, literally, a *purgation* or *lustrative sacrifice* the allusion is to a custom common among heathen nations in times of public calamity, who selected some unhappy men of the most abject and despicable character. These, after being maintained a whole year at the public expense, were then led out crowned with flowers, as was usual in sacrifices, and were devoted to appease or avert the anger of their deities, being either precipitated into the sea, or burnt alive, after which their ashes were thrown into the sea.

4 Eph. v 27. *That it* (the church of Christ) *should be holy and* WITHOUT BLEMISH, αμωμος, i c. so pure and spotless, so free from all censure, that even Momus himself (the fictitious deity of mirth and ridicule) could find nothing to carp at or ridicule.

IV. GENERAL RULES FOR THE INVESTIGATION OF EMPHASES.

A consideration of the affections by which the sacred authors were animated, when they committed their inspired communications to writing, as well as the scope and context of the passage under consideration, together with the nature of its subject, will always enable us to ascertain the *true* emphasis of words: but, as ingenious and fanciful minds are apt to discover them where they do not actually exist, it may not be irrelevant to offer a few leading hints respecting the particular investigation of emphases, selected from the great mass of observations, which have been collected by eminent biblical critics.

'1. *No emphases are to be sought in refined explanations of passages, or from etymology, both of them uncertain guides at the best; and which are*

---

¹ Dr. Lardner has collected and given at length various passages from Josephus (De Bell. Jud. lib. ii. c.10 and Ant. Jud lib. xvii c. 9.) and Philo (De Legat. ad Caium, p. 1024.), which confirm the above statement. See his Credibility, book 1. ch. ii. § 12.

too often carried to extremes by men of lively imaginations. *Neither will prepositions always enlarge or give additional force to the meaning of a word, particularly in the Greek language.*

We may instance in 1 Cor. xiii. 6., where we read that true charity rejoiceth not in iniquity, but rejoiceth (συγχαίρει) in the truth. Some commentators have conceived that this word is emphatic, and have rendered the passage *rejoiceth jointly* (with true believers) in the truth. But in this instance, as Schleusner has remarked from Hesychius, the Greek compound verb means no more than the simple verb χαίρω implies, viz. to be delighted or to rejoice in a thing. Our authorised version therefore fully expresses the apostle's meaning. But in Heb. xii. 2. the preposition is highly emphatic, and demands particular attention, in order to apprehend the full force and beauty of the passage, which is wholly *agonistical*, i. e. allusive to the antient foot-races. Having in the first verse exhorted Christians to divest themselves of every incumbrance, and to run with patience their Christian course, St. Paul adds, (v. 2.) *Looking unto Jesus the author and finisher of our faith.* The original word here rendered *looking* (ἀφορῶντες) [1], literally means to *look off* FROM every other object *to* some particular object placed full in view; as the reward destined to the victor in the olympic foot-race was placed immediately in view of the candidates. It is impossible to express the full import of this passage without the aid of a paraphrase. The whole clause may be thus rendered — *Wherefore, seeing we are also compassed about with so great a cloud of witnesses,* who (like the spectators at the antient olympic race) surround us on every side in a vast innumerable assembly, the spectators of our trial, *let us lay aside every* incumbering *weight,* and especially *the sin, which in present circumstances has the greatest advantage* [against us], or *the well circumstanced sin,* that which has every thing in its favour, time, place, and opportunity, more particularly, a disposition to relinquish or dissemble our profession of the Gospel for fear of sufferings; and let us *run with patience* and perseverance *the race which is set before us,* resolutely persisting in it, however long and painful it may be. *Looking off* from every object that would interrupt us in our career, and fixing our eyes *upon* (or *to*) *Jesus, the author* (or *leader*) *and finisher of our faith,* who called us out to this strenuous yet glorious enterprise, who animates us by his example, and supports us by his grace, until the season arrive, when he will bestow upon us the promised crown.[2]

2. *Further. Emphases are not to be sought in versions, which, however excellent they may in general be, are yet liable to error; consequently the derivation of emphases from them may lead us not merely to extravagant, but even to false expositions of Scripture.*

One instance will suffice to illustrate this remark. In Col. ii. 6. according to the authorised English version, we read thus, *As ye have therefore received Christ Jesus the Lord, so walk ye in him.* From this rendering of the Greek text many persons have laid much stress on the words *as* and *so* (which last is not to be found in the original), and have deduced a variety of inferences from them, viz. *as* ye received Jesus Christ in a spirit of faith, *so* walk ye in him; *as* ye received him in a spirit of humility, *so* walk ye in him, &c. Now all these inferences, though proper enough in themselves, are derived from *false emphases,* and are contrary to the apostle's meaning, who intended to say no such thing. His meaning, as Dr. Macknight has well translated the passage, is simply this — "*Since ye have received Christ Jesus the Lord, walk ye in him*" in other words, as the context plainly shows, "Since ye have embraced the doctrine of Christ, continue to hold it fast, and permit not yourselves to be turned aside by sophistical or Judaising teachers"[3]

3. *No emphases are to be sought merely in the plural number of words.*

We must be cautious, also, that we do not deduce emphasis merely from the use of the

---

[1] This word occurs in Josephus precisely in the very same meaning as it is used by the apostle. The Jewish historian, relating the aggressions of the Jews which led to the war with the Romans, says, among other things, that those who officiated in the temple-service, rejected the sacrifice for Cæsar and the Roman people. "And when many of the high priests and principal men besought them not to omit the sacrifice, which it was customary for them to offer for their princes, they would not be prevailed upon. These relied much upon their number, for the most flourishing part of the innovators assisted them," ΑΦΟΡΩΝΤΕΣ εἰς τὸν Ἐλεαζαρον, "*having the chief regard to Eleazar,* the governor of the temple;" *looking* TO HIM EXCLUSIVELY, by whom they had been instigated to those offensive measures. De Bell. Jud. lib. ii. c. xvii. § 2.

[2] See Braunius, Krebsius, Kypke, Ernesti, and also Drs. Doddridge, Macknight, and A. Clarke on Heb. xii. 1, 2 by whom every emphatic word in these two verses is particularly illustrated.

[3] See Drs. Macknight and A. Clarke on Col. ii. 6.

plural number; supposing that, where the plural is put instead of the singular, it necessarily denotes emphases. Thus ουρανος and ουρανοι simply mean *heaven*, yet Origen, following the trifling distinctions of some Jewish writers, has attempted to distinguish between them, and has announced the existence of several heavens each above the other.

4. *No emphases are to be sought in words where the abstract is put for the concrete.*

In the Old Testament the abstract is very frequently put for the concrete; that is, substantives are necessarily put in the place of adjectives, on account of the simplicity of the Hebrew language which has few or no adjectives. A similar mode of expression obtains in the New Testament. Thus, in Eph v. 8. we read, *Ye were sometimes* DARKNESS, σκοτος. In the parallel place, in iv. 18 the metonymy is thus expressed being DARKENED, εσκοτισμενοι, *in the understanding*, or, as it is rendered in an authorised version, having the understanding darkened. Numerous examples, in which the abstract is put for the concrete, will be found, *infra*, Book II. Chap. II. Sect. II. § 4.

5. *As every language abounds with* idioms [1], *or expressions peculiar to itself, which cannot be rendered verbatim into another language without violating its native purity, we should be careful not to look for emphases in such expressions.* [2]

"In the sacred books, and specially in the Hebraisms of the New Testament, we must take care not to seek for and recognise emphasis, merely in the idiom which is so very dissimilar to ours. Many persons, though acquainted with Hebrew, have often made this mistake but nothing is more fallacious. In the oriental languages many things *appear* hyperbolical, (if you translate them literally, that is, merely by the aid of common lexicons and etymology,) which are not in reality hyperbolical." [3]

CHAPTER II.

ON THE SUBSIDIARY MEANS FOR ASCERTAINING THE SENSE OF SCRIPTURE.

WORDS being the arbitrary signs of things, the *usus loquendi* denotes the sense which usage attaches to the words of any language. It is surprising that any attempts should have been made to find the sense of words in a dead language, by means different in their nature from those which we employ in order to find the sense of words in a living language. The meaning of a word must always be a simple matter of fact; and, of course, it is always to be established by appropriate and adequate testimony. The original languages of Scripture being to us dead languages, the *usus loquendi* in them is to be ascertained by the testimony of those who lived at the time when these

---

[1] On the Hebraisms, or Hebrew idioms peculiar to the Sacred Writings, see pp. 23—27. of the present volume.

[2] Bauer, Herm Sacr. pp 231—240. Ernesti Instit. Interp Nov Test. pp. 40—45. Mori Acroases in Ernesti, tom 1 pp 321—336 Aug. Pfeiffer, Herm. Sacr. c. vi. § 16—23. (Op tom pp. 649—651.) Wetstein, Libelli ad Crisin et Interp. Nov. Test. pp. 120—139 Viser, Herm Sacr Nov. Test. pars iii. pp 263—277. Bishop Marsh's Lectures, lect. xv. pp 43—49. Prof. Gerard has collected numerous valuable observations on the topics discussed in this and the two preceding sections, in his Institutes of Biblical Criticism, pp. 293—369. particularly in sect. iii. (pp. 300—314.) on the signification of words. J. B. Carpzovii Primæ Lineæ Herm. Sacræ, pp. 23. 40—45. The subject of emphases is copiously treated by Langius in his Hermeneutica Sacra, pp. 64—96.; by Rambach, in his Institutiones Hermeneuticæ Sacræ, lib. ii c. 8. pp. 317—362.; by Jahn, in his Enchiridion Herm. Generalis, pp. 127—135., by Chladenius, in his Institutiones Exegeticæ, pp 310—322; and by J. E Pfeiffer, in his Institutiones Herm. Sacr. pp. 594—569 Stuart's Elements of Interpretation, pp. 85—87.

[3] Stuart's Elements of Interpretation, p. 87.

languages were flourishing and in common use, and who well understood them. This testimony is either direct or indirect.

DIRECT TESTIMONY is to be obtained, in the first place, from those writers to whom the language, which is to be investigated by us, was vernacular, either from the same authors whom we interpret, or from their contemporaries; next from antient versions made while the language was spoken, and by individuals who were acquainted with it; thirdly, from Scholiasts and Glossographers; fourthly, from those who, though foreigners, had learned the language in question.

Where direct testimony fails, recourse must be had to INDIRECT TESTIMONY; under which head we may include the Context, Subject-Matter, Scope, Analogy of Languages, Analogy of Doctrine, Jewish Authors, the Greek Fathers, Historical Circumstances, and Commentators.[1] Some of these various aids are peculiar to the Old Testament, and others to the New Testament: to avoid unnecessary repetition, it is proposed to discuss them in the order pursued in the following Sections.

SECTION I.

DIRECT TESTIMONIES FOR ASCERTAINING THE USUS LOQUENDI.

§ 1. THE TESTIMONY OF CONTEMPORARY WRITERS.

THE most important testimony is afforded by those writers to whom the language to be investigated was vernacular: and where it is indubitable its evidence is abundantly sufficient. This testimony may be drawn from three sources, viz. 1. From the definitions of words; 2. From examples, and the nature of the subject; and, 3. From parallel passages.

I. With regard to DEFINITIONS, nothing more is necessary, than to take good care that the definition be well understood; and to consider how much weight the character of the writer who defines, may properly give to it.[2]

Professor Morus has collected various examples of definitions from profane writers, both Greek and Latin, which it is not necessary to adduce in this place: but the following definitions of certain words occurring in the New Testament are of importance for the right understanding of the sacred writers.

1. In Heb. v. 14. St. Paul says that he writes τοις τελειοις, to *the perfect;* and he there, with almost logical precision, defines the perfect to be *those who by reason of use have their senses exercised to discern both good and evil;* that is, those, who by long custom and conversation in the sacred writings, have so exercised and improved their faculties, that they can discern between good and bad, true and false doctrines In the whole of that passage, therefore, we are to understand the perfect, agreeably to St. Paul's definition.

---

[1] Bauer, Hermeneut. Sacra, pp. 77—79. Mori Acroases Hermeneuticæ, tom. i. pp. 75—77. Stuart's Elements of Interpretation, pp. 34, 35.
[2] Stuart's Elements of Interpretation, p. 35. Morus, tom. i. p. 79.

2. If we were at a loss to understand, in the style of the same apostle, what he means by the *body of Christ;* we may learn it from Eph. 1. 23., where it is defined by the *church:* thus, ...*the church, which is his body, the fulness of him that filleth all in all.*

3. Heb xi. 1. contains a definition of *faith;* which is there said to be *the substance of things hoped for, and the evidence of things not seen.*

II. EXAMPLES and the NATURE OF THE SUBJECT also show us the *usus loquendi* and force of words; but in order to judge correctly, and to make proper distinctions, a good understanding and considerable practice are highly necessary.

1. By *examples* is meant, that the writer who uses a particular word, though he does not directly define it, yet gives, in some one or more passages, an example of what it means, by exhibiting its qualities or showing the operation of it. Thus,

(1.) In order to explain the word δικαιοσυνη, *righteousness,* which is of very frequent occurrence in the New Testament, we must examine what *examples of righteousness* are added in each passage.

(2.) In Gal. iv. 3. St Paul uses the term στοιχεια του κοσμου, elements of the world, at first without an explanation. but afterwards we have an example of the meaning of it in Gal. iv. 9., where the expression is used of the religion and philosophy of the Jews and Gentiles which preceded the Christian dispensation, and includes the idea of incompleteness and imperfection.

2. The *Nature of the Subject,* in innumerable instances, helps to define which meaning of a word the writer attaches to it, in any particular passage.

For instance, χαρις, in our version usually rendered *grace,* denotes pardon of sin, divine benevolence, divine aid, temporal blessings, &c. Which of these senses it bears in any particular passage is to be determined from the nature of the subject.[1]

III. In order to ascertain the usus loquendi, and to investigate the meaning of a passage, recourse is in the next place to be had to the COMPARISON OF SIMILAR or PARALLEL PASSAGES: and as much caution is requisite in the application of this hermeneutic aid, it becomes necessary to institute a particular inquiry into its nature, and the most beneficial mode of employing it in the interpretation of the Bible.

1. " When, in any ordinary composition, a passage occurs of doubtful meaning with respect to the sentiment or doctrine it conveys, the obvious course of proceeding is, to examine what the author himself has in other parts of his work delivered upon the same subject; to weigh well the force of any particular expressions he is accustomed to use; and to inquire what there might be in the occasion or circumstances under which he wrote, tending to throw further light upon the immediate object he had in view. This is only to render common justice to the writer; it is necessary both for the discovery of his real meaning, and to secure him against any wanton charge of error or inconsistency. Now, if this may justly be required in any ordinary work of uninspired composition, how much more indispensable must it be when we sit in judgment upon the sacred volume; in which (if we acknowledge its divine original) it is impossible even to imagine a failure either in judgment or in integrity."[2]

---

[1] Mori Acroases, tom i. pp. 81—84. Stuart's Elements, p. 35.
[2] Bp. Vanmildert's Lectures, p. 190.

II. Sect. I. § 1.]   *Of ascertaining the Usus Loquendi.*   301

"God has been pleased, in sundry portions and in divers manners, to speak unto us in his word; but in all the books of Scripture we may trace an admirable unity of design, an intimate connection of parts, and a complete harmony of doctrines. In some instances the same truths are conveyed nearly in the same modes of expression; in other instances the same sentiments are clothed with beautiful varieties of language. While we are interested in discovering some of the indications of mental diversity among the sacred writers, we clearly perceive that the whole volume of revelation is distinguished by a certain characteristic style and phraseology altogether its own, and which, for simplicity, dignity, energy, and fulness, must be allowed to have no parallel. Now, if there be in the various parts of Scripture such important coincidences of sentiment, of language, and of idiom, it is evident that we proceed on just and rational principles, in comparing together passages that have some degree of resemblance, and in applying those, the meaning of which is clear, to the illustration of such as are involved in some degree of obscurity." [1]

The passages, which thus have some degree of resemblance, are termed PARALLEL PASSAGES; and the comparison of them is a most important help for interpreting such parts of Scripture as may appear to us obscure or uncertain; for, on almost every subject, there will be found a multitude of phrases, that, when diligently collated, will afford mutual illustration and support to each other; the truth which is more obscurely intimated in one place being expressed with greater precision in others. Thus, a part of the attributes or circumstances, relating to both persons and things, is stated in one text or passage, and part in another; so that it is only by searching out several passages, and connecting them together, that we can obtain a just apprehension of them. More particularly, the types of the Old Testament must be compared with their antitypes in the New (as Numb. xxi. 9. with John iii. 14.); predictions must be compared with the history of their accomplishment (as Isa. liii. the latter part of v. 12. with Mark xv. 27, 28. and Luke xxii. 37. and the former part of Isa. liii. 12. with Matt. xxvii. 57. Mark xv. 43. Luke xxiii. 50.), and the portion of Scripture, in which any point is specifically treated, ought to be chiefly attended to in the comparison, as Genesis, ch i. on the creation, Romans, ch. iii.—v. on the doctrine of justification, &c. &c. [2]

---

[1] Rev H F Burder's Sermon on the Duty and Means of ascertaining the Sense of Scripture, pp 17, 18.

[2] On the importance and benefit of consulting parallel passages, Bishop Horsley has several fine observations in his comment on Psal. xcvii. The whole passage is too long to extract, but the following sentences are so appropriate to the subject of this section, that the author deems any apology for their insertion unnecessary "*It should*," says his Lordship, "*be a rule with every one, who would read the Holy Scriptures with advantage and improvement, to compare every text which may seem either important for the doctrine it may contain, or remarkable for the turn of the expression, with the parallel passages in other parts of Holy Writ*, that is, with the passages in which the subject-matter is the same, the sense equivalent, or the turn of the expression similar These parallel passages are easily found by the marginal references in Bibles of the larger form."......... ." It is incredible to any one, who has not in some degree made the experiment, what a proficiency may be made in that knowledge which maketh wise unto salvation, by studying the Scriptures in this manner, without any other commentary or exposition than what the different parts of

The *foundation* of the parallelisms occurring in the Sacred Writings is the perpetual harmony of Scripture itself; which, though composed by various writers, yet proceeding from one and the same infallible source, cannot but agree in words as well as in things. Parallelisms are either *near* or *remote*: in the former case the parallel passages are sought from the same writer; in the latter from different writers. They are further termed *adequate*, when they affect the whole subject proposed in the text; and *inadequate*, when they affect it only in part: but the most usual division of the analogy of Scripture, or parallelisms, is into *verbal*, or parallelisms of words, and *real*, or parallelisms of things.

2. A *Verbal Parallelism* or *Analogy* is that in which, on comparing two or more places together, the same words and phrases, the same mode of argument, the same method of construction, and the same rhetorical figures, are respectively to be found. Of this description are the following instances.

(1.) *Parallel words and phrases.* — Thus, when the prophet Jeremiah, speaking of the human heart, says, that it is "deceitful above all things, and *desperately* wicked" (Jer. xvii. 9.), in order to understand the full import of the original word there rendered *desperately*, we must compare Jer. xv. 18. and Micah i. 9. where the same word occurs, and is rendered *desperate* or *incurable*. From which two passages it is obvious that the prophet's meaning was, that the deceitfulness and wickedness of the heart of man are so great that they cannot be healed or removed by any human art. Compare also Isa. xl. 11. and Ezek. xxxiv. 23. with John x. 11. 14, 15. Heb. xiii. 20. and 1 Pet. ii. 25. and v. 4.

(2.) *Parallel modes of arguing.* — Thus the apostles, Paul, James, and Peter, respectively support their exhortations to patience by the *example of Jesus Christ.* Compare Heb. xii. 2, 3. James v. 10, 11. and 1 Pet. ii. 21. On the contrary, dissuasives from sin are more strongly set forth in the Old and New Testaments, by urging that sinful courses were the *way of the heathen nations*. Compare Levit. xviii. 24. Jer. x. 2. and Matt. vi. 32.

(3.) *Of parallel constructions and figures* we have examples in Rom. viii. 3. 2 Cor. v. 21. and Heb. x. 6. in which passages respect-

---

the sacred volume mutually furnish for each other. *I will not scruple to assert that the most* ILLITERATE CHRISTIAN, *if he can but read his English Bible, and will take the pains to read it in this manner, will not only attain all that practical knowledge which is necessary to his salvation; but, by God's blessing, he will become learned in every thing relating to his religion in such degree, that he will not be liable to be misled either by the refined arguments or by the false assertions of those who endeavour to ingraft their own opinions upon the oracles of God.* He may safely be ignorant of all philosophy, except what is to be learned from the sacred books, which indeed contain the highest philosophy adapted to the lowest apprehensions. He may safely remain ignorant of all history, except so much of the history of the first ages of the Jewish and of the Christian church, as is to be gathered from the canonical books of the Old and New Testament. *Let him study these in the manner I recommend, and let him never cease to pray for the* ILLUMINATION OF THAT SPIRIT *by which these books were dictated, and the whole compass of abstruse philosophy, and recondite history, shall furnish no argument with which the perverse will of man shall be able to shake this* LEARNED CHRISTIAN's *faith.* The Bible, thus studied, will indeed prove to be what we Protestants esteem it — a certain and sufficient rule of faith and practice, a helmet of salvation, which alone may quench the fiery darts of the wicked." — Sermons on the Resurrection, &c. pp. 221—228.

ively, the Greek word ἁμαρτια, there translated sin, means *sacrifices or offerings for sin*, agreeably to the idiom of the Hebrew language, in which the same word elliptically signifies both *sin*, and *sin-offering*, which the Septuagint version invariably renders by ἁμαρτια in upwards of one hundred places. Dr. Whitby, on 2 Cor. v. 21., has pointed out a few instances; but Dr. A. Clarke (on the same text) has enumerated *all* the passages, which are, in fact, so many additional examples of verbal parallelisms. To this class some biblical critics refer those passages in which the same sentence is expressed not precisely in the same words, but in *similar* words, more full as well as more perspicuous, and concerning the force and meaning of which there can be no doubt. Such are the parallelisms of the sacred poets; which, from the light they throw on the poetical books of the Scriptures, demand a distinct consideration

Verbal Parallelisms are of great importance for ascertaining the meaning of words that rarely occur in the Bible, as well as of those which express peculiar doctrines or terms of religion, as *faith, repentance, new creature*, &c., likewise in explaining doubtful passages, and also the Hebraisms appearing in the New Testament.

3. A *Real Parallelism* or *Analogy* is, where the same thing or subject is treated of, either designedly or incidentally, in the same words, or in others which are more clear, copious, and full, and concerning whose force and meaning there can be no doubt. In comparing two passages, however, we must ascertain whether the same thing *is* really expressed more fully as well as more clearly, and also without any ambiguity whatever, otherwise little or no assistance can be obtained for illustrating obscure places. Real parallelisms are twofold — historical, and didactic or doctrinal.

(1.) *An Historical Parallelism of things* is, where the same thing or event is related: it is of great and constant use in order to understand aright the Four Gospels, in which the same things are for the most part related more fully by one Evangelist than by the others, according to the design with which the Gospels were respectively written.

Thus, the account of our Saviour's stilling the tempest in the sea of Genesareth is more copiously related by Saint Mark (iv 36—41) and Saint Luke (viii 22—25) than it is by Saint Matthew (viii. 24 26.). By comparing the several narratives of the Evangelists together, harmonies are constructed from their separate histories In like manner, the historical books of the Old Testament are mutually illustrated by comparing together the books of Samuel, Kings, and Chronicles. For instance, many passages in the book of Genesis are parallel to 1 Chron 1—ix, many parts of the books of Exodus, Leviticus, and Numbers are parallel to the book of Deuteronomy, the books of Samuel and Kings, to the two books of Chronicles, and, lastly, 2 Kings xviii 13—37 and 2 Chron. xxxii. are parallel with Isa xxxvi Dr Lightfoot and Mr Townsend have compiled very valuable harmonies of the Old Testament, in which the historical and prophetical passages are interwoven in the order of time, of which an account is given in the Appendix to this volume. [1]

(2.) A *Didactic or Doctrinal Parallelism of things* is, where the same thing is *taught*. this species of parallel is of the greatest importance for comprehending the doctrines inculcated in the Bible, which we should otherwise be liable to mistake or grossly pervert.

We have examples of it in all those Psalms which occur twice in the book of Psalms, as in Psal. xiv. compared with liii., xl. 13—17. with lxx., lvii. 7—11 with cviii. 1—5.; lx. 5—12. with cviii. 6—13.; and cxv. 4—8. with cxxxv. 15—18. Sometimes also a

---

[1] See the Appendix, p. 113.

hymn of David's, which occurs in the Book of Psalms, is to be found in some one of the historical books, as Psalm xcvi. compared with 1 Chron. xvi. 23—33 , Psalm cv. 1—15. with 1 Chron. xvi. 8—22 and Psal. cvi. 47, 48 with 1 Chron. xvi. 35, 36.

In like manner, in the New Testament, the same thing is taught nearly in the same words, as in the Epistle of Jude compared with 2 Pet. ch. ii. Frequently also the same doctrine is explained more fully in one place, which had been more concisely stated in another: such, for instance, are the superseding of the Mosaic dispensation by that of the Gospel, and all those passages which are parallel as to the thing or subject discussed though differing in words, so that, by comparing them, the scope of the doctrine inculcated will readily be collected. On the other hand, where the same subject or doctrine is delivered with more brevity, all the various passages must be diligently collated, and the doctrine elicited from them. Of this description are the numerous predictions, &c. relative to the future happiness of mankind, connected with the removal of the Jewish economy, and the conversion of the Gentiles to the Christian religion.

But the use of this parallelism will more fully appear from one or two instances. Let us then compare Gal. vi. 15 with Gal. v 6. 1 Cor. vii. 19. 2 Cor. v 17 and Rom. ii. 28, 29. In the former passage we read, *In Christ Jesus neither circumcision availeth any thing, nor uncircumcision, but a new creature*, or rather [there is] *a new creation*. In Gal. v 6. the apostle had briefly delivered the same doctrine in the following terms *In Christ Jesus neither circumcision availeth any thing, nor uncircumcision, but faith that worketh by love* — 1 Cor vii. 19. *Circumcision is nothing, nor uncircumcision, but the keeping of the commandments of God.* — 2 Cor. v 17 *Therefore, if any man be in Christ, he is a new creature*, or, more correctly, [there is] *a new creation old things are passed away, behold ! all things are become new.* — Rom. ii 28, 29 *He is not a Jew that is one outwardly,* i. e. he is not a genuine member of the church of God who has only an outward profession . *neither is that circumcision which is outward in the flesh But he is a Jew,* a true member of the church of God, *which is one inwardly, and circumcision is that of the heart, in the spirit,* and *not in the letter , whose praise is not of men, but of God.* From these passages it is evident that what Saint Paul, in Gal vi. 15. terms *a new creature,* or *creation,* he in Gal. v. 6. denominates *faith* that worketh by love, and in 1 Cor vii. 19. *keeping the commandments of God.* From this collation of passages, then, we perceive, that what the apostle intends by a *new creature* or *new creation,* is the entire conversion of the heart from sin to God ; and as creation is the proper work of an All-wise and Almighty Being, so this total change of heart, soul, and life, which takes place under the ministration of the Gospel, is effected by the power and grace of God, and is evidenced by that faith and obedience which are indispensably necessary to all Christians in order to salvation. [1]

Again in 2 Cor. i 21 God is said to have *anointed us* the parallel passage, where this expression is so explained as to give an idea of the thing intended, is 1 John ii. 20 , where true Christians are said to *have an unction from the Holy One, and to know all things;* and in v. 27 *the same anointing* is said to *teach all things.* Now, if the effect of this unction be that we should know all things, the anointing will be whatever brings knowledge to us, and therefore *teaching.* From this comparison of passages, therefore, we learn that by unction and anointing is intended the Holy Spirit, whose office is to teach all things, and to guide us into all truth (John xiv 26, and xvi. 13.), and whose gifts and graces are diffused throughout the church of Christ, and imparted to every living member of it. For his assistances are equally necessary to all, to the learned as well as the unlearned, to teachers as well as to hearers : he it is that enlightens our minds, purifies our hearts, and inclines our wills, not only beginning but carrying on and perfecting a new and spiritual life in our souls. The expression in v. 20. *and ye know all things*, is not to be understood in the largest sense, but must be limited to those things which are necessary to salvation. These every true Christian not only knows speculatively — that is, he not only has a notion of them in his mind — but he has also a practical and experimental knowledge and taste of them, which is productive of holy obedience This inestimable gift was purchased by the sufferings and death of Christ, who is here styled the *Holy One.* The words in v 27. *and ye need not that any man should teach you*, cannot be intended to set aside all outward teaching , but their meaning is, either that ye need not the teaching of any of those antichrists and false teachers mentioned in various parts of this epistle, or that ye need not that any one should teach you how to judge of those deceivers and their doctrines

4. Besides verbal and real parallelisms, there is a third species partaking of the nature of both, and which is of equal importance for understanding the Scriptures : This has been termed a *parallelism*

---

[1] Mori Acroases Hermeneuticæ, tom. i. p. 95. See also Macknight and Scott on the texts above cited.

of members it consists chiefly in a certain equality, resemblance, or parallelism, between the members of each period ; so that in two lines, or members of the same period, things shall answer to things, and words to words, as if fitted to each other by a kind of rule or measure.

The nature of this kind of parallelism, which is the grand characteristic of the poetical style of the Hebrews, being fully considered in a subsequent chapter [1], a few examples of its utility as an hermeneutical aid will only be necessary in this place.

In the poetical parts of the Old Testament, it sometimes happens that, in the alternate quatrain, the third line forms a continuous sense with the first, and the fourth with the second. Bishop Lowth has given a striking example of this variety of parallelism in his nineteenth prælection, from Deut. xxxii. 42. But as its distinguishing feature is not there sufficiently noted, Bishop Jebb adopts the following translation of Mr. Parkhurst:

> I will make mine arrows drunk with blood,
> And my sword shall devour flesh,
> With the blood of the slain and the captive ;
> From the hairy head of the enemy.

That is, reducing the stanza to a simple quatrain:

> I will make mine arrows drunk with blood :
> With the blood of the slain and the captive
> And my sword shall devour flesh ,
> From the hairy head of the enemy.

Again,

> From without the sword shall destroy ;
> And in the inmost apartments terror ;
> Both the young man and the virgin ;
> The suckling, with the man of grey hairs.
> Deut. xxxii. 25

" The youths and virgins," says Bishop Jebb, " let out of doors by the vigour and buoyancy natural at their time of life, fall victims to the sword in the streets of the city while infancy and old age, confined by helplessness and decreptitude to the inner chambers of the house, perish there by fear, before the sword can reach them."

Mr. Green, in his " Poetical Parts of the New Testament," observes that there is a similar hyperbaton in Isa. xxxiv. 6. And Dr Hales reduces to a similar form that remarkable prophecy, Gen. xlix. 10.:

> The sceptre shall not depart from Judah ,
> Nor a scribe of his offspring ,
> Until Shiloh shall come ,
> And [until] to him a congregation of peoples.

" That is, according to Dr. Hales, the sceptre, or civil government, shall not depart, till the coming or birth of Shiloh ; and the scribe, or expounder of the law, intimating ecclesiastical regimen, shall not depart, or cease, until there shall be formed a congregation of peoples, a church of Christian worshippers from various nations ; the former branch of this prophecy was fulfilled, when Augustus made his enrolment preparatory to the census throughout Judæa and Galilee, thereby degrading Judæa to a Roman province: the latter branch was fulfilled, at the sacking of Jerusalem by Titus; when the temple was destroyed, and the Jewish ritual abolished." [2]

---

[1] See Book II. Chap II. *infra*
[2] Jebb's Sacred Literature, pp. 29, 30.

By the application of this parallelism of members, Bishop Jebb has thrown considerable light upon a difficult passage in the eighty-fourth psalm, which he considers as an *introverted parallelism*.

> Blessed is the man whose strength is in Thee
> The passengers, in whose heart are the ways,
> In the valley of Baca make it a spring,
> The rain also filleth the pools,
> They go from strength to strength,
> He shall appear before God in Zion.
>
> Psal. lxxxiv. 5—7.

"The first and sixth lines are here considered, at once, as constructively parallel, and as affording a *continuous* sense: the intermediate four lines may be accounted parenthetical; the second, constructively parallel with the fifth, and the third with the fourth. The first line seems to contain the character of a confirmed proficient in religion, — *his strength is in God;* the sixth line, to describe his final beatification, — *he shall appear before God in Zion*. The intermediate quatrain may be regarded as descriptive of the intermediate course pursued by those who desire to be good and happy: they are passengers, but they know their destination, and they long for it; at a distance from the temple, (the mystical "sapientum templa serena,") they are anxious to arrive there, the very highways to Jerusalem are in their heart. And what is the consequence? Affection smooths all difficulties: the parched and sandy desert becomes a rich well-watered valley, and they cheerfully advance from strength to strength; from one degree of virtuous proficiency to another." [1]

One or two examples more will show the great importance of applying the poetical parallelism to the study of the New Testament.

> εσκοτισμενοι τη διανοια οντες·
> απηλλωτριωμενοι της ζωης του Θεου·
> δια την αγνοιαν την ουσαν εν αυτοις·
> δια την πωρωσιν της καρδιας αυτων
>
> Being darkened in the understanding;
> Being alienated from the life of God;
> Through the ignorance which is in them,
> Through the blindness of their hearts.
>
> Ephes. iv. 18.

That is, adjusting the parallelism:

> Being darkened in the understanding,
> Through the ignorance which is in them;
> Being alienated from the life of God,
> Through the blindness of their hearts.

Again,

> και εζητουν αυτον κρατησαι·
> και εφοβηθησαν τον οχλον;
> εγνωσαν γαρ, ότι προς αυτους την παραβολην ειπε·
> και αφεντες αυτον, απηλθον.

---

[1] Sacred Literature, p. 55. In p 56 Bishop Jebb has given a passage from Euthymius's Commentary on Psal. lxxxiv 7 which is so truly beautiful, that we cannot help inserting it Εκ δυναμεως εις δυναμιν εξ αρετης εις αρετην· οιον, εκ ταπεινοφροσυνης εις πενθος εκ δε πενθους εις κατανυξιν· και ουτως εκ ταυτης εις εκεινην προκοπτοντες, αναβησονται προς την ακρωρειαν δυναμιν δε την αρετην εκαλεσεν, ὡς ισχυροποιουντα τον μετιοντα αυτην· "From strength to strength; from virtue to virtue for example, from lowliness of mind to mourning; from mourning to contrition; and thus advancing from one attainment to another, they shall ascend the summit of the mountain. The psalmist calls virtue strength, because it makes him strong who attains it," — " Perhaps," the learned prelate remarks, " each gradation of goodness may be accounted, as it were a fortress or strong-hold upon the way a secure stage in the pilgrimage of virtue."

II. Sect. I. § 1.] *Of ascertaining the Usus Loquendi.* 307

> And they sought to seize him,
> And they feared the people,
> For they knew, that against them he spake the parable;
> And having left him, they departed.
> Mark xii. 12.

That is, adjusting the parallelism, and giving the particle καί, the three different senses, which Dr. Henry Owen has observed that it bears in this passage.

> And they sought to seize him;
> For they knew, that against them he spake the parable,
> But they feared the people;
> Therefore, having left him, they departed.[1]

---

5. As it requires particular attention and much practice in order to distinguish the different species of parallelisms, — especially the sententious or poetical parallelism, — the following hints are offered to the biblical student in the hope of enabling him to avail himself of them, and advantageously to apply them to the interpretation of the Scriptures.

(1.) *Ascertain the primary meaning of the passage under consideration.*

In 1 Cor. iv. 5. we read, *Judge nothing before the time, until the Lord come, who both will bring to light the hidden things of darkness, and will make manifest the counsels of the hearts.* Now, here is a parallelism of members, but the fundamental meaning is, that *God judges the counsels of men*, he therefore judges without respect of persons, and with unerring impartiality. The apostle's design was to show that it is impossible for men to perceive and judge the counsels of one another. Thus, again, words are also construed with words, and things with things, in order that an enumeration may be made of the species, kinds, or parts of the whole, as in the divine ode of the Virgin Mary contained in Luke i. 46—55, in which the *specific* displays of divine power are enumerated. God *hath put down the proud*, but *exalteth them of low degree*, &c. The diligent reader will observe, that this place describes the power of God, in whose hands is the distribution of prosperity and adversity, and that all these parts or species are, in an exposition, to be joined together with the proposition exhibiting the genus or kind, viz. that prosperity and adversity are in the hands of the Almighty.

(2.) *Although the Sacred Scriptures,* PRIMARILY *coming from God, are perfectly consistent, and harmonise throughout; yet, as they were* SECONDARILY *written by different authors, on various topics, and in different styles, those books and parts of books are, in the first instance, to be compared, which were composed by the same author, in the same language, and on a parallel subject.*

[i.] Thus, by comparing Psal. xxxviii. 10 with 1 Sam. xiv. 26, 27. (in which Jonathan having taken some honey for his refreshment, is said to have had *his eyes enlightened*), we shall readily apprehend the force of the psalmist's complaint, that *the light of his eyes was gone from him*, for the eyes of a person in good health are so strong, as to sparkle with the rays of light that fall upon them; whereas, when the constitution is worn by long sickness, or broken by grief, the eyes lose their vigour and brilliancy, and in cases of incipient blindness, the light gradually fails the eyes. In like manner, if we compare 1 Thess. v. 23. with Jude, verse 19. we shall find that the *spirit*, mentioned in the former passage, does not denote any *third* constituent part of man, distinct from the soul and body, but that it means the spiritual strength bestowed, through the grace of the Holy Spirit, in our renovation and sanctification; for the apostle Jude, speaking of false teachers,

---

[1] Jebb's Sacred Literature, p. 198. This elegant critic has thrown more light than all the commentators extant, on that very obscure passage, Matt. xv. 3—6 by exhibiting it in the form of an introverted parallelism (see pp 244—248.), and also on that very difficult portion of the New Testament — the song of Zacharias (Luke i. 67—79.) by dividing it according to the poetical parallelism See Sacred Literature, pp. 403—417.

describes them as *sensual*, NOT HAVING THE SPIRIT, that is as persons abandoned to follow their own evil ways, unrenewed and unsanctified by the Holy Spirit.

[ii.] But the propriety of this canon will particularly appear, if we compare the parallel passages of the same author, in preference to every other sacred writer. For instance, in Rom. iii. 24, Saint Paul, when treating of our justification in the sight of God, says, that we are justified freely by his grace: now that this is to be understood of the free favour of God towards us, and not of any quality wrought in us, is evident from Eph. ii. 4, 5. 2 Tim. i. 9. and Tit. iii. 5. 7. in which passages our salvation by Jesus Christ is expressly ascribed to the *great love wherewith God loved us — to his own purpose and grace,— and to his mercy and grace*.

(3.) *Besides the kindred dialects, much assistance will be derived, in studying the parallelisms of Scripture, from a diligent comparison of the Greek Septuagint version with the New Testament; as the latter was very frequently cited by Jesus Christ and his apostles, and was constantly used in the synagogues during the apostolic age, as well as by the Gentile converts to Judaism.*

Thus, the force of our Saviour's expression in Luke xii. 42. (giving a *portion of meat* σιτομετριον *in due season*) will best appear if we compare it with the Septuagint version of Gen. xlvii. 1, 2., where we are told that Joseph (when Pharaoh had constituted him intendant-general of Egypt) supplied his father and his brothers, and all his father's household, with a certain portion of corn for each person; εσιτομετρει αυτον, the very expression used by St. Luke. It was usual for the stewards of great families, in antient times, to measure out to each slave his allotted portion of corn every month. Again, in Luke xv. 13. the younger son is said to *have taken his journey into a far country*, απεδημησεν εις χωραν μακραν, an expression, Grotius remarks, which is singularly appropriate; for in the Septuagint version of Psal. lxxiii. 27. those who have wilfully cast off the fear of God are said μακρυνειν απο του Θεου ἑαυτους, to withdraw themselves afar from God.

(4.) *Whenever the mind is struck with any resemblance, in the first place consider whether it is a true resemblance, and whether the passages are sufficiently similar; that is, not only whether the same word, but also the same thing, answers together, in order to form a safe judgment concerning it.*

It often happens that *one* word has several distinct meanings, one of which obtains in one place, and one in another place. When, therefore, words of such various meanings present themselves, all those passages where they occur are not to be immediately considered as parallel, unless they have a similar power. Thus, if any one were to compare Jonah iv. 10. (where mention is made of the gourd which came up in a night, and perished in a night, and which in the original Hebrew is termed *the son of a night*,) with 1 Thess. v. 5, where Christians are called, not children of the night, but *children of the day*, it would be a spurious parallel.

(5.) *Where two parallel passages present themselves, the clearer and more copious place must be selected to illustrate one that is more briefly and obscurely expressed.*

The force and meaning of a word can never be ascertained from a single passage, but if there be a second passage on the same subject, we have a criterion by which to ascertain the writer's meaning. Or, if we consider the subject discussed by him, we shall find that he has in one part touched very slightly on topics which are elsewhere more fully explained, and in which he has omitted nothing that could more copiously illustrate the former place. In availing ourselves, therefore, of a parallel passage to elucidate any part of the inspired writings, it is evident that the clearer places, and those which treat more fully on a subject, are to be considered as fundamental passages, by which others are to be illustrated. Thus, in Hosea xii. 4. there is an allusion to the patriarch Jacob's wrestling with an angel of God; now this place would be extremely obscure, if the whole history of that transaction were not more amply related in Gen. xxxii. 24—31.

(6.) *Other things being equal, a nearer parallel is preferable to one that is more remote.*

If a writer elsewhere repeat the same forms of speech, and also discuss in another place a subject which he has but slightly touched in one place, it is better to explain that place from the same writer, than from parallel passages collected from others. But where a writer supplies nothing by which to illustrate himself, recourse must in that case be had to such as were contemporary with him, or nearly so, and from their compositions passages are to be collected. Thus Hosea, Isaiah, Micah, and Amos, having been nearly contemporary with each other, and having uttered predictions relative to nearly the same events, mutually elucidate each other, as the prophecy of Ezekiel illustrates that of Jeremiah, and *vice versâ* This rule will apply generally, unless the more remote writer define obscure places better, or continue and adorn the subject discussed.

(7.) *No assistance is to be derived from similar passages, the sense of which is uncertain.*

For if such passages be cited to explain another that is obscure, they will be of no use whatever, however similar they may be, but equally obscure. It is to little purpose, therefore, to accumulate similar passages where the same name of a tree, plant, herb, &c. is mentioned, and especially where there is no note or mark attached to it, for several of the birds, beasts, fishes, trees, plants, precious stones, and musical instruments, mentioned in the Scriptures, are either unknown to us, or cannot now be precisely distinguished [1]

(8.) *The exercise of comparison should be often repeated*

" To the observance of the principles above stated, frequent practice must be added, so that the interpreter may *easily* discern what passages are similar, and how he may rightly compare them, and judge of them. It will be very useful, here, to consult good interpreters, not only of the Scriptures, but of profane authors, that where they carry these principles into practice, and plainly make a right and skilful application of them, we may learn to imitate them, by attentively considering the manner in which they attain to the understanding of things which are obscure or ambiguous By *frequently* renewing this exercise, we may learn to go in the same path, in which they have travelled

The books of the New Testament present more inducement to repeat this exercise very frequently, than any other books For (1) They are of all books the most important. (2) They are not only all of the same idiom in general, but they have reference to the same subject, viz the developement of Christianity. They originated, too, from contemporary writers, possessed of views, feelings, and language that were alike. Hence, comparison has more force in illustrating the New Testament, than in the illustration of either Greek or Latin authors; many of whom, that agreed with each other in all the circumstances just stated, cannot be found But (3.) To all who admit that the same Holy Spirit guided the authors of the New Testament, and that their views of religion, in consequence of this, must have been *harmonious*, the inducement to comparison of various parts and passages with each other, in order to obtain a correct view of the whole, must be *very great*, and the additional force of the evidence arising from comparison, on account of the really harmonious views of the writers, must make this exercise an imperious duty of every theologian "[2]

(9.) *Many parallel passages should be compared.*

" To compare one passage only, is often insufficient, whether you are endeavouring to find the *usus loquendi* by the aid of parallel passages, or by testimony derived from the nature of the subject and from examples. Specially is this the case, when we are investigating the sense of words, that have a complex or generic meaning, made up of various parts In this case, comparisons should be made from numerous passages, until we perceive that what we are seeking is fully and entirely discovered

Suppose the word πιστις occurs in a particular passage, where you are doubtful what sense should be applied to it. First, you call to mind, that πιστις is a generic word, having several meanings related to each other, but still diverse, as species under the genus. You wish to determine how many *species* of meaning πιστις has, and in order to accomplish this, *many* passages where it is used must be compared, in order that you may know whether all the species are found. This being done, you proceed to compare them with the passage under investigation, and see which will fit it. And in this way all generic words must be investigated, before the generic idea can be determined."[3]

(10.) *It will be of great use to collect and reduce into alphabetical order all those similar passages in which the same forms of speech occur, and the same things are proposed in a different order of narration : but care must be taken to avoid the accumulation of numerous passages that are parallel to each other in forms of speech, or in things which are of themselves clear*

---

[1] See some instances of this observation in Mr. Pilkington's " Remarks on several Passages of Scripture," pp 83—90.
[2] Stuart's Elements of Interpretation, p. 40.
[3] Ibid. p. 41.

and certain: for such accumulations of parallel places savour more of a specious display of learning than real utility.¹

The best and most certain help by which to find out parallel passages is, unquestionably, the diligent and attentive perusal of the Scriptures, repeated after short intervals of time, and accompanied by the committal of the most difficult passages to writing, together with such other passages as are either similar in words or in things, and which tend to throw any light on obscure places. But, in instituting such parallelisms, care must be taken not to multiply references *unnecessarily* for mere show rather than for their practical utility, and also that they do not violate the analogy of faith. For instance, Rom iii 28. and James ii. 24. are not in every respect parallel to each other, because in the former passage Saint Paul is treating of justification *in the sight of God* — a doctrine which numerous passages of Scripture most clearly testify to be by faith alone, whereas Saint James is speaking of justification *in the sight of men*, who form their judgment of a man by his works.

The method here indicated is the only *effectual* way by which to ascertain parallel words and phrases, as well as parallelisms of things: it will indeed require a considerable portion of time and study, which *every one* may not perhaps be able to give, but individuals thus circumstanced may advantageously facilitate their researches by having recourse to editions of the Bible with parallel references, and to Concordances.²

§ 2. ANTIENT VERSIONS.

Observations on the respective Merits of the several Antient Versions. — Rules for consulting them to the best Advantage.

OF the Antient Versions of the Holy Scriptures, and their uses in sacred criticism, an account has already been given in pages 33—78, 186—190; and it may here be remarked, that, to those who are able to consult them, these versions afford a very valuable aid in the interpretation of the Bible: for they were the works of men, who enjoyed several advantages above the moderns, for understanding the original languages and the phraseology of Scripture. One or two instances will illustrate the propriety of this remark.

1. In the first promulgation of the Gospel to mankind (Gen. iii. 15.), God said to the serpent that beguiled our first parents, *And I will put enmity between thee and the woman, and between thy seed and her seed, and* IT (that is, the seed of the woman, as our authorised translation rightly expounds it,) *shall bruise thy head, and thou shalt bruise his heel.* But in the Anglo-Romish version, after the Latin Vulgate, (which has IPSA *conteret caput tuum,*) it is rendered, SHE *shall bruise his head,* as if a woman should do it; which the Romanists interpreting of the Virgin Mary, ascribe to her this great victory and triumph over sin

---

¹ Morus in Ernesti Inst Interpret. Nov. Test tom. i pp. 97—110 Bauer, Herm. Sacr. pp. 168—174. J. B Carpzov. Primæ Lineæ Herm. Sacr pp. 45—47. Pfeiffer, Hermeneut Sacr c xi. Franckii Prælect. Hermeneutt. pp. 95 *et seq*. 153. *et seq.* Rambach, Inst Herm. Sacræ, pp 362—384. 651, 652., also his Exercit. Herm. pp. 209—219 J. E Pfeiffer, Inst. Herm. Sacr. pp 278—305 Jahnii Enchiridion Herm. Generalis, pp. 81—94, and Chladenius's Institutiones Exegeticæ, pp. 399—406. Schæfer, Institutiones Scripturisticæ, pars ii. pp. 77—84 Dr. Gerard's Institutes of Biblical Criticism, pp 148—157. Arigler, Hermeneutica Biblica, pp. 181—194. Alber, Inst. Herm. Nov. Test. pp. 132—136

² For an account of the principal editions of the Bible with Parallel References, see the Appendix to this volume, pp. 74. 77., and for Concordances, see pp. 288—291.

and Satan, and are taught to say in their addresses to her, "Adoro et benedico sanctissimos pedes tuos, quibus antiqui serpentis caput calcâsti;" that is, "I adore and bless thy most holy feet, whereby thou hast bruised the head of the old serpent." That this rendering of the Romanists is erroneous, is proved by the Septuagint Greek version, by the Chaldee paraphrase, and by the Syriac version, all of which refer the pronoun IT to the *seed* of the woman, and not to the woman herself.[1]

2. As the expression *breaking bread*, mentioned in Acts ii. 46., ordinarily means taking food in the Jewish idiom, some expositors have understood that expression in this sense; but the old Syriac version, executed towards the close of the first or early in the second century, renders it *breaking of the Eucharist*. We are justified, therefore, in referring the term to the celebration of the Lord's supper among the first Christians (κατ' οικον) in a house appropriated to that purpose.

In applying antient versions, as an auxiliary, to the interpretation of Scripture, it is material to observe, that, since no version can be absolutely free from error, we ought not to rely implicitly on any one translation: but, if it be practicable, the aid of the cognate dialects should be united with reference to a version, in order that, by a comparison of both these helps, we may arrive at the knowledge of the genuine readings and meanings. From inattention to this obvious caution, many eminent men have at different times ascribed to particular versions a degree of authority to which they were by no means entitled. Thus, by many of the fathers, the Alexandrian interpreters were accounted to be divinely inspired, and consequently free from the possibility of mistake: a similar opinion was held by various eminent modern critics, particularly by Isaac Vossius, who asserted the Septuagint to be preferable to the Hebrew text, and to be absolutely free from error! The Church of Rome has fallen into the like mistake with respect to the Vulgate or Latin Version, which the Council of Trent declared to be the *only* authentic translation.

Further, *versions of versions*, that is, those translations which were not made *immediately* from the Hebrew Old Testament, or from the Greek New Testament, are of no authority in determining either the genuine text or meaning of the original, but only of that version from which they were taken. This remark applies particularly to the Anglo-Saxon, Old English, Spanish, French, and German translations, whether of the Old or New Testament; which, being made before the sixteenth century, were executed immediately from the Latin: and subsequently, even in those examples where they are unanimous in a reading, their united voices are of no more authority than that of the Latin Version alone.[2] In all cases, therefore, which require the aid of a version, either for the purpose of criticism or interpretation, recourse must be had to those translations,

---

[1] Bp. Beveridge's Works, vol. ii. p. 193. vol. ix. pp 233, 234.   Agier, Prophéties concernant Jésus Christ et l'Eglise, pp. 243, 244
[2] Michaelis, vol. ii. p 3.

which being more antient or better executed, are preferable to every other. And in this view the following will be found most deserving of attention, not only as uniting the two qualifications of antiquity and excellence, but also as being more generally accessible to students, being for the most part comprised in the Polyglott Bibles, which are to be found in almost every public library.

I. The *Alexandrian Version* is confessedly the most antient, and, with all its errors and imperfections, contains very much that is highly valuable, and on this account it has been used by nearly all the more antient interpreters. With the Septuagint should be consulted the fragments of the translations executed by Aquila, Symmachus, and Theodotion. The version of Aquila, in particular, exhibits a similar diction, as he was not very remote from the age of the apostles, and he has some things which may be of especial use in the interpretation of the New Testament. The version of Symmachus is also a valuable hermeneutic aid; as, by translating into pure Greek, he has facilitated the understanding of Hebrew.

II. The *Syriac Peschito*, whose fidelity as a version, independently of the excellence of its style, has received the highest commendations from Michaelis, is particularly serviceable for the interpretation of the New Testament.[1] Nor is its value inferior in the interpretation of the Old Testament. "Of all the antient Versions," says a living critic, "the Syriac is the most uniformly faithful and accurate; and as the language so nearly resembles the Hebrew, its value can scarcely be estimated too high.[2]

III. The *Latin Vulgate*, with the exception of the Psalms, deservedly claims the third place.

IV. The *Targums*, or Chaldee Paraphrases, though unequally executed, contain many things that are exceedingly useful, and necessary to be known, especially the paraphrases of Jonathan Ben Uzziel: they not only contribute essentially to the understanding of many difficult passages in the Old Testament, but also throw much light on the interpretation of the New Testament, as well as afford much advantage in arguing with the Jews, because they almost invariably view the prophecies in the same light as Christians do, as referring to the Messiah.[3] Extracts from them are to be found in all the larger commentaries, and also in the works of Dr. Lightfoot.

V. The other versions made immediately from the Hebrew and Greek originals follow next in order, particularly the Arabic translations of the Old Testament: but no certain dependence can be placed, as an authority, on the Latin translations of the Oriental versions, which are printed in the Polyglott Bibles.

It will not however be *necessary* to consult antient versions, except in passages that are really difficult, or unless a particular examination of them be instituted for some special object of inquiry.

---

[1] On the critical use of the Syriac version, the reader may consult G. B. Winer's Commentatio de Versionis N. T. Syriacæ Usu Critico cautè instituendo. Erlangæ, 1824.
[2] Mr. Holden's Translation of the Book of Proverbs, p. cviii.
[3] Hamilton's Introd. to Heb. Script. p. 192.

In this case not one or two versions merely should be consulted, but every version that is accessible should be referred to: and all such places should be compared together as are *parallel*, that is, those passages in which the same word or the same form of speaking respectively occurs; and, where any thing worthy of preservation offers itself, it will materially facilitate future studies to note it either in an interleaved Bible, or which perhaps is preferable, in an interleaved Lexicon. This practice will not only enable the biblical student to discover and correctly to appreciate the genius of a version, and the ability, or the reverse, with which it may be executed; but it will also supply many important helps for the interpretation of Scripture. As, however, some of the antient versions have been altered or interpolated in many places, great care must be taken to distinguish the modern amendments from the genuine text of the original antient translator. The various excellent concordances that are extant will afford great assistance in finding out such parallel words or phrases.

In order to ascertain how far the antient versions represent correctly the meaning of Hebrew or Greek words, the following rules will be found useful: —

1. *That meaning is to be taken and received as the true one, which all the versions give to a word, and which is also confirmed by the kindred dialects.*

Because, the number of testimonies worthy of credit being as great as possible, there can be no room left for doubt.

2. *All those significations, formerly given to Hebrew words, are to be considered as correctly given, which the Septuagint or other Greek translators express by the same or similar Greek words, although no trace of such meaning appear in any Oriental language:*

For, as no doubt can be entertained of the diligence and scrupulous learning of those translators, who can presume to measure the vast copiousness of the Arabic, Syriac, and other Oriental languages by the few books which in our time are extant in those languages? since no one is so ignorant as to suppose that all the riches of the Greek and Latin languages are comprised in the very numerous remains of classical literature with which our age happily abounds. With regard to the New Testament, " in cases where the sense is not affected by different readings, or the translator might have taken them for synonymous, the evidence of Greek manuscripts is to be preferred to that of an antient version The same preference is due to the manuscripts wherein the translator has omitted words that appeared of little importance, or a passage in the Greek original is attended with a difficulty which the translator was unable to solve, and therefore either omitted or altered according to the arbitrary dictates of his own judgment." [1]

3. *Where the versions differ in fixing the sense of a word, the more antient ones, being executed with the greater care and skill, are in the first place to be consulted, and preferred to all others:*

For, the nearer a translator approaches to the time when the original language was vernacular, we may readily infer that he has expressed with so much the greater fidelity the true signification of words, both primary and proper, as well as those which are derivative and translated. There are, however, some cases in which antient versions are of more authority than the original itself. Most of the translations of the New Testament, noticed in the preceding pages, surpass in antiquity the oldest Greek manuscripts now extant " and they lead to a discovery of the readings in the very antient manuscript that was used by the translator. By their means, rather than from the aid of our Greek manuscripts, none of which is prior to the fourth or fifth century, we arrive at the certain knowledge, that the antient writings have been transmitted from the earliest to the present age without

---

[1] Michaelis, vol ii. p. 3.

material alteration; and that our present text, if we except the passages that are rendered doubtful by an opposition in the readings, *is the same which proceeded from the hands of the apostles.* Whenever the reading can be precisely determined, which the translator found in his Greek manuscript, the version is of equal authority with a manuscript of that period but as it is sometimes difficult to acquire this absolute certainty, great caution is necessary in collecting readings from the antient versions."[1]

4. *A meaning given to a word by only one version, provided this be a good one, is by no means to be rejected; especially if it agree with the author's design and the order of his discourse:*

For, it is possible that the force and meaning of a word should be unknown to all other translators, and no trace of it be discoverable in the kindred dialects, and yet that it should be preserved and transmitted to posterity by *one* version. This remark applies chiefly to things which a translator has the best opportunity of understanding from local and other circumstances Thus the Alexandrian interpreters are the most ample testimony for every thing related in the Old Testament concerning Egypt, while others, who were natives of Palestine, and perhaps deeply skilled in Jewish literature, are the best guides we can follow in whatever belongs to that country.[2]

5. Lastly, "*Those versions" of the New Testament, " in which the Greek is rendered word for word, and the idioms of the original, though harsh and often unmeaning in another language, are still retained in a translation, are of more value in point of criticism than those which express the sense of the original in a manner more suitable to the language of the translator.*"

The value of the latter, as far as regards their critical application, decreases in proportion as the translator attends to purity and elegance, and of course deviates from his original. but their worth is greater in all other respects, as they are not only read with more pleasure, but understood in general with greater ease By means of the former we discover the words of the original, and even their arrangement. — but the latter are of no use in deciding on the authenticity of a reading, if the various readings of the passages in question make no alteration in the sense. No translation is more literal than the New Syriac, and none, therefore, leads to a more accurate discovery of the text in the antient manuscript whence the version was taken; but, setting this advantage aside, the Old Syriac is of much greater value than the New.[3]

---

§ 3. SCHOLIASTS AND GLOSSOGRAPHERS.

I. *Nature of Scholia.* — II. *And of Glossaries.* — III. *Rules for consulting them to advantage in the Interpretation of the Scriptures.*

WE have already stated that scholiasts and glossographers afford direct testimonies for finding out or fixing the meaning of words: it now remains that we briefly notice the nature of the assistance to be derived from these helps.

I. SCHOLIA are short notes on antient authors, and are of two kinds — *exegetical* or explanatory, and *grammatical.* The former briefly explain the *sense* of passages, and are, in fact, a species of commentary; the latter, which are here to be considered, illustrate the force and meaning of *words* by other words which are better

---

[1] Michaelis, vol. ii. p 2
[2] Jahn, Introduct ad Vet Fœd pp 116—122. Pictet, Theologie Chretienne, tom. i. pp. 151, 152. Bauer, Herm Sacr pp 147—162 301—309. J. P. Carpzov, Prim. Lin. Herm. pp.62—65. Ernesti, Inst Interp. N Test. p.57. Morus in Ernesti, tom. i. pp. 130, 131. Stuart's Elements, pp 43 64. Gerard's Institutes, pp. 107—111. Bishop Lowth's Isaiah, vol. i. pp. lxxxvii —xc 8vo. ed Pfeiffer, Herm. Sac. c. 14. (Op. tom. ii. pp. 663—664.) Arigler, Hermeneutica Biblica, pp. 102—107.
[3] Michaelis's Introduction, vol. ii. p. 3.

known. Such scholia are extant on most of the antient classics, as Homer, Thucydides, Sophocles, Aristophanes, Horace, Juvenal, Persius, &c. &c.

On the Old Testament, we believe, there are no antient scholia extant: but on the New Testament there are several collections, which present themselves under three classes.

1. *Scholia taken from the writings of the Greek fathers,* who in their homilies and commentaries have often briefly explained the force of particular words

The homilies of Chrysostom, in particular, abound with these scholia; and from his works, as well as those of Origen and other fathers, the more modern Greeks have extracted what those illustrious men had concisely stated relative to the meaning of words. Similar grammatical expositions, omitting whatever was rhetorical and doctrinal, have been collected from Chrysostom by Theodoret in a commentary on the fourteen Epistles of Saint Paul, by Theophylact, in an indifferent commentary on the four Evangelists; and, to mention no more, by Euthymius in a similar commentary executed with better judgment. There are extant numerous collections of this kind of explanations, made from the writings of the fathers, and known by the appellation of *Catenæ*[1], which follow the order of the books comprised in the New Testament. Many such scholia have been published by Matthæi in his edition of the New Testament.

2. *Scholia, written either in the margin, within the text, or at the end of manuscripts.*

Many of this description have been published separately by Wetstein in the notes to his elaborate edition of the Greek Testament, and particularly by Matthæi in his edition of the New Testament already noticed.

3. *Antient Scholia, which are also exegetical or explanatory*; these, in fact, are short commentaries, and, therefore, are discussed *infra*, in the Appendix to this volume.

II. A GLOSSARY differs from a Lexicon in this respect, that the former treats only of words that really require explanation, while the latter gives the general meaning of words. The authors of the most antient Glossaries are Hesychius, Suidas, Phavorinus, Photius, and Cyril of Alexandria. The celebrated Ernesti selected from the three first of these writers, and also from the *Etymologicon Magnum*, whatever related to the New Testament, and published the result of his researches at Leipsic, in 1786, in two octavo volumes; from which Schleusner has extracted the most valuable matter, and inserted it in his well known and excellent Greek Lexicon to the New Testament.

III. In estimating the value of scholiasts and glossographers, and also the weight of their testimony, for ascertaining the force and meaning of words, it is of importance to consider, first, whether they wrote from their own knowledge of the language, and have given us the result of their own learning, or whether they compiled from others Almost all the scholia now extant are compiled from Chrysostom, Origen, or some other fathers of the third and fourth centuries; if the scholiast have compiled from good authorities, his labours have a claim to our attention.

In proportion, therefore, to the learning of a scholiast (and the same remark will equally apply to the glossographer), he becomes the more deserving of our confidence. but this point can only be

---

[1] See an account of the principal Catenæ, *infra*, in the Appendix, pp. 193, 194.

determined by daily and constant use. The Greek fathers, for instance, are admirable interpreters of the New Testament, being intimately acquainted with its language; notwithstanding they are sometimes mistaken in the exposition of its Hebraisms. But the Latin fathers, many of whom were but indifferently skilled in Hebrew and Greek, are less to be depended on, and are, in fact, only wretched interpreters of comparatively ill-executed versions.

Again, our confidence in a scholiast, or in the author of a glossary, increases in proportion to his antiquity, at least in the explanation of every thing concerning antient history, rites, or civil life. But, in investigating the force and meaning of words, the antiquity of scholia and glossaries proves nothing; as their authors are liable to error, notwithstanding they lived near the time when the author flourished, whose writings they profess to elucidate. It not unfrequently happens that a more *recent* interpreter, availing himself of all former helps, perceives the force of words much better than one that is more antient, and is consequently enabled to elicit the sense more correctly. The result, therefore, of our inquiry into the relative value of scholiasts and compilers of glossaries is, that in perusing their labours, we must examine them for ourselves, and form our judgment accordingly, whether they have succeeded, or failed, in their attempts to explain an author.[1]

§ 4. ON THE TESTIMONY OF FOREIGNERS WHO HAVE ACQUIRED A LANGUAGE.

THE testimony of those who, though foreigners, have acquired a language, are an important help for ascertaining the Usus Loquendi. Thus, the writings of the Emperor Marcus Antoninus, and of Philo and Josephus, who were Jews, may be used to illustrate the meaning of Greek words; because, although foreigners, they well understood the Greek language. The productions of those writers, indeed, whom by way of distinction we commonly term *Pagan Writers*, are in various ways highly deserving the attention of the biblical student, for the confirmation they afford of the leading facts recorded in the sacred volume, and especially of the doctrines, institutions, and facts, upon which Christianity is founded, or to which its records indirectly relate. "Indeed it may not be unreasonably presumed, that the writings of Pagan antiquity have been providentially preserved with peculiar regard to this great object, since, notwithstanding numerous productions of past ages have perished, sufficient remains are still possessed, to unite the cause of heathen literature with that of religion, and to render the one subservient to the interests of the other."[2]

---

[1] Mori Acroases, tom 1. pp. 110—130. Angler, Hermeneutica Biblica, pp. 65. 115—119.
[2] Dr. Gray's Connection of Sacred and Profane Literature, vol. i. p. 3.

II. Sect. I. § 4.] *Of Ascertaining the Usus Loquendi.*

Of the value of the heathen writings in thus confirming the credibility of the Scriptures, very numerous instances have been given in the preceding volume. We have there seen that the heathen writings substantiate, by an independent and collateral report, many of the events, and the accomplishment of many of the prophecies recorded by the inspired writers; and that they establish the accuracy of many incidental circumstances which are interspersed throughout the Scriptures. " Above all, by the gradually perverted representations which they give of revealed doctrines, and institutions, they attest the actual communication of such truth from time to time; and pay the tribute of experience to the wisdom and necessity of a written revelation." Valuable as these testimonies, from the works of heathen authors, confessedly are, their uses are not confined to the confirmation of Scripture-facts; they also frequently contribute to elucidate the phraseology of the sacred writers. Two or three instances will illustrate this remark.

1. *Pagan writers use words and phrases coincident with, or analogous to those of the sacred writers, whose meaning they enable us to ascertain, or show us the force and propriety of their expressions.*

Thus, the sentiment and image of the prophet Isaiah,

> On what part will ye smite again, will ye add correction?
> The whole head is sick, and the whole heart faint.
>
> Isa i. 5. Bp Lowth's Translation.

Are exactly the same with those of Ovid, who, deploring his exile to Atticus, says that he is wounded by the continual strokes of fortune, so that there is no space left in him for another wound

> ——— Ego continuo fortunæ vulneror ictu:
> Vixque habet in nobis jam nova plaga locum
>
> Ovid. Epist. ex Ponto. lib. ii. ep. vii. 41, 42.

But the prophet's sentiment and image are still more strikingly illustrated by the following expressive line of Euripides, the great force and effect of which Longinus ascribes to its close and compressed structure, analogous to the sense which it expresses.

> Γεμω κακων δη κ' ουκετ' εσθ' οπη τεθη
> I am full of miseries there is no room for more.
>
> Eurip Herc. Furens, v. 1245.[1]

2. *Pagan writers often employ the same images with the sacred, so as to throw light on their import, and generally to set off their superior excellence.*

Thus, the same evangelical prophet, when predicting the blessed effects that should flow from the establishment of the Messiah's kingdom, says,

> They shall beat their swords into plough-shares,
> And their spears into pruning-hooks
> Nation shall not lift up sword against nation,
> Neither shall they learn war any more.
>
> Isa. ii 4.

The same prediction occurs in the same words, in Micah iv. 2. The description of well-established peace (Bp. Lowth remarks) by the image of *beating their swords into plough-shares, and their spears into pruning-hooks*, is very poetical. The Roman poets have employed the same image. Thus Martial has an epigram (lib. xiv. ep. xiv.) intitled *Falx ex ense* — the sword converted into a pruning-hook.

The prophet Joel has reversed this image, and applied it to war prevailing over peace.

> Beat your plough-shares into swords,
> And your pruning-hooks into spears.
>
> Joel iii. 10.

---

[1] Longinus, de Sublim. c. 40. Bp. Lowth's Isaiah, vol. ii. p. 9.

And so has the prince of the Roman poets:

> Non ullus aratro
> Dignus honos. squalent abductis arva colonis,
> Et curvæ rigidum falces conflantur in ensem.
> VIRGIL, Georg. lib. 1. 506—508.

> Dishonour'd lies the plough, the banish'd swains
> Are hurried from the uncultivated plains;
> The sickles into barbarous swords are beat.[1]

Additional examples, finely illustrative of the above remark, may be seen in Bishop Lowth's notes on Isa. viii 6—8. xi. 6—8 xx xxix. 4, 5. xxxii. 2. xlv. 2. and xlix. 2.

The great benefit which is to be derived from Jewish and Heathen profane authors, in elucidating the Scriptures, is excellently illustrated by the Rev. Dr. Gray [now Bishop of Bristol], in his

"Connexion between the Sacred Writings and the Literature of Jewish and Heathen Authors, particularly that of the Classical Ages, illustrated." London, 1819, in 2 vols. 8vo.

Grotius and other commentators have incidentally applied the productions of the classical writers to the elucidation of the Bible: but no one has done so much in this department of sacred literature, as Elsner, Raphelius, and Kypke, of whose publications an account is given in the Appendix to this volume.

SECTION II.

INDIRECT TESTIMONIES FOR ASCERTAINING THE USUS LOQUENDI.

THE usus loquendi cannot always be found with sufficient certainty by those *direct* means which have been discussed in the preceding section. Proper evidence is sometimes wanting; sometimes usage is variable or inconstant, even in the same age or in the same writer; or there is an ambiguity of language, or of grammatical forms; or an obscurity covers the thing or subject treated of; or novelty of language occurs; or a neglect of the usus loquendi, which sometimes happens even in the most careful writers. Other means must, therefore, be used, by which the true sense can be elicited. These *indirect* means it is the object of the present section to state and to illustrate.

---

§ 1. OF THE CONTEXT.

I. *The Context defined and illustrated.* — II. *Rules for investigating the Context.*

I. ANOTHER most important assistance, for investigating the meaning of words and phrases, is the consideration of the CONTEXT, or the comparison of the preceding and subsequent parts of a discourse.

1. If we analyse the words of an author, and take them out of their proper series, they may be so distorted as to mean any thing but what he intended to express. Since, therefore, words have several meanings, and

---

[1] Lowth's Isaiah, vol. ii, p. 29.

consequently, are to be taken in various acceptations, *a careful consideration of the preceding and subsequent parts will enable us to determine that signification, whether literal or figurative, which is best adapted to the passage in question.*

A few instances will illustrate this subject, and show not only the advantage, but also the necessity of attending to the context.

(1.) It has been questioned whether those words of the prophet Micaiah (1 Kings xxii. 15.) *Go and prosper, for the Lord shall deliver it* (Ramoth) *into the hand of the king,* are to be understood affirmatively according to their apparent meaning, or are to be taken in an ironical and contrary sense? That they are to be understood in the latter sense, the consideration of the context will plainly show, both from the prophet's intention, and from the prophetic denunciation afterwards made by him. Hence it may be inferred that some sort of ironical gesture accompanied Micaiah's prediction, which circumstance ought to be borne in mind by the interpreter of Scripture.[1]

(2.) Further, there is a difference of opinion whether the address of Job's wife (Job ii. 9.) is to be understood in a good sense, as *Bless* (or ascribe glory to) *God, and die*, or in a different signification, *Curse God, and die*, as it is rendered in our authorised version. Circumstances show that the last is the proper meaning, because as yet Job had not sinned with his lips, and, consequently, his wife had no ground for charging him with indulging a vain opinion of his integrity.

(3.) Job xli. Whether the leviathan is a whale or a crocodile has also divided the judgment of commentators. That the latter animal is intended is evident from the circumstances described in the context, which admirably agree with the crocodile, but can in no respect be applied to the whale: for instance, ch. xli. 17, &c. relative to the hardness of his skin, and v. 13—16. concerning his teeth and impenetrable scales.

(4.) Once more, it has been doubted whether our Lord's command to his disciples, *to provide neither gold nor silver in their purses* (Matt x. 9.) be a rule of perpetual observation. That it was only a temporary command is evident from the preceding and subsequent parts of the chapter, which prove *that* particular mission to have been only a temporary one; and that, as they were to go for a short time through Judea, and then to return to Jesus, he therefore forbade them to take any thing that would retard their progress.

2. *The context of a discourse or book, in the Scriptures, may comprise either one verse, a few verses, entire periods or sections, entire chapters, or whole books.*

Thus, if 1 Cor. x. 16. be the passage under examination, the preceding and subsequent parts of the epistle, which belong to it, are the eighth, ninth, and tenth chapters. If Isa. lii. be the chapter in question, the reader must not stop at the end of it, but continue his perusal to the twelfth verse of ch. liii., for these together form one subject or argument of prediction, in which the prophet is announcing to his countrymen the certainty of their deliverance and return from the Babylonish captivity. This entire portion ought, therefore, to be read at once, in order to apprehend fully the prophet's meaning. In like manner, the verses from v. 13. of ch. lii. to the end of ch. liii. form a new and entire section relative to the sufferings of the Messiah. Here, then, is a wrong division of chapters, to which no regard should be paid in examining the context of a book. Ch. lii. ought to include v. 12. of ch. liii. and ch. liii. ought to commence at v. 13. and be continued to the end of ch. liii. In like manner, the first verse of the fourth chapter of Saint Paul's Epistle to the Colossians ought to be joined to the third chapter: the slightest attention to this point will enable a diligent student to add numerous other examples.

3. *Sometimes a book of Scripture comprises only one subject or argument, in which case the whole of it must be referred to precedents and subsequents, and ought to be considered together.*

Of this description is Saint Paul's Epistle to the Ephesians, which consists of two parts, doctrinal and practical. The design of the doctrinal portion is to show, that although there was a difference between Jewish and Gentile believers, inasmuch as the former enjoyed a priority of time in point of expecting and acknowledging Christ, and through the free grace of God they were a church or congregation of believers before the Gentiles; yet that, *now*, the latter are become partakers of the same grace with them, and being thus admitted to this communion of grace, every *real* distinction between them is abolished; and, therefore, that both Jews and Gentiles together, form one body of the church under one head, even Jesus Christ. Other special doctrines indeed are incidentally mentioned;

---

[1] See a further illustration of this passage in Vol. I. p. 303.

but these are either adduced to explain and enforce the principal doctrine, or they are derived from it. The practical part or exhortation, which naturally flows from the doctrine inculcated, is concord and peace between Jew and Gentile, which the apostle enforces with great beauty and energy.[1]

To this head may also be referred the Psalms, each of which being separated from the other, and having no connection with the preceding or following psalm, for the most part comprises a distinct and entire subject. That some of the Psalms have been divided, and forcibly disjoined, which ought to have remained united, and to have formed one ode, is evident as well from the application of sacred criticism as from the subject matter. The number of the Psalms by no means corresponds, either in manuscripts or in the antient versions. Thus, in some manuscripts, the first and second Psalms are not reckoned at all, while in others the former is considered as part of the second Psalm that they are two distinct compositions, is evident from a comparison of the subject-matter of each Psalm. In the first Psalm the characters of the pious man and the sinner, as well as their respective ends, are contrasted: the second Psalm is prophetic of the Messiah's exaltation. The ninth and tenth Psalms are united together in the Septuagint version; while the hundred and sixteenth and hundred and forty seventh are, each, divided into two. The argument which pervades the forty-second and forty third Psalms plainly shows that they are properly but one divine ode, and are, therefore, rightly joined together in many manuscripts, although they occur as separate compositions in all our printed editions.[2]

II. In examining the context of a passage, it will be desirable,

1. *To investigate each word of every passage, and as the connection is formed by PARTICLES, these should always receive that signification which the subject-matter and context require.*

The Hebrew Concordances of Noldius and Taylor, and also Glassius's Philologia Sacra[3], will materially assist in ascertaining the force of the Hebrew particles, as will the elaborate work of Hoogeveen on the subject of the Greek particles.[4] Further, where particles are wanting, as they sometimes are, it is only by examining the argument and context that we can rightly supply them. For instance, the conditional conjunction is sometimes wanting, as in Gen xlii. 38., *and* [if] *mischief befall him by the way*[5], in Exod. iv 23 and [if] *thou refuse to let him go.* Particles of comparison also are frequently wanting, as in Gen. xvi 12, *he will be a wild man,* literally, *he will be a wild ass man*, that is, [like] *a wild ass.* How appropriately this description was given to the descendants of Ishmael, will readily appear by comparing the character of the wild ass in Job xxxix. 5—8. with the wandering, lawless, and freebooting lives of the Arabs of the Desert, as pourtrayed by all travellers. Psal xi 1. *Flee* [as] *sparrows to your mountain.* Psa. xii. 6. *The words of the Lord are pure words* [as] *silver tried in a furnace of earth.* Isaiah ix 18. *They shall mount up* [as or like] *the ascending of smoke.* Similar examples occur in the New Testament, as in John v. 17. *My Father worketh hitherto, and I work;* that is, as my Father worketh hitherto, so also do I work together with him. Sometimes particles are wanting both at the beginning and end of a sentence: thus Job xxiv. 19. [As] *drought and heat consume the snow,* so doth *the grave* those which *have sinned.* Jer. xvii 11. [As] *the partridge sitteth* on eggs, *and hatcheth not,* [so] *he that getteth riches, and not by right,* &c. Numerous similar instances occur in the book of Job, and especially in the Proverbs; where, it is but justice to our admirable authorised version to add, that the particles omitted are properly supplied in Italic characters, and thus complete the sense.

---

[1] Moldenhawer Introductio ad Libros Vet. et Nov Fœderis, p. 307. Professor Franck's Guide to the Reading of the Scriptures, translated by Mr Jacques, p 178. (1st edit.)

[2] They are considered, and translated, as *one* Psalm, by Bishop Horsley. See his Version of the Psalms, vol i. pp 110—114 and the notes

[3] See particularly, tract v.—viii on adverbs, prepositions, and conjunctions, tom. I. pp 561—556 ed Dathii

[4] Hoogeveen, Doctrina Particularum Græcarum, 2 vols 4to. 1769 Though treating of Greek particles generally, this elaborate work incidentally illustrates a great number of passages in the New Testament. A valuable abridgment of it, with the notes of various literati, was published by Professor Schutz at Leipsic in 1806, which has been handsomely reprinted at Glasgow, 1813. See also Dr. Macknight on the Epistles, vol. i. essay 4. § 74., to the end of that essay

[5] Purver rightly supplies it, and renders the passage thus, *and should death befall him in the way* in the authorised English version the conjunction *and* is omitted, and the conditional *if* is properly supplied.

II. Sect. II. § 1.]   *Of the Context.*   321

2. *Examine the entire passage with minute attention.*

Sometimes a single passage will require a whole chapter, or several of the preceding and following chapters, or even the entire book, to be perused, and that not once or twice, but several times. The advantage of this practice will be very great because, as the same thing is frequently stated more briefly in the former part of a book, which is more clearly and fully explained in the subsequent portion, such a perusal will render every thing plain to the meanest capacity. For instance, that otherwise difficult passage, Rom. ix. 18. *Therefore hath he mercy on whom he will have mercy, and whom he will he hardeneth*, will become perfectly clear by a close examination of the context, beginning at verse 18 of chapter viii. and reading to the end of the eleventh chapter; this portion of the epistle being most intimately connected. Disregarding this simple, and all but self-evident canon, some expositors have explained 1 Pet ii 8. as meaning that certain persons were *absolutely appointed* to destruction, a notion not only contradicting the whole tenor of Scripture, but also repugnant to every idea which we are there taught to entertain of the mercy and justice of God. An attentive consideration of the context and of the proper punctuation of the passage alluded to (for the most antient manuscripts have scarcely any points), would have prevented them from giving so repulsive an interpretation. The first epistle of Peter (it should be recollected) was addressed to believing Jews.[1] After congratulating them on their happiness in being called to the glorious privileges and hopes of the Gospel, he takes occasion to expatiate upon the sublime manner in which it was introduced, both by the prophets and apostles; and, having enforced his general exhortations to watchfulness, &c. by an affecting representation of our relation to God, our redemption by the precious blood of Christ, the vanity of all worldly enjoyments, and the excellence and perpetuity of the Gospel dispensation (ch. i. throughout); — he proceeds (ii. 1—12) to urge them by a representation of their Christian privileges, to receive the word of God with meekness, to continue in the exercise of faith in Christ as the great foundation of their eternal hopes, and to maintain such an exemplary conduct, as might adorn his Gospel among the unconverted Gentiles. *Wherefore*, says he, in consideration of the everlasting permanency and invariable certainty of the word of God, *laying aside all malice, and all guile, and hypocrisies, and envies, and all evil speakings*, which are so contrary to its benevolent design, with all simplicity, *as new born babes*[2] (or infants), who are regenerated by divine grace, *desire the sincere milk of the word, that ye may grow thereby* [*unto salvation*][3], *since* (or *seeing* that) *you have tasted that the Lord is gracious. To whom coming, as unto a living stone, disallowed indeed of men, but chosen of God, and precious; Ye also* (who believe,) *as living stones are built up a spiritual house, an holy priesthood, to offer up spiritual sacrifices by Jesus Christ. (Wherefore also it is contained in the Scripture, Behold I lay in Sion a chief corner-stone, elect, precious, and he that believeth on it* (confideth in it) *shall not be confounded, or ashamed). Unto* you, *therefore*, WHO BELIEVE *he is precious; but unto them that* DISBELIEVE απειθουσι[4],

---

[1] See this proved, *infra*, Vol. IV. Part II. Chap IV. Sect. III § III.

[2] This expression very emphatically denotes those who are newly converted or regenerated, as the apostle had said (1 Pet i 23.) the believing Jews were, through the *incorruptible word of God*. It is well known that the antient Jewish rabbies styled new proselytes to their religion, *little children* and *new-born babes*, and Peter, who was a Jew, very naturally adopts the same phraseology, when writing to Jewish converts to the Gospel.

[3] These words [*unto salvation*, εις σωτηριαν], though omitted in the common printed editions, are, by Griesbach, inserted in the text, *of which they form an integral part*. They are found in the Codices Alexandrinus, Vaticanus, and Ephremi (the three *oldest* manuscripts extant), in thirty-nine others of good authority, though of less antiquity; and also in the Old Syriac, the Philoxonian (or later) Syriac, the Arabic edited by Erpenius, the Coptic, Ethiopic, Armenian, Sclavonic, and Vulgate versions, and are quoted by Clemens Alexandrinus, Origen, Cyril, Joannes Damascenus, and Theophylact, among the *Greek Fathers*, and by the *Latin Fathers*, Jerome, Rufinus, Augustine, Gildas, Cassiodorus, and the venerable Bede. This reading is, therefore, undoubtedly *genuine*, and is of great importance It shows the reason *why* the believing Jews were regenerated, and also why they were to desire the unadulterated doctrines of the Gospel, viz that they *might thereby increase*, or *grow up*, *unto salvation* This was the *end* they should always have in view; and nothing could so effectually promote this end, as continually receiving the pure truth of God, praying for the fulfilment of its promises, and acting under its dictates.

[4] The verb απειθεω (whence the participle απειθουντες) and its derivative substantive απειθεια, signify such a *disbelief*, as constitutes the party guilty of obstinacy, or wilful refusal to credit a doctrine or narrative In the New Testament, it is *specially* used concerning those who obstinately persist in rejecting the doctrine of the Gospel, regardless of all the evidences that accompanied it. Thus, in John iii. 36. απειθων τω υιω, *he that disbelieveth the Son* is opposed to *him that believeth on the Son*, τω πιστευοντι εις τον υιον. So

the tone which the builders disallowed, the same is become the head of the corner, and a stone of stumbling, and a rock of offence. They DISBELIEVING THE WORD (τω λογω απειθουντες), that is, the word of the Gospel, which contains this testimony, stumble at this corner stone, whereunto they were appointed. But YE (believers, who rest your salvation on it) are a chosen generation, a royal priesthood, a peculiar people, &c. &c. Hence, it is evident, that the meaning of 1 Pet. ii. 8. is not, that God had ordained them to disobedience (for in that case their obedience would have been impossible, and their disobedience would have been no sin) but that God, the righteous judge of all the earth, had appointed or decreed, that destruction and eternal perdition should be the punishment of such disbelieving persons, who wilfully rejected all the evidences that Jesus Christ was the Messiah, the Saviour of the world. The mode of pointing above adopted, is that proposed by Drs John Taylor, Doddridge, and Macknight, and recognised by Griesbach in his critical edition of the Greek Testament, and is manifestly required by the context.

3. *A verse or passage must not be connected with a remote context, unless the latter agree better with it than a nearer context.*

Thus Rom. ii 16. although it makes a good sense if connected with the preceding verse, makes a much better when joined with verse 12. (the intermediate verses being read parenthetically as in the authorised version), and this shows it to be the true and proper context.

4. *Examine whether the writer continues his discourse, lest we suppose him to make a transition to another argument, when, in fact, he is prosecuting the same topic.*

Rom. v. 12. will furnish an illustration of this remark. From that verse to the end of the chapter Saint Paul produces a strong argument to prove, that as all men stood in need of the grace of God in Christ to redeem them from their sins, so this grace has been afforded equally to all, whether Jews or Gentiles. To perceive the full force, therefore, of the apostle's conclusion, we must read the *continuation* of his argument from verse 12. to the close of the chapter.

5. *The parentheses which occur in the sacred writings should be particularly regarded: but no parenthesis should be interposed without sufficient reason.*

Sometimes the grammatical construction, with which a sentence begins, is interrupted; and is again resumed by the writer after a larger or shorter digression. This is termed a parenthesis.

Parentheses being contrary to the genius and structure of the Hebrew language, are, comparatively, of rare occurrence in the Old Testament. In fact, as there is no sign whatever for it in Hebrew, the sense only can determine when it is to be used.

The prophetic writings, indeed, contain interruptions and interlocutions, particularly those of Jeremiah but we have an example of a real parenthesis in Zech. vii 7 The Jewish captives had sent to inquire of the prophet, whether their fasting should be continued on account of the burning of the temple, and the assassination of Gedaliah after a considerable digression, but closely connected with the question proposed, the prophet at length replies, in ch. viii 19. that the season formerly devoted to fasting should soon be spent in joy and gladness. The intermediate verses, therefore, from ch. vii 4. to ch viii. 17. are obviously parenthetical, though not marked as such in any of the modern versions, which we have had an opportunity to examine.

---

in Acts xiv 2 those Jews *who stirred up the* Gentiles, and made them evil affected towards the brethren, are termed οι απειθουντες Ιουδαιοι, *the disbelieving* (or, as it is not ill rendered in our authorised version), the *unbelieving* or wilfully incredulous *Jews*, who are opposed to the great multitude *both of the Jews and also of the Greeks, who believed,* πιστευσαι (verse 1.). The same verb is found in Acts xvii 5 and xix 9. Rom. xi 30, 31. and 1 Pet. iii. 1 (Gr.) in which last place Saint Peter exhorts wives, who believed the Gospel, to be in subjection to their husbands, that, if any, απειθουσι τω λογω, *disbelieve the word, they may also without the word be won* over to the Gospel, *by the exemplary conversation of the wives.* The lexicographer, Suidas, (as cited by Schleusner, *in voce,* to whom we are chiefly indebted for this note,) considers απειθειν as synonymous with απιστειν. Απειθειν δοτικη· απιστειν.

For examples, in which the derivative substantive απειθεια means *disbelief,* or contempt of the Christian doctrine, see Schleusner's Lexicon, *sub voce.*

II. Sect. II. § 1] *Of the Context.* 323

A remarkable instance of complicated parenthetic expression occurs in Dan. viii 2. *And I saw in vision, (and when I saw I was in Shushan,) and I saw (I was then by the waters of Ulai), and I lifted up my eyes, and saw and beheld!* &c. See other instances in Gen xxiv. 10. 2 Chron. xxxii. 9 Exod. xii. 15. Psal xlv. 6. Isa. lii 14. [1]

In the New Testament, however, parentheses are frequent, especially in the writings of Saint Paul; who, after making numerous digressions (all of them appropriate to, and illustrative of, his main subject), returns to the topic which he had begun to discuss. They are generally introduced in the following manner :

(1.) *Where the parenthesis is short, it is inserted without hesitation between two clauses which are grammatically connected, and then after the conclusion of the parenthesis, the latter clause proceeds, as if no interruption had taken place* Thus .

ı In Acts ı. 15. *Peter .... said (the number of names together was about an hundred and twenty, ἦν τε ὀχλος, &c), Men and brethren, &c*

ıı. Rom viii 19—21 The application of the parenthesis will render this very difficult passage perfectly easy. *The earnest expectation of the creation waiteth for the manifestation of the sons of God (ἡ γὰρ τῆς κτίσεως . . . ἡ κτίσις . . . was made subject to vanity, not willingly, but by reason of him who subjected it) in hope that the creation itself also shall be delivered from the bondage of corruption into the glorious liberty of the sons of God.* [2]

iii 1 Cor. xv. 52. *At the last trump · (for the trumpet shall sound .... and we shall be changed, σαλπιγγι γαρ, &c) for this corruptible must put on incorruption,* &c.

Similar parentheses occur in 2 Cor vi 2. x. 3, 4. Gal. ii. 8   A parenthesis of considerable length is in this way inserted in Rom. ii. 13—16. In cases of this kind the parenthesis is commonly indicated by the particles τε, γαρ, &c at its commencement. See the examples above adduced, and Rom 1. 20. xv. 3 , and Heb vii. 20, &c

(2) *When the parenthesis is longer, the principal word or words of the preceding clause are repeated with or without variation, after the parenthesis.*

ı 1 Cor viii 1—4 *Now as touching things offered unto idols (we know that we all have knowledge   Knowledge puffeth up, but charity edifieth, &c ..... as concerning those things that are offered in sacrifice unto idols) we know that an idol is nothing,* &c   Similar instances occur in John vi. 22—24 Eph. ii. 1—5 12—19. and Rev. iii. 8—10   and the *observant* student of the New Testament will easily be enabled to supply other examples. [3]

Another instance of the parenthesis we have in Phil i. 27. to chap. ii. 16. inclusive · in which the apostle discusses a subject, the proposition of which is contained in ch i. 27. ; and afterwards in ch ii. 17. he returns to the topic which he had been treating in the preceding chapter   " In conformity with this statement we find (ch. i 23.), that Saint Paul says, he is influenced by two things — a desire both of life and death , but he knows not which of these to choose. Death is the most desirable to himself, but the welfare of the Philippians requires rather that he may be spared a little longer , and, having this confidence, he is assured that his life will be lengthened, and that he shall see them again in person. Then, after the interruption which his discourse had received, he proceeds (ch. ii. 17) as follows   " Yea, and if I be offered upon the sacrifice and service of your faith, I joy and rejoice with you all." The intervening charge is happily and judiciously introduced by the apostle in order that the Philippians might not remit their exertions until his arrival, but contend for the faith of the Gospel with unity and humility ; as will be evident to those who examine the point with attention and candour." [4]

ii. To this class we may refer the following beautiful example of the parenthesis, in 2 Tim. i. 16—18.   The apostle acknowledging the intrepid affection of Onesiphorus — who, when timorous professors deserted him, stood by him and ministered to him — begins with a prayer for the good man's family , *The Lord grant mercy to the house of Onesiphorus, for he often refreshed me, and was not ashamed of my chain, but, being in Rome, very carefully sought me, and found me out*   Saint Paul then stops his period, and suspends his

---

[1] Stuart's Heb. Gram. § 244. p. 395.

[2] Those who are acquainted with the original language will, on consideration, easily perceive the justice of the above translation.   For the reasons on which it is founded, and for an able elucidation of the whole passage, see " Sermons preached at Welbeck Chapel, by the Rev. Thomas White," sermon xx. pp 363—380. Griesbach, and after him Vater, has printed in a parenthesis only the middle clause of verse 20. (" not willingly, but by reason of him who subjected it"); which certainly does not materially contribute to clear up the difficulty of this passage.

[3] Winer's Grammar to the Gr Test. p. 164   Some observations on Parentheses will be found in Franck's Guide to the Scriptures, pp. 188, 189. (Mr Jacques's Translation) 1st edit.

[4] Franck's Guide, p. 189.

sentence, to repeat his acknowledgments and prayer with renewed fervour and gratitude — (*The Lord grant that he may find mercy from the Lord in that day;*) *and in how many instances he ministered to me at Ephesus, you very well know.* If we peruse the choicest authors of Greece and Rome, we shall scarcely find, among their many parentheses and transpositions of style, one expressed in so pathetic and lively a manner, nor for a reason so substantial and unexceptionable.[1]

Additional instances might be offered, to show the importance of attending to parentheses in the examination of the context; but the preceding will abundantly suffice for this purpose. The author has been led to discuss them at greater length than may seem to have been requisite, from the circumstances, that less attention appears to be given to the parenthesis, than to any other species of punctuation, in the different works on the study of the Scriptures in our language, that have fallen under his notice.[2]

6. *No explanation must be admitted, but that which suits the context.*

In direct violation of this self-evident canon of interpretation, the church of Rome expounds Matt xviii. 17 *if a man neglect to hear the church, let him be unto thee as a heathen man and as a publican,* of the infallibility and final decisions of all doctrines by the (Roman) Catholic church. But what says the evangelist? Let us read the context. "*If,*" says our Lord, "*thy brother shall trespass against thee, go and tell him his fault between thee and him alone: if he shall hear thee, thou hast gained thy brother. But if he will not hear, take with thee one or two more, that in the mouth of one or two witnesses every word may be established. And if he shall neglect to hear them, tell it unto the church. but if he neglect to hear the church, let him be unto thee as an heathen man and a publican.* (verses 15—17.) That is, if a man have done you an injury, first admonish him privately of it, if that avail not, tell the church; — not the universal church dispersed throughout the world, but that particular church to which you both belong And if he will not reform upon such reproof, regard him no longer as a true Christian, but as a wicked man with whom you are to hold no religious communion, though, as a fellow-man, you owe him earnest and persevering good will and acts of kindness. Through the whole of this context there is not one word said about disobeying the determination of the Catholic church concerning a disputed doctrine, but about slighting the admonition of a particular church concerning known sin; and particular churches are owned to be fallible [3]

7. *Where no connection is to be found with the preceding and subsequent parts of a book, none should be sought.*

This observation applies solely to the Proverbs of Solomon, and chiefly to the tenth and following chapters, which form the second part of that book. and are composed of separate proverbs or distinct sentences, having no real or verbal connection whatever, though each individual maxim is pregnant with the most weighty instruction.[4]

From the preceding remarks it will be evident, that, although the comparison of the context will require both labour and unremitting diligence, yet these will be abundantly compensated by the increased degree of light which will thus be thrown upon otherwise obscure pas-

---

[1] Blackwall's Sacred Classics illustrated, vol i. pp. 68, 69. 3d edit.

[2] On the subject of parentheses, the reader is referred to the very valuable treatise of Christopher Wollius, De Parenthesi Sacrâ, at Leipsic, in 1726 4to. The same subject has also been discussed in the following works, viz Joh. Fr. Hirt, Dissertatio de Parenthesi, et generatim, et speciatim Sacrâ, 4to. Jena, 1745. Joh. Gottl. Lindner, Commentationes Duæ de Parenthesibus Johanneis, 4to. 1765. Ad Bened Spitzneri Commentatio Philologica de Parenthesi, Libris Sacris V et N T accommodata, 8vo Lipsiæ, 1773.

[3] Whitby on Matt xviii. 15—17. Bishop Porteus's Confutation of the Errors of the Church of Rome, pp 13, 14.

[4] J. B. Carpzov Prim. Lin. Herm. pp 36, 37. Bauer, Herm. Sacr. pp. 192—200. Pfeiffer, Herm. Sacr c. x. (op. tom. ii. pp. 656—658.) Franzius, Præf pp. 8—11. Tract. pp. 48—51. Morus, in Ernesti, tom i. pp 161—163. Viser, Herm Nov. Test. Sacr. pars iii. pp.189—194. Wetstein et Semler de Interpret. Nov. Test. pp. 116—190. Franckii Prælectiones Hermeneuticæ, pp. 61—94. Rambach, Inst. Herm. pp. 197—216. Jahnii Enchirid. Herm. Generalis, pp 51—71. Chladenii Institutiones Exegeticæ, pp 366—374 J E. Pfeifferi Institutiones Herm. Sacr. pp. 464—468. 507—534. Schæfer, Institutiones Scripturisticæ, pars ii. pp. 56—62. Arigler, Hermeneutica Biblica, pp. 148—165.

sages. The very elaborate treatise of Franzius, already referred to, will supply numerous examples of the Holy Scriptures which are rendered perfectly clear by the judicious consideration of the context.

§ 2. OF THE SUBJECT-MATTER.

ALTHOUGH, in interpreting words that have various meanings, some degree of uncertainty may exist as to which of their different senses is to be preferred; yet the ambiguity in such cases is not so great but that it may in general be removed, and the proper signification of the passage in question may be determined: for the SUBJECT-MATTER,—that is, the topic of which the author is treating—plainly shows the sense that is to be attached to any particular word. For there is a great variety of agents introduced in the Scriptures, whose words and actions are recorded.

Some parts of the Bible are written in a responsive or dialogue form, as the twenty-fourth Psalm, Isa. vi. 3. and Rom. iii. 1—9. And the sense of a text is frequently mistaken, by not observing who is the speaker, and what is the specific topic of which he treats; and also by not attending to the frequent and very elegant changes and successions of persons occurring in the Scriptures, and especially in the prophetic writings. One or two examples will illustrate the necessity of considering the subject-matter.

1. The Hebrew word בשר (BC-SHER) literally signifies the *skin*; by a metonymy, the *flesh* beneath the skin; and by a synecdoche it denotes *every animal*, especially man considered as infirm or weak, as in Jer. xvii. 5. *Cursed be the man that trusteth in man, and maketh* FLESH *his arm*, there are also several other meanings derived from these, which it is not material now to notice. But that the word *flesh* is to be understood of *man* only in Gen. vi 12 Psal. lxv 2. and Job x 4 will be evident on the slightest inspection of the subject-matter. *All flesh had corrupted his way* — that is, all men had wholly departed from the rule of righteousness, or had made their way of life abominable throughout the world And, in the Psalm above cited, who can doubt but that by the word *flesh* men are intended. *O thou that hearest prayer, unto thee shall all flesh*, that is, all mankind, *come*. In like manner also, in Job x 4 it is evident that *flesh* has the same meaning, if indeed the passage were at all obscure, the parallelism would explain it — *Hast thou the eyes of a man* (Heb. *of flesh*) ? or, *seest thou as man seest* ?

2. The first chapter of the prophecy of Isaiah affords an apposite elucidation of attending to the changes and successions of persons occurring in the Scriptures. Jehovah is there represented as impleading his disobedient people, Israel The prophet, with a boldness and majesty becoming the herald of the Most High, begins with summoning the whole creation to attend when Jehovah speaks. (ver. 2.) A charge of gross insensibility is in the next verse brought against the Jews, whose guilt is amplified (ver. 4.); and their obstinate wickedness highly aggravated the chastisements and judgments of God, though repeated till they had almost been left like Sodom and Gomorrah. (v. 5—9.) The incidental mention of those places leads the prophet to address the rulers and people of the Jews, under the character of the princes of Sodom and Gomorrah, in a style not less spirited and severe, than it is elegant and unexpected (10.) The vanity of trusting to the performance of the external rites and ceremonies of religion is then exposed (11—15.), and the necessity of repentance and reformation is strongly enjoined (16, 17), and urged by the most encouraging promises, as well as by the most awful threatenings. (18—20.) But, as neither of these produced the proper effect upon that people, who were the prophet's charge, he bitterly laments their degeneracy (21—23), and concludes with introducing the Almighty himself, declaring his purpose of inflicting such heavy judgments as would entirely cut off the wicked, and excite in the righteous, who should pass through the furnace, an everlasting shame and abhorrence of every thing connected with idolatry, the source of all their misery. (24—31.) The whole chapter, in loftiness of sentiment,

and style, affords a beautiful example of this great prophet's manner, whose writings, like his lips, are touched with hallowed fire.[1]

But it is not merely with reference to the meaning of particular passages that a consideration of the *subject-matter* becomes necessary to the right understanding of Scripture. It is further of the greatest importance in order to comprehend the various dispensations of God to man, which are contained in the sacred writings. For although the Bible comprises a great number of books, written at different times, yet they have a mutual connection with each other, and refer, in the Old Testament, with various but progressively increasing degrees of light and clearness, to a *future* Saviour, and in the New Testament to a *present* Saviour. With reference, therefore, to the several divine dispensations to man, the subject-matter of the whole Bible ought to be attentively considered: but, as each individual book embraces a particular subject, it will also be requisite carefully to weigh its subject-matter, in order to comprehend the design of the author. An analysis of each book will materially assist a reader of the Scriptures in forming a comprehensive view not only of its chief subject-matter, but will also show the methodical and orderly coherence of all the parts of the book with one another. Such an analysis the author has attempted in the fourth volume of this work. "Books," says an old writer, "looked upon *confusedly*, are but darkly and confusedly apprehended: but considered *distinctly*, as in these distinct analyses or resolutions into their principal parts, must needs be distinctly and much more clearly discerned."[2]

§ 3. OF THE SCOPE.

I. *The Scope defined — Importance of investing the Scope of a Book or Passage of Scripture.* — II. *Rules for investigating it.*

I. A CONSIDERATION of the SCOPE, or DESIGN, which the inspired author of any of the books of Scripture had in view, essentially facilitates the study of the Bible: because, as every writer had some design which he proposed to unfold, and as it is not to be supposed that he would express himself in terms foreign to that design, it therefore is but reasonable to admit that he made use of such words and phrases as were every way suited to his purpose. To be acquainted, therefore, with the scope of an author is to understand the chief part of his book. The scope, it has been well

---

[1] Bp Lowth's Isaiah, vol. ii. pp 4—27. 8vo. edit. Vitringa, in his comment on the same prophet, eminently excels in pointing out the rapid transitions of persons, places, and things Van Til, in his celebrated *Opus Analyticum*, has ably noticed various similar transitions in the Scriptures generally, and in the Psalms in particular, though in the last-mentioned book he has sometimes unnecessarily multiplied the speakers introduced. The value of Dr. Macknight's version and paraphrase of the epistle to the Romans is enhanced by his distinguishing between the objections brought by the Jew whom Saint Paul introduces as arguing with him, and the replies and conclusive reasonings of the Apostle.

[2] Roberts's Key to the Bible, pp. (11.) (12.) folio edit. 1665. See also Rambachii Institutiones Hermeneuticæ Sacræ, pp. 108—110. and Chladenius's Institutiones Exegeticæ, pp. 532. et seq.

observed, is the soul or spirit of a book; and, that being once ascertained, every argument and every word appears in its right place, and is perfectly intelligible: but, if the scope be not duly considered, every thing becomes obscure, however clear and obvious its meaning may really be.[1]

The scope of an author is either *general* or *special*, by the former we understand the design which he proposed to himself in writing his book; by the latter, we mean that design which he had in view, when writing particular sections, or even smaller portions, of his book or treatise.

The means, by which to ascertain the scope of a *particular* section or passage, being nearly the same with those which must be applied to the investigation of the *general* scope of a book, we shall briefly consider them together in the following observations.

II. The *Scope* of a book of Scripture, as well as of any particular section or passage, is to be collected from the writer's express mention of it, from its known occasion, from some conclusion expressly added at the end of an argument; from history, from attention to its general tenor, to the main subject and tendency of the several topics, and to the force of the leading expressions; and especially from repeated, studious, and connected perusals of the book itself.

1. *When the scope of a whole book, or of any particular portion of it, is expressly mentioned by the sacred writer, it should be carefully observed*

Of all criteria this is the most certain, by which to ascertain the scope of a book. Sometimes it is mentioned at its commencement, or towards its close, and sometimes it is intimated in other parts of the same book, rather obscurely, perhaps, yet in such a manner that a diligent and attentive reader may readily ascertain it. Thus the scope and end of the whole Bible, collectively is contained in its manifold utility, which St Paul expressly states in 2 Tim. iii. 16, 17 and also in Rom. xv 4. In like manner, the royal author of Ecclesiastes announces pretty clearly, at the beginning of his book, the subject he intends to discuss, viz. to show that all human affairs are vain, uncertain, frail, and imperfect; and, such being the case, he proceeds to inquire, *What profit hath a man of all his labour which he taketh under the sun?* (Eccl. i 2, 3) And towards the close of the same book (ch. xii. 8.) he repeats the same subject, the truth of which he had proved by experience. So, in the commencement of the book of Proverbs, Solomon distinctly announces their scope, (ch. i 1—4 6) — " *The Proverbs of Solomon, the Son of David king of Israel; — to know wisdom and instruction, to perceive the words of understanding to receive the instruction of wisdom, justice, judgment, and equity, to give subtilty to the simple, to the young man knowledge and discretion, to understand a proverb, and the interpretation; the words of the wise, and their dark sayings.*"— Saint John, also, towards the close of his gospel, announces his object in writing it to be, " *That ye might believe that Jesus is the Christ, the Son of God, and that, believing, ye might have life through his name.*" Therefore, all those discourses of our Lord, which are recorded almost exclusively by this evangelist and apostle, are to be read and considered with reference to this particular design · and, if this circumstance be kept in view, they will derive much additional force and beauty.

---

[1] " How unfair, how irrational, how arbitrary, is the mode of interpretation which many apply to the word of God? They insulate a passage, they fix on a sentence; they detach it from the paragraph to which it belongs, and explain it in a sense dictated only by the combination of the syllables or the words, in themselves considered. If the word of God be thus dissected or tortured, what language may it not seem to speak, what sentiments may it not appear to countenance, what fancy may it not be made to gratify? But would such a mode of interpretation be tolerated by any living author? Would such a method be endured in commenting on any of the admired productions of classical antiquity? Yet in this case it would be comparatively harmless, although utterly indefensible: but who can calculate the amount of injury which may be sustained by the cause of revealed truth, if its pure streams be thus defiled, and if it be contaminated even at the very fountain head?" Rev. H F Burder's Sermon on the Duty and Means of ascertaining the Genuine Sense of the Scriptures, p. 21.

Of the application of this rule to the illustration of a *particular* section, or the ascertaining of a *special* scope, the seventh chapter of Saint Paul's first epistle to the Corinthians will supply an example. — In that chapter, the object of which is to show that *it was not good to marry*, the apostle is replying to the queries which had been proposed to him by the Corinthian converts, and it is evident that his reply is continued through the whole chapter. But did he mean to insinuate *absolutely* that matrimony in itself was not good? By no means: on the contrary, it is clear from the scope of this section, given by Saint Paul in express words, that his design was not, in general, to prefer a state of celibacy to that of marriage; much less was it to teach that the living unmarried was either more holy or more acceptable to God; or that those who vow to lead a single life shall certainly obtain eternal salvation, as the church of Rome erroneously teaches from this place. But we perceive that he answered the question proposed to him with reference to the then existing circumstances of the Christian church. The apostle thought that a single life was preferable on account of the *present distress* — that is, the sufferings to which they were *then* liable. The persecutions to which they were exposed, when they came upon them, would be more grievous and afflictive to such as had a wife and children who were dear to them, than to those who were single; and, therefore, under such circumstances, the apostle recommends celibacy to those who had the gift of living chastely without marriage.

2. *The scope of the sacred writer may be ascertained from the known occasion on which his book was written.*

Thus, in the time of the apostles, there were many who disseminated errors, and defended Judaism; hence it became necessary that the apostles should frequently write against these errors, and oppose the defenders of Judaism. Such was the occasion of Saint Peter's second epistle; and this circumstance will also afford a key by which to ascertain the scope of many of the other epistolary writings. Of the same description also were many of the parables delivered by Jesus Christ. When any question was proposed to him, or he was reproached for holding intercourse with publicans and sinners, he availed himself of the occasion to reply, or to defend himself by a parable. Sometimes, also, when his disciples laboured under any mistakes, he kindly corrected their erroneous notions by parables.

The inscriptions prefixed to many of the Psalms, though some of them are evidently spurious, and consequently to be rejected, frequently indicate the occasion on which they were composed, and thus reflect considerable light upon their scope. Thus the scope of the 18th, 34th, and 3d Psalms is illustrated from their respective inscriptions, which distinctly assert upon what occasions they were composed by David. In like manner, many of the prophecies, which would otherwise be obscure, become perfectly clear when we understand the circumstances on account of which the predictions were uttered.

3. *The express conclusion, added by the writer at the end of an argument, demonstrates his general scope.*

Thus, in Rom. iii. 28. after a long discussion, Saint Paul adds this conclusion: — *Therefore we conclude, that a man is justified by faith without the deeds of the law.* Hence we perceive with what design the whole passage was written, and to which all the rest is to be referred. The conclusions interspersed through the epistles may easily be ascertained by means of the particles, "wherefore," "seeing that," "therefore," "then," &c. as well as by the circumstances directly mentioned or referred to. The principal conclusions, however, must be separated from those which are of comparatively less importance, and subordinate to the former. Thus, in the epistle to Philemon, our attention must chiefly be directed to verses 8 and 17, whence we collect that Saint Paul's design or scope was to reconcile Onesimus (who had been a runaway slave) to his master, and to restore him to the latter, a better person than he had before been. In the epistle to the Ephesians, the principal conclusions are, ch. ii 11, 12. and ch. iv. 1. 3 The subordinate or less principal conclusions are ch. i. 15. iii 13. iv 17. 25. v 1. 7. 15. 17. and vi. 13, 14. [1]

4. *A knowledge of the time when a book was written, and also of the state of the church at that time, will indicate the scope or intention of the author in writing such book.*

For instance, we learn from history, that during the time of the apostles there were numerous errors disseminated; and therefore they wrote many passages in their epistles with the express design of refuting such errors. An acquaintance with these historical particulars will enable us to determine with accuracy the scope of entire books as well as of detached passages.

---

[1] Franckii Manuductio, cap. iii. pp 87, 88. 292 or English edition, pp. 61. et seq. 177. et seq. Franckii Prælect. Herm. pp. 38. et seq.

Thus, the epistle of Saint James was written about the year of Christ 61, at which time the Christians were suffering persecution, and probably (as appears from ch. ii 6. and ch. v. 6.) not long before the apostle's martyrdom, which, Bishop Pearson thinks ¹, happened A. D. 62, in the eighth year of Nero's reign, when the destruction of the Jewish temple and polity was impending. (James v. 1. 8.) At the period referred to, there were in the church certain professing Christians, who in consequence of the sanguinary persecution then carried on against them both by Jews and Gentiles, were not only declining in faith and love, and indulging various sinful practices — for instance, undue respect of persons, (chapter ii verse 1 *et seq*) contempt of their poor brethren, (chapter ii. verse 9 *et seq*) and unbridled freedom of speech, (chapter iii. verse 3. *et seq*); but who also most shamefully abused to licentiousness the grace of God, which in the Gospel is promised to the penitent, and, disregarding holiness, boasted of a faith destitute of its appropriate fruits, viz of a bare assent to the doctrines of the Gospel, and boldly affirmed that this inoperative and dead faith was alone sufficient to obtain salvation (chapter ii. verse 17 *et seq*.) Hence we may easily perceive, that the apostle's scope was not to treat of the doctrine of justification; but, the state of the church requiring it, to correct those *errors in doctrine, and those sinful practices, which had crept into the church, and particularly to expose that fundamental error of a dead faith unproductive of good works.* This observation further shows the true way of reconciling the supposed contradiction between the apostles Paul and James, concerning the doctrine of salvation by faith. ²

5. *If, however, none of these subsidiary aids present themselves, it only remains that we REPEATEDLY AND DILIGENTLY STUDY THE ENTIRE BOOK, AS WELL AS THE WHOLE SUBJECT, AND CAREFULLY ASCERTAIN THE SCOPE FROM THEM, before we attempt an examination of any particular text.*

Thus we shall be enabled to understand the mind of its author, and to ascertain the main subject and tendency of the book or epistle which may be under consideration or if it have several views and purposes in it, not mutually dependent upon each other, nor in subordination to one chief end, we shall be enabled to discover what those different matters were, as also in what part the author concluded one and began another, and, if it be necessary to divide such book or epistle into parts, to ascertain their exact boundaries

But in this investigation of the scope, there is not always that clearness which leads to a certain interpretation: for sometimes there are *several* interpretations which sufficiently agree with the writer's design. In those places, for instance, where the coming of Christ is mentioned, it is not always determined whether it is his last advent to judge the world, or his coming to inflict punishment on the unbelieving Jews. In such cases the interpreter must be content with some degree of probability. There are, however, two or three cautions, in the consideration of the scope, to which it will be desirable to attend.

1. *Where, of two explanations, one is evidently contrary to the series of the discourse, the other must necessarily be preferred.*

In Psal xlii 2. the royal psalmist pathetically exclaims — *When shall I come and appear before God?* — This verse has, by some writers, been expounded thus, that a man may wish for death, in order that he may the sooner enjoy that state of future blessedness which is sometimes intended by the phrase *seeing God.* Now this exposition is manifestly contrary to the design of the Psalm; in which David, exiled from Jerusalem, and consequently from the house of God, through Absalom's unnatural rebellion, expresses his fervent desire of returning to Jerusalem, and beholding that happy day when he should again present himself before God in his holy tabernacle. In the fourth verse he mentions the sacred pleasure with which he had gone (or would repair, for some of the versions render the verb in the future tense) with the multitude to the house of God. There is, therefore, in this second sense a necessary and evident connection with the scope and series of the discourse.

In 1 Cor. iii. 17. we read, *If any man defile* (more correctly destroy) *the temple of God, him shall God destroy* The phrase *temple of God*, in this passage, is usually in-

---

[1] Annales Paulinæ, p 31.
[2] Jo. Henr. Michaelis Introductio Historico-Theologica in Jacobi Minoris Epistolam Catholicam, §§ viii. xi.

terpreted of the human body, and by its defilement is understood libidinous unchastity, which God will destroy by inflicting corresponding punishment on the libidinous man. This sense is certainly a good one, and is confirmed by a similar expression at the close of the sixth chapter. But, in the former part of the third chapter, the apostle had been giving the teachers of the Corinthian Christians an important caution to teach pure and salutary doctrines, together with that momentous doctrine — *Other foundation can no man lay than that is laid, which is Jesus Christ,* (v. 11) — and that they should not add false doctrines to it. After largely discussing this topic, he subsequently returns to it, and the passage above cited occurs intermediately. From this view of the scope it will be evident that by the temple of God is to be understood the Christian church, which, if any man defile, corrupt, or destroy, by disseminating false doctrines, God will destroy him also.

2. *Where a parallel passage plainly shows that another passage is to be understood in one particular sense, this must be adopted to the exclusion of every other sense, although it should be supported by the grammatical interpretation as well as by the scope.*

Thus, in Matt. v. 25. we read — "*Agree with thine adversary quickly, whilst thou art in the way with him, lest at any time the adversary deliver thee to the judge, and the judge deliver thee to the officer, and thou be cast into prison.*" This passage has been interpreted to refer either to a future state of existence, or to the present life. In the former sense, the *adversary* is God, the *judge*, Christ, the *officer*, death, and the *prison*, hell and eternal punishments. In the latter sense, the meaning of this passage simply is, " If thou hast a lawsuit, compromise it with the plaintiff, and thus prevent the necessity of prosecuting it before a judge: but if thou art headstrong, and wilt not compromise the affair, when it comes to be argued before the judge, he will be severe, and will decree that thou shalt pay the uttermost farthing." Now, both these expositions yield good senses, agreeing with the *scope*, and both contain a cogent argument that we should be easily appeased: but if we compare the parallel passage in Luke xii. 58, 59. we shall find the case thus stated — *When thou goest with thine adversary to the magistrate,* as thou art in the way, give diligence that thou mayest be delivered from him, lest he hale thee to the judge, and the judge deliver thee to the officer (τω πρακτορι, whose duty it was to levy fines imposed for violation of the law), and the officer on non-payment *cast thee into prison. I tell thee thou shalt not depart thence till thou hast paid the very last mite* — In this passage there is no reference whatever to a future state, nor to any punishments which will hereafter be inflicted on the implacable: and thus a single parallel text shows which of the two senses best agrees with the scope of the discourse, and consequently which of them is preferably to be adopted.[1]

---

§ 4. ANALOGY OF LANGUAGES.

I. *Analogy of Languages defined.* — *Its different Kinds.* — II. *Use of Grammatical Analogy.* — III. *Analogy of Kindred Languages.* — IV. *Hints for consulting this Analogy in the Interpretation of Scripture.* — V. *Foundation of Analogy in all Languages.*

I. ANALOGY of languages is an important aid in enabling us to judge of the signification of words.

Analogy means *similitude.* For instance, from the meaning attached to the forms of words, their position, connection, &c. in one, or rather in many cases, we agree to establish a similarity of meaning, where the phenomena are the same, in another. This analogy is the foundation of all the rules of grammar, and of all that is established and intelligible in language. The analogy of languages is

---

[1] Bauer, Herm. Sacr. pp. 201—204. J. B. Carpzov. Herm. Sacr. pp. 33—35. Ernesti, Institutio Interp. Nov. Test. pp. 61, 62. Mori Acroases in Ernesti, tom. i. pp. 150 —160. Franckii Prælect. Herm. pp. 29—61. Franckii Commentatio de Scopo Veteris et Novi Testamenti, Halæ, 1724, 8vo. Jahnii Enchiridion, pp. 69—71. Rambach, Inst. Herm. pp. 145—197. 234. 238—240. Chladenii Instit. Exeget. pp. 375—387. J. E. Pfeiffer, Inst. Herm. Sacr. pp. 147—151. 267—276. Schæfer, Institutiones Scripturisticæ, pars ii. pp. 62—68.

II. Sect. II. § 4.]   *Analogy of Kindred Languages.*   831

of different kinds, viz. 1. the *analogy of any particular language* (that is, of the same language with that which is to be interpreted), the principles of which are developed by grammarians. This kind of analogy has been termed *Grammatical Analogy*. 2. The *Analogy of Kindred Languages*.[1]

II. USE OF GRAMMATICAL ANALOGY.

Grammatical analogy is not only useful in finding the usus loquendi, but is also applicable to some doubtful cases; for instance, when the kind of meaning, generally considered, is evident, (by comparing other similar words, and methods of speaking concerning such things, appropriate to the language,) we may judge of the especial force or power of the word, by the aid of grammatical analogy.

1. In Col. ii. 23. occurs the word εθελοθρησκεια, in our version rendered *will-worship*. As there is no example of this word, its meaning must be sought from analogy by ascertaining the import of words compounded with εθελω. Of this description of words there are many examples. Thus, εθελοπροξενος, is one who takes upon him voluntarily to afford hospitality to strangers, in the name of a city: εθελοδουλος is one who offers himself to voluntary servitude: εθελουργος is one who labours of his own free will. From this analogy, we may collect that εθελοθρησκεια, in Col. ii. 23. means an affected or superstitious zeal for religion, which signification is confirmed by the argument of the apostle's discourse.

2 In 1 Pet v 5. where many critics have attached an emphatic sense to εγκομβωσασθαι, we must compare the other Greek phrases which relate to clothing or investing; and thus we shall see that the prepositions περι, αμφι, and εν, are used in composition without any accession of meaning to the verb thereby; for instance, ιματιον περιβαλλειν, αμφιβαλλειν, or εμβαλλειν, simply means to *put on a garment*. Consequently, εγκομβωσασθαι means no more than ενδυσασθαι, with which it is commuted by Clemens Romanus.[2] The meaning, therefore, of the apostle Peter's expression — *be clothed with humility* — is to *exhibit a modest behaviour*.

III. ANALOGY OF KINDRED LANGUAGES.

Another analogy is that of KINDRED LANGUAGES, either as descended from one common stock, as the Hebrew, Syriac, Chaldee, and Arabic; or derived the one from the other, as Latin and Greek.

Besides the critical use to which the Cognate or Kindred Languages[3] may be applied, they afford very considerable assistance in interpreting the Sacred Writings. They confirm by their own authority a Hebrew form of speech, already known to us from some other source: they supply the deficiencies of the Hebrew language, and make us fully acquainted with the force and meaning of obscure words and phrases, of which we must otherwise remain ignorant, by restoring the lost roots of words, as well as the primary and secondary meaning of such roots; by illustrating words, the meaning of which has hitherto been uncertain, and by unfolding the meanings of other words that are of less frequent occurrence, or are only once found in the Scriptures. Further, the cognate languages are the most successful, if not the only means of leading us to understand the meaning of phrases, or idiomatical combinations of words found

---

[1] Stuart's Elements, p. 50. Ernesti Institutio Interpretis Nov. Test. p. 65.
[2] Epist. I. p. 39. Mori Acroases, tom i pp 171, 172. Stuart's Elements, p. 51.
[3] See a notice of the Cognate Languages in pp. 80, 81, of the present volume.

in the Bible, and the meaning of which cannot be determined by it, but which, being agreeable to the genius of the original languages, are preserved in books written in them. Schultens, in his Origines Hebrææ [1], has illustrated a great number of passages from the Arabic, from whose work Bauer [2] and Dr. Gerard [3], have given many examples which do not admit of abridgment. Schleusner has also availed himself of the cognate dialects to illustrate many important passages of the New Testament. Of the various *modern* commentators on the Bible, no one perhaps has more successfully applied the kindred languages to its interpretation than Dr. Adam Clarke.

IV. In consulting the cognate languages, however, much care and attention are requisite, lest we should be led away by *any* verbal or *literal* resemblance that may strike the mind, and above all by *mere* etymologies, which, though in some instances they may be advantageously referred to, are often uncertain guides. The resemblance or analogy must be a *real* one. We must, therefore, compare not only similar *words* and *phrases*, but also similar *modes of speech*, which, though perhaps differing as to the etymology of the *words*, are yet evidently employed to designate the *same idea*. The following examples will illustrate this remark: —

1. In 1 Cor. iii. 15. St. Paul, speaking of certain Christian teachers at Corinth, observes, that "*if any man's work shall be burnt, he shall suffer loss, but he himself shall be saved ; yet so as by fire.*" On this passage, by a forced and erroneous construction, has the church of Rome erected the doctrine of purgatory, a place in which she pretends that the just, who depart out of this life, expiate certain offences that do not merit eternal damnation. Let us, however, consider the subject-matter of the apostle's discourse in his Epistle to the Corinthians. Reflecting on the divisions which were among them, and on that diversity of teachers who formed them into different parties, he compares these to various builders [4]; some of whom raised an edifice upon the only foundation, Jesus Christ, composed of *gold, silver,* and *precious stones;* in other words, who preached the pure, vital, and uncorrupted doctrines of the Gospel; while others, upon the same foundation, built *wood, hay, stubble,* that is, disseminated false, vain, and corrupt doctrines. Of both these structures, he says, (v. 13.) *Every man's work shall be made manifest ; for the day shall declare it, because it shall be revealed by fire ; and the fire shall try* (rather prove) *every man's work of what sort it is :* — either the day of the heavy trial of persecution, or rather the final judgment of God, shall try every man's work, search it as thoroughly as fire does things that are put into it. Then, adds the apostle, *if any man's work abide which he hath built thereupon,* if the doctrines he hath taught bear the test, as silver, gold, and precious stones abide in the fire, *he shall receive a reward.* But *if any man's work shall be burnt,* if, on that trial, it be found that he has in-

---

[1] Alberti Schultens Origines Hebrææ, sive Hebrææ Linguæ antiquissima Natura et Indoles, ex Arabiæ penetralibus revocata. Lugduni Batavorum, 1761, 4to.
[2] Bauer's Hermeneutica Sacra, pp. 90—144.
[3] Gerard's Institutes of Biblical Criticism, pp 58—70.
[4] Some writers have imagined that the apostle is speaking of the *materials*, that is, the persons, of which the church of God is composed, rather than of the *ministers* of the Gospel, whom he represents as architects in the heavenly building On a repeated consideration of the verses in question, the author is satisfied that the *latter* are intended and in this view of the subject he is supported by Mr. Locke, Dr. Doddridge, and other eminent critics.

troduced false or unsound doctrines, he shall be like a man, whose building being of wood, hay, and stubble, is consumed by the fire; all his pains in building are lost, and his works destroyed and gone. *But* (rather *yet*) if he be upon the whole a good man who hath built upon Christ as the foundation, and on the terms of the Gospel committed himself to him, *he himself shall be saved; yet so as by fire,* ως δια πυρος, that is, not without extreme hazard and difficulty, as a man is preserved from the flames of his house when he escapes naked through them, and thus narrowly saves his life, though with the loss of all his property. This expression is proverbial concerning persons who escape with great hazard out of imminent danger, and similar expressions are to be found in the Old Testament, as in Amos iv. 11.[1] and Zech. iii. 2, and also in the Epistle of Jude, ver. 23 Now, let this phrase be compared with the Latin words *ambustus* and *semiustus*. Livy, speaking of Lucius Æmilius Paulus, says, that he had very narrowly escaped being sentenced to punishment, *prope ambustus evaserat* (lib xxii. c. 35.); and again (c. 40.) the consul is represented as saying that he had, in his former consulate, escaped the flames of the popular rage not without being scorched, *se populare incendium semiustum evasisse*.[2] Here, also, though there is no *verbal* resemblance between the expression of Saint Paul and those of the Roman historian, yet the *real* analogy is very striking, and shows that the apostle employed a well known proverbial expression, referring solely to a narrow escape from difficulty, and not, as the Romanists erroneously assert, to the fire of purgatory, a doctrine which is justly characterised as " a fond thing, vainly invented, and grounded upon no warranty of Scripture, but rather repugnant to the word of God."[3]

2. The sentence in Gen. xlix. 10. *nor a lawgiver from between his feet,* has greatly exercised the ingenuity of commentators. It is at present considered as equivalent to *a teacher from his offspring*. But, without altogether rejecting this interpretation, we *may* derive some light on the venerable patriarch's meaning from the Greek writers, among whom the expression of Moses occurs in the *very same terms*. Thus, in the Theage of Plato, we have εκ των ποδων αποχωρησωμεν. In other writers the expression is εκ ποδων, or εκ ποδων γινεσθαι, which is equivalent to *e medio disce-*

---

[1] Grotius, in his note on this passage, has remarked that a similar mode of speaking obtained among the Greeks, Σωζεσθαι εκ πυρος, or εκ φλογγος, but he has not cited any examples Palairet cites the following passage from one of the orations of Aristides, who, speaking of Apelles, says that the gods saved him out ot the midst of the fire, ΕΚ ΜΕΣΟΥ ΠΤΡΟΣ τον ανδρα ΣΩΖΕΙΝ. Observationes Philologico-Criticæ in Nov. Test. p. 386. Some additional instances are given in Eisner's Observationes Sacræ in Novi Fœderis Libros, vol ii p. 78. See Bishop Porteus's Brief Confutation of the Errors of the Church of Rome, pp 48, 49. 12mo London, 1796; and Bishop Tomline's Elements of Christian Theology, vol ii. pp. 347—351, Drs. Whitby, Macknight, and A. Clarke, on 1 Cor iii. 15

[2] Cicero (Orat pro Milone, c. 5.) has the following passage — Declarant hujus *ambusti* tribuni plebis illæ intermortuæ conciones, quibus quotidie meam potentiam invidiose criminabatur" (tom vi. p. 91. edit. Bipont.); and in his second pleading against Verres, the following sentence, which is still more fully in point " Sic iste (Verres) multo sceleratior et nequior, quam ille Hadrianus, aliquanto etiam felicior fuit Ille quod ejus avaritiam cives Romani ferre non potuerant, Uticæ domi suæ vivus exustus est; idque ita illi merito accidisse existimatum est, ut lætarentur omnes neque ulla animadversio constitueretur *hic sociorum ambustus incendio, tamen ex illa flamma periculoque evolavit,*" &c (Cont Verr. Action ii. lib. 1. c. 27. tom. iii p 265.)

[3] Article xxii of the Anglican Church. The antiscriptural doctrine of purgatory is copiously and ably exposed by Mr. Fletcher in his " Lectures on the Principles and Institutions of the Roman Catholic Religion," (pp. 236—250) and more concisely, but with great force of argument, in the Rev Geo. Hamilton's " Tracts upon some leading Errors of the Church of Rome," (London, 1825,) pp. 73—81.

dere, e medio evadere, e conspectu abire, that is, to disappear.[1] The general meaning of Moses, therefore, may be, that a native *lawgiver,* or expounder of the law, teacher, or scribe (intimating the ecclesiastical polity of the Jews), should not be wanting to that people, until *Shiloh,* or the Messiah *come.* How accurately this prediction has been accomplished it is not necessary to show in this place.

3. In Matt. viii. 20. we read that Christ *had not where to lay his head:* which expression has been interpreted as meaning that he had literally no home of his own. But considerable light is thrown upon it by two passages from the Arabic History of Abulpharagius; in the first of which, having stated that Saladin had animated his soldiers to the storming of Tyre, he says, that *no place now remained to the Franks,* WHERE THEY COULD LAY THEIR HEAD, *except Tyre;* and again, after relating that the Arabs had stormed Acca, or Ptolemais, he says that NO PLACE WAS LEFT TO THE FRANKS, *on the coast of this* (the Mediterranean) *Sea,* WHERE THEY COULD LAY THEIR HEAD.[2] From these two passages *it is* evident that the evangelist's meaning is, that Jesus Christ had no secure and fixed place of residence.

V. FOUNDATION OF ANALOGY IN ALL LANGUAGES.

" No one can doubt that men are affected in nearly the same way, by objects of sense. Hence, those who speak of the same objects, perceived and contemplated in the same manner, although they may use language that differs in respect to etymology, yet must be supposed to have meant the same thing; and on this account, the one may be explained by the other.

Men are physically and mentally affected in the same manner, by very many objects; and of course, it may be presumed that they entertain and mean to express the same ideas concerning these objects, however various their *language* may be. Besides, *modes* of expression are often communicated from one people to another.

In general, this principle is of great extent, and of much use to the interpreter, in judging of the meaning of tropical language, and in avoiding fictitious emphasis. Accordingly, we find it resorted to, now and then, by good interpreters, with great profit. But it needs much and accurate knowledge of many tongues to use it discreetly; whence it is not to be wondered at, that its use is not very common among interpreters."[3]

The following general cautions, on the subject of comparing words and languages with each other, may be of some utility: they are abridged from Dr. H. C. A. Eichstädt's notes to Morus's Acroases Academicæ.

1. The meaning in each or any language is not to be resolved into the authority of Lexicons, but that of good writers.

2. Words, phrases, tropes, &c. of any antient language are to be

---

[1] Mori Acroases in Ernesti Instit. Interp. Nov. Test. vol i. p. 181.

[2] Abulpharagii Historia, pp 406. 591 cited by Ammon, in his notes on Ernesti's Instit. Interp. Nov Test. pp. 67, 68. The subject of the preceding section is briefly discussed by Ernesti, pp 65—70 and more at length in his Opera Philologica, pp. 173. *et seq.* and 277., as well as by Morus, in his Acroases, vol. i. pp 168—184. and particularly by G. G. Zemisch, in his Disputatio Philologica De Analogia Linguarum, Interpretationis subsidio, (Lipsiæ, 1758,) reprinted in Pott's and Ruperti's Sylloge Commentationum Theologicarum, vol. vii. pp. 185—221.

[3] Stuart's Elements, p. 53.

judged of by the rules of judging among those who spoke that language, and not by those which prevail in modern times, and which have originated from different habits and tastes.

3. Guard against drawing conclusions as to the meaning of words, in the same or different languages, from fanciful etymology, similarity or metathesis of letters, &c.

4. When the sense of words can be ascertained in any particular language, by the ordinary means, other languages, even kindred ones, should not be resorted to, except for the purpose of increased illustration or confirmation.

5. Take good care that *real* similitude exists, whenever comparison is made.[1]

§ 5. OF THE ANALOGY OF FAITH

I *The Analogy of Faith defined, and illustrated.*—II. *Its importance in studying the Sacred Writings.*—III. *Rules for investigating the Analogy of Faith.*

I. OF all the various aids that can be employed for investigating and ascertaining the sense of Scripture, the ANALOGY OF FAITH is one of the most important. We may define it to be *the constant and perpetual harmony of Scripture in the fundamental points of faith and practice*, deduced from those passages, in which they are discussed by the inspired penmen, either directly or expressly, and in clear, plain, and intelligible language. Or, more briefly, the analogy of faith may be defined to be that *proportion which the doctrines of the Gospel bear to each other*, or *the close connection between the truths of Revealed Religion.*

The *Analogy of Faith* is an expression borrowed from Saint Paul's Epistle to the Romans, (xii. 6.) where he exhorts those who *prophesy* in the church (that is, those who exercise the office of authoritatively expounding the Scriptures) to *prophesy according to the proportion*, or, as the word is in the original, the *analogy of faith*. To the same effect many commentators interpret Saint Peter's maxim, (2 Pet. i. 20.) that *no prophecy of Scripture is of any private*, or *self-interpretation;* implying that the sense of any prophecy is not to be determined by an abstract consideration of the passage itself, but by taking it in conjunction with other portions of Scripture relating to the subject, "comparing things spiritual with spiritual" (1 Cor. ii. 13.);—a rule which, though it be especially applicable to the prophetic writings, is also of general importance in the exposition of the sacred volume.[2]

---

[1] Mori Acroases, tom. i. pp 182—184. Ernesti Institutio Interpretis Nov. Test. pp. 65—70., and his Opera Philologica, pp. 171 et seq. and 277. Stuart's Elements, p. 58. The subject of the Analogy of Languages is also discussed at considerable length by G. G. Zemisch in his Disputatio Philologica de Analogia Linguarum Interpretationis Subsidio, (Lipsiæ, 1758, 4to.) reprinted in Pott's and Ruperti's Sylloge Commentationum Theologicarum, vol. vii pp. 185—221.

[2] Bishop Van Mildert's Bampton Lect. p.181. Pfeiffer, Herm. Sacr. c.xii. (Op. t.ii. p. 659.) Carpzov. Prim. Lin. Herm. Sacr. p. 28. It may here be remarked, that the New Testament presents *three* terms, which appear to be synonymous with the analogy of faith, viz. Rom. ii. 20. Μορφωσις της γνωσεως, και της αληθειας εν τω νομω, *the form of knowledge*, the grand scheme and draught of all true science, *and the system of eternal truth*

II. It is evident that God does not act without a design in the system of religion taught in the Gospel, any more than he does in the works of nature. Now this design must be uniform: for as in the system of the universe every part is proportioned to the whole, and is made subservient to it, so, in the system of the Gospel, all the various truths, doctrines, declarations, precepts, and promises, must correspond with and tend to the end designed. For instance, if any one interpret those texts of Scripture, which maintain our justification by faith only, or our salvation by free grace, in such a sense as to exclude the necessity of good works, this interpretation is to be rejected, because it contradicts the main design of Christianity, which is to save us *from* our sins (Matt. i. 21.), to make us holy as God is holy (1 Pet. i. 15.), and to cleanse us from all filthiness both of flesh and spirit. (2 Cor. vii. 1.) In the application, however, of the analogy of faith to the interpretation of the Scriptures, it is indispensably necessary that the inquirer *previously* understand the whole scheme of divine revelation; and that he do not entertain a predilection for a *part* only; without attention to this, he will be liable to error. If we come to the Scriptures with any pre-conceived opinions, and are more desirous to put that sense upon the text which coincides with our own sentiments rather than the truth, it then becomes the analogy of *our* faith rather than that of the whole system. This, Dr. Campbell remarks, was the very source of the blindness of the Jews in our Saviour's time: they searched the Scriptures very assiduously; but, in the disposition they entertained, they would never believe what that sacred volume testifies of Christ. The reason is obvious; their great rule of interpretation was *the analogy of faith*, or, in other words, the system of the Pharisean Scribes, the doctrine then in vogue, and in the profound veneration of which they had been educated. This is that veil by which the understandings of the Jews were darkened, even in reading the law, and of which Saint Paul observed that it remained unremoved in his day; and we cannot but remark that it remains unremoved in our own time.[1] There is, perhaps, scarcely a sect or denomination of Christians, whether of the Greek, Romish, or Protestant churches, but has some particular system or digest of tenets, by them termed the *analogy of faith*, which they individually hold in the greatest reverence; and all whose doctrines terminate in some assumed position, so that its partisans may not contradict themselves. When persons of this description, it has been well remarked, meet with passages in Scripture which they cannot readily explain, consistently with their hypothesis, they strive to solve the difficulty by the analogy of faith which they have themselves invented. But allowing all their assumptions to be founded in truth, it is by no means consonant with the principles of sound divinity, to interpret Scripture by the hypotheses of

---

in the law, — Rom. vi. 17. Τυπος διδαχης, the *form* or mould of *doctrine* into which the Christians were cast, — and 2 Tim. i. 17. Ὑποτυπωσις ὑγιαινοντων λογων, the *form of sound words*

[1] Dr. Campbell's translation of the Four Gospels, vol. i. dissert. iv. § 14. p. 116. 8d edit.

a church; because the sacred records are the *only proper media* of ascertaining theological truth.[1]

III. Such, then, being the importance of attending to the analogy of faith, it remains to state a few observations which may enable the student to apply it to the clearing up of obscure or difficult passages of Scripture.

1. *Wherever any doctrine is manifest, either from the whole tenor of divine revelation or from its scope, it must not be weakened or set aside by a few obscure passages.*

As the observance of this canon is necessary to every student of the inspired volume, so it ought especially to be regarded by those who are apt to interpret passages, which are not of themselves plain, by those opinions, of the belief of which they are already possessed, but for which they have little ground besides the mere sound of some texts, that appear, when first heard, to be favourable to their preconceived notions. Whereas, if such texts were compared with the scope of the sacred writers, they would be found to bear quite a different meaning. For instance, no truth is asserted more frequently in the Bible, and consequently is more certain in religion, than that God is good, not only to some individuals, but also toward all men. Thus, David says, (Psal. cxlv 9.) *The Lord is good to* ALL, *and his tender mercies are over* ALL *his works*, and Ezekiel, (xviii. 23.) *Have I any pleasure at all in the wicked that he should die, saith the Lord and not that he should turn from his ways and live?* Frequently also does the Almighty declare, both in the books of the law as well as in the prophets, and also in the New Testament, how earnestly he desires the sinner's return to him. See, among other passages, Deut. v 29. Ezek xviii 32 and xxxiii 11. Matt xxiii 37 John iii 16 1 Tim ii 4 Titus ii. 11. and 2 Pet iii 9. If, therefore, any passages occur which at first sight *appear* to contradict the goodness of God, as, for instance, that He has created some persons that he might damn them (as some have insinuated), in such case the very clear and certain doctrine relative to the goodness of God is not to be impugned, much less set aside, by these obscure places, which, on the contrary, ought to be illustrated by such passages as are more clear. Thus, in Prov. xvi. 4. according to most modern versions, we read, that *The Lord hath made all things for himself, yea even the wicked for the day of evil.* This passage has, by several eminent writers, been supposed to refer to the predestination of the elect and the reprobation of the wicked, but without any foundation Junius, Cocceius, Michaelis, Glassius, Pfeiffer, Turretin, Ostervald, Dr. Whitby, Dr S. Clarke, and other critics, have shown that this verse may be more correctly rendered, *The Lord hath made all things to answer to themselves*, or aptly to refer to one another, *yea even the wicked, for the evil day*, that is, to be the executioner of evil to others ᛫ on which account they are in Scripture termed the rod of Jehovah (Isa. x 5), and his sword. (Psal. xvii 13.) But there is no necessity for rejecting the received version, the plain and obvious sense of which is that there is nothing in the world which does not contribute to the glory of God, and promote the accomplishment of his adorable designs. The pious and the wicked alike conduce to this end; the wicked, whom God has destined to punishment *on account of their impiety*, serve to display his justice (see Job xxi 30.), and consequently to manifest his glory. " God," says Dr Gill (who was a strenuous advocate for the doctrines of election and reprobation), " made man neither to damn him nor to save him, but for his own glory, and that is secured whether in his salvation or damnation, nor did nor does God make men wicked He made man upright, and man has made himself wicked, and being so, God may justly appoint him to damnation for his wickedness, in doing which he glorifies his justice."[2]

2. *No doctrine can belong to the analogy of faith, which is founded on a* SINGLE *text*.

Every essential principle of religion is delivered in more than one place. Besides, single sentences are not to be detached from the places where they stand, but must be taken in connection with the whole discourse.

From disregard of this rule, the temporary direction of the apostle James (v. 14, 15.) has been perverted by the church of Rome, and rendered a permanent institution, from a mean of recovery, to a charm, when recovery is desperate, for the salvation of the soul. The mistake of the church of Rome, in founding what she calls the *sacrament of extreme*

---

[1] Franck's Guide to the Scriptures, p. 79. Franckii Prælect. Herm. p. 185.
[2] Gill in loc. See also J. E. Pfeiffer's Inst. Herm. Sacr pp. 134—136., and Twopenny's " Dissertations on some Parts of the Old and New Testaments," pp. 74—76.

unction upon this place, is very obvious; for the anointing here mentioned was applied to those whose *recovery* was *expected*, as appears from verse 16, where it is said that the Lord in answer to the prayer of faith shall raise up and restore the sick whereas in the Roman Catholic church, extreme unction is used where there is little, or no hope of recovery, and is called the *sacrament of the dying*.[1] The same remark is applicable to the popish system of auricular confession to a priest, which is attempted to be supported by James v. 16. and 1 John i. 9. neither of which passages has any reference whatever to the ministerial office In the former, confession of our faults is represented as the duty of the faithful to each other, and in the latter, as the duty of the penitent to God alone.

3. *The* WHOLE *system of revelation must be explained, so as to be consistent with itself.* — *When two passages* APPEAR *to be contradictory, if the sense of the one can be clearly ascertained, in such case that must regulate our interpretation of the other.*

Thus, in one passage, the apostle John says; *If we say that we have no sin, we deceive ourselves, and the truth is not in us If we confess our sins, he is faithful and just to forgive us our sins if we say we have not sinned, we make him a liar, and his word is not in us.* (1 John i. 8—10.) In another passage, the same apostle affirms. *Whosoever abideth in him, sinneth not. Whosoever is born of God, doth not commit sin, for his seed remaineth in him and he cannot sin, because he is born of God* (1 John iii. 6 9) This is an apparent contradiction, but the texts must be explained, so as to agree with one another. Now, from Scripture and experience, we are certain that the first passage must be literally understood. At the dedication of the temple, Solomon said, *If they sin against thee, and thou be angry, (for there is no man that sinneth not,)* 1 Kings viii. 46. And in Eccl. vii 20. *For there is not a just man upon the earth, that doeth good and sinneth not.* The explanation of the second passage, therefore, must be regulated by the established signification of the first, that both may agree. When it is affirmed that even good men cannot say, they have no sin; the apostle speaks of occasional acts, from which none are free. When Saint John says, that he who is born of God doth not commit sin, he evidently means, *habitually*, as the slave of sin, and this is incompatible with a state of grace. Both passages, therefore, agree, as the one refers to particular deeds, and the other to general practice and in this manner, must every seeming contradiction be removed. The passage, of which the literal sense can be established. must always regulate the interpretation of a different expression, so as to make it agree with fixed principles.

4. *An obscure, doubtful, ambiguous, or figurative text must never be interpreted in such a sense as to make it contradict a plain one.*

In explaining the Scriptures, consistency of sense and principles ought to be supported in all their several parts; and if any one part be so interpreted as to clash with another, such interpretation cannot be justified. Nor can it be otherwise corrected than by considering every doubtful or difficult text, first by itself, then with its context, and then by comparing it with other passages of Scripture, and thus bringing what may seem obscure into a consistency with what is plain and evident.

(1.) The doctrine of transubstantiation, inculcated by the church of Rome, is founded on a strictly literal interpretation of figurative expressions, *this is my body*, &c (Matt. xxvi. 26, &c) and (which has no relation to the supper,) *eat my flesh, drink my blood.* (John vi 51—58.) But independently of this, we may farther conclude that the sense put upon the words, "*this is my body*," by the church of Rome, cannot be the true one, being contrary to the express declaration of the New Testament history, from which it is evident that our Lord is ascended into Heaven, where he is to continue "*till the time of the restitution of all things*," (Acts iii 21.) that is, till his second coming to judgment How then can his body be in ten thousand several places on earth at one and the same time ? We may further add that, if the doctrine of transubstantiation be true, it will follow that our Saviour, when he instituted the sacrament of the Lord's Supper, did actually eat his own flesh and drink his own blood; a conclusion this, so obviously contradictory both to reason and to Scripture, that it is astonishing how any sensible and religious man can credit such a tenet.

(2.) Upon a similar literal interpretation of Matt. xvi. 18. *Thou art Peter, and upon this rock will I build my church*, the church of Rome has erected the claim of supremacy for Peter and his successors. Hence, building on Peter is explained away by some com-

---

[1] See Bishop Burnet on the 25th Article; Whitby, Benson, Macknight, and other commentators on this text; and Mr. Fletcher's Lectures on the Principles and Institutions of the Roman Catholic Religion, p 198. et seq. The Christian Guardian for 1823 (p. 305.) contains a good illustration of James v. 14, 15.

II. Sect. II. § 5.]   Of the Analogy of Faith.

mentators, as being contrary to the faith that Christ is the only foundation (1 Cor. iii. 11.) The most eminent of the antient fathers, as well as some of the early bishops or popes of Rome, particularly Gregory the Great, and likewise several of the most judicious modern commentators, respectively take this rock to be the profession of faith, which Peter had just made that *Christ was the Son of God*. The connection, however, shews that Peter is here plainly meant. *Thou art Peter,* says Christ; and *upon this rock,* that is, Peter, pointing to him, for thus it connects with the reason which follows for the name, in the same manner as the reason is given for that of Abraham in Gen. xvii 5. and of Israel in Gen xxxii 28. The Apostles are also called, in other parts of the New Testament, the foundation on which the church is built, as in Eph. ii 20. and Rev. xxi 14. as being the persons employed in erecting the church, by preaching. It is here promised that Peter should commence the building of it by his preaching, which was fulfilled by his first converting the Jews (Acts ii. 14—42.), and also the Gentiles (Acts x xv 7) This passage, therefore, gives no countenance to the papal supremacy, but the contrary, for this prerogative was personal and incommunicable.[1]

5. *Such passages as are expressed with brevity are to be expounded by those where the same doctrines or duties are expressed* MORE LARGELY *and fully.*

(1.) The doctrine of justification, for instance, is briefly stated in Phil. iii., but that momentous doctrine is professedly discussed in the Epistle to the Galatians, and especially in that to the Romans and according to the tenor of these, particularly Rom iii, all the other passages of Scripture that treat of justification, should be explained

(2.) Even slight variations will oftentimes serve for the purpose of reciprocal illustration. Thus the beatitudes related in the sixth chapter of Saint Luke's Gospel, though delivered at another time and in a different place, are the same with those delivered by our Lord in his sermon on the mount, and recorded in the fifth chapter of Saint Matthew's Gospel. Being, however, epitomised by the former Evangelist, they may be explained by the latter.

(3.) Further, the quotation from Isaiah vi. 9, 10. *Hear ye indeed, but understand not,* &c is contracted in Mark iv 12 Luke viii 10. and John xii. 40.; but it is given at large in Matt. xiii. 14, 15., and accordingly from this last cited Gospel, the sense of the prophet is most evident. Again, nothing is more certain than that God *hath no pleasure in wickedness,* or sin (Psal. v 4.), and, consequently, cannot be the cause of sin. When, therefore, any passages occur which *appear* to intimate the contrary, they must be so understood as not to impugn this important truth. The *hardening* of Pharaoh's heart, therefore, is not to be taken as the act of God, but that he permitted him to go on, following his own cruel schemes, regardless of the divine judgments.[2]

6. *" Where several doctrines of equal importance are proposed, and revealed with great clearness, we must be careful to give to each its full and equal weight."*

" Thus, that we are saved by the free grace of God, and through faith in Christ, is a doctrine too plainly affirmed by the sacred writers to be set aside by any contravening position for it is said, *By grace ye are saved through faith, and that not of yourselves ; it is the gift of God* (Eph. ii 8) But so, on the other hand, are the doctrines of repentance unto life, and of obedience unto salvation; for, again it is said, *Repent and be converted, that your sins may be blotted out,* (Acts iii. 19.) and, *If thou wilt enter into life, keep the commandments.* (Matt xix 17.) To set either of these truths at *variance* with the others, would be to frustrate the declared purpose of the Gospel, and to make it of none effect. Points thus clearly established, and from their very nature indispensable, must be made to correspond with each other, and the exposition, which best preserves them unimpaired and undiminished, will in any case be a safe interpretation, and most probably the true one. The analogy of faith will thus be kept entire, and will approve itself, in every respect, as becoming its divine author, and *worthy of all acceptation."* [3]

Some farther remarks might be offered in addition to the above rules; but as they fall more properly under consideration in the

---

[1] Barrow's Works, vol. i. p. 581. Grotius in loc. Elsley's Annotations, vol. i. pp. 273—275. Gerard's Institutes, p 163. See also the commencement of Bishop Burgess's Letter to his Clergy, entitled, *Christ, and not St Peter, the Rock of the Christian Church,* and especially Dr A. Clarke's Commentary on Matt xvi. 18.

[2] Franck's Guide, p 41. Pfeiffer, Herm. Sac. c xii. p. 659. and Critica Sacra, c. 5. § 15. (Op. t. ii. pp. 719, 720.) Gerard's Institutes, p. 161. J. E. Pfeiffer has given some additional examples, illustrating the preceding rule in his Inst. Herm. Sacr. pp. 142—144.

[3] Bishop Vanmildert's Bampton Lectures, p. 204.

subsequent part of this work, the preceding observations on the interpretations of Scripture by the analogy of faith will, perhaps, be found abundantly sufficient. It only remains to state, that valuable as this aid is for ascertaining the sense of Scripture, it must be used in *concurrence* with those which have been illustrated in the foregoing sections, and to subjoin a few cautions respecting the application of the analogy of faith, attention to which will enable us successfully to " *compare things spiritual with spiritual.*"

1. " Care," then, " must be taken, not to confound seeming with real analogies ; — not to rely upon merely verbal resemblances when the sense may require a different application, not to interpret what is parallel only in one respect, as if it were so in all ; not to give to any parallel passages so absolute a sway in our decisions as to over-rule the clear and evident meaning of the text under consideration ; and, above all, not to suffer an eagerness in multiplying proofs of this kind, to betray us into a neglect of the immediate context of the passage in question, upon which its signification must principally depend."[1] The occasion, coherence, and connection of the writing, the argument carrying on, as well as the scope and intent of the paragraph, and the correspondence of the type with its antitype, are all to be carefully remarked.

2. Further, " In forming the analogy of faith, all the plain texts relating to one subject or article ought to be taken together, impartially compared, the expressions of one of them restricted by those of another, and explained in mutual consistency; and that article deduced from them all in conjunction: not, as has been most commonly the practice, one set of texts selected, which have the same aspect, explained in their greatest possible rigour ; and all others, which look another way, neglected or explained away, and tortured into a compatibility with the opinion in that manner partially deduced."

3. Lastly, the analogy of faith, as applicable to the examination of particular passages, ought to be very short, simple, and purely scriptural; but most sects conceive it, as taking in all the complex peculiarities, and scholastic refinements, of their own favourite systems."[2]

Thus, as it has been remarked with equal truth and elegance[3], " by due attention to these principles, accompanied with the great moral requisites already shown to be indispensable, and with humble supplication to the throne of grace for a blessing on his labours, the diligent inquirer after Scripture truth may confidently hope for success. The design of every portion of Holy Writ, its harmony with the rest, and the divine perfection of the whole, will more and more fully be displayed. And thus will he be led, with increasing veneration and gratitude, to adore HIM, to whom every sacred book bears witness, and every divine dispensation led the way; even HIM who is *Alpha and Omega, the first and the last, Jesus Christ, the same yesterday, to-day, and for ever.*"[4]

---

[1] Bishop Vanmildert's Bampton Lect p. 215.
[2] Gerard's Institutes, p 161. The analogy of faith is copiously illustrated, in addition to the authorities already cited, by Franck, in his Prælect. Herm positio v. pp. 166—192.; by Rambach, in his Instit. Herm. Sacræ, lib ii c. 1. pp. 87—106 ; by Jahn in his Enchiridion Herm. Generalis, § 32 pp. 96—100.; by J E. Pfeiffer, in his Instit Herm. Sacræ, pp. 706—740., and by Chladenius, in his Institutiones Exegeticæ, pp. 406—430.
[3] By Bishop Vanmildert, Bampt. Lect. p. 216.
[4] Rev. i. 11, Heb. xiii. 8.

§ 6. ON THE ASSISTANCE TO BE DERIVED FROM JEWISH WRITINGS IN THE INTERPRETATION OF THE SCRIPTURES.

I. *The Apocryphal Books of the Old Testament.* — II. *The Talmud.* — 1. *The Misna.* — 2. *The Gemara* — *Jerusalem and Babylonish Talmuds.* — III. *The Writings of Philo Judæus and Josephus.* — *Account of them.*

BESIDES the various aids mentioned in the preceding sections, much important assistance is to be obtained, in the interpretation of the Holy Scriptures, from consulting the Apocryphal writings, and also the works of other Jewish authors, especially those of Josephus and Philo; which serve not only to explain the grammatical force and meaning of words, but also to confirm the facts, and to elucidate the customs, manners, and opinions of the Jews, which are either mentioned or incidentally referred to in the Old and New Testaments.

Of the writings of the Jews, the Targums or Chaldee Paraphrases, which have been noticed in a former page [1], are, perhaps, the most important; and next to them are the Apocryphal books of the Old Testament, and the Talmud.

I. The APOCRYPHAL BOOKS, as we have already had occasion to remark [2], are the productions of the Alexandrian Jews and their descendants. They are all curious, and some of them extremely valuable. It is to be regretted that the just rejection of these books from the scriptural canon by the reformed churches has occasioned the opposite extreme of an entire disregard to them in the minds of many serious and studious Christians. As a collection of very antient Jewish works, anterior to Christianity, as documents of history, and as lessons of prudence and often of piety, the Greek Apocryphal writings are highly deserving of notice; but, as elucidating the phraseology of the New Testament, they claim the frequent perusal of scholars, and especially of theological students. Kuinoel has applied these books to the illustration of the New Testament, with great success; and Dr. Bretschneider has also drawn many elucidations from the Apocryphal books in his Lexicon to the New Testament. The Apocryphal books of the New Testament exhibit a style in many respects partaking of the Hebraic-Greek idiom of the genuine books of the New Testament.

II. The TALMUD (a term which literally signifies *doctrine*) is a body of Jewish Laws, containing a digest of doctrines and precepts relative to religion and morality. The Talmud consists of two general parts, viz. The *Misna* or text, and the *Gemara* or commentary.

1. The MISNA (or *repetition*, as it literally signifies) is a collection of various traditions of the Jews, and of expositions of Scripture texts; which, they pretend, were delivered to Moses during his abode on the Mount, and transmitted from him, through Aaron, Eleazar, and Joshua, to the prophets, and by those to the men of

---
[1] See an account of the Targums in pp. 33—38, of the present volume.
[2] See Vol. I p. 496.

the Great Sanhedrin, from whom they passed in succession to Simeon (who took our Saviour in his arms), Gamaliel, and ultimately to Rabbi Jehuda, surnamed *Hakkadosh* or the Holy. By him this digest of oral law and traditions was completed, towards the close of the second century, after the labour of forty years. From this time it has been carefully handed down among the Jews, from generation to generation; and in many cases has been esteemed beyond the written law itself. The Misna consists of six books, each of which is entitled *order*, and is further divided into many treatises, amounting in all to sixty-three: these again are divided into chapters, and the chapters are further subdivided into sections or aphorisms.

2. The GEMARAS or Commentaries on the Misna are two-fold. —

(1.) The *Gemara of Jerusalem*, which in the opinion of Prideaux, Buxtorf, Carpzov, and other eminent critics, was compiled in the third century of the Christian æra; though, from its containing several barbarous words of Gothic or Vandalic extraction, father Morin refers it to the fifth century. This commentary is but little esteemed by the Jews.

(2.) The *Gemara of Babylon* was compiled in the sixth century, and is filled with the most absurd fables. It is held in the highest estimation by the Jews, by whom it is usually read and constantly consulted, as a sure guide in all questions of difficulty.

The Jews designate these commentaries by the term Gemara, or *perfection*, because they consider them as an explanation of the whole law, to which no further additions can be made, and after which nothing more can be desired. When the Misna or text, and the commentary compiled at Jerusalem, accompany each other, the whole is called the *Jerusalem Talmud*, and when the commentary which was made at Babylon is subjoined, it is denominated the *Babylonish Talmud*. The Talmud was collated for Dr. Kennicott's edition of the Hebrew Bible; and as the passages of Scripture therein contained were taken from manuscripts in existence from the second to the sixth century, they are so far authorities, as they show what were the readings of their day. These various readings, however, are neither very numerous nor of very great moment. Bauer states that Fromman did not discover more than *fourteen* in the Misna: and although Dr. Gill, who collated the Talmud for Dr. Kennicott, collected about a thousand instances, yet all these were not, in strictness, various lections. The Talmud, therefore, is chiefly useful for illustrating manners and customs noticed in the Scriptures.[1] Sometimes the passages cited from the Old Testament are

---

[1] Bauer, Crit. Sacr. pp. 340—343. Jahn, Introd ad Vet. Fœd. p. 174. Kennicott, Dissertatio Generalis, §§ 32—35 Leusden, Philologus Hebræo-mixtus, pp 90. et seq. In pp. 95—98. he has enumerated the principal contents of the Misna, but the best account of the Misna and its contents is given by Dr. Wotton, Discourses, vol. i. Disc 1. and ii. pp. 10—120 — See also Waehner's Antiquitates Ebræorum, vol. i. pp.256—340. — Pfeiffer, op tom. ii. pp. 852—855. De Rossi, Variæ Lectiones, tom. i. Proleg. canons 78—81 and Allen's Modern Judaism, pp. 21—64. Buddæus, in his Introductio ad Historiam Philosophiæ Ebræorum, pp. 116. et seq. has entered most fully into the merits of the Jewish Talmudical and Rabbinical writings.

exactly quoted; and sometimes many things are left out, or added in an arbitrary manner, in the same manner as some of the fathers have quoted from the New Testament.[1]

The *Rabbinical Writings* of the Jews are to be found chiefly in their *Commentaries* on the Old Testament.

As all these Jewish writings are both voluminous and scarce, many learned men have diligently collected from them the most material passages that tend to illustrate the Scriptures. An account of their labours, as well as of the editions of the Misna, Talmud, and Jewish Commentators, will be found in the Appendix to this volume, pp. 187—192.

The Misna, being compiled towards the close of the second century, may, for the most part, be regarded as a digest of the traditions received and practised by the Pharisees in the time of our Lord. Accordingly, different commentators have made considerable use of it in illustrating the narratives and allusions of the New Testament, as well as in explaining various passages of the Old Testament; particularly Ainsworth on the Pentateuch, Drs. Gill and Clarke in their entire comments on the Scriptures, Wetstein in his critical edition of the New Testament, and Koppe in his edition of the Greek Testament, who in his notes has abridged the works of all former writers on this topic.

In availing ourselves of the assistance to be derived from the Jewish writings, we must take care not to compare the expressions occurring in the New Testament *too strictly* with the Talmudical and Cabbalistical modes of speaking; as such comparisons, when carried too far, tend to obscure rather than to illustrate the sacred writings. Even our illustrious Lightfoot is said not to be free from error in this respect: and Dr. Gill has frequently incumbered his commentary with Rabbinical quotations. The best and safest rule, perhaps, by which to regulate our references to the Jewish writers themselves, as well as those who have made collections from their works, is the following precept delivered by Ernesti: — *We are to seek for help*, says he, *only in those cases where it is absolutely necessary, that is, where our knowledge of the Greek and Hebrew tongues affords no means of ascertaining an easy sense, and one that corresponds with the context.* The same distinguished scholar has further laid it down as a rule of universal application, that our principal information is to be sought from the Jewish writings, in every thing that relates to their sacred rites, forms of teaching and speaking; especially in the epistle to the Romans, which evidently shows its author to have been educated under Gamaliel.[2]

Some very important hints, on the utility of Jewish and Rabbinical literature in the interpretation of the New Testament, occur in

---

[1] On the alleged castigations and alterations of the Talmud by the Jews, the reader will find some curious information in Mr. Allen's Modern Judaism, pp. 61—64.

[2] Ernesti, Instit. Interp. Novi Testamenti, p 274. In the 5th vol. of Velthusen's, Kuinöel's, and Ruperti's Commentationes Theologicæ (pp. 117—197), there is a useful dissertation by M. Weise, De more Domini acceptos a magistris Judaicis loquendi ac diserendi modos sapienter emendandi.

the Rev. Dr. (now Bishop) Blomfield's discourse, intitled *A Reference to Jewish Tradition necessary to an Interpretation of the New Testament.* London, 1817, 8vo.

III. More valuable in every respect than the Talmudical and Rabbinical Writings, are the works of the two learned Jews, Philo and Josephus, which reflect so much light on the manners, customs, and opinions of their countrymen, as to demand a distinct notice.

1. PHILO, surnamed Judæus, in order to distinguish him from several other persons of the same name [1], was a Jew of Alexandria, descended from a noble and sacerdotal family, and pre-eminent among his contemporaries for his talents, eloquence, and wisdom. He was certainly born before the time of Jesus Christ, though the precise date has not been determined; some writers placing his birth twenty, and others thirty years before that event. The latter opinion appears to be the best supported, consequently Philo was about sixty years old at the time of the death of our Redeemer, and he lived for some years afterwards. He was of the sect of the Pharisees, and was deeply versed in the Scriptures of the Old Testament, which he read probably in the Septuagint version, being a Hellenistic Jew, unacquainted (it is supposed) with the Hebrew, and writing in the Greek language. Some eminent critics have imagined that he was a Christian, but this opinion is destitute of foundation: for we have no reason to think that Philo ever visited Judæa, or that he was acquainted with the important events which were there taking place. Indeed, as the Gospel was not extensively and openly promulgated out of Judæa, until ten years after the resurrection of Jesus Christ, and as there is not the most distant allusion to him — much less mention of him, — made in the New Testament, it cannot be supposed that this distinguished person was a convert to Christianity. The striking coincidences of sentiment, and more frequently of phraseology, which occur in the writings of Philo, with the language of Saint Paul and Saint John in the New Testament, are satisfactorily accounted for, by his being deeply versed in the Septuagint (or Alexandrian Greek) version of the Old Testament, with which those apostles were also intimately acquainted. The writings of Philo exhibit many quotations from the Old Testament, which serve to show how the text then stood in the Original Hebrew, or, at least, in the Septuagint Version: and although they contain many fanciful and mystical comments on the Old Testament, yet they abound with just sentiments eloquently expressed, and were highly esteemed by the primitive Christian Church. and his sentiments concerning the LOGOS, or WORD, bear so close a resemblance to those of the apostle John, as to have given rise to the opinion of some eminent men that he was a Christian. [2]

---

[1] Fabricius and his editor, Professor Harles, have given notices of *forty-seven* persons of the name of Philo. Bibliotheca Græca, vol. IV. pp. 750—754.

[2] The late Mr. Bryant has collected the passages of Philo concerning the Logos in his work intitled "The Sentiments of Philo Judæus concerning the Λογος or Word of God, together with large extracts from his Writings, compared with the Scriptures on many other particular and essential Doctrines of the Christian Religion." (8vo. London, 1776.) As this volume is now rarely to be met with, the reader will find the most material pas-

In the writings of Philo, we meet with accounts of many customs of the Jews; of their opinions, especially such as were derived from the oriental philosophy; and of facts particularly relating to their state under the Roman emperors, which are calculated to throw great light on many passages of the sacred writings.[1]

2. FLAVIUS JOSEPHUS was of sacerdotal extraction and of royal descent, and was born A.D. 37: he was alive in A.D. 96, but it is not known when he died. He received a liberal education among the Pharisees, after which he went to Rome, where he cultivated his talents to great advantage.[2] On his return to Judæa, he commanded the garrison appointed to defend Jotapata against the forces of Vespasian, which he bravely maintained during forty-seven days. Josephus being subsequently taken prisoner by Vespasian, was received into his favour; and was also greatly esteemed by Titus, whom he accompanied to the siege of Jerusalem, on the capture of which he obtained the sacred books and many favours for his countrymen. When Vespasian ascended the imperial throne, he gave Josephus a palace, together with the freedom of the city of Rome, and a grant of lands in Judæa. Titus conferred additional favours upon him, and Josephus out of gratitude assumed the name of Flavius. The writings of Josephus consist of, 1. Seven books, relating the *War of the Jews* against the Romans, which terminated in their total defeat, and the destruction of Jerusalem. This history was undertaken at the command of Vespasian, and was written first in Hebrew and afterwards in Greek: and so highly was the emperor pleased with it, that he authenticated it by putting his signature to it, and ordering it to be preserved in one of the public libraries; 2. Of the *Jewish Antiquities*, in twenty books, comprising the period from the origin of the world to the twelfth year of the reign of Nero (A.D. 66), when the Jews began to rebel against the Romans; 3. An account of his own *Life*, and 4. Two books vindicating the *Antiquity of the Jewish Nation against Apion* and others. The writings of Josephus contain accounts of many Jewish customs and opinions, and of the different sects that obtained among his countrymen; which very materially contribute to the illustration of the Scriptures. Particularly, they contain many facts relative to the civil and religious state of the Jews about the time of Christ: which being supposed, alluded to, or mentioned in various passages of the New Testament, enable us fully to enter into the meaning of those passages.[3] His accurate and minute

---

sages of Philo's writings, selected and faithfully translated in the Rev. Dr. J. P Smith's Scripture Testimony to the Messiah, vol i. pp. 420—445. Dr A Clarke has given *thirty-five* instances of the particular terms and doctrines found in Philo's works, with *parallel passages* from the New Testament, in his commentary, at the end of the first chapter of Saint John's Gospel

[1] Fabricii Bibliotheca Græca, à Harles, vol iv. pp. 720—750. Bp. Gray's Connexion between Sacred and Profane Literature, vol i. pp. 288—302. Dr. Smith's Scripture Testimony to the Messiah, vol. i. pp 417, 418 For the principal editions of Philo's Works, and the principal illustrations of Scripture derived from them, see the Appendix to this volume, pp. 187, 188. 191.

[2] It is highly probable that Josephus was the companion of St. Paul in his voyage to Rome, related in Acts xxvii. See Otti Spicilegium ex Josepho, pp. 336—338., and especially Bp. Gray's Connexion between Sacred and Profane Literature, vol i pp. 357—368.

[3] In all matters relating to the temple at Jerusalem, and to the religion of the Jews,

detail of many of the events of his own time, and, above all, of the Jewish war, and the siege and destruction of Jerusalem, affords us the means of perceiving the accomplishment of many of our Saviour's predictions, especially of his circumstantial prophecy respecting the utter subversion of the Jewish polity, nation, and religion. The testimony of Josephus is the more valuable, as it is an undesigned testimony, which cannot be suspected of fraud or partiality. The modern Jews have discovered this, and therefore a writer who is a principal ornament of their nation since the cessation of prophecy, is now not only neglected, but despised, and is superseded among the Jews by a forged history, composed by an author who lived more than eight centuries *after* the time of Josephus, and who has assumed the name of Josippon, or Joseph Ben Gorion. The plagiarisms and falsehoods of this pseudo-Josephus have been detected and exposed by Gagnier, Basnage, and especially by Dr. Lardner.[1]

Michaelis particularly recommends a diligent study of the works of Josephus, from the beginning of Herod's reign to the end of the Jewish antiquities, as affording the very best commentary on the Gospels and Acts[2]: and Morus[3] observes, that the Jewish historian is more valuable in illustrating the histories related in the New Testament than for elucidating its style. Our numerous references to his works in the third, as well as in the preceding volume of this work, sufficiently attest the advantages resulting from a diligent examination of them.[4] Josephus is jointly admired for his lively and animated style, the bold propriety of his expressions, the exactness of his descriptions, and the persuasive eloquence of his relations, on which accounts he has been termed the Livy of the Greek authors. Though a strict Pharisee, he has borne such a noble testimony to the spotless character of Jesus Christ, that Jerome considered and called him a Christian writer.[5]

---

there is a remarkable agreement between the authors of the New Testament and Josephus; who had in person beheld that sacred edifice, and was himself an eye-witness of the solemn rites performed there. Hence it is obvious, that his statements are unquestionably more worthy of credit than the unsupported assertions of the Talmudists, who did not flourish until long after the subversion of the city and temple, and of the whole Jewish polity, both sacred and civil. A single instance, out of many that might be adduced, will suffice to illustrate the importance of this remark. The Talmudical writers affirm that the priests only killed the paschal lambs, but Josephus (whose testimony is confirmed by Philo) relates that it was lawful for the master of every family to do it, without the intervention of any priest; and they further relate, that at the time of the passover, there were so many families at Jerusalem, that it was utterly impossible for the priests to kill the paschal lamb for every family. In the New Testament we read that Jesus Christ sent his disciples to a private house, that the passover might be prepared by its possessor and by them, without the presence of any priest, or previously taking the lamb to the temple. As the statements of Philo and Josephus are corroborated by the relation in the New Testament, they are undoubtedly correct.

[1] Jewish Testimonies, chap vi. Lardner's Works, 8vo. vol. vii. pp. 162—187., 4to vol. iii. pp 560—574.

[2] Introduction to the New Test. vol. iii. part i. pp. 339—341.

[3] Mori super Hermeneutica Novi Testamenti Acroases Academicæ, tom. ii. p 195.

[4] Bp. Gray has illustrated, at length, the benefit to be derived from the writings of Josephus, in the illustration of the Scriptures. See his Connection between Sacred and Profane Literature, vol. i pp. 303—390.

[5] See the *genuineness* of Josephus's Testimony concerning Jesus Christ established, in Vol I. pp 558—562. And for an account of the best editions of his works, and of elucidations of Scripture drawn from them, see the Appendix to this volume, pp. 188. 191.

§ 7. ON THE ASSISTANCE TO BE DERIVED FROM THE WRITINGS OF THE GREEK FATHERS, IN THE INTERPRETATION OF SCRIPTURE.

LEARNED men are by no means agreed as to the *persons*, to whom the venerable appellation of FATHERS OF THE CHRISTIAN CHURCH ought to be given. While some would confine it exclusively to the Apostles, or to those writers who lived in the century immediately succeeding them, others would extend it to those who flourished in the fifth and sixth centuries, and some even give the appellation of *fathers* to all those theologians who lived and wrote so lately as the twelfth century, or to the origin of Scholastic Theology. The most probable classification is that which would enrol among the fathers, those Christian doctors only, who flourished before the close of the sixth century · because, in the seventh and following centuries, the purity of Christian Doctrine was debased by the most absurd notions and degrading superstitions; and also because but few of those, who held the office of teachers of religion during the dark ages, conducted themselves in such a manner as to deserve the appellation of FATHERS OF THE CHURCH. Still less are the learned agreed as to the degree of *authority* to be conceded to the works of the Fathers of the Christian Church: by some they are depreciated beyond measure, while on the other hand they are estimated as repositories of every thing that is valuable in sacred literature.

It is, however, a singular circumstance, that, in almost all theological controversies, both parties are desirous of having the fathers on their side. Considering the question, then, without prejudice or predilection, we may safely assume, that the primitive fathers were men eminent for their piety and zeal, though occasionally deficient in learning and judgment; that they may be relied upon in general for their statements of facts, but not invariably for the constructions which they put upon them, unless in their expositions of the New Testament, with the language of which they were intimately acquainted; and that they are faithful reporters of the opinions of the Christian Church, but not always the most judicious interpreters of Scripture. As repositories, therefore, of Christian antiquity, as preachers of Christian virtue, and as defenders of the true Christian doctrine, they may still be very advantageously consulted; especially if we do not expect that from them which they could not have. The fathers applied themselves to the reading of the Scriptures with undivided attention, with intense thought, and with holy admiration, as to that which was alone worthy to be studied. No part of Scripture was neglected by them; they were so earnestly intent upon it, that not a jot or tittle escaped them. This, with the advantages which they had (especially the Ante-Nicene fathers) in point of languages and antiquities, could not fail to produce remarks which it must be very imprudent in any age to neglect. The mistakes, charged upon the fathers in their expositions of the Old Testament, originated in their being misled by the Septuagint version, which their ignorance of Hebrew, together with their contempt of the Jews, and their unwillingness to be taught that language by them, induced them to trust implicitly. And that excess of allegorical interpretation into which some of the antients ran, was probably occasioned by their studying, with a warm imagination, prophecies and types, parables and allusions, and by our Saviour's not developing the whole of his plan during his lifetime.

It is obvious that the contemporary friends of any body of men, *must* know the sentiments of those men more accurately and perfectly than even the most sagacious inquirers who flourish many ages posterior to them. Such of the primitive Fathers, therefore, as conversed with the Apostles, or with their immediate followers, are the most likely to know the true sense of their writings; and it is highly probable that the works of these Fathers must contain traits and sentiments strongly illustrative of the doctrines of the Bible. The use, then, which is to be made of their writings, is precisely that which a discreet lawyer would make of all the best contemporary authors, who lived when Magna Charta was obtained. If in that celebrated code of civil rights any thing appeared obscure and difficult to be understood, he would consult the best authors of the age who had written upon the same, or upon any collateral subject; and he would especially consult contemporary authors, or those who immediately followed, if any of them had undertaken to illustrate and explain the whole or any part of that invaluable instrument. Magna Charta is to us, as Englishmen, what the Word of God is to us as Christians: the one contains a copy of our civil rights and privileges; the other, of our religious privileges and duties. Nor is it any diminution of the just and absolute authority of the Holy Scriptures in our religious concerns, to consult the contemporary and subsequent writings of the Fathers, in order to see how the Bible was understood in the several ages in which they lived; any more than it would be a diminution of the just and absolute authority of Magna Charta, in our civil concerns, to consult the contemporary and subsequent writings of lawyers and historians, in order to see how it was understood in the several ages in which they lived. Similar to this is the conduct of every prudent person in all the common occupations and concerns of life. Accordingly, Christians in all ages, and of every denomination, have eagerly claimed the verdict of the Fathers in their own behalf: and no one ever lightly esteemed their testimony, but those whose principles and doctrines the writings of the Fathers condemned.[1]

The important testimony in behalf of the genuineness of the Sacred Writings of the New Testament, borne by the Fathers of the Christian church, and especially by the Greek Fathers, has been exhibited in detail in Vol. I. pp. 76—86.; and in pp. 192—195. of the present volume, the value of their writings as aids for determining various readings has been stated. It now remains to show, by one or two examples, the value of such of the fathers as are *not* professed commentators [2], in determining the meaning of words and phrases, and in whose writings passages of the Old and New Testaments *incidentally* occur, in such a connection or with such adjuncts, that we may clearly perceive what meaning was attached to them in the age when those fathers respectively flourished. Such interpretations we find in the writings

---

[1] Simpson's Plea for the Deity of Christ, p 438. Dr. Hey's Norrisian Lectures, vol. i. pp. 105—118. Quarterly Review, vol. xiii. pp. 188—188. See also some admirable observations of the learned Dr. Gregory Sharpe, in his Argument in Defence of Christianity, taken from the Concessions of the most antient Adversaries, pp. 90—99.

[2] The principal Commentaries of the Fathers are enumerated in the Appendix to this volume, pp. 192—195.

of Barnabas, Clemens Romanus, Ignatius, Justin Martyr, and others; where testimonies to the divinity of Christ have been collected by Mr. Burton. The evidence of the early Fathers on this fundamental topic of Christian doctrine (to omit others which might be adduced relative to the discipline and practice of the Christian church) is peculiarly important. for " if the doctrine of the real nature of Christ was corrupted in the three first centuries, the writings of that period must show the progress of that corruption." And, on the other hand, " if no variation appears in the opinions of Christians, during that period, but the Fathers of the three first centuries all deliver the same doctrine," and " with one consent speak of Christ as having existed from all eternity as very God, and that he took our human nature into the divine, we have surely good grounds for saying, that there never was a time when this was not the doctrine of the church, and that it was the true and genuine doctrine which the Apostles themselves preached." [1]

1. In John i 3. the work of creation is expressly ascribed to Jesus Christ. To evade the force of this testimony to his deity, Faustus Socinus affirms that τα παντα, *all things*, in this verse, means the moral world—the Christian church. but to this exposition there are two objections. *First*, a part of these τα παντα is in verse 10. represented as ὁ κοσμος, *the world;* a term no where applied in the New Testament to the Christian church, nor to men as morally amended by the Gospel. *Secondly*, this very world (ὁ κοσμος) which he created *did not know* or acknowledge him, αυτον ουκ εγνω: whereas the distinguishing trait of Christians is, that they know Christ; that they know the only true God and Jesus Christ whom he hath sent. Τα παντα, then, which the Logos created, means (as common usage and the exigency of the passage require) *the universe*, the worlds, material and immaterial.[2] In this passage, therefore, Jesus Christ is unquestionably called God ; and this interpretation of it is corroborated by the following passage of Irenæus, who wrote A. D. 185 : —

" Nor can any of those things, which have been made, and are in subjection, be compared to the Word of God, *by whom all things were made*. For that angels or archangels, or thrones or dominations, were appointed by him, who is God over all, and made by his Word, John has thus told us: for, after he had said of the Word of God, that he was in the Father, he added, *all things were made by him, and without him was not anything made.*"[3]

2. In Heb. i 2. God is said to have created the worlds by his Son — Δἰ οὗ και τους αιῶνας ἐποιησεν. To evade the force of this testimony, some opposers of our Lord's divinity expound αιῶνας, as meaning new times, or that God by Christ created anew the world of mankind. But the construction will not justify either of these renderings : for, it is evident, in the first place, from Heb. xi. 3. that αιῶνες does signify the worlds or world. Secondly, it is an undeniable fact that the tenth verse of this chapter does ascribe the creation of the world to Christ. Thirdly, that δια does not denote merely an instrumental cause, is evident from those passages in which it is also said of the Father, that all things were created δἰ αυτου, *by him*, (Heb. ii. 10. Rom. xi. 36.), as also from the fact that δια and

---

[1] Burton's Testimonies of the Ante-Nicene Fathers to the Divinity of Christ, Pref. p. viii.
[2] Stuart's Letters to Channing, p. 67.
[3] Irenæus, adv Hæres, lib. iii. c. 8. § 2. p. 185. Burton's Testimonies, p. 71. Mr. B.'s reasonings upon the above-cited passage of Irenæus are very powerful.

εκ are used interchangeably for each other. But as Heb. i. 1, 2 relates to the person through whom God instructed us, namely, the incarnate Logos or Word, the words *"by whom also he made the worlds"* must be understood thus : — God created the world by the same person through whom he hath spoken unto us, in as much as this person is God himself and one with the Father, *i. e.* He created the world by himself.[1] That this is the correct interpretation is confirmed by the testimony of Justin Martyr (who flourished about A.D. 150), or the author of the epistle to Diognetus, which is commonly ascribed to him. Speaking of the special revelation of his will which God had made to Christians, he says, "This is no earthly invention which has been handed down to them, neither is it a mortal notion which they are bent upon observing so carefully, nor have they a system of human mysteries committed to them : but the omnipotent and all-creative and invisible God hath Himself from heaven established amongst men the truth and the holy and incomprehensible word, and rooted it in their hearts : not, as you might suppose, by sending to men any of His servants, either an angel or a prince, or one of those who administer the affairs of earth, or one of those who have the management of heavenly things intrusted to them, but the *Framer and Creator of the universe himself, by whom He created the heavens, by whom He shut up the sea in its own bounds.*"[2]

On this passage, Mr. Burton remarks · — "We have here an express declaration that Jesus Christ was *the Framer and Creator of the World*. God created them by Jesus Christ, as is said in the Epistle to the Hebrews, i. 2., and if the words quoted above are not sufficiently strong to exclude the idea of God having employed any subordinate agent, we find in the very next chapter the expression of ' *God* the Lord and Creator of the universe, who made all things and arranged them in order.' Thus, according to Justin's own words, God created the world by His Son, and His Son, by whom He created them, was God."[3]

3. We have a striking confirmation of all those passages of the New Testament, in which the appellation and attributes of Deity are given to Jesus Christ, in the practice of the Christian church, mentioned by the father and ecclesiastical historian Eusebius ; who, opposing the followers of Artemon (who asserted the mere humanity of Christ), first appeals to the evidence of Scripture and to the works of Justin, Miltiades, Tatian, Clement, and many other fathers, in all of which divinity is ascribed to Christ, and then states the following fact · "Moreover, all the psalms and hymns of the brethren, *written from the beginning by the faithful, celebrate the praises of Christ the Word of God, and attribute* DIVINITY *to him.*"[4]

It were not difficult to add other examples : but the preceding may suffice to show the value of the Fathers, as aids for ascertaining the meaning of particular passages. The reader who is desirous of examining their important evidence on the cardinal Doctrine

---

[1] Schmucker's Biblical Theology, vol. i. pp. 425, 426.
[2] Epist. ad Diognet. c. 7. Burton's Testimonies, p. 47.
[3] Ibid. p. 48. Some other testimonies may be seen in the " Scripture Doctrine of the Trinity, briefly stated and defended," by the author of this Introduction, pp. 164—182. second edition.
[4] Euseb. Eccl. Hist. lib. v. c. 27, 28. Schmucker's Bib. Theol. vol. i. p. 413. The testimony of the heathen philosopher, Pliny, to the practice of the Christian Churches in a province of Asia Minor in his day must not be overlooked. *Carmen* CHRISTO *quasi Deo dicere secum invicem,* — they were wont to .. ... *sing among themselves alternately a hymn to* CHRIST *as* GOD. Epist. lib. x. Ep. 97.

of Christ's Divinity, is referred to Mr. Burton's "Testimonies," already cited: of whose elaborate and judicious work it has been truly said, that he "has brought before us a cloud of witnesses to prove that the faith delivered by our Lord to his Apostles, and by the Apostles to their successors, was essentially that which our Church professes and cherishes."[1]

§ 8. ON HISTORICAL CIRCUMSTANCES.

Historical Circumstances defined. — I. *Order.* — II. *Title.* — III. *Author.* — IV. *Date of the several Books of Scripture.* — V. *The Place where written.* — VI. *Occasion on which they were written.* — VII. *Antient Sacred and Profane History.* — VIII. *Chronology.* — IX. *Biblical Antiquities,* including, 1. *The Political, Ecclesiastical, and Civil State ;* — 2. *Coins, Medals, and other antient Remains ;* — 3 *Geography ;* — 4. *Genealogy,* 5. *Natural History ;* and 6. *Philosophical Sects and Learning of the Jews and other nations mentioned in the Scriptures.*

HISTORICAL CIRCUMSTANCES are an important help to the correct understanding of the sacred writers. Under this term are comprised — 1. The *Order ;* 2. The *Title ,* 3. The *Author ;* 4. The *Date* of each of the several books of Scripture; 5. The *Place* where it was written; 6. The *Occasion* upon which the several books were written; 7. *Antient Sacred and Profane History ;* 8. The *Chronology* or period of time embraced in the Scriptures generally, and of each book in particular; 9. *Biblical Antiquities,* including the Geography, Genealogy, Natural History and Philosophy, Learning, and Philosophical Sects, Manners, Customs, and Private Life of the Jews and other nations mentioned in the Bible. How important a knowledge of these particulars is, and how indispensably necessary to a correct interpretation of the inspired volume, we are now to consider.

I. A knowledge of the ORDER OF THE DIFFERENT BOOKS, especially such as are historical, will more readily assist the student to discover the order of the different histories and other matters discussed in them, as well as to trace the divine economy towards mankind under the Mosaic and Christian dispensations.

This aid, if judiciously exercised, opens the way to a deep acquaintance with the meaning of an author; but, when it is neglected, many things necessarily remain obscure and ambiguous.

II. The TITLES are further worthy of notice, because some of them announce the chief subject of the book; —

As *Genesis,* the generation of heaven and earth — *Exodus,* the departure of the Israelites from Egypt, &c.; while other titles denote the churches or particular persons for whose more immediate use some

---

[1] British Critic and Quarterly Theol. Review, Oct. 1837, p. 303.

parts of the Scriptures were composed, and thus afford light to particular passages.[1]

III. A knowledge of the AUTHOR of each book, together with the age in which he lived, his peculiar character, his sect or religion, and also his peculiar mode of thinking and style of writing, as well as the testimonies which his writings may contain concerning himself, is equally necessary to the historical interpretation of Scripture. Thus,

1. *The consideration of the testimonies concerning himself, which appear in the second epistle of St. Peter, will show that he was the author of that book.*

For he expressly says, 1. That he was present at the transfiguration of Jesus Christ (2 Pet. i 18), 2 That this was his second epistle to the believing Jews (iii. 1.), and that Paul was his beloved brother (iii. 15), all which circumstances quadrate with Peter. In like manner, the coincidence of style and of peculiar forms of expression, which exist between the second and third epistles of Saint John, and his other writings, prove that those epistles were written by him. Thus we shall be able to account for one writer's omitting some topics, and expatiating upon others — as Saint Mark's silence concerning actions honourable to Saint Peter, and enlarging on his faults, he being the companion of the latter, and writing from his information. A comparison of the style of the epistle to the Hebrews, with that of Saint Paul's other epistles, will show that he was the author of that admirable composition [2]

2. *In order to enter fully into the meaning of the sacred writers, especially of the New Testament, it is necessary that the reader in a manner identify himself with them, and invest himself with their affections or feelings; and also familiarise himself with the sentiments, &c. of those to whom the different books or epistles were addressed.*[3]

This canon is of considerable importance, as well in the investigation of words and phrases, as in the interpretation of the sacred volume, and particularly of the prayers and imprecations related or contained therein. If the assistance, which may be derived from a careful study of the affections and feelings of the inspired writers, be disregarded or neglected, it will be scarcely possible to avoid erroneous expositions of the Scriptures. Daily observation and experience prove how much of its energy and perspicuity familiar discourse derives from the affections of the speakers and also that the same words, when pronounced under the influence of different emotions, convey very different meanings. Franzius has paid particular attention to this subject in the examples adduced in his treatise *De Interpretatione Sacræ Scripturæ* · and Franck has written a distinct essay on the same topic, which, being already extant in our language, it is not necessary to abridge in this place.[4]

IV. Knowledge of the TIME when each book was written sometimes shows the reason and propriety of things said in it.[5]

Upon this principle, the solemn adjuration in 1 Thess. v. 27., which at first sight may seem unnecessary, may be explained. It is probable that, from the beginning of the Christian dispensation, the Scriptures of the

---

[1] Roberts's Clavis Bibliorum, pp (11.) (12.)

[2] This topic has been ably proved by Braunius, in his Commentarius in Epistolam ad Hebræos, pp. 10—21.; by Pritius, in his Introductio in Novum Testamentum, cap iv. § iii pp. 47, 48., and by Langius in his Commentatio de Vita et Epistolis Pauli, p 157. Le Clerc has some pertinent remarks on the same subject, in his Ars Critica, pars iii. sect. ii c. vi p. 372.

[3] Pritii Introductio ad N. Test. p. 612. Wetstein de Interpret Nov. Test pp 149—156. 8vo. edit. Franckii Prælectiones Hermeneuticæ, p. 192.

[4] See Mr Jaques's translation of Franck's Guide to the Reading and Study of the Scriptures, pp 141—175. 8vo. edit An enlarged edition of this essay is given by Franck himself in his Prælectiones Hermeneuticæ, pp. 198—250.; to which Rambach is partly indebted for his chapter De Investigatione Adfectuum. Inst. Herm Sacr. pp. 122—144 See also Chladenius's Instit. Exeget. pp. 25, et seq , and J. E. Pfeiffer's Inst. Herm. Sacr. pp. 251—260.

[5] Rambach, Inst. Herm. Sacr. p. 116.

Old Testament were read in every assembly for divine worship. Saint Paul, knowing the plenitude of the apostolic commission, now demands the same respect to be paid to his writings which had been given to those of the antient prophets: this, therefore, is a proper direction to be inserted in the *first* epistle written by him; and the manner, in which it is given, suggests an argument that the first Epistle to the Thessalonians was the earliest of his epistles. An accurate knowledge of the date of a book is further of peculiar importance in order to understand the prophecies and epistles: for not only will it illustrate several apparently obscure particulars in a prediction, but it will also enable us to ascertain and to confute a false application of such prediction. Grotius, in his preface to the second Epistle to the Thessalonians, has endeavoured to prove that the Emperor Caligula was the *man of sin*, and Simon Magus *the wicked one*, foretold in the second chapter of that epistle; and has fruitlessly laboured to show that it was written A. D. 38; but its true date, A. D. 52, explodes that application, as also Dr. Hammond's hypothesis that Simon Magus was the *man of sin*, and *the wicked one*.

V. Not unfrequently, the consideration of the PLACE, 1. Where any book was written; or, 2. Where any thing was said or done, will materially facilitate its historical interpretation, especially if regard be had, 3. To the NATURE OF THE PLACE, and the customs which obtained there.

1. For instance, it is evident that St. Paul's second Epistle to the Thessalonians was written, shortly after the first, at Corinth, and not at Athens, as its subscription would import, from this circumstance, viz. that Timothy and Silvanus or Silas, who joined him in his first letter, were still with him, and joined him in the second. (Compare 2 Thess. i. 1. with 1 Thess. iii. 6. and Acts xviii. 1—5.) And as in this epistle he desired the brethren to *pray that he might be delivered from unreasonable and wicked men* (2 Thess. iii. 2.), it is probable that he wrote it soon after the insurrection of the Jews at Corinth, in which they dragged him before Gallio the proconsul of Achaia, and accused him of *persuading men to worship contrary to the law.* (Acts xviii. 13.) But this consideration of the place where a book was written, will supply us with one or two observations that will more clearly illustrate some passages in the same epistle. Thus it is manifest from 2 Thess. iii. 8. that Saint Paul could appeal to his own personal labours for his subsistence with the greater confidence, as he had diligently prosecuted them at Corinth (compare Acts xviii. 3. with 1 Cor. ix. 11, 12, 13.): and, to mention no more examples, it is clear from 2 Thess. iii. 1, 2, that the great Apostle of the Gentiles experienced more difficulty in planting a Christian church at Corinth, and in some other places, than he did at Thessalonica. In a similar manner, numerous beautiful passages in his epistles to the Ephesians will be more fully understood, by knowing that they were written at Rome during his first captivity.

2. Our Lord's admirable discourse, recorded in the sixth chapter of St. John's Gospel, which so many disregarded, is said (v. 59.) to have been delivered in the synagogue at Capernaum, consequently in a public place, and in that very city which had witnessed the performance of so many of his miracles. And it is this circumstance of place which so highly aggravated the malice and unbelief of his hearers. (Compare Matt. xi. 23.)

3. The first Psalm being written in Palestine, the comparison (in v. 4.) of the ungodly to chaff driven away by the wind will become more evident, when it is recollected that the threshing-floors in that country were not

under cover as those in our modern barns are, but that they were formed in the open air, without the walls of cities, and in lofty situations, in order that the wheat might be the more effectually separated from the chaff by the action of the wind. (See Hosea xiii. 3.) In like manner, the knowledge of the nature of the Arabian desert, through which the children of Israel journeyed, is necessary to the correct understanding of many passages in the Books of Exodus, Numbers, and Deuteronomy, which were written in that desert.

VI. We find it to be no small help to the understanding of antient profane writings, if we can discover the OCCASION on which, as well as the time when, they were penned: and for want of such knowledge many passages in such writings are become obscure and unintelligible. The same may be observed in the books of the Old and New Testament (especially in the Book of Psalms and the Apostolical Epistles), the right understanding of the design of which, as well as of their phraseology, is most essentially promoted by a careful observance of the OCCASION upon which they were written.

To some of the Psalms, indeed, there is prefixed a notice of the occasion on which they were composed: and, by comparing these with one another, and with the sacred history, great light may be, and has been thrown upon the more difficult passages; and the meaning, beauty, and energy of many expressions have been set in a clearer point of view. But where no such titles are prefixed, the *occasion* must be sought from internal circumstances.

Psalm xlii. was evidently written by David, when he was in circumstances of the deepest affliction but if we compare it with the history of the conspiracy of Absalom, aided by Ahithophel, who had deserted the councils of his sovereign, as related in 2 Sam xv, and also with the character of the country whither David fled, we shall have a key to the meaning of that psalm, which will elucidate it with equal beauty and propriety.[1]

VII. ANTIENT SACRED AND PROFANE HISTORY.—An acquaintance with the history of the Israelites, as well as that of the Moabites, Ammonites, Philistines, Egyptians, Assyrians, Medes, Babylonians, Persians, Arabians, Greeks, Romans, and other antient nations, is of the greatest importance to the historical interpretation of the Bible: for, as the Jewish people were connected with those nations, either in a hostile or in a pacific manner, the knowledge of their history, customs, arts, and literature, becomes the more interesting; as it is well known that the Israelites, notwithstanding they were forbidden to have intercourse with the heathen, did nevertheless borrow and adopt some of their institutions. More particularly, regardless of the severe prohibitions delivered by Moses and the prophets against idolatry, how many idols did they borrow from the Gentiles at different times, previously to the great Babylonish captivity, and associate them in the worship of Jehovah! Their commercial intercourse with the Egyptians and Arabs, and especially with the Phœnicians, was very considerable · and, at the same time,

---

[1] Dr Randolph has very happily elucidated the whole of the forty-second Psalm, from an investigation of the occasion from internal circumstances, in a Dissertation, at the end of vol. I. of his View of Christianity, &c. Oxford, 1784. 8vo

they were almost incessantly at war with the Philistines, Moabites, and other neighbouring nations, and afterwards with the Assyrians and Egyptians, until they were finally conquered, and carried into captivity by the Assyrians and Babylonians. Further, the prophets, in their denunciations or predictions, not only address their admonitions and threatenings to the Israelites and Jews, but also frequently accost foreign nations, whom they menace with destruction. The writings of Isaiah, Jeremiah, and Ezekiel, contain very numerous predictions relative to the heathen nations, which would be utterly unintelligible without the aid of profane history. The same remark will apply to the divisions of time and forms of government that obtained at different periods, which cannot be ascertained from the perusal of the Sacred Writings merely.

In proportion, however, as the history of the antient nations of Asia becomes necessary to the interpretation of the Bible, it is to be regretted that it is for the most part involved in so much obscurity and confusion as to require no small labour before we can extricate it from the trammels of fable, and arrive at any thing like certainty. As the histories of antient Egypt have perished, with the exception of a few fragments preserved in the writings of Josephus, Eusebius, and other authors, our knowledge of the earliest state of that country (which is sufficiently confused and intricate) can only be derived from Herodotus, Diodorus, and some other Greek writers, who cannot always be depended on. The writings of Sanchoniatho, with the exception of a few fragments, as well as the works of Histiæus, and other Phœnician historians, have long since perished: and, for our accounts of the Assyrians, recourse must chiefly be had to the Scriptures themselves, as no confidence whatever can be placed in the narrations of Ctesias, whose fidelity and veracity have justly been questioned by Aristotle, Strabo, and Plutarch. The history of the Ammonites, Moabites, Idumæans, Philistines, and other petty neighbouring nations, who had no historians of their own, is involved in equal obscurity: for the little that is known of them, with certainty, we are exclusively indebted to the Holy Scriptures.

The sources, therefore, of that historical knowledge, which is so essential to an interpreter of the Sacred Writings, are, in the first place, the Old and New Testaments, and next the works of Josephus and profane authors. It is however to be observed, that where the latter speak of the Jews, they *wilfully misrepresent* them as is done by Justin and Tacitus. With a view to reconcile these various contradictions, and to overcome the difficulties thus interposed by the uncertainty of antient profane history, various learned men have at different times employed themselves in digesting the remains of antient history, and comparing it with the Scriptures, in order to illustrate them as much as possible and the Connections of Sacred and Profane History, by Drs. Shuckford, Prideaux, and Russell, Stackhouse's History of the Bible, and Dr. Lardner's Credibility of the Gospel History, are particularly worthy of notice. [1]

---

[1] An account of their valuable works is given in the Appendix to this volume.

VIII. CHRONOLOGY, or the science of computing and adjusting periods of time, is of the greatest importance towards understanding the historical parts of the Bible, not only as it shows the order and connection of the various events therein recorded, but likewise as it enables us to ascertain the accomplishment of many of the prophecies. Chronology is further of service to the biblical critic, as it sometimes leads to the discovery and correction of mistakes in numbers and dates, which have crept into particular texts. As considerable differences exist in the chronology of the Hebrew Scriptures, the Samaritan Pentateuch, the Septuagint version, and Josephus, different learned men have applied themselves to the investigation of these difficulties, and have communicated the result of their researches in elaborate systems. Some one of these, after examining their various claims, it will be desirable to have constantly at hand. The principal systems of Chronology are those of Cappel, Vossius, Archbishop Usher, Bedford, Jackson, and Dr. Hales; of which an account will be found in the Appendix to this volume.

IX. A knowledge of BIBLICAL ANTIQUITIES (including the Sacred and Profane History, Geography, Genealogy, Natural History, Coins, Medals, and other antient remains, and Philosophy, Learning and Philosophical Sects, Manners, Customs, and private Life, of the Jews and other nations mentioned in the Bible,) is indispensably necessary to the right understanding of the sacred volume.

1. What the peculiar rites, manners, and customs of the Hebrews and other nations actually were, that are either alluded to or mentioned in the Scriptures, can only be ascertained by the study of their POLITICAL, ECCLESIASTICAL, and CIVIL STATE; without an accurate knowledge of which, all interpretation must be both defective and imperfect.

If, in order to enter fully into the meaning, or correctly apprehend the various beauties of the Greek and Roman classics, it be necessary to be acquainted with the peculiar forms of government that prevailed — the powers of magistrates — modes of executing the laws — the punishments of criminals — tributes or other duties imposed on subjects — their military affairs — sacred rites and festivals — private life, manners, and amusements — commerce, measures, and weights, &c. &c. — how much greater difficulties will be interposed in *his* way, who attempts to interpret the Scriptures without a knowledge of these topics! For, as the customs and manners of the oriental people are widely different from those of the western nations, as further, their sacred rites differ most essentially from every thing with which we are acquainted, and as the Jews in particular, from the simplicity of their language, have drawn very numerous metaphors from the works of nature, from the ordinary occupations and arts of life, from religion and things connected with it, as well as from their national history; — there are many things recorded, both in the Old and New Testament, which must appear to Europeans either obscure, unintelligible, repulsive, or absurd, unless, forgetting our own peculiar habits and modes of thinking, we transport ourselves in a manner to the East, and diligently study the customs, whether political, sacred, or civil, which obtained there. In the third volume of this work, the author has attempted to compress the most important facts relative to biblical antiquities.

2. With regard to COINS, MEDALS, AND OTHER ANTIENT RE-MAINS, considered as a source of interpretation, a few remarks and illustrations may be here introduced. The examples given in Vol. I. pp. 205—216., as collateral testimonies to the credibility of the sacred writers, may indeed be considered as so many elucidations of the passages there referred to. Two or three additional instances shall now be subjoined, which will serve to show the important hermeneutical aid, which may be derived from these remains of antient art.

1. Acts xi. 26. *It came to pass that ...... the disciples were called* (Χρηματισαι) *Christians, first in Antioch.*

Commentators and critics are much divided in opinion concerning the origin of the appellation Christian Some are of opinion, that it was first invented by the enemies of religion, and was fixed upon the disciples of Christ as a stigma of reproach. In confirmation of this opinion, they refer to Acts xxvi 28 and 1 Pet. iv. 16 Others imagine, that the Christians themselves assumed this appellation. Others, with more propriety, conceive, that it was given to them by divine appointment, or by an oracle from God. In all other passages of the New Testament, where the word Χρηματιζω occurs, as well as in the Septuagint version [1], it uniformly means *warned by a divine oracle*: and when we consider, that it had been predicted by Isaiah (lxii. 2.) that the future church should *be called* by a NEW NAME, which the *mouth of the Lord shall name*; we shall be justified in adopting the third interpretation, and render the passage thus *And the disciples were called Christians by divine appointment first at Antioch.* The correctness of this interpretation is confirmed, not only by the fact, that the verb Χρηματιζω is used in this sense among Greek writers, and is especially understood concerning the manifestations of the heathen gods, in which responses were given to those who consulted them; but also by the fact of its occurring on an antient votive tablet found at Rome, which was formerly seen in the temple of Æsculapius, on an island in the Tiber· from which the following passages are selected :—

ΑΥΤΑΙΣ ΤΑΙΣ ΗΜΕΡΑΙΣ ΓΑΙΩΙ
ΤΙΝΙ ΤΥΦΛΩΙ ΕΧΡΗΜΑΤΙΣΕΝ (ὁ Θεος).

In those days (the god) DIVINELY ANSWERED (or gave an oracular response to), one Gaius, a blind man.

ΛΟΥΚΙΩΙ ΠΛΕΥΡΙΤΙΚΩΙ ....
ΕΧΡΗΜΑΤΙΣΕΝ Ο ΘΕΟΣ.

The God DIVINELY ANSWERED .. .... Lucius, who laboured under a pleurisy. [2]

2 John xi. 19. Εληλευθεισαν ΠΡΟΣ ΤΑΣ ΠΕΡΙ Μαρθαν και Μαριαν.

The expressions, οἱ περι τινα, and οἱ αμφι τινα, are used by the best Greek writers for the persons themselves the same mode of construction obtains in this passage of St John's Gospel, which is correctly rendered in our authorised version, *They came to Martha and Mary.* The same expression occurs in an inscription found at Olbiopolis ΕΠΙ ΑΡΧΟΝΤΟΣ ΜΑΡΚΟΥ ΟΥΛΠΙΟΥ ΠΥΡΡΟΥ ΑΡΣΗΧΟΥ, ΟΙ ΠΕΡΙ ΠΟΣΕΙΔΗΝ ΖΗΘΟΥ ΤΟ Γ ΑΓΟΡΟΝΟΜΟΙ, ΚΟΥΝΟΣ ΑΘΗΝΑΙΟΥ, &c. That is, during the archonship of Marcus Ulpius Pyrrhus [the son of] Arsechus, the Agoronomoi (or inspectors of markets) Poseides the son of Zethus for the third time, Kunus [the son of] Athenæus, &c. &c. [3]

3. Acts xix. 35. Commentators have been much perplexed concerning the functions of the Γραμματευς, or Town-clerk of Ephesus.

As the Ephesians were at this time solemnising games in honour of Diana (whose celebrated temple was erected at the common expense of all the cities of Asia) under the presidency of the Asiarchs, that is, principal officers or high priests chosen by the com-

---

[1] See Biel's Lexicon in LXX, voce Χρηματιζω.

[2] Gruteri Thesaurus Inscriptionum, p. lxxi. Munteri Symbolæ ad Interpretationem Nov. Test. ex Marmoribus, in Misc. Hafniensia, vol. i. part i. pp. 8, 9. The oracular responses above mentioned were given in the temple of Æsculapius, in the night-time, and for the most part to persons while asleep.

[3] Münter, Symbolæ, p. 23. It is, however, proper to remark, that the reading τας περι Μαρθαν και Μαριαν is not fully established. The Codex Bezæ *omits* the words τας περι, and the Codices Vaticanus, Ephremi, Regius 62 η (Stephani 8.), and Colbertinus, simply read προς την Μαρθαν και Μαριαν, *to Martha and Mary* : and the Syriac version has only the names of the two sisters. Münter, ibid. Winer's Grammar to the New Test. p. 54.

munity of Asia for that purpose, it is highly probable that this Γραμματευς was a person of greater authority than the clerk or recorder of Ephesus. Domninus, an antient author, cited by the chronologer Malela [1], (who, being a native of Ephesus, could not but be acquainted with the public transactions of his own city,) relates that, besides the Syriarch, there were the Alytarch, who represented Jupiter, the Γραμματευς, who represented Apollo, and the Amphitales, who represented Mercury, and that suitable honours were paid to them by all the people. Apuleius [2] also states, that a Γραμματευς presided over certain sacred rites in Egypt. The presumption, therefore, is, that the Γραμματευς of Ephesus was not a civil officer, as is commonly supposed, but a sacred officer and this presumption is converted into certainty by the fact that, among the various coins of that city, which are still extant, there are several containing the names of persons who bore the title of ΑΡΧΙΕΡΕΥΣ ΓΡΑΜΜΑΤΕΥΣ, or, High Priest-Scribe, particularly one which was struck during the triumvirate of Augustus, Anthony, and Lepidus (no very long time before the transaction related in Acts xix.), which has the following inscription

ΑΡΧΙΕΡΕΥΣ ΓΡΑΜ ΓΛΑΥΚΩΝ ΕΤΘΥΚΡΑΤΗΣ ΕΦΕΣΙΩΝ

Glaucon Euthycrates, the High Priest-Scribe of the Ephesians [3]

Now, as this officer was the representative of Apollo, who could be more proper to address the infuriated populace, or more likely to have weight and influence with them, and the force of an oracle in what he said to them, than that officer to whom they paid the honours due to Apollo? [4] The good sense of his address and the happy effect it produced upon the Ephesian populace, confirm this conclusion.

It were not difficult to adduce many additional instances, in which the comparatively untried application of coins and inscriptions is calculated to elucidate particular words and forms of expression in the New Testament but the preceding instances may suffice, and the student who is desirous of prosecuting this subject further will find ample materials in the publications of Bishop Munter, already cited.

In the application of Biblical Antiquities to the interpretation of the Sacred Writings, it is, however, of the utmost importance, that we should be guided by the exercise of a sober and cautious judgment, and by the influence of a correct taste; lest we ascribe to the inspired authors sentiments which perhaps never entered their minds, or imagine customs which never had any existence. From this mistake, that acute biblical critic, and most diligent investigator of oriental manners and customs, Michaelis, is not exempt.

In Prov x. 14. we read, *Wise men lay up knowledge*, that is, treasure it up, and reserve it for a proper opportunity to make use of it *but the mouth of the foolish is near destruction*, such an one is always talking, and seldom opens his mouth but it proves a present mischief to himself and others. By changing the points in the latter clause of this verse, Michaelis reads *the mouth of the foolish is as a censer near at hand (thuribulum propinquum)*, and he illustrates this expression by the oriental custom of offering perfumes to a guest, which (it is well known) is an intimation to him that it is time for him to depart. The sense, which this profound scholar puts upon the passage, is as follows: the foolish man alienates every one from him by his silly and insipid discourses. Is not this torturing words, and ascribing to the sacred penman an allusion which he never designed to make? [5]

But, more particularly,

(1.) *We should investigate the laws, opinions, and principles of those nations among whom the Hebrews resided for a long time, or with whom they held a close intercourse, and from whom it is probable they received some of them.*

From the long residence of the Hebrews in Egypt, it has been conjectured by some learned men that they derived by far the greater part of their institutions from the Egyptians: but this hypothesis appears untenable, to its full extent, the Israelites being separated from the

---

[1] Joan. Malela, p. 374, &c. Cited in Biscoe on the Acts, vol. i. p. 305.
[2] In Milesia undecima cited by Basnage, Annal. vol. i. p 673. Biscoe, p. 306.
[3] Rasche, Lexicon Rei Nummariæ, tom. ii. part i. col. 648.
[4] Biscoe on the Acts, vol. i, p 306.
[5] Bauer, Hermeneutica Sacra, p 275

Egyptians by their pastoral habits, which rendered them abominable in the eyes of the latter. At the same time, from their having passed four hundred years in that country, it is not unlikely that they derived *some* [1] things from their oppressors. A few instances will elucidate this remark.

1. Under the Jewish theocracy, the judges are represented as holy persons, and as sitting in the place of Jehovah [2] The Egyptians regarded their sovereigns in this light [3] Hence Michaelis, to whom we are indebted for this fact, conjectures that the Israelites just on their exit from Egypt, called their rulers *gods*, not only in poetry, but also in the common language of their laws, (see Exod. xxi. 6.) where the word *judges* is, in the original Hebrew, *gods* [4] Again, agriculture was the basis of the whole Mosaic polity; and it was probably from the Egyptians that the Jewish legislator borrowed the principle on which his polity was thus founded though indeed we find, that the state of the antient Romans was accidentally established on a similar plan [5] The priests, and especially the Levites, united the profession of ministers of religion with that of literati among the Jews, in the same manner as the Egyptian priests had partitioned literature among themselves, so that their institution was wholly Egyptian in its origin. [6] And, to mention no further instances of this kind, the molten calf which the Israelites required of Aaron, seems to have been an exact resemblance of the celebrated Egyptian god Apis, who was worshipped under the form of an ox [7]

2 At a subsequent period, during their captivity, some of the Jews appear to have imbibed the absurd notion of the Persians, that there were two supreme beings, an evil and a good one, representing light and darkness, and that according to the ascendancy of one or other of these, good and happiness prevailed among men, or evil and misery abounded. Such, at least, was the absurd opinion held by the person to whom Isaiah addressed his prophecy (ch. xlv.) and which he refutes in the most significant and pointed manner. [8]

3 In our Saviour's time the learning of the Greeks was cultivated by the Jews, who adopted the peculiar tenets of some of their most eminent philosophers. The Pharisees, it was well known, believed the immortality of the soul but it appears from Josephus, that their notion of such immortality was the Pythagorean metempsychosis [9] From the Pharisees this tenet was generally received by the Jewish people, and, notwithstanding the benefit derived from hearing the discourses and conversations of our Lord, it appears to have been held by some of his disciples.

(2.) *We must take care not to ascribe comparatively modern rites and customs to the antient Hebrews.*

From not attending to this rule, the Jewish teachers, and those Christian doctors who have implicitly followed them, have caused much perplexity in the antiquities of the Jews, having attributed to the antient Hebrews rites and ceremonies that did not exist till later

---

[1] That *all* the Hebrew institutions were of Egyptian origin is an hypothesis now generally abandoned, since the able refutation of it by the learned Herman Witsius, in his Ægyptiaca (Amstelodami, 1696, 4to.) and in his Miscellanea Sacra, tom. I pp 429 et seq.
[2] Deut. i 17 and xix 17.
[3] Diodorus Siculus, lib. i. c 90 "From this cause" (viz. gratitude to benefactors, among whom they reckoned such animals as were peculiarly useful to the country, and held them sacred,) "the Egyptians seem so to reverence their kings, and humbly to address them as if *they were gods*. They even believe that it is not without the peculiar care of Providence that they arrive at supreme power; and that those, who have the will and the power to perform deeds of the greatest benificence, are partakers of the divine nature."
[4] Michaelis's Commentaries on the Laws of Moses, vol. i p 192.
[5] Ibid. vol. i. p. 22. [6] Ibid. vol. i. p. 255.
[7] Schumacher, De Cultu Animalium inter Ægyptios et Judæos Commentatio, pp. 40—47. Our learned countryman, Spencer, in his work De Legibus Hebræorum, and Michaelis, in his commentaries above cited, have shown, in many additional examples, the striking resemblance between many of the institutions of the Israelites and those of the Egyptians.
[8] Vitringa, and Lowth, on Isaiah xiv. 7
[9] Josephus, De Bello Judaico, lib ii c 8. § 14. and Antiq. lib xviii. c. 1. § 3. The Pharisees held that every soul was immortal, but that only the souls of the righteous transmigrate into other bodies, while the souls of bad men are subject to eternal punishment At first sight, this account appears to contradict the statement of Saint Paul (Acts xxiv 15.) but the repugnancy is easily obviated, when it is considered that Josephus is speaking of the Pharisees only, but the Apostle of the Jews in general, and of himself in particular.

times; and, from not distinguishing the different ages, they have consequently confounded antient manners and customs with those which are of modern date. The Talmudists, and other Jewish writers, should not be consulted without the greatest caution; for, living as they did long after the destruction of the Jewish polity, they not only were imperfectly acquainted with it, but they likewise contradict each other, as well as Josephus and Philo, authors every way more worthy of confidence, as being contemporary with that event, not unfrequently indeed do they contradict the Scriptures themselves, and, indulging their own speculations, they produce commentaries which are truly ridiculous. The necessary consequence is, that those learned men, who have implicitly followed the Talmudists, have been precipitated into various errors. From these mistakes, not even Reland and Ikenius are exempt — two of the best writers, perhaps, who have applied themselves to the investigation of Jewish antiquities.[1]

(3.) *Lastly, our knowledge of Biblical Antiquities must be derived from pure sources.*

The first and most important source is unquestionably the Old and New Testaments; the careful collation of which will enable us to collect accounts of the modes of living which obtained among the antient Jews. Much light will further be obtained into the state of Jewish affairs, from consulting the Apocryphal books, among which the first book of Maccabees is particularly valuable. To these may be added the writings of Philo, Josephus, and the Talmudists. Further, a judicious comparison of the notions that obtained among antient, and comparatively uncultivated nations, with those entertained by the Hebrews or Jews, will, from their similitude, enable us to enter more fully into the meaning of the sacred writers. Thus many pleasing illustrations of patriarchal life and manners may be obtained by comparing the writings of Homer and Hesiod with the accounts given by Moses. The Iliad, for instance, illustrates Abraham's manner of dividing the sacrifice.[2] The patriarchal hospitality is similar to that described in the Odyssey.[3] How early a belief in the ministry of angels obtained among the heathen nations, is evident from comparing the account of Hesiod[4] with that of Moses[5], and it furnishes an additional proof to the many others, which have been collected by learned men, to show that all the knowledge of the antients was traditionally derived, though with innumerable corruptions, from the Hebrews.

Finally, if to these sources we add an acquaintance with the modern customs and manners which prevail in the East, as they are related by travellers of approved character, we shall have a sure and easy access to the knowledge of sacred antiquities: for, as the Orientals, from their tenacious adherence to old usages, are not likely to differ materially from their ancestors[6], we have no very great reason to be apprehensive, from comparing the manners, &c. of the modern Syrians, Arabs, and other inhabitants of the East, with those of the antient Hebrews, that we should attribute customs to them which never obtained among them. Where, indeed, any new usage does exist among the orientals, it may be discovered without much difficulty by men of learning and penetration. The interpretation of the Bible, therefore, is not a little facilitated by the perusal of the voyages and travels of those who have explored the East. Among these valuable contributors to the promotion of biblical science, the names of D'Arvieux, Maundrell, Thompson, Chardin, Shaw, Hasselquist, Pocock, Niebuhr, Seetzen, Dr. E. D. Clarke, Lord Valentia, Walpole, Ouseley, Morier, Light, Russell, Chateaubriand, Burckhardt, Buckingham, Belzoni, Dr. Richardson, the Rev. Mr. Jowett, Sir R. K. Porter, and others, are justly celebrated; but as many of their works are voluminous and costly, various writers have judiciously applied themselves to selecting and arranging the most material passages of their travels, which are calculated to elucidate the Holy Scriptures. In this department of sacred li-

---

[1] Schulzii Compendium Archæologiæ Hebraicæ, Prolegomena, p. xvii. Bauer, Herm. Sacr. p. 276.

[2] Homeri Ilias, lib. i. v. 460, 461. compared with Gen. xv. 9, 10. Mr. Trollope has happily applied the Homeric expressions to the elucidation of the Scriptures, in about four hundred instances, in his valuable edition of Homer with English Notes. London, 1827. 2 vols. 8vo.

[3] Gen. xviii. 6—8 compared with the Odyssey, lib. xiv. v. 71—76. 419—430.

[4] Opera et Dies, lib i v. 130—136.   [5] Gen. xxxii 1, 2.

[6] "The manners of the East," — it is remarked by one of the most intelligent of modern oriental travellers, — amidst all the changes of government and religion, are still the same. They are living impressions from an original mould; and, at every step, some object, some idiom, some dress, or some custom of common life, reminds the traveller of antient times; and confirms, above all, the beauty, the accuracy, and the propriety of the language and history of the Bible." Morier's Second Journey through Persia. Pref. p. viii.

terature, the compilations of Harmer, Burder, and the editor of Calmet's Dictionary of the Bible, are particularly distinguished Of these works, as well as of the principal writers on Jewish Antiquities, the reader will find a notice in the Appendix to this volume

3. Intimately connected with history and chronology is antient GEOGRAPHY, especially that of Palestine and the neighbouring countries; the knowledge of which, it is universally confessed, tends to illustrate almost innumerable passages of Scripture. The principal sources of sacred geography are the Scriptures themselves, and the antient Greek and other writers, who have treated on the different countries mentioned in the Bible, and to these may be added the voyages and travels of Chardin, Seetzen[1], and others, mentioned in the preceding page, who have explored the East, and whose narratives contain many very happy elucidations of the physical and political geography of the Bible. These sources have been diligently consulted by most of the learned men who have applied themselves to the illustration of this important topic. The principal works on sacred geography are those of Bochart, Michaelis, Spanheim, Reland, and Wells.[2]

4. Next to History and Geography, GENEALOGY holds an important place in the study of the Sacred Writings. The evidences of Christianity cannot be correctly, if at all understood, unless the genealogy of the Messiah, and his descent from Abraham and David, be distinctly traced. This is obvious from the prophecies, which, ages before his advent, determined the line of his descent; and left nothing to chance or importure on the important subject of the promised seed, that, in the fulness of time, was to "bruise the serpent's head," and by his one oblation of himself, once offered, was to make a full and perfect atonement for the sins of the whole world. Many neat genealogical tables are to be found in some of the earlier and larger editions of the Bible. Some of the most useful treatises on this subject are noticed in the Appendix.

5. Of equal importance with either of the preceding branches of knowledge is NATURAL HISTORY; by which alone many, otherwise obscure, passages of Scripture can be explained. Thus, frequent direct mention is made of animals, trees, plants, and precious stones; sometimes the Scripture expresses sentiments either in allusion to, or by metaphors taken from, some fact in natural history; and sometimes characters are described in allusion to natural objects; and without the knowledge of these, we cannot perceive the nature of the characters intended. Much information concerning this important topic may be derived from the labours of the oriental travellers already mentioned, and especially those of Shaw, Russell, Hasselquist, Forskül, and Niebuhr. The most successful investiga-

---

[1] The result of M Seetzen's researches, which were undertaken under the patronage of the Palestine Association for investigating the present state of the Holy Land, was published in a thin quarto tract, intitled "A brief Account of the Countries adjoining the lake of Tiberias, the Jordan, and the Dead Sea." Bath and London, 1810. Many places in Palestine, particularly beyond the Jordan, which are in great degree unknown, are satisfactorily described in this little tract.

[2] The writings of the above-noticed geographers and travellers have been consulted for the Summary of Biblical Geography and Antiquities, forming the third volume of this work.

tions of this interesting topic are to be found in the writings of Bochart, Celsius, Scheuchzer, Professor Paxton, and especially of the Rev. Dr. Harris, of Dorchester, Massachussetts.

6. Lastly, in perusing the sacred volume, the attentive reader cannot fail to be struck with allusions to PHILOSOPHICAL NOTIONS and SECTS, as well as to certain branches of learning, which were cultivated by the nations or people therein mentioned: it is impossible fully to apprehend the force, propriety, and beauty of these allusions without a knowledge of the notions, &c. referred to. A short sketch of the principal Jewish sects occurs in the third volume of this work; but the only writer, to the best of the author's recollection, who has discussed this subject in a separate treatise, is the learned and indefatigable Professor Buddeus, in his *Introductio ad Historiam Philosophiæ Hebræorum, Halæ*, 1720, 8vo.; of whose labours he has availed himself. The philosophical notions which obtained among the Jews are also incidentally treated in most of the larger commentaries, as well as in most of those works, which profess to be Introductions to the Bible.

§ 9. ON COMMENTARIES.

I. *Different Classes of Commentaries.* — II. *Nature of Scholia.* — III. *Of Commentaries strictly so called.* — IV. *Paraphrases.* — V. *Collections of Observations on Holy Writ.* — VI. *The Utility and Advantage of Commentaries.* — VII. *Design to be kept in view, when consulting them.* — VIII. *Rules for consulting Commentaries to the best advantage.*

I. THE labours of expositors and commentators have been divided into various classes, according to the nature of their different works; for, although few confine themselves to one method of interpretation, exclusively, yet each generally has some predominant character, by which he is peculiarly distinguished. Thus, some are,

1. Wholly *Spiritual* or *Figurative;* as Cocceius, and those foreign commentators who have followed his untenable system, viz. that the Scripture is every where to be taken in the fullest sense it will admit, and in our own country, Dr. Gill, Dr. Hawker, and some minor writers.

2. *Literal and Critical;* such are Ainsworth, Wetstein, Dr. Blayney, Bishop Patrick, Lowth, and Whitby, Calmet, Chais, Bishop Lowth, Archbishop Newcome, Wall, Dr. Campbell, Dr. Priestley, and others.

3. *Wholly Practical;* as Musculus, Zuingle, Baxter, Henry, Ostervald, Dr. Fawcett, the "Reformer's Bible," &c. &c.

4. Those who unite critical, philological, and practical observations: such are the commentaries of Dr. Dodd, Bishop Mant and Dr. D'Oyly, Poole, Scott, M. Martin, Dr. A. Clarke, Mr. Benson, &c. on the entire Bible, and the paraphrases of Pyle, and of Mr. Orton, on the Old Testament; on the New Testament, Dr. S. Clarke and Pyle, Dr. Doddridge, Mr. Locke, Dr. Benson, Dr. Macknight; Mr. Gilpin on the New Testament, &c. &c.

A more correct classification of expository writings may be into *Scholiasts, Commentators,* and *Paraphrasts*. whose united design is, to lead their readers to the right understanding of the author whom they undertake to explain. Hence their province is, to illustrate obscure passages, to reconcile apparent contradictions, to obviate difficulties, whether *verbal* or *real*, and, in short, to remove every thing that may tend to excite doubts in the minds of the readers of the Bible.

II. SCHOLIA, are short explanatory notes on the sacred writers; whose authors, termed *scholiasts*, particularly aim at brevity. In this kind of expository writings, obscure words and phrases are explained by such as are more clear; figurative by such as are proper; and the genuine force of each word and phrase is pointed out. Further, the allusions to antient manners and customs are illustrated, and whatever light may be thrown upon the sacred writer from history or geography, is carefully concentrated, and *concisely expressed* · nor does the scholiast fail to select and introduce the principal and most valuable various readings, whose excellence, antiquity, and genuineness, to the best of his judgment, give them a claim to be noticed. The discordant interpretations of difficult passages are stated and examined, and the most probable one is pointed out. These various topics, however, are rather touched upon, than treated at length: though no material passages are (or at least ought to be) left unnoticed, yet some very obscure and difficult passages are left to be discussed and expounded by more learned men. Such was the method, according to which the antient scholiasts composed their scholia, for illustrating Homer, Sophocles, Aristophanes, Horace, Virgil, and other Greek and Latin classics. and the same mode has been adopted by those Christian writers who have written scholia on the Bible.[1]

III. The various topics, which engage the attention of the scholiast, are also discussed, but more at length, by COMMENTATORS; whose observations form a series of perpetual annotations on the sacred writers, and who point out more clearly the train of their thoughts, as well as the coherence of their expressions, and all the various readings which are of any importance. The commentator, therefore, not only furnishes summaries of the argument, but also resolves the expressions of his author into their several parts, and shows in what respects they agree, as well as where they are apparently at variance. He further weighs and examines different passages, that admit of different interpretations; and while he offers his own views, he confirms them by proper arguments or proofs, and solves any doubts which may attend his own interpretation. Further, a judicious commentator will avoid all prolix, extraneous, and unnecessary discussions, as well as far-fetched explanations, and will bring every philological aid to bear upon passages that are in any degree difficult or obscure. Commentators *ought not* to omit a single passage that possesses more than ordinary difficulty, though the contrary is the

---

[1] Somewhat similar to Scholia are the *Questions* or Inquiries concerning particular books of Scripture, which were composed by antient ecclesiastical writers · they differ from Scholia in this respect, that questions are exclusively confined to the consideration of *some* difficult passages only, whose meaning was at that time an object of discussion, while it is the design of Scholia to notice *every* difficult or obscure passage with brevity and perspicuity. Augustine, among other biblical treatises, wrote two books of *Quæstiones Evangelicæ*, on the Gospels of Matthew and Saint Luke.

case with many, who expatiate very copiously on the more easy passages of Scripture, while they scarcely touch on those which are really difficult, if they do not altogether omit to treat of them. In a word, it is the commentator's province to remove every difficulty that can impede the biblical reader, and to produce whatever can facilitate his studies, by rendering the sense of the sacred writings more clear and easy to be apprehended.

IV. A PARAPHRASE is an exposition of the same thing in other words: the paraphrast, therefore, differs from the commentator in this respect, viz. that whatever is fully explained by the latter in his perpetual annotations, the former expounds by rendering the whole discourse, as well as every expression, of the sacred writer in equivalent terms; so that what is obscure is thus rendered more perspicuous, in one continued and unbroken narrative. *Provided the integrity of his author's sense be observed*, the paraphrast is at liberty to abridge what is narrated at length, to enlarge on what is written with brevity, to supply *supposed* omissions, to fill up chasms, to illustrate obscure and apparently involved passages, by plain, clear, and neatly turned expressions, to connect passages which seem too far asunder, or not disposed in order either of time or subject, and to arrange the whole in a regular series. These, indeed, it must be admitted, are important liberties, not to be taken with the Scriptures by *any* paraphrast without the utmost caution, and even then only in the most sparing manner. Paraphrases have been divided by Professor Rambach [1], and other writers on the interpretation of the Bible, into two classes — *historical* and *textual*. In the former class of paraphrases, the argument of a book or chapter is pursued historically; and the paraphrast endeavours to give his author's meaning in perspicuous language. In the latter instance, the paraphrast assumes, as it were, the person of the sacred writer, closely pursues the thread of his discourse, and aims at expressing every word and phrase, though in circumscribed limits, yet in terms that are both clear and obvious to the capacities of his readers. Hence it would appear, that a paraphrase is the most difficult species of expository writing; and, as the number of paraphrasts on the Scriptures is, comparatively, small (probably from this circumstance), the ingenious classification of them proposed by Rambach is not sufficiently important to render it necessary that we should form them into a separate class of interpreters. It is of infinitely greater moment to Bible readers, when purchasing works of this description, that they select those which are neither too prolix nor too expensive, and whose authors avoid every thing like party-spirit; neither extolling beyond measure any thing antient, merely because it is of remote antiquity, nor evincing a spirit of *dogmatical innovation*; but who, "rightly dividing the word of truth," while they express themselves in clear and perspicuous terms, show themselves to be well skilled both in the theory and application of sound principles of scriptural interpretation,

---

[1] Rambachii Institutiones Hermeneuticæ, pp. 706, 707.

and who have diligently availed themselves of every internal and external aid for ascertaining the sense of the sacred writers.

V. Closely allied to commentaries are the collections of OBSERVATIONS ILLUSTRATIVE OF THE SACRED WRITINGS, which have been formed of late years, and require to be consulted with similar cautions, and in the same manner. These books of observations are either grammatical and philological, or miscellaneous; sometimes they discuss only a few passages which are peculiarly difficult and obscure, and sometimes they appear in the form of a grammatical and philological commentary, following the order of the sacred books. On this account, as well as to facilitate reference, we have classed them with expositions of the Bible; of the best editions of all these, the reader will find some account in the Appendix to this volume, occasionally interspersed with concise bibliographical and critical observations.[1]

VI. Opinions widely different have been entertained respecting the utility and advantage resulting from commentaries, annotations, and other expositions of the Sacred Writings. By some, who admire nothing but their own meditations, and who hold all human helps in contempt, commentaries are despised altogether, as tending to found our faith on the opinions of men rather than on the divine oracles: while others, on the contrary, trusting exclusively to the expositions of some favourite commentators, receive as infallible whatever views or opinions they may choose to deliver, as *their* expositions of the Bible. The safest way in this case, as in all others, is to take the middle path, and occasionally to avail ourselves of the labours of commentators and expositors, while we diligently investigate the Scriptures for ourselves, without relying exclusively on our own wisdom, or being fascinated by the authority of a distinguished name.

The late eminent divine and theological tutor, Dr. Campbell, was of opinion that the Bible should be first read and studied *without* a commentary; but his advice was addressed to students who were *previously* acquainted with the originals: and though the design of the present work is to facilitate to studious inquirers the understanding of the Scriptures, yet the author presumes not to suppose that his labours will supersede the necessity of commentaries; or that he can furnish them with all that information which renders such works desirable to the generality of Bible readers. A sensible writer has observed, that the Bible is a *learned* book, not only because it is written in the learned languages, but also as containing allusions to various facts, circumstances, or customs of antiquity, which, to a common and unlettered reader, require explanation. So far, indeed, as relates to the way of salvation, "he that runs may read:" but there are many important points, if not of the first importance, in which we may properly avail ourselves of the labours of inquirers who have preceded us; especially in clearing difficulties, answering objections, and reconciling passages which at first sight appear contradictory.

Further, "the Bible is a large book, and we are under no small

---

[1] Arigler, Hermeneutica Biblica, pp. 256—263. Morus (Acroases, tom. ii. pp. 204—340) has given a detailed account of the various kinds of commentaries and commentators.

obligations to those who have collated its different parts — the New Testament with the Old, — the prophetic with the historical books, &c.; and to reject their assistance, in making the Scriptures their own interpreter, is to throw away the labours of many ages. As well might we reject all our historians, and insist on believing nothing but what we derive immediately from state papers, original records, or other documents, on which all history is founded." Once more, "the Bible is intended as a directory for our faith and practice. Now to have an experienced friend who has long been in the habit of perusing it with patient study and humble prayer, — to have *such* a friend at hand, to point out in every chapter what may be useful or important, and especially to disclose its latent beauties, may be no less desirable and useful, than it is, when travelling in a foreign country, to have with us a companion who has passed the same route, and is acquainted both with the road, and with the objects most worthy of notice. It is granted, however, that there are extremes; and that it is no less wrong to place *implicit* confidence in commentators, than it is to treat them with contempt: to derive advantage from them, we should treat them as commentators *only*, and *not* as inspired writers." [1]

VII. The USE to be made of interpreters and commentators is twofold:

FIRST, *that we may acquire from them a method of interpreting the Scriptures correctly.*

It is not sufficient that we be enabled rightly to understand the Bible ourselves, but it is essentially necessary that those who are destined for the sacred office should be able to explain it with facility, and also to communicate its sense and meaning with perspicuity to others. As, however, this faculty is not to be attained merely by studying rules for the interpretation of the Scriptures, habitual and constant practice must be superadded; and it will further prove of singular advantage to place before us some good expositors, as models for our imitation. In order to accomplish this desirable object, we must not accumulate and read every interpreter or commentator *indiscriminately* but should select one or two, or a *few* at most, of acknowledged character for learning and piety; and, by frequent perusal of them, as well as by studying their manner of expounding, should endeavour to form ourselves after them, until we are completely masters of their method. But the reading of commentaries will further assist us,

SECONDLY, *to understand whatever passages appear to us to be difficult and obscure.*

It is not to be denied that there are many passages in the Sacred Writings both difficult and obscure, in consequence of the various times when the different books were written, the different topics of which they treat, and their allusions to antient customs, &c. The helps, by which most of these difficulties may be removed, have already been stated in the course of the present work. But we cannot suppose that the solitary and unassisted researches even of the most learned expositor are adequate to the removal of every difficulty, or to the elucidation of every obscurity, or that he is not liable to mistake the sense of the sacred penman. By the united labours, however, of many learned and pious men, of different ages and countries, we are put in possession of *accumulated information* relative to the Bible, so that we may derive large accessions of important knowledge from the *judicious* use of the writings of commentators and expositors.

VIII. In order, then, that we may avail ourselves of their valuable labours to the utmost advantage, the following hints are submitted to the consideration of the reader.

1. *We should take care that the reading of commentators does not draw*

---

[1] The Christian Reader's Guide, by Thomas Williams. Part i. p. 82.

us away from studying the Scriptures for ourselves, from investigating their real meaning, and meditating on their important contents.

This would be to frustrate the very design for which commentaries are written, namely, to facilitate our labours, to direct us aright where we are in danger of falling into error, to remove doubts and difficulties which we are ourselves unable to solve, to reconcile apparently contradictory passages, and, in short, to elucidate whatever is obscure or unintelligible to us. In the first instance, therefore, no commentators should be consulted until we have previously investigated the Sacred Writings, for ourselves, making use of every grammatical and historical help, comparing the scope, context, parallel passages, the analogy of faith, &c., and even then commentaries should be resorted to only for the purpose of explaining what was not sufficiently clear, or of removing our doubts. This method of studying the sacred volume will, unquestionably, prove a slow one; but the student will proceed with certainty; and, if he have patience and resolution enough to persevere in it, he will ultimately attain greater proficiency in the knowledge of the Scriptures, than those who, disregarding this method, shall have recourse wholly to assistances of other kinds. From the mode of study here recommended, many advantages will result. In the first place, the mind will be gradually accustomed to habits of meditation without which we cannot reasonably hope to attain even a moderate, much less a profound knowledge of the Bible, — secondly, those truths will be more readily as well as indelibly impressed on the memory, which have thus been "marked, learned, and inwardly digested" in the mind by silent thought and reflection, — and, thirdly, by pursuing this method, we shall perceive our own progress in sacred literature more readily, than if (like idle drones in a bee-hive) we devour and exhaust the stores provided by the care and labour of others.[1]

2. *We should not inconsiderately assent to the interpretation of any expositor, or commentator, or yield a blind and servile obedience to his authority.*

The canon given by Saint Paul (1 Thess v. 21) — *Prove all things, hold fast that which is good*, — is therefore particularly worthy of our notice for since no man is an infallible judge of the sense of Scripture, not only the expositions given by commentators ought to be carefully examined, but we should also particularly investigate the proofs by which they support their interpretations, uninfluenced by the celebrity of their names, the semblance of ingenuity and novelty, the appearance of learning, or the *excellency of speech*.[2] Commentators, in fact, are witnesses, not judges · their authority is merely human and does not surpass the sphere of human belief. But we should not read, exclusively, commentators of a particular *school*, to which we are perhaps attached, and to whose opinions we subscribe; and though the writings of those who inculcate erroneous doctrines are to be received with the greatest suspicion, yet they are not to be altogether disregarded, as they *sometimes* contain valuable and important hints for the elucidation of difficult passages of Scripture. That he may not be misunderstood, the author will explain himself by a single example. The variety of erroneous *theological* notions, asserted in different publications by the late Dr. Priestley, has justly excited suspicions in the minds of all, who cherish a regard for what they conscientiously believe to be the peculiar doctrines of the Christian dispensation so that any theological or expository writings, bearing *his* name, are by them received with caution, and subjected to the most rigorous examination. His "*Notes on all the Books of Scripture*" are, nevertheless, well worthy of being consulted, for "though the doctor keeps his own creed (*Unitarianism*) continually in view, especially when considering those texts which other religious people adduce in favour of theirs, yet his work contains many invaluable notes and observations, particularly on the *philosophy, natural history, geography, and chronology* of the Scriptures · and to these subjects few men in Europe were better qualified to do justice."[3]

3. *The best commentators and interpreters only are to be read.*

So numerous are the commentaries at present extant on the Sacred Writings, that to notice them all would require a distinct volume. Not to mention the magnitude of their cost, the labour and fatigue of turning over and examining such a multitude of massy volumes, is sufficient to deter any one from the study of them and must necessarily prevent an ingenuous student from deriving any real advantage. For the perplexity of mind,

---

[1] Bauer, Herm Sacr. p. 302 Steph. Gausseni Dissertatio de Ratione Studii Theologici, pp. 25, 26 Dr. Henry Owen's Directions for young Students in Divinity p 37. 5th edit.

[2] C. D. Beckii Monogrammata Hermeneutices Librorum Novi Testamenti, pars i. pp 174, 175.

[3] Dr. A. Clarke, General Preface to vol. i. of his Commentary on the Bible, p. xi.

arising from so great a variety of conflicting opinions, will either disgust him altogether with sacred studies, or he will so bewilder himself, that he will not be able to determine which to follow or embrace.

Although the more antient commentators and expositors did not possess those peculiar facilities for interpreting the Scriptures, with which we are now happily favoured, yet they are not to be altogether despised by those, who may have leisure and opportunity to consult them, for the purpose of tracing the time when, and the authors by whom, particular expositions of certain passages were first introduced. The more antient Interpreters, being coeval or nearly so with the sacred writers, and also living in the neighbouring countries, are thus rendered good evidence, for the received sense of certain words in their day. Hence the Jews frequently throw much light on the meaning of Hebrew words and usages, as may be seen in the extracts from their writings which are to be found in all the larger commentaries: and in like manner the Greek fathers, the value of whose labours it has been the fashion unduly to depreciate, are excellent evidence for the meaning attached to Greek words, particularly in controversies relating to the deity of Jesus Christ, the reality and efficacy of his atonement, &c. And since there are *some expositions* of very important passages, in which all or nearly all expositors, both antient and modern, *are agreed*, these have a high claim to our attention. [1]

Of the more modern commentators, the *best only* must be selected, whom we may consult as guides: and those may be considered as the best commentators, who are most deeply furnished with the requisite critical skill; who most diligently investigate the literal sense, and do not attempt to establish a mystical sense until the literal sense is most clearly ascertained; who do not servilely copy the remarks of preceding commentators, but, while they avail themselves of every help for the interpretation of the Scriptures, elicit what appears to be the true meaning, and support it by such clear and cogent arguments, and state it with such perspicuity, as convinces the reader's judgment. To these acquirements, it is scarcely necessary to add, that *deep, yet sober piety and uprightness are indispensably necessary to a commentator on Holy Writ*.

On the subject of commentaries, it is an excellent advice of Ernesti's[2], that we shall find considerable advantage in making memoranda of the more difficult passages of the Sacred Writings, which have been variously explained by expositors, as well as of such passages as are particularly worthy of note, but concerning which our own researches, or those of others, have failed in procuring satisfactory information. Thus, whenever any *new* commentary falls into our hands, we can in a short time ascertain whether it contains any thing intrinsically new or valuable, or that may lead us to ascertain the genuine sense of a passage. By consulting commentators and expositors in this manner, we shall be able to distinguish ideas of things from ideas of sounds; and, thus becoming habituated to the investigation and consideration of the Sacred Writings, we shall, under divine teaching, be enabled to understand *the mind of the Spirit* in the Scriptures.

4. *Where it does not appear that either antient or modern interpreters had more knowledge than ourselves respecting particular passages; and where they offer only conjectures,— in such cases their expositions ought to be subjected to a strict examination. If their reasons are then found to be valid, we should give our assent to them: but, on the contrary, if they prove to be false, improbable, and insufficient, they must be altogether rejected.*

5. *Lastly, as there are some commentaries, which are either wholly compiled from the previous labours of others, or contain observations extracted from their writings, if any thing appear confused or perplexed in such commentaries, the original sources whence they were compiled must be referred to, and diligently consulted.*

---

[1] Bauer, Herm. Sacr. p. 304. Turretin de Interp. Sac. Scrip. p. 333.
[2] Institutio Interpretis Novi Testamenti, part iii. cap. ix. § 44. p. 306.

BOOK II.

ON THE SPECIAL INTERPRETATION OF SCRIPTURE.

HAVING stated and illustrated the general principles of interpretation in the preceding chapters, it remains that we show in what manner the sense, when discovered, is to be communicated, expounded, and applied. The consideration of this topic will lead us to notice the Interpretation of the *Figurative* and the *Poetical Language* of the Bible, and also the interpretation of *Spiritual* and *Typical, Prophetical, Doctrinal,* and *Moral* parts of the Bible, as well as the interpretation of the *Promises* and *Threatenings* contained in the Scriptures, and of *Passages alleged to be contradictory,* together with that *Inferential Reading,* and that *Practical Application* of them to the heart and conscience, without which all knowledge will be in vain. If, indeed, the previous investigation of the sense of Scripture be undertaken with those moral and devout qualifications which have been stated in the preceding volume[1], it is scarcely possible that we can fail to understand the meaning of the word of God.

CHAPTER I.

ON THE INTERPRETATION OF THE FIGURATIVE LANGUAGE OF SCRIPTURE.

FIGURATIVE language had its rise in the first ages of mankind: the scarcity of words occasioned them to be used for various purposes. and thus figurative terms, which constitute the beauty of language, arose from its poverty; and it is still the same in all uncivilised nations. Hence originated the metaphorical diction of the Indians, and the picture-writing of the Mexicans.

The Bible, though too commonly regarded as containing only lessons of morality and plain statements of facts, abounds with the most beautiful images, and with every ornament of which style is susceptible. Yet these very ornaments are sometimes occasions of difficulty; for the books, which contain the revelations of God, being more antient than any others now extant, are written either in the language used by mankind in the first ages, or in a language nearly allied to it. The style of these writings, therefore, being very different from that of modern compositions, to interpret them exactly as they are usually expounded, is without doubt to *mis*interpret them; accordingly, persons ignorant of the character of the primitive languages, have, by that method of interpretation, been

---

[1] See Vol. I. p. 491.

led to imagine that the Scriptures contain notions unworthy of God: and thus have not only exposed these venerable writings to the scorn of infidels, but have also framed to themselves erroneous notions in religion.[1] To prevent similar mistakes, and, it is hoped, to render more delightful the study of the sacred volume by an explanation of its figurative language, is the design of the present chapter.

Figures, in general, may be described to be that language, which is prompted either by the imagination or by the passions. Rhetoricians commonly divide them into two great classes, *figures of words* and *figures of thought*.

Figures of Words, are usually termed *tropes*, and consist in the advantageous alteration of a word or sentence, from its original and proper signification to another meaning; as in 2 Sam. xxiii. 3. *The rock of Israel spake to me.* Here the trope lies in the word *rock*, which is changed from its original sense, as intending one of the strongest works and most certain shelters in nature; and is employed to signify, that God, by his faithfulness and power, is the same security to the soul which trusts in him, as the rock is to the man who builds upon it, or flees for safety to its impenetrable recesses. So, in Luke xiii. 32. our Lord, speaking of Herod, says, *Go ye, and tell that fox:* here the word *fox* is diverted from its proper meaning, which is that of a beast of prey and of deep cunning, to denote a mischievous, cruel, and crafty tyrant; and the application of the term gives us a complete idea of his hypocrisy.

The other class, called Figures of Thought, supposes the words to be used in their literal and proper meaning, and the figure to consist in the turn of the thought; as is the case in exclamations, apostrophes, and comparisons, where, though we vary the words that are used, or translate them from one language into another, we may nevertheless still preserve the same figure in the thought. This distinction, however, Dr. Blair remarks, is of no great use, as nothing can be built upon it in practice: neither is it always very clear. It is of little importance, whether we give to some particular mode of expression the name of a trope, or of a figure, provided we remember that figurative language always imports some colouring of the imagination, or some emotion of passion expressed in our style: and, perhaps, *figures of imagination*, and *figures of passion*, might be a more useful distribution of the subject.[2]

Without regarding, therefore, the technical distinctions, which have been introduced by rhetorical writers, we shall first offer some hints by which to ascertain and correctly interpret the tropes and figures occurring in the Sacred Writings; and in the following sections we shall notice the principal of them, illustrated by examples, to which a diligent reader may easily subjoin others.

---

[1] Macknight on the Epistles, vol. iv. 4to., or vol vi 8vo. essay viii. sect. 1. On the right Interpretation of Scripture. The materials of this chapter are abridged chiefly from Professor Dathe's edition of Glassius's Philologia Sacra, lib. ii. forming the whole second volume of that elaborate work. See also Jahn's Enchiridion Hermeneuticæ Generalis, cap iv De Tropis Recte Interpretandis, pp 101—125, and Rambach's Institutiones Hermeneuticæ Sacræ, lib. iii. c ii. De Adminiculis Rhetoricis, pp. 429—440.

[2] Blair's Lectures, vol. i. p. 320.

SECTION I.

GENERAL OBSERVATIONS ON THE INTERPRETATION OF TROPES AND FIGURES.

" ALL languages are more or less figurative: but they are most so in their earliest state. Before language is provided with a stock of words, sufficient in their literal sense to express what is wanted, men are under the necessity of extending the use of words beyond the literal sense. But the application, when once begun, is not to be limited by the bounds of necessity. The imagination, always occupied with resemblances, which are the foundation of figures, disposes men to seek for figurative terms, where they might express themselves in literal terms. Figurative language presents a kind of picture to the mind, and thus delights while it instructs: whence its use, though more necessary when a language is poor and uncultivated, is never wholly laid aside, especially in the writings of orators and poets."[1] The language of the Scriptures is highly figurative, especially in the Old Testament. For this, two reasons have been assigned; *one* is, that the inhabitants of the East, naturally possessing warm and vivid imaginations, and living in a warm and fertile climate, surrounded by objects equally beautiful and agreeable, delight in a figurative style of expression: and as these circumstances easily impel their power of conceiving images, they fancy similitudes which are sometimes far fetched, and which to the chastised taste of European readers, do not always appear the most elegant. The *other* reason is, that many of the books of the Old Testament are poetical; now it is the privilege of a poet to illustrate the productions of his muse, and to render them more animated, by figures and images drawn from almost every subject that presents itself to his imagination. Hence David, Solomon, Isaiah, and other sacred poets, abound with figures, make rapid transitions from one to another, every where scattering flowers, and adorning their poems with metaphors, the real beauty of which, however, can only be appreciated by being acquainted with the country in which the sacred poets lived, its situation and peculiarities, and also with the manners of the inhabitants, and the idioms of their language.

The language of the New Testament, and especially the discourses and speeches of our Saviour, are not less figurative: "and numerous mistakes have been made by a literal application of what was figuratively meant. When our Saviour said to the Jews, 'Destroy this temple, and in three days I will raise it up,' the Jews understood the word *temple* in its natural sense, and asked him, Whether he could raise again in three days what had taken six-and-forty years to build? They did not perceive that his language was figurative, and that he spake of the temple of his body."[2]

In order, then, to understand fully the figurative language of the Scriptures, it is requisite, *first*, to ascertain and determine what is

---

[1] Bishop Marsh's Lectures, part iii. p. 69.   [2] Ibid.

really figurative, lest we take that to be literal which is figurative, as the disciples of our Lord and the Jews frequently did, or lest we pervert the literal meaning of words by a figurative interpretation; and, *secondly,* when we have ascertained what is really figurative, to interpret it correctly, and deliver its true sense. For this purpose, Ernesti has given the following general rule. — We may ascertain whether any expression is to be taken literally or figuratively, by recalling the thing spoken of to its internal or external sense, that is, by seeking out its internal or external meaning; and this may in general be readily ascertained. Hence it is, that in human compositions we are very rarely if ever in doubt, whether a thing be spoken literally or figuratively; because the thing or subject spoken of being human, and capable both of external and internal senses, may be recalled to a human sense, that is, to a sense intelligible by man. To understand this subject more particularly:

1. *The literal meaning of words must be retained, more in the historical books of Scripture, than in those which are poetical.*

For it is the duty of an historian to relate transactions, simply as they happened, while a poet has license to ornament his subject by the aid of figures, and to render it more lively by availing himself of similes and metaphors. Hence we find, that the style of narration in the historical books, is simple and *generally* devoid of ornament, while the poetical books abound with images borrowed from various objects not, indeed, that the historical books are *entirely* destitute of figurative expressions; for, whatever language men may use, they are so accustomed to this mode of expression, that they cannot fully convey their meaning in literal words, but are compelled by the force of habit to make use of such as are figurative. But we must not look for a figurative style in the historical books, and still less are historical narratives to be changed into allegories, and parables, unless these be obviously apparent. From inattention to this important rule, "some interpreters, in ancient and modern times, have turned into allegory the whole Jewish ceremonial law So, formerly and recently, the history of the creation of the world, the fall of man, the flood, the account of the tower of Babel, &c have been explained either as μυθοι, or as philosophical allegories, i.e philosophical speculations on these subjects, clothed in the garb of narration. By the same principles of exegesis, the gospels are treated as μυθοι, which exhibit an imaginary picture of a perfect character, in the person of Jesus. In a word, every narration in the Bible, of an occurrence which is of a miraculous nature in any respect, is μυθος; which means, as its abettors say, that some real fact or occurrence lies at the basis of the story, which is told agreeably to the very imperfect conceptions and philosophy of ancient times, or has been augmented and adorned by tradition and fancy.

But that such liberties with the language of Scripture are utterly incompatible with the sober principles of interpretation, is sufficiently manifest from the bare statement of them. The object of the interpreter is, *to find out what the sacred writers meant to say* This done, his task is performed. Party philosophy or scepticism cannot guide the interpretation of language." [1]

2. *The literal meaning of words is to be given up, if it be either improper, or involve an impossibility, or where words, properly taken, contain any thing contrary to the doctrinal or moral precepts delivered in other parts of Scripture.* [2]

(1.) The expressions in Jer. i 18. are necessarily to be understood figuratively. God is there represented as saying to the prophet, *I have made thee a defenced city, and*

---

[1] Stuart's Elements of Interpretation, p. 76. Mori Acroases, tom i pp. 281—291.

[2] "I hold it," says the learned and venerable Hooker, "for a most infallible rule in expositions of sacred Scripture, that, where a literal construction will stand, the farthest from the letter is commonly the worst There is nothing more dangerous than this licentious and deluding art, which changes the meaning of words, as alchemy doth or would do the substance of metals, making of any thing what it pleases, and bringing in the end all truth to nothing." Ecclesiastical Polity, Book v cc. 58—60. or p. 211. of Mr. Collinson's Analysis.

an iron pillar, and brazen walls against the whole land. Now, it is obvious that these expressions are figurative, because, if taken literally, they involve an impossibility. The general import of the divine promise is, that God would defend Jeremiah against all open assaults and secret contrivances of his enemies, who should no more be able to prevail against him than they could against an impregnable wall or fortress. So the literal sense of Isa. i. 25. is equally inapplicable, but in the following verse the prophet explains it in the proper words

(2.) In Psal. xviii 2 God is termed a *rock*, a *fortress*, a *deliverer*, a *buckler*, a *horn of salvation*, and a *high tower* · it is obvious that these predicates are metaphorically spoken of the Almighty

(3.) Matt. viii 22. *Let the dead bury their dead*, cannot possibly be applied to those who are really and naturally dead, and, consequently, must be understood figuratively, " Leave those who are spiritually dead to perform the rites of burial for such as are naturally dead " In Psal cxxx 1. David is said to have *cried unto the Lord out of the* DEPTHS, by which word we are metaphorically to understand a state of the deepest affliction; because it no where appears from Scripture, nor is it probable, that the Jewish monarch was ever thrown into the sea, even in his greatest adversity, as we read that the prophet Jonah was, who cried to the Lord out of the *depth*, or midst of the sea. (Jon. i. 15. 17 ii 2, 3 5) Similar expressions occur in 1 Cor iii 13. and Rev. vi. 13

(4.) The command of Jesus Christ, related in Matt xviii 8, 9. if interpreted literally, is directly at variance with the sixth commandment, (Exod. xx. 13.) and must consequently be understood figuratively. So, the declaration of Jesus Christ in John xiv. 28 (*My Father is greater than I*) is to be understood of himself, as he is man This is evident from the context and from the nature of his discourse. In John, xiv. 24. Christ tells his disciples that the Father had *sent* him, that is, in his quality of *Messiah*, he was sent by the Father to instruct and to save mankind Now as the *sender* is greater than he who is *sent* (xiii 16.), so, in this sense, is the Father greater than the Son It certainly requires very little argument, and no sophistry to reconcile this saying with the most orthodox notion of the deity of Christ, as he is repeatedly speaking of his divine and of his human nature Of the *former* he says, (John x. 30.) *I and the Father are one*, and of the *latter* he states with the same truth, *the Father is greater than I*

(5.) Whatever is repugnant to natural reason, cannot be the true meaning of the Scriptures, for God is the original of natural truth, as well as of that which comes by particular revelation. No proposition, therefore, which is repugnant to the fundamental principles of reason, can be the sense of any part of the word of God; hence the words of Christ,— *This is my body*, and *This is my blood*,— (Matt xxvi. 26 28) are not to be understood in that sense, which makes for the doctrine of transubstantiation, or, of the conversion of the bread and wine, in the sacrament of the Lord's Supper, into the actual body and blood of Christ. because it is impossible that contradictions should be true; and we cannot be more certain that any thing is true, than we are that *that* doctrine is false. Yet it is upon a forced and literal construction of our Lord's declaration, that the Romish church has, ever since the thirteenth century, erected and maintained the doctrine of transubstantiation. — a doctrine which is manifestly "repugnant to the plain words of Scripture, overthroweth the nature of a sacrament, and hath given occasion to many superstitions."[1] The expressions, "this is my body," and "this is my blood," (Matt. xxvi. 26, 28. and Mark xiv. 22 24 compared with Luke xxii 19, 20 and 1 Cor, xi. 24, 25.) by a well known metonomy simply mean, "this represents my body," and "this represents my blood " For, as these words were spoken *before* Christ's body was broken upon the cross, and *before* his blood was shed, he could not pronounce them with the intention that they should be taken and interpreted literally by his disciples nor do we find that they ever understood him thus If the words of institution had been spoken in *English* or *Latin* at first, there might perhaps have been some reason for supposing that our Saviour meant to be literally understood. But they were spoken in Syriac, in which, as well as in the Hebrew and Chaldee languages, there is no word which expresses to *signify*, *represent*, or *denote*. Hence it is that we find the expression *it is*, so frequently used in the Sacred Writings, for *it represents* or signifies Thus, in Gen. xvii. 10. 23. 26. this is [represents] *my covenant betwixt me and thee* So, in Gen. xli. 26, 27 *the seven good kine and the seven ill-favoured kine* ARE [represent] *seven years*. Exod. xii. 11. This is [represents] *the Lord's passover*. Dan vii 24 *The ten horns* ARE [denote] *ten kings*. 1 Cor. x. 4. *That rock* WAS [typified or represented] *Christ* Matt xiii 38, 39. *The field is* [denotes] *the world*, *the good seed* is [represents] *the children of the kingdom*; *the tares* ARE [represent] *the children of the wicked one*. *The enemy* is [represents] *the Devil*: *the harvest* is [signifies] *the end of the world*, *the reapers* ARE [represent] *Angels*. Similar modes of expression occur in Luke viii 9. xv 26. Gr. and John vii. 36. Gr. John vii. 36. and x. 6. Acts x. 17 Gal iv. 24 and Rev 1 20. It is further worthy of remark, that we have

---

[1] Art. xxviii. of the Confession of the Anglican Church.

a complete version of the Gospels in the Syriac language, which was executed at the commencement of the second if not at the close of the first century, and in them it is probable that we have the precise words spoken by our Lord on this occasion. Of the passage, Matt xxvi 26. 28. the Greek is a verbal translation nor would any man even in the present day, speaking in the same language, use, among the people to whom it was vernacular, other terms to express, "this represents my body," and "this represents my blood." It is evident, therefore, from the context, from parallel passages, and the scope of the passage, that the literal interpretation of Matt. xxvi. 26 28 must be abandoned, and with it necessarily falls the monstrous doctrine of transubstantiation

(6.) To *change day into night* (Job xvii. 12) is a moral impossibility, contrary to common sense, and must be a figurative expression. In Isa i 5, 6 the Jewish nation are described as being sorely *stricken* or chastised, like a man mortally wounded, and destitute both of medicine as well as of the means of cure. That this description is figurative, is evident from the context; for in the two following verses the prophet delineates the condition of the Jews in literal terms.

It is not, however, sufficient to know whether an expression be figurative or not, but, when this point is ascertained, another of equal importance presents itself, namely, to interpret metaphorical expressions by corresponding and appropriate terms. In order to accomplish this object, it is necessary,

3. *That we inquire in what respects the thing compared, and that with which it is compared, respectively agree, and also in what respects they have any affinity or resemblance*

For, as a similitude is concealed in every metaphor, it is only by diligent study that it can be elicited, by carefully observing the points of agreement between the proper or literal and the figurative meaning. For instance, the prophetic writers, and particularly Ezekiel, very frequently charge the Israelites with having committed adultery and played the harlot, and with deserting Jehovah, their husband. From the slightest inspection of these passages, it is evident that spiritual adultery, or idolatry, is intended. Now the origin of this metaphor is to be sought from one and the same notion, in which there is an agreement between adultery and the worship paid by the Israelites to strange gods. That notion or idea is unfaithfulness, by which as a wife deceives her husband, so they are represented as deceiving God, and as violating their fidelity, in forsaking him

To explain this general remark more particularly.

(1.) *The sense of a figurative passage will be known, if the resemblance between the things or objects compared be so clear as to be immediately perceived.*

Thus, if any one be said to *walk in the way of the ungodly*, or of the *godly*, we readily apprehend that the imitation of the conduct of those characters is the idea designed to be expressed In like manner, when any one is compared to a *lion*, who does not immediately understand that strength of limbs, firmness of nerve, and magnanimity, are the ideas intended to be conveyed? In Gen. xlix. 9. Judah is styled a *lion's whelp*, and is compared to a lion and lioness couching, whom no one dares to rouse. The warlike character and the conquests of this tribe are here prophetically described: but the full force of the passage will not be perceived, unless we know that a lion is, among the orientals, used figuratively to denote a hero, and also that a lion or lioness, when lying down after satisfying its hunger, will not attack any person Mr. Park has recorded an instance of his providential escape from a lion thus circumstanced, which he saw lying near the road, and passed unhurt. [1]

(2.) *As, in the sacred metaphors, one particular is generally the principal thing thereby exhibited, the sense of a metaphor will be illustrated by considering the context of a passage in which it occurs.*

This rule particularly applies to images, which do not always convey one and the same meaning. Thus, light and darkness not only denote happiness and misery, but also knowledge and ignorance, of which of these two significations is to be preferably adopted, the context alone can show In Psalm cxii. 4 we read · *Unto the upright there ariseth light in the darkness*. Bishop Horsley thinks that this is an allusion to what happened in Egypt, when the Israelites had light in all their dwellings in Goshen, while the rest of Egypt was

---

[1] Travels in the Interior of Africa, p 810. London, 1807, 8vo, or in Pinkerton's Collection of Voyages, vol. xvi. p. 848.

enveloped in darkness. Be this, however, as it may, since the design of the psalm in question is, to show the blessedness of the righteous and the final perdition of the ungodly, the context will plainly indicate that happiness is the idea intended in this verse; for, if we consult what precedes, we shall find that temporal prosperity is promised to the righteous, and that, among the particulars in which his prosperity is stated to consist, it is specified *that his seed shall be mighty upon earth, the generation of the upright shall be blessed, wealth and riches shall be in his house.* On the contrary, in Psal. xix. 8. where the commandment of Jehovah is said to *enlighten the eyes,* the idea of spiritual *knowledge* is intended, and this phrase corresponds to that in the preceding verse, where the testimony of Jehovah is said to *make wise the simple.* In the New Testament, light and darkness are of frequent occurrence, and in like manner designate a state of knowledge and a state of ignorance. It may be sufficient to refer to Luke i. 78, 79. Acts xxvi 18. Rom. i. 21. Eph iv. 18. and v. 8. 1 Pet. ii 9.

(3.) *The sense of a figurative expression is often known from the sacred writer's own explanation of it.*

In common with profane writers, whether in prose or verse, the inspired penmen of the Old Testament frequently subjoin to figurative expressions, proper or literal terms, and thus explain the meaning intended to be conveyed by the images they employ. Thus, in Esther viii. 16. it is said that *the Jews had light and gladness, and joy and honour,* here the explanatory synonymes mark the greatness of their prosperity and joy. In Psal. xcvii. 11. *light is said to be sown for the righteous;* the exposition immediately follows, *and joy for the upright in heart.* In like manner, when the prophet Hosea complains that a spirit of lasciviousness had driven the Israelites astray (Hos. iv. 12.) he explains his meaning not only by subjoining that they forsook their God, but in the following verse he states in clear and literal terms the eagerness with which they committed idolatry, *upon the tops of the mountains they sacrifice, and upon the hills they burn incense,* &c.

(4.) *The sense of a figurative expression may also be ascertained by consulting parallel passages; in which the same thing is expressed properly and literally, or in which the same word occurs, so that the sense may be readily apprehended.*

The Hebrew prophets very often represent Jehovah as holding in his hand a cup, and presenting it to men who are compelled to drink it up to the very dregs. The intoxicated stagger, and, falling prostrate on the ground, shamefully vomit forth the wine they have drunk. This metaphor is frequently repeated in various ways by the sacred poets, who sometimes only glance at it, while at others they more fully illustrate it. Compare Obad. 16. Nahum iii 11. Habak. ii. 16. Psal. lxxv. 8. Jer. xxv. 15—27. and Ezekiel xxiii. 33, 34. Now, if there were any doubt as to the meaning of the image occurring in these passages, its sense might be immediately ascertained by comparing the following parallel passage in Isaiah li. 17—23., in which the prophet portrays Jerusalem as a woman so intoxicated as to be unable to stand, but in which he introduces some words that clearly mark the sense of the metaphor. The passage itself, Bishop Lowth justly remarks, is poetry of the first order, sublimity of the highest proof.

Rouse thyself, rouse thyself up; arise, O Jerusalem!
Who hast drunken from the hand of JEHOVAH the cup of his fury;
The dregs of the cup of trembling thou hast drunken, thou hast wrung them out.
There is not one to lead her, of all the sons which she hath brought forth;
Neither is there one to support her by the hand, of all the sons which she hath educated.
These two things have befallen thee, who shall bemoan thee?
Desolation and destruction; the famine and the sword; who shall comfort thee?
Thy sons lie astounded; they are cast down
At the head of all the streets, like the oryx [1] taken in the toils;
Drenched to the full with the fury of JEHOVAH, with the rebuke of thy God.
Wherefore hear now this, O thou afflicted daughter;
And thou drunken, but not with wine.
Thus saith thy Lord JEHOVAH;
And thy God, who avengeth his people;
Behold I take from thy hand the cup of trembling;
The dregs of the cup of my fury
Thou shalt drink of it again no more.
But I will put it into the hand of them who oppress thee;

---

[1] Or wild bull.

Who said to thee, bow down thy body, that we may go over
And thou layedst down thy back, as the ground
And as the street to them that pass along.
                                    Bishop LOWTH's Version.

(5.) *Consider History.*

A consideration of events recorded in history will very frequently show, how far and in what sense any expression is to be understood figuratively. Thus many and various things are said relative to the coming of Christ, his kingdom, government, and adversaries. Now history informs us, that he came, at the destruction of Jerusalem, to rule and govern far and wide by the spreading of the Gospel. In Matt x 34. Christ says that he came not to send peace on earth, but *a sword*. In the parallel passage, Luke xii. 51, he says that he came to cause *division*. The general import of these two passages is, that he would cause discord, and as it were sow dissensions. But in what sense could the blessed Saviour mean that he would cause discord? We learn from history, that in consequence of the diffusion of the Christian religion, nations and families became divided, so that some embraced it while others rejected it, and the former were persecuted by the latter on account of their Christian profession. A further exposition of this passage is given in p. 382 *infra*.

(6.) *Consider the connection of doctrine, as well as the context of the figurative passage.*

A consideration of the connection of doctrine, as well as of the context, will often lead to the origin of the figurative expressions employed by the sacred writers, and consequently enable us to ascertain their meaning: for very frequently some word precedes or follows, or some synonyme is annexed, that plainly indicates whether the expression is to be taken properly or figuratively. For instance, the words *sin* and *iniquity*, which are of such frequent occurrence in the law of Moses, are tropically put for punishment: and that the phrase, *to bear one's sin* or *iniquity*, is equivalent to the suffering of the punishment due to sin, appears from the synonymous expressions of *being cut off from the people*, and *dying*, being very often annexed. As in Levit xix 8 Exodus xxviii 43. Numb xiv 34. and xviii 22. 32, &c Thus also diseases and infirmities are called sins, because they are considered as the punishment of sin, (as in Isa liii. 4. with Matt. viii. 17.) the figure in which passage is subsequently explained in verse 5. Compare also verse 12 and Psalm xxxviii 3—5. Ezek xxxiii. 10 and John iv. 2, 3. So likewise in Gen xxxi 42. 53. the context manifestly shows that *the fear of Isaac*, and *the fear of his father*, are put for Jehovah, the object of fear and reverence. Once more; when, in 1 Pet ii 5 9 believers are said to be living stones, a spiritual house, and a royal priesthood, as these expressions are derived from the Old Testament, we must recur to Exodus xix. 5, 6. in order to ascertain the full extent of their privileges. The general tenor of the Apostle's address then will be, "Consider yourselves as forming part of a nobler temple than that of the Jews, and in which a much more spiritual sacrifice is offered to God through Christ. — You, who have embraced the Gospel, are considered by God as inheritors of all those holy blessings which were promised to the Jews."

(7.) *In fixing the sense exhibited by a metaphor, the comparison ought never to be extended too far, or into any thing which cannot be properly applied to the person or thing represented.*

In other words, a comparison which ordinarily has but *one particular view*, ought not to be strained, in order to make it agree in other respects, where it is evident that there is not a similitude of ideas. For instance, in Isa xl. 6. we read *all flesh is grass*; that is, all mankind are liable to wither and decay, and will wither and decay like grass. But this metaphor would be tortured to a meaning, which, as it is foolish and absurd, we may be sure was never intended by the inspired writer, if we were to say that mankind were like grass, or were grass in colour or shape. What wild, and indeed what wicked abuse, would be made of the Scripture expression concerning our Lord that *he will come as a thief in the night* (Rev xvi 15), if we were not to confine the sense to the suddenness and surprisal of the thief, but should extend it to the temper and designs of the villain who breaks open houses in the night?[1] Hence, though one metaphor may be brought to signify *many* things with respect to some *different* qualities, and *diverse* attributes, it nevertheless is very evident that *that* sense ought chiefly to be attended to, which appears to be designed by the Spirit of God, and which is obviously figured out to us in the nature, form, or use of the thing, from which the metaphor is taken. Thus, Christ is called a *lion* (Rev. v 5) because he is noble, heroic, and invincible; Satan, the grand adversary of souls, is called a lion in

---

[1] Numerous similar instances are given by Glassius, Philologia Sacra, (edit. Dathii,) lib. ii. pp. 918—921.

1 Pet. v. 8. because he is rapacious, roaring, and devouring. And wicked men are termed *lions* in Job iv. 10, 11. and 2 Tim. iv. 17. because they are fierce, outrageous, and cruel to weaker men.

(8) *In the interpretation of figurative expressions generally, and those which particularly occur in the moral parts of Scripture, the meaning of such expressions ought to be regulated by those which are plain and clear.*

All mere maxims, whether plain or figurative, must be understood in a manner consistent with possibility and the rules of humanity. The rule just stated is especially applicable to the right interpretation of Matt. v. 38—42., which enjoins us not to retaliate, but to bear small injuries, and Matt vi. 19. 31. 34., which prohibits thoughtfulness about worldly concerns, which injunctions have been objected to, as being *impracticable* general duties, inconsistent with natural instinct and law, and altogether destructive of society. If, however, the present rule be kept in view, and if we attend to the auditors and occasion of this discourse and to the context, the true sense of the precepts before us will be evident.

The *auditors* were the multitude and the disciples of Christ, as appears from the context both preceding and following the sermon, and also from the conclusion of it.[1] The multitude and the disciples were likewise the auditors of the same, or a similar, discourse recorded by Luke.[2] They were both, therefore, intended for general instruction to all Christians. Particular appropriate instructions to his apostles, and to the seventy during his ministry, Christ gave to them when he sent them forth to preach and work miracles[3]; and upon other occasions when they were in private.[4] After Jesus had been delivering some similar instructions to those in the sermon on the mount, he tells Peter that they were designed for general use.[5] Our Lord, therefore, probably delivered the precepts we are considering in such language as was intelligible to the multitude. Now they, instead of viewing them as "impracticable, inconsistent with natural law, and destructive of society," expressed their great admiration of the wisdom and dignity with which he taught.[6]

The *occasion* of this sermon was, towards the beginning of his ministry, to teach the true nature of the Messiah's kingdom, to give laws suitable to it, and to correct the false and worldly notions of it, which the Jews in general entertained. They were filled with ideas of conquest, and revenge against the Romans, and of enriching themselves by plunder. But Christ, instead of countenancing a vindictive temper, enjoins lenity, forbearance, and kindness to those who injure us. These directions accord with the dispositions which, in the introduction to the sermon, he pronounces to be requisite to true happiness, with his plain injunctions to forgive injuries; with the general strain of his discourses, with the condition of humanity; and with the context, both in Matthew and Luke.[7] In connection with the precepts we are considering, in both Evangelists, "doing to others as we would have them do to us," and, "doing good to our enemies, in imitation of our heavenly Father," are enjoined. These plain comprehensive rules are introduced as including the figurative ones here specified, which point out small injuries. And *trivial* instances are here specified, probably to point out the necessity of extending a lenient and forbearing disposition to small circumstances, in order to pervade every social sentiment and action with the temper of kindness, and to prevent a vindictive spirit from insinuating itself by the smallest avenues into our hearts. That these commands are not to be taken *literally*, as enjoining the particular actions here specified, but the *disposition* of forgiveness and benevolence, is apparent, not only from its being usual in the East to put the action for the disposition[8], and from the manner in which the precepts are introduced, but also from our Lord's own conduct. For he mildly reproved the officer who struck him at his trial.[9] Though he had before *voluntarily* given himself up to the persons who were sent to take him, bade Peter sheath the sword with which he had maimed one of them, and himself miraculously cured him, yet even here he gently reproved them for the *manner* in which they came to apprehend him.[10] These instances of Christ's different behaviour under a variation of circumstances, show that he meant these precepts to be interpreted, according to the nature and reason of the case. He might express them the more strongly in order to contradict Ecclus xii. 4, 5. 7., and similar improper sentiments and practices which at

---

[1] Matt. v. 1, vii. 24. 28.; viii. 1. [2] Luke vi. 17. 47—49.; vii. 1.
[3] Matt. x. Mark vi. 7—11. Luke ix. 1—6., x. 1. 24.
[4] Matt. xiii. 10—23. 36—43. 51. John xiv—xvii.
[5] Luke xii. 41—48 [6] Matt. vii. 28, 29.
[7] Matt. v. 43—48. Luke vi. 27—36.
[8] Matt v. 38. Luke xxii. 36; xix. 13, 14. John xiii. 14, 15. 17.
[9] John xviii. 22, 23.
[10] Mark xiv. 48. Matt. xxvi. 55. Luke xxii. 50—53. John xviii. 10.

that time prevailed in Judæa. Neither did Paul act agreeably to the literal sense of the commands in question !

The injunction, *not to lay up treasures upon earth, but in heaven*[2], according to the Hebrew idiom, means, to prefer heavenly to earthly treasures. The reason given for it is, because, making earthly treasures the chief object, beclouds the moral eye, the guide of life, and is inconsistent with the love and service of God. Christ adds, "therefore take no thought," or as it should be translated, "be not anxious about food, drink, or clothing," but with moderate care only about them, trust the providence of your heavenly Father. Let your first and chief care be to do your duty. Do not anxiously anticipate the cares of the morrow. All this accords with our best natural sentiments, and with the other instructions of our Lord. The auditors, and occasion of the discourse, together with the language and connection in which the directions are given, show these to be the ideas which Jesus meant to convey.[3]

4. Lastly, *in explaining the figurative language of Scripture, care must be taken that we do not judge of the application of characters from modern usage; because the inhabitants of the East have very frequently attached a character to the idea expressed, widely different from that which usually presents itself to our views.*

The inhabitants of the East, from their lively imaginations, very often make use of far-fetched comparisons, and bring together things which, in our judgments, are the most dissimilar. Besides, since the Hebrew mode of living differed greatly from ours, and many things were in use and commended by the Israelites which to us are unknown, — we ought not to be surprised, if there be a very wide difference subsisting between the metaphorical expressions of the Hebrews, and those which are familiar to us, and if they should sometimes appear harsh, and seem to convey a different meaning from that which we are accustomed to receive. Thus, in Deut. xxxiii. 17 the glory of the *tribe* of Joseph is compared to the firstling of a bullock, in like manner Amos (iv 1.) compares the noble women of Israel to the kine of Bashan, and Hosea compares the Israelites to refractory kine that shake off the yoke. The patriarch Jacob, in his prophetic and valedictory address to his children (Gen xlix. 14) in which he foretells their own and their descendants' future condition, terms Issachar a *strong ass*, literally a *strong-boned* or *strong-limbed ass*. Now, if we take these metaphors according to their present sense, we shall greatly err. The ox tribe of animals, whose greatest beauty and strength lie in its horns, was held in very high honour among the antient nations, and was much esteemed on account of its aptitude for agricultural labour hence Moses specially enacts, that the ox should not be muzzled while treading out the corn. The ass tribe, in the East, is robust, and more handsome, as well as much quicker in its pace, than those animals are in our country; and therefore princes and persons of noble birth thought it no degradation to ride on asses. Hence, in the opinion of the inhabitants of the East, it is not reckoned disgraceful to be compared with oxen and asses; nor, if a metaphor be derived from those animals, do they intend to convey the same meaning which we should express by a figure drawn from them. In the comparison of the tribe of Joseph to the firstling of a bullock, the point of resemblance is *strength and power*.[4] In the comparison of the matrons of Samaria to the kine of Bashan, the point of resemblance is *luxury and wantonness, flowing from their abundance*[5]; in the comparison of Issachar to an ass, the point of resemblance is bodily *strength and vigour* for in that animal the Hebrews were accustomed to regard strength, though we usually associate with it the idea of slowness and stupidity.[6]

---

[1] Acts xxiii. 3 ; xvi. 37.   [2] Matt. vi. 19—34. John vi. 27.
[3] Blair on Christ's Sermon on the Mount Newcome's Observations on Christ, p 30. part i chap 1. sect 9.

[4] Mr. Brown has recorded a similar figure, which is in use at the present time at the court of the sultan of Dar Fûr, in Africa, where, during public audiences, a kind of hired encomiast stands at the monarch's right hand, crying out, "See the buffalo, the *offspring of a buffalo*, the bull of bulls, the elephant of a superior strength, the powerful Sultan Abd-el-rachmân-al-rashid!" Journey to Dar Fûr, chap. 1. *in fine*, or Pinkerton's Voyages, vol. xv. p. 122.

[5] The propriety of this comparison will appear when it is recollected that Bashan was celebrated for the richness of its pastures, and its breed of cattle. (See Numb. xxxii. 4 Deut. xxxii 14. and Ezek. xxxix. 18.) This region still retains its antient fertility; and its robust, handsome, and independent inhabitants are such as we may conceive its antient possessors to have been. See Buckingham's Travels in Palestine, pp 325—329.

[6] Bauer, Herm. Sacra, pp. 206. 210—213. 216—221. Ernesti, Instit. Interp. Nov. Test. pp. 99—110. Morus in Ernesti, tom I. pp. 260—300. Jahn, Enchirid. Hermeneut. pp. 100—119.

SECTION II.

ON THE INTERPRETATION OF THE METONYMIES OCCURRING IN THE SCRIPTURES.

Nature of a Metonymy. — 1. *Metonymy of the Cause* — 2. *Metonymy of the Effect.* — 3. *Metonymy of the Subject.* — 4. *Metonymy of the Adjunct, in which the Adjunct is put for the Subject.*

A METONYMY is a trope, by which we substitute one appellation for another [1], as the *cause* for the *effect*, the *effect* for the *cause*, the *subject* for the *adjunct*, or the *adjunct* for the *subject*.

A *Metonymy of the cause* is used in Scripture, when the person acting is put for the thing done, or the instrument by which a thing is done is put for the thing effected, or when a thing or action is put for the effect produced by that action.

A *Metonymy of the effect* occurs, when the effect is put for the efficient cause.

A *Metonymy of the subject* is, when the subject is put for the adjunct, that is, for some circumstance or appendage belonging to the subject: when the thing or place *containing* is put for the thing *contained* or placed; when the *possessor* is put for the thing *possessed*; when the *object* is put for the thing conversant about it; or when the thing signified is put for its sign.

A *Metonymy of the adjunct* is, when that which belongs to any thing serves to represent the thing itself.

1. METONYMY OF THE CAUSE.

I. *Frequently the person acting is put for the thing done.*

1. Thus, *Christ* is put for his *Doctrine* in Rom. xvi 9

Salute Urbanus our helper in Christ, that is, in preaching the doctrines of the Gospel, he having been a fellow-labourer with the apostles. Similar instances occur in 1 Cor. iv. 15. and Eph. iv 20.

2. The *Holy Spirit* is put for His *Effects*: as in 2 Cor. iii. 6.

Who hath made us able ministers of the new covenant, not of the letter but of the spirit; for the letter killeth, but the spirit giveth life. Here, by the word *letter* we are to understand the law written on tables of stone, which required perfect obedience, and which no man can perform because of the corruption of his nature, therefore the law or *letter killeth*, that is, can pronounce nothing but a sentence of condemnation and eternal death against man. But by the *spirit* is intended the saving doctrine of the Gospel, which derives its origin from the Holy Spirit, the Comforter, who teaches or instructs, and prepares man for eternal life. In the same sense, Jesus Christ says, John vi. 63. *The words that I speak, they are spirit and life*, that is, they are from the Spirit of God, and, if received with true faith, will lead to eternal life. A similar mode of expression occurs in Rom. viii. 2. Here, by *the law of the spirit of life* is meant the doctrine of the Gospel, because it is a peculiar instrument of the operation of the Holy Spirit, who, by a divine efficacy, changes the heart, and writes his law there, which now is not only inscribed on tablets or parchments, but also penetrates the very heart of man, and quickens the soul to spiritual motions and actions. [2]

3. The Holy Spirit is put for His *Operations:*

For renewing, Psal. li. 10. Ezek. xxxvi. 26, 27. compared with Eph. iv. 23. Rom.

---

[1] Quinctilian, lib. viii. c. vi. tom. ii. p. 103 ed. Bipont.
[2] Flaccus Illyricus, in Clav. Script. pars 1 col. 1162.

xii. 2. which passages imply nothing less than a radical change, both external or moral, and internal or spiritual, wrought in the soul by the influence of divine grace.

4. The Holy Spirit is put for *the Influences or Gifts of the Spirit*, as in 1 Thess. v. 19. *Quench not the Spirit.*

The similitude is borrowed from the antient altar of burnt-offering, in which the fire was to be kept continually burning. The Holy Spirit is here represented as a *fire*, because it is His province to enlighten, quicken, purify, and refine the soul, and to excite and maintain every pious and devout affection. The Christian, therefore, must not quench the sacred flame of the Holy Spirit in any of his *influences* by committing any act, uttering any word, or indulging any sensual or malevolent disposition, which may provoke Him to withdraw both His gifts and graces. Neither must the Christian extinguish the *gifts of the Spirit*, but keep them in constant exercise, as love, joy, peace, long-suffering, gentleness, goodness, fidelity, meekness, &c. So, in 2 Tim. i 6 Saint Paul's advice, *Stir up the gift of God which is in thee*, means *the gift of the Holy Spirit.* See also 1 Tim. iv. 14.

Again, when our Saviour " exhorts us to ask with confidence for spiritual aid, appealing to the conduct of men, he adds, ' *If ye then, being evil, know how to give good gifts unto your children, how much more shall your heavenly Father give the Holy Spirit to them that ask him ?*' (Luke xi. 13.) By which he would have us distinctly understand that if man, with all his imperfections and all his unkindness, can yet be tender-hearted to his children, and seasonably bestow on them beneficial gifts, much more will God, who is perfection and benignity itself, most assuredly impart the blessing of his Holy Spirit to those who earnestly and anxiously implore divine help, — that help which can illumine what is dark ; can strengthen what is irresolute , can restrain what is violent , can comfort what is afflicted ; in such a manner, and to such a degree, as may be requisite for the soul when struggling under different but difficult temptations, that help, without which man, unassisted, cannot persevere in rectitude of thought and action " [1]

5. *Spirit* also denotes a *Divine Power* or energy, reigning in the soul of a renewed man.

Compare Luke i. 46, 47. with 1 Thess v. 23.; and for other places, where the word *spirit* is put for the *new man* and *spiritual strength*, see Isa xxvi. 9. Ezek. xviii. 31. Matt. xxvi. 41. Rom i 9 1 Cor. v. 3—5. and vi 20. Gal. iii 3, &c

6. More especially the Holy Spirit is put for those *peculiar and extraordinary Gifts of the Spirit*, which, for various uses, whether public or private, spiritual or temporal, are bestowed on man.

Thus, in 2 Kings ii. 9. Elisha earnestly requests of Elijah, *Let a double portion of thy spirit rest upon me*, that is, an extraordinary measure of the gifts of prophecy, and of power in working miracles, which are here called the *portion of the spirit.* See also Numb. xi. 17. 25 Dan v 12 The prophet Daniel *had a more excellent spirit*, that is, a more eminent gift of the spirit, more knowledge, and more understanding.

7. The *Spirit* is also put for revelations, visions, or ecstasies, whether really from the Holy Spirit, or pretended to be so.

Ezek. xxxvii. 1. *The hand of the Lord carried me out in the spirit of the Lord*, that is, by a vision or rapture of spirit 2 Thess. ii 2. *That ye be not shaken in mind, — neither by spirit*, &c. that is, by revelations pretending to come from the spirit. Rev. i. 10 *I was in the spirit*, that is, in an ecstasy and peculiar revelation of the Holy Spirit, as is described in Rev. iv 2. xvii. 3. xxi 10 and 2 Cor. xii. 2. To this head may also be referred those passages, where spirit is put for doctrines, whether really revealed or pretended to be so as in 1 Tim iv. 1. where, by *seducing spirits* are intended false teachers who pretend to receive their doctrine from the Spirit of God; and 1 John iv. 1. where spirit is put for doctrine pretended to be received by the false teachers from God.

8. *Parents* or *Ancestors* are put for their *Posterity;* this mode of speaking is of very frequent occurrence in the Sacred Writings.

Thus *Shem*, *Japhet*, and *Canaan*, are put for their *posterity*, in Gen. ix. 27. Jacob and Israel for the *Israelites*, in Exod v. 2. Numb. xxiii 21. xxiv 5. 17. Deut. xxxiii 28. 1 Kings xviii. 17, 18. Psal. xiv. 7. and cxxxv 4. Amos vii 9. in which verse *Isaac*, as in verse 16. the *House of Isaac*, means the same people. The *seed of Abraham*, Isaac, and Jacob, (*of whom, according to the flesh, Christ came*, Rom. ix. 5.) is put for *Christ*

---

[1] Bishop Huntingford's Charge, intitled " Preparation for the Holy Order of Deacons," p. 14.

I. Sect. II.]   *On the Interpretation of Metonymies.*   381

himself, in Gen. xii. 3. xviii. 18. xxii. 18. xxvi. 4. xxviii. 14. and Gal. iii. 8., as is evident by comparing Acts iii. 25. and Gal. iii. 14. 16. In 2 Chron. xxv. 24. *Obededom* is put for his *descendants*, who, it appears from 1 Chron. xxvi. 15. were porters and keepers of the sacred treasures. In Ezek. xxxiv. 23. *David* is put for *David's Lord*, the illustrious Messiah.

9. The *Writer* or *Author* is put for his *Book* or *Work*:

As in Luke xvi. 29. xxiv. 27. Acts xv. 21. xxi. 21. and 2 Cor. iii. 15. in which passages *Moses* and the *Prophets* respectively mean the *Mosaic and Prophetic Writings*, composed by them under divine inspiration, and transmitted to posterity as the rule of faith.

To this first species of metonymy may be appropriately referred, FIRST, all those passages where the *soul of man* is put for his *life*, which is its effect, as in Gen. ix. 5. (Heb.) Exod. iv. 19. (Heb.) Lev. xvii. 11. Judg. ix. 17. (Heb.) 1 Sam. xxvi. 21. 1 Kings ii. 23. (Heb.) 2 Kings vii. 7. (Heb.) Psal. xxxiii. 19. xxxviii. 12. (Heb.) lvi. 13. Jer. xlv. 5. (Heb.) Lam. v. 9. (Heb.) Jonah ii. 6. (Heb.) Matt. ii. 20. (Gr.) x. 39. (Gr.) xvi. 25. (Gr.) xx. 28. (Gr.) John x. 17. (Gr.) xiii. 37, 38. (Gr.) xv. 13. (Gr.) &c. SECONDLY, those passages also, where the *soul* is put for the *will, affections, and desires*, which are its operations, as in the original of the following passages, where the metonymy is correctly rendered in our authorised version, viz. Gen. xxiii. 8.   Exod. xxiii. 9.   Deut. xxiii. 24. Psalm xvii. 10. xxvii. 12. xli 2. cv. 22.   Prov. xxiii. 2. and John x. 24. (literally, *hold our soul in suspense*). And, THIRDLY, all such passages where the *spirit* (which is frequently synonymous with the soul of man) is used to express the motions or affections of the soul, whether good or evil. Examples of this kind occur in Gen. xlv. 27. Numb. xiv. 24. Judg. viii. 3. where, in the Hebrew, *anger* is *soul*, as is *heart* in Exod. xxiii. 9. 2 Chron. xxi. 16. xxxvi. 22. Psal. lxxvi. 12. lxxvii. 3. Prov. i. 23. xviii. 14. xxix. 1. Eccles. vii. 9. Isa. xxix. 10. xxxvii. 7. Jer. li. 11. Ezek. xiii. 3. Dan. v. 20. Hag. i. 14. Hab. i. 11. Rom. xi. 8. (Gr.) 1 Cor. i. 12. (Gr.) &c.

II. *Sometimes the cause or instrument is put for the thing effected by it.* Thus,

1. The *Mouth*, the *Lips*, and the *Tongue*, are respectively put for the *Speech*.

Thus, Deut. xvii. 6. *by the mouth of two or three witnesses* (that is, their speech or testimony) *shall he that is worthy of death be put to death.* So Deut xix. 15 Matt xviii 16. Prov xxv. 15 *A soft tongue breaketh the bone*, that is, a mild and courteous way of speaking softens the hardest heart and most obstinate resolutions. Similar instances occur in Psal v 9. Prov. x. 20. Jer xviii 18. Acts ii. 4, 11. *Tongue* is also put for the *gift of foreign languages*, in Mark xvi 17. and 1 Cor. xiv. 19. Gen xi 1. *The whole earth was of one language*, (Heb *lip*,) *and of one speech* (Heb. *word*). In the book of Proverbs, the *lip* is very frequently put for *speech* See Prov. xii. 19. 22. xiv. 7. xvii. 7. xviii. 7. 20 Job xii 20. (Marginal renderings.)

2. The *Mouth* is also put for *Commandment* in Gen. xlv. 21. (marginal rendering) (Heb. *mouth*). Numb. iii. 16. 39. xx. 24. xxvii. 14. Deut. i. 26 43. and in Prov. v. 3. the *Palate* (marginal rendering) is also put for *Speech*.

3. The *Throat* is also put for *Loud Speaking*, in Isa. lviii. 1. *Cry aloud* (Heb. with the throat).

4. The *Hand* is ordinarily put for its *Writing*, 1 Cor. xvi. 21. Col. iv. 18.

By the same form of speech also *Labour* is put for *Wages*, or the fruit of labour, Ezek. xxiii 29., and *things that are sold*, for the *price* at which they are sold. Thus, in Matt xxvi. 9. it is said the ointment might have been sold for so much and given to the poor. See likewise Exod. xxi 21. The *sword* is put for *war* or *slaughter*. Exod. v. 3. Lev. xxvi. 6. Psal. cxliv. 10. Isa. i. 20. Jer. xlii. 11. Rom. viii. 35.

5. The *Sword, Famine,* and *Pestilence*, likewise respectively denote the effects of those scourges.

Ezek. vii. 15. *The sword is without, and the pestilence and the famine within;* that is, death and ruin are every where scattered by those terrible agents. So, in Matt. x. 34. *I came not to send peace (or temporal prosperity) but a sword*, that is, variance, death, and persecution. Our Saviour's meaning is, not that his coming was the *necessary* and proper cause of such unhappiness, but that so it should eventually happen on his appearance in our nature; because his kingdom was of another world, and, consequently, opposed to all the designs and interests of the present world. This remark will satisfactorily explain Luke xii. 51—53, where Jesus foretells the effects that would follow from preaching the Gospel.

2. METONYMY OF THE EFFECT.

III. *Sometimes, on the contrary, the effect is put for the cause.*

Thus, *God* is called *Salvation*, that is, the author of it, Exod. xv. 2, our *life* and the length of our days, Deut. xxx 20., our *strength*, Psal. xviii. 1. So, *Christ* is termed *Salvation*, Isa. xlix. 6. Luke ii. 30. — *Life*, John xi. 25. and the *resurrection* in the same place. See also Col iii 4 *Peace*, Eph. ii. 14. So he is said to be *made unto us wisdom, righteousness, sanctification, and redemption*, that is, the *author* of all these, in 1 Cor i. 30. So, in Luke xi 14 compared with Matt ix. 32., a *dumb devil* or demon is one that made the person whom he possessed, dumb. In like manner, the Gospel is called the *power of God unto salvation*, in Rom. i 16, that is, the instrument of his power. *Faith* is called our *Victory*, because by it we overcome the world, 1 John v. 4. That which is the means of sustaining or preserving life is called our *life*, Deut. xxiv. 6. or our *living*, Mark xii 44. Luke viii. 43. and xv. 12. So, *glad tidings*, are such as make glad, Rom. x. 15. A *lively hope* is that which revives or enlightens, 1 Pet. i. 3 — *Wine is a mocker, and strong drink is raging*, Prov. xx. 1., that is, they make men such. There is the same form of speech likewise in Heb vi 1. and ix. 14. where *dead works* are deadly works, that is, such as make men obnoxious to death Deut xxx. 15. *I have set before thee this day life and death*, that is, have clearly showed thee what is the cause and original of each John iii. 19. *This is the condemnation*, that is, the cause of it. Rom. vii 7 *Is the law sin?* that is, the cause of sin, in itself. Rom. viii. 6. *To be carnally minded is death*, that is, its cause, but to be *spiritually minded is life and peace*, or the cause of those blessings A like expression occurs in Rom. vi. 23. *Bread* is put for the *seed* of which bread is made, Eccl xi. 1. *Shame* is put for that which is the cause of it, or the idols worshipped by the Israelites, which proved their shame. Jer. iii. 24. Hos. ix. 10.

3. METONYMY OF THE SUBJECT.

IV. *Sometimes the subject is put for the adjunct, that is, for some circumstance or appendage belonging to or depending upon the subject.*

Thus, the HEART is frequently used for the *will and affections*, as in

Deut. iv. 29. vi. 5. x. 12 Psal ix 1. xxiv. 4. li 10. lxii 10 cv. 25. cxix 10. 32. 112 Prov xxi. 1. xxiii 26. Acts iv. 32 For the *understanding, mind, thoughts,* and *memory*, Deut iv 39 vi. 6 xi 16. 18 xxix. 4. 1 Sam. i 13. 2 Chron vi. 8. Job xxii. 22. Psal iv 4. lxiv. 6. Prov xix 21. xxviii 26. and Luke ii 51. For the *conscience*, 2 Sam. xxiv 10 2 Kings xxii. 19. Eccles vii 22. and 1 John iii. 20. and for the *desires of the soul* expressed in prayer, in Psal. lxii 8 Lam. ii. 19 The *reins* are also frequently put for the *thoughts*, as in Psal vii 9 xxvi. 2 li. 6 lxxiii 21. Prov. xxiii. 16 Jer. xi 20. xvii. 10 and xx. 12. So, the *new* or *inward* man is put for the condition or state of a regenerated soul, to which the *old* or *outward* man is opposed. See Rom. vi. 6. and xii. 2. Eph. iv 22. 24. 2 Cor v 17

V. *Sometimes the place or thing containing denotes that which is contained in such place or thing.*

Thus, the EARTH and the WORLD are frequently put for the *men that* dwell therein, as in Gen. vi. 11. Psal xcvi. 13. Hab. ii. 14. John i. 29. iii. 16, 17. xv. 18 and xvii. 21. 1 Cor. vi. 2. as also in very many passages In like manner, *countries, islands, cities,* and *houses*, are respectively put for their inhabitants, Gen. xli. 57. Psal. c. 1. cv. 38. Isa. xli. 1. 5. xlii. 4. xliii. 3. li. 5. Matt. iii. 5. viii. 34. xi. 21, 22, 23. Gen. vii. 1. Exod. i.

21. 2 Sam vii. 11. 1 Chron. x. 6. Acts x. 2 1 Tim. iii. 4. Heb. xi. 7. So the *houses* of *Levi* and *Israel* denote their several families. Exod ii 1. Ezek. iii. 1. The *basket*, Deut. xxviii. 5 17. is the fruit of the busket; a *table*, Psal xxiii 5. lxix. 22. and lxxviii. 19 denotes the meat placed on it, the *cup*, the wine or other liquor in it, Jer. xlix. 12. Ezek xxiii. 32. Matt. xxvi 27, 28. Mark xiv. 23. Luke xxii 17. 20. 1 Cor. x. 16. 21. and xi. 26, 27. ; *ships*, Isa xxiii. 1. 14. the men in them, the *grave*, those who are buried in it, as in Isa. xxxviii. 18 compared with verse 19. and in Psal. vi. 5. In like manner *heaven* is put for God himself, in Psal. lxxiii. 9. Matt xxi. 25. Luke xx. 4. and xv. 18

VI. *Sometimes the possessor of a thing is put for the thing possessed.*

Thus, Deut. ix. 1. *To possess nations greater and mightier than thyself*, means to possess the countries of the Gentiles. See also Psal. lxxix. 7. where *Jacob* means the land of the Israelites In like manner, the name *of God* is put for the oblations made to him Josh xiii. 33 with verse 14 Josh xviii. 7 and Deut. x. 9 *Christ* is put for his church (or believers, who are termed his peculiar people, Tit. ii. 14. 1 Pet. ii. 9) in Matt. xxv. 35 explained in verse 40. 1 Cor xii 12 ; and the afflictions of Christ are put for the afflictions of the faithful, in Col i. 24

VII. *Frequently the object is put for that which is conversant about it.*

Thus *glory* and *strength* are put for the celebration of the divine glory and strength, in Psal. viii. 2. explained by Matt. xxi. 16. , see also Psal. xcvi 7, 8 A *burthen* is a prediction of divine judgments or punishment about to be inflicted on sinners. Isa. xiii. 1. xv. 1. xvii 1. xix 1. xxi 1. xxii 1. and xxiii 1. *Promise* is put for faith which receives the gracious promise of God, in Rom ix 8. and Gal. iv. 28. *Sin* denotes a sacrifice for sin or sin-offering, Gen iv. 7 Exod xxx. 14. (Heb. *sin*) Lev. x 17. (Heb *sin*) Hos. iv. 8. Isa liii. 10. (Heb, *sin*) and 2 Cor. v. 21 [1]

VIII. *Sometimes the thing signified is put for the sign.*

So, the *strength of God*, in 1 Chron xvi 11 and Psal cv. 4 is the *ark*, which was a sign and symbol of the divine presence and strength, whence it is expressly called the *ark of the strength of God* in Psal cxxxii. 8 Thus, in Ezek. vii. 27. *desolation* denotes a mourning garment as a token of it.

IX. *When an action is said to be done, the meaning frequently is, that it is declared or permitted, or foretold that it shall be done.*

Thus, in the original of Lev. xiii. 3. the priests shall look on him *and pollute* him, in our version, *shall pronounce him unclean* or polluted. The original of Ezek. xiii. 22. is, by quickening or enlivening him, in our translation it is rendered by *promising him life* So Gen. xli. 13 *me he restored*, means, foretold or declared that I should be restored. Jer. iv. 10 *Ah Lord God ! thou hast greatly deceived this people*, that is, hast permitted them to be deceived by their false prophets Ezek. xiii 19. *to slay the souls which should not die*, denotes the prophesying falsely that they should die. So Jer. i. 10. *I have set thee over the nations to root out and to pull down*, that is, to prophesy or declare them pulled down Ezek xx. 25, 26 *I gave them statutes which were not good, and polluted them in their own gifts*, that is, I gave them up to themselves, and permitted them to receive such statutes of the heathen, and suffered them to pollute themselves in those very gifts, which, by the law, they were to dedicate to my service, and dealt with them accordingly. Hos vi 5. *I have hewn them by the prophets*, or foretold that they should be hewn or slain. So in Acts x 15 the original rendering is, *what God hath cleansed, that do not thou pollute* (compare Matt xv. 11), that is, as in our version, *call not thou common or defiled* Hence in Matt. xvi. 19. *whatsoever thou shalt bind or loose on earth,* &c. means whatsoever thou shalt declare to be my will on earth shall be confirmed in heaven. And in like manner the meaning of John xx 23. is, whose sins ye shall declare to be remitted or retained by the word of God [2] Matt. vi. 13. *lead us not into temptation,* that is, suffer us not to be overcome by temptation.

X. *Further, an action is said to be done, when the giving of an occasion for it is only intended.*

---

[1] Dr. A. Clarke, in his commentary on this verse, has adduced *one hundred and eight* instances from the Old and New Testaments, in which the word *sin* is put for a sin-offering · Dr. Whitby (in loc) has specified only twenty-two examples.

[2] On a forced interpretation of these two clauses (among others) has the papal church erected the dangerous notion that priests may grant particular absolution to individuals See it briefly but ably confuted in Bishop Porteus's Confutation of the Errors of the Church of Rome, pp. 44, 45.

Thus, the literal rendering of Jer. xxxvii. 23. is, *thou shalt burn this city*, that is (as translated in our version), shalt *cause it to be burnt*. Hence Jeroboam is recorded in 1 Kings xiv. 16. *to have made Israel to sin*, that is, to have occasioned it, by his example and command. In Acts i. 18. Judas is said to have *purchased a field*, that is, occasioned it to be purchased by the money which he cast down in the temple. Rom. xiv 15. *destroy not him*, that is, be not the cause or occasion of his destruction And in 1 Cor. vii 16 *whether thou shalt save thy husband*, means, whether thou shalt be the cause of his conversion, and, consequently, of his salvation.

---

4. *METONYMY OF THE ADJUNCT, IN WHICH THE ADJUNCT IS PUT FOR THE SUBJECT.*

XI. *Sometimes the accident, or that which is additional to a thing, is put for its subject in kind.*

The abstract is put for the concrete. So *grey hairs*, (Heb. *hoariness*, or *grey-headedness*) in Gen. xlii. 38. denote me, who am now an old man, grey and decrepit with age So also, *days*, and *multitude of years*, in Job xxxii. 7. are old men The *strength of Israel*, 1 Sam. xv 29 is the strong God of Israel. *Circumcision* and *uncircumcision*, in Rom. iii 30. signify the *circumcised* and *uncircumcised* The *election*, Rom. xi. 7 is the elect *Abomination*, in Gen xlvi. 34 and Luke xvi. 15 is an *abominable thing* A *curse*, Gal. iii 13. is accursed. *Light* and *darkness*, Eph. v 8. denote the enlightened and the ignorant.

XII. *Sometimes the thing contained is put for the thing containing it, and a thing deposited in a place for the place itself.*

Thus, Gen. xxviii. 22. means this place, where I have erected a pillar of stone, shall be God's house. Josh xv 19. Springs of water denote some portion of land, where there may be springs. Matt. ii. 11. *Treasures* are the cabinets or other vessels containing them. A similar expression occurs in Psal cxxxv 7. *Outer darkness*, in Matt. xxii 13 means *hell*, the place of outer darkness. Matt xxv 10 *Marriage* denotes the place where the nuptial feast was to be celebrated. Mark iii 11. *Unclean spirits* are men possessed by them. In Luke vi. 12. and Acts xvi 13 16. *Prayer* evidently means the place of prayer.[1] Rev viii 3 *Golden incense*, λιβανωτον, means a golden censer, and so it is rendered in our authorised English version.

XIII. *Time is likewise put for the things which are done or happen in time.*

This is to be understood both of the word *time* itself, and of names expressing portions of time, whether divided naturally or by human institution Thus, in 1 Chron. xii. 32. xxix. 30 Esth. i. 13 2 Tim. iii. 1. Deut. iv. 32. Mark xiv 35. and John xii 27. *times, day*, and *hour* respectively denote the transactions that took place in them. Again, *days* are said to be good or evil, according to the events which happen in them, as in Gen xlvii. 9. Eccles. vii 10. and Eph v. 16.; and that is called a person's day, in which any thing notorious or remarkable befalls him, whether it be good, as in Hos. i 11 and Luke xix. 42. 44 , or evil, as in Job xviii. 20. Psal cxxxvii 7. Ezek xxii 4. Obad 12. Micah vii 4 Psal xxxvii 13. *The days of the Lord*, in Job xxiv 1. Isa. xiii 6. Joel i. 15. and ii 1, 2. Amos v 20. Zeph i 14—16 18 and ii 2. respectively denote the days when divine punishments were to be inflicted, and hence, by way of eminence, the *day of the Lord* is appropriated to the *day of judgment*, in Joel ii 31. Acts ii 20. 1 Cor. i. 8 2 Thess ii 2, &c. In the same manner, the *harvest* and *summer* are put for the fruits gathered at those seasons Deut xxiv. 19. Isa xvi. 9 [Jer xl 10. Amos viii 1, 2. 2 Sam. xvi 2. in which three passages, as also in Isa xvi 9 the Hebrew is only *summer*] And also the *passover* is put for the lamb which was slain and eaten on that solemn festival Exod xii. 21. 2 Chron xxx. 17. Mark xiv. 12 14. Matt. xxvi. 17—19. Luke xxii 8 11 13. 15.

XIV. *In the Scriptures, things are sometimes named or described according to appearances, or to the opinion formed of them by men, and not as they are in their own nature.*

---

[1] Προσευχη. From 1 Macc. vii 37. it appears that the Jews had a similar place of prayer at Mizpah. See Wolfius, Rosenmuller, Schindler, and others, on Luke vi. 12.

Thus, Hananiah, the opponent of Jeremiah, is called a prophet, not because he was truly one, but was *reputed* to be one, Jer. xxviii. 1, 5 10. In Ezek. xxi. 3. the *righteous* mean those who had the semblance of piety, but really were not righteous. So in Matt. ix 13. Christ says, *I am not come to call the righteous,* (that is, such as are so in their own estimation,) *but sinners to repentance* See further Luke xviii. 9 and Rom. x 2, 3, &c.

In Luke ii. 48. Joseph is called the *father* of Christ, and in v. 41 is mentioned as one of his parents, because he was *reputed* to be his father, as the same evangelist states in ch iii. 23.[1] Compare John vi 42, &c. The preaching of the Gospel is in 1 Cor. i. 21. termed *foolishness*, not that it was really such, but was accounted to be so by its opponents. In like manner false teaching is called *another Gospel* in Gal. i. 6 and Epimenides, the Cretan philosopher, is termed a prophet in Tit i. 12 because his countrymen regarded him as such, and after his death offered sacrifices to him[2]

His enemies shall lick the dust, Psal. lxxii 9 means that they shall prostrate themselves so low towards the earth, that they shall seem to lick the dust. Similar expressions occur in Isa xlix. 23 Micah vii 17, &c. The phrase, *coming from a far country, and from the end of heaven,* in Isa xiii 5 is taken from the opinion which antiently obtained, and was founded on the appearance to the eye, viz that the *heavens* are not spherical but hemispherical, ending at the extremities of the earth, upon which the extremities of heaven appear to rest Hence the *ends of the earth* denote the remotest places. The same phrase occurs in Deut. iv 32. and xxx. 4. Neh. i. 9. Matt xxiv. 31.

XV. *Sometimes the action or affection, which is conversant about any object, or placed upon it, is put for the object itself.*

Thus, the *Senses* are put for the *objects* perceived by them, as *hearing* for doctrine or speech, in Isa xxviii 9 (marg. rend.) and liii 1. (Heb.) In John xii 38 and Rom. x 16 the Greek word ακοη, translated *report*, literally means hearing, and so it is rendered in Gal iii 2 5 Hearing is also put for fame or rumour in Psal. cxii 7 (Heb) Ezek. vii 26. Obad 1 Hab iii 2 (Heb.) Matt iv 24. xiv. 1. and xxiv 6 Mark i. 28 and xiii. 7, &c. The *Eye*, in the original of Numb xi. 7. Lev xiii 55. Prov. xxiii. 31. Ezek i. 4. viii. 2. and x. 9 is put for colours which are seen by the eye. *Faith* denotes the doctrine, received and believed by faith, in Acts vi 7. Gal. i 23. and iii. 23. 25 Eph. iv 5. 1 Tim iv. 1 Tit i 13. Jude iii Rev. ii. 13. — *Hope*, in Psal lxv. 5 and lxxi. 5. Jer. xiv 8. and xvii 7. 13 is God, in whom we have hope, or place our confidence. *Hope* also denotes Christ, or the benefits which we receive by him, in Acts xxvi 6—8. xxviii. 20. Col. i. 27 1 Tim. i. 1. *Hope* is sometimes also put for *men*, in whom we confide, or from whom we expect some good, as in Isa. xx. 5, 6. and for the thing hoped for, as in Prov. xiii. 12 Rom. viii. 24 and Gal. v. 5. in which last place *the hope of righteousness by faith* means eternal life, which is promised to the just by faith, and also in Tit ii. 13 — *Love* is put for the object of affection, Jer. ii. 33. and xii. 7. (marginal rendering) — *Desire,* Ezek. xxiv. 16. 21. is the thing desired. In like manner, the *lust* or desire of the eyes, 1 John ii. 16. is the object of the eyes which we eagerly desire. — So, *Fear* is put for the object that is feared, in Psal. liii. 5. Prov. i 26. Isa. viii. 13.

XVI. *Sometimes the sign is put for the thing signified.*

Thus, *Sovereign Power* and authority are expressed by a *Sceptre, Crown, Diadem, Throne,* and *Shutting and opening without resistance* in Gen. xlix. 10. Isa xxii. 22. Ezek xxi. 26 Zech x 11 and Rev. iii 7. War is denoted by bows, spears, chariots, and swords, Psal xlvi. 9. Lam. v 9 Ezek xxi. 3, 4. Matt. x. 34 So, to lift up the hand is sometimes to swear, Gen xiv 22 Deut xxxii. 40 , and sometimes to pray, Lam iii. 41 1 Tim ii 8. In like manner, to stretch forth the hand is to call for audience, Psal. xlv. 20 Prov. i 24

To *kiss* the hand, or to kiss another, is to yield reverence, Job xxxi. 27. 1 Sam. x. 1. Psal. ii 12. 1 Kings xix. 18 Hos. xiii. 2. To *bow the knee*, is to worship, Isa. xlv. 23. Phil. ii 10. Eph. iii. 14. To *give the hand*, or to *strike hands*, is to swear, join in *fellowship*, engage or become surety *for another*, Ezek xvii. 18. Gal ii 9. Job xvii. 3. Prov. vi. 1. To *put on sackcloth*, is to *mourn*, Psal lxix. 11. To *beat swords into plough-shares, and spears into pruning hooks* is *to live in peace and security,* Isa ii. 4.

---

[1] A similar mode of speech occurs in the Iliad, where Homer repeatedly calls Menelaus and Agamemnon, the sons of Atreus, though they were in reality the children of his son, Plisthenes, and, consequently, the grandchildren of Atreus. In consequence of their father's death, while they were very young, they were educated by their grandfather; who, from his attention to them, was universally acknowledged their protector and father. Hence arose their appellation of Atridæ, or sons of Atreus.

[2] Diog. Laert. lib. i. c. 10. § 11. tom. i. p. 123. ed. Longolii.

XVII. *Lastly, the names of things are often put for the things themselves.*

Thus, the *Name* of God denotes the *Almighty* himself, Psal. xx. 1. cxv. 1. Prov xviii. 10. Isa. xxx 27. Jer. x. 25. So, in Joel ii. 32. Acts ii. 21. and Rom. x. 13. the *name of the Lord* denotes Jesus Christ Names are likewise put for persons, Acts i. 15. Rev. iii. 4. and xi 13 (Gr) In like manner we find, that names are given to persons to express their state or condition, although they are not ordinarily called by such names, as in Isa i 26. *Thou shalt be called the city of righteousness* or justice, that is, thou shalt be so. Similar expressions occur in Isa. lxii. 4. and Jer. iii. 17.

SECTION III.

ON THE INTERPRETATION OF SCRIPTURE METAPHORS.

Nature of a Metaphor. — Sources of Scripture Metaphors. — I. The Works of Nature. — II. The Occupations, Customs, and Arts of Life. —III. Sacred Topics, or Religion and Things connected with it. — IV. Sacred History.

A METAPHOR is a trope, by which a word is diverted from its proper and genuine signification to another meaning, for the sake of comparison, or because there is some analogy between the similitude and the thing signified. Of all the figures of rhetoric, the metaphor is that which is most frequently employed, not only in the Scriptures, but likewise in every language; for, independently of the pleasure which it affords, it enriches the mind with *two* ideas at the *same* time, the *truth* and the *similitude*. Two passages will suffice to illustrate this definition. In Deut. xxxii. 42. we read, *I will make mine arrows drunk with blood, and my sword shall devour flesh*. Here, the *first* metaphor is borrowed from excessive and intemperate drinking, to intimate the very great effusion of blood, and the exceeding greatness of the ruin and destruction which would befall the disobedient Israelites: the *second* metaphor is drawn from the voracious appetite of an hungry beast, which in a lively manner presents to the mind the impossibility of their escaping the edge of the sword, when the wrath of God should be provoked. Again, in Psal. cxxxix. 2. we read, *Thou understandest my thoughts afar off.* In this verse the metaphor is taken from the prospect of a distant object: but in a proper sense the phrase assures us, that Jehovah, by his prescience, knows our thoughts, before they spring up in our souls.

In order to understand metaphors aright, it should be observed that the foundation of them consists in a likeness or similitude between the thing from which the metaphor is drawn, and that to which it is applied. When this resemblance is exhibited in one or in a few expressions, it is termed a single metaphor. When it is pursued with a variety of expressions, or there is a continued assemblage of metaphors, it is called an *allegory*. When it is couched in a short sentence, obscure and ambiguous, it is called a *riddle*. If it be conveyed in a short saying only, it is a *proverb*; and if the metaphorical representation be delivered in the form of a history, it is a *parable*. When the resemblance is far-fetched, — as *to see a voice*, (Rev. i. 12.)

it is termed a *catachresis*. This last-mentioned species of figure, however, is of less frequent occurrence in the Scriptures than any of the preceding.

The metaphor is of indispensable necessity in the Scriptures; for the sacred writers, having occasion to impart divine and spiritual things to man, could only do it by means of terms borrowed from sensible and material objects, as all our knowledge begins at our senses. Hence it is, especially in the poetical and prophetical parts of the Old Testament, that the sentiments, actions, and corporeal parts, not only of man, but also of inferior creatures, are ascribed to God himself; it being otherwise impossible for us to form any conception of his pure essence and incommunicable attributes. The various sources, whence the sacred writers have drawn their metaphors, have been discussed at great length by Bishop Lowth [1], and his annotator Michaelis, and also by Glassius [2]; from whose elaborate works the following observations are abridged. The sources of Scripture metaphors may be classed under the four following heads, viz. natural, artificial, sacred, and historical.

I. *The works of nature furnish the first and most copious, as well as the most pleasing source of images in the Sacred Writings.*

Thus the images of *light* and *darkness* are commonly made use of, in all languages, to denote prosperity and adversity; and an uncommon degree of light implies a proportionate degree of joy and prosperity, and *vice versâ*. Isa. xiii. 10. lix. 9. lx. 19, 20. xxx 26. Jer. xv. 9. Amos viii. 9. Micah iii. 6. Joel ii. 10. The same metaphors are also used to denote knowledge and ignorance. Isa. viii 20 ix. 2. Matt. iv. 16. Eph. v. 8. The sun, moon, and stars, figuratively represent kings, queens, and princes or rulers, as in Isa. xxiv. 23. Ezek. xxxii. 7.

"The lights of heaven," says a late pious and learned writer[3], "in their order are all applied to give us conceptions of God's power and the glory of his kingdom. In the lxxxivth Psalm (verse 11.) the Lord is said to be a sun and shield; a *sun* to give *light* to his people, and a *shield* to protect them from the power of darkness. Christ, in the language of the prophet, is the *sun* of righteousness; who, as the natural sun revives the grass and renews the year, brings on the acceptable year of the Lord, and is the great restorer of all things in the kingdom of grace, shining with the new light of life and immortality to those, who once sat in darkness and in the shadow of death. And the church has warning to receive him under this glorious character. *Arise, shine; for thy light is come, and the glory of the Lord is risen upon thee!* (Isa. lx. 1.) When he was manifested to the eyes of men, he called himself the *light* of the world, and promised to give the same light to those that follow him. In the absence of Christ as the personal light of the world, his place is supplied by the light of the Scripture, which is still a lamp unto our feet, and a light unto our paths. The word of prophecy is *as a light shining in a dark place;* and as we study by the light of a lamp, so we must give heed to this light, as if we would see things to come.

"The moon is used as an emblem of the church, which receives its light from Christ, as the moon from the sun: therefore the renovation

---

[1] In his Lectures on Hebrew Poetry, Lect vi.—ix
[2] Philologia Sacra, lib. ii. pp 916—1243. ed. Dathii
[3] The Rev. W. Jones, Lectures on the figurative Language of Scripture, Lect. ii. Works, vol iii. p. 25

of the moon signifies the renovation of the church. The angels or ruling ministers in the seven churches of Asia, (Rev. ii. and iii.) are signified by the *seven stars*, because his ministers hold forth the word of life, and their light shines before men in this mortal state, as the stars give light to the world in the night season; of which light Christians in general partake, and are therefore called children of the light."

Nothing is more grateful to the inhabitants of the East than springs, rivers, and rain: for, as showers rarely fall in their countries, the grass and flowers of the field become consumed by the intolerable heat, unless watered by showers or canals. Hence, flowing springs, copious showers, and nightly dews, which fertilise the fields, furnish them with a variety of pleasing images. Isa. xli. 18. and xxxv. 1. 6, 7. The blessings of the Gospel are delineated under the metaphors of dew, Isa. xxvi. 19., moderate rains, Hos. vi. 3., gentle streams and running waters, Isa. xxvii. 3. and xliv. 3. On the other hand, no metaphor is more frequent than that by which sudden and great calamities are expressed under the figure of a deluge of waters. With this metaphor the Hebrews appear to have been extremely familiar, as if it were directly taken from the nature and state of their country. Immediately before their eyes was the river Jordan[1], which annually overflowed its banks: for the snows of Lebanon and the neighbouring mountains, being melted in the beginning of summer, the waters of the river were often suddenly augmented by the descending torrents. The whole country, also, being mountainous, was exposed to frequent floods after the great periodical tempests of rain. To this David alludes, Psal. xlii. 7. Immoderate rains, hail, floods, inundations, and torrents, denote judgments and destruction, Isa. viii. 7. Jer. xlvii. 2. Ezek. xxxviii. 22.

To the class of metaphors derived from natural objects we may refer the *anthropopathy*, a metaphor by which things belonging to creatures, and especially to man, are ascribed to God, and the *prosopopœia* or personification, that is, the change of things to persons. Both these figures are nearly allied to the metaphor, and still more to the metonymy; but they are noticed in this place, as being upon the whole the most convenient arrangement.

1. In the consideration of *anthropopathies*, the two following important rules must be constantly kept in mind; viz.

[i.] *That we understand them in a way and manner suitable to the nature and majesty of the Almighty, refining them from all that imperfection with which they are debased in the creatures, and so attribute them to the Deity.*

Thus, when the members of a human body are ascribed to God, we are not to conceive of him as a venerable old man, sitting gravely in heaven to observe and censure the things done on earth; but must understand those perfections, of which such members in us are the instruments. The *eye*, for instance, being that member by which we discern or observe any thing, is employed to denote God's *perfect and exact knowledge of all things*, Job xxxiv. 21. Psal. xi 4. and Heb iv. 13., as also *his watchful providence*, Deut. xi. 12 1 Kings ix. 3. Psal xxxiv 15. In like manner, *ears* are attributed to him, to signify his *gracious acceptance* of his people's prayers, Psal. xxxi. 2 or the *exact notice* which he takes of the sins of others, James v. 4. By his *arm* we are to understand his *power and strength*, Exod. xv 16 which is also expressed by his *right hand*, Exod. xv 6. and Psal cxviii. 15, 16. So, his *work* is expressed by his fingers, Exod. viii. 19 and Psal. viii 3. and his *love* and compassion by his *bowels*, Isa lxiii. 15 Jer. xxxi. 20. Luke i. 78., *through the bowels of the mercy of our God* (διὰ σπλαγχνα), *whereby the day-spring from on high hath visited us* There are a thousand similar instances in the Scriptures

---

[1] Josh iii. 15. 1 Chron. xii. 15. Ecclus. xxiv. 26.

I. Sect. III.] *Interpretation of Scripture Metaphors.* 389

[ii.] Further when human affections are attributed to Jehovah, we must be careful not to interpret them in a manner that shall imply the least imperfection in Him; but must thereby conceive, (1.) Either *a pure act of his will, free from all perturbation to which men are liable*, or else, (2.) The effect of such human affections, the antecedent being put for the consequent, that is, one thing being expressed while another thing is understood, which is usually its effect, or at least follows it — a figure of very frequent occurrence in the Sacred Writings.

Thus, when God is said to repent, we are not to imagine any change of mind in Him with whom there is no variableness or shadow of turning, or any sorrow or trouble that is inconsistent with his perfect happiness, but, either his purpose to undo what he has done, or desist from what he is doing, which are the ordinary effects of repentance in man so that the change is not in the disposition of the Supreme Mind, but in the dispensations of his providence: as in Gen vi. 6 1 Sam. xv. 11. 35. 2 Sam. xxiv. 16. Psalm cvi. 45 Again, God is said in very many passages to be *angry*, to have *fury*, &c. in order to make us apprehend how much he hates sin, and will punish sinners. The same remark will apply to other affections which are attributed to Him

In a similar manner are we to understand all those passages in which *human actions* are ascribed to God, as in Gen xviii. 21. To *go down* and see what is done in Sodom, is to regard well, and proceed justly, orderly, and leisurely, to their punishment, though in the divine promise to *be with* Jacob, Gen xxviii. 15 it means that the divine favour and protection should accompany him all the way To *search the heart* and *try the reins*, is to discern exactly, as in Psal vii. 9 and Jer. xvii 10. — Lastly, *human relations* are likewise ascribed to God, to express the *properties* of such relations thus, he is called a *King*, Psal xcv 3. a *Father*, Psal. ciii 13. Rom. viii. 15. a *Husband*, Isa. liv. 5. Hosea ii. 19. a *Shepherd*, Psal xxiii, 1. to express his power and authority, his love, pity, tender care, and watchful providence.

2. Of the *prosopopœia* or personification, there are two kinds; one, when actions and character are attributed to fictitious, irrational, or even inanimate objects; the other, when a probable but fictitious speech is assigned to a real character:

[i.] The former, Bishop Lowth remarks, evidently partakes of the nature of the metaphor, and is by far the boldest of that class of figures: it is most frequently and successfully introduced by the sacred writers.

In Psalm lxxxv. 10 how admirable is the personification of the divine attributes!
Mercy and truth are met together;
Righteousness and peace have kissed each other.

How just, elegant, and splendid does it appear, if applied only (according to the literal sense) to the restoration of the Jewish nation from the Babylonish captivity ! But if we consider it in a most sacred and mystical sense, which is not obscurely shadowed under the ostensible image, viz. that of the method of redemption by the sacrifice and mediation of Jesus Christ, in which the divine perfections were so harmoniously displayed, it is beyond measure grand and elevated Again, what can be more sublime or graceful than the personification of wisdom, so frequently introduced in the Proverbs of Solomon, particularly in chapter viii verses 22—31 She is not only exhibited as the directress of human life and morals, as the inventress of arts, as the dispenser of honours and riches, as the source of true felicity, but also as the eternal daughter of the omnipotent Creator, and as the eternal associate in the divine counsels. Similar passages, exquisitely imagined, and from the boldness of the fiction, extremely forcible, occur in Job xvni. 13 xxviii. 22. Isa v. 14. xlvii. 1. 5. Lam. l, 1, 6. 17. Jer xlvii. 6, 7. Hos xiii. 14. and 1 Cor. xv. 54.[1]

[ii.] The second kind of prosopopœia, by which a probable but fictitious speech is assigned to a real person — though less calculated to excite admiration and approbation by its novelty, boldness, and variety, than the former, — is nevertheless possessed of great force, evidence, and authority. It would, as Bishop Lowth remarks, be an infinite task to specify every instance in the sacred poems, which on this occasion might

---

[1] The late benevolent and learned Mr. Gilpin has pointed out many very striking personifications and other metaphorical allusions used by Saint Paul. See his Sermons, vol iv. p. 405. et seq.

be referred to as worthy of notice; or to remark the easy, natural, bold, and sudden personifications; the dignity, importance, and impassioned severity of the characters. It would be difficult to describe the energy of that eloquence which is attributed to Jehovah himself, and which appears so suitable in all respects to the Divine Majesty; or to display the force and beauty of the language which is so admirably and peculiarly adapted to each character; the probability of the fiction; and the excellence of the imitation.

One example, therefore, must suffice for the present; one more perfect it is not possible to produce. It is expressive of the eager expectation of the mother of Sisera, from the inimitable ode of the prophetess Deborah (Judg. v. 28—30.)

The first sentences exhibit a striking picture of maternal solicitude, both in words and actions; and of a mind suspended and agitated between hope and fear

> Through the window she looked and cried out,
> The mother of Sisera, through the lattice:
> Wherefore is his chariot so long in coming?
> Wherefore linger the wheels of his chariot?

Immediately, impatient of his delay, she anticipates the consolations of her friends, and her mind being somewhat elevated, she boasts with all the levity of a fond female —

> (Vain in her hopes, and giddy with success,)
> Her wise ladies answer her;
> Yea, she returns answer to herself:
> Have they not found? — Have they not divided the spoil?

Let us now observe how well adapted every sentiment, every word, is to the character of the speaker. She takes no account of the slaughter of the enemy, of the valour and conduct of the conqueror, of the multitude of the captives, but

> Burns with a female thirst of prey and spoils.

Nothing is omitted which is calculated to attract and engage the passions of a vain and trifling woman — slaves, gold, and rich apparel. Nor is she satisfied with the bare enumeration of them, she repeats, she amplifies, she heightens every circumstance, she seems to have the very plunder in her immediate possession; she pauses and contemplates every particular —

> Have they not found? — Have they not divided the spoil?
> To every man a damsel, yea a damsel or two?
> To Sisera a spoil of divers colours?
> A spoil of needlework of divers colours,
> A spoil for the neck of divers colours of needlework on either side.

To add to the beauty of this passage, there is also an uncommon neatness in the versification, great force, accuracy, and perspicuity in the diction, the utmost elegance in the repetitions, which, notwithstanding their apparent redundancy, are conducted with the most perfect brevity. In the end, the fatal disappointment of female hope and credulity, tacitly insinuated by the sudden and unexpected apostrophe,

> So let all thine enemies perish, O JEHOVAH!

is expressed more forcibly by this very silence of the person who was just speaking, than it could possibly have been by all the powers of language.

But whoever wishes to understand the full force and excellence of this figure, as well as the elegant use of it in the Hebrew ode, must apply to Isaiah, whom we may justly pronounce to be the sublimest of poets. Bishop Lowth considers his fourteenth chapter, as the grandest specimen of that prophet's poetry, and as exemplifying almost every form of the prosopopœia, and indeed of all that constitutes the sublime in composition. An examination of this passage will be found in Vol. IV. Part I. Chap. V. Sect. IV. §IV.

II. *The Hebrews derived many of their figures from the ordinary occupations and customs of life, as well as from such arts as were practised at that time.*

I. Sect. III.]   *Interpretation of Scripture Metaphors.*   391

This source, indeed, is common to all nations; and in proportion as they are more polished, and cultivate more numerous arts, they are supplied with a greater variety of images. The whole course and method of common and domestic life among the antient Hebrews was simple in the highest degree. There did not exist that variety of studies and pursuits, of arts, conditions, and employments, which afterwards obtained among other nations. The Hebrews were a nation of husbandmen and shepherds: the patriarchs were possessed of great flocks and herds which they tended, though their descendants afterwards applied themselves to agriculture. Every Israelite, on the conquest of Canaan, received his allotted portion of land, which he cultivated, and which, as it could not be alienated by sale, descended without diminution to his posterity, who enjoyed unmolested the produce of his land and labour. Hence, very numerous metaphors in the Sacred Writings are derived from pastoral and rural occupations. Thus, kings are said to feed their people, who again are compared to a flock of sheep, which the shepherd conducts to pasture, and guards from danger. It would extend the limits of this section too far, to instance particularly with what embellishments of diction, derived from one low and trivial object (as it may appear to some) — the barn or threshing-floor — the sacred writers have added a lustre to the most sublime, and a force to the most important subjects. Yet the following passages we cannot omit to notice, on account of their uncommon force and beauty: —

Thus, Jehovah threshes out the heathen, and tramples them beneath his feet. (Hab. iii. 12.) He delivers the nations to Israel to be beaten in pieces by an indented flail, or to be crushed by their brazen hoofs (Joel iii. 14 (Heb.) Jer. li. 33. Isa. xxi. 10. Mic. iv. 13.) He scatters his enemies like chaff upon the mountains, and disperses them with the whirlwind of his indignation (Psal. lxxxiii. 13—15. Isa. xvii. 13.) But nothing can surpass the magnificent delineation of the Messiah coming to take vengeance on his adversaries expressed by imagery taken from the wine-press, which is of frequent occurrence with the sacred poets, and which no other poet has presumed to introduce. See Isa. lxiii. 1—3.

The pastoral and rural allusions in the New Testament are almost equally numerous with those of the Old Testament. Thus the world is compared to a *field*, the children of the kingdom to the *wheat*, and the children of the wicked to *tares*. (Matt. xiii. 38.) The end of the world is the *harvest*, and the angels are *reapers*. (Matt. xiii. 39.) A preacher of the word is the *sower*. (Matt. xiii. 3.) The word of God is the *seed*. The heart of man is the *ground* (Luke viii. 15. Heb. vi. 7.) The cares, riches, and pleasures of life are the *thorns*. (Luke viii. 14. Heb. vi. 8.) The preparation of the heart by repentance is *ploughing and breaking up the fallow ground* (Hos. x. 12.) Death, which cuts down the fairest flowers of the field, is a *mower* (Psal. xc. 6.) The minister, who serves under God in his husbandry, is the *labourer*. (Matt. ix. 37, 38. 1 Cor. iii. 9.) The wicked are *stubble*. (Isa. xlvii. 14.) And the temptations and trials of the godly are the *sifting of the wheat*. (Luke xxii. 31.)[1]

III. *Sacred Topics, that is to say, Religion, and Things connected with it, furnished many images to the sacred writers.*

Numerous and diversified sacred rites were enjoined to the Israelites by Moses, and their religious worship was conducted with great pomp and splendour.

Thus, the images derived from the temple and its magnificent service chiefly serve to denote the glory of the Christian church, the excellency of its worship, God's favour towards it, and his constant presence with it: the prophets speaking to the Jews in terms accommodated to their own ideas, as in Ezek. xxxvi. 25, 26. compared with Heb. viii. 10. Further, much of the Jewish law is employed in discriminating between things clean and unclean, in removing and making atonement for things polluted or proscribed; and under these ceremonies, as under a veil or covering, a meaning the most important and

---

[1] A Key to the Language of Prophecy, by the Rev. W. Jones, (Works, vol. v. p 282.) See also a Concise Dictionary of the Symbolical Language of Prophecy in the Appendix to Vol. IV.

sacred is concealed, as would appear from the nature of them, even if we had not other clear and explicit authority for this opinion. Among the rest are certain diseases and infirmities of the body, and some customs in themselves evidently indifferent; these, on a cursory view, seem light and trivial, but, when the reasons of them are properly investigated, they are found to be of considerable importance. We are not to wonder, then, if the sacred poets have recourse to these topics for imagery, even on the most momentous occasions; as when they display the universal depravity of the human heart, (Isa. lxiv 6) or upbraid their own people for the corruptness of their manners, (Isa i. 5, 6 16 Ezek. xxxvi. 17.) or when they deplore the abject state of the virgin, the daughter of Sion, polluted and exposed (Lam. i. 8, 9 17 and 11.) If we consider these metaphors, without any reference to the religion of their authors, they will doubtless appear in some degree disgusting and inelegant; but if we refer them to their genuine source, the peculiar rites of the Hebrews, they will not be found wanting either in force or dignity.

The pontifical vestments, which were extremely splendid, suggested a variety of images expressive of the glory both of the Jewish and Christian church. We have an instance of this in Ezek xvi 10. 13 18 and particularly in the following passage of the evangelical prophet —

> I will greatly rejoice in JEHOVAH
> My soul shall exult in my God,
> For he hath clothed me with the garments of salvation,
> He hath covered me with the mantle of righteousness,
> As the bridegroom decketh himself with a priestly crown,
> And as the bride adorneth herself with her costly jewels.
>   Isa. lxi. 10.

In this verse, the elegant Isaiah is describing, in his peculiar and magnificent manner, the exultation and glory of the church, after her triumphal restoration. Pursuing the allusion, he decorates her with the vestments of salvation, and clothes her in the robe of righteousness he afterwards compares the church to a bridegroom dressed for the marriage, to which comparison incredible dignity is added by the word *Ikohen*, a metaphor plainly taken from the priests' apparel, the force of which, therefore, no modern language can express. No imagery, Bishop Lowth further remarks, which the Hebrew writers could employ, was equally adapted with this to the display (as far as human powers can conceive or depict the subject) of the infinite majesty of God JEHOVAH is, therefore, introduced by the Psalmist as *clothed with glory and with strength*, (Psal. xciii 1.) and he is *girded with power*, (Psal. lxv. 6.) which are the very terms appropriated to the description of the dress and ornaments of the priests. The epistle to the Hebrews is an admirable comment on many parts of the Mosaic ritual

IV. *The Hebrews derived many of their Metaphors from Sacred History.*

Thus, as the devastation of the land of Israel is frequently represented by the restoration of antient chaos, (as in Jer. iv. 23—26. Isa. xxxiv. 4. 11. and Joel iii. 15, 16.) so the same event is sometimes expressed in metaphors suggested by the universal deluge (as in Isa. xxiv. 1. 18—20.), and also from the destruction of Sodom and Gomorrah. (Isa. xxxiv. 9.) See also Psal. xi. 6.

The departure of the Israelites from Egypt, while it affords materials for many magnificent descriptions, is commonly applied in a metaphorical manner, to represent other great deliverances: as in Isa. xi. 15, 16. xliii. 16—19. xlviii. 21. and li. 10. But the figurative application of the history of the Exodus is much plainer in the New Testament. There we see Zacharias, in his prophetical hymn, on occasion of the birth of John the Baptist, celebrating the blessings of the Christian redemption in terms borrowed from the past redemption of Israel out of Egypt.[1]

Lastly, when Jehovah is described as coming to execute judgment, to deliver the pious, and to destroy his enemies, or in any manner to display his divine power upon earth, the description is embellished from that tremendous scene which was exhibited on Mount Sinai[2] at the delivery

---

[1] This interesting and important topic is well illustrated in the "Lectures on the Figurative Language of Scripture," Lect vi —Jones's Works, vol. iii. pp. 92—100.
[2] See Exod. xix. 16. 18. Deut. iv. 11, 12.

of the law. Two sublime examples of this sort, to mention no more, occur in Psal. xviii. 7—15. and Mic. i. 3, 4.[1]

SECTION IV.

ON THE INTERPRETATION OF SCRIPTURE ALLEGORIES.

I. *The Allegory defined. — Different Species of Allegory.* — II. *Rules for the Interpretation of Scripture Allegories.*

ANOTHER branch of the figurative language of Scripture is the Allegory; which, under the literal sense of the words, conceals a foreign or distant meaning. Of this species of figure Bishop Lowth[2] has three kinds, viz.

1. The ALLEGORY[3] properly so called, and which he terms a *continued metaphor*, —

2. The PARABLE, or similitude, which is discussed in the following section; — and,

3. The MYSTICAL ALLEGORY, in which a double meaning is couched under the same words, or when the same prediction, according as it is differently interpreted, relates to different events, distant in time, and distinct in their nature.

The *Mystical Allegory* differs from the two first-mentioned species in the nature of its materials; it being allowable in the former to make use of imagery from different objects, while the mystical allegory is exclusively derived from things sacred. There is likewise this further distinction, that in those other forms of allegory, the exterior or ostensible imagery is fiction only; the truth lies altogether in the interior or remote sense, which is veiled as it were under this thin and pellucid covering. But, in the mystical allegory, each idea is equally agreeable to truth. The exterior or ostensible image is not a shadowy colouring of the interior sense, but is in itself a reality; and, although it sustains another character, it does not wholly lay aside its own. As, however, the interpretation of the mystical and typical parts of Scripture is treated of in a subsequent part of this

---

[1] The learned Professor Michaelis, in his additions to Bishop Lowth's ninth lecture, has endeavoured to prove that the sacred writers drew largely from poetic fable, which they derived from the Egyptians, in common with the Greeks and Romans As it respects the latter, his argument is convincing and satisfactory; but with regard to the Hebrews, as it depends chiefly on his *own* Latin versions, which (the excellent English translator of the Bishop's lectures remarks) are by no means so faithful to the original as our common version, his point does not appear to be demonstrated. On this account the present brief notice of Michaelis's hypothesis may be deemed sufficient : it is, however, adopted by Bauer in his Hermeneutica Sacra, pp. 209, 210

[2] Lectures on Hebrew Poetry, vol. 1 lect. x. and xxi.

[3] Αλληγωρια or *Allegory* is derived from αλλο αγορευται i. e *a different thing is said from that which is meant*. It differs from a metaphor, in that it is not confined to a word, but extends to a whole thought, or, it may be, to several thoughts. An allegory may be expressed moreover by pictures, by actions, as in Ezek. iii. iv. v. and Luke xxii. 36. — or by any significant thing.

volume[1] we shall, in the present section, direct our attention to the allegory, properly and strictly so called.

As every such allegory is a representation of real matters of fact under feigned names and feigned characters, it must be subjected to a two-fold examination. " We must first examine the immediate representation, and then consider what other representation it was intended to excite. Now, in most allegories the immediate representation is made in the form of a narrative; and since it is the object of an allegory to convey a moral, not an historical truth, the narrative itself is commonly fictitious. The immediate representation is of no further value, than as it leads to the ultimate representation. It is the application or moral of the allegory which constitutes its worth."[2] In the investigation, then, of an allegory, the following rules may assist us to determine its ultimate meaning: —

I. *Allegorical Senses of Scripture are not to be sought for, where the literal sense is plain and obvious.*

This rule is of the greatest importance; from not attending to it, the antient Jews, as the Therapeutæ, the author of the book of Wisdom, Josephus, and Philo, and, in imitation of them, Origen[3] and many of the fathers, (whose example has also been followed by some modern expositors,) have respectively turned even historical passages of Scripture into allegories, together with such other passages as already had a proper and literal sense. Hence many ridiculous interpretations have been imposed on passages of Scripture, the proper moral sense of which has been either greatly enervated, or entirely frittered away, by such misnamed spiritual expositions.

II. *The proper or literal meaning of the Words must be ascertained, before we attempt to explain an Allegory.*

For this purpose, the primary word itself must first be ascertained, and its force expressed, by an appropriate literal word, and to this sense all the other figurative words of the passage should be referred, and explained agreeably to it. The *primary* word in an allegory is that, which contains the foundation and reason why the passage under consideration is expressed by that particular image, and such primary word is to be ascertained both from the *scope* as well as from the *explanation* which may be subjoined, and also from the *subject* or *thing* itself which is treated of. Thus in 1 Cor. v. 6—8. the Apostle speaks of leaven in such a manner, that the whole of that passage contains an earnest exhortation to a holy life; for the context shows that the design of the allegorical admonition was, that the Corinthians should not be tainted with wickedness and depravity of life. The occasion of the allegory was their admittance of an incestuous person into the church at Corinth. Now, as the Apostle says, *Know ye not that a little leaven leaveneth the whole lump?* and accommodates the remaining sentence of the passage to the same image, the consideration of the primary word will readily lead us to this sense one man may be injurious to the whole congregation by his corrupt example. St Paul further adds an explanation of his meaning, when he says, *Let us keep the feast, not with old leaven, neither with the leaven of malice and wickedness,* &c. Here the meaning of ἑορτάζειν (keep the feast) is not to celebrate the festival of the passover as it literally means, but to serve and worship God in Christ, in other words, to be a sincere Christian, and in such a manner that, being cleansed from all former sins, we should serve and worship God in

---

[1] See Chapter III. infra, on the Mystical and Typical Interpretations of Scripture; and Chapter IV. Section III on the Double Sense of Prophecy.

[2] Bishop Marsh's Lectures, part iii. p. 80. The seventeenth and eighteenth lectures, in which the subject of figurative interpretation is ably discussed at considerable length, are particularly worthy of perusal.

[3] Dr. A. Clarke (note on Exod i. 22.) has given a curious specimen of Origen's mode of allegorising, to which the reader is referred on account of its length.

true holiness.[1] In like manner we are to understand the expression, *destroy this temple, and in three days I will raise it up* (John ii. 19.) The primary word *temple* must be changed into a proper or literal one, namely, the *body of Christ*, as the evangelical history suggests; and to this the rest of the passage must be referred.

III. *The Design of the whole Allegory must be investigated.*

The consideration of this rule will embrace a variety of particulars.

1. *In investigating the Design of an Allegory, the* CONTEXT *is first to be examined and considered*[2], *by comparing the preceding and subsequent parts of the discourse.*

In 2 Tim. ii. 20 we read thus *In a great house there are not only vessels of gold and silver, but also of wood and of earth, and some to honour and some to dishonour* Now, since the Apostle did not intend to say what these words literally mean of themselves, it is evident that he employed an allegory, the design of which is to be ascertained by the aid of the context. In the preceding verses, 15 and 16, he had exhorted Timothy to *study to show himself approved unto God, a workman that needeth not to be ashamed, rightly dividing the word of truth*, and to shun vain and profane babblings. Hence it appears that Saint Paul was speaking of the qualifications of a teacher The *great house* then, in which are vessels of several kinds, will signify the Christian church, in which are various teachers, and of different value In the *following* verses, 21. and 22., Timothy is exhorted to avoid novel doctrines, to separate himself from false teachers, and to make himself a vessel fitted for the master's use, prepared for every good work Here, again, the Apostle is not speaking literally of household goods, but of teachers. The design of the allegory, therefore, in the passage above cited, is to intimate, that, as in a great house there is a variety of utensils, some of a more precious and others of a coarser material, so in the church of God, which is the house of God, there are teachers of different characters and capacities Some of them, being faithful, are employed in the honourable work of leading men in the paths of truth and piety; while others, being unfaithful, are permitted to follow the dishonourable occupation of seducing those who love error, that the approved may be made manifest

2. *The* OCCASION *which gave rise to the Allegory, and which is indicated by the context, is also to be considered.*

Thus, in the Gospels, we meet with numerous instances of persons who asked questions of our Saviour, or who entertained erroneous notions. an allegory is delivered by way of reply, to correct the error, and at the same time to instruct the inquirer. In John vi. 25—65. many things are announced relative to the eating of bread these are to be understood of spiritual food, the doctrines of Christ, which are to be received for the same purpose as we take food, namely, that we may be nourished and supported. The *occasion* of this allegorical mode of speaking is related in verse 31. *Our fathers*, said the Jews, *did eat manna in the desert, as it is written, He gave them bread from heaven to eat. I*, says Christ, *am the living bread, which cometh down from heaven.* The meaning of the whole evidently is, that by eating the flesh of Christ we are to understand the same idea as is implied in eating bread, namely to derive support from it. The argument of our Lord, then, may be thus expressed — "The manna which our fathers did eat in the wilderness, could only preserve a mortal life. That is the true bread of life which qualifies every one who eats it for everlasting happiness. I call myself this bread, not only on account of my *doctrine*, which purifies the soul, and fits it for a state of happiness, but also because I shall give my own life to procure the life of the world"

---

[1] Mr. Gilpin has given the following lucid exposition of this, in some respects, difficult passage: — "I hear," says the Apostle to the Corinthians, that there hath been practised among you a very enormous kind of wickedness, which is not heard of even among Gentiles — that one of you hath had connection with his father's wife; and that others, instead of making it a cause of general mourning, and separating themselves from so vile a person, seem rather to defend him in his wickedness. — Though absent, I take upon me, through the authority of the Holy Ghost, to decide in this matter I command, therefore, that, on receipt of this epistle, you gather the congregation together, and in the name of Jesus Christ solemnly expel this person from your communion; that he may see the heinousness of his sin, and after a sincere repentance be restored to God's favour — Your defending him in his wickedness is an immediate step towards being corrupted yourselves. You are under a necessity, therefore, on your own account, to remove this pernicious example. Consider your blessed Saviour's death, and preserve yourselves as free as possible from sin, which was the cause of it." See the New Testament, vol. ii. p 165.

[2] On the investigation of the context, see pp. 318—324. *supra*.

3. *As the context frequently indicates the meaning of an Allegory, so likewise its* SCOPE *and* INTERPRETATION *are frequently pointed out by some explanation that is subjoined.*

In Luke v 29. it is related that our Lord sat down to eat with publicans and sinners. When questioned by the Pharisees for this conduct, he replied, *They that are whole need not a physician, but they that are sick* - and added the following explanation — I am not come to call the *righteous,* those who arrogantly presume themselves to be such, *but sinners to repentance* The scope, occasion, and explanation being severally known, the meaning of the allegory becomes evident Sometimes, however, this explanation of an allegory is conveyed in a single word, as in 1 Thess v 8. Here we are commanded to put on a breast-plate and helmet; it is added, by way of exposition, the breast-plate of faith and love, and the helmet of hope The sense of the figure is — Prepare yourself for your spiritual warfare with faith, love, and hope, lest you suffer loss.

4. *Sometimes the Allegory proposed is explained in its several parts by the person speaking.*

Thus, in Eph. vi 11—19. many things are said of the Christian's armour; and the girdle, breast-plate, greaves, shield, and sword, are distinctly specified. That these terms are allegorical is evident In the tenth verse the exhortation, *to be strong in the Lord, and in the power of his might,* precedes in the eleventh and following verses the apostle explains what he intended to be understood, in its several parts thus, the sword is the word of God, the girdle is integrity, the shield is faith, &c. In such passages as this, an explanation is desirable, otherwise the allegory it contains could not be interpreted upon any certain principle.

5. *Sometimes also the* CONTEXT *incidentally presents some proper word, by which the meaning of the whole allegory may be discerned.*

In John xii 35. our Lord says — *Yet a little a while is the light with you* A single proper word is almost immediately subjoined — *believe* in the light (Verse 36.) Hence it appears that by light is meant himself, the divine teacher · it is equally plain that to continue in darkness means to continue in ignorance Another instance occurs in Matt v 14 *Ye are the light of the world a city that is set on an hill cannot be hid,* &c. It is afterwards subjoined, *that men may see your good works, and glorify your Father which is in heaven.* From this expression, *good works,* which is the key to the whole passage, we perceive that our Lord's discourse treats of that example of a holy life and conversation, which it is the duty of Christians to set before others.

IV. *In the Explanation of an Allegorical Passage, Historical Circumstances should be consulted.*

For it sometimes happens that history alone can throw any light on the passage.

1. Thus, in John xxi 18. the evangelist evidently refers us to history for an explanation. Our Lord is there represented as saying to Peter — *When thou wast young thou girdedst thyself, and walkedst whither thou wouldest. but, when thou shalt be old, thou shalt stretch forth thy hands, and another shall gird thee, and carry thee whither thou wouldest not.* Thus, adds the historian, *spake he signifying by what death he should glorify God.* Now there is nothing related in the New Testament which can afford any clue to this passage but, if we consult ecclesiastical history, we shall find that Peter suffered a violent death; and thus every sentence becomes clear

2 So, in Matt. xiii. 31—34. the kingdom of God is likened unto a *grain of mustard seed* which gradually springs up and becomes a large plant, and also to *leaven,* which gradually ferments the whole mass, into which it is put. History shows that the church of Christ has arisen from small beginnings, and is spreading itself through the earth.

3. In Prov v. 15—18 we have the following beautiful allegory: — *Drink waters out of thine own cistern, and running waters out of thine own well Let thy fountains be dispersed abroad, and rivers of waters in the streets. Let them be only thine own, and not strangers with thee Let thy fountain be blessed, and rejoice with the wife of thy youth.* That this passage is allegorical, is evident from the same figure being continued through several sentences and verses Its sense is to be investigated both according to *the oriental mode of speaking,* (for the inhabitants of the East, who draw most of their metaphors from natural objects, are accustomed to compare their wives to a cistern or pool, whence rivers flow,) and also from the proper words subjoined towards the close, *rejoice with the wife of thy youth;* as likewise from the series of the discourse, since the author of the Book of Proverbs, in the beginning of this chapter, is dissuading from illicit intercourse. From these circumstances collectively considered, the sense of the allegory plainly is that no

man should follow strange women, but live content with the wife whom he hath espoused lest, influenced by his example, she should deviate from the path of virtue.

V. *The Nature of the Thing spoken of is also to be considered in the Exposition of an Allegory.*

It is necessary that the nature of the thing should be considered, in order that the *tendency* of every comparison may appear, and also the literal meaning which is concealed under the figurative expressions.

1. Thus in Matt v 13. we read, *Ye are the salt of the earth but if the salt have lost its savour, wherewith shall it be salted? It is thenceforth good for nothing but to be cast out, and to be trodden under foot of men* Now, what is the meaning of this admonition? What is the primary word? *Salt* But with what proper word can it be interpreted? Here the nature of the thing is to be consulted, which shows that it is the property of salt to render food savoury, as well as to correct the taste; hence it is clear in what sense the disciples are said to be the *salt of the earth*, for they were teachers by whom some were corrected and made better. The general meaning of the passage is; — Ye, who embrace my religion, like salt shall purify the world; but ye must first be pure yourselves.

2. In Luke v 36. the following passage occurs *No man putteth a piece of a new garment upon an old, if otherwise, then both the new maketh a rent, and the piece that was taken out of the new agreeth not with the old.* Nothing is adduced by way of explanation · in a preceding verse the Pharisees had asked Christ why his disciples did not fast, but lived more cheerfully than those of John. Our Saviour replied in the words above cited; nothing, then, can lead us to understand the passage but the nature of the subject. Now, in common life we know that no one voluntarily and readily acts indiscreetly, or in an unbecoming manner Therefore, says Christ, since no one in common life acts thus indiscreetly, neither do I require my disciples to do so, since there is no need for them to undergo such austerities. The time will come (verse 35) when they will fare hardly enough; then they will have sufficient trials. At present neither circumstances, time, nor place require it; things must be accommodated to circumstances The passage being thus considered, the meaning of the allegory becomes very evident.

VI. *Comparison is not to be extended to all the Circumstances of the Allegory.*

"Thus, in the parable of the good Samaritan, the point to be illustrated is, *the extent of the duty of beneficence.* Most of the circumstances in the parable go to make up merely the verisimilitude of the narration, so that it may give pleasure to him who hears or reads it. But how differently does the whole appear, when it comes to be interpreted by an allegoriser of the *mystic* schools! The man going down from Jerusalem to Jericho is Adam wandering in the wilderness of this world; the thieves, who robbed and wounded him, are evil spirits; the priest, who passed by without relieving him, is the Levitical Law; the Levite is good works; the good Samaritan is Christ; the oil and wine are grace, &c. What may not a parable be made to mean, if imagination is to supply the place of reason and philology? And what riddle or oracle of Delphos could be more equivocal, or of more multifarious significancy, than the Bible, if such exegesis be admissible? It is a miserable excuse, which interpreters make for themselves, that they render the Scriptures more edifying and significant by interpreting them in this manner. And are the Scriptures then to be made more significant than God has made them? Or to be mended by the skill of the interpreter so as to become *more edifying* than the Holy Spirit has made them? If there be a *semblance* of piety in such interpretations, a *semblance* is all. Real piety and humility appear to advantage in receiving the Scriptures as they are, and expounding them as simply and skilfully as the rules of language will render practicable, rather than by attempting to *amend and improve* the revelation which God has made." [1]

---

[1] Professor Stuart's Elements of Interpretation, translated from the Latin of Ernesti, p 80. Andover (North America), 1822. 12mo.

VII. *We must not explain one Part literally, and another Part figuratively.*

Thus, the whole of 1 Cor. iii. 9—13 is allegorical: a comparison is there instituted between the office of a teacher of religion, and that of a builder. Hence a Christian congregation is termed a building; its ministers are the architects, some of whom lay the foundation on which others build; some erect a superstructure of gold and silver; others of wood, hay, and stubble. The sense concealed under the allegory is apparent: a Christian congregation is instructed by teachers, some of whom communicate the first principles, others impart further knowledge, some deliver good and useful things (*the truth*) while others deliver useless things (*erroneous doctrines*, such as at that time prevailed in the Corinthian church). That day (the great day of judgment) will declare what superstructure a man has raised; that is, whether what he has taught be good or bad. And as fire is the test of gold, silver, precious stones, wood, hay, stubble, so the great day will be the test of every man's work. Though the whole of this passage is obviously allegorical, yet it is understood literally by the church of Rome, who has erected upon it her doctrine of the fire of purgatory. How contrary this doctrine is to every rule of right interpretation, is too plain to require any exposition.[1]

It falls not within the plan of this work to enumerate all the allegories occurring in the Sacred Writings; some have been incidentally mentioned in the present section; yet, before we proceed to other topics, we cannot but notice the admirable allegorical delineation of old age by Solomon, Eccl. xii. 2—6. It is, perhaps, one of the finest allegories in the Old Testament; the inconveniences of increasing years, the debility of mind and body, the torpor of the senses, are expressed most learnedly and elegantly indeed, but with some degree of obscurity, by different images derived from nature and common life; for by this enigmatical composition, Solomon, after the manner of the oriental sages, intended to put to trial the acuteness of his readers. It has on this account afforded much exercise to the ingenuity of the learned; many of whom have differently, it is true, but with much learning and penetration, explained the passage.

There is also in Isaiah (xxviii. 23—29.) an allegory, which, with no less elegance of imagery, is perhaps more simple and regular, as well as more just and complete in the colouring, than any of those above cited. In the passage referred to, the prophet is examining the design and manner of the divine judgments, and is inculcating the principle, that God adopts different modes of acting in the chastisement of the wicked, but that the most perfect wisdom is conspicuous in all; that he will, as before urged, "exact judgment by the line, and righteousness by the plummet;" that he ponders, with the most minute attention, the distinctions of times, characters, and circumstances, as well as every motive to lenity or severity. All this is expressed in a continued allegory, the imagery of which is taken

---

[1] Bauer, Herm. Sacr pp 221—226 Ernesti, Inst. Interp. Nov Test. pp 110, 111. Mori Acroases in Ernesti, tom i pp 301—313. Glassii Phil Sac. lib. ii pp. 1294—1304. Ramiresti de Prado, Pentecontarchus, c. 28. apud Fabricii Observationes Selectæ, pp. 173—179. J. E. Pfeiffer, Institutiones Herm, Sacr. pp. 740—753.

from the employments of agriculture and threshing, and is admirably adapted to the purpose.[1]

SECTION V.

ON THE INTERPRETATION OF SCRIPTURE PARABLES.

I. *Nature of a Parable.* — II. *Antiquity of this Mode of Instruction.* — III. *Rules for the Interpretation of Parables.* — IV. *Parables, why used by Jesus Christ.* — V. *Remarks on the distinguishing Excellencies of Christ's Parables, compared with the most celebrated Fables of Antiquity.*

I. A PARABLE (Παραβολη, from παραβαλλειν, to compare together[2],) is a similitude taken from natural things in order to instruct us in things spiritual. The word, however, is variously used in the Scriptures, to denote a *proverb* or short saying, (Luke iv. 23.) a *famous* or received *saying* (1 Sam. x. 12.[3] Ezek. xviii. 2.); a thing gravely spoken, and comprehending important matters in a few words (Job xxvii. 1. Numb. xxiii. 7. 18. xxiv. 3. 15. Psal. xlix. 4. and lxxviii. 2.); a *thing darkly* or figuratively *expressed* (Ezek. xx. 49. Matt. xv. 15.); a *visible type* or *emblem*, representing something different from and beyond itself (Heb. ix. 9. and xi. 19. Gr.) a *special instruction* (Luke xiv. 7.); and a *similitude* or *comparison.* (Matt. xxiv. 32. Mark iii. 23.[4])

According to Bishop Lowth, a parable is that kind of allegory which consists of a continued narration of a fictitious event, applied by way of simile to the illustration of some important truth. By the Greeks, allegories were called αινοι or *apologues*, and by the Romans *fabulæ* or *fables*[5]; and the writings of the Phrygian sage, or those composed in imitation of him, have acquired the greatest celebrity. Nor did our Saviour himself disdain to adopt the same method of instruction; of whose parables it is doubtful whether they excel most in wisdom and utility, or in sweetness, elegance, and perspicuity. As the appellation of PARABLE has been applied to his discourses of this kind, the term is now restricted from its former extensive signification to a more confined sense. This species of composition also

---

[1] Lowth's Prælectiones, No 10 or vol. i. p 230. of Dr Gregory's translation.

[2] A verbo παραβαλλειν, quod significat *conferre, comparare, assimilare* (cf Marc iv. 30.) ductum est nomen παραβολης; quod *similitudinem, collationem* Quinctilianus (Inst. Or. l. v. c. 11., l viii. c. 3. pp. 298 302. 470.) interpretatur, Seneca (Ep. lix.) *imaginem*. Itaque *collatio*, sive, ut Ciceronis (l. 1. de Invent. c 30.) definitione utamur, *oratio, rem cum re ex similitudine conferens*, Græco nomine parabola appellatur. Eo sensu Christus (Marc. iii. 23.) εν παραβολαις locutus dicitur, quando per varias *similitudines* (v. 24— 27) probavit se non Satanæ ope, sed altiore virtute dæmonia ejicere. G. C. Storr, De Parabolis Christi, in Opusc. Academic. vol. i. p 89. The whole disquisition, to which this section is largely indebted, is well worthy of perusal. See also Rambach, Institutiones Hermeneut p 187 et seq.; J. E Pfeiffer's Instit. Hermeneut. Sacr. pp. 753— 773. ; and Chladenius's Institutiones Exegeticæ, p. 190 et seq.

[3] In this and the other references to the Old Testament in the above paragraph, the original is משל (MASHAL), a parable.

[4] Glassii Phil. Sacr lib. ii. pp. 1304—1306. ed Dathii Parkhurst and Schleusner in voce παραβολη

[5] Storr, Opusc. Acad. vol. i. p. 89. et seq.

occurs very frequently in the prophetic poetry, and particularly in that of Ezekiel.

II. The use of parables is of very great antiquity. In the early ages of the world, when the art of reasoning was little known, and the minds of men were not accustomed to nice and curious speculations, we find that the most antient mode of instruction was by parable and fable: its advantages, indeed, are many and obvious. It has been remarked by an acute observer of men and morals, that " little reaches the understanding of the mass but through the medium of the senses. Their minds are not fitted for the reception of abstract truth. Dry argumentative instruction, therefore, is not proportioned to their capacity: the faculty, by which a right conclusion is drawn, is in them the most defective; they rather feel strongly than judge accurately: and their feelings are awakened by the impression made on their senses." [1] Hence, instruction by way of parable is naturally adapted to engage attention; it is easily comprehended, and suited to the meanest capacity; and while it opens the doctrine which it professes to conceal, it gives no alarm to our prejudices and passions; it communicates unwelcome truths in the least disagreeable manner; points out mistakes, and insinuates reproof with less offence and with greater efficacy than undisguised contradiction and open rebuke. Of this description, we may remark, are the parables related by Nathan to David (2 Sam. xii. 1—9.), and by the woman of Tekoah to the same monarch. (2 Sam. xiv. 1—13.) The New Testament abounds with similar examples. " By laying hold on the imagination, parable insinuates itself into the affections; and by the intercommunication of the faculties, the understanding is made to apprehend the truth which was proposed to the fancy." [2] In a word, this kind of instruction seizes us by surprise, and carries with it a force and conviction which are almost irresistible. It is no wonder, therefore, that parables were made the vehicle of national instruction in the most early times; that the prophets, especially Ezekiel, availed themselves of the same impressive mode of conveying instruction or reproof; and that our Lord, following the same example, also adopted it for the same important purposes.

'III. Although a parable has some things in common with an allegory, so that the same rules which apply to the latter are in some degree applicable to the former; yet, from its peculiar nature, it becomes necessary to consider the parable by itself, in order that we may understand and interpret it aright.

1. *The first excellence of a parable is, that it turns upon an image well known and applicable to the subject, the meaning of which is clear and definite: for this circumstance will give it that perspicuity which is essential to every species of allegory.*

How clearly this rule applies to the parables of our Lord, is obvious to every reader of the New Testament It may suffice to mention his parable of the *Ten Virgins* (Matt. xxv. 1—13.), which is a plain allusion to those things which were common at the Jewish marriages in those days. the whole parable, indeed, is made up of the rites used by the Orientals, as well as by the Roman people, at their nuptials, and all the particulars related in it were such as were commonly known to the Jews, because they were every day practised by some of them. In like manner the parables of the *lamp* (Luke viii. 16),

---

[1] Mrs. More's Christian Morals, vol. i. p. 106. [2] Ibid. p. 107.

of the *sower* and the seed, of the *tares*, of the *mustard seed*, of the *leaven*, of the *net cast into the sea*, all of which are related in Matt. xiii. as well as of the *householder* that planted a vineyard, and let it out to husbandmen (Matt. xxi. 33—41.) are all representations of usual and common occurrences, and such as the generality of our Saviour's hearers were daily conversant with, and they were, therefore, selected by him as being the most interesting and affecting.

If the parables of the sacred prophets be examined by this rule, they will not appear deficient, being in general founded upon such imagery as is frequently used, and similarly applied by way of metaphor and comparison in Hebrew poetry. Examples of this kind occur in the deceitful vineyard (Isa v 1—7), and in the useless vine which is given to the fire (Ezek xv and xix. 10—14), for, under this imagery, the ungrateful people of God are more than once described. Similar instances of opposite comparison present themselves in the parable of the lion's whelps falling into the pit (Ezek xix. 1—9) in which is displayed the captivity of the Jewish princes, and also in that of the fair, lofty, and flourishing cedar of Lebanon (Ezek. xxxi 3—17.), which once raised its head to the clouds, at length cut down and neglected —thus exhibiting, as in a picture, the prosperity and the fall of the king of Assyria. To these may be added one more example, namely, that in which the love of God towards his people, and their piety and fidelity to him, are expressed by an allusion to the solemn covenant of marriage. Ezekiel has pursued this image with uncommon freedom in two parables (Ezek xvi. and xxii.); and it has been alluded to by almost all the sacred poets.

2. *The image, however, must not only be apt and familiar, but must also be elegant and beautiful in itself, and all its parts must be perspicuous and pertinent; since it is the purpose of a parable, and especially of a poetic parable, not only to explain more perfectly some proposition, but frequently to give it animation and splendour.*

Of all these excellencies there cannot be more perfect examples than the parables which have just been specified to which we may add the well-known parables of Jotham (Judges ix 7—15), of Nathan (2 Sam. xii 1—14), and of the woman of Tekoah. (2 Sam xiv 4—7.) The admirably devised parable of Nathan is perhaps one of the finest specimens of the genuine pathetic style that can be found in the Old Testament, and David's eager condemnation of the unsuspected offender at the same time displays a striking instance of the delusion of sin and the blindness of self-love. "He, who had lived a whole year in the unrepented commission of one of the blackest crimes in the decalogue—and who, to secure to himself the object for which he had committed it, perpetrated another almost more heinous, and that with an hypocrisy suited to his character —he could in an instant denounce death on the imaginary offender for a fault comparatively trifling."—"*Seeing he saw not, and hearing, he heard not;*" he immediately saw the iniquity and barbarity of the rich man's proceedings, his heart was in a moment fired with indignation at the thought of it, "the vehemence of his resentment even overstepped the limits of his natural justice, in decreeing a punishment disproportioned to the crime, while he remained dead to his own delinquency. A pointed parable instantly surprised him into the most bitter self-reproach. A direct accusation might have inflamed him before he was thus prepared, and in the one case he might have punished the accuser, by whom, in the other, he was brought into the deepest self-abasement. The prudent prophet did not rashly reproach the king with the crime, which he wished him to condemn, but placed the fault at such a distance, and in such a point of view, that he first procured his impartial judgment, and afterwards his self-condemnation.—an important lesson, not only to the offender, but also to the reprover"[1]

3. Every parable is composed of three parts; 1. The *sensible similitude*, which has variously been termed the *bark* and the *protasis*, and consists in its literal sense;— 2. The *explanation* or *mystical sense*, also termed the *apodosis* and the *sap* or fruit, or the thing signified by the similitude proposed. This is frequently not expressed: for though our Saviour sometimes condescended to unveil the hidden sense, by disclosing the moral meaning of his parables (as in Matt. xiii. 3—8. 18—23. compared with Luke viii. 4—15. and Matt. xiii. 24—30. 36—43.); yet he usually left the application to those whom he designed to instruct by his doctrine. Of this description are the parables of the grain of mustard seed, of leaven, of the hidden treasure, and the pearl of great price

---
[1] Mrs More's Christian Morals, vol. i. p. 108.

(Matt. xiii 31—33. 44—46), between which and the kingdom of heaven a comparison is instituted, the mystical sense of which is to be sought in the similitudes themselves. 3. The third constituent part of a parable is the *root* or *scope* to which it tends.[1]

4. *For the right explanation and application of parables, their general scope and design must be ascertained.*

Where our Saviour has not himself interpreted a parable, its immediate scope and design are to be sought with great attention, this indeed will generally appear from the context, being either expressed at its commencement or at its conclusion, or it is sufficiently evident from the occasion on which it was delivered. More particularly, the scope of a parable may be ascertained,

(1.) *From the clear declaration prefixed to it,*

As in the parable of the rich glutton (Luke xii. 16—20.), which is prefaced by the following caution in verse 15. *Take heed and beware of covetousness, for a man's life consisteth not in the abundance of things which he possesseth.* Thus, in Luke xviii 2—8. the parable of the unjust judge is preceded by this declaration, which plainly points out one of its senses: *He spake a parable unto them, that men ought always to pray, and not to faint.* And again, in verse 9 *He spake this parable* (of the Pharisee and publican, verse 10—14.) *unto certain which trusted in themselves that they were righteous, and despised others.*

(2.) *From the declaration subjoined to a parable;*

Thus our Saviour concludes the parable of the unmerciful creditor, who would not forgive his debtor the minutest portion of his debt, though much had been forgiven him (Matt xviii. 23—35), by the following explanation — *So likewise shall my heavenly Father do also unto you, if ye forgive not every one his brother their trespasses* Similar declarations are annexed to the parables of the wedding feast (Matt. xxv. 13. Luke xiv 11.), of the rich glutton (Luke xii. 21), and of the unjust steward. (Luke xvi. 9.) The prophetic writings will furnish similar instances: thus Isaiah (v. 1—7) having delivered the parable of a vineyard — planted with the choicest vines, and cultivated with the utmost care, yet which produced only wild fruit — announces at its close, that by the vineyard were intended the Jews, and by the wild fruit their enormous wickedness, for which they deserved the severest judgments. Nathan, also, in the beautiful parable already cited, subjoined a declaration of its scope to the criminal sovereign. In the short parable, or apologue, communicated from Jehoash king of Israel to Amaziah king of Judah (2 Kings xiv. 9, 10), the application of it to the latter is explicitly stated at its conclusion

(3.) *Where no declaration is prefixed or subjoined to a parable, its scope must be collected from a consideration of the subject-matter, context, or the occasion on account of which the parable was delivered.*

Thus, in the parable of the barren fig-tree (Luke xiii. 6—9.), Jesus Christ has indicated nothing concerning its scope. But from the consideration of the context of his discourse, and of the occasion of the parable, we learn that it was designed to teach the Jews, that unless they repented within the space of time allotted to them by Infinite Mercy, severe punishments would await them, and their civil and religious polity be destroyed. The immediate occasion of the parable was, his disciples telling him of certain Galileans, who had come up to the temple at Jerusalem, to worship, and whose blood Pilate had mingled with their sacrifices On hearing this circumstance, Christ said, *Suppose ye, that these Galileans were sinners above all the Galileans, because they suffered these things? I tell you, nay But except ye repent, ye shall all likewise perish* Having repeated the last sentence a second time, he delivered the parable of the barren fig-tree.

In like manner, to the parable of the prodigal son nothing is prefixed or subjoined, but the relation occurs immediately after two others, in which it was declared that the return of penitent sinners affords joy in heaven. This, however, is an important topic, and will require to be more particularly considered From the observations already made on the general nature of parables, it will be easily perceived that the objects of our Lord's parables were various, such as the conveying either of instruction or reproof, the cor-

---

[1] In parabolis, si integre accipiantur, tria sunt; *radix, cortex*, et *medulla* sive *fructus*. *Radix* est scopus, in quem tendit parabola. *Cortex* est similitudo sensibilis, quæ adhibetur, et *suo sensu literali* constat. *Medulla* seu fructus est *sensus parabolæ mysticus*, seu ipsa res ad quam parabolæ fit accommodatio, seu quæ per similitudinem propositam significatur. Glassii *Philologia Sacra*, lib ii. pars i tr. 2 sect. 5. canon 3. col. 488 (Lipsiæ, 1725) It is not a little remarkable that the nine very useful canons for the interpretation of parables, by Glassius, should be altogether omitted in Professor Dathe's valuable edition of his work.

recting or preventing of errors; the instructing of men in the knowledge of some truths which could be viewed with advantage only at a distance, or of others, which would have startled them when plainly proposed. Further, there were truths which were necessary to be conveyed, respecting the establishment of his religion, and the conduct of his disciples on *occasion* of that event. These subjects required to be touched with a delicate hand; and a few instances will show that each of them was conducted with the highest grace and propriety.

Thus, the *worldly spirit* of the Pharisees is delicately yet strikingly reproved in the parables of the rich man whose grounds brought forth plentifully (Luke xii. 15—21.); which was spoken to show the folly of covetousness, — of the unjust steward (Luke xvi. 1.) to show the proper use of wealth, — and of the rich man and the beggar (Luke xvi. 19—31.), to show the danger of abusing it — The *selfishness* and bigotry of the same sect, which characteristic in some degree applied to the whole Jewish nation, who " trusted in themselves that they were righteous, and despised others," are convicted in the parables of the Pharisee and the Publican praying in the temple, of the two sons commanded to work in the vineyard, of the guest who chose the highest seat at the table, of the lost sheep and money, of the prodigal son, and of the good Samaritan. In several of these parables the comparative merit of the Jew and Gentile world is justly though faintly stated, on purpose to abase the pride of the one and to exalt the humble hopes of the other.

Another class of parables is designed to deliver some general lessons of wisdom and piety such are the parables of the ten virgins and the talents. The parables of the sower and of the tares, and many of the lesser parables, are designed to show the nature and progress of the Gospel dispensation, together with the opposition which would be made to it from the malice of Satan, and the folly and perverseness of mankind. With these are closely connected such parables as have for their object the rejection of the Jews, and the calling of the Gentiles: under this head are comprised the parables of the murmuring labourers, of the cruel and unjust husbandmen, the barren fig-tree, and the marriage-feast. By considering the occasions upon which these and other parables were delivered by the Redeemer of the world, we shall be enabled, not only to ascertain their scope and design, but also to perceive their wisdom, beauty, and propriety.

5. *Wherever the words of Jesus seem to be capable of different senses, we may with certainty conclude that to be the true one which lies most level to the apprehension of his auditors.*

Allowing for those figurative expressions which were so very frequent and familiar with them, and which, therefore, are no exceptions to this general rule, this necessary canon of interpretation, of all others, demands the most attention.

6. *As every parable has two senses, the* LITERAL *or external, and the* MYSTICAL *or internal sense, the literal sense must be first explained, in order that the correspondence between it and the mystical sense may be the more readily perceived.*

For instance, " the parable of the unforgiving servant represents, *literally*, that his lord forgave him a debt of ten thousand talents, — *mystically*, or spiritually, that God remits to the penitent the punishment of innumerable offences. *Literally*, it states that this servant, on his refusal to exercise forbearance towards his fellow-servant, was delivered over to the tormentors *mystically*, that God will inflict the severest judgments on all who do not forgive others their trespasses. The unity of sense in both interpretations is easily perceptible [1]." whence it follows that every parable must be consistent throughout, and that the literal sense must not be confounded with the mystical sense. Hence also it follows, that, since the scope and application of parables are the chief points to be regarded,

7. *It is not necessary, in the interpretation of parables, that we should anxiously insist upon every single word; nor ought we to expect too curious an adaptation or accommodation of it in every part to the spiritual meaning inculcated by it; for many circumstances are introduced into parables which are merely ornamental, and designed to make the similitude more pleasing and interesting.*

Inattention to this obvious rule has led many expositors into the most fanciful explanations: resemblances have been accumulated, which are for the most part futile, or at best of little use, and manifestly not included in the scope of the parable. Where, indeed, circumstantial resemblances (though merely ornamental) will admit of an easy and

---

[1] Bishop Vanmildert's Bampton Lectures, p 286.

natural application, they are by no means to be overlooked; and it is worthy of remark, that in those parables which our Lord himself explained to his disciples, there are few, if any, of the circumstantial points left unapplied, but here great judgment is necessary neither to do too little, nor to attempt too much.[1] In the application, then, of this rule, there are two points to be considered

(1.) *Persons are not to be compared with persons, but things with things; part is not to be compared with part, but the whole of the parable with itself.*

Thus, we read in Matt. xiii. 24. *The kingdom of heaven is likened unto a man which sowed good seed in his field* and in verse 45. *The kingdom of heaven is likened unto a merchant man seeking goodly pearls.* The similitude here is not with the men, but with the *seed* and the *pearl*; and the construction is to be the same as in verses 31. and 33, where the progress of the Gospel is compared to the grain of mustard-seed, and to leaven.

(2.) *In parables it is not necessary that all the actions of men, mentioned in them, should be just actions, that is to say, morally just and honest.*

For instance, the unjust steward (Luke xvi 1—8.) is not proposed either to justify his dishonesty, or as an example to us in cheating his lord (for that is merely ornamental, and introduced to fill up the story); but as an example of his care and prudence, in providing for the future. From the conduct of this man, our Lord took occasion to point out the management of worldly men, as an example of attention to his followers in their spiritual affairs, and at the same time added an impressive exhortation to make the things of this life subservient to their everlasting happiness; assuring them, that if they did not use temporal blessings as they ought, they could never be qualified to receive spiritual blessings. So again, in Luke xii 39. and Rev iii 3 the coming of Christ is compared to the coming of a thief, not in respect of theft, but of the sudden surprise. "It is not necessary," says a great master of eloquence, "that there should be a perfect resemblance of one thing in all respects to another; but it is necessary that a thing should bear a likeness to that with which it is compared."[2]

8. *Attention to historical circumstances, as well as an acquaintance with the nature and properties of the things whence the similitudes are taken, will essentially contribute to the interpretation of parables.*

(1.) Some of the parables related in the New Testament are supposed to be true histories. In the incidental circumstances of others, our Saviour evidently had a regard to historical propriety. Thus, the scene of that most beautiful and instructive parable of the good Samaritan (Luke x. 30—37.) is very appositely placed in that dangerous road which lay between Jerusalem and Jericho; no way being more frequented than this, both on account of its leading to Peræa, and especially because the classes or stations of the Priests and Levites were fixed at Jericho as well as at Jerusalem and hence it is that a Priest and a Levite are mentioned as travelling this way.[3] It further appears, that at this very time Judæa in general was overrun by robbers, and that the road between Jericho and Jerusalem (in which our Lord represents this robbery to have been committed) was particularly infested by banditti, whose depredations it favoured, as it lay through a dreary solitude. On account of these frequent robberies, we are informed by Jerome that it was called the *Bloody Way*.[4]

(2.) Again, in the parable of *a nobleman who went into a far country to receive for himself a kingdom, and to return* (Luke xix. 12.), our Lord alludes to a case, which, no long time before, had actually occurred in Judæa. Those who, by hereditary succession, or by interest, had pretensions to the Jewish throne, travelled to Rome, in order to have it confirmed to them. Herod the Great first went that long journey to obtain the kingdom of Judæa from Antony, in which he succeeded: and having *received the kingdom*[5], he afterwards travelled from Judæa to Rhodes, in order to obtain a confirmation of it from Cæsar, in which he was equally successful.[6] Archelaus, the son and successor of Herod, did the same, and to him our Lord most probably alluded. Every historical circumstance is beautifully interwoven by our Saviour in this instructive parable

(3.) Of the further benefit to be derived from history in the interpretation of parables, the similes in Matt. xiii. 31, 32. will afford a striking illustration. In these parables the progress of the Gospel is compared to a grain of mustard-seed, and to leaven. Nothing is subjoined to these verses, by way of explanation. What then is their scope? Jesus Christ was desirous of accustoming his disciples to parabolic instruction. From this design, how-

---

[1] Bishop Vanmildert's Bampton Lectures, p. 236.
[2] Non enim res tota toti rei necesse est similis sit; sed ad ipsum, ad quod conferetur, similitudinem habeat, oportet. Cicero ad Herennium, lib. iv. c. 48. tom. I. p. 122. edit. Bipont.
[3] Lightfoot, Hor. Heb in loc.   [4] Jerome, cited by Calmet, in loc.
[5] Josephus, Ant. Jud. lib. xiv. c xiv. §§ 4, 5.   [6] Ibid. lib. xv. c. vi. §§ 6, 7.

ever, we cannot collect the sense of the parables; we have, therefore, no other resource but *history*. Since, then, Jesus Christ is speaking of the progress of the Christian church, we must consult ecclesiastical history, which informs us that, from small beginnings, the church of Christ has grown into a vast congregation, that is, spread over the whole world. In order, however, that we may enter fully into the meaning of this parable of our Lord, it may not be irrelevant to observe that in eastern countries the mustard-plant (or at least, a species of the *sinapi*, which the orientals comprehended under that name,) attains a greater size than with us. It appears that the orientals were accustomed to give the denomination of *trees* to plants growing to the height of ten or twelve feet, and having branches in proportion.[1] To such a height the mustard-plant grows in Judæa, and its branches are so strong and well covered with leaves, as to afford shelter to the feathered tribe. Such is the image by which Jesus Christ represents the progress of his Gospel. *The kingdom of heaven*, said he, *is like to a grain of mustard-seed* — small and contemptible in its beginning, *which is indeed the least of all seeds*, that is, of all those seeds, with which the Jews were then acquainted — for our Lord's words are to be interpreted by popular use, and we learn from Matt. xvii. 20. that, *like a grain of mustard-seed* was a proverbial expression to denote a small quantity.) *but when it is grown, it becometh a tree, so that the birds of the air come and lodge in the branches thereof* Under this simple and beautiful figure does Jesus Christ describe the admirable developement of his Gospel from its origin to its final consummation.[2]

(4.) We have said that the understanding of parables is facilitated by an *acquaintance with the properties of the things whence the similitudes are derived*. Besides the diffusive effects of *leaven* already adverted to, which sufficiently indicate the certain spread of the Gospel, we may adduce an example from the prophet Jeremiah who parabolically describing a furious invader (xlix. 19.) says, *He shall come up like a lion from the swelling of Jordan against the habitation of the strong*. The propriety of this will appear, when it is known that in antient times the river Jordan was particularly infested with lions, which concealed themselves among the thick reeds upon its banks.[3] Let us then imagine one of these monarchs of the desert asleep among the thickets upon the banks of that river let us further suppose him to be suddenly awakened by the roaring, or dislodged by the overflowing of the rapid tumultuous torrent, and in his fury rushing into the upland country: and we shall perceive the admirable propriety and force of the prophet's allusion.

9. Lastly, *although in many of his parables Jesus Christ has delineated the future state of the church, yet he intended that they should convey some important moral precepts, of which we should never lose sight in interpreting parables.*

Thus, the parable of the sower (Matt. xiii 3—24 Mark iv. 3—20 and Luke viii. 4—16.) has a moral doctrine, for our Lord himself soon after subjoins the following important caution: *Take heed how ye hear.* Again, the parable of the tares (Matt. xiii. 24. *et seq.*) refers to the mixture of the wicked with the good in this world. When, therefore,

---

[1] See Lightfoot's and Schoettgenius's Horæ Hebraicæ et Talmudicæ, in Matt. xiii. 31, 32.

[2] As the common mustard (Sinapis nigra, L.) is an annual plant, which, in consequence of its herbaceous stem rarely attaining a greater height than three feet, cannot with propriety be termed δενδρον, a tree, commentators have been much perplexed in their attempts to explain our Lord's parable of the mustard tree. It has, however, been shown by an ingenious botanist, (Mr John Frost, F L S) that the plant intended by Jesus Christ is a species of Phytolacca, which grows abundantly in Palestine, and has the *smallest seed of any tree in that country*, but attains as great an altitude as any tree that flourishes there, and which possesses properties analogous to those of the Sinapis nigra. Mr. Frost is of opinion that the plant in question is most probably the *Phytolacca dodecandra* of Linnæus, (Journal of Science and the Arts, vol xx. pp. 57—59) In 1827 Mr. F. enlarged his communication to that Journal, and published it as a pamphlet, in octavo, with an engraving of the plant

[3] "After having descended," says Maundrell, "the outermost bank of Jordan, you go about a furlong upon a level strand, before you come to the immediate bank of the river. This second bank is so beset with bushes and trees, such as tamarisks, willows, oleanders, &c that you can see no water, till you have made your way through them. In this thicket antiently, and the same is reported of it at this day, several sorts of wild beasts were wont to harbour themselves, whose being washed out of the covert by the overflowings of the river gave occasion to that allusion, *He shall come up like a lion from the swelling of Jordan,*" &c Maundrell's Journey from Aleppo to Jerusalem, p 110. (London, 1810.) Agreeably to this account, Ammianus Marcellinus states, that "innumerable lions wander about among the reeds and copses on the borders of the rivers in Mesopotamia." Lib. xviii. c. 7 (tom. i. p. 177. edit Bipont)

our Lord intimated (in verses 27—29.) that it is not our province to judge those whom he has reserved for his own tribunal; and in the 30th verse added, *let both grow together*, he evidently implied that, since God tolerates incorrigible sinners, it is the duty of men to bear with them; the propagation of false doctrines is an offence against God, who alone is the judge and punisher of them;—man has no right to punish his brethren for their sentiments.[1] The parables which are delivered in the same chapter of Saint Matthew's Gospel, and also in Luke xiii. 19—21. delineate the excellence of the religion of Jesus, and are admirably adapted to inspire us with love and admiration for its Divine Author. Further, the parable of the labourers in the vineyard (Matt. xx. 1—17. besides predicting the future reception of the Gospel, teaches us that no one should despair of the divine mercy so long as he lives, and that God will bestow upon the faithful a larger measure of blessedness than they can venture to expect, and also that we should not be moved with envy, if others enjoy a greater portion of gifts or talents than are bestowed upon ourselves. In fact, as an able expositor[2] has remarked, since our Saviour's parables frequently have a double view, this parable seems not only to illustrate the case of the Jews and Gentiles, but also the case of all individuals of every nation, whom God accepts according to their improvement of the opportunities they have enjoyed. In like manner, the parable of the royal nuptials, related in Matt. xxii. verses 1—15. was designed chiefly to show the Jews, that the offers of grace which they rejected would be made to the Gentiles. But the latter part of it also seems intended to check the presumption of such as pretend to the divine favour without complying with the conditions on which it is promised. It was customary for the bridegroom to prepare vestments for his guests; and the man mentioned in verses 11—13 is said to have intruded without the requisite garment.[3]

IV. From the preceding remarks it will have been seen that parables are of more frequent occurrence in the New than in the Old Testament: and although some hints have been already offered[4], to account for the adoption of this mode of instruction; yet as some persons have taken occasion, from the prophecy of Isaiah (vi. 9, 10.), as cited by Matthew (xiii. 13—15.), to insinuate that our Lord spake in parables in order that the perverse Jews might *not* understand, it may not be irrelevant if we conclude the present strictures on parabolic instruction, with a few remarks on the reasons why it was adopted by our Lord.

1. The practice was familiar to the Jews in common with the other inhabitants of the East, as already stated: and some of our Lord's parables were probably taken from Jewish customs, as the royal nuptials (Matt. xxii. 1—15.), the rich glutton (Luke xvi. 19—31.), and the wise and foolish virgins (Matt. xxv. 1—13.).[5] This method of teaching, therefore, was intelligible to an attentive and inquiring auditory. See Matt. xv. 10. and Mark iv. 13.

2. It was customary for the disciples of the Jewish doctors, when

---

[1] It is with pleasure the author transcribes the following explicit declaration of the learned Roman Catholic writer, Viser. Having cited the passages above adduced, he says, *Facile apparet eos huic præcepto nequaquam satisfacere, qui vi, metu, ac minis, homines student a sua religione abducere.* Hermeneutica Sacra Nov. Test. pars ii. p. 131.

[2] Gilpin's Exposition of the New Test. vol. i. p. 78. note †.

[3] The authorities consulted for this section, independently of those already cited incidentally, are Ernesti, Instit. Interp Nov. Test. p 112.; Morus, in Ernesti, tom i. pp. 314. —320.; Bauer, Hermeneutica Sacra, pp 226—229.; Glassii Philologia Sacra, lib ii. part i. tract 2. sect. 5 canons 3—9. col 473—492., Turretin, de Interpret. Script. pp. 214, 215; Pfeiffer, Herm. Sacr c iii § 13 (Op tom ii. pp. 635, 636); Chladenius, Inst. Exeget. pp 190, 191, J. E. Pfeiffer, Inst Herm. Sacr. pp. 753—773.; Alber, Hermeneut Sacr. Nov Test. vol i pp. 50—56. Brouwer, de Parabolis Christi (Lug. Bat. 1825); and Scholten, Diatribe de Parabolis Christi (Lug. Bat 1827).

[4] See, p. 400. *supra*

[5] Sheringham, in Præf. ad Joma, cited by Whitby on Matt. xiii. 10. Lightfoot, in his Horæ Hebraicæ et Talmudicæ, has pointed out many Jewish sources whence it is probable that Jesus Christ took several of his parables.

they did not understand the meaning of their parables, to request an explanation from their teachers: in like manner, Christ's hearers might have applied to him, if they had not been *indisposed* to receive the doctrines he taught, and had they not preferred to be held in error by the Scribes and Pharisees, rather than to receive instruction from his lips.

3. Parabolic instruction was peculiarly well calculated to veil offensive truths or *hard sayings*, until, in due season, they should be disclosed with greater evidence and lustre, when they were able to hear and to bear them, lest they should revolt at the premature disclosure of the mystery. Compare Mark iv. 33. with John xvi. 12. 25.

4. It was a necessary screen from the malice of his inveterate enemies, the chief priests, Scribes and Pharisees; who would not have failed to take advantage of any *express* declaration which they might turn to his destruction (John x. 24.); but yet they could not lay hold of the most pointed parables, which, they were clear-sighted enough to perceive, were levelled against themselves. See Matt. xxi. 45. Mark xi. 12. and Luke xx. 19.[1]

5. The parables did not contain the fundamental precepts and doctrines of the Gospel, which were delivered in the audience of the people with sufficient perspicuity in Matt. v —vii. and elsewhere, but only the mysteries relative to its progress among both Jews and Gentiles.

6. Lastly, the Jews were addressed in parables, because, as their wickedness and perverseness *indisposed* them to receive profit from his more plain discourses, Jesus Christ would not vouchsafe to them a clearer knowledge of these events. To " have ears and hear not," is a proverbial expression, to describe men who are so wicked and slothful, that they either do not attend to, or *will not* follow the clearest intimations and convictions of their duty. See instances of this expression in Jer. v. 21. and Ezek. xii. 2.[2] To this remark we may add, with reference to the quotations from Isaiah vi. 9, 10. that it is common for God to speak, by his prophets, of events that would happen, in a manner as if he had enjoined them.[3]

V. Whoever attentively considers the character of our Saviour, merely as a moral teacher and instructor of mankind, will clearly perceive his superiority to the most distinguished teachers of antiquity. Through the whole of his Gospel, he discovers a deep and thorough insight into human nature, and seems intimately acquainted with all the subtle malignities and latent corruptions of the human heart, as well as with all the allusions and refinements of self-idolatry, and the windings and intricacies of self-deceit. How admirably the manner, in which he conveyed his instructions, was adapted to answer the end and design of them, we have already seen; we might indeed almost venture to appeal to his parables alone for the authenticity of our Lord's mission, as a divine teacher: all of them, indeed, are distin-

---

[1] Dr. Hales's New Analysis of Chronology, vol ii. p. 773.
[2] Grotius and Whitby on Matt xiii. 10. Dr. Whitby has collected passages showing the proverbial use of *having ears and hearing not*, from Philo (Alleg. lib ii. p 72 D. and lib. iii p. 850. E), and from Demosthenes. (Orat. in Aristogeton, sect. 127.)
[3] See Bishop Lowth's Note on Isa vi. 10

guished by a dignity of sentiment, and a simplicity of expression perfectly becoming the purity and excellence of that religion which he came to establish. The whole system of heathen mythology was the invention of the poets; a mere farrago of childish and romantic stories, chiefly calculated to amuse the vulgar. As the far greater part of their fables and allegories are founded on this fictitious history of the gods, so they were plainly subservient to the support of that system of idolatry and polytheism which the Gospel was designed to overthrow. If any secret meaning was conveyed under these allegorical representations, (which seems, however, to be very doubtful,) it was at any rate too refined and philosophical to be understood by the common people, whose religious knowledge and belief extended no farther than the literal sense of the words. The moral instruction, if any was intended, must be dug out of the rubbish of poetical images and superstitious conceits. And, as these were founded on a false system of the universe, and on unworthy sentiments of God, and his moral government, they could never contribute to the religious improvement of mankind either in knowledge or in practice. Let any man of true taste and judgment compare the abstruse allegories of Plato, or the monstrous fables of the Jewish Talmuds, with the parables of our Saviour, he will be at no loss which to prefer; while, tired and disgusted with the one, he will be struck with admiration at the beauty, elegance, and propriety of the other.

Further, the parables of Jesus far excel the fables of antiquity in clearness and perspicuity, which made them remarkably fit for the instruction of the ignorant and prejudiced, for whom they were originally designed. Our Saviour's images and allusions are not only taken from nature, but especially from those objects and occurrences which are most familiar to our observation and experience. It requires no laborious search, no stretch of imagination, to discover his meaning, in all cases where he intended instruction or reproof, as appears evident from the impressions immediately produced on the minds of his hearers, according to their different tempers and dispositions. Such of his parables, indeed, as predicted the nature and progress of the Gospel dispensation, and the opposition which it should meet from the malice of Satan and the folly of mankind [1], were purposely left to be explained by the events to which they refer, and with which they so exactly correspond, that their meaning soon became plain and obvious to all. It is, moreover, particularly worthy of observation, that the moral instructions conveyed by the parables of the Gospel, are of the most important nature, and essential to our duty and best interests. They do not serve merely to amuse the imagination, but to enlighten the understanding, and to purify the heart. They aim at no less an object than the happiness of mankind in a future and eternal state. The doctrines of the soul's immortality and a future judgment, are the ground-work of our Lord's parables; and to illustrate and confirm these fundamental principles, is their

---

[1] Of this description, for instance, are the parables of the sower, of the tares, and of the labourers in the vineyard.

main and leading design. They all terminate in this point, and describe the awful scenes of eternity, and the interesting consequences of that decisive trial, in a language, though simple and unadorned, yet amazingly striking and impressive. But the fabulous representations of the heathen poets on this subject, were more fitted to amuse than to instruct: they served rather to extinguish than revive the genuine sentiments of nature, and, consequently, to weaken the influence of this doctrine as a principle of virtuous conduct.

There is, also, a pleasing variety in the parables of Jesus. Some of them comprehend no dialogue, and scarcely any action, and are little more than a simple comparison between the subject to be investigated and something very well known. In others may be traced the outlines of a complete drama. The obscurity which may be thought to lie in some of them, wholly arises from our not clearly understanding *his character*, or that of his audience, or the occasion on which he spoke; except where the subject itself rendered some obscurity unavoidable.

Conciseness is another excellence of the parables of Christ. Scarce a single circumstance or expression can be taken away from any of them, without injuring the whole. They also comprehend the most extensive and important meaning in the shortest compass of narration; and afford at the same time the largest scope to the judgment and reflection of the reader. An extraordinary candour and charity likewise pervade all the parables of Jesus. He gives the most favourable representations of things. In the parable of the lost sheep, he supposes but one of a hundred to go astray; yet the good shepherd leaves the rest, to go in quest of this. In the parable of the ten virgins, he supposes the number of the wise to be equal to that of the foolish. In that of the prodigal, for one son that takes a riotous course, there is another that continued in his duty. In that of the ten talents, two are supposed to improve what is committed to them, for one that does not improve it. In the parable of the rich man and Lazarus, Abraham uses the term *Son* to the former, though in the place of punishment; and he is represented as still retaining kind regards to his brethren. A name is delicately withheld from the character that is blameable, while one is given to the good.

An exact propriety and decorum is observed in all the parables of Christ, and every thing that is spoken is suited to the character of the person who speaks it. His parables surpass all others, in being so natural and probable that they have the air of truth rather than of fiction.[1] Generosity and decorum are so strongly manifested in the character of the compassionate Samaritan, that the Jewish lawyer, whose prejudices and passions would be all excited by the very name, could not withhold his approbation of it. There is also great candour and propriety in the selection and adjustment of the two characters. Had a Jew or a Samaritan been represented as assisting a fellow-countryman, or a Jew assisting a Samaritan, the story would have been less convincing and impressive. " In the

---

[1] Law's Life of Christ, p. 325 note.

parable of the murmuring labourers, the proprietor of the vineyard assembles the labourers in the evening *all together* to receive their wages, begins to pay those who were called at the latest hour, and proceeds gradually to the first invited. This circumstance with the greatest propriety introduces their complaint. It also discovers candour and integrity in the judge, in allowing them to be witnesses of his distribution, in attentively hearing their objections, and calmly pointing out how groundless and unreasonable they were. In the parable of the barren fig-tree, the keeper of the vineyard is with great propriety and candour introduced as interceding earnestly for a further respite and trial to the tree, and enforcing his plea from weighty considerations." In what an amiable and proper light is the generous creditor in the parable represented, and with what natural simplicity. " Then the lord of that servant was moved with compassion, and loosed him, and forgave him the debt." What ingenuous sorrow appears in the character of the prodigal? What natural affection, generosity, and forwardness to forgive, in the parent?

Besides the regard paid by Jesus Christ to historical propriety in the incidental circumstances (which has been already noticed in pp. 404, 405.), it is a peculiar excellence of the parables of Christ, that the *actors* in them are not the inferior creatures, but *men*. He leads us sometimes to draw intruction from the inferior animals, and the process of things in the vegetable world, as well as nature in general. But men are the more proper *actors* in a scene, and *speakers* in a dialogue, formed for the instruction of mankind. Men add to the significance without diminishing the ease and familiarity of the narration. In the fables of Æsop, and of the Hindoos [1], as well as of the Jewish prophets, inferior creatures, and even vegetables are introduced as actors.

Another distinguishing character of our Lord's parables is, the frequent introduction of *his own character* into them, as the principal figure, and in views so various, important, and significant; for instance, the sower; the vine-dresser; the proprietor of an estate; the careful shepherd; the just master; the kind father; the splendid bridegroom; the potent nobleman; the heir of a kingdom; and the king upon his throne of glory judging the whole world of mankind. A striking contrast hence arises between the simplicity of the descriptions and the dignity of the speaker.

A further material circumstance which characterises the parables of Christ is, that he spake them just as occasions were offered; in the ordinary course of his conversation and instruction; privately as well as publicly; to his own disciples; to the multitude; and to the Pharisees and chief rulers. An accidental question or unexpected event, appears to have been the occasion of some of them. For instance, that of the good Samaritan, when he was asked, " Who is my neighbour?" that of the rich man, whose ground brought forth plentifully, when he was desired to determine a suit concerning an estate; that of the barren fig-tree, when he was told of the Galilæans

---

[1] See Wilkins's, or Sir W. Jones's Traslation of the Fables of Veshnoo-Sarma.

whom Pilate had massacred; that of a certain man who made a great supper, when he was present at a splendid entertainment; and those of the careful shepherd, the prodigal son, the unjust steward, and the inhuman rich Jew, when a great number of publicans and sinners, and of Pharisees and Scribes, happened to be present, and the latter murmured against him, and insulted him. No man, except Jesus, ever did speak in parables, unpremeditated, and on various occasions. No man is now capable of conveying instruction in the like manner. No instructor can ever presume to be equal to him, nor so much as to imitate or resemble him.

Again; the parables of our Lord were admirably adapted to the time when, the place in which, and the persons to whom, they were delivered; while they were also fitted for the general instruction of mankind in all ages. These compositions of Christ were likewise all original. Dr. Lightfoot and others have shown that Jesus often borrowed proverbs and phrases from the Jews. But an inspired teacher would not surely propose *whole parables*, that were in common use, for his own. Nor does it appear that any body used the parables of Christ before his time; for those which are alleged out of the Talmudical or other Jewish writers, were all penned some ages after his birth. For instance, the parable of the householder and the labourers [1], which is extant in the Jerusalem Gemara, was written an age and a half at least after the destruction of the temple. It is more probable, therefore, that it was written in imitation of Christ, than borrowed from any antient tradition. The same may be said of many others; as Matt. xviii. 17. out of the book of Musar; and of another parable like that, Matt. xxv. 1. of the ten virgins. [2]

If Jesus had borrowed whole parables, or discourses, it would scarcely have been remarked so often, that he spake as one who had authority, and not as the Scribes; nor would the extraordinary wisdom of his instructions have so much astonished his auditors. Further; the Scribes and Pharisees would have been glad to have exposed him by proclaiming to the people, that he was indebted to the Rabbis for what gained him the reputation of superior sagacity. This, also, would have been a plausible argument to have retorted upon him, when he opposed their traditions.

To conclude, it is a singular excellency in the Gospel parables, that, though they were for the most part occasional, and wisely adapted by our Saviour to the characters and circumstances of the persons to whom they were originally addressed, yet they contain most wholesome instructions and admonitions for all ages of the world, and for every future period of his church. They are at once excellently accommodated to the comprehensions of the vulgar, and capable of instructing and delighting the most learned and judicious. In short, *all* the parables of Christ " are beautiful; the truest delineation of human manners, embellished with all those graces which an unaffected lovely simplicity of diction is able to bestow, — graces beyond the reach of the most elaborate artifice of composition. But

---

[1] Matt. xx. 1—16.   [2] Le Clerc on Matt. xx. 15.

two of the number shine among the rest with unrivalled splendour; and we may safely challenge the genius of antiquity to produce, from all his stores of elegance and beauty, such specimens of pathetic unlaboured description, as the parables of the prodigal son and the good Samaritan."[1]

SECTION VI.

ON SCRIPTURE PROVERBS.

I. *Nature of Proverbs.* — *Prevalence of this mode of instruction.* — II. *Different kinds of Proverbs.*—III. *The Proverbs occurring in the New Testament, how to be interpreted.*

I. THE inhabitants of Palestine, in common with other oriental nations, were much in the use of PROVERBS, or detached aphorisms; that is, concise and sententious common sayings, founded on a close observance of men and manners.

This method of instruction is of very remote antiquity, and was adopted by those, who, by genius and reflection, exercised in the school of experience, had accumulated a stock of knowledge, which they were desirous of reducing into the most compendious form, and comprising, in a few maxims, such observations as they apprehended to be most essential to human happiness. Proverbial expressions were peculiarly adapted to a rude state of society, and more likely to produce effect than any other: for they professed not to dispute, but to command, — not to persuade, but to compel, they conducted men, not by circuitous argument, but led them immediately to the approbation and practice of integrity and virtue. That this kind of instruction, however, might not be altogether destitute of attraction, and lest it should disgust by an appearance of harshness and severity, the teachers of mankind added to their precepts the graces of harmony: and decorated them with metaphors, comparisons, allusions, and other embellishments of style.

Proverbial instruction was a favourite style of composition among the Jews, which continued to the latest ages of their literature; and obtained among them the appellation of *Mashalim* or parables, partly because it consisted of parables strictly so called (the nature of which has been discussed in the preceding section), and partly because it possessed uncommon force and authority over the minds of the auditors. The proverbs of the Old Testament are classed by Bishop Lowth among the didactic poetry of the Hebrews, of which many specimens are extant, particularly the book of Proverbs, composed by Solomon, of which an account is given in the subsequent part of this work.[2] The royal sage has, in one of his proverbs, himself ex-

---

[1] Dr. Gray's Delineation of the Parables, pp. 19. 21. (Edinburgh, 1814, 8vo.) Monthly Review, O. S. vol lvii. p. 196. Wakefield's Internal Evidences of Christianity, p 36. Simpson's Internal and Presumptive Evidences of Christianity, pp. 403—422.
[2] See Vol. IV. Part I. Chap. III. Sect. III

plained the principal excellencies of this form of composition; exhibiting at once a complete definition of a proverb, and a very happy specimen of what he describes:

> Apples of gold in a net-work of silver
> Is a word seasonably spoken
>
> Prov. xxv. 11.

Thus intimating, that grave and profound sentiments should be set off by a smooth and well-turned phraseology; as the appearance of the most beautiful and exquisitely-coloured fruit, or the imitation of it, perhaps, in the most precious materials, is improved by the circumstance of its shining (as through a veil) through the reticulations of a silver vessel exquisitely carved. In the above-cited passage he further insinuates, that it is not merely a neat turn and polished diction by which proverbs must be recommended; but that truth itself acquires additional beauty when partially discovered through the veil of elegant fiction and imagery.

1. The first excellence of a proverb is *Brevity*[1], without which it can retain neither its name nor its nature. The discriminating sentiment should be expressed in a few words, not exceeding ten or at most twelve words, otherwise it is no longer a proverb, but a declamation; and it should force itself upon the mind by a single effort, not by a tedious process. Accordingly, the language must be strong and condensed, rather omitting some circumstances which may appear necessary, than admitting any thing superfluous. Horace himself insists on this as one of the express rules of didactic poetry, and has assigned the reason on which it is founded:

> Short be the precept, which with ease is gained
> By docile minds, and faithfully retained.[2]

Solomon expresses the same sentiment in his own parabolic manner:

> The words of the wise are like goads,
> And like nails that are firmly fixed. Eccles. xii. 11.

That is, they instantaneously stimulate or affect the mind; they penetrate deeply and are firmly retained. Even the obscurity, which is generally attendant on excessive brevity, has its use; as it sharpens the understanding, keeps alive the attention, and exercises the genius by the labour of investigation, while no small gratification results from the acquisition of knowledge by our own efforts.

2. Another excellence, essential to a proverb, is *Elegance*; which is neither inconsistent with brevity, nor with some degree of obscurity. Elegance in this connection respects the sentiment, the imagery, and the diction: and those proverbs, which are the plainest, most obvious, and simple, or which contain nothing remarkable either in sentiment or style, are not to be considered as destitute of their peculiar elegance, if they possess only brevity, and that neat, compact

---

[1] "The brevity of this kind of composition," says an elegant critic of antient times, "and the condensing of much thought into a small compass, renders it more sententious, more sage, and expressive as in a small seed, the whole power of vegetation, which is to produce a tree, is contained. And if any writer should amplify the sentence, it would no longer be a proverb, but a declamation." DEMETRIUS PHALEREUS, Περι Ερμηνειας, sect. ix.

[2] Art of Poetry by Francis, verse 455.

form, and roundness of period, which alone are sufficient to constitute a proverb. Examples of this kind occur in the maxim of David, recorded in 1 Sam. xxiv. 13. and in that of Solomon, Prov. x. 12.[1]

II. Proverbs are divided into two classes, viz. 1. Entire SENTENCES; and, 2. Proverbial PHRASES, which by common usage are admitted into a sentence.

1. Examples of *Entire* PROVERBIAL SENTENCES occur in Gen x. 9. and xxii. 14. 1 Sam. x. 12. and xxiv. 13 2 Sam. v. 8. and xx. 18. Ezek. xvi. 44. and xviii. 2. Luke iv 23. John iv. 37. and 2 Peter ii 22, in which passages the inspired writers expressly state the sentences to have passed into proverbs.

2. Examples of PROVERBIAL PHRASES, which indeed cannot be correctly termed proverbs, but which have acquired their form and use, are to be found in Deut xxv. 4. 1 Kings xx. 11. 2 Chron. xxv. 9. Job vi. 5. xiv. 19. and xxviii. 18. Psal. xlii. 7. and lxii. 9. Of this description also is that beautiful and memorable sentence, THE FEAR OF THE LORD IS THE BEGINNING OF WISDOM, Psal. cxi. 10, which is repeated in Prov. i. 7. ix. 10. and in Job xxviii. 28. The book of *Proverbs* likewise contains very many similar sentences; from among which it may suffice to refer to Prov. i. 17. 32. iii. 12. vi. 6. 22. v. 5. 13. 19. 25. xi. 15. 22. 27. xii. 11. 15. xv. 2. 33. xvii. 1. 10. 19. 28. xix. 2. 24. xx. 4. 11. 14. 21. 25. xxii. 6. 13. xxv. 11. 16. 27. xxvi. 4. 10, 11. 14. 17. 28. xxvii. 6, 7, 8. 10. 14. 17. 22. xxviii. 21. So in the book of *Ecclesiastes*, ch. i. 15. 18. iv. 5 12. v. 2. 6. 8, 9, 10. vi. 9. vii. 17. ix. 4. 18. x. 1, 2. 8. 15. 19, 20. xi. 3, 4. 6, 7. xii. 12. And in the *Prophets*, Jer. xiii 23. xxiii. 28. Ezek. vii. 5. Micah vii. 5, 6. Habak. ii. 6. Mal. ii. 10, &c. And likewise in the *New Testament*, as in Matt. v. 13—15. vi. 3. 21. 34. vii. 2. 5. 16. ix. 12. 16. x. 10. 22 24. 26. xii. 34. xiii. 12. 57. xv. 14 xxiii. 24. xxiv. 28. Mark ix 50. Luke ix. 62 xii. 48. xxiii. 31. Acts ix. 5 xx. 35. 1 Cor. v. 6. x. 12. xv. 33. 2 Cor. ix. 6, 7. 2 Thess. iii. 10. Tit. i. 15.

III. The Proverbs occurring in the New Testament are to be explained, partly by the aid of similar passages from the Old Testament, and partly from the antient writings of the Jews, especially from the Talmud; whence it appears how much they were in use among that people, and that they were applied by Christ and his apostles, agreeably to common usage. The proverbs, contained in the Old and New Testaments, are collected and illustrated by Drusius, and Andreas Schottus, whose works are comprised in the ninth volume of the Critici Sacri, and also by Joachim Zehner, who has elucidated them by parallel passages from the fathers as well as from the heathen writers, in a treatise published at Leipsic in 1601. The proverbs which are found in the New Testament have been illustrated by Vorstius[2] and Viser[3], as well as by Lightfoot and Schoetgenius in their *Horæ Hebraicæ et Talmudicæ*, and by Buxtorf in his *Lexicon Chaldaicum Talmudicum et Rabbinicum*, from which last-

---

[1] Lowth, Prælect xxiv. pp. 312—318. (edit. 1763), or vol. ii. pp. 162—173. of Dr. Gregory's translation.

[2] Vorstius's Diatriba de Adagiis Novi Testamenti is printed in Crenius's Fasciculus Tertius Opusculorum quæ ad Historiam et Philologiam Sacram spectant. 18mo. Rotterdam, pp. 475—576.; and also in Fischer's second edition of Leusden, De Dilectis N. T. (8vo. Lipsiæ), pp. 168—252.

[3] Viser, Hermeneutica Sacra Novi Testamenti, part ii. sect. ix, cap. 2. pp 132—150.

mentioned works Rosenmüller, Kuinoel, Dr. Whitby, Dr. A. Clarke, and other commentators, both British and foreign, have derived their illustrations of the Jewish parables and proverbs.

SECTION VII.

CONCLUDING OBSERVATIONS ON THE FIGURATIVE LANGUAGE OF SCRIPTURE.

I. *Synecdoche.* — II. *Irony.* — III. *Hyperbole.* — IV. *Paronomasia.*

BESIDES the figures already discussed, and the right understanding of which is of the greatest importance for ascertaining the sense of Scripture, Glassius, and other writers, who have treated expressly on the tropes and figures of the Sacred Writings, have enumerated a great variety of other figures which are to be found in them. As, however, many of these are merely rhetorical; and though they are admirably calculated to show how vastly superior the inspired volume is to all the productions of the human mind, for the beauty and sublimity of its compositions, yet as it would lead us into too wide a field of discussion, were we to introduce such figures at length, our attention must be directed to a few of those *principal figures* which have not been mentioned in the preceding pages.

The most important of these figures, which remain to be noticed, are, 1. Synecdoche; 2. Irony, 3. the Hyperbole; and, 4. the Paronomasia.

I. *Synecdoche.*

A SYNECDOCHE is a trope in which, 1. The *whole* is put for a *part;* 2. A *part* is put for the whole; 3. A certain number for an uncertain one, 4. A *general* name for a *particular* one; and, 5. *Special* words for *general* ones. A very few examples will suffice to illustrate this figure.

1. *The whole is sometimes put for a part:*

As, the *world* for the *Roman empire*, which was but a small though very remarkable part of the world, in Acts xxiv. 5. and Rev iii 10 The *world* for the *earth*, which is a part of it, 2 Pet iii 6 Rom. i 8. 1 John v 19 Thus the whole person is put for a part, as *man* for the *soul*, Luke xvi 23. where the rich man, Abraham, and Lazarus, are respectively put for their souls; *man*, for the *body*, John xix. 42. xx 2. 13. with Luke xxiv 3, in which passages Jesus is put for his dead body. *Time* for a *part* of time, as Dan. ii 4. which simply means, we wish you a long life and reign Gen. xvii. 19. where the words *everlasting covenant* denote while the Jewish polity subsists, that is, until Messiah come (Gen. xlix. 10.) — See also Exod. xxi. 6. where the expression *for ever* means the year of jubilee.

To this class of Synecdoche may be referred those instances, in which the *plural* number is sometimes put for the *singular* - as the mountains of Ararat (Gen. viii. 4.), which term might refer to the bi topped form of that mountainous range. The cities where Lot dwelt, Gen xix. 29.; the sides of the house, Amos vi. 10.; the sides of the ship, Jonah i 5.; the ass and foal, on which Jesus Christ was set, Matt. xxi. 7. compared with Zech. ix. 9., the prophets, Mark i 2 John vi. 45. Acts xiii. 40.; in all which places only one of those things or persons mentioned is to be understood. So, children is put for child, Gen. xxi. 7. so daughters and sons' daughters, Gen xlvi. 7., when Jacob had but one daughter, (verse 15) and one grand-daughter (verse 17.). So the sons of Dan, (verse 23.) when he had but one. So the cities of Gilead are mentioned in Judg. xii 7, whereas Jephthah was buried in one city in that region. In like manner, by the sons of Jehoiada is intended only Zechariah, 2 Chron. xxiv. 25 compared with verses 20 and 21., and our Saviour speaks of himself in the plural number, John iii. 11.

2. *Sometimes the part for the whole.*

Thus in Gen. i. 5. 8. 13. 19. 23. 31. the *evening and morning*, being the principal parts of the day, are put for the entire day. So the *soul* comprehends the entire man, Acts xxvii. 37. See similar expressions in Gen. xii. 5. xvii. 14. Exod. xii. 19. Lev. iv. 2. Psal. iii. 2. xi. 1. xxv. 13. Isa. lviii. 5. Ezek. xviii. 4. Acts ii. 41, &c.

So, the *singular* number is sometimes put for the *plural.*

This chiefly takes place when the Scriptures speak of the multitude collectively, or of an entire species. Thus in Gen. iii. 8. *tree* in the Hebrew is put for *trees.* Exod. xiv. 17. (Heb.) *I will get me honour upon Pharaoh and upon all his host, upon his chariots, and upon his horsemen,* that is, the whole multitude of his chariots which are enumerated in verse 7. So in Exod. xv. 1. 21. *the horse and his rider* are put collectively for the horses and horsemen who were in the Egyptian army. So the *Hivite, Canaanite,* and *Hittite,* Exod. xxiii. 28., the ox and the ass, Isa. i. 3. the *stork,* the *turtle,* the *crane,* the *swallow,* Jer. viii. 7., the *palmer worm,* Joel i. 4 , *street,* Rev. xxi. 21 , are respectively put for the Hivites, oxen, storks, &c. &c. It is proper to remark, that in very many instances the learned and pious translators of our authorised version have justly rendered the singular words in the plural number where the sense evidently required it.

3. *Very frequently a certain or definite number is put for an uncertain and indefinite number.*

Thus we find *double* for *much* or sufficient, in Isa. xl. 2. lxi. 7. Jer. xvi. 18. Zech. ix. 12. Rev. xviii. 6. *Twice* for several times, in Psal. lxii. 11. *Five* for a few, 1 Cor. xiv. 19. in which verse ten thousand are put for many. *Ten* for many, Gen. xxxi. 7. and 1 Sam. i. 8. But most frequently we have *seven* for an indefinite number. See Gen. iv. 15 Lev. xxvi. 18. 21. 24. 28 Ruth iv 15. 1 Sam ii 5 Psal cxix. 164. Prov xxiv. 16. xxvi 25. Isa. iv. 1. Jer xv 9. Ezek xxxix. 9. 12. Zech. iii 9. Matt. xii. 45. *One hundred* for many, indefinitely, in Eccl v 3. viii. 12. Prov. xvii. 10 Matt xix 29 Luke viii. 8. A *thousand* for a great many, Exod. xx 6. xxxiv. 7. Deut.'i. 11. 1 Sam. xviii. 7. Psal. cxix. 72. *Ten thousand* for an immense number, 1 Sam. xviii 7 Psal. iii 6 , and *ten thousand thousand* for a countless host, in Numb x. 36 (Heb.) Dan. vii. 10. Rev v 11, &c.

4. A *general name* is put for a *particular* one,

As in Mark xvi. 15. where *every creature* means *all mankind*, as *flesh* also does in Gen. vi 12. Psal. cxlv 21. Isa. xl 5, 6. lxvi. 23. Matt. xxiv 22. Luke iii. 6. and Rom. iii 20.

5. *Sometimes special words or particular names are put for such as are general:*

Thus Jehovah is, in Psal. xlvi 9 said to *break the bow, and cut the spear in sunder, and to burn the chariot in the fire* that is, God destroys all the weapons of war, and blesses the world with peace. Again, in Dan. xii. 2. we read, *Many of them that sleep in the dust of the earth shall awake, some to everlasting life, and some to shame and everlasting contempt.* Here *many* is put for *all.* So *man*, generally, is put for all mankind, both male and female, Psal i. 1. Mark xvi 16 Numerous similar passages might be adduced. So, *father* is put for *any ancestor,* Psal. xxii. 4. xliv. 1. cvi 6 *Father* for *grandfather,* 2 Sam ix 7. Dan. v. 11. *Mother* for *grandmother,* 1 Kings xv. 10 13. compared with verses 2 8. *Brother* for *kinsman,* Gen xiii 8 and xiv 14. with Gen. xii. 5. Matt xii. 46. John vii 3. 5 In the same manner, *son* is put for any of the posterity, thus Laban is said to be Nahor's son, in Gen. xxix. 5 when he was the son of Bethuel, and grandson or nephew of Nahor. Compare Gen. xxii 20 23 with xxiv. 29. So Rebekah is called Abraham's brother's daughter, Gen xxiv 48 *Father* and *mother* it tend all superiors, Exod. xv 12. In like manner the Greeks, who are the most eminent of the heathen nations, are put for the whole Gentile world, in Rom. i. 16. Gal iii 28. and Col iii 11 So *bread* denotes all the necessaries of life, in Matt. vi. 11. and numerous other places The *fatherless* and *widows* are put for any who are in distress or affliction, Isa. i. 17. 23. James 1 27, &c.

II. *Irony.*

An IRONY is a figure, in which we speak one thing and design another, in order to give the greater force and vehemence to our

I. Sect. VII.] *Figurative Language of Scripture.* 417

meaning. An irony is distinguished from the real sentiments of the speaker or writer, by the accent, the air, the extravagance of the praise, the character of the person, or the nature of the discourse.

Very numerous instances of irony are to be found in the Scripture, which might be produced, but the following will suffice to show the nature of this figure.

Thus, the prophet Elijah speaks in irony to the priests of Baal — *Cry aloud, for he is a God, either he is talking, or he is pursuing, or he is on a journey, or, peradventure, he sleepeth, and must be awaked.* (1 Kings xviii 27) So the prophet Micah bids Ahab *go to battle against Ramoth-Gilead and prosper.* (1 Kings xxii 15) We meet with an irony in Job xii 2. *No doubt but ye are the people, and wisdom shall die with you.* That well known passage in Eccles xi 9 may also be considered as an irony. *Rejoice, O young man, in thy youth, and let thine heart cheer thee in the days of thy youth, and walk in the way of thine heart and in the sight of thine eyes.* Nay, the Almighty himself appears to speak ironically in Gen iii 22 *And the Lord God said, Behold the man is become as one of us, to know good and evil*, and also in Judges x 14. *Go and cry unto the gods which ye have chosen, let them deliver you in the time of your tribulation.* And in the same manner we may apprehend Christ's rebuke to the Jewish doctors, when he says (Mark vii. 9) *Full well ye reject the commandment of God, that ye may keep your own tradition*, where, by the word καλως, which our translators render *full well*, it is evident that our Saviour intends quite the contrary of what his language seems to import Saint Paul also has a fine example of irony in 1 Cor iv 8. *Now ye are full, now ye are rich, ye have reigned as kings without us, and I would to God ye did reign, that we also might reign with you.*

Under this figure we may include the SARCASM, which may be defined to be an irony in its superlative keenness and asperity. As an instance of this kind, we may consider the soldier's speech to our Lord; when, after they had arrayed him in mock majesty, they bowed the knee before him, and said, *Hail, King of the Jews.* (Matt. xxvii. 29.) So again, while our Redeemer was suspended on the cross, there where some who thus derided him, *Let Christ, the King of Israel, descend now from the cross, that we may see and believe.* (Mark xv. 32.)

III. *Hyperbole.*

This figure, in its representation of things or objects, either magnifies or diminishes them beyond or below their proper limits: it is common in all languages, and is of frequent occurrence in the Scripture.

Thus, things, which are very lofty, are said to reach up to heaven. Deut. i. 28. ix. 1. Psal. cvii. 26. So, things which are beyond the reach or capacity of man, are said to be in *heaven*, in the *deep*, or *beyond the sea*, Deut. xxx, 12. Rom x. 6, 7. So, a great quantity or number is commonly expressed by the *sand of the sea, the dust of the earth*, and *the stars of heaven*, Gen. xiii 16. xli. 49. Judges vii. 12. 1 Sam. xiii. 5. 1 Kings iv. 29. 2 Chron. i. 9 Jer. xv. 8. Heb. xi. 12. In like manner we meet, in Numb. xiii. 33. with *smaller than grasshoppers*, to denote extreme diminutiveness: 2 Sam. i. 23. *swifter than eagles*, to intimate extreme celerity. Judges v. 4. the *earth trembled*, verse 5. the mountains *melted*. 1 Kings i. 40. the earth *rent*. Psal. vi. 6. *I make my bed to swim*. Psal. cxix. 136. *rivers* of tears run down mine eyes. So we read of *angels' food*, Psal. lxxviii. 25. The *face of an angel*, in Acts vi. 15.; *the tongue of an angel*, in 1 Cor. xiii 1. See also Gal. i 8. and iv. 14. In Ezek xxi. 6. we read *sigh with the breaking of thy loins*, that is, most deeply. So in Luke xix. 40. we read that *the stones would cry out*, and in verse 44. they shall not leave in thee *one stone upon another;* that is, there shall be a total desolation.[1]

IV. *Paronomasia.*

PARONOMASIA is the name given to an expression, which contains two words, that are purposely chosen, so that they may resemble each other in *sound*, while they may differ in sense. It is a very favourite figure of rhetoric among the Hebrews, and is common among the oriental languages in general. Paronomasia differs from our rhyme, in as much as the words which constitute it do not necessarily stand at the end of parallelisms or strophes, but may be placed together in any part of a sentence, and are found in prose as well as in poetry. Professor Stuart [2] has given numerous examples of this figure in the Old Testament, which the limits of this work do not permit us to insert. The paronomasia also occurs very frequently in the New Testament, especially in the writings of Saint Paul, where it seems to be sometimes unpremeditated, and sometimes to be the result of design on the part of the writer. Professor Winer, to whom we are indebted for this paragraph, divides the paronomasia into two kinds, viz.

1. *Where words of a like sound are employed in the same sentence, without regard to their sense.*

In Rom. i. 29. we have πορνεια, πονηρια — φθονου, φονου — 31. ασυνετους, ασυνθετους — 1 Cor. ii 13. εν διδακτοις πνευματος, πνευματικοις πνευματικα συγκρινοντες — Luke xxi. 11. Και λιμοι και λοιμοι εσονται These instances of paronomasia can not be equivalently expressed in English.

In order to form a paronomasia of this kind, unusual words or forms of words are sometimes employed as in Gal v. 7. πειθεσθαι — ἡ πεισμονη.

2. *Where the words are not only the same in sound, but there is also a resemblance or antithesis in the sense.* Thus.

Gal iv. 17. Ζηλουσιν ὑμας, — ἱνα αυτους ζηλουτε. — *They* ZEALOUSLY AFFECT *you ...... that ye might* [ZEALOUSLY] *affect them*, that is, they earnestly desire to draw you over to their party, — that you may be devoted to their interests.

Rom. v. 19. Ὡσπερ δια της παρακοης του ἑνος ανθρωπου ἁμαρτωλοι κατεσταθησαν οἱ πολλοι, οὑτω και δια της ὑπακοης — *As by one man's* DISOBEDIENCE *many* [or multitudes] *were made sinners, so by the* OBEDIENCE *of one shall many* [or multitudes] *be made righteous.*

Other instances of this kind of paronomasia occur in Phil. iii. 2, 3. 2 Cor iv. 8. 2 Cor. v. 4. 2 Thess. iii. 11. Philem. 10. 20. Acts viii. 20. 1 Cor. iii 17. vi. 2. xi. 29 31. 2 Cor. x. 2 (Gr.)

In this manner a paronomasia is sometimes formed by repeating the same word in a different sense as in Matt. viii. 22 *Let the* DEAD *bury* their dead. See the proper import of this passage explained in page 373 *supra*.

Similar instances of paronomasia occur in the Greek Apocryphal writings of the Old Testament Compare particularly Dan. xiii. 54, 55.[3]

---

[1] Glassii Phil Sacr tom. ii. pp. 55, 56. 897—916. 1243—1276. 1283—1294. Turretin. de Interp S S. p 206

[2] Stuart's Hebrew Grammar, pp. 336, 337. (first edit.)

[3] Winer's Greek Grammar of the New Testament, pp. 161, 162 (Andover, 1825.)

CHAPTER II.

ON THE INTERPRETATION OF THE POETICAL PARTS OF SCRIPTURE.

I. *A large portion of the Old Testament proved to be poetical; — Cultivation of Poetry by the Hebrews.—* II. *The Sententious Parallelism, the Grand Characteristic of Hebrew Poetry.— Its origin and varieties.* 1. *Parallel Lines gradational; —* 2. *Parallel Lines antithetic; —* 3. *Parallel Lines constructive; —* 4. *Parallel Lines introverted.—* III. *The Poetical Dialect not confined to the Old Testament. — Reasons for expecting to find it in the New Testament.— Proofs of the existence of the Poetical Dialect there; —* 1. *From simple and direct quotations of single passages from the poetical parts of the Old Testament; —* 2. *From quotations of different passages, combined into one connected whole; —* 3. *And from quotations mingled with original matter —* IV. *Original Parallelisms occurring in the New Testament, —* 1 *Parallel Couplets;* 2. *Parallel Triplets ; —* 3. *Quatrains ; —* 4, 5. *Stanzas of five and six lines ;—* 6. *Stanzas of more than six parallel lines.—* V. *Other examples of the Poetical Parallelism in the New Testament ; —* 1. *Parallel Lines gradational; —* 2. *The Epanodos.—* VI. *Different kinds of Hebrew Poetry. —* 1. *Prophetic Poetry ; —* 2. *Elegiac Poetry ; —* 3. *Didactic Poetry, —* 4. *Lyric Poetry ; —* 5. *The Idyl ; —* 6. *Dramatic Poetry ;* 7. *Acrostic or Alphabetical Poetry. —* VII. *General Observations for better understanding the Compositions of the Sacred Poets.*

I. IT is obvious to the most cursory reader of the Holy Scriptures, that among the books of the Old Testament there is such an apparent diversity in style, as sufficiently discovers which of them are to be considered as poetical, and which are to be regarded as prose compositions While the historical books and legislative writings of Moses are evidently prosaic in their composition, the book of Job, the Psalms of David, the Song of Solomon, the Lamentations of Jeremiah, a great part of the prophetic writings, and several passages occasionally scattered through the historical books, bear the most plain and distinguishing marks of poetical writing.[1] We can have no reason to doubt that these were originally written in verse, or in some kind of measured numbers; though, as the antient pronunciation of the Hebrew language is now lost, we can only very imperfectly ascertain the nature of the Hebrew verse.

From the manner, however, in which Josephus, Origen, and Jerome have spoken of the Hebrew poetry, it should seem that in their time its beauty and rules were well known. Josephus repeatedly affirms[2] that the songs composed by Moses are in heroic verse, and that David composed several sorts of verses and songs, odes and

---

[1] In illustration of this remark, we may mention the song of Moses, at the Red Sea (Exod xv.), the prophecy of Balaam (Numb. xxiv. 18—24.), the song of Deborah, and Barak (Jud. v) Nor is it improbable that the *Book of the Wars of the Lord*, (Numb. xxi. 14.) and the *Book of Jasher*, (Josh. x. 13. 2 Sam i 18) were written in poetic measures.

[2] Antiq. Jud. lib. ii. c. 16. § 4, lib. iv. c. 8. § 44. and lib, vii. c. 12. § 3.

hymns, in honour of God: some of which were in trimeters or verses of three metrical feet, and others in pentameters or verses of five metrical feet. Origen and Eusebius are said to have espoused the same notion: and Jerome, probably influenced by the manner in which he found the poetical parts of the Old Testament exhibited in the manuscripts of the Septuagint version, fancied that he perceived iambic, alcaic, and sapphic verses in the Psalms, similar to those occurring in the works of Pindar and Horace: hexameters and pentameters in the Songs of Deuteronomy and Isaiah, the book of Job, and those of Solomon; and sapphic verses in the Lamentations of Jeremiah.[1] Among modern writers, the nature and genius of Hebrew poetry have been warmly contested[2]; but by no one have these subjects been illustrated with more elegance and ability than by the late eminently learned Bishop of London, Dr. Robert Lowth. In the third of his justly admired Lectures on Hebrew Poetry[3], he has collected much and very valuable information concerning the much litigated question, respecting the nature of Hebrew metre; but many of his arguments are successfully controverted by Bishop Jebb, in his Sacred Literature[4]; to which work, and to Bishop Lowth's Lectures, the reader is necessarily referred, as the discussion of this very difficult question would extend this chapter to an inordinate length. The construction, characteristics, and different kinds of Hebrew Poetry, including also the poetical

---

[1] Hieronymi, Præfat. in Chronic. Epist. 135. ad Paul. Urb. et Epist. ad Paulin. Comment. in Ezek. c. 30.

[2] Carpzov (Introd. ad Libros Canonicos Vet. Test. pars ii. pp. 28, 29.) has given a list of antient and modern writers who have treated on Hebrew Poetry, and in pp. 2—27. he has noticed the various discordant opinions on this topic. The hypothesis of Bishop Hare on Hebrew metre was refuted by Bishop Lowth at the end of his lectures, and also in his "Larger Confutation," published in 1766, in 8vo. in answer to Dr. Edwards's Latin Letter in defence of Hare's system, published in the preceding year. The general opinion of the learned world has coincided with the arguments of Lowth.

[3] The first edition of these Lectures appeared in 1753, in 4to., under the title of "De Sacra Poesi Hebræorum Prælectiones Academicæ." A second edition was printed by Bishop Lowth in 1763, in two volumes, octavo, the second volume, consisting of additions made by the celebrated Professor Michaelis, who had reprinted the Prælectiones at Gottingen. Several subsequent editions have issued from the Clarendon press, particularly a beautiful one in 1821, including (besides the additions of Michaelis) the further observations of Rosenmuller, (whose edition appeared at Leipsic in 1815,) Ritchei, and Weiss. In 1787, the late Dr. George Gregory printed his excellent English translation of Bishop Lowth's Lectures, in two octavo volumes, with some very important additional notes, which was reprinted in 1816. In 1787 M. Herder published at Leipsic two octavo volumes *On the Spirit of Hebrew Poetry*, from which a selection was translated and published in 1801, under the title of *Oriental Dialogues*. Both these publications are distinguished by that bold criticism, which for the last fifty or sixty years has characterised too many of those German divines, to whose researches in other respects biblical literature is so largely indebted. Sir William Jones has a few observations on Hebrew metres in his Poesos Asiaticæ Comment. cap. ii. (Works, vi. pp. 22—59.) See also "An Essay on Hebrew Poetry, Ancient and Modern. By Philip Sarchi, LL.D. London, 1824.," the latter portion of the volume, which treats on modern Hebrew poetry, is both curious and interesting. Professor Pareau has also given an abstract of the most material observations on Hebrew Poetry, in his Institutio Interpretis Veteris Testamenti, pp. 426—457.

[4] pp. 4—22. The title at length of this beautifully and correctly printed work is as follows: — "Sacred Literature: comprising a Review of the Principles of Composition, laid down by the late Robert Lowth, D.D. Lord Bishop of London, in his Prælections and Isaiah, and an Application of the Principles so reviewed to the Illustration of the New Testament. By John Jebb, A.M. [now D.D. and Bishop of Limerick.] London, 1820." 8vo.

style of the New Testament, are the subjects now to be considered: and our account of them is chiefly abridged from the Lectures of Bishop Lowth, and from his preliminary dissertation prefixed to his version of the prophet Isaiah, together with Bishop Jebb's elegant and instructive volume above cited.

The peculiar excellence of the HEBREW POETRY will appear when we consider that its origin and earliest application have been clearly traced to the service of religion. To celebrate in hymns and songs the praises of Jehovah — to decorate the worship of the Most High with all the charms and graces of harmony — to give force and energy to the devout affections — was the sublime employment of the sacred muses: and it is more than probable, that the very early use of sacred music in the public worship of the Hebrews, contributed not a little to the peculiar character of their poetry, and might impart to it that appropriate form, which, though chiefly adapted to this particular purpose, it nevertheless preserves on every other occasion. In the Old Testament we have ample evidence that music and poetry were cultivated from the earliest ages among the Hebrews. In the days of the Judges, mention is made of the schools or colleges of the prophets; in which the candidates for the prophetic office, under the direction of some superior prophet, being altogether removed from intercourse with the world, devoted themselves entirely to the exercises and study of religion: and though the sacred history affords us but little information concerning their institutes and discipline, yet it is manifest from 1 Sam. x. 5—10 and xix. 20—24., that a principal part of their occupation consisted in celebrating the praises of Jehovah in hymns and poetry, with choral chants accompanied with various musical instruments. But it was during the reign of David that music and poetry were carried to the greatest perfection. For the service of the tabernacle he appointed four thousand Levites, divided into twenty-four courses, and marshalled under several leaders, whose sole business it was to sing hymns, and to perform instrumental music in the public worship. Asaph, Heman, and Jeduthun were the chief directors of the music, and, from the titles of some of the psalms, we may infer that they also were excellent composers of hymns or sacred poems. In the first book of Chronicles (ch. xxv.) we have an account of the institutions of David: which were more costly, splendid, and magnificent than any that ever obtained in the public service of other nations.

II. According to Bishop Lowth there are four principal CHARACTERISTICS OF HEBREW POETRY, viz. — 1. The acrostical or alphabetical commencement of lines or stanzas;— 2. The admission of foreign words and certain particles, which seldom occur in prose composition, and which thus form a distinct poetical dialect; — 3. Its sententious, figurative, and sublime expressions; and, 4. Parallelism, the nature of which is fully illustrated in a subsequent page. But the existence of the three first of these characteristics has been disproved by Bishop Jebb, who observes that the grand characteristic of Hebrew poetry does *not* appear to belong peculiarly to the original language of the Old Testament as contra-distinguished from that of the New.

"It is not the acrostical, or regularly alphabetical commencement of lines or stanzas; for this occurs but in twelve poems of the Old Testament: it is not the introduction of foreign words, and of what grammarians call the paragogic, or redundant particles; for these licences, though frequent, are by no means universal, in the poetical books of Scripture; and they are occasionally admitted in passages merely historical and prosaic: it is not the rhyming termination of lines; for no trace of this artifice is discoverable in the alphabetical poems, the lines or stanzas of which are defined with infallible precision; and every attempt to force it on the text, has been accompanied by the most licentious mutilation of Scripture: and, finally, this grand characteristic is not the adoption of metre, properly so called, and analogous to the metre of the heathen classics; for the efforts of the learned, to discover such metre in any one poem of the Hebrews, have universally failed; and while we are morally certain, that, even though it were known and employed by the Jews, while their language was a living one, it is quite beyond recovery in the dead and unpronounceable state of that language; there are also strong reasons for believing, that, even in the most flourishing state of their literature, the Hebrew poets never used this decoration.

"Again, it is most certain, that the proper characteristic of Hebrew poetry is not elation, grandeur, or sublimity, either of thought or diction. In these qualities, indeed, a large portion of the poetical Scriptures, is not only distinguished, but unrivalled: but there are also many compositions in the Old Testament, indisputably poetical, which, in thought and expression, do not rise above the ordinary tone of just and clear conceptions, calmly, yet pointedly delivered."[1]

The grand, and, indeed, the sole characteristic of Hebrew Poetry, is what Bishop Lowth intitles PARALLELISM, that is, a certain equality, resemblance, or relationship, between the members of each period; so that in two lines, or members of the same period, things shall answer to things, and words to words, as if fitted to each other by a kind of rule or measure. Such is the general strain of the Hebrew poetry; instances of which occur in almost every part of the Old Testament, particularly in the ninety-sixth psalm.

It is in a great measure owing to this form of composition that our admirable authorised version, though executed in prose, retains so much of a poetical cast; for, that version being strictly word for word after the original, the form and order of the original sentences are preserved; which, by this artificial structure, this regular alternation and correspondence of parts, makes the ear sensible of a departure from the common style and tone of prose.

The origin of this form of poetical composition among the Hebrews, Bishop Lowth has satisfactorily deduced from the manner in which they were accustomed to sing or chant their sacred hymns. They were accompanied with music, and were alternately sung by opposite choirs: sometimes one choir performed the hymn itself, while the other sang a particular distich, which was regularly interposed at

---

[1] Bp. Jebb's Sacred Literature, pp. 4, 5.

stated intervals. In this manner we learn that Moses with the Israelites chanted the ode at the Red Sea (Exod. xv. 20, 21.); and the same order is observable in some of the psalms which are composed in this form. On some occasions, however, the musical performance was differently conducted, one of the choirs singing a single verse to the other, while the other constantly added a verse in some respect correspondent. Of this the following distich is an example: —

> Sing praises to Jehovah, for he is good,
> Because his mercy endureth for ever (Psal. cxxxvi. 1.)

Which Ezra informs us (iii. 10, 11.) was sung by the priests and Levites in alternate choirs, " after the ordinance of David, king of Israel;" as indeed may be collected from the hundred and thirty-sixth psalm itself, in which the latter verse sung by the latter choir forms a perpetual epode. Of the same nature is the song of the women concerning Saul and David (1 Sam. xviii. 7.); and in the very same manner does Isaiah describe the seraphin as chanting the praises of Jehovah — " they cried one to another," that is, alternately,

> Holy, holy, holy, Jehovah, God of hosts!
> The whole earth is filled with his glory! (Isa vi. 3.)

But the fullest example, perhaps, of this style of composition is to be found in the twenty-fourth psalm, composed on occasion of the induction of the ark to Mount Sion; the mode of performing which is particularly illustrated by Bishop Lowth [1], and must have had a most noble and impressive effect.

In determining the length of his lines, Bishop Lowth considers only that relation and proportion of one verse to another which arises from the correspondence of terms, and from the form of construction, whence results a rhythmus of propositions, and a harmony of sentences. From this correspondence of the verses one with another, arises a certain relation also between the composition of the verses, and the composition of the sentences, so that generally periods coincide with stanzas, members with verses, and pauses of the one with pauses of the other. This correspondence is called parallelism, the corresponding lines are called parallel lines, and the words or phrases answering one to another in the corresponding lines, parallel terms.

A single example will illustrate the above definition of parallelism: — In Luke i. 52, 53. we read, *He* (God) *hath put down the mighty from their seats, and exalted them of low degree. He hath filled the hungry with good things, and the rich he hath sent empty away.* In this passage the same *thing* is expressed, viz. that God changes the conditions of men · and this same *thing* is also expressed, in corresponding members that represent it in various points of view. Thus the Almighty changes adversity into prosperity, and prosperity into adversity. The *words answer to each other*, the mighty — those of low degree; put down — exalted; the hungry (or poor) — the rich; filled with good things — sent empty away. Lastly, the *things or*

---

[1] Lecture xxvii. Bishop Horsley, in his translation of the book of Psalms, has divided them so as to exhibit the construction of those divine compositions to the best possible advantage.

subjects stated answer to each other by a constrast sufficiently obvious: the former (the powerful and rich) are depressed; the latter (the humble and poor) are exalted.

The nature of parallelism, thus defined and illustrated, is sometimes so evident as to strike even a careless reader, and sometimes so subtle and obscure as to require considerable practice, and some familiarity with the system, in order to distribute the pauses and develope the different members of the sentences in probable order and connection. Thus, much doubt has arisen not only as to what books, but as to what parts of books, are to be accounted poetical. Sometimes, according to Dr. Jebb, it is continuous and unmixed, as in the Psalms, Proverbs, and Canticles; sometimes it characterises the main body of a work with a prosaic introduction and conclusion, as in the book of Job, — sometimes it predominates throughout a whole book with an occasional mixture of prose, as in most of the prophets; sometimes the general texture is prose, with an occasional mixture of verses, as in the historical books, and the book of Ecclesiastes.

This parallelism has hitherto been confined principally to the poetical books of the Old Testament; and to them chiefly, in the first edition of this work, the author had restricted it. Bishop Jebb, however, has demonstrated that this grand characteristic of Hebrew poetry pervades the New Testament as well as the Old.

The poetical parallelism has much variety and many gradations, being sometimes more accurate and manifest, sometimes more vague and obscure: it may, however, on the whole, be said to consist of four species, viz. Parallel Lines *Gradational*[1], Parallel Lines *Antithetic*, Parallel Lines *Synthetic*, and Parallel Lines *Introverted*.

1. PARALLEL LINES GRADATIONAL are those, in which the second or responsive clause so diversifies the preceding clause, as generally to rise above it, sometimes by a descending scale in the value of the related terms and periods, but in all cases with a marked distinction of meaning. This species of parallelism is the most frequent of all: it prevails chiefly in the shorter poems, in many of the psalms, and very frequently in the prophecies of Isaiah. Three or four instances will suffice to show the nature of parallel lines gradational. The first example shall be taken from the first psalm.

---

[1] Bishop Lowth has ranged the different kinds of parallelism under *three* classes only, viz. parallels synonymous, parallels antithetic, and parallels synthetic. The two last terms, it will be perceived, we have retained, and in lieu of parallels *synonymous* we have adopted the term *parallel lines gradational*. Bishop Jebb has assigned satisfactory reasons for changing the bishop's phraseology. According to Lowth, parallel lines synonymous are those which correspond one to another by expressing the same sentiment in different but nearly equivalent terms. But Bp. Jebb's proves, from an examination of the bishop's examples, that this definition does not hold good. he therefore proposes that of *cognate parallels*, as preferably applicable to this kind of parallels. (Sacred Literature, pp 34. —50.) A learned critic, however, has suggested the term *gradational parallelism*, as being most expressive, and also most applicable to the examples adduced by these eminent prelates. (British Critic for 1820, vol. xiv pp. 585, 586.) We have, therefore, adopted this term in the present chapter. Bp. Jebb had further considered the *introverted parallel* as a variety of the Hebrew parallelism; but as the same critic has assigned good reasons for constituting it a *distinct* class, we have availed ourselves of his authority, and have accordingly adopted it.

> O the happiness of that man,
> Who hath not walked in the counsel of the ungodly;
> And hath not stood in the way of sinners;
> And hath not sat in the seat of the scornful. (Psalm i. 1.)

"The exclamation with which the psalm opens, belongs equally to each line of the succeeding triplet. In the triplet itself, each line consists of three members; and the lines gradually rise, one above the other, not merely in their general sense, but specially, throughout their correspondent members. To *walk*, implies no more than casual intercourse; to *stand*, closer intimacy, to *sit*, fixed and permanent connection, the *counsel*, the ordinary place of meeting, or public resort, the *way*, the select and chosen footpath, the *seat*, the habitual and final resting-place, the *ungodly*, negatively wicked, *sinners*, positively wicked; the *scornful*, scoffers at the very name or notion of piety and goodness."[1]

The following passages will supply additional examples: —

> Who shall ascend the mountain of Jehovah?
> And who shall stand within his holy place?
> The clean of hands, and the pure in heart (Psalm xxiv. 3, 4.)

"To *ascend* marks progress, to *stand*, stability and confirmation the *mountain of Jehovah*, the site of the divine sanctuary; *his holy place*, the sanctuary itself. and in correspondence with the advance of the two lines which form the first couplet, there is an advance in the members of the third line *the clean of hands, and the pure in heart* - *the clean of hands, shall ascend the mountain of Jehovah. the pure in heart, shall stand within his holy place*"[2]

> O Jehovah, in thy strength the king shall rejoice;
> And in thy salvation, how greatly shall he exult!
> The desire of his heart, thou hast granted him,
> And the request of his lips, thou hast not denied. (Psalm xxi 1, 2.)

"The gradation of member above member, and line above line, in each couplet of this stanza, is undeniable "salvation" is an advance upon "strength," and "how greatly shall he exult," an advance upon "he shall rejoice:" again, "the request of the lips," is something beyond "the desire of the heart," — it is desire brought into act. The gradation in the last members of the last two lines may not be equally obvious; but it is by no means less certain "thou hast granted — thou hast not denied ." the negative form is here much stronger than the positive; for it is a received canon of biblical philology, that verbs of negation, or, what amounts to the same thing, adverbs of negation prefixed to verbs, have, in such cases, the force of expressing the opposite affirmative with peculiar emphasis. — for example, the Lord *will not hold him guiltless*, who taketh his name in vain: that is, WILL ASSUREDLY HOLD HIM GUILTY. Exod xx. 7."

The prophetic muse is no less elegant and correct. Isaiah especially abounds in beautiful instances of this mode of gradation Thus he says,

> Seek ye Jehovah, while he may be found,
> Call ye upon him, while he is near,
> Let the wicked forsake his way,
> And the unrighteous man his thoughts ·
> And let him return to Jehovah, and he will compassionate him;
> And unto our God, for he aboundeth in forgiveness (Isa lv. 6, 7)

"In the first line, men are invited to seek Jehovah, not knowing where he is, and on the bare intelligence that he *may be found*; in the second line, having found Jehovah, they are encouraged to call upon him, by the assurance that he is NEAR. In the third line, the wicked, the positive, and presumptuous sinner, is warned to forsake *his way*, his habitual course of iniquity; in the fourth line, the unrighteous, the negatively wicked, is called to renounce *the very thought of sinning* While in the last line, the appropriative and encouraging title OUR GOD, is substituted for the awful name of JEHOVAH; and simple *compassion* is heightened into *overflowing mercy and forgiveness* "[3]

In Isa. li. 1. 4. 7. there is another singularly fine example of moral gradation, which is admirably illustrated by Bishop Jebb[4], to whose "Sacred Literature" the reader is referred. But excellent as Isaiah confessedly is, he is not unrivalled in this kind of composition: the

---

[1] Bp. Jebb's Sacred Literature, p 41.
[2] Ibid. p. 40.
[3] Ibid. pp. 37, 38.
[4] Ibid. pp 46—49.

other prophets contain abundant examples; we shall, however, only adduce two instances. The first, which is from Hosea, is exquisitely pathetic, and will speak for itself: —

> How shall I give thee up, O Ephraim?
> Abandon thee, O Israel?
> How shall I make thee as Admah,
> Place thee in the condition of Zeboim?
> My heart is turned upon me;
> My bowels yearn all together.
> I will not execute the fury of mine anger
> I will not return to make destruction of Ephraim;
> For God I am, and not man;
> The Holy One in the midst of thee, although I am no frequenter of cities.
> Hosea xi. 8, 9. (Bp. Horsley's Translation.)

The other passage is from Joel, and is highly animated.

> Like mighty men shall they rush on,
> Like warriors shall they mount upon the wall,
> And, every one in his way, shall they march,
> And they shall not turn aside from their paths
> Joel ii 7.

The prophet is denouncing a terrible judgment on the land of Judah, by the devastation of locusts; and all naturalists and travellers, who have witnessed the desolation caused by those destructive insects, attest and confirm the fidelity of Joel's description of their progress and ravages.

2. PARALLEL LINES ANTITHETIC are those, in which two lines correspond one with another, by an opposition of terms and sentiments; when the second is contrasted with the first, sometimes in expressions, sometimes in sense only. This is not confined to any particular form. Accordingly the degrees of antithesis are various, from an exact contraposition of word to word, sentiment to sentiment, singulars to singulars, plurals to plurals, down to a general disparity, with something of a contrariety in the two propositions.

This species of parallelism is of less frequent occurrence in the prophetical poems of the Old Testament, especially those which are elevated in the style, and more connected in the parts; but it is admirably adapted to adages, aphorisms, proverbs, and detached sentences. Much, indeed, of the elegance, acuteness, and force, of a great number of the proverbs of Solomon, arises from the antithetic form, the opposition of diction, and sentiment, as in the following examples:

> A wise son rejoiceth his father:
> But a foolish son is the grief of his mother.
> Prov. x. 1.

Here every word has its opposite, the terms *father* and *mother* being relatively opposite;

> The memory of the just is a blessing
> But the name of the wicked shall rot.
> Prov x 7

In this instance there are only two antithetic terms, for *memory* and *name* are synonymous. See also Prov. xi. 24. xvi. 33. and xxix. 26

But, though the antithetic parallel be of comparatively rare occurrence in the superior kinds of Hebrew poetry, it is not inconsistent with them. Thus, we have a beautiful instance of it in the thanksgiving ode of Hannah, 1 Sam. ii. 4—7., and in some of the Psalms, as in Psalm xx. 7, 8. xxx. 5. and xxxvii. 10, 11. Isaiah, also, by means of it, without departing from his usual dignity, greatly increases the beauty of his composition.

> For the mountains shall be removed;
> And the hills shall be overthrown;
> But my kindness from thee shall not be removed;
> And the covenant of my peace shall not be overthrown
>
> Isa. liv. 10.

See likewise Isa. liv. 7, 8. ix. 10. and lxv. 13, 14.

3. PARALLEL LINES CONSTRUCTIVE are those, in which the parallelism consists only in the similar form of construction; in which word does not answer to word, and sentence to sentence, as equivalent or opposite: but there is a correspondence and equality between the different propositions, in respect of the shape and turn of the whole sentence, and of the constructive parts; such as noun answering to noun, verb to verb, member to member, negative to negative, interrogative to interrogative. This species of parallel includes all such as do not come within the two former classes. Accordingly, Bishop Lowth remarks, that the variety of this form is very great; the parallelism being sometimes more, sometimes less exact, and sometimes hardly at all apparent. The nineteenth psalm will furnish a beautiful instance of parallel lines constructive:

> The law of JEHOVAH is perfect, restoring the soul;
> The testimony of JEHOVAH is sure, making wise the simple,
> The precepts of JEHOVAH are right, rejoicing the heart
> The commandment of JEHOVAH is clear, enlightening the eyes
> The fear of JEHOVAH is pure, enduring for ever,
> The judgments of JEHOVAH are truth, they are just altogether,
> More desirable than gold, or than much fine gold,
> And sweeter than honey, or the dropping of honey-combs.
>
> Psal. xix. 7—11.

Additional instances of the constructive parallelism occur in Psalm cxlviii. 7—13. Job xii. 13—16 Isa xiv 4—9 and lviii. 5—8

Respecting the three preceding species of parallelism, Bishop Jebb remarks that, separately, "each kind admits many subordinate varieties, and that, in combinations of verses, the several kinds are perpetually intermingled; circumstances which at once enliven and beautify the composition, and frequently give peculiar distinctness and precision to the train of thought." He has illustrated this observation by some instances of such subordinate varieties. The six following are taken partly from his volume, and partly from the nineteenth of Bishop Lowth's Lectures on Hebrew Poetry. Thus:

(1.) Sometimes the lines are *bi-membral*; that is, they consist each of double members, or two propositions (or sentiments, as Lowth terms them).—For example,

> The nations raged; the kingdoms were moved,
> He uttered a voice, the earth was dissolved
> Be still, and know that I am God
> I will be exalted in the nations; I will be exalted in the earth.
>
> Psal. xlvi 6. 10.

> Bow thy heavens, O JEHOVAH, and descend,
> Touch the mountains and they shall smoke·
> Dart forth thy lightning, and scatter them,
> Shoot out thine arrows and destroy them.
>
> Psalm cxliv. 5, 6.

Isaiah has two striking instances of these bi-membral lines.

> When thou passest through waters, I am with thee;
> And through rivers, they shall not overwhelm thee.
> When thou walkest in the fire, thou shall not be scorched,
> And the flame shall not cleave to thee.
> Isa. xliii. 2.

> And they shall build houses, and shall inhabit them;
> And they shall plant vineyards, and shall eat the fruit thereof
> They shall not build, and another inhabit,
> They shall not plant, and another eat.
> Isa. lxv. 21, 22

(2) "Parallels are sometimes formed by a repetition of part of the first sentence:—

> My voice is unto God, and I cry aloud,
> My voice unto God, and he will hearken unto me
> I will remember the works of Jehovah;
> Yea, I will remember thy works of old.—
> The waters saw thee, O God,
> The waters saw thee, they were seized with anguish
> Psal. lxxviii. 1. 11 16.

(3.) "Sometimes, in the latter line, a part is to be supplied from the former, to complete the sentence:—

> The mighty dead tremble from beneath
> The waters, and they that dwell therein.
> Job xxvi 5.

(4.) "There are parallel triplets; where three lines correspond together, and form a kind of stanza; of which, however, only two lines are commonly synonymous:—

> The wicked shall see it, and it shall grieve him,
> He shall gnash with his teeth, and pine away,
> The desire of the wicked shall perish
> Psal. cxii 10."[1]

Another instance of parallel triplets occurs in Job iii. 4., and Micah vi. 15.

(5.) "There are parallels consisting of four lines; two distiches being so connected together by sound and construction, as to make one stanza:

> The ox knoweth his owner;
> And the ass the crib of his lord
> But Israel does not know,
> My people doth not consider.
> Isa i. 3. See also Psal xxvii. 1, 2.

In stanzas of four lines, sometimes the parallel lines answer to one another, alternately, the first to the third, and the second to the fourth:—

> As the heavens are high above the earth;
> So high is his goodness over them that fear him
> As remote as the east is from the west,
> So far hath he removed from us our transgressions.
> Psal. ciii 11, 12."[2]

Sometimes, however, in the alternate quatrain, by a peculiar artifice in the distribution of the sentences, the third line forms a continuous sense with the first, and the fourth with the second:—

---

[1] Bp. Jebb's Sacred Literature, pp. 27, 28.   [2] Ibid. p. 29.

> From the heavens JEHOVAH looketh down;
> He seeth all the children of men,
> From the seat of his rest he contemplateth
> All the inhabitants of the earth
>
> Psal xxxiii. 13, 14.

Isaiah with great elegance uses this form of composition:—

> For thy husband is thy Maker,
> JEHOVAH God of hosts is his name
> And thy Redeemer is the Holy One of Israel;
> The God of the whole earth shall he be called
>
> Isa liv. 5

(6) Some periods also may be considered as forming stanzas of five lines, in which the odd line or member usually either comes in between two distiches, or the line that is not parallel is generally placed between the two distiches, or, after two distiches, makes a full close.

> Who is wise, and will understand these things?
> Prudent, and will know them?
> For right are the ways of JEHOVAH
> And the just shall walk in them
> And the disobedient shall fall therein
>
> Hos. xiv. 9.

> Like as a lion growleth,
> Even the young lion over his prey,
> Though the whole company of shepherds be called together against him·
> At their voice he will not be terrified,
> Nor at their tumult will he be humbled
>
> Isa xxxi 4.

> Who establisheth the word of his servant
> And accomplisheth the counsel of his messenger;
> Who sayeth to Jerusalem, Thou shalt be inhabited,
> And to the cities of Judah, Ye shall be built,
> And her desolate places I will restore
>
> Isa xliv. 26.

The preceding are the chief varieties of the parallel lines, gradational, antithetic, and constructive a few others of less note are discussed both by Bishops Lowth and Jebb; for which the reader is necessarily referred to their respective works. We now proceed to notice,

4. PARALLEL LINES INTROVERTED. — These are stanzas so constructed, that, whatever be the number of lines, the first line shall be parallel with the last; the second with the penultimate or last but one; and so throughout, in an order that looks inward, or to borrow a military phrase, from flanks to centre. This may be called the *introverted parallelism.*

Bishop Jebb has illustrated this definition with several apposite examples, from which we have selected the three following.

> " My son, if thy heart be wise,
> My heart also shall rejoice,
> Yea, my reins shall rejoice;
> When thy lips speak right things.
>
> Prov. xxiii 15, 16.

> " And it shall come to pass in that day,
> JEHOVAH shall make a gathering of his fruit
> From the flood of the river;
> To the stream of Egypt:
> And ye shall be gleaned up, one by one;
> O ye sons of Israel,

> "And it shall come to pass in that day;
> The great trumpet shall be sounded
> And those shall come, who were perishing in the land of Assyria;
> And who were dispersed in the land of Egypt;
> And they shall bow themselves down before Jehovah,
> In the holy mountain, in Jerusalem.
> Isaiah xxvii. 13."

> "In these two stanzas of Isaiah, figuratively, in the first, and literally in the second, is predicted the return of the Jews from their several dispersions. The first line of each stanza is parallel with the sixth, the second with the fifth, and the third with the fourth; also on comparing the stanzas one with another, it is manifest, that they are constructed with the utmost precision of mutual correspondence, clause harmonising with clause, and line respectively with line; the first line of the first stanza with the first line of the second, and so throughout."

> "The idols of the heathen are silver and gold,
> The work of men's hand,
> They have mouths but they speak not,
> They have eyes but they see not,
> They have ears but they hear not;
> Neither is there any breath in their mouths;
> They who make them are like unto them,
> So are all they who put their trust in them.
> Psal cxxxv. 15—18."

The parallelisms here marked out are very accurate. In the first line of this example we have the idolatrous heathen; — in the eighth, those who put their trust in idols — in the second line the fabrication, — in the seventh, the fabricators, — in the third line, mouths without articulation; — in the sixth, mouths without breath; — in the fourth line, eyes without vision, and, in the fifth line, ears without the sense of hearing.

The parallelism of the extreme members, Bishop Jebb proceeds to state, may be rendered yet more evident, by reducing the passage into two quatrains; thus:

> The idols of the heathen are silver and gold;
> The work of men's hand,
> They who make them are like unto them;
> So are all they who put their trust in them.
>
> They have mouths, but they speak not,
> They have eyes but they see not,
> They have ears, but they hear not,
> Neither is there any breath in their mouths!

III. Such is the nature, and such are the species of the parallelisms, which are variously distributed throughout the Old Testament. With the exception of a few partial failures, it is worthy of remark, that the character and complexion of Hebrew poetry have been very competently preserved in that body of Greek translations, composed at different times, by different persons, and known under the name of the Septuagint version. Nor should it be omitted, that the Hebraic parallelism occurs also, with much variety, in the Apocrypha: the book of Ecclesiasticus, for example, is composed of pure parallelisms: the book of Wisdom, too, affords fine specimens of this manner, though it is commonly overlaid by the exuberant and vicious rhetoric of the Alexandrine Platonists; while, not to mention other parts of the Apocryphal writings, in Tobit and the books of Maccabees there are examples both of lyric and didactic poetry, clothed in parallelisms which will hardly shrink from comparison with several in the genuine Hebrew Scriptures. One other fact

---

[1] Sacred Literature, pp. 53, 54. 57, 58.

remains: namely, that in the sententious *formulæ* of the Rabbinical writers, the manner of Hebrew poetry is frequently observed, with much accuracy, though with a manifest declension of spirit.[1]

Such being the fact, we are authorised by analogy to expect a similar parallelism in the New Testament, particularly when the nature of that portion of the Holy Scriptures is considered. It is a work supplementary to and perfective of the Old Testament; composed under the same guidance that superintended the composition of the latter; written by native Jews, Hebrews of the Hebrews, — by men whose minds were moulded in the form of their own Sacred Writings, and whose sole stock of literature (with the exception of Paul, and probably also of Luke and James) was comprised in those very writings. Now, it is improbable in the extreme, that such men, when they came to write such a work, should, without any assignable motive, and in direct opposition to all other religious teachers of their nation, have estranged themselves from a manner, so pervading the noblest parts of the Hebrew Scriptures, as the sententious parallelism. But we are not left to analogical reasoning. The Greek style of the New Testament leads us to expect a construction similar to that which we find in the Old. The New Testament, as we have already shown[2], is not written in what is termed strictly classical Greek, but in a style of the same degree of purity as the Greek which was spoken in Macedonia, and that in which Polybius wrote his Roman History. From the intermixture of Oriental idioms and expressions with those which are properly Greek, the language of the New Testament has been termed *Hellenistic* or *Hebraic-Greek*. The difference in style and manner which subsists between the writers of the New Testament and the Greek classic authors is most strongly marked: and this difference is not confined to single words and combination of words, but pervades the whole structure of the composition: and in frequent instances, a poetical manner is observable, which not only is not known, but would not be tolerated in any modern production, purporting to be prose. This poetical style has been noticed briefly by Boecler, Ernesti, Michaelis, Schleusner, Dr. Campbell, and other critics, and also by the author of this work, in the first edition; but none of these writers were aware, to how great an extent it pervades the New Testament. It was reserved for Bishop Jebb, to whose "Sacred Literature" this chapter is so deeply indebted, to develope the existence of the poetical parallelism in the New Testament, and to place its numerous beauties in a point of view, equally novel and delightful to the biblical student.

The proofs of the existence of the poetical dialect in the New Testament, are disposed by this critic under the four following divisions; viz. 1. Simple and direct quotations, in the New Testament,

---

[1] Sacred Literature, p. 76. Bp. Jebb has illustrated the remarks in the text by numerous apposite examples from the apocryphal and rabbinical writings, for which the reader is referred to his work, pp. 84—90.

[2] See pp. 18—22. of this volume, for an account of the Greek style of the New Testament.

of single passages from the poetical parts of the Old Testament; — 2. Quotations of a more complex kind, when fragments are combined from different parts of the poetical Scriptures, and wrought up into one connected whole; and, 3. Quotations mingled with original matter. We shall give one or two examples of each of these proofs.

1. *Simple and direct Quotations of single passages from the poetical parts of the Old Testament, in which the parallelism has been preserved by the writers of the New Testament.*

και συ Βηθλεεμ, γη Ιουδα,
ουδαμως ελαχιστη ει εν τοις ηγεμοσιν Ιουδα.
εκ σου γαρ εξελευσεται ηγουμενος,
ὁςτις ποιμανει τον λαον μου τον Ισραηλ.

And thou, Bethlehem, territory of Judah,
Art by no means least among the captains of Judah.
For from thee shall come forth a leader,
Who will guide my people Israel
Matt ii. 6.

ὑιε μου, μη ολιγωρει παιδειας Κυριου,
μηδε εκλυου, ὑπ' αυτου ελεγχομενος :
ὁν γαρ αγαπα Κυριος, παιδευει·
μαςιγοι δε παντα ὑιον, ὁν παραδεχεται.

My son, despise not the chastening of the Lord ;
Nor faint when thou art rebuked by him ·
For whom the Lord loveth he chasteneth,
But scourgeth every son whom he receiveth.
Heb. xii. 5, 6.

This passage is taken from Proverbs iii 11, 12. thus rendered in our authorised translation

My son, despise not the chastening of the Lord ;
Neither be weary of his correction
For whom the Lord loveth, he correcteth,
Even as a father the son *in whom* he delighteth.

In this last line the parallelism is completely spoiled. But Bp. Jebb shows, that Saint Paul's reading is afforded without altering a letter in the Hebrew text, by a slight departure from the Masoretic punctuation. The original passage in Prov. iii. 11, 12 , therefore, may be thus rendered in strict conformity with the Apostle.

The chastening of JEHOVAH, my son do not despise,
Neither be weary at his rebuking
For, whom JEHOVAH loveth, he chasteneth,
But scourgeth the son in whom he delighteth.

In the corrected version of this quatrain, the parallelism is not only preserved, but there is also a beautiful climax in the sense, both of which are excellently illustrated by Bp. Jebb. [*]

2. *Quotations of a more complex kind, in which fragments are combined from different parts of the Poetical Scriptures, and wrought up into one connected or consistent whole.*

Of this class of quotations, the following is a short but satisfactory specimen .

ὁ οικος μου, οικος προσευχης κληθησεται πασι τοις εθνεσιν·
ὑμεις δε εποιησατε αυτον σπηλαιον ληστων.

My house shall be called the house of prayer for all the nations ,
But ye have made it a den of thieves.
Mark xi. 17.

---

[*] Sacred Literature, pp. 98 109—113. — In pp 99—108. other examples are given, with suitable philological illustrations.

This antithetical couplet is composed of two independent passages, very remotely connected in their subject-matter, of which the first stands in the Septuagint version of Isaiah lvi. 57 exactly as it is given above from Saint Mark's Gospel. The substance of the second line occurs in the prophet Jeremiah. (vii. 11.)

μη σπηλαιον ληστων ὁ οινος μου,
Is my house a den of thieves? ¹

ω βαθος πλουτου, και σοφιας, και γνωσεως Θεου·
ὡς ανεξερευνητα τα ϰριματα αυτου
ϰαι ανεξιχνιαστοι αἱ ὁδοι αυτου·
τις γαρ εγνω νουν Κυριου;
η τις συμβουλος αυτου εγενετο,
η τις προεδωκεν αυτω,
ϰαι ανταποδοθησεται αυτω;

O the depth of the riches, and the wisdom and the knowledge of God!
How inscrutable are his judgments,
And untraceable his ways!
For who hath known the mind of the Lord?
Or who hath been his counsellor?
Or who hath first given unto him,
And it shall be repaid him again?
            Rom. xi. 33—35.

On this passage Bishop Jebb remarks that, although the quotation is not always so uniformly direct as in the preceding example, yet the marks of imitation are unquestionable, the probable sources of imitation are numerous, the continuity of the parallelism is maintained unbroken and the style, both of thought and of expression, is remarkable alike for elegance, animation, and profundity. He supposes the Apostle to have had the following texts (which are given at length by Dr J) present in his recollection, when composing this noble epiphonema, Psal xxxvi. 6. Job xi. 7, 8. v 9. xxxvi. 22, 23, Jer. xxiii. 18. Isa. xl. 13 15. Job xxiii. 18 and xli. 2.

"The first line proposes the subject.

O the depth of the riches, and the wisdom and the knowledge of God!

"The notion of depth, as a quality attributed alike to God's riches, and wisdom, and knowledge, is first expanded in the next couplet.

How inscrutable are his judgments;
And untraceable his ways!

Riches, wisdom, and knowledge are then, in a fine epanodos, enlarged upon in the inverted order, first, knowledge·

For who hath known the mind of the Lord?

secondly, wisdom

Or who hath been his counsellor?

thirdly, riches

Or who hath first given unto him,
And it shall be repaid him again?

"Let, now, the most skilfully executed *cento* from the heathen classics, be compared with this finished scriptural Mosaic of St Paul the former, however, imposing at the first view, will, on closer inspection, infallibly betray its patch-work jointing, and incongruous materials, while the latter, like the beauties of creation, not only bears the microscopic glance, but, the more minutely it is examined the more fully its exquisite organization is disclosed. The Fathers, also, often quote and *combine* Scripture. let their complex quotations be contrasted with those of the Apostle; the result may be readily anticipated." ²

3 *Quotations mingled with original matter, in which one or more passages derived from the Hebrew Scriptures, are so connected and blended with original writing, that the compound forms one homogeneous whole;*

---

¹ Sacred Literature, p. 114.
² Ibid. pp. 114. 117. 120. Other examples of complex quotations are given in pp. 121—123.

the sententious parallelism equally pervaded all the component members, whether original or derived.

πας γαρ ὅς ἂν ἐπικαλεσηται το ονομα Κυριου σωθησεται;
πως ουν ἐπικαλεσονται εἰς ὃν ουκ ἐπιςευσαν;
πως δε πιςευσουσιν, ὃν ουκ ηκουσαν;
πως δε ακουσουσι χωρις κηρυσσοντος;
πως δε κηρυξουσιν ἐαν μη αποςαλωσι;
 ως γεγραπται·
ὡς ὡραιοι οἱ ποδες των εὐαγγελιζομενων εἰρηνην;
των εὐαγγελιζομενων τα αγαθα;

For whosoever shall call on the name of the Lord, shall be saved ·
But how shall they call on him, in whom they have not believed?
And how shall they believe in him, of whom they have not heard?
And how shall they hear without a preacher?
And how shall they preach, if they be not sent?
 As it is written,
How beautiful the feet of those who bring good tidings of peace!
Who bring good tidings, of good things! (Rom. x. 13—18.)

The first line of this passage is literally taken from the Septuagint version of Joel ii. 32., the next quotation is original, and affords an exact, though somewhat peculiar specimen of parallelism, its composition nearly resembling that of the logical sorites, in which the predicate of each preceding line becomes the subject of the line next in order. Similar instances of this logical construction occur in the prophetic writings, and abound in the epistles of St. Paul.[1] The last couplet is from Isa. lii. 7, the Septuagint rendering of which is both confused and inaccurate. St. Paul, however, has quoted so much as it answered his purpose to quote, but has carefully maintained the parallelism uninjured.

λιθον ὃν απεδοκιμασαν οἱ οἰκοδομουντες,
αὐτος ἐγενηθε εἰς κεφαλην γωνιας·
παρα Κυριου ἐγενετο αὐτη,
και ἐςι θαυμαςη ἐν οφθαλμοις ἡμων·
δια τουτο λεγω ὑμιν·
ὅτι αρθησεται αφ' ὑμων ἡ βασιλεια του Θεου,
και δοθησεται ἐθνει ποιουντι τους καρπους αὐτης;
και ὁ πεσων ἐπι τον λιθον τουτον, συνθλασθησεται,
ἐφ' ὃν δ' ἂν πεση, λικμησει αὐτον.

The stone which the builders rejected,
The same has become the head of the corner,
From the Lord hath this proceeded,
And it is marvellous in our eyes,
 Wherefore I say unto you
That from you shall be taken away the kingdom of God;
And it shall be given to a nation producing the fruits thereof:
And he who falleth upon this stone, shall be sorely bruised;
But upon whomsoever it shall fall, it will grind him to powder.
          Matt xxi. 42—44.

The first four lines are literally taken from the Septuagint version of Psalm cxviii. 22, 23. The last four are original, and Bp. Jebb asks, with great reason, whether the parallelism is not more striking in the latter portion, than in the former.[2]

 IV. The preceding examples will sufficiently exemplify the *manner* in which the inspired writers of the New Testament were accustomed to cite, abridge, amplify, and combine passages from the poetical parts of the Old Testament; and also to annex to, or inter-

---

[1] Sacred Literature, p 124. In p 125. and also in his nineteenth section, (pp. 388—390.) Bp. Jebb has given several of the instances above referred to.
[2] Ibid p 127. In pp 128—142. Bp. Jebb has given additional examples of this class of mingled quotations, one of which (Acts iv. 24—30.) is particularly worthy of the reader's attention, on account of the very striking evidence which it affords (on the principles of sententious parallelism) of the supreme Deity of Jesus Christ.

mingle with, their citations, parallelisms by no means less perfect, of their own original composition. These examples further corroborate the argument from analogy for the existence of the grand characteristic of Hebrew poesy, — the sententious parallelism, — in the New Testament. We shall, therefore, now proceed to give a few examples of the *original parallelisms*, which pervade that portion of the Holy Scriptures. They are divided by Bishop Jebb into, 1. Parallel couplets; — 2. Parallel Triplets; — 3. Quatrains, of which the lines are either directly, alternately, or inversely parallel: — 4, 5. Stanzas of five and six lines; — 6. Stanzas of more than six parallel lines.

1. Of PARALLEL COUPLETS the two following examples will give the reader an adequate idea:

τω αιτουντι δε, διδου·
και τον θελοντα απο σου δανεισθαι, με αποςραφης.

To him that asketh thee, give;
And him that would borrow from thee, turn not away.
Matt. v. 42.

μεγαλυνει ἡ ψυχη μου τον Κυριον·
Και ηγαλλιασε το πνευμα μου επι τω Θεω τω σωτηρι μου·

My soul doth magnify the Lord;
And my spirit hath exulted in God my Saviour.
Luke i. 46, 47. [1]

" The second line of the latter couplet, it is well observed, clearly rises above the first in all its terms, μεγαλυνω is simply to *magnify*, to praise; αγαλλιαω denotes *exultation* or *ecstasy*, ψυχη is the *animal soul*; πνευμα the *immortal spirit*; τον Κυριον is the simplest and most general expression of the Godhead, the *Lord* of all men, τω Θεω τω σωτηρι μου is a considerable amplification in terms, and personally appropriative in meaning, *the God who is* MY *Saviour*." [2]

2. PARALLEL TRIPLETS consist of three connected and correspondent lines, which are constructively parallel with each other, and form within themselves a distinct sentence or significant part of a sentence.

αἱ αλωπεκες φωλεους εχουσι·
και τα πετεινα του ουρανου κατασκηνωσεις·
ὁ δε υἱος του ανθρωπου ουκ εχει που την κεφαλην κλινη·

The foxes have dens;
And the birds of the air have nests,
But the Son of man hath not where to lay his head.
Matt. viii 20.

ὁ πιςευων εις τον υἱον, εχει ζωην αιωνιον·
ὁ δε απειθων τω υἱω, ουκ οψεται ζωην·
αλλ' ἡ οργη του Θεου μενει επ' αυτον.

He who believeth in the Son, hath life eternal;
But he who disobeyeth the Son, shall not see life;
But the wrath of God abideth on him.
John iii. 36.

In this passage, Bishop Jebb justly remarks, the translators of our authorised version " have not preserved the variation of the terms, ὁ πιςευων, ὁ απειθων rendering the former, 'he that believeth;' the latter, 'he that believeth not.' The variation, however, is most significant, and should, on no account, be overlooked as Dr. Doddridge well observes, ' the latter phrase explains the former, and shows, that the *faith* to which the

---

[1] Sacred Literature, p 143. In pp. 144—148. are given numerous other instances of parallel couplets.
[2] Ibid. p. 310.

promise of eternal life is annexed, is an effectual *principle* of sincere and unreserved obedience.' The descending series is magnificently awful. he who, with his heart *believeth in the Son*, is *already* in possession of eternal life. he, whatever may be his outward profession, whatever his theoretic or historical belief, who *obeyeth not the Son*, not only does not possess *eternal* life, he does not possess any thing worthy to be called *life at all*, nor, so persisting, ever can *possess*, for he shall not even *see* it. but this is not the whole, for, as eternal life is the *present possession* of the faithful, so the wrath of God is the *present* and *permanent* lot of the disobedient, it *abideth on him*."[1]

3. In QUATRAINS, two parallel couplets are so connected as to form one continued and distinct sentence; the pairs of lines being either directly, alternatively, or inversely parallel:

εαν τας εντολας μου τηρησητε,
μενειτε εν τη αγαπη μου·
καθως εγω τας εντολας του πατρος μου τετηρηκα,
και μενω αυτου εν τη αγαπη.

If ye keep my commandments,
Ye shall abide in my love;
Even as I have kept my Father's commandments,
And abide in his love.
                                  John xv. 10.

τις γαρ οιδεν ανθρωπων, τα του ανθρωπου,
ει μη το πνευμα του ανθρωπου το εν αυτω;
ουτω και τα του Θεου ουδεις οιδεν,
ει μη το πνευμα του Θεου.

For who of men, knoweth the depth of any man,
Save only the spirit of that man which is in him?
Even so, the depths of God knoweth no person;
Save only the spirit of God.
                                 1 Cor. ii. 11.

In this last cited passage, our authorised versions read *the things of a man, the things of the spirit of God*; an awkward mode of supplying the ellipsis, which ought to be filled up from the τα βαθη of the preceding verse. This ellipsis is supplied by Bishop Jebb from Dr. Macknight.

4. FIVE-LINED STANZAS admit of considerable varieties of structure, which it would exceed the limits of this work to specify. One or two instances must suffice to exemplify them.

ουχι δωδεκα εισιν ωραι της ημερας;
εαν τις περιπατη εν τη ημερα, ου προσκοπτει·
οτι το φως του κοσμου τουτου βλεπει:
εαν δε τις περιπατη εν τη νυκτι, προσκοπτει·
οτι το φως ουκ εστιν εν αυτω.

Are there not twelve hours in the day?
If a man walk in the day, he stumbleth not;
Because he seeth the light of this world
But if a man walk in the night he stumbleth,
Because the light is not in him.
                                John xi. 9, 10.

In this instance, the odd line or member (which commences the stanza) lays down a truth which is illustrated in the remaining four lines. A similar disposition is observable in the *first* of the two following stanzas, in which the odd line lays down the proposition to be illustrated, viz *By their fruits ye shall thoroughly know them*. In the *second* stanza, on the contrary, the odd lines make a full close, re-asserting with authority the same proposition, as undeniably established by the intermediate quatrains — *By their fruits*, THEREFORE, *ye shall thoroughly know them*.

---

[1] Sacred Literature, pp 149, 150. In pp. 151—167. are given numerous other examples, in which are interspersed some admirable quotations from the writings of the fathers.

[2] Ibid. p. 169. See also pp. 170—192. for further examples of the quatrain.

απο των καρπων αυτων επιγνωσεσθε αυτους·
μητι συλλεγουσιν απο ακανθων σταφυλην;
η απο τριβολων συκα;
ούτω παν δενδρον αγαθον καρπους καλους ποιει.
το δε σαπρον δενδρον καρπους πονηρους ποιει·
ου δυναται δενδρον αγαθον καρπους πονηρους ποιειν·
ουδε δενδρον σαπρον καρπους καλους ποιειν·
παν δενδρον μη ποιουν καρπον καλον,
εκκοπτεται και εις πυρ βαλλεται·
αραγε απο των καρπων αυτων επιγνωσεσθε αυτους.

> By their fruits ye shall thoroughly know them
> Do men gather from thorns the grape?
> Or from thistles the fig?
> Thus, every sound tree beareth good fruit;
> But every corrupt tree beareth evil fruit
>
> A sound tree cannot bear evil fruit;
> Nor a corrupt tree bear good fruit,
> Every tree not bearing good fruit,
> Is hewn down and cast into the fire
> By their fruits, therefore, ye shall thoroughly know them [1]
>
> Matt. vii. 16—20.

5. The SIX-LINED STANZAS likewise admit of a great variety of structure. Sometimes they consist of a quatrain, with a distich annexed: sometimes of two parallel couplets, with a third pair of parallel lines so distributed, that one occupies the centre, and the other the close, and occasionally of three couplets alternately parallel, the first, third, and fifth lines corresponding with one another, and, in like manner, the second, fourth, and sixth. Of these six-lined stanzas, Bishop Jebb has adduced numerous examples. We subjoin two.

οψιας γενομενης, λεγετε, ευδια,
πυρραζει γαρ ο ουρανος·
και πρωι, σημερον χειμων,
πυρραζει γαρ στυγναζων ο ουρανος·
υποκριται· το μεν προσωπον του ουρανου γινωσκετε διακρινειν·
τα δε σημεια των καιρων ου δυνασθε.

> When it is evening, ye say, "A calm!
> "For the sky is red"
> And in the morning, "To-day a tempest
> "For the sky is red and lowering"
> Hypocrites! the face of the sky ye know how to discern
> But ye cannot [discern] the signs of the times!
>
> Matt. xvi. 2, 3.

This stanza consists of a quatrain with a distich annexed. In the following passage, the stanza begins and ends with parallel lines, a parallel triplet intervening.'

εκεινος δε ο δουλος ο γνους το θελημα του κυριου έαυτου,
και μη έτοιμασας, μηδε ποιησας προς το θελημα αυτου,
    δαρησεται πολλας·
ο δε μη γνους,
ποιησας δε αξια πληγων,
    δαρησεται ολιγας.

> And that servant who knew the will of his lord,
> And who prepared not, neither did according to his will,
>   Shall be beaten with many stripes:

---

[1] Sacred Literature, p. 195.

And he who did not know,
And did things worthy of stripes,
Shall be beaten with few stripes.[1]
        Luke xii. 47, 48.

6. STANZAS OF MORE THAN SIX PARALLEL LINES.—It frequently happens that more than six parallel lines are so connected by unity of subject or by mutual relationship, as to form a distinct stanza. Of the numerous examples of this kind of distribution, given by Bishop Jebb, one specimen must suffice.

πας ουν ὁςις ακουει μου τους λογους τουτους, και ποιει αυτους,
ὁμοιωσω αυτον ανδρι φρονιμῳ,
ὁςις ῳκοδομησε την οικιαν αυτου επι την πετραν·
  και κατεβη ἡ βροχη,
  και ηλθον οἱ ποταμοι,
  και επνευσαν οἱ ανεμοι,
  και προσεπεσον τῃ οικιᾳ εκεινῃ,
και ουκ επεσε· τεθεμελιωτο γαρ επι την πετραν·

και πας ὁ ακουων μου τους λογους τουτους, και μη ποιων αυτους,
ὁμοιωθησεται ανδρι μωρῳ,
ὁςις ῳκοδομησε την οικιαν αυτου επι την αμμον·
  και κατεβη ἡ βροχη,
  και ηλθον οἱ ποταμοι,
  και επνευσαν οἱ ανεμοι,
  και προσεκοψαν τῃ οικιᾳ εκεινῃ,
και επεσε· και ην ἡ πτωσις αυτης μεγαλη.

  Whoever, therefore, heareth these my words, and doeth them,
  I will liken him to a prudent man,
  Who built his house upon the rock.
    And the rain descended,
    And the floods came,
    And the winds blew,
    And fell upon that house
  And it fell not, for it was founded upon the rock.

  And every one hearing these my words, and doing them not,
  Shall be likened to a foolish man,
  Who built his house upon the sand·
    And the rain descended,
    And the floods came,
    And the winds blew,
    And struck upon that house;
  And it fell, and the fall thereof was great.[q] Matt. vii. 24—27.

---

[1] Sacred Literature, pp 201. 204 We cannot withhold from our readers Bishop Jebb's beautiful remarks on the last cited passage. "The antithesis in this passage has prodigious moral depth he who sins *against* knowledge, though his sins were only sins of *omission*, shall be beaten with *many stripes*, but he who sins *without* knowledge, though his sins were sins of *commission*, shall be beaten only with *few* stripes. Mere negligence, against the light of conscience, shall be severely punished while an offence, in itself comparatively heinous, if committed ignorantly, and without light, shall be mildly dealt with. This merciful discrimination, however, is full of terror · for, whatever may be the case, respecting past, forsaken, and repented sins of ignorance, no man is intitled to take comfort to himself from this passage, respecting his present, or future course of life: the very thought of doing so, proves that the person entertaining that thought, has sufficient knowledge to place him beyond its favourable operation." Ibid. p. 205. Other examples of the six-lined stanza are given in pp. 204—211.

[q] Ibid. p. 211. In these two connected stanzas, the language may be justly termed *picturesque*. The marked transition in each of them from a long and measured movement, to short rapid lines, and the resumption, at the close, of a lengthened cadence, are peculiarly expressive. The continual return, too, in the shorter lines, of the copulative particle, (a return purely Hebraic, and foreign from classical usage,) has a fine effect:

Ch. II.]   *Poetical Parts of Scripture.*   439

V. Further, several stanzas are often so connected with each other as to form a paragraph or section. Luke xvi. 9—13. James iii. 1—12. iv. 6—10. and v. 1—6. and 1 John iv. 15—17. afford striking examples of this sort of distribution; for the detail and illustration of which we must refer our readers to Bishop Jebb's elegant and instructive volume, which has been so often cited. It only remains that we notice briefly the *gradational parallelism*, and the *epanodos*, in the New Testament, which he has discovered and elucidated.

1. PARALLEL LINES GRADATIONAL, (or, as Bishop Jebb terms them, COGNATE PARALLELISMS,) we have already remarked, are of most frequent occurrence in the poetical books of the Old Testament. The poetical parallelisms exhibited in the preceding pages, while they fully prove his position, that the poetical dialect pervades the New Testament, will prepare the reader to expect to find there similar instances of parallel lines gradational. The second example of parallel couplets, given in page 435. supra, affords a concise but beautiful specimen of the ascent or climax in the terms, clauses, or lines which constitute the parallelism. One or two additional instances, therefore, will suffice, to show the existence of the gradational parallelism in the New Testament.

> ὃν ὁ Κύριος Ἰησοῦς ἀναλώσει, τῷ πνεύματι ςόματος αὐτοῦ·
> καὶ καταργήσει τῇ ἐπιφανείᾳ τῆς παρουσίας αὐτοῦ.
>
> Whom the Lord Jesus will waste away, with the breath of his mouth,
> And will utterly destroy, with the bright appearance of his coming.
>   2 Thess. ii. 8.

"The first words, ὃν ὁ Κύριος Ἰησοῦς are common to both lines; ἀναλώσει implies no more, in this place, than *gradual decay*, καταργήσει denotes *total extermination;* while, in terror and magnificence, no less than in the effects assigned, *the breath of his mouth* must yield to *the bright appearance of his coming.* The first line seems to announce the ordinary diffusion, gradually to be effected, of Christian truth. the second, to foretell the extraordinary manifestation of the victorious Messiah, suddenly, and overwhelmingly, to take place in the last days." [1]

> εἰς ὁδὸν ἐθνῶν μὴ ἀπέλθητε·
> καὶ εἰς πόλιν Σαμαρειτῶν μὴ εἰσέλθητε·
> πορεύεσθε δὲ μᾶλλον πρὸς τὰ πρόβατα τὰ ἀπολωλότα οἴκου Ἰσραήλ.
>
> To the way of the Gentiles go not off;
> And to a city of the Samaritans, go not in;
> But proceed rather to the lost sheep of the house of Israel
>   Matt. x 5, 6

"This is a gradation in the scale of national and religious proximity; the *Gentiles,* the *Samaritans, Israel* In the remaining terms, there is a correspondent progress the *way,* or *road,* to foreign countries, a *city* of the Samaritans; the *house* of Israel, a phrase conveying the notion of HOME; *go not off,* — go not from Palestine, towards other nations; *go not in* to a city of the Samaritans; though in your progresses between Judæa and Galilee, you must pass by the walls of many Samaritan cities; but, however great your fatigue, and want of refreshment, *proceed rather* not merely to the house of Israel, but to *the lost sheep* of that house. Thus, by a beautiful gradation, the apostles are brought from the indefiniteness of a road leading to countries remote from their own, and people differing from themselves in habits, in language, and in faith, to the homefelt, individual, and endearing relationship of their own countrymen, children of the same covenant of promise, and additionally recommended to their tender compassion, as *morally lost.*

---

it gives an idea of danger, sudden, accumulated, and overwhelming. These are beauties which can be only retained in a literal traslation; and which a literal translation may exhibit very competently Ibid. p 214. In pp 215—248. the reader will find many other examples, intermingled with much just criticism and some fine quotations from the fathers.

[1] Sacred Literature, p. 312.

Bishop Jebb has given additional examples of the gradational parallelism from Matt. v. 45. vii. 1, 2. xx 26, 27 xxiv 17, 18 Mark iv. 24. Luke vi. 38. Rom. v. 7. James i. 17. iv 8. and v 5 Rev. ix. 6. and xxii. 14.

2. The nature of the INTROVERTED PARALLELISM, or *Parallel Lines Introverted*, has been stated in page 429., and confirmed by suitable examples Closely allied to this is a peculiarity or artifice of construction, which Bishop Jebb terms an *Epanodos*, and which he defines to be literally " *a going back*, speaking first to the second of two subjects proposed: or if the subjects be more than two, resuming them precisely in the inverted order, speaking first to the last, and last to the first." The *rationale* of this artifice of composition he explains more particularly in the following words : — " Two pair of terms or propositions, containing two important, but not equally important notions, are to be so distributed, as to bring out the sense in the strongest and most impressive manner : now, this result will be best attained, by commencing, and concluding, with the notion to which prominence is to be given, and by placing in the centre the less important notion, or that which, from the scope of the argument, is to be kept subordinate "[1] Having established the justice of this explanation by examples of epanodos, derived from the Scriptures, as well as from the best classic authors, Bishop Jebb has accumulated many examples proving its existence in the New Testament, the doctrines and precepts of which derive new force and beauty from the application of this figure. The length to which this chapter has unavoidably extended, forbids the introduction of more than one or two instances of the epanodos.

μη δωτε το ἅγιον τοις κυσι·
μηδε βαλητε τους μαργαριτας ὑμων εμπροσθεν των χοιρων·
μηποτε καταπατησωσιν αυτους εν τοις ποσιν αυτων.
και ςραφεντες ῥηξωσιν ὑμας

Give not that which is holy to the dogs,
Neither cast your pearls before the swine,
Lest they trample them under their feet;
And turn about and rend you
      Matt. vii. 6.

" The relation of the first line to the fourth, and that of the second to the third, have been noticed by almost all the commentators A minor circumstance is not altogether undeserving of attention the equal lengths, in the original, of each related pair of lines, the first and fourth lines being short, the second and third lines long. The sense of the passage becomes perfectly clear, on thus adjusting the parallelism

Give not that which is holy to the dogs;
Lest they turn about and rend you
Neither cast your pearls before the swine,
Lest they trample them under their feet.

" The more dangerous act of imprudence, with its fatal result, is placed first and last, so as to make and to leave, the deepest practical impression."[2]

Χριςου ευωδια εσμεν τω Θεω·
εν τοις σωζομενοις,
και εν τοις απολλυμενοις·
οἱς μεν οσμη θανατου, εις θανατον·
οἱς δε οσμη ζωης, εις ζωην.

We are a sweet odour of Christ,
To those who are saved,
And to those who perish;
To the one, indeed, an odour of death, unto death;
But to the other, an odour of life, unto life.[3]
      2 Cor. ii 15, 16.

---

[1] Sacred Literature, pp. 60, 335.   [2] Ibid. p. 339.   [3] Ibid. p. 344.

In this specimen of the epanodos, the painful part of the subject is kept subordinate; the agreeable is placed first and last.

The preceding examples are sufficient to show the existence of the grand characteristic of Hebrew poesy, — the sententious parallelism, with all its varieties, in the New Testament. The reader, who is desirous of further investigating this interesting topic (and what student who has accompanied the author of the present work thus far, will not eagerly prosecute it?) is necessarily referred to Bishop Jebb's "Sacred Literature," to which this chapter stands so deeply indebted; — a volume, of which it is but an act of bare justice in the writer of these pages to say, that, independently of the spirit of enlightened piety which pervades every part, it has the highest claims to the attention of EVERY biblical student for its numerous beautiful and philological criticisms and elucidations of the New Testament; for the interpretation of which this learned prelate has opened and developed a new and most important source, of which future commentators will, doubtless, gladly avail themselves.

VI. The sacred writers have left us DIFFERENT KINDS of poetical composition: they do not, however, appear to have cultivated either the *epic* or the *dramatic* species, unless we take these terms in a very wide sense, and refer to these classes those poems in which several interlocutors are introduced. Thus, M. Ilgen[1] and (after him) Dr. Good[2] conceive the book of Job to be a regular epic poem: while Messieurs Velthusen and Ammon think that the Song of Songs exhibits traces of a dramatic or melo-dramatic structure. Bishop Lowth, however, reduces the various productions of the Hebrew poets to the following classes; viz.

1. PROPHETIC POETRY. — Although some parts of the writings of the prophets are clearly in prose, of which instances occur in the prophecies of Isaiah, Jeremiah, Ezekiel, Jonah, and Daniel, yet the other books, constituting by far the larger portion of the prophetic writings, are classed by Bishop Lowth among the poetical productions of the Jews; and (with the exception of certain passages in Isaiah, Habakkuk, and Ezekiel, which appear to constitute complete poems of different kinds, odes as well as elegies) form a particular species of poesy, which he distinguishes by the appellation of *Prophetic.*

The predictions of the Hebrew Prophets are pre-eminently characterised by the sententious parallelism, which has been discussed and exemplified in the preceding pages. The prophetic poesy, however, is more ornamented, more splendid, and more florid than any other. It abounds more in imagery, at least that species of imagery, which, in the parabolic style, is of common and established acceptation, and which, by means of a settled analogy always preserved, is transferred from certain and definite objects to express indefinite and general ideas. Of all the images peculiar to the parabolic style, it most frequently introduces those which are taken from natural ob-

---

[1] Jobi, antiquissimi carminis Hebraici, Natura atque Virtutes, cap. iii, pp. 40—89.
[2] Introductory Dissertation to his version of the book of Job, p. xx

jects and sacred history: it abounds most in metaphors, allegories, comparisons, and even in copious and diffuse descriptions. It possesses all that genuine enthusiasm which is the natural attendant on inspiration; it excels in the brightness of imagination, and in clearness and energy of diction, and, consequently, rises to an uncommon pitch of sublimity, hence, also, it is often very happy in the expression and delineation of the passions, though more commonly employed in exciting them.[1]

The following passage from one of Balaam's prophecies (which Bishop Lowth ranks among the most exquisite specimens of Hebrew poetry), exhibits a prophetic poem complete in all its parts. It abounds in gay and splendid imagery, copied immediately from the tablet of nature, and is chiefly conspicuous for the glowing elegance of the style, and the form and diversity of the figures. The translation is that of the Rev. Dr. Hales.[2]

> How goodly are thy tents, O Jacob,
> And thy tabernacles, O Israel!
> As streams do they spread forth,
> As gardens by the river side;
> As sandal-trees which THE LORD hath planted,
> As cedar-trees beside the waters.
>
> There shall come forth a man of his seed,
> And shall rule over many nations
> And his kingdom shall be higher than Gog,
> And his kingdom shall be exalted.[3]
>
> (God brought him forth out of Egypt,
> He is to him as the strength of a unicorn)
> He shall devour the nations, his enemies,
> And shall break their bones,
> And pierce them through with his arrows.
>
> He lieth down as a lion,
> He coucheth as a lioness,
> Who shall rouse him?
> Blessed is he that blesseth thee,
> And cursed is he that curseth thee.

The eighteenth chapter and the three first verses of the nineteenth chapter of the Apocalypse present a noble instance of prophetic poesy, in no respect inferior to the finest productions of any of the Hebrew bards.[4]

---

[1] Bp. Lowth's Lectures on Hebrew Poetry, Lect. xviii. xix and xx.
[2] Analysis of Chronology, vol. ii. book i pp 224—226.
[3] In the rendering of this quatrain, Dr Hales has followed the Septuagint version, which he vindicates in a long note. In our authorised translation, made from the Masoretic text, the seventh verse of Numb xxiv. stands thus —

> He shall pour the water out of his buckets,
> And his seed *shall be* in many waters;
> And his king shall be higher than Agag,
> And his kingdom shall be exalted.

This is confessedly obscure. — Dr Boothroyd, in his New Version of the Old Testament, with a slight departure from the common rendering, translates the verse in the following manner —

> Water shall flow from the urn of Jacob,
> And his seed shall become as many waters;
> Their king shall be higher than Agag,
> And his kingdom more highly exalted.

[4] The passages above noticed are printed in Greek and English, divided so as to exhibit their poetical structure to the greatest advantage, in Dr. Jebb's Sacred Literature, pp. 452—459.

2. ELEGIAC POETRY. — Of this description are several passages in the prophetical books[1], as well as in the book of Job[2], and many of David's psalms that were composed on occasions of distress and mourning: the forty-second psalm in particular is in the highest degree tender and plaintive, and is one of the most beautiful specimens of the Hebrew elegy. The lamentation of David over his friend Jonathan (2 Sam. i. 17—27.) is another most beautiful elegy: but the most regular and perfect elegiac composition in the Scriptures, perhaps in the whole world, is the book intitled The Lamentations of Jeremiah, of which we have given a particular analysis, *infra*, Vol. IV. Part I. Chap. VI. Sect. II.

3. DIDACTIC POETRY is defined by Bishop Lowth to be that which delivers moral precepts in elegant and pointed verses, often illustrated by a comparison expressed or implied, similar to the Γνωμαι, or moral sentences, and adages, of the antient sages. Of this species of poetry the book of Proverbs is the principal instance. To this class may also be referred the book of Ecclesiastes.

4. Of LYRIC POETRY, or that which is intended to be accompanied with music, the Old Testament abounds with numerous examples. Besides a great number of hymns and songs which are dispersed through the historical and prophetical books, such as the ode of Moses at the Red Sea (Exod. xv.), his prophetic ode (Deut. xxxii.), the triumphal ode of Deborah (Judg. v.), the prayer of Habakkuk (iii.), and many similar pieces, the entire book of Psalms is to be considered as a collection of sacred odes, possessing every variety of form, and supported with the highest spirit of lyric poetry; — sometimes sprightly, cheerful, and triumphant; sometimes solemn and magnificent; and sometimes tender, soft, and pathetic.

5. Of the IDYL, or short pastoral poem[3], the historical psalms afford abundant instances. The seventy-eighth, hundred and fifth, hundred and sixth, hundred and thirty-sixth, and the hundred and thirty-ninth psalms, may be adduced as singularly beautiful specimens of the sacred idyl: to which may be added Isa. ix. 8.—x. 4.

6. Of DRAMATIC POETRY, Bishop Lowth[4] adduces examples in the book of Job and the Song of Solomon, understanding the term in a more extended sense than that in which it is usually received. Some critics, however, are of opinion, that the Song of Solomon is a collection of sacred idyls: and M. Bauer is disposed to consider the former book as approximating nearest to the *Mekàma*, that is, "the assemblies," moral discourses, or conversations of the celebrated Arabian poet Hariri.[5]

In another part of this work some reasons are offered in confirmation of this conjecture.

---

[1] See Amos v. 1, 2. 16. Jer ix. 17—22. Ezek. xxii. and xxxii.
[2] See Job iii. vi. vii. x. xiv xvii. xix. xxix xxx.
[3] Bishop Lowth defines an idyl to be a poem of moderate length, of a uniform middle style, chiefly distinguished for elegance and sweetness; regular and clear as to the plot, conduct, and arrangement
[4] Lowth, Prelect xviii —xxxiv.
[5] Bauer, Hermeneut. Sacr. p. 886.

Many of the psalms (and, according to Bishop Horsley[1], by far the greater part,) are a kind of dramatic ode, consisting of dialogues between persons sustaining certain characters. "In these dialogue-psalms, the persons are frequently the psalmist himself, or the chorus of priests and Levites, or the leader of the Levitical band, opening the ode with a proëm declarative of the subject, and very often closing the whole with a solemn admonition, drawn from what the other persons say."[2] The dramatic or dialogue form, which thus pervades the book of Psalms, admits of considerable variety. Its leading characteristic, however, is an alternate succession of parts, adapted to the purpose of alternate recitation by two semi-choruses in the Jewish worship. Bishop Jebb considers the sublime hymn of Zacharias (Luke i. 67—79.) as a dramatic ode of this description; and, in confirmation of his opinion, he remarks that Zacharias must have been familiar with this character of composition, both as a pious and literate Jew, much conversant with the devotional and lyric poetry of his country, and also as an officiating priest, accustomed to bear his part in the choral service of the temple. Dr. J. has accordingly printed that hymn in Greek and English, in the form of a dramatic ode: and by this mode of distribution has satisfactorily elucidated its true meaning and grammatical construction in many passages, which have hitherto in vain exercised the acumen of critics.[3]

To the preceding species of Hebrew poetry, we may add

7. The ACROSTIC or ALPHABETICAL POEMS. Bishop Lowth considered this form of poetry as one of the leading characteristics of the productions of the Hebrew muse: but this, we have seen[4], is not the fact. It may rather be viewed as a subordinate species, the form of which the Bishop thus defines: — The acrostic or alphabetical poem consists of twenty-two lines, or of twenty-two systems of lines, or periods, or stanzas, according to the number of the letters of the Hebrew alphabet; and every line, or every stanza, begins with each letter in its order, as it stands in the alphabet; that is, the first line, or first stanza, begins with א (*aleph*), the second with ב (*beth*), and so on. This was certainly intended for the assistance of the memory, and was chiefly employed in subjects of common use, as maxims of morality, and forms of devotion; which, being expressed in detached sentences, or aphorisms (the form in which the sages of the most antient times delivered their instructions), the inconvenience arising from the subject, the want of connection in the parts, and of a regular train of thought carried through the whole, was remedied by this artificial contrivance in the form. There are still extant in the books of the Old Testament twelve[5] of these poems: three of them perfectly alphabetical[6], in which every line is marked by its initial letter; the other nine less perfectly alphabetical, in which every stanza only is so distinguished. Of the three former

---

[1] Bishop Horsley's Book of Psalms translated from the Hebrew, Vol I. Pref. p. xv.
[2] See Vol. IV. Part I. Ch. III Sect. II. § II
[3] Sacred Literature, pp. 404—417. [4] See pp. 421, 422. *supra*.
[5] Psal. xxv. xxxiv. xxxvii. cxi. cxii. cxix. cxlv. Prov. xxxi. 10—91. Lam. i. ii. iii. iv.
[6] Psal. cxi. cxii. Lament. iii.

it is to be remarked, that not only every single line is distinguished by its initial letter, but that the whole poem is laid out into stanzas; two [1] of these poems each into ten stanzas, all of two lines, except the two last stanzas in each, which are of three lines; in these the sense and the construction manifestly point out the division into stanzas, and mark the limit of every stanza. The third [2] of these perfectly alphabetical poems consists of twenty-two stanzas of three lines: but in this the initial letter of every stanza is also the initial letter of every line of that stanza: so that both the lines and the stanzas are infallibly limited. And in all the three poems the pauses of the sentences coincide with the pauses of the lines and stanzas. It is also further to be observed of these three poems, that the lines, so determined by the initial letters in the same poem, are remarkably equal to one another in length, in the number of words nearly, and, probably, in the number of syllables; and that the lines of the same stanza have a remarkable congruity one with another, in the matter and the form, in the sense and the construction.

Of the other nine poems less perfectly alphabetical, in which the stanzas only are marked with initial letters, six [3] consist of stanzas of two lines, two [4] of stanzas of three lines, and one [5] of stanzas of four lines: not taking into the account at present some irregularities which in all probability are to be imputed to the mistakes of transcribers. And these stanzas likewise naturally divide themselves into their distinct lines, the sense and the construction plainly pointing out their limits: and the lines have the same congruity one with another in matter and form, as was above observed, in regard to the poems more perfectly alphabetical.

Another thing to be observed of the three poems perfectly alphabetical is, that in two [6] of them the lines are shorter than those of the third [7] by about one third part, or almost half; and of the other nine poems the stanzas only of which are alphabetical, that three [8] consist of the longer lines, and the six others of the shorter.

VII. We have already had occasion to remark, that the poetry of the Hebrews derives its chief excellence from its being dedicated to religion. Nothing can be conceived more elevated, more beautiful, or more elegant, than the compositions of the Hebrew bards; in which the sublimity of the subject is fully equalled by the energy of the language and the dignity of the style. Compared with them, the most brilliant productions of the Greek and Roman muses, who often employed themselves on frivolous or very trifling themes, are infinitely inferior in the scale of excellence. The Hebrew poet, who worshipped Jehovah as the sovereign of his people — who believed all the laws, whether sacred or civil, which he was bound to obey, to be of divine enactment — and who was taught that man was dependent upon God for every thing — meditated upon nothing but Jehovah; to Him he devoutly referred all things, and placed his supreme delight in celebrating the divine attributes and perfections.

---

[1] Psal. cxi. cxii. [2] Lament. iii.
[3] Psal. xxv. xxxiv. cxix. cxlv. Prov. xxxi. Lam. iv. [4] Lam. i. ii.
[5] Psal. xxxvii. [6] Psal. cxi. cxii. [7] Lament. iii. [8] Lam. i. ii. iv.

If, however, we would enter fully into the beauties of the sacred poets, there are two GENERAL OBSERVATIONS, which it will be necessary to keep in mind whenever we analyse or examine the Songs of Sion.

1. The first is, that *we carefully investigate their nature and genius.*

For, as the Hebrew poems, though various in their kinds, are each marked by a character peculiar to itself, and by which they are distinguished from each other, we shall be enabled to enter more fully into their elegance and beauty, if we have a correct view of their form and arrangement. For instance, if we wish critically to expound the Psalms, we ought to investigate the nature and properties of the Hebrew ode, as well as the form and structure of the Hebrew elegies, &c., and ascertain in what respects they differ from the odes, elegies, &c. of the Greek poets. In like manner, when studying the Proverbs of Solomon, we should recollect that the most antient kind of instruction was by means of moral sentences, in which the first principles of antient philosophy were contained; and, from a comparison of the Hebrew, Greek, and other gnomic sentences, we should investigate the principal characters of a proverb. In the book of Job are to be observed the unity of action, delineation of manners, the external form and construction of the poem, &c.

2. Further, in interpreting the compositions of the Hebrew bards, it ought not to be forgotten, that *the objects of our attention are the productions of poets, and of oriental poets in particular.*

It is therefore necessary that we should be acquainted with the country in which the poet lived, its situation and peculiarities, and also with the manners of the inhabitants, and the idiom of the language. Oriental poetry abounds with strong expressions, bold metaphors, glowing sentiments, and animated descriptions, pourtrayed in the most lively colours. Hence the words of the Hebrew poets are neither to be understood in too lax a sense, nor to be interpreted too literally. In the comparisons introduced by them, the point of resemblance between the object of comparison, and the thing with which it is compared, should be examined, but not strained too far; and the force of the personifications, allegories, or other figures that may be introduced, should be fully considered. Above all, it should be recollected, that as the sacred poets lived in the East, their ideas and manners were totally different from ours, and, consequently, are not to be considered according to *our* modes of thinking. From inattention to this circumstance the productions of the Hebrew muse have neither been correctly understood, nor their beauties duly felt and appreciated.

The reader will find some hints for the special study of the book of Psalms, in Vol IV. Part. I. Chap. III. Sect. II. § IX., and also a copious analysis of the book of Job, with observations for the better understanding of it, in Part I. Chap. III. Sect. I. §§ VIII. IX. X. of the same volume.

CHAPTER III.

ON THE SPIRITUAL INTERPRETATION OF THE SCRIPTURES.[1]

SECTION I.

GENERAL OBSERVATIONS ON THE SPIRITUAL INTERPRETATION OF THE SCRIPTURES.

IT has been a favourite notion with some divines, that the mystical or spiritual interpretation of the Scriptures had its first origin in the

---

[1] The present chapter is abridged from Rambach's Institutiones Hermeneuticæ Sacræ, pp. 67—82. compared with his "Commentatio Hermeneutica de Sensus Mystici Criteriis ex genuinis principiis deducta, necessariisque cautelis circumscripta." 8vo. Jenæ, 1728.

synagogue, and was thence adopted by our Lord and his apostles, when arguing with the Jews; and that from them it was received by the fathers of the Christian church, from whom it has been transmitted to us. The inference deduced by many of these eminently learned men is, that no such interpretation is admissible: while other commentators and critics have exaggerated and carried it to the extreme. But, if the argument against a thing from the possibility of its being abused be inadmissible in questions of a secular nature, it is equally inadmissible in the exposition of the Sacred Writings. All our ideas are admitted through the medium of the senses, and consequently refer in the first place to external objects: but no sooner are we convinced that we possess an immaterial soul or spirit, than we find occasion for other terms, or, for want of these, another application of the same terms to a different class of objects; and hence arises the necessity of resorting to figurative and spiritual interpretation. Now, the object of revelation being to make known things which " eye hath not seen nor ear heard, nor have entered into the heart of man to conceive," it seems hardly possible that the human mind should be capable of apprehending them, but through the medium of figurative language or mystical representations.

" The foundation of religion and virtue being laid in the mind and heart, the secret dispositions and genuine acts of which are invisible, and known only to a man's self, therefore the powers and operations of the mind can only be expressed in figurative terms and external symbols. The motives also and inducements to practice are spiritual, such as affect men in a way of moral influence, and not of natural efficiency; the principal of which are drawn from the consideration of a future state; and, consequently, *these* likewise must be represented by allegories and similitudes, taken from things most known and familiar here. And thus we find in Scripture the state of religion illustrated by all the beautiful images we can conceive; in which natural unity, order, and harmony consist, as regulated by the strictest and most exact rules of discipline, taken from those observed in the best ordered temporal government. In the interpretation of places, in which any of these images are contained, the principal regard is to be had to the *figurative* or *spiritual*, and not to the literal sense of the words. From not attending to which, have arisen absurd doctrines and inferences, which weak men have endeavoured to establish as scripture truths; whereas, in the other method of explication, the things are plain and easy to every one's capacity, make the deepest and most lasting impressions upon their minds, and have the greatest influence upon their practice. Of this nature are all the rites and ceremonies prescribed to the Jews, with relation to the external form of religious worship; every one of which was intended to show the obligation or recommend the practice of some moral duty, and was esteemed of no further use than as it produced that effect. And the same may be applied to the rewards and punishments peculiar to the Christian dispensation, which regard a future state. The rewards are set forth by those things, in which the generality of men take their greatest delight, and place their highest satisfaction of this life; and the punishments are such as are inflicted by human laws upon the worst of malefactors; but they can neither of them be understood in the *strictly literal* sense, but only by way of analogy, and corresponding in the general nature and intention of the thing, though very different in kind."[1]

But independently of the able argument *à priori*, here cited, in favour of the mediate, mystical, or spiritual interpretation of the Scriptures, unless such interpretation be admitted, we cannot avoid one of two great difficulties: for, either we must assert that the multitude of applications, made by Christ and his apostles, are fanciful and unauthorised, and wholly inadequate to prove the points for which they are quoted; or, on the other hand, we must believe that the obvious and natural sense of such passages was never intended, and that it was a mere illusion. The *Christian* will not assent to the former of these positions; the *philosopher* and the *critic* will not readily assent to the latter.[2] It has been erroneously supposed, that that this mediate, or mystical interpretation of Scripture is confined to the New Testament exclusively; we have, however, clear evidence of its adoption by some of the sacred writers of the Old Testament, and a few instances will suffice to prove its existence.

1. In Exod. xxviii. 38. Moses says, that the diadem or plate of gold, worn upon certain solemn festivals upon the high priest's forehead, signified that he bore in a vicarious and typical manner the sin of the holy things, and made an atonement for the imperfection of the Hebrew offerings and sacrifices.

2. In Lev. xxvi. 41. and Deut. x. 16. and xxx. 6., he mentions the circumcision of the heart, which was signified by the circumcision of the flesh. (Compare Jer iv. 4. vi. 10. and ix. 25, 26. with Exod. vi. 12. 30.)

3. Further, the great lawgiver of the Jews explains the historical and typical import of all their great festivals.

Thus, in Exod. xiii 13 and Numb iii. 12, 13. 44—51. and xviii 14—16, he shows the twofold meaning of the redemption of their first-born sons, viz. that the first-born of the Hebrews were preserved while Egypt groaned beneath the plague inflicted by divine vengeance, and that the first-born sons were formerly consecrated to the priesthood; which being afterwards transferred to the tribe of Levi, the first-born sons were exchanged for the Levites, and were thenceforth to be redeemed. The whole of the sacrificial law showed that the bloody sacrifices morally signified the punishment of the person for or by whom they were offered; and that the other sacred rites of the Hebrews should have a symbolical or spiritual import will be obvious to every one, who recollects the frequent use of symbols which obtained in Egypt, from which country Moses brought out the Hebrews.

The precepts delivered in the New Testament concerning the sacraments, plainly intimate that those very sacred rites were then about to receive their real accomplishment, and their symbolical or spiritual meaning is explained.

1. See, for instance, Rom. vi. 3—11. Col. ii. 12. 1 Cor. vi. 11. xi. 23—27. Eph. v. 26. and Tit. iii. 5. In which last passage baptism (by immersion in water probably) is said to signify not only the moral ablution of sin, but also the death and burial of guilty man, and (by his emersion from the water) his resurrection to a pious and virtuous life; in other words,

---

[1] Dr. John Clarke's Enquiry into the Origin of Evil, in the folio collection of Boyle's Lectures, vol. iii. p. 229.
[2] See Bishop Middleton on the Greek Article, p. 580. first edition.

III. Sect. II.] *Spiritual Interpretation of Scripture.* 449

our death unto sin and our obligation to walk in newness of life. The spiritual import of the Lord's supper is self-evident.

2. Lastly, Since we learn from the New Testament that some histories, which in themselves convey no peculiar meaning, must be interpreted allegorically or mystically (as Gal. iv. 22—24.), and that persons and things are there evidently types and emblems of the Christian dispensation, and its divine founder, as in Matt. xii. 40. John iii. 14, 15. 1 Cor. x. 4 and Heb. vii. 2, 3, it is plain that the mystical sense ought to be followed in the histories and prophecies[1] of the Old Testament, and especially in such passages as are referred to by the inspired writers of the New Testament, who having given us the key by which to unlock the mystical sense of Scripture, we not only may but ought *cautiously* and *diligently* to make use of it.

Where the inspired writers themselves direct us to such an interpretation, when otherwise we might not perceive its necessity, then we have an *absolute authority* for the exposition, which supersedes our own conjectures, and we are not only safe in abiding by that authority, but should be unwarranted in rejecting it.

SECTION II.

CANONS FOR THE SPIRITUAL INTERPRETATION OF SCRIPTURE.

THE Spiritual Interpretation of the Bible, " like all other good things, is liable to abuse; and that it hath been actually abused, both in antient and modern days, cannot be denied. He, who shall go about to apply, in this way, any passage, *before* he hath attained its literal meaning, may say in itself what is pious and true, but foreign to the text from which he endeavoureth to deduce it. St. Jerome, it is well known, when grown older and wiser, lamented that, in the fervours of a youthful fancy, he had spiritualised the prophecy of Obadiah, before he understood it. And it must be allowed that a due attention to the occasion and scope of the Psalms would have pared off many unseemly excrescences, which now deform the commentaries of St. Augustine and other fathers upon them. But these and other concessions of the same kind being made, as they are made very freely, men of sense will consider, that a principle is not therefore to be rejected, because it has been abused; *since human errors can never invalidate the truths of God.*"[2]

---

[1] On the *Double Sense of Prophecy*, see pp 469—471. *infra*.
[2] Bishop Horne's Commentary on the Psalms, vol. i. Preface. (Works, ii. p. x.) " The importance, then, of figurative and mystical interpretation can hardly be called in question The entire neglect of it must, in many cases, greatly vitiate expositions, however otherwise valuable for their erudition and judgment. In explaining the prophetical writings and the Mosaic ordinances, this defect will be most striking, since, in consequence of it, not only the spirit and force of many passages will almost wholly evaporate, but erroneous conceptions may be formed of their real purport and intention." Bp. Vanmildert's Bampton Lectures, p 240. Rambach has adduced several instances, which strongly confirm these solid observations, Institut Herm Sacr. p. 81.

The literal sense, it has been well observed, is, undoubtedly, first in point of *nature*, as well as in order of signification; and consequently, when investigating the meaning of any passage, this must be ascertained before we proceed to search out its mystical import: but the true and genuine mystical or spiritual sense excels the literal *in dignity*, the latter being only the medium of conveying the former, which is more evidently designed by the Holy Spirit. For instance, in Numb. xxi. 8, 9. compared with John iii. 14. the brazen serpent is said to have been lifted up, in order to signify the lifting up of Jesus Christ, the Saviour of the world, and, consequently, that the type might serve to designate the antitype.[1]

Though the true spiritual sense of a text is undoubtedly to be most highly esteemed, it by no means follows that we are to look for it in every passage of Scripture; it is not, however, to be inferred that spiritual interpretations are to be rejected, although they should not be clearly expressed. It may be considered as an axiom in sacred hermeneutics, that the SPIRITUAL MEANING OF A PASSAGE IS *there only* TO BE SOUGHT, WHERE IT IS EVIDENT, FROM *certain* CRITERIA, THAT SUCH MEANING WAS DESIGNED BY THE HOLY SPIRIT.

The criteria, by which to ascertain whether there is a latent spiritual meaning in any passage of Scripture, are two-fold: either they are *seated in the text itself*, or they are to be *found in some other passages*.

I. *Where the criteria are seated in the text, vestiges of a spiritual meaning are discernible, when things, which are affirmed concerning the person or thing immediately treated of, are so august and illustrious that they cannot in any way be applied to it, in the fullest sense of the words.*

The word of God is the word of truth: there is nothing superfluous, nothing deficient in it. The writings of the prophets, especially those of Isaiah, abound with instances of this kind. Thus, in the 14th, 40th, 41st, and 49th chapters of that evangelical prophet, the return of the Jews from the Babylonish captivity is announced in the most lofty and magnificent terms. He describes their way as levelled before them, valleys filled up, mountains reduced to plains, cedars and other shady trees, and fragrant herbs, as springing up to refresh them on their journey, and declares that they shall suffer neither hunger nor thirst during their return. The Jews, thus restored to their native land, he represents as a holy people, chosen by Jehovah, cleansed from all iniquity, and taught by God himself, &c. &c. Now, when we compare this description with the accounts actually given of their return to Palestine by Ezra and Nehemiah, we do not find any thing corresponding with the events so long and so beautifully predicted by Isaiah: neither do they represent the manners of the people as reformed, agreeably to the prophet's statement. On the contrary, their profligacy is frequently reproved by Ezra and Nehemiah in the most pointed terms, as well as by the prophet Haggai. In this description, therefore, of their deliverance from captivity, we must look beyond it to that infinitely higher deliverance, which in the fulness of time was accomplished by Jesus Christ: "who by himself once offered, hath thereby made a full, perfect, and suf-

---

[1] Rambach, Institutiones Hermeneuticæ Sacræ, p. 72.

ficient sacrifice, oblation, and atonement for the sins of the whole world," and thus, "hath opened the kingdom of heaven to all believers."

We proceed to show in what cases it will be proper to have recourse to other passages of Scripture.

II. *Where the spiritual meaning of a text is latent, the Holy Spirit (under whose direction the sacred penmen wrote) sometimes clearly and expressly asserts that one thing or person was divinely constituted or appointed to be a figure or symbol of another thing or person, in which case the* INDISPUTABLE TESTIMONY OF ETERNAL TRUTH *removes and cuts off every ground of doubt and uncertainty.*

For instance, if we compare Psalm cx. 4. with Heb. vii. 1. we shall find that *Melchisedec* was a type of Messiah, the great high-priest and king. So *Hagar and Sarah* were types of the Jewish and Christian churches. (Gal. iv. 22—24.) *Jonah* was a type of Christ's resurrection (Matt. xii. 40.) · the *manna*, of Christ himself, and of his heavenly doctrine. (John vi. 32.) The rock in the wilderness, whence water issued on being struck by Moses, represented Christ to the Israelites (1 Cor x. 4.); and the entrance of the high-priest into the Holy of Holies, on the day of expiation, with the blood of the victim, is expressly stated by Saint Paul to have prefigured the entrance of Jesus Christ into the presence of God, with his own blood. (Heb. ix. 7—20.)

III. *Sometimes, however, the mystical sense is intimated by the Holy Spirit in a more* OBSCURE *manner and without excluding the practice of sober and pious meditation, we are led by various intimations (which require very diligent observation and study) to the knowledge of the spiritual or mystical meaning. This chiefly occurs in the following cases.*

1. *When the antitype is proposed under figurative names taken from the Old Testament.*

Thus, in 1 Cor v. 7 Christ is called the Paschal Lamb — in 1 Cor xv 45. he is called the *last* Adam; the first Adam, therefore, was in some respect a type or figure of Christ, who in Ezekiel xxxiv. 23 is further called David. In like manner, the kingdom of Antichrist is mentioned under the appellations of Sodom, Egypt, and Babylon, in Rev. xi. 8. and xvi. 19

2. *When, by a manifest allusion of words and phrases, the Scripture refers one thing to another, or, when the arguments of the inspired writers either plainly intimate it to have a spiritual meaning, or when such meaning is tacitly implied.*

(1) Thus, from Isa. ix. 4., which alludes to the victory obtained by Gideon (Judges vii. 22.), we learn that this represents the victory which Christ should obtain by the preaching of the Gospel, as Vitringa has largely shown on this passage

(2) So, when St Paul is arguing against the Jews from the types of Sarah, Hagar, Melchisedec, &c he supposes that in these memorable Old Testament personages there were some things in which Christ and his mystical body the church were delineated, and that these things were admitted by his opponents: otherwise his argument would be inconclusive. Hence it follows, that Isaac, and other persons mentioned in the Old Testament, of whom there is no typical or spiritual signification given in the Scriptures, *in express terms*, were types of Christ in many things that happened to them, or were performed by them In like manner, St. Paul shows (1 Cor ix. 9, 10) that the precept in Deut xxv. 4. relative to the muzzling of oxen, has a higher spiritual meaning than is suggested by the mere letter of the command.

Such are the most important criteria, by which to ascertain whether a passage may require a spiritual interpretation, or not. But although these rules will afford essential assistance in enabling us to determine this point, it is another and equally important question, in what manner that interpretation is to be regulated.

In the consideration of this topic, it will be sufficient to remark, that the general principles already laid down[1], with respect to the figurative and allegorical interpretation of the Scriptures, are applicable to the spiritual exposition of the Sacred Writings. It only remains to add, that all mystical or spiritual interpretations must be such as really illustrate, not obscure or perplex the subject. Agreeably to the sound maxim adopted by divines, they must not be made the foundation of articles of faith, but must be offered only to explain or confirm what is elsewhere more clearly revealed[2]; and above all, they must on no account or pretext whatever, be sought after in matters of little moment.

In the spiritual interpretation of Scripture, there are two extremes to be avoided, viz. on the one hand, that we do not restrict such interpretation within too narrow limits; and, on the other hand, that we do not seek for mystical meanings in every passage, to the exclusion of its literal and common sense, when that sense is sufficiently clear and intelligible. The latter of these two extremes is that to which men have in every age been most liable. Hence it is that we find instances of it in the more antient Jewish doctors, especially in Philo, and among many of the fathers, as Cyprian, Jerome, Augustine, and others, and particularly in Origen, who appears to have derived his system of allegorising the Sacred Writings from the school of Plato. Nor are modern expositors altogether free from these extravagances.[3]

---

[1] See Chapter I Sections I III and IV pp 371—378 and 386—398 *supra*.

[2] "Est regula theologorum, *sensum mysticum non esse argumentativum*, hoc est, non suppeditare firma ac solida argumenta, quibus dogmata fidei modificentur." Rambach, Inst. Herm Sacr pp 72, 73

[3] Thus, Cocceius represented the *entire* history of the Old Testament as a mirror, which held forth an accurate view of the transactions and events that were to happen in the church under the New Testament dispensation, to the end of the world He further affirmed, that by far the greatest part of the antient prophecies foretold Christ's ministry and mediation, together with the rise, progress, and revolutions of the church, not only under the figure of persons and transactions, but in a literal manner, and by the sense of the words used in these predictions. And he laid it down as a fundamental rule of interpretation that the *words and phrases of Scripture are to be understood in* EVERY SENSE *of which they are susceptible* or, in other words, that *they signify in effect every thing which they can signify*. (Mosheim's Ecclesiastical History, vol. v p. 360 *et seq* edit. 1808.) These opinions have not been without their advocates in this country, and if our limits permitted, we could adduce numerous instances of evident misinterpretations of the Scriptures which have been occasioned by the adoption of them one or two, however, must suffice Thus, the Ten Commandments, or *Moral Law*, as they are usually termed, which the most pious and learned men in every age of the Christian church, have considered to be rules or precepts for regulating the manners or conduct of men, both towards God and towards one another, have been referred to Jesus Christ, under the mistaken idea that they *may* be read with a new interest by believers! (See an exposition of the Ten Commandments on the above principle, if such a perversion of sense and reason may be so called, in the Bible Magazine, vol. iv. pp 13, 14.) In like manner the first psalm, which, it is generally admitted, describes the respective happiness and misery of the pious and the wicked, according to the Cocceian hypothesis, has been applied to the Saviour of the world, in whom alone all the characters of goodness are made to centre, without any reference to its moral import! An ordinary reader, who peruses Isa. iv. 1., would naturally suppose that the prophet was predicting the calamities that should befall the impenitently wicked Jews, previously to the Babylonish captivity, which calamities he represents to be so great that *seven women shall take hold of one man*, that is, use importunity to be married, and

III. Sect. II.]   *Interpretation of Scripture.*   453

In these strictures, the author trusts he shall not be charged with improperly censuring "that fair and sober accommodation of the historical and parabolical parts to present times and circumstances, or to the elucidation of either the doctrines or precepts of Christianity, which is sanctioned by the word of God;" and which he has attempted to illustrate in the preceding criteria for ascertaining the mystical or spiritual meaning of the Scriptures. Such an accommodation, it is justly remarked, is perfectly allowable, and may be highly useful, and in some cases it is absolutely necessary. "Let every truly pious man, however, be aware of the danger of extending this principle beyond its natural and obvious application; lest he should wander himself, and lead others also astray from that clearly traced and well-beaten path in which we are assured that even ' a wayfaring man though a fool should not err.' Let no temptations, which vanity, a desire of popularity, or the more specious, but equally fallacious, plea of usefulness may present, seduce him from his tried way. *On the contrary, let him adhere with jealous care to the plain and unforced dictates of the word of God;* lest, by departing from the simplicity of the Gospel, he should inadvertently contribute to the adulteration of Christianity, and to the consequent injury which must thence arise to the spiritual interests of his fellow-creatures." [1]

IV. APPLICATION of the preceding principles to the spiritual interpretation of the Miracles recorded in the New Testament.

Although (as we have already observed) the design of miracles [2] is to mark the divine interposition, yet, when perusing the miracles recorded in the Sacred Writings, we are not to lose sight of the moral

---

that upon the hard and unusual conditions of maintaining themselves. But this simple and literal meaning of the passage, agreeably to the rule that the words of Scripture signify every thing which they can signify, has been distorted beyond measure, and, because in the *subsequent* verses of this chapter the prophet makes a transition to evangelical times, this first verse has been made to mean the rapid conversion of mankind to the Christian faith, the *seven women* are the converted persons, and the *one man* is Jesus Christ! A simple reference to the *context* and *subject-matter* of the prophecy would have shown that this verse properly belonged to the third chapter, and had no reference whatever to Gospel times. On the absurdity of the exposition just noticed, it is needless to make any comment. It is surpassed only by the reveries of a modern writer on the Continent, who has pushed the Coccelan hypothesis to the utmost bounds. According to his scheme, the incest of Lot and his daughters was permitted, only to be a sign of the salvation which the world was afterwards to receive from Jesus Christ, and *Joshua the son of Nun* signifies the same thing as *Jesus the son of Man !!!* Kanne's Christus im Alten Testament, that is, Christ in the Old Testament, or inquiries concerning the Adumbrations and Delineations of the Messiah. Nürnberg, 1818, 2 vols. 8vo. Happily this tissue of absurdity is locked up in a language that is read by few comparatively in this country. The author's knowledge of its existence is derived from the valuable periodical journal intitled Mélanges de Religion, de Morale, et de Critique Sacrée, published at Nismes, tome i. pp. 159, 160.

[1] Christian Observer for 1805, vol. iv. p 188 The two preceding pages of this journal contain some admirable remarks on the evils of spiritualising the Sacred Writings too much. The same topic is also further noticed in volume xvi for 1817, p. 319. et seq. Many important observations on the history and abuses of spiritual interpretation will be found in the late Rev J. J Conybeare's Bampton Lectures for 1824. The whole of Bishop Horne's Preface to his Commentary on the Psalms is equally worthy of perusal for its excellent observations on the same question. The misapplication and abuse of spiritual interpretation are also pointed out by Bishop Vanmildert, Bampton Lectures, p 241 et seq.

[2] The nature and evidence of miracles are discussed, in Vol I, pp. 221—298.

and religious instruction concealed under them, and especially under the miracles performed by our Saviour. "All his miracles," indeed, "were undoubtedly so many testimonies that he was sent from God: but they were much more than this, for they were all of such a kind, and attended with such circumstances, as give us an insight into the spiritual state of man, and the great work of his salvation." They were significant emblems of his designs, and figures aptly representing the benefits to be conferred by him upon mankind, and had in them a spiritual sense.

Thus, he cast out evil spirits, who, by the Divine Providence, were permitted to exert themselves at that time, and to possess many persons. By this act he showed that he came to destroy the empire of Satan, and seemed to foretell that, wheresoever his doctrine should prevail, idolatry and vice should be put to flight. — He gave sight to the blind, a miracle well suiting him who brought immortality to light, and taught truth to an ignorant world. *Lucem caliganti reddidit mundo*, applied by Quintus Curtius to a Roman emperor can be strictly applied to Christ, and to him alone No prophet ever did this miracle before him, as none ever made the religious discoveries which he made. Our Saviour himself leads us to this observation, and sets his miracle in the same view, saying, upon that occasion, *I am the light of the world ; I am come into this world, that they which see not might see*. He cured the deaf, and the dumb, and the lame, and the infirm, and cleansed the lepers, and healed all manner of sicknesses, to show at the same time that he was the physician of souls, which have their diseases corresponding in some manner to those of the body, and are deaf, and dumb, and impotent, and paralytic, and leprous in the spiritual sense — He fed the hungry multitudes by a miracle, which aptly represented his heavenly doctrine, and the Gospel preached to the poor, and which he himself so explains, saying, *I am the living bread which came down from heaven, if any man eat of this bread, he shall live for ever*. — He raised the dead, a miracle peculiarly suiting him, who at the last day should call forth all mankind to appear before him; and, therefore, when he raised Lazarus he uttered those majestic words. *I am the resurrection and the life ; he that believeth in me, though he were dead, yet shall he live*. — He performed some miracles upon persons who were not of his own nation, and it was so ordered by Divine Providence, that these persons, as the centurion, the Syrophœnician woman, the Samaritan leper, should show a greater degree of faith and of gratitude than the Jews to whom the same favours were granted. This was an indication that the Gospel would be more readily received by the Gentiles than by the Jews, and this our Saviour intimates, saying, when he had commended the centurion's faith, *Many shall come from the east and from the west, from the north and from the south, and shall sit down with Abraham and Isaac and Jacob in the kingdom of heaven, but the children of the kingdom shall be cast out into utter darkness*

It were easy to adduce other instances, but the preceding will suffice to establish the rule, especially as the spiritual import of the Christian miracles is particularly considered by every writer that has expressly illustrated them, but by no one with more sobriety than by Dr. Jortin, to whom we are indebted for most of the preceding illustrations.[1]

---

[1] See Dr. Jortin's Remarks on Ecclesiastical History, vol. i pp 267—275. (2d edit) See also Dr. Dodd's Discourses on the Miracles of the New Testament, and Dr. Collyer's Lectures on Scripture Miracles.

SECTION III.

ON THE INTERPRETATION OF TYPES.

I. *Nature of a Type.* — II. *Different Species of Types.* — 1. *Legal Types.* — 2. *Prophetical Types.* — 3. *Historical Types.* — III. *Rules for the Interpretation of Types.* — IV. *Remarks on the Interpretation of Symbols.*

I. A TYPE, in its primary and literal meaning, simply denotes a rough draught, or less accurate model, from which a more perfect image is made; but, in the sacred or theological sense of the term, a type may be defined to be a symbol of something future and distant, or an example prepared and evidently designed by God to prefigure that future thing. What is thus prefigured is called the *antitype*.[1]

1. The first characteristic of a type is its ADUMBRATION OF THE THING TYPIFIED.

One thing may adumbrate another, — either in something which it has in common with the other: as the Jewish victims by their death represented Christ, who in the fulness of time was to die for mankind: — or in a symbol of some property possessed by the other, as the images of the cherubim, placed in the inner sanctuary of the temple, beautifully represented the celerity of the angels of heaven, not indeed by any celerity of their own, but by wings of curious contrivance, which exhibited an appropriate symbol of swiftness: — or in any other way, in which the thing representing can be compared with the thing represented; as Melchisedec the priest of the Most High God represented Jesus Christ our priest. For though Melchisedec was not an eternal priest, yet the sacred writers have attributed to him a slender and shadowy appearance of eternity, by not mentioning the genealogy of the parents, the birth or death of so illustrious a man, as they commonly do in the case of other eminent persons, but under the divine direction concealing all these particulars.

2. The next requisite to constitute a type is, THAT IT BE PREPARED AND DESIGNED BY GOD TO REPRESENT ITS ANTITYPE [2]

This forms the distinction between a type and a simile: for many things are compared to others, which they were not made to resemble, for the purpose of representing them. For, though it is said that "all flesh is grass, and all the glory of man as the flower of grass" (1 Pet. i. 24.), no one can consider the tenuity of grass as a type of human weakness, or the flower of grass as a type of human glory. The same remark must be applied also to a metaphor, or that species of simile in which one thing is called by the name of another; for, though Herod from his cunning is called a *fox* (Luke xiii 32.), and Judah for his cou-

---

[1] Outram de Sacrificiis, lib i. c 18. or p. 215. of Mr. Allen's accurate translation. This work is of singular value to the divinity student, as affording, in a comparatively small compass, one of the most masterly vindications of the vicarious atonement of Christ that ever was published

[2] "It is essential," observes Bp. Vanmildert, "to a type, in the scriptural acceptation of the term, that there should be a competent evidence of the divine *intention* in the correspondence between it and the antitype, — a matter not left to the imagination of the expositor to discover, but resting on some solid proof from Scripture itself, that this was really the case." Bampton Lectures, p 239.

rage a *lion's whelp* (Gen xlix. 9.), yet no one supposes foxes to be types of Herod, or young lions types of Judah.

3. Our definition of a type includes also, that the OBJECT REPRESENTED BY IT IS SOMETHING FUTURE.

Those institutions of Moses, which partook of the nature of types, are called "a shadow of things to come" (Col. ii. 17.); and those things which happened unto the fathers for types are said to have been written for our admonition, "upon whom the ends of the world are come." (1 Cor. x. 1. 11.) In the same sense the Mosaic law, which abounded with numerous types, is declared to have had "a shadow of good things to come." (Heb. x. 1.) And those things which by the command of God were formerly transacted in the tabernacle, are described as prefiguring what was afterwards to be done in the heavenly sanctuary. (Heb. ix. 11, 12. 23, 24.) Hence it appears, that a type and a symbol differ from each other as a *genus* and *species*. The term *symbol* is equally applicable to that which represents a thing, past, present, or future: whereas the object represented by a *type* is invariably future. So that all the rites which signified to the Jews any virtues that they were to practise, ought to be called symbols rather than types; and those rites, if there were any, which were divinely appointed to represent things both present and future, may be regarded as both symbols and types; — symbols, as denoting things present; and types, as indicating things future.

4. We may further remark, that a type differs from a parable, in being grounded on a matter of fact, not on a fictitious narrative, but is much of the same nature in actions, or things and persons, as an allegory is in words; though allegories are frequently so plain, that it is scarcely possible for any man to mistake them; and thus it is, in many cases, with respect to types.

Where, indeed, there is only one type or resemblance, it is in some instances not so easily discernible; but where several circumstances concur, it is scarcely possible not to perceive the agreement subsisting between the type and the antitype. Thus, the ark was a type of baptism, the land of Canaan, of heaven, the elevation of the brazen serpent, and the prophet Jonah, of our Saviour's crucifixion and resurrection.

II. In the examination of the Sacred Writings, three SPECIES of types present themselves to our consideration; viz. *Legal Types*, or those contained in the Mosaic law; *Prophetical Types*, and *Historical Types*.

1. LEGAL TYPES. — It evidently appears, from comparing the history and economy of Moses with the whole of the New Testament, that the ritual law was typical of the Messiah and of Gospel blessings: and this point has been so clearly established by the great apostle of the Gentiles in his Epistle to the Hebrews, that it will suffice to adduce a very few examples, to show the nature of *Legal Types*.

Thus, the entire constitution, and offerings of the Levitical priesthood, typically prefigured Christ the great high priest (Heb. v. vii. viii.) and especially the ceremonies observed on the great day of atonement (Lev xvi. with Heb. ix. throughout, and x 1—22.) So, the passover and the paschal lamb typified the sacrifice of Jesus Christ (Exod. xii 3. *et seq.* with John xix 36. and 1 Cor. v. 7.); so, the feast of Pentecost, which commemorated the giving of the law on Mount Sinai, (Exod. xix. xx.) prefigured the effusion of the Holy Spirit on the apostles, who were thus enabled to promulgate the Gospel throughout the then known world. (Acts ii. 1—11.) And it has been conjectured ! that the feast of tabernacles typifies the final restoration of the Jews. In like manner, the privileges of the Jews were types of those enjoyed by all true Christians; "for their relation to God as his people, signified by the name *Israelite* (Rom ix. 4.), prefigured the more honourable relation, in which believers, the *true Israel*, stand to God. — Their *adoption* as the sons of God, and the privileges they were intitled to by that adoption, were types of believers being made partakers of the *divine nature* by the renewing of the Holy Ghost, and of their title to the inheritance of heaven. — The residence of the *glory*, first in the tabernacle and then in the temple, was a figure of the residence of God by His Spirit in the Christian church, His temple on earth, and of His eternal residence in that church brought to perfection in Heaven — The *covenant with Abraham* was the new or Gospel covenant, the blessings of which were typified by the temporal blessings promised to him and to his *natural seed* and the covenant *at Sinai*, whereby the Israelites, as the worshippers of the true God, were separated from the idolatrous nations, was an emblem of the final separation of the righteous from the wicked — In the *giving of the law*, and the formation of the Israelites into a nation or community, was represented the formation of the city of the living God, and of the general assembly of the church of the first-born — Lastly, the heavenly country, the habitation of the righteous, was typified by *Canaan*, a country given to the Israelites by God's promise." ²

2. PROPHETICAL TYPES are those, by which the divinely inspired prophets prefigured or signified things either present or future, by means of external symbols.

Of this description is the prophet Isaiah's going naked (that is, without his prophetic garment) and barefoot (Isa. xx. 2.), to prefigure the fatal destruction of the Egyptians and Ethiopians — The hiding of a girdle in a rock on the banks of the Euphrates, which, on being subsequently taken thence, proved to be rotten, to denote the destruction which would speedily befall the abandoned and ungrateful Jewish people (Jer. xiii 1 —7. compared with the following verses) — the abstaining from marriage (Jer xvi 2), mourning (ver 5), and feasting (ver 8), to indicate the woeful calamities denounced by Jehovah against his people for their sins. Similar calamities are prefigured by breaking a potter's vessel. (Jer. xviii. 2—10.) By making bonds and yokes (Jer. xxvii. 1—8.) is prefigured the subjugation of the kings of Edom, Moab, the Ammonites, Tyre, and Sidon, by Nebuchadnezzar and in like manner, Agabus's binding his own hands with Paul's girdle intimated the apostle's captivity at Jerusalem (Acts xxi 10, 11) ³

To this class of types may be referred *prophetical and typical visions* of future events some of these have their interpretation annexed as Jeremiah's vision of the almond-tree and a seething pot (Jer i. 11—16), Ezekiel's vision of the resurrection of dry bones (Ezek xxxvii.), with many similar instances recorded in the Sacred Writings. Other typical visions, however, will in all probability be explained only by their actual accomplishment, as Ezekiel's vision of the temple and holy city (ch xl to the end), and especially the Revelation of Saint John which will then be most clear and intelligible when the whole is fulfilled, as we can now plainly read the calling of the Gentiles in many parts of the Old Testament, which seemed so strange a thing, before it was accomplished, even to those who were well acquainted with the writings of the prophets. See an instance of this in Acts xi. 1—18.

3. HISTORICAL TYPES are the characters, actions, and fortunes of some eminent persons recorded in the Old Testament, so ordered by Divine Providence as to be exact prefigurations of the characters, actions, and fortunes of future persons who should arise under the Gospel dispensation.

In some instances, the persons whose characters and actions prefigured future events, were declared by Jehovah himself to be typical, long before the events which they prefigured came to pass these have been termed *innate*, or natural historical types; and these may be safely admitted But *inferred* types, or those in which typical persons were not known to be such, until after the things which they typified had actually happened, (and which can only be consequentially ascertained to be such by probabilities supposed to be agreeable to the analogy of faith,) cannot be too carefully avoided, notwithstanding

---

¹ By the Rev Dr. Elrington, Provost of Trinity College, Dublin. See the grounds of this conjecture ably supported in Dr. Graves's Lectures on the Pentateuch, vol. ii. pp. 393—395. notes.
² Dr. Macknight on Rom ix. 4. note 1.
³ Other examples of, and observations on, prophetical types may be seen in Dr. Nares's Warburtonian Lectures on the Prophecies concerning the Messiah, pp 70—86. 117—125

they have the sanction of some eminent expositors, because they are not supported by the authority of the inspired writers of the New Testament.[1]

III. From the preceding remarks and statements it will be obvious, that great caution is necessary in the INTERPRETATION OF TYPES; for unless we have the authority of the sacred writers themselves for it, we cannot conclude with certainty that this or that person or thing, which is mentioned in the Old Testament, is a type of Christ on account of the resemblance which we may perceive between them: but we may admit it as probable. "Whatever persons or things recorded in the *Old* Testament, were expressly declared by Christ, or by his apostles, to have been designed as prefigurations of persons or things relating to the *New* Testament, such persons or things so recorded in the *former*, are types of the persons or things with which they are compared in the *latter*. But if we assert, that a person or thing was designed to prefigure *another* person or thing, where no such prefiguration has been declared by *divine authority*, we make an assertion for which we neither *have*, nor can have, the slightest foundation. And even when comparisons *are* instituted in the New Testament between antecedent and subsequent persons or things, we must be careful to distinguish the examples, where a comparison is instituted merely for the sake of *illustration*, from the examples where such a *connection* is declared, as exists in the relation of *a type* to its antitype."[2] In the interpretation of types, therefore,

1. *There must be a fit application of the Type to the Antitype.*

"To constitute one thing the *type* of another, as the term is generally understood in reference to Scripture, something *more* is wanted than mere *resemblance*. The former must not only *resemble* the latter, but must have been *designed* to resemble the latter. It must have been so designed in its *original institution*. It must have been designed as something *preparatory* to the latter. The type, as well as the antitype, must have been pre-ordained; and they must have been pre-ordained as constituent parts of the same general scheme of Divine Providence. It is this *previous design* and this *pre-ordained connection*, which constitute the relation of type and antitype. Where *these* qualities fail, where the *previous design* and the *pre-ordained* connection are wanting, the relation between any two things, however similar in *themselves*, is not the relation of type to antitype."[3] In further explanation of this canon, it may be remarked, that in a type *every* circumstance is far from being typical, as in a parable there are several incidents, which are not to be considered as parts of the parable, nor to be insisted upon as such. From not considering the evident relation which ought to subsist between the type and the antitype, some fanciful expositors, under pretence that the tabernacle of Moses was a figure of the church or of heaven, have converted even the very *boards* and *nails* of it into *types*. Thus Cardinal Bellarmine[4] found the mass to be typified by Melchisedec's bringing forth *bread and wine*, he being a priest of the Most High God. The same great adversary of the Protestants (in his Treatise *de Laicis*) in like manner discovered that their secession under Luther "was typified by the secession of the ten tribes under Jeroboam, while the Lutherans, with equal reason, retorted that Jeroboam was a type of the Pope, and that the secession of Israel from Judah typified, not the secession of the Protestants under Luther, but the secession of the church of Rome from primitive Christianity. But, to whichever of the two events the

---

[1] The subject of historical types is copiously (but in some respects fancifully) elucidated by Huet in his Demonstratio Evangelica, cap. 170 vol. ii pp. 1056—1074. Amst. 1680, and by Dr. Macknight in his Essay on the right Interpretation of the Language of Scripture, in vol. iv or vi (4to. or 8vo.) of his translation of the Apostolical Epistles, Essay viii sect. I—5. The interpretation of types, generally, is vindicated by Alber, against the modern neologian divines on the Continent, in his Institutiones Hermeneuticæ Nov. Test. vol. i. pp. 68—85.
[2] Bishop Marsh's Lectures, part iii. p. 115.
[3] Ibid. part iii. p. 113.
[4] De Missa, lib. i. c. 9.

III. Sect. III.]   *On the Interpretation of Types.*   459

secession under Jeroboam may be supposed the most *similar* (if similarity exist there *at all* beyond the mere *act* of secession), we have no authority for pronouncing it a *type* of either. We have no *proof* of previous design and of pre-ordained connection between the subjects of comparison, we have no *proof* that the secession of the Israelites under Jeroboam was designed to prefigure any *other* secession whatever."[1] From the same inattention to considering the necessarily evident relation between the type and the antitype, the Hebrew monarch *Saul*, whose name is by interpretation *Death*, has been made a type of the moral law, which Saint Paul terms the "ministration of *death*." (2 Cor. iii. 7.) In like manner, the period, which elapsed between the anointing of David and the death of Saul, has been made to typify the time of Christ's ministry upon earth!! And the *long war between the house of Saul and the house of David*, (2 Sam. iii 1.) in which *David waxed stronger and stronger, and the house of Saul weaker and weaker*, has been represented as strikingly pourtrayed in the lengthened contests between the righteousness of faith and that of works, so often alluded to in the epistles, especially in those addressed to the Romans and Galatians!!![2]

It were no difficult task to adduce numerous similar examples of abuse in the interpretation of types; but the preceding will suffice to show the danger of falling into it, and the necessity of confining our attention to the strict relation between the type and the antitype. In further illustration of this canon it may be remarked, that in expounding typical passages two points should be always kept in mind, viz.

(1.) The TYPE *must in the first instance be explained according to its literal sense; and if any part of it appear to be obscure, such obscurity must be removed: as in the history of Jonah, who was swallowed by a great fish, and cast ashore on the third day.*

(2.) The ANALOGY *between the thing prefiguring and the thing prefigured must be* soberly *shown in all its parts.*

The criteria for ascertaining this analogy are to be found solely in the *Sacred Writings themselves*, for whenever the Holy Spirit refers any thing to analogy, either expressly or by implication, there we may rest assured that such analogy was designed by God. But further than this we cannot safely go.

2. *There is often more in the Type than in the Antitype.*

God designed one person or thing in the Old Testament to be a type or shadow of things to come, not in all things, but only in respect to *some particular thing* or things; hence we find many things in the type, that are inapplicable to the antitype. The use of this canon is shown in the epistle to the Hebrews, in which the ritual and sacrifices of the Old Testament are fairly accommodated to Jesus Christ the antitype, although there are many things in that priesthood which do not accord. Thus the priest was to offer sacrifice for his own sins (Heb. v. 3.), which is in no respect applicable to Christ. (Heb. vii. 27.) Again, the Mosaic priesthood is (vii. 18.) *weak and unprofitable*, neither of which characters can be applied to the Redeemer, *who continueth ever*, and *hath an unchangeable priesthood*. (vii. 24, 25.)

3. *Frequently there is more in the Antitype than in the Type.*

The reason of this canon is the same as that of the preceding rule: for, as no single type can express the life and particular actions of Christ, there is necessarily more in the antitype than can be found in the type itself; so that one type must signify one thing, and another type another thing. Thus, *one* goat could not typify Christ both in his death and resurrection, therefore two were appointed (Lev. xvi. 7.), one of which was offered, and prefigured his "full, perfect, and sufficient atonement;" while the other, which was dismissed, typified his triumph over death and the grave. In like manner, Moses was a type of Christ as a Deliverer, or Saviour, in bringing the children of Israel out of Egypt, and Joshua, in bringing them into Canaan, which was a type of heaven, — the true country of all sincere Christians.

4. *The wicked, as such, are* NOT *to be made Types of Christ.*

For how can a thing, which is bad in itself, prefigure or typify a thing that is good? Yet, for want of attending to this obvious and almost self-evident proposition, some[3] ex-

---

[1] Bp. Marsh's Lectures, part iii. p. 117.

[2] The reader who may be desirous of seeing the above extravagant *typifications* treated at length, will find them minutely stated, with other similar particulars equally extravagant, in the "Bible Magazine," vol. iv. pp 22—29.

[3] Azorius, the Spanish Jesuit, in his Institutiones Morales, lib. viii. c. 2., and Cornelius à Lapide, in Præfat. ad Pentateuch, canon 40.

positors have interpreted the adultery of David, and the incest of Amnon, as typical of the Messiah! and the oak on which Absalom was suspended by the hair of the head, has been made a type of the cross of Christ!¹ It is not, however, to be denied, that the punishments of some malefactors are *accommodated* to Christ as an antitype. Thus, Deut. xxi. 23. is by Saint Paul accommodated *typically* to him, Gal. iii. 13. Jonah, we have already observed, was a type of Christ, by his continuance three days and three nights in the belly of a great fish: but the point of resemblance is to be sought, not in his being there as the punishment of his disobedience to the divine command, but *in his coming forth, at the expiration of that time,* alive, and in perfect vigour; which coming forth prefigured the resurrection of Christ.

5. *In Types and Antitypes, an enallage or change sometimes takes place; as when the thing prefigured assumes the name of the type or figure; and, on the contrary, when the type of the thing represented assumes the name of the antitype.*

Of the first kind of enallage we have examples in Ezek. xxxiv 23. xxxvii. 24, 25 and Hos. iii. 5.; in which descriptions of Messiah's kingdom he is styled David; because as he was prefigured by David in many respects, so he was to descend from him. In like manner Christ is called a *lamb,* (John i. 29. 36 and Rev. xix. 7. 9.) because the paschal lamb was an eminent type of him. So, the Christian church is sometimes called Mount Sion and Jerusalem (Gal. iv. 26. Heb. xii. 22. Rev. xxi. 2.), because these places were types of her.

Of the second kind of enallage we have instances — 1. *In prophetical types,* in which the name of a person or thing, properly agreeing with the antitype, and for which the type was proposed, is given to any one as in Isa. vii. 3. and viii. 1—3. So, the wife of the prophet Hosea, and his legitimate children, are by the command of Jehovah termed a *wife of whoredoms,* and *children of whoredoms,* (Hos. i. 2.) on account of the Israelites, who were the antitype, and were guilty of spiritual whoredom or adultery. See Hos. i. 4. 6. 9.

2. *In historical types,* as when hanging was called in the Old Testament the curse of the Lord, because it was made a type of Christ, who was made a curse for our sins, as the apostle Paul argues in Gal. iii. 13.

6. *That we may not fall into extremes, in the interpretation of Types, we must, in every instance, proceed cautiously, " with fear and trembling," lest we imagine mysteries to exist where none were ever intended.*

No mystical or typical sense, therefore, ought to be put upon a plain passage of Scripture, the meaning of which is obvious and natural, unless it be evident from some other part of Scripture that the place is to be understood in a double sense. When Paul says, (Gal. iii. 24. Col. ii. 17.) that the *law was a schoolmaster to bring men to Christ,* and a *shadow of things to come,* we must instantly acknowledge that the ceremonial law in general was a type of the mysteries of the Gospel. Nothing can be more contrary to that sober judgment which is so strenuously urged by the apostle (Rom. xii. 3.), than to seek for types where there are not the smallest marks or traces of any, and that, too, by contradicting the plain and literal meaning of Scripture, and not unfrequently in direct opposition to common sense. " Should not the prudence and moderation of Christ and his apostles in this respect be imitated? Is it not pretending to be wiser than they were, to look for mysteries where they designed none? How unreasonable is it to lay an useless weight on the consciences of Christians, and to bear down the *true* and *revealed,* under the unwieldy burthen of traditional mysteries."²

IV. Closely connected with the interpretation of types is the ex-

---

¹ By Gretzer, De Cruce, lib. i. c. 6.

² Beausobre's Introduction to the New Testament. (Bishop Watson's Tracts, vol. iii. p. 140.) In the preceding observations on the interpretation of types, the author has chiefly been indebted to Glassii Philologia Sacra, lib. ii. part i. tract. ii. sect. iv. col. 442—472, which has been unaccountably *omitted* by Prof. Dathe in his otherwise truly valuable edition of that work, Langii Hermeneutica Sacra, pp. 97—119.; J. E. Pfeiffer, Inst. Herm. Sacr. pp. 775—795; Viser, Hermeneutica Sacra Novi Testamenti, part ii. pp. 184—188. The subject of types is particularly considered and ably illustrated in Dr. Outram de Sacrificiis, particularly lib. i. cap. 18. and lib. ii. c. 7. (pp. 217—228. 361—384. of Mr. Allen's translation already noticed); Mr. Faber's Horæ Mosaicæ, vol. ii. pp. 40—173., Bishop Chandler's Defence of Christianity from the Prophecies of the Old Testament, &c. chap. iii., and Mr. Wilson's popular Inquiry into the Doctrine of Scripture Types. Edinburgh, 1823. 8vo. But the fullest view of this subject is stated by Dr. Graves to be found in the Rev. Samuel Mather's work on the Figures and Types of the Old Testament. Dublin, 1683. 4to.

pounding of SYMBOLS; which, though often confounded with them, are nevertheless widely different in their nature. By *symbols*[1] we mean "certain representative marks, rather than express pictures; or, if pictures, such as were at the time *characters*, and, besides presenting to the eye the resemblance of a particular object, suggested a general idea to the mind. As, when a *horn* was made to denote *strength*, an *eye* and *sceptre*, *majesty*, and in numberless such instances; where the picture was not drawn to express merely the thing itself, but something else, which was, or was conceived to be, analogous to it. This more complex and ingenious form of picture-writing was much practised by the Egyptians, and is that which we know by the name of *Hieroglyphics*."[2]

It has been doubted whether symbolical language should be referred to figurative or spiritual interpretation; in the former case, it would have occupied a place in the discussion respecting the figurative language of Scripture; but, on consideration, it will appear that it is most nearly allied to mystical interpretation. For a symbol differs from a type in this respect, that the former represents something *past* or *present*, while a *type* represents something future. The images of the cherubim over the propitiatory were symbols, the bread and wine in the last supper also were symbols. The commanded sacrifice of Isaac was given for a type; the sacrifices of the law were types. So far, Bishop Warburton has remarked, symbols and types agree in their *genus*, that they are equally representations, but in their *species* they differ widely. It is not required, he further observes, that the *symbol* should partake of the *nature* of the thing represented: the cherubim shadowed out the celerity of angels, but not by any physical celerity of their own; the bread and wine shadowed out the body and blood of Christ, but not by any change in the elements. But *types* being, on the contrary, representations of *things future*, and so partaking of the nature of *prophecy*, were to convey information concerning the *nature* of the antitypes, or of the things represented; which they could not do but by the exhibition of their own nature. And hence we collect, that the command to offer Isaac, being the command to offer a *real sacrifice*, the death and sufferings of Christ, thereby represented, were a *real sacrifice*.[3]

As the same rules, which regulate the general interpretation of the tropes and figures occurring in the Scriptures, are equally applicable to the interpretation of symbols, it will be sufficient to refer to a former part of this volume[4], in which that topic is particularly discussed.

---

[1] Before an alphabet was invented, and what we call literary writing was formed into an art, men had no way to record their conceptions, or to convey them to others at a distance, but by setting down the figures and tropes of such things as were the objects of their contemplation. Hence, the way of writing in *picture* was as universal, and almost as early, as the way of speaking in *metaphor*, and from the same reason, the necessity of the thing. In process of time, and through many successive improvements, this rude and simple mode of picture-writing was succeeded by that of *symbols*, or was enlarged at least and enriched by it. Bishop Hurd's Introduction to the Study of the Prophecies, serm. ix. (Works, vol. v. p. 238.)

[2] Bishop Hurd's Introduction to the Study of the Prophecies, serm ix. (Works, vol. v. p. 239.)

[3] Divine Legation of Moses, book ix. ch. ii. (Works, vol. vi. p. 289. 8vo. edit.)

[4] See pp. 371—378. *supra*.

Much light will also be thrown upon the symbolical language of Scripture, by a careful collation of the writings of the prophets with each other; for "the symbolical language of the prophets is almost a science in itself. None can fully comprehend the depth, sublimity, and force of their writings, who are not thoroughly acquainted with the peculiar and appropriate imagery they were accustomed to use. This is the main key to many of the prophecies; and, without knowing how to apply it, the interpreter will often in vain essay to discover their hidden treasures."[1] Lastly, the diligent comparison of the New Testament with the Old will essentially contribute to illustrate the symbolical phraseology of the prophets. For instance, we learn what is intended by the *water* promised to the Israelites in Isa. xliv. 3, and to which the thirsty are invited in ch. lv. 1., from John iv. 10. and vii. 37—39.; where it is explained of the Holy Spirit and his gifts, which were afterwards to be dispensed.[2]

CHAPTER IV.

ON THE INTERPRETATION OF THE SCRIPTURE PROPHECIES.

SECTION I.

GENERAL RULES FOR ASCERTAINING THE SENSE OF THE PROPHETIC WRITINGS.

PROPHECY, or the prediction of future events, is justly considered as the highest evidence that can be given, of supernatural communion with the Deity. The force of the argument from prophecy, for proving the divine inspiration of the sacred records, has already been exhibited; and the cavils of objectors, from its alleged obscurity, has been obviated.[3] Difficulties, it is readily admitted, do exist in understanding the prophetic writings: but these are either owing to our ignorance of history and of the Scriptures, or because the prophecies themselves are yet unfulfilled. The latter can only be understood when the events foretold have actually been accomplished: but the former class of difficulties may be removed in many, if not in all, cases; and the knowledge, sense, and meaning of the prophets may, in a considerable degree, be attained by prayer, reading, and meditation, and by comparing Scripture with Scripture, especially with the writings of the New Testament, and

---

[1] Bp. Vanmildert's Lectures, p. 240.
[2] See a Concise Dictionary of the Symbolical Language of Prophecy, infra; Vol. IV. Index I.
[3] See Vol. I. pp. 299—363. For an account of the Prophets, see Vol. IV. Part I. Chap. IV. Sect. I., and for an analysis of their writings, with critical remarks thereon see also Vol. IV. Part I. Chap. IV. Sections II —IV.

particularly with the book of the Revelation.[1] With this view, the following general rules will be found useful in investigating the *sense and meaning* of the prophecies, as well as their *accomplishment*.

I. *As not any prophecy of Scripture is of self-interpretation*, (2 Pet. I. 20.) *or is its own interpreter*, "*the sense of the prophecy is to be sought in the events of the world, and in the harmony of the prophetic writings, rather than in the bare terms of any single prediction.*"[2]

In the consideration of this canon, the following circumstances should be carefully attended to:

(1.) *Consider well the times when the several prophets flourished, in what place and under what kings they uttered their predictions, the duration of their prophetic ministry, and their personal rank and condition, and, lastly, whatever can be known respecting their life and transactions.*

These particulars, indeed, cannot in every instance be ascertained, the circumstances relating to many of the prophets being very obscure but, where they can be known, it is necessary to attend to them, as this will materially contribute to the right understanding of the prophetic writings.[3] Thus, in order to understand correctly the prophecy of Isaiah, we should make ourselves acquainted with the state and condition of the people of Israel under the kings Amaziah, Uzziah, Jotham, Ahaz, and Hezekiah. With this view, the books of Kings (2 xiv.—xxi.) and 2 Chron. (xvi.—xxii.) ought to be repeatedly perused and studied, because they contain an accurate view of the state of those times.

(2.) *The situation of the particular places, of which the prophets speak, must also be kept in mind, as well as that of the neighbouring places, there being in the prophetic writings frequent allusions to the situation and antient names of places.*

When places are mentioned as lying north, south, east, or west, it is generally to be understood of their situation with respect to Judæa or Jerusalem, when the context does not plainly restrict the scene to some other place. For instance, Egypt and Arabia are every where called the land of the south, because they are situated to the south of Jerusalem. thus in Daniel (ch. xi.) the *king of the south* signifies the king of Egypt, and the *king of the north*, the monarch of Syria. The *sea* is often put for the west, the Mediterranean Sea being to the west of Judæa · by the *earth*, the prophets often mean the land of Judæa, and sometimes the great continent of all Asia and Africa, to which they had access by land and by the *isles of the sea*, they understood the places to which they sailed, particularly all Europe, and probably the islands and sea-coasts of the Mediterranean. The appellation of *sea* is also given to the great rivers Nile and Euphrates, which, overflowing their banks, appear like small seas or great lakes. The *Egyptian Sea*, with its *seven streams*, mentioned in Isa. xi. 15 is the Nile with its seven mouths: the *sea*, mentioned in Isa xxvii. 1 and Jer. li 36. is the Euphrates; and the *desert of the sea*, in Isa. xxi. 1 is the country of Babylon, watered by that river In like manner, the Jewish

---

[1] There is scarcely an expression in this book which is not taken out of Daniel or some other prophet, Sir Isaac Newton has observed, that it is written in the same style and language with the prophecies of Daniel, and has the same relation to them which they have to one another, so that all of them together make but one complete prophecy, and in like manner it consists of two parts, an introductory prophecy, and an interpretation thereof (Observations on the Apocalypse, chap ii. p 254) The style of the Revelations, says the profoundly learned Dr Lightfoot, "is very prophetical as to the things spoken, and very hebraizing as to the speaking of them Exceeding much of the old prophets' language and manner [is] adduced to intimate New Stories · and exceeding much of the Jews' language and allusion to their customs and opinions, thereby to speak the things more familiarly to be understood." Harmony of the New Testament, p. 154. (Lond 1655.) See also Langii Hermeneutica Sacra, pp. 148—150

[2] Bishop Horsley. This learned prelate has shown in his sermon on 2 Pet. i. 20. that the clause — *No prophecy of the Scripture is of any private interpretation* — may be more precisely thus expressed — "*Not any prophecy of Scripture is of self-interpretation*, or is its own interpreter because the Scripture prophecies are not detached predictions of separate independent events, but are united in a regular and entire system, all terminating in one great object, — the promulgation of the Gospel, and the complete establishment of the Messiah's kingdom " Sermons, vol. ii. pp. 13—16.

[3] On the chronological order, &c. of the prophets, see Vol. IV. Part I. Chap. IV. Sect. I.

people are described by several particular appellations, after the division of the kingdom in the reign of Jeroboam thus, the ten tribes, being distinct from the other two, and subject to a different king, until the time of the Assyrian captivity, are respectively called *Samaria*, *Ephraim*, and *Joseph*, because the city of *Samaria*, which was situated in the allotment of the tribe of *Ephraim*, who was the son of Joseph, was the metropolis of the kings of Israel. Compare Isa. vii 2 5 8, 9 Psal. lxxvi. 5. Hos vii. 11. Amos v. 15 and vi 6. They were also called Israel and Jacob, because they formed the greater part of Israel's, or Jacob's posterity The other two tribes of Judah and Benjamin are called the *kingdom of Judah*, the *house of David*, *Jerusalem* or *Sion* (Isa vii. 13 and xl 2. Psal cxxvi. 1. and Isa. lii. 8.), because those two tribes adhered to the family of David, from whose posterity their kings sprung, and the capital of their dominions was Jerusalem, within whose precincts was Mount Sion. After their return, however, from the Babylonish captivity, the names of Israel and Judah are promiscuously applied to all the descendants of the twelve tribes who were thus restored to their native country. This is the case in the writings of the prophets Haggai, Zechariah, and Malachi, who all flourished after that event. In addition to the situations and names of places, whatever relates to the history of those times must be ascertained, as far as is practicable, by consulting not only the historical books of Scripture, and the writings of Josephus, (whose statements must sometimes be taken with great caution, as he has not *always* related the sacred history with fidelity,) but also by comparing the narratives of Herodotus, Diodorus Siculus, and other profane historians, who have written on the affairs of the Chaldæans, Babylonians, Egyptians, Tyrians, Medes and Persians, and other Oriental nations, with whom the posterity of Jacob had any intercourse Quotations from these writers may be seen in all the larger commentaries on the Bible Dr. Prideaux's Connection of Sacred and Profane History, and Bishop Newton's Dissertations on the Prophecies, are both particularly valuable for the illustrations of the sacred predictions which they have respectively drawn from profane authors. In the Geographical Index, at the end of the third volume of this work, under the articles *Assyria*, *Babylon*, *Egypt*, *Media*, and *Persia*, we have given an Abstract of the Profane History of the East, from the time of Solomon until the Babylonish Captivity, to facilitate the better understanding of the history of the Hebrews described in the writings of the prophets.

(3.) *As the prophets treat not only of past transactions and present occurrences, but also foretell future events, in order to understand them, we must diligently consult the histories of the following ages, both sacred and profane, and carefully see whether we can trace in them the fulfilment of any prophecy.*

The event is the best interpreter of a prediction this inquiry into history, however, demands not only great labour, but also great industry and equal judgment, in order that the events may be referred to those prophecies with which they harmonise. These events must not be far-fetched; nor can they always be ascertained, because the circumstances alluded to by the prophets are often unknown to us, being yet future. Hence a considerable portion of the prophets, especially of the book of Revelation, is not only not understood, but *cannot* at present be comprehended Some conjectures, perhaps, may be offered but these should be advanced with caution as far as they throw light upon prophecy; and, where this is wanting, we must withhold our assent from such conjectures.

(4.) *The words and phrases of a prophecy must be explained, where they are obscure; if they be very intricate, every single word should be expounded, and, if the sense be involved in metaphorical and emblematical expressions (as very frequently is the case), these must be explained according to the principles already laid down.*

No strained or far-fetched interpretation, therefore, should be admitted; and that sense of any word or phrase is always to be preferred, which is the clearest and most precise.

(5) *Similar prophecies of the same event must be carefully compared, in order to elucidate more clearly the sense of the sacred predictions.*

For instance, after having ascertained the subject of the prophet's discourse and the sense of the words, Isa. liii. 5 (*He was wounded*, literally *pierced through*, for our transgressions,) may be compared with Psal. xxii. 16. (*They pierced my hands and my feet*), and with Zech. xii 10 (*They shall look on me whom they have pierced.*) In thus paralleling the prophecies, regard must be had to the predictions of *former* prophets, which are sometimes repeated with abridgment, or more distinctly explained by others, and also to the predictions of *subsequent* prophets, who sometimes repeat, with greater clearness and precision, former prophecies, which had been more obscurely announced.

II. *In order to understand the prophets, great attention should be paid to the prophetic style, which is highly figurative, and particularly abounds in metaphorical and hyperbolical expressions.*

By images borrowed from the natural world, the prophets often understand something in the world politic. Thus, as the sun, moon, stars, and heavenly bodies, denote kings, queens, rulers, and persons in great power, and the increase of splendour in those luminaries denotes increase of prosperity, as in Isa xxx. 26 and lx. 19. On the other hand, their darkening, setting, or falling, signifies a reverse of fortune, or the entire destruction of the potentate or kingdom to which they refer. In this manner the prophet Isaiah denounced the divine judgments on Babylon, (Isa xiii 10 13) and on Idumæa (xxxiv. 4—6), and Jeremiah, on the Jews and Jerusalem (Jer iv 23, 24). The destruction of Egypt is predicted in similar terms by Ezekiel (xxxii 7, 8), and also the terrible judgments that would befall the unbelieving Jews, by Joel (ii 28—31.) And Jesus Christ himself employed the same phraseology in foretelling the destruction of Jerusalem by the Romans (Matt. xxiv 29.)

In further illustration of this rule it may be observed, that the prophetical writings contain numerous figures and similitudes that appear strange to our habits and modes of thinking; but which in their times were perfectly familiar. These figures and similitudes, therefore, must not be interpreted according to our notions of things, but agreeably to the genius of Oriental writing. for instance, very numerous metaphors are taken from agriculture and the pastoral life, which were common pursuits among the Jews, some of the prophets themselves having been herdsmen or shepherds. However humble such employment may appear to us, they were not accounted servile at the time the prophets flourished. Other representations of events, that were to come to pass under the New Testament dispensation, are drawn from the sacred rites of the Jews. Thus, the conversion of Egypt to the Gospel is foretold (Isa. xix 19 21.) by *setting up an altar and offering sacrifice to the Lord*, and the conversion of the Gentiles in general (Mal i 11) by the offering up of incense. The service of God under the Gospel is set forth (Zech xiv. 16) *by going up to Jerusalem, and keeping the feast of tabernacles there*; and the abundant effusion of the Holy Spirit, in the miraculous gifts which attended the preaching of the Gospel, is represented (Joel ii 28.) *by prophesying, and dreaming dreams, and seeing visions*. In this passage the prophet did not intend to say, that these things should literally and actually take place under the Christian dispensation: but, in order that his meaning might be the better understood by those whom he addressed, he expressed the abundant measure of gifts and Gospel light by images drawn from those privileges which were at that time most highly valued by the Jews.

Although the prophets thus frequently employ words in a figurative or metaphorical meaning, yet we ought not, *without necessity*, to depart from the primitive sense of their expressions and that necessity exists, only when the plain and original sense is less proper, as well as less suitable to the subject and context, or contrary to other passages of Scripture. But, even in this case, we must carefully assign to each prophetical symbol its proper and definite meaning, and never vary from that meaning.

III. *As the greater part of the prophetic writings was first composed in verse, and still retains much of the air and cast of the original, an attention to the division of the lines, and to that peculiarity of Hebrew poetry by which the sense of one line or couplet so frequently corresponds with another, will frequently lead to the meaning of many passages; one line of a couplet, or member of a sentence, being generally a commentary on the other.*

Of this rule we have an example in Isa. xxxiv. 6.

> The Lord hath a sacrifice in Bozrah,
> And a great slaughter in the land of Idumæa.

Here the metaphor in the first verse is expressed in the same terms in the next the sacrifice in Bozrah means the great slaughter in the land of Idumæa, of which Bozrah was the capital. Similar instances occur in Isa. xliv. 3. and lxi 10. and in Micah vi. 6. in which the parallelism is more extended. Concerning the nature of Prophetic Poesy, see pp 441, 442 of the present volume.

IV. *Particular names are often put by the prophets for more general ones, in order that they may place the thing represented, as it were, before the eyes of their hearers: but in such passages they are not to be understood literally.*

Thus, in Joel iii. 4., *Tyre and Sidon, and all the coasts of Palestine*, are put, by way of poetical description, for all the enemies of the Jews, and the Greeks and Sabæans for distant nations. In like manner the prophet Amos (ch. ix. 12.), when speaking of the enemies of the Jews, mentions *the remnant of Edom, or the Idumæans*.

V. *It is usual with the prophets to express the same thing in a great variety of expressions; whence they abound in amplifications, each rising above the other in strength and beauty.*

For instance, when describing drought or famine, they accumulate together numerous epithets, to represent the sorrow that would accompany those calamities; on the other hand, when delineating plenty, they pourtray, in a great variety of expressions, the joy of the people possessed of abundance of grain; and in like manner, the horrors of war and the blessings of peace, the misery of the wicked and the blessedness of the righteous, are contrasted with numerous illustrations. It were unnecessary to cite examples, as we can scarcely open a single page of the prophetic writings without seeing instances; but in reading such passages it is not to be supposed that each individual phrase possesses a distinct and peculiar sense.

VI. *The order of time is not always to be looked for in the prophetic writings: for they frequently resume topics of which they have formerly treated, after other subjects have intervened, and again discuss them.*

Jeremiah and Ezekiel may, in particular, be cited as instances of this abruptness of style, who spoke of various things as they were moved by the Holy Spirit, and as occasion required; and whose discourses, being first dispersed, were afterwards collected together without regard to the order of time. In the midst of the mention of particular mercies promised to, or of judgments denounced against, the people of God, the prophets sometimes break forth into sublime predictions concerning the Messiah: these digressions appear extremely abrupt and incoherent to those who do not consider how seasonable the mention of Christ may be, in conjunction with that of the mercies of God, (of which he is the foundation and pinnacle, the ground and consummation,) and with the threats of the judgments of God, in which he was his people's grand consolation [1] A careful examination, however, of the plan and distribution of the different prophetical books will always enable the diligent reader to trace the arrangement and scope of the respective prophecies. Where, indeed, a new prediction or discourse is distinguished from a former one by a new title, as in Haggai i. 1. and ii. 10. 20.; it is an easy task to trace such an arrangement and scope: but where the prophets do not introduce any new titles (Hosea for instance) it becomes very difficult. Vitringa has laid it down as a canon [2], that in *continued* predictions, which are not distinguished one from another by titles or inscriptions, we should carefully attend both to the *beginning* and *end* of the prophetic sermon, as well as to the period of time in which the scene of the prophetic vision is fixed, and to the period in which it ends. This will tend to illustrate the sermons or discourses of Isaiah, in the forty-first and following chapters of his prophecy.

It is, however, probable that those prophecies — whose *terminus à quo* demonstrates the beginning of the time of Christ's kingdom, and the *terminus ad quem* the end of that time, — give a narration of the principal events that shall befall the church in a continued series, unless any thing intervene which may require us to go back to former times. Upon this foundation depends the interpretation of Isa. liv. 1. to lx. 22. The commencement of this prophecy unquestionably belongs to the beginning of Messiah's kingdom; the term or end falls upon the most flourishing state of that kingdom, which is to follow the conversion of the Jewish nation, and the vindication of the afflicted church; which deliverance, as well as the flourishing state of Christ's kingdom, are described in Isa. lix. 19—21. and lx. throughout.

VII. *The prophets often change both persons and tenses, sometimes speaking in their own persons, at other times representing God, his people, or their enemies, as respectively speaking, and without noticing the change of person; sometimes taking things past or present for things future, to denote the certainty of the events.*

Of this observation we have a signal instance in that very obscure prediction contained in Isa. xxi. 11, 12. which, according to Bishop Lowth's translation, is as follows:

---

[1] Boyle on the Style of the Holy Scriptures, Works, vol. ii. pp. 271.
[2] Typus Doctrinæ Propheticæ, p. 179.

THE ORACLE CONCERNING DUMAH.

A voice crieth unto me from Seir·
Watchman, what from the night?
Watchman, what from the night?
The watchman replieth
The morning cometh, and also the night.
If ye will inquire, inquire ye come again.

This prophecy, from the uncertainty of the occasion on which it was uttered, as well as from the brevity of the expression, is very obscure; but, if we observe the *transitions*, and carefully distinguish between the person *speaking* and the person *spoken to*, we shall be able to apprehend its general import. It expresses the inquiries, made of a prophet of Jehovah by a people who were in a very distressed and hazardous condition, concerning the fates which awaited them. The Edomites as well as the Jews were subdued by the Babylonians. They anxiously inquire of the prophet, how long their subjection is to last. He intimates that the Jews should be delivered from captivity, but not the Edomites. The transition being thus observed, the obscurity disappears.

Isa ix. 6., liii throughout, lxiii. throughout, Zech ix. 9. and Rev xvii 2 (to mention no other instances), may be adduced as examples of the *substitution of the past or present, in order to denote the certainty of things yet future* attention to the scope and context of the prophetic discourse will here also, as in the preceding rule, enable the reader to distinguish the various transitions with sufficient accuracy.[1]

It may here be further observed, that, in the computation of time, a *day* is used by the prophet to denote a *year*; a *week*, seven years; and that, when they speak of the *latter*, or *last days*, they invariably mean the days of the Messiah, or the time of the Gospel dispensation. The expression *that day*, often means the same time, and always some period at a distance.

VIII. *When the prophets received a commission to declare any thing, the message is sometimes expressed as if they had been appointed to do it themselves.*

This remark has, in substance, been already made. It is introduced again, in order to illustrate the phraseology of the prophetic writings. One or two additional examples will show the necessity of attending to it in interpreting the predictions of the Sacred Writings.

Thus, when Isaiah was sent to tell the Jews, that their heart would become fat, and their ears heavy, and that they would be guilty of shutting their eyes, so as not to understand and believe the truth, the message is thus expressed *Go and tell this people, hear ye indeed, but understand not, and see ye indeed, but perceive not.* This implies, that they would not employ the faculties which they possessed, so as to understand and believe the Gospel The reason of this is assigned *Make the heart of this people fat, and make their ears heavy, and shut their eyes, lest they see with their eyes and hear with their ears, and understand with their heart, and convert and be healed* (Isa. vi. 9, 10.). This is merely a prediction of what they would do: for when this prophetic declaration was accomplished, the Saviour quoted the passage, and expressed its genuine sense *In them is fulfilled the prophecy of Esaias, which saith For this people's heart is waxed gross and their ears are dull of hearing, and their eyes they have closed lest at any time, they should see with their eyes, and hear with their ears, and should understand with their heart, and should be converted, and I should heal them.* (Matt. xiii. 15.) This condition is still more explicitly stated in John iii 19. *This is the condemnation, that light is come into the world, and men loved darkness rather than light, because their deeds were evil. For every one that doeth evil, hateth the light, neither cometh to the light, lest his deeds should be reproved* The Lord said to Jeremiah, *I have put my words in thy mouth; see, I have this day set thee over the nations, to root out*

---

[1] This change of tense, however, is not exclusively confined to predictions of future events it is sometimes used by the prophets to represent duties as performed which ought to be done thus, in Mal 1. 6 *A son honours* (ought to honour) *his father.* But it is more frequently employed by the writers of the New Testament to express both our Christian privileges, and the duties to which they oblige us. Thus, Matt v. 13. *Ye are* (ought to be) *the salt of the earth.* Rom. ii. 4. *The goodness of God leadeth* (ought to lead) *thee to repentance* 2 Cor iii. 18 *We all with open face beholding* (enjoying the means of beholding) *as in a glass the glory of the Lord, are* (ought to be) *changed into the same image from glory to glory* Similar instances may be seen in 1 Cor. v. 7. Col. iii. 3. Heb. xiii 14. 1 Pet. i 6. 1 John ii. 15 iii. 9 and v. 4. 18. Dr. Taylor's Key to the Apostolic Writings, § 274. (Bishop Watson's Tracts, vol. iii. p 241.)

and to pull down, and to destroy, and to throw down, and to build, and to plant. (Jer. i 10.) The meaning of this message is, that the prophet was appointed to declare to the nations, that they should be rooted out, pulled down, and destroyed, and that others would be planted in their place, and built up. When Ezekiel beheld the glory of the God of Israel, he observes, that *it was according to the appearance of the vision which I saw, when I came* TO DESTROY THE CITY. (Ezek. xliii 3.) That is, when he came to prophesy that the city should be destroyed.

IX. *As symbolic actions and prophetic visions greatly resemble parables, and were employed for the same purpose, viz. more powerfully to instruct and engage the attention of the people, they must be interpreted in the same manner as parables.*[1]

We must therefore chiefly consider the scope and design of such symbolic actions and prophetic visions, without attempting too minute an explanation of all the poetical images and figures with which the sacred writers adorned their style. For instance, in Zech i 7—11, it is not necessary to inquire what is meant by the *man riding upon a red horse, and standing among the myrtle trees* this vision represents so many angels returning probably from the kingdoms over which they presided, to give to Jehovah an account of their expedition and ministry. The horses, it has been conjectured, denote their power and celerity, and the different colours the difference of their ministries. The scope of the vision, however, is sufficiently plain. the angels tell that all the earth was *sitting still and at rest*, the Persian empire and other nations connected with Judæa, enjoying peace at that time, though the Jews continued in an unsettled state.[2]

SECTION II.

OBSERVATIONS ON THE ACCOMPLISHMENT OF PROPHECY IN GENERAL.

A PROPHECY is demonstrated to be fulfilled when we can prove that the event has actually taken place, precisely according to the manner in which it was foretold, either from sacred history, where that is practicable, or from profane authors of unimpeachable veracity; whose characters stand so high, that they cannot possibly be suspected of having forged any thing to favour the idea of its accomplishment. In order to ascertain whether a prediction has been fulfilled, we must first endeavour to find out the general scheme of the prophecy in question, by a careful comparison of the parts with the whole, and with corresponding prophecies both earlier and later; and to classify the various things spoken of, lest the judgment be perplexed with a multitude of references. And, secondly, in our deductions from the prophecies thus arranged, those predictions, and their respective accomplishments, are principally to be selected and urged, which chiefly tend to remove all suspicion of their taking place by accident, or being foretold by some happy conjecture. Now this may be done, by showing the vast *distance of time* between the prophecy and the event foretold; the *agreement* of very many, even of the minutest circumstances, so that, when completed, the description determinately applies to the subject; and, lastly, the *dependence of actions* upon the uncertain will of man, or upon opportunity presenting itself: for *all* these things are of such a nature, that no unassisted

---

[1] On the construction of parabolic language, see pp. 400—406. of this volume.
[2] Archbishop Newcome on Zech. i. 7—11.

human intellect either can or could possibly foresee them. These two general observations being premised, we now proceed to offer a few canons by which to ascertain the accomplishment of prophecy.

I. *The same prophecies frequently have a double meaning, and refer to different events, the one near, the other remote; the one temporal, the other spiritual or perhaps eternal. The prophets thus having several events in view, their expressions may be partly applicable to one, and partly to another, and it is not always easy to mark the transitions. What has not been fulfilled in the first, we must apply to the second; and what has already been fulfilled, may often be considered as typical of what remains to be accomplished*

The double sense of prophecy has been opposed with much ingenuity by Mr. Whiston, Dr. Sykes, and Dr. Benson, in this country, and by Father Balthus in France, as well as by most of the German theologians, who severally contend that the antient prophecies contain only one sense but, that the rule above stated is correct, we apprehend will appear from the following remarks and illustrations.

1 "Throughout the whole of prophetical Scripture, a time of retribution and of vengeance on God's enemies is announced It is called '*the day of the Lord,*' '*the day of wrath and slaughter, of the Lord's anger, visitation and judgment,*' '*the great day;*' and '*the last day.*' At the same time it is to be observed, that this kind of description, and the same expressions, which are used to represent this great day, are also employed by the prophets to describe the fall and punishment of particular states and empires, of Babylon, by Isaiah (ch xiii), of Egypt, by Ezekiel (ch xxx 2—4 and xxxii 7, 8), of Jerusalem by Jeremiah, Joel, and by our Lord (Matt xxiv) and in many of these prophecies, the description of the calamity, which is to fall on any particular state or nation, is so blended and intermixed with that *general* destruction, which, in the final days of vengeance, will invade *all* the inhabitants of the earth, that the industry and skill of our ablest interpreters have been scarcely equal to separate and assort them Hence it has been concluded, by judicious divines, that these partial prophecies and particular instances of the divine vengeance, whose accomplishment we know to have taken place, are presented to us as types, certain tokens and forerunners, of some greater events which are also disclosed in them. To the dreadful time of universal vengeance, they all appear to look forward, beyond their first and more immediate object. Little, indeed, can we doubt that such is to be considered the use and application of these prophecies, since we see them thus applied by our Lord and his apostles." [1]

2. The second psalm is primarily an inauguration hymn, composed by David, the anointed of Jehovah, when crowned with victory, and placed triumphant on the sacred hill of Sion But, in Acts iv 25 the inspired apostles with one voice declare it to be descriptive of the exaltation of the Messiah, and of the opposition raised against the Gospel, both by Jews and Gentiles. — The latter part of the sixteenth psalm is spoken of David's person, and is, unquestionably, in its first and immediate sense, to be understood of him, and of his hope of rising after death to an endless life but it is equally clear from Acts ii 25—31. that it was spoken of Christ, the son of David, who was typified by that king and prophet. — The twenty-second psalm [2], though primarily intended of David

---

[1] Dr. Woodhouse on the Apocalypse, pp 172, 173 One of the most remarkable of these prophecies, he observes, is that splendid one of Isaiah, ch. xxxiv ; the importance and universality of which is to be collected from the manner in which it is introduced: "*All nations and people, the world and all things in it,*" are summoned to the audience. It represents "*the day of the Lord's vengeance,*" and the year of the *recompenses* for the controversy of Sion (ver. 8.), it descends on *all nations* and *their armies* (ver. 2.) The images of wrathful vengeance and utter dissolution are the same which are presented under the sixth seal in the Revelation of St John. (vi. 12—17.) The hosts of heaven are dissolved, the heavens are rolled together as a scroll of parchment; the stars fall like a leaf from a vine, or a fig from its tree. And yet *Idumæa* is mentioned by the prophet as the *particular* object of vengeance such seems to be the *typical* completion and *primary* application of this prophecy. but it has evidently a more sublime and future prospect, and in this sense the *whole world* is its object · and using the same symbols and figurative expressions with the prophecy of the sixth seal, with those of the fourteenth, fifteenth, and, above all, sixteenth chapters of the Apocalypse, and with others of the Old and New Testaments, it must, with them, be finally referred to the *great day* of the Lord's vengeance for its perfect completion." Ibid. p. 174

[2] Dr Randolph has a beautiful exposition of this psalm at the end of vol. i. of his View of Christ's Ministry, pp 503—515.

when he was in great distress and forsaken by God, is yet, secondarily and mystically, to be understood of our blessed Saviour during his passion upon the cross, and so it is applied by himself (Matt. xxvii 46) And it is further observable, that other passages of this psalm (v 8. 16. 18) are noticed by the Evangelist, as being fulfilled at that time (Matt. xxvii. 35. 43.), now it is certain that they could not be fulfilled unless they had been intended in this mysterious sense of Jesus Christ The forty-fifth psalm is, in the original, a *song of loves*, an epithalamium on the nuptials of King Solomon and the King of Egypt's daughter, but from Heb 1. 8. we are assured that it is addressed to Christ; and, therefore, in a remote and spiritual sense, it celebrates the majesty and glory of his kingdom, his mystical union with his church, and the admirable benefits that would be conferred upon her in the times of the Gospel.

It would be no difficult task to adduce many other psalms in which the double sense is most clearly to be discerned [1]: but we shall proceed to cite a few instances from the writings of the prophets.

(1.) Isa vii. 14. — In the *primary* but lower sense of this prophecy, the sign given was to assure Ahaz that the land of Judæa would speedily be delivered from the kings of Samaria and Damascus, by whom it was invaded But the introduction of the prophecy, the singular stress laid upon it, and the exact sense of the terms in which it was expressed, make it in a high degree probable that it had another and more important purpose and the event has clearly proved that the *sign given* had, secondarily and mystically, a respect to the miraculous birth of Christ, and to a deliverance much more momentous than that of Ahaz from his then present distressful situation. [2]

(2) Isa xi 6 — What is here said of the wolf dwelling with the lamb, &c is understood as having its first completion in the reign of Hezekiah, when profound peace was enjoyed after the troubles caused by Sennacherib; but its *second* and full completion is under the Gospel, whose power in changing the hearts, tempers, and lives of the worst of men, is here foretold and described by a singularly beautiful assemblage of images. Of this blessed power there has, in every age of Christianity, been a cloud of witnesses; although its most glorious æra predicted in this passage, may not yet be arrived. The latter part of the same chapter, in which there are many beautiful allusions to the Exodus from Egypt, seems to refer principally to the future restoration of the Jews from their several dispersions, and to that happy period when they and the Gentiles shall stand together under the banner of Jesus, and unite their zeal in extending the limits of his kingdom. This is a favourite theme with Isaiah, who is usually and justly designated the Evangelical Prophet, and who (ch xl.) predicted the deliverance of the Jews from the Babylonish captivity, and their restoration to the land of Canaan, — events which were primarily and literally accomplished, but which by the evangelist Matthew (iii 3) and by our Lord himself (Matt. xi 10. are said to have been fulfilled by John the Baptist's preaching in the wilderness of Judæa; and which, secondarily and spiritually, foretold the deliverance of mankind from the infinitely greater bondage of sin.

(3) Once more — Hos. xi 1. *Out of Egypt have I called my son*. This passage, in its literal sense, was meant of God's delivering the children of Israel out of Egypt; but, in its secondary and mystical sense, there can be no doubt that an allusion was intended by the Holy Spirit to the call of the infant Christ out of the same country. (Matt ii. 15)

Thus it is evident that many prophecies *must be taken in a double sense*, in order to understand their full import; and this twofold application of them, by our Lord and his apostles, is a full authority for us to consider and apply them in a similar way. In order to ascertain

---

[1] Bishop Horne, in the preface to his admirable commentary on the Psalms, has noticed a considerable number of those divine odes, which bear a double meaning, the propriety of which he has fully vindicated. Works, vol ii pp. x—xx See also Dr Apthorpe's Warburtonian "Discourses on Prophecy," vol. 1. pp 77—89, and Dr. Nares's Warburtonian Lectures, intitled "A Connected and Chronological View of the Prophecies relating to the Christian Church," pp. 155—162 176, 177. Almost the whole of the Psalms are applied by Bishop Horsley to the Messiah, in his "Book of Psalms translated from the Hebrew," 2 vols 8vo. But Bishop Marsh has endeavoured to show that there are no double meanings, or, as he terms them, *secondary senses*, in prophecy Lectures on Divinity, part iv lect. 22.

[2] There is a good philological illustration of this prediction in Dr. Randolph's Prælectiones Theologicæ, in vol. ii. (pp. 446. et seq) of his View of Christ's Ministry; and an elaborate vindication and explanation of it in the Abbé Hook's Religionis Naturalis et Revelatæ Principia, tom. ii. pp. 494—498

whether a prophecy is to be taken in a double sense, the following rules have been laid down by the celebrated Vitringa. [1]

(1.) That we may attain an accurate and distinct knowledge of the *subject* of a prediction, we must carefully attend to all the *attributes* and *characters* which are applied to the subject of the prophecy: if the subject be not specifically mentioned by *name*, it must be discovered by its characteristics; of this description are many of the prophecies concerning Christ, particularly Psalms ii. xxii. xlv. lx. Isa. liii. Zech. iii. 8. If the subject be named, we must inquire whether it is to be taken properly or mystically, or partly properly and partly mystically; as in Psalm lxxii.

(2.) We must not, however, depart from the literal sense of the subject, when called by its own proper name, if all the attributes, or the principal and more remarkable ones, agree to the subject of the prophecy. This rule will be found of considerable use in interpreting the prophecies concerning Israel, Judah, Tyre, Babylon, Egypt, and other countries and places.

(3.) If the attributes by no means agree with the subject expressed in a prophecy by its own name, we must direct our thoughts to another subject which corresponds to it, and which assumes a mystic name, on account of the agreement between the type and antitype. Examples of this occur in the prophecies concerning Edom (Isa. lxiii 1—6.), David (Ezek. xxxiv. 24—31.), and Elijah. (Mal. iv. 5.)

(4.) If, in prophecies, the subject be expressed by name, which may bear both a proper and a mystical interpretation, and the attributes of the prophetic discourse be of a mixed kind, so that some of them agree more strictly with the subject mystically taken, while others are more correctly predicated of it in a literal and grammatical sense. — in such cases, we must take the subject of the prophecy to be, not simple, but *complex:* and the prophet, actuated by divine illumination, expresses himself in such a manner as designedly to be understood of both senses, and to intimate to the reader that the mystical or allegorical sense is enveloped in the literal sense

Thus, many of the prophecies concerning Babylon, Edom, Egypt, and Tyre, contain such august and magnificent expressions, as, if taken properly, will admit of a very poor and barren exposition and, therefore, it must be presumed that the Holy Spirit designed something more, and to lead our minds to the mystical Babylon, &c In like manner, such grand things are sometimes spoken concerning the return of the Jews from the Babylonish captivity, and mention is made of such distinguished blessings being bestowed upon them, as necessarily lead us to look for a further and more complete fulfilment in the redemption by Jesus Christ, and the spiritual blessings of grace bestowed upon the people of God, under the Gospel dispensation. Isa. lii 1—3 and Jer iii 14—18, to cite no other examples, present very striking illustrations of this remark Hence it follows, that,

(5.) Prophecies of a general nature are applicable by accommodation to individuals, most of the things, which are spoken of the church, being equally applicable to her individual members.

(6.) Prophecies of a particular nature, on the other hand, admit, and often require, an extended sense: for instance, Edom, Moab, or any of the enemies of God's people, are often put for the whole; what is said of one being generally applicable to the rest. And, in like manner, what is said either to or concerning God's people, on any particular occasion, is of general application; as all, who stand in the same relation to God, have an interest in the same prophecies

---

[1] In his Typus Doctrinæ Propheticæ, cap. ii. Dr. Apthorpe has translated eighteen of Vitringa's canons (which are admirably illustrated by numerous examples in his valuable commentary on Isaiah) in his Lectures on Prophecy, vol i pp 90—106. Jahn has given several additional examples. Introd. ad Vet Fœdus, pp. 332—334.

(7.) In continued prophecies, which are not distinguished one from another, we should carefully attend, *first*, to the beginning and end of each discourse, and, *secondly*, to the epoch of time which commences the scene of the prophetic vision, and the term in which it ends.

The *first* observation is of principal use in the discourses of Isaiah, from the fortieth chapter to the end of the book. This distinction, often difficult and somewhat obscure, is of great moment in the interpretation of the prophecies, that we may not consider as a continued discourse what ought to be divided into several distinct topics. The *last* part of this canon is indispensable in explaining the Psalms and Prophetic Visions. See Psal. xxiv. 1. Isa. vi. 1.

II. *Predictions, denouncing judgments to come, do not in themselves speak the absolute futurity of the event, but only declare what is to be expected by the persons to whom they are made, and what will certainly come to pass, unless God in his mercy interpose between the threatening and the event.*

" So that comminations do speak only the *debitum pœnæ*, and the necessary obligation to punishment; but therein God doth not bind up himself as he doth in absolute promises, the reason is, because comminations confer no right to any, which absolute promises do, and therefore God is not bound to necessary performance of what he threatens. Indeed the guilt or obligation to punishment is necessary, where the offence hath been committed, to which the threatening was annexed: but the execution of that punishment doth still depend upon God's arbitrarious will, and therefore he may suspend or remove it upon serious addresses made to himself in order to it. For, since God was pleased not to take the present forfeiture of the first grand transgression, but made such a relaxation of that penal law, that conditions of pardon were admittable, notwithstanding sentence passed upon the malefactors, there is strong ground of presumption in human nature, that God's forbearance of mankind, notwithstanding sin, doth suppose his readiness to pardon offenders upon their repentance, and, therefore, that all particular threatenings of judgment to come do suppose incorrigibleness in those against whom they are pronounced; upon which the foundation of hope is built, that if timely repentance do intervene, God will remove those judgments which are threatened against them [1]." Of these conditional comminatory predictions we have examples in Jonah's preaching to the Ninevites (Jonah iii. 4—10.), and in Isaiah's denunciation of death to Hezekiah (Isa. xxxviii. 1.) See also a similar instance in Jer. xxxviii. 14—23.

III. *Predictions then express divine purposes, when many prophets in several ages concur in the same prediction.* —

" Because it is hardly seen but all those tacit conditions, which are supposed in general promises or comminations, may be altered in different ages: but, when the conditions alter, and the predictions continue the same, it is a stronger evidence that it is some immutable counsel of God, which is expressed in those predictions. And in this case one prediction confirms the foregoing, as the Jews say of prophets, ' one prophet that hath the testimony of another prophet, is supposed to be true:' but it must be with this supposition, that the other prophet was before approved to be a true prophet. Now, both these meet in the prophecies concerning our Saviour, for to him bear all the prophets witness, and in their several ages they had several things revealed to them concerning him: and the uniformity and perfect harmony of all these several prophecies by persons at so great distance from each other, and being of several interests and employments, and in several places, yet all giving light to each other, and exactly meeting at last in the accomplishment, do give us yet a further and clearer evidence, that all those several beams came from the same sun, when all those scattered rays were at last gathered into one body again at the appearance of the Sun of Righteousness in the world." [2]

---

[1] Stillingfleet's Origines Sacræ, book ii. chap vi. § 10. pp. 120, 121. 8th edit. Jahn, Enchiridion Hermeneuticæ Sacræ, pp. 148, 149.
[2] Stillingfleet's Orig Sac p. 120.

SECTION III.

OBSERVATIONS ON THE ACCOMPLISHMENT OF PROPHECIES CONCERNING THE MESSIAH IN PARTICULAR.[1]

I. *JESUS CHRIST being the great subject and end of Scripture revelation, we ought every where to search for Prophecies concerning him.*

We are assured by Christ himself that the Scriptures testify *of him* (John v. 39), and that in Moses, the Psalms, and Prophets, there are things concerning him (Luke xxiv. 25—27 44) further, we have the declaration of an inspired apostle, that to him give all the prophets witness (Acts x 43), and of an angel of God, that " *the testimony of Jesus is the spirit of prophecy* " (Rev. xix 10) It may, therefore, be remarked generally, that whatsoever is emphatically and characteristically spoken of some certain person, not called by his own name, in the psalms or prophetical books, so that each predicate can be fully demonstrated in no single subject of that or any other time, must be taken as said and predicted of the Messiah The twenty-second psalm, and the fifty-third chapter of Isaiah's prophecy, may be adduced as illustrations of this rule, which will not mislead any student or reader of the sacred volume. The four first remarks in p 471, may be advantageously employed in the application of this rule.

II. *The interpretation of the word of prophecy, made by Jesus Christ himself, and by his inspired apostles, is a rule and key by which to interpret correctly the prophecies cited or alluded to by them.*

The propriety of this canon must be obvious for as every one is the best interpreter of his own words, so the Holy Spirit (under whose influence the antient prophets wrote and spoke), in more recent prophecies, refers to former predictions, and often uses the same words, phrases, and images, thus leading us to understand the true sense of those oracles [2] For instance, the prophecy (in Isa viii. 14) that the Messiah would prove a stone of stumbling and a rock of offence, is more plainly repeated by Simeon (Luke ii 34.), and is shown to have been fulfilled by Paul (Rom ix 32, 33), and by Peter (1 Pet ii. 8.); and the sixteenth psalm is expressly applied to Jesus Christ by the latter of these apostles. (Acts ii 25—31.) [3]

III. *Where the prophets describe a golden age of felicity, they clearly foretell Gospel times: and particularly in the Prophecies and Psalms, whatever is predicated of a person not named, in terms expressive of such excellence, glory, and other characteristics, as are suitable in their just emphases to no other subject, must be interpreted as spoken and predicted of the Messiah.*

1. It is thus that the writers of the New Testament interpret and allege the antient prophecies, instances may be given in Deut xviii. 18 Psalms viii. xvi xxii xl. lxix. lxxviii cxviii 22, 23 Isa. iv 2. vii 14, 15. xlii 1 lui. Zech. iii 8. and xii. 10. It is worthy of remark that the writers of the New Testament directly apply to the SON OF GOD the most magnificent descriptions and attributes of the FATHER in the Old Testament, as in Psal. lxviii 18 cii 26, 27 Isa. xlv 22—24, which teach us to *acknowledge the mystery of God and the Father and of Christ, in whom are hid all the treasures of wisdom and knowledge.* (Col ii 2, 3)

2 At the time the prophets respectively flourished, the Israelites and Jews were, in general, notoriously wicked, although, even in the worst of times, there was a considerable number who feared Jehovah. Hence, while the prophets denounce national judgments upon the wicked (in which temporal afflictions the righteous would necessarily be involved), they at the same time hold out to the latter, to strengthen their trust in God, predictions of future and better times; and, with promises of some great and temporal deliverance, they invariably connect a display of the yet greater though future deliverance of the Messiah;

---

[1] Bishop Marsh (Divinity Lectures, part iv. lect. xx. and xxi.) has several admirable observations on the connection subsisting between the truth of Christianity and the prophecies relating to the Messiah nearly the whole of Lecture xxi. is occupied with examples of predictions literally and strictly *foretelling the coming of Christ*.

[2] Bishop Lowth has some fine remarks on this topic towards the close of his eleventh Lecture.

[3] The petty cavils and evasions of Ruperti and other modern commentators, who deny (without being able to disprove) the above canon, are well exposed by Dr. J. P. Smith, on the Person of Christ, vol. i. pp. 222, 223.

the peace and happiness which are to prevail in consequence of that deliverance, are pourtrayed in such a beautiful assemblage of images, and delineate so high a state of felicity, that, as there is no period in the history of the world, prior to the Christian dispensation, to which they can in any way be applied, these predictions of future happiness and peace must necessarily be understood exclusively to refer to Gospel times. Many passages might be adduced from the prophetic writings in confirmation of this rule. It will, however, suffice to adduce two instances from Isaiah, ch. ix. 2—7 and xi. 1—9. In the former of these passages, the peaceful kingdom of the Messiah is set forth, its extent and duration; and in the latter, the singular peace and happiness which should then prevail, are delineated in imagery of unequalled beauty and energy.[1]

IV. *Things foretold as universally or indefinitely to come to pass under the Gospel, are to be understood, — as they respect the duty, — of all persons, but, — as they respect the event, — only of God's people.*

Thus, when the peace, that is foretold to prevail in Gospel times, is stated to be so great that men should then *beat their swords into plough-shares, and their spears into pruning hooks, that nation should not lift up sword against nation, neither learn war any more* (Isa. ii. 4), and that *the wolf should lie down with the lamb, and the leopard with the kid* (Isa. xi. 6. and lxv. 25. with other passages that might be adduced), — all these highly figurative expressions are to be understood of the nature, design, and tendency of the Gospel, and what is the duty of all its professors, and what would actually take place in the Christian world, if all who profess the Christian doctrine did sincerely and cordially obey its dictates. And, so far as the Gospel does prevail upon any, it reclaims their wild and unruly natures, from being furious as wolves, they become meek as lambs, and from raging like lions, they become gentle and tender as kids: so far are they from hurting or injuring others, that they dare not entertain any the slightest thoughts of malevolence or revenge, towards their most inveterate enemies.

V. *As the antient prophecies concerning the Messiah are of two kinds, some of them relating to his first coming to suffer, while the rest of them concern his second coming to advance his kingdom, and restore the Jews; — in all these prophecies, we must carefully distinguish between his first coming in humiliation to accomplish his mediatorial work on the cross, and his second coming in glory to judgment.*

This distinction is sufficiently obvious in those passages which treat of either coming separately, as in Isa. vii. 14. ix. 6. liii. &c. which treat of his *first coming* in the flesh, and in Isa. ii. 10—21., which refers to his *second coming* to judgment. To the former must be referred all those passages which relate to his humiliation. But it is more difficult to distinguish each advent in those passages, in which the prophet makes an *immediate* transition from the one to the other. For instance, in Isa. xl. 1—9, the prediction relates to the first advent of Christ, but in v. 10. his second coming to judgment is noticed, express mention being made of the solemn work of retribution, which is peculiar to judgment. Again, in Jer. xxiii. 5—7. the promise of sending the Son of God into the world is in v. 8. joined with a prophecy concerning the conversion of the Jews, which is yet future. A similar instance of uniting the two advents of Christ occurs in Mal. iii. 1—5. By distinguishing, however, between them, we shall be better able to combat the objections of the Jews, who apply to the Messiah all those predictions which refer to a state of exaltation, while they overlook all those plain, though less numerous prophecies, in which is described Messiah's first coming in a state of humiliation.

Before we dismiss the important subject of prophecy, there are two cautions, which must uniformly be kept in view in studying the prophetic writings.

1. The first is, *that we do not apply passing events as actually fulfilling particular prophecies.*

It has justly been remarked, that " a commentator upon the predictions of Daniel and John can never be too much upon his guard against the fascinating idea, that he may expect to find *every passing event of his own day* there predicted. Before he ventures to introduce any exposition founded upon *present* circumstances, he ought to make it clearly appear that it both accords with the *chronological* order so carefully preserved in those prophecies,

---

[1] Rambach, Inst. Herm. pp. 175—177. J. P. Carpzov, Primæ Lineæ Hermeneuticæ, pp. 25, 26.

that it strictly harmonises with the *language of symbols*, and that it demonstrates every part of the prediction to tally *exactly* with its supposed accomplishments." [1]

2. The other caution is, that *we do not curiously pry beyond what is expressly written, or describe as fulfilled prophecies which are yet future*.

Such *secret things*, as unaccomplished prophecies, *belong unto the Lord* our God; and it is a vain waste of time to weary ourselves with conjectures respecting the *precise* mode of their accomplishment. Upon these points, when we go beyond what is written, we exceed our commission and it has almost invariably been found, that a commentator, who attempted to show *how* a prophecy was about to be fulfilled, was by the event convicted of error. We may safely and positively declare what will come to pass, and we may even say how it will come to pass, so long as we resolutely confine ourselves to the *explicit declarations of Scripture*, but to point out the *manner* in which an event will be accomplished, *any further than the word of God* hath revealed the manner of it, is to pry too curiously into what he hath purposely concealed, and to aim at becoming prophets, instead of contenting ourselves with being humble and fallible expositors of prophecy. What *the Bible* hath declared, that *we* may without hesitation declare beyond this, all is mere vague conjecture. [2]

On the subject of apparent contradictions between prophecies and their accomplishment, see Chap. VII. Sect. III. *infra*.[3]

CHAPTER V.

ON THE DOCTRINAL INTERPRETATION OF THE SCRIPTURES.

AS the Holy Scriptures contain the revealed will of God to man, they not only offer to our attention the most interesting histories and characters for our instruction by example, and the most sublime prophecies for the confirmation of our faith, but they likewise present to our serious study, *doctrinal truths* of the utmost importance. Some of these occur in the historical, poetical, and prophetical parts of the Bible: but they are chiefly to be found in the apostolic epistles which, though originally designed for the edification of particular

---

[1] Faber's Dissertation on the Prophecies, vol ii. pp 277.
[2] Ibid. vol i p 77.
[3] In addition to the writers cited in the course of this chapter, it may be stated that the fulfilment of prophecy is fully considered by Bishop Newton in his "Dissertations," 2 vols 8vo. See also Sir Isaac Newton's Observations on Daniel, and the Apocalypse, 4to. A. H Franckii Introductio ad Lectionem Prophetarum, (Halæ Magdeburgicæ, 1724 8vo) pp. 1—88. In pp 91—247. he has applied his general principles to the interpretation of the prophet Jonah, Glassii Philologia Sacr. lib. i. tract. IV. col. 311—324. 4to. edit. Lipsiæ, 1725), Rambachii Observationes Selectæ de Parallelismo Sacro, pp 219—235, and his Instit Hermeneuticæ Sacræ, pp. 741—745. 779—791. J. E. Pfeifferi, Inst. Herm. Sacr. pp. 79—81.; Langii Hermeneutica Sacra, pp. 133—150., Turretin de Sacræ Scripturæ Interpretatione, cap iv. pp. 244—255.; in pp. 256—295. he has given an admirable illustration of the principles laid down by him in the preceding chapter by expounding chapters i. and ii. of the prophecy of Joel, Pareau, Institutio Interpretis Veteris Testamenti, pp. 468—519, Principes Généraux pour l'Intelligence des Prophéties (Paris, 1763 8vo); Bishop Warburton's Divine Legation of Moses, book vi. (Works, vol vi. p. 47 *et seq.*), Dr. Hey's Norrisian Lectures, vol. i pp 235—240; Dr. Smith's View of the Prophets, 12mo; Bishop Hurd's Introduction to the Study of the Prophets (Works, vol. v., Dr. Macknight's Translation and Commentary on the Epistles, vol. iv (4to edit) or vi. (8vo edit. essay viii sect v.; Mr. Frere's Combined View of the Prophecies of Daniel, Esdras, and St John, 8vo, and the Rev Wm. Jones's Lectures on the Figurative Language of Scripture (Theol and Miscel. Works, vol. iv) These writers have all been consulted on the present occasion.

Christian churches or individuals, are nevertheless of *general application, and designed for the guidance of the universal church in every age*. For many of the fundamental doctrines of Christianity are more copiously treated in the epistles, which are not so particularly explained in the gospels: and as the authors of the several epistles wrote under the same divine inspiration as the evangelists, the epistles and gospels must be taken together, to complete the rule of Christian faith. The doctrinal interpretation, therefore, of the Sacred Writings is of paramount consequence; as by this means we are enabled to acquire a correct and saving knowledge of the will of God concerning us. In the prosecution of this important branch of sacred literature, the following observations are offered to the attention of the student.

I. *The meaning of the Sacred Writings is not to be determined according to modern notions and systems, but we must endeavour to carry ourselves back to the very times and places in which they were written, and realise the ideas and modes of thinking of the sacred writers.*

This rule is of the utmost importance for understanding the Scriptures; but is too commonly neglected by commentators and expositors, who, when applying themselves to the explanation of the Sacred Writings, have a preconceived system of doctrine which they seek in the Bible, and to which they refer every passage of Scripture. Thus they rather draw the Scriptures to *their* system of doctrine, than bring their doctrines to the standard of Scripture; a mode of interpretation which is altogether unjust, and utterly useless in the attainment of truth. The only way by which to understand the meaning of the sacred writers, and to distinguish between true and false doctrines, is, to lay aside all preconceived modern notions and systems, and to carry ourselves back to the very times and places in which the prophets and apostles wrote. In perusing the Bible, therefore, this rule must be most carefully attended to: — it is only an unbiassed mind that can attain the true and genuine sense of Scripture.[1]

II. *Regard must also be had to the peculiar state of the churches, cities, or persons, to whom particular epistles, especially those of Saint Paul, were addressed; as the knowledge of such state frequently leads to the particular occasion for which such epistle was written.*

"Although the general design of the whole of Scripture was the instruction of the world, and the edification of the church in every age, still there was an immediate and specific design with regard to every book. This appears particularly obvious in reference to the epistles. With the exception of those properly called catholic or general epistles, and of a few written to individuals, they were addressed to particular societies of Christians, and they were adapted to the exact state of those societies, whether consisting chiefly of Jewish or of Heathen converts; whether recently organised as churches, or in a state of flourishing maturity; whether closely cemented together by the strength of brotherly love, or distracted by the spirit of faction; whether steadfast in adherence to the truth, or inclining to the admission of error. Now, if these considerations were present to the mind of the inspired writer of an epistle,

---

[1] Turretin, de Interp. Sacr. Script. pp. 312-314. See also some sensible remarks on these perversions of the Sacred Writings in the Christian Observer for 1818, vol. xvii. p. 317.

and served to regulate the strain and the topics of his address, it is evident that they must by no means be disregarded by us in our attempts to ascertain the genuine and intended sense."[1] A knowledge, therefore, of the state of the particular churches, to which they addressed their epistles, is of the greatest importance, not only to enable us to ascertain the scope of any particular epistle, but also for the purpose of reconciling doctrinal passages, which, to a *cursory* reader, may at first sight appear contradictory.

For instance, the Galatian churches, not long after their members had been converted to the faith of the Gospel, were persuaded by some Judaising teachers that it was absolutely necessary they should be circumcised, and observe the entire law of Moses hence great dissensions arose among the Galatian Christians. These circumstances led Saint Paul to write his Epistle to them, the design of which was, to prove the Jewish ceremonial law to be no longer obligatory, to convince them of the moral and spiritual nature of the Gospel, and thus to restore mutual good-will among them

Again, Rom. xiv 5. and Gal. iv 10, 11. are *apparently* contradictory to each other. In the former passage we read — "*One man esteemeth one day above another, another esteemeth every day alike Let every man be fully persuaded in his own mind.*" The latter passage runs thus — "*Ye observe days, and months, and times, and years, I am afraid lest I have bestowed upon you labour in vain.*" Now, if we attend to the situation and character of the persons addressed, we shall easily be enabled to solve this seeming difficulty.

The Roman and Galatian churches were composed of both Jews and Gentiles; but they are not addressed promiscuously, neither are they the same description of people who are addressed in both passages. Those who "regarded days," among the Romans, were the *converted Jews*, who, having from their youth observed them as divine appointments, were with difficulty brought to lay them aside And as their attachment had its origin in a tender regard to divine authority, they were considered as "keeping the day unto the Lord," and great forbearance was enjoined upon the Gentile converts towards them in that matter Those, on the other hand, who, among the Galatians, "observed days, and months, and times," were *converted Gentiles*, as is manifest from the context, which describes them as having, in their unconverted state, "done service to them which by nature were no gods" (ch. iv 8.) These being perverted by certain Judaising teachers, were, contrary to the apostolic decision (Acts xv.), circumcised, and subjected themselves to the yoke of Jewish ceremonies Nor was this all; they were led to consider these things as necessary to justification and salvation, which were subversive of the doctrine of justification by faith in Jesus Christ (Acts xv. 1. Gal. v 4) These circumstances being considered, the different language of the Apostle is perfectly in character. Circumcision, and conformity to the law of Moses, in *Jewish converts*, was held to be lawful Even the apostle of the Gentiles himself "to the Jews became a Jew;" frequently, if not constantly, conforming to the Jewish laws And when writing to others, he expresses himself on this wise "Is any man called, being circumcised? let him not become uncircumcised. Is any called, in uncircumcision? let him not become circumcised Circumcision is nothing, and uncircumcision is nothing, but the keeping of the commandments of God" (1 Cor vii 18, 19.) But for *Gentiles*, who had no such things to allege in their favour, to go off from the liberty granted to them (Acts xv.), and entangle themselves under a yoke of bondage, and not only so, but to make it a term of justification was sufficient to excite a fear lest the labour which he had bestowed upon them was in vain.[2]

Braunius[3], Vitringa[4], and Buddeus[5] have happily illustrated numerous passages in Saint Paul's Epistles by attending to the circumstances mentioned in the above canon. The state of the Apocalyptic churches has also been well described by our learned countryman Smith[6], by Witsius[7], and especially by Ferdinand Stosch[8] Rambach, in his Introduction to the Epistle to the Romans, has elaborately investigated the state of the church at Rome, and applied it to the examination and scope of that epistle[9]

---

[1] Rev. H. F. Burder's Sermon on the Duty and Means of ascertaining the genuine Sense of the Scriptures, p. 19   [2] Fuller's Harmony of Scripture, pp. 44, 46.
[3] Selecta Sacra, lib i   [4] Observationes Sacræ, lib. iv. cc 7, 8.
[5] Jo Francisci Buddei Ecclesia Apostolica, sive de Statu Ecclesiæ Christianæ sub Apostolis Commentatio Historica-Dogmatica Jenæ, 1729. 8vo.
[6] In his "Remarks upon the Manners, Religion, and Government of the Turks, with a Survey of the Seven Churches of Asia," 8vo. 1678. The remarks had previously been printed in Latin in 1672, and again in an enlarged edition in 1674.
[7] Miscellanea Sacra, tom. i. p. 669
[8] Ferdinandi Stoschii Syntagma Dissertationum Septem de nominibus totidem Urbium Asiæ ad quos D Johannes in Apocalypsi Epistolas direxit, 8vo. Guelpherbyti, 1757.
[9] Jo. Jac. Rambachii Introductio Historico-Theologica in Epistolam Pauli ad Romanos. 8vo. Halæ, 1727.

478   *On the Doctrinal Interpretation of the Scriptures.*   [Part II.

III. *In order to understand any doctrinal book or passage of Scripture, we must attend to the controversies which were agitated at that time, and to which the sacred writers allude : for a key to the apostolic epistles is not to be sought in the modern controversies that divide Christians, and which were not only unknown, but also were not in existence at that time.*

The controversies which were discussed in the age of the apostles, are to be ascertained, partly from their writings, partly from the existing monuments of the primitive Christians, and likewise from some passages in the writings of the Rabbins.

From these it appears that the following were the principal questions then agitated, viz. What is the true way by which to please God, and thus to obtain eternal life — the observance of the Mosaic law, or faith and obedience as held forth in the Gospel? To this question the following was closely allied — Whether the observance of the Mosaic ceremonies was so absolutely necessary, that they were to be imposed on the converted Gentiles? The former question is *particularly* discussed in St Paul's Epistle to the Romans; the latter in the council held at Jerusalem (Acts xv. 1—31.), and *especially* in the Epistle to the Galatians.

Another question which was most warmly agitated, related to the calling of the Gentiles, which the Jews could by no means bear, as appears from numerous passages in the Gospels, Acts of the Apostles, and the Epistles. The apostles, therefore, found it necessary to assert that point, to confirm it by citing numerous prophecies from the Old Testament relative to the conversion of the Gentiles, and to vindicate it from the objections of the Jews : this has been done by Saint Paul in several chapters of his Epistle to the Romans, as well as in his Epistles to the Ephesians and Colossians, in which he proves that the Jewish ceremonies were superseded.

There were also some Jewish notions, which were refuted both by our Lord and by his apostles; for instance, that all Jews would certainly be saved. Turretin, to whom we are indebted for this observation, has adduced a passage from the Codex Sanhedrin, which affirmed that *every Jew had a portion in the future world*, and another from the Talmud, in which it is said that *Abraham is sitting near the gates of hell, and does not permit any Israelite, however wicked he may be, to descend into hell* [1] In opposition to such traditions as these, Jesus Christ thus solemnly warned them *Not every man that saith unto me, 'Lord, Lord,' shall enter into the kingdom of heaven, but he that doeth the will of my Father which is in heaven.* (Matt. vii. 21) This notion was also opposed at length by Saint Paul. (Rom ii 16. et seq.) Once more it appears from very many passages of the Jewish writers, that the Jews divided the precepts of the law into great and little, and taught that if a man observed *one such grand precept*, that would suffice to conciliate the favour of God, and would outweigh all his other actions. In opposition to this our Lord solemnly declares, that "whosoever shall break one of *these least commandments*, and shall teach men so, he shall be called (*shall be*) least in the kingdom of heaven" (Matt. v 19) : and Saint James also, "whosoever shall keep the whole law, and yet offend in *one point*, he is guilty of all." (Ja. ii 10.)

Further, many erroneous tenets were held and promulgated, in the time of the apostles, by persons calling themselves Christians. To these "oppositions of science falsely so called" (1 Tim. vi. 20.) there are numerous allusions in the Epistles, where such errors are refuted : for instance, Col ii 18. the worshipping of angels ; Col. ii. 20, 21 against the pretensions of extraordinary mortifications and abstinence , 1 Cor. viii. and 2 Cor vi. 16, &c against idols and eating things offered to them, &c The beginning of Saint John's Gospel, it is well known, was written to refute the false notions of Cerinthus.

IV. *The doctrinal books of Scripture, for instance, the Epistles, are not to be perused in detached portions or sections ; but they should be read through at once, with a close attention to the scope and tenor of the discourse, regardless of the divisions into chapters and verses, precisely in the same manner in which we would peruse the letters of Cicero, Pliny, or other antient writers.*

This reading should not be cursory or casual, but frequent and dili-

---
[1] De Sacr. Script. Interp. p. 316.

gent; and the Epistles should be repeatedly perused, until we become intimately acquainted with their contents.[1] Want of attention to the general scope and design of the doctrinal parts of Scripture, particularly of the Epistles, has been the source of many and great errors: "for, to pick out a verse or two, and criticise on a word or expression, and ground a doctrine thereon, without considering the main scope of the epistle and the occasion of writing it, is just as if a man should interpret antient statutes or records by two or three words or expressions in them, without regard to the true occasion upon which they were made, and without any manner of knowledge and insight into the history of the age in which they were written." The absurdity of such a conduct is too obvious to need further exposure.

Having already offered some hints for investigating the *scope* of a particular book or passage[2], it only remains to notice that there is this general difference observable between the scope of the *Gospels* and that of the *Epistles*, viz. The *former* represent the principles of Christianity *absolutely*, or as they are in themselves; while the *latter* represent them *relatively*, that is, as they respect the state of the world at that particular time.

V. *Where any doctrine is to be deduced from the Scriptures, it will be collected better, and with more precision, from those places in which it is professedly discussed, than from those in which it is noticed only incidentally or by way of inference.*

For instance, in the Epistles to the Romans and Galatians, the doctrine of justification by faith is fully treated and in those to the Ephesians and Colossians, the calling of the Gentiles and the abrogation of the ceremonial law are particularly illustrated. These must, therefore, be diligently compared together, in order to deduce those doctrines correctly.

VI. *Doctrines peculiar to a certain age are better ascertained from*

---

[1] Mr Locke has forcibly illustrated this remark by relating his own practice in studying the Epistles of Saint Paul After he had found by long experience that the ordinary way of reading a chapter, and then consulting commentators upon difficult passages, failed in leading him to the true sense of the Epistle, he says, " I saw plainly, after I began once to reflect on it, that if any one should now write me a letter as long as Saint Paul's to the Romans, concerning such a matter as that is, in a style as foreign, and expressions as dubious, as his seem to be, if I should divide it into fifteen or sixteen chapters, and read one of them to-day and another to-morrow, &c it was ten to one that I should never come to a full and clear comprehension of it. The way to understand the mind of him that wrote it, every one would agree, was to read the whole letter through from one end to the other, all at once, to see what was the main subject and tendency of it, or, if it had several parts and purposes in it, not dependent one of another, nor in a subordination to one chief aim and end, to discover what those different matters were, and where the author concluded one and began another, and if there were any necessity of dividing the Epistles into parts, to mark the boundaries of them " In the prosecution of this thought, Mr. Locke concluded it necessary for the understanding of any one of Saint Paul's Epistles to read it all through at one sitting, and to observe as well as he could, the drift and design of the writer Successive perusals in a similar way at length gave him a good general view of the Apostle's main purpose in writing the Epistle, the chief branches of his discourse, the arguments he used, and the disposition of the whole This, however, is not to be attained by one or two hasty readings. " It must be repeated again and again, *with a close attention to the tenor of the discourse, and a perfect neglect of the divisions into chapters and verses.* On the contrary, the safest way is, to suppose that the epistle has but one business and but one aim; until, by a frequent perusal of it, you are forced to see there are distinct independent matters in it, which will forwardly enough show themselves." Locke on the Epistles of Saint Paul, Preface. (Works, vol. ii. pp. 281, 282. 4to.)

[2] See pp. 327—330. *supra.*

writings belonging to that age, or the times immediately following, than from memorials or writings of a later date.

Thus, the ideas entertained by the patriarchs are better collected from the writings immediately concerning them — the book of Genesis, for instance — than from books written long afterwards, as the Apostolic Epistles. — Not that these are unworthy of credit (of such an insinuation the author trusts he shall be fully acquitted), but because the Apostles deduce inferences from passages of Scripture, according to the manner practised *in their own time;* which inferences, though truly correct, and every way worthy the assent of Christians, were not known at the time when such passages were first committed to writing [1]

VII. *Although the Scriptures sometimes speak of God after the manner of men, they are not to be understood literally, but must be taken in a sense worthy of God.*

This rule was not unknown to the Jews, with whom it was usual to say that the Scriptures speak of God *with the tongue of the sons of men* When, therefore, *human members, faculties, senses, and afflictions, are attributed to the Deity,* they are to be understood in a sense worthy of Him and the manner in which that sense is to be ascertained is twofold: 1. *From the light of nature,* which teaches us that all ideas of imperfection are to be removed from God, and, consequently, corporeity, and, 2. *From the comparison of other passages of Scripture,* in which it is written, that God is a spirit, that he cannot be represented by any figure, and that he is not a man that he should repent, &c. Numerous illustrations of this remark might be offered, were it necessary; but as this subject has already been discussed in a former chapter, it will be sufficient to give a reference to it. [2]

VIII. *No doctrine is admissible, or can be established from the Scriptures, that is either repugnant to them, or contrary to reason or to the analogy of faith.*

For instance, if the doctrine of transubstantiation were to be admitted, the evidence of our reason, as well as of our senses, could no longer be believed, and the consequence would be, that the arguments for the truth of the Christian religion, arising from the miracles and resurrection of Jesus Christ, would fall to the ground, and become of no effect whatever. Articles of revelation, indeed, may be above our reason, but no doctrine, which comes from God, can be irrational, or contrary to those moral truths, which are clearly perceived by the mind of man. We are sure, therefore, that any interpretation of revealed doctrines that is inconsistent with common sense, or with the established laws of morality, must be erroneous. The several parts of those doctrines, which are dispersed through the Scriptures, ought to be collected and explained so as to agree with one another, and form an intelligible and consistent scheme. The different parts of a revelation, which comes from God, must all be reconcileable with one another, and with sound reason. The prejudices of different denominations unfit them for understanding the passages, which are connected with the subjects of their disputations, but there are general principles that all parties adopt. and no text can be interpreted in a sense inconsistent with those articles which are universally received. This conformity, of every part to first principles, is commonly called the analogy of faith, the nature of which and the manner, in which it is to be applied to the interpretation of Scripture, are stated and explained in pp. 333—340.

---

[1] Turretin, p. 324.   [2] See pp. 388, 389. *supra.*

IX. *It is of great importance to the understanding of the doctrinal books of the New Testament, to attend to and distinctly to note the transitions of person which frequently occur, especially in Saint Paul's Epistles.*

The pronouns *I, We,* and *You*, are used by the apostles in such a variety of applications, that the understanding of their true meaning is often a key to many difficult passages.

Thus, by the pronoun *I,* Saint Paul sometimes means himself sometimes any Christian; sometimes a Jew, and sometimes any man, &c If the speaking of himself in the first person singular have these various meanings, his use of the plural *We* is with far greater latitude; for sometimes *we* means himself alone, sometimes those who were with him whom he makes partners to the Epistles (as in the two Epistles to the Corinthians, and in those to the Philippians and Colossians); sometimes with himself comprehending the other apostles, or preachers of the Gospel, or Christians Nay, he sometimes speaks in this way of the converted Jews, at others, of the converted Gentiles· sometimes he introduces the unregenerate as speaking in his own person, at other times he personifies false teachers or false Christians, whose names, however, he forbears to mention, lest he should give them offence In all these instances, his application of the above mentioned pronouns varies the meaning of the text, and causes it to be differently understood. Examples, illustrative of this remark, may be found in every page of Saint Paul's Epistles. Further, in the current of his discourse, he sometimes drops in the objections of others, and his answers to them, without any change in the scheme of his language, that might give notice of any other person speaking besides himself To discover this, requires great attention to the Apostle's scope and argument and yet, if it be neglected or overlooked, it will cause the reader greatly to mistake and misunderstand [1] his meaning, and will also render the sense very perplexed. Mr Locke, and Dr Macknight, in their elaborate works on the Epistles, are particularly useful in pointing out these various transitions of persons and subjects.

X. *In applying the Scriptures as a proof of any doctrine, it is necessary to ascertain, if all that is meant be expressed: or, if it be not expressed, what is necessarily implied, in order to complete the passage.*

Thus it is common (as we have already shown [2]) for the sacred writers to mention, only the principal part of any subject, for the whole.

In Rom x. 9. Paul says, *If thou shalt confess with thy mouth the Lord Jesus, and shalt believe in thine heart* THAT GOD HATH RAISED HIM FROM THE DEAD, *thou shalt be saved.* The resurrection of Christ is the only article which is mentioned here, because, by that miracle, God established the Saviour's authority, as a lawgiver, and confirmed all the doctrines which he taught. But there are other essential articles, which are necessary to be believed, in order to be saved, though they are not stated in the text. It is added, (ver. 13) *for whosoever shall call upon the name of the Lord shall be saved.* No *real* Christian can be so ignorant of the Gospel, as to suppose, that no more is necessary, in order to be saved, than to call upon the name of the Lord In this text, it is evident, that the Apostle mentions only a principal part of what is meant Now, from the context may be gathered the following particulars, as implied, though not expressed First, in the ninth verse it is affirmed, that in order to be saved, a man must believe in his heart. Secondly, he must confess with his mouth, *If thou shalt confess with thy mouth the Lord Jesus, and shalt believe in thine heart, that God hath raised him from the dead, thou shalt be saved* Confession implies more than profession. A true believer in Jesus Christ openly, and of his own accord, *professes* the articles of his belief; and when he is persecuted, and examined concerning his religion, he readily *confesses* the truth, as an evidence of his sincerity and faithfulness. Even this is not all that is necessary, in order to be saved; for it is added in the tenth verse, *with the heart man believeth* UNTO RIGHTEOUSNESS, *and with the mouth confession is made unto salvation* Faith acting on the heart, is productive of a righteous life, and thus the believer becomes a sincere worshipper of the Lord; *for whosoever will call on the name of the Lord shall be saved.* (ver 13.) In these different passages, it is evident, that a part is mentioned for the whole, and in order to understand all that is implied, the several parts must be collected and put together.

XI. *No article of faith can be established from metaphors, parables, or single obscure and figurative texts.*

---

[1] Locke's Preface to the Epistles (Works, vol. iii. p. 277.)
[2] See p. 415. *supra*.

The metaphorical language of the prophets, and figurative expressions which abound in the Scriptures, are calculated to promote the purposes of godliness by acting on the imagination, and by influencing a believer's conduct; but they never were intended to be a revelation of Gospel principles. Instead of deriving our knowledge of Christianity from parables and figurative passages, *an intimate acquaintance with the doctrines of the Gospel is necessary, in order to be capable of interpreting them*

The beautiful parable of the man who fell among thieves (Luke x 30—37, is evidently intended to influence the Jews to be benevolent and kind, like the good Samaritan Some writers have considered that parable to be a representation of Adam's fall, and of man's recovery, through the interposition and love of Jesus Christ But those, who embrace this opinion, did not learn these doctrines from the passage itself No person, who is wholly ignorant of Adam, and of Jesus Christ, could ever learn any thing concerning them, from what is related in this parable. The same observation is equally applicable to every other parable, and typical subject, in which the doctrines of the Gospel cannot be discovered by any person, who has not first learned them from other texts,

CHAPTER VI.

MORAL INTERPRETATION OF SCRIPTURE.

SECTION I.

ON THE INTERPRETATION OF THE MORAL PARTS OF SCRIPTURE.

HAVING already discussed the interpretation of the figurative, spiritual, typical, prophetical, and doctrinal parts of the Sacred Writings, it now remains that we consider the Moral Parts of Scripture. These, indeed, are to be interpreted precisely in the same manner as all other moral writings; regard being had to the peculiar circumstances of the sacred writers, viz. the age in which they wrote, the nation to which they belonged, their style, genius, &c. For, being natives of the East, they treat moral topics, after the oriental manner, in a highly figurative style, and with similitudes and figures considerably more far-fetched than is usual among Greek and Latin authors, or even among the moderns. Again, being for the most part persons in the common walks of life, they generally deliver their precepts in a popular manner, adapted to the capacities of those to whom they were addressed. In the examination of the moral parts of Scripture, the following more particular rules will be found useful.

I. *Moral propositions or discourses are not to be urged too far, but must be understood with a certain degree of latitude, and with various limitations.*

For want of attending to this canon, how many moral truths have been pushed to an extent, which causes them altogether to fail of the effect they were designed to produce! It is not to be denied that universal propositions may be offered: such are frequent in the Scriptures as well as in profane writers, and also in common life; but it is in explaining the expressions by which they are conveyed, that just limits ought to be applied, to prevent them from being urged too far. The nature of the thing, and various other circumstances will always afford a criterion by which to understand moral propositions with the requisite limitations. In order, however, that this subject may be better understood, and applied to the Scriptures, we will state a few of these limitations, and illustrate them by examples.

1. *Universal or indefinite moral propositions, often denote nothing more than the natural aptitude or tendency of a thing to produce a certain effect, even although that effect should not actually take place.*

Thus, when Solomon says that *a soft answer turneth away wrath*, (Prov. xv 1.) the best method of mitigating anger is pointed out, although the obstinacy or wickedness of man may produce a different result. In like manner, when St Peter says, *Who is he that will harm you, if ye be followers of that which is good ?* (1 Pet iii 13.) this expression is not to be understood as implying that good men shall *never* be ill-treated but it simply denotes the natural effect which a virtuous life will probably produce, viz many occasions of irritating men will be avoided, and, on the other hand, their friendship and favour will be conciliated.

2. *Universal or indefinite propositions denote only what generally or often takes place.*

As in Prov. xxii 6 *Train up a child in the way he should go and when he is old he will not depart from it.* Here the wise monarch intimates not what always takes place, but what is the frequent consequence of judicious education To this rule are to be referred all those propositions which treat of the manners, virtues, or vices of particular nations, conditions, or ages. Thus Saint Paul says, that the *Cretans are always liars* (Tit i 12.) Again, when the same apostle, pourtraying the struggles of an enlightened but unregenerate person, says — *I know that in me (that is, in my flesh) dwelleth no good thing*, (Rom vii. 18.) he does not mean to say that there is nothing morally good in man; but that no man is by nature *spiritually* good, or *good in the sight of God* [1]

3. *Universal or indefinite propositions frequently denote* DUTY, *or what* OUGHT *to be done, not what always does actually take place*

"It is the way of the Scriptures," says a late writer, "to speak to and of the visible members of the church of Christ, under such appellations and expressions as may seem, at first hearing, to imply that they are all of them truly righteous and holy persons Thus the apostles style those to whom they write, in general, *saints*, they speak of them as "sanctified in Christ Jesus, chosen of God, buried with Christ in baptism, risen again with him from the dead, sitting with him in heavenly places;" and particularly Saint Paul (Tit iii 5.) says, that they were "saved by the washing of regeneration," &c. The reason of which is, that they were visibly, by *obligation*, and by profession all this, which was thus represented to them, the more effectually to stir them up, and engage them to live according to their profession and obligation " [2]

By this rule also we may explain Mal. ii. 7 "*The priest's lips should keep knowledge*" which passage the advocates of the church of Rome urge, as asserting the infallibility of the priesthood. A simple inspection, however, of the following verse is sufficient to

---

[1] Similar to this is the language of the Liturgy of the Anglican church — " O God, ... because through the weakness of our mortal nature, we can do no *good* thing, without thou grant us the help of thy grace " (Collect for the first Sunday after Trinity.) On which Bishop Tomline remarks — "I have only to observe, that the good thing here mentioned, must mean *good in the sight of God* such an action our weak and unassisted nature will, unquestionably, not allow us to perform." (Refutation of Calvinism, pp 67, 68. 1st edit.) To the same purpose, in another place he observes — "The human nature is so weakened and vitiated by the sin of our first parents, that we cannot by our own natural strength prepare it, or put it into a proper state, for the reception of a saving faith, or for the performance of the spiritual worship required in the Gospel. this mental purification cannot be effected without divine assistance." (Ibid p. 54.) Again; "The grace of God prevents us Christians, that is, it goes before, it gives the first spring and rise to our endeavours, that we may have a good will; and when this good will is thus excited, the grace of God does not desert us, but it works with us when we have that good will."

"It is acknowledged that man has not the disposition, and, consequently, not the ability, to do what in the sight of God is good, till he is influenced by the Spirit of God." (Ibid. pp 60, 61)

[2] Bishop Bradford's Discourse concerning Baptismal and Spiritual Regeneration, p. 37. sixth edit. See also some excellent observations to the same effect in Dr. Macknight's Commentary on 1 John ii. 29.

refute this assertion, and to show that the prophet's words denote only the *duty* of the Jewish priesthood, not what the priests really did perform. The application of this rule will likewise explain Prov. xvi 10, 12, 13

4. *Many precepts are delivered generally and absolutely, concerning moral duties, which are only to be taken with certain limitations.*

For instance, when we are commanded *not to be angry*, we must understand, without a cause, and not beyond measure when we are forbidden *to avenge* ourselves, it is to be understood of *privately taking* revenge ; for the magistrate *beareth not the sword in vain, but is the minister of God, a revenger to execute wrath upon him that doeth evil* (Rom. xiii. 4.) Public vengeance, or punishment, therefore, is clearly not prohibited. Once more, though we are commanded in the Scriptures to *swear not all*, (as in Matt v 34.) and not to *forswear* ourselves, (Levit xix. 12) yet they do not forbid the use of oaths in cases where they can be made subservient to the support of truth and the interests of justice Moses says, *Thou shalt fear the Lord thy God, and serve him, and shall swear by his name.* (Deut. vi. 13) *Thou shalt swear*, says the prophet Jeremiah, *the Lord liveth in truth and and in judgment, and in righteousness.* (Jer. iv. 2) Our Saviour himself, when adjured by the high priest, in the name of the living God, to declare whether he was the *Christ the Son of God*, (Matt. xxvi 63, 64 Mark xiv 61, 62.) did not refuse to answer the question thus judicially proposed to him but he certainly would have remained silent if he had disapproved of all asseverations upon oath, or all such solemn invocations of, and appeals to, the name of God, in cases where the truth is doubtful or the testimony is suspected. The author of the epistle to the Hebrews says, that *an oath for confirmation is an end of all strife.* (Heb vi 16)[1]

II. *Principals include their accessaries, that is, whatever approaches or comes near to them, or has any tendency to them.*

Thus, where any sin is forbidden, we must be careful not only to avoid it, but also every thing of a similar nature, and whatever may prove an occasion of it, or imply our consent to it in others : and we must endeavour to dissuade or restrain others from it.

Compare Matt v 21—31 1 Thess. 5, 22 Jude 23. Ephes. v 11. 1 Cor viii 13. Levit xix. 17. James v 19, 20. So, where any duty is enjoined, all means and facilities, enabling either ourselves or others to discharge it, according to our respective places, capacities, or opportunities, are likewise enjoined See Gen xviii 19 Deut vi. 7. Heb x 23—25. Upon this ground our Lord makes the law and the prophets to depend upon a sincere affectionate love to God and man (Mark. xii. 30, 31 Luke x 27), because, where this prevails, we shall not *knowingly* be deficient in any duty or office which lies within our power, neither shall we willingly do any thing that may either directly or indirectly offend, or tend to the prejudice of mankind. See Rom. xii 17, 18. This observation will leave little room for the "evangelical counsels," or " counsels of perfection," as they are called by the Papists, who ground upon them their erroneous doctrine of supererogation.[2] Again, in whatever commandment we are forbidden to do any thing in our persons, as sinful, it equally restrains us from being *partakers* of other men's guilt, who do commit what we know is thereby forbidden. We must not, therefore, be either

---

[1] The reader will find some additional observations illustrative of the canon above given, in Archbp Tillotson's Works, vol ii. pp 62 158. (London, 1820.)

[2] " These ' *counsels of perfection*,' are rules which do not bind under the penalty of sin, but are only useful in carrying men to a greater degree of perfection than is necessary to salvation There is not the slightest authority in Scripture for these counsels of perfection · all the rules there prescribed for our conduct are given in the form of positive commands, as absolutely necessary, wherever they are applicable, to the attainment of eternal life, and the violation of every one of these commands is declared to be sin We are commanded to be ' perfect even as our Father which is in heaven is perfect,' (Matt v. 48), and so far from being able to exceed what is required for our salvation, the Gospel assures us, that after our utmost care and endeavours we shall still fall short of our whole duty . and that our deficiencies must be supplied by the abundant merits of our blessed Redeemer. We are directed to trust to the mercy of God, and to the mediation of Christ , and to ' work out our salvation with fear and trembling,' (Phil. ii 12) that is, with anxiety, lest we should not fulfil the conditions upon which it is offered Upon these grounds we may pronounce that works of supererogation are inconsistent with the nature of man, irreconcilable with the whole tenor and general principles of our religion, and *contrary to the express declarations of Scripture.*" Bishop Tomline's Elements of Christian Theology, vol ii. pp 281, 282. (8th edit.)

advising, assisting, encouraging, or in any shape a party with them in it: nay, we must not so much as give any countenance to the evil which they do, by excusing or making light of the crime, or by *hiding* their wickedness, lest by so doing *we* incur part of the blame and punishment, and thus deserve the character given by the psalmist — *When thou sawest a thief, then thou consentedst unto him, and hast been partaker with the adulterers.* (Psal. l. 18.)

III. *Negatives include affirmatives, and affirmatives include negatives. — in other words, where any duty is enjoined, the contrary sin is forbidden; and where any sin is forbidden, the contrary duty is enjoined.*

Thus, in Deut. vi. 13. where we are commanded to serve God, we are forbidden to serve any other. Therefore, in Matt. iv. 10. it is said, Him *only* shalt thou serve: and as honouring parents is required in the fifth commandment, (Exod. xx. 12.) so *cursing* them is forbidden. (Matt. xv. 4.) Stealing being prohibited in the eighth commandment, (Exod. xx. 15.) diligence in our calling is enjoined in Eph. iv. 28.

IV. *Negatives are binding at all times, but not affirmatives, that is, we must never do that which is forbidden, though good may ultimately come from it.* (Rom. iii. 8.) *We must not speak wickedly for God.* (Job xiii. 7.)

Such things, however, as are required of us, though they never cease to be our duty, are yet not to be done at *all* times: for instance, prayer, public worship, reproving others, visiting the sick, and other works of charity and mercy, will be our duty as long as we live, but, as we cannot perform these at *all* times, we must do sometimes one thing, sometimes another, as opportunity offers. Hence in the observance of negative precepts, Christian courage and Christian prudence are equally necessary; the *former*, that we may never, upon any occasion or pretence, do that which in positive precepts is pronounced to be evil; the *latter*, that we may discern the fittest times and seasons for doing every thing.

V. *When an action is either required or commended, or any promise is annexed to its performance: such action is supposed to be done from proper motives and in a proper manner.*

The giving of alms may be mentioned as an instance; which, if done from ostentatious motives, we are assured, is displeasing in the sight of God. Compare Matt. vi. 1—4.

VI. *When the favour of God or salvation is promised to any deed or duty, all the other duties of religion are supposed to be rightly performed.*

The giving of alms, as well as visiting the fatherless and widows in their affliction, (Jam. i. 27.) may be noticed as examples: such promise, therefore, is not to be so understood, as if one single Christian virtue were necessary to salvation, but that the particular virtue in question is one of several necessary and momentous virtues. The application of this rule will illustrate our Lord's declaration concerning a future judgment (Matt. xxv. 34—36.), where, though charitable actions only are mentioned, yet we know, from other passages of Scripture, that every idle word, as well as the secret thoughts of men, besides their actions, will be brought into judgment.

VII. *When a certain state or condition is pronounced blessed, or any promise is annexed to it, a suitable disposition of mind is supposed to prevail.*

Thus, when the poor or afflicted are pronounced to be blessed, it is because such persons, being poor and afflicted, are free from the sins usually attendant on unsanctified prosperity, and because they are, on the contrary, more humble and more obedient to God. If, however, they be not the *characters* described (as unquestionably there are many to whom the characters do not apply), the promise in that case does not belong to them. *Vice versâ*, when any state is pronounced to be wretched, it is on account of the sins or vices which generally attend it.

VIII. *Some precepts of moral prudence are given in the Scriptures, which nevertheless admit of exceptions, on account of some duties of benevolence or piety that ought to predominate.*

We may illustrate this rule by the often-repeated counsels of Solomon respecting becoming surety for another. (See Prov. vi. 1, 2 xi. 15. xvii. 18. and xx. 16.) In these passages he does not condemn suretyship, which, in many cases, is not only lawful, but, in some instances, even an act of justice, prudence, and charity [1]; but Solomon forbids his disciple to become surety *rashly* without considering for whom, or how far he binds himself, or how he could discharge the debt, if occasion should require it.

IX. *A change of circumstances changes moral things; therefore contrary things may be spoken together in moral things, on account of the difference of circumstances.*

Thus, in Prov. xxvi. 4, 5. we meet with two precepts that seem to be diametrically opposite to each other: *Answer not a fool according to his folly, lest thou be like unto him;* and *Answer a fool according to his folly, lest he be wise in his own conceit.* But if we attend carefully to the *reason* which the sacred writer subjoins to each precept, we shall be enabled satisfactorily to account for the apparent repugnancy in the counsels of the Israelitish monarch: and it will be evident that they form, not inconsistent, but *distinct*, rules of conduct, which are respectively to be observed according to the *difference of circumstances.* The following observations on the two verses just cited will materially illustrate their meaning.

A *fool*, in the sense of Scripture, means a wicked man, or one who acts contrary to the wisdom that is from above, and who is supposed to utter his foolishness in speech or writing. Doubtless there are different descriptions of these characters, and some may require to be answered, while others are best treated with silence. But the cases here seem to be one; both have respect to the same character, and both require to be answered. The whole difference lies in the *manner* in which the answer should be given.

" In the first instance, the term, ' according to his folly,' means *in a foolish manner,* as is manifest from the reason given; 'lest thou also be like unto him.' But in the second instance they mean, *in the manner in which his foolishness requires.* This also is plain from the reason given, ' lest he be wise in his own conceit.' A foolish speech is not a rule for our imitation; nevertheless our answer must be so framed by it, as to meet and repel it. Both these proverbs caution us against evils to which we are not a little addicted; the first, that of saying and doing to others *as they say* and do to us, rather than as *we would* they should say and do; the last, that of suffering the cause of truth or justice to be run down, while we, from a love of ease, stand by as unconcerned spectators. The

---

[1] Thus Judah became surety to his father, for his brother Benjamin (Gen. xliii. 9. xliv. 32.), and Paul to Philemon for Onesimus. (Philem. 18, 19.)

first of these proverbs is exemplified in the answer of Moses to the rebellious Israelites, the last in that of Job to his wife — It was a foolish speech which was addressed to the former :— ' Would God, that we had died when our brethren died before the Lord ! And why have ye brought up the congregation of the Lord into this wilderness, that we and our cattle should die there ?' Unhappily, this provoked Moses to speak unadvisably with his lips; saying, 'Hear now, ye rebels, must we fetch you water out of this rock ?' This was answering folly *in a foolish manner*, which he should not have done; and by which the servant of God became too much *like* them whom he opposed. — It was also a foolish saying of Job's wife, in the day of his distress; 'Curse God and die!' Job answered this speech, not in *the manner of it*, but in the manner *which it required.* 'What, shall we receive good at the hand of God, and shall we not receive evil ?' In all the answers of our Saviour to the Scribes and Pharisees, we may perceive that he never lost the possession of his soul for a single moment, and never answered *in the manner* of his opponents, so as to be *like unto them.* Yet neither did he decline to repel their folly, and so to abase their self-conceit." [1]

X. *Different ideas must be annexed to the names of virtues or vices, according to different ages and places.*

Thus, *holiness* and *purity* denote widely different things, in many parts of the Old Testament, from what they intend in the New, in the former, they are applied to persons and things dedicated to Jehovah; while in the latter, they are applied to all true Christians, who are called *saints* or holy, being made so through the illumination and renovation of the Holy Spirit, and because, being called with a high and holy calling, they are bound to evince the sincerity of their profession by a pure and holy life.

XI. *In investigating and interpreting those passages of Scripture, the argument of which is moral, — that is, passages in which holy and virtuous actions are commended, — but wicked and unholy ones are forbidden, the nature of the virtue enjoined, or of the sin prohibited, should be explained. We should also consider whether such passages are positive commands, or merely counsels or opinions, and by what motives or arguments the inspired writer supports his persuasions to virtue, and his dissuasives from sin or vice.*

In conducting this investigation, the parallel passages will be found of the greatest service. and in applying the writings of the New Testament as authority for practical institutions, it is necessary to distinguish those precepts or articles, which are circumstantial and temporary, from such as are essential to true religion, and therefore obligatory, in all ages. Not only are all the important laws of morality permanent, but all those general rules of conduct, and institutions which are evidently calculated in religion, to promote the good of mankind, and the glory of God. The situation of the first Christians, during the infancy of Christianity, required temporary regulations, which are not now binding on the Church. The controversy concerning holy days, and particular kinds of food, occasioned Paul to enjoin such temporary precepts, as suited the situation of the church when he wrote. Abstinence from the use of unclean beasts, in compliance with the opinions of the Jews, is not now necessary; but

---

[1] Fuller's Harmony of Scripture, pp.17, 18. Bishop Warburton has given an excellent illustration of the passage above explained, in one of his Sermons. See his Works, vol. x. Serm 21. pp. 61—78

a condescension to the very prejudices of weak brethren, in things indifferent, is at all times the duty of Christians. Those doctrines which were evidently adapted to the situation of Christ's disciples, when under persecution, do not apply to their conduct, when enjoying full liberty of conscience. Exhortations, which are restricted to particular cases, must not be applied as rules for general conduct.

Those directions, to be kind and hospitable to one another, in which the customs of eastern countries are mentioned, are not literally to be observed, by those among whom different manners prevail. Paul enjoins the saints, *to salute one another with a holy kiss.* (Rom. xvi. 16.) The Jews saluted one another, as an expression of sincere friendship. When Jesus Christ observed to Simon that he was deficient in kindness and affection, he said: *Thou gavest me no kiss, but this woman, since the time I came in, hath not ceased to kiss my feet.* (Luke vii 45.) The *disposition* is incumbent on saints, in all ages of the world; but not this *mode* of expressing it. In order to teach the disciples, how they ought to manifest their affection, for one another, by performing every office of friendship in their power, their Lord and Master *took a towel and girded himself, and began to wash the disciples' feet, and to wipe them with the towel wherewith he was girded; and said, If I then, your Lord and Master, have washed your feet, ye also ought to wash one another's feet.* (John xiii. 5. 14.) In those hot countries, after travelling in sandals, the washing of the feet was very refreshing, and an expression of the most tender care and regard: hence it is mentioned as an amiable part of the widow's character, that she hath *washed the saints' feet, and relieved the afflicted.* (1 Tim. v. 10.) It is evident, that this mode of expressing our love to one another, was not intended as a *permanent law*, but a direction adapted to the prevailing custom of the people, to whom it was originally given.

In concluding our remarks on the moral interpretation of the Sacred Writings, it is worthy of observation, that they contain two kinds of moral books and discourses, viz. 1. *Detached sentences*, such as occur in the book of Proverbs, in many of our Lord's sermons, and in several of the moral exhortations at the close of the apostolic epistles; and, 2. *Continuous and connected discourses*, such as are to be found in the book of Job. In the *former*, we are not to look for any order or arrangement, because they have been put together just as they presented themselves to the minds of their inspired authors: but, in the *latter*, we must carefully attend to the scope. Thus, the scope of the book of Job is specified in the second and third verses of the thirty-second chapter; *to this*, therefore, the whole book must be referred, without seeking for any mysteries.

The style also of the moral parts of Scripture, is highly figurative, abounding not only with bold hyperboles and prosopopæias, but also with antitheses and seeming paradoxes: the former must be explained agreeably to those general rules, for expounding the figurative language of Scripture, which have already been stated and illustrated [1]; and the latter must be interpreted and limited according to the nature of the thing; for instance, the beatitudes, as related by St. Matthew, (ch. v.) must be compared with those delivered

---

[1] See pp. 371—378, *supra*.

at a different time, as related by Saint Luke (ch. vi. 20. *et seq.*); and from this collation we shall be enabled to reconcile the seeming differences, and fully to understand the antithetic sayings of our Lord.

Lastly, as the moral sentences in the Scriptures are written in the very concise style peculiar to the Orientals, many passages are, in consequence, necessarily obscure, and therefore admit of various expositions. In such cases, that interpretation which is most obvious to the reader, will in general be sufficiently intelligible for all purposes of *practical edification*, and beyond this we need not be anxiously solicitous, if we should fail in ascertaining the precise meaning of every word in a proverb or moral sentence.

SECTION II.

ON THE INTERPRETATION OF THE PROMISES AND THREATENINGS OF SCRIPTURE.

A PROMISE, in the Scriptural sense of the term, is a declaration or assurance of the divine will, in which God signifies what particular blessings or good things he will freely bestow, as well as the evils which he will remove. The *promises*, therefore, differ from the *threatenings* of God, inasmuch as the former are declarations concerning good, while the latter are denunciations of evil only: at the same time it is to be observed, that promises seem to include threats, because, being in their very nature *conditional*, they imply the bestowment of the blessing promised, only on the condition being performed, which blessing is *tacitly* threatened to be withheld on non-compliance with such condition. Further, promises differ from the *commands* of God, because the latter are significations of the divine will concerning a *duty* enjoined to be performed, while promises relate to *mercy* to be received. As a considerable portion of the promises relates to the performance of moral and of pious duties, they might have been discussed under the preceding chapter: but, from the variety of topics which they embrace, it has been deemed preferable to give them a separate consideration.

There are four classes of promises mentioned in the Scriptures, particularly in the New Testament; viz. 1. Promises relating to the Messiah: 2. Promises relating to the church; 3. Promises of blessings, both temporal and spiritual, to the pious; and, 4. Promises encouraging to the exercise of the several graces and duties that compose the Christian character.[1] The two first of these classes,

---

[1] These promises are collected and printed at length, in a useful manual, published upwards of seventy years since, and intitled, *A Collection of the Promises of Scripture, arranged under proper Heads*. By Samuel Clarke, D D. Of this little manual, there are numerous cheap editions extant, which, having been chiefly printed at provincial presses, abound in errors of reference to the texts of Scriptures. The most recent edition is that published by Mr. William Carpenter, (London, 1825 18mo.), who has verified the references, corrected the errors that had crept into former impressions, and has made an addition of about two hundred promises, which enhance the value of this publication.

indeed, are many of them *predictions* as well as promises; consequently the same observations will apply to them, as are stated for the interpretation of Scripture prophecies[1]: but in regard to those promises which are directed to particular persons, or to the performance of particular duties, the following remarks are offered to the attention of the reader.

I. "*We must receive God's promises in such wise as they be generally set forth in the Holy Scripture.*"[2]

To us "the promises of God are general and conditional. The Gospel dispensation is described as a covenant between God and man, and the salvation of every individual is made to depend upon his observance of the proposed conditions. Men, as free agents, have it in their power to perform or not to perform these conditions: and God foresaw from eternity, who would and who would not perform them, that is, who will and who will not be saved at the day of judgment."[3] If, therefore, the promises of God be not fulfilled towards us, we may rest assured that the fault does not rest with Him "who cannot lie," but with ourselves, who have failed in complying with the conditions either tacitly or expressly annexed to them. We may, then, apply general promises to ourselves, not doubting that if we perform the condition expressed or implied, we shall enjoy the mercy promised: for, as all particulars are included in universals, it follows that a general promise is made a particular one to him, whose character corresponds with those to whom such general promise is made.

Matt. xi. 28. may be cited as an example: the *promise* here made is the giving of rest: the *characters* of the persons to whom it is made are distinctly specified, they are the *weary and heavy laden*, whether with the distresses of life, or with the sense of guilt (see Psal. xxxii 4. xxxviii 4.), or with the load of ceremonial observances, the condition required, is to *come unto Christ* by faith, in other words, to believe in him and become his disciples: and the menace *implied* is, that if they do not thus *come*[4], they will not find rest. Similar promises occur in John iii. 16. and 1 Tim. ii. 4.

---

[1] See pp 469—472 *supra.*

[2] Art. XVII of the Confession of the Anglican Church. Similar to this is the declaration of the Helvetic Confession, which in general symbolises with that of the British Church. " In the temptation concerning predestination, and which, perhaps, is more dangerous than any other, we should derive comfort from the consideration, that God's promises are *general to all that believe*—that he himself says, *Ask and ye shall receive — Every one that asks receives*" Chap. x towards the end, or in the valuable work intitled, " Primitive Truth, in a History of the Reformation, expressed by the Early Reformers in their Writings," p. 57.

[3] Bp. Tomline's Elements of Theology, vol ii p. 313 Similar to the above sentiments are those contained in the " Necessary Erudition of a Christian Man," (at the close of the introductory observations on " Faith,") a Manual of Christian Doctrine published in the year 1534: the value of which ought not to be lessened in our judgment by the circumstance of its not being purged of popish errors— " Although God's promises made in Christ be immutable, yet He maketh them not to us, but *with condition*, so that, His promise standing, we may yet fail of the promise *because we keep not our promise*. And therefore, if we assuredly reckon upon the state of our felicity, as grounded upon God's promise, and do not therewith remember, that no man shall be crowned, unless he lawfully fight, we shall triumph before the victory, and so shall look in vain for that, which is not otherwise promised but under a condition " On the subject of conditional promises, see also Tillotson's Works, vol. v pp. 185—193. 205, 206. vol. vi. p. 513 vol ix pp. 53, 54 and vol x p 119. and on the subject of conditional threatenings, see vol. vi. pp. 510, 511. (London, 1820.)

[4] Bp Horsley has the following animated and practical observations on this promise of our Saviour at the close of his 24th Sermon —" Come, therefore, unto him, all ye that are heavy laden with your sins By his own gracious voice he called you while on earth. By the voice of his ambassadors he continueth to call; he calleth you now by mine. Come unto him, and he shall give you rest — rest from the hard servitude of sin

II. *Such promises as were made in one case, may be applied in other cases of the same nature, consistently with the analogy of faith.*

It is in promises as in commands: they do not exclusively concern those to whom they were first made; but, being inserted in the Scriptures, they are made of public benefit. for *whatsoever things were written aforetime, were written for our use: that we, through patience and comfort of the Scriptures, might have hope.* (Rom. xv. 4.)

Thus, what was spoken to Joshua, on his going up against the Canaanites, lest he should be discouraged in that enterprise, is applied by Saint Paul as a remedy against covetousness or inordinate cares concerning the things of this life, it being a very comprehensive promise that God will never fail us nor forsake us. But if we were to apply the promises contained in Psal. xciv. 14. and Jer. xxxii. 40. and John x. 28. as promises of *absolute* and *indefectible* grace to believers, we should violate every rule of sober interpretation, as well as the analogy of faith. A distinction, however, must be taken between such of the promises in the Old Testament, particularly in the book of Psalms, as are of universal application, and such as were made to those Israelites and Jews who obeyed the law of God, which were strictly *temporal*. Of this description are all those promises of peace and prosperity in *this* world, which were *literally* suitable to the Jewish dispensation, God having encouraged them to obey his laws, by promises of peculiar peace and prosperity in the land of Canaan. Whereas now, under the Gospel dispensation, "godliness hath" indeed the "promise of the life that now is, as well as of that which is to come," (1 Tim. iv. 8.) but with an exception of the *cross*, when that may be best for us, in order to our future happiness in heaven. So that the promises in the Old Testament, of a *general* felicity in *this* life, are not so literally to be applied to Christians as they were to the Jews.[1]

III. *God has suited his promises to his precepts.*

By his *precepts* we see what is our *duty*, and what should be the *scope of our endeavours;* and by his *promises* we see what is our *inability*, what should be the *matter or object of our prayers*, and where we may be supplied with that grace which will enable us to discharge our duty. Compare Deut. x. 16 with Deut. xxx. 6 Eccles xii. 13. with Jer. xxxii. 40. Ezek. xviii. 31. with Ezek. xxxvi. 37. and Rom. vi. 12. with v. 14.

IV. *Where any thing is promised in case of obedience, the threatening of the contrary is implied in case of disobedience: and where there is a threatening of any thing in case of disobedience, a promise of the contrary is implied upon condition of obedience.*[2]

---

and appetite, and guilty fear. *That* yoke is heavy — *that* burthen is intolerable; *His* yoke is easy and *his* burthen light. But, come in sincerity, — dare not to come in hypocrisy and dissimulation. Think not that it will avail you in the last day, to have called yourselves Christians, to have been born and educated under the Gospel light — to have lived in the external communion of the church on earth — if, all the while, your hearts have holden no communion with its head in heaven If, instructed in Christianity, and professing to believe its doctrines, ye lead the lives of unbelievers, it will avail you nothing in the next, to have enjoyed in this world, like the Jews of old, advantages which ye despised — to have had the custody of a holy doctrine which never touched your hearts — of a pure commandment, by the light of which ye never walked. To those who disgrace the doctrine of their Saviour by the scandal of their lives, it will be of no avail to have vainly called him, 'Lord, Lord !'" Sermons, p. 490. 2d edit.

[1] Collyer's Sacred Interpreter, vol i p 336.
[2] Bp. Wilkins, in his admirable Discourse on the Gift of Preaching, has stated this rule in the following terms — "Every Scripture does affirm, command, or threaten not only that which is expressed in it, but likewise all that which is rightly deducible from it, though by mediate consequences." (Dr. Williams's Christian Preacher, p. 22.)

In illustration of this remark, it will be sufficient to refer to, and compare, Exod. xx 7. with Psal. xv. 1—4. and xxiv. 3, 4. and Exod. xx. 12. with Prov. xxx. 17.

There are, however, two important cautions to be attended to in the application of Scripture promises; viz. that we do not violate that connection or dependency which subsists between one promise and another; and that we do not invert that fixed order which is observable between them.

1. *The mutual connection or dependency subsisting between promises, must not be broken.*

As the duties enjoined by the moral law are copulative, and may not be disjoined in the obedience yielded to them (James ii 10.); so are the blessings of the promises, which may not be made use of as *severed* from each other, like unstringed pearls, but as *collected* into one entire chain. For instance, throughout the sacred volume, the promises of pardon and repentance are invariably connected together so that it would be presumptuous in any man to suppose that God will ever hearken to him who implores the one and neglects to seek the other. "He pardoneth and absolveth all them that truly repent and unfeignedly believe his holy word."

In like manner, in Psal. lxxxiv 11. the promise of *grace and glory* is so inseparably united, that no person can lay a just claim to the one, who is not previously made a partaker of the other. Bishop Horne's commentary on this verse is not more beautiful than just.[1]

2. *In applying the promises, their order and method should not be inverted, but be carefully observed.*

The promises, made by God in his word, have not inaptly been termed an ample storehouse of every kind of blessings, including both the mercies *of the life that now is, and of that which is to come.* There is, indeed, no good that can present itself as an object to our desires or thoughts, but the promises are a ground for faith to believe. and hope to expect the enjoyment of it but then our use and application of them must be *regular*, and suitable both to the *pattern* and *precept* which Christ has given us.

The *Pattern* or example referred to, we have in that most comprehensive prayer, emphatically termed *the Lord's prayer* (Matt vi 9—13), in which he shows what is chiefly to be desired by us, viz. the sanctification of his name in our hearts, the coming of his kingdom into our souls, and the doing of his will in our lives, all which are to be implored, before and above our daily bread We are not to be more anxious for food than for divine grace.

The *Precept* alluded to, we have in his sermon on the mount (Matt. vi 33). *Seek ye first the Kingdom of God and his righteousness, and all these things shall be added unto you.* The *soul* is of more worth than the *body*, as the body is more valuable than *raiment*, and therefore the principal care of every one should be, to secure his spiritual welfare, by interesting himself in the promises of life and eternal happiness. Here, however, a *method* must be observed, and the law of the Scripture must be exactly followed, which tells us (Psal. lxxxiv. 11) that God first gives grace and then glory. "As it is a sin to divide grace from glory, and to seek the one without the other, so is it also a sin to be *preposterous in our seeking*, to look *first* after happiness and *then* after holiness no man can be rightly solicitous about the crown, but he must first be careful about the race; nor can any be truly thoughtful about his interest in the promises of glory that doth not *first* make good his title to the promises of grace"[2]

---

[1] "Jesus Christ is our 'Lord' and our 'God' he is a 'sun' to enlighten and direct us in the way, and a 'shield' to protect us against the enemies of our salvation. He will give 'grace' to carry us on 'from strength to strength,' and 'glory' to crown us when we 'appear before him in Zion,' he will 'withhold' nothing that is 'good' and profitable for us in the course of our journey, and will himself be our reward, when we come to the end of it." Commentary on the Psalms, vol ii. (Works, vol. iii. p. 81)

[2] Dr. Spurstowe's Treatise on the Promises, pp. 62. 65. The whole volume will abundantly repay the trouble of perusing it. There is also an admirable discourse *on the Promises*, in the Sermons published by the late Rev Charles Buck · in which their divine origin, their suitability, number, clearness of expression, the *freeness* of their communication, and the certainty of their accomplishment, are stated and illustrated with equal ability and piety. See also Hoornbeck's Theologia Practica, pars I. lib, v. c. 2. pp. 468—477.

CHAPTER VII.

ON THE INTERPRETATION, AND MEANS OF HARMONISING PASSAGES OF SCRIPTURE, WHICH ARE ALLEGED TO BE CONTRADICTORY.

ALTHOUGH the sacred writers, being divinely inspired, were necessarily exempted from error in the important truths which they were commissioned to reveal to mankind, yet it is not to be concealed, that, on comparing Scripture with itself, some detached passages are to be found, which *appear* to be contradictory; and these have been a favourite topic of cavil with the enemies of Christianity from Spinosa down to Voltaire, and the opposers of Divine Revelation in our days, who have copied their objections. Unable to disprove or subvert the indisputable FACTS, on which Christianity is founded, and detesting the exemplary holiness of heart and life which it enjoins, its modern antagonists insidiously attempt to impugn the credibility of the sacred writers, by producing what *they* call contradictions. It is readily admitted that *real* contradictions are a just and sufficient proof that a book is not divinely inspired, whatever pretences it may make to such inspiration. In this way we prove, that the Koran of Mohammed could not be inspired, much as it is extolled by his admiring followers. The whole of that rhapsody was framed by the wily Arab to answer some particular exigencies.[1] If any new measure was to be proposed, — any objection against him or the religion which he wished to propagate, was to be answered, — any difficulty to be solved, — any discontent or offence among his people to be removed, — or any other thing done that could promote his designs, — his constant recourse was to the angel Gabriel, for a new revelation: and instantly he produced some addition to the Koran, which was to further the objects he had in view, so that by far the greater part of that book was composed on these or similar occasions to influence his followers to adopt the measures which he intended. Hence not a few real contradictions crept into the Koran; the existence of which is not denied by the Musulman commentators, who are not only very particular in stating the several occasions on which particular chapters were produced, but also where any contradiction occurs which they cannot solve, affirm that one of the contradictory passages is revoked. And they reckon in the Koran upwards of one hundred and fifty passages thus revoked. Now this fact is a full evidence that the compiler of that volume could not be inspired but no such thing can be alleged against the Scriptures. They were indeed given *at sundry times and in divers manners*, and the authors of them were inspired on particular occasions: but nothing was ever published as a part of it, which was afterwards revoked; nor is there any thing in them which *we* need to have annulled. Errors in the transcription of copies, as well as in printed editions and translations, do unquestionably exist: but the

---

[1] Prideaux's Life of Mohammed, pp 156, 159.

contradictions objected are only seeming, not real, nor do we know a single instance of such alleged contradictions, that is not capable of a rational solution. A little skill in criticism in the original languages of the Scriptures, their idioms and properties, (of which the modern opposers of revelation, it is well known, have for the most part been and are notoriously ignorant,) and in the times, occasions, and scopes of the several books, as well as in the antiquities and customs of those countries, which were the scenes of the transactions recorded, will clear the main difficulties.

To the person who *honestly* and *impartially* examines the various evidences for the divinity and inspiration of the Bible, (and it not only invites but commands investigation,) most of the *alleged* contradictions, which are discussed in the following pages, will appear frivolous: for they have been made and refuted nearly one hundred and fifty years since. But as they are now re-asserted, regardless of the satisfactory answers which have been given to them in various forms, both in this country and on the Continent, the author would deem his work imperfect if he were to suffer such objections to pass unnoticed, particularly as he has been called upon, through the public press, to consider, and to obviate them. Should the reader be led to think, that an undue portion of the present volume is appropriated to the interpretation of passages alleged to be contradictory, he is requested to bear in mind that, although the pretended contradictions, here considered, have for the most part been clothed in a few plausible sentences [1], yet their sophistry cannot be exposed without a laborious and minute examination.

Wherever, then, one text of Scripture seems to contradict another, we should, by a serious consideration of them, endeavour to discover their harmony; for the only way, by which to judge rightly of particular passages in any book, is, first, to ascertain whether the text be correct, and in the next place to consider its whole design, method, and style, and not to criticise some particular parts of it, without bestowing any attention upon the rest. Such is the method adopted by all who would investigate, with judgment, any difficult passages occurring in a profane author: and if a judicious and accurate writer is not to be lightly accused of contradicting himself for any seeming inconsistencies, but is to be reconciled with himself if possible, — unquestionably the same equitable principle of interpretation ought to be applied in the investigation of Scripture difficulties.

Some passages, indeed, are explained by the Scriptures themselves, which serve as a key to assist us in the elucidation of others.

---

[1] The late excellent Bishop Horne, upwards of forty years since, when speaking of the disingenuity of infidels in bringing forward objections against the Scriptures, has the following remarks· "Many and painful are the researches, usually necessary to be made for settling points of this kind. Pertness and ignorance may ask a question in *three* lines, which it will cost learning and ingenuity *thirty pages* to answer. When this is done, the same question shall be triumphantly asked again the next year, as if nothing had ever been written upon the subject. And as people in general, for one reason or other, like short objections better than long answers, in this mode of disputation (if it can be styled such) the odds must ever be against us, and we must be content with those for our friends, who have honesty and erudition, candour and patience, to study both sides of the question." Letters on Infidelity, p. 82 (Works, vol. vi pp 447, 448. 8vo. London, 1809.)

Thus, in one place it is said that *Jesus baptised*, and in another it is stated that *he baptised not* the former passage is explained to be intended not of baptism performed by himself, but by his disciples, who baptised in his name. Compare John iii. 22 with iv. 1, 2.

Frequently, also, a distinction of the different senses of words, as well as of the different subjects and times, will enable us to obviate the seeming discrepancy.

Thus, when it is said, *It is appointed unto all men once to die* (Heb ix 27), and elsewhere, *If a man keep* Christ's *saying, he shall never see death*, there is no contradiction; for, in the former place, *natural* death, the death of the body, is intended, and in the latter passage, *spiritual* or *eternal* death Again, when Moses says, *God rested on the seventh day from all his works* (Gen ii 2.), and Jesus says, *My Father worketh hitherto* 'John v. 17), there is no opposition or contradiction, for Moses is speaking of the works of creation, and Jesus of the works of providence So Samuel tells us God *will not repent* (1 Sam xv 29); and yet we read in other parts of the Old Testament that *It repented the* LORD *that he had made man on the earth* (Gen vi 6), and that he had *set up Saul* to be *king* (1 Sam. xv 11) But in these passages there is no real contradiction; repentance in the one place signifies a change of mind and counsel, from want of foresight of what would come to pass, and thus God cannot repent, but then he changes his course as men do when they change their minds, and so he may be said to repent In these, as well as in other instances, where personal qualities or feelings are ascribed to God, the Scriptures speak in condescension to our capacities, after the manner of men; nor can we speak of the Deity in any other manner, if we would speak intelligibly to the generality of mankind.

The contradictions which are alleged to exist in the Scriptures, may be referred to the following classes, viz.—seeming contradictions in historical passages — in chronology — between prophecies and their fulfilment — in points of doctrine and morality — in the quotations from the Old Testament in the New — between the sacred writers themselves — between the sacred writers and profane authors — and, lastly, seeming contradictions to philosophy and the nature of things.

SECTION I.

SEEMING CONTRADICTIONS IN HISTORICAL PASSAGES.

MOST of the seeming contradictions in Scripture are found in the historical parts, where their connection with the great subject or scope is less considerable; and they may not unfrequently be traced to the errors of transcribers or of the press. The apparent contradictions, in the historical passages of Scripture, arise from the different circumstances related,—from things being related in a different order by the sacred writers,—from differences in numbers,—and from differences in the relation of events in one place, and references to those events in another.

§ 1. *Seeming Contradictions in the different Circumstances related.*

These arise from various causes, as, the sources whence the inspired writers drew their relations, the different designs of the sacred writers, erroneous readings, obscure or ambiguous expressions, transpositions in the order of narrating, and sometimes from several of these causes combined.

1. *Apparent contradictions, in the different circumstances related, arise from the different sources whence the inspired writers drew their narratives.*

For instance, in the brief accounts recorded by Matthew and Mark respecting the birth and childhood of Jesus Christ, from whom could they have derived their information? They could not have become acquainted with those circumstances, unless from the particulars communicated by his relatives according to the flesh; and, as it has been frequently remarked, it is highly probable that they received their information from Mary and Joseph, or others of the family of Jesus. How easy, then, is it for some trifling variations to creep into such accounts of infancy as are preserved by oral relation: all of which, though differing, are nevertheless perfectly consistent with the truth! Again, during our Lord's three years' circuit in Palestine, Matthew and John were constantly his disciples and companions: the source of *their* narratives, therefore, was ocular testimony: while Luke and Mark, not having been Christ's disciples, related things as they were communicated to them by the apostles and others, who *from the beginning were eye-witnesses and ministers of the word*, as Saint Luke expressly states at the commencement of his Gospel.[1] Under such circumstances, how is it possible that some discrepancies should not appear in the writings of such persons? Yet these discrepancies, as we shall presently see, are so far from affecting their credibility as historians, that, on the contrary, they confirm their veracity and correctness. The same remark will apply to the history of our Lord's death and resurrection, as well as to the account of the sermon delivered on the mount and on the plain.

2. *Seeming contradictions, in the different circumstances related, may also arise, from the different designs which the sacred writers had in the composition of their narratives;* for the difference of design will necessarily lead to a corresponding selection of circumstances.

The consideration of this circumstance will remove the contradiction which modern opposers of the Scriptures have asserted to exist between the first and second chapters of the book of Genesis. The design of Moses, in the *first* chapter, was to give a *short* account of the orderly creation of all things, from the meanest to the noblest, in opposition to the absurd and contradictory notions which at that time prevailed among the Egyptians and other nations. In the *second* chapter, the sacred writer explains some things more at length, which in the preceding were narrated more briefly, because he would not interrupt the connection of his discourse concerning the six days' work of creation. He therefore more particularly relates the manner in which Eve was formed, and also further illustrates the creation of Adam. In thus recapitulating the history of creation, Moses describes the creation through its several stages, as the phenomena would have successively presented themselves to a spectator, had a spectator been in existence. Again, the design of the two books of Samuel, especially of the second book, is, to relate the various steps which conduced to the wonderful elevation of David from a low condition to the throne of Judah first, and after seven years and six months to that of Israel, together with the battles and occurrences which led to that great event, and secured to him the possession of his kingdom: and then at the close (2 Sam. xxiii. 8—39.) we have a catalogue to perpetuate the memory of those warriors who had been particularly instrumental in promoting the success and establishing the glory of their royal master. But in the first book of Chronicles the history of David begins with him as king, and immediately mentions the heroes of his armies, and then proceeds to an abridgment of the events of his reign. This difference of design will account for the variations occurring in the two principal chapters containing the history of those heroes: for in 1 Chron. xi. they are recorded in the beginning of David's reign, with Joab introduced at their head, and the reason assigned for his being so particularly distinguished; but in the concluding chapter of Samuel, when the history of David's reign had already been given, *there* the name of Joab is omitted, since no one could forget that he was David's *chief mighty man*, when he had been mentioned, in almost every page, as *captain general of the armies of Israel.*[2]

---

[1] On this subject compare Vol. IV. Part II. Chap. II. Sect. V.

[2] Dr. Kennicott's First Dissertation, pp 13—15. The subsequent part of this very learned volume is appropriated to an elaborate comparison of the discrepancies between 1 Chron. xi. and 2 Sam. v. and xxiii., to which the reader is referred.

VII. Sect. I. § 1.]   *Of Scripture, alleged to be Contradictory.*   497

The difference of design also will satisfactorily explain the seeming difference between the genealogies of our Saviour given by the evangelists Matthew and Luke from the public registers, and which comprise a period of four thousand years, from Adam to Joseph his reputed father, or to Mary his mother. The genealogy given by Saint Matthew was principally designed for the *Jews ;* and, therefore, it traces the pedigree of Jesus Christ, as the promised seed, downwards from Abraham to David, and from him through Solomon's line to Jacob the father of Joseph, who was the reputed or *legal* father of Christ. (Matt. i. 1—16.) That given by Saint Luke was intended for the *Gentiles,* and traces the pedigree upwards from Heli, the father of Mary, to David, through the line of his son Nathan, and from Nathan to Abraham, concurring with the former, and from Abraham up to Adam, who was the immediate " son of God," born without father or mother. (Luke iii. 23—38.) [1]

That Saint Luke gives the pedigree of Mary, the real mother of Christ, may be collected from the following reasons:

"1. The angel Gabriel, at the annunciation, told the virgin, that " God would give her divine Son the throne of *his father David"* (Luke i 32.); and this was necessary to be proved, by her genealogy, afterwards. 2. Mary is called by the Jews, בת עלי, " the daughter of Eli [2]," and by the early Christian writers, " the daughter of Joakim and Anna." But Joakim and Eliakim (as being derived from the names of God, יהוה, Iahoh, and אל, Eli) are sometimes interchanged. (2 Chron. xxxvi. 4.) Eli, therefore, or Heli, is the abridgment of Eliakim. Nor is it of any consequence that the Rabbins called him עלי, instead of אלי, the aspirates Aleph and Ain being frequently interchanged. 3. A similar case in point occurs elsewhere in the genealogy. After the Babylonish captivity, the two lines of Solomon and Nathan, the sons of David, unite in the generations of Salathiel and Zorobabel, and thence diverge again in the sons of the latter, Abiud and Resa. Hence, as Salathiel in Matthew, was the son of Jechoniah, or Jehoiachin, who was carried away into captivity by Nebuchadnezzar, so in Luke, Salathiel must have been the grandson of Neri, by his mother's side. 4 The evangelist himself has critically distinguished the *real* from the *legal* genealogy, by a parenthetical remark: Ἰησοῦς — ὼν ὡς ἐνομίζετο, υἱὸς Ἰωσήφ, [ἀλλ' ὄντως υἱὸς] τοῦ Ἡλὶ " Jesus — being (as was reputed), the son of Joseph, (but in reality) the son of Heli," or his grandson by the *mother's* side : for so should the ellipsis involved in the parenthesis be supplied " [3] This interpretation of the genealogy in Saint Luke's Gospel, if it be admitted, removes at once every difficulty; and (as Bishop Gleig has truly remarked) it is so natural and consistent with itself, that, we think, it can hardly be rejected, except by those who are determined, that " seeing they will not see, and hearing they will not understand."

---

[1] The view above given is confirmed and illustrated by Dr. Benson in his History of the first planting of the Christian religion, vol. i. pp. 259—263. 2d edit.
[2] Lightfoot on Luke iii 23.
[3] Dr Hales's Analysis, vol ii. book ii pp 699, 700. In pp. 700—704 he has considered and accounted for particular seeming discrepancies between the evangelists Matthew and Luke. But the fullest discussion of the subject is to be found in Dr. Barrett's Preliminary Dissertation prefixed to his edition of the Fragments of Saint Matthew's Gospel, from a Codex Rescriptus in Trinity College Library at Dublin. (*Evangelium secundum Matthæum ex Codice Rescripto in Bibliotheca Collegii Sanctæ Trinitatis juxta Dublin, &c.* 4to. Dublin, 1801) In this Dissertation he examines and notices the difficulties of the hypothesis proposed by Africanus, a father of the third century, preserved by Eusebius, (Hist. Eccl. lib i. c. 7.) and translated by Dr. Lardner (Works, vol ii. pp. 436—438 8vo. or vol. i pp. 416, 417. 4to.), and which Africanus professed to have received from some of our Lord's relatives. As Dr. Barrett's book is scarce, and comparatively little known, it may gratify the reader to learn that a copious and faithful abstract of it is given in the Eclectic Review for 1807, vol iii. part 2. pp. 586—594. 678—698. ; and also with some additional observations by Dr A. Clarke, at the end of his commentary on Luke iii. See also Mr. R. B. Green's " Table for exhibiting to the View, and impressing clearly on the Memory, the Genealogy of Jesus Christ, with Notes," &c. London, 1822. 8vo.

But the difference in the circumstances related, arising from the difference in design of the sacred writers, is to be found chiefly in those cases, where the same event is narrated very briefly by one evangelist, and is described more copiously by another.

An example of this kind we have in the account of our Lord's threefold temptation in the wilderness, which is related more at length by Matthew and Luke, while Mark has given a very brief epitome of that occurrence. But these variations, which arise from differences of design, do not present a *shadow* of contradiction or discrepancy: for it is well known that Saint Matthew wrote his Gospel a few years after our Lord's ascension, while the church wholly consisted of converts from Judaism. Saint Mark's Gospel, probably written at Rome, was adapted to the state of the church there, which consisted of a mixture of converts who had been Pagans and Jews. He inserts many direct or oblique explanations of passages in Saint Matthew's Gospel, in order to render them more intelligible to the converts from Paganism. The Gospel of Saint Luke was written for the immediate use of the converts from Heathenism; several parts of it appear to be particularly adapted to display the divine goodness to the Gentiles. Hence, he traces up Christ's lineage to Adam, to signify that he was THE SEED of the woman promised to our first parents, and the Saviour of all their posterity. He marks the æra of Christ's birth, and the time when John the Baptist began to announce the Gospel, by the reigns of the Roman emperors. Saint John, who wrote long after the other evangelists, appears to have designed his Gospel to be partly as a supplement to the others, in order to preserve several discourses of our Lord, or facts relating to him which had been omitted by the other evangelists, but chiefly to check the heresies which were beginning to appear in the church, and (as he himself declares, xx 31.) to establish the true doctrine concerning the divinity and mediatorial character of Christ.[1]

The differences, however, which thus subsist in the respective narratives of the Evangelists, do not in any degree whatever affect their credibility. The transactions related are still true and actual transactions, and capable of being readily comprehended, although there may be a trifling discrepancy in some particulars. We know, for instance, that a discourse was delivered by our Lord, so sublime, so replete with momentous instruction, that *the people were astonished at his doctrine*. But whether this discourse was delivered on a mountain or on a plain, is a matter of no moment whatever. In like manner, although there are *circumstantial* differences in the accounts of our Lord's resurrection from the dead, the thing itself may be known, and its truth ascertained.[2] A narrative is not to be rejected by reason of some *diversity* of circumstances with which it is related: for the character of human testimony is, *substantial* truth under circumstantial variety; but a close agreement induces suspicion of confederacy and fraud. Important variations, and even contradictions, are not always deemed sufficient to shake the credibility of a fact: and if this circumstance be allowed to operate in favour of profane historians, it ought at least to be admitted with equal weight in reference to the sacred writers. It were no difficult task to give numerous instances of differences between profane historians. Two or three may suffice. It is well known that Julius Cæsar wrote histories both of the civil war and of the war in Gaul: the same events are related by Dion Cassius, as well as by Plutarch in his lives of Pompey and Cæsar. The transactions recorded by Suetonius are also related by Dion, and many of them by Livy and Polybius. What discrepancies are discoverable between these writers! Yet Livy and Polybius are not considered

---

[1] The topic here briefly noticed is ably illustrated by the late Rev. Dr. Townson in his Discourses on the Four Gospels, chiefly with regard to the peculiar Design of each, &c. (Works, vol. i. pp. 1—274.)

[2] An abstract of the evidence for the fact of the Resurrection of Jesus Christ is given in Vol. I. pp. 268—285.

VII. Sect I. § 1.]   *Of Scripture, alleged to be Contradictory.*   499

as liars on this account, but we endeavour by various ways to harmonise their discordant narratives, conscious that, even when we fail, these discordancies do not affect the general credibility of their histories. Again, the embassy of the Jews to the emperor Claudian is placed by Philo in *harvest*, and by Josephus in *seed-time;* yet the existence of this embassy was never called in question. To come nearer to our own times: Lord Clarendon states that the Marquis of Argyle was condemned to be *hanged*, which sentence was executed on the same day: *four* other historians affirm that he was beheaded upon the *Monday*, having been condemned on the *preceding Saturday;* yet this contradiction never led any person to doubt, whether the Marquis was executed or not.

Much of the discrepancy in the Gospels arises from omission, which is always an uncertain ground of objection. Suetonius, Tacitus, and Dion Cassius, have all written an account of the reign of Tiberius; and each has omitted many things mentioned by the rest, yet their credit is not impeached. And these differences will be more numerous, when men do not write histories, but *memoirs* (which perhaps is the true name of the Gospels), that is, when they do *not* undertake to deliver, in the order of time, a regular account *of all* things of importance which the subject of the history said and did, but only such passages as were suggested by their *particular design* at the time of writing.[1] Further, as these seeming discordancies in the evangelical historians prove that they did not write in concert; so, from their agreeing in the principal and most material facts, we may infer that they wrote after the truth.

In Xiphilin and Theodosius, the two abbreviators of the historian Dion Cassius, may be observed the like agreement and disagreement; the one taking notice of many particulars which the other passes in silence, and both of them relating the chief and most remarkable events. And since, from their both frequently making use of the very same words and expressions, when they speak of the same thing, it is apparent that they both copied from the *same* original; so, no person was ever absurd enough to imagine that the particulars mentioned by the one were not taken out of Dion Cassius, merely because they were omitted by the other. And still more absurd would it be to say (as some modern opposers of revelation have said of the Evangelists), that the facts related by Theodosius are contradicted by Xiphilin, because the latter says nothing of them. But against the Evangelists, it seems, *all kinds* of arguments may not only be *employed* but applauded. The case, however, of the sacred historians is exactly parallel to that of these two abbreviators. The *latter* extracted the particulars, related in their several abridgments, from the history of Dion Cassius, as the *former* drew the materials of their Gospels from the life of Jesus Christ. Xiphilin and Theodosius transcribed their relations from a certain collection of facts contained in one and the same history; the four evangelists, from a certain recollection of facts contained in the life of *one* and the *same* person, laid before them by that same SPIRIT, which was to lead them into all truth. And why the fidelity of the *four* transcribers should be called in question for reasons which hold equally strong against the *two* abbreviators, we leave those to determine who lay such a weight upon the objection.[2]

3. A third source of apparent contradictions, in the different circumstances related, arises from *false readings, or from obscure and ambiguous expressions, or from transpositions in the order of relating, and sometimes*

---

[1] Mori Acroases in Ernesti Instit. Interp. Nov. Test. tom. ii. pp. 26—30. Paley's Evidences, vol. ii. pp. 274—279.
[2] West's Observations on the History of the Resurrection, p. 279.

from several of these causes combined.[1] The only way by which these seeming repugnancies may be reconciled, is to call in the aid of sacred criticism; which, when judiciously applied, will, in most instances, if not in every case, remove them.

Thus, in Gen. xxix. 1—8. we have a dialogue in which no man is mentioned but Jacob, the only living creatures present being three flocks of sheep: yet these are represented as conversing, rolling away the stone, and watering the sheep. This appearance of contradiction probably originated, first, in some transcriber writing הָעֲדָרִים (HADARIM), *flocks*, for הָרֹעִים (HAROIM), *shepherds*, in three places; and, secondly, from verse 3 expressing what *customarily* happened, not what then had actually taken place [2]; and this mistake, having obtained in some copy of high repute, has been transcribed into all the later manuscripts. That the above mistake has actually been made, appears from the Samaritan text of the Pentateuch, from the Arabic version in Bishop Walton's Polyglott, (which has preserved the true reading in verses 3 and 8) and from the Greek version. The true reading, therefore, as Houbigant and Dr Kennicott contend, is shepherds, not flocks, and the third verse should be read parenthetically.[3]

Having thus stated the various causes of apparent contradictions in the different circumstances related by the inspired writers, we shall proceed to illustrate the preceding remarks.

I. *The names of persons and places are respectively liable to change.*

Thus, the name of one person is sometimes given to another, either as they are types of them, — so *Christ* is called *David* (Ezek xxxiv. 23, 24.) and *Zerubbabel* (Hag. ii. 23.) — or, on account of some resemblance between them, as in Isa. i. 10 Ezek. xvi. 3. 46. Mal. iv. 5 compared with Matt xi. 14. and John i 21 Rev. ii 20. and xviii. 2. So *Hell* derives its name, in many languages, from the valley of the children of Hinnom, on account of the wickedness there committed, and the dreadful cries formerly heard in that place. In the like manner, the place of the great slaughter (Rev. xvi. 16) has its name from the place of the memorable battle where Josiah was slain, 2 Kings xxiii. 29.

II. *The name of the head of a tribe or nation is sometimes given to their posterity.*

Thus, Edom or Esau is put for the Edomites, who were the descendants of Esau, in Numb. xx 18. Gen xxxvi. 1 and Obadiah i 6 Very numerous similar examples are to be found in the Sacred Writings, which it is unnecessary to specify

III *Sometimes names remain after the reason for which they were given, or the thing whence they were taken, has ceased to exist.*

Aaron's rod, for instance, retained its name when changed into a serpent. Exod. vii. 12. So Matthew is called a publican, because he had formerly followed that calling. Simon the leper is so termed because he had formerly been afflicted with the leprosy, Matt. xxvi. 6. So it is said in Matt xi 5. that the blind see, and the deaf hear, that is, those who had been blind and deaf A similar instance occurs in Matt xxi 31. *The publicans and harlots enter into the kingdom of heaven*, that is, those who had been such, not those who continue so (Compare 1 Cor vi. 9)

IV. *The same persons or places sometimes have several names*

---

[1] Gerard's Institutes, p 426. § 1147. Jahnii Enchiridion Herm. Gen cap. vi. De Compositione Ειαπιοφανων, p. 137.

[2] The Vulgate version so renders verse 3. *Morisque erat ut cunctis ovibus* (lege *pastoribus*) *congregatis devolverent lapidem*, &c.

[3] Houbigant in loc. Dr. Kennicott's First Dissertation on the Hebrew text, pp 360—365. The proper version of the passage above referred to will be thus " Then Jacob went on his journey, and came into the land of the people of the east 2. And he looked, and behold a well in a field , and, lo, three *shepherds* were lying by it, for out of that well they watered their flocks , and a great stone was upon the well's mouth. (And there all the *shepherds usually* met together, and rolled the stone from the well's mouth, and watered the sheep; and put the stone again upon the well's mouth, in its place.) 4—7 And Jacob said, &c. &c. 8. And they said, We cannot until all the *shepherds* shall be gathered together, and roll the stone from the well's mouth; then we water the sheep.

Thus, Esau's wife is called Bashemath in Gen. xxvi 34. and Adah in Gen. xxxvi. 2 Gideon is called Jerubbaal in Judges vi. 32 and vii. 1. Zerubbabel and Sheshbazzar are the same person, Ezra i 8 and v. 14. compared with Hag. i. 14. and ii. 2. 21. Almost numberless similar instances might be adduced from the Old Testament: nor are examples wanting in the New. Thus, he who was nominated for the apostleship, is called Joseph, Barsabas, and Justus. (Acts i 25) Joses and Barnabas are the names of the same apostle. Simon, it is well known, was called Peter, and all the other apostles, except Saint John, had more names than one. In like manner, the same *places* are distinguished by several names; as Enmishphat and Kadesh, Gen. xiv 7. Hermon, Sirion, Shenir, Deut in 9. Magdala in Matt. xv 39. is termed Dalmanutha in Mark viii. 10. and the country of the Gergesenes, in Matt. viii 28, in Mark v. 1 called that of the Gadarenes

V. *Many persons and places also have the same name.*

There was one Bethlehem in the tribe of Zebulun, Josh xix. 15. and another in the tribe of Judah, Matt. ii. 6. Luke ii 4. There were two towns called *Cana*, Josh xix 28 John ii. 1 Several *Cæsareas*, Matt. xvi 13. Acts ix. 30. and xviii. 22. Several *Zechariahs*, as in 1 Chron. v 7. xv. 20. xxiv 25, &c. 2 Chron xvii. 7. xx. 14. Zech. i 1. Luke i. 5 Matt xxiii. 35. The Zechariah in this last cited passage, was probably the person mentioned in 2 Chron. xx 14. and the name of the father has been added *since*, by some transcriber, who took it from the title of the prophecy. Several *Herods*, as, 1. *Herod the Great*, in whose reign our Redeemer was incarnate, Matt ii 1. and by whom the infants at Bethlehem were massacred, Matt. ii.16. 2. *Herod Antipas*, surnamed the Tetrarch, Matt. xiv. 1. by whom John the Baptist was murdered, (verse 10.) and our Saviour was mocked and set at nought, Luke xxiii 11. · 3 *Herod Agrippa*, who slew the apostle James, Acts xii. 2. and miserably perished, verse 23 So, there are some names which appear to have been common to several, if not to all, the successive kings of a country Thus, Pharaoh was the general name of the kings of Egypt, Gen. xii 15. xxxix 1 Exodus i—xv. *passim*. 1 Kings iii 1. 2 Kings xxiii. 29. Isa xix, 11. Jer xxv 19 xliv 30. and xlvi. 17 and very frequently in the prophecy of Ezekiel; and that this was the constant title of the Egyptian kings, is further attested by Josephus [1] and Suidas [2] Artaxerxes was the common name of the whole race of Persian kings; as Abimelech was of the Philistines, Gen xx. 2 xxvi 8. compared with the title to Psal xxxiv, and Agag of the Amalekites, as may be inferred from Numb. xxiv 7. compared with 1 Sam xv. 8.

VI. *The differences in names occurring in the Scriptures, are sometimes occasioned by false readings, and can only be reconciled by correcting these;* but the true name may in such cases be distinguished from the erroneous one, by the usage of Scripture in other places, as well as from the Samaritan Pentateuch, the antient versions, and Josephus.[3]

The following instances will illustrate this remark. *Hadarezer*, 1 Chron xviii 3. ought to be Hadadezer, as in 2 Sam vii. 3 a Resh ר being mistaken for a Daleth ד.[4] *Joshebbassebet*, in 2 Sam xxii. 8 (marg rend) should be Jashobeam, as in 1 Chron. xi. 11. and xxvii. 2.[5] *Bathshua, the daughter of Ammiel*, in 1 Chron. iii 5 should be Bathsheba the daughter of Eliam, as in 2 Sam. xi. 5. the two last letters of the father's name being transposed, and the two first put last [6] *Azariah*, in 2 Kings xiv. 21. should be Uzziah, as in 2 Chron. xxvi. 1. and elsewhere; which reading is adopted, or nearly so, by the Arabic and Syriac versions.[7] *Jehoahaz*, in 2 Chron. xxi. 17. should be Ahazihu, or Ahaziah, as in 2 Kings viii. 24. and elsewhere.[8] The name of the great king Nebuchadnezzar is spelled seven different ways. [9]

---

[1] Antiq. l viii c. 6 § 2.   [2] Suidas, in voce.
[3] Gerard's Institutes, p. 427.
[4] Kennicott, Dissert. i pp 89, 90.   [5] Ibid. pp. 70—78.
[6] Ibid p 463.   [7] Ibid. pp 478—480.   [8] Ibid. pp 489, 490.
[9] Ibid. Dissert. ii. pp 503—505. concerning the variation of names, see further Kennicott's Remarks on Select Passages of the Old Testament, pp 23—26.

§ 2. *Apparent Contradictions, from Things being related in a different Order by the Sacred Writers.*

I. *The Scriptures being as it were a compendious record of important events, we are not to infer that these took place exactly in the order narrated; for frequently things are related together, between which many things intervened while they were transacting. Neither are we to conclude that a thing is not done, because it is not related in the history of other things happening in the same age.*

1. Thus, in Numb. xxxiii. we have a particular account of the journeyings of the Israelites, which are not noticed in their proper place in the book of Exodus. In the four Gospels especially, we find that each of the evangelists did not relate every word and thing; but one frequently omits what has been related by the rest, while that which has been briefly noticed by one, is recorded at length by the others, and two evangelists, when relating the same fact, do not always observe the order of time.

2. So, in John xii. 1—3 Jesus Christ is said to have been anointed at Bethany *six days before the passover;* yet Saint Matthew, (xxvi 2 6, 7) takes no notice of this remarkable circumstance till within two days of the feast "The reason is manifest. It was at this time that Judas offered to the chief-priests and elders to betray him; and the evangelist, intending to relate his treachery, returns to give an account of the event which prompted him to it. The rebuke which he received in the house of Simon, when he complained of the waste of ointment, had irritated his proud disaffected heart, and inspired him with sentiments of revenge The mention of the unction of our Saviour, which was preparatory to his burial, reminds us of another observation, which is of use in removing difficulties, namely, that two facts may much resemble each other, and yet not be the same. Although they differ, therefore, in some circumstances, while they agree in other, it is through haste and inattention that, on this account, we charge the Scriptures with contradiction The anointing of Christ, six days before the passover, is evidently different from the anointing recorded in the seventh chapter of Luke The two incidents agree, as both happened at table, and in the house of a person named Simon ; but on considering the passages, they appear to have taken place at different times." [1] Apparent contradictions of this kind are so numerous in the Gospels, that it would almost require a harmony of them to be constructed, were we here to specify them; and from these discrepancies have originated harmonies, or connected histories, compiled from the writings of the evangelists, in the structure of which different theories of arrangement have been adopted, in order to reconcile their seeming discrepancies. [2]

3. Other additional instances of things that are mentioned as having happened, but of which no notice is taken in the sacred histories, occur in Gen. xxxi 7, 8. the changing of Jacob's wages *ten times*, that is, frequently; in Psalm cv. 18. Joseph's feet being hurt with fetters; in Hosea xii. 4. Jacob's weeping; in Acts vii 25—30, several things concerning Moses, in Acts xx. 35 a saying of our Lord; in 1 Cor. xv 7 an appearance of Christ to St. James; in 2 Tim. iii 8. Jannes and Jambres withstanding Moses; in Heb ix 19 Moses sprinkling the book as well as the people with blood; and Heb. xii 21. a saying of Moses Jude 9. Michael's contending for the body of Moses; and verse 14 Enoch's prophecy; and in Rev ii. 14. Balaam teaching Balak to put a stumbling block before the children of Israel: all which things might be known by revelation, or by personal communication, as in the case of Christ's appearance to James, who was evidently living when Paul mentioned it, or by tradition, or by the history of those times, as some of the circumstances above adverted to are mentioned by Josephus.

II. *Things are not always recorded in the Scriptures exactly in the same method and order in which they were done; whence apparent contradictions*

---

[1] Dick's Essay on the Inspiration of the Scriptures, pp. 300, 301
[2] See an account of the principal Harmonies of the Gospels, pp 272—275 supra, and pp. 116—122. of the Appendix to this volume for editions of Harmonies.

VII. Sect. I. § 2.] *Of Scripture, alleged to be Contradictory.*   503.

arise, events being sometimes introduced by anticipation and sometimes by ὑστερωσις, in which the natural order is inverted, and things are related first which ought to appear last.

1. *Events introduced by anticipation.*

The creation of man in Gen. i 27; which, after several other things inserted, is related more at large, particularly the creation of Adam, in Gen. ii. 7. and of Eve, in verses 21—23 The death of Isaac (Gen. xxxv 29) is anticipated, as several transactions, especially those in chapters xxxvii and xxxviii. must have happened during his life it was probably thus anticipated, that the history of Joseph might not be disturbed. Isaac is supposed to have lived at least twelve years after Joseph was sold into Egypt In Exod. xvi. 33 we read of the keeping of the pot of manna, which was not done till many years after David's adventure with Goliath, related in 1 Sam. xvii., was prior to his solacing Saul with his music; and the latter story is recorded in 1 Sam xvi., the historian bringing together the *effect* of Saul's rejection, and the endowment of David with various graces, among which was, his pre-eminent skill on the harp. " It appears, indeed, from many circumstances of the story, that David's combat with Goliath was many years prior in time to Saul's madness, and to David's introduction to him as a musician In the first place, David was quite a youth when he engaged Goliath (1 Sam xvii 33 42) · when he was introduced to Saul, as a musician, he was of full age (xvi. 18.) Secondly, his combat with Goliath was his first appearance in public life (xvii. 56.); when he was introduced as a musician, he was a man of established character. (xvi 18) Thirdly, his combat with Goliath was his first military exploit. (xvii. 38, 39) He was a man of war when he was introduced as a musician. (xvi 18) He was unknown both to Saul and Abner when he fought Goliath He had not, therefore, yet been in the office of Saul's armour-bearer, or resident in any capacity at the court. Now, the just conclusion is, not that these twenty verses are an "interpolation" (as some critics have imagined [1]), but that the ten last verses of 1 Sam. xvi, which relate Saul's madness and David's introduction to the court upon that occasion, are misplaced. The true place for these ten verses seems to be between the ninth and tenth of the eighteenth chapter. Let these ten verses be removed to that place, and this seventeenth chapter be connected immediately with the thirteenth verse of chapter xvi. and the whole disorder and inconsistency that *appears* in the present narrative will be removed." [2] In Matt xxvi. 21. and Mark xiv. 18 our Saviour is recorded to have intimated by whom he was to be betrayed, *while* eating the passover; which Saint Luke (xxii 21) shows to have been *after* the institution of the Lord's Supper: the order of Luke therefore is the true one The imprisonment of John is set down in Luke iii. 19. *before* the baptism of Christ, whereas it happened *after* he had entered on his public ministry. The same occurrence is related by St Matthew and the other evangelists, per ὑστερολογιαν, on occasion of Herod's consternation.

2. *Events related first which ought to have been placed last.*

The calling of Abraham to depart from Ur in Chaldea, in Gen. xii. 1. for it preceded that departure which is related in ch. xi Compare Gen. xv. 7. with Acts vii. 3. The history of Judah, in Gen. xxxviii. for most of the particulars related happened before the sale of Joseph In Luke iv. 9. the carrying and placing of Christ on one of the battlements of the temple is related *after* his being transported to an exceeding high mountain; whereas it certainly preceded it, as appears from Matt. iv 5. 8. who has distinctly noted the order of the temptations [3]

III. *A thing is sometimes attributed to one who was formerly an example of any action.* See an instance of this in Jude, verse 11.

IV. *Actions or things are sometimes said to be done, when they are not*

---

[1] Particularly Mr Pilkington (Remarks on Scripture, pp. 62—68), and Dr. Kennicott. (Diss. ii on the Hebrew Text, pp 419—429.)

[2] Bp. Horsley's Biblical Criticisms, vol. i. p. 331. Mr. Townsend, in his Harmony of the Old Testament, has judiciously arranged the above chapters agreeably to Bp. H.'s suggestion, and has thus obviated a seeming contradiction, which has long since called forth the sarcasms of infidels

[3] Glassii Philologia Sacra, tom. i. pp. 668—671, edit Dathii.

already done, but upon the point of being accomplished, or (as we usually say), " as good as done."

And in this language Christ ordinarily spoke a little before his death, as in Matt xxvi. 24 the son of man *goeth*, &c verse 45. the son of man *is* betrayed. So Mark xiv. 41 Luke xxii 19, 20 which *is* given, which *is* shed, and verse 37. the things concerning me *have* an end A similar expression occurs in Isa ix 6. to us a child *is* born, to us a son *is* given, &c. and in Rev. xviii. 2. Babylon *is* fallen, *is* fallen.

V. *So, actions or things are said to be done, which are only* declared *to be done.*

Thus, in Gen xxvii 37. we read, *I have made him thy Lord*, that is, I have foretold that he shall be so Gen. xxxv 12 *The land which I gave Abraham and Isaac*, that is, promised or foretold should be theirs See like instances in Numb xvi. 7. Job v. 3. Jer. i 10. xv 1 and xxv. 15.

VI. *So, actions or things are said to be done, which only* seem *or are reputed to be done.*

Thus, in Josh. ii. 7 it is said, the men *pursued* after the spies ; that is, they believed they were doing so, at the very time when the spies were concealed.

VII. *So, a thing is said to be done by him who only* desires *or endeavours to accomplish it, or uses proper means for that purpose.*

See examples of this in Gen xxxvii. 21 Esther viii 5. Ezek. xxiv. 13. 1 Cor x. 33, &c.

---

§ 3. *Apparent Contradictions, arising from Differences in Numbers.*

Apparent contradictions in the Sacred Writings, arising from the difference of numbers, proceed from the Scriptures speaking in whole or round numbers, — from numbers being taken sometimes exclusively and sometimes inclusively, — from various readings, — and from the writers of the New Testament sometimes quoting numbers from the Alexandrian version, not from the Hebrew text.

I. *The Scriptures sometimes speak in whole, or, as we usually term them, round numbers; though an odd or imperfect number would be more exact.*

Thus, in Gen. xv. 13 it is foretold that his posterity should be enslaved in Egypt four hundred years. Moses (Exod. xii 40) states their sojourning to be four hundred and thirty years, as also does Paul, Gal. iii. 17. and Josephus.[1] In Acts vii 6. Stephen says, that the children of Israel sojourned in Egypt four hundred years, leaving out the odd tens. Though the Israelites themselves resided in Egypt only two hundred and some odd years, yet the full time of their peregrination was four hundred and thirty years, if we reckon from the calling of Abraham and his departure from Ur, until the Israelites quitted Egypt; and that this is the proper reckoning appears from the Samaritan copy of the Pentateuch; which, in all its printed editions and manuscripts, as well as the Septuagint version of the Pentateuch, reads the passage in Exod xii. 40 thus: *Now the sojourning of the children of Israel, and of their fathers, which they sojourned in the land of Canaan, and in the land of Egypt, was four hundred and thirty years*[2] In Numb xiv. 33 it is denounced to the murmuring Israelites that they should wander forty years in the wilderness: but if we compare Numb. xxxiii. with Josh. iv 19 we shall find that some days, if not weeks, were wanting to complete the number : but, forty years being a round and entire number, and because in so many years a few days were inconsiderable, therefore Moses delivers it in this manner The same remark applies to Judges xi. 26 relative to the sojourning of the Israelites in the land of the Amorites. The twelve apostles are also mentioned in 1 Cor xv. 5. though Judas was no more; and Abimelech is said to have slain seventy persons, though Jotham escaped. Compare Judges ix. 18. 56. with verse 5.

---

[1] Antiq. l iii. c 1. § 9   De Bell. Jud. l. v. c. 9. § 4
[2] Kennicott, Diss. ii. pp 396—398.

VII. Sect. I. § 3.]   *Of Scripture, alleged to be Contradictory.*   505

II. *Sometimes numbers are to be taken exclusively, and sometimes inclusively.*

Matt. xvii 1 Mark ix 2. Luke ix. 28. and John xx. 26. may be mentioned as examples of this remark   See them further explained in p. 511. § V. *infra.*

III. *Differences in numbers not unfrequently arise from false readings.*

As the Hebrews antiently used the letters of their alphabet to denote *numbers,* many of those numbers, which to us appear almost incredible in some places, and contradictory in others, are owing to mistakes in some of the similar letters. Thus, in 2 Kings viii. 26. we read that Ahaziah was *twenty-two* years old when he began to reign , but in 2 Chron xxii. 2 he is said to have been *forty-two years* old, which is impossible, as he could not be born *two years* before Jehoram his father, who was only forty years old.   *Twenty-two years*, therefore, is the proper reading, a Kaph ב, whose numeral power is twenty, being put for a Mem מ, whose numeral power is forty.   In like manner, in 2 Sam viii 4. and x. 18. we read seven hundred, which in 1 Chron. xviii. 4. and xix. 18. is seven thousand, the proper number.[1]

As the Jews antiently appear to have expressed numbers by marks analogous to our common figures, the corruption (and consequently the seeming contradiction) may be accounted for, from the transcribers having carelessly added or omitted a single cipher   Thus, in 1 Sam vi 19 we read that the Lord smote fifty thousand and seventy inhabitants of Bethshemesh for looking into the ark ; which number in the Arabic and Syriac versions, is five thousand and seventy. There is no doubt but that both these numbers are incorrect. Three of the MSS. collated by Dr. Kennicott (of the twelfth century) and Josephus, read simply *seventy* men, and omit 50,000. Seventy is evidently the true number : for, as Bethshemesh was but a " small village," it is improbable that it could contain so many as 50,000 inhabitants[2]   In 1 Kings iv. 26. we are told that Solomon had forty thousand stalls for horses, which number, in 2 Chron. ix. 25 is only four thousand, and is most probably correct, a cipher having been added[3] In 2 Chron xiii. 3 17. we meet with the following numbers, four hundred thousand, eight hundred thousand, and five hundred thousand, which in several of the old editions of the Vulgate Latin Bible, are forty thousand, eighty thousand, and fifty thousand : the latter are probably the true numbers.[4]

By the application of this rule, some critics have endeavoured to reconcile the difference relative to the hour of Christ's crucifixion, which by Mark (xv. 25) is stated to be the *third*, and by St. John (xix 14.) the *sixth* hour : for, as in antient times all numbers were written in manuscripts, not at length, but with numeral letters, it was easy for Γ, three, to be taken for ς, six. Of this opinion are Griesbach, in his elaborate edition of the New Testament, Semler, Rosenmuller, Doddridge, Whitby, Bengel, Cocceius, Beza, Erasmus, and by far the greater part of the most eminent critics.   What further renders this correction probable is, that besides the Codex Bezæ, and the Codex Stephani (of the eighth century), there are four other manuscripts which read τριτη *the third,* in John xix 14. as well as the Alexandrian Chronicle, which professes to cite accurate manuscripts — even the autograph copy of St John himself.   Such also is the opinion of Severus Antiochenus, Ammonius, and some others cited by Theophylact on the passage ; to whom must be added Nonnus, a Greek poet of Panopolis in Egypt, who flourished in the fifth century, and wrote a poetical paraphrase of the Gospel of St. John, and who also found τριτη in the manuscript used by him.[5]

IV. *Apparent contradictions in the numbers of the New Testament arise from the sacred writers sometimes quoting the numbers of the Septuagint or Alexandrian version, not those of the Hebrew Text.*

This is evidently the case in Acts vii.14. where Jacob's family is stated, at the time of his going into Egypt, to have consisted of *three-score and fifteen souls;* whereas

---

[1] Kennicott, Diss i. pp 96—99 462, 463 Diss. ii. p. 209. Other similar remarks are interspersed in the same elaborate volumes.

[2] Ibid. Diss. i. p. 532. Diss. ii p 208. Dr. A. Clarke, and Dr. Boothroyd on 1 Sam. vi. 19.

[3] Kennicott, Diss i p 532 Diss ii. p. 208.

[4] Ibid. Diss. i. pp. 532—534. Diss. ii. pp 196—218   Other examples occur in Diss. ii. p 219 *et seq*

[5] See Griesbach, Rosenmuller, Kuinoel, Doddridge, Whitby, Dr A. Clarke, and other commentators on the passage in question.

Moses, in Gen. xlvi 27. fixes it at *three-score and ten souls*. What further confirms this remark is, that the Septuagint version of Gen xlvi. 20 enumerates *five persons* more than the Hebrew, which, being added to the three-score and ten mentioned by Moses, exhibits the exact number, seventy-five.[1] To this we may add (although it does not strictly belong to numbers) the well-known passage, Luke iii. 36. where, in giving the genealogy of Jesus Christ, the evangelist notices a Cainan, whose name does not occur in the pedigree recorded by Moses, but which appears in the Septuagint version of Gen x 24 [2] On the subject of quotations from the Old Testament in the New, see pp. 204—270. *supra*

---

[1] Various other solutions have been given, in order to reconcile this seeming difference between the numbers of Jacob's family, as related in the Old and New Testaments the most *satisfactory* of all is the following one of Dr. Hales which by a critical comparison of Gen. xlvi 27. with Acts vii. 14 completely reconciles the apparent discrepancy

"Moses," he remarks, "states that, 'all the souls that came with Jacob into Egypt, *which issued from his loins* (except his sons' *wives*) were sixty-six souls,'" Gen. xlvi. 26. and this number is thus collected

Jacob's children, eleven sons and one daughter	12
Reuben's sons	4
Simeon's sons	6
Levi's sons	3
Judah's three sons and two grandsons	5
Issachar's sons	4
Zebulun's sons	3
Gad's sons	7
Asher's four sons and one daughter and two grandsons	7
Dan's son	1
Napthali's sons	4
Benjamin's sons	10
	66

"If to these sixty-six children, grandchildren, and great-grandchildren, we add Jacob himself, Joseph and his two sons born in Egypt, or four more, the amount is seventy, the whole number of Jacob's family which settled in Egypt. In this statement the *wives* of Jacob's sons, who formed part of the household, are omitted, but they amounted to nine; for of the twelve wives of the twelve sons, Judah's wife was dead (Gen xxxviii. 12.), and Simeon's also, as we may collect from his youngest son, Shaul, by a Canaanitess (xlvi. 19.), and Joseph's wife was already in Egypt These nine wives, therefore, added to the sixty-six, gave seventy-five souls, the whole amount of Jacob's household, that went down with him to Egypt; *critically* corresponding with the statement in the New Testament, that "Joseph sent for his father Jacob, and *all his kindred*, amounting to *seventy-five* souls."—the expression, *all his kindred*, including the wives who were Joseph's kindred, not only by affinity, but also by consanguinity, being probably of the families of Esau, Ishmael, or Keturah. Thus does the New Testament furnish an admirable commentary on the Old."

From the preceding list, compared with that of the births of Jacob's sons, it appears that some of them married remarkably early Thus Judah, Er, and Pharez, respectively married at the age of about fourteen years; Asher, and his fourth or youngest son (Beriah), under twenty, Benjamin about fifteen, and Joseph's sons and grandsons could not have been much above twenty years old when they married, in order that he should have great-grandchildren in the course of seventy-three years. What further confirms this statement is, that they *must have necessarily* married at a very early age (as we know is practised to this day in the East), to have produced, in the course of two hundred and fifteen years, at the time of their departure, no less than six hundred thousand men, above twenty years of age, exclusive of women and children, so that the whole population of the Israelites, who went out of Egypt, must have exceeded *two millions* Dr. Hales's New Analysis of Chronology, vol. ii. part i. pp. 159—162

[2] Dr. Hales has proved this second Cainan to be an interpolation in the Septuagint, New Analysis, vol. i. pp. 90—94.

§ 4. *Apparent Contradictions in the Relation of Events in one Passage, and References to them in another.*

These contradictions are of two kinds.

1. Sometimes events are referred to as having taken place, which are not noticed by the inspired historians; these apparent contradictions have already been considered in § 2. Obs. 1. p. 502.

2. Sometimes the reference appears contradictory to circumstances actually noticed in the history.

Thus, in Numb. xiv 30 it is said that none of the Israelites should come into the land of Canaan, *save Caleb and Joshua;* and yet, in Josh xiv. 1. and xxii 13 we read, that Eleazar and others entered into that land. But this seeming repugnance will disappear when it is recollected that nothing is more common in the most serious and considerate writers, than to speak of things by way of restriction and limitation, and yet to leave them to be understood with some latitude, which shall afterwards be expressed and explained when they treat of the same matter. So, here we read that none but Caleb and Joshua entered into the land of promise, this being spoken of *the chief leaders,* who had that privilege and honour: but if we consult other passages where this subject is more particularly related, we shall find that a more comprehensive meaning was not excluded. It is not to be supposed that the tribe of Levi were denied entrance into Canaan: because it is evident from the history that *they* did not murmur: and it is equally evident that against the murmurers only was the denunciation made, *that they should not see the land which God sware unto their fathers* (Numb. xiv. 22, 23.): therefore Eleazar and Phineas, being priests, are excepted. Again, the threatening cannot be intended to include those who were gone as spies into the land of Canaan, for they were not among the murmurers: and, consequently, the denunciation above mentioned could not apply to them. Thus, the statement in the book of numbers, is perfectly consistent with the facts recorded in the book of Joshua.

SECTION II.

APPARENT CONTRADICTIONS IN CHRONOLOGY.

CHRONOLOGY is a branch of learning, which is most difficult to be exactly adjusted, because it depends upon so many circumstances and comprehends so great a variety of events in all ages and nations, that with whatever punctuality the accounts of time might have been set down in the original manuscripts, yet the slightest change in one word or letter may cause a material variation in copies. Besides, the difference of the æras adopted in the computations of different countries, especially at great distances of time and place, is such, that the most exact chronology may easily be mistaken, and may be perplexed by those who endeavour to rectify what they conceive to be erroneous; for that which was exact at first is often made incorrect by him who thought it false before.[1] Chronological differences do undoubtedly exist in the Scriptures, as well as in profane historians; but these differences infer no uncertainty in the *matters*

---

[1] Jenkin on the Reasonableness and Certainty of the Christian Religion, vol ii p. 151. It would require too extensive an inquiry for the limits of this work, to enter into a detail of the various systems of chronology extant the most recent is the elaborate *Analysis* of Dr. Hales, in 3 vols. 4to. to which we can confidently refer the reader.

of fact themselves. It is a question yet undetermined, whether Rome was founded by Romulus or not, and it is a point equally litigated, in what year the building of that city commenced; yet, if the uncertainty of the time when any fact was done imply the uncertainty of the fact itself, the necessary inference must be, that it is uncertain whether Rome was built at all, or whether such a person as Romulus was ever in existence. Further, differences in chronology do not imply that the sacred historians were mistaken, but they arise from the mistakes of transcribers or expositors, which may be obviated by applying the various existing aids to the examination and reconciliation of the apparent contradictions in scriptural chronology.

I. *Seeming Contradictions in Chronology arise from not observing, that what had before been said in the general, is afterwards resumed in the particulars comprised under it.*

For, the total sum of any term of years being set down first, before the particulars have been insisted on and explained, has led some into mistake, by supposing that the particulars subsequently mentioned were not to be comprehended in it, but were to be reckoned distinctly as if they had happened afterwards in order of time, because they are *last* related in the course of the history. Thus, in Gen. xi 26. it is said that *Terah lived seventy years and begat* ABRAM · and in verse 32 that *the days of Terah were two hundred and five years; and Terah died in Haran.* But, in Gen xii. 4. it is related that *Abram was seventy and five years old when he departed out of Haran;* which is inconsistent, if we suppose Abram to have resided in Haran till the death of his father Terah. But, if we consider that the whole number of years, during which Terah lived, is set down in Gen. xi. 32. and that Abram's departure from Haran, which is related in Gen xii. 4. happened before his father's death, there will be no inconsistency; on the contrary, if Terah were only seventy years old when Abram was begotten, and if Abram were only seventy-five years old when he departed for Haran, it will be evident that Abram left his father Terah in Haran, where the latter lived after his son's departure, to the age of two hundred and five years, although during Terah's life, Abram occasionally returned to Haran, for his *final* removal did not take place until the death of his father, as we learn from Acts vii. 4. Now, if this way of relating the general first, which is afterwards particularly set forth, be attended to in the interpretation of the Scriptures, it will afford a natural and easy solution of many otherwise inexplicable difficulties Another explanation has been offered for the above apparent chronological difference, viz. that Abram was Terah's youngest son though first mentioned. What renders this solution probable is, that it is no unfrequent thing in Scripture, when any case of dignity or pre-eminence is to be distinguished, to place the *youngest* son before the eldest, though contrary to the usage of the Scriptures in other cases. Thus, Shem the second son of Noah is always placed first; Abram is placed before his two elder brothers Haran and Nahor; Isaac is placed before Ishmael; Jacob the youngest son of Isaac has the pre-eminence over Esau, and Moses is mentioned before his elder brother Aaron. Whatever chronological difficulties, therefore, arise upon this supposition, that the son first named must *necessarily* be the first-born, must consequently proceed from mistake.[1]

II. *Sometimes the principal number is set down, and the odd or smaller*

---

[1] Although the observations above given are sufficient to solve the chronological difficulty, it is proper to notice, that, instead of *two hundred and five years,* in Gen. xi. 32., the Samaritan Pentateuch reads *one hundred and forty-five years,* the adoption of which will remove the seeming contradiction According to the text (Gen xi 26.) Terah begat Abram, when he was seventy years old, and died in Haran (32.) when he was 205. Abram departed from Haran in his seventy-fifth year (Gen xii. 4.), and in Acts vii. 4. it is said that Terah died before Abram had departed from Haran. The age of Terah, when Abram was born, added to his age when he left Haran, makes only one hundred and forty-five years. Hence it is concluded that an error has crept into the text; and therefore De Dieu, and Drs. Kennicott, Geddes, and Boothroyd, adopt the reading of the Samaritan text in preference to that of the Hebrew.

number is omitted; which, being added to the principal number in some other place, causes a difference not to be reconciled but by considering that it is customary in the best authors not always to mention the smaller numbers, where the matter does not require it.

Of this we have evident proof in the Scriptures. Thus the Benjamites that were slain, are said in Judges xx 35. to be 25,100, but in verse 46 they are reckoned only at 25,000. So the evangelist Mark says, xvi 14., that Jesus Christ appeared to the *eleven* as they were sitting at meat, though Thomas was absent. The observation already made, on the use of round numbers in computations [1], will apply in the present instance, to which we might add numerous similar examples from profane writers Two or three, however, will suffice. One hundred acres of land were by the Romans called *centuria*, but in progress of time the same term was given to double that number of acres. [2] The *tribes*, into which the population of Rome was divided, were so denominated, because they were originally *three* in number, but the same appellation was retained though they were afterwards augmented to thirty-five, and in like manner the judges, styled *centumviri*, were at first five more than one hundred, and afterwards were nearly double that number [3], yet still they retained the same name. Since, then, it is evident that smaller numbers are sometimes omitted both in the Old and in the New Testament, as well as in profane writings, and the principal or great numbers only, whether more or less than the precise calculation, are set down, and at other times the smaller numbers are specified;—nay, that sometimes the original number multiplied retains the same denomination: therefore it is reasonable to make abatements, and not always to insist rigorously on precise numbers, in adjusting the accounts of scriptural chronology [4]

III. *As sons frequently reigned with their fathers, during the Hebrew monarchy, the reigns of the former are not unfrequently made, in some instances, to commence from their partnership with their fathers in the throne, and in others from the commencement of their sole government after their father's decease: consequently the time of the reign is sometimes noticed as it respects the father, sometimes as it respects the son, and sometimes as it includes both.*

Thus, Jotham is said (2 Kings xv. 33) to have reigned *sixteen* years, yet in the preceding verse 30 mention is made of his *twentieth* year. This repugnance is reconcileable in the following manner; Jotham reigned alone sixteen years only, but with his father Uzziah (who, being a leper, was, therefore, unfit for the sole government) four years before, which makes twenty in the whole. In like manner we read (2 Kings xiii 1) that, "in the *three-and-twentieth year* of Joash the son of Ahaziah king of Judah, Jehoahaz the son of Jehu began to reign over Israel in Samaria, and reigned seventeen years:" but in verse 10. of the same chapter it is related that, "in the *thirty-seventh* year of the same Joash began Jehoash the son of Jehoahaz to reign over Israel in Samaria" Now, if to the three-and-twenty years of Joash, mentioned in the first passage, we add the seventeen years of Jehoahaz, we come down to the thirty-ninth or fortieth year of Joash; when on the death of Jehoahaz, the reign of Jehoash may be supposed to have begun. Yet it is easy to assign the reason why the commencement of his reign is fixed two or three years earlier, in the thirty-seventh year of Joash, when his father must have been alive, by supposing that his father had admitted him as an associate in the government, two or three years before his death This solution is the more probable, as we find from the case of Jehoshaphat and his son (2 Kings viii. 16.) that in those

---

[1] See § 3. Remark I. p. 504
[2] *Centuriam* nunc dicimus (ut idem Varro ait) *ducentorum* jugerum modum olim autem ab *centum* jugeribus vocabatur *centuria* sed, mox duplicata nomen retinuit sicut *tribus* dictæ primum a partibus populi *tripartito* divisi, quæ tamen nunc multiplicatæ pristinum nomen possident Columella de Re Rust lib. v c. 1. tom ii p 199. ed Bipont. Ernesti, in his *Index Latinitatis Ciceronianæ*, article *Tribus*, has adduced several similar instances.
[3] In Pliny's time they were *one hundred and eighty* in number. Ep. lib. vi. ep 33.
[4] Jenkin's Reasonableness of Christianity, vol. ii. p. 157.

days such a practice was not uncommon."[1] The application of the rule above stated, will also remove the apparent contradiction between 2 Kings xxiv 8 and 2 Chron. xxxvi. 9. Jehoiachim being eight years old when he was associated in the government with his father, and eighteen years old when he began to reign alone. The application of this rule will reconcile many other seeming contradictions in the books of Kings and Chronicles: and will also clear up the difficulty respecting the fifteenth year of the emperor Tiberius mentioned in Luke iii 1. which has exercised the ingenuity of many eminent philologers who have endeavoured to settle the chronology of the New Testament Now, we learn from the Roman historians that the reign of Tiberius had *two* commencements: in the *first*, when he was admitted to a share in the empire (but without the title of emperor), in August of the year 764 from the foundation of the city of Rome, three years before the death of Augustus, and the *second* when he began to reign alone, after that emperor's decease. It is from the *first* of these commencements that the *fifteenth* year mentioned by Saint Luke is to be computed, who, as Tiberius did not assume the imperial title during the life of Augustus, makes use of a word, which precisely marks the nature of the power exercised by Tiberius, viz in the fifteenth year *της ἡγεμονιας of the administration of Tiberius Cæsar* Consequently, this fifteenth year began in August 778. And if John the Baptist entered on his ministry in the spring following, in the year of Rome 779, in the same year of Tiberius, and after he had preached about twelve months, baptised Jesus in the spring of 780, then Jesus (who was most probably born in September or October 749) would at his baptism be thirty-three years of age and some odd months, which perfectly agrees with what St. Luke says of his being at that time *about thirty years old*[2]

IV. *Seeming chronological contradictions arise from the sacred historians adopting different methods of computation, and assigning different duties to the same period.*

Thus, in Gen. xv. 13. it is announced to Abraham that his "seed should be a stranger in a land that was not theirs, and should serve them, and that they should afflict them four hundred years" But in Exod xii 40, 41 the sacred historian relates that "the sojourning of the children of Israel who dwelt in Egypt, was *four hundred and thirty* years. And it came to pass at the end of the *four hundred and thirty* years, even the self-same day it came to pass, that all the hosts of the Lord went out from the land of Egypt" Between these two passages there is an apparent contradiction: the truth is, that both are perfectly consistent, the computation being made from two different dates. In Gen. xv. 13. the time is calculated from the promise made to Abraham of a son, or from the birth of Isaac: and in Exod xii 40, 41. it is reckoned from his departure from "Ur of the Chaldees," his native country, in obedience to the command of Jehovah.[3]

By the application of this rule many commentators reconcile the difference between Mark xv. 25., who says the hour of Christ's crucifixion was the *third*, and John xxix. 14. who says it was about the *sixth* hour, that he was brought forth Notwithstanding the authorities above adduced[4], they observe that none of the antient translators read the *third* hour in John: they therefore solve the difficulty (imperfectly it must be confessed), by considering the day as divided into four parts answering to the four watches of the night. These coincided with the hours of three, six, nine, and twelve, or, in our way of reckoning, nine, twelve, three, and six, which also suited the solemn times of sacrifice and prayer in the temple: in

---

[1] Dick's Essay on the Inspiration of the Scriptures, p 299.

[2] Lardner's Credibility, part i. book ii chap. iii. (Works, vol i. pp. 389—392 8vo.) Doddridge's Family Expositor, vol. i. sect. 15. note (b). Macknight's Harmony, vol. i. Chronological Dissertations, No. iii That the solution above given is correct, see Dr. A Clarke's Chronological Table annexed to his Commentary on the Acts of the Apostles, p. ii.

[3] See p. 188 *supra*, where it is shown that the proper reading of Exod. xii 40. is, *Now the sojourning of the children of Israel* and of their fathers, *which they sojourned* in the land of Canaan and in the land of Egypt, *was four hundred* and thirty years. The reader who is desirous of seeing this subject fully discussed, is referred to Koppe's Dissertation, in Pott's and Ruperti's Sylloge Commentationum Theologicarum, vol. ii. pp. 255—274.

[4] See p. 505. *supra*.

cases, they argue, in which the Jews did not think it of consequence to ascertain the time with great accuracy, they did not regard the intermediate hours, but only those more noted divisions which happened to come nearest the time of the event spoken of Adopting this method of reconciliation, Dr. Campbell remarks, that Mark says *it was the third hour,* from which we have reason to conclude that the third hour was past John says it was *about the sixth hour,* from which he thinks it probable that the sixth hour was not yet come. " On this supposition, though the evangelists may by a fastidious reader be accused of want of precision in regard to dates, they will not by any judicious and candid critic be charged with falsehood or misrepresentation. Who would accuse two modern historians with contradicting each other, because in relating an event which had happened between ten and eleven in the forenoon, one had said it was past nine o'clock, the other that it was drawing towards noon "[1] From the evidence before him, we leave the reader to draw his own conclusions as to the reading which is preferably to be adopted. We apprehend that the weight of evidence will be found to preponderate in favour of the solution given in p. 505 *supra.*

V. *The terms of time in computation are sometimes taken* inclusively, *and at other times* exclusively.

Thus in Matt. xvii. 1. and Mark ix 2. we read that *after* six days *Jesus taketh Peter, James, and John his brother, and bringeth them up into an high mountain apart* But in Luke ix. 28 this is said *to come to pass* about an eight days *after;* which is perfectly consistent with what the other evangelists write. For Matthew and Mark speak *exclusively,* reckoning the six days between the time of our Saviour's discourse (which they are relating) and his transfiguration: but Luke *includes* the day on which he had that discourse, and the day of his transfiguration, and reckons them with the six intermediate days. So in John xx. 26. *eight days after* are probably to be understood inclusively; it being most likely on that day se'nnight on which Jesus Christ had before appeared to his disciples. It were unnecessary to subjoin additional examples of a mode of reckoning which obtains to this day in common speech, and in almost every writer, except those who professedly treat on chronology.

This mode of computation is not confined to the evangelical historians. The rabbins also observe, that the very first day of a year may stand in computation for that year[2]; and by this way of reckoning mistakes of years *current* for years *complete,* or vice versâ, in the successions of so many kings, and in the transactions of affairs for so long a time, as is narrated in the Scriptures, may amount to a considerable number of years. For this reason Thucydides says[3], that he computes the years of the Peloponnesian war, not by the magistrates who were annually chosen during that time, but by so many summers and winters: whereas Polybius, Josephus, and Plutarch, have been supposed to contradict themselves because they reckon, sometimes by *current* and sometimes by complete years.

The preceding, and various other ways by which disputes in chronology may be occasioned, are a sufficient argument to us, that they do not imply that there were, originally, chronological mistakes in the books themselves. And if mistakes might arise in so many and such various ways, without any error in the original writings;—if the same difficulties occur upon so very nice and intricate a subject in any or all the books which are extant in the world;—and if it could by no means be necessary, that books of divine authority should be either at first so penned as to be liable to no wrong interpretations, or be ever after preserved by miracle from all corruption, it is great rashness to deny the divine authority of the Scriptures, on account of any difficulties that may occur in chronology.

---

[1] Campbell on John xix 14 vol ii pp. 572, 573. 3d edit. 1807.
[2] Lightfoot's Harmony of the New Testament, § ix.
[3] Thucydidis Historia Belli Peloponnesiaci, lib. vi. c. 20. tom. iii. p. 237, 238. edit. Bipont.

SECTION III.

APPARENT CONTRADICTIONS BETWEEN PROPHECIES AND THEIR FULFILMENT.

I. "*When both a prediction and the event foretold in it are recorded in Scripture, there is sometimes an appearance of disagreement and inconsistency between them.*

"This appearance generally arises from some difficulty in understanding the true meaning of the prediction; it may be occasioned by any of those causes which produce the peculiar difficulties of the prophetic writings; and it is to be removed by the same means which serve for clearing these difficulties. It may proceed from any sort of obscurity or ambiguity in the expression, or from any uncertainty in the structure of a sentence."[1]

Thus, there is a seeming difference in Matt xii 40[2] between our Lord's prediction of the time he was to be in the grave, and the time during which his body was actually interred. Now this difference is naturally and easily obviated by considering, that it was the custom of the Orientals to reckon *any part* of a day of twenty-four hours for a whole day, and to say it was done after three or seven days, &c. if it were done on the third or seventh day from that last mentioned. Compare 1 Kings xx. 29. and Luke ii. 21. And, as the Hebrews had no word exactly answering to the Greek νυχθημερον to signify a natural day of twenty-four hours, they used night and day, or day and night, for it: so that to say a thing happened *after three days and three nights*, was the same as to say that it happened after three days, or on the third day. Compare Esther iv. 16 with v. 1. Gen. vii. 4. 12. 17. Exod. xxiv. 28 and Dan viii. 14.

II. *Apparent contradictions between prophecies and their accomplishment sometimes proceed from the figurative language of the prophets; which is taken, partly from the analogy between the world natural and an empire or kingdom considered as a world politic, and partly from sacred topics.*[3]

Hence it is that the prophets so frequently express what relates to the Christian dispensation and worship in terms borrowed from the Mosaic religion; of which instances may be seen in Isa ii. 2, 3. xix 19 and lvi 7. Jer iii 17. Zech. viii 22. and Mal. i. 11. For the religion of Moses being introductory to that of Jesus, and there being, consequently, a mutual dependency between the two religions, "it is reasonable to suppose that, previous to such an important change of the economy, some intimations would be given of its approach. And yet, to have done this in a way, that would have led the Jews to look with irreverence on a system under which not only themselves but their posterity were to live, would not have harmonised with our notions of the divine wisdom. A method was therefore to be invented, which, while it kept the people sincerely attached to the law, would dispose them, when the time was come, for the reception of a *better covenant* that was to be established on *better promises*. Now the spirit of prophecy, together with the language in which that prophecy was conveyed, fully accomplished both these purposes. By a contrivance only to be suggested by divine prescience, the same expressions, which in their primary and literal meaning were used to denote the fortunes and deliverances of the Jews, for the present consolation of that people, were so ordered, as in a secondary and figurative sense to adumbrate the sufferings and victories of the Messiah, for the future instruction of the church of Christ. Had no expedient of this sort been employed, we should have wanted *one* proof of the connection between the Mosaic and Christian religions: and, on the other hand, had the nature of the Messiah's kingdom been *plainly* described, the design of the national separation would have been defeated. But, when spiritual blessings were promised under the veil of temporal blessings, and in terms

---

[1] Gerard's Institutes of Biblical Criticism, p. 434.
[2] Doddridge, Macknight, &c. on Matt. xii. 40.
[3] Newton on Daniel, p. 16. edit. 1733.

familiar to the carnal expectations of the Jews, a proper degree of respect for the old system was preserved, at the same time that matters were gradually ripening for the introduction of the new: and the shadow of good things held forth obscurely in the law, prepared them to look forward to that happier day, when the very image itself should be presented in full splendour, and distinctly defined by the Gospel." [1]

III. *Apparent contradictions between prophecies and their accomplishment " may be occasioned by a prediction relating only to one part of a complex character or event, and on that account seeming to be inconsistent with other parts of it; and the appearance will be removed by taking in such predictions as relate to these other parts, and considering them all in connection."* [2]

Such seeming differences occur in the predictions relative to the exaltation and glory of the Messiah, compared with the prophecies concerning his previous sufferings. On this subject the reader may compare pp. 468—475 of the present volume. In Vol I. pp. 552—557 we have given a table of the chief predictions relative to the Messiah.

IV. *Seeming differences in the interpretation of prophecies also proceed partly from the difficulty of fixing the precise time of their fulfilment, and partly from the variety of opinions adopted by expositors; who, being dissatisfied with the views taken by their predecessors, are each solicitous to bring forward some new interpretation of his own.*

These differences, however, are no more an objection against prophecy, than they are against the truth of all history: and we may with equal propriety conclude that things never came to pass, because historians differ about the time when they were done, as that they were never predicted, because learned men vary in their modes of explaining the accomplishment of such predictions. Expositors may differ in the niceties of the chronological part, but in general circumstances they are agreed, hence, whoever will consult them may be greatly confirmed in the truth of the prophecies, upon this very consideration — that there is less difference in the explanation of the principal prophecies than there is in the comments upon most antient profane histories, and that those who differ in other matters, must have the greater evidence for that in which they agree. Although there may be a difficulty in calculating the precise time when some predictions were fulfilled, because it is disputed when the *computation* is to begin, or how some other circumstance is to be understood, yet all interpreters and expositors are agreed, concerning these very prophecies, that they *are* fulfilled. For instance, in Gen. xlix. 10. it is certain that the sceptre has departed from Judah, whether that prophecy is to be understood of the tribe of Judah, or of the Jewish nation who were denominated from that tribe. Although the later Jewish writers deny its application to the times of the Messiah, yet the elder writers *invariably* refer it to him; and it is certain that the city and sanctuary are destroyed, and that the sacrifice and oblation are entirely done away, though interpreters do not agree about the precise time and manner of the accomplishment of *every* particular. In a similar manner, the prophecy of Daniel respecting the *seventy weeks* is equally plain, and its accomplishment in the destruction of Jerusalem is certain; notwithstanding the differences of opinion in assigning the precise epocha of time. Plain matter of fact shows that these memorable predictions are fulfilled; and the only difference is concerning a single circumstance. To doubt, therefore, (as some of our modern self-styled philosophers do) of the fulfilment of prophecies, merely because we do not certainly know the exact time when each particular was accomplished, though we certainly know that they must have long since been fulfilled, is as unreasonable, as if a man should question the truth of history on account of the uncertainties which are to be found in chronology. The existence of Homer is not denied because it is uncertain when he lived; nor is the reality of the Trojan war the less certain because the time of the capture of Troy has been variously determined. History, it has been well remarked, relates what has happened, and prophecy foretells what shall come to pass; and an uncertainty in point of time no more affects the one than the other.

---

[1] Bishop Hallifax's Sermons on the Prophecies, Serm. 1.
[2] Gerard's Institutes, p. 435.

We may be uncertain of the time foretold by the prophet, and as uncertain of the time mentioned by the historian; but when all other circumstances agree, there is no reason why our uncertainty, as to the single circumstance of time, should be alleged against the credibility of either of them.[1]

V. *Some of the prophetic declarations are not predictions concerning things future, but simply commands relative to things which were to be performed, or they are conditional promises and threatenings, not absolute predictions; so that, if it subsequently appear that these were not executed, such non-performance cannot create any difficulty or repugnancy between the supposed prophecy and its fulfilment.*

We may illustrate this remark by reference to the fast observed by the Jews on the destruction of Jerusalem by Nebuchadnezzar: these fasts the prophet Zechariah (viii. 19.) in the name of Jehovah declares, are to be abolished, and converted into a joyous festival; but notwithstanding this declaration, we know that they continued afterwards to be observed. Another instance may be seen in 2 Kings viii. 10. Elisha's answer to Hazael; to which we may add the *seeming* assertion, that the last day was near, in Rom. xiii 11, 12 1 Cor. x. 11. 1 Thess iv. 15. Heb. ix. 26. James v 7, 8. 2 Pet iii. 12, 13. and 1 John ii. 18

VI. *Some of the prophetic promises appear to have been made to individuals, which, however, were not fulfilled in them.*

But between such prophecies and their fulfilment there is no real discordance: because they were accomplished in the posterity of the person to whom the promise was made. Thus, in Isaac's prophetic blessing of Jacob, it was announced (Gen xxvii. 29.) that he should be lord over his brethren. Now we know from the Sacred Writings that this never took effect in the person of Jacob; but it was fully verified in his posterity.

SECTION IV.

APPARENT CONTRADICTIONS IN DOCTRINE.

THESE arise from various causes; as contradictions from a mode of speaking which, to our apprehensions, is not sufficiently clear, — from the same term being used in different senses in different texts, — from the same word being used in apparently contradictory senses, — from the different designs of the sacred writers, — from the different ages in which the various sacred writers lived, and from the different degrees of their knowledge respecting the coming of the Messiah, and the religion to be instituted by him.

§ 1. *Seeming Contradictions from a mode of speaking which, to our apprehensions, is not sufficiently clear.*

It has been the practice of some writers to assert that the apostles, Saint Paul in particular, have argued both illogically and inconclusively; this assertion, however, falls to the ground of itself, when we consider the violent dislocations, to which writers of the school alluded to have resorted, in order to disprove what is self-evident from the Bible — the divinity and atonement of the Messiah. At the same time it is not to be concealed, that apparent contradictions do sometimes arise from a mode of speaking *which*, to OUR *apprehen-*

---

[1] Jenkin on the Reasonableness of the Christian Religion, vol. ii. pp. 178, 179.

sions, *does not seem sufficiently clear*. For instance, salvation is in one passage ascribed to *grace through faith*, which we are assured *is not of ourselves*, but is *the gift of God, — not of works, lest any man should boast* (Eph. ii. 8—10.); and in another Abraham is said to be *justified by faith without works* (Rom. iv. 2—6.); while in a third passage he is said to have been *justified by works*. (James ii. 21.) The apparent difference in these points of doctrine is occasioned by the fruits and effects being put for the cause. A little attention to the argument of the Apostle removes all difficulty. Saint Paul's object in the Epistle to the Romans was, to show, in opposition to the objections of the Jews, that how much soever Abraham excelled other men in righteousness during the course of his life, he had no cause for glorying before God; who justified, accepted, and covenanted with him, not for obedience, but for faith in the divine promise. Abraham believed God's word, and God accepted his faith, dealt with him as righteous, and became his God; in like manner as he now conducts himself towards all who truly repent, and unfeignedly believe his Gospel. Saint James, on the contrary, having encouraged the Christian converts to bear with patience the trials they should meet with, and improve them to the purposes of religion, presses upon them meekness and gentleness towards each other, as the *test of their sincerity;* and shows that *faith without love* is of no avail. Thus the doctrine asserted by each apostle is proved to be consistent, and the seeming repugnancy disappears. For the removal of difficulties arising from expressions not appearing sufficiently clear, the following observations will be found useful.

I. *A passage which is ambiguous, or which contains any unusual expression, must be interpreted agreeably to what is revealed more clearly and accurately in other parts of the Scriptures.*

Numerous instances might be adduced in illustration of this remark, in which bodily parts and passions are ascribed to God; which unusual modes of expression are to be explained in conformity with such other passages as remove the appearance of contradiction. Another example we have in Luke xiv. 13, 14. *When thou makest a feast, call the poor, the maimed, the lame, the blind, and thou shalt be blessed; for they cannot recompense thee, for thou shalt be recompensed at the resurrection of the just*. From this passage, some have inferred that the resurrection of the just *only* is intended, and, consequently, that the wicked shall certainly perish. There is, it is true, something unusual in this expression; but the doctrine of the resurrection of all mankind from the dead, which is so explicitly revealed in other parts of Scripture, being laid down and acknowledged, we readily perceive that our Saviour was speaking, in the passage under consideration, of acts of kindness done purely for the love of God, and on the recompense which He would bestow on them. But of the universal resurrection no notice is taken, nor is it denied that the wicked will receive *their* reward.

II. *A passage, in which a doctrine is slightly treated, must be explained by one where the subject is more largely discussed; and one single passage is not to be explained in contradiction to many others, but consistently with them.*

For instance, Jesus Christ in one place says, that he judges *no man*: in another, that he *will judge all men*: in one passage, that he is *not* come to judge the world; in another, that he *is* come for judgment. These seeming inconsistencies occur in the Gospel of Saint John, it becomes necessary, therefore, to find out some other passage that will reconcile them. Thus, in John xii. 47 he says, *I came not to judge the world;* and in ch. ix 39 he says, *For judgment I am come into this world.* In the latter passage he adds the cause of his thus coming,—namely, that they whose blindness proceeded from mere ignorance should be taught to see. while they who saw only through pride and prejudice should be left in their wilful blindness. Hence it appears, that our Lord was not speaking of the last judgment, from which we call God the judge of the living and of the dead, but that the tenor of his discourse was, to enable his hearers themselves to determine whether they were ignorant or not; for in the same chapter (verse 16) it is said that Jesus spoke these words to the Pharisees, who would not perceive their own ignorance, nor judge themselves. In the other passage (John xii. 47.) we read, *I came not to judge* (rather to *condemn*) the world, but to save the world,—not to make its inhabitants wretched, but to make them happy for time and for eternity, if they will be so wise as to listen to the proposals which I offer. Here the word *save* is plainly opposed to *condemn*: and that this is the proper meaning of the passage is evident from comparing chapter iii. verses 15—19.

The latter part of this rule the following passage will exemplify. In Gen xvii. 10—14 the observance of circumcision is commanded, in Acts xv the observance of that rite is affirmed not to be necessary. These propositions are apparently contradictory, Jesus Christ himself has determined them, Matt xi 13 *All the prophets, and the law, until John, prophesied*: intimating, as the context implies, that the observances of the law would thereafter cease.

III. *Between a general assertion in one text, and a restriction of it, or an exception to it, in another text, there is an appearance of contradiction which is sometimes removed by explaining the former with the proper limitations.*[1]

Several general expressions, in all languages, not only admit of, but also require a limitation; without which the true sense and meaning of many passages will not be understood. And, as the eastern nations indulged themselves most freely in the use of strong and figurative expressions, the Scriptures require more limitations, perhaps, than any other book.: as it respects the New Testament, St Paul mentions principles on which we may build our limitations : *I speak after the manner of men* (Rom. vi. 19) " It is manifest that he is excepted." (1 Cor xv. 27.)

Thus, in Mark x. 11, 12 and in Luke xvi. 18 divorce is absolutely forbidden. but in Matt v. 32 and xix. 9. it is allowed for adultery only. Yet in 1 Cor. vii 15 it seems to be allowed, though the Apostle does not authorise a second marriage

The precept, *Except we become as little children*, we shall *not enter into the kingdom of heaven* (Matt. xviii 3), cannot mean that we are not to speak distinctly, or to walk steadily : but obviously refers to the docility, and freedom from ambition and worldly thoughts, which characterise children.

The observations offered in pp. 415, 416, 417. *supra*, on the figures of speech, termed synechdoche, and hyperbole, may be applied in illustration of the preceding remark.

---

§ 2. *Apparent Contradictions from the same Terms being used in different and even contradictory Senses*

I. *Sometimes an apparent contradiction, in point of doctrine, arises from the same words being used in different senses in different texts.*

In this case the seeming repugnancy is to be removed by restricting the term properly in each text.

Thus, in some passages of the New Testament, we read that the kingdom of Christ is *eternal:* but in 1 Cor xv 24 it is said to have an *end:* in the latter passage, the *kingdom of Christ* means his mediatorial kingdom, which includes all the displays of his grace in saving sinners, and all his spiritual influence in governing the church visible on earth. By the eternal kingdom of Christ is intended the future state of eternal blessedness, which is so beautifully described as *an inheritance, incorruptible, undefiled, and that fadeth not away, reserved in heaven*, &c. (1 Pet. i. 4, 5)

In like manner, *It is appointed unto men once to die* (Heb. ix. 27.), that is, a temporal death : yet if any man keep Christ's sayings he *shall never see death* (John viii. 51.) that is, eternal death. *Hatred* of others is very sinful and odious (Tit iii. 3.),

---

[1] Gerard's Institutes, p. 436.

VII. Sect. IV. § 3.] *Of Scripture, alleged to be Contradictory.*   517

and yet to *hate* our nearest relations, that is, to love them *less* than we love Christ is a duty. (Luke xiv. 26. compared with Matt. x 37.) John the Baptist was *not* Elias (John i 21.), that is, not the prophet who lived under Ahab, but he was *the Elias* predicted by Malachi (Mal iv. 5, 6), that is, one in the spirit and power of the antient Elijah (Matt xi 11, 12. 14 Mark ix. 11—13. Luke i. 17)

So we cannot stand before God in the righteousness of our own *persons* (Psal. cxliii 2), but we may appeal to him for the righteousness of our *cause*, in matters of difference between ourselves and others (Psal xviii 20. xxxv. 27. Heb.)

II *Apparent contradictions, in points of doctrine, sometimes arise from the same word being used not only in different but also in contradictory senses.*

Thus in Joshua, xxiii. 5. the same Hebrew verb ירש (YARASH), which usually signifies to inherit or possess, also means to dispossess or disinherit. *He shall expel them* (from their inheritance) *from before you, and ye shall possess their land,* succeed to their inheritance In like manner, the word *sin* also denotes a *sin-offering* in Gen. iv. 7   2 Cor v 21. and in many other passages of Scripture. The Hebrew verb ברך (BARAK), to *bless*, has been supposed also to mean *curse;* and, contrary to the authority of antient versions, the lexicons (as the late eminently learned Mr. Parkhurst has proved) have given it the sense of cursing in the six following passages, 1 Kings xxi. 10. 13. Job i 5 11. and especially Job ii. 5. 9. The rendering of which last passage, he observes, should be thus :

Then said his wife unto him,
Dost thou yet retain thine integrity,
Blessing the Aleim (*God*) and dying, *or even unto death ?* ¹

The Greek language presents numerous similar examples of the same words having different senses. Thus Ειδωλον, in its primitive acceptation, bears a good sense, and simply means any representation or likeness of a thing , but it also most frequently denotes, in the New Testament, an image to which religious worship is given, whether it be intended of the *true* God, as in Acts vii 41. or of a *false* deity, as in Acts xv 20 1 Cor xii 2. and Rev. ix 20   So Περιεργος, which simply means *curious*, and its derivative περιεργαζομαι, are used in a worse sense, and denote impertinent curiosity in other persons' affairs, as in 1 Tim v. 13 and 2 Thess. iii. 11. So πλεονεκτειν, which primarily signifies to have more than another, also means to have more than one ought to possess, *to defraud and circumvent.* See 2 Cor. vii 2. xii 17, 18. and 1 Thess iv 6 (which last text denotes to defraud and injure by adultery, as numerous commentators, antient and modern, have already observed.) And μεθυειν, which (like the Hebrew verb שבר, Gen xliii 34.²) in its good sense denotes merely to *drink freely and to cheerfulness,* but not to intoxication (as in John ii. 10), is often taken in an ill sense, and means to be *drunken* Compare Matt. xxiv. 49. Acts ii 15 and 1 Thess v. 7. with Rev xvii 2. 6 ³

---

§ 3. *Apparent Contradictions, in Points of Doctrine, arising from the different Designs of the Sacred Writers.*

A kind of repugnancy sometimes arises from the different designs which the sacred writers had in view ; and this can only be removed by interpreting each passage agreeably to the writer's design.

---

¹ Parkhurst's Hebrew Lexicon, p 84 5th edition   Dr. Mason Good, in his accurate and elegant version of the book of Job, has adopted Mr. P.'s rendering, and confirmed its propriety by various examples; see particularly his notes, pp 5—9.

² They drank and were *merry* (literally *drank largely*) with him.

³ The Latin language presents us with many examples of the same words which have different meanings   It will suffice to specify two or three   *Sacer*, it is well known, signifies not only that which is holy, but also that which is most cursed and detestable. Thus, we have in Virgil (Æn. iii 57.) the well known words *auri sacra fames*   In our old English common law writers, *villanus* (villain) denotes a rustic of servile condition, but the English word is now exclusively a term of infamy.   So, *missa*, the mass, was at first an innocent word, signifying merely the service of the church, but has long since degenerated into a widely different meaning, and is given exclusively to the worship of the church of Rome.

It is obvious that the same person may express himself in various ways concerning one and the same thing, and in this case regard must be had to his intention. In Saint Paul's Epistles, for instance, we find the Apostle frequently arguing, but more or less severely, with those who rigorously urged a compliance with the Mosaic rites and ceremonies; in some passages he expresses himself more gently towards his opponents, in others, with greater severity, calling the opinions thus asserted *doctrines of devils*, and *profane and old wives' fables* (1 Tim. iv 1. 7.) To understand those passages aright, then, it is necessary that we distinguish the three fold design of the Apostle, according to the three different classes of advocates for the observance of the Mosaic ritual. 1. Against those who maintained the rites prescribed by Moses from *weakness of mind*, and could not persuade themselves that these ought to be abandoned, the Apostle argues with great lenity; compare Rom. xiv. throughout. 2. There were others, however, who, while they contended for and urged the external observance of the Mosaic law, expressed the utmost *contempt for the Christian religion*, which they either affirmed not to be true, or to be insufficient unless the observance of the law of Moses were superadded. Against this class of opponents, Saint Paul argues with much more severity, denying altogether the necessity of such observance; compare the Epistle to the Galatians. 3. There was another class of persons, who, to the external observance of the Mosaic ritual, joined certain philosophical notions borrowed from the Alexandrian school of philosophers, and which were received among the Therapeutæ. According to these, the highest wisdom consisted in a state of celibacy, mortification, and abstinence from animal food; against these crude opinions the Apostle argues vehemently, terming them profane and old wives' fables, and diabolical, that is the most pestilent doctrines. The perusal of Philo's treatise on the Therapeutæ will show what pretensions that sect made to wisdom and piety, which consisted in mortification and abstinence, and with what sovereign contempt they regarded all other persons. To this class of St. Paul's antagonists are to be referred 1 Tim. iv. throughout, and also Col. ii. verse 8. to the end.

On the best mode of ascertaining the design of any book or passage in the Sacred Writings, see pp 327—330. *supra*.

---

§ 4. *Apparent Contradictions, arising from the different Ages in which the Sacred Writers lived, and the different Degrees of Knowledge which they possessed.*

I. There is another class of doctrinal points, in which a species of repugnancy is produced by the *different ages in which the sacred writers lived*.

All expositors of the Scriptures are agreed in the summary of religious truths revealed in them, and that, from the book of Genesis to the Revelation of Saint John, this doctrine is constantly and unanimously delivered, viz. that there is one infinitely wise gracious, just, and eternal God; and that our salvation is of God through the atonement of the Messiah, &c. &c. But this doctrine is variously expressed, according as the ages, in which the writers lived, were more or less remote from the time when the Son of God was manifested in the flesh. Further, in the Old Testament, there are many very severe precepts relative to revenging of injuries on enemies, as well as many imprecations against the toes of David: no such precepts are to be found in the New Testament. Again, the law of revenge and retaliation, in the Mosaic system, is extremely severe, requiring eye for eye, hand for hand, tooth for tooth, &c. Widely different from this is the spirit of the Christian doctrine.

II. An apparent contradiction likewise is caused by the *different degrees of knowledge possessed by the sacred writers* relative to the happiness to be procured for man by Jesus Christ.

In the Old Testament this happiness is almost constantly described as being *external*: but in the New Testament all external considerations are dismissed, and it is affirmed to be *spiritual* or *internal*. Hence also it happens, that although the same worship of the same Jehovah is treated of in the books of the Old and New Testament, external worship is chiefly, though not exclusively, insisted upon in the former, but internal in the latter; in the Old Testament it is the *spirit of bondage*, but in the New it is the *spirit of adoption* In this gradual revelation of the divine will we see the wisdom and goodness of God; who graciously proportioned it to the capacities of men, and the disposition of their minds, to receive those intimations which he was pleased to communicate And, as the sacred writers accommodated themselves to the imperfect or more improved degrees of knowledge which existed at the times they wrote, so it appears that they adapted their precepts to the religious, civil, and domestic or private customs of their countrymen Hence it happens, that though religion in itself was always one and the same thing, yet the *manner* in which it was made known acquired some tinge,—

1. *From religious customs:* for as all the more antient people were accustomed to worship their own gods, agreeably to their own peculiar rites, so the Jews after their manner worshipped the only true God

2. *Civil customs* also imparted some degree of peculiarity to religion. For while one nation was separated from intercourse with others by its own customs, many things were spoken of God, as a national deity, more peculiarly appropriated to that nation: but, if that separation be removed, Jehovah is described as the common parent of all mankind.

3 Lastly, in the *domestic or private institutes* contained in the Mosaic law, there are many things derived from the manners and customs of their forefathers; this fact has been shown by the late Professor Michaelis, in his elaborate "Commentaries on the Law of Moses." In like manner the apostles accommodated themselves to the peculiar customs that obtained in different countries in their own age. How differently do they express themselves towards Jews and Heathens! Not only do they attend to religious, civil, and domestic or private manners and customs, but, in proportion as these underwent gradual changes, they explain many things more copiously, as well as more clearly, rejecting the veil of types, and despising those ceremonies in which the Jewish nation formerly delighted. An attentive consideration of these circumstances will contribute to clear up many apparent contradictions, as well as to solve very many of the objections brought by infidels against the Sacred Writings Let times and seasons be accurately distinguished, and perfect harmony will be found to subsist in the different books of Scripture.

SECTION V.

SEEMING CONTRADICTIONS TO MORALITY.

NOTWITHSTANDING it is generally admitted that the Holy Scriptures breathe a spirit of the purest and most diffusively benevolent morality; yet there are some passages which have been represented as giving countenance to immorality and cruelty. But these, when duly examined, will be found perfectly in unison with the purest principles of morality. The wide difference which subsists between antient and modern manners, *if fairly considered*, would alone be a sufficient reply to the indecencies, which are asserted to exist in the Bible.

Further, the characters and conduct of men, whom we find in all other respects commended in the Scriptures, are in some respects faulty; but these are, in such instances, by no means proposed for our imitation, and, consequently, give no sanction whatever to immorality: for several of these faults are either expressly condemned, or are briefly related or mentioned as matter of fact, without any intimation that they are either to be commended or imitated. The sacred writers, however, are only answerable for facts, not for the morality of actions. It is true that the Jewish history is stained with blood and cruelty; but so is the history of all other nations, (whose chroniclers, annalists, or other historians are not censured for their bare narration of the crimes of the individuals or nations,) and without the additional circumstance of being relieved by such histories of true piety and virtue as abound in the Scriptures. But it is worthy of remark, that the moral character of the Jewish nation was by no means so *uniformly* bad as the modern antagonists of divine revelation pretend. In some ages, their morals were much purer, and their piety more fervent, than at others. Such was the generation which first entered Canaan with Joshua, and such also the generations that lived during the reigns of their most pious monarchs. It is, moreover, to be considered, that the *mere* narration of any action, such as we find in the Old and New Testaments, implies neither the approbation nor the censure of it, but only declares that such a thing was done, and in such a manner; and the not concealing of these shows the simplicity and impartiality of the sacred writers, who spare no person whomsoever, not even when they themselves are concerned,—though the thing related should redound to their disgrace; — as in the case of Noah's drunkenness (Gen. ix. 21.), Jacob's deceiving of Isaac (Gen. xxvii.[1]) Peter's denial of Christ (Matt. xxvi. 69—75. and the parallel passages of the other evangelists): Paul's dispute with Peter (Gal. ii. 11—14.); and Paul's excuse of himself. (Acts xxiii. 5.)

The following are the principal passages which the recent advocates of

---

[1] From this circumstance God has been represented by infidels, as distinguishing his favourite Jacob, by a system of *fraud and lies* but the following considerations, by the late Bishop Horne, may assist us to form a right judgment of this matter.

"1st. The proposition of deceiving Isaac originated not with Jacob, but with Rebecca. Jacob remonstrated against it, as likely to bring a curse upon him, rather than a blessing, nor would consent to perform his part, till she engaged to take all the blame on herself— On me be thy curse, my son; only obey my voice.'

2dly. From this speech, and from the earnestness and solicitude discovered by Rebecca, it may not unfairly be presumed, that she had some special reason for what she did, that Isaac was about to take a wrong step in a concern of great moment, which ought to be prevented, and could be prevented by no other means.

3dly The rectitude of Rebecca's judgment seems evidently to have been recognised and allowed by Isaac, at the conclusion of the matter. For though he had blessed Jacob, intending to bless Esau, yet, as if recollecting himself, he confirmed and ratified that blessing in the strongest terms 'Yea, and he shall be blessed.' Still farther — at sending him away, he again repeated the benediction, in the most solemn and affecting manner; 'God give thee the blessing of Abraham!' It is hard to assign any other reason, why, if so disposed, upon discovering the fraud, he might not have reversed the proceeding. Nay, by the kind meeting of the brothers afterwards, one should be inclined to suppose, that Esau himself acquiesced at length in the propriety of what had been done.

4thly. If such were the case, Isaac was only deceived into what was right, and what himself acknowledged to be so in the conclusion. The deception was like those often practised by physicians for the benefit of their patients, and casuists must decide upon it in the same manner. The offence of Jacob is certainly alleviated, if not entirely taken off, by the circumstance of Rebecca pledging herself to bear the blame; as the conduct of Rebecca seems justified by that of Isaac ratifying and confirming to Jacob the blessing originally intended for Esau. Upon the whole, if there were any offence, it was one that might be forgiven, and if God, notwithstanding, continued to bless Jacob, he did forgive it, and had reasons for so doing." Bp. Horne's Works, vol. vi. pp. 477, 478.

infidelity have charged with being contradictions to morality; with how little pretext, the reader will be enabled to judge, by the candid examination and consideration of the remainder of this section.

1. *God's command to Abraham, to sacrifice Isaac,* (Gen. xxii.) *has been represented as a command to commit murder in its most horrid form, and, consequently, as inconsistent with the holiness of God to give.*

But this command may be satisfactorily vindicated, either by regarding it as a symbolical action [1], or (without this consideration) by resolving it into the divine sovereignty over the lives of his creatures. For, the Supreme Lord and Giver of Life has a right to take it away, and to command it to be taken away, whenever and in whatsoever manner he pleases. To offer a human victim to him, without his express warrant, would be to commit *murder*; but to do so by his command, would be an act of obedience. As the Almighty has a right to command, so his perfections lead us to infer, that he will command nothing but what is worthy of himself. The design of God, however, was to *prove* Abraham, in order that his faith, love, and obedience might be manifest, and not, in fact, that he should offer up Isaac.

2. *Jacob's vow* (Gen. xxviii. 20—22) *is asserted to be quite conditional, and as implying that if his God would clothe and feed him, he would serve him.*

This representation is not more unjust, than the manner in which it is stated is indecent. In order that this matter may be regarded in its proper light, it must be considered, that, immediately before the account which is given us of Jacob's vow, we are informed of a vision which he had when setting out on his journey to Padan-Aram, when God renewed to him the promises made to Abraham concerning the giving of the land of Canaan to his posterity, and that in his seed all nations of the earth should be blessed: at the same time assuring him, that he would be with him in all places whither he should go, and would bring him again into that land (12—15). In consequence of this vision Jacob made his vow the next morning, the design of which was, to express the sense he had of the divine goodness, and his confidence in God's gracious protection; and to declare his solemn resolution that if God would be with him and keep him in his way, and would give him *bread to eat* and *raiment to put on*, (which shows the moderation of his desires,) so that he should come again to his father's house in peace, he would after his return make an open and public acknowledgment of his gratitude and devotion to the Lord as his God; would set apart that place, where God had appeared to him, to his worship; and would devote to His service the tenth of all the substance which God should give him. Now such a conduct as this, instead of being impiously interested and craving (as some opposers of revelation have asserted), will appear to every one who judges candidly and impartially a great argument of the simplicity and goodness of Jacob's heart, and of a pious and well disposed mind: though undoubtedly it appears absurd to those who affirm — what however they cannot prove — that the Almighty does not concern himself with individuals of the human race.

3. *The objection, that God's commanding of the Israelites* (Exod. iii. 22. xii. 35.) *to borrow from the Egyptians what they never intended to restore, is not only an act of injustice, but favours theft,* is obviated by rendering the Hebrew verb שָׁאַל (SHAAL), *asked* or *demanded*, agreeably to its proper and literal meaning [2], which is given to it in all the antient versions, as well as in every modern translation, *our own excepted*.

4. *The hardening of Pharaoh's heart* (Exod. iv. 21. ix. 16.) *has been a fruitful source of malignant cavil with the adversaries of the Bible; some of whom have not hesitated to affirm that this single chapter is sufficient to destroy the authenticity of the entire Scriptures, while others, more decently and speciously, assert that a just God could not punish the Egyptian monarch for a hardness of heart of which he himself was evidently the cause.* This is the objection in all its force. Let us now see how little foundation there is for it.

---

[1] This is Bp Warburton's mode of solving the difficulty.
[2] It is the very word used in Psal. ii. 8. שְׁאַל (SHAAL). *Ask of me, and I will give thee the heathen for thine inheritance, and the uttermost parts of the earth for thy possession.*

" When we meet with an assertion apparently contrary to all the truth and equity in the world, it is but common justice to any writer, human or divine, to suppose, that we mistake his meaning, and that the expression employed to convey it is capable of an interpretation different from that which may at first present itself. We cannot, for a moment, imagine, that God secretly influences a man's will, or suggests any wicked stubborn resolution to his mind, and then punishes him for it We are, therefore, to consider, by what other means, not incompatible with his nature and attributes, he may be said, in a certain sense, and without impropriety, to harden a man's heart. There are many ways by which we may conceive this effect to be wrought, without running into the absurdity and impiety above mentioned The heart may be hardened by those very respites, miracles, and mercies, intended to soften it ; for if they do not soften it they will harden it — God is sometimes said to do that which he permits to be done by others, in the way of judgment and punishment: as when his people rejected his own righteous laws, he is said to have ' given them' the idolatrous ones of their heathen neighbours, ' statutes that were not good ' — The heart may be hardened by his withdrawing that grace it has long resisted ; men may be given up to a reprobate mind, as they *would* not see when they possessed the faculty of sight, the use of that faculty may be taken from them, and they may be abandoned to blindness But all this is judicial, and supposes previous voluntary wickedness, which it is designed to punish " [1]

Further, no person who *candidly* peruses the history of the transactions with Pharaoh, can deny that what the Almighty did to Pharaoh and the Egyptians had a tendency to soften rather than to harden his heart ; especially as it was not until after he had seen the miracles, and after the plagues had ceased, that he hardened himself and would not suffer the Israelites to depart. The threatened plagues were suspended on a condition with which he refused to comply, and then only were they inflicted. It is, moreover, well known that Hebrew verbs in the Hiphil conjugation signify to *permit* or to *suffer* to be done, as well as to *cause* to be done : hence nothing more is meant, than to leave a man to the bent and tendency of his own disposition. Thus Pharaoh was left, and he is said to have made his own heart stubborn against God HE *sinned yet more and hardened* HIS *heart* The proper rendering, therefore, of Exod. IV 21 is — *I will permit his heart to be so hardened that he will not let the people go* So in Exod IV 12 it ought to be translated, *Yet the* LORD *suffered the heart of Pharaoh to be so hardened that he hearkened not to them* And a more literal rendering of Exod IX 15, 16 would remove the discrepancy which seems at present to exist in our common version, which runs thus. — *For now I will stretch out my hand and smite thee with pestilence ; and thou shalt be cut off from the earth And in very deed for this cause have I raised thee up, for to show in thee my power, and that my name may be declared throughout all the earth* In the original Hebrew, the verbs are in the *past* tense and not in the *future*, as our authorised version improperly expresses them, by which means an apparent contradiction is produced · for neither Pharaoh nor his people were *smitten with pestilence*, nor was he by any kind of mortality *cut off from the earth* The first-born, it is true, were slain by a destroying angel, and Pharaoh himself was drowned in the Red Sea but there is no reference whatever to these judgments in the two verses in question. If the words be translated as they ought, in the subjunctive mood, or in the past instead of the *future*, this seeming contradiction to facts, as well as all ambiguity, will be avoided : For if now I HAD STRETCHED OUT שלחתי (SHALACHTI *had sent forth*) *my hand, and had smitten thee and thy people with the pestilence, thou* SHOULDEST HAVE BEEN *cut off from the earth But truly on this very account* have I caused thee to SUBSIST, *that I might cause thee to see my power and that my* NAME *might be declared throughout all the earth, or in all this land.* [2]

---

[1] Bp. Horne's Letters on Infidelity, Lett. XIV (Works, vol VI p. 481.)
[2] Ainsworth, Houbigant, Dathe, Schott and Winzer on Exod. IX. 15, 16 It is worthy of remark that the Septuagint Greek version of the Pentateuch (which confessedly is the best executed part of all that version), renders these two verses subjunctively, and is followed in this respect by Dr Boothroyd, who thus translates them — *Yea now* COULD *I stretch out my hand and smite thee and thy people with pestilence : so that thou* SHOULDEST *be cut off from the earth. And in very deed for this purpose have I preserved thee,* (Sept. ενεκεν τουτου διετηρηθης, *On this account thou hast been preserved,*) *that I may show to thee my power, and that my name* MAY *be declared through all the earth.* The case of Pharaoh is fully considered by Mr. Twopenny in his " Dissertations on some Parts of the Old and New Testaments," &c Diss. IV. pp. 38—54., and in Dr. Graves's Discourses on Calvinistic Predestination, pp. 295—304.

Thus God gave this impious king to know that it was in consequence of his especial providence, that both he and his people had not been already destroyed by means of the *past* plagues; but that God had preserved him for this very purpose, that he might have a further opportunity of showing Pharaoh His power in the remaining plagues, and of manifesting that He, Jehovah, was the only true God, for the full conviction of the Hebrews and Egyptians.[1]

Lastly, our authorised translation of Exod. vii. 13 (*and he* [that is, God] *hardened Pharaoh's heart*) is incorrect. It ought to have been, AND THE HEART OF PHARAOH WAS HARDENED, as the original is rendered by all the antient versions, without exception, and by the most judicious modern translations. The same phrase is *correctly* translated in our authorised version, in Exod. vii 22. viii 19. and ix 7.

The objections, therefore, which the opponents of the Bible have raised against it from the passages we have been considering, are thus proved to be utterly destitute of foundation.

5. Again, *visiting the sins of the fathers upon their children* (Exod. xx. 5.) has been charged as *injustice*.

But this objection disappears, the moment we are convinced that the reward and punishment here intended, are confined to the outward circumstances of prosperity and distress in the *present* life; because if (as was the case) such a sanction were necessary in the particular system by which God thought fit to govern the Jewish people, it is evident, that any inequality as to individuals, would be certainly and easily remedied in a future life (as in the particular instances recorded in Numb. xvi 27—33. and Josh. vii 24, 25), so that each should receive his final reward exactly according to his true appearance in the sight of God, and "thus the Judge of all the earth do right." It is only when children copy and improve on the crimes of their wicked parents, that they draw down upon their heads redoubled vengeance: so that the innocent *never* suffer for the guilty, except in such temporal calamities as necessarily result from their parents' crimes. As, when the profligacy of one generation involves the next in poverty, or the like. On the contrary, so benevolent is the God of Israel, that the eminent piety of one man is sometimes rewarded with blessings on thousands of his descendants. This was the case with Abraham and his descendants. Yet this is the God whom deists represent as cruel and vindictive.[2]

6. The extirpation of the Canaanites by the Jews, according to the divine command, is urged as an act of the greatest cruelty and injustice; but this objection falls to the ground when it is considered —

FIRST, That the Canaanites were unquestionably a most depraved and idolatrous race; and to have suffered them to remain and coalesce with the Israelites, would have been to sanction idolatry by encouraging their union with idolatrous nations. It *must* be admitted that God has a right to punish wicked nations by the infliction of judgments, such as pestilence, or famine, or by employing the sword of enemies; because we see that he actually does so in the course of his Providence; and we cannot see what essential difference there is between this and his giving a command to the Israelites to destroy the wicked Canaanites; for it is a notorious fact, that these latter were an abominably wicked people. "It is needless to enter into any proof of the depraved state of their morals; they were a wicked people in the time of Abraham, and even then were devoted to destruction by God; but their iniquity was not then full," that is, they were not yet arrived to such a height of profligacy and impiety as required their destruction. In the time of Moses, they were idolaters; sacrificers of their own crying and smiling infants; devourers of human flesh; addicted to unnatural lusts; immersed in the filthiness of all manner of vice. Now, it will be impossible to prove, that it was a proceeding contrary to God's moral justice to exterminate so wicked a people. He made the Israelites the executors of his vengeance. and, in doing this, he gave such an evident and terrible proof of his abomination of vice, as could not fail to strike the surrounding nations with astonishment and terror, and to impress on the minds of the Israelites what they were

---

[1] Dr. A. Clarke on Exod ix 16.

[2] Dr. Graves's Lectures on the Pentateuch, vol ii pp 172—185. See also Michaelis's Commentaries on the Laws of Moses, vol i pp. 45—47. Age of Infidelity, in answer to the Age of Reason, p. 52.

to expect, if they followed the example of the nations whom he commanded them to cut off. ' *Ye shall not commit any of these abominations, that the land spue not you out also, as it spued out the nations which were before you.*' (Lev xviii 28) How strong and descriptive this language! the vices of the inhabitants were so abominable, that the very land was sick of them, and forced to vomit them forth, as the stomach disgorges a deadly poison." [1]

SECONDLY, After the time of God's forbearance was expired, they had still the alternative, either to flee elsewhere, as, in fact, many of them did, or to surrender themselves, renounce their idolatries, and serve the God of Israel in which case it appears that there was mercy for them. Compare Deut xx 10—17. That the utter destruction here mentioned was to take place only in cases of obstinacy and resistance, may be inferred both from the reason of the denunciation, and also from the several facts attending its execution

(1.) The *reason* why they were to be cut off, is stated (Deut xx. 18) to be *that they teach you not to do after all their abominations ;* which reason would not hold good in case of their repentance and turning from their idols to worship the God of Israel.

(2) The *facts*, from which we argue, are the following After the conquest of the country, we are told (Josh. xi. 19, 20) that *There was not a city that made peace with the children of Israel, save the Hivites the inhabitants of Gibeon ; all other they took in battle For it was of the Lord to harden their hearts, that they should meet Israel in battle, that he* (i e Israel) *might destroy them utterly, and that they might have no favour, but that he* (Israel or the Israelites) *might destroy them* [2] Now this passage certainly implies that the Canaanites might have had peace, if they had thought proper to accept the proposed terms They rejected the first offers of peace, and were punished by Jehovah refusing them any further opportunities. The case of the Gibeonites seems so confirm this [3] in as much as it is difficult to conceive that the oath and covenant, made to them under the circumstances of deception, should have been so valid and sacred, if the order for their extinction admitted of no limitation. The preservation of Rahab also (Josh ii 12 —14 vi. 22, 23.), and a family of Bethel (Judg i 25), with some other instances, (1 Kings ix. 20, 21, &c), incline strongly to this exposition ; nor does it want the sanction of very respectable names among the critics and commentators, Jewish and Christian [4]

In the THIRD PLACE, The destruction is not to be attributed to Israel *wholly,* even as instruments The Lord himself, partly by storms and tempests, partly by noxious insects, and partly by injecting terror into the minds of the inhabitants, perhaps expelled and destroyed more than the Israelites themselves; the wonderful, and we may add the miraculous power of God, co-operating with them (Compare Exod xxiii. 27, 28. Josh. x 11, &c) Doubtless God might have destroyed these nations by earthquake, fire, storm, or plague, and no man surely would have disputed his justice or authority ? Then why should men dispute his equity in destroying them by the sword of war ? Or, if we admit for a moment the existence of invisible spirits, he might have sent an angel to destroy them, and would it be un-

---

[1] Bp. Watson's Apology for the Bible, in reply to the Age of Reason, Letter I p. 9. (London edit. 1820, 12mo.) The late Dr Paley has some admirable observations on the same topic, in his *Sermons on several subjects*, Serm xxix pp 429—443 And Dr. Graves has treated it at great length, and with his wonted accuracy Lect. on Pentateuch, vol. ii. pp 4—64

[2] The twentieth verse may, more literally, be rendered — *For it was of Jehovah* (or the will of Jehovah) *that they should be so courageous as to meet Israel in battle that they might utterly destroy them , that they might show to them no favour, but destroy them as Jehovah commanded Moses.*

[3] It may be objected, if the Israelites were to proclaim peace, whence the need of such policy in the Gibeonites ? The answer is easy . though they were to spare their lives, they were not to enter into any treaty of alliance with them. Here was their object, — to preserve their liberties and their city, which was not permitted ; hence they were made slaves, i. e. domestics to attend the menial offices of the tabernacle.

[4] Maimonides, Samson Micori, Moses de Kotzri, and Ben Nachman, among the Jews , among the Christians, Junius, Cunæus, Grotius, Placette, Selden and Le Clerc. See Findlay's Vindication of the Sacred Books against Voltaire, pp. 131—136, and Twopenny's Dissertations, pp. 103 – 113.

worthy of an angel to be the minister of his displeasure? Why, then, are Joshua and the Israelites to be *abused* on the same ground?

LASTLY, The Almighty has, in fact, executed judgments on mankind far more severe than this. Though the inhabitants of Canaan are reckoned seven or eight nations, their whole country was much less than England, and what is this to the drowning of the world? a fact, attested by all antient histories, divine and human, and confirmed by innumerable monuments.

These considerations will sufficiently justify Joshua and the other Hebrew worthies, who engaged in this war in obedience to the divine command. and unless we admit them in a great degree, we know not how any war at all can be justified, however necessary. If many of the people engaged in it from baser motives, we are not required to answer for their conduct. There will always be bad characters in an army, and we do not reckon the Jews to be a nation of pure saints! But the fact is, that it nowhere appears (nor can it be proved), that the Israelites in general contracted ferocious habits by this exterminating war. Few nations, if any, ever engaged less frequently, or in fewer offensive wars than Israel; and their agricultural habits, together with other circumstances, operated against such wars of ambition and conquest. If any individuals, or even the nation in some instances, did gratify a ferocious spirit, they proportionately violated their own laws, which enjoined love to neighbours, strangers, and enemies. The most remote shadow of proof cannot be adduced that Moses carried on war, under the pretext of religion. He made no proselytes by the sword, and neither he nor any other person mentioned with approbation in Scripture, made war on any nation beyond the borders of the promised land because they were idolaters.

7. The severity of Moses in ordering the extermination of the Midianites, (Numb. xxxi.) *can only be justified by the command. This the history asserts; but that assertion* (it has been insisted) *is contradicted by the nature of the case, because it is abhorrent from the Deity to require the destruction of his creatures, and more especially to require them to destroy one another.*

This is the objection in all its strength; only in this instance there is supposed to be equal cruelty in sparing as in destroying, because, while all the males were destroyed (children as well as adults), the female children and virgins were all to be spared, as it has been said, for prostitution. For the latter assertion, however, there is no foundation either in fact or in probability. It only proves that the objectors find it necessary to *exaggerate,* in order to produce the desired effect upon their readers, for the books of Moses no where allow the Israelites to debauch their female slaves. His law prohibited an Israelite even from marrying a captive, without delays and previous formalities, and if he afterwards divorced her, he was bound to set her at liberty ' because he had humbled her'" (Deut. xxi. 10—14.) They were, then, simply allowed to retain these captives as slaves, educating them in their families, and employing them as domestics. The destruction of the other Midianitish women, who were either married or debauched, is accounted for, by recollecting that they had enticed the Israelites to sin. It is a fact too well known to require additional proof in this place, that in the early heathen nations, numbers of lewd women were consecrated to fornication and idolatry, vestiges of which are still to be found among the dancing girls of Egypt and of India. Such, probably, were many of these women, and such, therefore, was their punishment. As to the males, they were appointed to destruction, that the nation might be extirpated, which was impossible while any of the male issue were preserved.

8. It is asserted that some of the Levitical laws have a manifest tendency to corrupt and defile the imagination; and the regulations in Deut. xxii. 13—21 *have been particularly urged as an instance of this sort.*

With regard to these regulations, and others of a similar kind, we may remark that what they require might be needful in the then situation of the Israelites, and yet it is not necessary that *we* should now curiously or impertinently scrutinise them. The people of Israel were naturally disposed to be jealous of their wives,

---

[1] Age of Infidelity, pp. 26—31.

and to defame them without any just cause, that they might have an excuse for putting them away, which would tend to produce many public mischiefs and disorders In this case, therefore, it was a wise and merciful institution, to provide a remedy by such sort of injunctions, by which the innocent might be vindicated Such signs of trial might never fail in that climate, though they might in some others So far indeed was it from being unworthy of God to leave such things upon record, that it may heighten our admiration both of his great wisdom and benignity in his management of that people, who were so extremely perverse, and so addicted to the extremes of lust and jealousy. If, therefore, the perusal of the passage in question excite improper thoughts in any one, the fault is in them, and not in the Scripture. Scarcely any thing can be mentioned, of which a bad use may not be made: things, the most sacred and divine may in this respect be strangely abused. Nor is it a better argument that the Scriptures were not written by inspiration of God, that there are some parts and passages of it, which may be abused by persons who are lasciviously disposed, than it is that the sun was not created by the Almighty, because its light *may* be used by wicked men as an auxiliary in perpetuating the crimes which they have meditated.

9. *The Mosaic law* (Deut. xiii.) *which punished idolatry with death, has been represented as cruel and unjust, and giving countenance to persecution for religious opinions.*

But it is manifest to any one, who will peruse the chapter in question with attention, that this law commanded only such Israelites to be put to death, as apostatised to idolatry and still continued members of their own community. And as their government was a *theocracy*, (in other words, God was the temporal king of Israel, and their kings were only his viceroys,) idolatry was, strictly, the political crime of *high treason*, which in every state is justly punishable with death It is further to be observed, that the Israelites were never commissioned to make war upon their neighbours, or exercise any violence towards any of them, in order to *compel* them to worship the God of Israel, nor to force them to it even after they were conquered (Deut xx. 10); nor were they empowered thus forcibly to attempt to recover any *native Israelite*, who should revolt to idolatry, and go to settle in a heathen country.

10 *The law in* Deut. xxi. 18—21. *has been stigmatised as being both inhuman and brutal, but with as little justice as any other part of the Mosaic institutes.*

The passage in question is as follows: — *If a man have a stubborn and rebellious son, which will not obey the voice of his father, nor the voice of his mother, and that when they have chastened him, will not hearken unto them, then shall his father and his mother lay hold on him, and bring him out unto the elders of his city and unto the gate of his place · and they shall say unto the elders of his city, This our son is stubborn and rebellious, he will not obey our voice; he is a glutton and a drunkard. And all the men of the city shall stone him with stones, that he die.* On this clause, we are to take notice, in the *first* place, of the character of the culprit, it is a *son*, — not a daughter; — a *stubborn* and *rebellious* son, a *glutton* and a *drunkard;* — in a word, a most profligate and abandoned character *Secondly*, his parents must reprove and correct him, *repeatedly*, and until there is *no* hope of amendment. *Thirdly*, the parents were the *only allowed prosecutors;* and it was required that they should *both* concur in bringing him to the magistrate, the power of life and death not being intrusted to the parents, as it afterwards was among the Greeks and Romans. *Lastly*, the magistrates were to investigate the case, which must be *fully proved*, so as to induce them to condemn the criminal, and order him to be put to death. Natural affection would almost always prevent the prosecution : the required proof would secure all, but the most atrociously criminal, from the hasty rage, or the deliberate malice of those few parents, who were capable of such desperate wickedness, as combining to murder their own children. We do not read of any instance, in the whole Jewish history, of this law having been carried into execution. If however, such an extraordinary event at any time occurred, it could not fail to excite general notice, and to produce a deep and lasting impression on the minds of both parents and children So that the solemn execution of one incorrigible criminal would be a most salutary warning to tens of thousands. The very existence of such a law would confirm greatly the authority of parents, and give energy to their admonitions; as well as fortify the minds of young persons against various temptations, and so prevent crimes. And it would constantly excite all parents, who attended to the law of Moses, to restrain, correct, and watch over their children, when young, to give them good instruction, set them a good example, and pray for them without ceasing; and to keep them as much as possible out of bad company, and from contracting bad habits.

This law, therefore, so harmless and beneficial in its operations, yet so contrary to human policy, proves, instead of invalidating, the divine original of that code, in which alone it is found.[1]

11. *From the conduct of Ehud* (Judges iii. 15—26.), *of Jael* (iv. 17—20.), *and from David's advice to Solomon concerning Joab and Shimei* (1 Kings ii. 5, 6. 8.), *it has been asserted that the Scriptures inculcate assassination.*

Nothing can be more false than this assertion. For, in the first place, the cases of Ehud and Jael are simply recorded as matters of fact, without any comment or observation whatever; and, therefore, they neither can nor ought to be represented as encouraging assassination.[2] The advice of David to Solomon, when on his death-bed, demands a more distinct consideration

And, in the first place, with regard to Joab, we remark that no attentive reader of the history of David, after his accession to the throne of Israel, can help observing how often it is noticed that the sons of Zeruiah were too strong for David; in other words, that they had too much power with the army for him to venture to punish their atrocious deeds; reasons of state deferred the punishment, and when those reasons were removed, it was proper to punish a deliberate murderer according to an express law David also knew that a man like Joab, who could brook no superior, might endanger the peace of the kingdom. He was now engaged to support Adonijah, and so far in actual rebellion. But it is to be observed that the Hebrew monarch does not advise Solomon to put Joab *absolutely* and *unconditionally* to death he charges him to *do according to his wisdom*, and the sum of his advice is in effect this:—"Though you have now pardoned Joab through policy, as I was myself compelled to do by the exigency of the times, and the predominant influence of the sons of Zeruiah; yet, should he offend *again*, act according to discretion, and then punish him, as a hoary-headed and confirmed traitor, with death."

Secondly, with respect to Shimei, David had fulfilled his promise He had only engaged that he would not put him to death on the day when Abishai had requested permission to do it (compare 2 Sam. xix 23 with 1 Kings ii 8.): and he left it to Solomon to treat him as he thought just, in reference to his future conduct David knew that he was Shimei still, and would so act as to bring on himself due punishment Solomon accordingly sent for Shimei, and commanded him to reside in Jerusalem, and not to depart thence, under pain of death on the day when he should pass over the brook Kishon, a condition to which Shimei thankfully acceded. (1 Kings ii 37, 38) Three years afterwards, the latter transgressed this convention, and went to Gath (verse 40), a suspicious quarter, in consequence of which Solomon, after charging him with the violation of his oath, commanded him to be put to death. (41—46)[3]

12. Again, *it has been asserted by some, that the law of Moses* (Levit. xxvii. 28), *concerning devoted things to be put to death, authorised human sacrifices and Jephthah's sacrificing his daughter* (Judg. xi. 34, &c.), *Samuel's hewing Agag in pieces before the Lord* (1 Sam. xv. 33), *and David's delivering seven of Saul's posterity to the Gibeonites to be put to death by them* (2 Sam. xxi. 2, &c.), *have been represented as instances of human sacrifices according to that law.*

---

[1] Age of Infidelity, p 24. Scott's Reply to Paine's Age of Reason, p. 18. London, 1820 12mo

[2] The cases of Ehud and of Jael are fully considered in Twopenny's Dissertations, pp. 133—140.

[3] See Dr Chandler's Life of David, vol. ii. pp. 444—481., where that monarch's conduct to Joab and Shimei is fully vindicated.

But as there are express prohibitions of sacrificing their children in Deut. xii 30, 31. Psal cvi 37, 38 Jer vii 31 and Ezek xvi 20, 21 ; so there not only is no direction to sacrifice any other human creature, nor are there any rites appointed for such sacrifice, but also it would have rendered the priest unclean, by touching a dead body, and the sacrifice of a man is expressly declared to be abominable in Isa lxvi 3 As no devoted thing could be sacrificed at all, the law in question cannot possibly relate to sacrifice, and is capable of a very different meaning For, although Josephus, and many commentators after him, are of opinion that Jephthah did really immolate his daughter, the probability is that she was not sacrificed And this will appear from the rendering of the conversive particle ו (*vau*), which the preceding considerations require to be taken disjunctively, and translated OR. instead of AND, 'both in Levit xxvii 28 ¹ and also in Judges xi 30, 31 ² What further confirms this rendering, and consequently reconciles these two passages, is, that Jephthah's rashness had time to cool, as his daughter went two months to bewail her *virginity*, that is, her consecration to God, which obliged her to remain single, without posterity. It is further said, that she went to bewail her *virginity*, not her *sacrifice* Besides, the Israelitish women went four times in every year to mourn or talk WITH (not *for*) the daughter of Jephthah, to lament her seclusion from the world, and the hardship of her situation as cut off from every domestic enjoyment Now, if in the course of two months no person could have suggested to Jephthah a ransom for his daughter, yet surely she must have been alive, though dead to him and his family (as his only child), and to the world by her seclusion, if the Israelitish women went to condole with her. It is further worthy of remark, that it is not afterwards said, that he actually *sacrificed* her, but that " *he did with her according to his vow* " The sacred historian subjoins, *she knew no man* · if she *were* sacrificed, this remark is frivolous, but if she were devoted to perpetual virginity, this idea coincides with the visits of the Israelitish women On the whole, we may safely conclude, that Jephthah's daughter was *not* sacrificed, but consecrated to a state of celibacy ³

With respect to the two other cases above mentioned, viz. the hewing of Agag in pieces before the Lord, and the delivery of seven of Saul's posterity to the Gibeonites, they have no reference whatever to sacrifices Agag, in particular, was put to death as a *criminal*, and not as a sacrifice ⁴

19 In 1 Sam xiii 14 David is called the *man after God's own heart.* And this phrase, as applied to him, has been a fertile source of sarcasm and reproach to many infidel writers, as if the Scriptures sanctioned adultery and murder.

But do they authorise those crimes ? By no means They are there reprehended, and the severest denunciations are pronounced against those who perpetrate them. In what sense then was he a *man after God's own heart*? ANSWER — In his strict attention to the law and worship of God, in his recognising, throughout his whole conduct, that Jehovah was king in Israel, and that he himself was only his vice-gerent ; in never attempting to alter any of those laws, or in the least degree to change the Israelitish constitution In all his *public official conduct* he acted according to the Divine Mind, and fulfilled the will of his Maker But the phrase

---

¹ That this passage should be so rendered, has been proved by Dr Hales It will then run thus — *Notwithstanding, no devoted thing, which a man shall devote unto* THE LORD, *of all that he hath,* [either] *of man or of beast, or of land of his own property, shall be sold or redeemed Every thing devoted is most holy unto the Lord.* New Analysis of Chronology, vol ii p 320 See the subject also treated, in an admirable manner in Dr Randolph's Sermon intitled Jephthah's Vow considered, in the second volume of his " View of our blessed Saviour's Ministry," &c pp. 166—195

² Which verses are to be translated thus — " *And Jephthah vowed a vow unto* THE LORD, *and said, If thou wilt surely give the children of Ammon into my hand, then it shall be that whatsoever cometh out of the doors of my house to meet me, when I return in peace from the children of Ammon, shall either be the Lord's,* OR *I will offer it up* [for] *a burnt-offering.*" New Analysis of Chronology, vol ii p 320

³ Hales, vol ii. pp 320—323 Calmet's Dictionary, vol. ii. pp. 158, &c. 4to edit Additions to Calmet Waterland's Scripture vindicated, on Judg ix. 18. (Works, vol. vi. pp 183—185.

⁴ Hales, vol. ii pp. 321. Du Voisin, Autorité des Livres de Moyse, p 405.

itself will, perhaps, be the best explained by the case of Samuel. Eli was rejected, and Samuel chosen in his place, just as David superseded Saul. On this occasion God said, *I will raise me up a faithful priest, that shall do according to* that *which is in mine heart.* (1 Sam. ii 35.) And is not he, who acts agreeably to the Divine Will, *a man after God's heart?* Further, it is worthy of remark, that this expression is never used in reference to his private or personal moral conduct. It is used wholly in reference to his uniform regard to the promotion of the interests of pure religion, notwithstanding all temptations to idolatry and persecution.[1]

14. *The conduct of David towards the Ammonites, in putting them under saws and harrows of iron, &c. on the capture of Rabbah, has been represented as an instance of diabolical and unparalleled cruelty.* (2 Sam. xii. 31.)

The cavils of the objectors, in this as in every other instance, are utterly unfounded: for if, instead of deducing their objections from translations, they had consulted the original passage, they would have seen that there was no ground whatever for their charges. The Hebrew prefix ב (beth), which is used throughout the verse in question, it is well known, signifies *to* as well as under; and to put the people to saws, harrows, axes, and the brick kilns, means no more than to employ them as slaves in the most menial and laborious offices, such as sawing, making iron harrows, hewing wood, and making bricks. This form of expression is an Anglicism as well as a Hebraism; and we still say, to put a person *to* the plough, *to* the anvil, &c. The passage objected to may be thus rendered *He* (David) *brought forth the people that were therein, and put them to saws, and to harrows of iron,* (or to *iron-mines,* for the original word means both,) *and to axes of iron, and made them pass through the brick-kiln.* The erroneous interpretation of this verse appears to have been taken from 1 Chron xx. 3 where David is said to have *cut them with saws and with harrows of iron, and with axes* · on which place it is to be observed that, instead of וישר (vayaseR) *he sawed* or *cut with saws,* seven of the manuscripts collated by Dr. Kennicott have וישם (vayaseM) he put them. 1 Chron. xx. 3., therefore, must be rendered in the same manner as 2 Sam xii 31.

15. *It has been asserted from* 1 Kings xxii. *that Jehovah kept false prophets as well as true ones.*

The most common attention to the context will show that this assertion is as false as it is malignant. For, *in the first place,* the four hundred prophets mentioned in that chapter (verse 6.) were pretended prophets whom the wicked king of Israel had in his pay, and who knew how to suit his humour and to flatter his vanity, all agreeing in the same fawning compliances and in the same treacherous counsels which pleased for the present, but ultimately proved fatal. They are emphatically termed by Micaiah (verse 23.) *Ahab's prophets,* notwithstanding they professed to be the Lord's prophets, prophesying in his name. And, *secondly,* the address of Micaiah to the two confederated kings in verses 19—23 is not a real representation of any thing done in the heavenly world, as if the Almighty were at a loss for expedients or had any hand in the sins of his creatures; but it is a mere parable, and only tells in figurative language what was in the womb of providence, the events which were shortly to take place, and the *permission*[2] on the part of God, for these agents to act. Micaiah did not choose to tell the angry and impious Ahab, that all his prophets were liars; but he represents the whole by this parable, and says the same truths in language equally forcible but less offensive.

16. The Scriptures represent the Almighty as a God of truth and faithfulness; but he is charged by the opposers of divine revelation with being guilty of falsehood, by *inspiring prophets with false messages,* and by *violating his promises.* The grossness of such assertions is sufficiently disgusting, but it is the duty of a Christian advocate fully to meet them, and to expose all their falsehood.

---

[1] See the Rev. Wm. Cleaver's Sermon on the Character of David King of Israel, in four Sermons annexed to Bp Cleaver's Seven Sermons on Select Subjects, pp. 377—399. and especially Dr. Chandler's Life of David, vol. i pp 321—330.

[2] That this is the meaning of 1 Kings xxii 22. is proved in the next remark,

In the first place, With regard to the charge of *inspiring prophets with false messages,* (which is founded on 1 Kings xxii 22, 23. Jer. iv. 10. and Ezek xiv. 9.) we remark that it is a known idiom of the Hebrew language, to express things in an imperative and active form, which are to be understood only permissively. So where *the devils besought* CHRIST *that he would suffer them to enter into the herd of swine, he said unto them, Go;* (Matt viii. 31) he did not command, but permitted them. And so in John xiii. 27 where our Saviour says to Judas, *What thou dost, do quickly,* we are not to understand that he commanded him to betray him, though that seemed to be expressed in the form. So likewise, here, where an evil spirit offered himself to be a lying spirit in the mouth of the prophet, and God says, *Go forth, and do so:* this only signifies a permission, not a command. And so (Jer iv. 10) where the prophet complains that God had greatly deceived the people, *saying, they should have peace, when the sword reacheth to the soul,* we are to understand this no otherwise, but that God permitted the false prophets to deceive them, prophesying peace to them, as appears by the history (Ezek xiv 9) *I the* LORD *have deceived that prophet,* that is, permitted him to be deceived, and to deceive the people, as a just judgment upon them for their infidelity with respect to his true prophets. This he threatens at the 5th verse, *I will take the house of Israel in their own heart, because they are all estranged from me through their idols ,* because they have chosen to themselves false gods, I will suffer them to be deceived with false prophets; and that this is the meaning, appears by the threatening added, *and I will stretch out my hand upon him, and I will destroy him from the midst of my people .* now God will not punish that of which he is the author.

That text, (Jer. xv. 7.) *Thou hast deceived me, and I was deceived,* signifies no more, but that he had mistaken the promise of God to him, who when he gave him his commission, told him he would be with him, by which he understood that no evil should come to him, and *now he was become a derision and the people mocked him ;* and in his passion and weakness, he breaks forth into this expression, *Thou hast deceived me, and I was deceived ;* whereas it was his own mistake of the meaning of God's promise, which was not, that he should not meet with scorn, and opposition, and persecution, but that they should not prevail against him, as we may see at the latter end of the first chapter [1]

Secondly, With respect to the assertion that the Almighty violates his promises, it has been objected that God did not give the children of Israel all the land which he promised to Abraham, as will appear by comparing Gen xviii 19, 20, with Josh. xiii. 1, &c and Judg ii 20, 21. In Gen xv. 18 God promised *to give Abraham and his seed such a land,* the bounds of which he describes in Josh. xiii 1. It is there said that *there remained very much land* yet unconquered, of which they had not got possession. And in Judg. ii. 20 it is said, that the people having not performed their part of the covenant, God would suspend the further performance of his promise, and *would not drive out* any more of the nations before them, and it is probable, that the Israelites never were possessed of the promised land in the full latitude, and extent of the promise.

Answer.—This covenant of God with Abraham was upon consideration of his past faith and obedience, though it seems that the full performance of it did likewise depend upon the future obedience of his posterity. In pursuance of his covenant, notwithstanding all the murmurs and rebellions of that people, God did bring them into the promised land, though they provoked him to destroy them many a time; because he remembered his covenant with Abraham. When they were possessed of it, God gave them a title to the rest, and would have assisted them in the conquest of it, if they had performed the condition required on their part, that is, continued faithful and obedient to him ; but they did not, and thereby discharged God from any further performance of his promise, and God, when he had done this, had fully performed the covenant he made with Abraham, so far as concerned his part, as appears by the acknowledgment of Joshua, even in a time when a great part of the land was unconquered (Josh. xxi 44), and of Solomon (1 Kings viii 56); yea, and had it not been that God had made this covenant, as well upon consideration of Abraham's faith and obedience, as upon condition of the future obedience of his posterity, the rebellions and disobedience of the people in the wilderness had released God wholly from the promise, and he would not have been unfaithful if he had utterly destroyed that people, and made a full end of them, and they had

---

[1] Tillotson's Works, vol. vi. p. 506. London, 1820.

never entered into that land; because a failure of the condition makes the obligation to cease; and that this condition was implied in the covenant with Abraham appears from Deut. vii 12, 13 xi 22, 23. and Judg. ii. 20 God gives this reason why he suspended the complete performance of his promise: *the anger of the* LORD *was hot against Israel, and he said, Because that this people hath transgressed my covenant which I commanded their fathers, and have not hearkened to my voice, I also will not henceforth drive out any of the nations which Joshua left when he died.*[1]

17. The destruction of *forty-two little children*, by Elisha, whom they had in sportive playfulness called *a bald head*, (it is said) was an act of cruelty and revenge.

It was no such thing. The original word in 2 Kings ii. 23, 24. נערים (NEARIM), which in our version is rendered little children, also means young persons who are grown up. Thus Isaac was called נער (NAAR) a lad, when he was *twenty-eight* years old, Joseph when he was *thirty;* and Rehoboam when he was *forty* years of age The town of Beth-el was one of the principal seats of Ahab's idolatry; and it is probable that these men came out of that city and insulted the prophet, at the instigation of the priests of Baal, exclaiming — *Ascend too, thou bald-head , ascend too, thou bald-head,* in allusion to Elijah's ascension to heaven; of which they had heard, but which they did not believe Elisha, it is said, *cursed them;* but he did not this from any petulant temper of his own He *cursed them in the name of the Lord,* that is, he declared in his name and authority the punishment which he would inflict upon them. Thus Elisha acted as a minister of the Supreme Governor of the world; and by his order and in his name he foretold the punishment which was about to be inflicted upon these profligate idolaters Had this denunciation proceeded from the angry resentment of the prophet only, and not from a divine impulse, such a signal event as the destruction of these profane young men of Beth-el would not have been the immediate consequence of it.

18. It is objected that many passages of the Old Testament ascribe to the Almighty human affections, passions, and actions, even those of the worst kind.

But these objections cease, when such passages are interpreted *figuratively,* as they ought to be, and when all those other passages of the Bible are duly considered, which most evidently convey the sublimest ideas of the Divine Majesty. The Holy Scriptures, it is true, in condescension to our limited capacities, and to the imperfections of human creatures and of human language, represent God as having the body, the passions, and the infirmities of a man. Thus, they make mention of his eyes and ears, his hands and feet, his sleeping and waking; they ascribe to him fierce anger and jealousy, grief and repentance, joy and desire. The simple language of the Hebrews might also be another reason for its abounding with such expressions But that no man might be so weak or so perverse as to take those expressions according to the letter, and entertain mean and unworthy thoughts of his Maker, the same Scriptures often add to those very descriptions something which manifestly shows us how they are to be understood, and reminds us that if God has a body, the heaven is his throne, and the earth, his footstool , if he has hands, they are hands which reach to the ends of the creation; if he has eyes, the darkness to them is no darkness; and from them nothing is hidden, and in other places we are told that he is perfect; that he is blessed or happy; that he is unchangeable; that he is every where present; that he is a spirit; that no man hath seen him or can see him , that he is incomprehensible; and that the most exalted notion which we can possibly frame of him, falls infinitely short of the truth.[2] One or two examples will illustrate the preceding remarks.

Thus, when God is said to *repent,* the expression simply means, that He does not execute that which seemed to *us* to have been his purpose; that he is pleased to do otherwise than his threatenings seemed openly to express, on account of some tacit condition implied in them. And this does not derogate either from the truth, or sincerity, or constancy, of God in his word It does not derogate

---

[1] Tillotson's Works, vol. vi. p 507 See also Waterland's Scripture Vindicated, on Ezek xiv 9 (Works, vol. vi. pp 257—264.)
[2] Jortin's Sermons, vol. i. p. 237.

from his *truth*, because he speaks what he really intends, unless something intervened to prevent the judgment threatened, upon which he resolved when he threatened to take off and stop his judgments. Nor does it derogate from his *sincerity*, for he has told us that his threatenings have such conditions implied in them: — nor from his *constancy* and immutability, because God does not change his counsel and purpose, but takes off the sentence, which he had passed with reserved conditions.

19. It has also been objected, that the book of Ecclesiastes contains some passages which savour of irreligion, and others which savour of immorality.

But the passages, thus excepted against, are either innocent when rightly interpreted; or else they express, — *not* the sentiments of Solomon, but the *false opinions* of others, whom he personates in order to confute them; — or, however, not his deliberate sentiments, but such hasty and wrong notions, as during the course of his inquiry after happiness, arose successively in his mind, and were on mature consideration rejected by him, that he might fix at last on the true basis, — the *conclusion of the whole matter*. which is to *fear God and keep his commandments. for God will bring every work into judgment, with every secret thing, whether it be good, or whether it be evil* (Eccl. xii. 13, 14.)

20. It has likewise been objected that the Song of Solomon, and the sixteenth and twenty-third chapters of Ezekiel's prophecy, contain passages offensive to common decency.

But this objection will fall to the ground by interpreting those parts allegorically, as almost all the commentators, from the earliest times, have unanimously done: and, likewise, by considering that the simplicity of the eastern nations made these phrases less offensive to them than they appeared to us; as, on the other hand, many things which are perfectly correct in our view, would appear far different in eastern climates. With respect to the Song of Solomon, in particular, it is to be remarked, 1. That most of the forms of speech, against which exceptions have been made, are mistranslations, and do not exist in the original: — And, 2. Admitting the correctness of these remarks, it may also be shown, that this book abounds with beautiful poetic images. There is, therefore, no just exception to supposing it allegorical, provided the allegory be not extravagant and inconsistent.

21. It is asserted, *that the imprecations contained in some of the prophetic parts of Scripture, and in the book of Psalms* (especially in the fifty-fifth and hundred and ninth psalms), *breathe a spirit of malice, are highly inconsistent with humanity, and highly vicious.*

These, however, are to be considered not as prayers, but as simple predictions; the imperative mood being put for the future tense agreeably to the known idiom, of the Hebrew language [1], and shown to be so put by the future being used in other parts of the prediction, as in Psalm xxviii 4, 5, and this idiom is more natural in prediction than in other kinds of composition, because it is the immediate result of combining idioms common in the prophetic style. For, as the prophets are often commanded to do a thing, when it is only intended that they should foretell it [2], so they often foretell a thing by commanding it to be done [3]; and they often express their predictions in an address to God [4], the union of which two idioms gives them the appearance of imprecations.

Of all those tremendous imprecations which appear in our common English version of Deut. xxvii 15—26., there is not one authorised by the original The Hebrew texts express no kind of *wish*, but are only so many denunciations of the

---

[1] Thus, Gen. xx. 7. if rendered *literally*, is *And he shall pray for thee, and* LIVE, that is, *thou shalt live*. A similar example occurs in Gen. xlii. 18. *This do and live*, that is, *ye shall live*, and in Gen xlv. 18. *I will give you the land of Egypt, and eat* (that is, *ye shall eat*) *the fat of the land*

[2] See examples of this mode of speech in Isa. vi 10. and Jer. i. 10.

[3] Isa. xlvii 1. *Come down* (that is, *thou shalt come down*) *and sit in the dust, O virgin daughter of Babylon,* (*thou shalt*) *sit on the ground*

[4] Isa. ix. 3. *Thou hast multiplied the nation, thou hast increased their joy, they joy* (that is, *they shall joy*) *before thee, according to the joy in harvest.* — Gerard's Institutes, p 448.

VII. Sect. V.] *Of Scripture, alleged to be Contradictory.* 533

displeasure of God against those who either were, or should be guilty of the sins therein mentioned, and of the judgments which they must expect to be inflicted upon them, unless prevented by a timely and sincere repentance. And agreeably to this view, the sacred texts should have been rendered " cursed they," or, " cursed *are* they," and not " cursed *be* they," in the sense of *Let them be* cursed; the word *be*, though inserted in our translation, having nothing answerable to it in the Hebrew.

It is further worthy of remark, that the fifty-fifth Psalm is a plain prophecy of the untimely fate of Ahithophel, and is so interpreted by the Chaldee paraphrase. The fifteenth verse should be rendered,

*Death shall suddenly seize upon them,
Alive* (that is, in their full strength and vigour) *shall they go down into Hades or the Grave.*

But the Septuagint has rendered it.

Ελθετω θανατος επ' αυτους
Και καταβητωσαν εις ἁδου ζωντες.

Let death come upon them,
Let them go down alive to the mansion of the dead.

And our common translation has it still worse.

Let death come hastily upon them;
And let them go down quick into hell.

In which rendering are two capital faults: 1. A most horrid curse is given to us instead of a prophecy and, 2. שאול (SHEOL), which signifies the *grave*, or *state of the dead*, is translated Hell, which is commonly, though erroneously, understood of the state and place of eternal punishment

The offence, which has also been taken against the supposed imprecations of the hundred and ninth Psalm, may be obviated in the manner above noticed, by rendering the verbs in the future tense, that is, literally as they are in the Hebrew. That Psalm contains a twofold prophecy, primarily of the fate of Doeg the Edomite, and secondarily of the traitor Judas; and to this last the apostle Peter has applied it in Acts i. 20. And it is further to be observed, that the imprecations in the hundred and ninth Psalm, are not the imprecations of David against his enemies, but of his enemies against him.[1]

The same idiom, which appears in the prophetic writings and Psalms, is also to be found in 1 Cor. xvi. 22. and 2 Tim iv. 14.

The former passage runs thus. — *If any man love not the Lord Jesus, let him be anathema maranatha* From 1 Cor. xii. 3. we find that the Jews, who pretended to be under the Spirit and teaching of God, called Jesus Christ αναθεμα or *accursed*, that is, a person devoted to destruction. In 1 Cor. xvi 22. Saint Paul retorts the whole upon themselves, and says, *If any man love not the Lord Jesus let* HIM *be* (that is, *he will* be) *accursed; the Lord will come.* This is not said in the way of imprecation, but as a *prediction* of what would certainly come upon the Jews if they did not repent; and of what *actually came* upon them, because they did not repent, but continued to *hate* and *execrate* the Saviour of the world, as well as a prediction of what still lies upon them because they continue to *hate* and *execrate* the Redeemer.

In 2 Tim. iv 14. we read *Alexander the coppersmith did me much evil; the Lord reward him according to his works;* which has the appearance of an imprecation. But instead of αποδωη *may the Lord reward*, αποδωσει *will reward* is the reading of the Codices Alexandrinus and Ephremi (which are of the best authority), the Codices Claromontanus, San Germanensis, Augiensis, also of those numbered by Griesbach,

---

[1] Williams's Dissertation on Scripture Imprecations, prefixed to " The Book of Psalms, as translated, paraphrased, or imitated by some of the most eminent English Poets." 8vo. 1781. Green's note on Psalm cix (Translation of the Psalms, 8vo. 1762.) The late Bishop Horsley also renders these imprecations as prophetic maledictions; though he considers that Psalm as denounced by Messiah against the Jewish nation. See also Dr. Randolph's Comment on Psalms cix. and lv in the second volume of his " View of our Saviour's Ministry," &c pp. 315—335.

6. 17. 31 37 67**. 71. 73 80 and of the MS. by Matthæi noted with the letter f.; — of the Coptic, Armenian, and Vulgate versions — and of Chrysostom, Theodoret, Eulogius as cited by Photius, Johannes Damascenus, Oecumenius, Augustine, and others among the fathers of the Christian Church. The reading of ἀποδώσει makes the sentence declaratory, — *The Lord* WILL REWARD *him according to his works* and, as it is supported by such satisfactory evidence, Griesbach has inserted it in his inner margin, as being nearly equal, if not preferable to the common reading An additional proof that this is the preferable lection is furnished by the fact, that it is in unison with the spirit and temper of the intrepid Apostle, Saint Paul; who, in the sixteenth verse, when speaking of his being deserted by every one, when (during his second imprisonment at Rome) he was first summoned to vindicate himself before the sanguinary emperor Nero, says, *Let it not be placed to their charge*, that is, Let them not have to reckon for it with the Supreme Judge, at the great day. This passage furnishes an additional example of canon 9, concerning various readings, which is given in pp 198, 199. *supra*.

22. The preceding examples, with two exceptions, have been taken from the Old Testament. So pure, indeed, is the morality of the New Testament, that the advocates of infidelity can find no other fault with it, than this, — that it carries the principle of *forbearance* too far, because, among other things, it inculcates the love of our enemies. Notwithstanding this involuntary testimony to its inimitable excellence, two passages have been singled out, as inculcating immorality, viz. Luke xvi. 8. and 1 Cor. ix. 5.

(1.) In Luke xvi. 8 we read, that *The lord commended the unjust steward* (who in the parable had been represented as having defrauded his master), *because he had done wisely*: and hence Jesus Christ has been unjustly charged with countenancing dishonesty. The whole of the context, however, shows, that it was the *master* or *lord of the steward*, and NOT Christ, who is represented as commending his conduct, and it is in consequence of his master's so commending him, that Jesus made the reflection, that *the children of this world are in their generation wiser than the children of light* The parable in question is to be interpreted *solely* in reference to the principal idea contained in it. and that idea is, from the conduct of a worldly minded man, to enforce upon the followers of Jesus Christ the necessity of their being at least as assiduous in pursuing the business of the next world, — the salvation of their souls, — as worldly minded men are in *their* management of the affairs of this world.

(2.) The interrogatory (1 Cor ix 5.) has been distorted into a charge of adultery against the apostle Paul. It would be a sufficient reply to this falsehood, to state that the whole of his conduct and sentiments completely disproves it. The purest benevolence, the severest reproofs of all sin, and the most exemplary discharge of all the civil, social, and relative duties pervade all his justly admired epistles. Let us, however, briefly consider this passage. It is sufficiently evident from the context, that at Corinth there were false teachers of Christianity, who questioned Paul's apostleship, and that he was obliged to conduct himself in the most circumspect manner, in order that they might not find any occasion against him Having vindicated his apostolic character and mission, and proved his right to have the necessaries of life supplied to him, if he had demanded them of those among whom he had laboured gratuitously, he says, — *Have we not power (authority or right) to lead about a sister, a wife, as well as other apostles, and as the brethren of the Lord and Cephas?* What is there in this passage, which can be construed into a sufficient proof of adultery in an English court of law? — When the Apostle speaks of his right to take with him a sister, a wife, he means, *first*, that he and all other apostles, and, consequently, all ministers of the Gospel had a RIGHT to marry: for it appears that James and Jude, who were *the brethren* or kinsmen *of the Lord*, were married: and we have infallible evidence that Peter (surnamed Cephas) was a married man, not only from this verse, but also from Matt. viii. 14 where his *mother-in law* is mentioned as being cured by Jesus Christ of a fever. And, *secondly*, we find that their wives were persons of the same faith; for less can never be implied in the word *sister*. It is further worthy of notice that Clement of Alexandria has particularly remarked that the apostles carried their *wives* about with them, " not as wives but as SISTERS, that they might minister to those who were mistresses of families; that so the doctrine of the Lord might, *without reprehension or evil suspicion*, enter the apartments of the women." And in giving his finished picture of a perfect Christian, he says — "Εσθιει και πινει, και ΓΑΜΕΙ .. ΕΙΚΟΝΑΣ εχει τους ΑΠΟΣΤΟΛΟΥΣ — *He eats and drinks and* MARRIES . *having the* APOSTLES *for his* EXAMPLE!"[1]

SECTION VI.

APPARENT CONTRADICTIONS BETWEEN THE SACRED WRITERS.

THERE are some facts recorded in one part of the Sacred Writings which seem to be repugnant to the statements contained in other parts of the Scriptures: and these apparent contradictions are to be found between different writers of the Old Testament, and also between the Old and the New Testament.

I. *In the Old Testament the following passages are objected to as contradictory.*

1. Gen. i and Gen. ii. have been affirmed to contradict each other.

They are perfectly consistent. In the first chapter, Moses gives a *general* account of the *whole* creation in six days, and then, carrying on his history, he proceeds to describe particularly the formation of Adam and Eve. In Gen. ii 3. it is said, that God *had rested from all his works which he had created and made*, that is, he ceased to make any more creatures, consequently, Adam was NOT made after this.

2. Gen vii. 12. *And the rain was upon the earth forty days and forty nights* } is said to be contradicted by { Gen vii 17. *The flood was forty days upon the earth.*

The words "*and forty nights*," in Gen vii 17. are lost from the Hebrew copies, but they are found in the Septuagint Greek version, and also in many MSS. of the Latin Vulgate version They ought to be restored to the text, which will read as follows, in perfect unison with Gen vii. 12 — *The flood was forty days and forty nights upon the earth.*

3 Gen. vii 24 *And the waters prevailed upon the earth an hundred and fifty days* } is said to be contradicted by { Gen. viii. 3 *The waters returned from off the earth continually, and after the end of the hundred and fifty days, the waters were abated.*

Gen viii. 3 ought to be rendered . — *The waters continually subsided from off the earth, and at the end of the hundred and fifty days, the waters were much abated* This rendering (which Dr Boothroyd has adopted in his new version of the Bible) completely removes the alleged contradiction.

4. Gen. viii. 4, 5. are affirmed to be repugnant.

Dr. Boothroyd renders them thus, which obviates that repugnancy: — The waters were much abated, *so that in the seventh month, on the seventeenth day of the month, the ark rested upon* one *of the mountains of Ararat And the waters were continually decreasing until the tenth month : and on the first day of the tenth month the tops of the mountains were visible.*

5. Gen vi. 19. vii. 2, 3. 8, 9. and 15. and viii. 20 are charged with being direct contradictions. A little attention to the context and connection of the passages in question will show their perfect consistency.

In Gen vi. 19—21 general orders are given to Noah to take into the ark with him, animals of every kind, *pairs of each.* In Gen. vii. 2. the number of pairs is stated, viz. *seven pairs* of clean beasts, and *two pairs* of beasts that are not clean; and (verse 3.) *of the fowls of the air that are clean, seven pairs, the male and the*

---

[1] Clementis Alexandrini Stromata, lib. vii. c. 2. cited by Dr. A Clarke in his Commentary on 1 Cor. ix. 5. — Clement was one of the most learned Greek Christian writers in the close of the second century. His Stromata were written A. D 193.

female, and of fowls that are not clean, two pairs, the male and his female[1] In vii 8, 9. and 15 the historian, relating what was done in obedience to the divine command, says generally, that *pairs* went with Noah into the ark; and in viii 20. it is stated, also, in general terms, that he offered sacrifices of every clean beast, and of every clean fowl. There is, therefore, no real contradiction between these several numbers. As animals were not used for food before the Deluge, it is probable that the distinction of beasts and fowls into clean and unclean was made with respect to sacrifices; the former being offered while the latter were not

6. On the alleged contradiction between Gen. xv. 13. Exod. xii. 40, 41. and Acts vii. 6. see p 504 *supra*.

7 Gen. xxii. 1 *It came to pass after these things, that God did tempt Abraham.* } apparently contradicts { James i. 13. *God cannot be tempted with evil, neither tempteth He any man.*

Temptation signifies nothing more than trial, any opposition or difficulty that may exercise our virtues, and make them known In this sense God may be said to *tempt* men, that is, he tries and proves them, and thus he tempted Abraham. Sometimes temptation means dangerous trials and enticements to sin. under which we are more likely to sink, than to overcome them. In this sense God *tempteth not any man;* nor, if we resist them, will He *suffer us to be tempted above what we are able*. (1 Cor x 13.)

8. From Gen. xxxi. 38. and 41. compared with Gen. xxxiv. it has been asserted that Dinah was only *six* years of age (instead of *sixteen*), when she was forcibly defiled by Shechem, and hence it is insinuated that the narrative is so contradictory as to be unworthy of credit.

This pretended difficulty, concerning the age of Dinah, originated in the supposition that that disastrous circumstance took place in the very same year when Jacob returned into Palestine So far, however, is the book of Genesis from dating it in that year, that, on the contrary, we learn from it, that Jacob resided in that country a long time. (Compare Gen. xxxiii 11 18. xxxiv 1 30. and xxxv 1. 28, 29) The best chronologists compute that the patriarch's residence, both at Succoth and at Shechem, was about ten years; and there is not a single word in the book of Genesis that affords any ground of contradiction or difficulty against this computation. Dinah, therefore, was about sixteen, or between sixteen and seventeen years of age; and her brothers Simeon and Levi, about twenty-two or twenty-three, (instead of twelve, as the opposers of the Bible falsely assert,) when the disastrous occurrence at Shechem obliged Jacob to quit that district or canton, and go to Bethel, whence he repaired to Mamre to his father Isaac. It is true, that Isaac's death, which is recorded at the close of Gen xxxv was subsequent to Joseph's departure into Egypt, though the latter is not related until the thirty-seventh chapter; but that Patriarch's decease was noticed in this place by anticipation, in order that the history of Joseph might not be interrupted. This mode of narrating facts, it is well known, is pursued by all historians who do not wish to be mere annalists, and by no means affects the date of the account of Dinah, which took place previously to Isaac's death, as well as the sale of Joseph. *The days of Isaac were a hundred and fourscore years;* he was one hundred and seventy-three years old when Dinah was violated, and one hundred and seventy-four when Joseph was sold into Egypt.

9. The land of Rameses, in Gen xlvii. 11. means, the land of Goshen, and not the capital of that district; it was probably so called in the time of Moses, from the city of Rameses, which the Israelites had built for Pharaoh. The Hebrew historian used an appellation well known to them. There is no improbability or contradiction whatever between Gen. xlvii. 11. and Exod. i. 11.

10. Gen. xlviii. 8 and 10. in the first of these verses, it is said, that *Israel beheld Joseph's sons;* and in the other, that *his eyes were dim, so that he could not see.*

---

[1] The above is the reading of the Samaritan Pentateuch, and of the Septuagint and Syriac versions. The rendering of the Hebrew text is imperfect — *Of fowls of the air also by sevens, the male and the female.* Bishop Newton's Works, vol. i. p. 168.

The meaning is, not that he could not see at all, but only that he could not plainly and distinctly see the objects which were before him. Therefore, though he beheld Ephraim and Manasseh, yet he could not *distinguish* them, until they were brought nigh to him. The declaration of Jacob to Joseph, in xlviii. 22. is *not* prophetic of the future, as a scoffing writer of the present day has asserted. From Gen. xxxiii. 19. we learn, that Jacob bought a piece of land from Hamor at Shechem; to which he doubtless alludes in Gen. xlviii. 22. *I have given to thee one portion above thy brethren, which I took out of the hand of the Amorite with my sword and with my bow.* It should seem that this spot had afterwards fallen into the hands of an Amorite family or tribe, after the destruction of the Shechemites, and that Jacob had retaken it from them by force of arms, though this transaction is no where else mentioned.

11. Reuel in Exod. ii. 18. is the same as *Raguel* in Numb. x. 29.

The Hebrew is the same in *both places*, consequently there is no contradiction. The reason of the seeming difference is, that the ע (oin or ain,) in רעואל, is sometimes used merely as a vowel, and sometimes as *g, ng,* and *gn*, and this is occasioned by the difficulty of the sound, which scarcely any European organs can enunciate. As pronounced by the Arabs, it strongly resembles the first effort made in the throat by gargling, *Raguel* is the worst method of pronouncing this word; Re-u-el, the first syllable being strongly accented, is nearer to the true sound. On a comparison, of all the places, where these relations of Moses are mentioned, it is evident that Re-u-el or Raguel was the father of Jethro, whose daughter Zipporah Moses married; and it is most probable that Hobab was the son of Jethro who accompanied the Israelites through the wilderness. (Compare Exod. iii.1 iv.18 and Numb x 29.) No solid objection *can* be made against this explanation from Reuel being called "*their father*," (Exod. ii. 18.) as this appellation frequently denotes any remote ancestor.[1] Aged men, uncles, and grandfathers are in the Scriptures sometimes called fathers Thus in Gen xxxi. 43 Laban calls his *grand*-children his *children*, and considers himself as their *father*, and in 2 Kings xiv. 3 David is called the father of Amaziah, though he was his remote ancestor

12 Exod iii 2. *And the angel of the* LORD *appeared unto him (Moses) in a flame of fire out of the midst of a bush.* is said to contradict Exod. iii. 4 *And when the* LORD *saw that he turned aside to see, God called unto him out of the midst of the bush*

In these two verses there is *no* contradiction whatever. On the subject of this and other divine appearances related in the Old Testament, (which both Jews and Christians believe, on the solid evidence of facts, though infidels, unable to refute them, dismiss them with scoffing,) the solid and incontestible solution is laid by Jesus Christ himself, who perfectly understood the whole affair of divine appearances, in John v. 37. *And the Father himself which hath sent me hath borne witness of me. Ye have neither heard his voice at any time, nor seen his shape.* (John i 18.) *No man hath seen God at any time.* He is *the invisible God, whom no man hath seen nor can see* It is often said, that the Lord, the Most High God, *appeared* to the patriarchs, to Moses, and to the prophets, the ancestors of the Jews but, according to Jesus Christ's rule, the appearance, form, or shape which they saw, was not the appearance of the Lord God himself, for never, at any time, did they see his shape. Again, it is often said, that the Most High God spake to the patriarchs, to Moses, and to the prophets, but our Lord affirms, that they never heard his voice at any time. How shall we reconcile this seeming inconsistency? The true solution according to the Scriptures, is this:— That the Lord God never spake or appeared in person, but always by a proxy, *nuncius*, or *messenger* who represented him and spake in his name and authority It was this messenger of Jehovah (or angel of Jehovah), who appeared unto Moses (Exod iii 2.), and who is called, in verse 4. JEHOVAH or Lord (whence it is evident that he was no created human being); and who spake to Moses, in verse 5. saying, *Draw not nigh hither, &c., I am the God of Abraham* (ver 6), and I AM THAT I AM. (ver. 14.) All which words were pronounced by an angel, but are true, not of the angel, but of God, whom he represented. So a herald reads a proclamation in the king's name and words, as if the king himself were speaking. The word ANGEL, both in the Greek language and in the Hebrew, signifies a *messenger* or *nuncius*, an *ambassador;* one who acts and speaks, not in his own name or behalf, but in the name, person, and behalf of him who sends him

---

[1] Dr. A. Clarke and Dr. Boothroyd on Exod. ii. 18.

Thus the word is frequently rendered in our authorised translation; and if it had always been rendered the *messenger* of the Lord, instead of *the angel* of the Lord, the case would have been very plain. But *angel*, being a Greek word, which the English reader does not understand, throws some obscurity upon such passages [1]

13. Exod. vii. 19—21. is apparently contradicted by Exodus vii. 22.

Both are reconciled by comparing verse 24. The Egyptians *digged round about the river for water to drink* and it seems that the water *thus obtained* was not bloody like that in the river, on this water, therefore, the magicians might operate. Again, though Moses was commissioned to turn into blood, not only the waters of the river Nile, but also those of their streams, rivers, ponds, and pools; yet, it seems evident from verse 20. that he did not proceed thus far, at least in the *first instance*, for it is there stated, that only the waters of the river were turned into blood. Afterwards, doubtless, the plague became *general*. At the commencement, therefore, of this plague, the magicians might obtain other water, to imitate the miracle; and it would not be difficult for them, by juggling tricks, to impart to it a bloody appearance, a fœtid smell, and a bad taste. On either of these grounds, there is no contradiction in the Mosaic account.

14. Exod. ix 6. ALL THE CATTLE OF EGYPT DIED; *but of the cattle of the children of Israel died not one* } is said to contradict { Exod ix 20. *He that feared the word of the Lord among the servants of Pharaoh made - - - - - HIS CATTLE flee into the houses.*

Nothing can be more evident than that universal terms are used in all languages in a limited sense; so that the word ALL, in verse 6 means, that all the cattle that did die, belonged to the Egyptians, and died in the field, while those in the houses escaped; or else that a great many of all sorts of cattle died, or, if we understand that all the cattle of the Egyptians perished as asserted in ix. 6, what was there to hinder them from obtaining others from the Israelites, not one of whose cattle died in the land of Goshen? This justifies the supposition that there was some respite or interval between the several plagues.

15. It has been asserted, that Exod. xx. 11. and Deut. v. 15. (both which passages enjoin the observance of the Sabbath), are at variance; and hence it has been inferred that Moses could not be the author of the Pentateuch.

But the enforcement of the *same* precept by *two different motives*, does not constitute two discordant precepts; and this is the case with the passages in question. In Exod. xx. 11 Moses urges the observance of the Sabbath, by a motive taken from the creation: and in the latter, by another derived from their exode or departure from bondage in Egypt.

16. Exod. xxxiii. 11. The LORD *spake unto Moses face to face.* } apparently contradicts { John i. 18. 1 John iv. 12. *No man hath seen God at any time*

The Almighty is said to have conversed with Moses, and Jacob to have *seen* him (Gen. xxxii. 30.) But this only signifies that God revealed himself to them in a more particular manner than to others: for *God is a Spirit whom no one hath seen or can see* (1 Tim. vi 16.), that is, as he is in Heaven. And when Moses besought this favour of God, he refused him, saying, *Thou canst not see my face, for there shall no man see me and live.* (Exod. xxxiii. 20.) The apostle John might, therefore, say, that *no man hath seen God at any time* The antient Christian writers (who certainly were more likely to understand the subject than we are) were generally agreed, that the person who appeared to Adam, Abraham, Moses, and the Prophets, was the Word of God, the Son of God, Jesus Christ.

17. In Levit. xvii 1—7. the Israelites were prohibited from slaughtering any clean animal, which they were permitted to eat, in any other place except upon the altar at the door of the tabernacle, whither they were to bring it, and to immolate it. The reason assigned for this prohibition in verse 7. is, that they should no longer offer sacrifice unto idols. But in Deut. xii. 15. 20—22. the Israelites, just before they en-

---

[1] Dr. J. Taylor's Scheme of Scripture Divinity, ch. xv. (Bp. Watson's Collection of Theological Tracts, vol. i. p. 65.)

VII. Sect. VI.] *Of Scripture, alleged to be Contradictory.* 539

tered Palestine, were permitted to slaughter oxen, sheep, or other clean animals at pleasure, in any part of the country, provided they did not regard them as sacrifices, and abstained from their blood, which the heathens, in their sacrifices, were accustomed to drink.

Between these two passages there is an apparent contradiction; but it may be readily accounted for, when we consider that the laws of Moses were necessarily regulated by the circumstances of the Israelites, and that they were not intended to be absolutely unalterable. The law in question might be observed in the wilderness, where the Israelites kept near together, and from their poverty, ate but little animal food: but in Palestine, and when their circumstances were improved, it would have been an intolerable grievance, for many of them lived at the distance of several days' journey from the sanctuary, at which alone offerings could be made; and they must, consequently, either have altogether denied themselves the use of the flesh of oxen, sheep, and goats, or else have travelled long journeys to present them at the altar before they could taste it. But, in fact, Moses himself shows that Lev xvii 1—7. was a *temporary law, intended only for their situation in the wilderness*, by the phrase " without or within the camp." And in the law last promulgated, (Deut xii. 15. 20—22.) in the fortieth year of their pilgrimage, just before their entrance into Palestine, he explicitly declares it repealed, as soon as they should abide there, permitting them to kill and eat the flesh of oxen, sheep, &c. any where, as already noticed. He tells them, that they might then eat them even *as the hart and the roe*, that is, with as full liberty, and likewise without the smallest idea of offering them; for the hart and the roe were not allowed to be brought to the altar.[1]

18. The promulgation of the Levitical law is said (Lev i. 1.) to have been made from the *tabernacle*, and in Lev. xxvii. 34. we read, *These are the commandments which the Lord commanded Moses in Mount* SINAI.

But there is no real contradiction here. The Hebrew preposition ב (beth) signifies *near* as well as *in*; the meaning, therefore, is, that these were added to the foregoing commandments, before the Israelites removed from the wilderness of Mount Sinai, or while they were *near* Mount Sinai. And if the objector had distinguished the time and place when the Levitical law was given, from the time when the moral law was promulgated, he would not have asserted the existence of a contradiction. The latter was given on Mount Sinai, in the *third* month of the *first* year after the departure of the Israelites from Egypt (Exod. xix. xx.) The tabernacle was raised on the first day of the first month of the *second* year after their departure; on which occasion Aaron and his sons were set apart to the sacerdotal office (Exod. xl. 2. 17—32.) To the ceremonies attendant on this consecration, the chief part of Leviticus belongs, and, from the manner in which this book begins, it is plainly a continuation of the preceding. Indeed the whole is but one law, though divided from a very antient period into five portions.

19 Numb. iv. 3 *From* THIRTY *years old and upwards, even until fifty years old.* } apparently contradicts { Numb viii 24. *From* TWENTY AND FIVE *years old and upwards, they shall go, &c*

These texts may be reconciled in two ways, either by recollecting that the Levites were obliged to spend five years in learning the duties of their ministry, before they were admitted to officiate; or that in the time of Moses, their consecration began at the twenty-fifth year of their age, but afterwards, during the time of David, at their twentieth year

20 Numb xiv 25 (Now the Amalekites *dwelled in the* VALLEY.) } is said to contradict { Numb. xiv. 45. Then the Amalekites CAME DOWN, and the Canaanites which dwelt in that hill

The twenty-fifth verse should be read without a parenthesis, and in the present tense *dwell*. The meaning simply is, that they at present lie in wait for you, at the bottom on the other side of the mountain. God, having consented not to destroy the people suddenly, gave them notice of their danger from the neigh-

[1] Michaelis's Commentaries on the Laws of Moses, vol. ii. pp. 414, 415. vol i pp. 28—33.

bouring people, who were lying in wait to give them battle. The Israelites presumed (verse 44.) to go up into the hill top, whence they were driven and discomfited by the Amalekites and Canaanites, who had posted themselves there. A detachment of the Amalekites who were encamped on the opposite foot of the hill, might easily ascend to succour their Canaanitish allies.

21 Numb. xxi. 2, 3. is said to be contradicted by the subsequent history of the conquest of Canaan.

But there is no reason why we should not understand the destruction of the Canaanites and their cities, as limited to those which they then took: for Joshua afterwards took the king of Arad (Josh. xii. 14.) See also Judg i 16, 17

22. In 1 Cor. x. 8. St. Paul tells us, that the number of persons who were cut off in the plague was *twenty three thousand;* but, in Numb. xxv. 9. Moses makes them not less than *twenty-four thousand*, because in this number he includes the thousand who were found guilty of idolatry, and were in consequence slain with the sword, whereas the Apostle speaks only of those who died of the pestilence.

23 From the law being mentioned in the book of Exodus, as delivered on Mount *Sinai*, and from Mount *Horeb* being mentioned as the place where it was delivered, in the book of Deuteronomy, without any notice being taken of Mount Sinai, it has been insinuated, that neither of these books are worthy of credit, especially because some injudicious persons have represented them in maps as two *distinct* mountains.

It is, however, well known that Sinai and Horeb are two different peaks of one and the *same range* of mountains; and hence it is, that what is in one passage of Scripture related as having been done at Horeb, is in another place said to have been done at Sinai, or in the wilderness of Sinai

24 Deut i. 9—18. is said to contradict Exod. xviii. 13—23. and Moses is asserted to have *conceived* the idea of setting judges and rulers over the people.

A little attention to the two passages would have satisfied the objector that Moses did *not* conceive any such idea. In Exod. xviii. 13—23 Jethro, his father-in law, having observed the great personal fatigue to which the Jewish legislator daily exposed himself, suggested to him the appointment of magistrates over thousands, hundreds, fifties, and tens, men of integrity and piety, to hear and determine minor questions between the people, subject, however, to the approbation of God. In verses 24—27. we read generally that Moses *hearkened to the voice of his father-in-law*, followed his counsel, with the approbation of God, and appointed the necessary officers In the first chapter of Deuteronomy, Moses is represented as alluding to this fact, but with this remarkable difference, that he not only says nothing of Jethro, but instead of representing himself as the person who selected those magistrates, he states that he had appealed to the people, and desired that they would elect them "There is a great and striking difference between these statements, but there is no contradiction Jethro suggested to Moses the appointment, he, probably after consulting God, as Jethro intimates, *if God shall thus command thee*, referred the matter to the people, and assigned the choice of the individuals to them; the persons thus selected he admitted to share his authority as subordinate judges Thus the two statements are perfectly consistent. But this is not all: their difference is most natural. In first recording the event, it was natural Moses should dwell on the first cause which led to it, and pass by the appeal to the people as a subordinate and less material part of the transaction; but in addressing the people, it was natural to notice the part they themselves had in the selection of those judges, in order to conciliate their regard and obedience. How naturally also does the pious legislator, in his public address, dwell on every circumstance which could improve his hearers in piety and virtue. The multitude of the people was the cause of the appointment of these judges How beautifully is this increase of the nation turned to an argument of gratitude to God ! How affectionate is the blessing with which the pious speaker interrupts the narrative, imploring God, that the multitude of his people may increase a thousand fold !

How admirably does he take occasion, from mentioning the judges, to inculcate the eternal principles of justice and piety, which should control their decisions! How remote is all this from art, forgery, and imposture! Surely here, if any where, we can trace the dictates of nature, truth, and piety." [1]

25. Deut. x. 6, 7. is affirmed to contradict Numb. xx. 23—29. and xxxiii 30. 37, 38.

But Dr Kennicott has shown that verses 6—9. of Deut x. are an interpolation, and ought to be inserted after Deut. ii 11 [2]. For reconciling this passage, where, Aaron is said to have died at Moserah, with Numb. xxxiii 31, 32 where his death is said to have taken place on Mount Hor, it is sufficient to remark that the same place frequently had different names; just as (we have seen) Horeb and Sinai were two peaks of the same ridge, so Moserah might have been a peak of Mount Hor, and interchanged with it. In Deut x., as it stands in our printed copies, there are several things omitted, which are preserved in the Samaritan copy, and remove the difficulty we otherwise find respecting the time and place of Aaron's death. The Samaritan copy may be thus translated: *"Thence they journeyed, and pitched their camp in Gudgodah; thence they journeyed, and pitched in Jobbatha, a land of springs and water. Thence they journeyed, and pitched in Abarnea. Thence they journeyed, and pitched in Ezion-geber Thence they journeyed, and pitched in the desert of Sin, which is Kadesh. Thence they journeyed, and pitched in Mount Hor, and there Aaron died,"* &c.

26. Deut. x. 22. is apparently contradicted by Acts vii. 14.

The family of Jacob are differently reckoned at their going into Egypt. In Deut. x. 22. Moses says, that they were *three score and ten*, that is to say, all who *came out of Jacob's loins* (Gen xlvi 26) *were three score and six*, besides himself, Joseph, and his two sons who were in Egypt before; which make three score and ten But in Acts vii 14 Stephen adds to these nine of his sons' wives, and thus makes the number three score and fifteen. The latter, though not of Jacob's blood, were of his *kindred*, as Stephen justly expresses it, being allied to him by marriage.

27. There is *no* "strange inconsistency" between Deut. xxxii. and Deut xxxiii.

The former is a sublime ode, which contains a defence of God against the Israelites, and unfolds the method of the divine judgments. In the latter chapter Moses takes his leave of the people, by pronouncing a blessing upon them generally, and upon each tribe in particular.

28. In Joshua x. 23. and 37. the Israelitish general is charged with killing the same king of Hebron *twice*.

The historian relates no such thing Hebron was a place of considerable note, and its inhabitants finding that their king had fallen in battle, elected another in his place. The second king was he whom Joshua slew, after he had taken the city and its dependencies, as related in verse 37

29. Josh. x. 15. is apparently contradicted by verse 43. of the same chapter.

In the former place he is said to have *returned and all Israel with him to Gilgal;* which he certainly did not do until the end of the expedition, (verse 43) where it is properly introduced. It is therefore either an interpolation, or must signify that Joshua *intended* to have returned, but changed his resolution, when he heard that the five kings had fled and hidden themselves in a cave at Makkedah. So Balak, king of Moab, is said (Josh xxiv 9) to have *warred against Israel*, that is, he intended to war against them

| 30. Josh xi. 19 *There was not a city that made peace with the children of Israel, save the Hivites, the inhabitants of Gibeon, all other they took in battle.* | is said to contradict | Josh xv. 63. *As for the Jebusites, the inhabitants of Jerusalem, the children of Judah could not drive them out, but the Jebusites dwell with the children of Judah unto this day.* |

---

[1] Dr Graves's Lectures on the Four last Books of the Pentateuch, vol. i p 87.
[2] Mr. Townsend has accordingly placed them so in his excellent Harmony of the Old Testament. See vol. i. p. 379.

There is no contradiction here. Although Jerusalem was taken and its king vanquished by Joshua, together with the land surrounding it (Josh. x. 5. 23. 42.) the fortress or strong hold of Zion continued in the hands of the Jebusites. And the Israelites not being able immediately to people all the cities they had taken, the Jebusites recovered possession of the city, whence the children of Judah expelled them after the death of Joshua (Judg. i. 8.) But the fortress of Mount Zion remained in their hands until the reign of David.

31. Josh. xxi. 43, 44. we read, *The Lord gave unto Israel all the land which he sware to give unto their fathers; and they possessed and dwelt therein. And the Lord gave them rest round about, according to all that he sware unto their fathers: and there stood not a man of all their enemies before them; the Lord delivered all their enemies into their hand.* This is asserted to be a direct contradiction to the preceding parts of this book; but it is assertion without proof.

The whole country was now divided by lot unto them; and their enemies were so completely discomfited, that there was not a single army of the Canaanites remaining to make head against them; and those who were left in the land served under tribute; and the tribute so paid by them, was the amplest proof of their complete subjugation.[1] Add to this, that the Israelites had as much of the land in *actual* possession as they could occupy; and as they increased, God enabled them to drive out the antient inhabitants, but in consequence of the infidelity of the Israelites, their enemies were often permitted to straiten them, and sometimes to prevail against them. It is also to be recollected, that God never promised to give them the land, or to maintain them but upon condition of obedience and so punctually did he fulfil this intention, that there is not a single instance upon record in which they were either straitened or subjugated, while they were obedient and faithful to their God. In this sense, therefore, it might most correctly and literally be said that *there failed not ought of any good thing which the Lord had spoken unto the house of Israel all came to pass.*—Nor will one word of his ever fail, while sun and moon endure.

32. In Judg. i. 19. we read, *The Lord was with Judah, and he drove out the inhabitants of the mountain, but could not drive out the inhabitants of the valley because they had chariots of iron.*

From this passage M. Voltaire and his copyists in this country have taken occasion to remark that it is difficult to conceive how the Lord of heaven and earth, who had so often changed the order and suspended the established laws of nature, in favour of his people, could not succeed against the inhabitants of a valley, because they had chariots of iron.

A little consideration, however, of the context of the passage will show that this mighty difficulty has as little foundation as all the rest which the ingenuity of the enemies of the Bible have imagined to exist. In the first place, then, it is to be observed, that when it is said HE *drove out the inhabitants of the mountain, but could not drive out the inhabitants of the valley;* the antecedent is Judah, not Jehovah; because Jehovah had often displayed much more eminent instances of his power; and he that effected the greater, could certainly have effected the less. In the second place, though it pleased God to give success to Judah in one instance, it does not necessarily follow, that therefore he should give it in all. So that there is no more absurdity in the passage, than there would be in the following speech, if such had been addressed to the sovereign by one of his commanders returned from America: "By the blessing of God upon your Majesty's arms, we overcame General Greene in the field; but we could not attack General Washington, because he was too strongly entrenched in his camp." There is no reason, therefore, for supposing, that "the Jews considered the God of Israel their protector as a local divinity, who was, in some instances more, and in others less powerful, than the gods of their enemies."[a]

---

[1] If payment of tribute be not an absolute proof of subjugation, the objector to the sacred historian might with equal truth have affirmed, that during the late war, in which Great Britain was engaged for her existence as an independent nation and government, her forces did not subdue the French West India Islands and the Dutch settlement at Batavia in 1812, because the antient inhabitants continued to remain in them, and to pay tribute.

[a] Bishop Horne's Works, vol. vi. p. 493.

33. Judg. vi. 1. is said to contradict Numb. xxxi. 10.

In the latter place, however, it is not said that *all* the Midianites were exterpated. Those who engaged the Israelites were discomfited, and their country was laid waste, that those who fled might have no encouragement to return thither. In the course of *two hundred years*, however, they might increase and become sufficiently formidable (as we read that they did in Judg vi. 1) to oppress the northern and eastern Israelites, especially when joined by the Amalekites and Ishmaelites, or *children of the east*, as their allies are termed in the third verse This remark will serve also to remove the contradiction alleged to exist between 1 Sam. xv. 7, 8., where the Amalekites are said to have been discomfited by the Israelites under Saul, and 1 Sam xxx. 1, 2., where they are said, twenty-three years afterwards, to have made a predatory incursion against Ziklag. The latter were, doubtless, a travelling predatory horde, similar to those who to this day live in the country where the Amalekites formerly dwelt, viz. Arabia

34. The account of Saul's death, related in 1 Sam. xxxi. 1—6. (whence it is copied, with some trifling difference, in 1 Chron. x.) is said to be contradicted by the account of the Amalekite, narrated in 2 Sam. i. 10.

The historian relates the fact as stated by the Amalekite himself, whose story bears every mark of being a fiction, formed in order to ingratiate himself with David as the next probable successor to the crown. (Compare 2 Sam. iv. 10.) There are always men of this description about camps, whose object is plunder, and for which they will strip the dead.

35. 2 Kings xxiv. 13. and xxv. 8—12 are stated to be contradictory.

If the objector had attended to the difference of *times*, he would have found the Scriptures perfectly consistent Nebuchadnezzar carried away the riches and furniture of the temple at *three* different times — *First*, in the third year of Jehoiachim (Dan. i 2), these were the vessels which his son Belshazzar profaned (Dan. v 2), and which Cyrus restored to the Jews (Ezra i. 7), to be set up in the temple, when rebuilt : — *Secondly*, in the reign of Jehoiachim he again took the city, and cut to pieces a great part of the vessels of gold which Solomon had made (2 Kings xxiv. 13), and, *thirdly*, in the eleventh year of Zedekiah, as related in 2 Kings xxv 13—17, he once more pillaged the temple.

36. Ezra ii. is apparently at variance with Nehemiah vii.

On the discrepancies occurring throughout these two chapters, the commentators must be consulted : it may suffice here to remark that the account contained in Ezra was taken in Chaldæa *before* the Jews commenced their return, and that, which is related in Nehemiah vii., *after* their arrival in Jerusalem. Some of them altering their minds and staying behind after they had given in their names to go, and others dying on the way, lessened part of the numbers in Nehemiah, as, on the contrary, some of them coming to them afterwards, made the numbers mentioned in the latter appear the greater.

But the principal and most numerous contradictions are to be found in the Old Testament between some parts of the second book of Samuel, and the books of Kings and Chronicles ; and chiefly relate to numbers, dates, names, and genealogies. The means by which some of these repugnancies may be reconciled have already been indicated [1]; in addition to which we may remark, that although the commentators generally present satisfactory solutions, yet many of the seeming differences may be easily reconciled on the principle that the books of Chronicles are *supplementary* to those of Kings, and hence they are termed in the Septuagint Παραλειπομενα, or things omitted. Besides, the language was slightly changed, after the captivity, from what it had previously been. The various places had received new names, or undergone sundry vicissitudes ; certain things were now better known to the returned Jews, under other appellations than those by which they had formerly been

---

[1] See pp. 495—512. of the present volume.

distinguished ; and from the materials before him, which often were not the same as those used by the abridgers of the histories of the kings, the author of the books of Chronicles takes those passages which seemed best adapted to his purpose, and most suitable to the time in which he wrote. It must also be considered, that he often elucidates obsolete and ambiguous words, in former books, by a different mode of spelling them, or by a different order of the words employed even when he does not use a distinct phraseology of narration, which he sometimes adopts The following are the most material passages of these books, which have been the subject of cavil to the modern advocates of infidelity.

37. In 1 Chron. xix. 7. the children of Ammon are said to have hired *thirty-two thousand chariots, and the king of Maachah and his people;* which appears an incredible number.

But the original word here rendered chariots does not always bear that meaning. it is a collective noun signifying *cavalry* or *riders* The meaning, therefore, is, that they hired thirty-two thousand Syrian auxiliaries, who were usually mounted on chariots or horses, but who occasionally also served as foot soldiers, which is perfectly in unison with 2 Sam. x 6, where the Syrian auxiliaries engaged by the Ammonites amount exactly to thirty-two thousand, besides a thousand men, whom they hired of the king of Maachah. and whom we may presume to be infantry.

38. 2 Sam xxiv 1. *Again the anger of the Lord was kindled against Israel,* and he moved David against them, *to say, Go number Israel and Judah.* } is said to contradict { 1 Chron xxi 4. *Satan stood up and provoked David to number Israel.*

It is not usual to mention the anger of God, without stating its cause : but as the first of these texts now stands, God is stated to be angry, and his anger leads him to move David to number the people. This numbering of the people, however, was not the cause, but the effect of his anger, the *cause* is stated in the second passage, which may be rendered — *an adversary* (perhaps one of David's wicked counsellors, for the Hebrew word שטן (*satan*) signifies an adversary) *stood up against Israel, and moved David to number Israel* At the time referred to, David probably coveted an extension of empire, and having through the suggestions of an adversary given way to this evil disposition, he could not well look to God for help, and, therefore, wished to know whether the thousands of Israel and Judah might be deemed equal to the conquest which he meditated His design was, to force all the Israelites to perform military service, and engage in the contests which his ambition had in view; and, as the people might resist this census, soldiers were employed to make it, who might not only put down resistance, but also suppress any disturbances that might arise Concerning the difference of numbers in this census, see Sect. VIII. 6. p 558 *infra*

39. In 2 Kings xvi. 9. it is said, that the king of Assyria *hearkened* unto Ahaz, but in 2 Chron. xxviii. 20. we read that he *distressed him, but strengthened him not.*

Both statements are true He *did* help him against the king of Syria, took Damascus, and delivered Ahaz from the power of the Syrians. But this service was of little value, for the Assyrian monarch did *not* assist Ahaz against the Edomites or Philistines, and he distressed him by taking the royal treasures and the treasures of the temple, and rendered him but little service for so great a sacrifice.[1]

The preceding are the chief passages in the Old Testament, in which differences have been imagined to exist. but with how little propriety the reader will be enabled to judge from a careful examination of the various passages themselves. It remains only that we notice a few passages in the New Testament which have also been the subject of cavil.

---

[1] This seeming contradiction is illustrated by what happened in our own nation The Britons invited the Saxons to help them against the Scots and Picts. The Saxons accordingly came and assisted them for a time, but at length they made themselves masters of the country.

40. Matthew xxvii. 9, 10. disagrees with Zechariah xi. 13.

Both may be reconciled by supposing the *name* of the prophet to have been originally omitted by the evangelist, and that the name of Jeremiah was inserted by some subsequent copyist. Jeremiah is *omitted* in two manuscripts of the twelfth century, in the Syriac, the later Persian, and modern Greek versions, and in some later copies. What renders it likely that the original reading was διὰ τοῦ προφήτου *by the prophet*, is, that Saint Matthew frequently omits the name of the prophet in his quotations. On this passage, see further p. 212. note ², in this volume.

41. Mark ii. 26. is at variance with 1 Sam. xxi. 1

Abiathar was not high priest at that time: but the expression may easily signify, in *the days of Abiathar*, who was afterwards high priest. Or, probably, both Ahimelech and Abiathar might officiate in the high priesthood, and the name of the office be indifferently applied to either.

42. The different manner in which the four evangelists have mentioned the superscription which was written over Jesus Christ when on the cross, was objected as a want of accuracy and truth by Dr. Middleton; and his objection has been copied by later writers.

But it is not improbable that it varied in each of the languages in which that accusation or superscription was written; for both Luke (xxiii. 38) and John xix. 20) say that it was written in Greek, Latin, and Hebrew. We may then reasonably suppose Matthew to have recited the Hebrew;

THIS IS
JESUS THE KING OF THE JEWS.

And John the Greek.

JESUS THE NAZARENE THE KING OF THE JEWS

If it should be asked, Why *the Nazarene* was omitted in the Hebrew, and we must assign a reason for Pilate's humour, perhaps we may thus account for it. He might be informed, that *Jesus* in Hebrew denoted *a Saviour*, and as it carried more appearance of such an appellative or general term by standing alone, he might choose by dropping the epithet *the Nazarene*, to leave the sense so ambiguous, that it might be thus understood:

THIS IS
A SAVIOUR THE KING OF THE JEWS.

Pilate, as little satisfied with the Jews as with himself on that day, meant the inscription, which was his own, as a dishonour to the nation; and thus set a momentous verity before them, with as much design of declaring it as Caiaphas had of prophesying, *That Jesus should die for the people*.² The ambiguity not holding in Greek, *the Nazarene* might be there inserted in scorn again of the Jews, by denominating their king from a city which they held in the utmost contempt.³

Let us now view the Latin. It is not assuming much to suppose, that Pilate would not concern himself with Hebrew names, nor risk an impropriety in speaking or writing them. It was thought essential to the dignity of a Roman magistrate in the times of the republic not to speak but in Latin on public occasions.⁴ Of which spirit Tiberius the emperor retained so much, that in an oration to the senate he apologised for using a Greek word, and once, when they were drawing up a decree, advised them to erase another that had been inserted in it.⁵ And though the magistrates in general were then become more condescending to the Greeks, they retained this point of state with regard to other nations, whose languages they esteemed barbarous, and would give themselves no trouble of acquiring. Pilate, indeed, according to Matthew, asked at our Lord's trial, *Whom will ye that I release unto you, Barabbas, or Jesus which is called Christ?* And again, *What shall I do then with Jesus which is called Christ?* But we judge this to be related, as the interpreter by whom he spake delivered it in Hebrew.⁶ For if the

---

¹ Pearson on the Creed, art. ii at the beginning
² John xi. 49—51.   ³ John i. 46
⁴ Valerius Maximus, b ii c 2. § 2.
⁵ Suetonius in Tiberio, c. 71. The two words were *Monopoly* and *Emblem*.
⁶ See Wolfius on Matt. xxvii. 2.

other evangelists have given his exact words, he never pronounced the name of Jesus, but spake of him all along by a periphrasis: *Will ye that I release unto you The King of the Jews? What will ye then that I shall do unto him whom ye call The King of the Jews?* Thus he acted in conference with the rulers, and then ordered a Latin inscription without mixture of foreign words, just as Mark repeats it:

THE KING OF THE JEWS:

Which is followed by Luke; only that he has brought down *This is* from above, as having a common reference to what stood under it:

THIS IS
THE KING OF THE JEWS:

Thus, it is evident that there were variations in the inscription, and that the Latin was the shortest: but it is equally evident that these variations are not discrepancies or contradictions in the narratives of the evangelists [1]

43. The alleged discrepancies in the genealogies recorded by Matthew (i.) and Luke (iii.) have already been considered in p 497. *supra*. In addition to the observations there adduced, the following solution of the supposed contradiction by Professor Hug, (founded on the law of the levirate [2],) is highly deserving of consideration, both from its novelty and its probability.

By that law, one and the same son might have two different fathers, one *real* and the other *legal*. Most of the apparent contradictions in the genealogies of Matthew and Luke disappear, since Salathiel might be declared to be the son of Jechonias as well as Neri, and since Zorobabel might appear in one filiation as the father of Abiud and in the other as the father of Rhesa. Thus, since one genealogy makes Jacob to be the father of Joseph, and the other makes Heli to be his father, he might be the son of *both*, viz of one by *nature*, and of the other by *law*. According to this solution, the design of the two evangelists in giving the genealogy of Jesus Christ, would have been to prove to the Jews, that the man who called himself the Messiah, was by his legal father Joseph, inscribed as a descendant of David in the genealogical tables, to which that nation attached so much importance and authority Indeed, in a country where a *legal* descent was the same as a *real* descent, and where an inscription in the genealogical tables was every thing; the Jews, to whom the apostles addressed themselves, were to be the sole judges, from the ancestors of Joseph, of the fulfilment of the prophecies relative to the family of the Messiah, and the descent of Mary was of no importance to them [3]

The following additional remarks of the late Bishop Horne, on the subject of the Jewish Genealogies, are likewise highly deserving of attention.

In the *first place*, Genealogies in general, and those of the Jews in particular, with their method of deriving them, and the confusion often arising from the circumstance of the same person being called by different names, or different persons by the same name, are in their nature, and must be to us, at this distance of time, matters of very complicated consideration, and it is no wonder they should be attended with difficulties and perplexities *Secondly*, The evangelists, in an affair of so much importance, and so open then to detection, had their been any thing wrong to be detected, would most assuredly be careful to give Christ's pedigree as it was found in the authentic tables, which, according to the custom of the nation, were preserved in the family, as is evident from Josephus, who says, "I give you this succession of our family, as I find it written in the public tables." *Thirdly*, As it was well known the Messiah must descend from David, the genealogical

---

[1] Dr Townson's Works, vol i. pp 200—202.

[2] By the *jus leviratus*, or law of the levirate, when a man died without issue, his nearest male relative was obliged to *raise up seed to him* accordingly, he married his widow, and the first born son, of that marriage, was reputed to be the son of the deceased, to whose name and rights he succeeded.

[3] Cellérier, Introduct. au Nouv. Test. pp. 332—334. Hug's Introd. to the New Test. vol. ii. pp. 266—272.

tables of that family would be kept with more than ordinary diligence and precision. *Fourthly*, Whatever cavils the modern Jews and others now make against the genealogies recorded by the Evangelists, the Jews their contemporaries never offered to find fault with, or to invalidate the accounts, given in the Gospels. As they wanted neither opportunity, materials, skill, nor malice to have done it, and it would have offered them so great an advantage against the Christians, this circumstance alone, as Dr. South well remarks, were we not now able to clear the point, ought with every sober and judicious person to have the force of a moral demonstration.[1]

44. Heb. ix. 4. is apparently contradictory to 1 Kings viii. 9.

From the text of the former book, it appears that the ark contained the several things therein specified: whereas, we learn from the latter, that it contained only the two tables of stone. The words Ἐν ᾗ, *in which* (*wherein* in the authorised translation), therefore, refer to the tabernacle, and not to the ark; and thus the difference is removed.

Lastly, Some of the differences between the Old and New Testaments arise from numbers and dates, and may be explained on the principles already laid down in pp. 504—511. *supra;* and others arise from the variances occurring in the quotations from the Old in the New Testament. But as these require a distinct consideration, the reader will find them fully discussed in pp. 256—270. of this volume.

SECTION VII.

SEEMING INCONSISTENCIES BETWEEN SACRED AND PROFANE WRITERS.

IT is not to be denied that the sacred Scriptures contain facts, which appear to be contradictory to the relations of the same facts by profane historians. But the objections which some would derive from these seeming inconsistencies, lose all their force, when the uncertainty and want of credibility in heathen historians are considered, as well as their want of authentic records of the times.[2] It may further be added, that the silence of the latter, concerning facts related by the inspired writers, cannot be regarded as contradicting them: because many of these facts are either too antient to come within the limits of profane histories, or are of such a description that they could not take notice of them.[3] The silence or omission even of many historians ought not to overturn the testimony of any one author, who positively relates a matter of fact· if, therefore, a fact related in the Scripture be contradicted by an historian who lived many centuries *after* the time when it took place, such contradiction ought to have no weight.

1. Justin, the abbreviator of Trogus Pompeius, who wrote at least eighteen hundred years *after* the time of Moses, relates that the Israelites were expelled from Egypt, because they had communicated the itch and leprosy to the Egyptians, who were apprehensive lest the contagion

---

[1] Bishop Horne's Works, vol. vi. p. 513.
[2] Bishop Stillingfleet has largely proved this point in the first book of his *Origines Sacræ*, pp. 1—65. edit. 1709, folio.
[3] On this subject, see Vol. I. pp. 198—203.

should spread; and that the Israelites having clandestinely carried away the sacred mysteries of the Egyptians, were pursued by the latter; who were compelled to return home by tempests.[1]

It is scarcely necessary to remark, how contrary this statement of the Roman historian is to that of the Jewish legislator, and when his credulity and want of information are properly weighed, the contradiction falls entirely to the ground. The same remark is applicable to the accounts of the Jewish nation given by the prejudiced historian Tacitus, which evidently betray the injurious representations of their avowed enemies. Dr Gray, who has given these accounts (for which we have not room) has observed that many of them had been *distinctly refuted* in the time of Tacitus by Josephus and other historians. They contain in themselves sufficient to show how full of errors they are: and while they exhibit much truth blended with falsehood, they tend to establish the former, without conferring any shadow of probability on the latter [2]

2. It has been thought impossible to raise so vast an empire as that of Assyria is described to have been by Herodotus and Ctesias (whose accounts contradict the relation of Moses), so early as within one hundred and fifty years after Noah.

But their accounts are, probably, exaggerated, and in many instances fictitious: and, according to the chronology of the LXX, as well as of the Samaritan Pentateuch, the origin of the Assyrian empire is carried to a much greater distance from the flood [3]

3. Joseph's division of the land of Egypt, which is recorded by Moses (Gen. xlvii.) has been represented as contradictory to the account of that country by Diodorus Siculus.

But on comparing the two narratives together, it will be found that the latter fully *supports* the sacred historian Diodorus[4] expressly affirms that *the lands were divided between the king, the priests, and the soldiery*, and Moses expressly says, that *they were divided between the king, the priests, and the people.* "Moses tells us that before the famine, all the lands of Egypt were in the hands of the king, the priests, and the people; but that this national calamity made a great revolution in property, and brought the whole possessions of the people into the king's hands, which must needs make a prodigious accession of power to the crown. But Joseph, in whom the office of high priest and patriot supported each other, and jointly concurred to the public service, prevented for some time the ill effects of this accession by his farming out the new domain to the old proprietors on very easy conditions. We may well suppose this wise disposition to have continued, till that *new king arose that knew not Joseph* (Exod 1 8), that is, would obliterate his memory, as averse to his system of policy. He, as it appears from Scripture, greatly affected a despotic government, to support which he first established a standing militia, and endowed it with the lands formerly belonging to the people, who now became a kind of villeins to this order, and were obliged to personal service, this and the priesthood being the orders of nobility in this powerful empire: and so considerable were they, that out of them, indifferently their kings were taken and elected Thus the property of Egypt became divided in the manner the Sicilian relates, and it is remarkable that from this time and not till now, we hear in Scripture of a standing militia, and of the king's six hundred chosen chariots," &c [5]

4. The destruction of Sennacherib's army which is ascribed to divine agency by the sacred historian, (2 Kings xix 35. 2 Chron xxxii. 21. and

---

[1] Justin Hist Philipp lib xxxvi. c. 2. p. 308 ed Bipont.
[2] See Dr Gray's Connection between Sacred and Profane Literature, vol 1. pp. 435—443. And also Du Voisin's Autorité des Livres de Moyse, pp 180—199
[3] Doddridge's Lectures, vol. ii. Lect. 146 § x. (Works, vol. v. p. 127) See also Dr Hales's Analysis of Chronology, vol ii. pp. 48—52.
[4] Bib. Historic l. i. c. 73
[5] Bishop Warburton's Divine Legation, book iv § 3. in fine. (Works, vol. iv. pp. 115, 116.)

Isaiah xxxvii 36.) was probably the *blast* or hot pestilential south wind called the *Simoom*, so well described by Mr. Bruce.[1]

The destruction of the same army before Pelusium, in the reign of Sethos king of Egypt, is attributed by Herodotus[2] to an immense number of mice, that infested the Assyrian camp by *night*, so that their quivers and bows, together with what secured their shields to their arms, were gnawed in pieces. It is particularly to be remarked that Herodotus calls the Assyrian king Sennacherib, as the Scriptures do: and that the time referred to in both is perfectly accordant. Hence it appears that it is the same fact to which Herodotus alludes, although much disguised in the relation, and thus the seeming contradiction between the sacred and profane historians is easily removed. The difference between them may be readily explained, when it is considered that Herodotus derived his information from the Egyptian priests, who cherished the greatest aversion from the nation and religion of the Jews, and, therefore, would relate nothing in such a manner as would give reputation to either.[3]

5. There are many, apparently considerable, contradictions of the Scriptures in the writings of Josephus.

But these, as well as his *omissions*[4], may be accounted for by his peculiar situation. His country was now in great distress; its constitution was overturned, and his countrymen in danger of extirpation, from the circumstance of their being confounded with the Christians, who were reputed to be a sect of the Jews, and at that time were suffering persecution. Josephus's deviations from Scripture, therefore, were made in order to accommodate his work to the taste of the Greeks and Romans.[5]

6. In consequence of this Jewish historian having omitted to notice the massacre of the infants at Bethlehem, which is related in Matt. ii. 16., the evangelical narrative has been pronounced a "fabrication," and "a tale that carries its own refutation with it."

This assertion was first made, we believe, by Voltaire, whose disregard of truth especially in matters connected with the sacred history, is sufficiently notorious. But the evidence for the reality of the fact, and, consequently, for the veracity of Matthew, is too strong to be subverted by any bold and unsupported assertions. For,

In the *first* place, The whole character which Josephus ascribes to Herod, is the most evident confirmation of the barbarous deed mentioned by the evangelist.

Secondly, The Gospel of Matthew was published about the year of our Lord 38, at which time there were doubtless persons living, who could, and (from the hostility then manifested against the the Christian faith) who would have contradicted his assertion if it had been false or erroneous: their silence is a tacit proof that the evangelist has stated the fact correctly. — But,

Thirdly, The reality of the fact itself (though mentioned in his usual scoffing manner) was *not denied* by the philosopher Celsus, one of the bitterest enemies of Christianity, who lived towards the close of the second century; and who would most unquestionably have denied it if he could.[6]

Fourthly, Matthew's narrative is confirmed by Macrobius, a heathen author, who

---

[1] Travels, vol. v pp. 80. 295 322, 323. 350—353.

[2] Book ii c 141.

[3] Prideaux's Connection, book i. sub anno 710. (Part i p. 25 edit 1720.) It is remarkable that the blast, which destroyed the Assyrians, happened at night, whereas the Simoom, usually blows in the day-time, and mostly about noon, being raised by the intense heat of the sun Dr. Hales's Analysis of Chronology, vol ii. p 467.

[4] Ottius has compiled a curious treatise, intitled *Prœtermissa à Josepho* it is a collection of sixty-eight articles, of which, in all probability, the Jewish historian could not be ignorant; but which he chose to omit for the reason above assigned. This treatise is appended to Ottius's very valuable Spicilegium sive Excerpta ex Flavio Josepho, pp. 527 —612.

[5] Divine Legation of Moses, book v. sect 4 (Warburton's Works, vol v. pp. 126— 128.) The bishop has given several instances at length, which we have not room to insert, see pp. 130—132.

[6] See the passages in Lardner's Works, vol viii. p 21. 8vo or vol. iv. p. 122. 4to.

lived about the end of the fourth century, and who mentions this massacre in the following terms: "Augustus," says he, "having been informed that Herod had ordered a son of his own to be killed, *among the male infants about two years old*, whom he had put to death in Syria," said, "it is better to be Herod's HOG than his SON."[1] Now, although Macrobius is far too modern to be produced as a valid evidence in this matter, unsupported by other circumstances, and although his story is magnified by an erroneous circumstance; yet the passage, cited from him, serves to prove how universally notorious was the murder of the children in Bethlehem, which was perpetrated by the orders of Herod.

Fifthly, With regard to the silence of Josephus, we may further remark, that no historian, not even an *annalist*, can be expected to record every event that occurs within the period of which he writes: besides, his silence may be satisfactorily accounted for. "Josephus was a firm Jew, and there was, therefore, a particular reason for his passing over this event; because he could not mention it, without giving the Christian cause a very great advantage. To write, that Herod, at the latter end of his reign, had put to death all the infants at Bethlehem, under two years of age, on occasion of a report that the king of the Jews had been lately born there, would have greatly gratified the Christians, whom Josephus hated; since it was well known that, about thirty years after the slaughter, and the latter end of Herod's reign, Jesus (who was said to be born at Bethlehem), being about thirty years of age, styled himself King of the Jews, and did many things, to say no more in proof of it." It seems utterly impossible that Josephus could have been ignorant of this event: his silence was more likely to have been, in this as in other instances, wilful and interested.[2]

Sixthly, Contemporary historians do not relate the same facts: Suetonius tells us many things which Tacitus has omitted; and Dion Cassius supplies the deficiencies of both.

Seventhly, It is unreasonable to make the silence of the Jewish historian an objection to the credibility of the sacred writer, while there is equal and even superior reason to confide in the fidelity of the latter.

Eighthly, Herod would naturally be disposed to take such precautions as he might think necessary without being scrupulous concerning the means

Ninthly, Voltaire, either from ignorance or dishonesty, asserts that fourteen thousand children must have lost their lives in this massacre If this were true, the silence of Josephus would indeed be a very important objection to the veracity of Matthew's narrative; and with this view Voltaire makes the assertion, who every where shows himself an inveterate enemy of revealed, and not seldom of natural religion also But as the children, whom Herod caused to be put to death (probably by assassins whom he kept in his pay), were only *males* of *two years old and under*, it is obvious, according to this statement, that more children must have been born annually in the village of Bethlehem, than there are either in Paris or London. Further, as Bethlehem was a very small place, scarcely two thousand persons existed in it and in its dependent district; consequently, in the massacre, not more than fifty at most could be slain. In the description of the life of such a tyrant as Herod was, this was so trifling an act of cruelty, that it was but of small consequence in the history of his sanguinary government

Lastly, As the male infants that were to be slain could easily be ascertained from the public tables of birth or genealogies, that circumstance will account for the reputed parents of our Saviour fleeing into Egypt, rather than into any city of Judæa.[3]

---

[1] Macrob. Saturn. lib. ii. c 4. The emperor, according to this writer, seems to have played upon the Greek words *υον* a *hog*, and *υιον* a *son*, the point of the saying perhaps consists in this, that Herod, professing Judaism, was by his religion prohibited from killing swine, or having any thing to do with their flesh; and, therefore, that his *hog* would have been safe where his *son* lost his life Macrobius, with singular propriety, states this massacre to have been perpetrated in Syria, because Judæa was at that time part of the province of Syria. Gilpin and Dr. A. Clarke on Matt. ii 16. The massacre of the infants is likewise noticed in a rabbinical work called Toldoth Jeshu, in the following passage. "And the king gave orders for putting to death every infant to be found in Bethlehem; and the king's messengers killed every infant according to the royal order." Dr. G. Sharpe's First Defence of Christianity, &c. p. 40.

[2] Townsend's Harmony of the New Testament, vol. i. pp. 77, 78

[3] Lardner's Credibility, part i. book ii. ch. ii. sect. 1 (Works, vol. i. pp. 329—338.

VII. Sect. VII.] *Of Scripture, alleged to be Contradictory.* 551

Any of these arguments would be sufficient to vindicate the evangelist's narrative; but, altogether, they form a cloud of witnesses, abundantly sufficient to overbalance the negative evidence attempted to be drawn from the silence of Josephus.

7. Luke ii. 2. is said to be contrary to historical fact, Saturninus and Volumnius being at that time the Roman presidents of Syria, and Cyrenius not being governor of that province until eleven years after the birth of Christ.

A slight attention to the situation of Judæa at that time, and a more correct rendering of the passage than is to be found in our English version, will easily reconcile the seeming difference between the sacred historian and Josephus

Towards the close of his reign, Herod the Great (who held his kingdom by a grant from Mark Antony with the consent of the senate, which had been confirmed by Augustus,) having incurred the emperor's displeasure, to whom his conduct had been misrepresented, Augustus issued a decree reducing Judæa to a Roman province, and *commanding* an enrolment, or register, to be made of every person's estate, dignity, age, employment, and office The making of this enrolment was confided to Cyrenius or Quirinius, a Roman senator, who was collector of the imperial revenue; but Herod having sent his trusty minister, Nicholas of Damascus, to Rome, the latter found means to undeceive the emperor, and soften his anger, in consequence of which the actual operation of the decree was suspended. *Eleven* years afterwards, however, it was carried into effect, on the deposition and banishment of Archelaus (Herod's son and successor), for maladministration, by Augustus, upon the complaint of the Jews, who, weary of the tyranny of the Herodian family, requested that Judæa might be made a Roman province. Cyrenius was now sent as president of Syria, with an armed force, to confiscate the property of Archelaus, and to complete the census, to which the Jewish people submitted. It was *this* establishment of the assessment or taxing under Cyrenius which was necessary to complete the Roman census, to which the evangelist alludes in the parenthetical remark occurring in Luke ii. 2, which may be more correctly written and translated thus: " *It came to pass in those days,*" that is, a few days before our Saviour's birth, " *that there went out a decree from Cæsar Augustus, that all the land*" [of Judæa, Galilee, Idumæa, &c under Herod's dominion] "*should be enrolled*¹" preparatory to a census or taxing; " *The taxing itself was first made when Cyrenius was governor of Syria*². " *And all went to be enrolled, every one to his own city* (Luke ii. 1—3.)

By the preceding construction, supported by the emendation in the note, the evangelist is critically reconciled with the varying accounts of

---

8vo. or pp 180—185 4to)   Volborth *Causa cur Josephus cædem puerorum Bethlemeticorum*, Matt. ii 16 *narratam silentio prætervert*, 4to. Gottingen, 1788, as analysed in the Monthly Review (O. S.) vol. lxxx, p 617   Schulzii Archæologia Hebraica, pp 52, 53. Colonia, La Religion Chretiénne autorisée par le Temoignage des Anciens Auteurs Paiens, pp. 117, 118.

¹ Απογραφεσθαι την ΟΙΚΟΥΜΗΝΗΝ, Luke ii 1 That ΟΙΚΟΥΜΗΝΗΝ signifies the land of Judæa, and not the whole Roman empire, see Vol III. p. 2.

² (Αὔτη ἡ απογραφη εγενετο ἡγεμονευοντος της Συριας Κυρηνιου)   In all the printed editions of the New Testament the first word in this verse is aspirated αὑτη, *thus*, as if it were the feminine of οὑτος   " But this," says Dr Hales, to whom we are indebted for the above elucidation, " materially injures the sense, as if the *enrolment* decreed in the first verse was the same as *this taxing* in the second ; whereas there was an interval of eleven years between the two   But in the most antient manuscripts, written in uncials or in capitals, without points or accents, the word is ambiguous, and may also be unaspirated αυτη, *self*, the feminine of αυτος , and both occur together in this same chapter, where the evangelist, speaking of Anna the prophetess, says, και αὐτη, αυτη τη ωρα επιστασα, ' And *this* [woman] coming in at *the instant itself*,' or at ' *the self-same hour*,' &c.   The ordinal πρωτη, first, is here understood adverbially, (see Bishop Middleton on the Greek Article, pp 304, 305) and connected with the verb εγενετο, ' *was made*,' or ' *took effect*,' signifying that the taxing itself *first took effect*, or was carried into execution, under the presidency of Cyrenius or Quirinius, which had been suspended from the time of his procuratorship "   Dr. Hales's Analysis of Chronology, vol. ii. pp. 705—710.

Josephus, Justin Martyr, and Tertullian, and an historical difficulty is solved, which has hitherto been considered as irreconcileable.[1]

Two other solutions, however, have been offered: which deserve to be noticed on account of their ingenuity.

(1.) The first is that of Mr Charles Thompson, late Secretary to the Congress of the United States, the learned translator of the Old and New Testaments from the Greek. He renders Luke ii 1, 2. in the following manner: " Now it happened in those days that an edict came forth from Cæsar Augustus that this whole inhabited land should be enrolled. *This was the first enrolment, it was made when Cyrenius was governor of Syria*." In a note on the passage in question, he observes, " There were two enrolments, the first merely for the purpose of *numbering* the inhabitants, and the second for assessing them. The first here spoken of, was in the reign of Herod the Great, when Cyrenius was deputy-governor of Syria. It was done according to communities and families, and all were obliged to repair to their respective cities or towns, to be enrolled in their several families, according to their genealogies. The second, which was after the death of Herod, was for the sake of *assessment*, and was made indiscriminately. This was the enrolment which offended the Jews, and excited tumults and insurrections, and brought on the war which terminated in the destruction of Jerusalem, and the utter dispersion of the Jews." From the rendering, thus supported, the praise of learning and ingenuity must not be withheld. Mr Thompson evidently considers the word η, which all other translators consider as an indefinite article prefixed to απογραφη (*enrolment*), as the third person singular of ην, the imperfect tense in the indicative mood of the verb ειμι, *I am*. It is well known that profane writers use η or ην indifferently as the third person singular; and if we could find a single parallel construction, in the New Testament, we should unquestionably give the preference to Mr. T.'s rendering.

(2.) The other solution is that offered by the learned editor of Calmet's Dictionary; who conjectures, that for the purposes of enrolment, Cyrenius, though not probably governor of Syria at the time of Christ's birth, might be associated with Saturninus, or, though now sent into Syria as an extraordinary officer, yet being afterwards governor of Syria, he might be called governor of Syria, as we call an officer during his life by the title he has borne, even after he has given up his commission. On a medal of Antioch appear the names of Saturninus and Volumnius, who were the emperor's chief officers in Syria. It would seem, therefore, that Volumnius was the colleague of Saturninus in the government of Syria, and procurator of the province, and that while Saturninus kept his court at Antioch, where he remained stationary, his associate Volumnius was engaged in other districts of the province as circumstances required. What we suppose of Volumnius we may also suppose of Cyrenius, who, after him, held the same office. Thus, the medal vindicates Josephus, who described Saturninus and Volumnius as governors of Syria, and it may justify both Saint Luke and Tertullian, of whom the former affirmed that Cyrenius, and the latter that Saturninus, executed the enrolment. It may also justify the evangelist, whose words the editor of Calmet thinks may be thus understood: " This was the first enrolment of Cyrenius, he being then governor of Syria, associated with Saturninus, and it should be dis-

---

[1] Dr. Campbell (Translation of the Four Gospels, vol. ii pp. 140 422—425) renders Luke ii. 2. in the following manner — '*This first register took effect when Cyrenius was president of Syria.*" But, as we have seen in the preceding note that πρωτη is here used adverbially, this version will not hold good. In confirmation of his rendering εγενετο " took effect," (which is adopted by Dr Hales,) Campbell refers to Matt v. 18. vi. 10. xviii 19. xxii 42. and 1 Cor xv 54. Dr. Lardner has proposed another solution of the above difference, (Credibility, part i book ii ch i Works, vol. i, pp. 248—329. 8vo. or pp. 136—179 4to.) which deserves to be noticed, because it has been adopted by Archdeacon Paley, (Evidences, vol. ii pp. 177, 178.) It is as follows —" *This was the first enrolment of Cyrenius governor of Syria*, that is, who was afterwards governor of Syria, and best known among the Jews by that title;" which title, belonging to him at the time of *writing the account*, was naturally subjoined to his name, although acquired after the transaction which the account describes. A similar solution is given by Alber. Hermeneut. Nov. Test. tom. ii. pp. 309, 310., and in Pritii Introd. in Nov. Test. p. 437.

tinguished from that which he made eleven years after, when he was the chief, the presidential governor of the same province."[1]

The reader will adopt which of the preceding solutions he may prefer either of them affords a sufficient explanation of the *seeming* contradiction between the Evangelist and Josephus, though, upon the whole, we think the rendering of Dr. Hales presents the most satisfactory elucidation.

8 In Luke iii. 19 Herod the tetrarch is said to have been reproved by John the Baptist for Herodias, his brother *Philip's* wife, whom he had forcibly taken away from her husband and married.

Now this is irreconcileable with profane history, which asserts his brother's name to have been *Herod* Hence it is probable that the name of *Philip* has crept into the text through the copyist's negligence, and ought to be omitted: Griesbach has omitted it in his text, but has inserted the word φιλιππου in the margin, with the mark of doubtful genuineness

9. Acts v. 36. *For before these days rose up Theudas,* &c Josephus's account of Theudas (Antiq. l. xx. c. 5. § 1.) referred to a transaction that occurred seven years *after* Gamaliel's speech, of which this text is a part.

The contradiction is removed by the probability that there might be *two* impostors of the same name: for there were four persons of the name of Simon within forty years, and three of *Judas* within ten years, all of whom were leaders of insurrections [2]

SECTION VIII.

ALLEGED CONTRADICTIONS TO PHILOSOPHY AND THE NATURE OF THINGS.

THE Scriptures often refer to matters of fact, which are *asserted* (though without any proof whatever) to be contradictory to philosophy and to the nature of things. A little consideration, however, will reconcile these alleged repugnances; for it has been well observed by different writers, who have treated on this subject, that the Scriptures were not written with the design of teaching us natural philosophy, but to make known the revealed will of God to man, and to teach us our duties and obligations to our great Creator and Redeemer. Therefore the sacred penman might make use of popular expressions and forms of speech, neither affirming nor denying their philosophical truth. All proverbial sayings and metaphorical expressions introduced by way of illustration or ornament, must be taken from received notions; but they are not, *therefore*, asserted in the philosophical sense by him who uses them, any more than the historical truth of parables and similitudes is supposed to be asserted. Further, to have employed philosophical terms and notions only. and to have rectified the vulgar conceptions of men concerning all the

---

[1] Calmet's Dictionary, vol i. article *Cyrenius*. Fragments Supplementary to Calmet, No. cxxiii p 37 Geographical Index and Sacred Geography, by the same editor, voce *Antioch*

[2] Dr **Lardner** has collected the passages in question relative to these impostors. Works, vol. i. pp. 409—413 See also Paley's Evidences, vol ii. pp. 179—181.

phenomena incidentally mentioned in the Scriptures, would have required a large system of philosophy, which would have rendered the Scriptures a book unfit for ordinary capacities, and the greater part of those for whom it is designed. If, indeed, revelation had introduced any the best founded system of modern physics, or if the Almighty Creator had been pleased to disclose the councils themselves of his infinite wisdom, what would have been the consequence? Philosophy would immediately have become matter of faith, and disbelief of any part of it a dangerous heresy. How many infidels would this or that man's fanciful hypothesis concerning the appearances of things have called forth! Besides, if the Scriptures had been made the vehicle for a refined system of natural philosophy, such a theory of nature would have seemed as strange and incredible to most men as miracles do; for there is scarcely any thing which more surprises men, unacquainted with philosophy, than philosophical discoveries. How incredible do the *motion* of the earth and the *rest* of the sun appear to all but philosophers, who are now fully convinced of the reality of these phenomena, while the rising and setting of the sun are terms as much in use with those who hold the doctrine of the earth's motion as with others. In fact, if we would be understood, we must continue to make use of this expression; but excepting this one instance, which is and ever will be in use, according to the vulgar conceptions of all nations and languages (notwithstanding any philosophical discoveries to the contrary), there is nothing in the Scriptures that is not strictly consistent with the present notions of philosophy. The discoveries both in chemistry and in physics, as well as in natural history, which have been made in later times, concur in many instances to confirm and elucidate the Sacred Writings. A few examples will illustrate the preceding observations.

1. No fact recorded in the Sacred Writings has been a more favourite subject of cavil with modern objectors, than the *account of the creation,* related in the two first chapters of the book of Genesis. Founding their cavils upon translations, instead of consulting the original Hebrew (which their ignorance completely disqualified them from doing), they have pretended that the Mosaic narrative is alike inconsistent with reason and with true philosophy. If, however, these writers had impartially considered the modern discoveries in philosophy, they would have found nothing to contradict, but on the contrary much — very much — to confirm the relation of Moses

" The *structure of the earth*," says one of the most profound geologists and practical philosophers of the present day [1], " and the mode of distribution of extraneous fossils or petrifactions, are so many direct evidences of the truth of the Scripture account of the formation of the earth; and they might be used as proofs of its author having been inspired, because the mineralogical facts discovered by *modern* naturalists were unknown to the sacred historian Even the periods of time, the six days of the Mosaic description, — are not inconsistent with our theories of the earth " Nor are the phenomena of the heavenly bodies at all contradictory to the Mosaic history. Modern opposers of revelation have objected that the historian talks of light before there was any such thing as the sun, and calls the

---

[1] Professor Jameson, in page v of his Preface to Mr. Kerr's translation of M. Cuvier's Essay on the Theory of the Earth.

moon a *great light*, when every one knows it to be an opaque body. But Moses seems to have known what philosophy did not till very lately discover, that the sun is not the original source of light, and, therefore, he does not call either the sun or the moon a *great light*, though he represents them both as great *luminaries* or *light-bearers*. Had these objectors looked into a Hebrew, Greek, or Latin Bible, they would have found that the word, which in Gen. 1. 3. our translators have properly rendered *light*, is different from that which in the fourteenth verse they have improperly rendered light also. In the third verse the original word is אור (*aur*), the Greek, φως, and the Vulgate Latin, *lux*, in the fourteenth verse the corresponding words are מארת (*mart*), φωστηρες, and *luminaria*. Each of the former set of words means that subtile, elastic matter, to which in English we give the name of *light;* each of the latter, the instruments, or means, by which light is transmitted to men. But surely the moon is as much an instrument of this kind, as the *reflector* placed behind the lamp of a light-house, for the purpose of transmitting to the mariner at sea the light of that lamp, which would otherwise have passed in an opposite direction to the land. Though the moon is not a light in itself, yet is that planet a light in its effects, as it reflects the light of the sun to us. And both the sun and moon are with great propriety called *great*,— not as being absolutely greater than all other stars and planets, but because they appear greater to *us*, and are of greater use and consequence to this world. And now, after all our improvements in philosophy and astronomy, we still speak of the light of the moon, as well as of the sun's motion, rising and setting. And the man, who in a moral, theological, or historical discourse, should use a different language, would only render himself ridiculous.

In like manner, had these objectors referred to the original Hebrew of Gen. 1. 6, 7, 8. (which in our English authorised version, as well as in other modern versions, is erroneously rendered *firmament*, after the Septuagint and Vulgate Latin version,) they would have rendered it *expanse;* and they might have known, that it meant the air or atmosphere around us, in which birds fly and clouds are formed, and that it had no reference whatever to a solid firmament, though such an idea was entertained by the antient Greek philosophers, who, with all their boasted wisdom, were nearly as ignorant of the works, as they were of the nature of God. And does not this circumambient air divide the waters from the waters, the waters of the sea from the waters which float above us in clouds and vapours? *For there is a multitude of waters in the heavens, and He causeth the vapours to ascend from the ends of the earth* (Jer x 13.)

Once more, Moses represents the earth at first in a state of *fluidity*. *The spirit of God*, says he, *moved upon the face* (or surface) *of the waters*. (Gen. 1. 2.) The apostle Peter also speaks of the earth as being formed out of a fluid. *The earth standing out of the water* (more correctly, consisting of water δι' ὕδατος συνεστωσα,) *and in the midst of the water.* The same tradition reached also some of the antient heathen philosophers, and Thales, in particular, one of the seven wise men and the wisest of them all, as Cicero informs us, said that all things were made out of water.[1] Others after him taught the same doctrine; and is it in the least degree contradicted or disproved by modern discoveries? On the contrary, is it not more and more confirmed and illustrated by them? It is well known that if a soft or elastic globular body be rapidly whirled round on its axis, the parts at the poles will be flattened, and the parts on the equator, midway between the north and south poles, will be raised up. This is precisely the shape of our earth, it has the figure of an oblate spheroid, a figure bearing a close resemblance to that of an orange. Now, if the earth was ever in a state of fluidity, its revolution round its axis must necessarily induce such a figure, because the greatest centrifugal force must necessarily be near the equatorial parts, and, consequently, there the fluid must rise and swell most. It has been *demonstrated* by experiment, that the earth is flattened at the poles and raised at the equator;[3] and thus do the Scriptures

---

[1] Princeps Thales, unus e septem cui sex reliquos concessisse primas ferunt ex aquas dixit constare omnia. Ciceronis Academic. Quæst. lib ii, c 37. Op tom. x. p. 118. edit. Bipont.

[2] The reader will find the sentiments of the philosophers above alluded to, in the notes to Grotius de Veritate, lib i c 16.

[3] This was first conjectured by Sir Isaac Newton, and confirmed by M Cassini and others, who measured several degrees of latitude at the equator and at the north pole, and found that the difference perfectly justified Sir Isaac Newton's conjecture, and, con-

and philosophy agree together and confirm each other. The Scriptures assert that the earth was in a state of fluidity; and philosophy evinces that it must have been in such a state from its very figure.

The account of the creation of man (Gen. i. 26, 27.) has been ridiculed by all opposers of revelation, but can they furnish us with one more likely to be the true one? Reason will tell us no better than history or tradition does, how man came into the world. This, therefore, is a subject of divine revelation, and until the objectors to revelation can give us a better account, we may safely affirm that the Mosaic history is perfectly consistent with every idea which right reason teaches us to entertain of the creation of man.

Lastly, objectors to the Scriptures have laid great stress upon the expression in Gen. ii. 3. — *God rested the seventh day from all his work*, as if it were alone sufficient to destroy the authority of the Mosaic writings. But no one, who impartially considers the noble account there given of the creation, that God is represented as having only spoken and it was done, can *reasonably* imagine, that the Almighty was tired with labour, as if he had moulded every thing with his hands, and that on the seventh day he lay or sat down for rest. *Hast thou not known*, says the Hebrew prophet Isaiah, — *hast thou not heard, that the everlasting God, the Creator of the ends of the earth, fainteth not, neither is weary?* (Isa. xl. 28.)

The objections drawn by infidel writers from the Mosaic narrative of the deluge have already been noticed in Vol. I. pp. 160, 161. 170—173.

2. The declaration of Moses in Deut. i. 10. that God had multiplied the Israelites as the *stars of heaven for multitude*, has been ridiculed, because to the apprehension of the objector "the number of the stars is infinite."

Let us, however, consider this subject. How many in number are the stars, which appear to the naked eye? For it is that which appears to the naked eye, which is to govern us in replying to this objection: for *God brought Abraham forth abroad*, — that is, out of doors, *and bade him look towards heaven* (Gen. xv. 5.), not with a telescope, but with his naked eyes. Now, let the objector go forth into the open air, and look up in the brightest and most favourable night, and count the stars. Not more than 3010 stars can be seen by the naked eye in both the northern and southern hemispheres; but at the time alluded to, the Israelites, independently of women and children, were more than six hundred thousand. Suppose, however, we even allow, from the late discoveries made by Sir Wm. Herschel and others with telescopes, which have magnified between thirty-five and thirty-six thousand times, that there *may be* seventy-five millions of stars visible by the aid of such instruments, which is the highest calculation ever made; yet still the divine word stands literally true. Matthew says (i. 17.) that the generations from Abraham to Christ were forty-two. Now we find at the second census, that the fighting men among the Hebrews amounted to 600,000; and the Israelites, who have never ceased to be a distinct people, have so multiplied that, if the aggregate number of them who have ever lived, could be ascertained, it would be found far to exceed the number of all the fixed stars taken together.[1]

3. The speaking of Balaam's ass (Numb. xxii. 28.) has been a standing jest to infidels in almost every age.

If the ass had opened her own mouth, and reproved the rash prophet, we might well be astonished. Maimonides and others have imagined that the matter was transacted in a vision. But it is evident, from the whole tenor of the narration, as well as from the declaration of an inspired writer (2 Pet. ii. 14—16.), that it is to be understood as a literal narrative of a real transaction. The ass, it has been observed, was enabled to utter such and such sounds, probably as parrots do, *without understanding them*: and, whatever may be said of the construction of the ass's mouth, and of the tongue and jaws being so formed as to be unfit for speaking, yet an adequate cause is assigned for this wonderful effect: for it is expressly said, that *the Lord opened the mouth of the ass*. The miracle was by no means needless or superfluous: it was very proper to convince Balaam, that the mouth and tongue

---

sequently, confirmed the truth of the Mosaic narrative. The result of the experiments, instituted to determine this point, proved, that the diameter of the earth at the *equator* is greater by more than *twenty three miles* than it is *at the poles*.

[1] Dr. A. Clarke's Commentary, on Deut. i. 10.

were under God's direction, and that the same divine power, which caused the dumb ass to speak contrary to its nature, could make him in like manner utter blessings contrary to his inclination. The fact is as consonant to reason as any other extraordinary operation, for all miracles are alike, and equally demand our assent, if properly attested. The giving of articulation to a brute is no more to the Deity, than the making of the blind to see, or the deaf to hear. And the reputed baseness of the instrument, of which God was pleased to make use, amounts merely to this, that (as the Apostle observes on another occasion) *God hath chosen the foolish things of the world to confound the wise.* (1 Cor. 1. 27.) There was, therefore, a fitness in the instrument used, for the more vile the means were, the fitter they were to confound the unrighteous prophet.

4. It has been affirmed that the circumstance of the sun and moon standing still, which is recorded in Joshua x. 12, is contrary to philosophy.

Let it, however, be recollected that the sacred historian expressly relates it as a *miracle* it is, therefore, impossible to account for it on philosophical principles, it must be resolved wholly into the power of God, who hearkened to the voice of a man to stop the luminaries, in their *diurnal* courses, or, perhaps, the earth's rotation, and by prolonging the day of battle to make them fight for Israel. From the circumstances of the narrative we may collect the time of the day and of the month when it happened, viz. soon after sun-rise, and when the moon was rather past the full.

"Joshua, when summoned by the Gibeonites to come to their succour against the confederate kings, went up from Gilgal *all night*, and came suddenly (we may conclude *about day-break*) upon the enemy, whom he discomfited with great slaughter, and chased along the way from Gibeon to Beth-horon, in a westerly direction, the Lord co-operating in their destruction by a tremendous shower of great hail-stones, which slew more than the sword of the Israelites, but did not touch the latter. In this situation the sun appeared to rise over Gibeon eastward, and the moon to set over Ajalon westward, near the Mediterranean Sea, in the tribe of Dan, when Joshua, moved by a divine impulse, uttered this invocation in the sight of Israel:—'*Sun,* stand thou still over Gibeon, and thou, *Moon,* in the valley of Ajalon.' So the sun stood still in the hemisphere [at its rising], and hasted not to go down [at its setting] about a whole day; which, in that climate, and shortly after the vernal equinox, might have been about thirteen hours long, thus giving him day-light for the destruction of his enemies for twenty-six hours, during which he took the city of Makkedah, and slew the five kings who hid themselves in a cave near it." (Josh x. 1—28.)[1]

The object of this miracle was of the most important and impressive nature. The sun and the moon, the two principal gods of the idolatrous heathen nations, were commanded to yield miraculous obedience to the chief servant of the true God; and thereby to contribute to the more effectual conquest of their own worshippers. It was a miracle of the same description as those which had been wrought in Egypt. With respect to the objections to the probability of this miracle, which originate in a consideration of its supposed consequences, it is justly observed by Bishop Watson, that "the machine of the universe is in the hand of God: he can stop the motion of any part or of the whole, with less trouble than either of us can stop a watch!" How absurd, then, are the reasonings of those men who believe in the existence of an omnipotent God, yet deny the possibility of the exertion of his power in other ways, than those which are known to their limited experience![2]

5. The beautiful poetical passage in Judges v. 20. has been stigmatised as a "species of Jewish rant and hyperbole."

A tempest meeting the enemy in the face discomfited them: and the torrent Kishon was so suddenly swelled by the rain (which common opinion ascribed to the planets), as to sweep away the greater part of Sisera's army in their precipitate flight. Hence the poetess calls it the *first* or the *prince* of torrents. The whole is

---

[1] Dr. Hales's New Analysis of Chronology, vol. i. p. 290. The reader, who is desirous of reading the different opinions of learned men, on the subject of this miracle, is referred to Mr Howlett's note on Josh. x. 12. (Comment on the Bible, vol. i.) and to an original and elaborate note of Dr. A. Clarke on the same passage.
[2] Townsend's Arrangement of the Old Testament, vol. i. p. 463. note.

exceedingly poetical, notwithstanding the censure of the opposers of revelation, whose cavils are characterised not more by want of taste, than by wilful ignorance and malignity of disposition.

6. It is said that such a number of inhabitants, as are stated to have dwelt in the land of Canaan, could not possibly have been supported there, viz. a million and a half of fighting men. (2 Sam. xxiv. 9. 1 Chron xxi. 5.)

To this it is to be answered, that if there be no mistake in the numbers (which probably are incorrect, as the Syriac version reads eight hundred thousand in 2 Sam. xxiv. 9. and 1 Chron xxi. 5.) this vast population is to be ascribed to the extraordinary fertility of the soil. Another solution of this apparent contradiction has been offered by a late writer [1], which is both ingenious and probable. "It appears," he observes, "from Chronicles, that there were twelve divisions of generals, who commanded monthly, and whose duty it was to keep guard near the king's person, each having a body of troops consisting of twenty-four thousand men, which jointly formed a grand army of two hundred and eighty thousand: and, as a separate body of twelve thousand men naturally attended on the twelve princes of the twelve tribes, mentioned in the same chapter, the whole will be three hundred thousand; which is the difference between the two last accounts of eight hundred thousand and of one million one hundred thousand [2] Whence may be deduced this natural solution as to the number of Israel. As to the men of Israel, the author of Samuel does not take notice of the three hundred thousand, because they were in the actual service of the king as a standing army, and, therefore, there was no need to number them · but the author of Chronicles joins them to the rest, saying expressly, כל ישראל, ' all those of Israel were one million one hundred thousand;' whereas the author of Samuel, who reckons only the eight hundred thousand, does not say כל ישראל ' all those of Israel,' but barely וחצי ישראל ' and Israel were,' &c It must also be observed, that, exclusively of the troops before mentioned, there was an army of observation on the frontiers of the Philistines' country, composed of thirty thousand men, as appears by 2 Sam vi. 1; which, it seems, were included in the number of five hundred thousand of the people of Judah, by the author of Samuel; but the author of Chronicles, who mentions only four hundred and seventy thousand, gives the number of that tribe exclusively of those thirty thousand men, because they were not all of the tribe of Judah: and therefore he does not say, כל יהודה ' all those of Judah,' as he had said כל ישראל ' all those of Israel,' but only יהודה ' and those of Judah' Thus both accounts may be reconciled, by only having recourse to other parts of Scripture, treating on the same subject; which will ever be found the best method of explaining difficult passages."

7. The number of cattle sacrificed at the dedication of Solomon's temple, has been objected to as incredible, viz. one hundred and twenty thousand sheep, and two and twenty thousand oxen. (1 Kings viii. 63.)

To this it may be replied, first, that all these were not offered in one day, much less on one altar. This solemn meeting continued fourteen days, viz. seven at the feast of tabernacles, and seven at the feast of dedication (1 Kings viii. 65.): and because the brazen altar was too little to receive the burnt offerings, Solomon by special permission from God, hallowed the middle of the court, that is, ordered other altars to be erected in the court of the priests, and perhaps in other places, which were to serve only during that solemnity, when such a vast number of sacrifices was to be offered. And, secondly, it is by no means improbable that there were some neighbouring princes, who paid Solomon their tribute in cattle, and who might supply victims for the extraordinary sacrifice above referred to See an instance of this kind in 2 Kings iii. 4.

The great number of beasts daily required in Solomon's kitchen, (1 Kings iv. 23) will by no means be found incredible, when we compare it with the accounts of the daily consumption of oriental courts in modern times, and the prodigious

---

[1] The editor of the quarto edition of Calmet's Dictionary of the Bible. See Fragments, No xxxvii. pp 62, 63.
[2] Vide Alichot Holam, p. 18.

number of servants of an Asiatic prince. Thus, Tavernier, in his description of the seraglio, said, that *five hundred sheep and lambs* were *daily* required for the persons belonging to the court of the sultan.[1]

8. It is urged that the treasures, mentioned in 1 Chron. xxix. 4—7. as amassed by David for the purpose of erecting a temple, are incredible; and that it was impossible that he could collect such a sum, which has been computed by M. le Clerc at eight hundred millions sterling, and which is thought to exceed all the gold of all the princes now upon earth put together.

But it is possible that there may be a corruption in the numbers: we are not so well acquainted with the weights mentioned, as to be able to ascertain with precision the then comparative value of the precious metals, nor what resources for obtaining them (now lost) there were at that time. Besides, it is probable that the *talent*, mentioned in the passage above cited, was the Syriac talent; according to which the amount collected by David would be £7,087,791.[2] And in an age like that in which David lived, when kings and princes were accustomed to hoard up vast quantities of gold and silver (as the oriental monarchs still do) it is by no means improbable that David and his princes, in their successful wars with the Philistines, Moabites, and Amalekites, and with the kings of Zobah, Syria, and Edom, might collect gold and silver to the above amount.

9. The circumstance of Elijah being fed by ravens (1 Kings xvii. 4.) has excited the profane scoffs of unbelievers, as an incredible thing; and they have attempted to be witty in their inquiries whence these unclean birds could have procured food for the prophet.

Had these writers, however, consulted the original word of this passage, and also other places where the same word occurs, they would have found that ערבים (orebim) signifies Arabian. Such is the meaning of the word in 2 Chron. xxi. 16 and in Neh. iv. 7. where our version correctly renders it Arabians. Now we learn from the *Beresheth Rabba* (a rabbinical commentary on the book of Genesis[3]), that there anciently was a town in the vicinity of Bethshan (where the prophet was commanded to conceal himself), and we are further informed by Jerome, a learned writer of the fourth century, that the *Orbim*, *inhabitants of a town, on the confines of the Arabs, gave nourishment to Elijah*[4] This testimony of Jerome is of great value, because he spent several years in the Holy Land, in order that he might acquire the most correct notion possible of the language and geography of the country, as well as of the customs and habits of the people, in order to enable him to understand, explain, and translate the Holy Scriptures. Although the common printed editions of the Latin Vulgate read *corvi*, crows or ravens, yet in 2 Chron xxi.16 and Neh iv. 7. Jerome properly renders the same word ערבים (orbim or orebim), the Arabians. What adds further weight to these testimonies is the fact, that the Arabic version considers the word as meaning a people, *Orabim*, and not ravens or fowls of any kind. We may also add, that the celebrated Jewish commentator, Jarchi, gives the same interpretation. How, indeed, (it has been well asked,) could the holy prophet receive his meat from such unclean animals as ravens are, contrary to that law of which he was so zealous and intrepid a defender? How could he know that these impure birds had not been resting among carcases and carrion, before they brought him his meat? Besides, Elijah was supplied with bread and flesh every morning and evening for a whole year. How can such a long and careful attendance be ascribed to ravens? It is therefore most likely, that some of the inhabitants of Oreb or Orbo furnished the prophet with food, being specially and divinely directed so to do.[5]

---

[1] Burder's Oriental Literature, vol 1 p 399

[2] The reader will find some elaborate and interesting calculations on this subject, in Dr. Brown's Antiquities of the Jews, vol. 1 pp. 149—153.

[3] Sect. 33 fol. 30. col 2.

[4] Orbim accolæ villæ in finibus Arabum, Eliæ dederunt alimenta.

[5] See Dr. A. Clarke on 1 Kings xvii and especially the Dissertation in De la Roche's Memoirs of Literature, vol. 1. pp 81—85; where the reader will find a full discussion of this subject. In the last cited work the testimonies of antient Jewish writers, confirming the view of it above given, are stated at length.

10. There is no contradiction between Job xxvi. 7. and Psal. xxiv. 2. and civ. 5.

In the first cited passage, Job says that God *hangeth the earth upon nothing* · and in Psal. xxiv. 2 it is said that Jehovah *hath founded the earth upon the seas, and established it upon the floods* and in Psal civ 5. that he hath *laid the foundations of the earth that it should not be removed for ever* All which expressions are philosophically correct. for the foundation of a pendulous globe can be nothing, but its centre, upon which all the parts lean and are supported by it; and the waters continually flowing through the bowels and concavities of the earth, from the depths of the sea, by a constant course and circulation, constitute an abyss in the lowermost parts of the earth *All the rivers run into the sea, yet the sea is not full : unto the place from whence the rivers come, thither they return again*. (Eccles 1. 7) So that, with great propriety of speech, the terraqueous globe is said to hang upon nothing, and the earth to be founded upon the seas, and established upon the floods, and (Psal cxxxvi 6) to *be stretched out above the waters* [1].

11. The *unicorn* רים (REIM), described in Job xxxix. 9. and alluded to in several other passages of Scripture, is the common rhinoceros, which is known, in Arabia, by the name of *reim* unto this day.

12. The circumstance of Jonah being in the belly of a *whale* (Jonah i. 17. Matt. xii. 40.) has been affirmed to be contrary to matter of fact , as the throat of a whale, it is well known, is capable of admitting little more than the arm of an ordinary man; and these fish are never found in the Mediterranean Sea.

But Bochart has long since proved that a great fish of the *shark* kind is here intended. It is a well attested fact that many of the shark species are not only of such a size and form as to be able, without any miracle, to swallow a man whole, but also that men have been found entire in their stomachs · and, since it is a fact well known to physiologists, that the stomach has no power over substances endued with vitality, this circumstance will account in part for the miraculous preservation of the prophet Jonah in the belly or stomach of the great fish, in which he was for three days and three nights Bochart is further of opinion, that the particular species of shark which followed the prophet Jonah, was the *squalus carcharias* or white shark, for its voracity termed *lamia* by some naturalists, and which is a native of the seas in hot climates, where it is the terror of navigators [a]

The preceding are the passages of Scripture, which have been principally excepted against, as being contrary to philosophy and the nature of things ; and yet, when all the circumstances of them are properly considered, there is nothing in them which may not be accounted for, and interpreted, on the principles of modern philosophy.

---

[1] Jenkin's Reasonableness of the Christian Religion, vol ii. p. 236.

[a] Bocharti Opera, tom. iii. col. 742 *et seq* Bochart's opinion has been adopted by Mr Parkhurst (Greek Lexicon, article Κητος), and is now generally received. See also Scripture illustrated by Natural History, &c Expository Index, p. 52 and the Fragments annexed to the quarto edition of Calmet's Dictionary, No cxlv p 103 Bishop Jebb, however, has urged several considerations (which are too long for insertion here, and the force of which it would impair to abridge,) showing that it probably was a whale, into the cavity of whose mouth Jonah was taken (Sacred Literature, pp 178—180) The observations which he has adduced from the natural history of the whale, are confirmed by the enterprising and experienced whale-fisher, Capt. Scoresby ; who states, that when the mouth of the *Bolæna Mysticetus*, or Great Common Whale, is open, " it presents a cavity as large as a room, and capable of containing a merchant ship's jolly-boat full of men, being six or eight feet wide, ten or twelve feet high (in front), and fifteen or sixteen feet long. (Scoresby's Account of the Arctic Regions, vol i p 455.) The only objection that can be offered to Dr Jebb's opinion, is, that there is no authentic instance on record of whales being found in the Mediterranean Sea.

CHAPTER VIII.
ON THE INFERENTIAL AND PRACTICAL READING OF SCRIPTURE.

SECTION I.
ON THE INFERENTIAL READING OF THE BIBLE.

I. *General Rules for the Deduction of Inferences.* — II. *Observations for ascertaining the Sources of Internal Inferences.* — III. *And also of External Inferences.*

I. THE sense of Scripture having been explained and ascertained, it only remains that we apply it to purposes of practical utility: which may be effected either by deducing inferences from texts, or by practically applying the Scriptures to our personal edification and salvation. By INFERENCES, we mean certain corollaries or conclusions legitimately deduced from words rightly explained· so that they who either hear or read them, may form correct views of Christian doctrine and Christian duty. And in this deduction of inferences we are warranted both by the genius of language, which, when correctly understood, not only means what the words uttered in themselves obviously imply, but also what may be deduced from them by legitimate consequences [1]; and likewise by the authority of Jesus Christ and his apostles, who have sanctioned this practice by their example. To illustrate this remark by a single instance. —

Our Lord (Matt. xxii. 23—32.), when disputing with the Sadducees, cited the declaration of Jehovah recorded in Exod. iii. 6. *I am the God of Abraham, Isaac, and Jacob:* and from thence he proved the *resurrection of the dead* inferentially, or by legitimate *consequence.* It should be observed, that Abraham had been dead upwards of three hundred years before these words were spoken to Moses, yet still Jehovah called himself the God of Abraham, &c. Jesus Christ properly remarked that God is not the God of the *dead,* (that word being equivalent to *eternal annihilation,* in the sense intended by the Sadducees, who held that the soul vanished with the body [2],) but of the *living*. whence it follows, that if he be the God of Abraham, Isaac, and Jacob, they have not altogether perished, but their bodies will be raised again from the dead, while their spirits or souls are alive with God, notwithstanding they have ceased for many centuries to exist among mortals. In the same reply, our Saviour further confuted, *inferentially,* another tenet of the Sadducees, viz. that there *is neither angel nor spirit,* by showing that the soul is not only immortal, but lives with God even while the body is detained in the dust of the earth, which body will afterwards be raised to life, and be united to the soul by the miraculous power of God.

The foundation of *inferential reading* is the perpetual harmony of sacred things; so that any one who has thoroughly considered

---

[1] Qui enim intelligit, quod loquitur, non modo *vim,* sed *ambitum* quoque verborum perspicit; ideoque id omne, quod ex iis legitime colligi potest, adprobare etiam meritò creditur. Buddei Elementa Philosophiæ Instrumentalis, part ii. cap. ii. § xxx. p. 246.

[2] Συναφανίξει τοις σωμασι. Joseph. Ant. Jud lib. xviii. c. 1. § 4. (al. c ii.)

and rightly understood a single doctrine, may hence easily deduce many others which depend upon it, as they are linked together in one continued chain. But, in order to conduct this kind of reading with advantage, it is necessary that we bring to it a *sober judgment*, capable of penetrating deeply into sacred truths, and of eliciting with indefatigable attention and patience, and also of deducing one truth from another by strong reasoning; and further, that the mind possess a sufficient knowledge of the *form of sound words in faith and love which is in Christ Jesus.* (2 Tim. 1. 13.) Without this knowledge, it will be impossible to make any beneficial progress in this branch of sacred literature, or to discover the exhaustless variety of important truths contained in the Sacred Writings. It will likewise be requisite to compare inferences when deduced, in order to ascertain whether they are correct, and are really worthy of that appellation. For this purpose the following rules may be advantageously consulted.

1. *Obvious or too common inferences must not be deduced, nor should they be expressed in the very words of Scripture.*

Thus, if from Matt. vi. 33. *Seek ye first the kingdom of God and his righteousness, and all these things shall be added unto you,* the following inferences be deduced — 1. The kingdom of God is to be sought in the first instance. 2. It is necessary that we seek the righteousness of God; and, 3. To him that thus seeks, all other things shall be added. Although these are in themselves weighty truths, yet they are expressed too plainly in the very words of Scripture, to be called inferences. They are, rather, truths seated in the text itself, than truths deduced from those words.

2. *Inferences must be deduced from the true and genuine sense of the words, not from a spurious sense, whether literal or mystical*

We have a striking violation of the sober and almost self-evident canon, in the inference deduced by cardinal Bellarmin, from a comparison of Acts x. 13. with John xxi 16. From the divine command, *Rise, Peter! kill and eat,* compared with our Lord's direction to the Apostle, *Feed my sheep,* he extorts this consequence, viz. that the functions of the Roman pontiff, as the successor of Peter, are two-fold — *to feed the church, and to put heretics to death!* It is scarcely necessary to add, that this inference is derived from putting a false and spurious sense upon those passages.

3. *Inferences are deduced more safely as well as more correctly from the originals, than from any version of the Scriptures.*

It is not uncommon, even in the best versions, to find meanings put upon the sacred text, which are totally foreign to the intention of the inspired penman. Thus, from Acts ii. 47. (*the Lord added to the church daily such as should be saved*), the papists have absurdly pretended to deduce the perpetuity and visibility of the (Roman Catholic) church; and, from the same text compared with Acts xiii. 48. (*as many as were ordained to eternal life believed*), some have inferred that those whom God adds to the church shall necessarily and absolutely be eternally saved. The question relative to indefectibility from grace is foreign to a practical work like this [1]: but, without throwing down the gauntlet

---

[1] "It may not be the most philosophical, but it *is probably the unsent opinion which we can adopt,* that the truth lies somewhere between the two rival systems of Calvin and Arminius; though I believe it to exceed the wit of man to point out the *exact* place where it *does* lie. We distinctly perceive the two extremities of the vast chain, which stretches across the whole expanse of the theological heavens; but its central links are enveloped in impenetrable clouds and thick darkness." (Mr Faber's Discourses, vol. i. pp 478, 479.) Archbishop Tillotson has a fine passage on this subject to the same effect (which is too long to be extracted), at the close of his hundred and seventh sermon. See his Works, vol. v. pp. 395, 396. Compare also vol. vii. pp. 99, 100. (London, 1820.) On this topic the author cannot withhold from his readers the following admirable observations of the late Bishop Horsley. Addressing the clergy of the diocese of Gloucester, he says, "I would entreat you of all things to avoid controversial arguments in the pulpit upon what are called the Calvinistic points; — the dark subject of predestination and

of controversy, we may remark, that these passages have *no relation whatever* to the doctrine of election, and that if the translators of our authorised version had rendered the original of Acts ii. 47. *literally*, as they have done in other parts of the New Testament [1], it would have run thus: —The Lord added daily to the church, τους σωζομενους, *the saved;* that is, those who were saved from their sins and prejudices; and so the passage is rendered by Drs. Whitby, Doddridge, and other eminent critics and divines. Further, if Acts xiii. 48. had been translated according to the *proper* meaning of τεταγμενοι, that verse would have run thus: — *As many as were disposed for eternal life, believed* which rendering is not only faithful to the original, but also to the *context* and *scope* of the sacred historian, who is relating the effects or consequences of the preaching of the Gospel to the Gentiles. For the Jews had contradicted Paul, and blasphemed, while the religious proselytes heard with profound attention, and cordially received the Gospel he preached to them; the *former* were, through their own stubbornness, utterly *indisposed* to receive that Gospel, while the *latter*, destitute of prejudice and prepossession, rejoiced to hear that the Gentiles were included in the covenant of salvation through Jesus Christ, and, therefore, in this good state or *disposition* of mind, they believed. Such is the plain and obvious meaning deducible from the consideration of the context and scope of the passage in question, and that the rendering above given is strictly conformable to the original Greek, is evident from the following considerations. In the first place, the word τεταγμενοι is *not* the word generally used in the New Testament to denote fore-ordination, or an eternal decree, but the verbs οριζω and προοριζω, which exactly answer to our English words *determine* and *predetermine*. Further, Dr. Hammond remarks, the verb τασσω or τατίω, (whence the participle τεταγμενος) and its compounds, are often employed in the sense of our military word *tactics*, by which is meant whatever relates to the *disposal* or marshalling of troops. (Compare Luke vii. 8. and Rom. xiii. 1. Gr) and hence, by analogy, it is applied to other things: — Thus, in 1 Cor xvi. 15. we read, " They devoted (εταξαν) themselves to the ministry of the saints." See also 1 Macc. v 27. and 2 Macc. xv. 20. (Gr); and particularly Acts xx. 13, where we read that Saint Paul went on foot to Assos, *for so he was* (διετεταγμενος) *disposed*. Similar expressions are to be found in the Greek classic writers.[2] But what confirms the preceding rendering of this text, is *the fact*, that it is so

election I mean, and the subordinate questions. *Differences of opinion upon these subjects have subsisted among the best Christians from the beginning, and will subsist, I am persuaded, to the end.* They seem to me to arise almost of necessity, from the inability of the human mind to reconcile the doctrine of a providence, irresistibly ruling all events, with the responsibility of man as a moral agent. And persons equally zealous for God's glory, have taken different sides of the question, according as their minds have been more forcibly impressed with awful notions of God's right of sovereignty on the one hand, or of his justice on the other. But in certain leading principles, Lutherans, Calvinists, Arminians, and we of the church of England are, I trust, all agreed: We are agreed in the fundamental doctrines of the Trinity; all believing in the united operation of the three persons, in their distinct offices in the accomplishment of man's redemption. We are all agreed that the fore-knowledge of God is — like himself — from all eternity, and absolute; that his providence is universal, controlling not only all the motions of matter, but all the thoughts and actions of intelligent beings of all orders, that, nevertheless, man has that degree of free agency which makes him justly responsible; that his sins are his own; and that, without holiness, no man shall see God. While we agree in these principles, I cannot see to what purpose we agitate endless disputes upon the dark — I had almost said — *presumptuous questions* upon the order of the divine decrees, as if there could be any internal energies of the divine mind, and about the manner of the communion between the Spirit of God and the Soul of the believer." (Bishop Horsley's Charge in 1800, pp. 32, 33. 4to.)

[1] It is worthy of remark that the participle σωζομενος occurs in four other places of the New Testament, in all which our translators give the true meaning. These are Luke xiii. 23. ει ολιγοι σωζομενοι, *are there few that* BE SAVED? — 1 Cor i. 18. τοις δε σωζομενοις ημιν, *but unto us* WHICH ARE SAVED — 2 Cor. ii. 15 εν τοις σωζομενοις, *in them* THAT ARE SAVED. — Rev. xxi. 24. τα εθνη των σωζομενων, *the nations of them*, WHICH ARE SAVED In none of these instances have the translators given the forced and arbitrary meaning above noticed, and no reason can be assigned why they should have so rendered Acts ii. 47.

[2] Dr. Hammond (on Acts xiii. 48.) has cited and commented on several passages which we have not room to state. He renders the word τεταγμενοι by *fitly disposed and qualified for*; Dr Wall, by *fit to receive;* and Mr. Thompson, the learned North American translator of the Scriptures from the Greek, by *fitly disposed*. Wolfius (Cur. Philol. in loc.) considers the phrase τεταγμενος εις as equivalent to ευθετος εις (Luke ix. 62.) in our version rendered *fit* (or, more correctly, *rightly disposed*) *for the kingdom of God*. Dr. Whitby

translated in the Old Syriac, the most antient of all the versions of the New Testament. This is of great moment, for that version was made at least four hundred years *before* the sense of this place was disputed by the different sects and parties of Christians " Meanwhile," says Dr Hammond, with equal truth and piety, " it must be remembered that these qualifications are not pretended to have been originally from themselves, but from *the preventing grace of God*, to which it is to be acknowledged due that they are ever pliable, or willing to follow Christ "

4. *Those inferences are always to be preferred which approach nearest to the scope of a passage.*

Thus, in John vi 37. Christ says, *Him that cometh unto me I will in nowise cast out.* From this clause the two following inferences have been deduced. 1. That Jesus Christ is a most certain asylum for all persons whose consciences are burthened 2. That Christians ought to receive those who are weak in faith, after the example of Christ, and to treat them with tenderness Now, though both these inferences are good in themselves, the first is most to be preferred, because it harmonises best with the scope of the passage, (compare verses 37—40) which is to show that Christ will reject none " that truly repent and unfeignedly believe" in him.

5. *Inferences ought to embrace useful truths, and such as are necessary to be known, on which the mind may meditate, and be led to a more intimate acquaintance with the doctrines of salvation, and with Christian morality.*

It were no difficult task to illustrate this remark by a variety of examples ; but this is rendered unnecessary by the admirable models presented in the valuable sermons of our most eminent divines, not to mention the excellent discourses of Masillon, Bossuet, Flechier, Claude, Saurin, Superville, Du Bosc, and other eminent foreign divines, both protestants and catholics. The reader, who is desirous of illustrations, will find many very apposite ones in Monsieur Claude's celebrated and elaborate Essay on the Composition of a Sermon.[1]

II. The *sources*, whence inferences are deducible, are divided by Professor Rambach (to whom we are almost wholly indebted for this chapter[2]) into two classes, viz *internal* and *external:* the former are *inherent* in the text, and flow from it, *considered in itself*, the latter are derived from a *comparison* of the text with *other passages and circumstances*.

To illustrate these definitions by a few examples : — The sources whence inferences may be deduced, are *internal*, or inherent in the text, when such consequences are formed, 1. From the affections of the sacred writer or speaker; 2. From words and their signification; 3. From the emphasis and force of words; and, 4. From the structure and order of the words contained in the sacred text.

1. *Inferences deduced from the affections of the writer or speaker, whether these are indicated in the text, or are left to the investigation of the interpreter.*

Thus, in Mark iii. 5 we read that Jesus Christ looked round about on those who op-

---

translates the word by *disposed*, and Dr. Doddridge by *determined*, in order to preserve the ambiguity of the word The meaning, he observes, of the sacred penman seems to be, that all who were deeply and seriously concerned about their eternal happiness, openly embraced the Gospel. And wherever this temper was, it was undoubtedly the effect of a divine operation on their hearts. See Whitby, Doddridge, Wall, Wetstein, Bengel, Rosenmuller, and especially Limborch, (Commentarius in Acta Apostolorum, pp. 183—186 folio, Rotterdam, 1711,) on Acts xiii. 48., and Krebsii Observationes in Nov. Test. ex Josepho, pp. 222—224. Compare also Franzius de Interpretatione Sacrarum Scripturarum, pp. 104—115.; Bp. Taylor's Works, vol. IX. p. 140.; and Bishop Wilson's Works, Sermon 57. Vol. II p. 272. folio edit. Bath, 1782.

[1] See particularly §§ 17—26. in Dr. Williams's edition of Claude's Essay, Christian Preacher, pp. 300—346.; or Mr. Simeon's much improved edition, Cambridge and London, 1827. 12mo.

[2] Institutiones Hermeneuticæ Sacræ, lib. IV. c. 3. pp 804—822.

VIII. Sect. I.] *On the Inferential Reading of the Bible.* 565

posed him with *anger, being grieved for the hardness of their hearts* - the anger here mentioned was no uneasy passion, but an excess of generous grief occasioned by their obstinate stupidity and blindness. From this passage the following conclusions may be drawn: 1 It is the duty of a Christian to sorrow, not only for his own sins, but also to be grieved for the sins of others. 2. All anger is not to be considered sinful 3. He does not bear the image of Christ, but rather that of Satan, who can either behold with indifference the wickedness of others, or rejoice in it 4 Nothing is more wretched than an obdurate heart, since it caused him, who is the source of all true joy, to be filled with grief on beholding it 5 Our indignation against wickedness must be tempered by compassion for the persons of the wicked.

2. Inferences deduced from words themselves, and their signification.

For instance, in Luke xxi 15 our Lord addressing his disciples, says, *I will give you a mouth and wisdom.* Inference 1 Christ, the eternal wisdom, is the source and spring of all true wisdom 2. *Will give.* They who attempt to procure wisdom by their own strength, without the aid of prayer, may justly be charged with presumption 3 *You.* No one stands more in need of the gift of divine wisdom than they who are intrusted with the charge of teaching others. 4. *A mouth,* or ready utterance The gift of eloquence is bestowed by God, as well as every other gift. *Wisdom.* It is possible for a man to acquire *cunning* by the mere force of corrupt nature, but nature cannot possibly confer true wisdom. 5 *And* Eloquence, when not united with wisdom, is of little utility in promoting the kingdom of Christ. From this last inference, it appears, that even the smallest particles sometimes afford matter from which we may deduce practical conclusions.

3. Inferences deduced from the emphasis and force of words.

We have an example in 1 Pet v. 5 *Be clothed with humility for God resisteth the proud.* Inference 1. *Humility* Christian humility does not reside in filthy or rent garments, but in a modest mind, that entertains humble views of itself. 2 *Be ye clothed,* εγκομβωσασθε, from εν, in, and κομβοω, to gather, or tie in a knot. The word means to clothe, properly, *with an outer ornamental garment, tied closely upon one with knots.* True humility is an ornament which decorates the mind much more than the most costly garment does the body 1 3 Humility is a garment with which we cover both our own virtues and the defects of others. 4. This ornament of humility, being exposed to many snares, must be most carefully guarded, and retained around us. 5. *The proud* υπερηφανοις, from υπερ, *above,* and φαινω, *to appear,* because such persons exalt themselves above others No sin is capable of being less concealed, or of escaping the observation of others, than pride 6 *God resisteth* αντιτασσεται, literally, SETTETH HIMSELF AS IN ARRAY *against, the proud man* this is a military term The inference deducible is, that while all other sinners retire, as it were, from the presence of God, and seek for shelter against his indignation, the proud man alone openly braves it.[2]

4. Inferences deduced from the order and structure of the words contained in the sacred text.

Thus, from Rom. xiv. 17. *The kingdom of God is righteousness, peace, and joy in the Holy Ghost,* the following inferences may be derived, according to the order of the words, which depends upon the connection and order of the subjects treated of 1 No constant and lasting *peace* of conscience is to be expected, unless we previously lay hold of the *righteousness* of Christ by faith. 2 They only possess a genuine and permanent *joy,* who being justified, cultivate *peace* with God through Jesus Christ 3 In vain do those persons boast of the *righteousness* of Christ, who still continue in a state of hostility and enmity with God and man. 4. A serene and peaceful conscience is the only source of spiritual joy.[3]

---

[1] Mr. Parkhurst's illustration of this truly emphatic word is too important and beautiful to be omitted. "On the whole," says he, "this expressive word, εγκομβωσασθε used by Saint Peter, implies that the humility of Christians, which is one of the most ornamental graces of their profession, should constantly *appear* in all their conversation, so as to *strike the eye of every beholder;* and that this amiable grace should be so *closely connected* with their persons, that no occurrence, temptation, or calamity should be able to *strip* them of it. — Faxit Deus !" Greek and English Lexicon, p 185. col 2. (5th edit.)

[2] It may be worth the reader's while to re-consider what has already been stated on the subject of emphatic words, which, in fact, are so many sources whence inferences may be judiciously deduced

[3] For a full illustration of this subject, we with pleasure refer the reader to an excellent discourse, in " Sermons on Subjects chiefly Practical, by the Rev John Jebb, A. M." (now Bishop of Limerick,) Serm. iv. pp. 71—98. London, 1816. 8vo.

III. The sources of inferences are *external*, when the conclusions are deduced from a comparison of the text, 1. With the state of the speaker; — 2. With the scope of the book or passage; — 3. With antecedents and consequents; or, in other words, with the context; — 4. With parallel passages, and other circumstances.

1. *Inferences deduced from the state of the writer or speaker.*

Thus, when Solomon, the wisest and richest of sovereigns, whose eager desire after the enjoyment of worldly vanities was so great, that he left none of them untried, and whose means of gratifying himself in every possible pleasure and delight were unbounded, — when he exclaims, (Eccl i. 2.) *Vanity of vanities, all is vanity,* the following inferences may be deduced from his words, compared with the state of his mind. (1.) Since the meanest artisan is not to be despised when speaking properly and opportunely of his own business, he must be more than usually stupid who does not give diligent attention when a most illustrious monarch is about to speak. (2.) How admirable is the wisdom of God, who, when it pleased him to select a person to proclaim and testify the vanity of all things human, made choice of one who had most deeply experienced how truly vain they were! (3.) When a sovereign, thus singularly possessed of glory, fame, human wisdom, riches, and every facility for the enjoyment of pleasures, proclaims the vanity of all these things, his testimony ought to be received by every one with great respect. (4.) Since princes, above all others, are exposed to the insidious wiles of pleasures, it is worthy of remark that God raised up one of their own rank to admonish them of their danger.

2. *Inferences deduced.*

(1.) *From the general scope of an entire book.* — For instance, let the following words of Jesus Christ (John viii. 51.) *Verily, verily, I say unto you, if a man keep my saying he shall never see death,* be compared with the *general scope* of the book, which is announced in John xx. 31. *These are written, that ye might believe that Jesus is the Christ, the Son of God, and that believing, ye might have life through his name.* From this collation the following inferences will flow. (i.) Faith in Christ is to be proved and shown by obedience to his word. (ii.) True faith cordially receives not only the merits of Christ, but also his words and precepts. And, (iii.) Whosoever is made, through faith, a partaker of spiritual life, shall also be freed from spiritual and eternal death.

(2.) *From the special scope of a particular passage.* — The particular scope of Jesus Christ in the passage above cited, (John viii. 51.) was to demonstrate that he was not possessed by an evil spirit, since the keeping of his words would procure eternal life for all who obey him, while Satan, on the contrary, leads men into sin, whose wages is *death,* or everlasting perdition. Hence we may deduce the subsequent inferences. (i.) That doctrine which produces such very salutary effects, cannot necessarily be false and diabolical. (ii.) Saving truths are to be proposed even to those who are guilty of calumniating them. (iii.) There is no nearer way, by which to liberate the mind from doubts formed against truth, than a ready obedience to acknowledged truth. (iv.) The precepts of Christ are to be regarded and obeyed, even though they should be ridiculed or defamed by the most learned men.

(3.) *From the very special scope of particular words or phrases* — The passage just referred to will supply us with another illustration. — For instance, should it be asked, (i.) Why our Lord prefixed to his declaration, a solemn asseveration similar to an oath? it is replied, because he perceived the very obstinate unbelief of his hearers, whence it may be inferred, that it is a shameful thing that Christ should find so little faith among men. (ii.) Should it be further inquired, why he prefixed a *double asseveration?* it is answered, in order that, by such repetition, he might silence the repeated calumnies of those who opposed him: hence, also, it may be inferred, that in proportion to the malice and effrontery of men in asserting calumnies, the greater zeal is required in vindicating truth. (iii.) Should it still be asked, why our Lord added the words, *I say unto you,* we reply, in opposition to the assertion of his enemies in the 48th verse, — *Say we not well, that thou hast a demon?* From which we may infer, that he who is desirous of knowing the truth, ought not only to attend to the stories invented and propagated by wicked men against the godly, but also to those things which Christ says of them, and they of him. Other instances might be adduced, but the preceding will suffice.

3. *Inferences deduced from a collation of the text with the context.*

In this case, the principal words of a text should be compared together, in order that inferences may be deduced from their mutual relation. (1.) Collate 1 Tim. i. 15. *It is a faithful saying,* with verse 4. *Neither give heed to fables. Inference.* The idle legends of the Jews (preserved in the Talmud), and the relations of the Gentiles concerning their deities, and the appearances *of the latter*, are compared to uncertain fables: but the narration in the Gospel concerning Jesus Christ is both certain, and worthy of being received with faith. (ii.) Collate also 1 Tim. i. 15 with verse 6. *Vain jangling*, or empty talking. *Inference*. God usually punishes those who *will not* believe the most certain words of the Gospel, by judicially giving them up to a voluntary belief of the most absurd and lying fables. (iii.) Compare the words, *Worthy of all acceptation*, (1 Tim i. 15) with verse 8. *The law is good. Inference.* The law, as given by God, is both good in itself and has a good tendency, though to a sinner it is so formidable as to put him to flight: but the Gospel recommends itself to the terrified conscience, as a saying or discourse every way worthy of credit.

4. *Inferences deduced from a collation of the text with parallel passages.*

The advantage resulting from such a comparison, in investigating the *sense* of a passage of Scripture, has already been stated and illustrated, and the observations and examples referred to, if considered with a particular view to the deduction of inferences, will supply the reader with numerous instances, whence he may draw various important corollaries. One instance, therefore, will suffice to exemplify the nature of the inferences deducible from a comparison of the text with parallel passages. In 2 Tim. i. 8 Saint Paul exhorts Timothy *not to be ashamed of the testimony of the Lord.* Compare this with Rom. i. 16. where he says, *I am not ashamed of the Gospel of Christ, for it is the power of God unto salvation to every one that believeth, to the Jew first, and also to the Greek;* and with Isa. xxviii. 16. and xlix 23. last clause, (cited in Rom x 11) where it is said, *Whosoever believeth in him* (Christ) *shall not be ashamed,* that is, confounded or disappointed of his hope From this collation the two following inferences may be derived (1.) Faithful ministers of the Gospel require nothing from others which they do not by their own experience know to be both possible and practicable. And, (2) All those, who have already believed, or do now or shall hereafter believe in Christ, have, in and through him, all the blessings foretold by the prophets all the promises of God, in (or through) him, being *yea*, that is, true in themselves, and *amen*, that is, faithfully fulfilled to all those who believe in Christ (2 Cor. i 20.)

IV. *A fifth external source of inferences, is the collation of the text with the consideration of the following external circumstances, viz.*

(1.) THE TIME *when the words or things were uttered or took place.*

Thus, in Matt xxvii. 52. we read that *many bodies of the saints which slept arose:* but when? After Christ's Resurrection, (v 53) not before (as Rambach himself, among other eminent divines, has supposed), for Christ himself was the *first fruits* of them that slept. (1 Cor. xv 20) The graves were opened at his death by the earthquake, and the bodies came out at his resurrection. *Inference.* The satisfactory efficacy of Christ's death was so great, that it opened a way to life to those who believed on him as the Messiah that was to come, as well as to those who believe in him subsequently to his incarnation and both are equally partakers of the benefits flowing from his resurrection.

(2.) THE PLACE *where the words were uttered.*

As in Matt xxvi. 39 42. *Not my will but thine be done!* Where did Christ utter this exclamation? In a garden *Inference* He who made an atonement for the sins of all mankind, voluntarily submitted himself, in the garden of passion, to the will of God from which man withdrew himself in a garden of pleasure.

(3.) THE OCCASION *upon which the words were spoken.*

Thus, in Matt. xvi. 3. Christ rebukes the Pharisees, *because they did not observe the signs of the times.* On what occasion? When they required him to show them a sign from heaven. *Inference.* Such are the blindness and corruption of men, that disregarding the signs exhibited to them by God himself, they frequently require new signs that are more agreeable to their own desires.

(4.) THE MANNER *in which a thing is done.*

Acts ix 9. During the blindness in which Saul continued for three days and three nights, God brought him to the knowledge of himself. *Inference.* Those, whom God vouchsafes to enlighten, he first convinces of their spiritual blindness [1]

---

[1] Professor Franck, in his Manuductio ad Lectionem Scripturæ Sacræ, cap. 3. (pp. 101—123. of Mr. Jacques's translation), has some very useful observations on inferential reading, illustrated with numerous instances different from those above given. See also Schaefer's Institutiones Scripturisticæ, pars ii. pp. 166—178.

Other instances, illustrating the sources whence inferences are deducible, might be offered, were they necessary, or were the preceding capable of being very soon exhausted. From the sources already stated and explained, various kinds of inferences may be derived, relating both to faith and practice. Thus, some may be deduced for the confirmation of faith, for exciting sentiments of love and gratitude, and for the support of hope: while others contribute to promote piety, Christian wisdom and prudence, and sacred eloquence; lastly, others are serviceable for doctrine, for reproof, for instruction, and for comfort. He, who adds *personal practice* to the diligent reading of the Scriptures, and meditates on the inferences deduced from them by learned and pious men, will abundantly experience the truth of the royal psalmist's observations, — *Thy commandment is exceeding broad,* and, *the entrance of thy words giveth light, it giveth understanding to the simple.* (Psal. cxix. 96. 130.) "The Scriptures," says the late eminent Bishop Horne, "are the appointed means of *enlightening* the mind with true and saving knowledge. They show us what we were, what we are, and what we shall be: they show us what God hath done for us, and what he expecteth us to do for him; they show us the adversaries we have to encounter, and how to encounter them with success; they show us the mercy and the justice of the Lord, the joys of heaven, and the pains of hell. Thus will they *give to the simple,* in a few days, an *understanding* of those matters, which philosophy, for whole centuries, sought in vain."

In conducting, however, the inferential reading above discussed, we must be careful not to trust to the mere effusions of a prurient or vivid fancy: inferences *legitimately deduced,* unquestionably do essentially promote the spiritual instruction and practical edification of the reader. "But when brought forward for the purpose of *interpretation* properly so called, they are to be viewed with caution, and even with mistrust. For scarcely is there a favourite opinion, which a fertile imagination may not thus extract from some portion of Scripture: and very different, nay contrary interpretations of this kind have often been made of the very same texts, according to men's various fancies or inventions." [1]

SECTION II.

ON THE PRACTICAL READING OF SCRIPTURE.

HAVING hitherto endeavoured to show how we may ascertain and apply the true sense of the Sacred Writings, it remains only to consider in what manner we may best reduce our knowledge to practice; for, if serious contemplation of the Scriptures, and *practice,* be united together, our real knowledge of the Bible must necessarily be increased, and will be rendered progressively more delightful. *If,* says Jesus Christ, *any man will do his* (God's) *will, he shall know*

---

[1] Bishop Vanmildert's Lectures, p. 247.

of the doctrine whether it be of God. (John vii. 17.) This is the chief end for which God has *revealed* his will to us (Deut. xxix. 29.); and all Scripture is profitable for this purpose, (2 Tim. iii. 16.) either directing us what we should do, or inciting and encouraging us to do it: it being written for our learning, that *we through patience and comfort of the Scriptures might have hope* (Rom. xv. 4.); that is, that by the strenuous exercise of that patience, which the consolations administered in Scripture so powerfully support, we might have an assured and joyful hope in the midst of all our tribulation. Even those things, which seem most notional and speculative, are reducible to practice. (Rom. i. 20, 21.) Those speculations, which we are enabled to form concerning the nature and attributes of God, grounded upon his works, ought to induce us to glorify him as such a God as his works declare him to be: and it is a manifest indication that our knowledge is not right, if it hath not this influence upon our conduct and conversation. (1 John ii. 3.)

The practical reading here referred to, is of such a nature, that the most illiterate person may prosecute it with advantage: for the application of Scripture which it enjoins, is connected with salvation: and, consequently, if the unlearned were incapable of making such application to themselves, it would be in vain to allow them to peruse the Sacred Writings.[1] After what has been stated in the preceding part of this volume, the author trusts he shall stand acquitted of undervaluing the knowledge of the original languages of the Scriptures, an acquaintance with which will suggest many weighty practical hints, that would not present themselves in a version. It is, however, sufficient, that every thing necessary to direct our faith, and regulate our practice, may easily be ascertained by the aid of translations. Of all modern versions, the present authorised English translation, is, upon the whole, undoubtedly the most accurate and faithful; the translators having seized the very spirit of the sacred writers, and having almost every where expressed their meaning with a pathos and energy that have never been rivalled by any subsequent versions either of the Old or the New Testament, or of detached books, although, in most of these, *particular passages* are rendered more happily, and with a closer regard to the genius and spirit of the divine originals.

The simplest practical application of the word of God will, unquestionably, prove the most beneficial: provided it be conducted with a due regard to those moral qualifications which have already been stated and enforced, as necessary to the right understanding of the Scriptures.[2] Should, however, any hints be required, the following may, perhaps, be consulted with advantage.[3]

---

[1] Franckii Manuductio, cap iv. p. 131 et seq ; or, p 124 et seq. of the English version

[2] See Vol. I p. 491. supra.

[3] These observations are selected and abridged from Rambach's Institutiones Hermeneuticæ, and Professor Franck's Brevis Institutio, Rationem tradens Sacram Scripturam in veram edificationem legendi, annexed to his Prælectiones Hermeneuticæ, 8vo Halæ Madgeburgicæ, 1717. Franck has treated the same topic nearly in a similar manner, in his Manuductio, already noticed, cap. iv.

I. *In reading the Scriptures, then, with a view to personal application, we should be careful that it be done with a pure intention.*

The Scribes and Pharisees, indeed, searched the Scriptures, yet without deriving any real benefit from them: they *thought* that they had in them eternal life yet they would not come to Christ that they might have life. (John v. 40.) He, however, who peruses the Sacred Volume, merely for the purpose of amusing himself with the histories it contains, or of beguiling time, or to tranquillise his conscience by the discharge of a mere external duty, is deficient in the *motive* with which he performs that duty, and cannot expect to derive from it either advantage or comfort amid the trials of life. Neither will it suffice to read the Scriptures with the mere design of becoming intimately acquainted with sacred truths, unless such reading be accompanied with a desire, that, through them, he may be convinced of his self-love, ambition, or other faults, to which he may be peculiarly exposed, and that by the assistance of divine grace, he may be enabled to root them out of his mind.

II. *In reading the Scriptures for this purpose, it will be advisable to select some appropriate lessons from its most useful parts, not being particularly solicitous concerning the exact connection or other critical niceties that may occur, (though at other times, as ability and opportunity offer, these are highly proper objects of inquiry,) but simply considering them in a devotional or practical view.*[1]

After ascertaining, therefore, the plain and obvious meaning of the lesson under examination, we should first consider the *present state of our minds*, and carefully compare it with the passage in question: next, we should inquire into the *causes of those faults* which such perusal may have disclosed to us, and should then look around for suitable remedies to correct the faults we have thus discovered.

III. *We should carefully distinguish between what the Scripture itself says, and what is only said in the Scripture, and, also, the times, places, and persons, when, where, and by whom any thing is recorded as having been said or done.*

In Mal. iii. 14. we meet with the following words: "It is in vain to serve God, and what profit is it that we have kept his ordinance?" And in 1 Cor. xv. 32. we meet with this maxim of profane men — "Let us eat and drink, for to-morrow we die." But, when we read these and similar passages, we must attend to the characters introduced, and remember that the persons who spoke thus were wicked men. Even those, whose piety is commended in the Sacred Volume, did not always act in strict conformity to it. Thus, when David vowed that he would utterly destroy Nabal's house, we must conclude that he sinned in making that vow. and the discourses of Job's friends, though in themselves extremely beautiful and instructive, are not in *every* respect to be approved, for we are informed by the sacred historian that God was wroth with them, because they had not spoken of him the thing that was right (Job xlii. 7.)

IV. *In every practical reading and application of the Scriptures to ourselves, our attention should be fixed on Jesus Christ, both as a gift, to be received by faith for salvation, and also as an exemplar, to be copied and imitated in our lives.*

---

[1] Doddridge's Rise and Progress of Religion, ch. xix. § 9. (Works, vol. i p 359. Leeds edit. 8vo)

We are not, however, to imitate him in all things. Some things he did by his divine power, and in those we *cannot* imitate him: other things he performed by his sovereign authority, in those we *must not* imitate him: other things also he performed by virtue of his office, as a Mediator, and in these we *may not*, we *cannot* follow him. But in his early piety, his obedience to his reputed earthly parents, his unwearied diligence in doing good, his humility, his unblameable conduct, his self-denial, his contentment under low circumstances, his frequency in private prayer, his affectionate thankfulness, his compassion to the wretched, his holy and edifying discourse, his free conversation, his patience, his readiness to forgive injuries, his sorrow for the sins of others, his zeal for the worship of God, his glorifying his heavenly Father, his impartiality in administering reproof, his universal obedience, and his love and practice of holiness, — in all these instances, Jesus Christ is the most perfect pattern for our imitation.[1] And the observation of these things, in a practical point of view, will be of singular use to us on this account; namely, that whatever sympathy and benevolence Christ displayed on earth, he retains the same in heaven, seeing that he is the same yesterday, to-day, and for ever, and that he ever liveth to make intercession for them that come unto God by him. For we have not an high priest that cannot be touched with the feeling of our infirmities, but [one who was] in all points tempted like as we are, so that we may now come with humble confidence to the throne of grace; assuring ourselves, that we shall find, from the true mercy-seat of God, sufficient help in all our distresses. (Heb. xiii. 8. vii. 25. and iv. 15, 16.) Jesus Christ, then, being our most perfect exemplar, (1 Cor. xi. 1.) the particular actions and general conduct of other men, as related in the Scriptures, should be regarded by us as models of imitation, only *so far as they are conformable to this standard.*

V. "*An example (that is, every good one) hath the force of a rule; all of them being* 'written for our admonition.' (1 Cor. x. 11.) *But then we must be careful to examine and discern whether the example be* extraordinary *or* ordinary, *according to which the application must be made.*"[2]

In illustration of this remark, it may be observed, 1. That in matters which were *extraordinary*, such as the killing of Eglon by Ehud, (Judg. iii. 21.) Elijah's killing the prophets of Baal, (1 Kings xviii. 40.) and his invoking fire from heaven, (2 Kings i. 10.) a conduct which, though approved in *him*, was condemned by our Lord in the apostles (Luke ix. 54, 55.); — 2. In matters that were *temporary;* such were many of the ceremonies observed by the Jews, the washing of his disciples' feet by our Lord, (John xiii. 14.) the celebration of love-feasts by the primitive

---

[1] The various features in the character of our Redeemer as man, which are enumerated above, are illustrated in an admirable, but little known tract of the pious commentator Burkitt (edited by the late Rev. Dr. Glasse), intitled "Jesus Christ, as Man, an inimitable pattern of religious virtue." 8vo. London, 1809 Having briefly, though perspicuously, illustrated the different subjects, the editor terminates his essay with the following caution, which is unhappily as applicable to the present time as when it was first written, "Take heed that ye do not so consider Christ for your pattern, as to *disown him* for your Saviour and Redeemer. God preserve us," he adds, "from this growing error, which stabs the heart of the Christian religion, in that it deprives us of the choicest benefits of Christ's death; namely, the expiation of sin by a proper satisfaction to the justice of God!"

[2] Bishop Wilkins on the Gift of Preaching, p. 23. of Dr. E. Williams's Christian Preacher See also some admirable observations on this subject in Bishop Taylor's Works, vol. xii. p. 452. *et seq.*

Printed in the USA
CPSIA information can be obtained
at www.ICGtesting.com
LVHW011228161023
761197LV00010B/207